W9-CTW-406

Contemporary
Literary Criticism

Guide to Gale Literary Criticism Series

For criticism on	Consult these Gale series
Authors now living or who died after December 31, 1959	*CONTEMPORARY LITERARY CRITICISM (CLC)*
Authors who died between 1900 and 1959	*TWENTIETH-CENTURY LITERARY CRITICISM (TCLC)*
Authors who died between 1800 and 1899	*NINETEENTH-CENTURY LITERATURE CRITICISM (NCLC)*
Authors who died between 1400 and 1799	*LITERATURE CRITICISM FROM 1400 TO 1800 (LC)* *SHAKESPEAREAN CRITICISM (SC)*
Authors who died before 1400	*CLASSICAL AND MEDIEVAL LITERATURE CRITICISM (CMLC)*
Black writers of the past two hundred years	*BLACK LITERATURE CRITICISM (BLC)*
Authors of books for children and young adults	*CHILDREN'S LITERATURE REVIEW (CLR)*
Dramatists	*DRAMA CRITICISM (DC)*
Hispanic writers of the late nineteenth and twentieth centuries	*HISPANIC LITERATURE CRITICISM (HLC)*
Native North American writers and orators of the eighteenth, nineteenth, and twentieth centuries	*NATIVE NORTH AMERICAN LITERATURE (NNAL)*
Poets	*POETRY CRITICISM (PC)*
Short story writers	*SHORT STORY CRITICISM (SSC)*
Major authors from the Renaissance to the present	*WORLD LITERATURE CRITICISM, 1500 TO THE PRESENT (WLC)*
Major authors and works from the Bible to the present	*WORLD LITERATURE CRITICISM SUPPLEMENT (WLCS)*

ISSN 0091-3421

Volume 104

Contemporary Literary Criticism

Excerpts from Criticism of the Works
of Today's Novelists, Poets, Playwrights,
Short Story Writers, Scriptwriters, and
Other Creative Writers

Deborah A. Schmitt
EDITOR

Jeffrey W. Hunter
CLC COORDINATOR

Tim Akers
Pamela S. Dear
Daniel Jones
John D. Jorgenson
Jerry Moore
Polly Vedder
Timothy White
Thomas Wiloch
Kathleen Wilson
ASSOCIATE EDITORS

GALE

DETROIT · NEW YORK · TORONTO · LONDON

Library of Congress Catalog Card Number 76-46132
ISBN 0-7876-1194-8
ISSN 0091-3421

Printed in the United States of America
10 9 8 7 6 5 4 3 2 1

Contents

Preface vii

Acknowledgments xi

Preface

A Comprehensive Information Source on Contemporary Literature

Named "one of the twenty-five most distinguished reference titles published during the past twenty-five years" by *Reference Quarterly,* the *Contemporary Literary Criticism (CLC)* series provides readers with critical commentary and general information on more than 2,000 authors now living or who died after December 31, 1959. Previous to the publication of the first volume of *CLC* in 1973, there was no ongoing digest monitoring scholarly and popular sources of critical opinion and explication of modern literature. *CLC,* therefore, has fulfilled an essential need, particularly since the complexity and variety of contemporary literature makes the function of criticism especially important to today's reader.

Scope of the Series

CLC presents significant passages from published criticism of works by creative writers. Since many of the authors covered by *CLC* inspire continual critical commentary, writers are often represented in more than one volume. There is, of course, no duplication of reprinted criticism.

Authors are selected for inclusion for a variety of reasons, among them the publication or dramatic production of a critically acclaimed new work, the reception of a major literary award, revival of interest in past writings, or the adaptation of a literary work to film or television.

Attention is also given to several other groups of writers-authors of considerable public interest—about whose work criticism is often difficult to locate. These include mystery and science fiction writers, literary and social critics, foreign writers, and authors who represent particular ethnic groups within the United States.

Format of the Book

Each *CLC* volume contains about 500 individual excerpts taken from hundreds of book review periodicals, general magazines, scholarly journals, monographs, and books. Entries include critical evaluations spanning from the beginning of an author's career to the most current commentary. Interviews, feature articles, and other published writings that offer insight into the author's works are also presented. Students, teachers, librarians, and researchers will find that the generous excerpts and supplementary material in *CLC* provide them with vital information required to write a term paper, analyze a poem, or lead a book discussion group. In addition, complete bibliographical citations note the original source and all of the information necessary for a term paper footnote or bibliography.

Features

A *CLC* author entry consists of the following elements:

- The **Author Heading** cites the author's name in the form under which the author has most commonly published, followed by birth date, and death date when applicable. Uncertainty as to a birth or death date is indicated by a question mark.

- A **Portrait** of the author is included when available.

- A brief **Biographical and Critical Introduction** to the author and his or her work precedes the excerpted criticism. The first line of the introduction provides the author's full name, pseudonyms (if applicable), nationality, and a listing of genres in which the author has written. To provide users with easier access to information, the biographical and critical essay included in each author entry is divided into four categories: "Introduction," "Biographical Information," "Major Works," and "Critical Reception." The introductions to single-work entries—entries that focus on well known and frequently studied books, short stories, and poems—are similarly organized to quickly provide readers with information on the plot and major characters of the work being discussed, its major themes, and its critical reception. Previous volumes of *CLC* in which the author has been featured are also listed in the introduction.

- A list of **Principal Works** notes the most important writings by the author. When foreign-language works have been translated into English, the English-language version of the title follows in brackets.

- The **Excerpted Criticism** represents various kinds of critical writing, ranging in form from the brief review to the scholarly exegesis. Essays are selected by the editors to reflect the spectrum of opinion about a specific work or about an author's literary career in general. The excerpts are presented chronologically, adding a useful perspective to the entry. All titles by the author featured in the entry are printed in boldface type, which enables the reader to easily identify the works being discussed. Publication information (such as publisher names and book prices) and parenthetical numerical references (such as footnotes or page and line references to specific editions of a work) have been deleted at the editor's discretion to provide smoother reading of the text.

- Critical essays are prefaced by **Explanatory Notes** as an additional aid to readers. These notes may provide several types of valuable information, including: the reputation of the critic, the importance of the work of criticism, the commentator's approach to the author's work, the purpose of the criticism, and changes in critical trends regarding the author.

- A complete **Bibliographical Citation** designed to help the user find the original essay or book precedes each excerpt.

- Whenever possible, a recent, previously unpublished **Author Interview** accompanies each entry.

- A concise **Further Reading** section appears at the end of entries on authors for whom a significant amount of criticism exists in addition to the pieces reprinted in *CLC*. Each citation in this section is accompanied by a descriptive annotation describing the content of that article. Materials included in this section are grouped under various headings (e.g., Biography, Bibliography, Criticism, and Interviews) to aid users in their search for additional information. Cross-references to other useful sources published by Gale Research in which the author has appeared are also included: *Authors in the News, Black Writers, Children's Literature Review, Contemporary Authors, Dictionary of Literary Biography, DISCovering Authors, Drama Criticism, Hispanic Literature Criticism, Hispanic Writers, Native North American Literature, Poetry Criticism, Something about the Author, Short Story Criticism, Contemporary Authors Autobiography Series,* and *Something about the Author Autobiography Series.*

Other Features

CLC also includes the following features:

- An **Acknowledgments** section lists the copyright holders who have granted permission to reprint material in this volume of *CLC*. It does not, however, list every book or periodical reprinted or consulted during the preparation of the volume.

- Each new volume of *CLC* includes a **Cumulative Topic Index,** which lists all literary topics treated in *CLC, NCLC, TCLC,* and *LC 1400-1800.*

- A **Cumulative Author Index** lists all the authors who have appeared in the various literary criticism series published by Gale Research, with cross-references to Gale's biographical and autobiographical series. A full listing of the series referenced there appears on the first page of the indexes of this volume. Readers will welcome this cumulated author index as a useful tool for locating an author within the various series. The index, which lists birth and death dates when available, will be particularly valuable for those authors who are identified with a certain period but whose death dates cause them to be placed in another, or for those authors whose careers span two periods. For example, Ernest Hemingway is found in *CLC,* yet F. Scott Fitzgerald, a writer often associated with him, is found in *Twentieth-Century Literary Criticism.*

- A **Cumulative Nationality Index** alphabetically lists all authors featured in *CLC* by nationality, followed by numbers corresponding to the volumes in which the authors appear.

- An alphabetical **Title Index** accompanies each volume of *CLC*. Listings are followed by the author's name and the corresponding page numbers where the titles are discussed. English translations of foreign titles and variations of titles are cross-referenced to the title under which a work was originally published. Titles of novels, novellas, dramas, films, record albums, and poetry, short story, and essay collections are printed in italics, while all individual poems, short stories, essays, and songs are printed in roman type within quotation marks; when published separately (e.g., T. S. Eliot's poem *The Waste Land),* the titles of long poems are printed in italics.

- In response to numerous suggestions from librarians, Gale has also produced a **Special Paperbound Edition** of the *CLC* title index. This annual cumulation, which alphabetically lists all titles reviewed in the series, is available to all customers and is typically published with every fifth volume of *CLC*. Additional copies of the index are available upon request. Librarians and patrons will welcome this separate index: it saves shelf space, is easy to use, and is recyclable upon receipt of the next edition.

Citing *Contemporary Literary Criticism*

When writing papers, students who quote directly from any volume in the Literary Criticism Series may use the following general forms to footnote reprinted criticism. The first example pertains to material drawn from periodicals, the second to material reprinted in books:

[1]Alfred Cismaru, "Making the Best of It," *The New Republic,* 207, No. 24, (December 7, 1992), 30, 32; excerpted and reprinted in *Contemporary Literary Criticism,* Vol. 85, ed. Christopher Giroux (Detroit: Gale Research, 1995), pp. 73-4.

[2]Yvor Winters, *The Post-Symbolist Methods* (Allen Swallow, 1967); excerpted and reprinted in *Contemporary Literary Criticism,* Vol. 85, ed. Christopher Giroux (Detroit: Gale Research, 1995), pp. 223-26.

Suggestions Are Welcome

The editors hope that readers will find *CLC* a useful reference tool and welcome comments about the work. Send comments and suggestions to: Editors, *Contemporary Literary Criticism,* Gale Research, Penobscot Building, Detroit, MI 48226-4094.

Acknowledgments

The editors wish to thank the copyright holders of the excerpted criticism included in this volume and the permissions managers of many book and magazine publishing companies for assisting us in securing reproduction rights. We are also grateful to the staffs of the Detroit Public Library, the Library of Congress, the University of Detroit Mercy Library, Wayne State University Purdy/Kresge Library Complex, and the University of Michigan Libraries for making their resources available to us. Following is a list of the copyright holders who have granted us permission to reproduce material in this volume of **CLC.** Every effort has been made to trace copyright, but if omissions have been made, please let us know.

COPYRIGHTED EXCERPTS IN *CLC*, VOLUME 104, WERE REPRODUCED FROM THE FOLLOWING PERIODICALS:

Américas, v. 47, January-February,1995. Copyright © 1995 *Américas*. Reproduced by permission.–*Analog*, v. CXIV, April, 1994 for a review of "The Innkeeper's Song" by Tom Easton. Reproduced by permission of the author.–*Book World--The Washington Post*, May 21, 1992; February 5, 1995, July 9, 1995. Copyright (c)1992, 1995 Washington Post Book World Service/Washington Post Writers Group. All reproduced with permission.–*Booklist*, v. 91, October 1, 1994. Copyright © 1994 by the American Library Association. Reproduced by permission of the publisher.–*Books in Canada*, v. 9, August-September, 1980 for "Brock's Muniments" by C. P. Stacey; v. 15, November, 1986 for "Tainted Victory" by Desmond Morton; v. 17, November, 1988 for "Of Ice and Men" by Christopher Moore; v. 24, November, 1995 for "The Great Recycler" by Anne Denoon. All reproduced by permission of the respective authors.–*Canadian Literature*, Spring, 1986 for "The Real Mr. Canada" by Lorna Irvine. Reproduced by permission of the author./ n. 67, 1992; n. 69, 1993; n. 72, 1993.Copyright © 1992, 1993 Canadian Children's Press. All reproduced by permission.–*Chicago Tribune–Books*, July 30, 1995 for "A Social History of Satan" by Rockwell Gray. Copyright (c) 1995, Chicago Tribune Company. All rights reserved. Reproduced by permission of the author.–*CLA Journal*, v. XXXVI, June, 1993. Copyright (c) 1993 by The College Language Association. Used by permission of The College Language Association.–*Commentary*, v. 69, June, 1980 for "Counter-Church" by Hyam Maccoby. Copyright (c) 1980 by the American Jewish Committee. All rights reserved. Reproduced by permission of the publisher and the author.–*Contemporary Sociology*, v. 21, March, 1992 for a review of "Moral Consciousness and Communicative Action" by Douglas Kellner; v. 22, May, 1994 for a review of "Postmetaphysical Thinking: Philosophical Essays" by William Outhwaite. Copyright (c) 1992, 1994 American Sociological Association. Both reproduced by permission of the publisher and the respective authors.–*Critique*, v. VIII, Fall, 1965; v. XIII, 1971; v. XIX, 1977. Copyright (c) 1965, 1971, 1977 Helen Dwight Reid Educational Foundation. All reproduced with permission of the Helen Dwight Reid Educational Foundation, published by Heldref Publications, 1319 18th Street, NW, Washington, DC 20036-1802.–*Extrapolation*, v. 20, Fall, 1979. Reproduced by permission.–*Fantasy Review*, v. 10, April, 1987 for a review of "The Folk of the Air" by Charles de Lint. Copyright (c) 1987 by Charles de Lint. Reproduced by permission of the author.–*Jewish Social Studies*, v. XXVIII, July, 1966. Copyright (c) 1966 by the Editors of Jewish Social Studies. Reproduced by permission.–*Locus*, v. 31, September, 1993 for a review of "The Inkeeper's Song" by Gary K. Wolfe. Reprinted by permission of the author.–*London Review of Books*, v. 11, December 21, 1985 for "Heavy Sledding" by Chauncey Loomis; v. 12, November 22, 1990 for "The New Restoration" by Onora O'Neill; v. 14, December 19, 1991 for "When the Going Gets Weird" by A. Craig Copetas; v. 15, May 13, 1993 for "Agreeing What's Right" by Peter Dews. All appear here by permission of the *London Review of Books* and the respective authors.–*Los Angeles Times Book Review*, September 11, 1983; June, 1992; December 9, 1996. Copyright (c) 1983, 1992, 1996 *Los Angeles Times*. All reproduced by permission.– *Maclean's Magazine*, v. 103, September 10, 1990. Copyright (c) 1990 by *Maclean's Magazine*. Reproduced by permission.–*Mississippi Quarterly*, v. XXVIII, Spring, 1975. Copyright (c) 1975 Mississippi State University. Reproduced by permission.–*Modern Fiction Studies*, v. XI, Winter, 1965; v. 25, Summer, 1979; v. 35, Winter, 1989. Copyright (c) 1965, 1979, 1989 by Purdue Research Foundation, West Lafayette, IN 47907. All rights reserved. All reproduced by permission of The Johns Hopkins University Press.–*Mythlore*, v. 15, Summer, 1989 for "Innocence and Experience and the Imagination in the World of Peter Beagle" by John Pennington. Reproduced by permission of the author.–*National Review*, v. XL, September 16, 1988. Copyright (c) 1988 by National Review, Inc.

Peter S. Beagle
1939-

(Full name Peter Soyer Beagle) American novelist, novella writer, short story writer, essayist, and screenwriter.

The following entry presents criticism of Beagle's work through 1997. For further information on his life and career, see *CLC,* Volume 7.

INTRODUCTION

Beagle is praised for his ability to develop characters, his use of incongruous humor, and his marriage of traditional fables with modern culture and settings. His novel *The Last Unicorn* (1968) is consistently cited by critics as a masterpiece in the fantasy genre.

Biographical Information

Beagle was born April 20, 1939, in New York City to Simon and Rebecca (Soyer) Beagle, both public school teachers. He grew up in a literary family; his grandfather wrote fantasy stories in Hebrew. Beagle published his first story in *Seventeen* magazine at the age of seventeen. He attended the University of Pittsburgh where he studied creative writing, receiving a B.A. in 1959. In 1960, at the age of twenty-one, he published his first novel, *A Fine and Private Place.* The work earned him critical praise and a Wallace Stegner Creative Writing Fellowship for study at Stanford. In 1964 Beagle married Enid Nordeen and adopted her three children. He described his journey via a motorscooter from New York City to his new home in California in the nonfiction book *I See by My Outfit* (1965). After his 1968 novel *The Last Unicorn,* which garnered great critical attention, Beagle produced no full-length fiction until 1987, when he published *The Folk of the Air.* During this period he published nonfiction articles, reviews, and books as well as a novella, *Lila the Werewolf* (1974). In 1980 he divorced his first wife, and in 1988 he married Padma Hejmadi.

Major Works

While Beagle's nonfiction work has varied in form and subject, his short stories and novels are centered in the fantasy genre. Beagle is particularly known for his placement of fables in contemporary settings, sophisticated character development, and witty dialogue. In *A Fine and Private Place* Beagle explores the issue of consciousness in life and death. The fantasy is about the relationship between a man who, though alive, has given up in life, and two ghosts who re-

gret their deaths. Beagle further develops the theme that true death is accepting the futility of life in his 1963 short story "Come, Lady Death." His novella *Lila the Werewolf* is a gothic fantasy set in New York City. His best known work, *The Last Unicorn,* is a mythopoeic fantasy, a heroic quest romance. The last female unicorn, who few people can recognize, represents imagination in the cynical world. She sets out to free the captive unicorns, falls in love with a prince, and has to kill the Red Bull in order to free the others and regain immortality. The work is both a new style of fantasy and a parody of the old quest romances. Beagle's *Folk of the Air,* a tale of witches and Californians pretending to be medievalists, resurrects the character Farrell from *Lila the Werewolf.* Beagle returns to his earlier theme of the nebulous relationship between life and death in *The Innkeeper's Song* (1993). His most noted works of nonfiction are *The California Feeling* (1969), *American Denim* (1975), and *The Garden of Earthly Delights* (1981). He also wrote the screenplay for the movie *The Dove* (1974) as well as screenplays for various television programs. Beagle received the Mythopoetic Fantasy Award in 1987 and the Locus Award in 1993.

Critical Reception

Critics agree that Beagle is a fantasy writer of distinction. He has been compared to such writers as Lewis Carroll, J. R. R. Tolkien, Hans Christian Andersen, James Branch Cabell, and Robert Nathan. Critics note his preoccupation with the human condition and his optimistic conclusions. David Van Becker, writing about *A Fine and Private Place*, states that numerous "passages illustrate Beagle's concern with the problems of human existence that give his fantasy worlds force and coherence." Raymond M. Olderman points out that *The Last Unicorn* focuses on the wonder and magic of life, in contrast to the works of other writers who focus on the bleaker aspects of existence. In addition, Beagle has been praised for his use of incongruity and humor, particularly within his witty dialogue. David Stevens, for instance, discusses the freshness and skill Beagle demonstrates in the dialogue of the butterfly in *The Last Unicorn*. Critics have noted as well Beagle's ability to merge new fantasy with old fables. Jean Tobin writes: "Beagle manages to give his readers fresh, contemporary versions of both the unicorn myth and the werewolf legend while retaining all the traditional and satisfying familiar elements of each."

PRINCIPAL WORKS

A Fine and Private Place (novel) 1960
I See by My Outfit (travel) 1965
The Last Unicorn (novel) 1968
The California Feeling: A Personal View [with Michael Bry] (essays) 1969
The Dove (screenplay) 1974
Lila the Werewolf (novella) 1974; revised edition, 1976
American Denim: A New Folk Art [with Baron Wolman] (nonfiction) 1975
The Fantasy Worlds of Peter S. Beagle (collection) 1978
The Lord of the Rings, Part One (screenplay) 1978
The Garden of Earthly Delights (nonfiction) 1981
The Last Unicorn (screenplay) 1982
The Folk of the Air (novel) 1987
The Innkeeper's Song (novel) 1993
The Unicorn Sonata (novel) 1996
The Magician of Karakosk, and Others (short stories) 1997

*This collection contains *A Fine and Private Place, The Last Unicorn, Lila the Werewolf,* and "Come, Lady Death."

CRITICISM

Edmund Fuller (review date 5 June 1962)

SOURCE: "Unique Recluse," in *New York Times Book Review,* June 5, 1962.

[*In the review below, Fuller describes* A Fine and Private Place *as imaginative and witty.*]

Peter S. Beagle makes a striking debut on several counts. With the first two paragraphs of *A Fine and Private Place* a style is established, a personality registered. We meet at once a talking raven, who is taking food (baloney) not to the prophet Elijah but to a retiring man named Jonathan Rebeck. This unique recluse had withdrawn in discouragement from a clamorous world some twenty years ago. He has lived ever since in an unattended mausoleum in a corner of Yorkchester, a vast interfaith cemetery in the upper Bronx. The raven has fed him all this while, as it explains, because "Ravens don't feel right without somebody to bring things to."

With the funeral of young Michael Morgan we discover that the dead haunt the cemetery for a time and that Mr. Rebeck has been sensitized by his strange life to the point where he can see and talk with them. Michael had been a disgruntled young history teacher and claims his wife poisoned him: later (through news fetched by the raven) we are able to follow her trial. Added to the cast are Laura, a faintly bitter ghost from a barren life, and Mrs. Klapper, a salty-tongued Bronx widow who, visiting her husband's mausoleum, discovers Mr. Rebeck and becomes a disturbing link to a world long rejected.

The ground rules in Mr. Beagle's conception of the afterlife are that the ghost is a permanent prisoner within the cemetery where the body is buried. This becomes a crucial point in the tender, wraith-like love story that develops between Michael and Laura. A disembodied love, in our literary climate, is about as original as a young man can be. The peculiar restriction becomes a key point in the climax which must not be spoiled by disclosure.

If the merit of the novel is seen early, so is one of its defects. There is a flaw in Mr. Beagle's taste. An occasional strident, inappropriate, irrelevant vulgarism makes one wince when it occurs in the fabric of so deft an artist. This simply has to be forgiven in the hope that it will be outgrown. Also, for all his crisp wit, Mr. Beagle is sentimental—his tenderness deteriorates to that level because his philosophical concept of death is shallow, making it the mere "junkyard" of the world. Yet the ghost of Morgan is forced to a painful self-knowledge somewhat inconsistent with the author's general image of death.

It is not fair to push too hard at the implications of so light a story, though they cannot be ignored. The great thing is that *A Fine and Private Place* has wit, charm and individuality—with a sense of style and structure notable in a first novel. Here is a sample of the author's touch:

> "Alarm clocks were going off in the city now. One after another, sometimes two or three together, they drove their small silver knives into the body of the great dream that sprawled naked on the housetops. Sensual, amiable, and defenseless as it was, it would still take a while to die."

The publishers invoke E.B. White and Robert Nathan in comparison. I think Peter DeVries might be closer. Be that as it may: watch Beagle.

Benedict Riely (review date 24 March 1968)

SOURCE: "The Dragon Has Gout," in *New York Times Book Review,* March 24, 1968, pp. 4, 8.

[*Below, Riely remarks on Beagle's skillful personification of animals in* The Last Unicorn.]

It is nothing to be surprised at that a man whose first novel [*A Fine and Private Place*] began with a raven stealing a sausage and bringing it to a dirty old man (Elijah?) who had lived for 19 years in a cemetery, should now write a novel about the last of the unicorns. The only rope that can hold a unicorn (one of his odd people tells me) is made of fish breath, bird spittle, a woman's beard, the miaowing of a cat, the sinews of a bear and—one thing more—mountain roots. Peter S. Beagle handles that rope as skillfully as a rodeo expert. He has given us a unicorn (female) in whose existence I find it easier to believe than I do in the existence of the fabulous running horse called Santa Claus, who won the English Derby and the Irish Derby in the same year and whom I once actually saw on a misty morning on the Curragh of Kildare.

That raven in the novel *A Fine and Private Place* was no relation to Poe's dismal, one-worded, repetitive bird. Indeed, in a story in which both the living and the dead talked with wisdom and eloquence, the raven was the best talker of them all. Oliver Goldsmith said, to the face of the Great Lexicographer, that if he (Johnson) tried to make fish talk in an apologue, he would make them talk like whales. Peter S. Beagle can make a raven talk marvelously in the style of Jimmy Durante.

The raven has a first cousin, at least, in the blue jay who flits and chatters briefly in *The Last Unicorn*. But the blue jay is a taciturn creature compared with the butterfly who meets the last unicorn when she is setting out to find her vanished brothers and sisters. The butterfly is, of course, the poet. The only reason why he, in a perverted and unknowing world, knows that the unicorn is a unicorn and not merely a white mare is, she sadly concludes, that "somebody once made up a song about unicorns, or a poem." And in a splendid speech the butterfly shows that, unlike some poets, he has carefully read contemporaries and predecessors: "Death takes what man would keep and leaves what man would lose. Blow, wind, and crack your cheeks. I warm my hands before the fire of life and get fourway relief." And so on.

A novel of this sort comes alive and stays alive on bright intensity of imagination, with style as a useful auxiliary. If the imagination is opulent enough the author can even exist without style, and a new myth may be created—as C.S. Lewis has noted in the case of George MacDonald. Now that I think of it, there is in *The Last Unicorn* the magic of living trees as there is in MacDonald's "Phantastes," and Mr. Beagle may have gone to school to the Scottish necromancer and also to the sardonic James Branch Cabell. He has both the opulence of imagination and the mastery of style.

Truth, with a searing double vision, and Purity got in the person of the unicorn, on a quest, through a sodden world, for a lost wonder. I raise my hat—or would if I had one—respectfully and enviously to the man who dreamed up Mommy Fortuna's (Hecate's) circus, where the unicorn is for a time entrapped. The barker cries: "Creatures of night, brought to light." The exhibits include a manticore, with the head of a man, the body of a lion, the tail of a scorpion, "captured at midnight eating werewolves to sweeten its breath"; a dragon (naturally), but a dragon that speaks 70 languages and is subject to gout. There is a satyr, who is really only a crippled ape; and Cerberus with his three heads and a healthy coat of vipers; and a portion of the Midgard serpent; and the frightful Harpy; and Elli, the worst monster of all, otherwise known as Old Age.

Schmendrick the Magician, who goes with the unicorn on her quest, is but a middling performer. But now and then the magic takes over, and sets him to do the most wonderful things. In the camp of Captain Cully of the Greenwood, Schmendrick—in a moment of sacred possession—brings back to earth Robin Hood and his men.

Which is the myth? Which is the reality? Captain Cully is a genial devil who has given thought to his public image, and written his own ballads about himself to insure himself a place in Child's famous ballad collection. He lived too early to be influenced by Alan Lomax. The guest goes on to meet King Haggard, a Grandet as big as Balzac, and the Red Bull who could have been sired by an animal from a place called Cooley.

If you're interested in unicorns—and who in his or her sane senses isn't?—this is your book. And as Schmendrick says to Molly Grue, who goes with him and the unicorn from the camp of Captain Cully:

"Haven't you ever been in a fairytale before?"

Granville Hicks (review date 30 March 1968)

SOURCE: "Of Wasteland, Fun Land and War," in *Saturday Review,* March 30, 1968, pp. 21-2.

[*In the following excerpt, Hicks argues that* The Last Unicorn *is a fable about imagination and the artist.*]

Peter Beagle's *The Last Unicorn* is frankly a fantasy, as was his first novel, *A Fine and Private Place*, which was published in the year he became twenty-one. (In the interval he brought out an unusual and amusing account of a transcontinental trip by motorscooter, *I See By My Outfit.*)

In the new novel the unicorn, learning from the talk of hunters that she may be the last of her species, sets out to discover what has happened to the others. En route she is captured by members of Mommy Fortuna's Midnight Carnival, and then freed by a melancholy magician named Schmendrick. She and the magician, who joins her in her search for King Haggard and the Red Bull, encounter a fifthrate Robin Hood, Captain Cully, and add to their party one of his followers, Molly Grue, who has recognized the unicorn. They come to King Haggard's barren country and to the city of Hagsgate, which, by exception and for sinister reasons, prospers. When the unicorn is attacked by the Red Bull, Schmendrick—who has begun to suspect that he may be a real magician after all—saves her by giving her a human form. Prince Lír falls in love with her in this form, and there are numerous complications before the unicorn frees all the other unicorns from the Red Bull.

It is a fable, of course, as well as a fantasy. The unicorn is a symbol of the imagination, and King Haggard's country is an image of a world in which the imagination has been destroyed, a wasteland. Schmendrick represents the artist; recognizing his failures, he learns that the power he craves comes and goes according to its own laws and is not under his control. Mommy Fortuna's Midnight Carnival, which raises profound questions about illusion and reality, is a place most of us have visited in our dreams.

Further interpretations are possible, but to me the fantasy is what counts. As he has shown before, Beagle has extraordinary inventive powers, and they make page after page a delight. Early on, for example, the unicorn is greeted by a butterfly who identifies himself as "a roving gambler." He says, "Death takes what man would keep, and leaves what

man would lose. Blow, wind, and crack your cheeks. I warm my hands before the fire of life and get four-way relief." Telling her about the Red Bull, he advises: "Let nothing you dismay; but don't be half-safe," and when he starts to leave, he says politely, "I must take the A train."

Captain Cully, who, as he tells Schmendrick, has had thirty-one ballads written about him, is desolate because none of them is included in Child's *English and Scottish Popular Ballads.* When they meet Prince Lír, Schmendrick is relieved, because now he is certain that they are operating in a proper fairy story, and the prince, falling in love with Lady Amalthea, the disguised unicorn, kills five dragons, vanquishes fifteen black knights, destroys witches, giants, and demons, "not to mention the winged horses, the basilisks and sea serpents, and all the rest of the livestock." There is less facetiousness as the story moves to its end, but there is considerable humor even in the midst of lively drama.

The book is rich not only in comic bits but also in passages of uncommon beauty. Beagle is a true magician with words, a master of prose and a deft practitioner in verse. He has been compared, not unreasonably, with Lewis Carroll and J.R.R. Tolkien, but he stands squarely and triumphantly on his own feet.

David Van Becker (essay date February 1975)

SOURCE: "Time, Space & Consciousness in the Fantasy of Peter S. Beagle," in *San Jose Studies,* Vol. 1, No. 1, February 1975, pp. 52-61.

[*In the following essay, Becker explores Beagle's manipulation of time and space.*]

In Peter Beagle's first novel, *A Fine and Private Place*, Jonathan Rebeck, the hero, has lived surreptitiously in a New York cemetery for nineteen years, aided by a talking raven who steals food for him from local stores. Rebeck would rather be dead, like the ghosts he talks with until they forget and fade from life. The kind and sociable Rebeck has become a reluctant teacher of the newly dead; he tells the ghosts Michael and Laura: "You'll drowse. . . . In time sleep won't mean anything to you. . . . it won't really matter." But Michael, a suicide who values life now that his is over, rejects the somnolent peace of Rebeck's art of dying, and he tells Laura to fight back—as he does—to remember the feeling of being alive: "Caring about things is much more important to the dead because it's all they have to keep them conscious. Without it they fade, dwindle, thin to the texture of a whisper. The same thing happens to people, but nobody notices it because their bodies act as masks. The dead have no masks."

These passages illustrate Beagle's concern with the problems of human existence that give his fantasy worlds force and coherence, but they do not fully convey the comic, inventive and richly particular texture of his writing. Nor do they fully reveal the ironic nature of Beagle's fantasy, which involves the reader's consciousness of space and time, of the real and the imaginary in fiction. Both *A Fine and Private Place* (published in 1960, the year Beagle turned twenty-one) and *The Last Unicorn* (1968) have talking animals as characters. But the animals are not merely delights of fantasy; they are the fantasist's technique for exploring the nature of reality in the modern world. The raven who brings Rebeck food, for instance, is a testy and tough-talking pragmatist, whose contempt for illusion is modified only by his need to preserve dignity. After grouchily delivering Rebeck a whole baloney, he says, "There are people . . . who give and people who take. . . . Ravens don't feel right without somebody to bring things to. . . . You think we brought Elijah food because we like him? He was a dirty old man with a beard."

In the first chapter of *The Last Unicorn*, the Unicorn leaves her forest of eternal spring to search for others like herself: she meets a butterfly, who says, "I am a roving gambler. How do you do?" From this zany acquaintance she gets the first help in her quest. The butterfly's disjointed conversation flutters with snatches of poetry, popular songs, and commercial slogans: "The sweet and bitter fool will presently appear. Christ, that my love were in my arms, and I in my bed again. . . . You can find your people if you are brave. . . . Let nothing you dismay, but don't be half-safe."

The raven and the butterfly are both traditional talking animals of fantasy and eccentrics like many of the helpers met by the heroes of folktales. But they simultaneously undercut the fiction, for their language in part refers not to the internal world of the story, but to some real context outside of it. The raven functions throughout *A Fine and Private Place* as a link between the cemetery and the "real" New York surrounding it; he also shows the limits of the fantasy in action, for he constantly opposes to the wishes and dreams of the other characters the indifference of the outside world. His last words in the story are to Rebeck, who is trying to avoid a difficult commitment: "Don't come sniffing around me, friend. I don't make decisions. I'm a bird."

The butterfly has a smaller but essential part at the beginning of *The Last Unicorn*. While providing a clue in the fairy-tale mystery of the vanished unicorns, his jumbled quotations refer to places and times outside the fantasy context and jar the reader into a complex participation in the fiction. This magical messenger, who says good-by by announcing politely, "I must take the A train," shifts us from the medieval fairy-tale world into our own memories and experiences. This anachronism not only creates irony and humor in the fantasy but tends to blur the distinction between the "reality" of everyday experience and the "illusion" of a story.

"What is reality?" I had written this absurd and important question while making notes before my conversation with Peter Beagle; when at one point I showed it to him, he said "O my God" in a soft voice of dismay (later he would say, "I have very little didact in me"). But he continued,

> . . . the thing that interests me most is the line between fantasy and realism, because they're both so arbitrary. The books I like always seem to shimmer back and forth between one and the other. And many books that are presented as realistic novels I find utterly fantastic, and a lot of books that are listed as fantasy seem very normal to me. . . .

Perhaps in an attempt to comprehend the line dividing them, Peter Beagle has moved back and forth between fantasy and realism as his writing has proceeded. After *A Fine and Private Place*—which he described as "a fantasy in a realistic setting"—he wrote *I See By My Outfit* (1964), a factual and wryly comic personal narrative of a trip from New York to California by motor scooter. He had previously published **"Come Lady Death"** in *The Atlantic Monthly* (1963), an exquisitely realized fantasy-parable set in eighteenth-century London. From 1964 to 1968 while working on his best-known book, the fairy-tale novel *The Last Unicorn*, Beagle was the chief book reviewer of *Holiday*. At the same time he was writing articles for other magazines, among them several frank and loving essays on family life and animals, as well as **"Cockfight,"** a realistic and sympathetic account of this sport and its fans in northern California. In 1967, when *Unicorn* was two-thirds finished, he and photographer Michael Bry began traveling, taking pictures and writing *The California Feeling: A Personal View* (1969), a series of essay-narratives with many beautiful and revealing photographs of the state's different regions and lifestyles. Since 1969 Beagle has written television and film scripts (including *The Dove*, a British film directed by Gregory Peck), *Lila the Werewolf*, a gothic fantasy novella set in modern New York, and a new novel, completed last summer and awaiting publication.

This variety of work has caused Beagle to feel uncomfortable at times about being classified as a writer of fantasy. I asked him about the domination of contemporary fiction by realism—"the great tradition" of critic F.R. Leavis:

> Well, that's where it was going in 1960 when I started publishing. It's always impressed me that I got reviewed as a serious novelist. . . . Because in

1960 when literature was so much in the grip of Leavis and Hemingway, I could so easily have been thrown into the back of the book with forty science fiction novelists that get reviewed about once a month by somebody who doesn't like science fiction. And the thing I like about 1974 is that all kinds of strange stuff is coming out that is not necessarily catagorizeable as pulp fiction or science fiction. . . . I don't know where literature is going anymore . . . but I am a lot more interested in the possibilities and the options for a young writer than I was in 1960. I just wrote fantasies because that was the way I thought, but I never expected to have even as much success as I've had. Fantasy writers didn't.

Although the critical categories seem to be breaking down, critics still make comparisons; Granville Hicks, writing about *The Last Unicorn* in *Saturday Review,* said Peter Beagle "stands squarely and triumphantly on his own feet," in the realm of fantasy, but Hicks also made the inevitable comparison to J.R.R. Tolkien and Lewis Carroll, a comparison reiterated on the back cover of the Dutch translation of *The Last Unicorn.* Later we were talking about the writers he felt close to. Beagle admires the Irish fantasist James Stephens and, especially, Joyce Cary. He continued:

> . . . Tolkien is not an influence of mine in fantasy, but I know he's there.

> *Question:* Do you like Peake? [Mervyn Peake, British writer and artist, author of the fantasy-epic *The Gormenghast Trilogy.*]

> *Beagle:* I like Peake a lot. . . . I'm probably closer to Peake than Tolkien. . . .

Once in a while you really know when someone is working your side of the street. . . . It's like reading the novelist Bulgakov. I read *The Master and Margarita* and there was this shiver of recognition. We're not doing the same thing; he's crazier than I am. . . .

When I first read reviews of *The Magus*—I respect John Fowles a lot, and I got a very unhappy feeling, damn it . . . he's in my territory and he has a very good mind and he's probably doing it very well. And I read *The Magus* and, no, that's not it. He blew it. . . . I didn't know whether I was relieved or unhappy. . . . Robert Nathan said in a letter . . . that he really had managed to call up the old gods, and then he backed off and explained them as rabbits out of a hat, and you can't do that.

Beagle regrets that Robert Nathan no longer receives the recognition he had in the early 1940's when *Portrait of Jenny* was translated into eight languages and made into a movie. Between 1919 and 1967 Nathan was, he said, "one of my great influences when I was in high school and college. . . . So when I started writing *A Fine and Private Place* I was taking off almost directly from Nathan's work." In *The California Feeling* he wrote, "I have learned important things from him—or at least started to learn them . . . such things as leanness and control. . . . Other writers have learned the same things from Hemingway or from Chekhov."

Another thing Beagle learned from Nathan—or more likely shared with him—was a way of perceiving, so that to him, "Certain things that seem unlikely or unnatural to other people seem very natural . . . and other things that seem very normal and daily for most people seem incredibly strange and fictional." Beagle especially admires in Robert Nathan the older writer's ability to "wander around in time."

> He's the only man I know of really who could effortlessly have a man on an airplane forced down in the Jordanian desert and have him aided . . . by a girl who may or may not be Merlin's Nimue, or she may be just a nice hippie girl he met at Stonehenge playing the guitar.

This concern with time, both as a dimension of human action and culture and as a fictional dimension to be explored flexibly in the consciousness of his characters and the awareness of the reader, is a central fact in Peter Beagle's fantasy. It reflects his awareness of himself:

> I was very conscious of time slips because having always felt—in a very vague kind of way—not out of any one particular time, just out of sync, out of place. I'm learning to live with it, actually to make a career out of it.

Peter Beagle's sense of temporal dislocation has been sharpened by his living in and writing about California. At the beginning of *The California Feeling* he wrote:

> A lot of the time, I don't even like the place. I don't like the politics, and I don't like the values behind the politics, and I don't like what's being done to the sky and the land and the water; and what I really don't like is that sense of having gotten here *almost* too late. . . . This is the California feeling, and . . . Juan Rodriquez Cabrillo, Joaquin Murietta, and John Muir undoubtedly suffered from it too. . . . But I came here from New York City, where you grow up knowing that there never was a golden time, that there was nothing to be too late for.

Beagle's portrait of his adopted state—like Michael Bry's fine photographs—alternates between and juxtaposes the past and the present: Gold Rush towns, the Monterey Jazz Festival, the Russian Fort Ross, Berkeley's student movements, the high Sierra, Caesar Chavez at Delano. This California feeling is a sense of beauty and of loss, of better yesterdays, just-missed possibilities, the end of the Frontier. The sad chapter on Los Angeles and Disneyland shows the end of the American dream in the banality of future shock.

But Beagle likes much of what is here, old and new. *The California Feeling* is the best portrait of California in the Sixties I expect to see. Giving a wealth of information on the many regions he visits, he talks to contemporary people against a past becoming legend. He sees compassionately and simultaneously the old lumberjacks and the new consciousness of the counter-culture, the Esalin Institute and Hearst Castle. Beagle here is something like one of his characters, whom he called "a collector of lost things." He has an unlikely sympathy for the baron of San Simeon, with his huge and miscellaneous collection of European art, because he "really tried . . . to incorporate it *all* into his own life." If we are too late for legend, there is still much worth keeping, like the seacoast north of Santa Cruz, a region pictured in a recent book for which Beagle wrote the introduction.

Legend is the common ground of fantasy writers of the present and mythmakers and poets of the past. Since the eighteenth century most writers in the "great tradition" of modern fiction have given up their claim in this older territory and have sought universal patterns in the structure of ordinary experience. The worlds of modern legendary fantasy have definite environments with their own history; C.S. Lewis calls his children's series the *Chronicles of Narnia,* and Tolkien's world parallels a mythical Middle-Earth to the prehistoric age of giants. Peake's rambling and ritualized castle has existed for seventy-seven generations. Such fantasy worlds usually have uniform natural laws and formal ethical and social structures—a code of fairyland that is essentially conservative and similar to the rules of Christian chivalry and courtly love which dominate the legendary fantasy of medieval romance. These closed worlds of legendary fantasy may be remote, but they also reflect the era of their creation: as several reviewers have observed, Tolkien's Hobbits are legendary fantasy versions of the conservative and rural British middle and working classes. They succeed in their exploits by muddling through with rather dull and virtuous perseverance, like the characters of John Buchan, who prosaically emerge from the same Edwardian ethos. The Oz books of L. Frank Baum were long suspect partly because he purposely ignored traditional legends and created a middle American agrarian fantasy utopia ruled by P.T. Barnum. Legendary fantasy is a once-upon-a-time folktale elaborated geographically and historically; it shades into saga and historical romance. In modern versions it often projects into the future perfect of science fiction or the past horrific of the gothic novel.

The complex sense of time in modern fiction may well have its origin in the gothic, in which a modern consciousness responds to terror out of the past, the return of the dead. Time shifts in most science fiction or fantasy are mere devices for arriving at another fictive world, like the convention of the dream vision. Only a few modern writers, such as Mark Twain and Virginia Woolf, use time in the structure of their fiction satirically or thematically. Peter Beagle's manipulation of time in fantasy goes beyond technique and becomes the means for defining states of human consciousness, will, and value. As his writing has matured, the idea of time has become increasingly important and has been used with increasing flexibility as he developed his ironic and sadly comic view of human character and fate. *A Fine and Private Place* presents a modern analog to a traditional folk tale theme, where the hero is suspended out of time, like Odysseus or Rip Van Winkle. Jonathan Rebeck voluntarily enters the cemetery where time stands still; like the ghosts, he is fading from life, rejecting involvement: "I don't want to be loved; it's a burden on me." Beagle's resolution complements his ironic and wistfully comic treatment of the theme; Rebeck is retrieved into the world of living time by the stout and warm-hearted widow Gertrude Klapper, the very opposite of the coy mistress implied by his title. The ghost of her husband helps Rebeck make up his mind: "You are a living man and you have deceived yourself. For a man there is no choice between worlds. There never was."

In *The Last Unicorn* the theme of time is pervasive, and it underlies a fantasy narration of rapid action and detailed characters. The setting is vaguely late medieval, and the story has a indefinite legendary framework: "I was deliberately taking the classic fairy tale structure, the classic fairy tale characters," Beagle told me, "and trying to do something else with them. I was saddling myself and aiding myself both with all the proper forms." But we see the "proper forms" of the traditional quest plot from many points of view at once, not only in the ironic inversions and multiple time-references within the story, but in the shifting of the reader's consciousness during fairy tale event, twentieth-century dialogue, ironic parody, and ingeniously relevant literary anachronisms. The Unicorn, an ingenue goddess whom most humans take to be a white mare, escapes from Mommy Fortuna's seedy Midnight Carnival—a traveling circus of sadly real animals, mythological monsters, and one true harpy. With Schmendrick, a schlemeil Mandrake who has been flunked out as a sorcerer's apprentice and cursed by his master with eternal youth, the Unicorn seeks King Haggard and the mysterious Red Bull, who holds the other unicorns captive in a wasteland where time stands still.

Schmendrick ("last of the red hot swamis") is captured by the scruffy brigand Captain Cully, whose band is a pathetic parody of Robin Hood's. Cully fabricates limping ballads of his exploits and hopes they will be collected by Professor Child (a real nineteenth-century ballad scholar). Schmendrick is forced to entertain the bandits, but his skills are comically inaccurate and trivial, disappointing his audience and himself. But at a crucial moment of frustrated anger he gives himself up to the magic and unknowingly calls up the real Robin Hood and his Merry Men, who silently and powerfully cross the clearing. The magician presents to the ragged company the images of their deepest desires. Their wild yearning is the distance between their fallen state and their ideal possibilities. This episode presents at once the real and the imaginary—the fictional present, the legendary past, the reader's memory, and true and false magic.

Here as elsewhere in Beagle's writing, the characters remain true to the story, but they are intelligent and self-conscious, and their speech constantly threatens the fictional framework. At a moment of decision in *The Last Unicorn,* when the Unicorn wants to keep her mortal human form and give up the quest, her lover Prince Lir says: "No. . . . the true secret of a hero lies in knowing the order of things. . . . The happy ending cannot come in the middle of the story." And near the end of the book, when the now King Lir rides homeward, Schmendrick says, "Great heroes need great sorrows and burdens, or half their greatness goes unnoticed. It is all part of the fairy tale."

Lila the Werewolf (1974), Peter Beagle's most recent story, is not a fairy tale at all, but a low-key novella set in New York with a deceptively straightforward opening:

> Lila Braun had been living with Farrell for three weeks before he found out she was a werewolf. They had met at a party when the moon was a few nights past the full. . . . Girls sometimes happened to Farrell like that.

Lila's psychobiological atavism is as inexorable as the moon: "First day, cramps; the second day, this. My introduction to womanhood." Lila "made a handsome wolf: tall and broad-chested . . . her coat was dark brown, showing red in the proper light." She kills only zoo animals and dogs, and is being treated by a psychiatrist. Farrell, "whose true gift was for acceptance," tells his friend Ben,

> If I break up with her now, she'll think I'm doing it because she's a werewolf. It's awkward, it feels nasty and middle class. . . . I don't want to mess up anyone's analysis. That's a sin against God.

But Farrell's complacency is shaken, and the story's naturalistic style (which reflects a viewpoint close to Farrell's) gives way to almost dream-like impressionism at the end in a nightmare chase all over Manhattan: Lila—pursued by Farrell, a loving dog-pack, her possessive mother, and a crazed Lithuanian building superintendent shooting silver bullets—barely escapes.

Lila comes close to uniting the realistic and fantastic tendencies in Peter Beagle's writing: in it, unknown but natural forces produce monstrosities of appearance or action, the inevitable intrusions of everyday life. But everything can be either accepted or ignored—as Farrell says, "Who wants to know what people turn into?" Lila's transformations of shape and time, her monthly reversions to a bloody past, are only more spectacular than Farrell's springtime changes of girl friends and his repetitive and inauthentic behavior towards them: "It's the same old mistake, except this time the girl's hangup is different. I'm doing it again." The uninvolved hero is stuck in time as much as Lila is, and his acceptance of her monstrosity is a reflection of his own; his self-awareness brings the world of fantasy closer to our own.

In one sense *Lila the Werewolf* is a study for Beagle's forthcoming novel, in which Farrell and Ben are major characters about ten years older. I asked him about the book, and he began with his character:

> Weird things happen to Farrell. . . . In this particular case he gets involved with a group of people who spend a great deal of their time reenacting the Middle Ages. . . . They are based on existing groups. And they make their own weapons, their own armour. . . . They have a hierarchy . . . a king chosen by armed combat. I saw a group like this, knew a few people in it, and began wondering what would happen if this got out of hand. . . . Farrell, in this incarnation, is a lute player. . . .

> And it has something to do with a hunger for old things. Farrell was a collector of lost things, doomed buildings, extinct species of animals. . . . The lute . . . has been his attempt at finding his way back. . . . He gets . . . into this league and becomes their minstrel.

The story, as it came out in our conversation, is a complex one, with conflicts within the league, murders of its members, and a series of notable characters: a fifteen-year-old witch who tries to control time, a teacher of medieval martial arts with an apocalyptic vision of personal violence, a goddess more powerful than the witch, and Farrell's girl friend Julie. While the league attempts to live back in the Middle Ages, identities from the past begin to inhabit Farrell's and Ben's bodies: Farrell begins to have the memories and dreams of a Provencal knight minstrel, and Ben becomes a ninth-century Viking. Time is only a state of consciousness, a context that might happen to any of us. The falconer of the league tells Farrell about it, Beagle told me, like this:

> 'I flip the falcon off my wrist and . . . she goes from my wrist, which is the real world, into her own world with the air and the sky. . . . It could be 100,000 years ago . . . where it's still very dark and scary under the trees and . . . civilization hasn't happened yet.' And he tries to explain to Farrell how close past, present, and future are.

Farrell and Ben help each other get straightened out in time at the end of the book, which is what happens to most people in Beagle's fiction. In previous stories, a character's spiritual nature was often revealed by his fantasy form or change: the transparency of ghosts, the brightness of the Unicorn's horn, and Lila's transformations indicate states of the psyche. The boyish and fumbling Schmendrick, for instance, is transformed into a "lean and lordly" magus after his mystic experience of compassion. Just as important are the changes in time: the unicorn's experience in mortality as a beautiful girl made her a sadder, wiser, and more powerful goddess on her return to the artifice of eternity. Jonathan Rebeck, Schmendrick, and Haggard's wasteland are all suspended in time until they are brought back into natural history.

Being somehow disoriented in time is the usual situation for most major characters at the beginning of Beagle's stories: they are not where they should be (or not when they should be); they seem alone, lost, powerless, or defeated. Rebeck, the ghosts, Mrs. Klapper, Schmendrick, Molly Grue, the Unicorn, Prince Lir, Lila, Farrell—all undervalue themselves, all are better than they seem. They are eirons, like the clever or virtuous heroes of traditional comedy who win at the end. When they realize their true nature, they are in tune with their proper time and have their proper shape.

Beagle's novels generally have happy endings in which the internal discrepancies are resolved. But the self-consciousness of his characters about their fictional roles and the anachronism of the frequent references outside the story maintain the ironies, at once isolating the fantasy world and drawing the reader closer to it. "We are in a fairy tale and must go where it goes"; "Robin and Marian are real, and we are the legend"; "The universe lies to our senses, and they lie to us, and how can we be anything but liars?" By such speeches the characters stimulate and echo our doubts about reality. The synchronicity of times and the simultaneity of the fabulous, the fictionally real, and our own actual memories keep us shimmering between scepticism and belief, comedy and compassion. We become aware of our imaginative possibilities.

The way to reconcile these ambiguities is magic. Within fantasy, the miracle worker transcends himself by hazarding everything: "Real magic can never be made by offering up someone else's liver," the Unicorn tells Mommy Fortuna. "You must tear out your own, and not expect to get it back."

The magician is impelled, as Beagle put it, by "a kind of hunger that casts out fear." Such hunger works for the writer, too:

> The nearest thing I have ever seen to magic, to witchcraft, is exactly that. And I've practiced it in the sense that I wanted more than anything to be a writer, and I didn't really care what I had to sacrifice in order to get that. As it happens I remained reasonably sane and turned out to have more of a capacity for real life than I expected. . . .

In the real working life of a writer, this creative power is related to craft, but goes beyond it: "language makes a good deal of my stories happen," he said, "which is why I can't plan too well." And the readiness is all, he explained:

> . . . on a good day you tap into something very strange. . . . There were a couple of scenes in the new novel . . . that I "heard" while I was doing something like washing the dishes. . . . I didn't know who was in them or who was talking but I heard the voices. Harold Pinter talks like that and . . . now I've come to believe him. . . .

> Much of what I do is craft. . . But every so often I just have to fall back on something that can be called . . . the unconscious, the universal, whatever, and that. . . I call the swamp. And it just belches out characters I've never met, things that never happened to me. . . . I've come to accept it and even to call on it on occasion.

"Much of what I do is craft." Beyond the swamp is Beagle's love of language, style, music, and structure. Much of the fantasy-interest and the irony in *The Last Unicorn* comes from its epigrammatic dialogue, songs, allusions, and prophecies, and the cross-references among them—the same aspects which gave the fairy tale its depth and solidity. Although Beagle said he did not plan well, *Unicorn* proves the contrary with its deftly arranged and interconnected incidents and its characters related to each other within a family of destiny. His stories exemplify his statement to me that good writing looks like Joe DiMaggio's effortless catch of a fly ball that someone else couldn't even get to.

Craft and the swamp, discipline and magic—Peter Beagle rightly sees himself as a traditional storyteller, "a descendant of Scheherazade . . . a long line of people who made up stories in the bazaar." For the singer of tales, the mythic figures and the fantasy magic—like the Muse who called it forth—are ways of describing the forces that transform human life. Within Beagle's fantasy worlds, the key to magic and to power over time and space is a quality of will: the ghosts' love beyond death, the Unicorns' willingness to risk all, Schmendrick's boundless compassion. But this "hunger that casts out fear" must be put in tune with time; will must result in timely and appropriate action.

The negative of magic is "the wanting of nothingness," the "willessness" Beagle found in the characters of John Barth, whose books he reviewed some years ago. The cemetery hermit Rebeck, the fading ghosts, and Farrell in different ways share this non-involvement, a paralysis of the will. The bored and weary King Haggard's "greed without desire" is an extreme form of what Beagle called the "life-denying or life-avoiding thing." These figures are all suspended in time in their stories, cast out of their own history.

The magic of self-realization and harmony with the tempo and myth of one's life has its costs even in fantasy. Beagle's stories often end for his characters in a sad and comic blend of triumph and regret, and for the reader in an ironic recognition of the evanescence of fantasy and the complexity of his own imaginative responses. Beagle's fantasy speaks to the modern reader aware of relativity, the vast unconsciousness within and without, the renaissance of myth, the community of man and environment, the irony of history. Marianne Moore said poetry gives us imaginary gardens with real toads in them. Peter Beagle gives us imaginary times and places with real characters who reflect ourselves. And some of us are unicorns.

Don Parry Norford (essay date 1977)

SOURCE: "Reality and Illusion in Peter Beagle's *The Last Unicorn*," in *Critique,* Vol. XIX, No. 2, 1977, pp. 93-104.

[*In the following essay, Norford discusses the symbolism of the characters in* The Last Unicorn.]

A cheeky and didactic squirrel in Peter S. Beagle's *A Fine and Private Place* (1960) tells the cynical raven that "there is poetry in the meanest of lives, and if we leave it unsought we leave ourselves unrealized. A life without food, without shelter, without love, a life lived in the rain—this is nothing beside a life without poetry." He is so preachy that one sympathizes with the weary raven: "If I was a hawk, I'd eat you in two bites." Beagle is much more subtle and complex in *The Last Unicorn* (1968), but the theme is the same: "the main message of the allegory is that there is magic in being human." The symbol of the magic is the unicorn, who is "the

dream we have forgotten how to see, the thing whose absence makes our world a waste land; she is renewal and rebirth, the lost fertility and potency of life."

Significantly, the unicorn, in her mortal form as the Lady Amalthea, inspires Prince Lir to write poetry: she is what Jung calls an anima figure, the eternal feminine that leads us on into art as well as life. In *The Last Unicorn* magic and poetry are closely related. The outlaw, Captain Cully, writes ballads about himself which he hopes will be collected by Child, to raise his tawdry and lying life to the reality of a Robin Hood; to become a legend, to have one's life become poetry, is to achieve a form of immortality, to transform a true life of lies into what Octavio Paz has called the "lying life of truths." Although Cully pretends to be Robin Hood, he will not acknowledge the "real" Robin whom Schmendrick conjures up: "It was a lie, like all magic! There is no such person as Robin Hood!" Molly Grue, however, like the rest of Cully's band, runs after Robin and his men, thirsting for the true, the real: "'Nay, Cully, you have it backward,' she called to him. 'There's no such a person as you, or me, or any of us. Robin and Marian are real, and we are the legend'." In Keats's terms, then, beauty is truth, truth beauty. Poetry is more real than life—and yet at the same time a magical evocation or illusion; just as our life is real, or true, yet also false—a constant betrayal of ourselves, our deepest hopes, convictions, and potentialities.

Though the unicorn inspires poetry and may even symbolize what might popularly be called the beauty and poetry of life, she herself, before her experience of mortality, is as cold and aloof, as remote from human passion, as the attic figures on Keats's Grecian urn. Alone in her lilac wood, indifferent to time and the round of birth and death, she lives in a cold pastoral that is yet a friend to man, the source of enchantment in the world. As in Keats, a strange kinship exists between cold pastoral and warm, breathing human imperfection. Perhaps for this reason the aging and bitter Molly Grue enjoys a special intimacy with the unicorn. The jealous Schmendrick asserts that "Unicorns are for beginnings . . . for innocence and purity, for newness. Unicorns are for young girls." To which Molly replies, "You don't know much about unicorns." Poetry is immortal, yet its raison d'etre is love, suffering, and death. Early in the novel the unicorn meets a rakish butterfly who seems in some ways like the squirrel of *A Fine and Private Place*. This flighty, spacy butterfly, who evidently was once a bookworm, quotes indiscriminately snatches of poetry, songs, slogans, and commercials, confusing past and present, the sublime and the ridiculous. In contrast to the immortal unicorn, the butterfly seems to symbolize Time, who has a wallet at his back wherein he puts alms for oblivion, jumbling everything together regardless of quality. A butterfly is a creature of a day, transient, ephemeral. As the unicorn says, "All they know are songs and poetry, and anything else they hear. They mean well, but they can't keep things straight. And why should they? They die so soon." Here poetry, of which the unicorn seems rather contemptuous, is related to the vulgar and tawdry, to time and death. The butterfly episode suggests that poetry is found in the ruins of time, in the meanest of lives, something the unicorn is as yet unable to appreciate.

Later on, when the unicorn finally drives the Red Bull into the sea, "her horn was light again, burning and shivering like a butterfly." Before her experience as a mortal girl, her horn remained dark, and she fled from the Red Bull: as merely immortal she could not defeat him. But as a woman she loses her magical beauty, begins to fall in love, and therefore becomes subject to time. As Haggard says, "I will catch you at last if you love much more." Only when Prince Lir throws himself in front of the charging bull in an attempt to save her and is trampled to death does the unicorn achieve the power to defeat the bull. Letting out "an ugly, squawking wail of sorrow and loss and rage, such as no immortal creature ever gave," she charges, her horn lighting up like a butterfly, and she paradoxically triumphs over the dark power of time with which the Red Bull is associated. Earlier, just after she had been transformed into a girl and could feel her body rotting all around her, she cried "How can anything that is going to die be real? How can it be truly beautiful?" Schmendrick corrects her: "Whatever can die is beautiful—more beautiful than a unicorn, who lives forever, and who is the most beautiful creature in the world." We shall see that his statement implies the interdependence of such opposites as reality and illusion, eternity and time, life and death. The truth of one does not negate, but paradoxically affirms, the equal truth of the other. But let us now examine the significance of Mommy Fortuna, King Haggard, and the Red Bull.

The problem of what is real is closely connected in the novel with the question of time. Surely, one definition of "real" is what endures, what transcends the vicissitudes of time. In Plato's allegory of the cave, the sense world is compared to a cave of flickering illusions: reality is found only in the sunlit world of the intelligential, which is always the same. Two of Cully's outlaws, returning disillusioned from their pursuit of Robin Hood, express a Platonic pessimism about the possibility of knowledge in the phenomenal world, complaining about the deceitfulness of the senses: "The universe lies to our senses, and they lie to us, and how can we ourselves be anything but liars? For myself, I trust neither message nor messenger; neither what I am told, nor what I see. There may be truth somewhere, but it never gets down to me." Mommy Fortuna, as her name suggests, seems to be the presiding deity of the network of illusion that makes up this world. Like the medieval goddess Fortuna, she is associated with the irrational whirls of the wheel of fortune, which raises up and throws down indiscriminately: "Here is there, and high is low; / All may be undone. / What is true, no two men know— / What is gone is gone." Mommy Fortuna, imper-

sonating the Norse deity Elli—Old Age—sings this haunting song, a song indeed of disillusioned old age—of time and mortality. Nothing remains the same; all things are in flux. Young girls "never become anything more than silly old women."

King Haggard, the male counterpart of Mommy Fortuna, has known all the pleasures of life, yet they have not made him happy because they are ephemeral: what is gone is gone. Thus he takes a perverse pleasure in doing without pleasure. One of his serving men recounts Haggard's hatred for good food: "'It is an illusion,' says he, 'and an expense. Live as I do, undeceived'." Later Haggard tells the Lady Amalthea, "But I always knew that nothing was worth the investment of my heart, because nothing lasts, and I was right, and so I was always old." Likewise, the villagers of Hagsgate, though blooming and prosperous, cannot delight in their good fortune, knowing it will end. Drinn tells Schmendrick that because of the curse they have not taken a moment's joy in their wealth—"or in anything else—for joy is just one more thing to lose." For all these people, particularly Haggard, joy and beauty are illusions; like the unicorn they associate the real with the enduring

If, then, the universe lies to our senses, if nothing is what it seems, how can we be anything but liars? If nothing is true, then we must be content with falsehood. Thus Haggard dismisses his real magician, Mabruk, and hires the inept Schmendrick. Even Mommy Fortuna has had to settle for the "homemade horrors" of the Midnight Carnival because she cannot be a real witch. Like Captain Cully, she leads a false life, longing for the true; and so also does Schmendrick, who performs cheap tricks while awaiting the birth of his true power as a magician. Since in this lying world people can understand only lies, they cannot see the unicorn, mistaking her for a white mare. When Mommy Fortuna captures the unicorn, she must cast a spell of illusion upon her so that, paradoxically, people will recognize the unicorn as real: "These days, it takes a cheap carnival witch to make folk recognize a real unicorn."

The gulls who gawk at Mommy Fortuna's Midnight Carnival, confusing the true and the false, substance and shadow, resemble the prisoners in Plato's cave. At first glance these spectators seem a contrast to Haggard, who tries to live without illusions. Yet Haggard also thinks that time is real and so is bound by the illusions of *maya*. Like Elli he seems the personification of Old Age. Mommy Fortuna, whose other name is Elli, may be the Mistress of Illusion, the Goddess *Maya,* the maternal power who spins the web of world illusion by which men perceive the material world as real. Because they are ignorant of the true nature of reality, visitors to the Midnight Carnival mistake poor mangy animals for mythical monstrosities, who may symbolize apocalyptic dreams of bliss or horror sprung from the oppression of mortality. The monsters satisfy the craving for wonder, even if in a perverted way.

Thus as Schmendrick says, "Belief makes all the difference to magic like Mommy Fortuna's. Why, if that troop of witlings withdrew their wonder, there'd be nothing left of all her witchery but the sound of a spider weeping." Schmendrick is speaking specifically of the spider, Arachne, who is different from the other animals in the carnival because she believes in the illusion which Mommy Fortuna projects upon her web, believes that her web is of cosmic dimensions, holding the world together. The spectators wonder at her web, "which was like a fisherman's net with the dripping moon in it. Each of them took it for a real web, but only the spider believed that it held the real moon." Of course, the moon has sometimes been envisaged in primitive myth as an immense spider, for the moon by its rhythms weaves the web of mortal life. The spider's web, therefore, can be related to *maya,* the world illusion of Mommy Fortuna; however, the web is here believed to hold the moon rather than be identified with it.

The moon symbolism in the novel is complex. First, we should note that the unicorn is consistently related to the moon: "The moon was gone, but to the magician's eyes the unicorn was the moon, cold and white and very old, lighting his way to safety or to madness." The smile of the Lady Amalthea seems to Prince Lir "like the new moon, a slender bend of brightness on the edge of the unseen." The image of the spider's web holding the moon calls to mind some lines from the song the bored princess sings in her lackadaisical ritual to call a unicorn: "I am a king's daughter, / And if I cared to care, / The moon that has no mistress / Would flutter in my hair," and in turn harks back to the description of Maid Marian: "The woman's heavy hair shone with a secret, like a cloud that hides the moon." A cloud seems to hide the moon whenever the harpy appears, the destructive harpy being a polar opposite to the unicorn, whose mortal name, Amalthea, evokes the cornucopia, the overflowing horn of plenty. At the end of the novel, when the Lady Amalthea goes through the clock, we are told that "She entered the clock and vanished as the moon passes behind clouds." The clock, of course, symbolizes time, which clouds perception of the immortal moon. The spider's web, a woman's hair, and clouds all may be associated with the mortal, time-bound realm, which seeks to embrace or embody the ideal or the "real," the beauty and wonder of life. To have the moonflutter in your hair, or to hold it in your web, is to have intimations of immortality, to transcend mortal existence—or perhaps more accurately, to transfigure mortal existence.

The spider, however, is deluded. Schmendrick says that the truth melts Mommy Fortuna's magic, that she never should have meddled with a real harpy or real unicorn. At night, we are told, "All the beasts were asleep, save the spider, who wove, and the harpy, who waited." Here spider and harpy represent forces of creation and destruction; because the spider's creation is governed by Mommy Fortuna, the truth symbolized by the harpy—the iron force of brute reality, the cynicism and hatred that befoul and bestink—destroys any possibility of incarnating the moon. The harpy ravages the Midnight Carnival, leaving only "the tiny, dry sound of a spider weeping."

Rather strangely, the unicorn seems joyful in confronting the harpy, crying out, "not in terror but in wonder, 'Oh, you are like me'." Each sees herself reflected in the other, circling each other "like a double star, and under the shrunken sky there was nothing real but the two of them." Even the harpy laughs with delight as she attacks. Perhaps their joy comes from finally confronting something real, even if an enemy: the joy of battle against a worthy foe. Yet something more is implied: each reflects the other, and they are like a double star, halves of the same reality. The unicorn, we have seen, is associated with the moon, and the harpy with clouds, yet when the harpy gathers her power in, "as a crouching wave draws sand and water roaring down the beach," a "bloodshot moon burst out of the clouds," the color of "swollen gold," the same color as the harpy. So both unicorn and harpy are associated with the moon; and the harpy is associated with the ebb tide, the retreating ocean drawing sand and water back into its depths. We recall that Haggard has imprisoned the unicorns in the sea: he "has them all now drifting in and out on the tides for his delight—all but one."

The polarity of unicorn and harpy is not developed; more important, and parallel, is that between unicorn and the Red Bull, who also is related to the moon and tides. At the beginning of her quest to find the other unicorns, the unicorn lies awake at night, "waiting to see the vast form of the Red Bull come charging out of the moon"; and when the bull actually appears, he comes "like the moon, the sullen, swollen hunter's moon. She could feel the shock of the livid horns in her side, as though he had already struck." The unicorn's horn heals; the bull's horns wound, and the bull's neck "swells like a wave." Bulls are associated with the sea in Greek mythology: Poseidon and various river-gods often took the form of a bull. Here, too, the Red Bull finally retreats into the dark depths of the sea, causing a tidal wave that frees the unicorns and destroys Haggard's castle. The unicorn, particularly her eyes, is also associated with the sea: "Slowly the deep, secret sea returned to the Lady Amalthea's eyes, filling them until they were as old and dark and unknowable and indescribable as the sea"; and the other unicorns resemble sea foam as the huge wave dashes upon shore. As the harpy and unicorn circle each other like a double star, so also do bull and unicorn: "Smoke and fire, spray and storm, they came on together."

The harpy and the Red Bull seem to represent two kinds of cosmic force. The harpy may be the active power of rage, hatred—what Freud called *thanatos,* the aggressive, destructive, death-instinct. The Red Bull is more difficult to define, associated with Fear, the fear of pain and loss that keeps one from life and makes the world a wasteland. The harpy can kill the unicorn, but the Red Bull can make her forget what she is; the same thing almost happens to the Lady Amalthea in Haggard's castle as mortal lineaments gradually erase her immortal beauty and cloud her memory. Like Plato's fallen soul, she forgets the reality of the pure forms. The Red Bull is the color of blood, "the blood that stirs under an old wound that never really healed," "the red darkness you see when you close your eyes in pain." He is blind and hates the light, his "raging ignorance" filling the universe. He is as "invincible as the night itself." The unicorn acknowledges that he is too strong: "There was no end to his strength, and no beginning. He is older than I." The bull does inspire fear but has more to him: Haggard says that the bull "serves anyone who has no fear—and I have no more fear than I have rest." Perhaps not only fear keeps Haggard from life, but greed, the blind desire to possess, to hoard unicorns in the sea. According to the witch's prophecy Haggard's castle will one day sink into the sea when his greed causes the sea to overflow; and the Red Bull, the symbol of greed, fulfills the prophecy. Of course, fear—the fear of losing—is closely related to greed; and both forces arise, in a way, from the dread of time.

Like the spider trying to hold the moon in her web, Haggard wants to possess all the unicorns, "for my need is very great." So he has the Red Bull catch them and drive them into the sea, where they drift in and out on the tides for his enjoyment. The ebb and flow of the tides resembles the whirling wheel of fortune: "Here is there, and high is low; / All may be undone." Drifting in the sea, the unicorns are imprisoned by time, their immortality transmuted into an existence "hopeless and eternal." The ebb and flow of existence in time is eternal—and hopeless. That is why Haggard says that "I always knew that nothing was worth the investment of my heart, because nothing lasts." The skull who guards the way to the Red Bull says that Haggard scrambled the works of the clock "one day when he was trying to grab hold of time as it swung by." Since Haggard cannot live in the moment or stop the flow of time, all his joys inevitably turn cold and dull as he guards them: "All things die when I pick them up." The essence of Haggard is recognized by Schmendrick "I'm not poor Haggard, to lose my heart's desire in the having of it."

The episode of the skull and the clock deals explicitly with the problem of time and shows, ironically, that Haggard suffers from the greatest illusion of all—that time is real. As the butterfly informed the unicorn about the Red Bull, so in Haggard's castle a cat suddenly speaks to Molly Grue, telling her that "When the wine drinks itself, . . . when the skull speaks, when the clock strikes the right time—only then will you find the tunnel that leads to the Red Bull's lair." Each of these prophecies involves a paradox or contradiction, the last of which is the easiest to understand. The skull tells Molly and the others that the way to the bull is through the clock: "You simply walk through the clock and there you are." To walk through the clock demonstrates that, as the skull says, time is an illusion. When he was alive the skull thought that time was as real and solid as himself, but now he knows that "You can strike your own time, and start the count anywhere. When you understand that—then any time at all will be the right time for you." Ironically, a skull, an obvious emblem of mortality, says this. That the skull should speak at all illustrates that mortality is not what it seems to be. One of the conditions for passing through the clock is that the skull must be smashed. In a way, then, mortality leads to the knowledge of immortality yet must be overcome before one can actually find fulfillment. The episode is closely related to that in which the butterfly, another emblem of mortality, sets the unicorn on the trail of the bull, and to that where the unicorn is transformed into a girl and asks the anguishing question, "How can anything that is going to die be real? How can it be truly beautiful?"

Schmendrick, we have seen, replies that "Whatever can die is beautiful—more beautiful than a unicorn, who lives forever, and who is the most beautiful creature in the world," and he knows because he has known both mortal and immortal existence. His life turns out to be the inversion of the unicorn's: he started as mortal, was granted immortality by his master Nikos until he could overcome his vast incompetence as a magician and find his true power, and finally became mortal again when he becomes a real magician. The unicorn, of course, was immortal, became mortal, and regained her immortal form. As an immortal, Schmendrick has been false, a tawdry purveyor of cheap tricks, for the most part. He becomes true—or real—only when he becomes mortal. When he speaks the magic words that transform the Lady Amalthea back into a unicorn, "he felt his immortality fall from him like armor, or like a shroud." He has been dead, and now is alive again—and we see what he means when he says that whatever can die is more beautiful than a unicorn: mortal existence is more beautiful, more poignant, because of its very brevity. Moreover, the brevity, the pain and sorrow of mortality, leads to the knowledge that beauty is truth, truth beauty. Schmendrick and the unicorn both regain their true lives, their reality, though the reality of one is mortal, the other immortal. Apparently, the immortal and mortal, joy and sorrow, life and death, are equally real halves of the same whole: you cannot have one without the other. Time is indeed an illusion, yet Prince Lir says that "Things must happen when it is time for them to happen. . . . The happy ending cannot come in the middle of the story." So time also is real. Beagle has constructed the story so that every statement has its counterstatement. The result is a paradoxical coincidence of opposites: life and death, eternal and temporal, are inextricably mingled.

For this reason the unicorn can defeat the Red Bull only when she suffers anguish for the loss of Prince Lir, for the very depths of despair express the beauty, the reality, of love and joy—the fact that "We can love but what we lose— / What is gone is gone." Her rage is an affirmation of mortal life that renews the immortal light of her horn, which burns and shivers like a mortal butterfly. With such enraged affirmation the tide turns, and the Red Bull is driven into the sea.

Schmendrick comes into his true power only by suffering in the same way as the unicorn. Throughout the book he has been rather aloof and uncommitted, infected—as indeed are most of the characters—by a Haggard-like cynicism and despair; but when he sees Lir's heroic death, buried reserves of emotion are unleashed:

> Wonder and love and great sorrow shook Schmendrick the Magician then, and came together inside him and filled him, filled him until he felt himself brimming and flowing with something that was none of these. He did not believe it, but it came to him anyway, as it had touched him twice before and left him more barren than he had been. . . . There was too much to hold, too much ever to use; and still he found himself weeping with the pain of his impossible greed. He thought, or said, or sang, *I did not know that I was so empty, to be so full.*

The brimming and flowing of Schmendrick's power resembles the ebb and flow of the tides which imprison the unicorns. His power "comes and goes." When it comes he is filled to overflowing; when it goes he is empty—and all the more empty for the very fullness he has known. After speaking the magic words that transform the unicorn into a girl, Schmendrick finds that "the emptiness rushed back with a thunderclap that threw him on his face." His relation to his power is much like Haggard's to the Red Bull. Both are filled with "impossible greed." Several times the question is raised: does Haggard control the bull or does the bull control Haggard? Such also is the question with Schmendrick's power over which he has little control and which possesses him when it will. Haggard also knows the alternation of fullness and emptiness: the unicorns fill him with joy; but he realizes that "great power cannot give me whatever it is that I really want." Both Schmendrick and Haggard must face emptiness, the void: "But no power stirred or spoke in him [Schmendrick]; he could hear nothing but the far, thin howling of emptiness against his ear; as old King Haggard must have heard it waking and sleeping, and never another sound."

Here we come to the core of the novel and the key to the significance of unicorn and Red Bull. The unicorn represents fullness, the overflowing horn of plenty, the bounty and beauty of life; the Red Bull, however, represents emptiness, dread, the pain and sorrow of life. The Red Bull lives in a cavern beneath Haggard's castle, filling the empty place in the depths of Haggard's being. The bull expands to fill whatever space is left empty, driving the unicorns into the sea, where they ebb and flow. Now the moon, of course, governs tides; and both unicorn and bull are related to the moon, which also goes through phases of fullness and emptiness. Fullness and emptiness are halves of the same lunar whole, apparently opposed yet ultimately one: "*I did not know that I was so empty, to be so full.*"

The significance of the first condition for passing through the clock may now be understood. When the wine drinks itself, they may go beyond the clock. Molly brings along some water in a flask since there is no wine, hoping that Schmendrick can imitate Christ's turning water into wine! He tries a spell, seems to smell a faint bouquet of wine, yet finds the flask empty when he turns it over. Nevertheless, the skull drinks from the flask and "gurgled and sighed and smacked. 'Ah,' it said at last, 'ah, that was the real stuff, that was *wine*!'." Here the themes of reality and illusion, and fullness and emptiness come together: emptiness is fullness, illusion becomes reality. A saying of Jesus in the apocryphal Gospel of Thomas is to the effect that "when you make the inner as the outer, and outer as the inner, and the upper as the lower, and when you make male and female into a single one, so that the male shall not be male and the female (shall not) be female, then shall you enter (the Kingdom)." So also with emptiness and fullness: when they are seen as identical, each real yet also illusory, then one can go beyond time. The unicorns are the sea foam, moments of joy and transfiguration, tossed up by the dark depths of life. We float upon the abyss, yet the imperishable can be embodied in the perishable if one can forsake greed, the desire to fill emptiness. Beagle seems to say that if we can let go, surrender ourselves to that "destructive element" which is life, then the waves will bear us up. To let go, however, requires an act of faith, a commitment of the heart, the kind of faith that turns the tepid water of life into wine, transmutes emptiness into fullness. If we can see with the eyes of wonder—"O, wonder! / . . . O brave new world / That has such people in't," then we can bring about the rebirth of the wasteland.

At the end of the novel the two realms of eternity and time have mingled: the unicorns are freed from the sea, bringing the fullness of rebirth to the land; henceforth, the immortal, though almost as fugitive and elusive as it was in the sea, will still bless the land invisibly. Even so, Prince Lir loses his love, withered despite the blooming of his land, and the unicorn, again immortal, regrets the loss of her mortal form, for she "might have lived happily ever after with the prince."

We are thus left with a poignant and paradoxical sense of the separation between two realms that we have seen are one. "Eternity is time, / Time, eternity. / To see the two as opposites / Is mind's perversity." Yet "mind's perversity" seems to tinge the conclusion of *The Last Unicorn*. A hero, says Lir, must live in time, and so must lovers. The unicorn disappears into her cold pastoral, as unfitted for it now as Lir is, at least temporarily, for his life as king. Each pole has nourished the other, longs for the other, but is debarred from final and complete union by the polarities of mortal existence: "And therefore her Decrees of Steel / Us as the distant Poles have plac'd, / (Though Loves whole World on us doth wheel) / Not by themselves to be embrac'd."

David Stevens (essay date Fall 1979)

SOURCE: "Incongruity in a World of Illusion: Patterns of Humor in Peter Beagle's *The Last Unicorn*," in *Extrapolation*, Vol. 20, No. 3, Fall, 1979, pp. 230-37.

[In the essay below, Stevens argues that Beagle uses humor to manipulate the tone of The Last Unicorn.*]*

While humor is peripheral to much fantasy, it is central to Peter Beagle's *The Last Unicorn*. Beagle creates a quasi-medieval universe with built-in anachronisms to serve as the setting for his fairy tale that is at once high romance and self-parody. He presents a serious theme, that we are what people think us and we become what we pretend to be, with a comic technique, and much of the success of the novel can be traced to its humor.

Beagle leaves no doubt about his comic intentions very early in the novel. Before any of the important mortal characters are introduced, the unicorn meets a butterfly. While some important exposition is presented, the main purpose of the encounter seems to be humorous. In Beagle's world butterflies can talk, but all they can do is repeat what they have heard. This butterfly has apparently heard a lot of popular songs, a lot of television commercials, and a lot of Shakespeare and other medieval and Renaissance English poetry. Its speech is a combination of these elements, and the juxtaposition of the ridiculous and the sublime is very funny:

> "Death takes what man would keep," said the butterfly, "and leaves what man would lose. Blow, wind, and crack your cheeks. I warm my hands before the fire of life and get four-way relief."

The other speeches from this brief section are just as incongruous. Responding to the unicorn's question, "Do you know who I am?" the butterfly cheerfully pulls a few appropriate lines from its memory: "Excellent well, you're a fishmonger. You're my everything, you are my sunshine, you are old and gray and full of sleep, you're my pickle-face, consumptive Mary Jane." In response to nothing at all, but merely to pass the time, the butterfly leaps into the following soliloquy:

> One, two, three o'lairy ... Not, I'll not, carrion comfort, look down that lonesome road. For, oh, what damned minutes tells he o'er who dotes, yet doubts. Hasten, Mirth, and bring with thee a host of furious fancies whereof I am commander, which will be on sale for three days only at bargain summer prices. I love you, oh, the horror, the horror, and aroint thee, witch, aroint thee, indeed and truly you've chosen a bad place to be lame in, willow, willow, willow.

It almost seems natural that, preparing to leave, the butterfly says: "I must take the A train."

If the incongruities in the speech of the butterfly are rather obvious, they are only the beginnings of Beagle's skillful use of incongruity for comic effect. We first learn the main character's name, for example, in the following manner: "'I am called Schmendrick the Magician,' he answered." "Schmendrick," of course, is a Yiddish word, meaning roughly "bungler," from the same general group as "schlemiel." This in itself is funny, but the magician says the opposite of what we expect when he adds, "You won't have heard of me."

Beagle's general use of incongruity is well illustrated in the following expository passage, where everything that is mentioned is twisted into the opposite of what is expected:

> He made an entire sow out of a sow's ear; turned a sermon into a stone, a glass of water into a handful of water, a five of spades into a twelve of spades, and a rabbit into a goldfish that drowned. Each time he conjured up confusion, he glanced at the unicorn with eyes that said, "Oh, but *you* know what I really did." Once he changed a dead rose into a seed. The unicorn liked, that, even though it did turn out to be a radish seed.

In most cases the incongruity involves an item that lowers the high, heroic tone that has been established: the incongruity deflates the puffed-up prose. In one instance, however, during the sequence in the camp of Captain Cully, a self-appointed Robin Hood, the incongruity serves to inflate the level. Jack Jingly, a member of the band of "merry" outlaws, says of the other men: "Cooped up in the greenwood all day, they need a little relaxing, a little catharsis, like." It is also in the camp of Captain Cully that Schmendrick, to flatter his host, reels off a series of romantic escapades that he has heard of in connection with the Captain and then reveals to us that he "had never heard of Captain Cully before that very evening, but he had a good grounding in Anglo-Saxon folklore and knew the type."

Beagle uses songs with incongruous elements throughout the novel, and it is partly through them that the theme is revealed. Captain Cully is so concerned with songs about himself that he has written thirty-one of his own, and is constantly on the look-out for Mr. Child, in order to be properly classified and annotated. Cully has one of them sung to Schmendrick, whom he half-believes to be Mr. Child, and stanzas two and three (of the twenty-five!) show us Beagle's technique:

> "What news, what news, my pretty young man?
> What ails ye, that ye sigh so deep?
> Is it for the loss of your lady fair?
> Or are ye but scabbit in your greep?"

> "I am nae scabbit, whatever that means,
> And my greep is as well as greep may be,
> But I do sigh for my lady fair
> Whom my three brothers ha' riven from me."

The two songs with incongruous elements that most clearly reveal Beagle's theme are Prince Lír's song to the Lady Amalthea, and Schmendrick and Molly's song as they go away together at the end of the novel. Both deserve citing at length.

> When I was a young man, and very well thought of,
> I couldn't ask aught that the ladies denied.
> I nibbled their hearts like a handful of raisins,
> And I never spoke love but I knew that I lied.

> And I said to myself, "Ah, none of them know
> The secret I shelter and savor and save.
> I wait for the one who will see through my seeming,
> And I'll know when I love by the way I behave."

> The years drifted over like clouds in the heavens;
> The ladies went by me like snow on the wind.
> I charmed and I cheated, deceived and dissembled,
> And I sinned, and I sinned, and I sinned, and I sinned.

> But I said to myself, "Ah, they none of them see
> There's a part of me pure as the whisk of a wave.
> My lady is late, but she'll find I've been faithful,
> And I'll know when I love by the way I behave."

> At last came a lady both knowing and tender,
> Saying, "You're not at all what they take you to be."
> I betrayed her before she had quite finished speaking,

And she swallowed cold poison and jumped in the sea.

> And I say to myself, when there's time for a word,
> As I gracefully grow more debauched and depraved,
> "Ah, love may be strong, but a habit is stronger,
> And I knew when I loved by the way I behaved."

The point is reinforced in Schmendrick and Molly's song, which is the last thing that we read in the novel:

> "I am no king, and I am no lord,
> And I am no soldier at arms," said he.
> "I'm none but a harper, and a very poor harper,
> That am come hither to wed with ye."

> "If you were a lord, you should be my lord,
> And the same if you were a thief," said she.
> "And if you are a harper, you shall be my harper,
> For it makes no matter to me, to me,
> For it makes no matter to me."

> "But what if it prove that I am no harper?
> That I lied for your love most monstrously?"
> "Why, then I'll teach you to play and sing,
> For I dearly love a good harp," said she.

The theme is clearly stated by Schmendrick earlier in the novel, using a technique that is elsewhere used for comic effect: verse as prose, Schmendrick is speaking to the unicorn:

> "It's a rare man who is taken for what he truly is," he said. "There is much misjudgment in the world. Now I knew you for a unicorn when I first saw you, and I know that I am your friend. Yet you take me for a clown, or a clod, or a betrayer, and so I must be if you see me so. The magic on you is only magic and will vanish as soon as you are free, but the enchantment of error that you put on me I must wear forever in your eyes. We are not always what we seem, and hardly ever what we dream. Still I have read, or heard it sung, that un[i]corns when time was young, could tell the difference 'twixt the two—the false shining and the true, the lips' laugh and the heart's rue."

The running gag is a favorite comic device, and Beagle makes good use of it. Speaking disparagingly about the power of Mommy Fortuna's magic, Schmendrick says: "She can't turn cream into butter." A few pages later, Rukh tells Schmendrick: "You can't turn cream into butter." When Schmendrick later meets Molly Grue, she cheerfully deflates his ego by asserting the same thing: "You can't turn cream into butter." And finally, King Haggard, speaking to the Lady Amalthea about Schmendrick, quite independently comes to the not-so-surprising conclusion: "I don't think he could turn cream into butter." The running gag has run its course, each iteration delighting the reader more than the last.

By far the most important mode of humor used in the novel is anticlimax—a sudden drop from the dignified or important in thought or expression to the commonplace or trivial. Beagle uses this technique literally dozens of times, beginning on the first page with the description of the unicorn: "and the long horn above her eyes shown and shivered with its own seashell light even in the deepest midnight. She had killed dragons with it, and healed a king whose poisoned wound would not close, and knocked down ripe chestnuts for bear cubs." While perhaps not the most hilarious example that could be chosen, it certainly indicates that this will be a novel that does not take itself too seriously.

Schmendrick is responsible for many of the anticlimactic lines, which seems perfectly appropriate since the character resembles an out-of-work stand-up comic down on his luck. For example, when he introduces himself to the unicorn, he says: ". . . For I too am real. I am Schmendrick, the magician, the last of the red-hot swamis, and I am older than I look." Speaking of their destination, Schmendrick explains its origins like this:

> "Haggard's fortress . . . Haggard's dire keep. A witch built it for him, they say, but he wouldn't pay her for her work, so she put a curse on the castle. She swore that one day it would sink into the sea with Haggard, when his greed caused the sea to overflow. Then she gave a fearful shriek, the way they do, and vanished in a sulphurous puff. Haggard moved in right away. He said no tyrant's castle was complete without a curse."

Approaching Hagsgate, Schmendrick seems surprised: "It must be Hagsgate, and yet there's no smell of sorcery, no air of black magic. But why the legends, then, why the fables and fairy tales? Very confusing, especially when you've had half a turnip for dinner."

We can always count on Schmendrick to break the mood. Having had too much to drink, he sounds as if he could be on the Johnny Carson show:

> "You don't know what a real curse is. Let me tell you *my* troubles." Easy tears suddenly glittered in his eyes. "To begin with, my mother never liked me. She pretended, but I knew—"

Later, when the questing group is followed out of Hagsgate, Schmendrick tries to figure out why: "Perhaps Drinn has started to feel guilty about underpaying his poisoner. . . . Perhaps his conscience is keeping him awake. Anything is pos-

sible. Perhaps I have feathers." Finally, at what could be a tender moment, Schmendrick advises the Lady Amalthea: "You are truly human now. You can love, and fear, and forbid things to be what they are, and overact."

But anticlimax is not limited to Schmendrick's speech. Molly, too, can change the mood with a word or two. After Schmendrick has turned the unicorn into the Lady Amalthea, he is explaining how he carries the true magic: "I am a bearer. . . . I am a dwelling, I am a messenger." Without missing a beat Molly says: "You are an idiot." Speaking about the need for wine to fulfill the riddle that will finally lead them to the Red Bull, Molly says to Schmendrick: "I thought if you had some water to start with. . . Well, it's been done. It's not as though you'd have to make up something new. I'd never ask that of you."

The Lady Amalthea even gets into the act, as unlike that sweet and beautiful lady as that may sound. Trying to mislead King Haggard she says: "The Red Bull. But why do you think I have come to steal the Bull? I have no kingdom to keep, and no wish for conquest. What would I do with him? How much does he eat?" In a rare moment of candor, Prince Lír, too, uses anticlimax with the Lady Amalthea: "I became a hero to serve you, and all that is like you. Also to find some way of starting a conversation."

Minor characters as well use this comic device to good effect. Captain Cully, for example, wants to pump Schmendrick for news about Cully's reputation in the wide world. He phrases his dinner invitation this way: "Come to the fire and tell us your tale. How do they speak of me in your country? What have you heard of dashing Captain Cully and his band of freemen? Have a taco." The cat who tells Molly how to get to the Red Bull seems very mysterious—until the last line:

> "When the wine drinks itself," he said, "when the skull speaks, when the clock strikes the right time— only then will you find the tunnel that leads to the Red Bull's lair." He tucked his paws under his chest and added, "There's trick to it, of course."

Naturally, the skull the cat spoke of speaks, and just as naturally it uses anticlimax. When speaking to Schmendrick, the skull remarks: "Matter can neither be created nor destroyed. . . . Not by most magicians anyway." And while sounding the alarm for King Haggard, the skull shrieks: "Help ho, the king! Guards, to me! Here are burglars, bandits, moss-troopers, kidnapers, housebreakers, murderers, character assassins, plagiarists! King Haggard! Ho, King Haggard!"

It seems clear that this comic device is not being used for character delineation but simply for humorous effect. This belief is confirmed by the number of uses of anticlimax in narrative and expository passages where there is no dialogue. For example, the confrontation between the followers from Hagsgate and Schmendrick and company goes like this:

> The magician stood erect, menacing the attackers with demons, metamorphoses, paralyzing ailments, and secret judo holds. Molly picked up a rock.

A typical evening in King Haggard's castle is described as follows:

> And in the evenings, before she went to bed, she usually read over Prince Lír's new poems to the Lady Amalthea, and praised them, and corrected the spelling.

Finally, Molly's typical day is described:

> Molly Grue cooked and laundered, scrubbed stone, mended armor and sharpened swords; she chopped wood, milled flour, groomed horses and cleaned their stalls, melted down stolen gold and silver for the king's coffers, and made bricks without straw.

All of these uses of humor seem to have a common effect: they break the empathic bond that the reader might form with the characters by drawing attention to themselves as devices of the author. There is no subtlety here, but a purposive and carefully planned exaggeration. The mechanics of the form are being laid bare, and the writer's technique revealed. The basic critical question must by *why,* and the answer can be found in one final pattern of incongruity existing in the text: a consistent pattern of self-parody. *The Last Unicorn* is cast in the form of a fairy tale, and throughout the novel the various characters (but especially Schmendrick) make observations about the form and how their story fits it.

For example, in Hagsgate Drinn describes Prince Lír's birth like this:

> "I stood by the strange cradle for a long time, pondering while the snow fell and the cats purred prophecy."

He stopped, and Molly Grue said eagerly, "You took the child home with you, of course, and raised it as your own." Drinn laid his hands palm up on the table.

> "I chased the cats away," he said, "and went home alone. . . . I know the birth of a hero when I see it," he said, "Omens and portents, snakes in the nursery. Had it not been for the cats, I might have

chanced the child, but they made it so obvious, so mythological."

Molly, talking to Schmendrick about the apparent cruelty of leaving the child to die in the snow, says: "They deserve their fate, they deserve worse. To leave a child out in the snow—" Schmendrick, of course, knows better, and replies: "Well, if they hadn't, he couldn't have grown up to be a prince. Haven't you ever been in a fairy tale before?" And on the next page he says: "It's a great relief to find out about Prince Lír. I've been waiting for this tale to turn up a leading man."

Another reference to the story within the story occurs shortly after Schmendrick turns the unicorn into a human being:

> "You're in the story with the rest of us now, and you must go with it, whether you will or no. If you want to find your people, if you want to become a unicorn again, then you must follow the fairy tale to King Haggard's castle, and wherever else it chooses to take you. The story cannot end without the princess."

The exaggeration that we saw in Beagle's description of Molly's typical day is enlarged upon in Prince Lír's discussion with Molly about his deeds:

> "I have swum four rivers, each in full flood and none less than a mile wide. I have climbed seven mountains never before climbed, slept three nights in the Marsh of the Hanged Men, and walked alive out of that forest where the flowers burn your eyes and the nightingales sing poison. I have ended my betrothal to the princess I had agreed to marry—and if you don't think that was a heroic deed, you don't know her mother. I have vanquished exactly fifteen black knights waiting by fifteen fords in their black pavilions, challenging all who came to cross. And I've long since lost count of the witches in the thorny woods, the giants, the demons disguised as damsels; the glass hills, fatal riddles, and terrible tasks; the magic apples, rings, lamps, potions, swords, cloaks, boots, neckties, and nightcaps. Not to mention the winged horses, the basilisks and sea serpents, and all the rest of the livestock."

Any one of these deeds, of course, would be sufficient to win the hand of the fair lady in the average fairy tale—but this is far from the average fairy tale. Prince Lír knows the way things, are, and he tells the Lady Amalthea:

> "My lady. . . . I am a hero. It is a trade, no more, like weaving or brewing, and like them it has its own tricks and knacks and small arts. There are ways of perceiving witches, and of knowing poison

streams; there are certain weak spots that all dragons have, and certain riddles that hooded strangers tend to set you. But the true secret of being a hero lies in knowing the order of things. The swineherd cannot already be wed to the princess when he embarks on his adventures, nor can the boy knock on the witch's door when she is away on vacation. The wicked uncle cannot be found out and foiled before he does something wicked. Things must happen when it is time for them to happen. Quests may not simply be abandoned; prophesies may not be left to rot like unpicked fruit; unicorns may go unrescued for a long time, but not forever. The happy ending cannot come in the middle of the story."

After he becomes King, Lír says to Schmendrick: "A hero is entitled to his happy ending, when it comes at last." But since Lír cannot have the Lady Amalthea, a substitute must arrive, and Beagle obliges. Just before Schmendrick and Molly ride off into the sunset, "out of this story and into another," a damsel in distress (apparently out of another story, but certainly in need of a hero) rides up, saying:

> "A rescue! a rescue, *au secours*! An ye be a man
> of mettle and sympathy, aid me now. I hight the
> Princess Alison Jocelyn, daughter to good King
> Giles, and him foully murdered by his brother, the
> bloody Duke Wulf, who hath ta'en my three broth-
> ers, the Princes Corin, Colin, and Calvin, and cast
> them into a fell prison as hostages that I will wed
> with his fat son, the Lord Dudley, but I bribed the
> sentinel and sopped the dogs—"

Shmendrick replies, apparently keeping a straight face: "Fair princess, the man you want just went that way."

Schmendrick and Molly and the other refuse to take themselves seriously, and so the reader doesn't take them seriously either. Beagle has carefully and lovingly created a work that satirizes and glorifies its form, much in the same way that the music of P.D.Q. Bach satirizes and pays homage to baroque music. Various forms of incongruity play a major role in the success of the enterprise.

Jean Tobin (essay date 1986)

SOURCE: "Werewolves and Unicorns: Fabulous Beasts in Peter Beagle's Fiction," in *Forms of the Fantastic: Selected Essays from the Third International Conference on the Fantastic in Literature and Film,* edited by Jan Hokenson and Howard Pearce, Greenwood Press, 1986, pp. 181-89.

[*In the following essay, Tobin examines Beagle's use of myths about unicorns and werewolves in such works as* The Last Unicorn *and* Lila the Werewolf.]

"Would you call this age a good one for unicorns?" asks the elder of two hunters riding through the first pages of Peter Beagle's *Last Unicorn;* "Times change," the other mutters. By the end of a brief conversation, the elder has made a judgment. Breaking out of the lilac wood, he shouts back over his shoulder as if he knows the listening unicorn can overhear: "Stay where you are, poor beast. This is no world for you." Elders in fairy tales are wise, and the hunter may be right. This world—our world—*is* no world for unicorns. Indubitably, people believed in the existence of unicorns for a thousand years and more, but they do no longer. Belief in unicorns, in werewolves—indeed in a whole menagerie of mythical and legendary beasts—vanished over two hundred years ago with the coming of the Enlightenment. People on the streets of San Francisco and New York, Indianapolis, and Miami know about but do not believe in either werewolves or unicorns. How, then, in such an age, for such an audience, does any contemporary writer create a compelling novel or short story based on a myth? A good number of writers have done it, of course, but among them Peter Beagle is one of the very best. In *The Last Unicorn* (1968) and *Lila the Werewolf* (1974), Beagle manages to give his readers fresh, contemporary versions of both the unicorn myth and the werewolf legend while retaining all the traditional and satisfying familiar elements of each.

In *The Last Unicorn,* Beagle's fabulous beast both looks and acts like unicorns in the classical and Christian accounts. Marvelously, she meets physical criteria from both versions of the myth. As she first appears, looking nothing "like a horned horse, as unicorns are often pictured, being smaller and cloven-hoofed," she is one of the caprine unicorns reported in the *Physiologus,* or "The Bestiary," a collection of moralistic animal tales gathered in third-century Alexandria and popularized throughout Europe during the next thousand years. When perceived by unsuspecting villagers merely as a "white mare with strange eyes," however, Beagle's lovely last unicorn is equally one of the equine unicorns of earlier, classical accounts. The physician Ctesias first wrote of such creatures, on his return home to Greece in 398 B.C. after seventeen years in the Persian court, that "their bodies are white . . . and their eyes dark blue. . . . The animal is exceedingly swift and powerful." The last unicorn has the mane given to her by Aelian, who wrote in the *Historia Animalium* that "this animal is as large as a full-grown horse, and it has a mane, tawny hair, feet like those of the elephant, and the tail of a goat." Hunters in *The Last Unicorn* even repeat the elder Pliny's somewhat later description of the unicorn as having characteristics of horse, deer, elephant, and bear, with "a deep bellowing voice, and a single black horn." Only when she is frightened, however, does the last unicorn's seashell horn turn black, and then "even Molly Grue" is unable to prevent herself from recognizing the unicorn's absurdity "when the shining has gone out of her."

The last unicorn meets other traditional criteria as well. Her single horn has the curative powers first given it by Ctesias; she has memories of the unicorn hunts described in "The Bestiary." In this European and Christian account, the unicorn, symbolic of Christ, is vulnerable to capture only by chaste young maidens, symbolic of the Virgin Mary. In the past, Beagle's unicorn recalls, "I went to them all and laid my head in their laps," but now she allows herself to be touched only by Molly Grue, who though bedraggled is pure in heart, and whose name is the common form of Mary. There are other traces of the medieval unicorn hunt in *The Last Unicorn*, for one of the hunters retells a family story of how a unicorn came to his grandmother, who was generally afraid of large animals; and later in the fairy tale, recalling the virginity test long associated with the unicorn myth, an anxious princess intent on marriage and her indifferent prince are seen flourishing a golden bridle and calling unicorns. However, even though most unicorns, as symbols of Christ, are male and even symbols of male potency, the last unicorn is female. From the moment the unicorn appeared to him, according to Beagle, "she was female."

Beagle's werewolf is similarly female, but female werewolves are more common. In both novels considered here, Beagle shows the fabulous beast being transformed into a young girl, for in *The Last Unicorn* the unicorn becomes the Lady Amalthea, the beautiful, gentle, chaste maiden required by the legend. In *Lila the Werewolf*, however, the werewolf becomes Lila. As sexuality is often part of the werewolf legend, Beagle emphasizes this element by merging it with the Talmudic tradition of Lilith, a vampire-like nocturnal female demon. In addition, in Beagle's long story, all the standard elements of the Central European werewolf legend are present, or at least mentioned: stakes in the heart, wolf bane, bags of garlic, "cold iron, silver, oak, running water," the drinking of blood and howling at the full moon. In using all this ancient and traditional material, however, Beagle recreates his werewolf—and his unicorn—in narratives that are new and compelling for contemporary audiences.

In both *The Last Unicorn* and *Lila the Werewolf*, Beagle places his fabulous beasts in a recognizably modern landscape, and this in a world almost without wonder, where unicorns and werewolves are generally acknowledged not to exist. This paradox is most obvious in *Lila the Werewolf*, in which Beagle's werewolf, Lila, is a girl from the Bronx who began turning into a wolf monthly; under the full moon, with the onset of puberty, and who now lives in an apartment on Ninety-Eighth Street with an accommodating young

man called Farrell. When Farrell first sees that Lila is a werewolf, three weeks after they have begun living together, he breathes in "the wild smell of the wolf" and finds it difficult to simultaneously accept the two realities: "That smell and the Miro prints on the walls." Even when Farrell later that morning goes up on the roof and discovers that the Russian wolfhound he has been dog-sitting is dead, bloodless, its throat torn out of its body, he has difficulty finding a place for real werewolves in his modern consciousness: "The coffeepot was still chuckling when he came back into the apartment, which struck him as very odd, you could have either werewolves or Pyrex nine-cup percolators in the world, but not both, surely." A major part of the reader's delight in *Lila the Werewolf* comes from precisely this juxtaposition of two realities, from seeing the entire, totally familiar Central European legend—even to the use of a silver bullet to kill a werewolf—newly worked out in the context of an equally familiar, and very realistic, modern American city. Throughout the story, Beagle insists upon juxtaposing the marvelous with mundane details and ordinary places: His characters converse sensibly about werewolves in the Automat; his werewolf is hunted down Columbus Avenue and Riverside Drive, through Central Park and near Lincoln Center; the Lithuanian—or Latvian—building superintendent who shoots at Lila with the silver bullet is fined by the New York police for possessing an unlicensed handgun. Werewolves, as we all know, do not exist in New York or in other large American cities; but in Beagle's *Lila the Werewolf*, at least one werewolf, Lila, most improbably but realistically does.

In *The Last Unicorn*, Beagle places his fabulous beast in a less realistic but no less modern setting. When Beagle sends his last unicorn off in quest for all the lost unicorns, he has her leave her lilac wood, where time has passed her by, and traverse the landscape of the modern world. The unicorn may travel through fairy-tale villages and towns, be detained a short while at Mommy Fortuna's Midnight Carnival, and wander through the Greenwood; but these realms of the imagination are now sadly diminished, and always her destination is Haggard's kingdom. When she—and companions Molly Grue and magician Schmendrick—reach Haggard's realm, they find a parched, barren, wintry land, where nothing grows and children are neither desired nor born. We as twentieth-century readers recognize the place, for we have been here often before. More than any other in the twentieth century, the landscape that has lingered in our minds is T.S. Eliot's image of spiritual sterility and physical desolation—the Waste Land. Later in the fairy tale, as if in confirmation of this thought, Haggard's successor is justly informed that his kingship is over a wasteland that has always had only one king: "fear." Indeed, the kingdom has been "wasteland in Haggard's time."

As the years of the twentieth century have worn on, and the mud and trenches of World War I have been supplanted by the cratered battlefields of World War II and eventually by the defoliated jungles of Vietnam, Eliot's image of a barren, unproductive land has lost none of its power. Countless writers have used the image since the publication of *The Waste Land* in 1922: The most memorable early use is probably F. Scott Fitzgerald's creation of the Valley of Ashes in *The Great Gatsby* (1925), but among later works dominated by the image—so argues Raymond Olderman in *Beyond the Wasteland* (1973)—are novels by writers as various as Ken Kesey, Stanley Elkin, John Barth, Joseph Heller, Thomas Pynchon, John Hawkes, and Kurt Vonnegut. Indisputably, the Waste Land is a twentieth-century landscape. It is strange to see a unicorn in the Waste Land.

In publishing his long poem, it will be remembered, Eliot acknowledged his debt to James G. Frazer's *Golden Bough* (1890) and Jessie L. Weston's *From Ritual to Romance* (1920). Both works have to do with myth. Frazer investigated vegetation myths and rituals celebrating the death and resurrection of primitive gods intimately related to the seasons. Weston applied Frazer's insights to trace the legend of the Holy Grail back to its source in those mystery religions originating in vegetation myths, and examined the medieval versions portraying an ailing and sexually impotent fisher king ruling over a cursed, barren land to be saved only by a questing knight. The Waste Land of the twentieth century, Eliot suggests, is similarly much in need of renewal, in part because myth and ritual have lost their power to lend wonder to our daily lives. Almost by definition, then, the presence of the Waste Land in Beagle's book suggests that in *The Last Unicorn* is a world where myth has lost its potency—where unicorns, for instance, are not generally acknowledged to exist. The narrative supports this surmise. As the younger hunter insists in the opening pages, "Unicorns are long gone . . . if, indeed, they ever were." The villagers and townspeople in Beagle's book are recognizably like ourselves. They see no unicorns in their world; they experience little wonder.

Thus, in *The Last Unicorn*, as in *Lila the Werewolf*, Beagle places his fabulous animals not only within recognizably modern landscapes, but also among characters to whom he has given modern consciousness. One expects contemporary attitudes from the realistic New Yorkers in *Lila the Werewolf*. When Farrell shouts his story of werewolves to his friend, Ben, above the clatter of the Automat, no one expects the New Yorkers to look up, because nothing can surprise New Yorkers; and besides, as Beagle accurately points out, "New Yorkers never eavesdrop. . . . [They] hear only what they simply cannot help hearing." But it is startling while reading a fairy tale like *The Last Unicorn* to hear one character tell another in blunt disbelief that neither of them knows anything about unicorns: "for I've read the same books and heard the same stories, and I've never seen one either." Beagle's fairy-tale characters share our modern

knowledge of the origins of myths and legends as well as our lack of wonder regarding their content—such as werewolves and unicorns. Schmendrick talks to the unicorn herself about how "the whole silly myth got started" with the rhinoceros. Captain Cully, who lives in the Greenwood with his band of unmerry men, lets Molly know that Robin Hood, as mere myth, demonstrates how "heroic folk-figures [are] synthesized out of need." In a brief lecture he explains that, since our need for heroes cannot be filled by men of ordinary size, "a legend grows around a grain of truth, like a pearl."

Like other characters in and readers of twentieth-century literature, the characters of *The Last Unicorn* find that their knowledge of myths, legends, and fairy tales forces them to acknowledge the present lack of heroes. As a nameless townsman grumbles about the loss of "old standards" and "values." Some may carry an honorable title—Magician, Prince, Witch—but they are self-consciously aware they do not fill the roles. Schmendrick tells the unicorn, describing how he entertains carnival-goers with "miniature magic, sleight of hand . . . accompanied by persuasive patter." Schmendrick humbly admits that he welcomes the appearance of Prince Lír because he has "been waiting for this tale to turn up a leading man." But Prince Lír is merely the fat fiancé who idly flipped through a magazine while his princess unsuccessfully sang for unicorns. Prince Lír may be tall, but being also flabby and lazy he is no hero. Molly Grue, who lives in the Greenwood with Captain Cully, greets Schmendrick in a caustic, curiously modern, self-deprecating way: "Dress and dirty hair tattered alike, bare feet bleeding and beslimed, she gave him a bat's grin. 'Surprise', she said. 'It's Maid Marian'." Even the witch, Mommy Fortuna, is disillusioned that her youthful dreams of evil have ended in "meager magic, sprung of stupidity."

Some of Beagle's characters are still blindly self-promoting, of course. Mistaking Schmendrick for the wandering Child collecting songs for his *English and Scottish Popular Ballads,* Cully reveals his hopes "to be collected, to be verified, annotated, to have variant versions, even to have one's authenticity doubted." Mistrusting the folk, Cully has written thirty-one ballads himself; he now urges his minstrel to practice for the day when he will be "field-recorded." Those characters in Beagle's *Last Unicorn* who have looked at themselves with clear eyes, however, are shamefaced at their unheroic stature. Only ordinary, they know they do not measure up to their dreams.

All of the characters need the last unicorn, and a very few recognize her. Schmendrick the magician and the witch, Mommy Fortuna, accustomed to enchantment, know her for what she is: "a rare creature," "myth," "memory." King Haggard knows, and in his greed would pen her up in an attempt to keep her elusive beauty forever. Molly, too, recognizes the unicorn, first scolding, then weeping that the unicorn has come "now, when I am *this*." Molly serves the unicorn, becoming her handmaiden. Almost no one else, however, truly sees the unicorn, who is bewildered that unicorns are not merely forgotten but not seen at all or seen as "something else." The last unicorn knows then that human beings and the world have changed "because the unicorns are gone."

In *Lila the Werewolf,* Beagle's New Yorkers, equally ordinary sorts, react variously to the mythical creature in their midst. Only one, the Lithuanian—or Latvian—building superintendent, recognizes her for a werewolf while she is in the guise of Lila. He drops the chair he is carrying, cowers, and makes the sign of the cross. Telling his friend, Ben, about the superintendent's terror, Farrell remarks, "I guess if you believe in werewolves and vampires, you probably recognize them right away. I don't believe in them at all, and I live with one." Apparently having little belief in myth, most of the dog owners who witness the werewolf slashing at their Pomeranians and Chihuahuas on West End Avenue just before dawn are less able to admit to themselves what they have seen. Adjusting a mythical experience to their modern expectations, most call Lila a "killer dog," although some insist she is a wolf. Beagle comments further. "As for the people who had actually seen the wolf turn into a young girl when the sunlight touched her, most of them managed not to have seen it, though they never really forgot. There were a few who knew quite well what they had seen, and never forgot it either, but they never said anything."

The people who know Lila well—Farrell; her mother, Bernice; her psychiatrist, Schechtman; and, at second hand, Ben—accept the fact that Lila is a werewolf as easily and with as much certainty as characters in any Lithuanian forest, but for their own contemporary reasons. Farrell, whose "gift was for acceptance," tells Ben he hates confrontations: "If I break up with her now, she'll think I'm doing it because she's a werewolf. It's awkward, it feels nasty and middle-class." Ben scolds Farrell—"You see why nobody has any respect for liberals anymore?"—but takes more than werewolves on faith for friendship's sake: "If there's such a thing as werewolves, the other stuff must be real too." The psychiatrist, as variously reported, explains it in his own terms: "Lila's shrink says she has a rejection thing, very deep-seated," says Farrell; "Dr. Schechtman says it's a sex thing," says Lila; "[It is] Dad's fault," according to Lila's stereotypical Jewish mother, who worries about how and when her daughter will get married. Lila herself sees being a werewolf in terms of the monthly inconvenience: "I missed a lot of things. Like I never could go to the riding camp, and I still want to. And the senior play, when I was in high school . . . they changed the evening, and I had to say I was sick." Eventually, as Bernice spitefully reports to Farrell, Lila marries a Stanford research psychologist. In response to

Farrell's hesitant question, Bernice crows: "Does he know? . . . He's proud of it—he thinks it's wonderful! It's his field!"

The effect of these modern New Yorkers' bland tolerance for werewolves is to neutralize the power of myth in their lives. They ignore, or accept, or explain, or investigate the phenomenon, but are unchanged by it. This is not to say that Beagle—or his narrator—is unaware of myth's power. Beagle even intensifies it, by adroitly combining the werewolf myth with elements of Talmudic traditions. As mentioned, his werewolf Lila is also Lilith, that nocturnal female vampire long associated with lustful sexuality in Jewish folklore. The smell of Lila's lovemaking joins with the smell of the wolf as "wild, heavy zoo smells, warm and raw and fearful, the sweeter for being savage." Sexual disgust is strong in *Lila the Werewolf,* particularly when as a werewolf Lila goes into heat and runs in the streets of New York with a mangy pack of dogs. "The hell with it," even Farrell says then; "She wants to mess around, let her mess around." As werewolf and as Lilith, Beagle's Lila eventually turns on her dog lovers, for the blood.

Beagle allows his narrative to gain power from other myths. His building superintendent, for example, pursuing Lila through the city by underground passageways, "using the keys that only superintendents have to take elevators down to black sub-sub-basements," becomes momentarily a modern equivalent to Pluto, pursuing his Persephone. At that moment, the spirit of Demeter is briefly revealed in Lila's mother, for as Beagle describes her, with "her plum colored hair all loose, one arm lifted, and her orange mouth pursed in a bellow, she was no longer Bernice but a wronged fertility goddess getting set to blast the harvest."

But it is Beagle and his narrator who perceive such power. The usual reaction of the New Yorkers is to make the mythical and marvelous reassuringly mundane. Farrell's early response is characteristic:

> The thing is, it's still only Lila, not Lon Chaney or somebody. Look, she goes to her psychiatrist three afternoons a week, and she's got her guitar lesson one night a week, and her pottery class one night, and she cooks eggplant maybe twice a week. She calls her mother every Friday night, and one night a month she turns into a wolf. You see what I'm getting at? It's still Lila, whatever she does, and I just can't get terribly shook about it.

In the end, Farrell is largely unchanged by living with a werewolf. She fit into a pattern in his life, after all: "It's the same good old mistake," he thought at the time, "except this time the girl's hangup is different." Four years later, he feels wistful about Lila, for he is living with a girl with a "really strange hangup." Thus, the characters of *Lila the Werewolf* attest to the continued presence of myth in our lives, but not to its power.

In contrast, by the end of *The Last Unicorn,* not only Beagle but also his major characters triumphantly assert the power of myth. However diminished that power may seem in our present age, it is real, as is the power of the imagination and love and beauty. One of Beagle's best images for the *seemingly* diminished power of myth occurs in Mommy Fortuna's Midnight Carnival. The witch—now akin to mere superstition rather than powerful good or bad fortune—has caged the epic creatures of Greek myths and Norse sagas. Gesturing toward the cages, Schmendrick tells the unicorn, "Look at your fellow legends and tell me what you see." She stares disbelievingly at a dog, an old ape with a twisted foot, a crocodile, and a lion beneath signs marked Cerberus, Satyr, Dragon, and Manticore. Then she sees in each cage a "second figure" produced by magic. The lion was "tiny and absurd" compared to the Manticore. "Yet they were the same creature." Fittingly, before the unicorn continues on her quest, the caged creatures of the imagination are freed.

Later in the journey, while the diminished and very ordinary characters of Beagle's Greenwood—Cully, Willie Gentle, shrill Molly Grue, and the unmerry men—look on, Schmendrick calls up the heroes of medieval ballad and legend in his first act of real magic; and Robin Hood, Alan-a-Dale, Maid Marian, Will Scarlet, and the others stride silently across the clearing at more than human size. Even as Cully denies that Robin Hood exists, Molly rebukes him, saying that the reverse is true; they themselves do not exist. "Robin and Marian are real, and we are the legend." Much later, it is Schmendrick who informs Molly that they are controlled by the plot of the fairy tale they are in, that it is the unicorn who is "real."

The power of the unicorn is such that even those who cannot see her truly are altered by her presence: "there were women who woke weeping from dreams of her." The mayor's men, sent to capture her, do not know why, later, "they laughed with wonder in the middle of very serious events, and so came to be considered frivolous sorts." As for the three who accompany the unicorn on her quest—inept Schmendrick, unlovely Molly, and flabby Lír—they believe and work, lose weight, and eventually grow in stature, until they become characters fit for a fairy tale: powerful Magician, fair Beloved, heroic Prince. The power of the unicorn, of beauty, when accompanied by the imagination and aided by love and by self-sacrifice, is great. Together, the four do battle with greed in the guise of King Haggard—who is real—and with fear—which is not, but seems so—in the guise of the terrifying Red Bull. Beagle allows them to triumph and, more affirmative than Eliot and more certain of the power of myth in our lives, lets all the found and freed unicorns sweep in a wave across the parched Waste Land,

bringing green leaves and spring flowers to that scene of twentieth-century desolation.

The Last Unicorn is a young man's book. Even six years later, Beagle had something very different to say about myth in *Lila the Werewolf.* But in both book and long story, he succeeds in presenting ancient and fabulous beasts in fresh and significant ways for a twentieth-century audience.

Gerald Jonas (review date 18 January 1987)

SOURCE: A review of *The Folk of the Air,* in *New York Times Book Review,* January 18, 1987, p. 33.

[*In the review below, Jonas praises* The Folk of the Air *as a dazzling work that demands a sequel.*]

The Folk of the Air by Peter S. Beagle, a fantasy novel set in contemporary California, mixes science and the supernatural so seamlessly that the bedazzled reader soon ceases to care which is which. Certainly none of the characters in this book stay up nights worrying about such distinctions.

The woman known as Sia is a psychotherapist of sorts who lives in a house with an indeterminate number of windows; describing her chents as "the displaced ones," she adds, "You can be uprooted from imaginary places too, you know." Joe Farrell, an attractive drifter who plays a mean lute when the mood strikes him, readily identifies himself as a man born out of his time; he would have preferred the heyday of the gallard, the pavanne and the madrigal. Farrell's old friend Ben is a scholar with a more than academic interest in the Vikings. Together with Ben and an old girlfriend, Farrell is caught up in the antics of the League for Archaic Pleasures, whose members masquerade on weekends as medieval lords and ladies and witches and bards. Farrell's refusal to deny the evidence of his senses makes him an unusually reliable guide to events that keep stretching the conventional coordinates of reality.

Mr. Beagle (whose 1968 novel *The Last Unicorn* is generally considered a landmark in modern fantastic literature) knows how to use language to keep the reader from peering too closely at the machinery of a tale. Here, he pokes fun at the "Classic Comics talk" of his make-believe medievalists, before drawing blood from the all too solid flesh beneath their outlandish gear. Farrell's encounters with supernatural forces are cunningly described in metaphors lifted from modern science. When Sia is compelled to reveal her power the epiphany is manifested as "a single blinding silence like a star, endlessly devouring itself." The plot unfolds at a languorous but inexorable pace that seems entirely appropriate to the matters at hand. The ending manages to be satisfying in itself while pointing the way to a sequel that I, for one, eagerly await.

Suzy McKee Charnas (review date 1 February 1987)

SOURCE: A review of *The Folk of the Air*, in *Los Angeles Times Book Review*, February 1, 1987, pp. 1, 9.

[*In the review below, Charnas argues that despite minor problems with its structure and plot,* The Folk of the Air *is well written and superior to Beagle's earlier novels.*]

Like the hero of this book, who returns to friends from his wanderings, Peter Beagle returns, with *The Folk of the Air*, to the company of publishing novelists. Beagle's first two novels, *A Fine and Private Place* and *The Last Unicorn*, were fantasies that won great popular response in the '60s No further books have come from this author for 18 years.

About 10 years ago at a fantasy and science fiction convention, I heard him read aloud from a work-in-progress that, rumor had it, he was having great trouble completing. Now here is the finished book at last, and it is a humdinger.

The Folk of the Air, also a fantasy, begins by firmly anchoring its hero in the real world. Joe Farrell, a wandering musician, arrives in the college town of Avicenna on the California coast in a bizarre and funny scene involving a hold-up attempt by a preppy hitchhiker and bandit. Avicenna itself is bright with real sunlight, complete with creeps and crazies and expensive gentrification.

Joe moves in with an old college buddy, and runs into a former sweetheart. The buddy, Ben, lives with an unglamorous (in the fashion sense only) but mysteriously attractive older woman psychologist named Sia, who counsels her clients at home.

Joe's recurrent old flame, Julie, is deeply involved in the League for Archaic Pleasures, an association of people whose consuming hobby is to re-create for themselves the atmosphere of a highly romanticized past (the League is clearly modeled on the real-life Society for Creative Anachronism). The European Age of Chivalry is the preferred period, but anyone, from Samurai to Saracen, can join so long as they play by the rules and speak in the Sir Walter Scott-Prince Valiant style that all, even the children, affect. Among other things, the book is a sympathetic study of characters who suffer from various sorts and degrees of discomfort in our time, and who long for real or imagined ages past.

Joe soon realizes that Sia is an ancient personage of immense

power. And one member of the League, a teen-age girl, is not merely playing at being a medieval witch called Aiffe; she is a witch, a modern child with magical powers that she is honing and proving at the League's revels, wars and tourneys.

The two strongest characters in the book are these opposing sorceresses. Sia is a lovely, knotty, enigmatic creation, and in Aiffe Beagle has caught precisely a certain sort of awful adolescent girl, full of need, greed and vanity.

Under the tutelage of a demonic boy whom she has conjured out of the air, Aiffe casts increasingly destructive—and increasingly effective—spells, to the dismay and danger of Joe and his friends. The conjured boy has plans of his own, which lead in the end to a magical duel to the death.

Beagle's language is rich, his deployment of it deft and fluid, and his eye for detail wonderfully keen. Scenes set at the doings of the League sparkle with wry, affectionate humor, and the magic of Aiffe and Sia is wild and disorienting, as magic should be. Using the multicultural reality of his setting to the full, Beagle gives us characters of diverse backgrounds and magic of Africa and Asia as well as that of Europe—very refreshing.

Invoking any kind of convincing magic in a realistic setting—even one as inherently fantastical as a California college town—is no mean feat. Beagle does it splendidly.

There are problems: A few of the many (perhaps too many) prominent characters fail to come convincingly to life. A subplot about Ben's seizures of soul-exchange with a 9th-Century Viking doesn't quite work. At times, the writing was too rich for this reader, tending to clog with adjectives and similes (given Beagle's descriptive gifts, the temptation to overindulge is understandable). Some loose ends remain, most of them to do with the rules of Sia's relationship to our world, her strengths and weaknesses. But Beagle is so good that we forget about the rules. In fact, he is a far better writer now than he was when he wrote *The Last Unicorn*. The vein of sentimental cuteness that marred both earlier books is absent here.

The Folk of the Air rises easily above its flaws. It's an entertaining and engrossing read, crammed with interesting people and magical surprises. Welcome back, Mr. Beagle, and may there be many more books to come.

Charles de Lint (review date April 1987)

SOURCE: "Well Worth the Wait," in *Fantasy Review*, Vol. 10, No. 3, April, 1987, p. 33.

[In the review below, de Lint remarks favorably on The Folk of the Air.*]*

For some twenty-seven years, Peter S. Beagle has been a voice to be reckoned with in the fantasy field, a reputation based solely upon two novels, *A Fine and Private Place* and *The Last Unicorn*, and two short stories, *Lila the Werewolf* and "Come, Lady Death." It's been almost nineteen years since we've had a novel from him. *The Folk of the Air*, which apparently took fourteen years to write, now rectifies that dearth. And it's well worth the wait.

Joe Farrell, the protagonist from *Lila the Werewolf*, returns as the central viewpoint character of *The Folk of the Air*. Arriving in San Francisco to visit his old friend Ben, Farrell soon becomes involved with an old girlfriend Julie, the League for Archaic Pleasures (a group of medievalists along the lines of the Society for Creative Anachronism), and Ben's lover Sia, an enigmatic woman who lives in a house that has rooms and corridors which come and go.

Both Ben and Julie belong to the League—which Farrell also joins on the strength of his lute-playing. But all's not well within the League. A young witch named Aiffe has powers that are more than playacting, while Ben appears to be possessed by the spirit of an ancient Viking at the League's gatherings. To further complicate matters, Ben's lover Sia is not all she seems to be: she never leaves her curious house; and, when Aiffe tries to summon a demon, what appears instead is a young man from out of limbo who has a vendetta against Sia.

Beagle's wonderful prose is what carries his work, and it has been sorely missed these last two decades. It has elements of James Thurber, James Stevens, and T.H. White, but mostly it's Beagle's own, moving from a matter-of-fact recounting of events to superb analogies and whimsical asides. The characterizations are all very good, and Beagle's mix of fantasy elements with those of the real world makes for a perfect blend.

Any lover of fantasy, or simply of good writing, will be doing him or herself a great disservice if they pass this one up. Highly recommended.

Colin Greenland (review date 20 November 1987)

SOURCE: A Review of *The Folk of the Air*, in *New Statesman*, Vol. 114, No. 29,561, November 20, 1987, p. 31.

[Below, Greenland argues that The Folk of the Air *"lacks the mordant Jewish irony" that was present in* A Fine and Private Place.*]*

In (and out of) progress since 1971, and featuring Farrell, hero of a story from 1969, Peter S. Beagle's comeback novel *The Folk of the Air* is also somewhat concerned with old hippies. The protraction has not been good for it. Though this book has much of Beagle's former lyrical expansiveness and wry, lugubrious caricature in sidelights, it mostly lacks the mordant Jewish irony that, in *A Fine and Private Place* especially, co-ordinated the various purples of the prose. The titular Folk are a group of Californian Creative Anachronists, who put on medieval dress, talk like Robin Hood movies, and hold banquets, jousts, wars and so on. Initially scornful, Farrell, a rootless lutenist, rapidly becomes assimilated to their fraternity, just as it is taken over by a teenage witch and her brat demon boyfriend. Luckily Farrell's landlady is a retired goddess.

Beagle acknowledges the perversity of the League for Archaic Pleasures, the insecurity beneath the helms and wimples, but he so much wants it to be all right he allows their army to repulse a surprise attack by five real medieval mercenaries conjured through time, and lose only one man.

It's hard to tell whether this leniency, this new mellowness in the face of the preposterous, is because Beagle approves of these people or because he believes many of his old readers may now *be* these people.

John Pennington (essay date Summer 1989)

SOURCE: "Innocence and Experience and the Imagination in the World of Peter Beagle," in *Mythlore*, Vol. 15, No. 4, Summer, 1989, pp. 10-16.

[In the following essay, Pennington applies William Blake's philosophy of contraries to understand Beagle's work and its critical reception.]

"Without Contraries is no progression. Attraction and Repulsion, Reason and Energy, Love and Hate, are necessary to Human existence," writes William Blake in his radical and paradoxical *The Marriage of Heaven and Hell*, a marriage that prompted C.S. Lewis to annul in *The Great Divorce*. In Blake's universe opposites attract and repel and inform one another. As Martin Nurmi explains;

> A human world must be informed by opposed yet positive and complementary forces which, when allowed to interact without external restraint, impart to life a motion and a tension that make it creative.

This dialectic is extremely complex, for unlike Yin and Yang which separates light from dark, good from evil into balancing forces (a philosophy at the heart of many of Ursula Le

Guin's fantasies and science fiction tales), Blake's philosophy encompasses contraries as simultaneous entities; these oppositions become the touchstone to the imagination and to creativity. *Songs of Innocence and Experience,* Blake's most accessible work, is also structured upon contraries: innocence and experience, the lamb and the tiger, the echoing green and London, the shepherd and the bard. The prelapsarian world of innocence, however, needs the influence of the experienced world since the Fall; otherwise, innocence becomes a victim of experience, as attested by the chimney sweeper's hopeful and naive rationalization for his pitiable condition. Experience, partly born from rigid and binding reason, blights innocence, but this too is essential. Mary Lynn Johnson and John Grant suggest that

> in the reader's mind the claims of Innocence and Experience should be weighed against each other; it is possible for the reader to share with the artist a vision that encompasses both and allows for the growth that comes out of continual strife of contraries.

In a sense, Blake's mythology is anti-romantic and highly realistic. "Opposition is true Friendship," writes Blake in *The Marriage:* "From these contraries spring what the religious call Good and Evil. Good is the passive that obeys Reason. Evil is the active springing from Energy. "Yet such good and evil are symbiotic, and our preconceived notions of these dichotomies must be modified and refined to encapsulate a more realistic design.

This overly succinct and limited synopsis of Blake's mythology points to the archetypal patterns that are the bases of romance, fairy and folktale, and fantasy. Brain Attebery claims that

> more than realistic fiction, it [fantasy] can clarify philosophical and moral conflicts, embodying them in story lines that may not be directly applicable to our own complex and muddied lives but which can please or inspire because of their open and evident design. This is one of the most important accomplishments at which fantasy can aim, to give comprehensible form to life, death, good, and evil; this has always been the primary aim of the earliest kind of fantasy, the folktale.

And R.E. Foust contends that

> it is by the unambiguity of this core encounter between Good and Evil that fantasy, unlike realism, asserts its mythic intentions: it conserves by reasoning ancient social ideals of decency, order, and proscribed behavior.

Attebery and Foust identify, it seems, the more conservative and simplistic design and function of much fantasy—good versus evil, often a cut-and-dry separation where good prevails over evil, a structure that C.S. Lewis and Tolkien basically follow. There are, however, more complex fantasies which muddle these polarities and explore the tenuous relationship between good and evil, fantasies that subscribe to Blake's theory of contraries.

In his review essay on *The Lord of the Rings,* Peter S. Beagle argues that the forces that power Tolkien's trilogy are similar to those that control our daily lives—"history, chance, and desire." "*The Lord of the Rings,*" continues Beagle,

> is a tale of Frodo's journey through a long nightmare of greed and terrible energy, of his education in both fear and true beauty, and of final loss of the world he seeks to save. In a sense, his growing knowledge has eaten up the joy and the innocent strength that made him, of all the wise and magic people he encounters, the only one fit to bear the Ring.

Beagle's diction—*energy, knowledge, innocent*—is peculiarly Blakean, and in Beagle's fantasy world we can see Blake's contraries at work. Reason and Energy. Love and Hate. Good and Evil. Innocence and Experience. These opposites are what keep Beagle's imaginative world alive, and in *The Last Unicorn,* his most sustained fantasy, such contraries are the key that keeps the work progressing.

The Last Unicorn has received overwhelming praise. As the blurb on my edition claims, it is "one of the world's most beloved fantasies," even made into a successful, though overly childish, animated feature film. Robert H. Boyer and Kenneth J. Zahorski believe that "if there were a 'ten best' list of modern fantasy, *The Last Unicorn* would certainly be on it." And that would include a list of such luminaries as Tolkien, Lewis, Williams, Le guin. Yet some critics are unimpressed with Beagle's creation, most notably C.N. Manlove and Brian Attebery. Manlove considers *The Last Unicorn* an anemic work, and though Attebery praises moments of the work—Mommy Fortuna's Midnight Carnival, the barren Hagsgate, the sea-enslaved unicorns, and the Red Bull—he feels that "its characters and imagery go flying off in all directions, without reference to the patterns of significance that should command." His major complaint is that Beagle's attempt at a "literary homage" to Tolkien misfires because he is unable to find a proper balance between Thurberesque humor and Tolkienesque grandeur:

> The graft fails to take, and the two components draw apart, the magic into sentimentality and the modern voice into embarrassed joking. . . . But

Beagle does not gather these things into a satisfying whole because he lacks faith in them.

The Last Unicorn is certainly an unusual fantasy, hovering between humor and pathos, but these two strains are conscious selections. Another way to view *The Last Unicorn* is to read it as a homage and a parody simultaneously, to see it as encompassing contradictory "visions" not unlike Blake's cosmos. Beagle creates in *The Last Unicorn* a new breed of fantasy that is dependent upon traditional fairytale structures and themes but one that also undercuts these and forges into new fantasy territory. Beagle's precursors? George MacDonald, Lewis Carroll, James Thurber.

To define fantasy is to open Pandora's box—near chaos reigns. Tolkien, Todorov, Brooke-Rose, Rabkin, Irwin, Swinfen, Jackson, to only name a few have all attempted to define fantasy; each study has its own merits, but as in any kind of classification and definition, these studies are limited to the select few fantasies that "fit" an individual theory. Definition of fantasy becomes exclusive, myopic, often useless as a literary tool. This is the central concern of Kathryn Hume in *Fantasy and Mimesis,* an engrossing study of fantasy in relation to realism. Hume intends to be more inclusive in her definition of fantasy; she contends

> that literature is the product of two impulses. These are *mimesis,* felt as the desire to imitate, to describe events, people, situations, and objects with such verisimilitude that others can share your experience; and *fantasy,* the desire to change givens and later reality—out of boredom, play, vision, longing for something lacking, or need for metaphoric images that will bypass the audience's verbal defences.

In his recent fantasy *The Folk of the Air,* Beagle takes literally Hume's conception of literature and tries to fuse the realistic with the fantastic, with definitely mixed results. Hume identifies two strains of fantasy that help us begin to categorize *The Last Unicorn.* One strain is the fantasy of *vision* which "aims to disturb us by dislodging us from our settled sense of reality, and tries to engage our emotions on behalf of this new version of the real." A fantasy of vision can achieve this end by "manipulating our literary expectations, giving us a different presentation of reality than we expect from the form or story (as Gardner does in *Grendel*)." The fantasy of *revision,* on the other hand, "lays out plans for revising reality, for shaping futures"; this type of fantasy focuses on man and the cosmos—on man's relation with himself and the world—and works more on the didactic level, for

> we are given the grounds for saying that one action is good while another is bad—or effective and ineffective, or proper and improper. One can assimi-

late an experience readily if one can classify and relate it to other experiences. A didactic system gives us that framework, and with it, prescriptions for our own responses and action. This guidance helps lessen the indigestibility of chaotic experience.

The fantasy of vision is "expressive" and "expects only reaction," while the fantasy of revision is "didactic" and pushes "the reader from passive agreement to action." As these definitions imply, the fantasy of vision is diametrically opposed to the fantasy of revision—one explodes our notion of a coherent reality, the other rearranges it into an easily accessible form. Lewis could be pigeon-holed as a revisionist, Borges as a visionist.

The Last Unicorn incorporates these contradictory strains of fantasy—the work is both vision and revision—and this may point to Attebery's complaint: *The Last Unicorn* does indeed meld together disparate narrative approaches. On the visionist level, *The Last Unicorn* is a metafictional or metafantastical tale that consciously analyzes itself as a literary creation. Beagle undercuts, parodies, and revises traditional fairy-tale structures into a modern schematic that accounts more effectively for Blakean contraries. On the revisionist level, though, Beagle ironically provides us with a foundation to lay good and evil, innocence and experience together, provides us with a framework that accounts for man and the universe. Beagle's fantasy of vision works more on the structural level, his fantasy of revision on the thematic level, and this tension manifests itself throughout the fantasy. Schmendrick claims in *The Last Unicorn,*

> For only to a magician is the world forever fluid, infinitely mutable and entirely new. Only he knows the secret of change, only he knows truly that all things are crouched in eagerness to become something else, and it is from this universal tension that he draws his power.

From contraries or universal tension comes potentiality and progression, as Blake well knew, and Beagle in *The Last Unicorn* is the literary magician who takes two kinds of cream and churns them magnificently into a powerful and tasty bit of butter.

The best analysis of *The Last Unicorn* is undoubtedly R.E. Foust's "Fabulous Paradigm: Fantasy, Meta-Fantasy, and Peter S. Beagle's *The Last Unicorn.*" "Peter Beagle is the most neglected American fictionist of more than ordinary talent to reach creative maturity in the 1960s," claims Foust perhaps a bit too eagerly. Barth, Barthelme, Coover, Gass, Pynchon—Foust places Beagle in such ranks. His thesis is that Beagle's fantasy is

> a paradigmatic instance of an assured transition now

in process from the 'metafictions' of the sixties to the more recent imagination of the fabulous that heralds, it may be, the next evolutionary stage in the development of the novel.

Foust analyzes Beagle's "linguistic playfulness"—"language, then, is highly anachronistic, alliterative, synaethetic, onomatopoeic, metaphoric, and metonymic"—and shows how Beagle collapses mythic and historical temporality, what Foust labels "extra-(con)-textuality." *The Last Unicorn* reflects a timelessness both internal and external to the text which

> signifies Beagle's attempt to augment the reader's skeptical historical attention with both the linear and the mythic tempos of the narrative for the sake of extrapolating from their impacting an extra-textual sense of mythic or timeless possibility.

He ends his study by defining such fantasists as Beagle's as an alteration between "the realistic and the anti-novel":

> It is an extended fictional narrative prose, paying strict attention to deep and repeated verisimilar dislocations, which attempts to deliver the reader into a fictive realm ruled over by heart's desire—by mutability and potency—for the ethical purpose of re-creating and energizing the reader's sense of culturally shared value.

Here we have, it seems, an analogy to the visionist and revisionist fantasy which weaves its spell through opposition. Beagle's metafantasy—the visionist stage—exposes and explores the fictional reality of fairy tales. Such self-reflexivity makes *The Last Unicorn* a new type of fantasy that is a powerful vision for the modern world.

Patricia Waugh posits that

> metafictional novels tend to be constructed on the principle of a fundamental and sustained opposition: the construction of a fictional illusion (as in traditional realism) and the laying bare of that illusion,

and Robert Scholes theorizes that experimental fabulation"—a type of metafiction—assumes

> "that the positivistic basis for traditional realism had been eroded, and that reality, if it could be caught at all, would require a whole new set of fictional skills.

Blake's experimentation with poetic and narrative structures, his blending of the verbal with the visual, his undercutting and parody of Swedenborg's *Treatise Concerning Heaven*

and Hell, for example, could classify his *Marriage,* on one level, as a metafictional work. Beagle's strategy is similar: he wants to exhaust the traditional fairy-tale structures and imbue them with new life—to make modern—and he achieves this through metafictional means. In *The Last Unicorn* characters write and revise their own story, aware that they are part of a fairy tale, similar to Escher's hands that draw each other into being.

Disgruntled over his inability to contain and redirect magic, Schmendrick thinks, "The magic knows what it wants to do. . . But I never know what it knows. Not at the right time, anyway. I'd write it a letter, if I knew were it lived." This allusion to the writing process is a touchstone to Schmendrick's quest to rewrite his fairy tale into a happy ending, and to Beagle's goal to create a new type of fairy tale. *The Last Unicorn* begins as a traditional fairy tale—a unicorn, once upon a time, in an Edenic garden. Immediately, though, the narrative is placed in a larger framework, one antagonistic to the fairy tale. Hunters appear in the wood and debate the reality of unicorns: "'Unicorns are long gone,' the second man said. 'If, indeed, they ever were. This is a forest like any other'." The hunter's conception of a unicorn is

> "only from books and tales and song. . . . You know no more about unicorns that I do, for I've read the same books and heard the same stories, and I've never seen one either." One hunter remarks, "You don't have to have a golden bridle to catch a unicorn; that part's the fairy tale."

Beagle creates a complex web—characters discuss the nature of fairy tales while they are part of a fairy tale. The hunters allude to Pliny and the Chinese myths about unicorns, yet they are part of this very myth. Fiction becomes reality, even though the characters are unaware that they are part of the very fairy tale.

The unicorn's encounter with the rambling butterfly also reinforces this theme. Giving us a catalogue of such disparate elements from Yeats, Conrad, popular songs, and television commercials, the butterfly represents the medium between the myth and reality, between the timelessness of fairy tales and the timebound world of literature and television. Thus the butterfly is transcendent, able to exist within myth and outside in the real, parallel to the way the hunters can discuss fairy tales as they are part of one. The butterfly is self-conscious of both perspectives, and when the unicorn challenges the butterfly to guess her name, it responds, "Rumplestiltskin," now using traditional folktale material for its means. When the butterfly defines *unicorn*—"Unicorn. Old French, unicorne. Latin, unicornis. Literally, one-horned: *unus,* one and *cornu,* a horn. A fabulous animal resembling a horse with one horn"—it parodies the definition of a horse found in *Hard Times* and pinpoints the structural tension of

The Last Unicorn: real versus mythical, literary versus extraliterary. Fiction is fleshed into life, life is fleshed into fiction.

Another use of metafictional devices in the fantasy is Beagle's use of the story-within-the story technique to foreshadow and comment on future action. Schmendrick tells us about his mentor Nikos who changed a unicorn into a young man; this "fiction" will shortly become reality. Captain Cully, a rough parody of the Robin Hood myth, consciously tries to insert himself into legend and myth. He boasts,

> One always hopes, of course, even now—to be collected, to be verified, annotated, to have variant versions, even to have one's authenticity doubted . . . well, well, never mind.

This hilarious debunking of academia also raises the question of literary authenticity within the tale itself, and, of course, the Captain, for all his poems and legends, is not the real thing, and Schemendrick calls up the real Robin Hood to show Cully precisely this. Myth again becomes reality within a fictional creation. As Molly understands, "Nay, Cully, you have it backwards. There's no such person as you, or me, or any of us. Robin and Marian are real, and we are the legend!" Beagle reinvents myth here; it takes on reality and becomes more real than the fictional reality we are reading. Text is replaced by subtext, or as Waugh explains,

> One way of reinforcing the notion of literary fiction as an alternative world is the use of literary and mythical allusion which remind the reader of the existence of this world outside everyday time and space, of its thorough-going textuality and intertextuality.

Other instances in the fantasy show fiction becoming real, or the literary characters in *The Last Unicorn* becoming fiction: the poems of Captain Cully that try to place him into the world of myth; the poem a young maiden sings in hopes of calling up a unicorn (the same poem Lady Amalthea will sing); the legend of Hagsgate that is created to prevent the curse from becoming reality—

> "Those dark tales of Hagsgate that you spoke of— we invented them ourselves, and spread them as widely as we could to make certain that we would have few visitors."

The cumulative effect of these instances is to disturb our notion of what is real and unreal, and Beagle succeeds by disturbing our literary expectations.

By far the most sustained use of metafictional techniques is the character's awareness that they are part of a fairy tale in which they can determine the outcome. As we as readers are challenged to juggle this extra-(con)-textuality, so are the characters. Schmendrick and Molly are the two polar characters who represent various attitudes towards their status as fictional characters. Schmendrick understands that he is in a fairy tale, and he is always looking for plot lines to keep the tale progressing, and he understands that certain triggers must be present in a fairy tale. He tells Molly, who complains about the citizens who abandoned a young child,

> Well, if they hadn't, he couldn't have grown up to be a prince. Haven't you ever been in a fairy tale before? The hero has to make a prophecy come true, and the villain is the one who has to stop him— though in another kind of story, it's more often true the other way around. . . . I've been waiting for this tale to turn up a leading man.

Molly, however, feels that only the unicorn is real, others just an illusion: "Haggard and Lir and Drinn and you and I—we are in a fairy tale, and must go where it goes. But she is real She is real." So real, it appears, that she transcends the fairy tale. But Schmendrick manipulates the tale, and his transformation of the unicorn into Lady Amalthea, who then becomes a traditional fairy-tale princess, ironically inserts the unicorn into the myth.

This is the importance of the first unicorn-Red Bull encounter. Schmendrick begins to revise the fairy tale. Because he changes the unicorn into the princess, the fairy tale must be adjusted to account for this. As he explains to Lady Amalthea,

> You're in the story with the rest of us now, and you must go with it, whether you will or no. If you want to find your people, if you want to become a unicorn again, then you must follow the fairy tale to King Haggard's castle, and wherever else it chooses to take you. The story cannot end without the princess.

In a sense, two separate tales—that of the unicorn, and that of Schmendrick and Molly—are fused together.

The fairy tale, then, begins again with different parameters, and those parameters from old tales are no longer useful to this tale. A new tale must be written. Once they arrive at Haggard's castle, there is a debate as to how the tale should end; conventionally with Lir and Amalthea marrying, or non-conventionally with the hero and heroine remaining apart. Lir tends to represent the conventional, and Beagle satirizes this by having Lir exaggerated as a hero. He complains, "For her sake, I have become a hero," yet his deeds have no effect on Lady Amalthea, for she has never been in such a tale before. "I have swum four rivers, each in full flood and none less than a mile wide," admits Lir.

> I have climbed seven mountains never before climbed, slept three nights in the Marsh of the Hanged men, and walked live out of that forest where the flowers burn your eyes and the nightingales sing poison. I have. . . .

And the catalogue goes on . . . and on. Lir even resorts to writing love poems to Lady Amalthea:

> He was sitting on a stool in the corner, evidently writing another poem. "Gazelle," he murmured, tapping his pen against this lips. "Demoiselle, citadel, asphodel, philomel, parallel. . . " He chose "farewell," and scribbled rapidly.

Lir says, "It's hard to give up being a hero, once you get used to it." He learns how to be a romantic hero, albeit a foolish and silly one, but Lady Amalthea is entirely new to the game and it takes her a while to feel comfortable with her role as princess. When she approaches the castle with Molly and Schmendrick, a sentinel notices her specialness:

> She has a newness. Everything is for the first time. See how she moves, how she walks, how she turns her head—all for the first time anyone has done these things before.

The climax of *The Last Unicorn* revolves around the battle between the unicorn and the Red Bull, and, as importantly, between the traditional and the new: the characters must decide *how* to end their tale, and the fate of the unicorn is really up to them. As Lady Amalthea, the unicorn has forgotten her true being, and she wishes to remain as a mortal and be with Lir. Schmendrick says resignedly,

> You can love, and fear, and forbid things to be what they are, and overact. Let it end here then, let the quest end. . . . Marry the prince and live happily ever after.

Lady Amalthea learns her role only too well. It is, ironically, Lir who finally acts like a true hero, not a parody of one; he realizes the importance of a true ending, and he will not condone an ending that allows for the unicorn to remain mortal:

> But the true secret of being a hero lies in knowing the order of things. . . . Things must happen when it is time for them to happen. Quests may not simply be abandoned; prophecies may not be left to rot like unpicked fruit; unicorns may go unrescued for a long time, but not forever. The happy ending cannot come in the middle of the story.

Though Molly wants the tale to end, she is unable to persuade Schmendrick to help. He says, "I have no concern for regulated rescues and official happy endings. That's Lir." And when Lir chastises Schmendrick for his inability to help the unicorn in her battle with the Red Bull, Schmendrick admits with "sad mockery in his voice": "That's what heroes are for." Lir's selfless sacrifice for the unicorn gives the unicorn the power to drive the Red Bull into the sea, thus freeing the trapped unicorns. Prince Lir restores magic back into the world, he fulfills the age-old prophecy, and he does this by consciously inserting himself in the fairy tale—he finally understands what it means to be a hero in a fairy tale.

Yet the tale cannot quite end here, for Beagle intends for his characters to return back to their old tales and resume their old adventures. Schmendrick tells Lir,

> Your true task has just begun, and you may not know in your life if you have succeeded in it. . . . As for her, she is a story with no ending, happy or sad. She can never belong to anything mortal enough to want her.

Lir, then, must become part of another unfinished tale and find his happy ending. When Schmendrick and Molly, on their way to their own tale, meet Alison Jocelyn, a damsel in dire distress, Schmendrick sends her to Lir ("'I send all my princesses to him'") so that Lir's tale can end on a traditional happy note, but he understands that in their current fairy tale such endings are not appropriate. He reasons, "Great heroes need great sorrows and burdens, or half their greatness goes unnoticed. It is all part of the fairy tale."

Schmendrick and Molly. They too are just beginning their tale, and Beagle has them go "away together, out of this story and into another." Each character can now go on with his or her story, the unicorn the magic that will hover over the tales. The metafictional dimension to *The Last Unicorn* draws attention to the literary merits of the fairy tale, reworking conventional structures into an original one, breathing new life into an old form. Beagle expands fairy-tale discourse; his fantasy of vision speaks more loudly and clearly to a modern world far, far away from the land of the fantastic imagination.

For all his debunking of fairy-tale form, however, Beagle still relies on the archetypal pattern of good versus evil to emphasize his thematic concerns. *The Last Unicorn* is also a fantasy of revision which provides "programs for improving reality." Near the end of the tale, Schmendrick realizes: *"I did not know that I was so empty, to be so full."* This metaphor of emptiness-fullness mirrors the central theme of the work, that good and evil, innocence and experience are vital to one's understanding of one's self and the world. Raymond Olderman argues,

Beagle gives us recognition of life's pains and sorrows, but only a symbolically ponderous threat of annihilation; he emphasizes, instead, the balance of caring and loving with a world of wonder, [asking us] to revalue by making us see anew. The rediscovery of wonder in the world may ultimately be the best our decade [the 70s] can offer as a substitute for a truly accepted mythology to move us out of the waste land.

The revisionist strain in the fantasy categorizes and provides for us strategies for living.

The Last Unicorn is about the importance of innocence and the imagination in a fallen world, an innocence, it must be noted, based on experience, a quality of this fallen world. Like Blake, Beagle emphasizes the fearful symmetry between innocence and experience. The unicorn is untainted innocence, the Red Bull pure corrupted experience; Molly and Schmendrick are innocents on their way to experience. The tale progresses precisely because the unicorn, Molly, and Schmendrick meet Mommy Fortuna, Haggard, and the Red Bull.

At the beginning of the fantasy we are immersed in a world of innocence, a prelapsarian world of magic. The unicorn's wood is an enchanted wood where "it was always spring." It is Edenic. The hunters represent the realm of experience and they invade the unicorn's wood, one disbelieving in magic and unicorns, the other certainly undecided. One hunter gives warning, however: "This is no world for you. Stay in your forest, and keep your trees and green and your friends long-lived." But they bring temptation to the unicorn; she begins to wonder where her other "friends" truly are. Her curiosity spurs her to leave the unfallen world for the fallen one. In the experienced world none but a select few, those pure of heart, can recognize the unicorn. As the princess who attempts to call a unicorn states:

> If there really were such things as unicorns, one would have to come to me. I called as sweetly as anyone could, and I had the golden bridle. And of course I am pure and untouched.

Sure! But she only pretends to believe, for in her world there is no room for unicorns. The unicorn is welcomed to the world of experience.

Her first dangerous encounter in the new world is with Mommy Fortuna's Midnight Carnival where "creatures of night, [are] brought to light." Mommy Fortuna's carnival is based on illusion; she weaves her "spells of seeming" so that people believe that they are actually seeing caged mythological beasts—a manticore, dragon, satyr, Cerbeus, Midgard Serpent, Arachne. But all these are actually mundane—a

dog, crocodile, lion, etc. Mommy Fortuna must ironically cast spells on the unicorn and the harpy even though they are real; the world is too fallen to identify the magical. This world is dangerous, not because people are unable to see through appearances, but because such a demented person as Mommy can see though illusion. After all, she is able to do what is virtually impossible—capture a unicorn and a harpy. The unicorn's magical defences are not powerful enough to protect her completely in this world. Mommy Fortuna's capture and caging of the unicorn is symbolic for her imprisonment of the imagination. The cage represents the experienced world that binds and chains innocence and stifles creativity; it will trap her forever if allowed:

> The cage began to grow smaller.... Already she could not turn around. The bars were drawing in, pitiless as the tide or the morning, and they would shear through her until they surrounded her heart, which they would keep a prisoner forever.

An interesting addition to the carnival is the harpy. Don Norford suggests that the harpy reflects the "active power of rage, hatred—what Freud called *thanatos,* the aggressive, destructive, death instinct," and by extension, then, the unicorn represents the contrary—love, compassion, passivity, creation. That both creatures are from the magical realm is significant, for these opposing forces are part of the natural structure. Its imprisonment is also unnatural, and Beagle may be suggesting that such destructiveness is a result of being denied freedom, for only those destroyed by the harpy try to run away. The unicorn explains, "You must never run from anything immortal. It attracts their attention." The precarious balance between unicorn and harpy is essential for the imagination.

Immortality and mortality is another tension that is explored in *The Last Unicorn*.

> I am a king's daughter
> And I grow old within
> The prison of my person,
> The shackles of my skin.

This poem becomes a motif, later sung by Lady Amalthea. Like the cage, the body is also a container of immortality, and the unicorn becomes trapped into mortality. By being mortal, the unicorn begins to forget that she is immortal; she forgets her innocence. But her loss of immortality results in a gain of humanity, and she learns about love. She is changed forever, as she explains:

> I have been mortal, and some part of me is mortal yet. I am full of tears and hunger and the fear of death, though I cannot weep, and I want nothing, and I cannot die. I am not like the others now, for

no unicorn was ever born who could regret, but I do. I regret.

Here we have an interesting revision of the Adam and Eve story: the unicorn is thrust back into her prelapsarian world having tasted from the tree of knowledge—she knows goodness and evil, her innocence is informed by experience, and she must live forever with the burden of such knowledge. Original sin also touches the unicorn.

In contrast to the unicorn-Lady Amalthea metamorphosis is the Haggard-Red Bull transformation. There is little of merit to these creatures, except that they force the others to act wisely. The Red Bull represents Haggard's subconscious selfish desires—his "eyes were the same color as the horns of the Red Bull. "He was the color of blood," writes Beagle of the Red Bull, "but not springing blood of the heart but the blood that stirs under an old wound that never really healed." Contrast: the redness of the bull to the whiteness of the unicorn, the bull's destructiveness to the unicorn's ability to heal. The Red Bull is amorphous, having "no shape at all, but a swirling darkness, the red darkness you see when you close your eyes in pain. The horns had become the two sharpest towers of old King Haggard's crazy castle." Norford finds the Red Bull "associated with Fear, the fear of pain and loss that keeps one from life and makes the world a wasteland." It "represents emptiness, dread, the pain and sorrow of life" while the "unicorn represents fullness, the overflowing horn of plenty, the bounty and beauty of life." The Red Bull is a void, a hollowness that reflects Haggard and Hagsgate's barrenness; it symbolizes caged experience, as Lady Amalthea represents caged innocence. In *The Book of Urizen,* Blake explores the cosmogony myth of Urizen whose fear of the imagination forces him to use reason to contain it, thus separating himself in two. Haggard is like Urizen; he is fearful of unrestrained energy and creativity and joy, so he redirects this energy into the Red Bull who then hunts down the unicorn and traps them in the sea. Whereas the harpy is natural, the Red Bull is man-made, a creature not unlike that in *The Forbidden Planet.* Rintrah, the keeper of the wasteland in *The Marriage of Heaven and Hell,* "roars & shakes his fires in the burdened air" and drives "the just man into barren climes"; he is a prototype for the Red Bull.

Haggard's loss of humanity is parallel to the unicorn's acquisition of humanity. One survives, the other is destroyed. Good defeats Evil, but not without a price. Everyone's world is changed: Hagsgate will now become barren as the land becomes fertile, Prince Lir will become the King; a new age begins. The world is on the mend, and the ending is a tentative happy one, the Red Bull as always an ominous presence. But in Beagle's world, and in Blake's, these opposing forces are important: Haggard and the Red Bull force Schmendrick and Prince Lir to find their true selves, and the unicorn has

a knowledge that may make her more magical than ever, for she is now universal—immortal, mortal; innocent, experienced. Beagle's revisionist fantasy teaches us that opposition is true friendship, that his fairy tale is complex enough to account for such contraries.

The Last Unicorn is Beagle's masterpiece, a truly original fantasy. It challenges us to revise our conception of literature and reality, and it presents avenues so we can travel wisely. He takes two strains of fantasy—vision and revision—and meshes them together to make a whole that is more powerful that the parts. Norford concludes his study by saying, "Apparently, the immortal and mortal, joy and sorrow, life and death, are equally real halves of the same whole: you cannot have one without the other." This synthesis of opposites recalls Blake's contraries. Brian Attebery proposes that

> the American writer [of fantasy] must find some way of reentering the ancient storytelling guild: he must validate his claim to the archetypes that are the tools of the trade. To do so, he must find an archetypal analogy for his own land—an American fairyland—to which those old world magical motifs may be drawn.

In *The Last Unicorn* Beagle enters this guild by creating an original fantasy of vision and revision; he plays with metafictional structures and recombines the archetypal patters of fairy tales into a vision that is specifically modern. And American. For all are equal, all have the potentiality for good (and evil), all are free to choose, and even the evil that permeates much of the world can be redirected. Without the Red Bull we can have no unicorns, for in Beagle's world without contraries is no progression.

Gary K. Wolfe (review date September 1993)

SOURCE: A review of *The Innkeeper's Song,* in *Locus,* September, 1993, pp. 23-4.

[*In the review below, Wolfe compares* The Innkeeper's Song *to Beagle's earlier works and concludes that* The Last Unicorn *is Beagle's best fantasy but that* The Innkeeper's Song *is his best novel.*]

A couple of months ago, Peter Beagle said in a *Locus* interview that *The Last Unicorn* might well go on dominating his work, and he's probably right: it became an instant classic for its grace, wit, complexity, and accessibility. It's not surprising that many readers, including myself, found 1987's *The Folk of the Air* a little thin by comparison with what we'd hoped for after such a long wait. By now, Beagle must certainly be accustomed to readers wanting another *Unicorn,* just as Woody Allen has to live with fans who want him to do more funny movies. His new novel, *The Innkeeper's Song,* is likely to confound everyone's expectations. Its basic premise—a war between two nearly all-powerful wizards—seems the stuff of supermarket fantasy, but it's a fantasy in the same way that Clint Eastwood's *Unforgiven* is a western, and it draws the same kind of power from setting, character, and memory. *The Last Unicorn* may always be Beagle's best fantasy, but *The Innkeeper's Song,* based on an enigmatic song Beagle wrote some years ago, is his best *novel.*

If I seem to be invoking filmmakers to describe this novel, there's a reason: Beagle has been doing a lot of film work in recent years, and perhaps as a result this contains some of the most strikingly visual of his writing. The love of language is still evident, but it's no longer as playful, and his gritty, dark setting, lightly sketched in as it is, is among the most memorable worlds in recent fantasy. What is surprising is that Beagle achieves this with a minimum of self-conscious world-building, and without the aid of the omniscient narrative voice he has used in the past. Instead, he offers no fewer than six major narrators and four minor ones, each with a distinct voice and perspective, and each with his or her own story. This technique of describing a common crisis in the lives of several characters through a kind of volleyball point of view is difficult enough to bring off in mainstream fiction—Ernest Gaines' *A Gathering of Old Men* is an example—but in fantasy, where so much of the nature of the fictive world must be revealed by indirection, it's a positive *tour de force.*

All these characters' stories converge during one summer when three mysterious women arrive at a rural inn called the Gaff and Slasher, pursued by the forlorn lover of one of the women, Lukassa, who had earlier drowned and been resurrected by Lal, a swordswoman and sailor with some supernatural powers. The third woman is Nyateneri, who it turns out is also being pursued by some genuinely chilling assassins. (Nyateneri also provides us with an effectively startling surprise during a sexual escapade that is one of the book's several set-pieces of narrative technique.) Accompanying the women is a fox who can change into a jolly old man, and the chapters told in the fox's quirky voice at times call to mind the butterfly's speeches in *The Last Unicorn.* The innkeeper himself, the gruff and exasperated Karsh, is another wonderful voice, and one which serves to ground the narrative with periodic doses of no-nonsense realism.

Other characters include Karsh's stable boy Rosseth, who falls in love with all three of the women visitors; Tikat, Lukassa's devoted lover; and the two wizards, who are the only major characters who never narrate chapters. The older wizard, the former teacher of Lal and Nyateneri, is sheltered at the inn while the two women undertake a quest to find his enemy and former pupil Arshadin. The quest ends surprisingly badly—heroics don't always add up to much in Beagle's world, though they're impressively portrayed—and the final apocalyptic battle returns the action to the inn itself, and gives a surprising and satisfying role to the drowned woman Lukassa. By the end, all the pieces and voices fit together in a tapestry that is both rich and simple, filled with both genuine hope and genuine regrets. Unexpected though it is, given his previous work, *The Innkeeper's Song* may be the novel that we've all been hoping Beagle will write, and it may be some sort of classic.

Gerald Jonas (review date 14 November 1993)

SOURCE: A review of *The Innkeeper's Song,* in *New York Times Book Review,* November 14, 1993, p. 74.

[*In the following favorable review, Jonas discusses* The Innkeeper's Song, *asserting that in Beagle's hands "even the most timeworn material shines again."*]

As Webster's Third New International Dictionary confirms, the word "fantasy" has a long and honorable lineage. Its ancestry can be traced back to the Greek *phantazein,* "to make visible, present to the mind," which is derived from *phaos,* the Greek word for light, and akin to the Sanskrit *bhati,* "it shines." Sadly, most books marketed today under the label of fantasy do a disservice to this proud etymology. Instead of fresh wonders made visible, fantasy as a commercial genre has come to mean endlessly recycled adventures of sword-wielding heroes and spell-casting wizards, recounted in a pseudopoetic prose as dreary and predictable as the characters and settings. This makes the achievement of Peter S. Beagle in *The Innkeeper's Song* all the more remarkable. In his capable hands even the most timeworn material shines again.

Mr. Beagle, whose 1968 novel, *The Last Unicorn,* is something of a classic in the field, sets his story of love and loss in familiar territory—a preindustrial world in which the levers of power are manipulated, for good or ill, by people known as wizards or magicians. Three women—one black, one brown and one paler than a corpse—take a room in a village inn. Their coming is no accident. Two of the women are former pupils of a magician who is locked in a deadly duel with his greatest protégé; the pale woman has been called back from the dead by an act of gratuitous kindness that will have profound consequences.

No hint is given of how this world is related to our own or how its magic is related to our science, but it is clear from the outset that the exercise of power here follows rules every bit as exacting as those of physics or chemistry, and as baffling to those who lack the requisite knowledge. The story, rich in incident but no more complicated than it need be, is told from multiple points of view: the three women, a young man consumed by love, the innkeeper, his servants and a "fox" who is sometimes a "man" but who turns out to be neither. The only characters who do not speak in the first person are the dueling magicians; they provide the occasion for the story, not its focus.

While Mr. Beagle distinguishes the various speakers by more or less subtle shifts of tone, all share an unaffected eloquence that we recognize as the voice of the natural storyteller. On shooting white-water rapids: "Crosslegged as always, drenched with bitterly stinging spray, her neck and shoulders so bruised that she could only look ahead, she eased our boat through that wildness like a needle through folds of silk." On the bad taste left in the mouth by speaking a language associated with past evils: "That tongue has been dead for five centuries, which is not nearly long enough." On the power of magicians: "Magicians never lock their doors."

If the author of a fantasy like this has done his job well, he has earned the right to a summation, a moral if you will. Mr. Beagle's is characteristically complex: "Love each other from the day we are born to the day we die, we are still strangers every minute, and nobody should forget that even though we have to."

Tom Easton (review date April 1994)

SOURCE: A review of *The Innkeeper's Song,* in *Analog,* Vol. CXIV, No. 5, April, 1994, pp. 166-68.

[*In the review below, Easton remarks favorably on* The Innkeeper's Song.]

Peter S. Beagle is well known for beautifully crafted fantasies—think of *The Last Unicorn* and *The Folk of the Air*—that offer rather different takes on familiar themes. It is thus a great pleasure to find that he has produced a new novel, ***The Innkeeper's Song***.

Beagle's numerous fans undoubtedly grabbed the book as soon as they saw it on the bookstore shelf. For those of you who resisted temptation but have been wondering whether those who succumbed got their money's worth, let me assure you they did.

The tale is constructed as if, many years later, its several characters are relating what happened to an interviewer, perhaps the novelist, perhaps the reader, perhaps just a stranger who has joined them at their table in the inn. Why are they talking? Well, perhaps someone sang the title song—

> "There came three ladies at sundown:
> one was as brown as bread is brown,
> one was black, with a sailor's sway,
> and one was pale as the moon by day."

—And they hinted that they were the ladies, the innkeeper, the potboy, the stableboy, or even the fox. The interviewer said, "Mmm?" and they answered, "Buy me a drink, and I'll tell you. . . ."

The prologue sets up the situation: Two lovers, soon to be married, are strolling. They pause on the village bridge, where winter rains have rotted a railing that gives way. The bride-to-be, Lukassa, drowns. The groom-to-be, Tikat, tries to save her but fails, and then neither he nor his fellow villagers can find Lucassa's body. Yet that night, while he sits forlornly on the bank, a strange woman appears, says a few words, and raises Lukassa from her watery grave. Sadly, she ignores her bereft lover, turning and leaving with the stranger. Tikat, of course, follows desperately.

Now the characters begin to speak for themselves. Here is the stableboy, Rosseth, who meets three women—black, brown, white—on their way to the inn, with a fox in a saddle bag. Here is the innkeeper, Karsh, a fat tyrant who is sure his new guests will be the ruin of him. Tikat again, starving in the wilderness until a man in a red coat points the way. The women, black Lal, Sailor Lal, who feels drawn by dreams to the aid of an old friend, a wizard; and Nyateneri, in flight from a strange convent that sends assassins after its apostates and also linked to the wizard.

Once everyone is at the inn, the search for the wizard begins. Alas, he has vanished, and only the recently dead Lukassa can read the signs of struggle with a rival and demons. They learn more—the wizard is doomed, his foe is a one-time student whom no one can defeat even though he is now dead, his fate is one of horror and peril to all the world. Yet when the final confrontation arrives, there proves to be hope after all. One of those at the inn has the power to draw the wizard back from death. Another has the power to draw that one as well. And a third turns out to be a *deus ex machina* in disguise with so much strength one cannot help but wonder why it did not intervene sooner.

Am I too cryptic? Tough. If I am more precise I will surely spoil your fun, for it is in the disguises that Beagle conceals his hand. The innkeeper, for instance, is a rather nicer fellow than he seems at first, and his tyranny has a solid foundation in guilt. One of the women is. . . well. And the fox. . . hmmm. I dare not say.

This is the kind of novel that absorbs you. Beagle tells the tale at one remove, but he still convinces you of its reality, and you are so reluctant to let him go at the end that, "Stay!" you cry. "Have another drink! And say, about that fox, what was his history? And what happened after?"

But there's no sequel promised. To his credit, Beagle always leaves you wanting more. I commend him and all his works unto you.

FURTHER READING

Criticism

Gutcheon, Beth. Review of *American Denim: A New Folk Art,* by Peter S. Beagle and Baron Wolman. *New York Times Book Review* (18 January 1976): 6.
Describes Beagle's text that accompanies the photographs as entertaining, pertinent, and well-crafted.

Hicks, Granville. "Visit to a Happy Haunting Ground." *Saturday Review* XLIII, No. 22 (28 May 1960): 18.
Argues that while *A Fine and Private Place* is not a first rate work, it is well-written and engaging.

Miller, Faren. Review of *The Innkeeper's Song,* by Peter S. Beagle. *Locus* 31, No. 4 (October 1993): 59.
Describes *The Innkeeper's Song* as deeply moving and lyrical.

Review of *The Garden of Earthly Delights,* Peter S. Beagle. *New York Times Book Review* (20 June 1982): 31.
Considers Beagle's book a good introduction to the work of the Flemish painter Hieronymus Bosch.

Olderman, Raymond M. "Out of the Waste Land: Peter S. Beagle, *The Last Unicorn.*" In *Beyond the Waste Land: A Study of the American Novel in the Nineteen-Sixties,* pp. 220-42. New Haven, CT: Yale University Press, 1972.
Discusses the wasteland imagery in *The Last Unicorn* and notes that Beagle's optimistic work breaks with the 1960s tradition.

Schlobin, Roger C. "The Survival of the Fool in Modern Heroic Fantasy." In *Aspects of Fantasy: Selected Essays from the Second International Conference on the Fantastic in Literature and Film,* edited by William Coyle, pp. 123-30. Westport, CT: Greenwood Press, 1986.
Schlobin considers examples from *The Last Unicorn* in his discussion of the role of the fool in fantasy literature.

Wolfe, Gary K. "1993: The Year in Review." *Locus* 32, No. 2 (February 1994): 37.
Praises *The Innkeeper's Song* as the most accomplished fantasy novel of 1993.

Additional coverage of Beagle's life and career is contained in the following sources published by Gale: *Contemporary Authors,* Vols. 9-12R; *Contemporary Authors New Revision Series,* Vols. 4 and 51; *Dictionary of Literary Biography Yearbook: 1980;* and *Something about the Author,* Vol. 60.

Pierre Berton
1920-

(Has also written under pseudonym Lisa Kroniuk.) Canadian journalist, historian, novelist, biographer, satirist, and children's writer.

The following entry presents criticism of Berton's work through 1997.

INTRODUCTION

One of Canada's best-selling authors, Berton has written over forty books on a wide variety of topics, most notably Canadian history. His historical works have drawn praise from reviewers for their engaging narrative style and their ability to make complex events and issues accessible to readers. Many academic critics, however, have faulted Berton for overdramatizing events and introducing historical inaccuracies, arguing that "serious" historians are overlooked while he "popularizes" history.

Biographical Information

Born July 12, 1920, in Whitehorse, a small town in the Yukon Territory, Pierre Berton spent his childhood in the rugged Canadian frontier. After graduating with a B.A. from the University of British Columbia in 1941, he became Canada's youngest city editor at the Vancouver *News-Herald,* where he remained for one year before joining the Canadian army. After four years of service, Berton returned to Vancouver, taking a position with the Vancouver *Sun* as a feature writer. In 1947 he moved to Toronto to work as an assistant editor with *Maclean's,* where he eventually rose to managing editor, a position he held until 1958. During this time, Berton began producing his first books, including *The Mysterious North* (1956) and *Klondike: The Life and Death of the Last Great Gold Rush* (1958), both of which earned the Governor General's Literary Award. It was during this time also that Berton began his work in television, eventually becoming a panelist on such programs as *Close-Up* and *Front Page Challenge.* When *Maclean's* objected to his television work, he took a position with the Toronto *Star,* writing a daily column from 1958 until 1962. Berton collected many of these columns into books such as *Just Add Water and Stir* (1959), *Adventures of a Columnist* (1960), and *Fast, Fast, Fast Relief* (1962). Although he continued his television work after leaving the *Star,* Berton devoted most of his time to his writing, producing nearly a book a year. Even in his late seventies, Berton continues to publish regularly. He

and his wife of over fifty years, the former Janet Walker, live in Kleinburg, Ontario.

Major Works

Berton's histories are characteristically easy-reading narratives that utilize an anecdotal approach. His most notable works, such as *Klondike, The Last Spike* (1971), and his books on the War of 1812, focus on the development of Canada during the nineteenth century. Central in that development is the birth of a Canadian national identity, which Berton feels is essential considering Canada's proximity to the United States. Berton makes clear the importance of differentiation between American and Canadian cultural makeup in *Hollywood's Canada: The Americanization of Our National Image* (1975), in which he criticizes the depiction of Canada in film, and *Why We Act Like Canadians: A Personal Exploration of Our National Character* (1982). Some of Berton's other works include collections of articles from his days as a journalist, a children's book, and a novel, written under the pseudonym Lisa Kroniuk, about sexual fantasies.

Critical Reception

Most of Berton's books have met with enormous popular appeal. Credited with creating a "new Canadian mythology," his historical accounts have made Canadian history accessible to a mass audience by presenting exhaustive research in a readable narrative. Many academic critics, however, fault Berton's work for some historical inaccuracies and the "publicity hype" it has received, claiming that work done by "serious" historians is overlooked as a result. In response to their attempts to distinguish between "popular" history and "serious" history, Berton responds, "History is history. Good history is good history. I don't make any distinctions." These detractors, however, have admitted that Berton's work is well written, and credit it for striking a "deeply responsive chord in Canada's reading public."

PRINCIPAL WORKS

The Mysterious North (nonfiction) 1956
Klondike: The Life and Death of the Last Great Gold Rush (history) 1958
Just Add Water and Stir (nonfiction) 1959
Adventures of a Columnist (nonfiction) 1960
The Secret World of Og (juvenile) 1961
Fast, Fast, Fast Relief (nonfiction) 1962
The Last Spike (history) 1971
Hollywood's Canada: The Americanization of Our National Image (nonfiction) 1975
The Dionne Years: A Thirties Melodrama (nonfiction) 1977
The Invasion of Canada, 1812-1813 (history) 1980
Flames Across the Border: The Canadian-American Tragedy, 1813-1814 (history) 1981
Why We Act Like Canadians: A Personal Exploration of Our National Character (nonfiction) 1982
*Masquerade (novel) 1985
Vimy (history) 1986
Starting Out, volume 1: 1920-1947 (autobiography) 1987
My Times: Living With History, 1947-1995 (autobiography) 1995
The Great Lakes (nonfiction) 1997

*This book was published under the pseudonym Lisa Kroniuk.

CRITICISM

Trevor Lloyd (review date 26 February 1956)

SOURCE: "Polar Challenge and Assault," in *The New York Times Book Review,* February 26, 1956, pp. 7, 27.

[*In the following review, Lloyd provides a brief summary of Berton's* The Mysterious North.]

To many people there is a perplexing similarity between the Arctic and Antarctic. Both come to mind as a mélange of ice and snow, penguins, polar bears, sledge dogs, blizzards, Eskimos, igloos and pack-ice and as the goal of infrequent but invariably heroic polar expeditions. Giant ice-breakers leave Boston for one in April and for the other in October, so that by some freak of geography we are provided with frigid and harrowing reports on a year-round basis.

All such confusion should now cease, even for readers who get no farther than the wrappers of these two excellent books. The jacket of Pierre Berton's **The Mysterious North** shows a mine shaft, a grinning native dance mask, a reindeer and a compass needle pointing steadfastly to the north, all superimposed on a map of Canada. By contrast, *The Antarctic Challenged* is wrapped in a photograph of ice floes, with a few barely distinguishable seals drowsing in the foreground. The striking antithesis is a fair one. Today, the Far North is a constantly broadening economic frontier, fairly bursting with activity. The Far South is five million square miles of ice-encrusted land surrounded by ice-filled seas.

Lord Mountevans in *The Antarctic Challenged* sets out to relate the story of Antarctic exploration in nontechnical language, and in this he succeeds admirably. His sixteen chapters provide an introduction to the geography and wildlife of the Far South, and summarize the most important expeditions that have visited the region in the last 170 years. All the great names, from Capt. James Cook to Admiral Richard E. Byrd are met with, and the author often uses their own accounts to highlight his narrative. Speaking of Antarctica, which he had sailed around but barely seen, Cook, who was once a Yorkshire grocer's apprentice, said with his customary terseness: "To judge the bulk by the sample, it would not be worth the discovery"—and many later explorers have agreed with him.

Yet the author shows that this forlorn and blizzard-swept land has attracted more than its share of great men, commemorated in such names as Wilkes' Land, Bellinghausen Sea, Ross Shelf Ice and Mawson. There, too, are patches of "holy ground" such as Little America, first seen by Sir James Clark Ross in 1841, revisited by Capt. Robert F. Scott sixty years later, named "Bay of Whales" by Shackleton and still later used by Roald Amundsen as the base "Framheim" from which he launched his successful assault on the South Pole.

Lord Mountevans has many advantages as an historian of the Antarctic, not the least that he combines personal experience gained half a century ago with long study of the very different ways of modern polar travelers, for whom he has the highest regard. During the next two years, world-wide attention will focus on Antarctica, where a coordinated scientific assault is to be made by expeditions from a dozen nations. *The Antarctic Challenged* provides fine background reading for this, and is all the better for being written in the breezy style of the sailor, and with broad international sympathy all too often absent from histories of the polar regions.

Pierre Berton is a second-generation sourdough, born in the Yukon and schooled in its pioneer ways, but now managing editor of Maclean's Magazine. That he has not allowed his Toronto surroundings to obscure his love of the North is revealed by a photograph which shows him dressed in a fur-rimmed parka and with a week's stubble on his face. His book is an astonishingly comprehensive and thoroughly reliable account of northern Canada today, and it is very entertainingly written.

The Mysterious North rolls back the northern frontier in a region by region description. Here are semi-technical discussions of permafrost, gabbro, drumlins, glaciers and the like, along with a guided tour to "Headless Valley," the story of a mad trapper, accounts of hair-raising rescues by bush pilots and a tale from days not so long ago when an Eskimo was free to expedite his ancient mother-in-law on her way to the Hereafter.

The book is far more than a potpourri of travelers' tales from North of 53. It contains a systematic account of the resources of the far North and the problems that confront those who endeavor to exploit them. Missionaries, traders, administrators, miners and not least the native Indians and Eskimos have played a part in the minor revolution of the past decade. Clearly the days of fur-trapping as a basic means of livelihood are ending, while mining does not yet provide an adequate alternative. Still minerals such as oil, uranium, gold and iron, now being mined profitably, probably hold the key to the future.

Perhaps the deciding factor in development of the North will not be its undoubted resources but the accident of location between the United States and the Soviet Union. Because of this, three radar screens are being built between Alaska and the Atlantic, and one of them, the Distant Early Warning Line, has in the last year started the biggest northern boom of all time. Its construction has already called for immense tonnages of air freight, including 50,000-pound roadgraders dropped by parachute, and the author reports that Coca-Cola now flows as freely in the Arctic as ice water.

This massive assault on a largely unexplored region will assuredly end, in one way or another, the many problems surrounding the future of the native people, some of whom still live close to the Stone Age. Now there will be work and plenty for every Eskimo who can adjust himself to eating hamburgers, driving tractors and working a forty-hour week.

The Antarctic Challenge and *The Mysterious North* are provided with good maps and with many splendid photographs.

Bruce Hutchison (review date 10 March 1956)

SOURCE: "From Yukon to Ungava," in *The Saturday Review,* Vol. XXXIX, No. 10, March 10, 1956, p. 20.

[*In the following review, Hutchison praises* The Mysterious North *as an engaging work of nonfiction.*]

As a skilled professional reporter and a reckless amateur of exploration Pierre Berton has written in *The Mysterious North* a book with an unusual, perhaps a unique, virtue in its field: it sees the Canadian North whole. Many other books have examined parts of it in greater detail. Few if any, can have surveyed it in such a wide sweep and engaging style.

No such survey would have been possible in a single lifetime before the day of the airplane. Mr. Berton has used automobiles, trains, horses, dogsleds, and his own legs on various side journeys, but for the most part he has flown, dropping down at any place which seemed to promise interesting copy. The result is a mural stretched from the Yukon to Ungava, a painting of bold brush strokes, gaudy background colors, and some rare human figures in the foreground.

For this formidable undertaking the author was equipped by his birth in Whitehorse, his youth in the dwindling gold town of Dawson City, the perpetual travels of his manhood as a magazine writer, and, most of all, by his passionate love of the North.

A boy who grew up next door to Robert W. Service and floated down the Yukon River with his parents almost before he could walk thought of the North as a single piece, centered around the gutted placer fields of the Klondike. But he has found that there really is no North, except as a geographical expression, that dozens of separate climates, terrains, and races occupy an unimaginable area where Texas or the British Isles could be stowed away unnoticed. To speak of the North as a single region, the author says, is like lumping Scotland and Serbia together because both belong to Europe. In fact the mountainous Yukon, the oozing Mackenzie River basin, the rusty Labrador Peninsula, with its hills of iron, or the glistening fjords of Baffin Island might be on separate continents. They are unified only by the nationality of Canada and imaginary lines of latitude.

Variety is one part of the northern mystery but only one part. All travelers have felt, like Mr. Berton, the mystery of the land itself, its beauty, brutality, and loneliness. Few have equaled his descriptive talents. His pen makes the mystery palpable and appalling.

Still deeper is the mystery of human life throughout the North now in process of rapid change, thanks to the airplane. All the familiar figures of fiction appear in this factual book—the starving trapper, the mad prospector, the devoted missionary, the happy Eskimo, the tragic Indian—and many unlikely newcomers who in a few remote mining towns and military bases, are importing civilization overnight by air.

Mr. Berton's swarming narrative is enlivened by a series of unknown epics, the adventures of nameless men and not a few of the author's own narrow escapes—for example, his mad flight into Headless Valley, which was long described as a tropical oasis and haunt of homicidal stone-age Indians but turned out to be perhaps the finest mountain and river scenery on the continent, innocent of any habitation.

If he has a strong anecdotal talent and knows how to bring obscure characters to life, Mr. Berton knows how to invoke the grandeur and the history of the planet's northern slope.

The reader who is interested in the geological story of this land, the emergence of America's highest mountains, the rise of its largest inland seas, the advance and retreat of the ice, the deposit of oil in the vast central plateau and minerals throughout the horseshoe of the Precambrian Shield, will find it told here in layman's language. The armchair explorer will confront spectacles beyond the reach of the camera.

The book is chiefly valuable, however, as a total assessment of the North in all its aspects, by an accomplished writer and a Northern man. Since the economic gravity of Canada and the defense system of America are now tilting northward in Russia's direction Mr. Berton's report is not only a lively record of travel but a timely social document.

Mordecai Richler (review date 12 November 1972)

SOURCE: A review of *The Impossible Railway,* in *The New York Times Book Review,* November 12, 1972, p. 48.

[*In the following review, Richler calls* The Impossible Railway *a "considerable triumph," praising Berton for his ability to make a complex story "readable."*]

Canada, threatened within by French Canadian separatists and without by rampaging American investment, is presently in a truculent and soul-searching mood. Its writers, their nationalist zeal often outstripping their talent, are bent on myth-making. Turned inward, they are prospecting the past for those heroic tales that helped forge the nation or at least de-

fine how it differs from the other, sometimes insufferably overshadowing, America.

In this, as in any stake-claiming race, many of the searchers, ill-equipped, are inevitably panning fool's gold. Others are salting shallow pit-heads, inflating the stock for nationalistic consumption. But a few are surfacing with valuable, even essential, mythological ore.

Among them, the indefatigable Pierre Berton is unexcelled. Following ***Klondike,*** his compulsive account of the gold rush, he has struck an even richer vein a veritable bonanza, with ***The Impossible Railway,*** the saga, richly detailed (yet never at the sacrifice of its narrative drive) of the building of the Canadian Pacific Railway. A marvelous story in its own right, something of a cliffhanger, it anticipates, as Berton readily grasps without belaboring the point, the major problem that bedevils Canada even now: American domination.

The Canadian Pacific Railway, the longest in the world, was undertaken in 1871, when Canada was only four shaky years old, its population no more than four million. Its construction, initially promised in order to lure British Columbia, then still a colony, into the new Confederation, was the surpassing vision of a brilliant, charming, but alcoholic Prime Minister, John A. MacDonald. It was also almost his ruin, temporarily washing him out of office on a wave of bribery and swindles, culminating in the Pacific Scandal.

The railway remained essential, however, if Canada, comprised of isolated settlements with conflicting interests, was to be knit into a nation. It was, like Sir John A. himself, resurrected. It had to be built if it were to become possible for Canadians to journey from Atlantic to Pacific without being obliged to dip dependently into the United States.

It was impractical, a seemingly economic enterprise, ever teetering on the verge of bankruptcy, and threatening to sink the Government with it. But it was also absolutely necessary if Canada was to opt for true independence, piercing impassable Selkirks, and so transforming itself from a nest of settlements on the St. Lawrence lowlands into a nation that spanned two oceans. And Sir John A., a Yankee hater born, was determined that it would be an all-Canadian enterprise. "We shall not be trampled upon and ridden over," he declared, "as we have been in the past, by foreign capitalists."

And yet—and yet—though this impossible project was dominated by the industrious Scots of Montreal, the unrivaled manipulators of the great banks and financial houses, it was seen through, all along the line, by American contractors. They were the engineers.

And, in a tale that abounds with outsize characters, Rocky Mountain surveyors of astonishing courage and eccentricity, imaginative financiers with unflinching nerve, adventurers, opportunists, and even a saintly French Canadian priest, the largest and easily the most important is the American engineer of German and Dutch extraction, William Cornelius Van Horne, who did in fact eventually become a Canadian, and was knighted in 1894. The fascinating Van Horne was rather more than the driving, ebullient engineer who, miraculously, built the 2,500 mile railway in less than five years. He was also a gourmet, all-night poker player, violinist and astute geologist. A most appealing Victorian. Years after the railway was completed, he said: "I get all I can; I drink all I can; I smoke all I can, and I don't give a damn for anything."

It is Pierre Berton's considerable triumph that, working from primary sources, unpublished diaries, and letters as well as public documents, he has rendered a horrendously complex story so readable, moving with ease from Parliament Hill to the Riel Rebellion, from the boardrooms of financial houses to the end of track, where the Irish navvies, the Swedes, the French-Canadian and Chinese coolies were being conned by camp following whiskey-peddlers and whores.

If the building of the C.P.R. is a story rich in political chicanery, sharp dealing and profiteering, it is, for all that, heroic. One of the great railway and nation-building stories told, warts and all, with the gusto it so richly deserves.

Jeff Greenfield (review date 10 December 1978)

SOURCE: "Quint-Hype," in *The New York Times Book Review,* December 10, 1978, p. 16.

[*In the following review, Greenfield provides a brief summary of* The Dionne Years.]

To a generation surrounded by worldwide depression, poverty and the rise of fascism, the birth of the Dionne quintuplets in May 1934 was less a curious diversion than a badly needed affirmation of the human spirit. From a farmhouse in northern Ontario, news of the birth of the five identical infants, each weighing little more than a pound, gradually spread worldwide to become the biggest story of the decade. Everyone within reach of newspapers, radio and movie newsreels knew of Oliva and Elzire Dionne; of Dr. Allan Roy Dafoe, who fulfilled the dream of Charlie Brown's Linus by becoming "a world-famous humble country doctor"; of every change of weight and strength.

The quints, however, were more than a fascinating story. They were a marketable, multimillion-dollar commodity. The Chicago World's Fair wanted them as an exhibit, to hype disappointing attendance. Manufacturers and advertisers wanted them to help them sell milk, clothing, baby food. Newspapers, magazines, newsreel and motion picture companies wanted them as celebrities. And ordinary citizens, by the hundreds of thousands, wanted to see them in person. There was, then, a worldwide public hunger for "quint-hype" and a series of mechanisms eager to profit from the feeding of that hunger. The depressing, inevitable result of this mix is the subject of this riveting book, which is a fair-minded yet inspiring look at massive media hype.

The tale told by Pierre Berton, a Canadian writer and broadcaster, strains credulity; it is as if Richard Condon had superseded his own generous limits of plausibility. The quints were removed from the care of their uneducated French-Canadian parents and raised for nine years in a nursery-compound that attracted enough tourists to save Ontario from bankruptcy. The press that attacked the Dionne parents for cashing in on their fame built up Dr. Dafoe as a humanitarian indifferent to wealth and fame, even as the doctor was pulling down enormous fees for speaking around the nation. The care of the quints became part of the French-English conflict in Canada, until the English-speaking Dafoe was removed from his role as one of their guardians and the quints returned to their parents—to what they later called "the saddest home we have ever known." The unhappy fate of the three surviving quints—one is amazed to find that both they and their parents are still alive—seems to have been dictated by the circumstances of their birth and fame.

It is tempting to say that such an event could not occur today; that we are far more sophisticated in the ways of media hype. Let us look to the list of forthcoming books and movies, to the shelves of books by Watergate conspirators, sexual deviates of every calling, soon-to-be-heard Son of Sam tapes—and ask how well we have coped with the power of the media machine to shape and ruin human beings by its sheer omnipresence.

C. P. Stacey (review date August-September 1980)

SOURCE: A review of *The Invasion of Canada, Volume One: 1812-13,* in *Books in Canada,* Vol. 9, No. 7, August-September, 1980, pp. 7-8.

[*In the following review, Stacey addresses a number of shortcomings in Berton's* The Invasion of Canada, *claiming that "as a history of the war [it] leaves much to be desired."*]

Pierre Berton does not tell us just why he has undertaken to write what is clearly going to be quite a long book on the War of 1812. One more book, one might say; for there is a large literature on this war and historians and near-historians have produced a good many books and articles about it in recent years. Inevitably, Berton is threshing old wheat and he has not been able to find much that is new to say. But there is a certain perennial interest in this strange conflict among North Americans, and he and his publishers evidently feel that it is enough to support this considerable literary enterprise.

Interest among North Americans. This was essentially a war between Britain and the United States that was fought mainly in Canada. (To call it "the war that Canada won," as Berton does in the beginning, is foolish and he goes on to explain that he knows it.) Yet the English, who were a main party to the war, have never heard of it, and the Americans and the Canadians have quite different conceptions of it. American popular history has tended to represent it mainly as a naval war, fought on the oceans, in which a few American frigates humiliated the Royal Navy. Canadian legend centres on land battles, chiefly on the Niagara frontier, in which the gallant Canadian militia supposedly played a leading part in vanquishing the proud invader. This is myth; if the defence had been left to the Canadians, it wouldn't have lasted a month. It was the British professionals in their scarlet coats (*not* crimson, please, Pierre) who provided the leadership and bore the brunt. These old tales, no doubt, are still not extinct; so perhaps there is room for a popular book, based as this one is on careful research in the contemporary documents, to bring to the masses (if they can be prevailed upon to read it) some knowledge of the actual facts as writers and readers of history have known them for years.

The author and his helpers have done a great deal of investigation, as his bibliography and references testify. Nevertheless, as a history of the war *The Invasion of Canada* leaves much to be desired. Its approach, not surprisingly, is anecdotal, and on the analytical side it falls short. Some things are overdone; others are almost entirely missing. It may be, as Berton says, that the Indians have had less than their due from some writers, but he errs in the opposite direction; we are inundated with Indians throughout. (Indians, of course, are much in the public eye at the moment.) On the other hand, the naval forces on the Great Lakes—the real key to victory in warfare on the Canadian frontier—are very inadequately dealt with; the Provincial Marine, which made Sir Isaac Brock's successful defence of Canada in 1812 possible, is mentioned only incidentally, and is not even in the index. The nature of the land forces on each side is likewise never fully explained. In Canada Berton talks about "the militia" but never tells us the nature of the force or of the laws that created it; Brock's innovation on the eve of war, the law setting up the volunteer "flank companies" that gave him the most effective militia units that fought under him, is not mentioned. And the author has a tendency to interpret the early 19th century in terms of 1980. He seems astonished to discover that Brock "despised democracy"—in other words,

that he was typical of his time, class, and country. One might as well attack the poor general for never having voted NDP.

Anecdotal, I said, the book is, and Berton is a skilful anecdotist. On the most important anecdote in the book, however, his researchers have slipped a bit. He quotes the Kingston *Gazette* (incidentally, *it* was actually quoting the York *Gazette*) as writing of Brock's fall at Queenston Heights, "'Push on brave York Volunteers,' [they] being then near him, they were the last words of the dying Hero." He is quite right in saying that these words cannot have been addressed to the York Volunteers, for they were not yet on the field when Brock was killed; he is right in saying that it is well established that Brock said nothing after he was hit; but he is not right in saying that if the words were said at all it could only have been when he passed the Volunteers as he rode towards Queenston. He has missed a letter dated two days after the battle and printed in the Quebec *Mercury.* The writer, probably himself a Volunteer officer, says, "The York volunteers to whom he was particularly partial, have the honor of claiming his last words; immediately before he received his death wound he cried out, to some person near him to push on the York volunteers, which were the last words he uttered." It is quite possible that this is the true version.

Berton is not the first to point out that the leaders of the militia in 1812 later became the leaders of the Family Compact (whom he seems to think of as pretty villainous, as per the school histories of half a century ago). But is he really right in saying that Brock's Monument on Queenston Heights is merely a "symbol" of the Compact? I wonder whether the thousands of people from all over Upper Canada who converged on Queenston on July 30, 1840, to make plans for a new and finer monument to replace the one that had been bombed were really there for political reasons? I would prefer to think of Chief Justice John Beverley Robinson, who was there and was a leader in the movement, not as a political figure in this connection but rather as the hero-worshipping militia subaltern who followed Brock to the capture of Detroit and who met his body being carried back as he and his company of the Volunteers pounded into Queenston on the bloody morning of Oct. 13, 1812, and who never forgot him. And I suspect that those crowds of Canadians who assembled in 1840 were moved not by political motives but by the continuing power of the legend of the Hero of Upper Canada, and by gratitude to the memory of the man who had, beyond all question, saved the province from conquest. It takes more than politicians to create such waves of feeling. Especially, I suspect, in Canada.

This is a long-winded book. The present volume (the first of two) gets us only to January, 1813, covering eight months of a 2 1/2-year war. Berton often goes into enormous detail, particularly on the American side. He and his helpers have dug deeply into the accounts the assailants of 1812 left behind them—they are almost all in print, somewhere or other—and he quotes fairly relentlessly. His own lively style and skilful organization are sometimes almost swept away in the flood of early American rhetoric. The documents familiar as brief quotations in the old textbooks are given here *in extenso*. The book's title, one speculates, was chosen with intention; the emphasis is rather more on the invasion of Canada than on the defence. One notes that it was "printed in the United States of America." Is it a fair assumption that this time the Great Canadian Storyteller and The Canadian Publishers are out to crack the Great American Market? Well, if they are, good luck to them.

John Yohalem (review date 22 February 1981)

SOURCE: A review of *The Invasion of Canada, Volume One: 1812-13*, in *The new York Times Book Review*, February 22, 1981, pp. 18-19.

[*In the following brief review, Yohalem credits Breton for providing a "rousing" historical novel.*]

Pierre Berton, a Canadian journalist with 18 works of non-fiction to his credit, writes popular history as it should more often be written, exciting but carefully documented, in a clear, somewhat classical style. His subject is our (but not Canada's) most pointless war, the War of 1812, a tragicomedy of bungled maneuvers and fouled communications carried out with a farcical gentility that soon degenerated into savagery.

Neither side wished to fight. The Americans were grossly unprepared, but didn't realize it, thanks to the 30 years of back-patting that followed the Revolution. The British had their hands full fighting most of Europe—indeed, President Madison said he would never have declared war if he had thought Napoleon would lose. Only the brutalized and disinherited Indians wanted to fight—for the British and against the land-hungry Americans mostly—and only the Indians got nothing out of it.

The Americans got two war-hero Presidents, Harrison and Jackson. But the Canadians, as is usually forgotten south of the border, got a national myth. (Mr. Berton has the wise historian's healthy respect for the power of myth.) A sparsely populated land in which an entrenched aristocracy ruled an apathetic yeomanry, mostly American or French in origin and loyalty, Canada seemed likely to drift into the Union rather than remain loyal to a distant colonial office. This did not occur, Mr. Berton convincingly asserts, thanks to the national sentiment aroused by the incompetent but bloody American attempt to force union.

He tells the complicated story of the first year of the war and its antecedents in the present tense: "The articles of surrender stipulate that the Americans must leave the fort before the British enter. A confused melee follows. The American soldiers are in a turmoil, some crying openly, a few of the officers breaking their swords and some of the soldiers their muskets rather than surrender them. Others cry 'Treason!' and 'Treachery!' and heap curses and imprecations on their general's head. One of the Ohio volunteers tries to stab Macdonell." The evidence for scenes like this are drawn from the innumerable archives, letters, journals and recollections that survive on both sides.

The Invasion of Canada is much more rousing than most historical novels. The maps are many, clear and informative. The second volume will appear in 1983.

George Woodcock (review date October 1981)

SOURCE: "Berton's Judgements on the Horror of War," in *Quill & Quire*, Vol. 47, No. 10, October, 1981, p. 33.

[*In the following review, Woodcock claims that Berton has "passed the test for good history writing" by providing a "richer, deeper, and . . . truer" view of the War of 1812.*]

The real shape or intent of a book is never truly revealed to us until we have read the last chapter or, in longer works, the final volume. And it is near the end of *Flames Across the Border, 1813-1814*, the second part of his account of the War of 1812, that one really recognizes what differentiates Pierre Berton's kind of history from the works of most academic historians. It is not merely the intense populism of Berton's approach, though the small people are here again in their dozens, the private soldiers, the women defending their possessions, the anonymous farmers gratuitously killed, the Indians who are faceless terrors to their enemies. It is also his deep moralism. For, as his account of this foolish and unnecessary conflict draws to an end one realizes that, as certainly as Tolstoy in *War and Peace*, Berton is making his judgments on the phenomenon of war and on the political pretensions from which it emerges.

"Men will write," Berton remarks, "that the War of 1812 was the making of the United States: for the first time she was taken seriously in Europe; that it was also the making of Canada: her people were taught pride through a common resistance to the invaders: that bloody and insane though it may have been, Lundy's Lane and Stoney Creek produced the famous undefended border between the two nations.

"True, But in terms of human misery and the human waste—the tall ships shattered by cannonball and grape; the barns and mills gutted by fire; villages put to the torch, grain fields ravaged, homes looted, breadwinners shackled and imprisoned; and thousands dead from cannon shot and musket fire, gangrene, typhus, ague, or simple exposure, can anyone truly say on this crisp Christmas Eve that the game was ever worth the candle?"

True, that is a question, but a rhetorical one, and like most such questions it really admits of only one answer. What in our hearts can we say but "no!" But that, it seems to me, is the answer Berton, as surely as Tolstoy, is intent we should make to war of any kind. Few academic historians—for Donald Creighton was a notable exception—would lead us so firmly towards a moral conclusion. And this, I suppose, is what marks off the way a man of imagination as distinct from a man of mere scholarship, responds to the facts with which he deals. He cannot leave them as mere facts. He composes them into a picture, detailed and panoramic though it may be, and the very fact of shaping brings a judgement that is implicit from the beginning, but slowly emerges into articulateness as the facts build on each other, until in the end, if the author makes an explicit statement, as Berton does, the reader is at least prepared for the lesson he is being taught, and may well agree.

[In *Flames Across the Border, 1913-1814*,] as in *The Invasion of Canada*, his earlier volume, Berton gives us a fascinating gallery of portraits, in which the common people caught in the web of war are as mordantly visualized as the incompetents and megalomaniacs who had the illusion of pulling the strings of destiny.
—*George Woodcock*

What we enjoy from reading history is perhaps not so much the lessons it may have to teach us—which most men are inclined to forget pretty quickly—as its power to recreate a past that time has stolen from us but which we feel has in some way determined the kind of life we are living in the present. Quite apart from our moral judgements of the War of 1812, of the ineptness or callousness of its commanders, of the triviality of its aims in comparison with the suffering and destruction it caused, we are interested in the patterns of these battles of long ago, which Berton visualizes and narrates so clearly, and in these people who are our spiritual— even if not our physical—ancestors because they have helped to shape the world in which we live, the Canada that is still, as Berton remarks, so attached to the "comfortable, orderly, secure, paternalistic". As in *The Invasion of Canada*, his earlier volume, Berton gives us a fascinating gallery of portraits, in which the common people caught in the web of war are as mordantly visualized as the incompetents and mega-

lomaniacs who had the illusion of pulling the strings of destiny.

Berton's is the kind of history that has little room for heroics, for the posturings of men who think themselves great. But it still has room for true heroes, and just as the image of Isaac Brock seems to breathe through *The Invasion of Canada*, so does that of Tecumseh through *Flames Across the Border*, even though he is dead and spirited away from the battlefield by the time the book is half way through. For, as Berton remarks, Tecumseh and a few of his fellow Indians were almost the only people in the War of 1812 who fought for an ideal, for the freedom to continue their ancient way of life, and they were the real losers in the war, betrayed by the British, destined to be destroyed as tribal societies by the Americans. In the process they helped to preserve Canada from American domination, but that was not their aim, which was doomed when Tecumseh died.

"But in death as in life," as Berton says, "there is only one Tecumseh. His last resting place like so much of his career, is a mystery; but his memory will be for ever green."

The final test of good history writing is whether it changes our view of the past it deals with. I know I shall never again look on the War of 1812 as I did before I read Berton's two books. My view is now richer, deeper and, I think, truer.

Lorna Irvine (essay date Spring 1986)

SOURCE: "The Real Mr. Canada," in *Canadian Literature*, No. 108, Spring, 1986, pp. 68-79.

[*In the following essay, Irvine discusses Berton's development of a "Canadian approach to the confidence game tradition that so dominates the folklore and culture of the United States."*]

Early in July of 1985, Pierre Berton staged a game of "To Tell the Truth" at an apparently typical press party. The mystery guests were three women in masks; the panelists, Canadian historian William Kilbourn, Dinah Christie, and Berton himself. The object of the game was to discover which of the three women was Lisa Kroniuk, the author of *Masquerade: Fifteen Variations on a Theme of Sexual Fantasy*. The novel bears on the back cover a description of the author: "Lisa Kroniuk emigrated to Canada several years ago and now lives in the West. A single mother, she has one daughter, Lara. This is her second novel; an earlier work was published in Eastern Europe, on the theme of sexual ambiguity. She writes: 'I am myself part of the masquerade'."

When the "To Tell the Truth" game arrived at its famous question, "Will the real Lisa Kroniuk please stand up?", to people's astonishment, Pierre Berton rose. He, it turns out, is the novel's author. He had kept his secret well. Jack McClelland, *Masquerade*'s publisher as well as Berton's long-time publisher, friend, and business partner, claims to have been kept in the dark during the two years of the project's maturing. So does Janet Berton, the author's wife. Berton described the experience for Sandy Naiman of *The Toronto Sun*: "'I got the idea during a period of jet lag in London. . . . It had never occurred to me to write a novel. I'm not a novelist. But I got the idea of a bordello that ran fantasies and I started fiddling with it when I was on vacation in the Caribbean'." The book received little attention. For Pierre Berton, author of thirty books (other than *Masquerade*), three-time winner of the Governor General's Award for Non-Fiction, possessor of ten honorary degrees and fifteen other awards, an author who has topped the Canadian best-sellers list with books like *The Comfortable Pew*, and *The Smug Minority*, a well-known television personality, the man who has made the Yukon famous and who has, some think single-handedly, created Canadian history, writing an ignored novel about sexual fantasies is an unusual experience.

Considering his prolific publishing record, is it appropriate to begin a discussion of Pierre Berton's work with an apparent aberration like *Masquerade*? His publishers and his agent insist that the book is completely different from anything Berton has written heretofore. However, apart from the fact that it is listed as a novel, and Berton is essentially a writer of non-fiction, *Masquerade* is a most revealing piece of writing, tying in neatly with what is perhaps Berton's most significant popular role: the establishing, elucidating, and developing of a specifically Canadian approach to the confidence game tradition that so dominates the folklore and culture of the United States. This is not a popular argument to make. Canadians have long prided themselves on their superiority to American selling techniques, and among anglophones at least, the stereotypical British dislike of self-promotion—indeed of any kind of promotion at all—has encouraged the belief in Canadian reserve. This fiction has among other misconceptions worked against the accepting of any specifically Canadian popular culture; the tendency has been, until very recently, to denounce all forms of popular or mass manipulative culture as American.

To suggest that the thoroughly Canadian Pierre Berton has developed, in content, but more important, in his style of writing and the method of selling, a pattern that can be connected with cultural conning, implies that Canada has its own game mentality, and that erasing it by calling it American is inaccurate. Nonetheless, such erasure has a long history. Thomas Haliburton's Sam Slick was a Yankee; about him, Robert McDougall writes: "Sam's democratic brashness, his

'calculatin' shrewdness, his colossal assurance and resourcefulness in argument, his readiness with homespun comments, with anecdotes and tall tales—all these traits were already connected with popular conceptions of the Yankee character." Susanna Moodie employs the stereotype: "No thin, weasel-faced Yankee was he, looking as if he had lived upon 'cute ideas and speculations all his life," while her sister, Catherine Parr Traill, comments disparagingly on "annoying Yankee manners." The disease "spreading up from the south" that creeps through Margaret Atwood's *Surfacing* is none other than American commercialism. Denial and projection seem, then, conventionally to characterize Canadian approaches to the low art of selling.

Obviously, *Masquerade* is a con, and as such, tells us something about Pierre Berton's own use of the tradition of tricksters and gamesmen. The title is the first hint that trickery is occurring. Indeed, the fantasies stress, one after the other, the counterfeiting of fiction. They are not particularly erotic. The connecting link is a business operation, a bordello, run by a "Momma" who has been financially, and imaginatively, backed by a Magician who might come from the work of Robertson Davies. The business is designed to cater to people's sexual fantasies while keeping, as one of the concluding stories states, "within the bounds of good taste," within the normal, rather than the abnormal, one is tempted to say, the Canadian rather than the American. To carry out the fantasies are Erika, the perennial schoolgirl, Candace, the nurse, beautiful male Julio, loved by men, Lara, the Bitch of Berlin, Raven, whose specialty is necrophilia, Andrea, the jungle girl, the three nuns, Flame, Lola and Bibi, Alix, the schoolmarm, and finally Turk, the simple-minded truck driver who has to be locked into his truck to keep him from wandering off. With this cast, Berton creates fifteen fantasies that begin and end with the same client, Marcus, who, we are told in the first fantasy, "*was* in a rut. He longed to get away, perhaps to some South Sea island where the wind was warm and the women willing. He longed for an adventure—any adventure—even if it meant flirting with death."

Although I am not interested in describing the specific fantasies, I want to investigate several of Berton's themes, his narrative technique and, what I think is of most interest, his role as a representative of Canada, a role only obliquely realized in *Masquerade*. Several of the stories of *Masquerade*, like many individual stories in *Klondike*, *The National Dream*, *The Last Spike*, *The Invasion of Canada*, *Flames Across the Border* and, *The Promised Land*, focus on and demonstrate, not just trickery or illusion (the whole book does that), but the setting up of actual confidence games. In "Momma's Reverie," Momma describes the game: "In a seduction, or a confidence game (is there really any difference? Momma asks herself), both players take on roles, the seduced as well as the seducer, the mark as well as the trickster. Bolstered by the flattery of one, the other sees herself with new eyes, gains confidence, falls in love with the image that has been constructed for her." It is a theme that has earlier received Berton's attention. In a book published in the 1960's, *The Big Sell*—a collection of his newspaper columns—Berton discusses classic confidence games: "Any student of the classic confidence games must be struck by the several parallels they present with some modern big-sell techniques. The confidence man sells nothing but himself, of course, while the salesman peddles more tangible merchandise; but the psychological techniques each employs are remarkably similar." Con artists, as Berton is well aware, need to be masters of detail. A friend of his, an accomplished con artist, tells Berton that con artists expend the most energy establishing the credibility of a story. Apart from the fact that trickery inevitably connects with any writer's job—to create illusion—an author who attracts a mass audience has necessarily developed particularly sophisticated selling techniques. As Berton said in one interview (apparently in reference to all his books): "I wouldn't be writing this stuff if there weren't the market for it."

Anecdotes dominate the selling techniques of good confidence men, anecdotes that frequently debunk or make accessible characters and events in fact quite distant. This aspect of Berton's work leads a reviewer of *The Promised Land* to state: "there's an overemphasis on scandal and corruption, and not enough about farming the land, getting the crop to market, early frost, loneliness. One might have hoped for a little less debunking." This reviewer is asking for factual, rather than anecdotal, material. But Berton has made his name precisely by telling tall tales, by creating vivid, if unworthy, characters, by reporting, in various guises and from different perspectives, all the ways in which Canadians have manipulated themselves into the present. Melville's confidence man has Canadian brothers.

The psychology of conning fascinates Berton. In *Klondike,* he investigates people who, in the role of either yeggs or con artists, are consumed by greed. At its height, the gold rush disproved any Horatio Alger myth of success (that is, hard work as superior to luck). People aimed to get rich as quickly as possible. Incredible devices were invented—and sold. Dawson's entertainments, Berton tells us, were established to "extract as much gold as possible from the audience." People worked under false names; some fortunes were exhausted in a few weeks; others were made overnight. Soapy Smith, the dictator of Skagway, built up a career from nothing; he was a "man of considerable imagination and dry humour" who contrived to appear on the side of law and order but who, in fact, made his fortune from taking money away from others. And he had the down-home personality of an effective confidence man; people liked him. The whole of *Klondike* elaborates on stories about this kind of person. Indeed, the book itself, perhaps an example of what it is about, continues to make its author considerable money.

> **Berton has made his name precisely by telling tall tales, by creating vivid, if unworthy, characters, by reporting, in various guises and from different perspectives, all the ways in which Canadians have manipulated themselves into the present. Melville's confidence man has Canadian brothers.**
> **—Lorna Irvine**

Klondike concentrates on the gold rush, a particularly symbolic example of greed. But from different perspectives, each of the other three books of the tetralogy (*The National Dream, The Last Spike,* and *The Promised Land*) reveals the author's interest in bargaining, if not in downright cheating among the principal makers of Canada's past. *The National Dream* elucidates, with anecdotal delight, proliferating land deals, alcoholic but immensely personable Prime Ministers, and a public growing fat on materialistic fantasies, while *The Last Spike* illustrates in detail a short-sighted but greedy Canadian west. No longer interested in growing crops, when land can be marketed much more profitably, Canadians are shown cheating the Indians, while the company stores develop increasingly fast methods of making a buck. *The Promised Land,* published last year, concentrates its whole attention, as its title announces, on land: not solid earth, the kind farmers plough, but ephemeral fantasies.

In *The Confidence Man in American Literature,* a fascinating psychological and cultural analysis of the meaning of conning in American life, Gary Lindberg argues that, at least in the settling of the American West, "Nation building . . . turns out to be a massive game of confidence." He continues: "in speculation, as in confidence games more generally, all belongings and winnings became mere parts of the game. The reality was drained out of domestic life, material objects and labor." This phenomenon is precisely what Berton investigates in *The Promised Land.* In the Prologue, he tells us that "This is a book about dreams and illusions, escape and survival, triumph and despair," and goes on to describe various searches for utopia in the continuous flow of people from the old world to the new, all too easily promised, land.

Newspapers became major agents in the game of selling people land and populating the west (and Berton, a newspaperman himself, understands newspaper games). Suppression of information was customary, as it inevitably is in any kind of manipulation. The nightmares of journeys in extremely cold weather were hushed up; for example, attempts were made to ban the publication of Manitoba's winter temperatures. Berton makes clear too that self-interest was the motivating force behind settlement: the word "ethnic" was not in use in the nineteenth century; "there were no discussions about 'roots,' no talk of 'multiculturalism,' little pandering to national cultures, and certainly no reference to a Canadian mosaic." According to Berton, assimilation was the key word. Indeed, many of the Europeans who peopled the west of Canada were themselves in the grip of dreams that all too often were formed because of trickery. The Doukhobors followed a peculiarly destructive path, and evangelical groups from Scotland were sold on Canada by preachers—themselves masters of the art of conning—like the Rev. Isaac Barr:

> Barr, Barr, wily old Barr
> He'll do you as much as he can.
> You bet he will collar
> Your very last dollar
> In the valley of Sask-atchewan.

Great Britain continued to advertise Canada as the land of opportunity, while in fact using Canada as a dumping ground for her own undesirables.

The politics of the west frequently exacerbated (or perhaps reflected) the problem; politicians like Clifford Sifton, Minister of the Interior under Prime Minister Laurier, a character of apparent fascination to Berton, who makes him the central character of *The Promised Land*, demonstrate the connections between political corruption and confidence trickery. Sifton, like any manipulator, wanted to get rich, and used political power to do so. In a review of this book, William French extends the example: "Sifton's methods of attracting settlers provide a forceful examination of modern marketing techniques. He was selling an idea—the idea that the Canadian West was the promised land, that free homesteads and hard work would bring undreamed-of material success."

An example from more recent history is Berton's less well-known book about the Dionne quintuplets, *The Dionne Years*. The book is certainly cultural history and points to the use made of the Quints in the battle between the French and the English. But Berton's real interest is in the ways successful marketing techniques can move an unknown product (the backwoods, northern Ontario Dionne family) into the international limelight. Again, too, Berton spends considerable time elucidating the psychology of the doctor who delivered the quints and who made himself a substantial fortune as a result. Although initially an apparently simple country doctor, he became adept at selling his personality and, of course, his story. What emerges from the book, too, is what begins to seem standard Canadian response to marketing: while complaining about "cheap American publicity," and attempting a neutral Canadian stance, the Canadians involved with Quintland were raking in fortunes, by selling the Quints' pictures to advertising firms, tourists, and other Canadians—hardly a neutral undertaking.

Many such examples occur in Berton's books. Nonetheless, the confidence mentality plays an ambivalent role in the Canadian consciousness. The economically powerful United States makes Canada's differences about money particularly problematic. Economic metaphors are frequently used (Canadians sell out to the United States; Americans buy Canadians). Enraged by American economic dominance, Canadian nationalist Robin Mathews lashes out at susceptible Canadians: "Colonies are places that are *done* to rather than doing or doing to. . . . The people are under perpetual pressure to adopt the beliefs and ideology of the powerful country that manipulates them." Mathews later claims: "The human product of the liberal ideology is the Robber Baron of free enterprise and the cop-out hippie/yippie of the so-called 'counter-culture.' . . . It teaches the Canadian to scorn history, to reject communal values." One can certainly detect a long history of British snobbery here. But in a somewhat less hysterical way, a good number of Canadians want to believe that Canada is a less gullible, less outrageously vulgar, less materialistic, less self-advertising country than the United States. Berton is no exception. He seems, then, an interesting example of the ambivalence that permeates Canada's effort to differentiate itself from American business. He is interested in the confidence mentality, in the selling of his own books as well as in their content and style; he emphasizes anecdotes and tall tales, uses the present tense, which makes the reader participate more fully in the action, and loudly sells ideas.

But Berton also openly castigates American techniques. In *Why We Act Like Canadians*, a book structured as a dialogue between Berton and Uncle Sam, he describes Canadians as virtually immune to manipulation of the confidence kind. Institutions like the Hudson's Bay Company he paints as paternal protectors rather than exploiters of the population, and argues that Canadians have always been more interested in public good than in private property. Important extensions of these ideas occur in *Hollywood's Canada*, where Berton casts the Americans as manipulators and con artists, translating Canadian characters such as the Royal Canadian Mounted Policeman, the French Canadian, the Metis, the Canadian Indian into items saleable to an American public. According to Berton, it "didn't occur to Hollywood and it didn't occur to Canadian audiences either, that the Canadian concept of order imposed from above clashed with the American idea of rough frontier justice." In the American Preface to *Flames Across the Border*, Berton hammers away at the same differences ("America's heritage is revolutionary; Canada's is colonial"), and summarizes the differences in national qualities: "American ebullience, Canadian reserve. The Americans went wild over minor triumphs, the Canadians remained phlegmatic over major ones." Like many other Canadians, Berton insists on dividing Americans and Canadians specifically in terms of their ability to promote themselves and others.

Berton is fascinated by slick talking and by selling, and associates characteristics related to confidence trickery with Canadian development. Rhetorically, he uses confidence tricks that have worked to make him one of the best-selling writers in Canada. He understands the psychology of his largely Canadian audiences, who enjoy both the anecdotal (his work seems more oral than literary) style and the quantity of factual information he offers. As one Canadian to whom I recently spoke said: "Nobody would know anything about Canadian history if Berton were not around to popularize it." The assumptions he makes are various; he does not always assume his audience's gullibility—he is in fact a much more committed Canadian than that—but he is in the business of selling ideas and, often, of persuading others to change their minds. In a book like *Why We Act Like Canadians*, he adopts the voice of a manipulator, addressing a naive audience, in this case, a pretended American one (the book in fact is meant for the educating of a Canadian audience; Americans find it most offensive). He frequently assumes a helpful, comradely persona, employing considerable repetition and assiduously establishing his own honesty. *The Wild Frontier* begins inclusively: "We are all the creatures of the wilderness, the children of frontiers"; the author's Note at the end of *Klondike* announces that "My whole life has been conditioned by the Klondike"; all of *Drifting Home* is an establishing of familial and cultural roots, and, in an epigraph to the first chapter of the cookbook he co-edited with his wife (*The Centennial Food Guide*), he assures the reader that "The male editor of this book unconditionally guarantees this soup. In twenty years of marriage he has drunk bathtubfuls of it."

Berton consistently plays as well, on the human desire for variety, shifting his persona as he shifts his game strategies. His dramatic shift into the role of a female Polish novelist draws particular attention to this facility. But his performance ranges over an extremely wide area, from the children's story, *The World of Og* (based on episodes and characters in his own family); to the cookbook; to numerous, snappy newspaper columns (collected in *Just Add Water and Stir, Fast, Fast, Fast Relief*, and *Adventures of a Columnist*); to the promotion of tourism (for example, *The New City: A Prejudiced View of Toronto, Drifting Home*); to exposés of public corruption or hypocrisy (*The Big Sell, My War With the Twentieth Century, The Comfortable Pew, The Smug Minority*); to popular Canadian histories (the western tetralogy, the books on the War of 1812); and to commentaries on popular culture (*The Dionne Years, The Cool Crazy Committed World of the Sixties, Hollywood's Canada*). Part of the appeal of these books is nostalgic: they encourage Canadian longings for past glories and, what is more important, satisfy some of these desires with historical and cultural information and dramatic anecdotes. The popular style that Berton uses—parabolic, anecdotal, a traditional selling style—simplifies the oblique lessons of history and gives

narrative coherence to disparate facts. The popular histories particularly elicit our confidence.

On the other hand, Berton's ambivalence about the merchant mentality persists. Like other Canadians, he attempts to project the more unpleasant effects of mercantile persuasion on to the Americans. This inclination is, I believe, characteristically Canadian and, while reflected in the artifacts of Canada's popular culture, is most noticeable in their reception. In Berton's work, the Canadian confidence game simultaneously demonstrates and repels trickery, while Canada and various Canadians appear confusingly as both active and passive, as both persuaders and gulls, as both perpetrators and victims. This ambivalent stance is peculiarly paralyzing, at least when one is talking about Canadian popular culture. Yet, like the United States, Canada's is a new world culture. Gary Lindberg believes that confidence games tell us something about the psychology of societies newly forming and in flux. He argues that repeated moving has

> made many Americans restless, unstable, thirsty for novelty. It has loosened family and community bonds and has encouraged people to dwell imaginatively in the future. Institutions that depend on stable residence, like primogeniture and apprenticeship, have lost their power, and personal facility has been given a correspondingly wider field. In social relations this ceaseless movement has weakened the familiar patterns of identification. Instead of relying on family background, class habits, inherited manners, many Americans have had to confront each other as mere claimants.

Canadians cannot avoid these phenomena.

At the same time, Canada, at least hypothetically, seems particularly sensitive to communal demands, quite likely for geographical and economic reasons. The themes Berton most emphasizes in Canadian development (the importance of authority in Canada and the preference for arbitration over revolution), are themes that create tension between individual and group undertakings. Berton seems torn between the two. His own family matters to him; and he is certainly concerned about his country. According to most analysts of it, the confidence tradition in American culture emphasizes distinctive individualism. In certain ways, Berton delineates for Canada a more group-oriented conning, games that pertain to broad segments of Canadian culture.

He also undertakes to give Canada a frontier past that seems to contradict Canadian denials about its existence: he shows, in books like *The Mysterious North, Klondike*, and *The Wild Frontier*, how Canadians, like other people, are attracted to the mystery and danger of frontiers where they can test their courage. This largely masculine undertaking—

Berton does describe women on the frontier, but mostly he is concerned with male adventure—often, as Lindberg also demonstrates, goes hand in hand with confidence trickery, with the susceptibilities of changing cultures. Yet here too, Berton's ambivalence persists. Although he seems to be constructing a less passive, rough and tumble, carousing, bad-boy image of Canada—some Canadian historians stereotypically reflect Canada in female metaphors—he also preserves Canada's difference from the United States in passive-active dichotomies. In *Why We Act Like Canadians* he writes: "We were never a community of rebels, escaping from the clutches of a foreign monarch. . . . Basking in the security and paternalism that our constitutional phraseology suggests, we sought gradually and through a minimum of bloodshed to achieve our own form of independence." Berton's ambivalence does not, of course, lessen the significance of frontier conning. In fact, the paternalistic, authoritarian culture that Berton posits as Canada's seems particularly amenable to manipulation. As soon as someone establishes authority, victims appear to play the game. Even the dislike of physical violence that accompanies particular kinds of authoritarianism encourages the mental rather than physical struggles characteristic of confidence games.

Finally, ambivalent Canadian attitudes to rigid class systems give further room for confidence trickery. Confidence men seem classless, eliminating cultural differences by conning rich and poor alike. Furthermore, like many Canadians, the confidence man is not interested in abrupt or radical changes in society. Lindberg emphasizes that he "does not provide an outlet for unruliness, nor does he disrupt the social bounds. He is a culturally representative figure, not a marginal one, and his message is that the boundaries are already fluid, that there is ample space between his society's official rules and its actual tolerances." Berton operates on just such fluid boundaries.

In his literary study of confidence men, John Blair argues that the confidence man "serves as figure for the writer whose artistic medium must manipulate pretenses and falsehoods even in order to probe the nature of the true and false in the larger world." Thus we return to *Masquerade*. Broadly interpreted, Blair's observation is no doubt true. But it is not just that Berton is a writer. It is that he is predominantly interested in masquerades, in the playing of roles, in trickery. As Momma says: "in life costume is everything. Costume is a two-way mirror. It casts a reflection. The role player sees his image staring back at him in the eyes of others, and the role becomes the reality." Furthermore, Berton is a remarkably popular writer; his manipulation of his material and of his audience allows him to play games, as well as to instruct. He reminds Canadians of their materialism, of their willingness to be manipulators as well as victims. Survival may, as Atwood claims, be a significant Canadian theme. But Canadian victims, at least according to Berton, are amply bal-

anced by persuaders who know what the game is, and how to play it. These too, he insists, are Canadians.

Desmond Morton (review date November 1986)

SOURCE: "Tainted Victory," in *Books in Canada,* Vol. 15, No. 8, November 1986, pp. 21-3.

[*In the following review, Morton criticizes* Vimy, *stating that it is "laden with errors and inaccuracies."*]

Nations, claimed the French historian Ernest Renan, are not created by speaking the same language or even by occupying the same territory. They are made by people who have done great things together in the past and who expect to do great things together in the future.

Even at the time, the Canadians who captured Vimy Ridge in 1917 knew that they had done a great thing. The bodies of close to 50,000 French and British soldiers who had died in earlier attempts seemed warning enough that the Germans could hold the ridge as long as they chose. For months, through the coldest winter Europe had known in decades, Canadians tunnelled and dragged supplies and raided enemy trenches. Generals and staff officers, who had been salesmen, editors, and professors only a couple of years earlier, plotted and planned. Finally, in the wake of the most effective artillery barrage the war had so far seen, 49 battalions of Canadian infantry walked forward through snow and mud to do the impossible deed.

Vimy is the battle Canadians associate with the First World War, as Australians remember Gallipoli or Broodeeinde, or the Americans Belleau Wood. It was not the complete, dramatic victory the British would achieve at Messines a few months later, or that Caadians and Australians would deliver at Amiens in August, 1918; it was a triumph Canadians needed to share with no one. Never before had all four divisions of the Canadian Corps advanced in line on a single objective. In the battalions were French and English, Poles, Germans, Ukrainians, Japanese Canadians, native Canadians and representatives of every other ethnic fragment of the transcontinental Dominion.

There are few painless or perfect victories. Of the 38,000 men who advanced on Vimy, close to 10,000 would fall dead or wounded. Only three of the four divisions reached their objectives on that cold Easter Monday; not until the fourth day could the 4th Division's Brigadier General Edward Hilliam report from the final German stronghold, "I am King of the Pimple."

Worse, Vimy was not a great thing Canadians had done together. In Montreal that spring, recruiting parties for the Canadian Expeditionary Force were jeered; in most of Canada, they were merely ignored. Replacing the casualties of Vimy forced the conscription crisis of 1917. The scar tissue on the wounds to our national unity is still tender 70 years later.

At the time, the conflict at home was only hinted at to the victors of Vimy, much as soldiers themselves gave their families only rare glimpses of the horrors of their experiences in war. For them, Vimy had an unquestioned national significance. It coincided not only with the new professionalism of the corps and an unfamiliar wealth of shells, guns, and other military material but also with the dominance of the Canadian-born in what had been largely a contingent of British emigrés.

Even before historians suggested that April 9, 1917, was the moment when Canada was transformed from colony to nation, the Canadians at Vimy felt it in their bones. It was a feeling even the frugal, unimaginative government of William Lyon Mackenzie King was forced to respect when, a decade later, it authorized the memorial that now towers over the Douai Plain.

As the faithful chronicler of our national epics, Pierre Berton has turned to Vimy as naturally as he rediscovered the War of 1812, the building of the CPR, and the settlement of the Canadian West. He has brought to the task his usual narrative skill, an enthusiasm for odd characters and bizarre anecdotes and sufficient righteous indignation at war and its horrors to reassure readers who fear the Rambo disease.

Berton's researchers have assembled scores of books and pamphlets by proud participants, and they have mustered a few dozen nonagenarian survivors and grilled them on their memories. The result, proclaims Professor William Kilbourn from the book's back cover, is "one of the most moving accounts of war and battle ever written."

Frankly, in the name of sales or friendship, Kilbourn overreaches himself. There are more accurate and interesting accounts of the battle, notably by the internationally known but locally ignored Canadian historian, Donald Goodspeed. The enthusiasm of Berton and his researchers reveals an embarrassing shortage of knowledge about the Canadian Expeditionary Force and the First World War. Errors speckle the pages. It would not have detracted from the author's lively prose to recognize that an artillery brigade in 1917 was very different from an infantry brigade, or that the 75th Battalion (now the Toronto Scottish) had nothing much to do with the thriving city that was named Mississauga only in 1967. Lloyd George favoured the Australian, John Monash, over Canada's Arthur Currie as a colonial successor to the generals he despised. The British began the war with two machine guns per battalion, not per division.

Frequent repetition does not guarantee truth. A generation ago, Charles Stacey demolished the beloved Canadian folk-myth that Sam Hughes thumped Lord Kitchener's desk for the sake of preserving a united Canadian contingent. Berton gives this and many other dubious legends a second life.

The unhappy fact is that *Vimy* is laden with errors and inaccuracies, none of which are needed for a lively narrative. Who cares? Berton, and the friends whose editorial puffs decorate his back cover—Richard Rohmer, Peter Newman, June Callwood—may dismiss such criticisms as the jealousy of academic nit-pickers. The marketplace may give them confidence. In *Vimy,* Pierre Berton has given book-buyers what most of them want: a good read and a help with the Christmas shopping list.

There is no evidence that Berton's readers want accuracy as much as they relish his colourful sermons on human folly and national achievement. They will learn much to excite and inspire them. In turn, the dollars he earns do as much as the rest of Ontario's taxpayers put together to keep McClelland & Stewart in business.

And someday a better book will be written.

Christopher Moore (review date November 1988)

SOURCE: "Of Ice and Men," in *Books in Canada,* Vol. 17, No. 8, November, 1988, p. 30.

[*In the following excerpt, Moore cites a number of Berton's "strengths" as a historian, but notes that "a few sloppinesses have crept in" to* The Arctic Grail.]

The North West Passage, for all practical purposes, did not exist—that much was clear by 1700. But in 1818 the Royal Navy had run out of other navies to fight, and it decided to take on the North. The pursuit of what Pierre Berton calls the "Arctic Grail" began.

Seeking the elusive passage, the navy found a maze of icechoked channels where big naval vessels were the worst possible vehicle of exploration. Yet year after year, the navy sent ships and crews, with little or no special preparation, to bury themselves in the Arctic ice, then hope to get out before scurvy and starvation took over. Naval men refused to make any accommodation to the Arctic. They clung to their own brass-polishing subculture, and would no more take advice from Arctic whalers and northern fur traders than from the Inuit.

> **Berton's strengths as a historian are those that made him a master journalist: identifying the big story, getting the facts, and laying them out in clear, vigorous prose with strongly evoked protagonists and good common-sense judgements.**
> —*Christopher Moore*

The navy's heroic stupidity culminated in Sir John Franklin's expedition of 1845. Franklin managed to bury two ships and 129 men more deeply than eer in Arctic ice—so successfully that no one ever saw them again. Franklin created one of those sentimental tragedies Englishmen loved, and it took ten frantic years and 50 expeditions to find where he had gone.

When the navy had proved what everyone knew, attention turned to a new grail, the North Pole. Brash Americans and methodical Scandinavians rushed in to compete, but the cold, distant pole defied them all. Finally in 1909 two separate American expeditions claimed victory. It now appears that both were frauds. No one, it seems, has ever reached the North Pole and returned unaided. The polar grail remains beyond reach, concludes Pierre Berton.

Berton's strengths as a historian are those that made him a master journalist: identifying the big story, getting the facts, and laying them out in clear, vigorous prose with strongly evoked protagonists and good common-sense judgements. All those strengths are evident in *The Arctic Grail*, and he needs them. Arctic exploration was often the work of vainglorious and incompetent men, but a Berton history needs heroes. With these the only heroes available, he has to steer a narrow passage between cautious debunking and qualified admiration.

There's another problem: most of the Arctic explorers turn out to be the same person. Question: which of the British explorersis a repressed, obsessed, middle-aged naval careerist with an odd marriage? Answer: all of the above. The Americans are all egomaniacal self-promoters, and the Scandinavians are, well, very Scandinavian. Berton uses all his narrative skill to guide us through their endless battles with cold, darkness, hunger, and each other. In a long book, a few sloppinesses have crept in. John Richardson could hardly have been a friend of Robert Burns, who died when he was nine. Surprisingly, there are lapses into jargon (tripe-de-roche, polynya), and the native people are mostly called Eskimo, sometimes Innuit, and once Inuit. The route maps are excellent, but the murky illustrations are haphazardly chosen. Where is the Arctic Council painting that is discussed in the text?

"Whose Arctic is it?" asks Berton at the close. He calls the British voyages the basis of Canadian sovereignty, and cites all their names on the map to prove it. But Frobisher Bay is already Iqaluit, and Franklin District will one day be Nunavut. Real Canadian sovereignty in the North came with the laborious imposition of Canadian policing and administration after 1900—a sovereignty still challenged by foreign submarines and tankers, and by the reassertion of native title.

The Arctic Grail closes on a plea to include the Inuit in northern history. Sadly, Berton has been almost completely unable to do this himself. He tells us the explorers failed to perceive the natives, but he notices only those few who played Sancho Panza to some explorer's Quixote.

Could he have done more? He tells how Robert McClure abandoned HMS *Investigator* at Banks Island in 1853, but not how the *Investigator* made the local Inuit rich. Coming so often to harvest precious wood and copper from the wreck, they wiped out the Banks Island musk-ox, which did not return for a century. McClure never knew that most lasting result of his voyage. Neither will Berton's readers. There is an ethnographic literature, not wholly valueless, that documents Inuit worlds. Who better than Berton to lead Canadians into them? But that might have meant challenging his readers—and Berton is cautious about that. He has given us an adventure thick with colour and drama. Are we asking too much to ask for more?

Charles Davies (review date November 1988)

SOURCE: "Death in the North," in *Quill & Quire*, Vol. 54, No. 11, November, 1988, p. 2.

[*In the following review, Davies focuses on Berton's depiction of Sir John Franklin in* The Arctic Grail.]

Judging by appearances, there was never a less likely hero than Sir John Franklin. For most of his adult life Franklin was balding, overweight, and out of shape. He struck his fellow officers in the Royal Navy as being overly sensitive. He winced at floggings—a fairly common occurrence in 19th century naval service—and he fared poorly in confrontational situations. "Chicanery made him ill," his son-in-law, Philip Gell, would later write, "and so paralysed him that when he had to deal with it he was scarcely himself." Today, Franklin would be considered a wimp.

Nor was he a sophisticate in intellectual or spiritual affairs. He was horribly uncomfortable in drawing-room conversations and scarcely more relaxed in his correspondence. During their courtship, his first wife, poet Eleanor Anne Porden, reproached him for failing to address her in his letters by anything more intimate than "my dearest friend." His approach to religion was equally backward; in modern terms, he might be likened to a born-again Christian.

Yet Franklin, who had first gone to sea at the age of 12, had an extraordinary naval record. He had been on active duty in three of the great sea engagements of the Napoleonic Wars—including the Battle of Trafalgar—and surviveda shipwreck off Australia's Great Barrier Reef.

None of this, however, has anything to do with his enduring fame. What sealed his reputation, as Pierre Berton tells us in *The Arctic Grail*, was the fact that in 1845, at the age of 61, he took 134 men in two barque-rigged sailing ships (replete with such essentials as button polish and crested silverware) and disappeared somewhere in the area of King William Island. By losing his way (and in the process, his life) Franklin rose to a kind of sainthood. His disappearance triggered an 11-year search that filled in vast sections of the Arctic map, though few of the search parties yielded traces of the explorer's fate.

Berton treats Franklin's final expedition as the pivotal dramatic incident in the great age of Arctic exploration. From 1818, when the British Navy's Sir John Ross first attempted to find the Northwest Passage, until 1908, when American Robert Peary made his last expedition to the North Pole, Arctic exploration was something akin to a national obsession in Great Britain. Berton chronicles all the great voyages in this, his 34th book, and he fits them smoothly into the context of an age. Like that other magnificent Victorian adventure, the search for the source of the Nile River, expeditions to the Arctic created heroes suitable for an empire that spanned the globe.

In this romantic context, Franklin's failings could easily be forgotten. In a *New York Times* article of the period, Franklin was described as "one of the ablest, oldest and bravest men who had trodden that perilous path." The search for his expedition was, likewise, "as noble an epic as that which has immortalized the fall of Troy or the conquest of Jerusalem."

The reality, as Berton details in this exhaustively researched and seamlessly written narrative account, was much different. The hardships of Arctic exploration were almost indescribable. After waiting out the endless winter months of darkness and deadly cold, the members of these pioneering expeditions faced raging gales, rapidly changing weather conditions, and brutal physical labour. It was not uncommon for men to pull sledges weighing several hundred pounds across ice floes for days, only to discover that they had actually lost ground because of ice movements. But most explorers, including Franklin, learned to make the best of things, bringing along the accoutrements of civilization and passing the barren winter months with amateur theatricals.

No matter how remote an outpost might be, it was nevertheless a tiny island of English civilization.

Ironically, this imperial attitude contributed to Franklin's downfall and limited the progress of many other expeditions. The British Navy, arrogant in the extreme, sent out expeditions time after time in unsuitable ships, manned by sailors in inadequate clothing (English woollens rather than Arctic furs). The ships invariably carried ample supplies of the wrong kind of food. Salted meat kept the explorers' bellies full but made it unnecessary to seek out the fresh meat or native foods that would have prevented the single greatest curse of each enterprise: scurvy.

Berton concludes that most of the crew likely succumbed to scurvy and the resulting dementia (even though recent evidence makes clear that lead poisoning from improperly soldered tin cans was also a factor). But what Berton is implying in this intensely readable book is that the most famous of all Arctic explorers really died of stupidity. In 1858, the veteran naval explorer Leopold M'Clintock stumbled across graphic evidence of Franklin's folly on the northwest coast of King William Island. He found a 28-foot boat, weighing about 700 or 800 pounds, on top of a sledge weighing another 650 pounds. Franklin's men, most likely weakened by scurvy and other illnesses, had dragged this grotesque contraption across the ice. What astounded M'Clintock, though, was the collection of books, cutlery, clothing, and other sundries the men had piled on the sledge. There was, Berton writes, "everything, in short, that civilized nineteenth century travellers considered necessary for their comfort and well-being." Ozymandias himself couldn't have left more telling mementoes of his passing.

Roland Huntford (review date 20 November 1988)

SOURCE: "Going to Extremes," in *The New York Times Book Review*, November 20, 1988, pp. 1, 44-5.

[*In the following review, Huntford provides an overview of Breton's* The Arctic Grail, *praising it as a "highly readable compendium of northern exploration."*]

The view from space has made familiar the image of the world; but within living memory, its surface was still imperfectly known. The polar regions were the last great blanks upon the map, and the 19th century was haunted by the drive to fill them in. Since the Arctic was more accessible, that is where attempts were concentrated first. These events coalesce into an intricate saga which it is the purpose of this book to relate.

Pierre Berton, a Canadian historian and the author of *The*

Mysterious North, takes the quest for the North Pole and the Northwest Passage as a theme to unify the tale of Arctic exploration from the end of the Napoleonic wars to the first decade of this century. He dovetails the various expeditions to bring narrative order to a complex succession of events. He has produced a highly readable compendium of northern exploration, and a much-needed one, too.

The North Pole and the Northwest Passage represented the conquest of the unknown. Both captivated the public at the time. The North Pole was an obvious symbol of the ultimate. The Northwest Passage had a more convoluted significance. It was a route between the Atlantic and the Pacific, around the top f the North American continent, sought since the 16th century by northern Europeans as a shortcut to the East. By the time of its 19th-century revival, the quest for the Northwest Passage had become an end in itself—a romantic harking back to the glories of the Elizabethan age. In Mr. Berton's words, his book is "as much about *explorers* as it is about *exploring.*" And rightly so. They are all there, the assorted rogues, idealists, escapists, heroes, bunglers and occasional man of talent who trooped into the snows.

There is kindly old Sir John Franklin, seeking the Northwest Passage in 1845 and innocently leading his men to death, every one. There is his indomitable wife, Jane, consummately playing the role of Victorian widow, seeing that expeditions went out to search for her husband. There is Elisha Kent Kahe, the American doctor who went on one of those searches and whose twin obsessions were the Arctic and Margaret Fox, probably the original medium. "Remember then," he wrote her, "that Doctor Kane of the Arctic Seas loved Maggie Fox of the spirit rappings." In that direction, at least, Kane had no illusions; Miss Fox produced her effects by cracking her double-jointed toes. Far from the world of spirit rappings, there is the Norwegian, Roald Amundsen, finally navigating the Northwest Passage in 1903 with a minimum of fuss.

What drove these disparate characters to high latitudes? Mr. Berton sensibly does not give an answer pat. He does give one hint in the title of the book. The symbolism of the Holy Grail is connected with the power of illusion in driving men on. Mr. Berton also implies that an obsessive personality may be part of the pattern.

In the background, more easily identifiable motives lurk. For the first half of the 19th century. Arctic exploration was virtually a British preserve. Most expeditions were naval ones. Partly, it was to find work for redundant officers after the Napoleonic wars. Partly, too, it was to promote the westward march of Empire, for the Northwest Passage lay largely in the Canadian Arctic. Above all, it was to keep Russia in check. For Russia held Alaska then and, whatever her regime, was proceeding, as usual, with her organic drive to expand.

The Royal Navy secured British and, later, Canadian sovereignty in the Arctic. It was accompanied by staggering ineptitude and unnecessary loss of life. That holds the moral of this book. The Royal Navy stumbled from one debacle to the other because it clung to unsuitable methods and refused to adapt to an unfamiliar environment.

"Badly and hastily organized with a smugness and an arrogance that in hindsight seem almost criminal," Mr. Berton writes of one naval expedition, "this band of amateurs set off blithely, as so many had before it, without any real idea of what they were facing." In half a century, the Navy learned almost nothing in the snows, repeating the same old mistakes. There was no attempt to learn from the Eskimos, who clearly had learned how to survive in a barely habitable environment. Dogs were not used, and man-hauling was the order of the day. Clothing was tight, stiff, unsuitable and made of broadcloth and wool instead of fur. Innovation was despised. Mr. Berton quotes one member of a naval expedition who brought snowshoes and suffered "laughter and derision from the gallant but very inexperienced officers." Scurvy ravaged expedition after expedition, despite the example of the native peoples who were manifestly exempt.

It is a familiar tale. In the heyday of Empire the British, wherever they went, somehow contrived to live as uncomfortably and unhealthily as they possibly could. Their tragedy was that they dragged their environment with them, and staunchly refused to adapt. Worse still, among them, they did number polar travellers without equal. There was, for instance, Dr. John Rae (Amundsen's hero), an Orkneyman working for the Hudson's Bay Company, who had learned from the native peoples. But Rae and his like were ignored by the polar establishment. It was one outcome of a depressing worship of mediocrity.

It is a disturbing echo of larger issues. Britain was sinking into intellectual isolation. The Royal Navy, which after Trafalgar stood supreme, was decaying from within. Flair and initiative, the backbone of the Nelson tradition, were rapidly being bred out. The culmination in the snows, as Mr. Berton repeatedly points out, was Scott's disastrous rout by Amundsen at the South Pole—predictable, and predicted, even at the time. It was a paradigm of the collapse of British power.

In the Far North, during the second half of the 19th century, the British, symbolically enough, faded from the picture, to be replaced by the Americans. That also brought drama, but of a different kind. There was, for example, Charles Francis Hall, a high school dropout and owner of the little Cincinnati News, who sold out, tried to reach the North Pole and suffered death by arsenic. There was Adolphus Washington Greely who, in 1882, wrested the record for the Farthest North from the British, after they had held it for three centuries; they were never to recover this distinction. But on Greely's expedition, only 6 of 23 men survived, he executed one man for stealing food and there was cannibalism, too.

Technically, there was little wrong with these Americans. They were adaptable. They learned from the indigenous tribes—Hall was one of the few white men deliberately to live like the Eskimos. They admired success and were alien to the British cult of the glorious failure. Their flaws were impetuosity, impatience, a desire for quick results, so that their technical virtuosity was almost to no avail. It all ended with Cook and Peary, both masters of polar travel, each claiming to have conquered the North Pole for the United States, but neither of whom Mr. Berton happens to believe.

Mr. Berton reserves his admiration for the Norwegians. Their achievements were out of all proportion to their numbers. There was Fridtjof Nansen, who in 1888 made the first crossing of Greenland and, a few years later, achieved a sensational Farthest North by allowing his ship to be frozen in and drifting with the pack. There was Otto Sverdrup, who in four seasons discovered 100,000 square miles of new territory in the Canadian Arctic. There was Roald Amundsen, whom Mr. Berton calls the Norwegians' "crowning ornament": double victor of the Northwest Passage and finally the South Pole.

These men were notably efficient and achieved what they did with little loss of life. They were, in Mr. Berton's words, "a different breed from the hidebound British and the impetuous Americans. They were, after all, a subarctic people, used to cold weather and high winds, familiar with skis, sledges, and dogs. They were also immensely practical." They were also, be it added, individualists to a man, but free of the heroic delusion.

In the end, Mr. Berton's real heroes are the Eskimos. They are not commemorated on the maps, but the European explorers are. "The squat little men," as he puts it, "who fed John Ross's company in the Gulf of Boothia . . . who taught Rae, Hall, and Peary how to exist under polar conditions, gave no thought to such white concepts as fame, ambition or immortality." There is in this an all-too-familiar note of Western self-abnegation.

Implicit in *The Arctic Grail* is yet another chapter, for better or worse, of the Western European conquest of the globe. It is the movement that began with the blaze of the Renaissance in Italy five centuries ago and spread out in all spheres of human endeavor. Exploration, in the sense of sheer restlessness to find out what lies over the horizon, is a Western phenomenon. Those men who, with varying success, pitted

themselves against the hostile polar environment were the heirs of the Renaissance, the heart of which was the promotion of the individual and the discovery of the world. They represent our kind of civilization, of which, in spite of everything, we should still be proud. This book suggests as much.

Chauncey Loomis (review date 21 December 1989)

SOURCE: "Heavy Sledding," in *London Review of Books,* Vol. 11, December 21, 1989, pp. 22-3.

[*In the following review, Loomis notes Berton's eye for detail and his ability to make difficult material appealing to readers.*]

In the 19th century, Canada's Arctic Archipelago proved to be an explorer's nightmare, a maze of straits, channels, gulfs, inlets, sounds, shoals, peninsulas and islands that confounded even the best navigators. Looking at its jigsaw configurations on a modern map, we can understand why its uncharted straits and channels were often mistaken by the pessimistic for dead-end inlets, its inlets by the optimistic for straits and channels—its islands for peninsulas, its peninsulas for islands. Exacerbating the problem was ice, especially floe and pack ice. Protean and shifting, it also could be fatally solid, and it made the geography of the Arctic unstable: a passage clear one week could be clogged the next, and even accurate charts could be made useless by the ice. The Archipelago was a daunting place to find your way around in.

A writer setting out to tell the story of 19th-century Arctic exploration faces a maze almost as shifting and as daunting as the Archipelago itself. Especially during the search for the Franklin Expedition at mid-century, the story is complex. In the decade between 1848, when the search for Franklin began, and 1859, when M'Clintock discovered some grisly remains on King William Iland, almost thirty naval and overland expeditions joined the search. A writer has to juggle the names of explorers, famous in their day, but now known only to Arctic buffs, such as John and James Clark Ross, Rae, Pullen, Collinson, M'Clure, Austin, Ommanney, Richardson, Penny, DeHaven, Kane, Forsyth, Bellot, Kennedy, Belcher, Inglefield. M'Clintock—and names of ships, such as *Plover, Herald, Enterprise, Investigator, Resolute, Intrepid, Assistance, Pioneer, Lady Franklin, Sophia, Felix, Advance, Rescue, Prince Albert, Isabel, Phoenix, Talbot, Fox.* Then there are innumerable place-names, often the names of powerful personages scattered around the Arctic wastes like confetti and made confusing by repetition: Viscount Melville Sound, Melville Island, Melville Peninsula, Victoria Island, Victoria Strait, Prince of Wales Strait, Prince Regent Inlet, Prince Albert Sound (penetrating, it might be noted, deep into Victoria Island), Barrow Strait, Cornwallis Island, Bathurst Island, Boothia Peninsula (Felix Booth, the distiller and patron of Arctic exploration—there also is a Gulf of Boothia and a Cape Felix). Space and time become logistical problems: the writer has to move this explorer here, and that explorer there, in such and such ships, at such and such times, and then explain why they did or did not encounter each other. The danger of narrative confusion is great, and even greater is the danger of narrative monotony.

The latest writer to tell the story is Pierre Berton in *The Arctic Grail.* Berton accepts the challenge with a boldness worthy of a Robert M'Clure or a James Clark Ross. Not only does he tell the story of the Franklin Expedition and the search for it, he tells the story of *all* Arctic exploration in the 19th century in three overlapping stages: the search for the North-West Passage, the search for Franklin, and the attempt to reach the North Pole. The story has the scope, the heroism, the grandeur of a saga, and it also has the absurdity that is latent in any saga looked at with a cool eye. Berton sees both sides of it—and that is one of the many strengths of his book. Assisted by the plenitude of mini-maps scattered throughout the text (an excellent piece of book design), he tells the story clearly, informing the reader of who was where when, but avoiding the tedium and confusion that often accompanies such exposition. He uses much unpublished manuscript material, especially private journals and letters, and also much 19th-century periodical literature, handling both with intelligence and imagination. He puts the exploration into historical context by commenting on the motives that impelled it, and by demonstrating public and private responses to it. He has a unifying thesis: throughout the book his focus is on the terrible cost paid for cultural arrogance and inflexibility (especially the arrogance and inflexibility of naval establishments) in the face of such an austere and fickle environment as the Arctic. The thesis is not original, but it is sound and inevitable when the story is viewed with the imaginative common sense that he demonstrates in the book.

In a postscript, Berton rightly comments that *The Arctic Grail* is 'as much about *explorers* as it is about *exploring*'. He is deft in brief characterisation, an art that vivifies the entire work. Explorers who were just names in most earlier books become men with private lives and defined personalities in his. At the very outset he demonstrates this skill. There is Edward Parry, son of a cultivated and fashionable doctor in Bath—well-educated, intelligent, pious—a team-player very quick to use his charm and his connections to his own advantage, but also courageous and steadfast. There is John Ross; Parry's commander on his first venture into the Arctic, of relatively humble stock, a quirky intellectual Scot, proud, individualistic, and badly humiliated by a mistake on that venture that he never lived down. There is John Barrow, Second Secretary of the Admiralty (who always

acted, according to Ross, like the First Secretary) and the power behind British Arctic exploration for four decades—of humble stock and attracted to persons, like Parry, more to the manor born, stubborn in defending his own often wrong ideas, high-handed in his use of power. And there is William Scoresby, a whaling captain and brilliant amateur scientist who knew more about the Arctic than all of the others put together. In the opening pages, Berton plays these men off against each other: Barrow in power, not liking John Ross and simply refusing to listen to the knowledgeable Scoresby, but taking Parry as his protégé; Scoresby, disdained by Barrow, denied any sort of naval command and forced to stand on the sidelines watching the amateurs do their thing; Ross, seeing mountains up Lancaster Sound where no mountains exist and turning his expedition back; Parry, second in command, not protesting at the time, but taking full advantage of Ross's error after the fact, and proving Ross wrong on his own expedition a year later. When Parry returned triumphant from his own expedition, one of the first letters of congratulation he received was from his former commander John Ross, who had good reason to dislike Parry because Parry had been openly critical of his command after they had returned to England. Writing to his parents, Parry sarcastically said that he should frame the letter and put it in the British Museum, and he noted that he would reply civilly, but in such a way as 'to prevent the possibility of his bringing on a correspondence, which is the game he now wants to play'. Such a glimpse into the private thinking of a man like Parry confirms the truth of Berton's assertion that in Arctic exploration 'personality and temperament were as significant as seamanship,' and that important aspects of the personality and temperament often were concealed from the public. Parry acted the paragon among explorers, but he also was a shrewd player of power games.

The importance of unpublished manuscript material in achieving something like a whole instead of a partial truth is well demonstrated in *The Arctic Grail* by the story of Elisha Kent Kane's 1853-1855 expedition ('The Second United States Grinnell Expedition'). Well-educated, handsome, frail (he suffered from rheumatic fever) but nevertheless remarkably tough, Kane made himself famous partly by his books on his two expeditions. Elegantly written and gorgeously illustrated, they enjoyed immense circulation, and Kane became a *beau idéal* in his country. After his death in Havana at the age of 36, his body was carried in state by train and boat from New Orleans to Philadelphia; the obsequies observed by communities along the way can be compared to those lavished on Lincoln's funeral train. The Second United States Grinnell Expedition had been a grinding ordeal. Ostensibly, its purpose was to search for Franklin, but Kane obviously hoped to find the 'Open Polar Sea' that many still believed lay beyond the encircling rim of ice—and perhaps even to reach the North Pole. Instead, he and his crew ended up virtually marooned on the west coast of Greenland for more than two years. The story is not entirely one of noble endurance, although Kane soft-peddles the nastiness. Frictions on board led to open rebellion and desertion several times. Kane rather coolly describes one such incident, when eight men separated from the expedition to sledge south. The implication is that Kane, although he disagreed with the plan, willingly acquiesced to it and wished the men a heartfelt godspeed. Actually, in his private journal he was pouring out hatred on them:

> I cannot but feel that some of them will return broken down and suffering to seek a refuge on board. They shall have it to the halving of our last chip-but-but-but-if I ever live to get home-*home*! And should I meet *Dr Hayes* or *Mr Bonsall* or *Mister Sonntag*—let them look out for their skins. If I don't live to thrash them, why then, brother John, seek a solitary orchard and maull [sic] them for me. Don't honour them with a bullet and let the mauling be solitary save to the principals. It would hurt your Character to be wrestling with such low-minded sneaks.

Berton also quotes passages from the unpublished papers of John Wall Wilson, Kane's sailing master, who despised Kane and wrote that he was 'peevish, coarse, sometimes insulting . . . the most self-conceited man I ever saw.'

Berton's purpose is not to debunk heroes and heroism, but he knows that under sustained pressure (duration is crucial here, and was a crucial element in all 19th-century explorations—most expeditions took years rather than months), human beings often do lose control, at least temporarily. In *The Arctic Grail*, images of Elisha Kent Kane and of the other men who were caught up in the Polar passion are complex, or at least as complex as they can be when each individual has to be treated briefly as only one part of the saga. Berton avoids the sense of rushing over the surface; at times, indeed, he seems almost leisurely in his treatment of detail. For example, he cares enough about the individuality of the explorers to inform us about their love lives—Parry's unsuccessful pursuit of various young ladies, the stodgy Franklin's surprising marriages to two forceful and highly intelligent women, Kane's weird affair with the famous 'spirit rapper' Margaret Fox. This humanising detail makes them, in a subtle way, not less but more heroic. Fallible human beings, sometimes even weak and neurotic, not romantically conceived supermen, lived through those terrible ordeals.

Berton's eye for selected detail also strengthens his commentary on the historical and cultural implications of 19th-century Arctic exploration. His ideas here are not particularly original, but he gives them clearer and more forceful expression than they have been given in the past. One theme is the pig-headed stubbornness of the Admiralty in refusing to adjust its methods to the environment—in particular, by ignoring techniques of travel and survival that could have been learned from the Inuit. Many other writers have made the same point, but Berton's exposition is more effective. One of his best examples is drawn from late in the century, when the Navy should have learned from its past mistakes. When the Nares Expedition set out for the Pole in 1875, its leaders had been given the advice of George Rae among others. Rae was the most accomplished British traveller in the Arctic; he had lived with Inuit, and he had been willing to learn from them. For several pages, Berton quotes Rae's advice and describes how it was ignored. Rae urged that they learn how to make snow houses, citing some subtle advantages: 'When you use snow as a shelter your breath instead of condensing on your bedding gets condensed on the walls of the snow house, and therefore your bedding is relieved from nearly the whole of this.' An additional benefit of the snow house is, of course, that it does not have to be carried. The Nares Expedition manhauled heavy tents and paid a terrible price.

Berton sees that the flaws of the Navy were not just its own, but were cultural, and that behind the refusal to learn from the Inuit was an ethnocentric, even racist arrogance. And he sees that the arrogance was fed partly by the fuel of misguided and anachronistic chivalric idealism—an idealism that presumably separated civilised men from barbarians like the Inuit. Again, his eye for detail strengthens his argument. The manhauling of heavy naval (as against light Inuit) sledges was one of the most deadly flaws in the Navy's methods of Arctic exploration.

> Strangely, to the English there was something noble, something romantic, about strong young men marching in harness through the Arctic wastes, enduring incredible hardships with a smile on their lips and a song in their hearts. They were like the knights of old, breaking new paths, facing unknown perils in their search for the Grail. The parallel is by no means inexact, for M'Clintock had given his sledges names that suggest knightly virtues—Inflexible, Hotspur, Perseverance, Resolute. Each sledge proudly carried a banner of heraldic design and each had its own motto ('Never Despair' . . . 'Faithful and Firm'), some even in Latin.

Inevitably in such a survey as *The Arctic Grail*, things are missing. In particular, one wishes Berton has commented more on aesthetic responses to the Arctic, and that the book were better illustrated: the small maps are excellent, but the other illustrations are second-rate, both in choice and in quality of reproduction. Berton does not even mention that George Back was an almost professional artist and graphics were an important aspect of Arctic exploration in the 19th century. Many of the explorers, like Back, were competent draughtsmen, and their sketches became the basis of work done by professional artists and illustrators; illustrations in widely-circulated books, magazines and newspapers, as well as paintings and dioramas that attracted large audiences to popular displays, gave the public the chilling and dramatic images of the Arctic that linger on today.

Berton writes in the tradition of a master, Alan Moorehead. He is more facile than Moorehead and perhaps more superficial, looser and perhaps more pointed in shaping his material, but he shares Moorehead's ability to assimilate masses of material to select what is telling, and to cast it into an appealing narrative without excessive distortion or oversimplification. He makes available to the common reader a saga that might otherwise be forgotten by all but historians. The drunken poet in Thomas Keneally's *The Survivor* berates the Antarctic explorer Ramsey for being so laconic about his experiences: 'What's the use of getting involved in a bloody saga if you won't tell a poet about it?' Berton may not be a poet, but he is a fluent writer of narrative prose, and *The Arctic Grail* is the best survey of 19th-century Arctic exploration yet written.

William Barr has translated and edited Heinrich Klutschak's *Als Eskimo unter den Eskimos* as *Overland to Starvation Cove*. Klutschak was a member of the Schwatka Expedition in 1878-80, and during part of the expedition travelled by himself with Inuit. His account, published in 1881, is valuable primarily as a description of Inuit life as observed by an intelligent and sympathetic outsider, its thrust made clear by the original title *As an Eskimo among the Eskimos*. Klutschak was not a professional anthropologist, but his observations were keen enough to earn the respect and gratitude some years later of the first true ethnographer to live with Inuit, Franz Boas. The translation and republication of such a work is important mainly to scholars and Arctic buffs, but its importance is indeed great to them.

Owen Beattie's and John Geiger's *Frozen in Time* is an account of Beattie's rather sensational researches into the causes of the Franklin disaster. The book is an 'as told to' story. Apparently Beattie has told Geiger the story, and Geiger has written it. After Beattie, an anthropologist, found high levels of lead in the bones of some of the Franklin victims scattered about King William Island, he received permission to exhume the bodies of three members of the expedition who had died on Beechey Island during the first winter of the expedition. Most of the book is a description of Beattie's own trips and of the exhumations, and the text is accompanied by some repellent photographs of the bodies.

The exhumed bodies also had a high lead content, and

Beattie argues that the entire expedition was poisoned by faulty lead soldering in the tins that held much of the expedition's food supplies. Lead poisoning can lead to erratic behaviour and bad judgment—and this, according to Beattie, explains why the Franklin expedition make so many mistakes. The argument cannot be dismissed, but it has problems. First of all, we don't really know what happened to the Franklin Expedition—what the situation was, or what the reasoning was behind some of the decisions that were made—and so it is hard to specify just what the mistakes were. Often cited is the sheer madness of men on the verge of death hauling heavy boats over the ice loaded with such things as silverware and teak desks—but such madness can also be attributed to naval discipline and the sort of quixotic stupidity that Berton describes in *The Arctic Grail*. A more serious flaw lies in a missing statistic. Beattie makes much out of the fact that Inuit bones near the Franklin bones did not have a high lead content. That's interesting, but a more important statistic would be the lead content in Englishmen in general in the 19th century, and Beattie offers no such statistic. At one point in the book, he mentions that they might have had more lead in their systems than they do today, but he rapidly drops the subject. If in fact the average English homebody did have a high content of lead during that period, then probably the tin cans on the Franklin Expedition were not the cause of the disaster. I confess, however, that I was sufficiently persuaded by his description of the effects of lead poisoning to entertain the possibility that all of England suffered it in the century—that maybe the entire island was high on lead and stark raving mad.

Victor Dwyer (review date 10 September 1990)

SOURCE: "Look Back in Anger," in *Maclean's,* Vol. 103, No. 37, September 10, 1990, pp. 79-80.

[*In the following review, Dwyer praises* The Great Depression, 1929 to 1939, *stating that it is "arguably [Berton's] best book."*]

After producing 35 titles, and at the venerable age of 70, Pierre Berton has written his first angry book. Canada's most-read author has taken on the Great Depression, and the project has made him furious. "It's my first book that really made me mad as I wrote it," he said in an interview. "I suddenly realized that a lot of what happened back then was appalling. It was a surprise, and I think that helped me to write a better book." Berton's 36th work, *The Great Depression, 1929 to 1939,* excoriates prime ministers William Lyon Mackenzie King and R.B. Bennett, business giants including the Eatons, and the press for a callous disregard for ordinary Canadians during those dark years. Said Berton: "I've done all the research, I've soaked it up, and I believe I've earned the right to say I think that this guy was an idiot and this guy was a clown." He added: "I've been accused of creating Canadian heroes. It's never been my purpose. In any case, the villains are much more interesting."

A gripping and often disturbing survey of the century's leanest years, *The Great Depression* is arguably Berton's best book. It crowns a career that has yielded some of the most popular titles produced in Canada, 15 of them looing back to the country's roots. Ever since the appearance of his first Canadian history book, *Klondike* (1958), which told the story of the Yukon gold rush of 1898, Berton has topped the domestic best-seller lists with lively glimpses into the past.

Among his most popular books have been *The Last Spike* (1971), about the building of the Canadian Pacific Railroad, *The Dionne Years* (1977), which told the story of Canada's Dionne quintuplets, and *Vimy* (1986), an examination of the First World War battle in which the Canadian corps captured France's Vimy Ridge. But the restlessly curious—and highly nationalistic—author has also turned his attention to such disparate subjects as the Anglican Church, in *The Comfortable Pew* (1965), and the U.S. movie industry's misrepresentation of Canada, in *Hollywood's Canada* (1975).

For Berton, the effort has been financially rewarding. Mindful of his past success in the bookstores, Toronto-based McClelland & Stewart gave the author a $610,000 advance for *The Great Depression* and an upcoming series of four books about the history of Niagara Falls. And the millionaire author, who lives in Kleinburg, Ont., just north of Toronto, with his wife, Janet (they have eight grown children), will receive royalties of at least 15 per cent on sales of those five books—an arrangement that could net him well over $500,000 if they sell briskly. Said Berton of his publishers: "They treat me well, but then, I treat them pretty well, too." Indeed, the 75,000-copy first printing of *The Great Depression* reflects the publishing house's confidence in Berton.

His success has been the result of hard work and determination. "Just the basic research for my books routinely takes six months," Berton told *Maclean's*. "Those first months of research are really terribly depressing—because you don't think you have a story. It's not till you get in really deep that you get to the interesting stuff." In the case of *The Great Depression*, that groundwork, which the author carried out with the help of his full-time assistant, Barbara Sears, involved such daunting tasks as reading the 8,000-page report of the 1935 Regina Riot Inquiry Commission. The hefty document was an examination of the causes of a riot that broke out between the police and several hundred relief-camp workers travelling from Vancouver to Ottawa, where they had planned to stage a protest rally.

Berton also put advertisements in newspapers to find people who had interesting stories to tell about the Depression. The author then travelled across Canada for dozens of interviews, including one with octogenarian Steve Brodie of Victoria, who recounted crossing the country in a boxcar 75 times because he could not find a steady job.

Berton himself was relatively untouched by the Depression. In 1929, when the stock market crashed, he was a nine-year-old living in the Yukon, where the events to the south had only a mild impact. The following year, his father, Francis, retired from his job as a civil servant in the North and moved the family to Toronto. Then, in 1932, the family relocated to Victoria, where Pierre went to high school and college. With his father's small pension, the Bertons lived a modest but comfortable life. "Frankly," said Berton, "for me, in many ways the Thirties was a wonderful time."

As the author plunged into his research, he realized just how devastating the era was for a lot of other Canadians. "What I didn't want to do was color the book with too much nostalgia," he said, "because, for most people, it wasn't a good time." Describing the "mindless optimism" that prevailed in "an overdeveloped, overstocked country" in the 1920s, *The Great Depression* vividly captures the abject terror that gripped ordinary people when the stock markets collapsed and the capitalist system ground to a halt.

Like Berton's best historical works, the book's strength lies in his ability to blend detailed accounts of influential personalities, events and movements with stories about the lives of everyday Canadians. There are scores of fascinating anecdotes, including the story of Toronto bookkeeper Lottie Nugent, who invested her life savings, and borrowed heavily, to play the market. A few months later, unable to repay her loans, she calmly entered her room in a downtown boarding house and killed herself by turning on the gas.

Despite the hard times that followed the crash, many of Canada's political and economic leaders chose to ignore the misery experienced by many of their fellow Canadians—and Berton seems to take pleasure in describing the elite's shortcomings in scathing detail. He portrays the Liberal Mackenzie King as alternately smug and hypocritical in the face of great decisions. In his diary entry for Jan. 1, 1930—three months after the crash—King thanked God "with all my heart for protecting me through the year now drawing to a close."

Although the Prime Minister enthused in his journals about the "spirit of mutual aid" that informed his Christian beliefs, he steadfastly refused to match those sentiments with adequate federal money for the victims of the crash. In fact, he wrote elsewhere in his diary that he hoped those who still had their jobs would be selfish enough to ignore the jobless and would not add their voices to the growing chorus demanding unemployment benefits.

Berton paints an equally unflattering picture of the country's private employers, who, he maintains, exploited the vulnerability of their workforce to profit from the Depression. The New York City-based Woolworth chain of department stores, for one, formulated a policy of keeping its female employees on call, "never knowing," Berton writes, "when they would be offered work, and unable to look for other jobs." In 1932, the company demanded, and got, a 10-per-cent wage cut from its employees—while showing a net profit of $1.8 million.

The T. Eaton Co., meanwhile, made it impossible for some of its employees to take rests at its Toronto clothing factory. Winnifred Wells, who worked as an "examiner" there, testified to the Royal Commission on Price Spreads in 1935 that, since the Depression, Eaton's had removed the stool that she would occasionally use to take brief breaks. She reported that she hated going home on the streetcar, "because if I sat down I could not get up again, my knees and my legs would be so stiff." In Quebec, several of the biggest garment manufacturers implemented industry-wide blacklists of employees who had been fired for complaining of being paid below the legal minimum wage.

For many of the millions who could not find work, conditions were even worse. In 1932, unemployment reached a staggering 36 per cent in Ontario. To single men, the government of Conservative Prime Minister R.B. Bennett, who led the country from 1930 to 1935, offered what Berton terms "the gift of 20 cents a day" to work in one of dozens of relief camps spread across the Canadian countryside. Breeding grounds of bacteria and disease, the poorly funded camps were virtual prisons for the men who lived in them. They were finally closed after King's re-election in 1936—but only after the bloody Regina Riot of the previous year, in which the RCMP shot 12 unarmed former relief-camp inmates on their way to a protest in Ottawa. Writes Berton: "Although the Canadian government tried to make it appear that the relief camps were part of a plan to save the youth of the country, the real reason was to save the country from its youth—to get the jobless out of the way and prevent revolution."

According to Berton, the fight against real and alleged Communists became a routine excuse for federal, provincial and local governments to trample on democratic rights. Individuals labelled "Communist" by the federal authorities were routinely deported—including some of German descent who ended up in Hitler's death camps. Berton recounts that one man, Hans Kist, was sent back to his native Germany by government officials after he participated in a strike in Fraser Mills, B.C. The Nazis, agreeing with Canada's assessment of Kist as a "thoroughgoing troublemaker," tortured him to death.

City officials in Sudbury, Ont., banned all meetings of more than two persons after Communists there tried to organize nickel miners in 1930. Seven years later, Quebec Premier Maurice Duplessis introduced the notorious padlock law, which gave police in that province the power to lock any building used for what officials considered to be "Communist gatherings."

Not until the book's closing chapter does Berton's anger at the ineptitude and hypocrisy of such men as King and Bennett reach its peak. Priming for war, King suddenly became generous with the public purse. Interspersing the narrative with earlier quotes by both Bennett and King about the danger of spending public money for the common good, Berton demonstrates his genuine contempt for those former Canadian leaders. Relating a story of two former relief-camp workers who meet on a warship heading for Germany, Berton spells out the sad irony of their situation: "The government had once paid them 20 cents a day and treated them as bums. Now it was paying 6 1/2 times as much and treating them as heroes."

Although *The Great Depression* presents a searing attack on governmental and economic elites, Berton says that he did not set out to write a political tract—"It's not a left-wing book, but you can't write a book about the Depression without being considered left-wing, because the right-wingers were in charge, and they bungled it." He added, "Those are the facts; it's about time this book was written."

With passion and fury, Pierre Berton has cast a harsh light on one of the darkest corners of Canada's past. The country's image of itself may never be quite the same.

Anna Chiota (review date 1992)

SOURCE: "Berton's Canadian History," in *Canadian Children's Literature*, No. 67, 1992, pp. 75-7.

[*In the following review, Chiota discusses the value of Breton's work as an academic resource for students.*]

Two of a four part set, these titles feature the events and people involved in military confrontations along the Great Lakes border during the War of 1812. *Canada Under Siege* covers the attacks on York and Fort George, the battles of Stoney Creek and Beaver Dams, and the legendary walk of Laura Secord. *Revenge of the Tribes* highlights the events and attitudes that prompted the Indians to throw their support and force behind the Canadian and British cause. Other titles not reviewed cover battles at Detroit and Queenston Heights.

Berton covers this historical material in a manner both vivid and engaging. As adults have been drawn to his popularized histories, so too should a younger readership. The third-person narrative form, interspersed with direct quotations, draws the reader into history. One cannot help but sympathise with the soldiers when the physical conditions they had to endure are described in the following manner: "Harnessed five to a sleigh, [the soldiers] hauled their equipment through snow and water for eleven days . . . Provisions and men were soon soaked through. The days were bad but the nights were a horror." The military leaders and individual soldiers are given human faces in some broad portrayals that are not always flattering or uncritical. Human error, failings or procrastination determine the course of the war as much as bravery, decisiveness, and heroic acts. Pierre Berton, the storyteller, excels in weaving the facts, events and people of the period into compelling stories.

As well, there is no lack of factual detail, and peppered throughout the text are maps and illustrations highlighting military features such as attack routes, weaponry, and uniforms. A good index makes the information accessible if the books are being used for historical study. On the same note, an eleven-page overview of the war appears at the beginning of each title in the series and gives a broad perspective connecting the individual events to the general development of Canadian history. While useful, the repetition of this relatively lengthy preface in each slender volume is perhaps unnecessary.

In his historical analysis, Berton presents the War of 1812 as a civil war, a "war fought by men and women on both sides of a border that all had ignored until hostilities broke out. . . ." With many settlers being former Americans or related to such, this fact is relevant in determining the sentiment of civilians or even the militia, but one wonders how strongly it applied to the British and American military leaders and the regular army. This approach also has little relevance to the Indians who participated and to whom Berton assigns an integral role. Their support of the British and Canadian cause resulted from the American policy to undertake the total destruction of the Indians as signalled by the Battle of Tippecanoe. In turn, such Indian leaders as Tecumseh, were "determined to lead the forces of his confederacy across the border to fight beside the British against the common enemy."

A second theme that Berton attempts to develop is one of the war as a foundation of Canadian nationalism. Having repelled the giant from the south in defense of their settlements, Canadians "developed both a sense of pride and sense of community" that in future would forge a nation. This view

loses a little of the glory when at times he shows that victory often came through luck, bad weather or some other prosaic event. As well, Berton is a little inconsistent when he refers to the "real victors, who, being Indians, were really losers." The intent to provide some continuity is admirable, but at times the result is strained.

Overall, there is little doubt that this series will be successful. It provides the excitement of a good adventure story with a wealth of historical data. These titles also fill a gap that should provide some curriculum support. One should note that the "Battles of the War of 1812" is actually a subset of another series entitled *Adventures in Canadian History* that will cover topics from the war to the opening of the Canadian West and is targeted for children twelve and up.

Robert Nicholas Bérard (review date 1993)

SOURCE: "At Once Too Staid and Melodramatic: Berton's Canadian History," in *Canadian Children's Literature,* No. 69, 1993, pp. 40-2.

[*In the following review, Bérard criticizes Berton's work as too detail-oriented to serve as good historical fiction, and too melodramatic to serve as a key source for historical analysis.*]

These two books are the first in a series of "Adventures in Canadian History" to be written for McClelland & Stewart by Pierre Berton. A third volume devoted to the War of 1812, *The Revenge of the Tribes,* has also been published, as well as three additional titles, dealing with the opening of the West and the North. The publishers have, no doubt, made a prudent investment in this series. There is a dearth of well-written Canadian history aimed at young people, particularly at the twelve-to-fourteen year age group for which this series has been prepared. The clear type and the low price of these books will make them particularly attractive for purchase by schools and libraries. Finally, who better to interpret the history of Canada, particularly the story of the War of 1812, to young people than Canada's most prolific and popular pop historian, Pierre Berton? A decade ago, Berton won substantial critical acclaim from academic historians as well as the general public for *The Invasion of Canada* (1980) and *Flames Across the Border* (1981), his treatment of the War of 1812 for an adult readership. He knows his subject, and he is, perhaps, Canada's most widely-read author.

Unfortunately, the likely commercial success of these volumes and their value as classroom resources must be set against the disappointment that will be felt by many teachers of history that such a talented writer has done so little with his material. Despite Berton's best efforts to bring into high relief the drama and irony of the North American aspect of the Napoleonic Wars, the books are staid and flat, too heavily laden with the minutiae of textbook history to be compelling historical fiction and too breathless and melodramatic to be a key source for historical analysis.

Both books open with a common introduction to "the peculiar war," which Berton characterizes as a "civil war" fought in large measure by people who did not want to fight each other. The author summarizes his view that this indecisive conflict, whose follies and excesses he repeatedly notices, yielded little benefit to either the Americans or the Indian nations which found themselves drawn into battle but was a decisive event in Canadian history, one which "marked the first faint stirrings of a Canadian nation." It is significant that Berton says very little about the War of 1812 in Québec and nothing about the Atlantic region. It lends support to the idea that, in the perspective of many of our intelligentsia, the "Canadian nation" bears a striking resemblance to Upper Canada.

Berton has taken pains to ensure that he has got his facts straight, even to the point of drawing his dialogue from contemporary sources, and this constitutes one of the strengths of the books. He has also tried to avoid the partisan chauvinism that marks many older histories of the War of 1812. He has sought and found heroes and villains, the silly and the sagacious, on both sides in the conflict, although he leaves little doubt about his favourites; and each individual figure, from the brave, gallant Isaac Brock to the equally-noble Shawnee chief Tecumseh to the "pompous, self-important" American general Alexander Smyth is presented as less complex than we might expect. Berton also pursues his long-standing concern—see his *Why We Act Like Canadians* (1982)—with distinguishing the Canadian from the American national character through contrasts in historical experience. Thus, in *The Capture of Detroit,* he contrasts the relatively peaceful and law-abiding "pioneer" community of Upper Canada with the intemperate and violent "frontier" society to the south: "No Daniel Boones stalked the Canadian forests, ready to knock off an Injun with a Kentucky rifle or do battle over an imagined slight." It will be a matter of little consequence if Americans find the comparison inaccurate or overdrawn, but the publishers may well expect serious criticism from aboriginal groups who will no doubt take issue with Berton's references to drinking and scalping.

A major drawback, for many readers, will be the narrow military, even strategic focus of much of the books. To be fair, Berton does try to describe the nature of Upper Canadian society and community life, but more often he lapses into overlong descriptions of armaments and battle plans which may not engage the interest of more than a minority

of adolescent boys. It is too difficult to find the links between these events and the lives of contemporary Canadian teenagers to make these books a popular choice on drugstore shelves. At the same time, Berton raises some provocative questions about war and heroism. Although some may find the language a bit strong, Berton's descriptions of the horrors of the conflict—"Blood and brains spattered the walls and the gowns of some women who had sought refuge nearby"—underscore his determination to avoid excess glorification of war. He also invites a reappraisal of the American general William Hull, sentenced to death by a military court for cowardice in his surrender of Detroit, an act which averted an almost certain slaughter of American soldiers and civilians.

Berton's narrative is, in general, forceful, although the text is littered with annoying metrically-correct parentheticals—thus, John Norton, military leader of a Mohawk band, is referred to in *The Death of Isaac Brock* as "a strapping six-foot (two m) Scot"—and miles and kilometers appear randomly throughout. The author displays his recognized skill at deploying characters and events for maximum surprise and impact, and he never condescends to younger readers. In fact, while reading, one can almost hear Berton's pleasant and familiar voice narrating a CBC documentary on the events described. Unfortunately, the comparison that comes immediately to mind is with the acclaimed American Public Broadcasting System's award-winning documentary series, *The Civil War.* It was the genius of that production to relate a massive military conflict in an age more different from our own than most people immediately recognize to the concerns of ordinary people. That series set a standard for popular history that Pierre Berton perhaps could, but has not in these volumes, attained.

Eric Henderson (review date 1993)

SOURCE: "Footnotes in Canadian History," in *Canadian Children's Literature,* No. 72, 1993, pp. 78-80.

[*In the following review, Henderson criticizes Berton's Canadian historical series for children, arguing that many of the titles deal with events and issues only marginally significant in Canadian history.*]

Pierre Berton's series of popular history books for twelve- to fourteen-year-olds, "Adventures in Canadian History," keeps expanding, even as their "Canadian content" shrinks. While earlier titles in the series chronicled significant moments in the building of a nation (notably Berton's four books on The War of 1812), some of the more recent ones have had little to do with Canada at all. For example, *Dr. Kane of the Arctic Seas,* the third in the "Exploring the

North" series, tells the story of an American from Philadelphia who searches for a lost Englishman in the seas off the Greenland coast. The connection with Canada is tenuous at best.

Indeed, it seems as though Berton is driven in his choice of subjects less by their historical relevance than by the personal appeal of a character. Berton likes stories of the Promised Land, stories of ambitious mavericks doomed to disillusionment who engage in wild, idealistic quests for honour, fame or wealth—the search for Klondike gold and for the fabled North West Passage to the East are the subjects of two series within the larger "Adventures in Canadian History" series.

That these questers weren't Canadians or that their exploits weren't formative events in Canada's history seems incidental to the interest Berton creates in his roguish, sometimes cruel, but always persistent characters, such as Robert John McClure (the discoverer of the North West Passage in *Trapped in the Arctic*) and Dr. Elisha Kent Kane, both of whom lead expeditions into the polar regions, braving ferocious hardships and driving their crews to the brink of death to satisfy vaulting ambitions.

In *A Prairie Nightmare*, Berton describes the plight of 2,000 Britains who become dupes of a scheme by the Christian missionary Isaac Montgomery Barr to start an all-British colony in the area of the Saskatchewan-Alberta border. Barr, more interested in personal profit than the plan's practicality, convinces his "flock" that harsh prairie life is much like the pastoral agrarian life of rural England they are leaving behind.

Barr is a representative Berton "anti-hero," one whose ambitious cravings have consequences beyond those he intended. Barr's Colony of naïve tenderfeet eventually prospers to become the site of the city of Lloydminster. Berton's interest here, as in his popular adult histories, is in the role personal ambition played in Canada's development.

Still, with the exception of *Steel Across the Plains*, about the building of the Canadian Pacific Railway from Winnipeg to Calgary, the later books in the series remain examples of Canadian marginalia, stories of flawed and flaky individuals, rather than nation-builders. Essentially, they are footnotes to Canadian history.

Invariably, the characters who occupy centre stage in Berton's histories are British, and to a lesser degree, Americans, perhaps giving young readers the impression that the contribution of people of other nationalities to Canada's unfolding nationhood has been minimal to non-existent.

One also notices a disturbing tendency toward racial stereo-typing. Whenever Swedes appear in the two books on the Klondike gold rush and in *Steel Across the Prairies*, they are described as bear-like, hard-drinking oafs; "feelings of superiority" accounted for the inability of the British to survive in the Far North, according to Berton in *Parry of the Arctic*.

Americans, too, or "Yanks," as Berton refers to them at one point in *The Klondike Stampede*, are victims of similar stereotyping. Americans objected to the interference of the Mounties as they crossed into Canada to take part in the 1897 Gold Rush. "In keeping with the American tradition of individualism . . . they wanted to drown themselves if they wished," says Berton, engaging here in a train of censorious moralizing also present elsewhere. In *A Prairie Nightmare*, for example, he cautions his young readers to "remember . . . that even today Canadians sometimes want to reject new arrivals because they seem unsuitable for life in Canada."

Each book is accompanied by drawings and maps. Occasionally, the illustrations reveal an inconsistency with the text. For example, two maps in *Jane Franklin's Obsession* purport to show the area of the Arctic charted by Sir John Franklin. But in the first map, showing the known Arctic before Franklin, King William Island (where Franklin was believed to have disappeared) is drawn as an island, and Berton has already noted that Franklin believed it to be a peninsula.

One drawing in *Parry of the Arctic* is a scene from a high-spirited theatrical performance held on board Parry's ship, the Fury. Berton has described the ship's isolation, a gloomy landscape without birds, animals or "cheerful natives." Yet Inuit appear prominently in the drawing, gesticulating in bafflement at the Englishmen's on-stage antics.

Berton's ability to animate the past through his portrayal of strong, magnetic characters is, perhaps, his major trademark. Many of the books in the "Adventures in Canadian History" series succeed in this aim and will undoubtedly maintain the interest of young readers who would ordinarily never read history outside of the classroom.

But if these books are ever to be used as tools for learning, they need to focus more sharply on significant events in Canadian history. In addition, Berton should try to convey greater historical authenticity. Far more useful than the somewhat pretentious indices that accompany the short books would be a list of recommend readings for students.

Such a bibliographic resource would not only enable Berton's readers to pursue an interest that developed out of their reading, but would also allow students and teachers alike to examine what Berton calls his "unimpeachable," though unnamed, historical sources.

Anne Denoon (review date November 1995)

SOURCE: "The Great Recycler," in *Books in Canada,* Vol. 24, pp. 29, 32.

[*In the following brief review, Denoon notes some "minor irritants" in the second volume of Berton's autobiography, but states that they are "counterbalanced" by "snappy writing."*]

Pierre Berton's sixtieth published book picks up where ***Starting Out***, his first volume of autobiography left off, and begins with his arrival in Toronto in 1947. The postwar metropolis he evokes in ***My Times*** was still essentially the Good, with delusions of worldclassness decades away. The journalistic band Berton joined may seem equally quaint to younger readers: an alcohol-fuelled, almost all-male, visible-minority-free milieu in which only the widespread anti-Semitism of the time allowed personal tolerance to be put on the line.

(The modern types, including Berton, who formed a co-operative community in rural Kleinburg in 1948 inverted the then commonplace "restrictive" clause to exclude known bigots, but he does not record whether any Jews joined.)

In the book's engaging early chapters, one of which is aptly entitled "Hustling," the young Berton is driven to extraordinary feats of journalistic endurance not only by innate ambition, but also by rapidly escalating domestic responsibilities. He became, as he puts it, a "jack-of-all-writing-trades," churning out magazine articles, film and theatre scripts, government pamphlets, and anything else that paid or kept his name in print. Add his first books, his daily(!) newspaper column, the start of his enduring career as a radio and television personality, and you have the familiar, ubiquitous Pierre Berton of the 1960s onward.

Unfortunately, once success arrives—by his reckoning, about ten years ater his arrival in Toronto—*My Times* turns into a sometimes tedious chronicle of triumphs. Berton's unabashed enjoyment of fame and notoriety is rather endearing; after all, honest arrogance, to which Berton candidly admits, is more appealing than false modesty. But, over more than four hundred pages, the accumulation of such blush-inducing quotations as "he is one of the most fascinating, talented, and interesting persons in Canada" does take its toll. And while a certain amount of "and then I wrote" is unavoidable in a journalistic memoir, perhaps only the Great Recycler (an epithet he cheerfully accepts) would reprint a newspaper column from the early 60s almost in its entirety.

Another minor irritant is his refinement of the art of namedropping, in which well-known people are introduced by their familiar diminutives (Pat Watson, Bill Mitchell, Bob McMichael, Betsey Kilbourn . . .) so that the reader may miss a beat before belated recognition comes.

Still, memorable anecdotes (visiting Robert Service in his Monaco villa, for one) and snappy writing counterbalance such annoyances. Although most of ***My Times*** is short on introspection (a defect in an autobiography, but probably an asset in a career like the indefatigable Berton's), the epilogue finds him in elegiac mode. For Berton, as for other liberal crusaders of his generation, being publicly called a racist during the brouhaha surrounding the 1994 Writing Through Race conference was an experience that seems almost to have broken his spirit. But only almost, for he leaves the final verdict on his achievements to his faithful readers and fans, and ***My Times*** is really for them.

Stephen Smith (review date July 1996)

SOURCE: "Berton's Really Not Funny," in *Quill & Quire,* July, 1996, p. 50.

[*In the following brief review, Smith criticizes Berton's failed attempts at satire in* Farewell to the Twentieth Century: A Compendium of the Absurd.]

What I was going to do was make a humorous approach to Pierre Berton's purportedly funny ***Farewell to the Twentieth Century: A Compendium of the Absurd***. What I had in mind was a piece poking jocosely at the book's general—what to call it?—imperfection, showing by clever example that this was a balloon that never had any air in it, and how sad is *that*? Light on the feet, quick to the point, winkish in a benevolent way that said nothing harsher than *while somebody may find this to be a funny book, and while I could respect their choice in doing so in the spirit of pluralism, they should not try to contact me because we'd have nothing much to talk about:* that's what I was thinking as I made a way through Berton.

What I wasn't banking on was defeat. I'm talking Montcalm here on the plains at Quebec: *utter* defeat (though without the loss of a continental toehold). I can't remember the last time I got to the end of a book feeling so vanquished, so much like the book itself—hilarity-free. After ***Farewell to the Twentieth Century***, I had no humour left in me, just an abdominal emptied-out feeling that woke me up wheezing in the night.

What Berton meant to do in the 50 or so short pieces herein was satirize us where we sit late in the century and show us in North America to be muddled, hopelessly foibled folk. There's one about James Bond standing trial for sexual harassment. There's one about the crazy old population explosion. There's one—a real chestnut—about new regulations for the CRTC. As the bok jacket helpfully points out, "Berton uses a number of literary devices to make his points: *Fables, First-person reports, History as it might be written in the future, Found documents. . . .*" What it doesn't report is that while Berton deals now and then in potentially funny properties, he always finds a way of flattening them to particle-board with a style that might best be classified as deadpan bulldozer.

What it might look like from where you sit is that I just don't know funny. Listen, apart from this bout with Berton, I've never had a problem that way. Give me a page of Bill Richardson or Ian Frazier or Garrison Keillor or Flann O'Brien or *anyone* not trying to force the issue and I'll curdle a cat laughing. There. That's better: I've got some feeling back in my sense of humour. With any luck, I'll be up to some light grinning this weekend.

FURTHER READING

Blodgett, E. D. "After Pierre Berton What? In Search of a Canadian Literature." *Essays on Canadian Writing* 30 (Winter 1984-85): 60-80.

Discusses Canadian literature as a distinct field of study.

Jürgen Habermas
1929-

German social philosopher and cultural critic.

The following entry presents criticism of Habermas's work through 1996.

INTRODUCTION

Widely regarded as the most influential philosopher in late-twentieth-century Germany, Habermas has focused his career on the nature of the public realm. His scholarly writings have influenced a broad range of disciplines, including philosophy, social theory, hermeneutics, anthropology, linguistics, ethics, educational theory, and public policy. Beginning with *Strukturwandel der Offenlichkeit* (1962; *The Structural Transformation of the Public Sphere*), Habermas has produced major works on the development of public discourse, the relation between radical theory and political practice, the conflicting influences informing human understanding, crises of legitimacy in the modern state and capitalist society, social evolution, and communicative social action. Habermas's best-known and most accomplished theory is a synthesis of linguistic philosophy and sociological systems theory. In addition he has formulated what has come to be called "discourse ethics," a normative philosophy which postulates how moral consensus is achieved through public discussion by a community of rational, self-interested subjects. Habermas's dense essays possess a sharp critical edge that requires reflection about a wide range of contemporary political, cultural, and theoretical issues. Often characterized as a modern proponent of the *philosophe* of the Enlightenment, Habermas also has publicly denounced violations of civil rights and historical revisionism of the Holocaust. Douglas Kellner has remarked that Habermas is "very much a public intellectual who involves himself in the key social and political debates of the day."

Biographical Information

Born June 18, 1929, in Düsseldorf and raised in Nazi Germany, Habermas was deeply affected by the moral and political unrest of his youth. After World War II, he attended the universities at Göttingen, Zürich, and Bonn, where he received his Ph.D. in 1954. During the late 1950s, he turned radical while serving as Theodor Adorno's assistant at the University of Frankfurt, where he studied the works of Karl Marx and Sigmund Freud. Written as his "habilitation" (a dissertation qualifying a person to become a professor) at Marburg in 1961, the widely acclaimed *Structural Transformation of the Public Sphere* established Habermas's repu-

tation as a social scientist, endearing him to the Leftist student movement and earning him a lecturing position in philosophy at the University of Heidelberg in 1962. The next year he published the essay collection *Theorie und Praxis* (1963; *Theory and Practice*). Habermas left Heidelberg in 1964, taking a position as professor of philosophy and sociology at Frankfurt where he met and began associations with members of the so-called Frankfurt School of critical theory—Adorno, Max Horkheimer, and Herbert Marcuse. Here, Habermas wrote the pivotal *Erkenntnis und Interesse* (1968; *Knowledge and Human Interests*) and *Toward A Rational Society* (1970), both of which granted him recognition as the new theoretical force of Frankfurt. In 1971, he assumed the directorship of the Max-Planck-Institut in Starnberg, where he produced *Philosophisch-politische Profile* (1971), *Legitimationsprobleme im Spätkapitalismus* (1973; *Legitimation Crisis*), and *Communication and the Evolution of Society* (1979). By 1982 Habermas had achieved renown as a great philosopher, especially with the publication of his two-volume masterpiece, *Theorie des kommunikativen Handelns* (1982; *The Theory of Communicative Action*). Habermas resumed teaching philosophy and sociology at Frankfurt in 1983, and since then he has continued to lecture and write; among his recent publications are *Moralbewusstsein und Kommunikatives Handeln* (1983; *Moral Consciousness and Communicative Action*), *The Philosophical Discourse of Modernity* (1987), *Nachmetaphysisches Denken* (1988; *Postmetaphysical Thinking*), *The New Conservatism* (1990), and *Faktizität und Geltung* (1992; *Between Facts and Norms*).

Major Works

Habermas's scholarly writings strive for a comprehensive critical theory of contemporary society. *The Structural Transformation of the Public Sphere* traces the development and eclipse of the public sphere in modern society and contains the seeds of Habermas's formulation of discourse ethics and communicative action. The essays collected in *Theory and Practice* elaborate the relation between theory and practice through criticism of positivism, reason, philosophy, and politics. *Zur Logik der Sozialwissenschaften* (1967; *On the Logic of the Social Sciences*) compares and analyzes positivistic, functional, and behaviorist approaches and historical, narrative, and hermeneutical approaches to social theory, demonstrating the limitations and inadequacies of each approach. Habermas's first systematic development of his ideas, *Knowledge and Human Interests* formulates a tripartite cognitive theory comprising the "technical interest" of the empirical-analytical sciences; the "practical interest" of the historical-hermeneutical sciences; and the "emancipatory interest" of critical social sciences. *Legitimation Crisis* treats crises of economic life, motivation, rationality, and legitimacy in advanced capitalist societies. *Communication and the Evolution of Society* contains Habermas's revision of Marxist historical materialism in terms of his theory of communicative action. *The Theory of Communicative Action* interprets Habermas's theories of social action and of modernity in the context of the classic theoretical positions of Marx, Max Weber, George Mead, and Talcott Parsons, among others. The articles in *Moral Consciousness and Communicative Action* present Habermas's evolved positions in philosophy, the social sciences, and ethics, while defending a notion of critical rationality rooted in his theories of communicative action and discourse ethics. Illuminating some key themes found in his previous works, *Postmetaphysical Thinking* focuses on the nature of reason and the question of metaphysics, attempting to hold a middle position that is postmetaphysical without relinquishing the role of reason and philosophy. *Between Facts and Norms* addresses the question of political legitimacy by developing new understandings of law, democracy, and the relationship between them in terms of "deliberative politics." However, Habermas's works often speak to audiences who do not follow his basic work in philosophy or social theory. He practices the communicational ethics that he defends theoretically by contributing pieces to a range of contemporary cultural and political debates. *Toward a Rational Society* features essays on student protests of the 1960s, the democratization of German universities, the role of technology and science as ideology, and the "scientization" of politics and public opinion. The biographical sketches in *Philosophical-Political Profiles* focus on select twentieth-century philosophers, notably Martin Heidegger, Walter Benjamin, and Hannah Arendt. The lectures in the *Philosophical Discourse of Modernity* engage the current debates about modernity versus postmodernity in light of the critical theories of such writers as Freidrich Nietzsche, Michel Foucault, and Jacques Derrida. *The New Conservatism* reflects on contemporary neoconservatism and recent German debate about its Nazi past. Critics usually concede that the interview collections *Autonomy and Solidarity* (1986) and *The Past as Future* (1994) offer "a marvelous point of entry" into Habermas's thought, as Martin Jay put it.

Critical Reception

Since he began to formulate his discourse ethics in the 1970s, Habermas has often been accused, from various directions, of confusing a principle of political democracy with one of morality. Peter Dews has observed that "Habermas, when sympathetically interpreted, has failed to capture philosophically our core sense of morality, while offering a compel-

ling basis for the regulation of public issues through discussion and collective decision-making." Jay perhaps has summarized best the critical reaction to Habermas's thought: "To his admirers, Habermas has accomplished a much-needed reconstruction of historical materialism by incorporating insights ranging from ordinary language philosophy and hermeneutics to developmental psychology and sociological systems theory. To his detractors, the result has been an amalgam of ill-fitting elements that merits comparison more to Rube Goldberg than with that of Marx." Yet Onora O'Neill has concluded that Habermas's achievement demonstrates that "philosophical writing may be *engagé* without being ephemeral."

PRINCIPAL WORKS

Das Absolut und die Geschichte: Von der Zwiespaltigkeit in Schellings Denken (philosophy) 1954

Strukturwandel der Offenlichkeit [*The Structural Transformation of the Public Sphere*] (social philosophy) 1962

Theorie und Praxis [*Theory and Practice*] (essays) 1963; revised and expanded, 1971

Zur Logik der Sozialwissenschaften [*On the Logic of the Social Sciences*] (essays) 1967; revised and expanded, 1970

Erkenntnis und Interesse [*Knowledge and Human Interests*] (social philosophy) 1968

**Technik und Wissenschaft als "Ideologie"* (essays) 1968

**Protestbewegung und Hochschulreform* (essays) 1969

Arbeit, Erkenntnis, Fortschritt (essays) 1970

Toward A Rational Society: Student Protest, Science, and Politics (essays) 1970

†*Philosophisch-politische Profile* (biographical sketches) 1971

Theorie der Gesellschaft oder Sozialtechnologie: Was Leistet die Systemforschung? 1971

†*Kultur und Kritik* (essays) 1973

Legitimationsprobleme im Spätkapitalismus [*Legitimation Crisis*] (social philosophy) 1973

‡*Zur Rekonstruktion des historischen Materialismus* (essays) 1976

Communication and the Evolution of Society (essays) 1979

Theorie des kommunikativen Handelns I-II 2 vols. [*The Theory of Communicative Action*] (philosophy) 1982

Moralbewusstsein und Kommunikatives Handeln [*Moral Consciousness and Communicative Action*] (essays) 1983

Philosophical-Political Profiles (essays) 1983

Vorstudien und Erganzungen zur Theorie des Kommunikativen Handelns 1984

Autonomy and Solidarity: Interviews with Jurgen Habermas (interviews) 1986; expanded edition, 1994

The Philosophical Discourse of Modernity: Twelve Lectures
    (lectures) 1987
Nachmetaphysisches Denken [*Postmetaphysical Thinking:*
    Philosophical Essays] (essays) 1988
The New Conservatism: Cultural Criticism and the Histo-
    rians' Debate (essays) 1990
Faktizität und Geltung: Beiträge zur Diskurstheorie des
    Techts und des demokratischen Rechtsstaats [*Between*
    Facts and Norms: Contributions to a Discourse Theory
    of Law and Democracy] (social philosophy) 1992
Justification and Application: Remarks on Discourse Eth-
    ics (essays) 1993
The Past as Future (interviews) 1994

*Selected essays from these works appear in *Toward a Rational
Society.*
†Selected essays from these works appear in *Philosophical-
Political Profiles.*
‡Selected essays from this work appear in *Communication and the
Evolution of Society.*

CRITICISM

Jürgen Habermas with Boris Frankel (interview date November 1973)

SOURCE: "Habermas Talking: An Interview," in *Theory and Society,* No. 1, 1974, pp. 37-58.

[*In the following interview originally conducted in November, 1973, Habermas discusses the place of socio-political, Marxist, and psychoanalytic theories in his own linguistic and epistemological philosophy, addressing various critiques of his historical materialist analysis.*]

It was at Frankfurt University that Jürgen Habermas made his reputation as the new theoretical force continuing the tradition of the Horkheimer-Adorno-Marcuse brand of Critical Theory. It was also at Frankfurt that Habermas' popularity with the Left student movement changed dramatically from mutual support to bitter condemnation from many students. In recent years, owing to a combination of new trends in the German Left and also his own retreat into research work at Starnberg, Habermas has become more and more isolated from German Left activists. On the one hand, he is roundly (but unfairly) condemned as a "cop-out" by many elements of the existing student movement who still retain incorrect memories of his role in the student-administration confrontation at Frankfurt. Habermas did *not* call the police in at Frankfurt (in fact he strongly opposed this move behind the scenes but could not bring himself to publicly criticize Adorno due to his personal friendship and justifiably great concern over Adorno's deteriorating health), but he did criticize various student tactics as being short-

sighted and counter-productive which earned him abundant criticism from many students. On the other hand, he has never been loved by the academic establishment as well as being almost universally excluded from Marxist ranks in Germany and abroad (with the notable exception of Marxists such as the Praxis group in Yugoslavia).

While not wishing to exonerate or apologize for Habermas' activities during the recent past, a large degree of confusion, accusation and misinterpretation concerning his theoretical work, derives from the non-conventional approach he has undertaken to historical materialist analysis. The peculiar position of Habermas is that he confronts contemporary Marxism not merely with the German-Continental theoretical tradition, but also with an intimate knowledge of Anglo-American philosophy, social and natural science. It is not an exaggeration to say that his knowledge is encyclopaedic and hence the grand project of a brilliant reformulation of historical materialism is only intelligible in the light of the familiarity with the two (Continental and Anglo-American) dominant, and conventionally regarded (almost everywhere) as irreconcilable traditions.

In confronting these two dominant traditions, Habermas' work assumes a misleading conventional, academic appearance because a large part of it until now has been in the form of an immanent critique of bourgeois sociology, linguistic philosophy, systems theory, and various forms of neo-positivism. Perhaps the largest single reason for many of the Left to be suspicious and hostile to Habermas stems from his attempts to develop a Communication Theory of Society. As one who previously shared his hostility to Habermas, it is easy to understand why most Marxists continue to feel this way. First, there is the matter of acquiring Habermas' works in English or French. No translations of his work have been published in French, although two books will be out in the near future; and in English we are on the average about five years behind his recent publications. More than 10 years after its publication in German English readers are now able to read ***Theorie und Praxis***. The abridged English version could give rise to further misinterpretations of Habermas' Marxism as there is inadequate note made of the fact that Habermas no longer holds certain views on political economy which appear especially in the chapter entitled "Between Philosophy and Science: Marxism as Critique". Although he has attached a brief list of more recent Marxist analysis, readers should refer to his more recent book ***Legitimationsprobleme im Spätkapitalismus*** (1973) in order to understand his present analysis. Added to this delay in translations is Habermas' own unfinished development of the Communication Theory of Society which largely exists in unpublished manuscripts. The second, and equally important fact, is that one almost immediately has suspicion about any so-called "Communication Theory". The concept is somewhat confusing in that one inevitably has images of either a McLuhan type of bourgeois apologetics in the form of a communication theory concerned with technological determinism and media etc., or else one thinks of Habermas as just another idealist working in the sociology of language, phenomenology, or symbolic universes, etc., which are becoming so dominant in the bourgeois academic world. Consequently, Habermas' work is basically misconceived as the latest form of idealist aberration which seeks to reduce all problems to that of problems concerning the language of communication, and thereby diverting us away from the historical analysis of class struggle, imperialism, and capitalist forces of production. As Habermas states, nothing could be further from the truth or the intention of his work.

In his isolation from most of the German Left, Habermas is quietly but impressively working and directing a series of substantial analyses of various facets of advanced capitalist societies. Current projects being developed are those concerning the role of the state in capitalist society, capitalist policies and investment in Third World countries, ecology and capitalism, alternative science and technology theories, the relation of science to state and industry, and socialization problems dealing with conflict and apathy. (Two of these projects are summarized in the journal *Working Papers on the Kapitalistate*, no.1, 1973.)

> **Habermas has no desire to debunk Marx or to point with bourgeois glee that Marx is obsolete and so forth. His intention is in fact the very opposite.**
> —*Boris Frankel*

Habermas' own epistemological critique, rather than being merely another sophisticated form of Hegelian idealism in new clothes, is, in fact, the only body of writing which substantially exposes and undermines linguistic philosophy's attempts to debunk Marxist ideas such as ideology and false consciousness. In contrast to other Marxists who provide a limited critique of linguistic and hermeneutic philosophy from an "external" position, i.e. they criticize the latter for its trivialization of social reality, e.g. all dogs have tails, or for being fundamentally ahistorical, Habermas acknowledges the contributions made by linguistic philosophy and thereby establishes his penetrating critique. By incorporating the insights of linguistic and hermeneutic philosophy into historical materialism, Habermas endeavours to transcend the philosophic problem of "consciousness" which has hitherto constituted the background against which the relationship between ideology and "false consciousness" has been thrashed out between Marxists and bourgeois theorists. As true or false consciousness is articulated verbally, Habermas is concerned to analyse the historical materialist conditions of everyday discourse in order to show how not only the

class nature of social relations manifests itself within everyday language, but also the emancipatory notions of freedom and justice. This interest in the manner in which material conditions have distorted communication (verbal and behavioural), also accounts for his utilization of psychoanalysis in order to grasp the hidden, unconscious and suppressed activity of individuals distorted by class societies.

Communication is not conceived by Habermas as something which is exclusively verbal, but rather his Communication Theory rests upon an extremely solid philosophical anthropology. This "materialist phenomenology of mind" is a brilliant attempt to articulate in unambiguous and non-reductionist terms, the anthropological assumptions behind Marx's concept of "sensuous activity". Only by elucidating the linguistic aspect of the reproduction of social life, can the images, plans, programs and organization of a free society be realized without perpetrating the explicit and implicit repression so prevalent at the moment. Regardless of whether Althusser and others are correct about alienation (or the Feuerbachian problematic) not being present in Marx's mature work, one thing is clear, we can not ignore or dilute into other analytic categories the epistemological assumptions about human competences and the manner in which social reality is constituted and reconstituted. If Althusser has done us the service of criticizing those Marxists who reduce forces and relations of production to "historicist" questions of human "essence", Habermas' strength lies precisely in avoiding the other extreme—reducing all symbolic interactions to questions concerning the forces of production and labour processes.

Habermas has no desire to debunk Marx or to point with bourgeois glee that Marx is obsolete and so forth. His intention is in fact the very opposite. In probing the epistemological assumptions of Marx's work, Habermas wishes to make explicit that which has been implicit, and to eradicate or make unambiguous that which is objectivistic and scientist (in the positivist and naturalist sense). If it is "no accident" that the Second and Third Internationals both shared crude, mechanistic and scientist notions of historical materialism, then Marx's works cannot be treated either as a sacred cow or a biblical fountain for the solution of every new theoretical and practical development. Nor can Marx's notion that knowledge is historical only be given lip service. In utilizing the insights of linguistic philosophy and other twentieth century developments in social and scientific theory, Habermas is not indulging in fanciful eclecticism but rather trying to strengthen historical materialism against contemporary bourgeois attacks.

Moreover, his work provides us with what is perhaps the most decisive critique of "Hegelian Marxism" of which, ironically, he is regarded to be a leading exponent. By distinguishing between knowledge which involves a relationship between a subject and an object (empirical-analytic sciences), and that knowledge which involves a relationship between one subject and another subject (dialectical-hermeneutic sciences), Habermas is able to make an immanent critique of objective idealism and objective materialism. The Lukácsian and Horkheimer-Adorno-Marcusian concepts of reification and instrumental rationality are subtly shown to be responsible for the various idealizations, pessimism, or romanticism, which characterizes their theoretical work. It is not merely that Habermas calls for more detailed analysis of the forces and relations of production, which Lukács and the old Frankfurt School failed to do, but that he shows how the notions of rationality which Lukács, et al. shared with Marx were inadequate to clearly distinguish the continuity and discontinuity between domination and emancipation.

Habermas is a probing and first-rate thinker who raises long term questions concerning the nature of science, technology, division of labour, etc., in capitalist and future socialist societies. Any serious Marxist cannot avoid confronting these fundamental questions if the qualitative differences between capitalism and socialism are not to be blurred in vague romantic or eschatological visions. This is not to say that Habermas is trying to circumscribe or predict the potentialities and organization of the future, but it does mean that he is not trying to avoid fundamental problems which are so frequently subsumed under the all pervasive answer—"we don't know what will happen when the first human phase of history begins".

While this is not the place to give a summary of Habermas' work, it cannot be overstressed that he is *not* an idealist concerned with only linguistics and epistemology, but that he is trying to develop a historical materialist analysis which helps to bring about a society free from domination and repression, or what he calls distorted communication. It is simply not true, as Göran Therborn claims, that Habermas replaces the proletariat with science, and the forces and relations of production with Parsonsian categories of labour and interaction. While it is true that he uses Parsons in a critical sense, his categories of labour and interaction cannot be confused or reduced to merely new equivalents for the forces and relations of production. Habermas' long term ("transcendental") perspective is a quality which makes his work significant, but at the same time irritating and "idealist" to those involved in the immediate problems of day-to-day class struggle. This long term perspective is also responsible for Habermas' political attitudes; in aiming for large scale success, he places his hopes in the Jusos' (the younger Social Democrats) strategy of the "long march through the institutions". Actually, he supports the work done by many radical groups but his own personal predisposition to intellectual work cuts him off from the spontaneity and immediacy of activism. In the German situation of a minority Social Demo-

cratic Party depending on fragile support from conservative Free Democrats, plus the absence of a large Left, it is not surprising that Habermas is not overconfident about large scale Left success in the next ten or more years. Still, he does not exclude the possibility of unexpected contingent crises which could affect the present capitalist situation; in the meantime he sees his usefulness in building up a solid body of Marxist analysis and in trying to change legitimating beliefs in social institutions such as schools and public institutions. One thing is clear, Habermas offers little in the way of immediate strategy and tactics; he is not an activist and will most probably never be one. It is also true, as Therborn points out, that many fashionable "reformist" sociologists will find Habermas attractive. This is partly due to the current concern with methodological problems being discussed in universities, and also partly due to Habermas' own decision to answer his critics via an academic dialogue. However, the quality and pertinence of a man's thought is not determined solely by those who utilize merely a part of a great thinker's horizons. It should be made clear that Habermas is committed to a socialist revolution even though he is occasionally courageous enough to express a scepticism about its form and future which others have kept to themselves. I believe that Habermas' contributions will outlive those academic "leeches" who presently cling to him for the wrong reasons as well those Marxist sectarians who oppose him for the wrong reasons. Hopefully, the Marxist Left will make an effort to comprehend what he is all about and judge Habermas' work on the adequacy of its analysis rather than dogmatically ignoring it because of intolerant labelling. The self-reflection needed to eliminate domination is not to be relegated to the priorities of tomorrow; distorted communication is not a characteristic which is confined to the ranks of the non-Marxist population.

. . . . .

[*Frankel:*] *You talk about the "subsystems" of purposive rational action and communicative action. To what extent do you subscribe to Parsons' understanding of "system"?*

[Habermas:] I think that I use the term "subsystem" in two different contexts, the first context is familiar to sociological discourse. Take for instance some passages from ***Technik und Wissenschaft als Ideologie*** (1968) where I differentiate, on the one hand, between those subsystems which mainly serve functions of pattern maintenance and integration such as the family, or face to face relationships or educational settings and so forth, and on the other hand, those social systems which mainly serve goal attainment and adaptation, i.e. the economic or administrative system. Actions of the purposive rational type play a much more important role in the economic and more formalized social systems, while communicative action "overweighs" or is more important in the other types of social systems. I think that if you have a concrete piece of social interaction you will have in any case, both types of action, namely, a communicative action which is guided by norms, and on the other hand, attached in a way, or embedded *in* this interaction are what Parsons calls "tasks"—I mean elements of actions which can be reconstructed as instrumental actions or as purposive rational actions; there are only extreme situations in which you may have a pure type of either communicative or purposive rational action. For instance, if you play chess then you intentionally follow a setting in which I think you pursue a type of rational choice behaviour. In my sociological analyses I make use, of course, of the usual concept of "system" and "subsystems"; e.g. I try to analyse empirically if there are systematic limitations to the planning capacities of state bureaucracies then my focus is the administrative system. Here I don't see any problem. I only want to say that you can order subsystems on a scale, that is, from a point where you have almost exclusively a subsystem in which communication governs the whole process, to another point, where you have systems in which you have exclusively almost a type of purposive rational behaviour.

So this is one context in which I use the categories of purposive rational action and communicative action. The other context is when I speak on a rather anthropological level: when I try to analyse the constituents of social systems in general, then I refer to basic human competences. One dimension of analysis is instrumental action, and another dimension of analysis is communication, which presupposes the structure of intersubjectivity in which you can either act communicatively or have a discourse, or something like this. So there are two uses of the terms which I would like to distinguish; rather a sociological way of speaking about systems and subsystems of communicative versus purposive rational behaviour, on the one hand, and a more anthropological way of speaking when I am analysing only basic components of what can be conceived as the socio-cultural form of life.

So in other words it is not correct to say that you subscribe to Parsons' general conception of the "social system".

That is correct. In my last book on *Legitimationsprobleme im Spätkapitalismus* (1973) there is a first part in which I discuss the strengths and weaknesses of the "systems" approach. There I try to explain that we have to combine in a systematic manner the "systems" approach with an approach which has so far been explicated, rather in phenomenological traditions, I mean the "*Lebenswelt*" analysis. I think that we have to put together both aspects, "system" aspect and "*Lebenswelt*" aspect into one integrated analysis.

Do you feel close to the work that the ethnomethodologists are doing?

No. I think that the ethnomethodologists as well as the phenomenologists are isolating only one aspect in the same manner as the "system" theorists are isolating the other aspect. I distinguish myself from both approaches, maintaining that we have to employ a framework which is capable of integrating both aspects mentioned.

Various interpretations have been made of your work **Knowledge and Human Interests.** *Could you clarify a few misconceptions by illustrating the "technical interest of control" inherent in the empirical-analytic sciences with reference to a "scientific" theory such as Darwin's theory of the evolution of the species? In what sense is the latter theory only a theory for "instrumental action"?*

I think in no sense. Since the evolution theory has a methodological status which is quite different from a normal theory in, say, physics, I think that the categorical framework in which the evolution theory has been developed since Darwin presupposes some references to a pre-understanding of the *human* world and not only of nature. The whole concept of adaptation and selection presupposes some elements which are more characteristic for the human sciences than for the empirical-analytic sciences, strictly speaking. So in my opinion, the evolution theory is no example of an empirical-analytic science at all. But as far as bio-chemical theories about mutations go into this evolution theory, we have, of course, a usual empirical-analytic theory. However, this is not what is characteristic for the design of the evolution theory. This is only a component of the evolution theory which may be quite indifferent or independent of the evolution theory. Modern genetics is not dependent on the evolution theory framework. Modern genetics is, I propose, a strictly objectifying theory which make no use of concepts inherently related to our pre-understanding of what social life or cultural life is.

But would you then say that modern genetic theory has an inherent interest in control, e.g. being able to control certain genetic formations?

No. I think that we must not confuse a psychological meaning of interest with its epistemological meaning. I don't want to maintain that any part of natural science has been developed in the researcher's subjective interest of making technical use of the final output or scientific informations. Well, we have some parts of natural science, e.g. agricultural science at the time of Liebig, which indicate a type of theory formation induced from outside practical interests; but this is not the usual way of theoretical development. I only want to maintain that the very logical and meta-theoretical structure of theories and informations predetermines their possible application. I take this concept of *Erkenntnis Interesse* in order to explain why you can use, for instance, nomological knowledge only in the way of technical application, whereas you can make use of, let's say historical knowledge, only in the way of affecting the self-understanding of acting and interacting and speaking people. But this type of connection between the formal structure of knowledge and the structure of possible contexts of use, this connection is an indicator of the practical impact of any human knowledge. My attempt to explain this in reference to the relationship between cognition and interest (*Erkenntnis Interesse*) is, of course, an attempt to show that human knowledge is not something which is developed in an area completely disentangled, or disconnected from life-practice. That means that I doubt that there can be a realm of pure theory, although I want to stress that of course there are structural differences between realms of action and experience, on the one hand, and realms of discourse (and theoretical discourse) where your main task is to check truth claims and not to implement new aims of praxis and action.

If you say that we must not confuse the psychological and external meaning attached to science with the epistemology used in the empirical-analytic sciences, what implication does this have for the possibility of a new humane science that Marcuse talks about?

There are two versions of this Marcusean idea of a new science. The first, and stronger version, is that there might be a possibility to develop a type of science which is generically different from what we have now; so that due to its very structure this new science could not be applied in the exploitation of nature. This idea is a very romantic idea. I don't want to be impolite to Marcuse, but I'm convinced that this idea has no real base. The other version is that there might be a change in the relationship between the scientific system and its environment, moreover, its political environment. A change, so that in the future the developments in the science system might be stronger and stronger influenced, and after all *guided* by political aims and by a discursively formed, politically reasonable will.

But in your essay on the "scientization of politics" you say that "responsible scientists, disregarding their professional or official roles, cross the boundaries of their inner scientific world and address themselves directly to public opinion when they want either to avert practical consequences . . . or to criticize specific research investments in terms of their social effects." What do you mean by this "inner scientific world" and is this only applicable to contemporary scientific activity?

I don't think that we can go back behind a given level of the division of labour. So, I don't think that we can just demand that scientists should de-differentiate their several roles which they have anyway—that is, as a scientist, as a citizen, as a family member and so on. This, I think, would not make much sense to me. But there can be political and or-

ganizational steps, or pushes in the direction of raising the political consciousness of scientists so that they can first at their working place, try to get influence, efficient influence on the direction and course of their investigations; that means that on the level of co-determination, self-determination and self-administration of scientific institutes, universities, etc., there can be a political organization of the decision-making processes within the scientific community which might have some impact on the directions and overall priorities of research development.

Do you see the possibility of a new form of society which overcomes the distinction between pure scientific theory and everyday life? For instance, what do you think of the attempts made in China to integrate scientific work directly into the work place itself?

I suppose these attempts are meaningful for a more humane application of science and a more stimulating input into science from practical life. But I don't think that a serious progress in theory formation can be gained or made more rapid by these types of de-differentiations. I think that these attempts produce much more closer connections and interactions between science and different areas of political and professional practice, but they wouldn't abolish scientific theoretical work.

But would these attempts substantially alter pure theoretical problems?

It is difficult to answer these questions in general. These attempts are in any case relevant for sensitizing the scientist, making them aware of the political content of their work, especially in those fields, e.g. physics, which up until now seem to be quite distant from social practices. On the other hand, we have in recent years seen some attempts of action research in the social sciences, for instance, in educational research or in industrial sociology which are designed to continue immediately research and political action; it is sometimes meaningful but I don't think that these attempts have an impact on the development of social theory so that the whole course of theory formation would be changed. I don't believe that. I don't want to exclude it from the very beginning, but I am sceptical in the long run.

Moving to your other basic concept of "communicative action"; one writer has queried the inherent interest in mutual understanding in a "cultural-science" such as law which is based on a large amount of empirical-analytic theory and is also used as a means of technical control. Do you think that this is a legitimate critique of the relationship between "communicative action" and the human sciences, or a basic misunderstanding of your work?

I would say that the *praktische Interesse* or epistemological interest of improving mutual understanding and preserving intersubjectivity of understanding, that this interest is related to the hermeneutic sciences, strictly speaking, I am thinking of literary criticism, of the work of historians, the history of literature and so on. For these sciences, which we can call hermeneutic sciences, I would maintain that the only context of application which you could imagine is that of influencing, of changing and maintaining a self-understanding of a relevant group which is mainly determined by prevailing traditions. So that the group and ego identity of speaking and acting subjects and groups of those subjects cannot be maintained except if you grant some basic consensus about general interpretations of their world and their surroundings. This is already the case before you enter any science. But there is some type of science, which, on the level of discourse, articulates and controls this type of self-understanding; so you can say that these hermeneutic sciences are designed for a scientifically controlled continuation or revision of dominant traditions. The epistemological interest of mutual-understanding is, e.g. involved in interpreting the dominant tradition of legal theories underlying concepts of justice. On the other hand, if you take criminal sociology, that is, an empirical theory about the causes of juvenile delinquency, then you have a type of social theory which is different from the interpretative activity of the hermeneutic sciences. In the social sciences we have a peculiar combination of hermeneutic and empirical-analytic methods and I have tried to explain this in terms of the nature of social systems which are characterised by systematically distorted communication. These types of social systems are in a way nature, pseudo-nature. In these systems interactions are determined by an institutional setting which is not freely accessible to the consciousness of the actors; they are acting under the violence of intentions which are not immediately their own. These are the latent intentions of social systems acting, so to say, behind the back of the individual actors: and because of this nature or pseudo-nature of social systems characterized by violence and domination, we are bound to develop theoretical frameworks which are designed to grasp both aspects—the subjective aspect of, let me say, the cultural components and the intentionality of social systems on the one hand, and also the quasi-natural aspect of social systems which are "unseen", which are "withdrawn" from what is immediately accessible to the consciousness of the actors. One can of course study the historical background of juvenile delinquency, but as soon as you try to get a theory of the social determinants of juvenile delinquency, you are leaving the field of the strictly interpretative sciences. Then you cannot rely solely on the documents of delinquency or the contents of the consciousness of young people who are on trial. You can of course, attempt to develop a strictly behavioural theory in order to explain the whole thing, let me say a learning type of theory, but there is only a limited range of applicability for this type of objectifying behavioural theory. To my opinion, a more promising approach would be the attempt to have a socialization theory using psychoanalytic hypotheses as well as actual social theory hypotheses so that you can have a theory basically depending on the paradigm of systematically distorted communication. Using our example of juvenile delinquency, we could examine the type of communication which is dominant in a family in which the socialization process of the young child—i.e. how it gains its linguistic, cognitive and communicative competences—results in the child being driven into a deviant direction. So that when the child is grown up his or her competences are deficient; given empirical circumstances, the solution of some stressful problems may be crime or mental disease, and sometimes, even much more useful things like political protest.

Moving to another area, one that has been subject to many accusations and interpretations, namely your analysis of Marx. As I understand you, one of the primary motives for developing your Communication Theory of Society was the desire to reformulate historical materialism on a more explicit and comprehensive basis by: (a) developing the symbolic realm of human interaction which Marx only treated briefly or implicitly, and (b) eliminating the objectivistic and scientistic elements in Marx's categorical self-understanding of historical materialism. However, while you indicate that Marx had a basic misconception of historical materialism at the categorical level, you also argue that in his actual material investigations, e.g. Class Struggles in France, *Marx always took into account "social practice that encompasses both work and interaction". If this is true, in what sense do you think that your epistemological "reformulation" of historical materialism would enable us to actually practice historical materialism in a "broader" way than what you claim Marx already achieved in his concrete analyses?*

This is an important question since I think you are quite right—there are many people who have the suspicion that I favour epistemological work *instead* of sociological work, and of course, I have not the slightest idea of this kind: I don't have this intention. I think that epistemological analysis can of course provide us with some insights which have an impact on the general course of Marxist empirical analysis; once you get rid of the idea that materialism doesn't mean reducing all social phenomena to production and work processes, in the strict sense, then you can better escape the pitfalls, several pitfalls of dogmatism. Therefore, I think that epistemological analysis might be a help in avoiding the dogmatist self-understanding of Marxist traditions, especially the Soviet type of Marxism. These are considerations on a meta-level, but nevertheless an important palliative or preservation against false argumentation.

(interruption) There are many contemporary Marxists who desire to read the three volumes of Capital *on the basis that*

only in doing an intensive reading of Capital *will one be able to distil the so called "science" of capitalism and the "science" of history. Would you regard such a reading of* Capital *to be indicative of the type of epistemological errors which you wish to avoid?*

No, it depends on the context. If you think of those groups who confine their intellectual activity to interpreting the three volumes of *Capital,* then I at least would have the suspicion that their analysis would fall short of what we have to do now in analysing late capitalism. There is no doubt that we have to read and to reread, and to interpret Marx again and again, but this is not enough—we have to apply what we have learned in *Capital.* In trying to apply the labour theory of value we have, in my opinion, to realize that we can no longer move sufficiently within the range of just this type of theory. My main argument (which I have developed in ***Legitimationsprobleme im Spätkapitalismus***) is that we have now a new amount of a new type of work which I like to call "*reflexive Arbeit*", reflective work, which is the work of scientists, engineers, teachers, etc., and is designed in the first instance to improve the productivity of labour. Now we have capital which is invested in the area of science, technology, education, and so on, in order to boost the productivity of labour, resulting in, economically speaking, a rising rate of surplus value and in the cheapening of the constant elements of capital. This capital investment in reflective labour is therefore a counter-tendency against the fall in the rate of profit already remarked about by Marx. But the difference between late capitalism and liberal capitalism, or one relevant difference, is that we now incorporate these activities into the economic processes while at the time of Marx, this type of reflective work could be conceived of as an external input just as some natural resources such as water, etc. were. So that even if you argue on the basis of the premises of the labour theory of value, you can show that with the economic institutionalization and exploitation of science and technology, the whole mode of surplus value production was changed by a new type of capital which I would like to call with Jim O'Connor, the indirect productive type of capital. So my basic thesis is that the mode of surplus value production changed from the base, where we have the production of absolute surplus value, over the base where we have the production of relative surplus value, to a position where we now have the production of relative surplus value by engaging indirect productive type of labour which is not immediately productive in terms of the labour theory of value, but indirectly productive by producing informations and qualifications which in turn improve the productivity of labour and thereby affect the rate of surplus value and the price of the constant elements in capital. This is basically my argument for the inapplicability of the labour theory of value under the conditions of late capitalism; this means that we now have to come to a Marxist analysis of late capitalism which is no longer bound strictly to Marx's premises of

the labour theory of value, but which is still Marxist in the sense that the general hypotheses about the working of late capitalism are taken from historical materialism. This introduces my second answer to your question about the impact of epistemological analysis. Since today we have no longer a self-sustaining economic system in relation to the state and the cultural system, since we now have an integrated system in which the state is no longer only an agent of the ruling class, but where things are much more complicated, we are now compelled to leave the level of analysis which is indicated by Marx's critique of political economy, and we have to go back, so to say, to the level of that analysis which Marx called historical materialism—this is the level of class struggle and the interaction of the political system and the economic system and so on. Going back to this level, I think we now have to get to a reformulation, to a clarification of historical materialism for which it is quite important to have a clear idea about the relationship between productive forces and productive relationships. This is an issue which might be clarified by such epistemological investigations.

One of the differences you see between liberal capitalism and late capitalism is that "politics is no longer only a phenomenon of the superstructure . . . society and the state are no longer in the relationship that Marxian theory had defined as that of base and superstructure." The implication here is that you understand Marx's analysis to be an economic determinist theory of the relationship between base and superstructure. Is this true?

Insofar as he is working as an economist, let's say in *Capital,* Marx's methodological premise, in my opinion, is that in liberal competitive capitalism the economic system is self-sustaining, at least in the following way that you can explain any process in the total social system finally in terms of economic processes. This is no longer true.

Concerning this new relationship between the state and the economic system, Nikos Poulantzas criticized the idea of viewing the state as merely a crisis manager; would this critique affect in any way Claus Offe's and your analysis of the state in late capitalism?

There are two different aspects which one can analyse in the development of the state apparatus. One is of course its planning capacity and under this viewpoint you can try to show systematic limits in the resources upon which this "crisis manager" is depending. There are two resources, namely, fiscal resources (economic resources) and legitimation. On both sides you can try to show that the demand of the state which is necessary in order to fulfil its crisis management functions, is larger than the supply from the economic or the cultural system respectively. My opinion is that we may well have a legitimation crisis. That means that the cultural system—traditions and agencies of socialization which are relevant for the generation of necessary motives as well as the motives needed to uphold the educational and political systems—that these modes of structures are now no longer in accordance with what is demanded from the political or the economic system. This means that there is an evolution of cultural systems, value systems, moral systems, etc. which is just not sensitive to the imperatives of the economic and political systems; but that this cultural development is following an inherent logic so that there arises certain irreversible discrepancies. For instance, if you take moral systems then you can, without great difficulties show that the only type of moral systems which are still credible today are of a universalistic type. If you have to refer to these universalistic morals, then you get into many difficulties if you want to legitimate a class society or a society which is still based on a pattern of distribution and dominance which is class dependent. This is another example of the importance of epistemological analysis since, on this epistemological level, we can rehabilitate in a way the relative autonomy of culture in relation to economy. But on the other hand, coming back to Poulantzas' critique, we can also analyse the state under the aspect of actions and group activities and phenomena which are identifiable on the level of interactions. This is quite another aspect, and on this level we might analyse the actual class struggles, the fights between different factions of capital and unions, etc. And I don't see that these two aspects are mutually exclusive, but they are both legitimate theoretical levels. So I'm not quite sure that the Poulantzas objection would disturb me very much.

In your critique of Freud's scientistic self-misunderstanding of metapsychology (the energy model), you state that "at the human level we never encounter any needs that are not already interpreted linguistically and symbolically affixed to potential actions". Hence your reinterpretation of biological instincts into "symbols" which are either suppressed (i.e. producing distorted or repressed behaviour) or freed (i.e. non-repressed communicative action which has self-reflectively abolished historical constraint imposed internally and externally). But if biological instinctual repression has now been understood by you to be only intelligible in its "symbolic" form, i.e. through linguistic mediation, what does one make of Mitscherlich's argument that aggression cannot be conceived in monist terms as being either completely endogenous or completely cultural?

This is actually a difficult question, but let me say just why I don't think that it worries me so much. I would like to discuss this on a methodological level. If you want to have an area in which you speak about drives, just drives, then go ahead and show me how you can succeed. Taking the Freudian example, it is evident by now, and it has been evident at any time, that there is no sufficient operationalization of this concept of drive and energy. So that all hypotheses which Freud calls "economic" hypotheses, are in a way in the open

air and nobody knows how to relate them to empirical data except in the very situation of the analyst and the patient. And if you enter the latter situation, then of course the frame of reference is quite different; there you cannot look at drives or energy potentials or changes of energy and so on, but what you have is *verbal* material. This is what I was arguing for, that you have to reformulate the structural model of Freud in terms of a communication model—a model of historical communication. If you do so, then of course you have to pay a price; the price is that you can only speak about the intelligible needs, that means needs which in principle are capable of being represented on the level of verbal communication.

But would you acknowledge that there are influential non-verbal drives?

What I retain from this "energetic" aspect of Freud is, that I think that drives are something real in distorting verbal communication, they have some force in destroying an individual's capacity to act; but I cannot account for this without referring to a communication frame. If we try to examine the disruption of the normal business of communication, one can try to get indicators of the severity, of the intensity of disruption; for instance, we know that some people are just neurotic and others have something else causing their distorted activity. But it is complicated to find reliable indicators. If we have something which is negatively fixable, then you must start from suppositions about a normal state of affairs; only then you can measure the deviant states. This is what Freud did; you establish that there is something destroyed and how severely it is destroyed only by comparing the given behavior with a state of say, ego strength or undistorted communication. If you don't have this positive aspect, it is much more complicated, I mean, than perhaps we have to write poems about it in order to grasp it.

You have been criticized as being a "reformist" who only desires greater "discussion" and "participation" in existing institutions but not their total overhaul. What does "radical reformism" mean in the present context of Western capitalist countries and does this assume that a "crisis-collapse" theory of capitalism is not applicable any more (if it ever was)?

I think that a crisis theory is no longer applicable only in one sense, namely, that we have a theory of economic crisis which allows us to predict that there must be—in a middle range perspective—a breakdown of capitalism. I don't think so. But I think that there might be crises because of other reasons; for instance, a legitimation crisis, and in any case, there might be a breakdown of capitalism because of stringent conditions: there is not so much imagination needed in order to think of shortcomings which indeed leave no way out for capitalism. What is "radical reformism"? An attempt to use the institutions of present day capitalism in order to challenge and to test the basic or kernel institutions of this system. In regard to the German Federal Republic today, this is the strategy of the Jusos (Young Social Democrats) who, on the one hand, at least this is their programme, try to push the Social Democratic Party in the direction of reforms which are no longer compatible with the now-a-days functioning of the economic system. That is that they push their Party in the direction of programmes which would not only mean a much higher proportion of taxes, but also changed priorities that could only be implemented by the control of investment decisions, etc. The reformistic flavour or aspect of this strategy is mainly that the Jusos only need to take literally what we can find in the problematic references of the more liberal or "progressive" established politicians, that is, to take these issues and to pursue them consequently without any concern for the vested interests of economically and politically dominating groups. This is one side of this strategy, and the other side is to get a larger part of the population mobilized on those issues which are strictly political ones. The main field of activities of the Jusos until now has been communal policies, regional planning, transport and health service issues, etc. Of course, much more could be done, and is being done by other groups within the factories, with the workers who are pushed to think about real working conditions, and real gains in terms of self-determination more than in terms of social rewards of the conventional type, e.g. more money and free time.

So you would see the Jusos as the group with the appropriate political and theoretical programme, or would there be other German groups you admire as well?

Theoretical programme is another question. I mean, there are many groups which are dedicated to the analysis of late capitalism, but I don't see any group which has succeeded in developing Marx's theory to a point which could be regarded as in a way sufficient. But practically, of course, there are many ways and you have to take into consideration the empirical reference system. If you ask me how to proceed within present day Western Germany then I would be inclined to say that the strategy which seems to me to be most promising is that of the Jusos. But on the tactical level I think that there are other groups who are more successful within the factories and in organizing wild cat strikes or in pushing the workers' demands forward into political dimensions, or even in trying to influence the established unions which are not in any case just an element of the establishment. Now the unions have been pushed by the wild cat strikes in the summer and the uneven development between wages and prices, to go ahead towards contracts which for the first time include issues of immediate working conditions. This is a new thing which might have an effect on the consciousness of the workers who can now learn to make another category of demands.

But do you see in the next five or ten years any serious dislocations within capitalism which would require a different form of organizational strategy than that of the long term strategy employed by the Jusos?

I don't know. This would require a much more detailed analysis for each country which I am not capable of doing. For instance, one could imagine that Mitterand would be the next president of France, this possibility cannot be excluded, and one has to analyse closely, empirically, what this would mean to have a Popular Front government in France. Something will happen, perhaps only a "social-democratization" of France, maybe, but may be it could be the beginning of an even more radical development. Similar things could happen in Italy; there is at least a middle range perspective that the Communists could take power in the government. But in Germany my hope is more modest, and my hope is that we have a Social Democratic government for the next twenty years—a government which is so well established that after four or eight years it can even govern without the Free Democrats so that the Party leadership is in a much weaker position against the demands of the left wing. Until now, in any case, the Party leadership is happy to say that "you see we have to take consideration of our coalition partner, etc."; but one can imagine a process which changes things and then no doubt we will have a much more severe polarization than we have at present. In this case, things get very difficult to predict. If we have a polarized situation many things can happen; one indicator, at least in present day Western Germany, of at least the possibility of a middle range radicalization is that quite openly in the press it is discussed that there is a need to prevent a situation which is similar to Allende's just before the coup. I don't want to say that I'm very hopeful and so on, but if there are hopes at all, I think they are to be expected in this long term dimension rather than in a more dramatic one.

So essentially you would work through existing social democratic parties and hope to radicalize these.

Not parties. It is actually only the case in Germany that we don't have another way. But in France and Italy you do have other means. The radicalization of the Social Democratic Party in Germany is the only possible medium that we have so far for large scale success. I mean, there is no indication that the Communists in Germany can gain more than five per cent of the vote, and then I would ask—what would this mean? In Germany we have a special situation because of the two Germanies and this is another aspect about which I can only speculate. If we succeed in "de-hostilizing" the other part of Germany, then there will smoothly appear very new possibilities of coalitions. Both left wings can perhaps some day form a kind of cooperation—a "hidden" coalition among intellectuals of both parts is already coming about.

When you say left wing, do you mean the ruling party in the D.D.R. with its form of communism?

No, I mean the "left" opposition within the D.D.R. could in a way cooperate with left opposition groups in the Federal Republic and this would create a unique situation.

But wouldn't this be a very long term proposition given the very limited possibility of seeing any left opposition within the D.D.R. being free to organize politically?

You see, Sakharov is already at the phone of our most popular television station; there are tendencies... I'm only speculating on the possibilities. In Russia things are different of course, the samizdat people are by our standards right wing or so, nevertheless their function in Russia is not different from a left wing opposition.

How would you see your own role as a radical in advanced capitalist society; do you think a theorist should concentrate on theory?

Under the general viewpoint I take this to be a serious opportunity for intellectuals and scientists to try to join community groups, radical professional groups (or to create them), or even to go into the factories to try to get into contact with active labour groups there. This is a possibility. The other aspect is, who can, and who should make this contribution; this question is very much biographically touched and tinged. Since we don't have a situation which pinpoints one possibility as the most promising or real one, e.g. we don't have a situation of a counter-push facing the whole left as Chile had before the fall of Allende, therefore we are left with a wide range of options. I myself have taken the option to work within a research institute and this is then an option for a division of labour which forbids an engagement which takes more than a small part of one's working time. Of course, it depends then on contingent circumstances, how much you nevertheless feel inclined to take a stand on certain issues and to join longer ranging things. I have left the university (Frankfurt) and this means that I can no longer continue my activities on Hochschul Politik which I have presumed so far; it wouldn't be credible if I tried to continue this. But there are other issues; for the last two years I was very much detached from almost anything, I must admit, now I see that I will get involved into curriculum issues for high schools. Then I'm involved in matters of science policy—first in the formal setting which means in a council attached to the science ministry, and in a more informal setting I'm occasionally joining a group of Jusos people who are periodically meeting with the science minister. The interest in high school curriculae serves the func-

tion to defend a pretty radical first push in setting up new curriculae. I think that these material questions of what the children will learn are relevant if the hypothesis is correct that the educational system will be the promising locus of creating legitimation and motivational problems in this capitalist system. Regarding science policy, the immediate thing is to politicize the whole area of science policy with the aim to disconnect the present policy making in this area from a very well established and channelized influence coming, not from industry in general, but from the technically high developed industries such as electronics. So this might be possible within the present setting of the Social Democratic Party, but of course it depends on very contingent developments. Another, and even more relevant possibility would be to engage in the long term programme of the Social Democratic Party which projects middle range policies which might well be incompatible with capitalist institutions. This might be at least a base on which the inner Party opposition could be effectively organized during the next five or ten years. I know these are very undramatic and very reformist, perhaps even ineffective attempts, but for alternatives I think I am either a little bit old or I have well taken priorities.

Concerning these priorities, how would you see your present investment of energy into your research projects?

I see our research projects as an input into a social science which should be capable of a critical analysis of late capitalism with practical consequences. It's trivial, but this is a standing demand upon any Marxist that you must have a theoretical approach which is just. I don't see, at least in the Federal Republic, any other place or group where endeavours are made in the same direction which are more promising than ours.

Would you still call yourself a Marxist?

Oh yes. I protested some months ago in *Der Spiegel* where this new epilogue to **Knowledge and Human Interests** was taken as an excuse for telling the people that I'm far out of any Marxist field; I wrote to them saying that I don't see why I should not be regarded as a Marxist. I think that in Germany it is very important to have people, or to get the whole scene accustomed to Marxists, even if, as Brecht would say, they are part of the establishment. This is only one single aspect of "radical reformism"; step by step people must get used to the view that the Marxist analysis is a serious one and that Marxists are not only "wild and coloured beasts" out there in the D.D.R. or in Russia or China. In France we have this acceptance of Marxists for a long period, at least they are part of a very different climate—you have for instance a very strong Communist Party at the back of the Marxist intellectual scene. I think this change of attitude to Marxists in Germany is one, perhaps not a necessary, but a useful condition for changing the base of the only party we have if we want to change a society like ours. On the other hand, I must say that to think of revolution raises a lot of questions. One question is whether there can be any type of revolutionary, i.e. rapid and violent classical change, of a system which is so complex as ours is, without a breakdown which is self-defeating in any case—that is a breakdown of basic functions of the system beginning with fuel and ending in water, etc. Of course this view has motivational aspects and perhaps you cannot mobilize energies without binding them to revolutionary pictures; but then we are at the place where Sorel was.

But we really don't know what kind of disintegration will take place?

That is correct. One can of course speak of long term enduring revolutionary processes transforming individuals in a way in which there is no difference left between a radical reformist position and the so called revolutionary one. These are converging conceptions.

Martin Jay (review date 9 November 1986)

SOURCE: "Standing Up to Paris and Bitburg," in *The New York Times Book Review,* November 9, 1986, p. 26.

[*In the following review, Jay suggests that* Autonomy and Solidarity *"provides a marvelous point of entry" into Habermas's thought.*]

One of the major ironies of contemporary thought is surely the fact that a champion of enlightened rationality is now more likely to speak German than French. No one represents this reversal of roles more clearly than the Frankfurt philosopher and sociologist Jürgen Habermas. Vigorously defending what he calls the "uncompleted project of modernity" as an emancipatory learning process, he has come squarely into conflict with French poststructuralists such as Jacques Derrida and Jean-François Lyotard.

> **At a time when theorizing on a grand scale is increasingly out of favor, Mr. Habermas has spun out a highly abstract model of social development that bears comparison with those of such 19th-century predecessors as Hegel and Marx.**
> **—*Martin Jay***

Mr. Habermas's targets, to be sure, have also been domestic, as evidenced by his courageous intervention in the Ger-

man debate following President Reagan's visit to Bitburg cemetery over the "normalization" of the Nazi past by certain German historians. But in the main, he has taken aim recently at the postmodernist, poststructuralist onslaught from Paris, whose repercussions have been felt in the British-American world as well.

Mr. Habermas's nuanced and complicated attempt to vindicate the legacy of the Enlightenment, in which he includes Marxism in certain of its forms, has been carried out in a series of ambitiously conceived studies. Beginning in 1962 with a widely discussed treatise on the transformation of the realm of public discourse, he has produced major works on radical theory and political practice, the competing interests underlying human cognition, crimes in the legitimacy of the modern state, social evolution and communicative social action.

At a time when theorizing on a grand scale is increasingly out of favor, Mr. Habermas has spun out a highly abstract model of social development that bears comparison with those of such 19th-century predecessors as Hegel and Marx. To his admirers, Mr. Habermas has accomplished a much-needed reconstruction of historical materialism by incorporating insights ranging from ordinary language philosophy and hermeneutics to developmental psychology and sociological systems theory. To his detractors, the result has been an amalgam of ill-fitting elements that merits comparison more with the work of Rube Goldberg than with that of Marx.

Happily, Mr. Habermas himself has been eager to help in the task of elucidating his work by responding to his critics. In so doing, he has exemplified his commitment to the communicative, rational discourse he identifies as the Enlightenment's most potent legacy. He has also given a stream of interviews on a wide range of subjects. The most important of these, conducted between 1977 and 1984 in Israel, Holland, Italy, Germany and England, have now been collected [in *Autonomy and Solidarity*] under the auspices of the English journal *New Left Review,* and trenchantly introduced by Peter Dews, an editor for the journal.

The interviews supplement and 'clarify' Mr. Habermas's more formal writings in several ways. Probing his intellectual roots, the interviewers shed liht on his relationship with the older members of the Frankfurt School—Max Horkheimer, Theodor W. Adorno and Herbert Marcuse, whose Critical Theory he has substantially revised. Insistent on exploring his political agenda, they elicit hitherto unavailable information about Mr. Habermas's membership in the Hitler Youth, his political re-education during the American occupation, his initial allegiance to and then temporary estrangement from the German New Left, and his re-entry into political life during the so-called German Autumn of 1977, when there were signs of a new authoritarianism in response to terrorism.

Soliciting his views on a series of contemporary topics, from the Green Party and Eurocommunism to neoconservatism and the women's movement, they allow him to demonstrate the applicability of his grand theory to the issues of the day. And along the way, they help to dispel versions of his position disseminated by critics too impatient to struggle with his forbiddingly dense and lengthy *oeuvre*.

The Habermas who emerges from these pages is a genuinely attractive figure, flexible, tough-minded, self-critical and deeply committed to the project of human emancipation. That such a grandiose goal might still seem even remotely worth fighting for, despite all the voices now cynically raised against it, is due in no small measure to Mr. Habermas's work and example.

Repudiating the spirit of Bitburg, which counsels compromise in the remembrance of evil, he has been no less adamant in rejecting counsels of resignation in the present, no matter what the latest intellectual fashions from Paris. However much one may contest various aspects of his work, it is chilling to imagine the current theoretical and political landscape without Mr. Habermas's towering figure. *Autonomy and Solidarity* provides a marvelous point of entry into the thought of the outstanding German *philosophe* of our day.

Onora O'Neill (review date 22 November 1990)

SOURCE: "The New Restoration," in *London Review of Books,* Vol. 12, No. 22, November 22, 1990, p. 13.

[*In the review below, O'Neill examines various themes of* The New Conservatism *in terms of Habermas's engagement with contemporary cultural and political debates, concluding that his work proves that "philosophical writing may be* engagé *without being ephemeral."*]

Should philosophers be politically committed, *engagés* in the manner of Socrates or of Sartre? Or should they adopt an aloof and distanced posture, like Plato after his early political disappointments, who views concern with this-worldly affairs as (at best) a conscientious return from the heights to 'the cave'? Jürgen Habermas and John Rawls are surely the two most distinguished political philosophers of our day, and their work exhibits many parallels: but on this deeply political matter they are worlds apart.

John Rawls's writing is scrupulously, evenly distant from political and cultural controversy. Although he is quite ex-plicit about the historical and cultural context of his own theory of justice, which he sees as specifically tied to and designed for a modern world that lacks consensus on ultimate values, and although his theory has definite practical import, he does not engage with current political and cultural debates. His writings focus relentlessly on the fundamental task of vindicating and articulating a complex account of justice. The enormous public influence that these writings have had, at least within the US, is not because Rawls's own writing reaches a wide audience, but because Rawlsian positions and arguments have been appropriated and developed in the debates of lawyers, policy-makers and other professionals. In these debates Rawls is invoked by many who think that Utilitarians don't care enough about rights or that neo-conservatives care too much about property rights—hence too little about welfare or the poor.

Jürgen Habermas's relations to his public—or rather publics—are quite different. His intellectual reputation, like Rawls's rests centrally on a corpus of philosophical and theoretical work, most of it long translated, if not yet widely appreciated, in the English-speaking world. However, Habermas also often speaks directly to audiences who don't follow his basic work in philosophy or social theory. He practises the communicational ethics that he defends theoretically by contributing pieces to a range of contemporary cultural and political debates. From time to time Suhrkamp publish selections of these shorter writings; and the pieces in *The New Conservatism* are mostly translations from writings published in Volumes V and VI of the Suhrkamp collections. Some pieces have been translated before, but none is easily available in English. Where the translations are new or have been revised, an attempt has been made to retain not only Habermas's paragraphing and metaphors but his sentence structure and punctuation. Unsurprisingly one result is wilfully inelegant, if serviceable English.

The thematic unity of the volume is greater than its mixed provenance suggests. Nearly all of these writings reflect on political and cultural currents of the Eighties, and in many Habermas tries both to make intelligible and to criticise the neo-conservatism which dominated the decade in the German as in the English-speakin world. Habermas's central line of thought diagnoses the neo-conservatisms of the last decade as a selective repudiation of the secular and universal ideals of the Enlightenment: the new conservatives combine 'an affirmative stance towards *social* modernity and the devaluation of *cultural* modernity'. They endorse processes of modernisation in the organisation of economy, polity and administration, yet repudiate them in the sphere of culture, where they reject democratic and secular ideals and seek a reinstatement of tradition. In British terms, this amounts to relishing the Big Bang while wanting to restore Victorian values: 'a disenchanted modernity has to be satisfied by a process of re-enchantment.'

Yearnings for re-enchantment demand that 'the legacy of tradition ... be preserved in as static a form as possible.' Where preservation and stasis are not enough to keep cultural modernisation at bay, a bit of judicious restoration, or even nostalgic invention, of traditions may be called for. Accordingly, most neo-conservatives hark back to and even try to 'improve' on religious and other traditions. Others of them, who don't find cultural restoration a plausible option, are led from a distaste for the modernisation of culture into a restless array of eclectic, aestheticised Post-Modernisms. Habermas dubs anti-traditionalists who are also cultural anti-modernists 'Young Conservatives', and his translator has kept the term with an insouciance which may amuse British readers, but which is not after all so implausible: yuppie conservatism, too, endorses the economic and administrative ideals of the Enlightenment, but substitutes a variegated consumerism for its moral and cultural ideals. Traditionalists and Post-Modernists may then join a common neo-conservative cause on the basis of a shared hostility to the legacy and ideals of the Enlightenment, combined with a shared acceptance of its economic, administrative and political implications.

The search for re-enchantment has taken varied forms, and while Habermas's analyses are by no means confined to the German case, many of the pieces in this volume trace the *Sonderweg* of German neo-conservatism in the post-war period, and in particular in the late Seventies and the Eighties. The conservative project of affirming and reviving tradition became a more controversial and bitter affair in a culture whose traditions had not only included Wilhelmine values but had led to Auschwitz. Faced with flawed traditions, cultural neo-conservatives may be tempted to help their project along by denying past realities or minimising past horrors.

A resolute refusal to forget those horrors had become a point of honour to the generation of Germans who define themselves as 68-ers, many of whom look to Habermas as their spokesman. Nonetheless, some German historians writing in the mid-Eighties manifested their conservative cultural sympathies by a willingness to revise previous accounts of Nazi war crimes. The revisionists took an apologetic and normalising approach to the Nazi period, blaming the initial descent into what they chauvinistically termed 'Asian' barbarities on the provocations of earlier Bolshevik strategies, and by implication condoning Nazi atrocities as an explicable response to other people's behaviour. Habermas's response in the last pieces included in this volume is not to defend Bolshevik barbarities, but to insist—with a passionate sobriety—that Germans should not gloss over those of their own past.

Given the furore caused in Britain earlier this year by Nicholas Ridley's speculations on the German character, it is worth quoting Habermas's position at some length: 'After Auschwitz our national self-consciousness can be derived only from the better traditions of our history, a history that is not unexamined but appropriated critically. The context of our national life, which once permitted incomparable injury to the substance of human solidarity, can be continued and further developed only in the light of a gaze educated by the moral catastrophe, a gaze that is, in a word, suspicious. Otherwise we cannot respect ourselves and cannot expect [?respect] from others.' In Habermas's account, Ridley's mistake would not lie in the concern he showed about the German past, but in his assumption that what is awry is 'the German character', rather than the neo-conservative, tendency to endorse specific elements of that past. Ironically, the very neo-conservatism that mars the writing of those German historians who took an accommodating view of the Nazi past also lurks in Ridley's position. Ridley was all for economic development, provided it was 'not in my backyard'. This nimby politics, too, accepts universal rules and market imperatives—the economic, political and administrative project of modernity—but rejects cultural modernisation in favour of enclaves of tradition and privilege, which are said to be demanded by fixities of character and tradition.

The 'Historians' Debate' in which these issues were fought out provides the context of several pieces in this book. Other manifestations of neo-conservative thought are dealt with separately. Habermas dissects architectural disputes, in which traditionalists and Post-Modernists have combined to mount a neo-conservative attack on Modernism. He takes a look at religious revivalism in the US. He analyses the sources of the renewed flowering of hostility to intellectuals in Germany. (British and American corroborations might be added.) He offers a guide to the controversies surrounding the relationship between Heidegger's Nazism and his philosophy. He probes the Eighties revival of interest in Carl Schmitt's realist jurisprudence where constitutionalism is endorsed at the expense of democracy.

These case-studies may persuade many readers that Habermas is able to provide a penetrating diagnosis of the structure of neo-conservatism. However, some will still wonder what he thinks is so wrong with neo-conservatism. Isn't the attempt to secure economic growth, prosperity and (some) human rights, while also hanging onto the particularities of culture and tradition very understandable? Isn't the fear that processes of modernisation end up imposing uniformities—a fear evident in current discussions of moves towards European unity—entirely reasonable? And if we think it is, wouldn't it make sense to espouse neo-conservatism?

The lectures and essays in *The New Conservatism* offer only parts of answers to these questions. The most convincing reason Habermas offers for rejecting neo-conservatism is that it is internally incoherent. The spread of universal principles of market, politics and administration is itself a cause of the destruction of traditional forms of life and culture: hence a politics that demands economic and political modernisation cannot also embrace cultural conservatism. In British terms, the party of the market cannot also be the party of the traditional family. Habermas points out many cases in which this stark choice is obscured and evaded by a rhetoric of resentment that identifies other villains and accuses them of causing cultural and moral disorder. He points out some of the popular scapegoats, such as left-wing intellectuals and educators; the list can be richly extended by drawing on the demonology of the neo-conservative decade in the English-speaking world, which includes feminists, loony lefties, working mothers, welfare cheats and a large number of other citizens. Meanwhile the real dynamic of modernisation proceeds unchecked, administrative and market forces penetrate more and more spheres of life, and cultural traditions crumble.

If the two elements of neo-conservatism cannot be combined, there will be hard choices, and on this these short writings leave much open. We could imagine a completed and consistent modernisation across all spheres of life; various self-limiting forms of modernisation which deliberately leave some domains to the contingencies of life, and which may be compatible with elements of traditionalism; and also (although this is harder) a retrenchment of modernisation. (Some Greens may offer an account of what this would entail.) Accounts of alternatives to neo-conservatism can, however, be found in Habermas's more systematic writings.

This volume mainly offers English-speaking readers a diagnosis rather than a remedy, but, in the UK at least, the symptoms it diagnoses are very recognisable: the neo-conservative decade is still alive and unhealthy in these parts, if not only in these parts. In the wake of last year's transformations, demands for economic and political modernisation and for cultural and national restoration jostle throughout the continent of Europe. Habermas's discussion of German predicaments in the Eighties speak to European dilemmas of the Nineties. Writings that began as occasional pieces dealing with the issues of the moment have turned out—in ways that Habermas would regret—to have a lasting relevance, and incidentally to show that philosophical writing may be *engagé* without being ephemeral.

Douglas Kellner (review date March 1992)

SOURCE: A review of *Moral Consciousness and Communicative Action* and *The New Conservatism,* in *Contemporary Sociology,* Vol. 21, No. 2, March, 1992, pp. 278-79.

[*In the following review, Kellner outlines the main concerns of Habermas's thought in* Moral Consciousness and Communicative Action *and* The New Conservatism.]

Jürgen Habermas's *New Conservatism* and *Moral Consciousness and Communicative Action* are collections of his recent essays on his major political and theoretical concerns of the 1980s. *The New Conservatism* assembles articles which provide critiques of recent forms of conservative thought, while the articles in *Moral Consciousness and Communicative Action* present his latest positions in philosophy, the social sciences, and ethics. Together, these collections provide an excellent survey of Habermas's intellectual and political concerns of the last decade.

> **Habermas follows Adorno and the Frankfurt school in stressing the need continually to work through and reappropriate the past critically without forgetting its horrors or rationalizing away its crimes.**
> **—Douglas Kellner**

On the whole, Habermas is a deft practitioner of the art of political polemics. His essays are clearly written, accessible to a broad public, and possess a sharp critical edge that requires reflection about a wide range of contemporary political and theoretical issues. Most of the articles published in *The New Conservatism* were first published in Germany's leading cultural and political journals, and one—on the crisis of the welfare state and exhaustion of utopian energies—was even first delivered as a lecture to the Spanish parliament in 1984. Habermas is thus very much a public intellectual who involves himself in the key social and political debates of the day. This stance is grounded in the tradition of the Frankfurt school, which attempted to merge theory and politics, and is also inspired by the Marxian tradition of ideology critique.

In *The New Conservatism,* Habermas polemicizes against rightist thought in the Weimar Republic and Third Reich, as well as against contemporary conservatism. His sharpest attacks are directed against the thought of German philosopher Martin Heidegger, political theorist Carl Schmitt, and the contemporary renewals of a rightist conservatism which covertly apologizes for National Socialism in the so-called historians' debate. Several essays contain Habermas's answer to recent historians like Michael Sturmer, who believe that history should provide that "higher source of meaning, which, after [the decline of] religion, only the nation and patriotism were able to provide." Habermas also polemicizes against recent German histories of the Third Reich which downplay the crimes of the German army and the horrors of the holocaust. Habermas follows Adorno and the Frankfurt school in stressing the need continually to work through and reappropriate the past critically without forgetting its horrors or rationalizing away its crimes.

Most of the essays in *The New Conservatism* deal with recent and contemporary German history, and in these essays Habermas appears as the conscience of the critical liberal and Social Democratic Left. He also appears in both collections as a resolute defender of Enlightenment reason against its critics. Habermas links attacks on reason with conservatie ideology and is deeply concerned about the renaissance of conservatism, which has played a pernicious role in German history. For instance, in response to the recent revelations that Heidegger was much more actively involved in National Socialism than previously known, Habermas is concerned to demonstrate the kinship between Heidegger's philosophy and the worldview of fascism. For Habermas, it is not just Heidegger's political links with National Socialism that are at stake in the so-called Heidegger controversy, but his very philosophy, which, like fascism, attacks reason, democracy, and modernity itself.

Likewise, Habermas criticizes Carl Schmitt's concept of the political as "the collectively organized self-assertion of a 'politically existing' people against external and internal enemies." He also sees Schmitt's decisionism, his rejection of the norms of critical reason, as dangerous. For Schmitt, sovereignty rests in the "decision power" of "he who decides in the exceptional situation." Such positions obviously legitimate totalitarian domination and state political violence, as was obvious in the use of Schmitt' ideas in the Third Reich. Habermas also critically engages the thought of Daniel Bell and of contemporary German conservatives, such as Arnold Gehlen, detecting inconsistencies in these affirmations of economic modernity and rejections of modern culture and defending cultural modernity against conservative cultural criticism.

Throughout his political and philosophical essays, Habermas is concerned to hold on to the notion of critical rationality and believes that precisely this concept is rejected in the decisionism of Heidegger and Schmitt and the defense of traditional morality of old and new conservatism. Against these positions, Habermas defends a notion of critical rationality rooted in his theories of communicative action and a discourse ethics. This theme stands at the center of *Moral Consciousness and Communicative Action.* For Habermas, philosophy is a "stand in" (*Platzhalter*) for "empirical theories with strong universalistic claims." Rejecting the notion that philosophy is an usher (*Platzanweiser*) and judge, Habermas assigns philosophy the more modest role of mediating among the claims of practical, theoretical, and aesthetic reason and serving as a "place holder" for empirically grounded theories. Habermas's philosophy draws strongly on

the social sciences, and his model for a universalistic science with strong empirical foundations is Kohlberg's theory of moral development.

The subtext of many of Habermas's essays is his philosophical reflections on modernity and his defense of critical rationality as a legacy of modernity worth defending. Thus he rejects the postmodern claims of a break or rupture in history, as well as postmodern attacks on rationality and modernity. In general, Habermas interprets the contemporary French postmodern theory inspired by Nietzsche and Heidegger as a form of irrationalism and aestheticized subjectivism that engages in a total rejection of modernity.

This interpretation of postmodern theory, which associates it ultimately with fascism, has produced a heated debate, as has Habermas's labeling Derrida, Foucault, Lyotard, and other French postmodern thinkers as "young conservatives." There is little in these French theorists, however, that is conservative, and this labeling misfires and covers over the linkages between some aspects of postmodern theory and the Frankfurt school tradition in which Habermas is rooted. Habermas does, to be sure, find sympathetic elements in the late Foucault, but he has yet to undertake a systematic interrogation of postmodern theorists to discern both their contributions and their limitations for social theory today. Habermas is more concerned with their attacks on reason and modernity and thus fails to appreciate the ways that some postmodern theorists help conceptualize new trends within the contemporary media, computer, and high-tech society in which we find ourselves.

David Weberman (review date July 1992)

SOURCE: A review of *Moral Consciousness and Communicative Action,* in *The Philosophical Review,* Vol. 101, No. 3, July, 1992, pp. 924-26.

[*In the following review, Weberman explains Habermas's contribution to the field of discourse ethics, defining his methodology and its application to ethics.*]

[*Moral Consciousness and Communicative Action*] is a well-translated edition of a book that first appeared in 1983. It has been expanded to include a fifth, more recent essay. The last three essays (two of which are short treatises in themselves) address pivotal issues in ethical theory, such as cognitivism, justification, Kantianism, and moral psychology. They contain the most definitive statement yet of Habermas's original contribution to the field: discourse ethics. It should be noted that analytic moral philosophers will find this book both accessible and relevant.

The first two essays deal more generally with the legitimate aims of philosophy and social science, but they also clarify the methodological assumptions underlying Habermas's ethics. Habermas argues that philosophy should no longer regard itself as an entirely distinct type of aprioristic inquiry serving as the judge and usher (*Platzanweiser*) for all purported claims to truth. This repudiation of foundationalism and dethronement of philosophy is said to follow from the historicity of our cognitive achievements and the impossibility of *ultimate* justification (moral and epistemological). Although it has led some to abandon all attempts at justification, Habermas is at great pains not to give up ship. Against Rorty, he argues: "Even a philosophy that has been taught its limits by pragmatism and hermeneutics will not be able to find a resting place in edifying conversation *outside* the sciences without immediately being drawn back into argumentation, that is, justificatory discourse." Sharing many of Rorty's premises, Habermas nevertheless arrives at different conclusions. He proposes not the abandonment, but the transformation of philosophy.

Habermas's transformed philosophy attempts to steer a middle course between aprioristic foundationalism and relativistic contextualism. Absolutely unwilling to restrict the evaluation of standards of rationality and morality to the bounds of a given culture, he engages in a "rational reconstruction" of the transcendental conditions of the various kinds of competence that we possess. What makes this different from foundationalism is that these transcendental conditions are "weak"—that is, historically contingent and (in part) empirically discoverable and falsifiable. The point is to discover in these conditions criteria for the rational assessment of moral and theoretical questions. This is the method; we can now turn to its deployment in ethics.

The treatment of ethics in this book can be divided into five parts: (1) the defense of ethical cognitivism; (2) the formulation and justification of the principle of universalization; (3) the appeal made to moral psychology; (4) the role of discourse in determining universalizability; and (5) the nonsubstantive, procedural character of moral theory.

(1) Habermas has long opposed ethical skepticism and subjectivism. Here he argues that moral rightness is not a naturalistic property, but a "higher-level" predicate like truth. However, this does not mean that moral judgmets are true in the same way as empirical propositions. Moral judgments have their own kind of legitimacy that derives from the reasoning inherent in moral argumentation.

(2) For Habermas, moral argumentation must be based on a Kantian-like principle of universalization. His version of that principle, (U), requires that a valid norm be not only consistently universalizable, but also acceptable to *all* concerned parties. This stronger stipulation is motivated by the recognition that any one person's test for universalizability will be parochial to that person's preferences.

Habermas's justification of (U) takes the form of a "transcendental-pragmatic" argument that "show(s) that the principle of universalization... is implied by the presuppositions of argumentation in general" such that participation in argumentation accompanied by the disavowal of some such principle constitutes a "performative contradiction." Habermas maintains that implicit in argumentation are procedural rules that require equal opportunities for all participants and that the recognition of such rules "amounts to implicitly acknowledging (U)." Habermas mentions but does not lay to rest two problems with this derivation. First, individuals are free to opt out of argumentation. Second, recognizing certain rules of argumentation would not seem to entail recognizing similar rules for action. Whatever the cogency of the argument, Habermas says that it does not provide an ultimate justification or Kantian-like deduction of (U), but only shows that there are no plausible alternatives to (U). On his account, (U) has only "hypothetical" status, meaning that its universality and interpretation must be empirically corroborated. What remains puzzling are Habermas's reasons for not taking his argument to be as strong as any demonstration of necessary presuppositions and for thinking that it requires empirical confirmation.

(3) Habermas seeks further grounding for (U) in Kohlberg's theory of moral development, in which the possession of universal ethical principles represents the highest stage of moral consciousness. Yet it is hard to see how facts about psychological moral development are supposed to corroborate Habermas's philosophical argument aside from mapping onto or "fit(ting) into the same pattern," especially since Habermas concedes that "the empirical theory presupposes the validity of the normative theory it uses" and that the two stand in a "relationship of mutual dependence." In fact, Habermas's discussion serves principally to illuminate, reinterpret, and undergird Kohlberg's theoretical framework, and not the other way round.

(4) Perhaps the most original feature of Habermas's ethics is his insistence on the role of discourse. His strong formulation of the principle of universalization resembles the impartiality demanded by Rawls's veil of ignorance. However, Habermas argues that the test of universalizability "cannot be handled monologically but require[s] . . . a process of discursive will formation . . . a 'real' process of argumentation." In the last, more recent essay, Habermas defends discourse ethics against various criticisms including those leveled by Hegel against Kant (formalism, abstractness).

(5) Despite his departure from Kant's formalism through the inclusion of discourse, Habermas concedes and embraces a different kind of formalism. Discourse ethics is and must re-

main a procedural theory or a minimalist ethics that cannot provide "substantive guidelines" to questions concerning the good life. In accordance with liberalism and in recognition of the difference between cultures, Habermas leaves substantive moral issues to be decided by the actual process of public discourse.

Frederick J. Antczak (review date November 1992)

SOURCE: A review of *Moral Consciousness and Communicative Action,* in *The Quarterly Journal of Speech,* Vol. 78, No. 4, November, 1992, pp. 510-11.

[*In the review below, Antczak summarizes Habermas's theory of communication ethics and various potential objections from the communication scholars' perspective.*]

It is a truism now accepted even by some philosophers that modern medicine saved ethics, that moral theory had been mired in the same concerns with ever-diminishing returns until it confronted the new problems that emerged from the advances in medical practice, with consequences that significantly changed both ethics and medicine. It's hardly shocking when powerful new technologies applied in urgent practical questions reinvigorate standing issues and open further productive lines of thought; what's surprising is that nothing similar has happened to that other practice where momentous transformations have been changing the ways we approach issues of the highest public and personal importance—the practice of communication.

Many have seen Jürgen Habermas's theory of communicative action as presaging just such a change. Over more than twenty years he has been articulating a theory of communication that attempts to provide society with a self-understanding that is both critical and emancipatory. Characterizing positivist science as insensitive to its own practice-based meanings, and hermeneutic inquiry as unable to transcend embeddedness in the authority of tradition, Habermas has sought to develop claims that are both sufficiently sensitive to practical meaning and transcendentally grounded. In [*Moral Consciousness and Communicative Action*], his latest book, he attempts to demonstrate the relevance of communicative action for moral theory.

Habermas articulates a theory of normative justification that advances a sharply Kantian distinction: moral theory is concerned strictly with the Right and is separate from the larger field of questions sometimes treated as part of ethics, all those variously concerning the Good. But Habermas attempts to get beyond Kant's problematic reliance on the individual moral actor in a manner that seems to hold special promise for communication scholars: not by replacing that actor with a Rawlsian "veil" that blinds individuals to their identities and interests, but with a communication procedure that removes the onus from the individual moral actor and places it on communicative action—on participatory argument. This seems a promising move: a uniting of ethics and communication in a relation at least as intimate as that of ethics and medicine.

Habermas bases his theory of normative justification on two principles. The "Principle of Universalization" establishes that "*all* affected can accept the consequences and the side effects its *general* observance can be anticipated to have for the satisfaction of *everyone's* interests (and these consequences are preferred to those of known alternative possibilities for regulation)." The "Principle of Discourse Ethics" mandates that "only those norms can claim to be valid that meet (or could meet) with the approval of all affected in the capacity *as participants in a practical discourse*" (chapter 3). But for either of these principles to make sense, the participants must see argumentation as fundamentally cooperative, not competitive. The purpose of argument is either to reach a new consensus on questions of right or wrong, or to reaffirm a consensus that has been disrupted.

For this procedure to reach normative justification, participants must be "competent" to partake in argument as he has defined it. Habermas bases his notion of competence on the developmental theories of Kohlberg and Piaget. All people, regardless of culture, pass through the same stages of moral (Kohlberg) and intellectual (Piaget) development. These stages are distinct, hierarchical, irreversible, chronological in nature, and tied to perspectives on the world. A competent participant in argument must have moved into the "postconventional stages" of moral development—a move beyond adherence to culturally structured norms.

Argument in this mode is a reflexive act of communication. Participants in the argument inherently have the competence to partake in three roles during the process: that of the actor expressing his or her experience in the lived world; that of the critic who is able to distance herself form the lived world; providing an "objectivating" viewpoint toward the world; and that of the participant in an interpersonal relationship within the legitimate world of norm-conformative behavior (chapter 4). The interplay of these roles constitutes Habermas's procedure of normative justification, the procedure for testing the validity of claims of "rightness."

Habermas attempts to anticipate and answer his critics; disappointingly, the objections he chooses to engage are matters of philosophy, not necessarily those of scholars of practical communication. One of these concerns the core element of The Principle of Universalization: the requirement that *all* consent. Habermas attempts to transcend Kant's individual justification by transferring that justification to a process involving all. Yet Habermas disclaims responsibility for advancing any mechanism of ensuring, however abstractly, the participation of *all*—thereby evading exactly the sorts of practical nexus with the lived world that has been so productive for ethics and medicine. Instead he seems to redefine "all" circularly, as all who conceivably "could" participate in a system which neither he in his theory nor we members of the all in our communicative practices have a responsibility to change, much less perfect. While Habermas has argued that hermeneutic inquiry leads to a limited form of understanding because of its contented embeddedness in the hermeneutic circle, it is not clear from his own arguments that Habermas systematically eliminates the possibility of his own contented embeddedness, his own kind of circularity.

Even when he successfully defends his position against philosophers, Habermas does not attempt to address the kinds of concerns that communication scholars might be more inclined to pursue. Many of us may question the universalist abstractions of this approach, holding that questions of morality—even those drawn so narrowly as to include only questions of normative Right—cannot be separated from the specific contextual arenas in which they occur. Not all of us have accepted the Speech-Act approach to language that allows him to make distinctions like the one between interactive communicative behavior and strategic communicative behavior, a distinction he treats as marvelously clean and unproblematic; many have raised doubts about the "rational" model that envelops the Speech-Act approach. Others among us would have trouble with the assumption that the purpose of argument is to reach or reaffirm consensus. We have in our midst critics of Kohlberg and Piaget, who find controversial the rigidity of developmental stages, their necessary sequence and hierarchy; the controversy may be especially widespread on the possibility and degree to which persons may step outside their own cultures and be able to formulate ethically meaningful critiques of those cultures. Finally, some of the philosophical and theological literature that has stoked the recent revival of communication ethics casts doubt on the assumption that it is either necessary or possible to separate out and privilege questions about the Right from questions about the Good.

But this book is meant primarily to address philosophers; it does not attempt to speak to the concerns of argumentation theorists in the field of communication or of those scholars practically interested in revitalizing the public sphere. Fair enough. There is still much for us to consider and adapt here. But perhaps the most important issue the book poses is whether we can best revitalize ethics—and our own discipline in the bargain—by yearning to be philosophers, or by doing what *we* do: understanding the meaning and moment of actual communication practices, however culturally embedded, however far—perhaps usefully far—from transcendence.

Peter Dews (review date 13 May 1993)

SOURCE: "Agreeing What's Right," in *London Review of Books,* Vol. 15, No. 9, May 13, 1993, pp. 26-7.

[*In the review below, Dews detects a change in Habermas's discourse ethics in* Faktizität und Geltung, *offering a thematic analysis of the philosophical principles addressed in the book.*]

On 9 November last year, the anniversary of Kristallnacht, the philosopher Manfred Frank was invited to give the principal address at the memorial service which is held annually in the Paulskirche in Frankfurt. The Paulskirche was the home of the first democratically elected German national assembly, which flourished briefly amidst the revolutions of 1848-9, and, in keeping with this setting, Frank refused to limit himself to a 'retrospective ritual of mourning'. Rather, he used the occasion to consider contemporary events in Germany, in particular the rise of a violently xenophobic right-wing element, whose activities claimed 17 lives in 1992, and the reaction of the established political parties to it. Central to this reaction has been the attempt to limit the right of political asylum enshrined in Article 16 of the Grundgesetz, the German constitution. The provisional agreement reached between the main political parties on 6 December 1992 foresees abolishing this right for applicants arriving from an EC country or from any 'safe third country' deemed to have satisfactory asylum procedures of its own. Since Poland and the Czech Republic fall into this category, these measures will effectively cut off the flow of applicants, the vast majority of whom reach Germany by land.

Frank suggested that in Germany an ethnic rather than political definition of the nation, and an excessive concern with national unity and security, had repeatedly overridden the protection of individual freedoms, and had hindered the development of an appropriate conception of democracy: 'The predominant conception of the essence of democracy is expressed in the demand that politics should bow to pressure from the streets.' To illustrate this he quoted leading protagonists in the current *Asyldebatte* from both the Right and the Left. He then reached for a shocking comparison: 'Goebbels's populism invented a fitting jingle for what happens when one adapts to the unqualified feelings of the populace: "Our thinking was simple, because the people are simple. Our thinking was primitive, because the people are primitive."' At this point many members of the audience, including the entire Christian Democrat contingent, walked out. Subsequently, all the parties in the Frankfurt Parliament (including the Greens) repudiated the speaker, and the furore occupied the local press for a fortnight afterwards.

These events illustrate the drawback of one possible interpretation of *Faktizität und Geltung,* Jürgen Habermas's new book on the philosophy of law and the theory of the constitutional state. Under the headline 'Jürgen Habermas makes peace with the constitutional state', a pre-publication review in *Der Spiegel* sought to present the book as an old leftist's recantation in response to the collapse of Communism, and his belated return to the fold of liberal democracy. But one of the deepest motivations of Habermas's work has been an anxiety that the institutions and practices of the modern democratic state may not be sufficiently firmly anchored in the traditions of German thought and politics. He is convinced that the emancipatory potential of such a state needs to be defended against the powerful current in German philosophy and culture which views democratic ideals as—at best—helpless before, and—at worst—a positive symptom of, the spiritual desolation of modernity. It is not surprising, therefore, that Habermas should have sprung to Frank's defence. In a highly combative article in *Die Zeit* he denounced the German government's increasing tendency to contemplate altering, or simply bypassing, the constitution, for the sake of Germany's self-assertion as a 'normal' nation-state. This 'D-Mark patriotism' is, in Habermas's view, an attempt to compensate for the 'normative deficits' of a bungled reunification process, with its disastrous social consequences, particularly in the East. He repeated the argument he has made before: instead of what amounted to an administrative incorporation, through provisions contained in the Grundgesetz of the old Bundesrepublik, the reunited Germany should have had the opportunity to conclude a new 'social contract' in the form of a new constitution.

Faktizität und Geltung ('Facility and Validity') provides the philosophical background to these political arguments. The book's title indicates the main direction in which Habermas's thinking has moved in the last decade, since he began to work more intensively on a universalist foundation of morality in the tradition of Kant. Ever since the Sixties, he has contended that human communication is necessarily framed by 'relations of recognition' between language-users, and that such recognition always involves, implicitly at least, commitment to a search for consensus. Naturally, Habermas does not deny that it is always possible for individuals to use language 'strategically', in order to mislead, intimidate or exclude others. But even in this case the expectation that communication will convey verifiable truths and justifiable imperatives is being obliquely exploited. The requirement that speakers provide grounds for their claims and assertions, when these do not initially appear convincing, is ultimately not culturally determined, but is built into the necessary conditions of communication, and provides the basis for a conception of the rightness of moral norms. Such norms are objectively 'right' when they result from a consensus attained through free and equal discussion by all concerned in the light of their respective interests (this is the principle of what has come to be known as 'discourse ethics').

Since he began to formulate this approach in the Seventies, Habermas has often been accused, from various directions, of confusing a principle of political democracy with one of morality. It has been argued, by his colleague Albrecht Wellmer, for example, that moral convictions are anchored in the personality at a level which stops them from being readily altered, even in the light of discussion, whereas collectively agreed norms, though the obligation to obey them may have a 'weak' moral force, can change in the light of shifting opinions or circumstances. In Kantian terms, immoral actions are those which, as rational agents, we cannot even coherently will, let alone fail to agree on. It has also been argued (by feminist critics inspired by Carol Gilligan's *In a Different Voice*) that moral awareness involves an attentiveness to individuals in their uniqueness, and a concern with the sustaining of personal relationships, which are not susceptible to universal regulation. The conclusion of both these lines of argument is often that Habermas, when sympathetically interpreted, has failed to capture philosophically our core sense of morality, while offering a compelling basis for the regulation of public issues through discussion and collective decision-making.

In *Faktizität und Geltung* Habermas takes the major step of accepting, at least in a qualified form, the force of this criticism. He begins from the historical consideration that, in modern societies, a morality based on universal principles progressively separates itself from those forms of ethical practice which are tied to specific social roles and expectations. As a result, what has been referred to, since Hegel, as *Sittlichkeit* degenerates into mere convention. Habermas still insists on this, despite the objections of his critics, communitarian in the United States, Neo-Aristotelian in Germany, that even modern morality ultimately derives what force it has from communally shared convictions. But while Habermas has resisted this move, and continues to defend the formal priority of a universalist point of view, he now also stresses its corresponding weaknesses. First, the complexity of the situations that moral agents need to adjudge generates a 'cognitive indeterminacy' which can make excessive demands on the individual. Second, to be effective this morality must be transformed, from a form of social knowledge, into the driving force of the individual conscience. (An additional difficulty here is that the moral agent is disadvantaged if others don't follow the same norms, as he or she is entitled to expect.) Third, the level of social organisation required if some moral duties are to be fulfilled—for example, aid for disaster-struck regions of the world—often lies far beyond the reach of individual initiative.

On these grounds, Habermas argues, it is clear that a post-conventional morality requires the complementary form of law. Law enables a society to regulate interactions without having to rely directly on the motivations of its members;

indeed it vastly increases the scope for strategic action, yet in a manner still ultimately anchored in the principle of a communicative consensus. Law, in other words, generates a higher-level reflexive social facticity, which compensates for the increasing risks posed by those conflicts which arise when traditional life-worlds splinter, and the space for the pursuit of individual interests expands.

Habermas wants to emphasise, however, that law must also satisfy expectations of legitimacy; if it is to fulfil its socially integrative roles, it must be generated through a democratic procedure, in which all concerned can, in principle, take part. From this he draws the conclusion that his general principle of 'discursive grounding' ('Those norms of action are valid, which all who may be concerned could accept in a rational discourse') separates into two distinct principles, a 'principle of morality' (which specifies the aim of consensus, taking into account all relevant interests) and a new 'principle of democracy'. This second principle is contrasted with the first: 'Whereas the moral principle operates at the level of the *internal* constitution of a particular form of argumentation, the principle of democracy relates to the level of the *external* (effective) institutionalisation enabling equal participation in the discursive formation of will and opinion, which in its turn takes place within legally guaranteed forms of communication.'

In Habermas's view, this 'principle of democracy' provides a means of resolving the dispute represented paradigmatically by Kant and Rousseau: does the autonomy of the private individual come before the 'public autonomy' of the citizen, or are the subjective freedoms central to liberal political thought themselves bestowed by an act of collective self-definition? Habermas proposes a 'logical genesis' for the system of rights—a more modest version of the dizzying feats of deduction of his German Idealist predecessors—in which the subjective right to the greatest possible freedom of action compatible with equal freedom for others is understood as a condition of participation in a law-governed polity. Since such a polity must also define a status for its associates, offer guarantees of this status, and legitimate its content collectively, a spiralling movement of internalisation generates further basic rights: of recognised membership of the community, of protection and redress, of political expression and participation. Underpinning all these are rights to the preservation of the social, technical and ecological bases of life itself. All such a derivation presupposes, according to Habermas, is 'an intuitive understanding of the discourse principle, and the concept of the form of law'.

Even during his most abstract excursions, Habermas remains aware that a purely normative conception of law is likely to fall prey to idealist illusions, misconceiving an institution essentially torn between facticity and validity. He therefore seeks to bring into his picture the sceptical results of that 'sociological disenchantment' which sees law as a self-contained system, interacting with other social systems, or simply as an implement of unequally shared power. Habermas's social theory as a whole is based on a fundamental distinction between a 'life-world', organised primarily through tacit consensus, and the systems of state administration and the market economy, which use money and power to co-ordinate actions without the need to gain agreement. In *The Theory of Communicative Action,* Habermas analysed contemporary developments in terms of a distinction between law as 'institution', ultimately anchored in the moral expectations of the life-world, and law as 'steering medium', or an administrative mechanism intermeshed with those processes of bureaucratisation and monetarisation which 'colonise' the life-world. From such a standpoint the crucial question is how the legislative process can be brought under the democratic control which, according to Habermas, the modern concept of law intrinsically implies. *The Theory of Communicative Action* bequeathed us the problem of how the life-world can 'steer' such systems, and limit their intrusions, without disrupting their functioning.

To address this problem Habermas has recourse here to the category of the 'public sphere' (*Öffentlichkeit*). This concept, first developed in *The Structural Transformation of the Public Sphere* (1962), provides a sketchmap of Habermas's entire intellectual itinerary, and is the key to his conception of the continuing emancipatory content of democratic ideals. The public sphere consists of both the direct and the mediated discussions of 'critically reasoning' individuals, who thereby form public opinion, and are thus able to exert pressure on the political system, without being formally part of it. Already in the early Sixties, Habermas had appreciated that, under contemporary conditions, only groups and organisations providing internal forums for discussion could hope to withstand the blizzard of advertising, public relations and the mass media, an insight seemingly confirmed by more recent developments, such as the emergence of the 'new social movements'. Accordingly, in this book, Habermas intertwines the concept of the 'public sphere' with that of 'civil society', a more recent term for those spontaneous movements and associations beyond the reach of the state which bring new problems and perspectives to political attention. He emphasises the 'dual politics' characteristic of such movements, which do not seek simply to influence the political system, as traditional interest groups do, but also to hold open new spaces of communication.

In this way Habermas seeks to span the gulf between the 'anarchistic' core of communicative action, which leaves no truth-claim in principle unchallenged, and the remote, inflexible mechanisms of the modern state. Is this conception convincing? He does not conceal the mass of evidence suggesting the extent to which the manipulated, media-saturated public sphere destroys the potential for an effective democratic opinion to form. Statistics such as those indicating that the average length of the sound-bites of presidential candidates on American television has declined from 42.3 seconds in 1968 to 9.8 seconds in 1988, seem to confirm the worst apprehensions of **Structural Transformation.** One could also argue that Habermas's enthusiasm for the 'post-Marxist' category of 'civil society', already tarnished by the latest developments in Eastern Europe, seriously underplays the continuing role of social class as a factor in determining access to channels of political influence. In **Faktizität and Geltung** he is obliged to appeal, rather weakly, to the 'normative self-understanding of the mass media', as informing and facilitating public discussion, in order to convince his readers that issues of sufficient common concern will eventually obtain a hearing. Even then, however, he stresses that it is only crises which are capable of mobilising people successfully. Can such sporadic movements really be said to constitute 'communicative practices of self-determination'? And how are the democratic impulses of civil society to be distinguished effectively from that pressure from the streets whose role in German politics, as we have seen, Habermas so fears?

To these political concerns can be added reservations about the philosophical bases of Habermas's conception of a *Rechtsgemeinschaft*. He believes his theory can help to resolve the problem of the oscillation between the goals of formal equality and of compensatory intervention, which has become explicit in recent legal discussion, and which he illustrates by discussing feminist debates. The problem highlighted by feminist critics is that welfare-state intervention simply assumes what the needs of specific groups are, and makes allowance for these as 'deviations' from a norm which is not itself neutral. The solution, Habermas suggests, cannot be to return to a 'formal' liberalism, which has irretrievably lost its innocence, but rather to move to a 'proceduralist' paradigm, where social groups themselves can bring forward the relevant interpretations of their needs and aspirations. In the light of this move: 'a programme of law proves to be discriminatory when it is insensitive to the freedom-limiting side-effects of actual inequality, and paternalistic when insensitive to the freedom-limiting side-effects of the state-organised compensation for these inequalities.'

There is no critique here of law as such. Yet ten years ago, in **The Theory of Communicative Action,** Habermas described the increasing intrusion of law into the life-world as 'deworlding', or as isolating and antagonising individuals, and disrupting a social integration essentially grounded in values, norms and processes of understanding. Habermas now renounces this conception of an unavoidable dilemma whereby a simultaneous process of emancipation and colonisation is the result of encroaching 'legalisation' (*Verrechtlichung*). Yet it's fair to ask whether his earlier in-

sights may not have been suppressed by his current, more positive evaluation of law.

In *Kampf um Anerkennung* ('Struggle for Recognition'), Axel Honneth, a younger representative of the Frankfurt School tradition, suggests that the recognition of individuals as subjects of universal legal rights is not sufficient if they are to achieve an undistorted sense of selfhood. Individuals also require acknowledgment of their contribution to the general welfare if they are to value as well as respect themselves, and it is only this reciprocally endowed sense of worth which makes forms of social solidarity possible. From such a standpoint, the intrusion of law must have a damaging effect, because what is at stake is not merely the maximisation of freedom, in terms of individual autonomy and political participation, as Habermas's formulation suggests. One can see this from the feminist critiques of state intervention which Habermas himself discusses. What is at issue here is not simply whether such intervention restricts the freedom of women, but rather that it treats women as anomalies, and does not reflect an appropriate, non-androcentric valuing of their specific contributions to society. What is ultimately required, therefore, is not merely further legal reform, but a change in the values which organise the possibilities of social solidarity.

Habermas suggests at several points in this book that, in contemporary societies, the resources most urgently in need of protection are not economic or administrative, but rather those of a 'social solidarity which is currently disintegrating'. It is doubtful, however, whether the 'project of the realisation of law' alone, whatever content it is imbued with, is sufficient to combat this disintegration. Indeed, Habermas himself has recently made clear that a concern with rights, which enable self-determination, must be balanced by sentiments of solidarity, which enable self-realisation: '*Justice* is connected with the equal freedoms of unique and self-determining individuals, whereas *solidarity* is connected with the well-being of one's fellows, who are bound together in an intersubjectively shared form of life—and thus also with the sustaining of the integrity of this form of life itself.'

Habermas goes on to emphasise, of course, that solidarity cannot be restricted to the internal relations of one social group, closing itself against others, but must be construed in a universalist spirit. In this case, however, a philosophical space appears to be opened up by his own argument for an enquiry into the fundamental structures of the human form of life, as the locus of the 'archaic, binding energies' which drive even this expanded, cosmopolitan solidarity. The need for such an investigation is perhaps suggested by Habermas's blunt declaration, in a recent interview, that 'emancipation—if the word is given an unambiguous interpretation—makes human beings more independent, but not automatically happier.' Against the background of German history, his reluctance to provide even an outline of how the striving for solidarity might be fulfilled is understandable. But this very reluctance risks discouraging and dampening emancipatory impulses. An attempt to explore what is essential to the integrity of human life-forms in general might enable more to be said about the goals which could inspire collective self-determination, without damaging that steadfast, subtle universalism which has been the hallmark of Habermas's massive contribution to contemporary philosophical debate.

William Outhwaite (review date May 1994)

SOURCE: A review of *Autonomy and Solidarity* and *Postmetaphysical Thinking,* in *Contemporary Sociology,* Vol. 23, No. 3, May, 1994, pp. 456-58.

[*Below, Outhwaite detects Habermas's "practical-political concerns" in* Autonomy and Solidarity *and outlines his philosophical approach in* Postmetaphysical Thinking.]

The first edition of ***Autonomy and Solidarity: Interviews with Jürgen Habermas,*** published in 1986, rapidly established itself as the fast track into an understanding of Habermas's life and work, as well as an indispensable complement to his own massive oeuvre and the equally massive accretion of secondary literature which surrounds it. This new edition contains five further interviews from the period 1985-90, and Peter Dews has extended his excellent introduction with a new postscript.

As Dews notes, Habermas is now giving more and more interviews. Dews has therefore had to be more selective this time, choosing some of the interviews from ***Eine Art Schadensabwicklung*** (1987) and ***Die nachholende Revolution*** (1990) which best illustrate Habermas's relation to earlier critical theory, his assessment of contemporary German society and intellectual life, and his work on morality, law, and democratic theory which recently came to a head in ***Faktizität und Geltung*** (1992).

Some parts of the interviews serve directly as summaries and close discussions of specific works or bodies of work by Habermas; this is true particularly of the written interview with *New Left Review* entitled **"A Philosophico-Political Profile,"** of **"Dialectics of Rationalization,"** and of the final essay in the new edition, **"Discourse Ethics, Law and Sittlichkeit."** But these and the others also range more widely: A particular virtue of the interview format is that it encourages juxtapositions of distinct, yet related, themes of a kind which would look peculiar in a more formal text.

One of the striking aspects of Habermas's work is that despite its massive scholarship—his tendency not just to bor-row themes from a very wide variety of disciplines and approaches but to immerse himself thoroughly in their various discourses—a set of persisting practical-political concerns can also be seen to run right through his work. So, for example, his assessment of his relationship to earlier critical theory, something which he seems not to have reflected on explicitly, or at least publicly, in his earlier work, is closely bound up with his judgments of the political culture of the German Federal Republic. These in turn, documented in his "political writings," such as those from which these interviews are mostly taken and which he sees as distinct from his more theoretical work, are intimately linked with his concerns about how to secure a genuinely democratic political culture in contemporary societies—which itself is a kind of red thread running through from his early work on students' political orientations and the "structural change" in the contemporary public sphere, through his critique of technocracy in the 1960s, to his current focus on legal and democratic theory. The interviews bring out these connections in a uniquely vivid way. They also are an arena in which Habermas can be seen to comment on issues of international politics which have been strikingly absent from the rest of his work so far. And as he disarmingly put it at the end of the written *NLR* interview of 1984, "I should not talk about socialism only in interviews."

Peter Dews rightly contrasts "the steady development of Habermas's project" with the "theoretical gyrations" found in much contemporary French thought. Habermas began his scholarly career in the 1950s with an acute sense of the difficulties of contiuing the central themes of neo-Marxism in the postwar period. Having initially conceptualized his project as a modified philosophy of history, Habermas came in the 1970s to seek an alternative foundation in an analysis of the presuppositions of linguistic communication and a resultant theory of communicative action. . . . This in turn led Habermas to develop and defend, in writings through the 1980s, a "discourse ethics" addressed in the last interview in this collection and, most recently, by a massive attempt to theorize the complex relations between "facticity and validity" in legal and democratic theory.

Postmetaphysical Thinking (*Nachmetaphysisches Denken*) is well translated and usefully introduced by W. M. Hohengarten. For the English-language version, Habermas has replaced two essays originally published in English and a review essay on the work of the philosopher Dieter Henrich with the paper **"Peirce and Communication."**

In these essays, Habermas develops and illustrates his conception of a philosophical approach which has abandoned what he variously characterizes as metaphysics, the philosophy of the subject, and the philosophy of consciousness, but avoids the jump into poststructuralist or postmodern skepticism. In a narrow sense, the term "postmetaphysical" means that philosophy gives up the attempt to compete with or transcend the individual sciences, adopting instead a more modest ancillary and collaborative role. This change of orientation goes along with a shift of focus from consciousness to language (in analytical philosophy, structuralism, and even Habermas's own theory) from abstract universalism to an awareness of context and culture and finally to a sense of the rootedness of our cognitive activities in our life practice—in, for example, pragmatist philosophy, cognitive psychology, and the sociology of knowledge.

Attempts to rehabilitate metaphysics, whether in the traditional mode of transcendental philosophy, as in the work of Dieter Henrich, or in more innovative and fashionable variants building on Heidegger's later philosophy, attribute to philosophy a privileged method and domain which it can no longer aspire to without anachronism. In opposition to this love-hate relationship to metaphysics found in some contemporary philosophy, a more genuinely antimetaphysical radical contextualism is represented by Richard Rorty's neopragmatism. But where Rorty claims that we cannot mean by truth anything more than truth "for us," though we can aim to extend the scope of "us" by pursuing intersubjective agreement, Habermas argues that we could not understand the way we criticize and modify our established standards of rationality and justification if we did not take seriously the idea of a possible consensus which would transcend the opposition of us and them.

In social theory, Habermas argues, the current valorization of contradiction and difference derives partly from a still unclarified relation to metaphysics, but even more to a recognition of the complexity, differentiation, and decenteredness of modern societies, in which the state no longer acts as a center for social functions and *"everything* appears to have become part of the periphery." Yet we cannot sustain our own self-understanding without a corresponding image of our societies and their possible futures; even a decentered society needs as a reference point "the projected unity of an intersubjectively formed common will." Thus Habermas aims "to make plausible a weak yet not defeatist concept of linguistically embodied reason" which preserves from the metaphysical tradition the ideas of the rational understanding of reality and the unconstrained harmony of individual and society in a way which is skeptical and fallibilist enough to fit the reality of the contemporary situation.

The essays in this volume range widely, from the themes summarized above to a dense essay on the theory of meaning which leads into the foundation of Habermas's theory of communicative action and an "excursion" into literary criticism which examines the notion of levels of reality in the work of Italo Calvino. More directly sociological concerns are addressed in the essays on Peirce and **"Mead's Theory of Subjectivity,"** which bring out Habermas's cre-

ative incorporation of the pragmatist tradition. The Mead essay concludes with some fascinating conjectures about the interrelations between individuation and socialization, and individualism and social constraint, in contemporary welfare capitalism.

Per Fjelstad (review date November 1994)

SOURCE: A review of *Postmetaphysical Thinking* and *Philosophical Interventions in the Unfinished Project of Enlightenment,* in *The Quarterly Journal of Speech,* Vol. 80, No. 4, November, 1994, pp. 500-03.

[*In the following review of a festschrift dedicated to Habermas and* Postmetaphysical Thinking, *Fjelstad examines the "communicative implications" of Habermas's notion of "the self-hood of the individual" in the philosopher's book.*]

Jürgen Habermas has afforded the self-hood of individuals a remarkably central place in his philosophy of social life. This commitment is not always evident, given Habermas's better known attention to the ideal of universal consensus and to the pragmatics of *general* social norms. Still, his communicative model equally values claims to truth, rightness, and truthfulness. By claiming truthfulness, communicators assume responsibility for the selves they proclaim to be. Two recent books, one a collection of essays by Habermas, the other a festschrift dedicated to him on his sixtieth birthday, develop the communicative implications of such self-hood in a way not discernible in earlier works by and about the theorist.

On its surface, *Philosophical Interventions in the Unfinished Project of the Enlightenment* thematizes self-hood, as all honorific works do, by celebrating the person and life of Jürgen Habermas. At issue generically are the implications of his work: its consistency and inconsistencies; its development over time; and its relationship as a whole to the ideas and agendas of other writers. Yet the contributors refrain, as one would expect, from dwelling on the person or the personality of Habermas. They take his work as a starting point from which to develop and question epistemological premises. Habermas's particular accomplishments are present by being absent, assumed and implied in the rationales of these original essays. The Habermas reader will recognize those theoretical traces, underplayed as they are, and see the many things that can be done with such beginnings.

The first essays in *Philosophical Interventions* trace lines of philosophical heritage. Michael Theunissen shows that the intellectual tradition Plato inherited despised processes of development; philosophy spurned signs and semblances of life. Dieter Henrich finds in the work of Friedrich Jacobi an emerging theory of the acting subject. Charles Taylor distinguishes between acultural and cultural theories of modernity to explain the particular inward-turning of the self in modern western society: reason disciplines the "self" in isolation from body and cosmos; the self engages in a reflexive search for personal identity and inner being. Taylor suggests that recent theories of subjectivity and agency grew out of that cultural tradition.

In the next section of the festschrift, Ernst Tugenhat, Karl-Otto Apel, Albrecht Wellmer and Peter Bürger extend and apply Habermas's theoretical principles. Wellmer, for instance, broadens the requirements for comprehending validity claims beyond the structural conditions Habermas proposed. In addition to knowledge of illocutionary form, Wellmer describes a knowledge of situational and pragmatic substance. He suggests that conditions of acceptability vary according to the content that speakers assert. Similarly, the normative knowledge built into advice is deeply situational; such evaluation is not an "*additional* validity claim" (emphasis in original). Rather it is a "normative understanding of the situation that the speaker relies on without thematizing it". Wellmer proposes a theory of validity inherently rhetorical.

In the final section of the festschrift, Thomas McCarthy, Martin Jay, Richard Bernstin and Herbert Schnädelbach defend Habermas against, and expose him to, certain postmodern critiques. Jay examines Habermas's criterion of performative consistency, a standard Habermas invokes most obviously when accusing others of using reason to debunk the validity of reason. A performative contradiction exists "when whatever is being claimed is at odds with the presuppositions or implications of the act of claiming it". While Jay professes a lingering fascination with the possibly unresolvable contradictoriness of actual life, he defends Habermas's zeal for performative consistency against challenges by Michel Foucault, Rodolphe Gasché and Paul de Man. Jay upholds Habermas's claim that *parole* may have a discernible structure and his distinction between literary and philosophical rhetorics. These guidelines could hold communicative agency to the criterion of consistency, even if the individuating constructs of subjectivity and consciousness evaporate as illusory.

These essays form a frame for reading Habermas. They historicize and theorize the problem of human subjectivity, especially as this informs perceptions of action. They review and develop the pragmatic communicative norms that Habermas used to judge validity. They summarize challenges that postmodern theories pose for the Enlightenment project, particularly for Habermas's variant thereof. The essays function as testament to Habermas's influence and to the provocative fertility of his thought. They sketch a philosophy as much concerned with human action and interaction as with the ideals of truth and validity.

The editors of the festschrift selected primarily philosophers to be contributors. One author out of eleven is a historian; one other is an art critic. Given the breadth of Habermas's readership, this concentration of expertise positions the book narrowly. It canonizes Habermas in the philosophical literature, while down playing the cross-disciplinary value of his work. The book also assumes extensive knowledge of Habermas's writings, especially if readers are to appreciate the way the essays frame and extend Habermas's work.

Habermas's own philosophical reflections, first published in 1988 and now in translation, serve a different function and address a different readership. [*Postmetaphysical Thinking*] studies the "aging of modernity". Modern philosophy, that effort early this century to break with the totalizing tradition of metaphysics, is itself undergoing change. Habermas suggests that philosophy, like recent architecture, might also be returning to the "historical decoration" and "ornamentation" it once so proudly had disclaimed. Insofar as philosophers find themselves on that road, they may need to reask what today still constitutes "postmetaphysical thinking".

Habermas reviews the tradition of metaphysical philosophy since Kant. This tradition grounds subjectivity in a subject's "relation to, and understanding, of itself". Habermas refers to Dieter Henrich, a contributor to the festschrift reviewed above, as a contemporary illustration of the metaphysical orientation. Henrich inquires "how a life that is *conscious* and originarily [sic] at home with itself can be maintained". Metaphysical thinkers account for the tenability of consciousness, in fact the possibility of moral consciousness and common sense, in a world transformed by the successes of specialized sciences.

Habermas goes on to list three ways that the philosophical illumination of common sense has been affected by the onset of modernity. Philosophy no longer stands as the source or measure of rationality in relation to other existing fields of inquiry. It must restrict its claim of knowledge to theoretical issues rather than pedagogical, moral, or practical ones. It must restrict its judgment of lifeworlds to the general structures that these all share. Thus while philosophy still can pursue metaphysical lines of inquiry, in the sense that these assess the conditions of possibility for consciousness and common sense, these assessments will gain or lose their validity within a modernist field of inquiry that rejects proofs merely intellective.

Habermas affirms Henrich's preference for metaphysical analyses of self-reflexivity over its apparent opposite, naturalism. Applying this metaphysical orientation to the analysis to communication systems requires a shift of attention to the *interactive* reflexivity of utterances. This paradigm shift resolves the dilemma of the self being able to recognize itself only by objectifying itself. Instead the self belongs to a performative relationship established when "the speaker takes up the second-person perspective of a hearer toward the speaker". Postmetaphysical thought defines itself primarily as procedural, as language-analytical, and as the activity of situating reason in the world.

Habermas reviews the "turn to pragmatics" in modern theories of language and communication. He refers to Karl Bühler's trichotomy between functional modes of linguistic meaning: expression, representation, and appeal. He contends that contemporary theories of meaning focus singularly upon one or another of those functions. Habermas claims that his theory treats the functions in conjunction with one another.

In a special essay added to this English translation, Habermas observes that Charles Sanders Peirce had an early interest in the intersubjectivity implied by exchangable personal pronouns. Instead of following that route, however, Peirce developed a theory of semiotics in which consciousness and purpose were incidental to interpretation. Peirce explained the openness and flexibility of language by subsuming it in the larger evolutionary process of semiotics. Habermas argues that Peirce strayed from his original insight that language was performative. Thus he eliminated those features that make human communication specifically human, features that make individuality and unique utterances desirable accomplishments.

Habermas then takes up his theory that individuality is a developmental complement to sociality. He suggests that the One and the Many have always stood, and should stand, in a philosophically productive relationship to one another. Still the nature of this relationship is neither clear nor obvious. The metaphysical tradition identifies all particulars by subsuming them to universals and thus constrains the modes in which someone can be individual: "No place remains for the ego *qua* individual person between the ego as something universal and the ego as something particular".

Modern theories of subjectivity allow Habermas to join the particularities of the Many and the generality of the One in an evolving communicative dynamic. Neither the One nor the Many exists outside history. Thus the presumed universality of reason is precarious and at risk. Habermas compares its stability to the "rocking hull" of a ship: "it does not go under the sea of contingencies, even if shuddering in high seas is the only mode in which it 'copes' with these contingencies".

Habermas takes Mead's theory of social formation to define the subjectivity of individuals in and through their relationship to others. Mead pictures individuation "as a linguistically mediated process of socialization and the simultaneous constitution of a life-history that is conscious of itself". This formation of individuality is not just any manifestation of selfhood. Performative interaction demands a specifically "nonconventional ego-identity". The speaker "cannot *in actu* rid himself of his irreplaceability, cannot take refuge in the anonymity of a third person, but must lay claim to recognition as an individuated being". Being an "I" in a communicative interaction necessarily signifies more than the ability to adopt a role.

The individual takes responsibility in speech for his or her own life history. In fact, an idealization of individuality comes into play related to "the guarantee I consciously give, in light of a considered individual life project, for the continuity of my life history". Constitutive features of that ideal are irreplaceability, autonomy, spontaneity, and responsibility for a life history. This ideal of individuality, obviously unmet in actual communicative experience, belongs implicitly and necessarily to the pragmatic structure of language.

Ulrich Beck's social analysis (*Risikogesellschaft*, Frankfurt, 1986), finds that contemporary society increasingly requires people to shape themselves in multiple and fragmented dimensions of social life. Following Beck's communicatively derived criterion of individuality, Habermas concludes that such society singularizes, i.e. atomizes, but does not individualize persons or choices.

Habermas's ideal of selfhood should not predestine a culture to be "individualistic" in any way opposite to being "collectivistic". Habermas exposes that dichotomy as false by locating the possibility of individuation in the communicative function of socialization. The speaker develops a conception of a self who can act, an "I", only through communicative performances in which the speaker gleans renderings from others about their perceptions of the speaker's own and individual "me". These renderings, however, that contribute to the reflectively knowable contours of the acting self, are only communicable, and thus realizable, in the language available for normative and descriptive generalizations. Individuation thus is a consequence, not an opposite, of increased abstraction in a culture.

Habermas's theory enriches and orients analyses of communication. It provides a linguistic model for linking everyday communication with theoretically self-reflective discourse. Rather than excluding one another, these forms of communication belong to a gradated map of the same basic activity. On the basis of this model, Habermas's theory offers the prospect of universal pragmatic standards against which critics might evaluate the legitimacy of communicative practices.

Habermas's theory remains underdeveloped, particularly when showing the communicative basis for normative standards. Habermas bases many of his claims about inter-subjectivity on the symmetrical reciprocity of pronouns and on the structurally analyzable pragmatics of speech acts. One is left wondering how fully Habermas's model will be sustained by empirical analyses and supported by other theories of communicative interaction. Until such work is done, however, Habermas's attempt to idealize contexts for subjective expression will remain alluring. His theory should interest us, both because of what it develops and what it leaves for communication scholars to do.

The two books reviewed here propose a mode of reflective discourse that is pragmatically philosophical. The authors neither privilege the word "rhetoric" nor expound on the incomparable uniqueness of situations. Instead they privilege a mode of discourse that abstracts and generalizes, one that posits the possibility of universal communicative norms. Even so, this philosophy calls for an engagement of our subjectivity that is highly personal, irreplaceable and socially formed. The philosophy beckons us to reevaluate the place of persons within the larger project of knowing.

Such thinking about the subject's position in speech imbues all communicative action with implicit accountability. The speaker takes on responsibility, not only to acknowledge relevant social norms and objective facts, but also, in her presentation of self, to be herself. The theories suggested here allow one to explain interest in personal "authenticity" without debunking that interest as decadent or glamorizing it as redemptive.

Dieter Misgeld (review date March 1995)

SOURCE: A review of *Justification and Application,* in *The Review of Metaphysics,* Vol. XLVIII, No. 3, March, 1995, pp. 657-58.

[*In the review below, Misgeld describes the themes of* Justification and Application.]

In all of his works Habermas pursues the elucidation of the modern age ("modernity") and of the principles and processes constitutive of it. The affirmation of modernity and its critique are integral to the elucidation. [***Justification and Application***] also pursues these themes. It is a collection of four recently published essays, all dealing with the issue of ethics, and concludes with a long and informative interview. There is also a lengthy, useful introduction by the translator. The translation is adequate, even good. The theme of the essays is the possibility of a "discourse theory of morality." This theory is largely a form of deontological cognitivist

metaethics defending a "universalistic concept of morality." The essays fit together thematically and are more lucid than a few earlier writings by Habermas on the same topic.

The first essay introduces a distinction between ethical and moral discourse, singling out the second as the discourse in which universal moral judgments can be justifiably made. Essays 2 and 3 more or less cover the same terrain, developing a critique of contemporary contextualist and other moral theories (including those of Alasdair MacIntyre, Charles Taylor, Bernard Williams, John Rawls, Karl O. Apel). Essay 2 (**"Remarks on Discourse Ethics"**) is the more important of the two It largely reads like a lecture, in which Habermas discusses his well known and controversial theories of validity—claims, rationality, and justification of the moral point of view as a communications—theoretically restated form of Kantian cognitive ethics. He also pays attention to a variety of more specific problems, such as the relation between rights, and duties and the "primacy of the right over the good." Most of all, he draws a firm line between philosophical ethics as a theory of justification, clarifying the moral point of view, on the one hand, and "discourses of application," which determine the appropriateness of a universal norm to a particular situation, on the other.

Moral theory is part of the emancipatory history of modernity, insofar as some of its forms contributed to liberating public consciousness (in some societies) from dependence on specific cultural traditions and forms of life. They help call these traditions and ways of life into question. Discourse ethics attempts to radicalize this critical impulse by arguing that disputed norms can only be shown to be valid if they can command the voluntary assent of all affected by the norm. Thus a public process of criticism and debate is given pride of place in the resolution of moral disputes.

In his final essay, Habermas draws the conclusion that a discourse theory of morality is postmetaphysical. It gives primacy to the right to call conceptions of justice (and sometimes also those of the good) before the "tribunal of justificatory discourse," even if it cannot give an ultimate or unconditional reason for being moral. Modernity is affirmed as the epoch which has made it possible to approach questions of principles and norms as *open* questions. But it also encourages an argumentational and public process of seeking the *correct* solution to these questions. According to Habermas, recalling the Kantian tradition helps us to recover this will to rational justification.

Richard A. Posner (review date 6 May 1996)

SOURCE: "Law's Reason," in *The New Republic,* Vol. 214, May 6, 1996, pp. 26-30.

[*In the following review, Posner details Habermas's central laim in* Between Facts and Norms, *concluding with two criticisms and two questions.*]

Jürgen Habermas, who is professor emeritus of philosophy at Frankfurt University and is widely regarded as Germany's leading philosopher and social thinker, was a month short of his sixteenth birthday when Hitler's Reich collapsed. Shocked to learn of the Nazi atrocities, and free from any complicity in them, Habermas proceeded through the West German university system appalled by its unapologetic continuity with the past. Its philosophy departments, staffed mainly by professors who had served uncomplainingly during the Nazi period, looked up to Heidegger—whom Habermas has sarcastically described as the "felicitously de-Nazified Heidegger"—as the lodestar of German philosophy.

From these early experiences Habermas acquired a lifelong un-German distaste for the idea of German nationhood, for the German philosophical tradition insofar as it nourishes nationalism and political extremism of the right or the left (Habermas is a social democrat but not a socialist or a "Green"), and for totalizing theories of a religious or other metaphysical cast. He refuses to refer to the uniting of the two Germanies as the reunification of Germany, since that would imply a preexisting unity unfortunately sundered. He prefers to describe what happened in 1989 as the liberation of a people, the East Germans, who since 1933 had been denied civil liberties and the other legacies of the Enlightenment. He derides "the longing of many intellectuals for a lost German identity" as "kitsch," and says that "philosophers are not teachers of the nation. They can sometimes—if only rarely—be useful people."

For inspiration Habermas reaches back to Kant, who preceded the concept of a German nation and constructed his moral and political philosophy on universalistic foundations. But Habermas does not believe that Kant can simply be dusted off and put back into service. Kant and the other thinkers of the Enlightenment grounded their philosophy in metaphysical ideas that are unavailable in our predominantly secular, morally heterogeneous, socially complex, relativist and historicist era, in which "normative certainties must be maintained without metasocial guarantees." In place of the idea that each of us can use our God-given reason to construct an avenue of access to ultimate scientific and moral truths, Habermas has borrowed from the American pragmatist philosopher Charles Sanders Peirce and greatly elaborated the idea that truth, whether of a scientific, moral or political character, is most usefully regarded as what a community of rational, disinterested, undominated inquirers would arrive at if given all the time in the world. Communities of inquirers do not have all the time in the world, so the agreements they do arrive at are incomplete (non-unanimous), tentative and revisable: "the decision reached by the majority only represents a caesura in an ongoing discussion." But they are the best that we can hope for; and they are good enough.

Habermas calls this the theory of "communicative action" or "discourse theory," which "grounds the fallibilist assumption that results issuing from proper procedure are more or less reasonable." Being procedural rather than substantive, the theory supports his project of rejecting totalizing visions. Its aim is securing the preconditions for rational inquiry rather than anticipating the end of that inquiry. It is therefore interested in equality of incomes, say, not as a goal that might be derived from utlitarianism or Marxism or some other comprehensive moral or political theory, but only insofar as some measure of equality may be necessary to prevent the rationality of political debate from being distorted by money or may be adopted as the outcome of a political process founded on rational discourse. This approach bears the stamp of John Dewey, like Peirce an advocate of "epistemic" or "deliberative" democracy—the idea that truth, or, more precisely, warranted assertibility, can be modeled as the outcome of a "vote" of a community of free, equal and rational inquirers. The process must be protected, but it would be presumptuous under modern pluralist conditions to prescribe the outcome.

Discourse theory, as the subtitle of [***Between Facts and Norms***] suggests, is the master concept of this ambitious work of jurisprudence. But almost as important is the German jurisprudential tradition, or rather its limitations. That tradition is organized around the concepts of *Rechtsstaat* and *Sozialstaat* (Justice State and Social State). The first is the idea that government must operate exclusively through laws that in their administration by judges and other officials, as well as in their formulation by legislatures, abstract from the unique situations of particular persons or classes. Laws that enforce property rights regardless of consequence and without consideration of competing goals or interests are illustrative, for they are laws out of which every element of equitable discretion has been wrung. (And so plea bargaining is improper, which is still the official position in Germany, as in Europe generally.) Such a rigid conception of the rule of law eventually proved politically unrealistic and was modified in the direction of the *Sozialstaat*, which seeks to make "material," that is, operational, the merely "formal" rights created by the *Rechtsstaat*, and thus to narrow the gap between legal and social justice. It does this by creating flexibly administered entitlements—bureaucratically rather than judicially enforced—to public services, such as education.

Missing from both concepts is any reference to democracy; and this is the gap that Habermas believes discourse theory can fill. Formulated by Kant in eighteenth-century Prussia, an absolute monarchy at a time when England was already a constitutional monarchy, the *Rechtsstaat* is a theory of limited government rather than a theory of popular government, a theory, that is, in which the legitimacy of the law is grounded not in popular consent but solely in "the abstract rule structure of legal statues, the autonomy of the judiciary, as well as the fact that administration is bound by law and has a 'rational' construction." And the *Sozialstaat*, originating in Bismarck's authoritarian Reich, was paternalistic rather than popular, a device for diffusing social tensions. As Habermas points out, it has bred welfare dependency and other dysfunctions, and it is permanently in tension with the generalizing, abstract, formal, nondiscretionary character of *Rechtsstaat* norms.

Habermas's main criticism of the German legal tradition is that it failed to grasp the importance of democratic legitimacy. Yet he recognizes that the idea of legitimating law by reference to democracy is paradoxical. He is strongly committed to the core ideas of the *Rechtsstaat* and the *Sozialstaat*—that law is supposed to protect the people from the government and the weak people from the strong people. In a democracy, however, the people are the government, so how can the law protect the people from the government? And democracy means majority rule, which is the rule of the stronger, or at least the more numerous; and majorities sometimes like to coerce minorities.

The only grounding for a legitimate legal system in the modern world, and the only basis for law that survives Habermas's criticisms, is democracy. He claims to be able to dissolve the tension between democracy and law by approaching democracy from the direction of discourse theory.
—*Richard A. Posner*

Habermas's attempt to reconcile democracy with law begins with the proposition that law is, on the one hand, a part of social reality and, on the other hand, a part of the normative (moral) order, but that it is not fully one or the other. Among the reasons law is not simply a subset of moral duties is that it binds only the people who happen to be subject to a given legal system. And it employs coercion and thus secures the compliance even of people for whom law, or a particular law, is not morally obligating. It constrains only behavior, and thus "enforces norm-conformative behavior while leaving motives and attitudes open." Indeed, it "complements morality by relieving the individual of the cognitive burdens of forming her own moral judgments." It even creates a space in which people can opt out of certain moral duties—the duty to engage in communicative action, for example. For Habermas is emphatic that "legally granted liberties entitle one to *drop out* of communicative action"

and thus to live the unexamined life or the thoroughly private life. But at the same time he believes that law is not effective unless most people obey it not because they are coerced or bribed to do so, but because they accept the moral authority of the law. Law thus has two sides: "its positivity and its claim to rational acceptance." "Social rights," for example, "signify, from a *functionalist* viewpoint, the installation of welfare bureaucracies, whereas from a *normative* viewpoint they grant compensatory claims to a just share of social wealth."

But how is moral authority imparted to law? Habermas believes that all but one of the possible ways are disreputable (such as the tradition of the German *Volk*) or, since we live in a "post-metaphysical" world, unavailable. Habermas counts among modern "metaphysicians" of the law both John Rawls and Ronald Dworkin. Neither considers himself to hold a metaphysical conception of justice or law, but both their conceptions have substantive foundations and entailments, and, according to Habermas, "in a pluralistic society, the theory of justice can expect to be accepted by citizens only if it limits itself to a conception that is postmetaphysical in the strict sense, that is, only if it avoids taking sides in the contest of competing forms of life and worldviews." At the other end of the spectrum are the positivists, such as H. L. A. Hart, who give "priority to a narrowly conceived institutional history purged of any suprapositive validity basis," attributing "hard cases" (cases in which reason or justice clashes with rules validated by having been properly enacted by legally competent institutions) to "an unavoidable vagueness in ordinary language" that gives judges "a discretionary leeway" which they fill out "with extralegal preferences."

The only grounding for a legitimate legal system in the modern world, and the only basis for law that survives Habermas's criticisms, is democracy. He claims to be able to dissolve the tension between democracy and law by approaching democracy from the direction of discourse theory. Unlike populist or plebiscitary democracy, epistemic or deliberative democracy, which is the democracy of inquirers, presupposes both the negative liberties associated with the *Rechtsstaat* and the positive liberties associated with the *Sozialstaat*. If people are either intimidated or desperate, they will not be able to participate rationally in political debate. If they are neither, they will be able to participate rationally and the laws will be legitimate because produced by rational discourse. The laws secure the conditions for epistemic democracy, and epistemic democracy in turn secures the legitimacy of the laws. This is he book's central claim.

Habermas realizes that modeling the political process as a system of fully rational, fully disinterested inquiry may appear to be hopelessly unrealistic. Interest groups, the selective and distorting attentions of the media, public ignorance and apathy, and other interrelated social phenomena that neither the *Rechtsstaat* nor the *Sozialstaat* limits—indeed, that the *Rechtsstaat* fosters by creating the preconditions of capitalist development—deflect the political process from the deliberative ideal. Habermas wants to limit these distorting influences. Borrowing a leaf from the American constitutional theorist John Hart Ely, he considers the central (and virtually the only) task of constitutional law to be to secure "equal opportunities for the political use of communicative freedoms." His criticism of Ely is that Ely takes it for granted that we know what "democracy" is; he has no theory. Habermas's criticism of other American constitutional theories is that they are undemocratic. They cast the Supreme Court in the role of "a pedagogical guardian or regent" of an incompetent "sovereign," the people. "The addressees of law would not be able to understand themselves as its authors if the legislator [or judge] were to discover human rights as pregiven moral facts that merely need to be enacted as positive law."

Consistent with these criticisms, Habermas, who is no utopian dreamer, believes that there is too much hand-wringing over the imperfections of political democracy. The fact that political parties are coalitions of disparate interests makes it difficult for a politician to formulate his appeal for votes in terms limited to the narrow interests of the members of his coalition. He is constrained to speak in broader terms of principle, and this forces the voting public, too, to think in terms of principle. It may even nudge the politician into taking a public-spirited position for the sake of consistency: "concealing publicly indefensible interests behind pretended moral or ethical reasons necessitates self-bindings that . . . lead to the inclusion of others' interests."

And people form their views about political questions not only by listening to politicians and media pundits, but also by reflection on personal and social experiences acquired in the family, at work, in political or cultural movements, and in other voluntary non-political associations. This competition in points of view enables people to form political opinions that are authentically their own. Habermas rejects the view that people are "'cultural dopes' who are manipulated by the [television] programs offered to them." Yet he is not so naïve as to suppose that self-interest can be eliminated from the political process. Quite the contrary, it is because of the "weak motivating force of good reasons" that law has its irreducible "factive" as well as normative component. "Bargaining processes are tailored for situations in which social power relations cannot be neutralized in the way rational discourses presuppose." Compromises arrived at through bargaining rather than consensus are legitimate so long as the bargaining interests have equal power and therefore "equal chances of prevailing." This is another basis for

redistributive policies viewed not as ends in themselves but as procedural preconditions for legitimate law.

Habermas intimates, without quite saying, that the political process in democratic nations such as the United States and Germany is sufficiently deliberative, in part because of the network of positive and negative liberties that are among the essential conditions of democratic deliberation, to impart the minimum necessary legitimacy to the legal systems of these nations. So while he is concerned about the influence of moneyed interests and other "normatively unfiltered interest positions" on the political process, and would like to see that influence reduced, the tone of Habermas's **Between Facts and Norms** is moderate and hopeful.

This will not endear him to radicals. His response to the claim by radical feminists that it is not enough for the law to give women the same rights as men is that the law should make sure that women have the political and economic independence necessary to enable them to participate actively in the political process. He is unwilling to prescribe a particular outcome of that process, and he is mindful of the downside of legal activism. "What is meant to promote the equal status of women in general often benefits only one category of (already privileged) women at the cost of another category, because gender-specific inequalities are correlated in a complex and obscure manner with membership in other underprivileged groups."

I have described, summarized and quoted at such length in order to make a little more accessible a book that, in its density, its abstractness, its unfamiliar terminology (such as "lifeworld," "autopoiesis," "thematize" and "materialized law"), its lengthy discussions of obscure German legal and social theorists, and its translation into a clumsy, Teutonic-sounding English, makes inordinate demands on an American reader. It is unfortunate that the book is so difficult. It is a fascinating synthesis of Continental and Anglo-American legal theory, and it is full of interesting insights, acute criticisms and striking passages, such as the observation that the parties to Hobbes's social contract "transfer their unrestricted liberties to a state authority, which gathers up the scattered anarchic potentials for violence and puts them to work for the disciplinary enforcement of legally restricted liberties."

I have two criticisms and two questions. The first criticism is that the book exaggerates the extent to which legislative enactments or even judicial decisions can be regarded as the outcome of rational discourse. The subject matter of the law is often, perhaps typically, too emotional or too freighted with uncertainty (or both) for the participants in the enacting or decisional process to be able to reach even tentative agreement. Peirce, a scientist as well as a philosopher, modeled his ideal of the deliberating community on the scientific community, in which the criteria of validity are agreed upon and operational, enabling the community to reach the nirvana of "observer independence," where people having different values and perspectives are brought into an uncoerced agreement.

The political community is not like that. The criteria for decisions are contested and vague. The outcomes of legislative "deliberations" usually reflect compromises between bargaining interests with unequal power or opportunistic coalitions (as when religious fundamentalists and radical feminists agree to support a ban on pornography), or divergent estimates of consequences, as when both liberals and conservatives agree to reduce sentencing discretion, the former in the hope that it will reduce unjust disparities and discriminations, the latter in the hope that it will lead to longer sentences. Unbridgeable gaps in values and perceptions are visible in many split judicial decisions as well. Habermas thinks it very important to equalize bargaining power between groups, but does not explain how that can be done or even what "equal bargaining power" means.

When stakes are high and information is sparse, people do not simply yield to the weight of argument. Habermas himself warns against "avant-gardism," the "consensually veiled domination of intellectual spokespersons. Powerful in word, they grab for themselves the very power they profess to dissolve in the medium of the word." Elsewhere he distinguishes between "discourse," where agreement is secured through the force of argument, and aesthetic evaluations, which are not expected to convince all doubters even if there is no time limit on deliberation. Political and judicial disagreements—in my view, contrary to Habermas's—are more often of this kind than of the discourse kind, where disagreement would dissolve if only deliberation continued long enough.

It would be odd to insist, for example, that the prohibition of police torture be justified by a weighing of the arguments pro and con. The reasons that are given for the prohibition—that it makes the police lazy, or brutalizes them, or produces false information—are makeweights that do not really "outweigh" the fact that torture is a generally effective method of eliciting information. The revulsion against the practice can be rationalized in highfalutin' terms, by defining a human essence that torture violates, but actually the revulsion is based on history, or emotion, or how we are brought up (to be squeamish), rather than on arguments. This doesn't mean it isn't a reliable basis for action. But academia selects for people who attach unusual weight to arguments. Only academics can be *argued* into becoming, say, vegetarians.

Torture, like slavery, is an easy case, because at the moment it has no advocates. Many of the issues that are on the legislative and judicial agendas today can be resolved neither by a convergence of values nor by discourse, but only by power, or by the sorts of nonrational persuasions, or emotional demonstrations or manipulations, that produce religious-style conversions and other Gestalt switches, or by giving people information that corrects misconceptions. Only the last of these has a secure footing in discourse theory, though Habermas himself does not exhibit an interest in facts.

My second criticism is that Habermas's lack of concreteness makes it difficult to determine whether discourse theory has any practical significance. Habermas thinks that it is vital, in the interest of discourse, to place "curbs on the power of the media." But he does not explain what those curbs might be, or how they would be consistent with the preservation of freedom of expression—one of the liberties that undergirds the democratic legitimacy of the law—or why curbs are necessary, given the increasing competitiveness and diversity of the media and his own rejection of the view that people are cultural dopes. He favors liberal immigration policies on the pragmatic ground that multiplying perspectives aids the search for truth and justice. But he does not consider the effect on the likelihood of forging consensus of admitting large numbers of people whose values were shaped in societies that do not believe in the resolution of conflict by deliberative means. People from different "lifeworlds" have difficulty communicating, let along achieving even temporary consensus.

Not only is Habermas weak on particulars; he never makes clear how much deviation from the tenets of discourse theory a political system can be permitted without losing its legitimacy. Which brings me to the first of my two questions. What exactly is the problem to which Habermas's theory of law is the solution? He might answer that it is the problem of law's legitimacy. I am not sure that there is such a problem in the United States or most other wealthy countries. He says that "law must do more than simply meet the functional requirements of a complex society; it must also satisfy the precarious conditions of a social integration that ultimately takes place through the achievements of mutual understanding on the part of communicatively acting subjects." Yet if law meets "the functional requirements of a complex society" by providing a reasonably predictable, adaptable and just framework for peaceful social interactions, where "just" means nothing more pretentious than consistent with durable public opinion, who is going to raise an issue of legitimacy about the framework, that is, about the law itself?

Particular laws, particular judicial decisions and particular enforcement decisions and institutional details will sometimes be challenged as illegitimate. An example would be a decision by a judge who had been bribed, or, more subtly, a judicial decision that rested on arguments that the legal culture ruled out of bounds for judges. Particular groups in society may feel disserved, even discriminated against, by the people who enforce and administer the law. These retail issues of legitimacy can be serious, but they do not seem to be illuminated by discourse theory. The wholesale issue—the legitimacy of *the law*—does not arise. A successful practice does not require foundations. That is the abiding lesson of pragmatism.

An entire legal system could be illegitimate even though most people were unaware of the fact. But if the system is legitimate (as Habermas believes) *and* no one of consequence doubts this, then what precisely is the point of trying to prove it? But before discounting Habermas's book as academic in the pejorative sense, we should recall its cultural context. Habermas's universalism speaks far more to the German situation than to that of most other developed nations, including the United States. Americans do not need to be instructed in the values of diversity, the unavailability of "metaphysical" groundings for political principles, the importance of democracy, or the preconditions for legitimate political institutions. These things are the features of our "lifeworld," the taken-for-granted background of discussion and debate.

The Germany in which Habermas grew up, by contrast, did not have a secure, untroubled relation to diversity, democracy, reason or law. That Germany seemed dangerously susceptible to totalizing visions, stifling cultural conformity, ethnocentrism, irrationalism, political extremism and, in law, to excessive formalism on the one hand and excessive paternalism on the other. Against all these tendencies, which are much weaker fifty years after the fall of Hitler but have been given a shot in the arm by the unification of the two Germanies, **Between Facts and Norms** is a powerful polemic. We Americans are fortunate in not needing it so badly.

Maybe Kant was wrong. Maybe jurisprudence is an unavoidably ethnocentric enterprise. If so, my second question need not arise. That question is, how can law be democracy's foundation and democracy be law's foundation? It is a circle without a beginning or a foundation. How much easier it would be just to say that in our system, which is also the system of our peer nations such as Germany, law and democracy exist in a creative, mutually supporting and stable tension.

Cass R. Sunstein (review date 18 August 1996)

SOURCE: "Democracy Isn't What You Think," in *The New York Times Book Review,* August 18, 1996, p. 18.

[*Below, Sunstein reviews the question of political legitimacy addressed in* Between Facts and Norms, *especially Habermas's concept of "deliberative democracy."*]

Most people know that the Constitution's First Amendment provides the rights to freedom of speech and to the free exercise of religion. But in the first Congress some people seriously proposed that the First Amendment should contain another right: the right on the part of constituents "to instruct" their representatives how to vote. The first Congress ultimately rejected the proposal. Roger Sherman made the central argument against it. In Sherman's view, representatives had a "duty to meet others from the different parts of the Union, and consult. . . . If they were to be guided by instructions, there would be no use in deliberation." A right to instruct "would destroy the object of the meeting."

By rejecting the right to instruct, the first Congress affirmed a distinctive concept of politics. It favored what might be called a deliberative democracy, in which representatives would be accountable to the people but also operate as part of a process that prized discussion and reflection about potential courses of action.

Jürgen Habermas is one of the most important political philosophers of the 20th century: he has been preoccupied for much of his life with the problem of political legitimacy. Under what circumstances is it legitimate for political authorities, mere human beings, to exercise power over other human beings? It is unsurprising that a German philosopher—in his teens during the Nazi period and a witness to countless other atrocities since—should direct his attention to this question. Mr. Habermas thinks that the question is especially urgent in an era that is "postmetaphysical," in the sense that it has lost the sense that we have wholly external foundations by which to ground our judgments and choices. Whether or not we believe that God exists, it seems clear that as citizens in a heterogeneous society we must proceed on the understanding that our choices are our own. But even as he insists on this point, Mr. Habermas draws a line against modern irrationalists, many of them—like Michel Foucault and Jacques Derrida—influential within the modern academy. Mr. Habermas says, tellingly, that those who oppose reason and the Enlightenment can give no account of the basis for their own rhetoric, which seems inspired by the Enlightenment commitment to human liberation.

In his influential past work, Mr. Habermas offered a "theory of communicative action" whose centerpiece is the "ideal speech situation." In the ideal speech situation, all participants have equal power, attempt to reach understanding, do not act manipulatively or strategically, and understand their obligation to offer reasons. In this situation, outcomes depend on what he calls "the unforced force of the better argument."

This is abstract stuff, and for many years Americans, Germans and many others have been interested in the real-world implications of Mr. Habermas's work. For example: Can we derive a set of rights from those ideas? Real-world politics is far from the ideal speech situation; might that notion bear on the obligations of the mass media, on issues of race and sex, on campaign finance law? Mr. Habermas's new book, ***Between Facts and Norms,*** is both the culmination of a lifetime of thought about political legitimacy and his effort to bring his argument closer down to earth by developing new understandings of law, democracy and the relationship between them.

Much of Mr. Habermas's analysis urns on an exploration of two accounts of democracy, which he labels "liberal" and "civic republican." Under the liberal account, rooted in the work of Thomas Hobbes, politics is a process of bargaining, a matter of aggregating private interests. Liberals define citizens as holders of negative rights against the state. In the liberal view, politics is a struggle among interest groups for position and power. The civic republican account, rooted in Aristotle and Rousseau, is very different: politics is not a mere matter of protecting our selfish interests but instead an effort to choose and implement our shared ideals. Civic republicans see rights not as negative constraints on government, but as promoting participation in political practices through which citizens become authors of their own community. Consider the right to free speech and the right to vote. For civic republicans, politics is a matter of discussion and self-legislation, in which people participate not in bargaining and compromise but in forms of reflection and talk.

The organizing theme of the book is Mr. Habermas's rejection of both views and his effort to defend instead what he calls "deliberative politics" or "deliberative democracy." This is emphatically a procedural ideal. It is intended to give form to the notion of an ideal speech situation. Like civic republicans, deliberative democrats place a high premium on reason-giving in the public domain. But like liberals, they favor a firm boundary between the state and the society, and they insist on a robust set of constraints on what the government can do. Mr. Habermas sees majority rule not as a mere statistical affair, an effort to tally up votes, but instead as a large social process by which people discuss matters, understand one another, try to persuade each other and modify their views to meet counterarguments. In this way we form our beliefs and even our desires.

The deliberative conception of democracy anchors Mr. Habermas's theory of political legitimacy. For him, democracy does not exist to secure rights with which we have been endowed by our Creator; nor is it simply a way to allow us to throw the rascals out; nor is it a mechanism for processes of accommodation, compromise and the exercise of power.

Democracy, ideally conceived is a process by which people do not implement their preferences but consult and deliberate about what values and what options are best.

Mr. Habermas's argument sees constitutional law as institutionalizing the presuppositions of a system of discussion by which legitimate lawmaking is made possible. Thus his account of fundamental rights includes the right to "equal opportunities to participate in processes of opinion and will-formation in which citizens exercise their *political autonomy* and through which they generate legitimate law."

Mr. Habermas thinks that the principal goal of a court, interpreting a constitution, should be to protect the procedural preconditions for deliberative democracy. The point suggests an especially aggressive role for courts when democratic processes do not fit with the aspirations to deliberation and democracy—for example, when people are excluded from politics, or when outcomes reflect power and pressure rather than reason. This is how Mr. Habermas tries to reconcile the tension between law and democracy, seeing them not as opposed but instead as mutually supportive. Law can create the preconditions for democracy, by insuring freedom of speech, voting rights, political equality and so forth. Democratic ideals can inform the appropriate content of law.

Mr. Habermas isn't a lot of fun to read (despite a clear translation from the German by William Rehg). He offers little in the way of summary and guide-posts to help readers see the main lines of argument. His analysis is abstract, turgid and filled with short, puzzling discussions of a dazzling variety of German and American thinkers. The book raises substantive questions, too. What Mr. Habermas calls the liberal account of democracy does not capture the liberal political tradition; John Stuart Mill, John Dewey and John Rawls—to name three prominent liberals—are, in their ways, deliberative democrats too. And Mr. Habermas does not do a great deal to address the predictable concern that deliberative democracy should be constrained by a robust set of rights on what even a deliberative public might do.

For those interested in a deliberative approach to democracy, much future work lies not in abstractions but in more concrete thinking designed to help with concrete problems. American democracy, for example, is far from deliberative, and we might ask how to make it more so. Can the mass media—even the Internet—be harnessed to promote political deliberation? How can a deliberative democracy operate when there are huge disparities in both wealth and education? What sorts of constraints should be imposed on the permissible substance and form of public talk? Should we strengthen local democracy? Mr. Habermas does not much take up these issues.

But this is a work of political philosophy, dealing with the foundations of democratic theory, and as such it has great value, above all because of its careful exposition of deliberative democracy and the potential for productive interactions between democracy and law. The 20th century is ending at a time when democratic aspirations are proliferating throughout the globe; Jürgen Habermas has provided one of the best and, I think, most enduring accounts of the values that underlie those aspirations.

Timothy Dykstal (review date Fall 1996)

SOURCE: A review of *The Past as Future*, in *Southern Humanities Review,* Vol. 30, Fall, 1996, pp. 375-79.

[In the review below, Dykstal questions Habermas's standard of "the norm" in The Past as Future.*]*

Conversation is indispensable to Jürgen Habermas. In the German philosopher's "theory of communicative action," the values that sustain a good conversation—that is, one that produces greater understanding—are perhaps the only transhistorical imperative that we have. We speak in order to be understood, and we can use that desire for understanding to criticize whatever—from material deprivations to immaterial, or ideological, distortions—would defeat it. Given the indispensability of conversation to Habermas, this interview with the German journalist Michael Haller, conducted between the close of 1990 and March 1991, and covering such topics as the Persian Gulf War, German unification, and the future of Europe, is something of an event. Habermas has given interviews before, but none as extensive or, paradoxically, as carefully articulated: paradoxically because, as Haller explains in his preface, the interview "was ultimately conducted by correspondence." If *The Past as Future* is not an actual conversation, then, it is still a dialogue, still benefitting from the "eminent capability and productivity of socially circulating everyday speech," which, as Habermas asserts, "is the only faculty that has grown adequate to extraordinarily complex tasks precisely because it remained nonspecialized, because it hasn't been forced to specialize." Habermas' interview with Haller exhibits the "unwavering, insistent thinking" called for by his mentor Adorno, but in "everyday," nonspecialized speech that makes his thought available to what he would call the "lifeworld."

The risk of the interview form, as Habermas worries more than Haller, however, is its sheer topicality. Habermas admits that he "was not enthusiastic" when his German publisher proposed issuing the interview in paperback, because "the rapid pace of current events"—including, since the first edition, the collapse of the Soviet Union and the outbreak of civil war in Yugoslavia—"had certainly not slowed," and he supplements the 1991 edition with a lecture on the so-

called "asylum debate" in Germany and an afterword. Yet Habermas need not have worried that his thoughts on contemporary topics would become so quickly dated: the situation of Germany (on which he and Haller naturally focus), looking back to a barely usable past and ahead to an uncertain future (made even more uncertain after unification), could stand for the situation of nearly every Western nation at the end of the Cold War. Habermas takes the title of the interview from an election slogan of German chancellor Helmut Kohl's ruling Christian Democratic party; he complains that the CDU's maxim "the past as future" encourages Germans to say, "Let's get it [that is, the past] over with," just as Konrad Adenauer and others "repressed" the immediate Nazi past after World War II. Habermas, however, by way of imagining a future, would have Germans "work through" their past: in this case, the immediate past of a divided Germany and the legacy of repression left by the former German Democratic Republic. Although Habermas emphasizes the particularism of the German situation—the sense of Germany as a nation, he explains, "emerged from the context of a war of liberation [from Napoleon], and thus remained ensnared in passionate notions of the uniqueness of culture and identity"—other nations are engaged in the same wrestlings with their pasts as his. Indeed, Habermas' description of the editors of the right-wing *Frankfurter Allgemeine Zeitung* who, "[a]rmed with saber-rattling ideas from the old young-conservative attic," are "ready to put paid to the '68ers," sounds remarkably like the new young conservatives in the United States who are ready to dismantle the 1960s counter-culture.

Habermas deploys his theory of communicative action against those postmodern skeptics who, suspicious of the claim of reason, sense "behind every universal validity claim the dogmatic will to domination of a cunningly concealed particularism." The desire for understanding that Habermas detects in conversation may, as Haller objects, lead to "sweeping" validity claims, but it cannot produce too-particular ones: we desire to understand the other as much as to be understood by him or her. But Haller also objects that Habermas has too idealistic a view of ordinary conversation. He points out (and Habermas concedes) that *their* dialogue is more "reasonable" than the passionate, topical debates taking place in the public sphere. There, people trade interests rather than ideas; there, "[i]t's rare for anyone to demand the better argument." How can practical "compromise building" serve as a theory for a saving rationality? Habermas replies that "these compromises are also rational, in the sense of a moral and practical procedural rationality," and that every sticking-point on the way to compromise building "can only be decided in a discourse about questions of justice." In other words, even the most practical debate appeals to local (or "procedural") standards of fairness, and, when compromise building breaks down, it can be built back up again only by grander, more theoretical debates about just how fair, or how universal, those standards really are. Allowing for the passions that sometimes inhibit debate, Habermas concludes, "I never say that people *want* to act communicatively, but that they *have to*."

A theory like Habermas' that concerns itself with what human beings have in common rather than, as is the academic fashion, with what makes them different, risks being accused of what Haller calls a "false universalism." Habermas is, after all, attempting to define what is "normative" in human behavior, even if his norm is limited to the expectations that we bring to the conversational table, and any definition of what is normal, as the philosophical discourse of postmodernity has taught us, excludes as much as it includes. Yet Habermas modestly claims that he is no master thinker, and he is sensitive to the crimes committed in the name of "normalcy" by those less modest than he. When the German public, or some factions of it, greet unification with the sigh, "we have finally become normal again," Habermas not only wonders about the moral ambiguity of the adverb "again"—are those sighing in relief referring to a Germany previously "united" by National Socialism?—he also worries that the rush to normalcy appeals, paradoxically, to a German "special consciousness" that would exclude from the newly unified nation political refugees and other immigrants from Eastern Europe, the Middle East, and Asia. Habermas' future can only be multicultural: his normalcy must come from that "overlapping consensus" that John Rawls finds among world moral and religious traditions, not from drawing the physical and ethnic borders around "Germany" ever tighter.

Habermas also guards against the accusation of false universalism by focusing his search for what is normative on the process of communicative action rather than the product. This is why testing his theory against the case of German unification, as Haller insists that he do, is so appropriate, for the product of unification—a nation-state not divided against itself—would seem to merit Habermas' approval. But Habermas is clearly uneasy about what he perceives as "the normative deficits of unification." In their rush to bring the GDR into the fold, Habermas protests, West German Chancellor Helmut Kohl and his burgher allies "managed to outmaneuver both the deeply divided opposition and the public sphere." They saw the unification process as merely the legal and administrative tinkering necessary to make what was already a "self-running economic mechanism" run more efficiently; they did *not* see it as an opportunity to persuade the German public of their own "better argument" for bringing the two Germanies together. In the process—or, rather, in the *lack* of a process—Kohl and his allies shortchanged, and may have irreparably damaged, "incalculable and exhaustible moral and cultural resources": those democratic traditions that Habermas is bold enough to attribute to Western rationality. Only public debate about ideas, not private or unconscious appeals to an-

cient ethnic and linguistic bonds, can create a unified nation of "citizens." Habermas may welcome the product of German unification, but doubts that the process by which it was achieved can forever sustain the ideals to which its leaders continue cynically to appeal.

For Habermas, in short, the process is the norm. But to state this is also to expose the weakness in his theory, a weakness that the German situation, if not necessarily Haller's scrutiny of it, reveals. One can imagine a German nation-state that has met the normative requirements of the unification process—that has discussed all that Habermas thinks it should discuss—and is yet repressive. Conversely, one can name certain democratic ideals—the right to dissent comes to mind—that the process of communicative action, with its emphasis on consensus, does not yield. There are norms that can be derived from the ideal speech act; there are also norms that have nothing to do with how we should treat one another in conversation, norms that may be called on to set things right when communicative action produces a result that, although agreed on by all parties, is still wrong. Terry Eagleton has compared Habermas' theory to the process of psychoanalysis, and, at certain times during this interview, the comparison is apt: discussing the tendency in the Western media to shy away from the crimes against humanity perpetrated by the Stasi, the East German secret police, Habermas—quoting Richard Schröder, a former leader of the resistance to the old regime—says that Westerners "have to let us [Easterners] tell them how it was, and at least listen, even if it's hard." Such a process may be therapeutic, but it is not emancipating: it may lessen the pain of the past, but it cannot prevent the crimes of the future. The skills that communicative action depends on—honest speaking and empathetic listening—are process skills; they do nothing to improve the ultimate product.

But, again, Habermas does not claim that his theory of communicative action *can* provide ultimate standards of worth. Since the shining moment of the public sphere, which he locates in early eighteenth-century Europe (and especially in England), the lifeworld has been "structurally transformed" into a series of specialized disciplines, each with its own standards of validity and each with its own ideas about how to meet those standards. Within the disciplines, the products of each can be improved; across the disciplines, standards of worth do not apply. At the conclusion of *The Past as Future,* it is clear that Habermas' hope for a post-unification politics, like his hope for a postmodern philosophy (previously expressed in his synoptic article **"Philosophy as Stand-In and Interpreter"**), is that it will function as a kind of mediator between the disciplines, or between the previously mentioned ethnic and linguistic communities. In politics, he envisions a Europe made up of both smaller and larger structural units, with the smaller defined by the sacred truths that divide them, and the larger units (perhaps as large as an entire European Union) defined by the democratic traditions—the communicative actions—that bring them together. In philosophy, Habermas envisions not a new metanarrative but only ways to practice "a little more solidarity." That conclusion ought to chasten those critics who would see him instituting, in the bleak vision of *Dialectic of Enlightenment,* a new world order of totalizing reason.

FURTHER READING

Criticism

Bauman, Zygmunt. "The Adventure of Modernity." *Times Literary Supplement,* No. 4376 (13 February 1987): 155.
    Favorably reviews *Autonomy and Solidarity,* identifying Habermas's work as "a staunch and resolute defence of the essential values and ambitions of modernity."

McCarthy, Thomas. "Kantian Constuctivism and Reconstructivism: Rawls and Habermas in Dialogue." *Ethics* 105, No. 1 (October 1994): 44-63.
    Dialectical comparison of John Rawl's theory of justice and Habermas's moral and political theory.

Poster, Mark. "Postmodernity and the Politics of Multiculturalism: The Lyotard-Habermas Debate over Social Theory." *Modern Fiction Studies* 38, No. 3 (Autumn 1992): 567-80.
    Discusses the pros and cons of "Habermassian universalism . . . and postmodernist differentialism."

Rosenfeld, Michael. "Law as Discourse: Bridging the Gap between Democracy and Rights." *Harvard Law Review* 108, No. 5 (March 1995): 1163-189.
    Contextualizes Habermas's discourse theory of law within contemporary legal, moral, and political philosophy. Rosenfeld investigates how theory relates democracy to rights, both ideally as a paradigm and practically as the role of judicial review in a constitutional democracy.

Review of *The Past as Future. Social Forces* 73, No. 3 (March 1995): 1191.
    States that "the book ably emphasizes the remarkable breadth of Habermas's concerns and the contemporary relevance of his thought."

"From Historicism to Marxist Humanism." *Times Literary Supplement,* No. 3510 (5 June 1969): 597-600.
    Overview of Habermas's early works—*Theory and Practice, Knowledge and Human Interests,* and *On the Logic of the Social Sciences*—situated in the context of mid-century German thought.

Additional coverage of Habermas's life and career is contained in the following sources published by Gale: *Contemporary Authors,* Vol. 109, and *Contemporary Issues Criticism,* Vol. 1.

Everything That Rises Must Converge
Flannery O'Connor

(Full name Mary Flannery O'Connor) American short story writer, novelist, and essayist.

The following entry presents criticism of O'Connor's short story collection *Everything That Rises Must Converge* (1965). For further information on O'Connor's life and career, see *CLC,* Volumes 1, 2, 3, 6, 10, 13, 15, 21, and 66.

INTRODUCTION

The title of O'Connor's *Everything That Rises Must Converge* is taken from Pierre Teilhard de Chardin's *The Phenomenon of Man.* The stories in the collection revolve around characters who are not prepared to accept God's grace. O'Connor's genre is very specific; she is a southern Catholic writer whose work is infused with southern and religious imagery.

Plot and Major Characters

Many of the characters in *Everything That Rises Must Converge* are similar types. The protagonist of the title story, Julian, is an educated, seemingly liberal, would-be writer who has had to resort to selling typewriters to make a living. He lives with his mother, another O'Connor archetype, a pretentious southern woman who is living in reduced circumstances. She struggles to keep her dignity and to dominate her son, for whom she has sacrificed everything. "The Enduring Chill" features Asbury, another would-be writer forced to move in with his mother. Like Julian, Asbury feels he has risen above the Southern environment in which he was raised. Also reminiscent of Julian, he is a would-be liberal whose attempts to befriend the African-American workers on his mother's dairy farm is more of a rebellion against his mother than a true affection or concern for the workers. The pompous middle-class woman is another frequent character in these stories. Represented by Julian's mother in the title story, Mrs. Turpin in "Revelation," and Mrs. May in "Greenleaf," each woman discovers that her belief in her own virtue and goodness is not enough for true grace. Simply avoiding evil is not enough for redemption in O'Connor's world. Intellectuals are also portrayed with little sympathy by O'Connor. Sheppard in "The Lame Shall Enter First" believes that intelligence and a good home life is enough to save Rufus, a club-footed juvenile delinquent whom he takes in and tries to redeem. Sheppard's blind devotion to ideas and intelligence causes him to be duped by Rufus and to lose his own son, Norton.

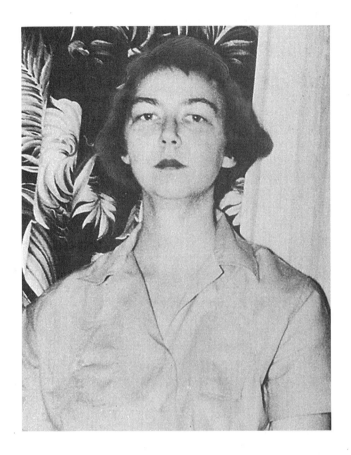

Major Themes

The major theme of *Everything That Rises Must Converge* is derived from Pierre Teilhard de Chardin's *The Phenomenon of Man.* In that work, the author asserts that all matter and spirit will eventually converge at what he refers to as the Omega point. The stories from this collection are about man's resistance to this convergence. O'Connor's characters use different methods to avoid convergence or union with mankind, including isolating themselves in intellectualism like Julian and Sheppard, or clinging to a romanticized version of the past like Julian's mother. It is only through the destruction of pride and false identities that O'Connor's characters have a chance at convergence or redemption, hence the violent climaxes of many of the stories: Julian loses his sense of superiority over and separation from his mother as he watches her die from a stroke; Sheppard realizes the error of his judgement when he finds his son hanging in the attic. Other themes in *Everything That Rises Must Converge* include Christians struggling to keep their faith and finding redemption in an increasingly secularized and technologically advancing world. A final theme in this collection focuses on capturing the changes of the South of the 1950s and 1960s. O'Connor traces her characters' relationship to the New South, delineating the continuing evolution of the region.

Critical Reception

Most critics discuss the relationship of *Everything That Rises Must Converge* to the ideas of Pierre Teilhard de Chardin. The title's obvious allusion to Teilhard de Chardin's work is commonly accepted; however, reviewers disagree about O'Connor's intentions. Some argue that she accepts Teilhard de Chardin's ideas, and the stories are her attempt to portray true convergence. Others, including Robert Fitzgerald in the Introduction to the work, assert that O'Connor uses the title ironically. Reviewers often note the irony and humor in the stories. In addition, many critics praise her storywriting skill and her ability to convey colloquialism and rural southern dialogue. Critics often discuss the grotesque and violent images in the stories, but many point out that the images are not gratuitous. Due to the imagery and setting of the stories, reviewers note a resemblance to the work of William Faulkner, but several assert that O'Connor's work is more representative of the New South than Faulkner's.

PRINCIPAL WORKS

Wise Blood (novel) 1952
A Good Man Is Hard to Find and Other Stories (short stories) 1955
The Violent Bear It Away (novel) 1960
Everything That Rises Must Converge (short stories) 1965
Mystery and Manners: Occasional Prose [edited by Sally and Robert Fitzgerald] (nonfiction) 1969
The Complete Stories of Flannery O'Connor (short stories) 1971
The Habit of Being: Letters of Flannery O'Connor (letters) 1979
The Presence of Grace and Other Book Reviews [compiled by Leo J. Zuber, edited by Carter W. Martin] (essays) 1983
Flannery O'Connor: Collected Works (fiction, criticism, letters) 1988
Flannery O'Connor: The Growing Craft—A Synoptic Variorum Edition of The Geranium, An Exile in the East, Getting Home, Judgement Day (short stories) 1993

CRITICISM

Granville Hicks (review date 29 May 1965)

SOURCE: "A Cold, Hard Look at Humankind," in *Saturday Review,* Vol. XLVIII, No. 2, May 29, 1965, pp. 23-4.

[*In the following review, Hicks discusses the lack of compassion in the stories in O'Connor's* Everything That Rises Must Converge.]

Flannery O'Connor died last summer in her fortieth year, having published two novels and a collection of short stories. She left enough short stories to make another collection, which has just been published: ***Everything That Rises Must Converge.***

Already a kind of Flannery O'Connor legend is taking shape. Much has been written about her since her death, and *Esprit,* published by the University of Scranton, has devoted most of an issue to praise of her work by distinguished men and women of letters. Certain themes are emphasized: her devotion to Catholicism, the toughness of character that permitted her to survive and to triumph as a writer while living on an isolated Georgia farm, the courage with which she endured a crippling and incurable disease, her constant preoccupation with her craft.

Certain of Flannery O'Connor's virtues—particularly her courage and her craftsmanship—cannot be exaggerated, but she was not, as some of her admirers seem to suggest, a candidate for sainthood. She was a devout and proud Catholic: "I am no disbeliever in spiritual purpose and no vague believer," she wrote in her essay in *The Living Novel,* and, "I see from the standpoint of Christian orthodoxy." Yet she refused to conform to the literary standards set up by many priests and laymen in the name of the Church. (See, for instance, the text of one of her lectures printed in *Greyfriar,* published by Siena College, Loudonville, New York.) She insisted on expressing her orthodoxy in her own way.

Similarly, although she was an extraordinarily independent young woman, living a kind of life that few contemporary writers would put up with, she was by no means a solitary. Friends and admirers visited her in Milledgeville, and she was cordial with them, even making small talk when that seemed called for, in the best Southern manner. She corresponded with literary people she found congenial, and her letters were lively and often gay. (*Shenandoah* for the winter of 1965 prints a collection of letters written to Richard H. Stern that reveal sides of Flannery O'Connor few people saw.) Difficult as travel was for her, she spoke at many colleges. She was in the world as much as she wanted to be, as much as was consonant with the state of her health and her integrity as a writer.

She grew steadily in her art, and the best of the stories in ***Everything That Rises*** are the best things she ever wrote. They are superb, and they are terrible. She took a cold, hard look at human beings, and she set down with marvelous precision what she saw.

In the title story we have a pretentious, empty-headed woman who is struggling to dominate her son, for whom, as she frequently reminds him, she has sacrificed everything. The reader's sympathies are at first altogether with the son, but slowly, ruthlessly, Miss O'Connor strips him bare. He is weak, selfish, confused, afraid of the freedom he pretends to desire. The unhappy resolution of the situation comes by way of a Negro woman, who is herself arrogant, bitter, and violent.

Miss O'Connor shows us a number of these pompous, self-satisfied, middle-class women. In **"Revelation"** she holds up for our appalled gaze a peculiarly outrageous specimen, and then contrives a situation in which the woman sees herself as we see her. In **"Greenleaf"** a hard-working, narrow-minded woman, who thinks of herself as the epitome of virtue, is pitted against a shiftless farmer, and loses the struggle.

The weak intellectual also appears in several stories. ("Intellectual" was not a flattering term in her vocabulary; in one of her letters to Stern in Chicago she speaks of his being "in that cold place among them interlekchuls.") She was particularly distrustful of the rationalistic reformer, the do-gooder. She revealed her sentiments in her portrayal of Rayber in *The Violent Bear It Away,* but her study of the type in the story called **"The Lame Shall Enter First"** is even more dismaying. A social worker, a widower, befriends an intelligent but badly behaved boy of the streets, even putting him ahead of his own son. Gradually the reader comes to understand the futility and wickedness of the reformer's conduct, and the twist of the screw comes when he himself is forced to understand—too late.

There is violence in most of the stories, but it rarely seems to be dragged in for its own sake. Violence is an integral part of the world Miss O'Connor is describing, an inevitable consequence of the evil she portrays. In another horrible story, **"A View of the Woods,"** an old man and his grand-daughter, who are exactly alike in their meanness, are brought into physical conflict, which becomes grotesque and terrible.

She may not have been a saint, but she was one of the best writers of short stories this era has seen.
—*Granville Hicks*

I find almost no compassion in these stories. In **"Judgment Day"** Miss O'Connor seems to be sorry for the old man who has been transplanted from his Georgia farm to his daughter's New York City apartment, but she is not sorry for many of her characters. I was devastated by the fate of the reformer in **"The Lame Shall Enter First,"** but Miss O'Connor appears to believe that he got what he deserved. I see him as a man who made mistakes but in the end was to be pitied. Miss O'Connor, I think, saw him as a man who rejected Divine Grace and could expect nothing but hellfire. (The urchin the man tries to befriend knows himself to be a child of Satan, but to the man that is all nonsense.)

I am not saying that Miss O'Connor's Catholicism was responsible for the harshness of her judgments; but the harshness, which probably had many causes, was compatible with her religion as she conceived it. The evil of unredeemed human nature was part of her dogma, and she saw plenty of evidence of it. She was not a pessimist, of course, because she believed there was a way of salvation, but I know of no pessimist who has painted a darker picture of the world we live in.

What are we who are not believers in her sense to make of this? Simply that she set down what she saw. We may have pity where she did not, but we cannot deny the testimony of her eyes. Again and again the reader is brought up short by the precision with which she communicates her insights. She appears to be a rather simple, even casual, sort of writer, but the more one analyzes her stories, the more one is impressed by her artistry. She may not have been a saint, but she was one of the best writers of short stories this era has seen.

Walter Sullivan (September 1965)

SOURCE: "Flannery O'Connor, Sin, and Grace: *Everything That Rises Must Converge,*" in *The Hollins Critic,* Vol. II, No. 4, September, 1965, pp. 1-8, 10.

[*In the following essay, Sullivan asserts that O'Connor is more successful in carrying out her themes in her short fiction than in her novels, because she is unable to sustain the images and relationships in the longer form.*]

The stories in *Everything That Rises Must Converge* are the last fruits of Flannery O'Connor's particular genius; and though one or two of them display an uncertainty that must have been the result of her deteriorating health, they are for the most part successful extensions of her earlier fiction. God-ridden and violent—six of the nine end in something like mayhem—they work their own small counter reformation in a faithless world. Flannery O'Connor's limitations were numerous and her range was narrow: she repeated herself frequently and she ignored an impressively large spectrum of human experience. But what she did well, she did with exquisite competence: her ear for dialogue, her eye for human gestures were as good as anybody's ever were: and her vision was as clear and direct and as annoyingly precious as that of an Old Testament prophet or one of the more irascible Christian saints.

Her concern was solely with the vulgarities of this world and the perfections of the other—perfections that had to be taken on faith, for the postulations and descriptions of them in her work are at best somewhat tawdry. She wrote of man separated from the true source of his being, lost, he thinks and often hopes, to God; and of a God whose habits are strange beyond knowing, but Who gets His way in the end. That she was a Southerner and wrote about the South may have been a fortunate coincidence. The South furnished her the kind of flagrant images her theme and her style demanded, and Southern dialogue augmented and perhaps even sharpened her wit. But the South as locale and source was quite peripheral. She once wrote Robert Fitzgerald, "I would like to go to California for about two minutes to further these researches [into the ways of the vulgar]. . . . Did you see that picture of Roy Rogers' horse attending a church service in Pasadena?" Had she been born in Brooklyn or Los Angeles, the surface agonies of her work would have been altered: perhaps they would have been weakened: but the essential delineations of her fiction, the mythic impulse itself would, I believe, have been essentially unchanged.

As a novelist, she was not successful. She could never fill a booklength canvas: the colors thinned out, the relationships weakened, the images became, before the denouement, rigid and brittle. The weakness obviously was not in her theme, which was big enough to fill the world, powerful enough to shape some of the greatest of all literary careers in the past, and in our own time those of Eliot and Mauriac and Graham Greene and William Golding. What went wrong was technical. Flannery O'Connor used to be fond of saying that the way she wrote a story was "to follow the scent like an old hound dog." At first glance, one might conclude that her novels were written with too little forethought. *Wise Blood* is full of loose ends: the theme dribbles away through the holes in the structure. According to Fitzgerald, the idea for having Hazel Motes blind himself came to O'Connor when, stuck at the crucial point in her manuscript, she read *Oedipus* for the first time. Then the earlier parts of the novel had to be reworked to prepare for the ending.

But a lot of novels get written and rewritten this way. And some novels of real power have ends as loose as that left by Enoch Emery who is last seen disappearing into the night in his ape's suit. Except for Haze, all the characters fade off—Hawkes and Sabbath and Hoover Shoates. The landlady fills the void in the last chapter. But what Motes means to do, and what O'Connor meant for us to understand concerning what he does, seem clear enough. Driven by the

Christ he cannot escape from, the "ragged figure" who "moves from tree to tree in the back of his mind," and motions "him to turn around and come off into the dark where he was not sure of his footing," he murders his double, the false prophet of his own false religion and therefore kills that part of himself. Then by blinding himself, he exhibits the strength of belief that Hawkes was unable to muster: he redeems Hawkes' failure and turns his vision totally inward away from this world, toward the Christ who exists in the inner darkness.

A better case can be made for *The Violent Bear It Away.* The beginning is extraordinarily powerful: the old man dies at the breakfast table, the boy abandons the partially dug grave, gets drunk and burns the house down. The lines of the conflict are clearly drawn between the scientific attitude—which is to say, the new gnosticism—of Rayber and the gift of Christian grace which Tarwater has not been able to escape. That Tarwater is a reluctant vessel enhances the drama of the novel: he does the work of God in spite of himself and a part of the resolution of the story is his understanding of his role and his acceptance of it. Having been abused by a homosexual, he has a vision of a burning bush, and a message comes to him: GO WARN THE CHILDREN OF GOD OF THE TERRIBLE SPEED OF MERCY. And in the final scene he is moving toward the darkened city where the "children of God" lie sleeping.

The characters here are fewer than in *Wise Blood,* which is in itself a kind of virtue: every novelist needs to learn what he can do without. The plot is rounded off neatly. The old man has been buried by some Negroes. The feeble-minded child has been baptized and drowned. The prophet's will has been done: Rayber is defeated. The scent has been true and truly followed and all ought to be well, but the novel remains, for me at least, unsatisfactory. The difficulty does not lie in faulty concept or structure: the scenes balance out nicely and the pace is sure. The trouble, I think, is with the characters: brilliantly drawn and fascinating and symbolically significant as they are, they will not hold up through a long piece of fiction. They are too thin, in the final analysis, and too much alike.

Yet, the characters, the clothes they wear, the gestures they make, the lines they speak, the thoughts they think are what make Flannery O'Connor's work so magnificently vivid and so totally memorable. The dialogue ranges from the outrageous to the absolutely predictable, the latter done so well that it never fails to delight. For example, in **"The Life You Save May Be Your Own,"** Mr. Shiftlet says, "There's one of these here doctors in Atlanta that's taken a knife and cut the human heart—the human heart . . . out of a man's chest and held it in his hand . . . and studied it like it was a day old chicken, and lady . . . he don't know no more about it than you or me."

Or take this passage from **"The Displaced Person."**

> "They came from over the water," Mrs. Shortley said with a wave of her arm. "They're what is called Displaced Persons."
>
> "Displaced Persons," he said. "Well now. I declare. What do that mean?"
>
> "It means they ain't where they were born at and there's nowhere for them to go—like if you was run out of here and wouldn't nobody have you."
>
> "It seems like they here, though," the old man said in a reflective voice.
>
> "If they here, they somewhere."
>
> "Sho is," the other agreed. "They here."
>
> The illogic of Negro thinking always irked Mrs. Shortley. "They ain't where they belong to be at," she said.

Again in **"The Life You Save,"** Shiftlet offers the old woman a stick of chewing gum, "but she only raised her upper lip to indicate she had no teeth." In ***The Violent Bear It Away,*** Tarwater makes a face suitable for an idiot to fool the truant officer, the old man lies down in his coffin to try it out—his fat stomach protrudes over the top—and the wire to Rayber's hearing aid characterizes the quality of his intelligence. All this is very fine, supported as it is with O'Connor's keen sense of the world in its various aspects: the buildings and sidewalks and trolley cars of the city, the fields and trees and clouds—many clouds—and barns and houses and pigs and cows and peacocks. Her people function richly as images and frequently they evolve into symbols.

In **"A Good Man is Hard to Find,"** the Misfit represents the plight of man from the beginning of Christian history to the modern age, and he sets forth the dilemma with such blunt clarity that it cannot be misread. Jesus was truly God or he was not: between being God and not being God there is no middle ground. If He were, then He must be followed. If He were not, then all men are free to work out their own destinies and the terms of their own happiness for themselves. The Misfit is aware of his own helplessness. Life is a mystery to him: the ways of fate are inscrutable: he denies flatly that he is a good man, and he expects neither human charity nor the mercy of God. He knows only that he does not know, and his awareness is the beginning of all wisdom, the first step toward faith.

It is an awareness that the grandmother and the other characters in the story do not share. "You're a good man!" she says to Red Sammy Butts, owner of the roadside restaurant, and he readily agrees. But he is not: nor is she a good woman: nor are Bailey or his wife or his children good. Their belief in their own virtue is a sign of their moral blindness. In pride they have separated themselves from God, putting their trust in modern technology: in paved roads and automobiles (Red Sammy gave two men credit because they were driving a Chrysler); in advertising messages along the highway and tapdancing lessons for children and in motels and pampered cats. **"A Good Man is Hard to Find"** makes clear—as does ***Wise Blood***—that the characters in Flannery O'Connor's work may not be distinguished as good or bad, or as guilty or innocent. All are guilty; all are evil. The distinctions are between those who know of God's mercy and those who do not, between those who think they can save themselves, either for this life or for the next, and those who are driven, in spite of their own failings, to do God's purpose. In the general retreat from piety, man and the conditions under which he lives have been perverted.

It was Flannery O'Connor's contention that the strange characters who populate her world are essentially no different from you and me. That they are drawn more extravagantly, she would admit, but she claimed that this was necessary because of our depravity: for the morally blind, the message of redemption must be writ large. This is not to say that she conceived of her art as a didactic enterprise: but rather that like all writers of all persuasions, she wrote out of her own ontological view which remained orthodox and Catholic, while the society in which she lived and for which she wrote became more profane and more heretical every day. She could no sooner have stopped writing about God than Camus could have ceased being an existentialist. She was committed and she had to shout to be heard.

But in writing, as in all other human endeavors, one pays his money and makes his choice. He gives up something to get something, and to get the outrageously drawn, spiritually tormented character, it is necessary to sacrifice the subtlety that long fiction demands. Complex characterization is the *sine qua non* of the novel: the characters must not only have epiphanies: they must change and develop in terms of what they have done and seen. It was the nature of Flannery O'Connor's fictional vision that discovery on the part of her people was all. When one has witnessed the flaming bush or the tongues of fire or the descending dove, the change is final and absolute and whatever happens thereafter is anticlimax. This is why the characters in O'Connor's novels fade and become static and often bore us with their sameness before we are done with the book. But fulfilling their proper roles—that is of revelation, discovery—in the short stories, they are not boring and they do what they were conceived to do.

In the society which is defined by the grandmother and the Misfit, the central conflict is between those who are driven by God and those who believe in their own self-sufficiency. This idea was put forth in **Wise Blood,** but the struggle took place too much inside the mind of Motes, and O'Connor's efforts at finding images for her values were not entirely successful. In the heavily ironic **"Good Country People,"** the conflict is between two of the godless. Hulga, the Ph.D. in philosophy, is deprived of her wooden leg by Pointer, the Bible salesman, when she will not submit to his advances. But more than this, she is robbed forever of her belief in the final efficacy of the rational process. This issue is fully joined, as I indicated earlier, in *The Violent Bear It Away:* Rayber believes in the social sciences, their theories, their statistics. To him, all mysticism is superstition, nothing is finally unexplainable, and man is the product of his environment. That the latter may not be quite true is made clear from the outset by the presence of Rayber's idiot son. But Rayber sees Bishop as the kind of mistake of nature that will ultimately be eradicated in the course of scientific advancement. All things will sooner or later be subject to the control of man. Tarwater, the unwilling instrument of grace, represents the super-rational quality of the Christian impulse. Determined not to do what his uncle, the prophet, had set for him to do, he does so anyway. Every step he takes away from the task of baptising Bishop takes him closer to that very act. All his bad temper, his country cunning and his determination to be and to act to suit himself avail no more than Rayber's educated scheming. God snatches whom He will and sets His will in motion.

One of the most successful stories in *Everything That Rises,* and in my judgment one of the best pieces Flannery O'Connor ever wrote, is a shorter and somewhat more realistic reworking of *The Violent Bear It Away.* The characters in **"The Lame Shall Enter First"** are three: Sheppard, city recreational director and volunteer counselor at the reformatory; Norton, his son who still grieves over the death of his mother; and Rufus Johnson, a fourteen-year-old, Bible reading criminal with a club foot. Like Rayber, Sheppard knows the answers to everything. When he discovers, during his ministrations at the reformatory, that Rufus has an I.Q. of 140, he determines to rehabilitate him, hard nut that he is. "Where there was intelligence, anything was possible." Immediately on seeing the boy, Sheppard discovers the source of Rufus' delinquency. "The case was clear to Sheppard instantly. His mischief was compensation for the foot."

To know everything is to be able to solve everything, and therefore Sheppard sets out to rearrange life for the mutual benefit of Rufus and Norton, who, being an only child, is selfish and needs to learn to share. Reluctantly, Rufus comes to live with Sheppard, but he does nothing to make himself pleasant. Where Sheppard is kind, Rufus is surly. He betrays Sheppard's trust in many ways, the most important of which is by corrupting Norton. He disputes Sheppard's claim that when one is dead he is simply gone, that the entry into the grave is final. Rufus knows himself to be evil, and if he does not repent he will go to hell, but the good go to heaven and everybody—including Norton's mother—goes somewhere.

Sheppard points out that a belief in God or Satan is incompatible with the "space age," and in order to turn the minds of the boys from superstition to healthy reality, he installs a telescope at the attic window. Sheppard tells the boys to look at the moon: they may go there someday: they may become astronauts. But Rufus is more interested in what will happen to the soul after death, and Norton thinks what he sees in the sky is his mother. Norton kills himself in the end, preferring death to life—or rather, preferring the life to come that he has learned about from Rufus to the drab logical existence he has lived with Sheppard. The victory here belongs to Rufus, who is lame and evil and conscious of both. He takes pride in his club foot, not because it explains his character or causes him to be forgiven his trespasses, but because it represents to him something of the burden of being human, the lameness of soul, the weight of sinfulness that we all must endure.

In spite of its typical O'Connor grimness, **"The Lame Shall Enter First"** comes to a more optimistic conclusion than does *The Violent Bear It Away.* Sheppard has his epiphany. When Johnson has finally been carried off to the police station, Sheppard reflects that he has nothing to reproach himself with. "I did more for him [Johnson] than I did for my own child."

> Slowly his face drained of color. It became almost grey beneath the white halo of his hair. The sentence echoed in his mind, each syllable like a dull blow. His mouth twisted and he closed his eyes against the revelation. Norton's face rose before him, empty, forlorn, his left eye listing almost imperceptibly toward the outer rim as if it could not bear a full view of grief. His heart constricted with a repulsion for himself so clear and intense that he gasped for breath. He had stuffed his own emptiness with good works like a glutton. He had ignored his own child to feed his vision of himself. He saw the clear-eyed Devil, the sounder of hearts, leering at him from the eyes of Johnson. His image of himself shrivelled until everything was black before him. He sat there paralyzed, aghast.

Jacques Maritain says, in *Art and Scholasticism,* "A reign of the heart which is not first of all a reign of truth, a revival of Christianity which is not first of all theological, disguises suicide as love." This is to say, in a more complex and sophisticated fashion, that the road to hell is paved with good intentions. And who in Flannery O'Connor's work is without his good intentions? Only those who are conscious of their own evil. Only those who are driven by the grace of God. Julian in the title story of *Everything That Rises* is charity itself in his view toward the world at large; but his mother, in whose house he lives, is the object of his scorn and hatred. He despises her for her stupidity which is real and for her narrowness: she is against integration. On the bus, Julian sits beside Negroes and makes conversation with them, not because he loves his fellow man, but to annoy his mother. Later, she patronizingly offers a penny to a little Negro boy, is knocked down by the boy's mother and Julian is delighted. But like Sheppard, he too in the end is forced to see his own guilt.

Once more, in the same volume, the same theme is introduced in **"The Enduring Chill."** The story opens with Asbury's return from New York where he has been living and trying to write, to his mother's farm in Georgia where he thinks he will die. He has come because illness has forced him to come, and he has in his possession the only piece of writing he was ever able successfully to finish: a long statement of his grievances, an indictment blaming his mother for all his failures, his weaknesses, his unfulfilled desires: he holds her accountable for every miserable thing that has ever happened to him. The source of his present misery, however, is his previous disobedience of one of her rules for conduct in the dairy. Earlier he was home to do research on a play he was writing about "The Negro." To get close to his subject matter, he worked in the dairy with his mother's hired men, and here to prove his solidarity with the other race, he suggested that they all drink milk together. The Negroes would not, but Asbury did, and now he has undulant fever.

The end of **"The Enduring Chill"** and the end of life as Asbury has heretofore led it are marked by the descent of the Holy Ghost, the sign of God's mercy. But until this point all of Asbury's affection for mankind has been as vague and directionless in his mind as are the outlines of the lecture on Zen Buddhism he attended in New York. Negroes for him are not human beings, but "The Negro," and he shows kindness to those on the farm that he may learn more about them for the advancement of his own projects. He abhors his mother and his sister, the priest and the doctor who try to help him. But God snatches him away. Of such is our hope.

Of the nineteen stories by Flannery O'Connor so far published—I am told that at least one has not yet been printed—nine end in the violent deaths of one or more persons. Three others end in or present near the end physical assaults that result in a greater or less degree of bodily injury. Of the remaining seven, one ends in arson, another in the theft of a wooden leg, another in car theft and wife abandonment. The other four leave their characters considerably shaken but in reasonable case. Each of the novels contains a murder and

taken together, they portray a wide range of lesser offences, including sexual immorality, ordinary and otherwise, voyeurism, mummy stealing, self-mutilation, assault with a deadly weapon, moonshining, vandalism and police brutality. All this, performed by characters who are for the most part neither bright nor beautiful, is the stuff of Flannery O'Connor's comic view.

Her apparent preoccupation with death and violence, her laughter at the bloated and sinful ignorance of mankind informed her continuing argument with the majority view. Believing as she did in a hereafter, she did not think, as most of us do, that death is the worst thing that can happen to a human being. I do not mean that she held life cheap, but rather that she saw it in its grandest perspective. Nor did she conceive of earthly happiness and comfort as the ends of man. The old lady in **"The Comforts of Home"** brings a whore into the house with her own son because she believes that nobody deserves punishment. This is the other kind of sentimental, self-serving charity, the obverse of that practiced by Sheppard and Asbury. Both kinds result from a misunderstanding of ultimate truth. But so much of even the apparent worst of O'Connor is funny, because, as Kierkegaard made clear, under the omniscience of God, the position of all men is ironic: measured against eternity, the world is but a dream.

In her work the strain of hope is strong. **"Revelation"** stands not necessarily as the best story she ever wrote, but as a kind of final statement, a rounding off of her fiction taken as a whole. O'Connor's version of the ship of mankind is a doctor's office and here sits Mrs. Turpin surrounded by the various types of humanity: the old and the young, the white and, briefly, the black, the educated and the uneducated, trash and aristocrat and good country people. Mrs. Turpin's thoughts are mostly on differences, on how, if Jesus has asked her to choose, she would have come to earth as a Negro of the right sort before she would have come as a trashy white person. The conversation is of human distinctions and of the race question, and from the beginning a silent girl with a bad complexion and a Wellesley degree regards her with loathing from behind a book. Finally, while Mrs. Turpin is in the act of thanking Jesus for making her who she is and putting her where she is, the girl attacks her and calls her an old wart hog from hell.

Mrs. Turpin's satisfaction with herself is broken: for her the scuffle in the doctor's office has shaken the scheme of things: her concept of herself and her relationships with both God and man have been called into question. She has a vision at the end.

> She saw the streak as a vast swinging bridge extended upward from the earth through a field of living fire. Upon it a vast horde of souls were rumbling

toward heaven. There were whole companies of white trash, clean for the first time in their lives, and bands of black niggers in white robes, and battalions of freaks and lunatics shouting and clapping and leaping like frogs. And bringing up the end of the procession was a tribe of people whom she recognized at once as those who, like herself and Claud, had always had a little of everything and the God-given wit to use it right. . . . They were marching behind the others with great dignity, accountable as they had always been for good order and common sense and respectable behavior. They alone were on key. Yet she could see by their shocked and altered faces that even their virtues were being burned away.

So no one escapes the need for grace: even the virtues of this world, being worldly, are corrupt. But it is easy to guess what Mrs. Turpin sees. Passing before her is that gallery of rogues and lunatics who are the *personae* of Flannery O'Connor's work—all of them loved from the beginning, and all of them saved now by God's mercy, terrible and sure.

Webster Schott (review date 13 September 1965)

SOURCE: "Flannery O'Connor: Faith's Stepchild," in *The Nation,* Vol. 201, No. 7, September 13, 1965, pp. 142-44, 146.

[*In the following review, Schott discusses O'Connor's Catholicism and asserts that "in Flannery O'Connor's stories evil is man's inevitable fate."*]

After reading Flannery O'Connor's final stories I ended the night listening to the mathematical music of the baroque. Order had to be restored, the monsters exorcised from the imagination and pressed back into her fiction.

> **Like an expert on one function of the spleen, [O'Connor] chose a small territory of soil and soul and treated it as though nothing else really existed.**
> —*Webster Schott*

Losers all, her characters act out the Gothic rituals of defeat and destruction in the nightmare American South. And if Miss O'Connor's god was ever aware of them (a problem to return to eventually), he is now obliviously sawing logs in heaven, as Pär Lagerkvist suggested in *The Eternal Smile.* Let them kill and be killed or grind their teeth in anticipation.

There are nine stories here, all episodes of fatal error and ironic retribution—modern Old Testament scenes in eschatology as the earth binds winding sheets around her failures. First a fat white woman, beaten to the pavement for offering a Negro boy a penny at the end of a bus ride, dies of a stroke or heart attack. Next a farm spinster is gored to death by the bull she commanded her hired man to shoot. A progress-crazed old farmer in **"A View of the Woods"** pounds his 9-year-old granddaughter's skull against rocks until her "eyes were fixed in a glare that did not take him in"; then he staggers suicidally into a lake as immense as his guilt. In **"The Comforts of Home"** a son accidentally shoots his mother; he was aiming at their slut boarder. In **"The Lame Shall Enter First"** a child hangs himself after seeing his dead mother waving from a distant star. In **"Judgment Day,"** the only story placed in the North, an ancient Southern D.P. headed home to die gets as far as the stairs and expires; the Negro in the next apartment shoves the corpse's head, arms and legs through the spokes of a staircase as if in a stock. The last three stories settle for purgatory: an invalid intellectual returns to Georgia and waits for the water-stain holy ghost to descend from the ceiling above his bed. A maniacal ex-sailor, with a Byzantine Jesus tattooed on his back, wails against a tree, unrecognized, like Christ crucified. A self-righteous hog raiser, deranged by accusation and assault, sees a vision of herself at the very end of a heavenly procession led by white trash, bands of "black niggers in white robes and battalions of freaks and lunatics shouting and clapping and leaping like frogs."

Flannery O'Connor ventured into the world. She was born and reared in Georgia, and died there a year ago at the age of 38. But she lived as an adult in New York City, Connecticut and Iowa City, where she studied in Paul Engle's Writer's Workshop. She lectured and read in at least five states and visited France and Italy. Yet all her fiction—these stories; her first collection, *A Good Man Is Hard to Find;* her two novels, *Wise Blood* and *The Violent Bear It Away*—rise out of the Baptist South. Their recurring ethos is that hereditary conflict of wills one imagines warring behind closed doors as he drives lost at twilight on a back road near the battlefield at Vicksburg. Like an expert on one function of the spleen, she chose a small territory of soil and soul and treated it as though nothing else really existed. Human behavior beyond distorted Christianity, outside the lower social orders of the rural South and the domestic arrangements of widowed parents and their children, is perceived as if by accident.

She had only a few ideas, but messianic feelings about them. Children and parents, rarely husbands and wives or brothers and sisters, strike at one another. The family unit—not society as a whole—opens the trap to dysfunction and cataclysm. Only the land, trees and sky possess beauty. Her adults look like mistakes; even her children are ugly. Love enters her stories as the comprehension of loss after death of a child or parent.

Her chief characters belong to the genus Southern Neanderthal. Their minds are pre-Darwinian and post-Christian. The only belief that might make a difference in their lives is Baptist literalism. Like astrology, it's nonfunctional, but provides a defensive reflex system against thought. Miss O'Connor's Negroes are "niggers," endowed with physical strength, great fears and animal survival powers. Her intellectuals—a college professor, schoolteacher, social worker, three failed writers and a Wellesley girl—create special hells. They know about paperback books, psychic compensation, electric blankets, racial equality, but nothing about themselves. Educated atheists, they can claim no more stability than the red-necked semi-literates they loathe. Flannery O'Connor's reality is destiny out of control, choices made after alternatives have been frozen. To begin one of her stories is to anticipate its end. The only questions are how the dreadful punishment for living will be delivered and in what manner her savage sense of humor will delay the agony.

"If nothing happened, there's no story," Flannery O'Connor once said to Robert Fitzgerald. Events take place, words are spoken in her stories for reasons her characters would not understand. Buried in their psychic histories, black flowers of chaos bloom because Miss O'Connor creates them. The tattooed Parker marries a woman he does not love. The social worker, Sheppard, persists at rehabilitating a psychopathic youth even though the boy is destroying his own son. Her characters aspire to the impossible out of mysterious inner needs. We believe in them because Flannery O'Connor's visionary logic descends on us like a clamp. Intelligence says wait. But the emotions follow her to exhaustion. She had the fictionalist's only requisite gift—a genius for deception.

"I think the first thing you need to realize about fiction," she wrote to one of her nun correspondents, "is . . . the writer [tries] to see an action, or a series of actions, clearly. To make anyone see a thing, you have to say straight out what it is, you have to describe it with the greatest accuracy. The fiction writer is concerned with the way the world looks first of all."

The phenomena of sight obsessed her. Events and revelations come in strings of optical epiphanies. What her characters see and how they see it, the colors of their eyes and the reflections in them, their visions in crisis or at the instant of death, the play of hues and shadows in trees and sky, reinforce what we feel about the core-man inside the shell.

Before the reducing class at the Y, the fat woman's sky-blue eyes in the title story are "as innocent and untouched by experience as they must have been when she was ten." Crumpled like a blimp after the handbag blitzkreig, she seeps

into death. "One eye, large and staring, moved slightly to the left as if it had become unmoored. The other remained fixed on him [her son], raked his face again, found nothing and closed." Lights drift farther away the faster the youth runs for help. Darkness and his sins sweep him back to her.

Windows to the soul, eyes signal preludes and clues to action and meaning. Visions and vistas serve as codas. The "same pale slate color as the ocean," O.E. Parker's eyes "reflected the innocent spaces around him as if they were a microcosm of the mysterious sea." The Jesus tattooed on his back as a desperate gesture to make contact with his wife has "eyes to be obeyed." His wife cannot recognize the Jesus. "He don't *look*. . . . No man shall see his face." She watches Parker, crying like a baby against the pecan tree, welts forming on the face of his tattooed Christ, and "her eyes hardened still more." As the horns pierce her body, Mrs. May in **"Greenleaf"** had "the look of a person whose sight has been suddenly restored but who finds the light unbearable." Smell, sound, kinesthesis orient Miss O'Connor's characters. Vision directs them; emotional stimuli enter through their eyes. Their frustrating pasts, obliquely bared, turn their responses into acts of hostility, hatred, violence. Curiously, all are denied the sensuality of sex. To introduce the erotic would have taken Miss O'Connor outside the psychophysical graveyard. She was, apparently, never in love.

Flannery O'Connor is everywhere in her stories. She entered fiction by way of painting and cartooning, which partly accounts for the visual intensity. Many of her characters struggle to walk or move in their states of shock; she herself used crutches when these stories were written. Like most of her characters, the continuous personal presence in her life was one parent—her widowed mother. One sees the spinster author sitting in bed, paring her fingernails and watching the peacocks on her farm, tolerating the ministrations, wandering through visions of violence in the distances surrounding her. Along with physical pain, sight was the most intense sensual experience available to her. Enlarged by a medieval religious attraction to the manifestations of evil, sight gave her art its phantasmagorial reality.

The most imaginatively endowed Roman Catholic writer the United States has developed, Flannery O'Connor once said of the eucharistic symbol, "If it were only a symbol, I'd say to hell with it." She received the last sacraments before her death in Milledgeville. She went to mass every day when she lived with Robert Fitzgerald and his wife in Connecticut in 1949 and 1950. When lupus (the disease that eventually killed her) got worse in 1957, she went to Lourdes and then to Rome for an audience with Pius XII. At Notre Dame that year she had said: "The Catholic sacramental view of life is one that maintains and supports at every turn the vision that the storyteller must have if he is going to write fiction of any depth." She chose the title of this book from Teilhard de Chardin, the evolutionist Jesuit theologian who theorized that matter and spirit would eventually converge at "point omega." Judging from Fitzgerald's introduction and the evidence of the stories, she did it for ironic effect. Flannery O'Connor must have viewed Chardin as another "interleckchul" and Vatican II an "Eyetalian" conspiracy against the blood of Christ and the one true faith.

Her Catholicism belongs, it seems to me, somewhere near the time of the Inquisition. The village priest in **"The Enduring Chill"** is a hard-of-hearing country bumpkin. "You will never learn to be good unless you pray regularly," he says when Asbury Fox asks him what he thinks of James Joyce. Ignatius Vogle, S.J., appears briefly in the same story to suggest the "real probability of the New Man, assisted, of course, by the Third Person of the Trinity." Very cool, he has the same trouble as Asbury and looks beyond the cross. He's too damned smart.

On three occasions in the Gospel according to John, Jesus calls the devil "the ruler of this world," and in Flannery O'Connor's stories evil is man's inevitable fate. Helplessly enveloped by satanic emanations, her characters sense the poisons, breathe deeper and sink. "Pride is the queen and mother of all vices," Thomas Aquinas said with rhetorical affection. The loss of Paradise was the price Adam and Eve paid for their pride. In every story, Flannery O'Connor's characters aspire beyond their capabilities. Asbury tries to write and can't. He attempts to liberate Negroes and instead gets undulant fever and his mother's banalities. Sheppard, in **"The Lame Shall Enter First,"** cannot possibly rehabilitate a monster who has the intelligence of a near-genius and the will to destroy his child. Thomas, another would-be writer living on his vanity and his mother, in **"The Comforts of Home,"** stumbles into matricide when he exceeds his psychological potentialities. O.E. Parker tries to have himself tattooed out of anxiety—his solitary fate—and into love. He goes down the emotional drain with Jesus on his back.

Vanity corrupts Christian belief, selfless intention, personal sacrifice. "To help anybody out that needed it was her philosophy in life," Mrs. Turpin tells herself in **"Revelation."** In the doctor's waiting room as she says, "Thank you, Jesus, for making everything the way it is," she gets socked in the eye and thrown to the floor. Grandpa Fortune tries for wealth and progress and succeeds at murder. The boy Norton acquires a belief in God and hangs himself over it; the delinquent Johnson believes so strongly in the Bible that he tears out a page, eats it and goes on in his life of crime.

According to Christian orthodoxy, everything is inverted in Flannery O'Connor's stories. No one can find happiness or salvation. No one acquires the grace she speaks of. Her South is Salem metamorphosed; it would take a Second Coming to give her people hope.

In one of her letters to the novelist, Richard G. Stern, Flannery O'Connor said to look up John Hawkes in Providence because he was a good writer. Despite her attacks on existentialists, she saw the world in the same distorted and sinister form as did Hawkes. She dramatized Sartre's hell of other people. She confirmed James Purdy's conviction that love is impossible in the present. Pagan Christian symbols and practices frame her work. Ignorant fundamentalism, not Catholic pageantry and transubstantiation, haunts the preachers and believers in her stories and novels. Why, one wonders, could she not write at length about Catholics? Why did she choose as her larger models the misshapen Oral Robertses of the South? She selected those properties of Christianity that served to justify her black reality. The emerging Catholic theology that implies the visitation of Christ may have regenerated matter and dignified all of life was anti-art and personally intolerable. It denied her particular vision of hell on earth. She talked about free will, the sacramental view, redemption by Christ. But her characters have no real choice—only faint glimmers of possibilities lost.

Flannery O'Connor's work is filled with irony—small hope turned to great despair, rewards transformed into punishments, seriousness mocked by comedy, vanity in modesty, hate in place of love, grotesquery disguised as simplicity. But the delicious irony probably escaped her.

Based on the most depressing features of Christianity, the consignment of man to the evil forces within him and the denial of an evolving intelligence to help himself, her stories created a small universe. As patterns of thought her work suggests the absolute theological dead end enlightened Catholicism is struggling to escape. Artistically her fiction is the most extraordinary thing to happen to the American short story since Ernest Hemingway.

Reality is fantastic. Violence does bear life away. Sometimes. Myopic in her vision, Flannery O'Connor was among those few writers who raise the questions worth thinking about after the lights are out and the children are safely in bed: What is reality? What are the possibilities for hope? How much can man endure?

Irving Howe (review date 30 September 1965)

SOURCE: "Flannery O'Connor's Stories," in *The New York Review of Books,* Vol. V, No. 4, September 30, 1965, pp. 16-7.

[In the following review, Howe praises O'Connor's storywriting ability and her collection Everything That Rises Must Converge, *but complains that, except for two stories, O'Connor's work is missing the unexpected revelation that he finds endearing in other great stories.]*

On and off these last months I have been fussing in my mind with Miss O'Connor's stories, unable to reach that certainty of judgment which, we all know, is the established trade mark of the modern critic. The skill and ambition of these stories are not lost upon me, yet I hesitate fully to join in the kind of praise they have won from respected critics.

At first I feared my distance from Miss O'Connor's religious beliefs might be corrupting my judgment, but while one cannot, in the nature of things, offer guarantees, the trouble does not seem to reside in the famous "problem of belief." Miss O'Connor was a serious Catholic, and what she called "the Catholic sacramental view of life" is certainly a controlling force in her stories. But it is not the only nor always the dominant one, since she could bring into play resources of worldliness such as one might find in the work of a good many sophisticated modern writers. Miss O'Connor's religious convictions certainly operate throughout most of her stories, but at so deep a level, as so much more than mere subject matter of fixed point of view, that the skeptical reader is spared the problem of an explicit confrontation with "the Catholic sacramental view of life." Except for an occasional phrase, which serves partly as a rhetorical signal that more than ordinary verisimilitude is at stake, there are no unavoidable pressures to consider these stories in a strictly religious context. They stand securely on their own, as renderings and criticisms of human experience.

And as such, they merit a considerable respect. The writing is firm, economical, complex: we are engaged with an intelligence, not merely a talent. Miss O'Connor has a precise ear for rural colloquialism and lower-class mangling of speech; she can be slyly amusing in regard to the genteel segments of the Southern middle class, partly because she knows them with an assurance beyond sentiment or hatred. She has brought under control that addiction to Gothic hijinks which, to my taste, marred her early work (though it won her the applause of critics for whom any mode of representation they take to be anti-realistic is a token of daring and virtue). Touches of Gothic survive in these late stories, but no longer in a programmatic or obsessional way, and no longer on the assumption that to proclaim the wonders of the strange is to escape the determined limits of familiar life. What these touches of Gothic now do is to provide a shock in the otherwise even flow of narrative, thereby raising its pitch and tensing its movement.

What then is wrong? For most of Miss O'Connor's readers, nothing at all. For this reviewer, a tricky problem in method and tone, about which there is no need to pretend certainty.

Miss O'Connor's title story has been much admired, and with reason. An aging Confederate lady, fat, rather stupid and crazed with fantasies of status, keeps battling with her emancipated son Julian, an idle would-be writer. Julian expends ingenuities of nastiness in assaulting his mother, but most of his attacks fall harmlessly upon the walls of her genteel incomprehension. Unavoidably their personal conflict becomes entangled with "the Negro problem": polite racism against a blocked and untested fury for Justice.

Mother and son encounter a "cute" Negro child, upon whom the woman decides to bestow a coin. But there is another mother, an infuriated black giantess who hates such gestures of condescension. The Negro woman strikes the white one, and Julian, as his mother lies sprawling on the sidewalk, gloats: "You got exactly what you deserved." But then, while mother and son start for home, she bewildered and he delighted, the mother collapses, this time from a stroke, and Julian must shed the convenient mask of "emancipation" to recognize his fright, his dependence, and his loss. "The tide of darkness seemed to sweep him back to her, postponing from moment to moment his entry into the world of guilt and horror."

The story is unquestionably effective. We grasp the ways in which the son's intellectual superiority rests upon his emotional dependence, and the mother's social stupidity coexists with a maternal selflessness. Their quarrels are symptoms of a soured family romance, but the romance cuts far deeper than the quarrels. As true motives are revealed and protective beliefs dissolved, ironies and complexities fall into place: which is precisely what, in a good sophisticated modern story, they are supposed to do.

Yet that is all this story is: good sophisticated modern, but lacking in that resonance Miss O'Connor clearly hoped it might have. Why? One clue is a recurrent insecurity of tone, jarring sentences in which Miss O'Connor slips from the poise of irony to the smallness of sarcasm, thereby betraying an unresolved hostility to whatever it is she takes Julian to represent. . . . Repeated several times in these stories, this pattern of feeling seems quite in excess of what the theme might require or the characters plausibly evoke. One can only suppose that it is a hostility rooted in Miss O'Connor's own experience and the kind of literary education she received (intellectuality admired but intellectuals distrusted). Repeatedly she associates the values she respects with an especially obnoxious kind of youthful callowness, while reserving some final wisdom of experience for the foolish and obtuse, the unbearable parents.

In thus shaping her materials Miss O'Connor clearly intends

us to savor a cluster of ironies; her sensibility as a writer of fiction was formed in a milieu where irony took on an almost totemic value. But there can be, as in much contemporary writing there is, a deep failure of ironic perception in a writer's unequivocal commitment to irony. Mustered with the regularity of battalions on parade, complex ironies have a way of crystallizing into simple and even smug conclusions. Everything becomes subject to ironic discount except the principle of irony itself.

Let me try to be more concrete. Reading the title story, one quickly begins to see the end toward which it moves and indeed must move. The climax is then realized effectively enough—except for the serious flaw that it is a climax which has already been anticipated a number of pages earlier, where it seems already present, visible and complete, in the preparatory action. One doesn't, to be sure, know that the Negro woman will strike the white woman; but more important, one does know that some kind of ironic reversal will occur in the relationship between mother and son. There is pleasure to be had in watching Miss O'Connor work it all out, but no surprise, for there has been no significant turning upon the premises from which the action has emerged. The story is entirely harmonious with the writer's intent, characterized by what might be called the clarity of limitation. Miss O'Connor is in control of the narrative line from beginning to end, and by the standards of many critics, that is the consummation of her art.

But is it? When I think of stories by contemporary writers which live in my mind—Delmore Schwartz's "In Dreams Begin Responsibilities," Norman Mailer's "The Man Who Studied Yoga," Bernard Malamud's "The Magic Barrel"—I find myself moved by something more than control. In such stories there comes a moment when the unexpected happens, a perception, an insight, a confrontation which may not be in accord with the writer's original intention and may not be strictly required by the logic of the action, but which nevertheless caps the entire story. This moment of revelation gains part of its power from a sharp and sudden brush against the writer's evident plan of meaning; it calls into question all "structural analysis"; the writer seems to be shaken by the demands of his own imagination, so that the material of the story "acts back" upon him.

This final release beyond craft and control, and sometimes, to be honest, beyond clarity, is what I find missing in most of Miss O'Connor's stories. And the reason, I would surmise, is that only toward the end of her career had she fully discovered the possibilities of craft, possibilities she exercised with a scrupulous enjoyment but limited effect. She reached that mastery of means which allows a writer to seek a more elusive and perilous kind of mastery, and in two of these stories, **"Revelation"** and **"Parker's Back,"** she began to break past the fences of her skill and her ideas.

Like **"Everything That Rises Must Converge," "Revelation"** starts as a clash between generations, old against new South. The setting is a doctor's office, where gradations of social rank are brilliantly located through inflections of speech. Mr. and Mrs. Turpin, an elderly and hopelessly respectable farm couple, encounter a Southern lady, also waiting for the doctor; the lady has with her an acne-pocked and ill-tempered daughter who goes to "Wellesley College," the one "in Massachusetts." Mrs. Turpin trades fatuous pleasantries with the lady about the recent cussedness of the Negroes (though the lady adds, "I couldn't do without my good colored friends"). Meanwhile a poor-white slattern tries to break into the conversation and transform genteel racism into open hatred, but she is coolly pushed aside. Mrs. Turpin, straining her imagination, decides to place the slattern even lower than Negroes on her private scale of virtue. The talk continues, the comedy heightens, but to the "emancipated" daughter from Wellesley College it becomes intolerable. Enraged by every word she hears, the girl bites Mrs. Turpin and then curses her with the magnificent words, "Go back to hell where you came from, you old wart hog." The girl is dragged off to a hospital; Mrs. Turpin staggers home.

Now, thus far the story has followed a pattern close to that of **"Everything That Rises Must Converge,"** but in **"Revelation"** Miss O'Connor is not content with easy triumphs: she follows Mrs. Turpin home to the farm, to the bed on which she uneasily rests and the pigpen she angrily hoses down. For Mrs. Turpin has been shaken by the girl's curse, as if indeed it were a kind of "revelation." In an astonishing passage, Mrs. Turpin cries out to God: "What do you send me a message like that for? . . . How am I a hog and me both? How am I saved and from hell too?" Her rank is broken, her righteousness undone, and a terrible prospect unfolds itself of a heavenly injustice beyond propriety or comprehension:

> A visionary light settled in her eyes. She saw the streak as a vast swinging bridge extending upward from the earth through a field of living fire. Upon it a vast horde of souls were rumbling toward heaven. There were whole companies of white-trash, clean for the first time in their lives, and bands of black niggers in white robes, and battalions of freaks and lunatics shouting and leaping like frogs. And bringing up the end of the procession was a tribe of people whom she recognized at once as those who, like herself. . ., had always had a little of everything and the God-given wit to use it right. . . . They were marching behind the others with great dignity, accountable as they had always been for good order and common sense and respectable behavior. They alone were on key. Yet she could see by their shocked and altered faces that even their virtues were being burned away.

This is not the kind of last-minute acquisition of understanding with which literature has so often tried to get around life. It is a vision of irremediable disorder, or God's ingratitude; the white trash, the niggers, the leaping lunatics will all march to heaven ahead of Mrs. Turpin. Something remarkable has happened here, beyond the cautions of planning and schemes of irony: "How am I a hog and me both?"

It is intolerable that a woman who could write such a story should have died at the age of thirty-nine.

Patricia Kane (review date Fall 1965)

SOURCE: "Flannery O'Connor's *Everything That Rises Must Converge*," in *Critique*, Vol. VIII, No. 1, Fall, 1965, pp. 85-91.

[*In the following review, Kane discusses the distinctive qualities of three stories from O'Connor's* Everything That Rises Must Converge—*"The Lame Shall Enter First," "A View of the Woods," and "Everything That Rises Must Converge."*]

Reviewing the last book of the talented Flannery O'Connor is an awesome task. It seems fitting to praise the quality of her life, the extraordinary spirit that animated Miss O'Connor through her long and painful illness. Such is Robert Fitzgerald's splendid introduction to *Everything That Rises Must Converge.* Fitzgerald movingly evokes the woman who wrote the stories and suggests a continuity in the totality of her work. I shall attempt neither. It requires a personal acquaintance like Fitzgerald's to convey all Miss O'Connor's gifts for living as well as for writing. But the stories here collected can be confronted, admired, and recommended.

The nine stories, all but one of which have previously appeared in various journals, have some common concerns. There are similarities in theme, method, and characterization among them, as there are resemblances to earlier works. But the similarities strike me less than the distinctive qualities of each story as an entity. A conflict may resemble that between generations in other stories, a character's style of language or of life may remind one of other O'Connor characters, but each story has its internal logic and special interest apart from the patterns in the total work. Thus I shall focus primarily on three especially fine stories.

"The Lame Shall Enter First" dissects a smug social worker who neglects his son in order to try to restore a delinquent boy whose intelligence he admires. He fails with the delinquent boy just as he fails with his son because his self-image as a noble selfless agent of truth and goodness conceals from him his failure to love until a blinding recognition comes too late to help either boy.

As the story opens, Sheppard watches his ten-year old son Norton and contemplates with distaste a face that he believes reveals the mediocrity of a person who will never learn to be good or unselfish. Sheppard tells Norton about a boy he has counseled at the reformatory, a volunteer job that Sheppard performs for "the satisfaction of knowing that he was helping boys that no one else cared about." Sheppard's failure to recognize that no one cares about his son is one of several ironies implicit in the scene. He sympathizes with the boy, named Rufus, because his mother is in prison, but when Norton cries in grief for his dead mother, Sheppard feels disgust for a grief that he sees as selfish. Sheppard speaks feelingly about Rufus's deformed foot, but remains oblivious to his son's needs, as one word tellingly suggests. To one of his father's sermons about Rufus's needs, Norton replies "lamely." Sheppard, who prides himself on his understanding of the debilitating effects of physical lameness, cannot recognize how his rejection has maimed his son.

Rufus comes to live with Sheppard and Norton, but he opposes Sheppard's efforts to help him. Their conflict focuses on Rufus's insistence that he is bad because Satan has him in his power. Sheppard grows angry at the persistence of a belief that he considers unintelligent. He tries to encourage Rufus's intellectual gifts by buying a telescope that he mounts in the attic. Rufus shows less interest in it than Norton does, but Sheppard ignores his son's attempts to please him. When Norton eagerly listens to Rufus's religious beliefs, Sheppard feels that it is Rufus's "way of trying to annoy him," but decides not to feel annoyed since "Norton was not bright enough to be damaged much" and "Heaven and hell were for the mediocre, and he was that if he was anything." Sheppard's concern about what he considers a stupid belief centers on Rufus's tenacious clinging to it; he abandons his son to error. In this, as in other episodes, Sheppard's expressed liking for goodness is revealed as less a factor than his attraction to intelligence that he can direct. To the person of neither boy does Sheppard respond.

Rufus opposes Sheppard by continuing his vandalism. After he apparently erred in thinking Rufus guilty in one incident, Sheppard resolutely insists on Rufus's innocence. So intent is he on winning Rufus's trust that he continues to neglect his son. In one such instance, after the boys have gone to bed, Sheppard talks with Rufus and leaves him, saying "good night, son." Across the hall, Norton lies in his bed and beckons his father to come in. Sheppard ignores his son because he fears that Rufus will feel that he does not trust him and is consulting Norton about his story. He walks away, thinking happily about the next day when he will take Rufus to get a new corrective shoe. Meanwhile, Norton "sat for some time looking at the spot where his father had stood."

The next day, Sheppard continues to neglect Norton so that his attention to Rufus and his shoe will not be divided. But Rufus refuses the shoe and tells Sheppard that he has committed the crimes that the police suspect him of. Confronted with this betrayal, Sheppard is chilled by hatred.

The next evening, Rufus defies Sheppard by reading the Bible at the table, by jubilantly shouting at Sheppard, "the devil has you in his power," and by leaving his house deliberately to be caught at a crime. Norton goes to the attic to look through the telescope. When he tells his father that he sees his mother among the stars, Sheppard orders him to stop being foolish and leaves him. Confronted with Rufus, whom the police bring and who says that he prefers prison to Sheppard's home because Sheppard is not a Christian, Sheppard tells the police: "I did more for him than I did for my own child." He makes a last attempt to reason with Rufus, telling him that he is not evil, that he need not compensate for his foot with crime. Rufus snarls that his foot has nothing to do with his crime and that only Jesus can save him, not a "lying stinking atheist."

Sheppard's phrase "I did more for him than I did for my own child" repeats itself in his mind, at first as consolation, then as "the voice of his accuser." When he realizes that "he had ignored his own child to feed his vision of himself," his self-image "shrivelled until everything was black before him." He thinks of the light of his son's face as his salvation and races to tell him that he loves him and will not fail him again. But he finds Norton in the attic "hung in the jungle of shadows, just below the beam from which he had launched his flight into space."

Sheppard's failure is thus explicit at the end. The consequence is shocking in its horror, but it has been prepared for by the texture of the story. For example, descriptions of the dullness or brightness of Norton's eyes suggest his condition and, in retrospect, prepare for his end. In the opening scene, his eyes look forward but are not engaged by what his father says. His eyes are a pale blue, "as if they might have faded" like a shirt, and one of them "listed, almost imperceptibly, toward the outer rim." After his father tells him about Rufus, Norton's eyes brighten slightly when he hopes that Rufus will not come. In his tearful grief for his mother, his eyes become slits. After his grief leads to vomiting and his father speaks kindly about it, he looks blindly at him. When he first listens to Rufus's account of heaven and hell, Norton's eyes "appeared to grow hollow" as he thinks of his mother. His response to Sheppard's explanation that his mother exists only as her spirit lives in others is to harden his pale eyes in disbelief. But to Rufus's comment that his mother is in the sky somewhere, Norton soon responds by looking intently through the telescope. Norton's sense that he has lost his father is poignantly evoked in the episode in which he looks at the space where Sheppard has stood and

ignored him, until "his gaze became aimless." The void is filled with Rufus's religion. As Rufus tells Sheppard that he has stolen a Bible, Norton's eyes have an excited sheen, he looks alert, and his eyes are brighter. Norton's eyes glitter with pleasure as he announces that he plans to be a space man. He looks intently through the telescope and with "an unnatural brightness about his eyes," tells his father that he sees his mother. That brightness is the last description of Norton's eyes, but in his moment of revelation, Sheppard realizes that Norton's eye lists "as if it could not bear a full view of grief." Sheppard then sees "the clear-eyed devil, the sounder of hearts, leering at him" with Rufus's eyes. He understands his son's eyes too late.

Sheppard's final awareness comes through a do-gooder cliche: I did more for Rufus than I did for my own son. That this should introduce an understanding too late is ironically appropriate for a person whose language frequently sounds like a bad text book in social work. He hides his neglect of his child behind a platitudinous wish that the child would cease to be selfish. He is opposed by the cliches of revival religion. Through the two sets of language he comes to understand, with simple, concrete immediacy, that he "had stuffed his own emptiness with good works like a glutton." But when this insight comes he can only stand in the shadows of his attic "like a man on the edge of a pit."

Less complex understandings come to characters in other stories in this collection, but the consequences frequently are as devastating and as irreversible. **"A View of the Woods"** brings an old man and his granddaughter who have been apparent allies against her parents to an opposition that ends in death for both. The grandfather's final vision reveals that the progress he has believed in cannot save him.

Mr. Fortune and his double, his nine-year old granddaughter Mary Fortune Pitts, spend most of their time together, usually watching building taking place on land that once was part of Fortune's farm. Fortune sells parts of his land for two reasons: he believes in progress, and he enjoys annoying his son-in-law, who is farming the land. Fortune dislikes his son-in-law generally and particularly because he sees him as the kind of "fool that would let a cow pasture interfere with progress," whereas Fortune is "a man of advanced vision." A rift comes between Fortune and the child when he decides to sell that part of the farm used as a lawn and pasture. Mary Fortune wants to keep it so that they can continue to have a view of the woods. After Fortune sells it, she defies him. He decides that he will have to beat her. When he does, she fights back, saying that she will kill anyone who beats her. Angered, he kills her by pounding her head on a rock. Then he dies of a heart attack.

The conflict between Fortune and the child is not a simple conflict of age and youth: it reflects a difference in values.

The two share a liking for watching bulldozers and other machinery, but they differ utterly on the matter of the beauty of woods. In a reversal of a stereotyped assignment of roles, the child stands for the agrarian past, for the beauty of nature, the grandfather for the urban present, for the utility of stores and gasoline stations. The man who buys the land intends to put a gasoline station on the road that probably will soon be paved. Fortune considers how handy it will be to have such services near-by. He sees nothing ugly in the buyer's present site of business, which is replete with junked cars, roadside billboards, and a dance hall. When Mary Fortune surprises him with regard for the view of the woods, Fortune is honestly bewildered. All he sees is a profusion of weeds and "the sullen line of black pine woods, . . . the gray-blue line of more distant woods and beyond that nothing but the sky, entirely blank except for one of two threadbare clouds." The child, on the other hand, looks at this scene "as if it were a person that she preferred to him." Fortune is shaken enough by her response to look at the view several times that afternoon. But he can see only woods, not beauty. He hopes to win over the child who, as the double he has taught his tricks and to whom he has willed the farm, is his future—a future that has no room for sentimental attachment to anything so common as pine woods. But she is his double in stubborn opposition as well as looks. Each kills the other in defense of his integrity, his values.

Two visions of the old man link his granddaughter to the woods. He has thought of her as "thoroughly of his clay" and her face as "a little red mirror." Thus when he sees red in the woods, he is seeing her death although he fails to realize it. In that first vision, "the gaunt trunks appeared to be raised in a pool of red light that gushed from the almost hidden sun setting behind them." Fortune feels briefly that he is "out of the rattle of everything that led to the future . . . and held there in the midst of an uncomfortable mystery." It seems "as if someone were wounded behind the woods and the trees were bathed in blood." Fortune closes his eyes against the vision, but he still sees "hellish red trunks . . . in a black wood." The trees are figuratively bathed with blood when he kills Mary Fortune in "an ugly red bald spot" surrounded by pine trees. As he lies dying, Fortune feels as if he is running toward the lake to escape the ugly pines. But at the lake, he realizes that he cannot swim and escape the gaunt trees that "had thickened into mysterious files." When he looks for help, all he sees is a machine, a "huge yellow monster that sat to the side, as stationary as he was, gorging itself on clay." Fortune cannot escape the pines, as he could not escape Mary Fortune's fury. His refuge, a place that he has welcomed as part of the progressive future, offers only another image of himself as a machine gorging itself on clay—just as Fortune has destroyed "his clay," i.e., his double, and thus himself and his future.

A new awareness comes also to the central character in "Everything That Rises Must Converge." The conflict in this story, between an adult son and his mother, resembles the conflict in other stories in this collection (**"Greenleaf," "The Comforts of Home,"** and **"The Enduring Chill"**); there are also resemblances in its wry comment about a futile reaching out toward Negroes (**"The Enduring Chill"** and **"Judgment Day"**), and in its depiction of a character who wants another to face what he thinks of as reality (**"Parker's Back," "The Enduring Chill,"** and **"Revelation"**). The story abounds in the humor that often characterizes Miss O'Connor's work. The several strands are apparent as the story opens. Julian resentfully contemplates accompanying his mother on the bus, which she will not ride alone since they have been desegregated. She is going to a reducing class "designed for working girls over fifty, who weighed from 165 to 200 pounds," but Julian's mother says that "ladies did not tell their age or weight." As she prepares to go, she talks about her new hat, wondering if she should have bought such an expensive one. She concludes with trite expressions characteristic of her, "you only live once and paying a little more for it, I at least won't meet myself coming and going."

She meets herself, or rather a Negro woman wearing a hat exactly like hers, on the bus trip to her class. The hats the two women wear are hideous: "A purple velvet flap down on one side of it and stood up on the other; the rest of it was green and looked like a cushion with the stuffing out." Julian's mother has been wearing her hat "like a banner of her imaginary dignity;" the Negro woman has her own dignity. Julian hopes that the episode will teach his mother something about reality, but to his dismay, his mother only finds it funny. The lesson will have more finality for both of them. After they leave the bus, Julian's mother offers the Negro woman's child a penny, as is her custom. The Negro expresses her outrage at what she considers condescension by hitting the white woman with such force that she falls. The preposterous hat falls off; Julian's mother struggles to her feet and dies within the hour. Too late Julian realizes his love for his mother and enters "the world of guilt and sorrow."

Before he suspects that his mother is dying, Julian taunts her by calling her attacker her black double and insisting that she must face a reality in which her manners and graciousness are valueless. But Julian himself is his mother's double and begins to learn that his own defenses may be inadequate. Julian has felt smugly satisfied with his values and resentful of his mother's sense of identity. He believes that only he understands their family heritage and would suit the decayed mansion that had belonged to the family during his mother's girlhood. He congratulates himself because "in spite of growing up dominated by a small mind, he had ended up with a large one." As proof of his superiority, he tries to start a conversation with a Negro man who boards the bus. When the Negro ignores him, he daydreams about confronting his mother with a cultivated Negro. To his discomfort, his mother establishes contact with the Negro child, whom she finds attractive. As his mother dies, killed by a Negro far different from the polished ones of Julian's daydreams, he can only run futilely for help, but his feet are numb and seem to carry him nowhere. He feels a tide of darkness sweeping him back to his mother. Although the Negro woman who unknowingly killed Julian's mother may be suggested by the title, *converge* also has the sense of uniting in a common interest: it is Julian who must converge. Perhaps he will in the world of sorrow and guilt that is his heritage at the end of the story.

The stories of *Everything That Rises Must Converge* will bear comparison with the high standard set in Miss O'Connor's earlier work. Much might be said of the ways in which these stories, like the earlier ones, show Miss O'Connor to be the Catholic and Southern writer that she called herself. While not denying the importance of such matters, I feel that they can obscure other qualities and that the stories can and should be seen in the particular before useful generalizations emerge. *Everything That Rises Must Converge* deserves scrutiny as a document in Flannery O'Connor's life and work, but it also merits praise for the sheer pleasure of good reading that it offers us.

Robert Fitzgerald (essay date 1965)

SOURCE: "Introduction," in *Everything That Rises Must Converge,* by Flannery O'Connor, Farrar, Straus and Giroux, 1956, pp. vii-xxxiv.

[*In the following introduction, Fitzgerald provides an overview of O'Connor's career and the themes present in the stories in* Everything That Rises Must Converge.]

She was a girl who started with a gift for cartooning and satire, and found in herself a far greater gift, unique in her time and place, a marvel. She kept going deeper (this is a phrase she used) until making up stories becam, for her, a way of testing and defining and conveying that superior knowledge that must be called religious. It must be called religious but with no false note in our voices, because her writing will make any false note that is applied to it very clear indeed. Bearing hard upon motives and manners, her stories as moralities cut in every direction and sometimes go to the bone of regional and social truth. But we are not likely to state what they show as well as they show it. We can stay on the safe side by affirming, what is true and usefully borne in mind, that making up stories was her craft, her pleasure and her vocation, that her work from first to last is imaginative writing, often comic writing, superbly achieved and always to be enjoyed as that. We had better let our awareness of the knowledge in her stories grow quietly without forcing it, for nothing could be worse than to treat them straight off as problems for exegesis or texts to preach on.

The new severely cut slab of marble bearing her name and the dates March 25, 1925—August 3, 1964, lies in the family plot on a bare elevated place in the Milledgeville cemetery, beside another slab of identical shape marking the grave of her father, but his has also a soldier's headstone for Edward F. O'Connor, Jr., Lt. 325th Infantry, 82nd Division, who died February 1st, 1941. I have been out there with her mother to note it all and to say my heart's prayer as I should, though generally I feel as I gather Flannery felt about cemeteries, that they and all they contain are just as well left in God's keeping and that one had better commune with persons, living or dead, than with gravestones and the silent earth. Milledgeville on a mild winter day without leafiness or bloom suggests no less remarkably than in the dogwood season (when I came before) the strict amenity of the older South, or at least this is what I make of there being so many pillared white houses. It was, after all, the capital of Georgia until after the War Between the States.

At the Cline house in town I have been out on the front porch, hatless and coatless in the sun, between the solid handcarved columns, fluted and two stories high, that were hoisted in place when the house was built in 1820 and the slaves, they say, were making by hand the bricks for the house and the openwork walls around the garden. Peter Cline acquired this place in 1886. He was a prominent man, in our American phrase, for many years mayor of the town, and he married successively two sisters, Kate L. and Margaret Ida Treanor. By the former he had seven children and by the latter nine, of whom Regina, Flannery's mother, was the seventh. All of these people were old Georgia Catholics. The first Mass in Milledgeville had been celebrated in the apartment of Hugh Treanor, father of Kate and Ida, in the Newell Hotel in 1847. Mrs. Hugh Treanor gave the plot of ground for the little church that was built in 1874.

From the house in town to the farm called Andalusia is about five miles on the Eatonton-Atlanta highway. A quarter of a mile off the road on rising ground, the white farmhouse looks narrow and steeply roofed with a screen porch across the front of it and a white watertank on very tall stilts behind. The driveway cuts through a red clay bank and curves gently uphill until it swerves around back of the house where there is a roof running out from over the kitchen door to make a broad shelter, and beyond this there are three cedar trees, one with a strong straight bough about eight feet off the grass. The grass is sleeted white by droppings from the peacocks that roost at night on the bough. In the background off to the left is the low darkly weathered clapboard house with a low open porch where the Negroes live and beyond it the barn with farm machinery in the yard. From the carport you see geese going by in single file and there are swans preening in the middle distance; you also see the peacocks proceeding sedate and dainty through the shrubbery to denude it of berries and through the flowerbeds to denude them of buds. There are maybe a dozen or twenty peacocks in sight, fabulous in throat and crest, to say nothing of the billowy tensile train behind. Between the fowls of this farmyard and the writings of Flannery O'Connor, who bought and cared for them and loved to look at them, I do not at all mind drawing a certain parallel, to wit, that if you miss the beauty of plain geese the peacocks will knock your eye out.

I have been in the dining-room looking at old photographs with Regina. There is a big one of Flannery at about two, in profile, sitting crosslegged on a bed and frowning at a large book with an elegantly curled page lit within by reflected light. There is another of her father, a robust amused young man, looking very much the Legion Commander that he was, sitting like the hub of a wheel with his five gay younger brothers beside and behind him. They were a Savannah family, the O'Connors, and Ed, as Flannery always called him, had been in the real estate business there, and Flannery was born and lived her childhood there in a tall narrow brownstone house, going to St. Vincent's parochial school and later to the Sacred Heart. There is a studio photograph of the child at five or six, standing on a bench beside her mother, who is an absolute beauty with a heart-shaped face and large grey eyes and dark hair smoothly drawn down from the part. That would be about 1930 or '31 in Savannah. They moved to the Cline house in Milledgeville toward the end of the decade when Mr. O'Connor was ill with a fatal disease called lupus for which no effective treatment was then known. Flannery in her turn would suffer it and die of it or its consequences.

I have also been in the front room on the other side of the house, Flannery's bedroom, where she worked. Her aluminum crutches, acquired in 1955, are standing against the mantel. The bed is narrow and covered by a plain spread. It has a tall severe wooden headboard. At the foot is one of those moveable tray stands used in hospitals. On the low table to the right of the bed there is a small pile of books covered in black leather, three books in all, on top a Sunday missal, below that a breviary, below that a Holy Bible. To the left of the bed is her work desk, facing away from the front windows, facing the back of a wardrobe that is shoved up against it, no doubt to give her as nearly as possible nothing to look at while she worked. Behind it on a table under the window is a new electric typewriter still unused, still in the corklight plastic box it came in. There are a lot of books in plain bookcases of various sizes around the interior walls. Her painting of a rooster's angry head, on a circular wooden plaque, glares from the top of the tallest bookcase.

In the hall, in the dining-room, and in the comfortable small living-room of the "addition" they built in 1959, the paintings on the walls are all Flannery's, all done during the last thirteen years when she lived, in more or less infirmity, at the farm. They are simple but beautiful paintings of flowers in bowls, of cows under trees, of the Negro house under the bare trees of winter. I use this word "beautiful" with all possible premeditation. Once when I was working at a university I was asked with a couple of my friends who taught there to take part in a symposium on Flannery's work, a symposium which I expected would be favorable if critical, but it turned out that one of my friends didn't like her work at all because he thought it lacked a sense of natural beauty and human beauty. Troubled by this, I looked in the stories again and took a sentence from **"The Artificial Nigger"** to say what I felt she perceived not only in natural things but in her characters: "The trees were full of silver-white sunlight, and even the meanest of them sparkled." Surely even the meanest of them do. I observed that in the violent tale called **"A Good Man is Hard to Find"** the least heroic of the characters was able, on his way to be shot, to shout a reassurance to his mother (though supporting himself against a tree) and that his wife, asked if she would like to follow him, murmured "Yes, thank you," as she got up with her baby and her broken shoulder. These were beautiful actions, I argued, though as brief as beautiful actions usually are.

To come back to the paintings, they are not only skilled in the application of paint but soundly composed and bold and sensitive in color and revelatory of their subjects, casual as the whole business was for her. She went deeper in this art as well. I know because I have looked through a sheaf of drawings she made before she was twenty when she was going to the Georgia Woman's College in Milledgeville and doing linoleum cut cartoons for the college paper, *Colonnade.* In one of the sketches one fish is saying to another, "You can go jump out of the lake," an idea in which I can hear, already, the authentic O'Connor humor. In the linoleum cuts the line was always strong and decisive with an energy and angularity that recall the pen drawings of George Price, drawings that in fact she admired. For the yearbook, *Spectrum,* for 1945, when she graduated, she tried a rounder kind of comic drawing, not so good. She was editor of the literary magazine, *The Corinthian,* that year and so clearly on her way to being a writer that one of her teachers took the initiative in getting her a fellowship to the Writers' Workshop at the University of Iowa. She began to publish before she got her M.A. there in 1947. After one more year at Iowa, she worked on her writing at Yaddo and in New York.

My wife and I met her early in 1949 when she was not yet twenty-four. A friend of ours brought her to our apartment in New York to bear him out in something he had to tell, and she did this with some difficulty, frowning and struggling softly in her drawl to put whatever it was exactly the way it was. She sat facing the windows and the March light over the East River. We saw a shy Georgia girl, her face heart-shaped and pale and glum, with fine eyes that could stop frowning and open brilliantly upon everything. We had not then read her first stories, but we knew that Mr. Ransom had said of them that they were *written.* Before she left that day we had a glimpse of her penetration and her scornful humor, and during the spring we saw her again and saw the furnished room where she lived and worked in a drab apartment hotel on the upper West Side. Among the writing people who were our friends Flannery, as a devout Catholic, was something of a curiosity (they were curiosities to her, too). She could make things fiercely plain, as in her comment, now legendary, on an interesting discussion of the Eucharistic Symbol: "If it were only a symbol, I'd say to hell with it."

The manner in which Flannery came to live with us that year was this. Having two small children and the promise of more, we were looking for a home in the country, and in July we found and bought one, a stone and timber house that lay back in a wilderness of laurel and second-growth oak on a hilltop in Connecticut. Over the garage part of the house was a separate bedroom and bathroom with a stairway of its own, suitable for a boarder. We badly needed a boarder, and Flannery volunteered. Our new house had character but no good joinery or other luxury, and the O'Connor study-bedroom was austere. The only piece of furniture I can distinctly remember was a Sears Roebuck dresser that my wife and I had painted a bright sky blue. The walls were of beaverboard on which we had rolled a coat or two of paint, vainly hoping to make them smooth. Between beaverboard and timbering the fieldmice pattered as the nights turned frosty, and our boarder's device against them was to push in pins on which they might hurt their feet, as she said. She reassured us a few years later that she had not had to put layers of New York *Times* between her blankets that winter. I know for a fact that she had to stuff newspaper in the window cracks; we did, too. We all stayed healthy, nevertheless.

The working day as we set it up that fall began with early Mass in Georgetown, four miles away. My wife and I took turns making this drive with our boarder while one of us remained to amuse the infants and get breakfast. After her egg the boarder would disappear up the back stairs. She would reappear about noon in her sweater, blue jeans and loafers, looking slender and almost tall, and would take her daily walk, a half mile or so down the hill to the mailbox and back. No one lingered over lunch, but in the evening when the children had been fed and quieted for the night we would put a small pitcher of martinis to soak and call the boarder. Our talks then and at the dinner table were long and lighthearted, and they were our movies, our concerts, and our theatre.

Flannery was out to be a writer on her own and had no plans to go back to live in Georgia. Her reminiscences, however,

were almost all of her home town and countryside, and they were told with gusto. We heard a great deal even then about the farm outside Milledgeville which her mother had inherited from a brother, Flannery's Uncle Bernard, and was already managing with hired help, though she lived in town. The Negroes included, and still do, Jack and Louise and their boarder, Shot. Flannery would shake with laughter over some of their remarks and those of other country characters. We heard comparatively little about Iowa City, though one of the friends she had made there, Robie Macauley, won our pleased attention that year by bringing out a new edition of the Tietjens novels of Ford. Our boarder corresponded with a number of other young writers, wandering souls, from whose letters she would sometimes read us a passage of bravado.

I owe to Flannery my first reading of *Miss Lonelyhearts* that winter, as I owe her also my reading of *As I Lay Dying.* These are the only two works of fiction that I can remember her urging on me, and it is pretty clear from her work that they were close to her heart as a writer. So was Lardner. Literary criticism in general was not, but one essay that we all read and liked was Andrew Lytle's classic piece on Caroline Gordon, whom we knew and who later gave Flannery a lot of close and valuable counsel. We read and passed on to one another Newman and Acton and Father Hughes' history of the Church. At the college where I was working, an hour's drive away, I took up the *Divine Comedy* with some students, and I am almost sure I lent Flannery the Binyon version. Though she deprecated her French, now and again she would read some, and once carried off one of those appetizing volumes of Faguet from which I had learned about all I knew of old French literature. The interior life interested her, but less at that time than later as material for fiction. She maintained, for example, that Harry in *The Family Reunion* actually had pushed his wife overboard, against a theory that he had done so only in his mind. "If nothing happened, there's no story."

Meanwhile the typescript of yellow second sheets piled up in the room over the garage. Her first hero, Hazel Motes, had been imagined for a story that she published in the *Sewanee,* and this story, thinned out and toned down, was the opening of the novel she worked on now. The central episodes with Enoch Emery and Hoover Shoates (a name we all celebrated) were written in the winter and spring. In the summer of 1950, when she had reached an impasse with Haze and didn't know how to finish him off, she read for the first time the Oedipus plays. She went on then to end her story with the self-blinding of Motes, and she had to rework the body of the novel to prepare for it.

So that year passed in our wilderness. The leaves turned, the rains came, the woods were bared, the snows fell and glittered, fenders were belted by broken chains, the winter stars shone out. In the early mornings we had the liturgies of All Hallows, All Souls, Advent, Christmas, Epiphany. The diaper truck and the milk truck slogged in and slogged out. We worked on at our jobs through thaws and buds, through the May flies, and into summer, when we could take our evening ease in deckchairs on the grass. In May we had a third child to be baptised, this one held by Flannery O'Connor as Godmother. Standing with her was Robert Giroux, who had become her editor (he too had met her in 1949) and later was to become her publisher. She was now one of the family, and no doubt the coolest and funniest one. She often entertained a child in her room or took one for a walk, and she introduced me to the idea and the Southern expression of *cutting a switch* to meet infant provocation—a useful recourse then and later. She was sure that we grown-ups were known to the children in private as "he," "she" and "the other one."

In the second autumn I had reason to be especially glad of our boarder's company at home, because I had to be away on a job half the week. But in December, just after the long labor of typing out her first draft, Flannery told us with amusement of a heaviness in her typing arms. When this got worse, we took her to the doctor at Wilton Corners. Rheumatoid arthritis, he was afraid it was, but he advised her to have a hospital check-up in Georgia when she went home for Christmas. On the train going south she became desperately ill. She did not have arthritis but a related disease, lupus, the disease that had killed her father.

For the rest of that winter and spring she was mostly in Emory Hospital in Atlanta, and very sick indeed. Disseminated lupus, as it is technically called, is an auto-immune disease in the same general group as arthritis and rheumatic fever. The trouble is that the body forms antibodies to its own tissues. It is primarily a blood vessel disease and can affect any organ; it can affect the bones. I have these details from Dr. Arthur J. Merrill in Atlanta, who pulled Flannery through that first onset with blood transfusions and was able then to arrest the disease with injections of a cortisone derivative, ACTH, in those days still in the experimental stage. Her hair all fell out after the high fevers, her face became terribly swollen, and he had to dehydrate her and put her on a salt-free diet. It is a fair indication of how sick she was that, until summer, we had no letter from her at all but corresponded through her mother. When at last Dr. Merrill let her go home she was too weak to climb stairs, and Regina O'Connor, deciding to take her to the farm, made a home there which was to be hers and Flannery's for thirteen years.

It must have been in late spring or early summer that Giroux accepted the first complete draft of the manuscript of **Wise Blood** for publication at Harcourt, Brace, for I find an undated letter from Regina referring to this, and to attempts at revision that Flannery had been making before a recurrence of high fever sent her back to Emory. When this particular

bout was over she slowly improved for the rest of the year and began to write to us regularly. In September she reported being down to two moderate shots a day from four large ones. "The large doses of ACTH send you off in a rocket and are scarcely less disagreeable than the disease, so I am happy to be shut of them. I am working on the end of the book while a lady around here types the first part of it. . . . I have twenty-one brown ducks with blue wing bars."

She sent the retyped manuscript to us and we forwarded it, at her request, to Caroline Gordon, who had read Flannery's few stories with intense interest. "She sent it back to me," Flannery wrote later, "with some nine pages of comments and she certainly increased my education thereby. So I am doing some more things to it and then I mean to send it off for the LAST time. . . . I have got me five geese." A little later: "Enclosed is Opus Nauseous No. 1. I had to read it over after it came from the typist's and that was like spending the day eating a horse blanket. . . . Do you think Mrs. Tate would [read it again]? All the changes are efforts after what she suggested in that letter and I am much obliged to her."

One of Caroline's main points was that the style of the narrator should be more consistently distinct from the style of the characters, and I believe that Flannery saw the rightness of this and learned quickly when and when not to use a kind of indirect discourse in the country idiom she loved. Before the first of the year the publishers had the manuscript in its final form, and it was published in May, 1952. The reviewers, by and large, didn't know what to make of it. I don't think anyone even spotted the bond with Nathanael West. Isaac Rosenfeld in *The New Republic* objected that since the hero was plain crazy it was difficult to take his religious predicament seriously. But Rosenfeld and everyone else knew that a strong new writer was at large.

Flannery had announced in December that she aimed to visit us sometime in 1952. "I am only a little stiff in the heels so far this winter and am taking a new kind of ACTH, put up in glue. . . ." This worked so well that in the course of the spring she decided to come in June. Reactions to her grisly book around Milledgeville were of course all that could have been expected. One of the kin delighted her with a telling and memorable remark: "I wish you could have found some other way to portray your talents." In May she wrote: "My current literary assignment (from Regina) is to write an introduction for Cousin Katie 'so she won't be shocked,' to be *pasted* on the inside of her book. This piece has to be in the tone of the Sacred Heart Messenger and carry the burden of contemporary critical thought. I keep putting it off."

She came, looking ravaged but pretty, with short soft new curls. She was still on the salt-free diet, so my wife gave her cress and herbs. It proved to be a difficult summer. We now had four small children and were taking a small Negro slum child for a two week country holiday. I had to go off on a six week job in the Middle West. Our D.P., an old shepherdess from Gorizia, after being helpful for a year, had learned from Croatian acquaintances of the comparative delights of life in Jersey City, and had begun to turn nasty. Before I got back, my wife was ill and Flannery, herself on the verge of a relapse, had to return to Milledgeville. She took the Negro child, Loretta, with her as far as New York. I'm afraid she had no high opinion of our quixotic hospitality to Loretta, who, she wrote to me, "might have been controllable if there had been a U.S. marshal in the house." My wife says this was pure Georgia rhetoric on Flannery's part, Loretta having been too shy during her visit to do anything but stand around caressing the blond heads of our young. Flannery had picked up a virus infection, which aroused her lupus, and Dr. Merrill had to put her dose of ACTH up temporarily from .25 cc. to 1 cc. a day. As to this, she wrote, "I have gotten a kind of Guggenheim. The ACTH has been reduced from $19.50 per bottle to $7.50." Soon she was better, up, and working, "and have just ordered myself a pair of peafowl and four peachicks from Florida...."

That year, in spite of illness, she did a lot of writing, some of it as good in its way as she would ever do. The story entitled **"The Life You Save May Be Your Own,"** an inimitably funny one that is also a triumph over Erskine Caldwell and a thing of great beauty, I remember reading in manuscript on the road to Indiana. She showed us, too, the opening of a second novel, so powerful that we felt, one and all, that since it would be very hard to sustain it might have to be toned down. It was later, a little, and became part of *The Violent Bear It Away.* She wrote **"The River."** In the fall John Crowe Ransom invited her to apply for a Kenyon Review Fellowship, and she applied, she said, "before the envelope was opened good." By Christmas she knew that she had it. "I reckon most of this money will go to blood and ACTH and books, with a few sideline researches into the ways of the vulgar. I would like to go to California for about two minutes to further these researches, though at times I feel that a feeling for the vulgar is my natural talent and don't need any particular encouragement. Did you see the picture of Roy Rogers' horse attending a church service in Pasadena?"

News and other items in the press of our favored land were always a solace to her. She turned eagerly for years to the testimonial ads for a patent medicine called HADACOL, and these she would often pass on, especially after we moved to Europe late in '53 and were cut off from the savor of American life. Early that year, when she began to receive her fellowship money, she reported a mild change in the interest shown her work by the countryside. "My kinfolks think I am a commercial writer now and really they are very proud of me. My uncle Louis is always bringing a message from

somebody at the King Hdw. Co. who has read *Wise Blood.* The last was: ask her why she don't write about some nice people. Louis says, I told them you wrote what *paid.* . . . I am doing fairly well these days, though I am practically baldheaded on top and have a watermelon face. . . ."

In another letter of about the same time I find: "The Maple Oats really send me. I mean they are a heap of improvement over saltless oatmeal, horse biscuit, stewed kleenex, and the other delicacies that I have been eating. . . . The novel seems to be doing very well. I have a nice gangster in it named Rufus Florida Johnson. . . ." Disappearing from the novel, he turned up a long time later in one of the stories in this volume. Dr. Merrill, whom she liked and called "the scientist," told her in the summer that she was "doing better than anybody else has that has what I got," and she flew up to see us in August. It was our last meeting as a family for five years.

The correspondence for 1954 begins: "I got word the other day that I had been reappointed a Kenyon Fellow, so that means the Rockerfellers [the Foundation supplied funds for the fellowships] will see to my blood and ACTH for another year and I will have to keep on praying for the repose of John D.'s soul. . . . Today I got a letter from one Jimmie Crum of Los Angeles, California, who has just read *Wise Blood* and wants to know what happened to the guy in the ape suit. . . . I am also corresponding with the secretary of the Chef's National Magazine, the Culinary Review. . . ." She was acquiring what she called a "gret" reading public. She would soon have enough short stories for a collection. And her disease had apparently been checked. Late in the year, however, we heard of a new ailment in a letter to my wife: "I am walking with a cane these days which gives me a great air of distinction. . . . I now feel that it makes very little difference what you call it. As the niggers say, I have the misery." In the same letter: "I have finally got off the ms. for my collection and it is scheduled to appear in May. Without your kind permission I have taken the liberty of dedicating (grand verb) it to you and Robert. This is because you all are my adopted kin. . . . Nine stories about original sin, with my compliments. . . ."

The misery referred to in this letter turned out to be disheartening enough. Either her disease or the drug that controlled it, or both, caused a softening or deterioration of the bones, her jaw bones and also her leg bones at the hip. Finally, a year later, the doctor put her on crutches. At more or less the same time, though, she was able—thank God—to switch from ACTH to a new wonder drug, taken in tablets, in tiny doses, and "for the first time in four years don't have to give myself shots or conserve on salt." Meanwhile her book of stories, *A Good Man Is Hard To Find,* went into a third printing. Early in '56 she learned that Gallimard was publishing *Wise Blood* in Paris in an expert translation by

Maurice Coindreau. She found herself now and hence-forward a woman-of-letters. And in fact she and her devoted and keenwitted mother, who learned thoroughly to understand what Flannery was up to, became an effective team. Regina ran the farm and guarded Flannery's limited strength and saw to it that she had her mornings free for writing. At noon they would drive in to town for the mail and most often have lunch at the Sanford House, where behind the white pillars there is excellent cooking, and over the mantel there is a photograph of General Lee. In the afternoon Flannery could take the air on her crutches and feed her various fowl. She wrote that she had sixteen peachickens and her sense of well-being was at its height.

The new drug and the crutches increased Flannery's mobility so much that she began to accept invitations to give talks and readings at relatively distant points. After the isolated life in Connecticut and the confinement of her illness, these trips—and in the next six or seven years she made a score of them—brought her into the world again and gave her a whole new range of acquaintances. In her talks she had wonderful things to say. I didn't quite realize this—I just wanted to see her—when I got her to come to Notre Dame in the spring of '57 (I was working there on temporary leave, self-accorded, from the job I had in hand in Italy). I met her in Chicago and flew down with her to South Bend. She seemed frail but steady, no longer disfigured by any swelling, and her hair had grown long again. She managed her light crutches with distaste but some dexterity. Her audience that evening was already instructed in a number of topics of concern to her, but it was better instructed when she finished. I have this paper before me now, and can remember my pleasure as she read it out, intent upon it, hanging on her crutches at the lectern, courteous and earnest and dissolvent of nonsense.

"I doubt if the texture of Southern life is any more grotesque than that of the rest of the nation, but it does seem evident that the Southern writer is particularly adept at recognizing the grotesque; and to recognize the grotesque, you have to have some notion of what is not grotesque and why. . . ."

"Southern culture has fostered a type of imagination that has been influenced by Christianity of a not too unorthodox kind and by a strong devotion to the Bible, which has kept our minds attached to the concrete and the living symbol. . . ."

"The Catholic sacramental view of life is one that maintains and supports at every turn the vision that the story teller must have if he is going to write fiction of any depth. . . ."

"The Church, far from restricting the Catholic writer, generally provides him with more advantages than he is able or willing to turn to account; and usually, his sorry productions are a result, not of restrictions that the Church has imposed, but of restrictions that he has failed to impose on himself. Freedom is of no use without taste and without the ordinary competence to follow the particular laws of what we have been given to do. . . ."

Toward the end of the year she wrote to us (we were living in Liguria) that Cousin Katie in Savannah wished to give her and her mother a trip to Lourdes with a company of pilgrims from Savannah. Dr. Merrill permitted this on condition that she depart from the "tour" to rest with us for a week. So in April I brought her and Mrs. O'Connor down to our place from Milan, and after the visit my wife went along to Lourdes to help with the languages and details of travel. Flannery dreaded the possibility of a miracle at Lourdes, and she forced herself to the piety of the bath for her mother's sake and Cousin Katie's; she also accompanied the pilgrims to Rome for an audience with Pope Pius XII, who received her with interest and gave her a special blessing. On May 11, home again, she wrote: "I enjoyed most seeing you all and the Pope. . . ." There was no miracle but what seemed a small favor: her bone trouble got no worse.

For the rest of that year she worked on the new novel. Early in '59 she had finished a draft at about the time the Ford Foundation gave her (as also to me, a bolt from the blue) one of eleven grants for creative writing. Her hip and her general condition now allowed her to drive around Milledgeville "all over the place in the automobile just like a bloody adult." We had some correspondence about the novel, in particular about reworking the character of Rayber who had been, she said, "the trouble all along." She made the middle section more dramatic by adding the episode of the girl revivalist. By mid-October it was done, and it was brought out by her present publisher in May, 1960.

I saw Flannery twice again, once on a visit to the farm when the dogwood was flowering in April, 1961, and then at the Smith College commencement in 1963 when she received an honorary degree. The serenity of the natural scene on these occasions now frames for me the serenity of our old boarder, who had fought a good fight and been illuminated by it. In '63 as in '56 she won the first prize in the annual O. Henry short story collection, and she was working on a third novel. But early in '64 her great respite came to an end. She had to have an abdominal operation. In the aftermath of this her lupus returned, in April, and proved uncontrollable. In May, as I learned later, Caroline Gordon found her looking wan and wasted. She was in the Piedmont Hospital in Atlanta for a month in May and June. I heard nothing of this and had no notion that she was seriously ill until a note came from her with a new anecdote of farm life and the single sentence: "Ask Sally to pray that the lupus don't finish me off too quick." Late in July she was taken to the

Milledgeville hospital with a severe kidney failure, and she died there in a coma on the morning of August 3.

> The black sky was underpinned with long silver streaks that looked like scaffolding and depth on depth behind it were thousands of stars that all seemed to be moving very slowly as if they were about some vast construction work that involved the whole order of the universe and would take all time to complete. No one was paying any attention to the sky. The stores in Taulkinham stayed open on Thursday nights so that people could have an extra opportunity to see what was for sale.
>
> (*Wise Blood*)

A catchword when Flannery O'Connor began to write was the German *angst,* and it seemed that Auden had hit it off in one of his titles as the "Age of Anxiety." The last word in attitudes was the Existentialist one, resting on the perception that beyond any immediate situation there is possibly nothing—nothing beyond, nothing behind, nada. Now, our country family in 1949 and 1950 believed on excellent grounds that beyond the immediate there was practically everything, like the stars over Taulkinham—the past, the future, and the Creator thereof. But the horror of recent human predicaments had not been lost on us. Flannery felt that an artist who was a Catholic should face all the truth down to the worst of it. If she worried about the side effects of the ungenteel imagination, she took heart that year from Mauriac's dictum about "purifying the source"—the creative spirit—rather than damming or diverting the stream.

The fiction writer presents mystery through manners, grace through nature, but when he finishes, there always has to be left over that sense of Mystery which cannot be accounted for by any human formula.
—*Flannery O'Connor*

In *Wise Blood* she did parody the Existentialist point of view, as Bernard Cheney has said (in the *Sewanee Review* for Autumn, 1964), but the parody was very serious. In this and in most of her later writing she gave to the godless a force proportionate to the force it actually has: in episode after episode, as in the world, as in ourselves, it wins. We can all hear our disbelief, picked out of the air we breathe, when Hazel Motes says, "I'm going to preach there was no Fall because there was nothing to fall from and no Redemption becase there was no Fall and no Judgment because there wasn't the first two. Nothing matters but that Jesus was a liar." And in whom is *angst* so dead that he never feels, as Haze puts it: "Where you came from is gone, where you

thought you were going to never was there, and where you are is no good unless you can get away from it."

Note the velocity and rightness of these sentences. Many pages and a number of stories by this writer have the same perfection, and the novels have it in sections though they narrowly miss it as wholes. I am speaking now of merits achieved in the reader's interest: no unliving words, the realization of character by exquisitely chosen speech and interior speech and behavior, the action moving at the right speed so that no part of the situation is left out or blurred and the violent thing, though surprising, happens after due preparation, because it has to. Along with her gifts, patient toil and discipline brought about these merits, and a further question can be asked about that: Why? What was the standard to which the writer felt herself answerable? Well, in 1957 she said:

> The serious fiction writer will think that any story that can be entirely explained by the adequate motivation of the characters or by a believable imitation of a way of life or by a proper theology, will not be a large enough story for him to occupy himself with. This is not to say that he doesn't have to be concerned with adequate motivation or accurate reference or a right theology; he does; but he has to be concerned with them only because the meaning of his story does not begin except at a depth where these things have been exhausted. The fiction writer presents mystery through manners, grace through nature, but when he finishes, there always has to be left over that sense of Mystery which cannot be accounted for by any human formula.

This is an open and moving statement of a certain end for literary art. The end, and some of the terms used here, seem to me similar to those of another Christian writer who died recently, T.S. Eliot. I do not propose any confusion between a London man of letters who wrote verse and criticism and a Southern woman who wrote fiction, for indeed they lived a world apart. Only at the horizon, one might say, do the lines each pursued come together; but the horizon is an important level. It is also important that they were similarly moved toward serious art, being early and much possessed by death as a reality, a strong spiritual sensation, giving odd clarity to the appearances they saw through or saw beyond. In her case as in his, if anyone at first found the writing startling he could pertinently remind himself how startling it was going to be to lose his own body, that Ancient Classic. Sensibility in both produced a wariness of beautiful letters and, in the writing, a concision of effect.

When it comes to seeing the skull beneath the skin, we may remark that the heroes of both O'Connor novels are so perceived within the first few pages, and her published work begins and ends with coffin dreams. Her *memento mori* is no less authentic for being often hilarious, devastating to a secular world and all it cherishes. The O'Connor equivalent for Eliot's drowned Phoenician sailor ("Consider Phlebas, who was once handsome and tall as you") is a museum piece, the shrunken corpse that the idiot Enoch Emery in *Wise Blood* proposes as the new humanist jesus.

> "See theter notice," Enoch said in a church whisper, pointing to a typewritten card at the man's foot, "it says he was once as tall as you or me. Some A-rabs did it to him in six months. . . ."

And there is a classic exchange in **"The Life You Save May Be Your Own"**:

> "Why listen, lady," said Mr. Shiftlet with a grin of delight, "the monks of old slept in their coffins."
>
> "They wasn't as advanced as we are," the old woman said.

The state of being as advanced as we are had been, of course, blasted to glory in *The Waste Land* before Flannery made her version, a translation, as it were, into American (**"The Vacant Lot"**). To take what used to be called low life and picture it as farcically empty, raging with energy, and at the same time, *sub specie aeternitatis*, full of meaning: this was the point of *Sweeney Agonistes* and the point of many pages of O'Connor. As for our monuments, those of a decent godless people, surely the asphalt road and the thousand lost golf balls are not a patch on images like that of the hillside covered with used car bodies, in *The Violent Bear It Away:*

> In the indistinct darkness, they seemed to be drowning into the ground, to be about half-submerged already. The city hung in front of them on the side of the mountain as if it were a larger part of the same pile, not yet buried so deep. The fire had gone out of it and it appeared settled into its unbreakable parts.

Death is not the only one of the Last Things present in the O'Connor stories; Judgment is there, too. On the pride of contemporary man, in particular on flying as his greatest achievement, Tarwater in *The Violent* has a prophet's opinion:

> "I wouldn't give you nothing for no airplane. A buzzard can fly."

Christ the tiger, a phrase in Eliot, is a force felt in O'Connor. So is the impulse to renounce the blessèd face, and to renounce the voice. In her work we are shown that vices are fathered by our heroism, virtues forced upon us by our impudent crimes, and that neither fear nor courage saves us (we are saved by grace, if at all, though courage may dispose us toward grace). Her best stories do the work that Eliot wished his plays to do, raising anagogical meaning over literal action. He may have felt this himself, for though he rarely read fiction I am told that a few years before he died he read her stories and exclaimed in admiration at them.

The title of the present book comes from Teilhard de Chardin, whose works Flannery O'Connor had been reading at least since early 1961 when she recommended them to me. It is a title taken in full respect and with profound and necessary irony. For Teilhard's vision of the "omega point" virtually at the end of time, or at any rate of a time-span rightly conceivable by paleontologist or geologist alone, has appealed to people to whom it may seem to offer one more path past the Crucifixion. That could be corrected by no sense of life better than by O'Connor's. Quite as austere in its way as his, her vision will hold us down to earth where the clashes of blind wills and the low dodges of the heart permit any rising or convergence only at the cost of agony. At that cost, yes, a little.

The better a poem or piece of fiction, the more corrective or indeed destructive it is likely to be of any fatuous happiness in abstractions. "Rising" and "convergence" in these stories, as the title story at once makes clear, are shown in classes, generations, and colors. What each story has to say is what it shows. If we are aware that the meaning of the stories is to be sought in the stories and well apprehended in the stories alone, we may try a few rough and cautious statements about them. Thus the title story shows, amid much else in a particular action of particular persons, young and old and black and white to be practically sealed off against one another, struggling but hardly upward or together in a welter of petty feelings and cross purposes, resolved only slightly even by the tragic blow. "Slightly," however, may mean a great deal in the economy of this writer. The story is one of those, like **"The Artificial Nigger"** in her first collection and **"Revelation"** in this, in which the low-keyed and calibrated style is allowed a moment of elevation.

What is wrong in this story we feel to be diffused throughout the persons and in the predicament itself, but in at least two of the stories, and those among the latest and most elaborate, the malign is more concentrated in one personage. I do not mean *il maligno*, as the Italians call the devil. There are few better representations of the devil in fiction than Tarwater's friend, as overheard and finally embodied in *The Violent;* but in these two stories, **"The Comforts of Home"** and **"The Lame Shall Enter First,"** the personage in question is not quite that. He need not be, since the souls to be attacked are comparatively feeble. Brainless and brainy depravity are enough, respectively, to bring down in ruin an irritable academic and a self-regarding do-gooder. The latter story is clearly a second effort with the three figures of the novel, Tarwater, Rayber and Bishop, who are here reworked, more neatly in some respects, as Johnson, Shepard and Norton.

Other similarities link various stories to one another and to earlier stories. There is a family resemblance between Julian in the title story, Wesley in **"Greenleaf,"** Asbury in **"The Enduring Chill"** and Thomas in **"The Comforts of Home."** The Wellesley girl in **"Revelation"** is related to all these and to the girl in **"Good Country People."** In the various mothers of the stories there are facets of Mrs. McIntyre in **"The Displaced Person."** Parker in **"Parker's Back"** has some of the traits of a latter-day Hazel Motes. The critic will note these recurrent types and situations. He will note too that the setting remains the same, Southern and rural as he will say, and that large classes of contemporary experience, as of industry and war and office work and foreign travel, are barely touched if touched at all. But in saying how the stories are limited and how they are not, the sensitive critic will have a care. For one thing, it is evident that the writer deliberately and indeed indifferently, almost defiantly, restricted her horizontal range; a pasture scene and a fortress wall of pine woods reappear like a signature in story after story. The same is true of her social range and range of idiom. But these restrictions, like the very humility of her style, are all deceptive. The true range of the stories is vertical and Dantesque in what is taken in, in scale of implication. As to the style, there is also more to say.

She would be sardonic over the word *ascesis,* but it seems to me a good one for the peculiar discipline of the O'Connor style. How much has been refrained from, and how much else has been cut out and thrown away, in order that the bald narrative sentences should present just what they present and in just this order! What counts is the passion by which the stories were formed, the depth, as Virginia Woolf said of Milton, at which the options were taken. Beyond incidental phrasing and images, beauty lies in the strong invention and execution of the things, as in objects expertly forged or cast or stamped, with edges, not waxen and worn or softly moulded.

If we look for pleasure of a secondary kind such as we take in the shadings and suffusions of Henry James, I suggest that this is given in these stories by the comedy. There is quite a gamut of it, running from something very like cartooning to an irony dry and refined, especially in the treatment of the most serious matters. John Crowe Ransom was the first reader known to me to realize and say that Flannery O'Connor was one of our few tragic writers, a fact that we will not miss now in reading **"The Displaced Person"** in the first volume or **"The Comforts of Home"** in this. But it is far from the whole story. On the tragic scene, each time, the presence of her humor is like the presence of grace. Has

not tragicomedy at least since Dante been the most Christian of *genres?*

I do not want to claim too much for these stories, or to imply that every story comes off equally well. That would be unfaithful to her own conscience and sense of fact. Let the good critic rejoice in the field for discrimination these stories offer him. Before I turn them over to him and to the reader, I should like to offer a reflection or two on the late masterpiece called **"Revelation."** One of its excellences is to present through a chance collection in a doctor's waiting-room a picture of a whole "section"—realized, that is, in the human beings who compose it, each marvelously and irreducibly what he or she is. For one example of the rendering, which is faultless, consider this:

> A grotesque revolving shadow passed across the curtain behind her and was thrown palely on the opposite wall. Then a bicycle clattered down against the outside of the building. The door opened and a colored boy glided in with a tray from the drug store. It had two large red and white paper cups on it with tops on them. He was a tall, very black boy in discolored white pants and a green nylon shirt. He was chewing gum slowly, as if to music. He set the tray down in the office opening next to the fern and stuck his head through to look for the secretary. She was not in there. He rested his arms on the ledge and waited, his narrow bottom stuck out, swaying slowly to the left and right. He raised a hand over his head and scratched the base of his skull.

Not only do we see this boy for the rest of our lives; for an instant we hear him think. But the greater excellence of the story is to bring about a rising and a convergence, a movement of spirit in Ruby Turpin that is her rising to a terrible occasion, and a convergence between her and the violent agent of this change.

The terms of the struggle are intensely local, as they will be in all such struggles, but we need not be too shy about seeing through them to the meaning that lies beyond at the usual mysterious depth. How else but at a mysterious depth can we understand a pretty notion like the Soul of the South? What the struggle requires of Mrs. Turpin is courage and humility, that is clear enough. Perhaps as a reward for these, her eyes are opened. And the ascent that she sees at the end, in an astonishment like the astonishment of the new dead, takes place against that field of stars that moved beyond Taulkinham in *Wise Blood* and that hold for a small boy, in another of these stories, the lost presence of his mother.

Patricia Dinneen Maida (essay date Fall 1970)

SOURCE: "'Convergence' in Flannery O'Connor's 'Everything That Rises Must Converge,'" in *Studies in Short Fiction*, Vol. VII, No. 4, Fall, 1970, pp. 549-55.

[*In the following essay, Dinneen Maida discusses the idea of convergence in O'Connor's "Everything That Rises Must Converge" and asserts that O'Connor shows man his inadequacies.*]

Flannery O'Connor's fiction continues to provoke interest and critical analysis. The title story of her posthumous collection of short stories, ***Everything That Rises Must Converge,*** has been among those stories that have received attention lately. But no one has yet examined the implications of the title. Robert Fitzgerald tells us that Miss O'Connor got the idea for the title when she read Teilhard de Chardin's *The Phenomenon of Man* in 1961.

Typical of an O'Connor work, this story has meaning on several levels; especially, the allusion to Chardin's theory of "convergence" offers an enriching dimension to the story. Essentially, it describes an experience of a mother and son that changes the course of their lives. Measured against the background of Southern middle-class values, the mother-son relationship has social and also personal implications. But, on a larger scale, the story depicts the plight of all mankind. Furthermore, as one considers the allusion in the title, the universality of Miss O'Connor's message becomes even more evident—as does the intensity of her vision and her aesthetic.

The focus of the story is on the disparate values of Julian and his mother, epitomized by the bourgeois hat she chooses to wear on her weekly trip to an equally bourgeois event, a reducing class at the "Y." More provoked than usual because he considers the hat ugly, Julian sullenly accompanies her on the bus ride downtown. His mother, a descendent of an old Southern family, lives on past glories that give her a sense of self-importance. Thus as she goes to her reducing class, she tells Julian: "Most of them in it are not our kind of people, . . . but I can be gracious to anybody. I know who I am." In his retort Julian sums up the attitude of his generation: "They don't give a damn for your graciousness. . . . Knowing who you are is good for one generation only. You haven't the foggiest idea where you stand now or who you are." His mother, however, is convinced of her ability to communicate amiably: when boarding the bus, she "entered with a little smile, as if she were going into a drawing room where everyone had been waiting for her." In contrast, Julian maintains an icy reserve.

Integration emerges as the divisive issue. When Julian and his mother first board the bus, there are no Negro passengers. But when a Negro man enters shortly afterwards, the atmosphere becomes tense. As one might expect, Julian's mother does not see any value in integration, whereas Julian favors it. He purports to be a liberal; yet he acts primarily out of retaliation against the old system rather than out of genuine concern for the Negro. We are told that "when he got on a bus by himself, he made it a point to sit down by a Negro in reparation as it were for his mother's sins." His sense of guilt proves to be a negative force; for although he has tried to make friends with Negroes, he has never succeeded. Even during the bus ride when he attempts to converse with a Negro, he is ignored, his ingenuousness apparently sensed by those he approaches.

Julian's cynicism shuts him off from any human association. His chief asset, his intelligence, is misdirected: he freely scorns the limitations of others and assumes a superior stance. During the bus ride he indulges in his favorite pastime:

> Behind the newspaper Julian was withdrawing into the inner compartment of his mind where he spent most of his time. This was a kind of mental bubble in which he established himself when he could not bear to be a part of what was going on around him. From it he could see out and judge but in it he was safe from any kind of penetration from without. It was the only place where he felt free of the general idiocy of his fellows.

Ironically, he had convinced himself that he was a success—even though with a college degree he held a menial job instead of becoming the writer he had once hoped to be.

The bus and its passengers form a microcosm, and the events that occur in the course of the ride comprise a kind of sociodrama. As Julian's mother, bedecked in her new hat, chats with those around her, Julian remains distant and uninvolved. However, when a Negro woman and her son board the bus, the situation changes. Suddenly all eyes focus on the Negro woman, who happens to be wearing a hat identical to that of Julian's mother. Both women are shocked at first, but Julian is delighted: "He could not believe that Fate had thrust upon his mother such a lesson. He gave a loud chuckle so that she would look at him and see that he saw." But she recovers and is able to laugh, while the Negro woman remains visibly upset. When the two pairs of mothers and sons emerge from the bus at the same stop, Julian's mother cannot resist the impulse to offer the Negro boy a coin—despite Julian's protests. This act provokes such anger in the boy's mother that she strikes Julian's mother with her handbag. As Julian attempts to help his mother up from the pavement, he realizes that the shock of the experience has caused her to suffer a stroke—thus she actually becomes victim to the outdated code by which she has lived. The patronizing act of offering a coin is completely natural to her, yet offensive to the Negro. Her lack of touch with reality is dramatically exhibited after the stroke when she reverts to former times completely: "Tell Grandpa to come get me." For Julian, however, the shock he experiences at his mother's condition seems to open his eyes at long last to "the world of guilt and sorrow."

Because Julian, unlike anyone else in the story, is distinguished by name, the story focuses on him and his development. Everyone else functions in relation to and for the sake of the learning experience that eventually becomes meaningful to him. On a larger scale, moreover, the story has mythic and universal proportions in terms of the treatment of how an individual faces reality and attains maturity. For Julian, maturity becomes a possibility only after his faulty vision is corrected. When he witnesses the assault on his mother and its subsequent effect, he experiences a form of shock therapy that forces him out of the "mental bubble" of his own psyche.

Julian's situation reflects the particular O'Connor combination of comedy and tragic irony. On the bus as he recalls experiences of trying to make friends with Negroes, his responses are genuinely funny. When he recounts his disillusionment in discovering that his distinguished looking Negro acquaintance is an undertaker, when he imagines his mother desperately ill and his being able to secure only a Negro doctor for her, when he dreams of bringing home a "suspiciously Negroid" fiancée—the comedy runs high.

But as one considers the bitter irony of the situation, the nature of the humor changes. The lesson that he had hoped his mother would learn turns out to be meant for him; the confrontation of the two women with identical hats is comical, but the comedy is quickly reversed. In a discussion of the author's unique comedy, Cheney contends that this kind of humor might be called "metaphysical humor." He describes the effect in this way: "She begins with familiar surfaces that seem secular at the outset and in a secular tone of satire or humor. Before you know it, the naturalistic situation has become metaphysical, and the action appropriate to it comes with a surprise, an unaccountability that is humorous, however shocking." It is metaphysical in the sense that such humor calls into question the nature of being: man, the universe, and the relationship of the two. The hat, a symbol of the self-image, and the convergence of the two women with identical hats poses several questions: What is the significance of the individual's self-image? What common qualities do all men share? How does one relate to the world and others in it?

The "convergence" of the hats and the personalities of the respective owners is a violent clash—unpredictable and shocking. Nevertheless, the timing and circumstances work together to produce a kind of epiphany for Julian. And this kind of epiphany seems to be conceived and produced by the author. The title of the story offers a key to a more complete understanding of the epiphany or convergence process in an O'Connor short story. From the structure of the story it becomes evident that the rising action culminates in a crisis, a convergence of opposing forces, causing a dramatic and decisive change.

In addition, an understanding of the origin of the title of the story reveals a link between content and form. In a commentary on *The Phenomenon of Man,* Miss O'Connor tells why the work is meaningful to her:

> It is a search for human significance in the evolutionary process. Because Teilhard is both a man of science and a believer, the scientist and the theologian will require considerable time to sift and evaluate his thought, but the poet, whose sight is essentially prophetic, will at once recognize in Teilhard a kindred intelligence. His is a scientific expression of what the poet attempts to do: penetrate matter until spirit is revealed in it. Teilhard's vision sweeps forward without detaching itself at any point from the earth.

Chardin's vision seems to correspond with her own vision as she attempts to penetrate matter until spirit is reached and without detaching herself from the earth at any point. Penetration of matter occurs in an O'Connor story at the moment of crisis. Thus in the scene in which Julian witnesses the assault of his mother, the effect of physical violence produces a spiritual equivalent—Julian is forced to take stock of his soul. In fact, the theme of the story might be considered "a search for human significance in the evolutionary process."

> **"Everything That Rises Must Converge" is a simple story told in almost stark language. But the combination of realism and the grotesque with simplicity and starkness effects a unique intensity.**
> —*Patricia Dinneen Maida*

Chardin conceives of evolution as a constantly emerging spiral culminating at the center with God. In the tradition of the Christian humanist, he affirms the value of the individual by emphasizing his role as an intelligent being capable of cooperating with his Creator through grace—a term used for the communication of love between God and man. Chardin describes grace as "Christic energy," an illuminating force operative on the minds of men. The individual realizes his potential as a person through self-awareness, which is the ultimate effect of grace. In its entirety, Chardin's treatise is optimistic: he looks forward to the time when love will unite all individuals in the harmony of their humanity to produce a renewal of the natural order.

In contrast, Flannery O'Connor's view does not appear to be quite so optimistic: **"Everything That Rises Must Converge"** describes a bus ride in which there is no real communication between people, no understanding, and no harmony. How does this correspond with Chardin's prophecy of harmony between men at the point of convergence? The crux of the difference lies in perspectives: Chardin looks to the future; Miss O'Connor is concerned with the present and its consequences in the future. In other words, a mother and son boarding a bus in a Southern town at the present time are important individuals; the way they live their lives is also important. Why? Because, as Chardin would agree, each man has the potential to fulfill himself as a human being. In his introduction to ***Everything That Rises Must Converge,*** Fitzgerald says that Miss O'Connor uses the title "in full respect and with profound and necessary irony." The irony, however, is not directed at erring mankind or at Chardin's optimism; it is in the contrast between what man has the potential to become and what he actually achieves. For example, Julian deludes himself into thinking that no one means anything to him; he shuts himself off from his fellows and becomes the victim of his own egotism. In his immediate situation he is his own worst enemy and the cause of his own failure; but ultimately, he is less than a man—and, in this sense, his position is tragic. However, he does receive a revelation that may "redeem" him; that is, make him the man he could be.

The difference between the convergence described by Chardin and that which occurs in Miss O'Connor's story is ironic only in the contrast between the real and the ideal. Julian does experience a kind of convergence: his distorted vision is corrected (if not permanently, at least for a time): he does receive the opportunity to revamp his life. Consider how Julian arrives at his moment of truth: he does not seek it, nor does he achieve it himself through thoughtful deliberation. The means are external to him, gratuitous, though compelling. Chardin would call this a form of "Christic energy" or grace through which the individual is brought into closer communication with the source of truth. Miss O'Connor seems to be describing the same process, though in fictional terms. In discussing grace and its presentation in fiction, she said, "Part of the complexity for the Catholic fiction writer will be the presence of grace as it appears in nature, and what matters for him here is that his faith not become detached from his dramatic sense and from his vision of what is." This statement explains her focus on the present; it also reveals the basis of her aesthetic.

In his study of Flannery O'Connor, Hyman contends that "any discussion of her theology can only be preliminary to, not a substitute for, aesthetic analysis and evaluation." Aes-

thetically, Miss O'Connor strived to produce a view of reality in the most direct and concrete terms. **"Everything That Rises Must Converge"** is a simple story told in almost stark language. But the combination of realism and the grotesque with simplicity and starkness effects a unique intensity. Consider, for example, the way realistic and grotesque elements form the imagery of the story. As mother and son begin their trip, "the sky was a dying violet and the houses stood out darkly against it, bulbous liver-colored monstrosities of a uniform ugliness, though no two were alike." Even the hat, which plays such a focal part in the conflict, is especially hideous: "A purple velvet flap came down on one side of it and stood up on the other; the rest of it was green and looked like a cushion with the stuffing out." Julian is hypersensitive: color and form possess an emotional equivalent for him. Thus when the Negro woman sits next to him on the bus, he is acutely aware of her: "He was conscious of a kind of bristling next to him, a muted growling like that of an angry cat. He could not see anything but the red pocketbook upright on the bulging green thighs." The correlation between color and emotion is also evident when he looks at his mother after she recognizes the hat on the other woman: "She turned her eyes on him slowly. The blue in them seemed to have turned a bruised purple. For a moment he had an uncomfortable sense of her innocence." But the ultimate horror awaits him after his mother has suffered the stroke: "Her face was fiercely distorted. One eye, large and staring, moved slightly to the left as if it had become unmoored. The other remained fixed on him, raked his face again, found nothing and closed." Miss O'Connor does not flood her work with details; she is highly selective—choosing only those aspects that are most revealing. She does not cringe at ugliness; in fact, she seems compelled to highlight it when it is essential to meaning.

Julian has the potential to fulfill himself as a person and to be of use to a society in need of reform. Until his mother's stroke, he has no impetus to change his outlook; consequently, it takes a disaster to move him. The world in which he lives is grotesque, and perhaps the way in which he comes to his self-realization is appropriately grotesque. But the glimmer of hope shines only after he has been illuminated by the experience. Considering man's "progress" in human development, Flannery O'Connor seems to be painting the most vivid picture possible to show mankind where his inadequacies lie and to open his eyes to some painful truth. Through her keen, selective way of compressing the most significant material into a clear and simple structure, the message comes across with power and shocking clarity.

Marion Montgomery (essay date 1971)

SOURCE: "On Flannery O'Connor's 'Everything That Rises

Must Converge,'" in *Critique,* Vol. XIII, No. 2, 1971, pp. 15-29.

[*In the following essay, Montgomery refers to a superficial analysis of O'Connor's "Everything That Rises Must Converge," and proceeds to analyze the story on a deeper level.*]

Flannery O'Connor's **"Everything That Rises Must Converge"** first appeared in *New World Writing Number 17,* in 1961, from which it was selected for inclusion in both *Best American Short Stories of 1962* and *Prize Stories of 1963: the O. Henry Awards.* It appeared posthumously, as the title story of the final collection of her fiction, in 1965. It has, in consequence, had special attention called to it over a period of years and has received critical, if sometimes puzzled, readings at a number of hands. Predictably, much (though not all) of that attention has centered upon the topical materials it uses, the "racial" problem which seems the focus of the conflict between the story's "Southern mother" and her liberal son. That sort of attention is one of the inevitable by-products of the turmoils that have engaged us since the story's initial publication, turmoils that fulfill Unamuno's prophecy that soon we would be dying in the streets of sentimentality. In the interest of getting beyond the topical materials of the story, to those qualities of it that will make it endure in our literature, I should like to examine it in some detail, starting, as seems most economical, with a particularly superficial evaluation of it which Miss O'Connor called to my attention.

When the story appeared as first prize winner of the 1963 *O. Henry Awards,* it was remarked in one of those primary sources of Miss O'Connor's raw material, the Atlanta *Journal-Constitution:*

> . . . her basic plot line is provocative and witty: an old-guard Southern lady, afraid to ride the buses without her son since integration, parades out for an evening dressed in a new and expensive hat. On the bus she encounters a Negro woman in the same hat.

> Unfortunately the denouement of the story (the good Southern lady drops dead) is uncomfortable. It is pushed just too far.

An Olympian, anonymous evaluation, by one who has not even noticed that Julian is the protagonist. Almost two years later, when the posthumous collection appeared, there followed a praiseful review of the collection in which its author was caled "the most gallant writer, male or female in our contemporary culture," in which review Julian's mother is again specifically identified as the story's "protagonist."

One no longer expects to discover incisive reviews in news-

papers, more's the pity, and these notices themselves are of little importance except that they show forth a good bit of the context from which Miss O'Connor drew the materials of her fiction. She had immediate access to her "Christ-haunted" figures through local radio programs; one need only canvass the location stations between 11:00 A.M. and 2:00 P.M. during the week and on Sunday mornings to hear the voices of her prophets, though not their substance, and to see what a true ear she had for that speaking voice. But she used as well the Atlanta daily papers (called by rural Georgians as often as not "them lying Atlanta papers"). In them, for instance, she could see every Saturday a fundamentalist column, run as a paid advertisement with the title "Why Do the Heathen Rage," the title she had given the novel she left unfinished. There was also on Saturday the famous Pickrick ads of Lester Maddox, with their outrageous turns of wit in the midst of absurdities. But these were only a part of what interested Miss O'Connor in the newspapers. There were also displays of the mind of her Julians and Sheppards and Raybers, in the editorial columns and on the book review page. As to what was constantly available to her, consider these excerpts from a regular column. It is a Sheppard's or a Rayber's version of **"A Good Man Is Hard to Find,"** underlining by contrast Miss O'Connor's sharpness in reading that particular "Southern" mind:

> Sixteen-year-old Dixie Radcliff, daughter of an Amesville, Ohio, clergyman, is in jail, classified as an adult charged with being an accessory to murder. She is a tenderhearted child who doesn't like to see anyone hurt. Because of this feminine revulsion to seeing people hurt, she remained in the car while her friend and lover, young Donald Boggs, killed four men. Donald, she says, was considerate. He did not ask Dixie to do more than tie the victims' hands behind their backs. He then took them away from the car so that Dixie would not see the killing. . . .

> There is no particular moral to draw from this sordid, pitiful story. That Don is a dangerous criminal, with a compulsion to kill, and that he is uninhibited by any sense of fear or moral conviction is plain. That Dixie Radcliff is a retarded child is plain. . . .

> Dixie will offend most those who say that children become delinquent today because of a lack of religious influence about the home. Dixie Radcliff grew up, apparently, with a religious influence about her like her clothes or skin. . . . She must have heard papa preach, pound the pulpit and flog the devil and his works a thousand times or more. . . .

> . . . The psychiatrists who worked over Dixie found

she knew quite well all that was going on and knew it was wrong and wicked.

Was the motivation of Don Boggs (and Dixie) something in their genes—or in their environment—or both?

We never will know. So we will send them both to jail and forget about it.

That Miss O'Connor's Raburs and Sheppards are with us as decisively as our Misfits is, I think, sufficiently evidenced by these excerpts from a Pulitzer winner's remarks, remarks that are vaguely disturbed by an anticipation of the fundamentalist reaction and by society's lack of primary concern for Don and Dixie over their hapless victims. The statement that Dixie is clearly retarded does not fit with the assertions of the psychiatrists. Nor does it seem to reside in the columnist's awareness that he has in fact drawn a moral from the story: namely, that parents and environment are either or both responsible for the unhappy plight of Don and Dixie. The columnist's position is that of a determinist, and if the grandmother in Miss O'Connor's story faces her Misfit with the same excuses for evil, she is able to do so from what she has absorbed from the Raburs and Sheppards who have inherited from the priest position of authority in moral matters, with the media as effective pulpit. (Still she was reared with a sounder understanding of evil as she finally admits.)

It is easier of course to make gestures of compassion or brotherhood in the daily press than to deal directly with our Dixies or Dons whom Miss O'Connor translates as a Misfit or Rufus Johnson. What she shows in the inescapable confrontations is, first, the stock responses such as the grandmother's or the columnist's or Sheppard's. Then she presses those responses, through the presence of antagonists, to the point where the response proves inadequate. The modern innocent so confronted is forced to acknowledge the existence of evil and of an older innocence, as the first step toward recovery. This we see in the grandmother's development following her encounter with the Misfit, but the same procedure is used in **"Everything That Rises Must Converge"** with an important exception. Here the central character is not a country grandma moved to Atlanta, but an aspiring candidate for the *intelligentsia*. Also the confrontation and the stock response to the confrontation occur in the same character. That is, Julian is, in effect, two presences in the story, the Julian who assumes himself aloof and detached from the human condition by virtue of his superior intellect and the Julian who destroys his mother before our eyes. The climax of the story occurs at a point where he recognizes his participation in the catastrophe that has occurred. I think we may make the point clear by first looking at the point of view Miss O'Connor has chosen, a point of view

which led the newspaper reviewers to mistake the mother as the central character.

From the first sentence of the story we have it established that this is Julian's story, though with a sufficient freedom in the related point of view to allow the author an occasional intrusion. "Her doctor had told Julian's mother that she must lose twenty pounds on account of her blood pressure, so on Wednesday nights Julian had to take her downtown on the bus for a reducing class at the Y." It is always *Julian's mother;* she is given no name. And we see her through Julian's eyes. The rest of the first paragraph, for instance, carries as if in Julian's sardonic mind, indirect reflections of his mother's words. Who else would speak of herself as one of "the working girls over fifty"? And there is a mimicry of his mother by Julian in such an indirect statement as this: ". . . because the reducing class was one of her few pleasures, necessary for her health, and *free,* she said Julian could at least put himself out to take her, considering all she did for him." The first paragraph concludes with a statement which is not quite neutral on the author's part, a statement we are to carry with us into the action: "Julian did not like to consider all she did for him, but every Wednesday night he braced himself and took her." The *but* indicates that on Wednesdays the consideration is inescapable, but also that Julian is capable of the minor sacrifice of venturing into the world from his generally safe withdrawal into "a kind of mental bubble." With the story so focused that we as readers are aware that we watch Julian watching his mother, the action is ready to proceed, with relatively few intrusions of the author from this point.

Our reading of Julian's mother, then, is made for us by him, so that one might very well see "the basic plot line" as dealing with "an old-guard Southern lady, afraid to ride the buses," as our anonymous reviewer put it. But our author gives a careful control of our reading, particularly in the imagery Julian chooses to describe his mother. Julian's distortions are those that a self-elected superior intellect is capable of making through self-deception; he is an intellect capable of surface distinctions but not those fundamental ones such as that between childish and child-like. In short, Julian takes himself to be liberated, older than his mother since he is more modern. He feels burdened by his retarded mother and so is free to enjoy the pleasure of his chosen martyrdom to her small desires. Still, there is no one available to him capable of appreciating him, and so no one to know, other than himself, the constancy of his sacrifice. While the mother doesn't hesitate to declare her sacrifices for him openly, he only acts out the pain of his own with expressions of pain and boredom. Standing slouched in the doorway, unwilling audience to her self-torture over paying $7.50 for a hideous green and purple hat, he is "waiting like Saint Sebastian for the arrows." He sees himself "sacrificed to her pleasure," and a little later finds himself depressed "as if in the midst of martyrdom he had lost his faith." In the bus, which he hates to ride more than she, since it brings him close to people, he sits by a Negro "in reparation as it were for his mother's sins." The disparity between his reading of his situation and our seeing that situation for what it is, is sufficient to put us on our guard in evaluating the mother.

Nevertheless, she too is full of a language disproportionate to her position, as he points out with pleasure. She repeats the cliches on the general decay of her civilization, recalling the days when her family was substantial. Her arguments are inherited, rather than learned as are Julian's, for Julian has, in his view of the matter, gotten on his own a first-rate education from a third-rate college, with the result that he is free. That is, he is already "as disenchanted with [life] as a man of fifty." His mother, in his account of the matter, is living a hundred years in the past, ignoring the immediate circumstances of her existence. It is rather obvious from what has been so far said that Julian is not only the central character of the story, but in many respects a less spectacular version of the Misfit. Disillusioned with life, he wants to be no closer than three miles to his nearest neighbor, as he says. That failing, since his ancestral "mansion" is lost to him, the only pleasure he gets from life is meanness, specifically that of torturing his mother by reminding her of the new world she lives in. But unlike the Misfit, his meanness is paralysed force, gesture without motions. He cannot make a decisively destructive move, since that would require his own self-shattering involvement. Actually it is he who lives in the past, though only his own private past, for he can deal only in abstractions fed by reverie and memory. Through reverie he builds a fantasy version of the world as he would have it be, which is of course not the one he actually inhabits.

Thus it is that he sees his mother as childish. Her eyes, "sky blue, were as innocent and untouched by experience as they must have been when she was ten." Again, "she might have been a little girl that he had to take to town." He detaches accidents from essence, and mistakes them for essence. A pseudo-existentialist, he builds a fairyland, that "magnificent ersatz of the science of Phenomena" Maritain declares existentialism to be. For, unlike Sartre's Orestes, Julian's destruction of his mother is not deliberate. He mistakes self-justification for self-affirmation. It is a relatively simple matter then to make the mother be what it is comfortable to him to suppose her. From being simply as innocent as when she was ten, she becomes eventually an obnoxious child whom "he could with pleasure have slapped." She becomes so through the exercise of his withdrawal, leading him finally to feel "completely detached from her."

But words, even when poorly used or deliberately distorted, have a way of redounding upon the user. It is thus with the terms Julian uses in his careless abstractions. In addition to the metaphors of his mother as child and himself as martyr, there is also the metaphor of evil that slowly worms its way into his language. At the bus stop, he finds in himself "an evil urge to break her spirit." Neither *evil* nor *spirit* here carries full meaning, for he intends only to express his impulse to embarrass her in public. He sets about that petty meanness out of a vanity which sees as his own most "miraculous" triumph that "instead of being blinded by love for her as she was for him, he had cut himself emotionally free of her and could see her with complete objectivity. He was not dominated by his mother." Love is at this point no more than an emotional attachment as seen with the intellectual freedom Julian professes; so too is evil. And so the possibility of catastrophe is remote indeed to his thinking as he sets about harassing his mother. Thus, when he gives the woman with protruding teeth and canvas sandals "a malevolent" look, he is practicing his revenge upon the mother at a level very close to June Starr's sticking out her tongue at Red Sammy's wife. He is more nearly naughty than malevolent. His childishness is fed by his satisfaction in seeing "injustice in daily operation," since that observance "confirmed his view that with few exceptions there was no one worth knowing within a radius of three hundred miles." It is this state of withdrawal that we must be aware of in seeing his actions on the bus. When he sits down by the Negro man, he stares across at his mother "making his eyes the eyes of a stranger." His tension lifts "as if he had openly declared war on her," which of course he has, thus making his withdrawal from the world possible. His only reaction to those about him is that of hate, but his expression of that hate is capable only of irritating, except in the case of that one person in his world who loves him, his mother.

It is in respect to that love that the story's title is to be read. For in the first instance *convergence* carries the sense Hardy gives it in "The Convergence of the Twain." It is only after the devastating collision Julian experiences that any rising may be said to occur. The collision is presented initially in the comical exchange of sons, Julian for the small Negro boy, on the bus. One notices, as Julian sees the large Negro woman get on the bus, that she has a hat identical to that his mother wears. But Julian, observing the accident of color, does not notice it. He can connect nothing with nothing. As in the grandmother's first encounter with the Misfit, Julian is aware only that there is something vaguely familiar about her, the huge woman waiting for tokens. When it finally dawns on him that it is the hat that is familiar, he thinks the problem solved. It is only begun. Feeling triumphant, he awaits his mother's recognition of the hat, for it seems the chance he has waited to teach her "a lesson that would last for awhile." But the real shocker is that he discovers his own likeness to the Negress, the ironic exchange of sons becoming ultimately more terrifying that he anticipated. We see this by observing the Negro mother in comparison to what we know of Julian, ours being an advantage scarcely available to Julian. Though he is very much annoyed by her physical presence as she crowds him in his seat, he doesn't look at her, preferring rather to visualize her as she stood waiting for tokens a few minutes earlier. His is a retreat into the memory such as he accuses his mother of, and in that retreat he realizes that it is the hat that is familiar. It is at this point of recognition that he sees his mother's eyes once more and interprets them. "The blue in them seemed to have turned a bruised purple. For a moment he had an uncomfortable sense of her innocence, but it lasted only a second before principle rescued him." Principle, as abstraction imposed upon the concrete circumstances, rather than derived from them, delays for the moment the threat of the abyss to Julian. He sees that his mother "would feel" the symbolic significance of the purple hat but not "realize" it, as he, Julian, is capable of doing. His mother is to him just like the Negro woman in the world his mother refuses to acknowledge.

But that is merely reverie's abstraction on Julian's part, for the Negro woman is very much unlike his mother. The facts of her size and color are accidental dissimilarities which Julian's sophistication removes, but there is an essential unlikeness to his mother that underlines the strange woman's kinship to Julian. She, like Julian, is unaware of the possibilities of love. The Negro child, Carver, acts toward Julian's mother to the discomfort of the Negro mother, but with an innocence that Julian can't claim for his childishness. When the mother has snatched the child back, he presently escapes back to "his love," Julian's mother. Afterward the Negro woman slaps the "obnoxious child" as Julian only imagines doing to his mother. When the game of Peek-a-boo starts between Julian's mother and Carver, Carver's mother threatens to "knock the living Jesus" out of the child. And later, we see her carry the child down the bus steps by its arm as if it were a thing and not a child. She then shakes Carver angrily for his conspiracy of love.

At this point we might reconsider Julian's mother as an "old-guard Southern lady." It is perfectly true that her words are such as to make her appear condescending to her "inferiors" when they are black. And she sees little difference between herself and such people as the white woman with the protruding teeth, a person with far fewer historical credentials than she, this last failure one which Julian is very much embarrassed by. But there is a more fundamental rightness about Julian's mother than her inherited manners and social cliches reveal. So long as Julian is allowed to deal with the surfaces—with her stock words and responses to the immediate social situation—he is safe to enjoy his pretended indignation within his mental bubble. He can make a surface response to surface existence. It is when he is forced to go deeper that horror intrudes, as when for a moment he glimpses a child-like innocence in his mother's blue eyes, from which horror "principle" rescues him back to his portrait of her as childish. Eventually, though, a "terrible intu-

ition" gets the better of him as he realizes that his mother will give Carver a coin. "The gesture would be as natural to her as breathing." He, rather than his mother, can feel now the symbolic significance of her act, though he is not yet ready to "realize it." For the world Julian insists upon as changed from the world he takes his mother to dwell in is the world of time untouched by that transcendent love that begins to threaten him. Julian's and the Negro woman's world is one in which a penny is hardly an acceptable substitute for a nickel, or any gift at all suitable since it represents an intrusion that can only seem condescension of the Haves to the Have-nots. Julian's is that world of history out of the eighteenth century in which Progress and Change have removed the obstacle of "Original Sin" through an intellectual exercise. Julian's mother cannot make distinctions of minor significance, as her son is capable of doing with his college-trained mind. But being child-like, she can make major distinctions, even as Carver can. The mother's gesture of love with the penny has removed from it any concern for the worldly value of her gift. It is a bright coin, given with an affection misunderstood by both Julian and Carver's mother. In the world made by a George Washington Carver with synthetics on the one hand and by Sartre with synthetic existence on the other (the worlds pursued by the Negress and Julian respectively) things and actions have a value in respect to their surfaces. *Action* and *thing* precede *essence* and *intrinsic value.* In such a world, where the possibilities of love are ignored, things and actions are ultimately only mechanical. Thus it is to be expected that the Negro woman explodes "like a piece of machinery," striking Julian's mother with the lumpy pocket book. And Julian, a more subtle machine of his own making, is like a clock, capable of telling only the present confused moment. He is trapped by history, his mother's and his own.

> The convergence in the story ["Everything That Rises Must Converge"] then, at its most fundamental level, is not that of one person with another but of Julian with the world of guilt and sorrow, the world in which *procedures* have replaced *manners,* both of which are surface aspects of that world.
>
> —*Marion Montgomery*

His mother lying on the ground before him, the Negro woman retreating with Carver "staring wide-eyed over her shoulder," Julian picks up his old theme. "That was your black double," he says. He reads the significance of the event to her: "The old manners are obsolete and your graciousness is not worth a damn." But for the first time he remembers bitterly "the house that was lost to him." In his earlier remembrance it has been a *mansion* as contrasted to his mother's word *house.* Now when he insists to her "You aren't who you think you are," the words begin immediately to redound upon him. For now his mother's blue and innocent eyes become "shadowed and confused." He does not try "to conceal his irritation," and so there is no sign of love in his face. That is why she looks at him "trying to determine his identity." He begins to abandon his separateness ("Are *we* walking [home].") Still, when she ignores him, he reads her the stock lesson of our moment of time. The Negro woman is "the whole colored race" rising up against such people as his mother. The mistake Julian is incapable of seeing is that the Negro woman is more than the colored race; she is the human race, to which he himself belongs through the burden of man's being a spiritual mulatto. The mother's earlier words, simple-minded in Julian's view, that she feels sorry for "the ones that are half white" since "They're tragic" take on theological symbolism still beyond his ken. In the presence of his mother dying, he sees her eyes, one moving as if "unmoored," the other fixing on him and finding "nothing." It is the final terrible mirror to his being which he has fleetingly seen reflected in the Negro woman on the bus. But now he cannot deny his own condition by any act of abstraction, by "principle," his old means of escaping his emptiness. His mother's return to her childhood at the moment of death, her acting "just like a child" as Julian says, leads her to call for "Grandpa" and then for her old nurse "Caroline." Only at this point does Julian realize her serious condition. But his reaction is in regard to his own safety rather than hers. Stunned, he is aware of "a tide of darkness" that seems to be "sweeping her from him." The word *mother* no longer suffices, and it is the beginning of a new Julian when he calls out his frightened "Mamma, Mamma!"

The story, then, is one in which Julian discovers, though he does not understad it, the necessity of putting aside childishness to become a little child. It recalls those errors of our childhood in which we take pleasure in our superiority over those younger than we. That superiority we take, with pride, to be a measure of our intellectual station. But the shocking revelation comes as we realize that the pinnacle of this moment's superiority on which we rise is tomorrow's dark valley out of which it is difficult to see. Or in another figure also appropriate to our story we play childishly with our supposed inferiors, as Julian does: we hold up before a mirror a message only we can decipher in its backwardness since we were privy to its writing. Or we write the mirror image and hold it up to be reflected aright for others to read with awe and wonder at our cleverness. What is shattering to us is the larger mystery of our own life which includes childishness but which our intellect cannot comprehend. Thus Julian delights in the mirror reflection of his mother in the Negress, only to discover the dark woman a truer image of himself, the denier of love. Thus too those metaphors of love and hate play mirror tricks as they grow larger than their childish use by Julian, so that "true culture" appears no

longer simply "in the mind" as he insists early. Perhaps it is "in the heart." as his mother insisted." Setting out with "the evil urge to break her spirit," he has finally succeeded in breaking his own.

The convergence in the story then, at its most fundamental level, is not that of one person with another but of Julian with the world of guilt and sorrow, the world in which *procedures* have replaced *manners,* both of which are surface aspects of that world. For, while the *spectacle* of the convergence of Julian's mother with the Negro mother is indeed a convergence in a "violent form," as one critic of the story puts it, the most violent collision is within Julian, with effects Aristotle declared necessary to complex tragedy. The tragedy is Julian's, in which he recognizes that he has destroyed that which he loved through his blindness. He has so carefully set himself off from his mother that, through the pretenses of intellect, he is as far removed from her as Oedipus from Jocasta. But the Christian implications of Julian's tragedy separate him from Oedipus. Guilt and sorrow come of knowing that one has spurned love. Already the possibilities of grace are present as he cries out to her with the voice of a child. Whether he will perform a more significant expiation on his own behalf than the childish gesture he pretends for his mother's sins—his sitting by the Negro man in the bus—is left suspended. What we do know is that, as if repeating an error of his namesake (St. Julian the Hospitaller of the Saints' legends), he has, through the childishness of intellectualism, made himself capable of a mistake of identity. And like Oedipus and St. Julian he has been an instrument in the destruction of his parent. As he goes crying to any person who might happen along in his dark night, the tide of darkness seems to sweep him back to his mother lying on the ground dead. But in his favor, he is opposing that tide of darkness which would postpone "from moment to moment his entry into the world of guilt and sorrow." He has at the least arrived, as Eliot would say, at the starting place, as Miss O'Connor's characters so often do, and has recognized it for the first time. He is now ready to profit from those words of Teilhard which give the story its title, but they are words which must not be read as Teilhard would have them in his evolutionary vision. For in Teilhard there is no place for guilt and sorrow since human existence has had removed from it that taint of original sin which this story certainly assumes as real. It is a Dantean reading of Teilhard's words that we are called upon to make:

> Remain true to yourself, but move ever upward toward greater consciousness and greater love! At the summit you will find yourself united with all those who, from every direction, have made the same ascent. *For everything that rises must converge."*

John F. Desmond (essay date Autumn 1972)

SOURCE: "The Lessons of History: Flannery O'Connor's 'Everything That Rises Must Converge,'" in *The Flannery O'Connor Bulletin,* Vol. I, Autumn, 1972, pp. 39-45.

[In the following essay, Desmond discusses the influence of Pierre Teilhard de Chardin's ideas about human history and redemption on O'Connor's "Everything That Rises Must Converge."]

This vision of human history developed by Pierre Teilhard de Chardin—a synthesis of biological and psychological evolution and the Christian conception of historical redemption—is one which strongly appealed to Flannery O'Connor and influenced much of her later work. In *The Phenomenon of Man* Teilhard describes the process of evolution as one which follows a law of increased complexification and convergence toward greater consciousness as the inevitable outcome of the evolutionary process. For Teilhard, the drive toward synthesis is caused by the energy of union—love—and he warned strongly against isolation or refusal of reconciliation in any form, racial or individual. Teilhard sees the energy of union as an Omega point which is the source and object of love, and to the theist Omega is God. The central position of Christianity in this perspective, with its beliefs in a personal God and its own universality, is that the actuality of Omega is achieved through Christ's Incarnation, uniting Himself organically with human history, with all matter and all psychism. Attempts at isolation from corporate human history—from the universal bond of fallen yet redeemed mankind—are in fact attempts to deny the concrete reality of suffering, grace, and redemptive love in favor of a specious "innocence" that projects one outside or above the redemptive process. Such a stance is, of course, the classic one of pride.

In a letter to this writer in December 1963, Miss O'Connor acknowledged the influence of Chardin and remarked that "what he attempted appeals to my imagination." While Miss O'Connor could agree with Teilhard's vision of history and its apotheosis in Christ, she could not, as she often said, let her Christian beliefs distort what she actually saw going on in the world around her. And what she actually saw were not only prideful refusals of redemptive grace on the part of man, but the more fundamental refusal to admit any *need* for redemption. Convergence means the universal drive toward spiritual union amog men, through love. However, Miss O'Connor shows this drive as one which is everywhere resisted, by characters who choose various forms of isolation and immunity—such as retreat into abstract intellectualism or into a romanticized past—to escape the demands of concrete union and growth. For redemption includes the total, corporate community of humankind, and through pride these characters implicitly and explicitly try to deny their place in this process. Consequently, they resist "convergence," and because of this the initial action which must occur is the de-

struction of their false identities and false, detached "place" of immunity. Because of their hardened isolation, it takes an apocalyptic-like violence to penetrate their shell, but this violent encounter can, though not necessarily, work mysteriously to open the character to see and accept his true place and identity in redemption history. Some characters retreat from this terrible knowledge, but even these are chastened so that they cannot return to their former "innocent" state. Such knowledge is the purpose of the violent convergence in **"Everything That Rises Must Converge,"** where Miss O'Connor dramatized particular cases of modern pride typologically as part of her vision of history.

In the story the violent convergence occurs between a stout Negro woman and an aristocratically inclined white woman, whose son Julian witnesses the impact. The encounter between the two women dramatizes the violent forces which erupt in a clash whose racial manifestations are the terms of deeper spiritual conflict. Both women, as well as Julian, are guilty of a denial of love and charity because of their prideful isolation.

The relationship between Julian and his mother is the central focus throughout the story, and the irony of their relationship derives from the fact that while she is a product of the now-faded aristocratic past, Julian's mother has adapted somewhat to their present "reduced" condition. It is Julian's indulgence of her *as a figure from the past,* made in his own image, that is as much responsible for her gesture of condescension toward the Negroes as her own pride. A pseudo-intellectual, Julian espouses the gospel of liberalism—toleration of all—but in truth his liberalism is only a reactionary response to his own ambivalent feelings toward his family history. He has created his own idealized view of this past and sustains it through the attachment to his mother, but his real dependence upon her is hidden from his eyes by the blinder he wears—an *apparent* hatred of what she represents. Thus Julian's so-called progressivism, based upon intellectual and cultural elitism (he wishes to associate with intelligent, liberal Negroes) rather than a recognition of spiritual equality, is specious and in fact much akin to his mother's own aristocratic pretensions. He uses his liberalism simply as a means of revenge against a past he both falsely idealizes and nostalgically admires. Both mother and son are dissociated from reality, from history, and they must be returned to the real at a terrible cost.

The weekly trips made by Julian's mother to the YWCA "Reducing Class," a comic symbol of both their reduced circumstances (she was formerly a "Godhigh") and the "Fall" from pride which awaits her, underscore the fact that she is slightly more adaptable to present realities than her son wishes to believe. Yet she is also possessed of an exalting pride. What distinguishes her from "common" humanity is the ridiculous purple and green hat she wears, and though she thinks the hat too expensive and wants to return it, it is Julian, significantly, who insists that she keep it. Thus her son fosters the indulgent pride whereby she assumes an aristocratic stance above common humanity, epitomized in the salesgirl's remark, "with that hat, you won't meet yourself coming and going." Nevertheless, she is willing to live in the decayed neighborhood, whereas Julian, a typewriter salesman with literary ambitions, dreams of isolating himself from society in a place "three miles" from any neighbors.

Possessed of a sense of identity that her son lacks, Julian's mother nevertheless suffers a moral blindness manifested in her nostalgic affection for the past. To her, the world is in "a mess," though she still can appear gracious to other women in the reducing class while convinced of her superiority. Julian's belief that she is "out of touch" with the present is accurate; yet ironically it is through his belief in her as a representative of the past that he sustains his own false identity—"innocently" detached from reality and aristocratically superior in his condemnation of her limitations. Her view of equality and social evolution through integration—convergence and reconciliation—is one of retrenchment and moral isolation. "It's simply not realistic. They should rise, yes, but on their own side of the fence." Sentimentally, she recalls her visits to the Godhigh plantation before its decline. Observing this, Julian concludes that his mother's adaptability to present circumstances is simply due to her insensitivity; yet the real basis of his irritation with her is the fact that in her adaptability she does not conform to the idealized image of her he uses to support his own retreat from the real present. When she insists that her family retained self-respect in spite of reduced circumstances, Julian's own nostalgia is revealed.

> "Doubtless that decayed mansion reminded them," Julian muttered. He never spoke of it without contempt or thought of it without longing. He had seen it once when he was a child before it had been sold. The double stairways had rotted and been torn down. Negroes were living in it. But it remained in his mind as his mother had known it. It appeared in his dreams regularly. He would stand on the wide porch, listening to the rustle of oak leaves, then wander through the high-ceilinged hall into the parlor that opened onto it and gaze at the worn rugs and faded draperies. It occurred to him that it was he, not she, who could have appreciated it.

After they have boarded the bus together, Julian retreats into a "mental bubble" while his mother discusses the race question with two other women passengers. From his detached perspective, ironically. Julian sees his mother as living in a "fantasy world," while she believes accurately that her son is inexperienced in the "real world." As a further irony,

Julian sees himself as liberated from her, when in fact he is vitally dependent upon her as the scapegoat for his own intellectual and moral self-righteousness. When a sophisticated Negro passenger boards the bus, Julian's postured "toleration" is revealed when he unsuccessfully tries to engage the Negro in conversation by borrowing matches, though a NO SMOKING sign is posted clearly. When the Negro isolates himself behind a newspaper, Julian recalls his other attempts to become acquainted with "the better types" and imagines the revenge he could perpetrate against his mother's bigotry by bringing a Negro woman home as his fiancee. His "fantasy" ends when the large, fierce-looking Negro woman boards the bus with the child, Carver, and the stage is set for the violent convergence and Julian's shattering epiphany.

The bond between Julian's mother and the Negro woman, both isolated and proud, is of course symbolized by the identical hats which the women wear. Furthermore the fact that the Negro child sits with Julian's mother and the woman next to Julian, separated by the aisle, signifies their moral kinship and the incipient theme of convergence. Recognizing the equality implied by their similar hats, Julian's mother appears "as if sickened at some awful confrontation," while her son blindly gloats at her humiliation. Nevertheless, she suppresses her indignation by assuming a comical attitude toward the likeness, as if "a monkey" were wearing the hat. The real link between the two women is established through the child Carver—whose name suggests the difficult process by which suffering is transformed through Christ-like love—and both women fail in this opportunity provided by his presence to transcend intolerance. Julian's mother sees the child as "cute" and smiles at him patronizingly, anticipating her disastrous gesture of condescension later when she offers Carver a penny. The Negro woman, on the other hand, pulls him across the aisle to her as if "snatching him from contagion," and threatens to "knock the living Jesus" out of him if he doesn't behave. The two women are identical in their blind moral isolation, and their encounter erupts inevitably into violence when Julian's mother's offer of money is answered by the Negro woman's blow.

For Julian, the defeat of his mother is a momentary triumph, a confirmation of his self-righteousness and intellectual "hatred" of her values. Yet while the effect of the violent convergence upon his mother is a fatal heart attack on the way "home"—she is retreating into the romanticized past as she dies, calling for her childhood Negro maid—her death also reveals Julian's shallowness and "innocent" detachment from the real. Ironically, his mother now becomes "the past" he has not only seen her as representing but from which he has created his own reproachless, false progressivism; and the false identity this provided him is suddenly destroyed by her death. He must face the "void" alone. His perversion of her real values and his own prideful isolation have fostered a moral adolescence in which he has had no mature spiritual identity, and now alone, "the tide of darkness seemed to sweep him back to her, postponing from moment to moment his entry into the world of guilt and sorrow."

The death of his mother brings Julian for the first time face to face with the reality of history—the "world of guilt and sorrow"—and unprepared in his innocence, he wishes to retreat from this terrible knowledge. The god he has served has been the idolatrous one of self, his gospel one of social progress through strictly human means, which Miss O'Connor found woefully inadequate to overcome the real human condition of the Fall. Only Redemption through Christ could transform the "world of guilt and sorrow" and cause man's humble acceptance of his true place in the slow working out of the redemptive plan through the wounds of history and man's acceptance of the healing grace that can truly unite mankind.

Preston M. Browning Jr. (essay date 1974)

SOURCE: *"Everything That Rises Must Converge,"* in *Flannery O'Connor,* Southern Illinois University Press, 1974, pp. 99-130.

[*In the following essay, Browning asserts that in O'Connor's* Everything That Rises Must Converge, *"she recognized that the recovery of depth, or being, was possible only by stripping the masks from men whose fraudulent righteousness had rendered them too complacent even to be damned."*]

In Flannery O'Connor's posthumous volume of stories, *Everything That Rises Must Converge,* subject and setting are very much a part of the contemporary South. Economic growth is under way, and its partisans are feverishly engaged as midwives to "progress" (**"A View of the Woods"**); racial integration is a fact increasingly difficult to ignore, and white Southerners of all classes are forced to assume some attitude toward it (**"Everything That Rises Must Converge"**). The upheavals wrought by World War II and the Korean conflict have unsettled class lines, and the sons of tenant farmers are on their way to becoming "society" (**"Greenleaf"**); the dispersion of poor whites throughout the urban North is well advanced, constituting opportunity for many of the young but exile in an alien and hostile land for the elderly (**"Judgement Day"**). And, as in the novel, *The Violent Bear It Away,* the techniques of modern psychology are being liberally applied by social worker-types reared on progressive philosophies (**"The Lame Shall Enter First"**). Wherever one turns in these stories, he encounters evidence of Flannery O'Connor's sensitivity to the changes which her region was undergoing during the late 1950s and early 1960s.

As always, Miss O'Connor brought to these subjects an intelligence keenly alive to the complexities of the human mind—its subterfuges, its self-deceptions, its seemingly inexhaustible capacity for rationalization. In her two novels and in such early stories as **"Good Country People," "The Life You Save May Be Your Own,"** and **"The Artificial Nigger,"** she had demonstrated an astonishingly mature grasp of the dynamics of human psychology. Yet something new (in degree if not in kind) seems to distinguish the stories of the second collection: an almost clinical understanding of certain forms of neurosis. The title story, for example, is a virtual case study of what psychoanalysts would describe as denial and projection.

The narrative itself is simple enough: Julian and his mother travel by bus to the Y in order that she may attend a reducing class. Contemptuous of his mother, from whose values and prejudices he thinks he has freed himself, Julian attempts unsuccessfully to befriend a Negro man and indulges in malicious glee when a large Negro woman boards the bus wearing a hat identical to the one his mother has on. As they leave the bus together, Mrs. Chestny offers a penny to the Negro woman's small son and is knocked to the sidewalk by the infuriated Negress. After pointing out to his mother that she has been taught a proper lesson, Julian discovers that she is dying and runs for help in a last futile effort to delay his entrance in the "world of guilt and sorrow."

Like many of the sad young men of Flannery O'Connor's last stories, the protagonist of **"Everything That Rises Must Converge"** wants desperately to distinguish himself from everything in the South which he finds morally, intellectually, and aesthetically repugnant: its racism, its nostalgia for the glorious past, its (to him) petty concern with manners, its barren intellectual life, its insufferably banal social intercourse. (Julian is cast from the same mold that produced the rebellious "artistic" or "intellectual" sons of **"The Enduring Chill," "The Comforts of Home,"** and **"Greenleaf."** Julian, Asbury, Thomas, and Wesley make up a quartet of angry, frustrated individuals caught in "late adolescent" impotence so acute that they can direct their hostility only against their protective, and oftentimes patronizing and controlling mothers.)

Julian wants to be different, and since everything about the South which affronts his sense of decency and decorum is symbolized by his mother, Julian wants especially to be different from his mother. Merely being different, however, is not sufficient; his hatred for all that his mother epitomizes is so venomous that he must constantly insult it. As it is impossible to insult the entire Southern ethos, Julian is reduced to the expediency of humiliating and insulting his mother. But Julian's relation to his mother, like his relation to the South itself, is less unambiguous than he would like to imagine. What he thinks he detests, he also loves and longs for.

What he believes he is totally free of, he is, in fact, fearfully dependent upon.

While Miss O'Connor undoubtedly portrays the bad faith of Julian as the more damning, it must be conceded that there is something exasperating about his mother. She is one of those legendary Southern matrons of "aristocratic" birth who, though forced to live in relative poverty, continues to insist upon a distinction which she believes birth has conferred upon her. Though she must use the now-integrated public transportation system and must associate at the YWCA with women of a lower social class, she insists that because she "knows who she is,'" she "'can be gracious to anybody.'" Indeed, it is this assumption that the glue which holds society together is a certain politeness and openness of manner—almost always, however, practiced with a degree of unconscious condescension—which enables Julian's mother to face the unpleasant alterations in her external circumstances with a calm and cheerful assurance that she herself at least has not changed. It is her ardent faith in the primacy of manners, in fact, which is one of the sources of the conflict between Julian and his mother. She insists that authentic culture is "'in the heart . . . and in how you do things and how you do things is because of who you *are*.'" Julian's attitude provides the starkest contrast, since he maintains that with the new fluidity of class structure, his mother's graciousness counts for nothing. "'Knowing who you are is good for one generation only,'" he declares. "'You haven't the foggiest idea where you stand now or who you are.'"

Naturally, Julian is convinced that he knows where *he* is. Yet he is in fact far more pitifully confused than his mother. In him Flannery O'Connor has drawn a devastating portrait of the young white "liberal" Southerner who is doing all of the supposedly right things for the wrong reasons. Conceited in his assurance that he is free of his mother's prejudices and her unrealistic attachment to a dead past, Julian betrays in every gesture and word his thoroughly ambivalent attitudes toward the principal objects of her bigotry (Negroes) and her nostalgia (the ancestral home). How small the distance is he has put between himself and the heritage which he condemns is suggested in this description of his feelings about the family mansion he had once seen as a child.

> He never spoke of it without contempt or thought of it without longing. He had seen it once. . . . The double stairways had rotted and been torn down. Negroes were living [in] it. But it remained in his mind as his mother had known it. It appeared in his dreams regularly. . . . He preferred its threadbare elegance to anything he could name.

In some way reminiscent of Quentin Compson's tortured exclamation at the conclusion of *Absalom, Absalom!*, "I don't hate it, I don't hate it" (the "it" referring to the South),

Julian's reveries reflect much of the ambivalence but little of the profundity of Quentin's attitude toward the traditional South. For, whereas Quentin stands much closer to the great decisive events which have shaped Southern history and must grapple existentially with their meaning, as well as with the meaning of his own family's former glory and present decadence, Julian is a child of the 1950s and sixties, and, as such, faces the quite different problem of establishing personal identity in a South for which neither the grandeur nor the guilt of the past are ever-present, haunting realities. Yet the tradition which his mother represents, while attenuated and diluted, is nonetheless a factor with which he must reckon. Wishing to assert his independence from his mother, he vehemently proclaims his independence of the cultural heritage from which she derives *her* identity. But as he finds his present life and surroundings drab and humiliating, he is forced against his conscious will to identify with that very way of life which he can neither appropriate completely, as his mother thinks she has done, nor repudiate completely, as he would like to believe he has done.

The confusion of his attitude toward the Southern past is recapitulated and underscored in his ambivalent feelings toward his mother, whom he considers a child, "innocent and untouched by experience," for whose protection he must sacrifice himself. Remote as Julian's mother's world may be from reality, Julian's own fantasy world is even more remote. With his arrogant sense of superiority ("he realized he was too intelligent to be a success"), Julian's habitual way of dealing with the unpleasant aspects of life is to retreat "into the inner compartment of his mind . . . a kind of mental bubble" from which he may judge the intellectual bankruptcy of the rest of mankind. Somewhat like Hulga and very much like Asbury of **"The Enduring Chill,"** Wesley of **"Greenleaf,"** and Thomas of **"The Comforts of Home,"** Julian suffers from a form of neurosis in which his idealized image is threatened by self-doubt and self-pity and can be protected only by maintaining an uncommitted and superior attitude toward the world. At the same time subjecting the world to withering scorn for its failures and fearing to engage the world in creative struggle, Julian withdraws into his bubble where the self is free to judge without making itself vulnerable to judgment.

The viability of Julian's defensive psychological mechanism largely depends upon the availability of someone whom he can continuously belittle and scorn and whose stupidity and phoniness (as judged by him) can serve to point up, by contrast, his own supposedly enlightened and authentic existence. And that person is his mother. But while Julian thus needs his mother, she also poses a constant threat, to the extent that she is able to withstand his attacks and, through simply being what she is, to insinuate the possibility of some radical discrepancy between his idealized image and the actuality of his life. Ultimately, therefore, he must attempt to destroy her or destroy *for* her that system of values which makes her life possible.

On the bus an opportunity of attack presents itself when a white woman moves from a seat next to one just occupied by a Negro man. Ostensibly to "convey his sympathy" but actually to embarrass his mother, Julian crosses the aisle to the vacated seat. Now so situated that he can stare at her as though he were a stranger, Julian experiences a release of tension such as might accompany a declaration of war. Julian now fantasizes about various ways of hurting his mother, though always the conscious intention is "to teach her a lesson." Interestingly, all of his schemes involve Negroes or causes related to Negroes.

Here brief reflection upon Julian's "liberalism" should help to illumine the moral and psychological ramifications of the story. It is clear that Julian uses his putative tolerance and freedom from racial bias as a weapon in the struggle with his mother. What is far worse, he *uses Negroes* for the same purpose. Significantly, Julian has "never been successful in making Negro friends"; the reason for his failure is not difficult to locate, since he all too obviously wishes only to accumulate "some of the better types, . . . ones that looked like professors or ministers or lawyers" to bolster his always tenuous hold upon his self-image as a liberated representative of the "new South." Julian's own latent prejudice begins to show itself when a huge, fierce-looking Negro woman, who could not possibly be mistaken for a member of the Negro intelligentsia, boards the bus and settles in a seat next to his. Julian is "annoyed." Quickly his annoyance turns to elation as he sees the symbolic appropriateness of the two women having "swapped sons" when the woman's small child sits next to his mother. Julian's triumph is completed when he notices that the Negro woman's hat is an exact match of the one his mother is wearing for the first time.

Reveling briefly in his mother's distress, Julian discovers their true relationship after she has been struck to the ground by the hostile Negro woman. Attempting to reinforce the "lesson" with what sounds like a rehearsed lecture, Julian assures his mother that the fury she has just witnessed is not that of a single "uppity Negro woman" but rather that of "the whole colored race which will no longer take your condescending pennies." His speech is lost on his mother, who, calling for "Grampa" and Caroline (the Negro mammy who had cared for her as a child), willingly submits to "a tide of darkness" which carries her swiftly back to the ordered world of childhood and thence to death. Julian, who had moments before wished to prove to his mother she could not expect to be forever dependent upon him, is compelled at last to recognize how total has been his dependence upon her. Crying "Mamma, Mamma!" he throws himself beside her, but "Mamma," whose gaze had earlier scanned his face but rec-

ognized nothing there, lies motionless. Last seen racing toward lights which appear to recede beyond his grasp, Julian postpones momentarily "his entry into the world of guilt and sorrow." On this unmistakable Hawthornesque note the chronicle of another American Adam is concluded.

For a number of reasons the choice of this story to open the collection was a happy one. Like the stories examined in the chapter on *A Good Man Is Hard to Find* and like most of the stories in this volume, **"Everything That Rises Must Converge"** focuses upon the existential dilemmas of the self—its anxiety before the truth of its condition, the contemptible dodges it employs to deceive itself, and the inescapable surge of guilt as the shock of awareness is delivered. But in this tale the social context is broadened, thereby providing a connecting thread to the last story in *A Good Man Is Hard to Find,* **"The Displaced Person,"** in which race relations play a significant role, as well as pointing forward to the other pieces in the present volume, in most of which there is a heightened consciousness of the social ambience within which the awakened individual must live in the presence of grace. Both the title and the story's action give evidence of Flannery O'Connor's growing interest in the movement of the isolated self toward union with others; and while many commentators have maintained that Miss O'Connor uses the line borrowed from Teilhard de Chardin ironically, I find myself in agreement with those critics who contend that in the narrative of Julian and his mother there is a true convergence, although not a simple one. As the title suggests, the story concerns both rising and converging. Before their bus ride, Julian's mother had spoken of the propriety of Negroes rising, "but on their side of the fence." Her encounter with the outraged woman attests to the rising which has already occurred, as well as the fragility of the fence and the difficulty of maintaining it. But a convergence, albeit a violent one, does take place, and there are numerous hints besides the obvious one of the identical hats, that Julian's mother and the Negro woman are more alike than either would care to admit. If nothing else, the story's action foreshadows a convergence such as that envisaged by Teilhard, who speaks of "courage and resourcefulness" as necessary ingredients in the struggle to overcome "the forces of isolationism, even of repulsion, which seem to drive [men] apart rather than draw them together." Though the results of this particular convergence are quite the opposite of those anticipated by Teilhard when mankind achieves its unity in Christ, and though it would seem that here there is only reinforced isolation and repulsion, emphasis should perhaps be placed upon the pain and cost of both rising and converging. Such emphasis is certainly congruent with Miss O'Connor's belief that redemption is never easy and always involves suffering. The frustration and anger of the Negro woman *and* her courage imply a depth of spirit out of which might someday come the "resourcefulness" requisite for genuine convergence.

But since it is Julian, not the Negro mother, who is the main character, it is his rising and convergence which is central. As in other renditions of the fortunate fall, Julian's calamity will eventually lead, so all the evidence indicates, to "growth of consciousness," to raised sight, to a risen spirit. According to Teilhard de Chardin, growth toward unity with others is the spiritual direction of evolution and is a process to which those with "expanded consciousness" contribute. It is, moreover, the true end of man. "To be fully ourselves it is in . . . the direction of convergence with all the rest, that we must advance—towards the 'other.'" Teilhard distinguishes between individuality and personhood and asserts that the latter can be achieved only by "uniting together. . . . The true ego grows in inverse proportion to 'egoism.'" Insofar as Julian is able to replace his defensive idealized image with a realistic view of the self which obviates the necessity of belittling others in order to enhance the value of the self, to this extent will it be possible for him to attain personhood, a "true ego" capable of proper self-love and proper love of others. The capacity to develop such an ego is the psychological equivalent of the Christian's faith in man's ability to be radically altered by grace, and in the volume as a whole this capacity emerges as a central concern.

One critic offers a useful clue to the basis of these stories' commonly acknowledged excellence when he observes that "[i]t is as though in the struggle against her illness [Flannery O'Connor] had come to locate grotesqueness and grace in the common life of men and that she had no more time or talent to waste on merely being odd or bizarre." Here one may feel compelled to demur, since today most critics agree that even in her earliest fiction Flannery O'Connor spent little of her time on the *merely* odd or bizarre. Yet this reviewer has put his finger on something real and important in the development of Miss O'Connor's talent: in the last stories she has apparently left behind the blatant melodrama of, say, **"A Good Man is Hard to Find."** Her Misfits are no longer psychopathic killers or voyeuristic Bible salesmen. They are instead the ineffectual sons of well-meaning but exasperating mothers. Or they are the emotionally disturbed Wellesley student and the self-righteous Mrs. Turpin of **"Revelation."** Exceptions there are, two or three stories which demonstrate Flannery O'Connor's penchant for the extreme situation and the exaggerated character—for instance, **"Parker's Back"** and **"The Lame Shall Enter First."** But for the most part she did seem to find her imagination creating less extravagantly fanciful characters than Tom T. Shiftlet or Manley Pointer or Hazel Motes. More often than not, too, it is in the "common life of men" that she located the workings of grace. Which is not to say that there is anything commonplace or tame about the stories in *Everything That Rises;* on the contrary, here is abundant grotesquerie and violence. Instead of abandoning altogether her taste for melodrama, "she severely disciplined it to weight the consequences of perverse will and crooked passions,"

the result being that in such a story as **"A View of the Woods,"** what appears as a more or less harmless and humorous contest of wills detonates into a fury of destruction, and self-destruction, even as the comic surface is preserved almost to the very end.

The action is easily summarized: an old man, Mark Fortune, permits his son-in-law Pitts, whom he detests, to farm his property; but, from time to time, largely to provoke his daughter and her family, Mr. Fortune sells off a lot. The only member of the Pitts family the old man can tolerate is the youngest daughter, Mary Fortune, who bears an uncanny likeness to her grandfather and whom he considers virtually an extension of himself. These two form an invincible alliance against the Pitts clan until the old man conceives the idea of selling the land directly in front of the house. Since Mary Fortune has heretofore shared his enthusiasm for "progress," the old man assumes that she will be free of what is to him an irrational Pitts attachment to the land. To his dismay he learns that on this issue Mary Fortune sides with her family, and, in the story's denouement, he attempts to punish her physically for opposing his scheme. Having counted on neither her ferocity nor her strength, the old man finds himself overpowered by the girl, and it is only when she releases her hold that he is able to subdue her. Inadvertently, he strikes her head against a rock, killing her, and then himself dies of a heart attack.

This bare outline, of course, provides no indication of the comedy of the piece. Neither does it allow for more than a hint of its tragic dimensions. Presumably it was a failure to discern these tragic elements which led Stanley Hyman to the otherwise mystifying conclusion that the ending involves "the unnecessary multiple death of Jacobean drama." Obviously, if Miss O'Connor intended this as merely a comic story, the deaths are not only unnecessary but downright inappropriate. What seems to be the case, however, is that **"A View of the Woods"** is an example of that modern genre which Flannery O'Connor practices with considerable success—the story with a comic (or "absurd") surface beneath which lies a feeling for the human reality which approaches the tragic.

Mark Fortune, the story's protagonist, most certainly exhibits traits usually associated with the hero of traditional tragedy. He is a man whose sense of self is magnified to the point of becoming monstrous. He cannot tolerate criticism, claims a godlike omniscience with respect to the thoughts and feelings of others, meets opposition with unhesitating action and unswerving faith in the correctness of his judgment. He considers himself on the side of Fate or the gods (in this case, "progress") and aspires to immortal glory (a town to be named after him). His excessive and misplaced confidence in the justice of his cause and in the power of his will to implement that cause leads to events which shatter his project and destroy both himself and the chosen agent of his dream. Finally, in the moment of death, Mark Fortune, the proud tyrant of a cherished if insignificant kingdom, perceives both the mocking emptiness of his life and the fatality which has lain hidden behind the façade of his willful rationalizations and self-justifications. Mark Fortune is no Oedipus or Hamlet, and perhaps he lacks the tragic (or tragicomic) potential of even a Hazel Motes. Yet he is anything but a "perfect comic" character, and his violent death is, as I shall show, the only fitting conclusion (dramatically as well as morally) to this story of monstrous egotism and haughty disdain for the feelings and rights of others.

An extremely self-centered and possessive man, Mr. Fortune had apparently resented his daughter's marrying—at any rate, marrying the "idiot" Pitts. Hence, when she comes home with her none-too-successful husband and seven children, "she [comes] back like any other tenant." Of Mary Fortune, he makes a conspicuous exception as she has "his intelligence, his strong will, and his push and drive." But his feeling for her transcends mere respect or affection. For in the nine-year-old child Mr. Fortune sees so much of himself that she represents for him the hope of an almost literal reincarnation. When he is dead and can no longer torment the Pittses, Mary Fortune, he thinks, will perpetuate that source of gratification, since he has secretly left his property in trust to her.

From the old man's standpoint, one thing only mars this relationship. This is Pitts's periodic, sadistic beating of Mary Fortune for no apparent cause, and Mr. Fortune is enraged and made physically ill each time it occurs. For he conceives Pitts's aggression to be directed toward him, as clearly it is; "This was Pitts's revenge on him. It was as if it were *he* that Pitts was driving down the road to beat and as if *he* were the one submitting to it." And each time he confronts Mary Fortune with her "cowardice," her failure to defy her father, the child emphatically repudiates his accusation, stoutly maintaining that no one has beaten her and that "'if anyone did [she'd] kill him.'" Considering the extreme pain which Mary Fortune's humiliation and suffering cause him, it is a reasonable assumption that the old man's motives in taunting Pitts are colored by a tinge of masochism. But, whatever his unconscious motives, his conscious hatred of Pitts grows with each brutal assault upon Mary Fortune, causing him to seek ever more devilish ways of inflicting pain upon the child's father.

Clearly, affronting Pitts and his "tribe" satisfies some deep psychological need in the old man. So too does any act which reinforces his conviction that he, unlike the dull and backward Pitts, is on the side of "progress." Thus his eagerness to see a town arise on his property. As a beginning, he intends to sell the "lawn" to the owner of one of those combination roadside businesses—gas station, country store,

dance hall and junk yard—which dot the Southern landscape. Tilman signifies for Mr. Fortune the resourceful man who goes boldly forward to meet the future, "the kind . . . who was never just in line with progress but always a little ahead of it." The narrator's description of the man is more sinister and more revealing: Tilman normally sits at the counter with folded hands, "his insignificant head weaving snake-fashion above them." Mr. Fortune may believe, when he signs the deed of sale, that he is dealing with an enlightened apostle of progress, but Flannery O'Connor suggests, rather too obviously perhaps, that he is signing a pact with the devil.

What is soon made evident is that he is signing his own death warrant as well. For in his refusal to heed his granddaughter's initial complaint that the "lawn" not only makes possible a view of the woods but also provides space where "[her] daddy grazes his calves," there is a foreshadowing of the fatal miscalculation which is destined to demolish all of Mr. Fortune's grand hopes. For the child is like him in so many ways that he is quite incapable of believing that, in this instance, her sympathies are with her "daddy." The irony of his position is perfect, since it is those very qualities which he most admires in the child—her independent spirit, her strong will, her obstinacy—which compel her to oppose him when he forces her to choose ("'Are you a Fortune,' he said, 'or are you a Pitts? Make up your mind'") between her family and him. In forcing this choice he is, in effect, asking her to submerge her individuality in his, something her spirited, self-assertive nature will not permit. Thus she responds to his challenge by saying she is "'Mary—Fortune—Pitts,'" or, in other words, herself: a Pitts, with an abundance of Fortune temperament, but finally MARY—an independent self which transcends categories and clans. The old man's shouted reply, "'Well I am PURE Fortune!'" is later echoed by the child as she sits astride his chest, having just administered him a savage pummeling: "The old man looked up into his own image. It was triumphant and hostile. 'You been whipped,' it said, 'by me' and then it added, bearing down on each word, 'and I'm PURE Pitts.'" Enraged to hear his "own image" claiming to be everything that the loathes, the old man takes the child by the throat and pounds her head on the ground, after which he "stare[s] at his conquered image."

The language of this and other passages intensifies the impression of Mark Fortune as a deeply troubled and divided man. His inordinate identification with the child clearly indicates that she fills the role of his double. Yet, when their basic interests conflict, he learns to his dismay that she embodies not only that part of himself which he admires but also another, unacknowledged and suppressed aspect of his humanity. The child stands for a quality of imagination and sensibility which can recognize in ordinary pine trees some of the glory and wonder of nature, the loss of which no amount of "progress" can compensate for. That quality, atrophied and nearly extinct in himself, still lives feebly on in the deepest recesses of his unconscious mind, and when it threatens to interfere with his conscious purposes, he acts (as if by compulsion) to destroy it. Hence his killing of Mary Fortune, while not a consciously willed act, corresponds to a profound conflict within his unconscious. Her death symbolizes a violent extirpation of a part of himself and it is indeed his own "conquered image" which he beholds as he stares at his lifeless granddaughter.

The story's imagery illumines this division within the old man's psyche. There are two primary and opposing patterns, corresponding to the two dimensions of Mr. Fortune's self. The first of these patterns consists of images of mechanisms, is associated with the old man's belief in progress, and is represented chiefly by the earth-moving machine which is digging an artificial lake. This machine is portrayed as if it were some living, mindless creature compelled endlessly to devour and then disgorge the earth. Like her grandfather, Mary Fortune is enthralled by its activities; both are depicted as "looking down into the red pit, watching the big disembodied gullet gorge itself on the clay, then, with the sound of a deep sustained nausea and a slow mechanical revulsion, turn and spit it up." The machine seems intended to symbolize a malignancy, a repulsive disease in the old man or in the dream of progress to which he is so compulsively committed. Its description as a "disembodied gullet" conjures up a picture of grotesque, unnatural voraciousness, while the phrases "sustained nausea" and "mechanical revulsion" suggest a form of nonintelligent resistance to the ceaseless gorging. Interestingly, there are links between the two symbols of "progress," the machine and the Snopes-like Tilman: both are portrayed as reptilian (Tilman as snake, the earth mover as perhaps mechanical dinosaur), both as devourers without intelligent purpose. Correspondingly, the old man's obsessive pursuit of the future, in utter disregard of the feelings of those closest to him, is an analogue of the mindless rapacity of the machine.

The images of the second pattern are drawn from nature, the central image in this configuration being the woods themselves. In contrast to the machine, the woods are pictured as lifelike, virtually human. The distinction is established early: the already examined passage describing the machine is from the story's third paragraph; in the first paragraph the reader is told that the lake construction is "bordered on [one] side by a black line of woods which appeared at both ends of the view to walk across the water." Near the middle of the story, Mary Fortune rejects her grandfather's efforts at reconciliation, all the while staring across the front lot to the distant trees and looking "into this scene *as if it were a person* that she preferred to him" [emphasis added]. Disgusted with her behavior, Mr. Fortune enters the house for his afternoon rest. Twice he goes to the window and each time sees "just woods."

The third time he got up to look at the woods, . . . the gaunt trunks appeared to be raised in a pool of red light that gushed from the almost hidden sun setting behind them. The old man stared for some time, as if for a prolonged instant he were caught up out of the rattle of everything that led to the future and were held there in the midst of an uncomfortable mystery that he had not apprehended before. He saw it, in his hallucination, as if someone were wounded behind the woods and the trees were bathed in blood. After a few minutes this unpleasant vision was broken by the presence of Pitts's pick-up truck grinding to a halt below the window.

In this crucial passage it becomes apparent that, through the medium of the woods, some elemental and persistent component of reality is attempting to communicate with the old man and that he finds this inchoate communication unsettling and threatening. His fixation upon the future is momentarily suspended as a force deep within himself enters into a kind of mystical communion with a force in nature. But the mystery is too "uncomfortable" to be long endured, and the old man is soon snatched back into the safe and familiar world of mechanism by the "grinding" of Pitts's truck. The experience, however, has penetrated his defenses, the magnitude of its threat being disclosed by the extravagance of the rationalizations to which he is driven later that evening.

The conflict symbolized by the machine/woods opposition is brought to a climax in the final paragraph. Mary Fortune lies motionless on the ground; next to her lies the old man, whose heart, threatening to give way throughout the narrative, at last succumbs to the excitement of his violent encounter with the child. Again a "vision" forces itself upon his imagination and this time he perceives, too late, the meaning of the trees and machine and, thus, the meaning of his life. Feeling himself pulled along toward the water and desperate to escape the encircling woods (always, in an O'Connor story, a sign of the presence of grace), the old man imagines himself about to be enfolded by the lake's miniature waves. He remembers that he cannot swim, and then the trees, which earlier had seemed "ugly," begin to thicken "into mysterious dark files" and march away "across the water," leaving him utterly alone "except for one huge yellow monster . . . gorging itself on clay."

The significance of the "huge yellow monster" is evident; the symbolism of the trees requires further investigation. Sister Bernetta Quinn has written that "the woods . . . represent those moments of grace, of inspiration, which come to all of us from time to time." But since the old man rejects this grace, to him the woods are "first of all a vision of hell." This conclusion is undoubtedly suggested by the consummation of the old man's vision on the previous afternoon when, after looking at the woods three times, he returns to bed and then "against [his] closed lids hellish red trunks [rise] up in a black wood." Moments earlier, however, the "uncomfortable mystery" had been bodied forth in a different guise: "He saw it . . . as if someone were wounded behind the woods and the trees were bathed in blood." In this trope and in the incident when Mary Fortune stares at the woods as though she were seeing a person, the trees take on attributes of the human. But, as Sister Bernetta's remarks imply, we seem here to be dealing with the human extended to that limit of height or depth where "human" and "divine" meet and fuse. The moment in history when this meeting was most radically concretized is recalled, I think, in the imagery of "the gaunt trees [which appear] to be raised in a pool of red light that gushed from the almost hidden sun. . . ." But, whether it is Christ's crucifixion which is being recollected in the figure of the trees "bathed in blood" or Mary Fortune's or his own death which is being foreshadowed, the story's ending leaves no doubt that in repudiating the trees and the "grace" which they symbolize, Mr. Fortune has chosen for himself a lonely, despairing death.

This ending may be melodramatic; but, then, so also is that of *Doctor Faustus.* And the vision of damnation, while patently more modern than that of Marlowe's play, is scarcely less terrifying. The comparison, in fact, is not altogether gratuitous. For, like Faustus in his uncompromising pursuit of knowledge and power, Mr. Fortune allows his blind passion for the dream of "progress" to destroy the agents necessary for the realization of that dream—Mary Fortune and himself. But his true tragedy (and again the analogy with Faustus is surprisingly apt) resides in the fact that his dream is of such a nature that its "success" depends upon the destruction of a faculty within himself which, though suppressed and underdeveloped, is nevertheless essential for his existence as a whole human being. Only in his dying moments, when the "gaunt trees" have "thickened into mysterious dark files," only when these signs of the deep mystery surrounding man's life (and invulnerable to his rapacious gorging) have deserted him, does Mark Fortune come to a full recognition of the sterility and dehumanized bleakness of his dream.

Almost every critic who has commented on Flannery O'Connor's novella **"The Lame Shall Enter First"** has noted its similarities to *The Violent Bear It Away,* published two years earlier. In the shorter work the trio of characters from the novel—Rayber, Bishop, and Tarwater—are metamorphosed into a social worker, Sheppard, his not overly bright child, Norton, and Rufus Johnson, a clubfooted juvenile delinquent with a missionary zeal to expose his "tin Jesus" benefactor for the sham that he is. As in the novel, the child dies, the rebellious teen-ager wins the struggle with the "positivist" adult, while the latter discovers, in a convulsive moment of self-revelation, the hollowness of his soul.

In other ways, too, the works are alike: Sheppard shares Rayber's belief in the power of rational understanding over irrational impulse, and the action of the story is generated, in large part, by his effort to prove true Rayber's dictum that "[w]hat we understand we can control." Rufus, the recalcitrant youth, like Tarwater, has imbibed from a fanatical grandfather a great religious passion, though in his case the satanical and criminal element is overt and pronounced. To Sheppard's bland assertions that Rufus can make of himself anything he sets his mind to, the boy retorts, tauntingly and mockingly, "'Satan . . . has me in his power.'" Rufus also differs from Tarwater in another respect, for he is without any ambivalence toward his would-be "savior": from the beginning he feels only contempt, and when he does occasionally express toward Sheppard some slight trust and affection, he is all the while slyly baiting a trap.

There are other important ways in which the two works differ, one of the chief being the nature of the central conflict in each. As we saw, the Rayber-Tarwater conflict involves principally the clash of a positivist world view and an understanding of reality which allows for something "left over" after man's abstracting intellect has exhausted its potency. This theme is also present in **"The Lame Shall Enter First,"** but the novella is much more than a simple reworking of the material of the novel. At bottom, the conflict of the later story is the conflict of faith versus works, even though the faith is a demonic one and the works are secular in character.

As his name suggests, Sheppard is a man desirous of being a pastor, though not of course in the conventional sense. For Christianity or any other system of religious belief he feels nothing but scorn. At the reformatory where he devotes his Saturdays to counseling wayward boys, he encounters his first prospective follower, Rufus Johnson—a wild, sullen, Satan-dominated grandson of a zealous "prophet." Rufus seems a compulsive criminal, and since he has a monstrous clubfoot, Sheppard immediately concludes that the boy's rebellion can be explained simply as compensation for feelings of inferiority. Sheppard also learns that Rufus has been brutally beaten by his grandfather and subjected to general neglect; therefore, when Rufus is paroled, Sheppard determines to befriend the boy, hoping to win his confidence and affection by giving him the "advantages" of a home and a loving parent.

As the story unfolds, the ambiguity of Sheppard's motives quickly becomes apparent. Not only does he consider himself a kind of surrogate priest, listening to the "confessions" of troubled teen-agers in a narrow, cramped office at the reformatory, but, having turned what he calls his unselfishness into a surrogate religion, he makes a fetish of self-denial, sleeping in "an ascetic-looking iron bed" in an uncarpeted room. For his work at the reformatory he receives no monetary compensation, and it is obvious that, in order for Sheppard to derive from it the psychic benefits he needs, his work must be done without pay. In this way he can maintain the fiction that he is "helping boys no one else care[s] about" and "receiving nothing" in return.

Driven as he is by the need to have continually before him an image of himself as "good" and unselfish, Sheppard is constantly annoyed by his son Norton, who hoards money and understands only one sense of sharing—his being given part of something that belongs to someone else. Sheppard contemplates with disgust the likelihood of Norton becoming a banker or, even worse, the manager of a loan company; and since Norton appears to be decidedly inferior to Rufus in intelligence, Sheppard virtually dismisses his son as an object worthy of his attention. Norton thereafter becomes a pawn in the struggle which develops between Sheppard and Rufus, once the delinquent accepts Sheppard's invitation to come and share their home.

The story's opening scene unveils Sheppard's confused attitudes toward the two boys. As the father sits eating breakfast cereal "mechanically," Norton wanders about the kitchen in search of a breakfast of his own—stale cake spread with peanut butter and ketchup. Sheppard lectures the boy on Rufus's pitiable condition (his mother is in the penitentiary and he must search for food in garbage cans) and suggests to Norton that he share his hoarded wealth with the delinquent, perhaps buying him a new shoe for his clubfoot. The boy is threatened, becomes agitated, and vomits—"a limp sweet batter." Sheppard is overcome by a sense of the injustice of things—the intelligent Rufus "deprived of everything from birth" and the uninspiring "average or below average" Norton who "had had every advantage." Of course, far from having had every advantage, Norton is utterly starved for love, love which Sheppard is incapable of giving him for two distinct but related reasons. First, Sheppard's need to be good and unselfish is so obsessive that it can only be satisfied when he helps those who have no right to expect his help. Given his psychological make-up, Sheppard is inevitably blind to the needs of those closest to him; he neglects Norton, because his desire to be "good" springs from an emptiness in himself which can only be filled by gratuitous deeds of charity in behalf of the world's suffering and underprivileged. His son Norton has a claim upon him, and hence no particular "merit" attaches to anything he may do for the boy. Thus he feels deep sympathy for Rufus who must scavenge for his food, but none at all for his own child who must make a breakfast of ketchup and stale cake. He laments the fate of a boy whose mother is in the penitentiary, but is without pity for his own son's longing for his dead mother. He is sensitive to the psychological scarring which he imagines Johnson's clubfoot has caused, while oblivious to the desperate loneliness of Norton.

The second reason for Sheppard's failure as a father is that, treating the human and the intellectual as interchangeable quantities, he imposes upon the living reality of his child an abstract image; then he responds to the image he has created rather than to the actual boy. Norton *is* selfish and he is (or appears to be) dull. But he is dull largely because of Sheppard's refusal to treat him as a significant human being. (It is important to note that Rufus awakens much that is repressed in Norton, who seems brighter, livelier toward the story's end; even Sheppard, myopic as he is, discovers in Norton's eyes an alertness which he had not noticed before.)

As he fails to see Norton except as a creation of his mind, so also does Sheppard refuse to see the real Rufus. The flesh and blood Rufus tells him that he commits crimes because he's "good at it," but Sheppard insists upon interpreting the boy's behavior according to textbook psychology. Rufus declares that he is in Satan's power, but because his intellectual system has made no provision for the demonic, Sheppard must reject this notion with an outraged cry of "'Rubbish!'" And, when Rufus speaks of heaven and hell as real places to which people go in an afterlife, Sheppard responds by assuring Rufus that he considers him "too intelligent" to believe such nonsense. Because Sheppard has attempted to force reality to conform to an intellectual construct of his own creation, intelligence is for him the decisive factor of human existence. Therefore, Rufus is a more "interesting" specimen of humanity than Norton.

It is his inordinate faith in reason which prevents Sheppard from understanding the power of feeling. He knows, of course, that Rufus possesses feelings of aggression; but because of his *idée fixe* that the source of these feelings is the clubfoot, Sheppard is incapable of taking seriously the boy's outrage at his self-righteousness and his propensity for playing God. Most importantly, Sheppard's obtuseness extends to his own feelings and to the motivation for his behavior. Convinced as he is that he is "good" and that he is "'stronger than [Rufus],'" Sheppard is shocked when he discovers that he can hate and is utterly confounded by the realization that, before the determined lucidity of Rufus's vision of damnation-with-the-possibility-of-salvation, his own self-serving "goodness" is as fragile as a paper doll's house.

The depth of Sheppard's confusion about his own feelings is revealed in the first episode involving Rufus and the police. Just prior to the arrival of the officers who come to arrest Rufus for a "smash job," Sheppard discovers the boy's absence and decides that his method of dealing with his protégé has been less successful than he had anticipated: "He had been over-lenient, too concerned to have Johnson like him. He felt a twinge of guilt." For a moment Sheppard determines to lay down strict rules for Rufus. But when he realizes that Rufus's response will be merely another assertion of independence and a threat to walk out, Sheppard panics: "Oh my God, he thought. He could not bring it to that. He would have to be firm but not make an issue of it." Sheppard obviously is much "too concerned to have Johnson like him" to force the unambiguous understanding which the boy might respect. Yet the twinge of guilt is sufficient to cause Sheppard to fail Rufus at the one point in the story when the boy's confidence might have been won. As the police prepare to take Rufus off to jail, the boy denies knowledge of the crime and turns to his benefactor and protector and asks, "You believe me, don't you?"

There was an appeal in his voice that Sheppard had not heard there before.

This was crucial. The boy would have to learn that he could not be protected when he was guilty. "You'll have to go with him, Rufus," he said.

"You're going to let him take me and I tell you I ain't done a thing?" Johnson said shrilly.

Sheppard's face became harder as his sense of injury grew. The boy had failed him even before he had had a chance to give him the shoe. They were to have got it tomorrow. *All his regret turned suddenly on the shoe; his irritation at the sight of Johnson doubled* [emphasis added].

In Sheppard, Miss O'Connor has created a classic example of one form of "bad faith" as defined in existentialist philosophy—the detached observer or manipulator who refuses to acknowledge that he is part of the problem he is trying to analyze.
—*Preston M. Browning Jr.*

Rufus *is* guilty, and, as we subsequently learn, he wants Sheppard to vouch for him so that he can ultimately compromise and expose this man who is determined to "save" him. The significance of this episode should not be underestimated, since it renders unmistakably clear that weakness in Sheppard which makes him an easy prey for Johnson's malice: Sheppard is so completely a captive of his confused feelings and his voracious hunger for ego satisfaction that he is incapable of dealing with any situation except in terms of its capacity to minister to his psychological needs. Thus, out of shame, he abdicates the little authority he has heretofore maintained over the boy, when he learns the following day that the police have arrested someone else for the crime and are releasing Rufus. Later, when Johnson rejects the new shoe with the scornful comment, "'I don't need no new shoe. . . .' 'And when I do, I got ways of getting my own,'" Sheppard's response to this new rebuff confirms our image

of him as a man totally incapable of responding to life except on the level of childish demands for ego gratification and equally childish petulance when those demands are frustrated.

He wanted to recover his good humor, *but every time he thought of the rejected shoe, he felt a new charge of irritation.* He did not trust himself even to look at Johnson. He realized that the boy had refused the shoe because he was insecure. Johnson had been frightened by his own gratitude. . . . *Grudgingly, Sheppard felt a slight return of sympathy for the boy.* In a few minutes, he lowered his paper and looked at him [emphases added].

Here by skillfully interweaving Sheppard's attempted analysis of Johnson's psychological problems and intimations of Sheppard's failure to see his own psychological shortcomings as equally damaging, Flannery O'Connor underscores this mock-pastor's moral and spiritual blindness. In Sheppard, Miss O'Connor has created a classic example of one form of "bad faith" as defined in existentialist philosophy—the detached observer or manipulator who refuses to acknowledge that he is part of the problem he is trying to analyze.

Because he treats the boy with a condescension rooted in nothing more substantial than his limitless faith in reason, Sheppard's image of himself is destined to be shaken to its very foundations when he discovers the implacable reality of Johnson's dedication to evil. Like many of Miss O'Connor's earlier protagonists, both among the positivists and the positive thinkers, Sheppard commits the fatal error of supposing that good and evil are only words, denoting alternative conditioned responses to social reality. From this it follows that he should assume that it is intelligence which can free man (Rufus) from "evil" responses, just as he believes that he himself is too intelligent to be evil. Hence, because he considers Rufus endowed with intelligence equal to his own, he persists in maintaining—in the face of mounting evidence to the contrary—that the boy is "too intelligent" to commit the crimes which the police attribute to him. Only at the last, when Rufus has confessed to being the culprit, has allowed himself to be caught, and has (falsely) accused Sheppard o making "[i]morr'l suggestions"—only then does Sheppard recognize the impotence of his philosophy that man can make of himself anything he wishes, by virtue of intellect alone.

In one respect, Sheppard is correct about Rufus; the boy *is* intelligent, so much so, in fact, that he immediately perceives that Sheppard's supposedly humanitarian interest in others is in reality a form of self-aggrandizement (cf. Julian of **"Everything That Rises"**). Therefore, Rufus insists upon being what he is, rather than a creature of Sheppard's theories.

He is obstinate, vindictive, malicious, ungrateful, unregenerate—all these and more. In him we encounter once again the criminal-compulsive who so often serves as a spokesman for the author's most deeply felt convictions. Like that earlier prototype, The Misfit, Rufus declares that man faces a choice between Jesus and the devil; but Rufus's faith in both the divine and the satanic is less anxiety-ridden, more rooted in positive conviction. He revels in his depravity while at the same time maintaining that "'[n]obody can save [him] but Jesus'" and that if and when he does repent, he is going "'to be a preacher,'" because "'If you're going to do it, it's no sense in doing it halfway.'" Here Rufus sounds very much like Tarwater, whom he resembles in other respects, principally, I think, in the clarity of his understanding of the relation of act and consequence and in his unswerving insistence upon the primacy of will over reason.

Near the story's conclusion, as Johnson is about to be taken off to jail, he shouts: "'I lie and steal because I'm good at it! My foot don't have a thing to do with it! The lame shall enter first! The halt'll be gathered together. When I get ready to be saved, Jesus'll save me, not that lying stinking atheist.'" This outburst causes Sheppard to reflect: "'I have nothing to reproach myself with.'" Then, as he counts over his "selfless" acts of devotion to the cause of "sav[ing] Johnson for some decent kind of service," there reverberates through his mind, like the drumbeat of an attacking enemy force, the words, "'I did more for him than I did for my own child.'" Immediately, in a crescendo of revelation, Sheppard hears the "jubilant voice" of Rufus shouting, "'Satan has you in his power,'" and at that moment, in the boy's mocking eyes, Sheppard sees an image of "the clear-eyed Devil," malicious and triumphant.

> Norton's face rose before him, empty, forlorn. . . .
> His heart constricted with a repulsion for himself
> so clear and intense that he gasped for breath. He
> had stuffed his own emptiness with good works like
> a glutton. He had ignored his own child to feed his
> vision of himself. . . . His image of himself shriv-
> elled until everything was black before him. He sat
> there paralyzed, aghast.

At this instant, Sheppard experiences a wave of "agonizing love" for his son, only to discover the boy hanging from a rafter in the attic where "he had launched his flight into space."

Sheppard's failure as a human being is figured here with exquisite irony, since it had been his ambition that his son become an astronaut, conquering space and exploring the stars. But Norton has responded instead to Rufus's very concrete, vivid and immediate faith in heaven and hell, remaining impervious to Sheppard's lectures about the glories of science and man's penetration of the darkness of the universe. Af-

firming his own humanity, Norton chooses to join his mother, whom he believes he has sighted in heaven (through the telescope Sheppard had bought principally to interest Rufus in science!), in preference to continuing his empty existence with the man who has given him "every advantage." It is Sheppard who at last begins to penetrate the darkness, not of outer space but of his own heart. Perhaps Sheppard is too much of a caricature to be fully believable; and perhaps for this reason he cannot be considered a tragic figure. Yet this story has about it an ironic fatality as beautifully contrived and as inexorable as that of any Greek tragedy.

Not the least of the virtues of this tale is the clarity with which Flannery O'Connor has portrayed the manner in which a passionate belief in the truth of the divine Word may exist *simultaneously* with a passionate commitment to the demonic principle. (Rufus swallows a page from the Bible and cries, "'I've eaten it like Ezekiel and it was honey to my mouth!'" On the other hand, the success of his lying and stealing is a source of immense satisfaction to him, and he assumes the role of Satan's helper with a gusto which is breathtaking.) Rufus has been described as "a basic figure in modern existentialist literature—the criminal who is seeking God," and has been compared to Dostoevsky's Raskolnikov. The comparison is in many respects apt, not so much because of a resemblance uniting the two characters as such, but because of the basic similarity of the religious or metaphysical questions explored in *Crime and Punishment* and in Flannery O'Connor's novella. Rufus's clubfoot clearly symbolizes a crisis of the spirit not unlike that by which Dostoevsky's hero is afflicted, and the experiences of both Raskolnikov and Rufus suggest that at certain stages in the disintegration of a spiritual tradition, it is only through apparent dedication to the devil and through motiveless crime that a new, authentic humanity can be born.

This notion of commitment to the satanic principle illumines certain features of Miss O'Connor's work that have long been problematic. That the devil plays a conspicuous role in her fiction there is no denying, and one sympathetic commentator has suggested that Flannery O'Connor's authorial voice and that of her devil often appear indistinguishable. From this observation John Hawkes concluded that, whether she was conscious of it or not, "as writer [Flannery O'Connor] was on the devil's side." Granting the truth of Hawkes's description of her authorial stance as sometimes "black," and of the creative impulse in her writing as often "so unflagging and so unpredictable as to become, in a sense, 'immoral,'" I believe Miss O'Connor's attraction to the demonic can better be explained as part of that metaphysical enterprise mentioned in Chapter One—the quest of being and the Holy. For it appears to have been one of her cardinal beliefs that without a recovery of the demonic there could be no true "rediscovery of man." As we have seen in our examination of such characters as Mrs. Cope, the grandmother, and Sheppard, O'Connor's fiction projects an image of man who has lost so completely his capacity for apprehending true evil that he is equally incapable of recognizing true good. And his addiction to superficial and platitudinous conceptions of both good and evil seems the consequence of a loss even more profound—the experience of the self as grounded in being.

Both O'Connor's positivists and her positive thinkers, then, like the "faithless pilgrims" of Conrad's *Heart of Darkness,* suffer from a malaise which is, at bottom, ontological. Dispossessed both of their original innocence and of their postlapsarian knowledge, they seek, however unconsciously, a way back into being. But the way to being is fraught with peril, since it entails confronting the irrational and destructive aspects of the self, facing up to the ugliness and cruelty of life, exploring that foul "dungeon of the heart," which Hawthorne, Dostoevsky and other spiritual forefathers of Flannery O'Connor considered of the essence of human existence but which centuries of moralistic Christianity and bourgeois culture have tended to deny or obscure.

Thus when Flannery O'Connor set out to represent "the conflict between an attraction for the Holy and the disbelief in it which we breathe in with the air of the times," she in fact created a body of fiction one of whose major accomplishments is to present a persuasive dramatic case for the reality of the demonic. But belief in the demonic is only one step from belief in the Holy, for the two stand, so Paul Tillich has argued, in dialectical relation to each other. ("The divine," Tillich states, "embraces itself and the demonic," and he talks of "divine holiness" and "demonic holiness.") Flannery O'Connor's intention, apparently, was to render intelligible the concept of demonic holiness as a way of affirming the reality of holiness itself, and in so doing to bear witness to some depth reality, some "ground of Being" (to borrow another phrase from Tillich), where both the demonic and the Holy reside and out of which man's own being emerges.

Flannery O'Connor, it might finally be argued, sought to recover the depth dimension of existence in order to adumbrate an answer to the "ontological void" posited by Ionesco and other contemporary artists and philosophers. But she recognized that the recovery of depth, or being, was possible only by stripping the masks from men whose fraudulent righteousness had rendered them too complacent even to be damned. Therefore her strategy as a writer was to make as vivid as possible the reality of the demonic, to celebrate, as it were, "spiritual crime," to employ the shock of evil over and over again, in the hope that, finally, by plunging into those fearful psychic depths she might bring up some evidence that, in a time marked by moral chaos and ontological deprivation, it was yet being, not absurdity, which would have the last word.

John V. McDermott (essay date Spring 1975)

SOURCE: "Julian's Journey into Hell: Flannery O'Connor's Allegory of Pride," in *Mississippi Quarterly: The Journal of Southern Culture,* Vol. XXVIII, No. 2, Spring, 1975, pp. 171-9.

[In the following essay, McDermott discusses Julian and his loss of faith in O'Connor's "Everything That Rises Must Converge."]

In Flannery O'Connor's abrasive allegory **"Everything That Rises Must Converge,"** Julian Chestny runs vainly from his soul's imminent dissolution as the story reaches its inevitable climax. The fact that Julian "had lost his faith" is proven conclusively in the story's final scenes, where "his entry into the world of guilt and sorrow" is nothing less than his entrance into the world of hell, and where his pride, now dethroned, seeks to flee from the crippling abject image it finally has of itself.

The essential inevitability of the climax is an integral part of the studied structure of the work, which in its compactly interwoven, parable-like form makes one realize that nearly every incident is symbolic in action, and that there is in fact a chain reaction, imperative in essence, where one sees one action precipitate another, in an unremittingly lethal fashion, for the unfortunate characters who are involved in its enactment.

In opposition to the profoundly pessimistic conclusion concerning the final, pitiful condition of Julian's soul that I have reached are Leon V. Driskell and Joan T. Brittain, who grow rather optimistic and feel that "Julian . . . [when] brought face to face with his own weaknesses must learn to acknowledge reality" and that consequently "the moment of truth can offer nothing but hope."

But to judge the story in this way is to deny completely Miss O'Connor's recognition of "the interpenetration of the real and the ideal" and the fact that she did not divide "the world into [the] ideal and reality." If this is so, then to judge her story on the singular level of "transcendence" is to pronounce the separation "of the real and the ideal" rather than to stress their "interpenetration." To think of the story in these terms is to place it strictly in "the province of thought," and in doing that we must deny every word, thought and deed that makes the story what it is—an allegory that reveals how man, through excessive pride, may lose all touch with reality and, in the subsequent process, destroy himself.

Certainly to ignore "Julian's treatment of his mother [as] beside the point" is to ignore the major theme of the story, which shows Julian, as the personification of pride, dooming himself because of the gradual and insidious inversion of his living soul; for rather than reaching out to others, he turns more and more toward the center of himself as the story progresses. His role in his mother's death causes him finally to move not on a "horizontal . . . treadmill" toward de Chardin's "point omega" but rather in a self-centered, solitary orbit where his pride-driven soul can only ultimately disintegrate in its terrifying, lonely subjectivity. His words and actions after his mother's death clearly reveal his knowledge of himself as a "cause" in her death, and his knowledge of this makes him frighteningly aware of the "evil" within himself. His reactions are inconsistent with any idea of "transcendence" where, at the point of full "convergence or growth" such ideas as "cause and effect . . . 'good' and 'evil'" have no meaning. In contrast, these reactions are filled with ominous portent.

Another critic who feels optimistic about Julian's final fate is Carter W. Martin, who says that Julian "crosses over into maturity and knowledge" as the story concludes. It is my contention, however, that Julian fits into the category of those of Miss O'Connor's characters whom Sister Bertrande D.C. Meyers describes as "people with a defective sense of spiritual purpose," and thematically the story itself seems to center on the idea of "'un-Redemption,' the warping evil of unaided human nature." As Robert Drake perceptively notes, Miss O'Connor's "characters prepare their own ends. . . . She refuses to let them off the hook by interfering with the consequences of their actions." Julian, I feel, is one of the characters whom Miss O'Connor "refuses to let . . . off the hook." His pride is so consuming that it prevents him from seeing the erosive effect it has on his spirit. It is not so much that he "painfully discovers . . . the history of the world progresses at the same time in the line of evil and in the line of good"; rather, his terror at the end is caused by the shock of his realization that he does not truly know himself. His self-righteous self-image having been destroyed by the sudden, jarring awareness of what he has done to his mother, he is left with only the figure and appearance of a man. He finally sees himself in the naked light of truth and cringes at the sight, since, in his case, the truth represents the corrosive and hideous alternates of beauty and goodness.

To comprehend the story fully and give it its just due one must keep in mind Miss O'Connor's precise use of "anagogical vision," that insight which enables her "to see different levels of reality in one image or one situation." In considering one of the story's significant final scenes, the "nothing" that Mrs. Chestny sees, as her eyes "rake" her son's soul, is the equivalent of the total absence of goodness in Julian's now vacuous spirit. His life spirit, having been warped by pride, has become irreparably shattered, and his pathetic cry for help is without true fervor or substance; it is, as Miss O'Connor writes, "thin, scarcely a tread of sound." In this mournful conclusion we see the "lights" drift-

ing from him and "the tide of darkness" sweeping him up. He has indeed become one of the living dead.

Because Julian has lost his soul, his physical nature reacts without purpose ("his feet moved numbly as if they carried him nowhere"), and it is as if his pride, having risen and converged upon itself, suddenly realized the hollow void upon which it had built itself. Indeed his pride throughout the story was simply the mask, or "mental bubble," which had helped him escape the reality of himself. It was the castle of illusion he could go to without walking "with his hands . . . in his pockets and his head" (if not literally, at least psychologically) down. It was the fantasy world he fled to, to escape from his binding feelings of self-inadequacy. Indeed throughout the entire story he moves about in a climate "saturated in depression."

In reaching a conclusion such as the one I have drawn, one must first remember Julian's initial reaction to his mother's frightening collapse. We are made not only to see but to hear his bitter reaction: "He stood over her for a minute, gritting his teeth . . . 'You got exactly what you deserved, . . . now get up.'" And in the terrifying moment before her final breath Julian's seemingly tender call of "Darling, sweetheart, wait!" is met by his mother's unerring eye, the eye of the "heart" which "remained fixed on him, raked his face again, found nothing and closed." Thus the empty reality which he had become was unbearable to his mother. She realized his cries were generated, not out of his love for her, but out of fear for his own hopeless state. She recognized that he was devoid of life because love for him, like "darling" and "sweetheart," were merely hollow sounds. He runs in terror at the end from the fleeting monstrous image he glimpses of himself, and, like his mother, closes his eyes to it. His "postponing from moment to moment" will evolve into a perpetual state for him. He has become at the end a completely lost soul.

If one is to see Julian clearly, however, he must note the close association Julian has with the black woman. As an allegorical figure she represents very dramatically the violent and acrimonious nature of Julian's seethingly hostile mind. Josephine Hendin is correct when she says "the black woman . . . fulfills Julian's fantasies of revolt," for the woman is simply the personification of his active and malignant imagination.

From the beginning the black woman is at one with him in spirit. They both reflect strong and obvious contempt for their fellow man: "The downward tilt of her large lower lip was like a warning sign: DON'T TAMPER WITH ME." This is simply the counterpart of Julian, whom we see "establish himself in . . . a kind of mental bubble . . . when he could not bear to be a part of what was going on around him." His pernicious imagination which "began to imagine various unlikely ways by which he could teach [his mother] a lesson" makes him a kindred spirit to the black woman. She personifies the insidious gradations of his angry mind. "He was conscious of a kind of bristling next to him, a muted growling like that of an angry cat." And whereas she reflects man's inclination to react in violent passion, Julian, on the level of idle fantasy, represents man's equally treacherous tendency to destroy by passive indifference. "He studied [his mother] coldly. . . . He felt completely detached from her. At that moment he could with pleasure have slapped at her as he would have slapped a particularly obnoxious child in his charge." But what Julian only thinks, the black woman finally does, for as the symbol of his violent imagination, she rumbles "like a volcano about to become active." The frenzied woman's attack is indeed shocking to his mother, but it is not this woman's act of violence that causes Mrs. Chestny's final collapse; rather, it is Julian's reaction to the attack—"You got exactly what you deserved"—that totally destroys her spirit. Searching for the familial reality of love, Mrs. Chestny let "her eyes [rake] his face, [but] she found nothing familiar about him." Later, and with the author's obvious emphasis, we read that she "raked his face again [but] she found nothing and closed [her eyes]." The black woman, then, is basically the allegorical figure of Julian's fury, which he has always prided himself in being in rigid control of, like the martyr St. Sebastian.

In considering Julian's plight one must take careful note that the spirit of evil has not, like some powerful incarnate force, overcome this pathetic figure against his will. Rather, he has obviously exercised free choice. We note that on the fateful bus ride it was his deliberate choice to leave his mother's side, and thereby later afford the Negro woman the opportunity to sit by his side. "Julian rose, crossed the aisle, and sat down in the place of the woman with the canvas sandals. From this position, he looked serenely across at his mother. . . . He stared at her, making his eyes the eyes of a stranger. He felt his tension suddenly lift as if he had openly declared war on her"; at this moment he was indeed preparing his own end.

In considering the precise role of the Negro woman in the story Miss Hendin feels that she may be considered a "heroine" who reaches "a sudden, cataclysmic maturity." She feels that Julian is "powerless before the black woman's violence." But this is true only to the extent that his will has finally surrendered to his dark, angry thoughts. He is not "powerless" because he is the black woman's fearful enemy; rather he is "powerless" because he is her true ally. She represents, in indelible terms, the volcanic part of his nature that has finally erupted and converged upon his reason. That is why his mother fails to recognize him, and why, after her death, he refuses to recognize himself.

In keeping with the sustained symbolism of the story, we note

the subtle biblical references to the devil that further ally Julian to the Negro woman: "He was tilted out of his fantasy again as the bus stopped. The door opened with a sucking hiss and out of the dark a . . . sullen-looking colored woman got on." A short time later we note that just before leaving the bus, Julian reacts to his mother's desire "to give the little boy a nickel. . . . 'No!' Julian hissed. 'No.'" And finally we see them leave the bus together: "He reached up and pulled the cord. The woman reached up and pulled it at the same time." Thus as the allegorical embodiment of his anguished mind, the Negro woman acts in perfect consonance with him.

In touching on the true spiritual level of the story, we see that Miss O'Connor is not interested in forced brotherhood, in integration on the physical, surface level where men are forced by executive order to bend their wills to the laws of the land. In his essay on Miss O'Connor, Stanley Edgar Hyman stresses the theme of social integration by saying that "the characters, a travesty segregationist mother and a travesty integrationist son, are not adequate to the finely structured action." And later, "Integrationism is savagely travestied as sentimental and fatuous in Julian . . . and the opposing view just as savagely travestied in the mother." But this interpretation, I feel, tends to belabor the obvious and ignore the allegorical intent of the story, for Miss O'Connor is interested only in a true integration of the spirit, an integration, freely given, by which man allies himself to his fellow man out of love. What one sees in this story is exactly the opposite. Here the atmosphere is permeated not by love, but by an imperative chain of selfishness and fear, which produces in each man's heart a feeling of hatred, born out of wounded pride; for when one thinks only of the self, there can be no reciprocity of affection. Each person on the bus tries desperately to shield and preserve his own self-image, but in so doing tends to isolate himself. "The Negro . . . immediately unfolded a newspaper and obscured himself behind it"; "[t]he woman with the red and white canvas sandals had risen at the same time the Negro sat down and had gone further back in the bus. . . ."; "Julian rose, crossed the aisle, and sat down in the place of the woman with the canvas sandals." Each person then tends to display and personify distrust, fear and hatred, and Julian's desire to sit by the Negro's side is motivated not by brotherly love, but by his desire to "declare war" on his mother.

The story, in keeping with its oppressive tone and theme, begins and ends in darkness. The entire landscape is bathed in colors pertinent to the theme of Christian death. We read that "the sky was a dying violet and the houses stood out darkly against it" and, in the dire conclusion that immediately precedes Mrs. Chestny's physical death and Julian's spiritual demise, that "Rising above them on either side were black apartment buildings, marked with irregular rectangles of light." And then, in the very next sentence, we see what can only be interpreted as a final, comprehensive symbol of man's divided heart: "At the end of the block a man came out of a door and walked off in the opposite direction," leaving Julian and his mother to their isolated problem. This gesture is indeed symbolic of what happens when man locks himself in his own world and takes pernicious delight in excluding others. And it is fairly evident that throughout the story Julian's wounded pride thrived on offending others by excluding them. We see he longed to feel "free of the general idiocy of his fellows," but he focused and intensified this feeling of antipathy on his mother; "he had ceased to recognize her existence." To his great sorrow, she later does the same thing to him; "trying to determine his identity . . . , she found nothing familiar about him." She finally closes her eyes on him, and, in guilt, he tries to do the same thing to himself. His earlier taunt to his mother, "You aren't who you think you are" proves ironically and direfully prophetic when finally applied to himself. He is at the end a man without a "voice" or "identity"; he has become "nothing" where it elicits the deepest pain—in his own mind.

Robert D. Denham (essay date Autumn 1975)

SOURCE: "The World of Guilt and Sorrow: Flannery O'Connor's 'Everything That Rises Must Converge,'" in *The Flannery O'Connor Bulletin,* Vol. IV, Autumn, 1975, pp. 42-51.

[*In the following essay, Denham discusses O'Connor's "Everything That Rises Must Converge" as a journey towards Julian's growth, and asserts that the bus scene serves to make Julian unsympathetic and provides the means for the story's climax.*]

"In the act of writing," says Flannery O'Connor, "one sees that the way a thing is made controls and is inseparable from the whole meaning of it. The form of a story gives it meaning which any other form would change." She adds that unless the reader "is able, in some degree, to apprehend the form, he will never apprehend anything else about the work, except what is extrinsic to it as literature." These statements imply a neatly capsulated set of principles for one kind of critical inquiry, the kind which seeks to explain a fictional whole not only in terms of its parts but also in relation to the reader's apprehension of the story's shaping principle. Miss O'Connor's brief statement, in fact, closely parallels R. S. Crane's Neo-Aristotelian argument about causal inquiry as a method of criticism. Crane contends that in order to speak critically about any one part of literary work it is first necessary to determine its "essential cause." This cause, he argues, is the writer's primary intuition of form, an intuition which will enable him to synthesize his materials into a unified whole and which, in turn, will correspond to the reader's

experience of the work. In other words, we cannot determine the function of the individual parts of a story without a prior induction from the story itself of a shaping principle which, in what Crane calls "imitative" works, has the power to affect our emotions in a certain way. The starting point, therefore, in this kind of inquiry, would be a description of the moral and emotional qualities which characterize our experience as readers, the assumption being that if we have read carefully and sensitively, our experience will coincide closely with the shaping principle of the whole. This is what Miss O'Connor means, I think, when she says that we must be able to "apprehend the form" before we can "apprehend anything else about the work"; which is to say that the relationship between the way a thing is made and its shaping form is an integral one. It is this shaping form, according to Crane, which we as readers, by reasoning backward from effect to cause, can use to make explicit the function of any part of a well-made story.

Flannery O'Connor's **"Everything That Rises Must Converge"** can be read from the perspective of these general principles. This is not to suggest, of course, that other views are not possible. Perhaps the most frequent readings of the story have derived from the thematic perspective and have aimed to show the relationship of O'Connor's fiction to something else. Although thematic principles and analogical methods make for legitimate critical inquiry, they are not calculated to shed much light on the particular shape of an individual story as this is reconstructed by formal analysis. All I am suggesting therefore, is that we can account for the form which gives the story meaning by beginning with the plot as experienced, that is, by beginning with the affective reaction which our experience of the story forces upon us. If we then take this response as related to the synthesizing or shaping of the whole, we can use it to explain some of the narrative choices Flannery O'Connor made in developing the story.

Our experience of **"Everything That Rises"** is primarily a reversal of our expectations and desires for the principal characters and a change in attitude toward them. Standing at the center of the action is Julian, a disheartened, cynical, confused, misanthropic young man. He habitually uses his sense of moral superiority to elevate himself and thereby judge the inadequacies of others. Playing the intellectual sophisticate, he sees his task as instructing the unenlightened, especially his mother, in the ways of "true culture"; and for Julian true culture is always defined in terms of "the mind." He is, in short, a self-pitying malcontent who enjoys the role of martyr and who treats his mother with an unrelenting contempt, offering her no love or sympathy and delighting in her discomfort. Only twice does he waver from what he is shown everywhere else to be: first, in one of his initial reveries, when he longs for the old Chestny mansion; and later, on the bus, when he senses his mother's innocence. But in each case the real Julian quickly emerges.

> In the act of writing, one sees that the way a thing is made controls and is inseparable from the whole meaning of it. The form of a story gives it meaning which any other form would change.
> —*Flannery O'Connor*

Julian's mother, on the other hand, is a poor, struggling widow, who has sacrificed her own well-being for her son's education and who sees him now, with diploma in hand, reduced to peddling typewriters. Naive in outlook and understanding, she sees her identity in terms of a glamorous but lost past, truth in terms of the platitudinous cliché, "true culture" in terms of "the heart," and success in terms of social melioration. Her concern is genuine but her vision is limited.

These are the two characters whose conflict Miss O'Connor plays out before us in three scenes. In the first scene, Julian's depression, occasioned by his mother's rather outlandish garb, erupts eventually into a string of contemptuous rejoinders at her efforts at conversation. At every point mother and son are diametrically opposed, whether the issue be the purple and green hat, or the remembrance of things past, or the "rise" of the Negro. The conflict is developed further in the bus scene, where their attitudes about the racial question, prepared for in scene one, become the central issue. Here, Julian's gambit with the Negro man having failed, talk subsides as mother and son engage in a game of glances. The narrator's intrusions into Julian's mind at this point show us most clearly the shallowness and pretension of his intellectualism. His efforts to atone for his mother's racial prejudice are sham, since his motivation to dramatize her pettiness precludes any humane concern, even though he postures such concern. The climax of the second episode, and of the story itself, comes in the encounter with the Negro woman, everything that rises converging figuratively in the recognition by Julian's mother that she and the Negro woman are wearing the same hat; and converging literally, moments later, with the impact of the black woman's fist.

What occurs in the final moving scene is Julian's discovery: the recognition which issues in his change of character. His perverse intellectualism suddenly pales before the stark reality of his mother's death; so that his futile, yet tender, cry to her, just before she crumples to the pavement, makes mockery of his earlier testimony that "instead of being blinded by love for her as she was for him, he had cut himself emotionally free from her and could see her with complete objectivity." But now, the terrifying moment becomes

for Julian an epiphany, dissolving the vanity in his assertion of emotional freedom and melting his contempt. His cries for help suggest not merely the panic of the moment, effacing his earlier claim of fearlessness; they suggest also his desperate awareness of the dark state of his own soul. The final words of the narrator, which show Julian on the threshold of "the world of guilt and sorrow," make explicit his discovery. Recognition and reversal are coincident, and the change which comes from Julian's new knowledge is imminent.

What Flannery O'Connor has done in the final moving scene is crucial in the description of our overall experience of the story; for it is here that what I have referred to as the reversal of our expectations, desires, and attitudes is forced upon us. By carefully controlling our feelings about the two characters, Miss O'Connor has turned upside down what we have been made to feel up to this point. Our experience is one of *agreeable astonishment,* in that a young man, who has knowingly done evil and yet who is unaware of the pretension in his moral posturing, encounters a shocking event that changes his moral nature: it alters the attitude toward the evil he has done wittingly and deflates his unconscious moral egoism. Our experience, in the first place, is *agreeable,* in that an unsympathetic character, one whose actions and thoughts have aroused our moral indignation, has changed in such a way that our reaction of vexed displeasure toward him has become understanding; our disapprobation, sympathy. In short, the change in Julian's character is for the better, and we are gratified by the moral reversal. Our experience, in the second place, is one of *astonishment,* in that within Julian's character there has been too much which is unredeemed for us to desire this moral change and too little which is redeeming for us to expect it. Rather, what we expect and desire until the reversal occurs is something quite singular: the belief that poetic justice will be served if Julian is somehow punished.

In the case of Julian's mother, we experience quite the opposite effect: something neither unexpected nor agreeable. Her moral nature throughout the story has caused reactions more sympathetic than our response to Julian; and this is due to the fact that her shortcomings are less vicious and blameworthy, since they derive from unconscious prejudice and naivete. In other words, she is more innocent than Julian, and our feeling toward her at the end is one of pathos. She is a pitiable, unknowing victim, struck down before moral change becomes an option. And thus our response to her fate is the reverse of that satisfaction we find in Julian's imminent new understanding.

Precisely what happens to Julian's mother is significant, for it qualifies our reaction not only to her fate but also, and more importantly, to Julian's. I have spoken of the death of Julian's mother, even though there is no explicit statement to this effect. But we must assume, I think, that when her eye closes having raked Julian's face and found nothing, she does die, or at least that she is to die shortly. What happens to Julian—his imminent entry into the world of guilt and sorrow—is difficult to explain unless we draw this inference. To approach the question from the other end: Given the narrator's statement that Julian is shortly to become sorrowful and guilty, what are the causes in the action which explain this effect? To have Julian's mother suffer only a stroke is not enough to account for the change; for although the narrator expresses at one point Julian's qualms about pushing his mother to the extent that a stroke would result, he is possessed throughout by a malevolent desire to see her suffer, to teach her a lesson in morality by hurting her, even by directly inflicting the pain himself ("he could with pleasure have slapped her"); so that a heart attack alone is insufficient cause for Julian's final reaction. In other words, if death does not ensue, then Julian gets more or less what he desired all along; and if this were the case, we would be forced to imagine the last lines of the story informing us of something quite different, like Julian's re-entry into his world of moral pride and smug self-esteem. To see Julian's mother suffer anything less than death is sufficient justification for his sadness, at most, but hardly for guilt and sorrow. In short, to assume that his mother does not die is to call into question Flannery O'Connor's artistry.

If our reaction to the moral and emotional qualities of the story as a whole corresponds to the shaping principle or form, then, as I have argued, the various parts of the whole should contribute to this essential cause. Take, for example, the scene on the bus. How does this part of the story help to develop the shaping cause? Comprised of three separate episodes (each marked by someone boarding the bus), the scene serves two primary functions: first, it further develops Julian's character and thereby makes possible the complication of the conflict between him and his mother; and second, it provides a means for achieving the narrative climax.

In the first scene of the story Julian's character is presented only in outline. He is depressed about the prospects of tagging along with his mother, gloomy about what the future holds for him, possessed by mixed feeling (contempt and longing) regarding the ancestral heritage in which his mother takes such pride, and overcome by self-pity to the point of having a martyr complex. Clearly, this sketch of Julian's character must be developed if we are to explain the conclusion to the story and our reaction to it. It is not surprising, then, that this becomes one of Miss O'Connor's chief aims in the bus scene. And it is especially because of this scene that Julian emerges as a highly unsympathetic character. His malevolence and misanthropy and moral pretension are particularly heightened, especially in those places where the narrator gives us extended inside views.

It is significant, I think, that after Julian's abortive attempt at conversing with the Negro man, he utters not one word for the remainder of the scene; for this, coupled with his fantasies, indicates the kind of passive character he is and contrasts sharply with the later, genuine outburst to his stricken mother. It is also in this scene that we see that Julian's views of himself are precisely the wrong views. Some such process of artistic reasoning as just described seems to have guided Miss O'Connor in developing Julian's character in this scene. The form of the whole, created by that intuition of hers which works to shape the total effect, demands that she endow her characters with certain moral traits. I am suggesting that Julian must possess those qualities developed in the bus scene for our experience of the effect to be what it in fact is; so that creating these traits in Julian's character is one of her chief accomplishments in this scene.

If the form of the story requires that Julian embody these necessary moral qualities, it also demands particular kinds of probable incidents. Reasoning *a posteriori,* we can see that with the entrance of the Negro woman and her son, Flannery O'Connor has introduced the means for reaching the story's climax. It seems likely that by this point in the story she must have had some conception of a conclusion which would call for a sudden, shocking event, resulting in the heart attack and subsequent death of Julian's mother. Some violent action *could* be used to achieve this effect. It is highly unlikely, however, that Julian, passive dreamer that he is, would be capable of perpetrating any violence upon his mother. Other characters, therefore, will be needed as a means to this end.

If these are reasonable assumptions, Miss O'Connor's problem now becomes that of determining some point of dissension or conflict which will lead to the violent action. Her introduction of the Negro woman and her son, with the ingenious little game of musical bus-seats and son-swapping that ensues, is a perfect solution; for this will bring the racial issue clearly to the fore. And given the kind of woman Julian's mother has already been shown to be, the conclusion of the scene is practically inevitable. We have already seen her condescending racial attitudes—initially, in her discussion with Julian in the first scene, and later in her brief dialogue with the woman with protruding teeth—so that we expect her to display the same kind of unthinking attitude toward the Negro woman and her son. And we are also prepared to encounter some blundering expression of this patronizing manner, given the disposition of some of her previous remarks about "darkies," "colored friends," "mixed feelings," and the like.

Julian's mother, of course, obliges our expectations in both cases, the immediate result being the blow to the face, and the ultimate effect being death and Julian's subsequent change. The racial issue itself, which is so prominent throughout, should not be construed as the story's shaping principle. It is simply a means necessary for the climax and final effect: the Negro woman disappears when she has served her function, just as the Negro man, having performed his fictional duty, is made conveniently to disembark when Miss O'Connor's front seats get a bit too crowded. My conclusion is this: Given the form of the whole, which I have defined experientially in terms of the achieved effect, the two chief things accomplished by the bus scene are both probable and necessary: making Julian into a morally unsympathetic character and providing a means for the story's climax. As Flannery O'Connor herself has said, "I try to satisfy those necessities that make themselves felt in the work itself."

Finally, it should be observed that Julian's mother has also made a discovery in having to confront, shockingly, the truth of Julian's one correct claim: her condescending and patronizing attitude toward Negroes. But her discovery issues in the tragedy and irony of death: tragedy, from Julian's perspective, since it is only through the loss of his mother that he can enter his new life; and fateful irony from his mother's perspective, since her irresponsibility, though more innocent than his, is not allowed the same potential for change. Whereas she has been shown throughout to be ludicrous and pathetic and even pitiable, she embodies at the end, in her lurch toward death, what Yeats called "a vision of terror." We respond accordingly. Julian, on the other hand, for whom we have been able to muster little sympathy, has now become a young man whose desperate cries give us sympathetic joy in his change and more than a modest optimism for his future. The story, then, is finally Julian's story. His mother's death becomes the terrible means by which he can grow toward maturity. And the beginning of this growth is what the story is all about.

Dorothy Tuck McFarland (essay date 1976)

SOURCE: "*Everything That Rises Must Converge,*" in *Flannery O'Connor,* Frederick Ungar Publishing Co., 1976, pp. 43-71.

[*In the following essay, Tuck McFarland analyzes the different instances of rising and convergence in the stories from O'Connor's* Everything That Rises Must Converge.]

The stories in O'Connor's second collection reflect her concern with questions implicitly raised by the rather gnomic title **"Everything That Rises Must Converge."** The phrase comes from the work of Pierre Teilhard de Chardin, a Jesuit paleontologist-philosopher. Teilhard hypothesized that evolution, far from stopping with the emergence of *homo sapiens,* continues to progress toward higher levels of con-

sciousness, and that its ultimate goal is pure consciousness, which is Being itself, or God.

Teilhard's concept of the progress of evolution, actual and predicted, can best be visualized as a globe. At the base of the globe—the beginning of the evolutionary process—lines radiate outward and upward, representing the diversification of many forms of life which are moving upward toward greater levels of biological complexity. At the midpoint of the globe the diversification stops and one species—man—comes to dominate the earth. Moving from the midpoint of the globe upward, the lines begin to converge as they approach the topmost pole, the evolutionary destination that Teilhard called the Omega point. The converging lines now represent individual human consciousnesses which, as they rise, grow closer and closer together.

One aspect of this convergence can be seen in the increased intercommunication and interdependence of men in modern mass society. The increasingly complex interaction of men, Teilhard believed, tends to generate fresh bursts of evolutionary energy that produce still higher levels of consciousness, and these increases in consciousness find material expression in new technological breakthroughs. Teilhard, however, did not equate rising in consciousness solely with social or intellectual or scientific advances; he saw these achievements as manifestations of an increase in consciousness that was primarily a growing toward the fullness of Being—God—that is the source of all life.

O'Connor certainly regarded an increase in consciousness—which in her stories is signified by an increase in vision—to be a growing toward Being. However, her characters typically resist this kind of rising and the spiritual convergence with others that accompanies it. This has led some commentators to conclude that O'Connor's use of the title **"Everything That Rises Must Converge"** is largely, if not completely, ironic. (According to one critic, nothing rises in the title story but Julian's mother's blood pressure.) It is true that O'Connor deliberately plays off the meaning of the title against numerous metaphors of non-convergent rising, and especially against her characters' desire to rise without convergence; for instance, the "rising" of Negroes is acceptable to Julian's mother only as long as there is no convergence: "they should rise, yes, but on their own side of the fence." The thrust of most of the stories, however, is to bring the protagonist to a vision of himself as he really is, and thus to make possible a true rising toward Being. That this rising is inevitably painful does not discredit its validity; rather, it emphasizes (as Teilhard's conception does not) the tension between the evolutionary thrust toward Being and the human warp that resists it—the warp which O'Connor would have called original sin.

Julian, the protagonist of the title story, considers the position in which he finds himself to be monumentally beneath his dignity. He is taking his mother, who is overweight and has high blood pressure, to her reducing class at the Y, because she will not ride the buses by herself at night now that they have been integrated. As he waits for her while she adjusts a hideous green and purple hat, he feels as if his sensibilities are suffering martyrdom; leaning against the door frame, he seems to be "waiting like Saint Sebastian for the arrows to begin piercing him."

A would-be intellectual, Julian likes to think that he has raised himself, by his own efforts, above his mother's anachronistic values and above the intellectual sterility of his environment. This rising implies no convergence. Although he has fantasies about making friends with Negroes (to express his liberal views and annoy his conventional Southern mother), he has no real desire for convergence with anyone. He thinks of himself in proud isolation from others, retreating into an "inner compartment" of his mind whenever "he could not bear to be a part of what was going on around him." His idea of an ideal home is one where the nearest neighbors are three miles away on either side.

Whatever signs of convergence of social classes or races are evident in the story are dealt with by the characters in ways that minimize any real meeting. Julian's mother believes she can "go anywhere"—i.e., mix in any kind of social situation—because she is a descendant of a once-proud family: "if you know who you are, you can go anywhere." When a Negro woman gets on the bus wearing a hat identical to her own, she is dismayed by this sign of identity between them. She handles the situation by reducing the other woman to a subhuman level and seeing the implied relationship between them as a comic impossibility: "She kept her eyes on the woman and an amused smile came over her face as if the woman were a monkey that had stolen her hat." She thinks the Negro woman's child is "cute," and attempts to give the little boy a "shiny new penny" as they get off the bus. The woman, outraged at this sign of white condescension, literally converges with her and batters her in the face with her enormous handbag. Julian's mother, knocked to the ground, suffers a stroke.

Thus far, the metaphors of rising and convergence in the story seem to be purely ironic. Julian's mother's death, however, does bring about a rising in consciousness in Julian, and the nearness of death brings her to a real desire for convergence with a beloved Negro nurse of her childhood. The motions of true rising in both characters come about through an apparent descent, a regression back to childhood. Julian, in the midst of an angry tirade at his mother, finally becomes aware of what is happening to her. Shocked out of his self-justifying and isolating "adult" behavior by this realization, he is precipitated back into his childhood love for her: "'Mother!' he cried. 'Darling, sweetheart, wait!' Crumpling,

she fell to the pavement. He dashed forward and fell at her side, crying, 'Mamma, Mamma!'" She, too, regresses to childhood, calling out for her old Negro nurse Caroline to come and get her. Unable to accept the convergence of social equality with Negroes in life, she nevertheless turns to the memory of a Negro with a true motion of convergence as she is dying.

The shock of his mother's dying brings Julian not only into contact with his buried love for her but also to the verge of realizing his repeated betrayals and denials of that love. The story has an almost tragic force in its evocation of the horror attendant upon Julian's dawning discovery of his blindness of what he has been and done. His all-too-human reluctance to be fully illuminated, and the nature of the illumination that is awaiting him, are beautifully suggested in the final lines of the story. O'Connor describes him seeming to be swept back toward his mother, toward his childhood connection with her, by a "tide of darkness" that "postpon[es] from moment to moment his entry into the world of guilt and sorrow."

In **"The Enduring Chill"** O'Connor uses conventional religious imagery for comic purposes but finally reveals in the imagery an unexpected and terrifying reality. Asbury, the protagonist, is another would-be writer who believes himself to be far superior to the Southern environment in which he was raised. As the story opens, he has just come back from New York City to his mother's dairy farm, believing he has a fatal illness. Wanting to bring his mother to a realization of how her commonplace life has stifled his artistic talent, he plans to leave her a lengthy letter—"such a letter as Kafka had addressed to his father"—to be read after his death. His attitude toward death is full of romantic posturings; he believes that "he had failed his god, Art, but he had been a faithful servant and Art was sending him Death."

His life, too, is full of posturings. Before his illness he had attempted a ludicrous "communion" with the Negro hands on his mother's farm by smoking with them and trying to get them to share a glass of unpasteurized milk with him in the dairy. Now, convinced he is dying, he badgers his mother into sending for a Jesuit priest because he wants to talk to "a man of culture" and he believes Jesuits to be sophisticated and worldly, and also because he knows it will annoy his Methodist mother. The priest, who turns out to be Irish and orthodox, brusquely turns aside Asbury's attempts to initiate a literary discussion and (in one of the funniest scenes in the O'Connor canon) examines him on his catechism. Finding Asbury deplorably ignorant, he exhorts him to ask God to send him the Holy Ghost. Asbury, furious at this turn of affairs, retorts to the priest that "the Holy Ghost is the last thing I'm looking for!"

When his illness is finally diagnosed as undulant fever (which is recurrent but not fatal), contracted by drinking the unpasteurized milk, Asbury's pretentious illusions about himself suffer a terrible blow. Instead of a romantic death, he is condemned to the terrifying reality of living and seeing himself clearly for what he really is. His eyes look "shocked clean as if they had been prepared for some awful vision about to come down on him." As that vision comes, an image made by water stains on the ceiling above his head—which has seemed to Asbury since childhood to be a "fierce bird" with icicles hanging from its wings—seems suddenly to be in motion. O'Connor identifies the bird with the Holy Ghost, traditionally imaged as a dove and the agent of spiritual illumination:

> Asbury blanched and the last film of illusion was torn as if by a whirlwind from his eyes. He saw that for the rest of his days, frail, racked, but enduring, he would live in the face of a purifying terror. A feeble cry, a last impossible protest escaped him. But the Holy Ghost, emblazoned in ice instead of fire, continued, implacable, to descend.

O'Connor uses allusions from classical mythology to suggest the deeper levels of meaning present in **"Greenleaf."** Even the names of the protagonist, Mrs. May, and her tenants, the Greenleafs, suggest the springtime of the world and the ancient rites of fertility associated with that season. Mrs. May's character, however, is in ironic contrast to her name, for there is nothing yielding, receptive, or springlike about her. She runs her farm with an "iron hand." She pits herself against her tenants, the Greenleafs, who embody for her all that is shiftless and irresponsible, who live "like the lilies of the field." She fears that Mr. Greenleaf will wear her down by sheer attrition if she doesn't keep her "foot on his neck all the time." She sees the "rising" of the Greenleaf boys (they now own a prosperous farm after being educated on the G.I. bill) as a threat of unwelcome convergence. "And in twenty years . . . do you know what those people will be?" she asks her sons. "*Society,*" she replies blackly. However, she consoles herself with the thought that "no matter how far they *go,* they *came* from that." "That" is slovenly, uncouth Mrs. Greenleaf, who conducts "prayer healings" in the woods, moaning and crying over buried newspaper clippings recounting the atrocities of the world. Mrs. May's rejection of *that*—all that is primitive, unsocialized, mysterious, powerful—is even more adamant than her refusal to consider any offspring of the Greenleafs socially acceptable.

As is usual in the O'Connor canon, the mysterious, chthonic forces of nature are symbols of divinity, and Mrs. May's relentless resistance to these forces suggests that the primary convergence she is attempting to avoid is union with God. The specific embodiment of the divine in the story is a "scrub" bull belonging to the Greenleaf sons. The bull, who likes to "bust loose" (suggesting the uncontainable power of divinity), appears at the opening of the story eating a hole in the hedge outside Mrs. May's bedroom window. The hedge (like the wall of trees surrounding her property) is a symbol of the metaphoric walls behind which Mrs. May isolates herself, and the bull is a destroyer of such defenses. His symbolic role as divine lover is made quite explicit early in the story. Standing outside her window, he is likened to "some patient god come down to woo her." Crowned with a wreath of hedge that has slipped over his horns, he is also implicitly associated with the garlanded victim of ancient sacrifice.

The threat that the bull represents to Mrs. May is expressed largely through sexual metaphors. On the naturalistic level, she is afraid that this "scrub" bull will get in with her wellbred dairy cows and "ruin the breeding schedule." She has the same fear in regard to the Greenleafs themselves; she is afraid that her ill-tempered sons (who seem capable of doing anything in order to annoy her) will marry "trash" like Mrs. Greenleaf and "ruin everything I've done."

Basically, Mrs. May's fears of the bull and the Greenleafs represent her anxiety about the intrusion of that which is vaster than she into her well-controlled life; she is afraid of being overpowered, either by the forces of nature or those transcending nature. Inasmuch as both the bull and the Greenleafs symbolize these forces, Mrs. May directs all her energies to keeping both the bull and the Greenleafs under her control.

When the bull repeatedly breaks out of his pen, and the Greenleaf boys display no eagerness to come and get him, Mrs. May decides to make Mr. Greenleaf shoot him. She orders Mr. Greenleaf to get his gun and drive out to the pasture with her. When the bull runs into the woods, she sits on the front bumper of the car and waits for Mr. Greenleaf to drive the bull back into the pasture. When the bull—who does not like cars—comes out of the woods, he gallops toward Mrs. May with "a gay rocking gait as if he were overjoyed to find her again." The imagery again suggests that the bull is both a lover and a destroyer of defensive walls. Charging toward her, he "buried his head in her lap, like a wild tormented lover. . . . One of his horns sank until it pierced her heart and the other curved around her side and held her in an unbreakable grip." The tree line surrounding the pasture—symbolic of her outermost wall of defense—now appears to her as a "dark wound in a world that was nothing but sky." That wound is analogous to the wound the bull makes in the wall of her body as he penetrates to the very core of her being—her heart.

This "convergence" with the bull and all he symbolizes brings Mrs. May to an overwhelming illumination: "she had the look of a person whose sight has been suddenly restored but who finds the light unbearable." The bull, the divine lover whose embrace is death to the walled-in and controlling self, becomes the sacrificial victim as Mr. Greenleaf runs up and shoots him "four times through the eye." (The analogy between the bull and Christ, who is traditionally the divine Bridegroom as well as the sacrificial victim on the cross, is too close to be overlooked.) United with the bull in death, Mrs. May seems to accept her divine suitor; as the bull's huge body sinks to the ground, Mrs. May is pulled forward so that, loverlike, she seems to be "bent over whispering some last discovery into the animal's ear."

Even more than Mrs. May, old Mr. Fortune, the protagonist of **"A View of the Woods,"** is determined to resist convergence. In the consequences of his resistance, O'Connor may be suggesting that convergence—with others and, ultimately, with God—is demanded of man, and his unrelenting refusal of it makes him experience what is potentially a source of joy as the pain of hell. This is hinted at in Mr. Fortune's response to the woods. The view of the woods, and the cow pasture that commands it, have much the same function as the bull in **"Greenleaf."** They embody something non-utilitarian and gratuitous, something charged with mysterious power. They appear under different aspects according to how they are regarded. To the Pitts children in the story, who love the pasture, it is "where we play," and the view of the woods is of immense importance. To old Mr. Fortune, who cannot see letting trees and a pasture stand in the way of progress, the woods embody an "uncomfortable mystery" that he finds distinctly unpleasant. As he stares at the woods at sunset, the red light of the setting sun makes it seem to him "as if someone were ounded behind the woods and the trees were bathed in blood." To his eyes, the vision of the woods is "hellish."

Mr. Fortune is an old man who sees the advent of "progress" in his rural neighborhood as a means of maintaining his position of dominance over his family. He is of the opinion that "[a]nyone over sixty years of age is in an uneasy position unless he controls the greater interest." When an artificial lake is created adjacent to his property, he is able to sell off lakefront lots, thus both strengthening his financial position and causing considerable pain to his despised son-in-law, Pitts, who farms the old man's land and wants to buy it himself. Mr. Fortune's attitude toward his family—with one exception—is that of enormous contempt. The one exception is his granddaughter, Mary Fortune Pitts, who bears a strong resemblance to him and whom he sees as an extension of himself.

Mr. Fortune has decided to sell the pasture in front of his house as a site for a gas station, partly in the expectation of seeing his rural environment grow into a modern town, and partly for the pleasure of annoying his son-in-law. To his surprise and consternation, Mary Fortune—who heretofore has always supported him in his enterprises—strenuously objects to the sale because "We won't be able to see the woods across the road." Moreover, she adds, "My daddy grazes his calves on that lot." The child's loyalty to her father infuriates the old man, partly because it is loyalty to someone other than himself and partly because it is given to Pitts, who, for no apparent reason, beats her. She inexplicably submits to these beatings, though she denies to the old man that they take place. She even boasts that "Nobody's ever put a hand on me and if anybody did, I'd kill him."

As her name suggests, Mary Fortune Pitts embodies the union of Fortune and Pitts. In addition to her physical resemblance to her grandfather, she shares his fascination with signs of progress, particularly the construction of a fishing club on the shores of the artificial lake. She is, however, (though Mr. Fortune would like to overlook this) also a Pitts, as is reflected in her name, in her intense commitment to the view of the woods, and in her loyalty to her father. To Mr. Fortune, the convergence of Fortune and Pitts is abhorrent. As Mary Fortune's stubborn loyalty to the view of the woods and her father's calf pasture makes the Pitts in her more apparent, Mr. Fortune attempts to force her to choose between them: "Are you a Fortune," he asks her, "or are you a Pitts? Make up your mind."

Mr. Fortune's rejection of the importance of the view of the woods, and his refusal to accept the Pitts in Mary Fortune, have dire consequences. O'Connor suggests the spiritual dimensions of those consequences in the way she describes Tilman, the man to whom Mr. Fortune sells the pasture. Tilman has a triangular face, very narrow green eyes, and a head that weaves "snake-fashion" above his body. Tilman's serpentine appearance suggests that Mr. Fortune is completing a deal with the devil.

When the sale is concluded Mary Fortune bursts into the room in a fury and begins hurling pop bottles at Tilman. Mr. Fortune, appalled at her behavior, decides he has been too lenient with her and takes her out in the woods to whip her. However, she will not consent to be beaten by him; she attacks him, overcomes him, and crows in triumph, "You been whipped . . . by me . . . and I'm PURE Pitts." Mr. Fortune is so outraged to see "his own image" call itself Pitts that he strikes her head against a rock, asserting "There's not an ounce of Pitts in me." Having done literally what he intended to do metaphorically—kill the Pitts in the child—he suffers a fatal heart attack.

As he is dying he has a hallucinatory vision: he believes he is running out of the mysterious and threatening woods toward the artificial lake. When he reaches it he realizes that he can go no further, for he has no boat and he cannot swim. Only the trees, the very things he is trying to escape from, seem able to move on beyond the lake: "On both sides of him he saw that the gaunt trees had thickened into mysterious dark files that were marching across the water and away into the distance." He himself is stopped at the shore of the lake, the construction site where he had sat with Mary Fortune and watched the yellow machines of progress eating a hole in what had been a cow pasture. The hopelessness of the situation to which his choices have brought him is suggested in the final line of the story:

> He looked around desperately for someone to help him but the place was deserted except for one huge yellow monster [an earth-moving machine] which sat to the side, as stationary as he was, gorging itself on clay.

In **"The Comforts of Home"** the action that starts the story moving is an act of charity on the part of the protagonist's mother that represents a true movement toward convergence: she has taken an amoral and incorrigible girl who calls herself Star Drake (née Sarah Ham) into the home she shares with her son Thomas. She undertakes this quixotic act of charity because, as she tells Thomas, "I keep thinking it might be you. . . . If it were you, how do you think I'd feel if nobody took you in? What if you were a nimpermaniac [sic] and not a brilliant smart person and you did what you couldn't help and. . . ." To Thomas, a good man devoted to order and moderation, being identified in any way with the "little slut" is insufferable; hearing his mother thus link his condition, even in the realm of remote possibility, with that of Sarah Ham, Thomas feels "a deep unbearable loathing for himself, as if he were slowly turning into the girl."

The motions toward convergence that are embodied in his mother's actions and attitudes are seen by Thomas, who is the point-of-view character, to be excessive, foolhardy, useless, and destructive of the peace of their home. And, though Thomas's outrage and frustration at the loss of his comforts of home are portrayed in a comic light, Thomas himself is presented as a character whose views it is possible to take seriously. His desire to get Sarah Ham out of the house seems eminently understandable and even justifiable, as does his furious refusal of any kind of convergence with her— whether that of ordinary politeness, or the convergence of the sexual encounter that she openly invites, or the spiritual convergence implied in his mother's repeated "it might be you."

Though Thomas's refusal of convergence with the girl grows out of his loathing for the corruption and moral disorder she embodies, his desire to get rid of her leads him to an undesired convergence with the evil spirit of his deceased father. Thomas had not been able to endure his ruthless and dishonest father when he was alive, but as his exasperation grows and his mother persists in her course of "daredevil charity," he remembers that his father would have put an end to any such nonsense before it got started. The voice of his father begins to rasp in his head: "Numbskull, the old man said, put your foot down now. Show her who's boss before she shows you." The evil nature of Thomas's father is suggested in the description of him taking up a squatting position in Thomas's mind; the image recalls that of Satan in Milton's *Paradise Lost,* squatting in the form of a toad at the ear of Eve.

Thomas initially resists the tempter's suggestions. "Several ideas for getting rid of her had entered his head but each of these had been suggestions whose moral tone indicated that they had come from a mind akin to his father's, and Thomas had rejected them." However, after Sarah Ham has been in the house for a week, during which time she has histrionically (and ineffectively) cut her wrists, entered Thomas's study in his absence and taken his gun from his desk drawer, and entered his bedroom unclothed at night, Thomas delivers an ultimatum to his mother: either the girl goes or he goes. When this does not work, he finally capitulates to his father's suggestions that he see the sheriff—a man "as easily dishonest" as his father—and get her arrested for stealing his gun.

Having arranged for the sheriff to come and search her room for the gun, Thomas returns home and finds, to his dismay, that the gun is back in his desk drawer where it belongs. Frantic, he gives in to his father's commands to plant it in her handbag. Caught in the act by the girl and accused by her in the presence of his mother, Thomas (prompted by the voice of his father) delivers a counter-accusation: "The dirty criminal slut stole my gun!" Furious, the girl lunges at him and Thomas, again responding to his father's promptings, fires. But his mother has thrown herself between them to protect the girl, and the shot kills her instead. At that moment the door opens and the sheriff, unnoticed by Thomas and the girl, surveys the scene. The story concludes with his interpretation of what he sees: "the fellow had intended all along to kill his mother and pin it on the girl. . . . As he scrutinized the scene, further insights were flashed to him. Over her body, the killer and the slut were about to collapse into each other's arms."

The convergence with the girl that Thomas was so determined to avoid is thus brought about by his own actions. This convergence is emphasized by the sheriff, who assumes a sexual relationship between Thomas and the girl and sees them, in addition, as partners in crime. In actual fact the sheriff's interpretation of the scene is grossly inaccurate— the furthest thing from Thomas's mind was to kill his mother, whom he loved, and embrace the detested girl; however, the sheriff's view does accurately manifest some important symbolic realities. Thomas's planting of his gun in the girl's purse is, symbolically, a sexual act; the phallic symbolism of the gun and the description of the "skin-like feel" of the purse—which, when opened, emits an odor of the girl—are only too obvious. He has thus symbolically united himself with her; moreover, he has also joined her (as the sheriff thought) in criminality, for Thomas's intent in planting the gun was plainly dishonest. He and the girl have not committed the same crime, but his actions have demonstrated that he is more like the girl than he has been willing to acknowledge. It is not true that he has "No bad inclinations, nothing bad [he was] born with."

In O'Connor's theological view, the "something bad" one is born with, which one cannot help, is original sin. O'Connor evidently felt that the man who is good by secular humanitarian or ethical standards tends to disbelieve in any inherent evil in himself; this she saw to be a major obstacle to a true rising in consciousness, to vision, and to true convergence. True rising, she implies, begins with the recognition of oneself as a non-privileged member of sinful and suffering humanity, and true convergence involves union with what is most despised.

Sheppard of **"The Lame Shall Enter First"** is, like Thomas, a man who disbelieves in the existence of evil in himself. Even more than Thomas, Sheppard disbelieves in the reality of evil qua evil. In the course of counseling inmates at the reformatory, Sheppard comes across Rufus Johnson, a 14-year-old delinquent with a record of malicious mischief, an I.Q. of 140, and a club foot. Sheppard's explanation of Johnson's behavior is psychological: "His mischief was compensation for the foot." Johnson—raised by a fundamentalist grandfather—counters Sheppard's view with his own uncompromising belief that he does what he does because of Satan: "He has me in his power." Because of the boy's superior intellectual capacity, Sheppard is eager to "save" Johnson and to prove to him that he is "not evil" but only "mortally confused."

Sheppard values intelligence, goodness, and the amelioration of social ills. He is deeply disappointed in his own son, ten-year-old Norton, who is mediocre in intellect and uninterested in sharing what he has with poor children or with the disadvantaged Johnson. What Sheppard does not realize is that Norton, who has all the material advantages, feels himself more radically disadvantaged than Johnson. Norton's mother is dead and the boy's grief is inconsolable. He fears he has irrevocably lost her, for Sheppard—contemptuous of stories of heaven and hell, which he feels are "for the mediocre"—has told him that she no longer exists. Sheppard is incapable of grasping what the thought of his mother's nonexistence means to Norton; when he tells Norton about Johnson's disadvantages, he lists the fact that Johnson's mother is in the penitentiary. At this Norton breaks down and howls: "'If she was in the penitentiary,' he began in a kind of racking bellow, 'I could go to seeeeee her.'" Later, when Johnson talks to Norton about heaven and hell,

Sheppard observes with disgust that Norton "would rather she be in hell than nowhere." Sheppard's values are thus shown to be inadequate to meet the needs of his son. Indeed, his values cause him to reject his son and to commit the betrayal of love that is high on O'Connor's list of major sins.

If we look at Sheppard's values in terms of "rising" and "convergence," we see that he values rising very highly indeed; he wants both Johnson and Norton to rise to high levels of intellectual ability and social goodness. Imagistically, Sheppard's interest in rising is expressed in terms of his particular ambition for the boys: he wants them to study the stars through a telescope and rise to the heights of the physical heavens in space travel. This intellectual rising, however, implies no convergence. Similarly, Sheppard's conception of goodness leads to isolation rather than to convergence. He conceives of his goodness as an "armor of kindness and patience" which protects him from Johnson's insults. The image suggests that the effect of his goodness is to make him insensitive to the reality of Johnson's malice, but also—such being the nature of armor—to the reality of Norton's grief and need for love.

Sheppard is convinced that he can save Johnson by the force of his own goodness. Johnson, however, is equally determined to prove to Sheppard that he, Johnson, is evil and that Sheppard cannot save him. Part of Sheppard's program to save Johnson involves getting him a new orthopedic shoe. Though he allows himself to be fitted for the shoe, when it is ready he refuses to accept it. His deformed foot in its ugly, battered shoe is a visible symbol of his spiritual condition, and he will not accept Sheppard's attempt to deny the symbolic significance of the deformity by improving on its physical appearance.

The breakdown of Sheppard's faith in his own goodness and in his ability to be Johnson's savior is brought about through Johnson's deliberate malice. Johnson continues to commit acts of vandalism, though he at first denies them in a malicious effort to get Sheppard to trust him. When Sheppard has been sufficiently taken in, Johnson flaunts his crimes before him. Johnson also befriends poor Norton, apparently with the intention of annoying Sheppard by teaching the boy about heaven and hell and Jesus. Almost certainly, however, in telling the grief-stricken Norton that his mother is in heaven and that he, Norton, would go to heaven if he were to die right now, Johnson is deliberately setting the child up to kill himself.

Johnson is motivated not only by sheer malice but by outrage at what he perceives to be Sheppard's violation of truth. Early in the story, when Norton had attempted to defend his father by saying he was good, Johnson burst out, "I don't care if he's good or not. He ain't *right!*" Later, when Sheppard was reasserting his determination to save him, claiming that the "good will triumph," Johnson retorted, "Not when it ain't true. . . . Not when it ain't right." Truth, for Johnson, is fundamentally religious: that there is a heaven and a hell, that the Bible is true, and that nobody is capable of saving him—when he gets ready to be saved—but Jesus.

Sheppard, however, is convinced that Johnson does not really believe these religious truths: "I flushed that out of your head in the reformatory. I saved you from that, at least." Johnson's final actions in the story grow out of his furious determination to prove to Sheppard that he does, indeed, believe them, and to confront Sheppard with the truth. Johnson commits another act of vandalism, allows himself to be caught, and demands to be taken to Sheppard. In the presence of the policemen who have brought him, Johnson declares that he committed his vandalism to "show up that big tin Jesus! . . . He thinks he's God. . . . The devil has him in his power." He asserts that a natural inclination to evil, not maladjustment, is at the root of his behavior. "I lie and steal because I'm good at it!" he shouts at Sheppard. "My foot don't have a thing to do with it."

Sheppard, pained, defends himself: "I did more for him than I did for my own child. I hoped to save him and I failed, but it was an honorable failure. I have nothing to reproach myself with." Sheppard's defense contains his own condemnation: "I did more for him than I did for my own child." Finally, hearing his words echoing in his ears, he sees the truth of what he is saying: "He had stuffed his own emptiness with good works like a glutton. He had ignored his own child to feed his vision of himself." The agent of this revelation is "the clear-eyed Devil, the sounder of hearts," whom he sees "leering at him from the eyes of Johnson." With this rising in consciousness, Sheppard experiences a true desire for convergence; he feels a "rush of agonizing love" for Norton and hurries to tell him "that he loved him, that he would never fail him again." Norton, however, has sought rising and convergence elsewhere; believing that he has seen his mother in the heavens through the telescope that Sheppard bought to interest the boys in space travel, Norton has hanged himself to get to heaven where she is, and Sheppard finds him dangling from the beam "from which he had launched his flight into space."

Mrs. Turpin, the protagonist of **"Revelation,"** is, like Sheppard, convinced of her own goodness. Mrs. Turpin is a good Christian woman who looks after the poor, works for the church, and thanks Jesus effusively for making her what she is—and not "a nigger or white trash or ugly." Mrs. Turpin's failure of charity, despite her works of charity, is obvious as she sums up the other patients in the doctor's waiting room in which the story opens. Sizing up a "stylish lady" as one of her own kind and striking up a conversation with her, Mrs. Turpin reveals, through her words and thoughts, her interior judgements on the others present. Her

veiled racism and social snobbery, her cheerful complacency, and her unabashed pride in her good disposition are too much for the stylish lady's daughter, a fat, scowling girl who has obviously had to suffer much of the same sort of thing from her mother. The girl responds to Mrs. Turpin's remarks with ugly looks until finally, provoked beyond endurance, she flings a book at Mrs. Turpin's head and lunges at her throat. "Go back to hell where you came from, you old wart hog," the girl whispers to her fiercely.

Hog imagery has already been introduced in the conversation between Mrs. Turpin and the stylish lady. Mrs. Turpin mentioned the hogs she raises in a concrete-floored pig parlor. Responding to an unwelcome interruption by a "whitetrash woman," who declares hogs to be "Nasty stinking things, a-gruntin and a-rootin all over the place," Mrs. Turpin coldly replied that her hogs are washed down every day with a hose and are "cleaner than some children I've seen." ("Cleaner by far than that child right there," [the "whitetrash" woman's child] she added to herself.)

O'Connor uses hogs in this story (and elsewhere) as symbols of unredeemed human nature. As no amount of external cleanliness can fundamentally change hog nature, so no amount of external goodness can fundamentally change human nature, which, in O'Connor's view, is contaminated with evil—whether it be the consciously chosen evil of Johnson or the more subtle evil of pride and self-righteousness displayed by Sheppard and Mrs. Turpin.

Evil seems a strong word to apply to a character like Mrs. Turpin, who, for all her pride and complacency, is surely not a "bad" woman. Yet O'Connor obviously felt that Mrs. Turpin's belief in her own goodness was, if anything, more of an obstacle to the salvation of her soul than an outright commitment to evil. Thomas Merton reflects on this paradox: "Truly the great problem is the salvation of those who, being good, think they have no further need to be saved and imagine their task is to make others 'good' like themselves."

Mrs. Turpin is at first shocked and indignant at the injustice of what has happened to her. Why should she, a hardworking, respectable, church-going woman, be singled out for such a message when there was "trash in the room to whom it might justly have been applied"? At the same time, however, Mrs. Turpin senses that the girl "knew her in some intense and personal way, beyond time and place and condition," and the message, unpleasant as it is, has for her the force of divine revelation.

After pondering the girl's words with increasing wrath and indignation all afternoon, Mrs. Turpin marches down to the pig parlor on her farm and contemplates her hogs. "What do you send me a message like that for?" she demands of God. "How am I a hog and me both? How am I saved and from hell too?" She rails at God with increasing sarcasm until, with a final surge of fury, she roars, "Who do you think you are?" An echo of her own words comes back to her, like an answer, out of the silence.

Who does she think she is? The imagery surrounding this scene suggests that Mrs. Turpin considers herself the equal of God. The sun, that perennial symbol of God in O'Connor's fiction, seems comically obedient to Mrs. Turpin's presumption, and hangs over the tree line in an attitude almost exactly imitative of her own position on the fence of the pig parlor: "The sun was behind the wood, very red, looking over the paling of trees like a farmer inspecting his own hogs." While this image embodies Mrs. Turpin's assumption of the equality between her and God, it also suggests that the true relation between them is that God is the farmer, the world is His farm, and Mrs. Turpin is one of the "hogs"—humanity—at which He is gazing. His gaze—His light, symbolically the infusion of His grace into the world—is transforming; in the light of the setting sun the pigs are suffused with a red glow, and appear to "pant with a secret life." Mrs. Turpin, too, is touched by this transforming light, and life flows into her. "Like a monumental statue coming to life," she bends her head and gazes, "as if through the very heart of mystery, down into the pig parlor at the hogs."

The mystery of humanity, as O'Connor saw it, is that it is rooted in earth, yet bathed in God's light that fills it with secret life, the life of grace that is in no way dependent on worthiness or on the scale of human values Mrs. Turpin cherishes. The irrelevance of social values in the sphere of grace is manifested in the vision that is given to her as she lifts her eyes from the pigs and gazes at the purple streak in the sky left like a trail by the setting sun:

> She saw the streak as a vast swinging bridge extending upward from the earth through a field of living fire. Upon it a vast horde of souls were rumbling toward heaven. There were whole companies of white-trash, clean for the first time in their lives, and bands of black niggers in white robes, and battalions of freaks and lunatics shouting and clapping and leaping like frogs. And bringing up the end of the procession was a tribe of people whom she recognized at once as those who, like herself and Claud [her husband], had always had a little of everything and the God-given wit to use it right. . . . They were marching behind the others with great dignity, accountable as they had always been for good order and common sense and respectable behavior. They alone were on key. Yet she could see by their shocked and altered faces that even their virtues were being burned away.

For her to rise, to follow even at the end of the heaven-bound procession, it is necessary for her virtues to be burned away, for her to see herself as no more worthy of God's grace than the Negroes and white trash and freaks and lunatics she habitually looks down upon. Good works, in O'Connor's view, do not redeem; they only prevent Mrs. Turpin from seeing that she shares in the poverty and limitation and evil proclivities common to all humanity. She is not capable of lifting herself out of this condition by her own efforts; indeed, her efforts to do so only compound evil by making her think herself superior to others and thus reinforcing social inequality, pride, and complacency. "Rising" comes about by grace, and by Mrs. Turpin's response of openness to it. Appropriately enough, the instrument of grace—the ugly girl who hurled a book at Mrs. Turpin's head and declared that lady's kinship with hogs and hell—is named Mary Grace.

In O'Connor's stories, a character's refusal of convergence with others is an externalization of a deeper refusal to accept convergence with Being. A character's desire to remain autonomous and in control of things prevents his surrender to the transcendent—to that which is greater than he, which is uncontrollable, which is, in the words of **"Parker's Back,"** "to be obeyed." Expressed in other stories in naturalistic symbols—the bull, the sun, the woods—in **"Parker's Back,"** transcendent Being is embodied in the face of a Byzantine Christ that is tattooed on the back of the protagonist, O.E. Parker.

A man who is otherwise as "ordinary as a loaf of bread," Parker was stirred with a mysterious longing when, at the age of fourteen, he saw at a fair a man covered from head to foot with tattoos that formed "a single intricate design of brilliant color." This initial response of wonder to what is to Parker a thing of beauty makes him literally a marked man, for ever afterward he has been subject to an unrest that can be assuaged only by the acquisition of a new tattoo. However, the total effect, on him, is "not of one intricate arabesque of colors but of something haphazard and botched."

Parker's frustrated longing for the perfection of aesthetic form grows more acute as the space on the front of his body is used up and the single, intricate effect is not achieved. His dissatisfaction provokes him to actions he does not understand, notably his marriage to Sarah Ruth Cates, the daughter of a Straight Gospel preacher. Sarah Ruth, a plain-looking woman, thinks his tattoos are a "heap of vanity." She spends most of her time telling him "what the judgement seat of God will be like for him if he doesn't change his ways."

Though he is unimpressed with Sarah Ruth's religious convictions, Parker is driven to consider getting a tattoo with a religious subject in order to get Sarah Ruth to look at it. Parker feels strongly that his tattoos are to be looked at. To have a tattoo on his back, where he cannot see it, seems to him sheer foolishness if Sarah Ruth will not look at it either. It is against her religion, however, to contemplate anything in the natural world as a sign or symbol of the transcendent; to do so, she thinks, is idolatrous. To her way of thinking, religion is entirely spiritual, entirely disembodied.

In O'Connor's view, however, the natural world is the medium of divine revelation. Thus when Parker, preoccupied by his need for a new tattoo and unable to think of one "that will bring Sarah Ruth to heel," runs his tractor into a big tree in the middle of a hayfield, the result is not simply a comic catastrophe but an event with supernatural significance. Parker is knocked out of his shoes and the tree bursts into flame. The flaming tree is implicitly for Parker what the burning bush was for Moses: a manifestation of the divine Presence. Struck with holy terror, Parker crawls backward toward his truck and drives straight to the city and to the tattoo parlor. There, trembling, he picks out the head of a Byzantine Christ with "all-demanding eyes" to be tattooed on his back.

The image of Christ on his back has literally the effect of a sacrament; though it is a symbol, it acts on Parker as if it were Christ Himself. Parker seeks out his pool-hall buddies but, unable to take their friendly razzing about his new tattoo, he gets into a fight and finds himself thrown out into the alley. O'Connor compares the pool hall, and the "nerve-shattering" calm that descends on it after Parker's ejection, to the ship "from which Jonah had been cast into the sea." The comparison suggests that Parker's motive in going to the pool hall in the first place was, like Jonah's, an attempt to evade a prophetic mission. Jonah had been called by God to preach to the city of Nineveh. Parker's prophetic mission is not so specific, but he does have a prophetic name—Obadiah Elihue—which he has kept a secret, using only the initials O.E.

Sitting in the alley outside the pool hall, Parker inspects his soul, the depths of his being that he had thought "was not at all important to him but which appeared to be necessary in spite of his opinion." His soul is in the process of being transformed from a "spider web of facts and lies" to "a single intricate arabesque of brilliant color" by the image of Christ that is now forever on his back.

That Parker is becoming a "new man" in Christ is emphasized in the description of his trip home: "It was as if he were himself but a stranger to himself, driving into a new country though everything he saw was familiar to him, even at night." Moreover, his attitude toward Sarah Ruth has changed radically; from wondering, in the opening of the story, why he had married her in the first place and why he did not leave her in the second, he comes to look to her as a source of guidance, and to want to please her. Bewildered at the effect the "all-demanding eyes" of the Christ on his back are having on him, he drives home to Sarah Ruth, con-

fidently expecting that she "would know what he had to do . . . and she would at least be pleased. It seemed to him that, all along, that was what he wanted, to please her."

When he arrives home, Parker finds the door barricaded against him. When he identifies himself as O.E., Sarah Ruth denies she knows any O.E. and demands to know who he is. Just as the sun comes up, shooting a "tree of light" (reminiscent of the earlier tree of flame) over the horizon, Parker answers that he is "Obadiah Elihue." All at once he feels the light (here, as in **"Revelation,"** a symbol of divine grace) pouring through him, "turning his spider-web soul into a perfect arabesque of colors, a garden of trees and birds and beasts." Sarah Ruth, however, is unmoved by the new tattoo that has accomplished the transformation of the designs on his body from "something haphazard and botched" into an aesthetic unity. When Parker tells her that the tattoo is a picture of God, she is outraged. "'Idolatry!' Sarah Ruth screamed. 'Idolatry! . . . I can put up with lies and vanity but I don't want no idolater in this house!'" She picks up a broom and proceeds to beat Parker on the back "until she had nearly knocked him senseless and large welts had formed on the face of the tattooed Christ. Then he staggered up and made for the door."

In this image O'Connor graphically conveys the suffering of Christ incarnate in humanity, and expresses her belief that convergence with Christ means union with Christ's suffering, not escape from suffering into some abstract realm of spiritual bliss. And here also, as in the title story, Flannery O'Connor emphasizes that the rising in consciousness that precedes true convergence is expressed not through an increase in external power or dominance over others but, paradoxically, in a descent into vulnerability, into suffering, into weakness, into man's essential poverty. The story concludes with the image of the prophet, Obadiah Elihue, having been driven out of the house by his harridan wife, "leaning against the tree, crying like a baby."

In the last three stories in this collection, O'Connor began to go beyond the point at which, heretofore, she had characteristically ended her stories: the violent conclusion that implicitly contained a revelation capable of bringing the protagonist to see himself as he really is. **"Revelation,"** the third from the last story, is transitional; the story continues, after Mary Grace's violent attack on Mrs. Turpin, to explore Mrs. Turpin's struggle to respond to the girl's message, but it does not go beyond Mrs. Turpin's tacit acceptance of the vision of herself bringing up the rear of the horde of souls trooping into heaven. What happens to a character after that acceptance is suggested in **"Parker's Back"**; Parker accepts the Christ on his back and his prophetic name, and the unexpected result is that he finds himself beaten and weeping underneath a tree. He has begun, the imagery suggests, to participate in the sufferings of Christ.

In **"Judgement Day,"** the last story in the collection, old Tanner, the protagonist, has begun before the story opens to accept a convergence with the lowly and the suffering, symbolized by his relationship with his Negro friend Coleman. In old Tanner's situation O'Connor suggests that acceptance of convergence inevitably brings one "down" in the world—down into helplessness, into suffering, into the lot of the most disadvantaged members of humanity. At the opening of **"Judgement Day"** old Tanner is already reduced to a state of childlike weakness and dependency. Enfeebled by a stroke, he is living in unhappy exile with his daughter in her New York City apartment. In the course of the action he experiences violent rejection, suffering, and finally death. His death is not a means by which a revelation of something he had vigorously resisted is forced upon him, as is the case in most of the earlier stories in this collection. Rather, it is the means of completing, both literally and symbolically, the journey "home" that he was determined to set out on at the beginning of the story.

"Home" is one of the dominant images in the story. Literally, it is Corinth, Georgia, where old Tanner lived all his life until his "high and mighty" daughter found him living in a shack with his Negro friend Coleman. Scandalized that he had come to "settle in with niggers," she urged him to come and live with her in New York City. Despite the fact that her opinion of his living situation "shamed" him, Tanner might not have gone with her had he not, that same day, discovered that the land on which he and Coleman had built their shack had been bought by a pompous Negro doctor. The doctor, Foley, let him know that if Tanner wanted to stay, he would have to accept a reversal of the traditional Negro-white roles. Unwilling to operate a still for the doctor and be "a nigger's white nigger," Tanner had gone north with his daughter. Once in New York, however, he regretted his choice: "If he had known it was a question of this—sitting here looking out of this window all day in this no-place, or just running a still for a nigger, he would have run the still for the nigger." He was not in New York a week before he had decided to take the bus back to Georgia as soon as his next monthly pension check arrived.

Before Tanner's check arrived, a Negro moved into the apartment next door. Tanner's daughter warned him not to "go over there trying to get friendly with him." In the crowded city "convergence" is a physical reality, but "all stripes of foreigner" living together in a "pigeon-hutch" of an apartment building does not bring spiritual convergence. Tanner's daughter expresses what O'Connor felt to be the urban secular refusal of convergence: "you mind your business and they'll mind theirs. That's the way people were meant to get along in this world."

Tanner, however, lonesome himself and confident that "the nigger would like to talk to someone who understood him,"

waited for his new neighbor in the hallway and tried to make friends with him. To the city-bred Negro, however, Tanner's style of friendliness smacked of white patronage. Enraged at Tanner's repeated approaches, and at Tanner's addressing him as "Preacher" (the Negro is an actor and an atheist), he slammed the old man against the wall. The assault gave Tanner a stroke, and the medical expenses ate up his pension check.

Thus prevented from getting home on his own power, Tanner made his daughter promise to have him shipped home to Georgia when he dies. Relieved, he slept peacefully for a while and dreamed of arriving home in his coffin and surprising his friends, Coleman and Hooten the station agent, by springing up and shouting, "'Judgement Day! Judgement Day! Don't you two fools know it's Judgement Day?'" As this fantasy indicates, Tanner equates "home," with all its particulars (Corinth, Coleman, Hooten), with heaven on the Day of Judgement, when the dead will be raised and the just will live eternally with God. Judgement Day is thus the equivalent of Teilhard's "Omega point," at which all created consciousness will be united with Being itself, with God.

Tanner's daughter, however, had no intention of keeping her promise. When Tanner learned of this—he overheard her telling her husband that she would have the old man buried in New York—he made up his mind to get home himself, "dead or alive." When the story opens, he is waiting for his daughter to go out shopping so that he can slip out of the apartment, hire a cab to take him to the train yards, and get aboard a southbound freight. He has written a note and pinned it in his pocket: "IF FOUND DEAD SHIP EXPRESS COLLECT TO COLEMAN PARRUM, CORINTH, GEORGIA." Barely able to walk, he gets as far as the head of the stairs before his legs fail him and he pitches down the steep staircase. He is found there by the Negro actor and his disdainful wife. Believing that he has reached home and that the coffin containing his body is being unloaded from the train, Tanner murmurs, "Coleman?" The Negro actor interprets this as a contemptuous epithet—"coal man"—and, mocking the old man, he pulls Tanner's hat down his over his face and thrusts his head and arms through the spokes of the bannister.

This violent convergence with a hostile Negro on the physical level brings about, on the spiritual level, a convergence with "otherness"—what is not oneself, and especially what is feared and despised as alien and inferior. Tanner's final convergence with the "negative image of himself" is suggested through the position of his body on the stairs. That position recalls an image that had come to him thirty years before, when he first met Coleman. Then he had been a lone white man bossing a team of unruly Negroes at an isolated sawmill. A man with a reputation for being able to "handle" Negroes, Tanner disarmed the half-drunk and potentially dangerous Coleman by whittling a pair of spectacles out of a piece of bark and giving them to him:

"What you see through those glasses?"

"See a man."

"What kind of a man?"

"See the man make theseyer glasses."

"Is he white or black?"

"He white!" the Negro said as if only at that moment was his vision sufficiently improved to detect it. "Yessuh, he white!" he said.

"Well, you treat him like he was white," Tanner said.

The spectacles enabled Coleman to "see" and accept Tanner in the traditional white man's role; but they also gave Tanner a momentary glimpse of a different vision. When Coleman put them on and looked at him and

grinned, or grimaced, Tanner could not tell which . . . he had an instant's sensation of seeing before him a negative image of himself, as if clownishness and captivity had been their common lot. The vision failed him before he could decipher it.

The subsequent events of Tanner's life brought him increasingly closer to realizing that "common lot." He lost his property and lived with Coleman on terms of at least economic equality in the shack they built together. Then, in New York, he became willing to accept the reversal of traditional roles and work for the Negro doctor. Finally, in the circumstances of his death, he takes on the traditional Negro posture of "clownishness and captivity." The position of his body in death is that of a man confined and offered up to public mockery: his feet dangle over the stairwell "like those of a man in the stocks."

This is apparently an image of total defeat. Tanner has not got where he was going. The atheistic Negro has derided Tanner's belief in Judgement Day as the day of the resurrection of the dead and has asserted that the only judgement day is the day of death: "Ain't no judgement day, old man. Cept this. Maybe this here judgement day for you." Tanner's daughter carries out her intention to have him buried in New York. Yet the concluding paragraph of the story suggests that out of these apparent defeats, Tanner has achieved the ultimate convergence. After his daughter has had him buried, she cannot sleep at night, and she finally has him dug up and shipped to Corinth. That Tanner does, at last, arrive at

his literal home suggests that he also arrives at his ontological home, union with God, imaged in the story as heaven on Judgement Day.

John Ower (essay date Winter 1986)

SOURCE: "The Penny and the Nickel in 'Everything That Rises Must Converge,'" in *Studies in Short Fiction,* Vol. 23, No. 1, Winter, 1986, pp. 107-10.

[*In the following essay, Ower discusses the symbolism of the coin Julian's mother gives to the young boy in "Everything That Rises Must Converge."*]

In O'Connor's story, the violent climactic "convergence" of black and white races is precipitated by Julian's mother offering a coin to a little Negro boy. Her customary gift to black children is a nickel, but she has been able to find only a cent in her pocketbook. That the fateful coin is a penny, and that it is newly minted, are both emphasized by O'Connor through being twice mentioned. The author thereby hints the significance with regard to **"Everything that Rises. . ."** of the Lincoln cent and Jefferson nickel (the two coins current in 1961 when O'Connor's story was written). The designs of these pieces suggest a nexus of meanings relating to the social, racial and religious themes of **"Everything that Rises. . . ."**

The obverse of the Lincoln cent bears the portrait of its namesake, to the left of which is the motto "LIBERTY." The chief feature of the reverse is a representation of the Lincoln Memorial. These three details have an obvious relevance to O'Connor's sympathetic concern with the "rise" of Southern blacks from slavery towards true freedom and socio-economic equality. Thus, the features of the Lincoln cent just mentioned suggest (1) the freeing of Negroes by the "Great Emancipator" and (2), by extension, the activity of the Federal Government in O'Connor's own day to ensure the rights of Southern blacks. Regarding the second, the Supreme Court decision of 1954 and its aftereffects (including the sit-ins of 1960) constitute the immediate historical background for the action of **"Everything that Rises. . . ."** The story suggests how the crumbling of the "Jim Crow" system was making possible a new "liberty" for Negroes in the South. Blacks have gained both a greater physical freedom in their world and increased opportunities for socio-economic mobility. This twofold access of "liberty" is exemplified by the well-dressed Negro man with the briefcase who sits with the whites at the front of the bus. The new possibilities for betterment opening to blacks are intimated not only by the abovementioned details of the Lincoln cent but also by its "bright," shiny freshness.

Julian's mother is unaware of the ways her "new penny" suggests the historical "rise" of Southern blacks, and would be dismayed if she recognized such implications. She represents the reactionary element among white Southerners who want to reverse history with respect to race relations. Julian's mother would like to return to the days of segregation ("They should rise, yes, but on their own side of the fence.") and seemingly even to the era of slavery ("[Blacks] were better off when they were [slaves].""). The retrograde desire of Julian's mother to reduce Negroes to their antebellum servitude stands in ironic contrast to her penny as recalling Lincoln's emancipation of blacks. Furthermore, the date on the obverse of the "new" (presumably 1961) cent is exactly a century after the start of the Civil War, and almost a hundred years after the Emancipation Proclamation (1863). The 1961 date thus underlines just how antiquated are the racial views of Julian's mother.

As opposed to the Lincoln cent, the Jefferson nickel in part suggests the conservative and patrician outlook of Julian's mother, the quasi-mythical old South in which she psychologically dwells. In particular, Jefferson's life strikingly parallels that of the aristocratic grandfather whom Julian's mother so reveres. Both men were slaveholding plantation owners, and both were governors of their home states. It is by virtue of such distinguished ancestry that Julian's mother identifies with the antebellum Southern aristocracy, to whom she romantically attributes a lofty preeminence balanced by "graciousness." That combination of qualities is suggested by the palladian architecture of Jefferson's "stately home" Monticello, depicted on the reverse of the nickel. Monticello further ties in with the Godhigh country mansion as a symbol of the aristocratic heritage and accompanying social pretensions of Julian's mother. Just as the somewhat Olympian Monticello suggests the superior position of the white aristocracy in a class and racially stratified order, so does the plan of the Godhigh house (the owners being elevated above the black cooks who work on the ground floor). It is from such an apparently secure social eminence that Julian's mother looks down on Negroes with a blend of snobbish condescension, "graciousness" and paternalistic benevolence. That set of attitudes is expressed by Julian's mother in bestowing small change upon black children. The Jefferson nickel is especially appropriate as the usual coin for such largesse because it implies the identification with the old Southern aristocracy that largely determines the racial views of Julian's mother.

However, the aforementioned connotations of the Jefferson nickel are in contrast with meanings implied by the motto "LIBERTY" on the obverse of the coin. The slogan brings to mind Jefferson's chief fame as a champion of democratic ideals. In relation to **"Everything that Rises. . . ,"** Jefferson's advocacy of "liberty" and equality is (1) basically antithetical to the cherished social assumptions and racial views of Julian's mother and (2) essentially in keeping with

the movement towards freedom and equality for blacks implied by the Lincoln cent. Concerning the second point, Jefferson although a slaveholder himself found the South's "peculiar institution" morally repugnant. He accordingly devoted considerable effort to advocating the gradual emancipation of Negroes, and he likewise freed some of his own blacks at his death. Jefferson's enlightened attitudes towards slavery, which anticipate Lincoln's Emancipation Proclamation, are diametrically opposed to those of Julian's mother. Far from seeing slavery as morally repellant, she believes that blacks were "better off" in servitude, and is proud that an ancestor owned two hundred Negroes. Such sentiments are undercut through the Jefferson nickel by implicit contrast with the views of one of America's foremost political and social thinkers.

Another detail of both the Lincoln cent and Jefferson nickel which is relevant to **"Everything that Rises . . ."** is the motto "E PLURIBUS UNIM" ("Out of many, one"). While the slogan is intended to refer to the U.S. as a nation federated out of various states, it also suggests the American ideal of a unified society tolerantly encompassing racial and ethnic diversity. Both possible meanings of "E PLURIBUS UNIM" are germane to the racial situation that existed in the South in 1961. Since the main impetus towards desegregation came from the U.S. Federal Government, the resistance of Southern white reactionaries threatened to create strife not just between the races, but also between Dixie and the rest of the nation. The first of these potential conflicts is suggested in **"Everything that Rises. . ."** when the black woman assaults Julian's mother. The second is implied by the Lincoln cent as recalling the Civil War. In opposition to both possible evils, the motto "E PLURIBUS UNIM" indicates how the South should accept the will of the Federal authorities and help create a society where the races can co-exist in harmony.

The motto "E PLURIBUS UNIM" also ties in with the theology of Teilhard de Chardin that influenced O'Connor when writing **"Everything that Rises. . . ."** Teilhard maintains in *The Phenomenon of Man* that an eschatological evolution is moving the human race from "diversity to ultimate unity." Such a "convergence" will be completed at "Omega point" with the oneness of all men in Christ. In order for convergence to occur, individuals must surrender their "personal or racial egotism" and join with one another in love. Teilhard's convergence of mankind from "diversity to ultimate unity" is of course brought to mind by the motto "E PLURIBUS UNIM." The slogan would thus for O'Connor relate both to God's plan for unifying all men and to U.S. history, suggesting the two are connected. More specifically, O'Connor evidently saw the progress of race relations in the South since the Civil War as part of the convergence of all humanity towards Omega point. The segregationist views of Julian's mother and her like accordingly constitute a sinful resistance to God's redemptive plan for mankind. That opposition is caused in the case of Julian's mother by a "personal . . . [and] racial egotism" arising from her pride of ancestry and class status. Such "egotism" is suggested by the name Godhigh borne by Julian's grandmother. The name stands in neat ironic antithesis to the motto "IN GOD WE TRUST" on the Lincoln cent and Jefferson nickel, a slogan which implies a humble self-surrender to the divine plan moving man towards convergence.

In **"Everything that Rises. . . ,"** the penny and the nickel thus relate the racial situation in the South of 1961 to a larger cultural, historical and spiritual context. On the one hand, the Lincoln cent suggests a century of political, social and economic progress elevating blacks towards a final Teilhardian convergence with whites. On the other hand, the Jefferson nickel most obviously intimates a conservative, aristocratic mentality contributing to Southern white resistance to integration. The ultimate defeat of such reaction is implied when Julian's mother cannot find a nickel to give the little black boy. O'Connor is suggesting that the old South called to mind by the five cent piece is gone forever. The "new penny" Julian's mother does discover indicates the time has come for Southern whites to accept social change, abandon their obsolete racial views, and relate to Negroes in a radically different way. Instead, Julian's mother stubbornly clings to a quasi-mythical past and refuses to accept the realities of the present. This wrongheaded strategy is seen when she tries to use the coin suggesting a new order in a way appropriate to the old. The violent rejection of the "condescending" penny by the black woman is for Julian's mother an appropriate, if ultimately tragic, initiation into verities she so willfully denies.

Jeffrey J. Folks (essay date Spring 1986)

SOURCE: "The Mechanical in *Everything That Rises Must Converge*," in *The Southern Literary Journal*, Vol. XVIII, No. 2, Spring, 1986, pp. 14-26.

[*In the following essay, Folks discusses O'Connor's relationship to the Southern literary tradition and to the industrialization of the South as expressed in the stories in* Everything That Rises Must Converge.]

To many critics, the views of Flannery O'Connor on science and technology have seemed self-evident. The modern faith in science was the extension of a Post-Reformation reliance on Nominalism, a philosophical position that O'Connor never ceased to question. More damaging than pure science, the popular belief in technology as a panacea had led the twentieth century away from religious faith and toward belief in a future paradise to be brought about by technology.

As Jane C. Keller insisted, O'Connor's empiricists had erected barriers between themselves and the recognition of the universe as the work of God. In the figure of Sheppard, Thomas Carlson saw "the supreme exponent of Pelegianism," a character who "tries to render the material thing spiritual through technology, a kind of latter-day alchemy."

Certainly O'Connor's writing has provided ample evidence that the concept of mechanization is to be viewed in opposition to the religious message of her works. In a letter of March 17, 1956, to Shirley Abbott, O'Connor expressed her rejection of the strictly empirical approach: "It is popular to believe that in order to see clearly one must believe nothing. This may work well enough if you are observing cells under a microscope. It will not work if you are writing fiction. For the fiction writer, to believe nothing is to see nothing." Speaking of the sweeping impact of mechanization on the South and its effect on the southern writer, O'Connor stated in "The Regional Writer": "The present state of the South is one wherein nothing can be taken for granted, one in which our identity is obscured and in doubt." As a result of this sort of comment, one might well conclude that O'Connor's orthodox Catholicism, attested by her own statements and the great majority of her critics, has set her in opposition to the modern forces of science and technology. According to this interpretation, modernization, as represented by a host of characters from Sheppard to Rayber to Mrs. McIntyre, may be read as the clear villain in each of her works. The representation of the machine carries with it an implied negative cast, and the extent to which characters such as Mr. Head or Parker are depicted as "mechanical" indicates the working out of the destructive effects of a nominalist philosophy.

> **Certainly O'Connor's writing has provided ample evidence that the concept of mechanization is to be viewed in opposition to the religious message of her works.**
> **—*Jeffrey J. Folks***

In view of the frequency with which this reading is repeated, it is striking to find that O'Connor had an extensive interest in natural and social science. While she implied at one point that science has led to the decline of Biblical knowledge and Bible reading, she admired Teilhard de Chardin as a scientist and a Christian, and in a review of his work, she spoke scathingly of "a caricature of Christianity . . . which sees human perfection as consisting in escape from the world and from nature." As O'Connor's book reviews indicate, O'Connor nurtured an open-minded interest in psychology; she praised *Cross Currents* for printing "the best that can be found on religious subjects as they impinge on the modern world, or on modern discoveries as they impinge on the Judeo-Christian tradition."

One can trace the tension in O'Connor's writing between the traditionalist eager to decry the abuses of modernization, as when she describes the mass media as a "diet of fantasy," and the sophisticated modern, aware of the latest advances in psychiatry and philosophy. One suspects that this internal struggle between traditionalist and modern underlies her comment singling out a quotation from Baron von Hügel: "'how thin and abstract, or how strained and unattentive, the religion of most women becomes, owing to their elimination of religious materials and divinely intended tensions!'" Though certain of her readers have sought to disregard the battling of "divinely intended tensions" in her fiction, her fictional treatment of the changing South benefited enormously from her appreciation of the need to preserve these tensions in her stories. The outright dismissal of mechanization would have resulted, as she recognized, in a very thin and "inattentive" body of fiction; more important to O'Connor, it would have mitigated against a clear-sighted application of religious truths to the modern world. O'Connor came to recognize that the predictable revulsion of the southern traditionalist to the "evil" of science was a failure of vision, a narrow-sighted disregard for the world of sense experience. Her marginal lining of a passage in George Tavard's *Transience and Permanence: The Nature of Theology According to St. Bonaventure* highlighted the statement "that sense forms the first degree of the way to God and has thus a momentous religious value." The emphasis of the concrete image as the starting point of vision is indeed fundamental in O'Connor's aesthetics, but the assumption that she arrived at this aesthetic position out of a deductive process of reading medieval exegesis or theology seems entirely inconsistent with what we know about the emergence of her narrative art. Rather, her reading in Catholic and non-Catholic theology, philosophy, and social science must have confirmed ideas on aesthetic practice that had already been formed long before any serious theological study occurred. Whether her recognition of the value of concrete writing was the result of the influence of the New Criticism, a movement that deeply marked her work, or was the working out of her own psychological needs during her narrative apprenticeship is a question that will probably be impossible to answer conclusively. That she was influenced by the ideas of Allen Tate and particularly by the advice of Caroline Gordon, that she had read a number of New Critical texts, and that she was trained in a school of writing which was New Critical in emphasis can be demonstrated.

More pertinent to the issue of this study is the result of O'Connor's remarkable shaping of an aesthetic theory that demanded complete fidelity to the naturalistic facts of the objective world while it sought to express supranaturalistic insights. O'Connor had been trained from the inception of her writing career in an aesthetic theory that excluded the rhetoric of transcendence, an aesthetic that Faulkner only partially practiced and that Tate worked toward throughout his career only to abandon at the end; but in O'Connor's case the realistic bias in her aesthetic conflicted sharply with her intention to write a form of moral fable. From one perspective, we can see that *Wise Blood* is the perfect example of the Jamesian novel, written with strict control of the point of view and a density of specification that fell clearly within the New Critical understanding of Jamesian theory as interpreted by Percy Lubbock, and later by Brooks and Warren, Booth, Schorer, and others. Nonetheless, in other respects O'Connor's first novel reveals intentions that fall outside the tradition of James, for while the technique of O'Connor's writing, the careful limitation to the point of view of individualized characters and the accretion of specific details, are convincingly Jamesian, the larger shaping of her fictions is wildly subversive of the middle-class assumptions about motivation and behavior that are equally a part of the aesthetic of New Criticism and its understanding of literature. Without intending to downplay O'Connor's *ultimate* compassion for the Mrs. Mays of her fiction, one can see that the "secure" untroubled matrons and bachelors whose "faith" is grounded more than anything on illusive commonplaces of bourgeois language are the targets of her often virulent satire. Her character by and large is not the fully rounded "intelligence" whose consciousness is gradually revealed but the representative figure closer to caricature. The Jamesian technique, predicated on the aesthetic assumption of complexity, only serves to exacerbate the sense of a debased idiom.

Furthermore, in an amazing strategy of aesthetic indirection, O'Connor has created fiction which ultimately confirms the sexless and often friendless middle-aged heroines and heroes by insisting that their limitation is the basis of a spiritual search, a pattern that neatly parallels the dialectic of O'Connor's aesthetic: with the legacy of a Jamesian aesthetic of self-effacement and limitation, O'Connor opens her fiction to the corrosive effects of satire and ambiguity, only to end with a seemingly more secure confirmation of her aesthetic origins. I would say "seemingly," because to many of her readers and to O'Connor herself, the interpretation of her fiction is clouded by psychological forces that pull in the opposite direction of her orthodox intention.

The issue of mechanization is crucial to this process of aesthetic reevaluation and formulation. Growing up in the postwar South at the point of its greatest industrial transformation and social change, O'Connor observed a radically different land from that of earlier southern writers. When Faulkner wrote of the machine, he still had the agrarian ways very much in mind if not as a viable future, at least as an experienced past. Almost all of his characters could remember with some nostalgia the pre-industrial South in which the automobile was a rarity. Even Allen Tate, who outlived O'Connor by fifteen years, grew up in a southern cultural milieu which was centered mythically if not actually in the agrarian past. For O'Connor, perhaps because she was a woman and because of her illness, the modernization of her region was a more compelling, inescapable reality. The transformation of the physical landscape of the South and the concurrent transfiguration of human manners and values became O'Connor's primary subject, and the enormous pressures of dealing with this material led to shifts in the aesthetic which O'Connor inherited from her predecessors. With O'Connor the southern aesthetic for the first time fully accepted mechanization as the permanent and inescapable destiny of the region. Whatever theological fable O'Connor felt compelled to satisfy on the symbolic level of her stories, the concrete reality out of which she writes is the fact of sweeping social change with all the dislocation, destruction, and excitement it brings about. O'Connor is writing a fiction of "outrage," as Ihab Hassan recognizes, in which there is "a radical threat to man's nature." In this Post-Modernist fiction, the sense of outrage arises not out of time, as it does in the writing of Modernists, but from space, so that the southern landscape becomes a metaphor for violence.

Although the outrage of which Hassan writes is present in all O'Connor's books, the stories that comprise *Everything That Rises Must Converge,* written toward the end of her life, contain the greatest sense of a mechanical world. As several critics have noted, these stories center on the conflict between parents and children, and this conflict, as Claire Katz states, resembles the larger global struggle of technological society "to assert the magnitude of the individual against the engulfing enormity of a technological society which fragments social roles, shatters community, and splits off those qualities of warmth, intimacy and mutual dependence which nourish a sense of identity." According to Katz, "the environment becomes a projection of sadistic impulses and fears," yet there is no sense of any attempt or even wish to flee from the technological landscape. Instead, its sadistic power to corrode human feeling and to unveil illusions about the meaningfulness of human life is willingly embraced by the characters and by the author. The extent to which O'Connor relished the technological landscape is implied in her description of the New South as "a society that is rich in contradiction, rich in contrast, and particularly rich in its speech."

One might argue, as Katz has, that the nourishment that O'Connor received from the barren landscape of the New South is the result of a Freudian necessity to repress and violate the Ego: "Her peculiar insistence on absolute powerlessness as a condition of salvation so that any assertion of autonomy elicits violence with a vengeance ... suggest[s] that at the center of her work is a psychological demand which overshadows her religious intent." Despite the accuracy of much of what Katz has to say, one can recognize the need for "absolute powerlessness," I think, without attributing it to a Freudian conflict of unspecified origin. A more convincing argument may be made for the *aesthetic* necessity of experiencing barrenness and powerlessness. The timing of O'Connor's arrival as a fiction writer required her participation in a southern literary tradition which had become dominated by New Criticism with its bias toward a Jamesian theory of narrative. At the same time, her coming to adulthood coincided with the period of greatest technological change in the South, so that the *only* authentic subject for her art was modernization. It was not necessarily a projection of O'Connor's psychological need to experience violation.

The New South, in which O'Connor was among the first generation to grow up, was much changed from the South of the young William Faulkner. The southern phenomenon of industrialization was also different from that of the North, in which the industrial and urban experience was long familiar. Certainly one would have to return to the writing of Emerson or Melville to find recorded the fresh sense of outrage with which the southerners of O'Connor's generation write of the machine, an outrage that helps to explain why the machine is so often associated with the startling epiphanies at the end of her stories. Indeed, the "sadistic" landscape is the source of the "richest" humor, a paradoxical comedy that arises from our relief at admitting what we already know: that human beings are often little more "human" than machines. In her treatment of the New South, the Faulknerian portrayal of the destruction of the wilderness or the ghastly rise of the Snopeses in the social order is inconceivable because the distortions of landscape and social order brought about by mechanization are intrinsic to O'Connor's world: the mechanical is so closely connected with the human condition as to make consciousness for any length of time unbearable *without* the recognition that we have been reduced to insensibility and repetition.

More fully than in either of her previous books, O'Connor presents an unremittingly mechanical world in *Everything That Rises Must Converge.* The shift toward the use of males as central intelligences may be connected with the intention to present the milieu of machinery and technological knowledge, although the farming operations of Mrs. May and Mrs. Turpin reflect a fully developed appreciation of the "benefits" of technology. If a maturing of O'Connor's aesthetic has taken place in this collection, as I believe it has, it is toward an appreciation of the richness of the "barrenness" of technology. O'Connor's satire of mechanization is no longer as overtly funny as it had been in *A Good Man Is Hard to Find* because O'Connor has meditated the distinction, raised by philosophers such as Jacques Maritain, between "Making" or productive action unrelated to the *use* of its product, and the modern sense of "making" as industrial production. While Mrs. Turpin's pride in the cleanliness of her swine is certainly grotesque, her understanding of the farming operation is not entirely overwhelmed by the technological emphasis on *ends*. Her appreciation of a certain aesthetic of hog-farming, however comic it is made to seem by O'Connor's narrator, lies somewhere between the Scholasticist notion of use-less and the Modern use-ful forms of Action. The best stories in this collection—**"Greenleaf,"** **"Parker's Back,"** and **"A View of the Woods"** among them—are equally unresolved: they lead us neither to embrace nor reject industrialization but to marvel at the ambiguities of the human condition in its fundamental mechanicalness. Carlson's reading of **"Parker's Back"**—that "Parker intuitively grasps and rationally rejects . . . the union of spirit and matter, for the natural has no lasting meaning except to the degree that it is informed by the supernatural"—does not recognize that Parker's "search" is carried out *through* the mechanical world of the tattoo parlor and the pool hall. Certainly, the tattoo parlor has functioned aesthetically as more than "the false temple": it is the landscape that is as necessary to Parker's understanding of himself as was Dante's mountain called Purgatory. Similarly, Mr. Fortune is more than "the modern fortune hunter, unable to accept nature for what she is rather than for what he can get out of her." By accepting the Post-Modernist landscape as her necessary canvas, O'Connor has recognized that to some extent the attitude of mechanized culture toward nature will always be "what he can get out of her" and this recognition has indelibly marked her aesthetic.

Even Sheppard, perhaps the most "hopeless" of O'Connor's protagonists, reflects the maturity of the Post-Modernist aesthetic. Though we are tempted to label him as one of O'Connor's "intellectuals," a moral ingénue who has fled the complexity of human life for a self-assured life of rationalization, Sheppard arrives at the most tragic sort of knowledge only *because* he has been immersed in the technological culture. His occupational specialization in testing, his belief that an IQ score measures the worth of a person, his faith that a special shoe, the product of medical technology, will bolster the image of a juvenile delinquent who sees the world as grotesquely evil are examples of technological society's most fervid expressions of compassion. Sheppard's act of making a telescope available to Rufus Johnson is an attempt to free the boy's perception from cultural limitation.

The physical world is inherently "mechanical" to O'Connor, and Sheppard is beginning at the proper point in the journey to self-understanding. Restricted in his own physical senses, inhibited by his hypersensitivity to touch and smell, Sheppard lives with a child who moves like a "mechanical toy" and has taken on a delinquent rebel whose reflexive criminal acts assume no sense of freedom, an adolescent whose insults Sheppard describes accurately as "part of the boy's defensive mechanism." Rufus Johnson is almost a

parody of the modern, a grotesque double of Sheppard himself, for he cynically advances the traditionalist religious rhetoric of his father only to further his own destructive whimsy. The point is that Rufus is the distortion of modernity, while Sheppard is the true modern, sincere in his intentions if uncertain of his direction. A rural transplant to the city who is cynical of "progress" but unable to live within the limitations of a pre-modern culture which his father's Fundamentalism evokes, Rufus lives with a despair which is expressed in his comment to Norton that "'if you live long enough, you'll go to hell.'"

The major action of the story is Sheppard's gradual awakening to the mechanism of the world in which he lives, and the key symbol for this mechanism is the telescope. Unlike Rufus, who sees the telescope as a possession, an object of selfishness, and unlike Norton, who naively assumes that the instrument is the means to sight his lost mother, Sheppard feels that the telescope is a means of instruction. O'onnor's depiction of Sheppard as "instructor" is not predominately ironic, for he truly desires to teach Rufus and Norton about the future society in which they will live, including the possibility of space travel, and his purchase of the machine is intended to lead to a reformation of Rufus's character. O'Connor's hints that the telescope will lead to self-instruction do not diminish Sheppard's stature as a seeker of knowledge.

His search for knowledge intensifies during his visits to the brace shop, of which the description, like the symbolic interiors of Hawthorne's fiction, grimly symbolizes the human condition of suffering. Forced by the store clerk's complicitory wink to become an accomplice in fitting the shoe to Rufus's foot, Sheppard is struck by the accidental quality of human suffering, and the extent to which the natural failing of the human body is intensified by the mechanical lack of feeling with which it is treated. "'In this shoe,'" the clerk comments, "'he won't know he don't have a normal foot.'" Soon afterwards, Sheppard begins to see himself more accurately in the "distorting mirrors" of Rufus's eyes. Sheppard's own voice becomes increasingly mechanical and his efforts to save Rufus are now "involuntary," indications of a greater understanding of just how difficult the sort of freedom he seeks may be. What Sheppard understands at the conclusion of the story is the difficulty of maintaining his idealism, the moral sincerity that makes him a "shepherd," at the same time that he participates fully in a modern technological culture, working with its necessarily limited possibilities for human freedom and creative action. He has not abandoned his quest to "reach for the stars," even on the night when he finds his only son hanging from the telescope which symbolizes his belief in self-development. Instead, Sheppard has only arrived at the stage where his self-instruction has led to a merging of his positivist assumptions with a broader understanding of the future direction of human life. He has not worked "through" his faith in science but found that it coincides with a knowledge that transcends questions of immediate means. Sheppard's new understanding will never free him from the mechanical element in life, but it will lead to an appreciative humor in which the mechanical nature of life is the object of comic pleasure.

The vision of progress in **"A View of the Woods"** again surveys the region's transition toward the industrial New South. Once again, the effort to portray the effects of this transformation mark O'Connor's aesthetic strategies more importantly than anything else in the story. By no means a "satire" of the New South or an attempt to suggest a return to the simpler ways of the agrarian life, the story succeeds aesthetically because it does not "promote" alternatives. It oes, however, require the reader to move emotionally into the mechanical heart of the technological society and to replicate the spatial "barrenness" which the modern human condition has imposed.

> **The rural southerner in O'Connor's tales is usually hypocritically attracted to the machine culture that he or she claims to despise.**
> —*Jeffrey J. Folks*

Repetition, the most important feature of technological life, is a motif throughout the story from its early description of the digging machine which would "gorge itself on clay, then, with the sound of a deep sustained nausea and a slow mechanical revulsion, turn and spit it up" to the exact mirroring of the grandfather's face in Mary Fortune's. The persistent but ultimately unsuccessful effort of Mr. Fortune to comprehend modernity is the central action, for like many of O'Connor's works, the story traces the arrival of the southern countryman at the entrance to modern culture. Fascinated by the machine and by the notion of "progress" which it represents—more awed of course than the sophisticated city dweller would be by these mechanical wonders—Mr. Fortune fails the other human beings around him, however, not because he has abandoned agrarianism for modernity, but because he has not understood modernity well enough. In an important sense, his failure is that he has not come far enough into the technological society. Like the protagonist of **"Parker's Back"** and other stories of rural immigrants to the city, Mr. Fortune clings inordinately to agrarian concepts of human free will and to sentimentalized ideas of human worth—illusions that have increasingly little application in an urban industrial South. Thinking that progress is his "ally" against a stubbornly independent son-in-law, Mr. Fortune plays into the hands of an enemy which he does not understand.

The sense of Mr. Fortune's misunderstanding of progress is paralleled by the larger community's clouding of the whole notion of urbanization. The fishing camp which is the basis for the new "town" of Fortune, Georgia, is the product of the urban misprision that the pastoral world provides a retreat from an urban workplace which is unliveable but inevitable. The comforts which city dwellers hope to find in the country are based on the mythic illusion that the country offers a simpler life than the city and that the pastoral landscape is the healing retreat for those who have suffered the woes of city life, a notion that O'Connor always dismissed with brisk irony.

Like Sarah Ruth, the fundamentalist wife whose narrow demands of morality seem irresistibly attractive to Parker, the rural southerner in O'Connor's tales is usually hypocritically attracted to the machine culture that he or she claims to despise: Sarah Ruth, who first notices Parker standing beside his broken-down vehicle on the roadside, later insists on a civil wedding ceremony in the Country Ordinary's office. Her insistence on the ugliness of the human body is an expression of her alienation from any satisfactory human identity beyond the mechanical idiom of the fundamentalist, and her final violent rejection of the "idolatrous" Byzantine Christ tattooed on Parker's back indicates a severance of religious rootedness in the past, not the comfortable religious traditionalism that it seems.

Mr. Fortune is among the most significant of O'Connor's advocates of progress. Because he is essentially a countryman without real experience of industrialization, Mr. Fortune is all too susceptible to the allure of the machine, so much so that he wishes to merge with it: sitting in his car with Mary's feet on his shoulders, he seemed "as if he were no more than a part of the automobile." Despite this merging, he understands industrialization in a very imperfect way, for he sees it through the distorting lens of the myth of progress. Much as the railroad appeared to the nineteenth-century American, the bulldozer seems to Mr. Fortune the awe-inspiring savior. Mr. Fortune is one of those "afflicted with the doctrine of the perfectibility of human nature by its own efforts" that O'Connor describes in **"The Teaching of Literature."** As such, he is unusually disturbed by the "natural" fallenness of his son-in-law, whose beatings are inflicted without apparent cause on his favorite granddaughter.

The crucial scene in the story is the beating which Mr. Fortune himself attempts to inflict on Mary. His granddaughter's violent resistance implies that the beating which he inflicts is of a different order than that administered by her father. In fact, Mr. Fortune beats the girl to extract an admission that she is a replication of his attitudes and behavior—that she is the exact product of his training. Most significantly, he wishes Mary to subscribe to his faith in the myth of progress by denying that her father has the right to beat her.

Mary does not recognize her father's violence as "beating" because she understands that the human condition is inherently flawed, or in O'Connor's words that "a sense of loss is natural to us." Coming of a later generation which is quite at home with mechanization and has seen its mark on the landscape with open eyes, Mary Fortune is willing to humor her grandfather's belief in progress up to the point when he decides to spoil the view of the woods by selling her father's cow pasture to erect a filling station. Although she can hardly have any sentimentalized notions of the nature of rural life, Mary insists on preserving the "view," the vision of a transcendent value beyond the reach of a strictly mechanistic philosophy. Even after the tragedy of accidentally killing his granddaughter, Mr. Fortune is still unable to grasp Mary's understanding of mechanism. The conclusion of the story, with the rows of trees marching away across the lake, implies that the need for a transcendent view evades Mr. Fortune even at the end of his life.

Mr. Fortune is consequently in a much worse condition than many of O'Connor's protagonists because there is no recognition on his part of the myth of progress as a myth. Though it is in fact no "monster," the bulldozer appears as such to Mr. Fortune at the end because he failed to humanize the machine by accepting it for what it is. He is still responding to the myth of the machine as savior, so the mechanical beating that he receives from his granddaughter ("five claws in the flesh of his upper arm where she was hanging from while her feet mechanically battered his knees and her free fist pounded him again and again in the chest," is the appropriate mirroring of his own distorting vision. To this limited extent he has managed to inscribe his self on another, the granddaughter who is his favorite only because she appears to acquiesce to his ideas.

Mr. Fortune becomes a truly grotesque figure not because he is the proponent of progress, but because he knows so little about the modern industrial culture. Understanding none of the larger psychic and emotional implications of technological society, he has adopted the machine as a kind of toy, and his taking Mary to watch the bulldozer dig up the earth reminds one of a childish sort of play. The extraordinary sadness of the story derives from the fact that Mr. Fortune is so much the product of an outdated generation that once exuberantly hailed the machine as the sign of a utopian age. In the modern South, Mr. Fortune is bound to be a lonely exponent of this enthusiasm.

In **"A View of the Woods,"** O'Connor's purpose is not to satirize the industrialization of the South but to explore the necessity of the mechanical element in human society. O'Connor understands that flight from mechanism is more damaging than the machine itself, which has no power to harm those who understand it. More important, the mechanical plays a key role in O'Connor's comic aesthetic. The machine is not just a neutral force to be controlled by humane purposes—it is the best representative symbol for the repetitive, mechanical element in which human beings live most of the time. Typically, human beings resemble machines in O'Connor's fiction, because as she views everyday life, the "normal" condition is one of insensitivity and automatism. However, if "mechanical" describes the normal condition of human society, it is also the basic trope in O'Connor's fictional aesthetic. To be "mechanical" is to be in a condition which is capable of warmth, humor, and compassion; it is also to be in a perpetual condition of need, just as Parker ("heavy and earnest, as ordinary as a loaf of bread") standing before the tattooed man at the fair feels a "peculiar unease" about "the fact that he existed." Unlike the Modernist generation of writers who viewed the machine by and large as a monstrous intrusion into the normal human society in which meaningful action was possible, O'Connor has depicted the mechanical level of reality as the primary and normative subject for her art. The artistic challenge that O'Connor set for herself was to portray the response of southerners to modernization without allowing herself to regress to thinking in terms of the agrarian myth. O'Connor was in no sense a traditionalist whose work calls for a return to a simpler, agrarian community. Her art is more severely realistic in its treatment of the psychological reactions of southerners to change than that of her predecessors, for her recognition of mechanization as the inevitable, permanent condition of human society permits no recourse to escape through a mythic history of pastoral. Instead, O'Connor's realism is the aesthetic foundation for a comic art in which the concrete details of mechanization are the source of her greatest humor.

Alice Hall Petry (essay date Spring 1987)

SOURCE: "Julian and O'Connor's 'Everything That Rises Must Converge,'" in *Studies in American Fiction,* Vol. 15, No. 1, Spring, 1987, pp. 101-08.

[*In the following essay, Hall Petry compares Julian from O'Connor's "Everything That Rises Must Converge" to the Roman Emperor Julian the Apostate and discusses their rejection of Christianity.*]

In a brief note published in 1978, Mary Frances Hopkins argues that critics of Flannery O'Connor's **"Everything That Rises Must Converge"** should desist from imposing the name "Mrs. Chestny" on Julian's mother. "No author names characters more deftly than does O'Connor, with all the deadliness of a Thackeray or Waugh but with none of the weaknesses inherent in their lack of subtlety," so the omission of a name for the mother is not an oversight but rather a statement in itself. As much as there is a studied purpose behind O'Connor's decision to give her character the generic label of "Julian's mother," so too there is a rationale underlying the name of the son: Julian. Marion Montgomery sees it as evocative of St. Julian the Hospitaller, while a more suggestive explanation is offered by Josephine Hendin. She perceives a connection between the fictional Julian and the emperor Julian the Apostate (AD 331 or 332 to AD 363), remembered to this day for his vigorous campaign to rid the Roman Empire of its official religion, Christianity, and to reinstate the paganism of the ancient Greeks. Writes Hendin, "Julian's relation to his mother and the past she represents is implied in his name. He is an apostate Julian raised to be a gentleman. . . . Although raised as a Christian, . . . Julian still yearns after the old gods, or, more specifically, the old Godhighs." Hendin takes the matter no further, unfortunately, for the connections between the Julian of O'Connor's story and Flavius Claudius Julianus are too numerous to be coincidental. More to the point, these connections help to guide the reader's responses to this most analyzed and enigmatic story.

In terms of their personal situations and temperaments, the fictional and the historical Julian have much in common. Each was born to the purple, albeit this proved to be a mixed blessing for both. The Julian of O'Connor's story is perpetually reminded by his mother of his aristocratic background: "'Your great-grandfather was a former governor of this state. . . . Your grandfather was a prosperous landowner. Your grandmother was a Godhigh.'" This is cold comfort for Julian, whose knowledge of his aristocratic background serves only to intensify his bitterness that this blue-blooded youth must sell typewriters for a living and accompany his mother on weekly trips to the YWCA. Julian the Apostate found his own aristocratic links problematic at best, deadly at worst. Although eventually he would be designated Caesar (AD 355) and then acclaimed Emperor during the Gallic campaigns (AD 360), Julian spent his entire childhood and adolescence under house arrest at a series of private homes and fortresses scattered throughout the Roman Empire. The power struggles of the fourth century hit close to home: His father and brother had been slaughtered before his eyes by his older cousin, the emperor Constantius, who spared the five-year-old Julian but kept him surrounded by guards and spies until he reluctantly named him Caesar to replace Julian's older brother, the Caesar Gallus, whom Constantius had murdered in AD 354. The point would not be lost on a writer such as O'Connor, who utilizes "estrangement within the family" as a major source of "sublimated violence and overt feuding" in her stories. Such familial internecine strife is particularly evident in **"Everything That Rises,"** and no better model for verbal and physical violence directed against blood relatives could be found than the personal and historical situation of Julian the Apostate. Fourth-century Rome was characterized by political turmoil, bloody religious clashes, a costly policy of military aggression, and

severe inflation. Whether one attributes this situation to climactic change, birth control, or low-level lead poisoning from the city's water system, the fact remains that Julian the Apostate lived in a world where old standards, old values, and the secure old lifestyle had been obliterated. To someone living in the South of the early 1960s, chaotic fourth-century Rome would be an apt emblem of the turmoil attendant upon the Civil Rights Movement, as Congress attempted to deal legislatively with social and economic changes which had been underway for a century and accelerated by a series of international wars. As Julian's mother laments, "'the world is in such a mess,'" and under the circumstances it is not surprising that familial strife, especially between generations representing the Old South and the New, would come to the fore. No wonder either that both the fictional and the historical Julian cultivated salient features of their personalities to establish their identities and to ensure survival in a world turned upside down.

Both Julians became withdrawn. O'Connor's Julian longs to live "where the nearest neighbors would be three miles away on either side," and it is his habit to withdraw "into the inner compartment of his mind where he spent most of his time. This was a kind of mental bubble in which he established himself. . . . From it he could see out and judge but in it he was safe from any kind of penetration from without." His sole companion is his mother, whom he can barely tolerate, and there is no mention of friends. The contemporaries of the Apostate record that he was singularly reserved and had "the air of being withdrawn in an inner world." He had no friends, his only close associate having been the eunuch Mardonios, a teacher whom he regarded as a mother figure. His marriage to Helena, sister of the murderous Constantius, was a political arrangement. The death in childbirth of Helena and their infant son had no impact whatsoever on Julian and, according to his contemporary biographer Libanius, "had it not been for that single encounter . . . Julian 'would have ended his days knowing nothing of human sexual intercourse save by report.'" The Apostate's chastity may have had a religious basis, but it was widely perceived as part of a lifelong pattern of asocial self-denial verging on self-destruction. He ate little and slept on straw; his death in battle from a Persian spear was regarded as suicide, since seasoned officers of the Roman army were not wont to dismiss their own bodyguards and go into battle without armor. The self-denying Apostate is thus an ironically monumental prototype for O'Connor's Julian, who apparently has no girlfriend, no friends to help him after the death of his mother, and a histrionic impulse to feel like Saint Sebastian, "pinned to the door frame, waiting . . . for the arrows to begin piercing him" simply because he must accompany his mother on a short bus trip. The self-destructiveness of the Apostate raises the question of whether O'Connor's Julian deliberately (consciously or otherwise) instigated the death of his mother. Certainly he knew that she had high blood pressure, he could plainly see her face turning "unnaturally red," and her death would leave him totally alone. Hence his torment of her would be in keeping with the pattern of asocial behavior and self-denial which characterized both himself and his historical namesake. And inasmuch as his identity is inextricably linked with hers (she has no name: just "Julian's mother"), her death would be a type of suicide for him.

Of course, an impulse towards self-destruction can stem from any number of factors, but, for both Julians, it may be symptomatic of their inability to deal effectively with reality. It is understandable how each man—his personal identity, social standing, family, and nation tottering—might turn some of his frustration inward rather than face directly the problems of the real world, especially when the source of distress either is murderous (cousin Constantius) or intangible (the "convergence" of various elements of American society at mid-century). Besides self-destructiveness, other modes of dealing with (or evading) harsh reality are evident in the two Julians. Both embodied and nurtured a childlike quality. Historian Robert Browning, for example, feels that in many ways the Emperor Julian, even after establishing himself as a canny politician and courageous army officer, was like "a child without experience" thanks to a life spent in isolation. In O'Connor's story, Julian's mother is quite correct that her son "was still growing up. . . . She said he didn't yet know a thing about 'life,' that he hadn't even entered the real world," and his childlike status is particularly evident in his close associations with little Carver, the son of his mother's "black double." Hence withdrawal from society, whether self-induced or imposed from without, leads to an immaturity that can serve as an effective buffer between the self and society.

Another way of responding to harsh reality is to become immersed in fantasies and dreams. Reportedly the Apostate turned from the Christianity of his youth to paganism in part because of a series of dreams in which he felt the gods were guiding him to greatness; indeed, his decision to do battle against the heavily-armed, elephant-mounted Persians minus his armor is said to have been his response to signs from the gods that they would favor him no longer. O'Connor's Julian fantasizes extensively about befriending educated Negroes, abandoning his mother at the bus stop, becoming engaged to a Black girl, anything that would enable him to evade the immediate world.

A less readily apparent mode of responding to an unpleasant reality is to lose oneself in the world of books, even to become a kind of perpetual student. The Apostate "had a very high regard for learning" and was exceptionally well-read in both Christian and pagan (ancient Greek) texts; he even brought his library with him on military campaigns and immersed himself in reading rather than consort with his officers. He also was a facile writer, best-known for his

"Against the Galileans" tract ["Galileans" being his pejorative term for Christians]. Likewise, O'Connor's Julian acquired, "on his own initiative," a "first-rate education" at a "third-rate college," habitually reads newspapers, and longs to be a writer. But the intelligence and education of both Julians are misdirected, subverted, and perhaps even overrated. The generally sympathetic Browning, for example, notes that in "Against the Galileans" the Apostate "is repetitive and woolly, unable to distinguish between the fundamental and the trivial. Throughout his life he tried hard to be a great thinker and a great writer, although nature had not fitted him to be either." The "woolly" mind of the Apostate helps clarify how the reader is to respond to O'Connor's Julian, an important issue since the story is told from his point of view. The example of the Apostate confirms the reader's suspicions that Julian hides behind newspapers rather than read them, and that his asking a Black for matches when he does not even smoke betokens true woolly-mindedness more than liberal zeal. It is difficult, of course, not to sympathize with someone whose mother may be charitably termed "exasperating," but O'Connor counters the reader's impulse to sympathize with Julian by drawing parallels with his ancient Roman namesake, "Julian the Wicked," a man so reprehensible that, 1600 years after his death, Christianity "still shudders at his memory."

One of the elements that renders the Apostate reprehensible is that he used noble means for evil ends: He cultivated his tendency towards intellectualism and then channelled his considerable knowledge and reasoning ability into undermining his own faith and destroying that of others. For all his passion for dreams, the Apostate approached paganism in a coldly rational way: The gods had promised him success; success had come; ergo, continue to worship the gods, and impel others to do the same. Further, he equated paganism with Hellenism and Hellenism with all the best that civilization had to offer. It was quite rational, therefore, to destroy the upstart religion that embodied no culture of its own and which seemed to extol the emotional at the expense of the practical: "Basically [the Apostate] supposed that it was a matter of explanation. If the absurdities of Christian doctrine and the duplicity and hypocrisy of Christian practice were pointed out, people could not fail to be impressed by them and would return to the religion of their ancestors in some form." O'Connor's Julian assumes the same approach. He regards his mother's devotion to the past as irrational, a refutation of logic. When she speaks emotionally of Julian's Chestny and Godhigh ancestors, he responds rationally: "'Will you look around you,' he said tensely, 'and see where you are now?'" While he insists that "true culture is in the mind, the *mind*," she insists that "'it's in the heart,'" a response which would have been untenable to the cynical Apostate, who demanded "rational acceptance" as an emperor rather than the "unthinking, emotional loyalty" of his people. Smugly satisfied with their education and disdainful of emotions, the two Julians are so similar in temperament that historians and literary critics alike frequently seem to be discussing the "other Julian." What Classical historian Browning writes of the Apostate is certainly true for both Julians: He was "a bookish, . . . sober young man, a little inclined to priggishness and more than a little pleased with himself." Likewise, what Patricia Dinneen Maida writes of O'Connor's character applies equally well to the Apostate: "Julian's cynicism shuts him off from any human association. His chief asset, his intelligence, is misdirected: he freely scorns the limitations of others and assumes a superior stance." Biographies of the Apostate and critical studies of **"Everything That Rises"** repeatedly characterize the two Julians as cynics, as misanthropes, as dissemblers. It is in fact their fundamental duplicity—a duplicity facilitated by their misguided capacity for rational thought and their misdirected knowledge—which is perhaps the most suggestive similarity between the two Julians.

The duplicity of the two Julians is most apparent in their ostensible support for social minorities. The Apostate, for example, after pretending to be a good Christian for a decade, suddenly revealed himself to be a pagan and embarked on a campaign to rebuild the Temple at Jerusalem, which had been destroyed by Vespasian and Titus 300 years earlier. His campaign earned him the title of *restaurator templorum,* and he has had "a good reputation with Jews ever since." But Julianus disliked Jews intensely, as his personal writings testify. His impulse to rebuild the Temple was insistently political, a coolly calculated, purely rational means of consolidating his personal position and, above all, of "unsettling and discrediting his Christian enemies." The situation is identical to that of Julian and the Blacks in **"Everything That Rises."** Julian appears to be open-minded and selfless; he goes to great lengths to befriend Blacks, although "he had never been successful at making any Negro friends." But as John R. May recognizes, Julian "wants to hurt his mother more than make amends to God or Negroes," precisely as the Apostate sought to hurt Christians more than make amends to Jews.

What passes for a highly liberal, pro-minority stance may appear to be an immersion in reality, but, in fact, it is part of the pattern of avoiding reality. Both Julians are essentially reactionary. The Apostate, faced with an empire in turmoil at all levels, "took refuge in a return to a past which, like so many historical pasts, was in part mythical." For the Apostate, that partly mythical past was the pagan world of the Hellenes, a model of orderliness where the cosmos was parceled out to pantheon of gods who provided personal, practical advice through the medium of dreams. It appealed strongly to his love of reason and was quite unlike the state religion of Christianity, which he regarded as illogical, hypocritical, and effeminate in its emphasis on a loving, forgiving God. The "part mythical" past to which O'Connor's

Julian longs to return is the Old South signified by the family mansion: "He never . . . thought of it without longing. . . . It remained in his mind as his mother had known it. It appeared in his dreams regularly." For all his ostensible support of civil rights and his verbal rejection of the segregated world of the Old South—"He never spoke of [the mansion] without contempt"—Julian's stance is false. The world he longs for is that of his grandparents and great-grandparents, in which he would have a secure, superior position, and in which that bottom rail would remain firmly at the bottom. For all their seeming liberalism and insistence upon reason, then, both Julians had a reactionary impulse that ventured upon sentimentalism. So much for cool rationalism.

But reactionism is rarely a long-term solution to widespread, accelerated change, and for both Julians, a dramatic encounter with harsh reality ends their respective stories. The Apostate, feeling abandoned by the pagan gods who previously had guided his good fortune through dreams, apparently deliberately allowed himself to be killed in battle. It is generally held that his dying words—"Vicisti, Galilea" ["Thou hast triumphed, Galilean"]—were his acknowledgment not simply that his empire-wide policy of reinstating paganism had failed, but that it had failed due to the rightness of Christianity: the evil Julian finally saw the light. In view of the parallels between the two Julians, the Apostate's conversion to Christianity when faced with adversity tends to confirm that **"Everything That Rises,"** much touted as O'Connor's one attempt to deal with what she termed "That Issue," is more a story about the individual acceptance of Christianity in the increasingly secularized United States of the twentieth century than a story of racial tolerance. Carter W. Martin is doubtless correct that, although she does not express herself directly concerning God or faith, the mother is a "right-thinking Christian." Hence, Julian's rejection of her may be perceived as a rejection of Christianity which, in its way, is as virulent as that of the Apostate. But at the end of the story, Julian is about to make "his entry into the world of guilt and sorrow" and, for the Roman Catholic O'Connor, that "is the only world there is." From the traditional Christian perspective, the ending of the story is insistently affirmative in that the Galilean has triumphed once again.

Julian the Apostate proved to be "a Christian *malgré lui,*" and this suggests that the close connections between O'Connor's Julian and his historical namesake have implications for other works by O'Connor. What Miles Orvell has identified as "the Rayber type" in her fiction, a character noted for "a desperate liberal zeal, a predictably thwarted sexual or married life, and an impulse toward self-martyrdom," may more profitably be termed "the Apostate type." In her creation of Rayber, Haze Motes, Joy-Hulga, and a host of others who use intellectualism, reason, and formal learning in their doomed attempts to deny Christ, Flannery

O'Connor evidently found confirmation—if not direct inspiration—in the remarkable story of Julian the Apostate.

Alice Hall Petry (essay date Spring 1987)

SOURCE: "O'Connor's *Everything That Rises Must Converge*," in *The Explicator*, Vol. 45, No. 3, Spring, 1987, pp. 51-4.

[*In the following essay, Hall Petry describes the place of the YWCA in O'Connor's "Everything That Rises Must Converge."*]

As Patricia Dinneen Maida has pointed out, Flannery O'Connor "does not flood her work with details; she is highly selective—choosing only those aspects that are most revealing." The justice of this observation in regard to **"Everything That Rises Must Converge"** was confirmed recently by John Ower, who argues persuasively that Julian's mother's having to offer a penny to the little Black boy in lieu of a nickel illustrates the ascendancy of Lincolnesque racial tolerance over Jeffersonian segregation in the South of the Civil Rights Movement. O'Connor's capacity to utilize detail symbolically in **"Everything That Rises"** is evident even in the destination of Julian's mother: the local "Y." Mentioned no less than five times in this brief story, the Y serves as a gauge of the degeneration of the mother's Old South family and, concomitantly, of the breakdown of old, church-related values in the United States of the mid-twentieth century.

As Julian's mother is wont to point out, she is related to the Godhighs and the Chestnys, prominent families of the Old South whose former status is conveyed nicely by the high-ceilinged, double-staircased mansion which Julian had seen as a child, and of which he still dreams regularly. But with the end of the plantation system, the mother's glorious ancestry is meaningless: she has had to work to put her son through a third-rate college, she apparently does not own a car (hence the dreaded, fatal ride on the integrated bus), and she lives in a poor neighborhood which had been fashionable forty years earlier. One of the most telling indicators of her loss of socioeconomic status is, however, also one of the most subtle: she participates in a program at the YWCA.

As Maida notes, a reducing class at the Y is a "bourgeois event"; but more than this, it suggests how much Julian's mother, and the socioeconomic system she represents, has declined by the early 1960s. The Young Women's Christian Association has been functioning in some form in the United States since 1866; the national organization of the "Young Women's Christian Association of the United States of America" was effected in 1906. From the beginning, it was

a group whose local chapters were organized and financed by the very wealthy, including Grace Hoadley Dodge (1856-1914), the daughter and great-granddaughter of prominent American philanthropists. The civic-minded Miss Dodge managed to supplement her own generous personal contributions by soliciting enormous gifts from captains of industry such as George W. Vanderbilt, and YWCA chapters spread throughout the United States, including the rapidly industrializing post-World War I South. In the late nineteenth- and early twentieth-centuries, then, a woman with the family background of Julian's mother would have been an organizer and financial supporter of the YWCA; but to actually participate in the programs would have been unheard-of, since the Association was intended specifically to benefit "young women of the operative classes"—that is, young women who were either immigrants or poor native-born country girls seeking employment in large cities, and who were "dependent on their own exertion for support." That the reducing class Julian's mother attends is for "working girls over fifty" is thus not only a transparent joke on the self-image of a middle-aged woman (i.e., a fifty-plus "girl") but alo a sad commentary on Julian's mother having become one of the desperate members of "the operative classes": with the loss of the Godhigh/Chestny plantation, she is simply another poor, naive country girl trying to survive in a hostile urban environment. And the hat and gloves she pathetically wears to the Y—those emblems of wealth and respectability of women such as Grace Dodge—serve only to underscore her socioeconomic decline.

At the same time that it sought to help working girls on a personal level, the YWCA of the United States was a surprisingly important force in national and international affairs. At the turn of the century the YWCA, under the leadership of its "industrial secretary" Florence Simms, was actively involved in exposing the poor working conditions of women and children and campaigning for legislation to improve those conditions. Through the publication of books, pamphlets, and magazines (such as *Association Monthly*, begun in 1907) and a series of well-publicized national conventions and international conferences, the YWCA called for America's participation in the World Court and the League of Nations; sought the modification of divorce laws, improved Sino-American relations, and world-wide disarmament; advocated sex education as early as 1913; and, through the platform known as the "Social Ideals of the Churches," campaigned vigorously for labor unions—a bold move at a time (1920) when anything resembling Bolshevism was anathema. In short, in its early years, the YWCA never shrank from controversial social issues and often was a pioneer in facing and correcting social problems. That stance was perhaps best illustrated by the 1915 convention in Louisville, Kentucky, in which Black and white members of the YWCA met to discuss ways to improve race relations in the United States. In fine, had **"Everything That Rises"** been written in 1915, that YWCA to which she travels throughout the story might well have been the common meeting-ground of Julian's mother and her "black double"; but only 45 years after the pioneering interracial convention in Louisville, the YWCA had declined to the point where, far from being a center of racial understanding and integration, it was essentially a free health club for poor white women. The Black woman, after all, gets off at the same bus stop as Julian's mother, but there is nothing to suggest that she, too, is headed for the Y. And much as the YWCA had lost its earlier status as a force for racial understanding, it also had lost its status as a source of practical help: although the Y is only four blocks from where his mother collapses, Julian does not go there for help; and, unlike the early days when the YWCA would literally send its members to factories to conduct prayer meetings for the working women, no one from the Y comes to Julian's mother's aid. Where only a few years before the Y would have been the first source of aid for a desperate woman, by the early 1960s, it was as meaningless and impersonal as the gymnasium to which it had been reduced. The startling decline of the once powerful, liberal, and comforting YWCA parallels the decline of the Old South—and the old America—embodied in Julian's mother. As Driskell and Brittain observe, "the world around her has changed drastically and no longer represents the values she endorses."

The aspect of the YWCA's decline which would most have disturbed a writer such as O'Connor, however, is its secularization, for she knew only too well that the average American of the twentieth century was out of touch with Christianity. From its inception, the YWCA was regarded as the "handmaid of the Church"; in the early years, "The Sunday afternoon 'gospel meeting' was the heart of the whole organization; always there were Bible classes, and mission study extended the interest beyond the local community and out into the world," while the improved working conditions and wages of the working girls were seen not as ends in themselves, but as means of generating "true piety in themselves and others." But as early as World War I, the religious dimension of the Association was losing ground—a phenomenon noted with dismay by YWCA leaders, who nonetheless recognized that it was part of a nation-wide move towards secularization: "The period extending from the day when Bible study was taken for granted as being all-important to the day when there might be no Bible study in the program of a local Association shows changes, not only in the Association, but in religion in general." Those changes were reflected in the requirements for admission to membership in the YWCA. To join the nineteenth-century "Ladies' Christian Association," a woman had to prove herself a member "in good standing of an Evangelical church"; by 1926, church membership was no longer a requirement, and the declaration that "I desire to enter the Christian fellowship of the Association" was deemed adequate for mem-

bership. Small wonder that the gymnasium, a standard feature of even the earliest YWCA chapters since bodily health was seen as conducive to spiritual health, became divorced form its Christian context: for many Americans after mid-century, "the Y" is synonymous with "the gym." Indeed, the secularization of the YWCA is conveyed dramatically by its nicknames. To its earliest members, the young Women's Christian Association was known informally as "the Association." That emphasis on Christian sisterhood is obscured by the popular abbreviation "YWCA," and it is completely lost by the Association's slangy contemporary nickname, "the Y"—a term with an implied emphasis on youth. It is ironically appropriate, then, that a "working girl over fifty" in youth-minded America would go to the Y for a reducing class, apparently oblivious to the Association's tradition of Christian living and racial understanding. For O'Connor, Julian's mother would be painfully typical of most mid-century Americans, who neither understand nor appreciate the meaning and purpose of the original Young Women's Christian Association. As such, Julian's mother's situation—like the degeneration of the YWCA into a gymnasium—is a gauge of the secularization of American life and the loss of the "old" values and standards.

David Jauss (essay date Winter 1988)

SOURCE: "Flannery O'Connor's Inverted Saint's Legend," in *Studies in Short Fiction*, Vol. 25, No. 1, Winter, 1988, pp. 76-8.

[*In the following essay, Jauss asserts that in "Everything That Rises Must Converge" the name of the protagonist is an allusion to St. Julian Hospitator, and that "By subtly calling our attention to St. Julian and the story of his life, O'Connor transforms this story of a tragic bus trip to the Y into an ironic, inverted saint's legend."*]

As many critics have noted, Flannery O'Connor's stories are populated with characters who bear symbolic names. Many of these names are so overtly symbolic that we wouldn't be surprised to encounter them in an allegory by Bunyan or Spenser: witness, among the many examples, Joy, Mrs. Hopewell, and Mrs. Freeman from **"Good Country People"**; Mr. Paradise from **"The River"**; Mr. Fortune from **"A View of the Woods"**; Sheppard from **"The Lame Shall Enter First"**; and, of course, the Misfit from **"A Good Man is Hard to Find."** Other names, such as Mrs. May and Mr. Greenleaf from **"Greenleaf,"** are only slightly less overt in their symbolism. But at least one of O'Connor's symbolic names is subtle and obscure enough to have escaped critical notice. I am referring to Julian, the protagonist of **"Everything that Rises Must Converge."** As both the story's events and its references to sainthood and martyrdom suggest, Julian's name is an ironic allusion to St. Julian Hospitator. By subtly calling our attention to St. Julian and the story of his life, O'Connor transforms this story of a tragic bus trip to the Y into an ironic, inverted saint's legend.

Early in the story, O'Connor establishes the idea that Julian is an inverted saint by comparing him to Saint Sebastian "waiting . . . for the arrows to begin piercing him" and by describing his weekly chore of taking his mother downtown to the Y as a "martyrdom." These religious allusions are obviously, even heavy-handedly, ironic. Julian is clearly no Saint Sebastian. He is not waiting to give his life for his faith (indeed, he has no faith); he is merely waiting for his mother to quit fussing with her new hat. And he is not a martyr but a persecutor, for he cruelly drives his mother toward a fatal stroke. The ironic discrepancy between Julian and Saint Sebastian's "martyrdoms" clearly suggests that Julian is anything but saintly. By inverting the legend of St. Julian in her story's plot, O'Connor not only extends this suggestion but also explains precisely *why* Julian fails to achieve salvation.

A devout, even a fierce, Roman Catholic, O'Connor may have encountered the story of St. Julian Hospitator in any of a number of works of hagiography, but most likely she discovered it in a tale by one of her favorite authors, Gustave Flaubert. Flaubert's "The Legend of St. Julian Hospitator" was based on standard versions of the legend found in Jacopo da Voragine's *Golden Legend* and the thirteenth-century *Legend of St. Julian,* as well as on the stained-glass window at Rouen Cathedral depicting the saint's life that Flaubert mentions at the end of his tale. Briefly, all of these sources describe Julian's youthful cruelty to people and animals, his parricide (he murders his mother and father in his bed, mistaking them for his wife and a lover), and his attempt to do penance for his sins by "spending his life in the service of others," in particular by helping travelers cross a dangerous river. The legend concludes with him ferrying a leper across the river during a hail storm, then taking him into his hut for the night. Although the leper is so contagious that everything he touches is instantly covered with scaly pustules, Julian shows no concern for his own health and sacrifices everything he has for the leper. When the leper says, "I am hungry," Julian gives him the last of his food. When he says, "I am thirsty," Julian gives him all of his remaining water. And finally, when the leper complains that he is cold, Julian gives him his bed, then lies down on him to warm him, "mouth to mouth, breast to breast." Through this act of compassionate union—what we might call "convergence"—with a repellent stranger, Julian is redeemed: the leper turns into Christ, and Julian rises to heaven in His arms.

Like his saintly counterpart, O'Connor's Julian serves as a "ferryman"—he helps his mother not from one side of a dan-

gerous river to the other but from their home to the Y—and he is a parricide, for he mercilessly drives her blood pressure up until she suffers the stroke he has previously and unsympathetically imagined her having. But O'Connor reverses the order of her story's parallels with the saint's legend and inverts their significance. Whereas the saint first murders his mother, then expiates his guilt by selflessly risking his life to help strangers make a dangerous passage, O'Connor's Julian browbeats his mother into a fatal stroke *after* he selfishly refuses to help her make her simpler journey safely. And whereas St. Julian treats even the most noxious of strangers as someone deserving of love and sympathy, Julian treats his own mother as if she were "a stranger." Given these inversions, it is not surprising that the two stories end in ironically opposed ways. While the legend of St. Julian ends with his rising to heaven, O'Connor's inverted saint's legend ends with Julian "postponing from moment to moment his entry into the world of guilt and sorrow," the world that St. Julian has transcended by sacrificing himself for others. Julian ends, then, where the saint began.

As all of this suggests, Julian fails to "rise" because he refuses to "converge" with his mother as St. Julian converged with the leper. He fails to recognize Christ in his mother and treats her like a leper, discriminating against her in a crueller way than she, with her condescending gift of a penny to a black boy, discriminates against blacks. He fails, too, O'Connor implies, to realize what St. Julian did: that every act, even if it's as mundane as giving someone a crust of black bread or taking one's mother to the Y on the bus, is an opportunity for redemption.

On the surface, **"Everything that Rises Must Converge"** is, until the apocalyptic ending, a relatively mundane account of a bus trip. But because of the story's subtly ironic parallels with the legend of St. Julian, its everyday, worldly events become charged with religious significance. At issue is not merely Julian's relationship with his mother but his very salvation. While the parallels to the saint's legend serve the purpose of ironic deflation—St. Julian becomes ordinary Julian, his boat a bus, and the dangerous river the streets of our modern world—they also serve to suggest that Julian could achieve salvation through something as ordinary as "ferrying" his mother to the Y, provided he did so with self-abnegation and compassion. By inverting the legend of St. Julian, O'Connor forcefully communicates both Julian's failure to achieve redemption and the spiritual perils and possibilities implicit in the most common and mundane acts.

Alice Hall Petry (essay date Summer 1989)

SOURCE: "Miss O'Connor and Mrs. Mitchell: The Example

of 'Everything That Rises,'" in *The Southern Quarterly,* Vol. XXVII, No. 4, Summer, 1989, pp. 5-15.

[In the following essay, Hall Petry outlines allusions to Margaret Mitchell's Gone With the Wind *found in O'Connor's "Everything That Rises Must Converge."]*

Flannery O'Connor knew only too well that she could not assume her audience brought a solid background in Christianity to their readings of her fiction. It was part of the price she paid for being an insistently Roman Catholic writer in the increasingly secularized United States of the mid-twentieth century. One element which she could count on being familiar to any American reader from any socioeconomic or educational stratum was, however, Margaret Mitchell's *Gone with the Wind.* That familiarity enabled O'Connor to incorporate into her fiction various echoes of Mitchell's novel, echoes sometimes transparent and sometimes subtle, sometimes parodic and sometimes serious. In **"A Late Encounter with the Enemy,"** for example, the reference to the "preemy" of twelve years before indicates that "General" George Poker Sash had attended the world premiere of the novel's movie version in Atlanta in 1939. Sadly, Sash's finest hour had come not during the Civil War, but during the premiere of the movie which, seventy-five years later, had romanticized and popularized the conflict. Likewise, in **"A Good Man Is Hard to Find"** the grandmother tells little John Wesley that the plantation is "Gone With the Wind. Ha. Ha," her pallid joke pointing, once again, to the pervasive acceptance of Mitchell's rendering of the most painful era in southern history. One O'Connor story which has a special kinship with Mitchell's classic story is **"Everything That Rises Must Converge."** Taken together, these echoes of *Gone with the Wind*—some blatant parallels, some ironic reversals—underscore the story's thesis that Julian's and his mother's responses to life in the South of the civil rights movement are unreasonable and, ultimately, self-destructive precisely because those responses are based upon actions and values popularized by Mitchell's book. Even worse, in several instances, actions and values are pathetic distortions of what Mitchell presents in *Gone with the Wind.*

A clear connection between **"Everything That Rises Must Converge"** and *Gone with the Wind* is the mother's hat. As Patricia Dinneen Maida points out, O'Connor is "highly selective" in her choice of details; John Ower confirms this by arguing the importance of the mother offering little Carver a new Lincoln penny in lieu of a Jefferson nickel. Of course, the ugly hat which the mother has purchased for an outrageous $7.50, a hat identical to that of the large black woman, will help confirm that they are "doubles" and, thereby, will make a statement about racial equality. But there is more to the hat than this. Note O'Connor's careful description of it, presented twice: "It was a hideous hat. A purple velvet flap came down on one side of it and stood up on the other; the

rest of it was green and looked like a cushion with the stuffing out. [Julian] decided it was less comical than jaunty and pathetic." The purple of the hat suggests bruising. Thus it is very appropriate for a woman whose eyes seem bruised and whose face looks purple as her son torments her, and who will literally be struck to the ground by an overstuffed purse. Less obvious is the irony that her black double has no doubt suffered the bruises of psychological and physical abuse during her life in the South, bruises which are less apparent to whites who, for generations, have been conditioned to believe that blacks have less sensitivity to blows than whites. In addition, various commentators have pointed out that the color purple has religious associations, most notably Easter redemption and penance. At the same time, the antipodal orientations conveyed by the purple flap—"down on one side . . . up on the other"—graphically depict the twin socioeconomic movements in the South: the downward movement of aristocratic families like the Godhighs and the Chestnys, and the upward movement of "upwardly mobile" blacks who, because of improved economic status, have "as much freedom to pursue absurdity as the whites." In part, then, the hat's purple flap renders semiotically the impact of the civil rights movement on southern society. Less clear, however, is why the rest of the hat is green and looks "like a cushion with the stuffing out"—less clear, that is, unless one remembers *Gone with the Wind.* Overwhelmed by the familial and regional crises engendered by the Civil War, the widowed Scarlett O'Hara is all the more personally dismayed by the attire of Emmie Slattery, a "poor white trash" neighbor who has suddenly stepped up economically by marrying the underhanded Jonas Wilkerson, and who is considering buying Tara: "And what a cunning hat! Bonnets must be out of style, for this hat was only an absurd flat red velvet affair, perched on top of [Emmie's] head like a stiffened pancake." The velvet pancake, however "absurd," does not go unnoticed by Scarlett's creative self, for shortly thereafter the threadbare mistress of Tara, desperate for $300 more for municipal taxes, resolves to construct a new outfit out of household goods and coerce the sum out of Rhett Butler. With the help of Mammy, Scarlett makes a dazzling dress out of the mansion's "moss-green velvet curtains" and a petticoat out of the satin linings of the parterres; her pantalets are trimmed with pieces of Tara's lace curtains. Even the plantation's rooster surrenders his "gorgeous bronze and green-black tail feathers" to decorate the green velvet hat. Ashley Wilkes is duly moved: "he had never known such gallantry as the gallantry of Scarlett O'Hara going forth to conquer the world in her mother's velvet curtains and the tail feathers of a rooster." As Dorothy Walters points out, the fact that Julian's mother's hat looks like a cushion without its stuffing makes her "instantaneously ridiculous. . . . Imagery deflates ego. What the character conveys is not what he intends," but if one remembers the Scarlett O'Hara connection, it is clear that the hat suggests the mother's desperate bid for dignity, for a Scarlett O'Hara-type "gallantry," as much as it does a deflation of her ego. True, Julian's mother did not actually make her hat out of a cushion, but it is entirely possible that, at some level, Julian's mother—herself a widow from a good southern family down on her luck—may have been identifying with the plucky Scarlett, using her as a role model of a lady who survives by making do with what she has. Indeed one could say of Scarlett just as readily as of Julian's mother that she "had struggled fiercely to feed and clothe and put [her child] through school," and Scarlett eventually does attain the economic and social prominence that Julian's mother can only dream of through her son, a would-be writer. Perhaps Scarlett's own makeshift outfit looked as "jaunty and pathetic" as the hat of Julian's mother; but it surely was unique (Scarlett would never "meet [her]self coming and going"), and the encounter with Rhett ultimately led to her successful business career. The redoubtable Scarlett must have been a role model for many women in the same situation as Julian's mother, so the hat—"hideous," "atrocious," "preposterous"—may be seen as her pathetic attempt to emulate not simply a southern belle in dire straits, but the most famous belle of them all. Whether Julian's mother consciously has Scarlett in mind is a moot point. What matters is that she is conducting herself like a romanticized fictional character from a book set a century before. Times, however, have changed.

Nothing illustrates these changing times more readily than the issue of ladyhood, an issue which permeates both **"Everything That Rises Must Converge"** and *Gone with the Wind.* Julian's mother insisted that "ladies did not tell their age or weight"; she was "one of the few members of the Y reducing class who arrived in hat and gloves"; and she entered the bus "with a little smile, as if she were going into a drawing room where everyone had been waiting for her." Julian's mother, in short, regards herself as the consummate lady. It is precisely here that she parts company most glaringly with Scarlett, who herself "found the road to ladyhood hard." Scarlett scorns those well-bred women, financially ruined by the Civil War, who cling desperately to the manners and trappings of the ante-bellum South. "She knew she should believe devoutly, as they did, that a born lady remained a lady, even if reduced to poverty, but *she could not make herself believe it* now" (emphasis added). For all her self-imagined kinship with archetypal belles like Scarlett, Julian's mother is actually more akin to these pathetic women who cannot give up the past. True, Scarlett creates for herself a magnificent outfit, one befitting a lady; but she does it only because she needs the $300 from Rhett. If not for this emergency, she would have continued wearing the slippers reinforced with carpeting and the "raggedy," much mended dress which her harsh postwar life on Tara demanded. She is practical and has no illusions about herself or about what she must do to survive. Julian's mother, however, is but a pale copy of Scarlett. She was practical enough to finance Julian's college education, and she realizes that the $7.50 she paid for the hat should be put towards the gas bill; but she only sent him to a third-rate college, and she capitulates with notable ease to her son's suggestion that she forget the bill and keep the hat. Likewise, she lives in a poor neighborhood only because forty years before it was "fashionable," whereas Scarlett would never fool herself into thinking that past glory had any true bearing on one's current situation. She wants to retain Tara, after all, out of principle and as a matter of family pride, not because it is chic.

The situations of Scarlett and Julian's mother are, of course, superficially similar, and one can see why the example of *Gone with the Wind* would appeal to a middle-aged southern woman of "good" family in the early 1960s. Scarlett is trying to survive in a South undergoing social, economic and racial upheavals due to the Civil War, while Julian's mother is trying to survive in a South undergoing similar upheavals caused by the civil rights movement, World War II and the Korean conflict. Julian's mother states repeatedly that "'the world is in such a mess,'" and that "'the bottom rail is on the top.'" This is precisely how Scarlett perceives her own world: "Ellen's [Scarlett's mother's] ordered world was gone and a brutal world had taken its place, a world wherein every standard, every value had changed." Scarlett's immediate response to this realization is chillingly like Julian's: she blames her mother. Scarlett's Julian-like cynicism and rudeness

> helped her to forget her own bitterness that everything her mother had told her about life was wrong. Nothing her mother had taught her was of any value whatsoever now and Scarlett's heart was sore and puzzled. It did not occur to her that Ellen could not have foreseen the collapse of the civilization in which she raised her daughters, could not have anticipated the disappearing of the places in society for which she trained them so well. It did not occur to her that Ellen had looked down a vista of placid future years, all like the uneventful years of her own life, when she had taught her to be gentle and gracious, honorable and kind, modest and truthful. Life treated women well when they learned those lessons, said Ellen.

Scarlett's resentment towards Ellen O'Hara may help explain Julian's own palpable contempt for his mother. She represents a world, a lifestyle that Julian wants but can never attain, and he bullies her like Scarlett bullies her sisters, wishing he could slap his mother and hoping that some black would help him "to teach her a lesson." But where the resilient Scarlett eventually comes to forgive her mother for the loss of her world, Julian cannot forgive his. He literally torments her to death.

For Scarlett, Julian and his mother, the focal point of the

world they have lost is the ancestral mansion. Julian's great-grandfather had a plantation and two hundred slaves, and Julian dreams of it "regularly. He would stand on the wide porch, listening to the rustle of oak leaves, then wander through the high-ceilinged hall into the parlor that opened onto it and gaze at the worn rugs and faded draperies." But Julian's memory of it is marred: "The double stairways had rotted and been torn down. Negroes were living in it." The prospect of the family mansion undergoing such a reversal is also what haunts Scarlett. Part of the reason she so fears the purchase of Tara by its former overseer for his wife Emmie (the local "dirty tow-headed slut") is that "these low common creatures [would be] living in this house, bragging to their low common friends how they had turned the proud O'Haras out. Perhaps they'd even bring negroes here to dine and sleep." But, once again, Scarlett differs significantly from Julian and his mother: she is truly adaptable. To save Tara, "she changed swiftly to meet this new world for which she was not prepared," even taking advantage of her status as a "lady"—a status which, as noted, she does not take too seriously—to cheat male customers in her lumber business. Julian and his mother utterly lack Scarlett's imagination and resourcefulness, although they have both deluded themselves into thinking they do possess these qualities. As Sister Kathleen Feeley notes, Julian's mother, "secure in her private stronghold . . . can afford to be 'adaptable' to present conditions, such as associating at the YWCA with women who are not in her social class." However, this is hardly "adaptability" as the enterprising and non-sentimental Scarlett would understand it. Nothing illustrates this inability to adapt more graphically than the death of Julian's mother at the end of the story.

The death scene itself echoes *Gone with the Wind.* Ellen, Scarlett's mother, dying of typhoid, had regressed to her childhood: "'she think she a lil gal back in Savannah,'" and called for her long-dead sweetheart, Philippe. Likewise, Julian's mother regresses to her secure childhood and calls for her mammy Caroline, a request which indicates that, "for all its defects, the older generation had more genuine personal feeling for Negroes than [Julian's] with its heartless liberalism." The death of Julian's mother results from her "loss of illusion" and, concomitantly, her awareness that she can never adapt to the newly-revealed reality: it is "more than she can bear, but mercifully her mind *breaks*" (emphasis added)—a perfect verb to use since, like a brittle stick, Julian's mother responds to the stress of her realization by "breaking" physically and psychologically. Her son, albeit physically alive, is psychically shattered, pathetically calling "Mamma!" as he enters "the world of guilt and sorrow." In sharp contrast, Scarlett is like a reed. She bends under duress, adjusts, survives.

What Julian's mother could not accept, and what Julian had only deluded himself into believing that he did accept, is not that everything rises, but that everything that rises must *converge.* Hence her insistence that it's fine if blacks rise as long as they stay on their side of the fence, and her dismay over mulattoes, those emblems of the process of racial convergence. The fact that the black woman wore an identical hat (O'Connor takes care to describe it twice) is another blatant emblem of convergence, which Julian's mother had tried to deny "by reducing the other woman to a subhuman level and seeing the implied relationship between them as a comic impossibility"—that is, by responding as if the black woman "were a monkey that had stolen her hat." It is reminiscent of Scarlett's shocked reaction to Emmie's dressing like a lady (which she is not). Scarlett's response to the convergence which she sees around her in postwar Georgia is more constructive: she accepts what she must and changes what she can. Scarlett must often swallow her pride, lerning the lumber business from scratch and even, in effect, offering herself to Rhett in exchange for negotiable currency. But survive and thrive she does, and "ladylike" behavior be damned. And if it turned out that ladylike behavior could be damned so readily in 1865, what could be more pathetic than trying to retain it in 1960?

The superficial similarities in their situations may have led Julian's mother to emulate Scarlett, consciously or otherwise. But as Kathryn Lee Seidel argues, Scarlett is "both conventional and unique," as is evident from her green eyes. Writes Seidel: "Of all the belles I have studied, she is the only one with green eyes. By assigning Scarlett this eye color, Mitchell both acknowledges and overturns this small detail of the belle stereotype. It is a technique Mitchell uses masterfully throughout the novel; with it, *she compliments her audience's knowledge of and affection for the stereotype, but uses it for her own purposes*" (emphasis added). O'Connor is using an identical technique in her presentation of Julian's blue-eyed mother, who evidently has extracted selectively for emulation only the most conventional, most romantic aspects of southern womanhood that were popularized by *Gone with the Wind.* Without the "unique" qualities that are so vital in the characterization of Scarlett (her personal toughness, imagination, adaptability), the emulation of those conventional aspects is pathetic—and especially so in a middle-aged woman living a century after the Civil War. No doubt Julian's mother would be flattered to see the connection between herself and Scarlett O'Hara signified by the cushion-like hat; and no doubt Scarlett herself would find that connection a grim commentary on the self-image of Julian's mother.

There is no copy of *Gone with the Wind* in Flannery O'Connor's personal library; but in view of her considerable knowledge of southern literature, it is difficult to believe that she had never read Mitchell's novel. And one can surmise readily which features of it would be of special interest to O'Connor: the Georgia setting; the lovely description of ante-bellum Tara surrounded by flocks of turkeys and geese, birds being, of course, a life-long love of O'Connor's; the startling scene wherein Scarlett's father—like O'Connor, an Irish Catholic living in Protestant Georgia—is given a Church of England funeral (the ignorant mourners "thought it the Catholic ceremony and immediately rearranged their first opinion that the Catholic services were cold and Popish"); even the references to Milledgeville, O'Connor's hometown (e.g., Scarlett admits to Mammy, "'I know so few Milledgeville folks'"). It is far more to the point, however, that O'Connor could readily assume that other American readers and movie-goers, of whatever faith or region, would be familiar with Mitchell's story and would respond to echoes of it in her writings. As is illustrated by the case of **"Everything That Rises Must Converge,"** those echoes could be used, comically or otherwise, to help guide our responses to the often enigmatic fiction of Flannery O'Connor.

Harbour Winn (essay date Summer 1990)

SOURCE: *"Everything That Rises Must Converge: O'Connor's Seven-Story Cycle,"* in *Renascence,* Vol. XLII, No. 4, Summer, 1990, pp. 187-212.

[*In the following essay, Winn asserts that O'Connor's* Everything That Rises Must Converge *is a short story cycle in which "O'Connor varies the location of her limited omniscient point of view and interweaves parallel thematic patterns to link together the seven stories."*]

In modern fiction, writers have combined the aesthetics of the novel and the short story to construct grouping of interrelated stories that are too finely patterned to be described as a mere collection of stories and too dependent on individual components to be described as a novel. Among the names proposed for this new genre, Forrest Ingram's suggestion of "short story cycle" in *Representative Short Story Cycles of the Twentieth Century* most clearly represents its nature. He defines a short story cycle as "a book of short stories so linked to each other by their author that the reader's successive experience on various levels of the pattern of the whole significantly modifies his experience of each of its component parts." In this hybrid, writers combine the essential differences between the short story and the novel: each individual story within a cycle focuses upon a single moment of peculiar significance in the life of its protagonist, yet the sequence of stories traces a number of peak moments in a series of events.

Even though critical treatments of short story cycles have generally failed to illuminate their complex interrelationships, they have recognized that such obvious structural patterns as recurring characters or settings establish that the stories of a collection are interconnected. For example, it is apparent that the recurrence of Aram in Saroyan's *My Name Is Aram* and Fidelman in Malamud's *Pictures of Fidelman* groups together these stories just as the common locale of Dublin in Joyce's *Dubliners* and New Orleans in Cable's *Old Creole Days* links those collections. In the spectrum of the short story cycle genre, however, Flannery O'Connor's *Everything That Rises Must Converge* represents the type of series of interconnected stories whose strands of unity are least apparent. Amidst the diversity of characters and settings that comprise the book, O'Connor, like Kafka in *A Hunger Artist* and Camus in *Exile and the Kingdom,* ties together the stories through similarly treated themes and motifs.

O'Connor's *Everything That Rises Must Converge* poses additional difficulty because of the misconception surrounding its composition. Published posthumously in 1965, the standard edition consists of nine stories. Shortly before her death in 1964, however, O'Connor wrote to her publisher proposing that the book contain eight stories, one of which, **"The Partridge Festival,"** she ultimately withdrew. While Robert Giroux, her publisher, and Robert Fitzgerald, her literary executor, fulfilled her intention in this instance, upon discovering two stories she had been working on shortly before her death, they seem to have disregarded her plan for the collection by adding them as the eighth and ninth stories, **"Parker's Back"** and **"Judgement Day."** Any attempt to discuss the book as a cycle, therefore, must assume that it is composed of only the first seven stories. Fitzgerald has since admitted the validity of such an assumption and illuminated O'Connor's cyclic intention by acknowledging that she had planned the order of the seven stories in the collection and intended it for publication in that order. A consideration of the relationship of the excluded story and the two added stories to the cycle, however, can reinforce an understanding of the distinctive interconnecting strands grouping together the seven included stories.

Since most critics of the book have not been aware of O'Connor's intention, they have regarded *Everything That Rises Must Converge* as a collecton of nine rather than seven stories and thus failed to consider the actual make-up of the work itself. Of the seven book-length studies on O'Connor, for example, only one author, Josephine Hendrin, seems to have known of this misconception. Hendrin, however, discusses only six of the stories as a group, for she treats **"The Lame Shall Enter First"** in a chapter on *The Violent Bear It Away.* Nevertheless, with only two exceptions critics have not even considered the nine stories as a series of interconnected pieces; one typical critical observation summarizes the prevailing attitude to the collection: "The nine stories . . . have some common concerns. There are similarities in theme, method, and characterization among them, as there are resemblances to earlier works. But the similarities strike me less than the distinctive qualities of each story as an entity."

That O'Connor did not arrange the seven stories chronologically according to the date of their composition or publication shows that she brought them together to illuminate or comment upon one another through juxtaposition or association. Each of the seven had been published previously in magazines over a period of eight years: **"Greenleaf"** in 1956; **"A View of the Woods"** in 1957; **"The Enduring Chill"** in 1958; **"The Comforts of Home"** in 1960; **"Everything That Rises Must Converge"** in 1961; **"The Lame Shall Enter First"** in 1962; **"Revelation"** in 1964. In bringing together these stories for the cycle, O'Connor seems to have aimed for a much looser structure than, for example, Faulkner intended in *The Unvanquished,* for unlike him she did not revise any of the stories to make their interconnectedness more apparent. Instead, she seems to have viewed **"Revelation,"** both the final story in the cycle and the last one written, as reiterating and concluding the patterns of thematic concern developed throughout the first six stories.

The parallel compositional history of O'Connor's other short story collection, *A Good Man Is Hard To Find,* which also can be considered a cycle, indicates that the process of arrangement in *Everything That Rises Must Converge* was not accidental. In the earlier work, O'Connor also arranged already-published stories in a significant order, the opening story bearing the same title as the cycle, and the final story, **"The Displaced Person,"** strategically placed to conclude themes raised throughout the previous pieces. One critic, Burke, notes that like Joyce's *Dubliners* "the order of the stories is meaningful in both of Miss O'Connor's collections." O'Connor's own description of her writing habits while working on the first of her two novels, *Wise Blood,* can perhaps partly explain the process by which two unified cycles emerged from stories already written on similar themes: "I must tell you how I work. I don't have my novel outlined and I have to write to discover what I am doing. Like the old lady, I don't know so well what I think until I see what I say; then I have to say it over again." Whether or not *Wise Blood* can even be considered a novel has been questioned by some on the grounds that it is too episodic and fragmentary. O'Connor herself stated: "I am not writing a conventional novel." Melvin Friedman regards it as more a "tightly knit collection of stories" than a conventional novel:

> Four of the fourteen chapters were earlier published separately, which reinforces the sense of short stories being strung together to form a novel. The first edition, published by Harcourt, Brace, in fact leaves blank pages between chapters almost begging that we come to a complete endstop before proceeding to the next division.

Although more conventionally constructed, O'Connor's second novel, *The Violent Bear It Away,* contains a strong picaresque element and was also reshaped from shorter fiction published earlier. While most critics indicate that such observations on the episodic quality of her novels and their compositional history indicate that O'Connor was essentially a short story writer and not a novelist, those descriptions also point to O'Connor's affinity for the cyclic method of structuring.

O'Connor expresses her Catholic world view of man's need for the sudden manifestation of grace offered the protagonists in the cycle by including physical sickness in each story to emphasize the disease of spiritual emptiness.
—Harbour Winn

One of the most salient means for penetrating the structural unity of *Everything That Rises Must Converge* lies in exploring the implications of its title. On one level the title can simply refer to O'Connor's classical method of constructing her stories through the rising action of conflict between two characters who either converge or collide at the climax of the story. The title contains far richer implications, however, for it refers to the convergence or collision throughout the seven stories of the rising Southern Blacks with white Southerners, the rising lower class with the upper class, and the rising younger generation with the older generation. But even these explanations do not approach the central underlying implication. The title comes from the writings of the French Jesuit theologian-scientist-poet, Pierre Teilhard de Chardin, whom O'Connor greatly admired. For example, when asked by the editors of *The American Scholar* in 1961 to single out "what . . . were the outstanding books of the past three decades," O'Connor designated Teilhard's *The Phenomenon of Man* with this comment:

> It is a search for human significance in the evolutionary process. Because Teilhard is both a man of science and a believer, the scientist and the theologian will require considerable time to sift and evaluate his thought, but the poet, whose sight is essentially prophetic, will at once recognize in Teilhard a kindred intelligence. His is a scientific expression of what the poet attempts to do: penetrate matter until spirit is revealed in it. Teilhard's vision sweeps forward without detaching itself at any point from the earth.

Teilhard's vision seems to correspond with O'Connor's, for the central element of each centers around belief in a world penetrated by spirit. In his evolutionary system Teilhard sees the continuing movement of diverse species into higher and higher forms of consciousness until, ultimately, they combine or converge upon one another at what he calls the Omega Point, the stage at which spirit and matter exist in equal proportion and blend together as one. According to Teilhard, the individual must grow from egoism to self-awareness and love for human history to evolve toward Omega:

> To be fully ourselves it is in the opposite direction, in the direction of convergence with all the rest, that we must advance—towards the "other!" The goal of ourselves, the acme of our originality is not our individuality but our person; and according to the evolutionary structure of the world, we can only find our person by uniting together. There is no mind without synthesis. The same law holds good from top to bottom. The true ego grows in inverse proportion to "egoism."

In this rejection of egoism as limiting being, Teilhard emphasizes man's capacity through love to rise to higher levels of consciousness where psychic convergences with others can transform the universe: "Remain true to yourself, but move ever upward toward greater consciousness and greater love! At the summit you will find yourself united with all those who, from every direction, have made the same ascent. *For everything that rises must converge.*"

Throughout the seven stories of the cycle O'Connor dramatizes this struggle of rising to higher consciousness by focusing on characters whose egoism distorts their perception, blinding them to the transforming power of the divine at work in the world. Declaring that "for me the meaning of life is centered in our Redemption by Christ," O'Connor expresses her Catholic world view of man's need for the sudden manifestation of grace offered the protagonists in the cycle by including physical sickness in each story to emphasize the disease of spiritual emptiness. Ironically, however, the potential moment of epiphany does not usually trigger self-awareness, for the narrow-minded, self-righteous protagonists of all but the final story collide rather than converge with this possibility for growth; instead of recognizing their tainted nature and participating in a collective effort to transform the secular into an ultimately divine order, they rationalize to maintain their self-righteous pose in a profane existence that serves as a microcosm for their Godless world. The successive exploration of this pattern in varying contexts from story to story provides a structural basis for the cycle.

It is principally through her use of point of view that O'Connor manages to avoid mere repetition with this pattern in the seven stories. Using indirect interior monologue much as Jane Austen did, she in a sense perches on top of the shoulders of the protagonist of a story in order to approximate the workings of the character's mind; the subtle shifting from objective narration to a character's idiom allows her to penetrate, throughout the cycle, the grotesque irony of the protagonist who reveals the self-righteous obsession with which he unknowingly confronts the world. The opening of **"The Comforts of Home"** illustrates this technique: "Thomas withdrew to the side of the window and with his hands between the wall and the curtain he looked down on the driveway where the car had stopped. His mother and the little slut were getting out of it." The objective description of the narrator in the first sentence subtly switches to Thomas's indirect interior monologue in the second sentence through the use of the derogatory phrase describing the girl his mother is bringing home; the cumulative effect of similar passages characterizes the pseudo-intellectual arrogance with which Thomas confronts reality. Throughout the cycle self-inflation manifests itself especially in the tension between generations in a number of ways: intellectually, socially, racially, morally, and religiously. O'Connor varies this basic situation in each story by shifting the location of her point of view from one generation to the other in successive stories in order to examine fully the dimensions of this recurrent pattern. For example, in **"Everything That Rises Must Converge,"** she tells the story through the indirect interior monologue of a son in conflict with his mother; and in the next story, **"Greenleaf,"** she shifts the point of view to a mother whose relationship with her sons and reality corresponds to that of the mother of the first story. This shifting of point of view from parent to child occurs in the succeeding stories until, in the final one, **"Revelation,"** the point of view centers on a third person who observes and is affected by the conflict between a mother and daughter.

The opening story of the cycle, **"Everything That Rises Must Converge,"** establishes some of the basic trademarks of O'Connor's fiction: the vivid use of color in the description of Julian's mother's hat to emphasize the grotesque quality of a character; the Southern setting in which the sound of idioms, speech patterns, and clichés capture the flavor of the region; the dramatic opening in the midst of an action whose background is not filled in until later in the story; the relentless use of verbal, dramatic, and situational irony to tear apart the protagonist's facade of pious respectability; and the building toward a carefully foreshadowed violent climax often resulting in death. The story, however, also introduces the character types, the technical use of parallelism or twinning, and the thematic conflicts present particularly throughout this cycle.

The parasitic relationship between Julian and his mother establishes the prototype for parent and child figures in subsequent stories. College educated, Julian prides himself on his cultural sophistication, racial liberalism, and ability to perceive his mother's genteel affectation and racial paternalism. Realizing that the governing principle of his mother's fantasy world "was to sacrifice herself for him after she had first created the necessity to do so by making a mess of things," he revels in the thrill of his own self-assurance that in spite of her he has "turned out so well":

> In spite of going to only a third-rate college, he had, on his own initiative, come out with a first-rate education; in spite of growing up dominated by a small mind, he had ended up with a large one; in spite of all her foolish views, he was free of prejudice and unafraid to face facts. Most miraculous of all, instead of being blinded by love for her as she was for him, he had cut himself emotionally free of her and could see her with complete objectivity. He was not dominated by his mother.

Ironically, however, Julian's pompous assumptions prove to be only self-deceptions, for his every action reflects his dependence on his mother. To maintain his delusion while still living with his mother who partly supports him until he can become a successful writer, he fabricates a martyr role that allows him to comply with his mother's ways and yet think he remains aloof from them. The ludicrous quality of his rationalizing is revealed when the narrator describes him awaiting his mother's departure in the opening with "his hands behind him, . . . pinned to the door frame, waiting like Saint Sebastian for the arrows to begin piercing him." While accompanying her to the YWCA his attention is consumed by the petty need to annoy her in every way possible: he mocks her class pretensions by removing his necktie and taunts her segregationist views by going out of his way to move to a seat on the bus next to a Negro. When he imagines means by which he might capitalize on her bigotry to "teach her a lesson," he reveals his sterile imagination as well as his own deep-rooted racism by resorting to such hypothetical clichés of white racism as the horror of being treated by a Negro doctor or of intermarriage. Throughout his fantasies his own racial hostility emerges as even more dehumanizing than his mother's, for he prides himself on favoring integration while she at least admits that she does not. His liberal facade discloses that he is concerned with the racial question only insofar as it confirms his misanthropic self-righteousness: racial "injustice in daily operation" gives "him a certain satisfaction," for it confirms "his view that with a few exceptions there was no one worth knowing within a radius of three hundred miles." And while he outwardly scorns his mother's dream of her ancestral mansion, he secretly longs for the leisure life rooted in the institution of slavery that it represents.

Although Julian's mother's moral platitudes reflect her small-mindedness and her suffocating love contributes to her son's immaturity, she has a clearer understanding of the world she lives in. In uncanny fashion she often makes statements that contain more truth than she realizes. For example, without realizing the degree to which Julian is still dependent on her, she says he "didn't yet know a thing about 'life,' that he hadn't even entered the real world." Even though she appears more sympathetic juxtaposed to Julian, O'Connor's tone never becomes sentimental, for the mother's obsession with respectability and pride in her genealogy cripple her efficacy as an individual and parent.

The dramatic conflict of the story builds toward its climax through O'Connor's paralleling of objects and persons. When a Negro woman and child board a bus, Julian becomes elated when he realizes that she is wearing the same hideous hat as his mother who had earlier prided herself on its being one of a kind. O'Connor emphasizes her twinning intent by repeating the exact description of Julian's mother's hat in particularizing the grotesqueness of the Negro woman's: "A purple velvet flap came down on one side of it and stood up on the other; the rest of it was green and looked like a cushion with the stuffing out." In addition to the hat, the two mothers parallel each other in that both are overweight, concerned for their own son's welfare, and insensitive to each other—the one through hate and the other through condescension. When the woman sits by Julian and her son sits by his mother, Julian sees that symbolically they "had in a sense, swapped sons." Dumbfounded, he can hardly believe that "Fate had thrust upon his mother such a lesson." After his mother's paternalistic offering of the penny precipitates her violent confrontation with the Negro woman, Julian makes sure that she understands her lesson by explaining its meaning even though her shocked state increases the susceptibility to a stroke, given her high blood pressure:

> "Don't think that was just an uppity Negro woman," he said. "That was the whole colored race which will no longer take your condescending pennies. That was your black double. . . . What all this means," he said, "is that the old world is gone. The old manners are obsolete and your graciousness is not worth a damn."

The confrontation, however, proves both psychologically and physically too jarring to lead her to a higher level of self-awareness, for as she collapses she reverts back to her childhood plantation life whose passing she had never accepted. Ironically, then, Julian learns that the lesson has proven costly, for as he bends over her crumpled body his dependence surfaces in the childlike manner in which he addresses her: "Darling, sweetheart"; "Mamma, Mamma." The full implications of O'Connor's technique of twinning now become apparent: just as the parallelism with the Negro woman shattered Julian's mother's social pretensions, so, too, does the parallelism with a four-year-old child disclose Julian's hidden dependence. Both childishly attempt against their mother's wishes to gain the attention of a person of the opposite race and, in a sense, exchange mothers when they sit beside the other's mother on the bus. The "*mental bubble in which he established himself when he could not bear to be a part of what was going on around him*" (italics mine) bursts, leaving Julian alone with the realization that his security depended on the existence of his now-dead mother. The heavily connotative diction of the final two sentences of the story indicates that rather than rising to maturity and knowledge Julian will always be weighted down in a life tormented by guilt and horror: "The lights drifted farther away the faster he ran and his feet moved numbly as if they carried him nowhere. The tide of darkness seemed to sweep him back to her, postponing from moment to moment his entry into the world of guilt and sorrow." The brutality that characterizes Julian's relationship with his mother serves as the prototype for the subsequent exploration of conflict between generations throughout the cycle.

In "**Greenleaf**," O'Connor essentially repeats the themes of "**Everything That Rises Must Converge**" while shifting to the mother's point of view and emphasizing the role of the agent of destruction rather than the son's. Like Julian's mother, Mrs. May speaks in clichés, preoccupies herself with monetary concerns, and prides herself that as a widow she has sacrificed herself for the betterment of her sons. In her obsession with maintaining social status she, too, uses others—poor whites instead of Blacks—as a vehicle for rationalizing her innate sense of superiority. For example, when the Greenleaf boys were younger she patronizingly handed down to them her own sons' old clothes and toys. She also senses that her higher position in society is threatened, for the rising of Greenleaf's practical and educated sons promises to displace her own land and family just as Julian's mother's ancestral home was taken over by Negroes. Aspects of an older Julian appear in each of Mrs. May's bachelor sons, both in their thirties, who still live at home: as a misanthropic professor, Wesley indulges in sterile intellectualism; as an insurance salesman to Negroes, Scofield exploits them for his own benefit. Both respond to her overprotectiveness with the same petty contempt and impotent rage that Julian had hurled at his mother. Scofield, for example, strikes his mother where she is most vulnerable by threatening to marry a poor white who would thus inherit his mother's farm.

O'Connor parallels parents and children in this story also. As a family on the rise, the Greenleafs—their name indicating ripeness—contrast with the Mays, a family in decline. Unlike Scofield and Wesley, Greenleaf's two sons, O.T. and E.T., are competent, married with three children each, and educated in agriculture. Whereas Wesley talks about Paris and Rome but never even goes to Atlanta, and Scofield was only a Private First Class at the end of his military service, the Greenleaf boys both became sergeants overseas where they met their French wives. Refusing to admit that the

Greenleaf sons will eventually usurp the land and social position she hopes to maintain for her own sons, Mrs. May continually combats Greenleaf's innuendos to that effect. O'Connor also contrasts Mrs. May's religious attitudes with Mrs. Greenleaf's. Although the latter's primitive "prayer healing" appears grotesque and superstitious, it originates from the genuine conviction that her concern for suffering mankind carries some efficacy. On the other hand, Mrs. May is repulsed by this emotional outpouring directed at strangers, for she believes religion should be left at the church door and used only for such social ends as meeting prospective wives for her sons.

O'Connor develops the agent of the violent climax in "**Greenleaf**" more elaborately than in the first story, for, unlike the Negro woman, the bull acquires several levels of symbolism. On one level, it reflects an extension of the twinning technique: the bull—a scrub bull and therefore of inferior stock—poses a threat to the breeding habits of Mrs. May's herd just as the virility of the Greenleafs—whom Mrs. May thinks of as "scrub human"—threatens her conservative sense of a static class society. The bull gnaws at her hedges just as she feels that the Greenleafs have been gradually displacing her over the last fifteen years; the bull patiently waits for her until finally charging in anger just as Greenleaf has followed her demands patiently until finally losing his temper on the day she is killed. The bull is associated with the reproductive energy of the sun in her dream the night before her death just as the Greenleaf's modern milk parlor is filled with sunlight. The bull also symbolizes supernatural and reproductive forces moving Mrs. May toward regeneration: the hedge wreath that adorns the tip of his horns looks "like a menacing prickly crown"; the bull, described in the traditional religious imagery of Christ as bridegroom, listens at her bedroom window "like some patient god come down to woo her" and yet "like an uncouth country suitor"; at the end it buries its head in her lap "like a wild tormented lover." In O'Connor's Catholic world view, therefore, the bull ultimately symbolizes the life-affirming intrusion of grace which Mrs. May is free to accept or reject.

The "mental bubble" in which Mrs. May lives, however, will not permit her to recognize the clouded vision through which she perceives reality. Just as Julian's attempt to teach his mothe a lesson backfires, so does Mrs. May's attempt to get even with Greenleaf by showing that his son's lack of respect for him necessitates his killing their bull. Ironically, it is she who discovers the truth of the empty threat that she had earlier hurled at her sons, "you'll find out what *Reality* is when it's too late." Like Julian's mother who becomes disoriented at the moment of death, Mrs. May stands immobile in "freezing unbelief" like someone "whose sight had been suddenly restored but who finds the light unbearable." Any glimpse of self-revelation that penetrates her egoism is rejected, and the violent impact of the bull simply amounts to a collision that ends in death rather than a convergence with the divine that could effect a rising to a new level of consciousness. That her death occurs so violently stresses the degree to which O'Connor thinks that the ego must be jolted to perhaps glimpse the potential moment of epiphany.

In the opening of the next story, **"A View of the Woods,"** O'Connor signals the continuation of her exploration of the narrow-minded self-righteousness of Mrs. May in the protagonist, Fortune, for he is first described as sitting on the bumper of his car in a tree-surrounded clearing just as Mrs. May sat on the hood of her car in the tree-surrounded field where the bull charged at the end of **"Greenleaf."** Older than Mrs. May, Fortune has had to face what Mrs. May only dreaded, the threat of a poor white like Greenleaf inheriting his property, for the man his daughter married against his wishes farms his land. To assert his sense of class superiority over Pitts, his son-in-law, who like Greenleaf has seven children, Fortune repeatedly sells prize pasture land to businessmen set upon developing the area for commercial interests rather than to Pitts. To insure, moreover, that Pitts does not inherit his land, he secretly arranges in his will to leave everything in trust to his favorite grandchild, Mary Fortune Pitts, with his lawyer as executor—an act parallel to Mrs. May's decision to entail her property so that her sons could not leave it to their wives if they married. Ironically, however, the proud attempts of both to perpetuate their wills after death are defeated, for the Greenleafs clearly are in the ascendance and Mary's death will provide Pitts with the property by default.

Although Fortune's daughter—like Julian, Scofield, and Wesley—feels bound by duty to tolerate her father, O'Connor shifts the emphasis of the conflict between generations from parent and child to grandparent and child in this story. In spite of the seventy-year gap in age, Fortune and Mary are spiritually close in their strength of will. Furthermore, O'Connor's twinning technique makes Fortune and Mary parallel figures: physically, Mary's face is "a small replica of the old man's," and temperamentally she possesses his same stubborn pride in resisting his determination to sell the lawn between the house and the highway. Only this recalcitrance and the seemingly willing acquiescence in allowing her father to whip her interfere with Fortune's conception of her as his double. To eliminate these imperfections he decides to teach her a lesson that, as with Julian in **"Everything That Rises Must Converge,"** ironically reveals that he shares the faults he accuses Pitts of having: "a nasty temper and . . . unreasonable resentments." In the violent struggle with Mary in which he assumes the punitive role of Pitts that he so detests, Fortune's exclamation that "this ought to teach you a good lesson" rings hollow as he looks "down into the face that was his own but had dared to call itself Pitts." The spirit that he had intended to inculcate into

Mary rages so violently when she kicks and claws him that he must strangle her in defense, only to suffer a stroke himself from the physical ordeal and the shock that his ever-spiraling capacity to rationalize his singularity has been deflated by his common identity with the character stains of Pitts.

In **"A View of the Woods"** O'Connor also elaborates on a theme only tangentially included elsewhere in the cycle: her questioning whether the progress of modern civilization proves that man spirals ever upward toward greater spiritual consciousness. Whereas the urban highrises that the bus journeys through in **"Everything That Rises Must Converge"** reveal the nightmare of the modern city, and the uniformity of the Greenleaf twins who seem "like one man in two skins" and live in a modern, warehouse-like home represents the hollowness of the middle class of the future, Fortune's conviction that he would not "let a cow pasture interfere with progress" signals the industrial exploitation and commercial dominance of modern life. Fortune's wedding of his patriotic cliches with "his duty to sell the lot . . . to insure the future" demonstrates the devitalization of the linguistic basis upon which American ideals are articulated. Envisioning the displacement of the woods by supermarkets, highways, and motels within five years, Fortune rationalizes the sensibility of selling the lawn plot because of the wealth and fame he will achieve as the founder and developer of a new vacation area. The Satanic overtones surrounding the entrepreneur who purchases the plot to build a gas station reinforce O'Connor's attitude; the spiritual emptiness of his combination country store, filling station, and dance hall is deftly suggested "by a field of old used- car bodies" and a line of tombstones for sale that border it on either side. The "huge yellow monster" bulldozer systematically "gorging itself on clay" at the beginning and ending of the story symbolizes Fortune's rationalistic pursuit of his unnatural designs on both Mary and the woods.

By locating her limited omniscient point of view in the younger member of the generational conflict in **"The Enduring Chill,"** O'Connor explores similar situations from a different angle: like Mrs. May in **"Greenleaf,"** Asbury's widowed mother has put her two children through college by running a dairy farm; like Fortune toward his daughter and son-in-law in **"A View of the Woods,"** Asbury plans to triumph over his mother through his death. Returning home after attending college in the North and failing to succeed in as an artist in New York City, Asbury follows the same self-righteous pattern of O'Connor's other pseudo-intellectuals in his determination to introduce his mother to "reality" in order to "assist her in the process of growing up." Convinced that he suffers from a fatal disease promising imminent death, he hopes to accomplish this lesson through a lengthy letter to be read after his burial, accusing her of ruining his imagination and talent without destroying "the desire for these things." His equation of this letter with Kafka's letter to his father, as well as the attempt to simulate a Yeatsian style in its writing, deflate his pretentious, self-serving critical faculty. The picture in his room of "a maiden chained to a rock" epitomizes the sterile cliches in which his romantic self-pity envisions his fate.

The root of Asbury's inability to adjust to reality, however, lies not so much in his pose as an artist as in his dependency on his mother. Like Julian of **"Everything That Rises Must Converge,"** except that he has attempted rather than merely projected an artistic career, Asbury struggles to combat the domineering mother set upon insuring that her child remains an appendage of herself. From the opening of the story, when in response to his mother's suggestion that he remove his coat he defensively shouts, "I'm old enough to know when I want to take my coat off," to the conclusion, all his actions stem from his need to defy her: he attempts to weaken her power by encouraging the Black dairy workers, Morgan and Randall, to break her smoking ban in the milk house; he irritates her Protestant mistrust of Catholicism by asking her to send for a Jesuit when he thinks he is dying. Even his approaching death, which he regards as "his greatest triumph" and a gift from "his god, Art to compensate for his artistic failure, was precipitated by his vain attempt to convince Morgan and Randall to break his mother's major rule by following his example and drinking unpasteurized milk. The significant experience he imagines death holds for him never arries, for his supposedly fatal illness is eventually diagnosed as undulant fever whose symptoms will recur periodically, ironically promising that he, rather than his mother, will be left with an "enduring chill." Compared to the tragic portrayal of Fortune's projected triumph through his death in **"A View of the Woods,"** O'Connor's treatment in **"The Enduring Chill"** proves devastatingly comic.

O'Connor also imparts to the title another level of meaning through her development of the manifestation of the supernatural. Although Father Finn's formulaic apologetics are satirized along with Asbury's fashionable agnosticism, Goetz's Eastern philosophy, and Father Vogle's corrupt asceticism, he does diagnose Asbury's spiritual dilemma: "The Holy Ghost will not come until you see yourself as you are— a lazy ignorant conceited youth." The reference to the Holy Ghost, who is frequently represented in religious imagery as a bird, can be paralleled to Asbury's earlier figurative association of his imagination with a hawk and his illusion that the water stains on the ceiling above his bed resemble "a fierce bird with spread wings" and an icicle in its beak. The continued presence of the bird above him which he felt "was there for some purpose" functions, like the bull in **"Greenleaf,"** as the ever-available agent through which grace can be revealed. Just as the emblem of his imagination is encaged within his derivative writing style, however, the Holy Spirit descends ultimately "emblazoned in ice in-

stead of fire," because Asbury's agnostic pose leads him to collide rather than converge with this manifestation of the divine; his spiritual as well as artistic "mental bubbles" burst, leaving him frozen like Julian in his incapacity to realize the implications of his revelation.

In the fifth and sixth stories, **"The Comforts of Home"** and **"The Lame Shall Enter First,"** O'Connor focuses on the conflict generated by a parent's decision to bring home a delinquent to attempt rehabilitation. In both instances, however, the intruder proves incorrigible while upsetting the domestic tranquility and threatening the security of an only child. In **"The Comforts of Home"** Thomas and his mother resemble the parent-child types recurrent throughout the cycle: a bachelor at thirty-five, the pseudo-intellectual Thomas writes for the local Historical Society and still resides at the home of his widowed mother for whom he feels simultaneously both love and hate. Her decision to return home from her paternalistic jail visit bringing a nymphomaniac, Star Drake, to whom she has taken a box of candy— "her favorite nice thing to do"—unsettles Thomas, who condescendingly labels Star Drake a "moral moron" and petulantly warns that he will leave if she remains. When his mother's excessive sentimentalism leads her to conclude that she would not send Thomas back to jail if he had suffered like Star Drake and that the girl can thus share their home, Thomas, realizing that he cannot forfeit the comforts of home, wallows in comparing his own impotent efforts to remove the girl with the ruthless authority his father would have successfully exerted. In the resulting conflict O'Connor explores the Freudian implications of the parent-child types recurrent throughout the cycle: Thomas's Oedipal fantasy, his repressed desire for Star Drake, and his overcompensation for the failure to assume a masculine role.

On another level, though, O'Connor continues from **"The Enduring Chill"** her treatment of the sterility of the overly rationalistic view of life. She makes fun of the professional attempts of the psychiatrists and lawyer to categorize Star Drake's condition by satirically noting their verdict: she "was a psychopathic personality, not insane enough for the asylum, not criminal enough for the jail, not stable enough for society." She develops her theme through Thomas, who parallels Asbury in regarding the devil as "only a manner of speaking," but contrasts with Asbury's agnosticism in his Pelagian belief that Star Drake represents "blameless corruption because there was no responsible faculty behind it." Soon, however, he realizes the fatuity of accounting for her as an "unendurable form of innocence," for she unsettles his sense of order by disturbing him in a way that lies beyond "his power of analysis." On the other hand, his mother seems to advance beyond the simplicity of her sentimentalism and to realize the tainted nature of man, for the experience of Star Drake plunges her, like Mrs. Greenleaf, "into mourning for the world." When Thomas cannot mature beyond his rationalistic need to discern a world perfectly ordered for good and learn to accept O'Connor's belief in man's need of God's grace, he damns not only Star Drake "but the entire order of the universe that made her possible." In his desperation at the end he fires at Star Drake, hoping that the blast will "bring an end to evil in the world" and restore the "peace of perfect order." His shot, however, only multiplies the disorder, and the arrival of the sheriff whose brain works "instantly like a calculating machine" only reinforces the absurdity of attempting to account for experience through reason alone.

In **"The Lame Shall Enter First,"** O'Connor transfers the limited omniscient point of view and the brunt of the irony to the parent and develops more fully a similar triangle of characters involved in the same plot situation. A widower of one year, Sheppard is more excited about what "*he* could do" (italics mine) for a fourteen-year-old delinquent, Rufus Johnson, than for his neglected ten-year-old son, Norton, who has not yet adjusted to his mother's death—a fact that Sheppard, unable to account for rationally, concludes reflects his son's selfishness. Very much aware that he is "busy helping other people" during his volunteer counseling at the reformatory, Sheppard is drawn toward the delinquent not out of sentimentality like Thomas's mother but because Rufus, the most intelligent and deprived boy he has worked with, represents a vehicle through which he can self-righteously demonstrate the efficacy and kindness of his good works. When all efforts to improve Rufus are met with resistance, Sheppard continually rationalizes to avoid confronting his own limitations and ineffectiveness. When the boy shows hostility toward him, he concludes that Rufus is only upholding his own pride by pretending not to like him; when the boy seems bored, Sheppard self-contentedly reflects in his inflated manner that Rufus is secretly learning the essential thing: "that his benefactor was impervious to insult and that there were no cracks in his armor of kindness and patience"; when the boy mocks Sheppard's efforts by breaking into a home, he decides as Fortune did with Mary that he only needs to be firmer to teach Rufus "that he could not treat with impunity someone who had shown him nothing but kindness."

O'Connor's satiric depiction of the Pelagian conception of man is continued and more fully developed in this story in Sheppard. Steeped in the modern theories of counseling and social work, Sheppard rationalizes that Rufus's delinquency results from his unfortunate backwoods upbringing by his fundamentalist grandfather and his abrupt transplantation to the city. To counteract these deterministic forces that have misshapen his values, Sheppard resorts to such secular means as encyclopedias, a telescope, new clothes, and a good home life to rehabilitate Rufus. In all his attempts to save him, however, he can never acknowledge what for O'Connor is the essential prerequisite for reform, God's grace; instead,

when Rufus warns that only Jesus can save him, Sheppard appeals to the boy's intelligence, claiming that the Bible is only "'for cowards, people who are afraid to stand on their own feet and figure things out for themselves.'" Even when at one point he feels "a momentary full despair as if he were faced with some elemental warping of nature that had happened too long ago to be corrected now," he refuses to ascribe Rufus's defects to any cause that cannot be altered by man. His rationalizations that Rufus's incorrigible behavior was compensation for his club foot, O'Connor's symbol for original sin, and that an orthopedic shoe can rectify the deformity epitomize for O'Connor the absurdity of his secular optimism. Even at the end when Rufus threatens Sheppard's position in the community by telling a newspaper reporter about his atheistic beliefs, Sheppard clings to the same view, telling Rufus: "You're not evil, you're mortally confused. You don't have to make up for that foot, you don't have to. . . ." Rufus, however, has proven to be a more formidable opponent to Sheppard than Star Drake was to Thomas, and Sheppard appears to be on the brink of revelation after Rufus is taken away, for the litany-like repetition of "I did more for him than I did for my own child" does seem to burst the "mental bubble" of his self-righteous claim that "I have nothing to reproach myself with." The epiphany is aborted, though, and, like Mrs. May who at the moment of death resembled "a person whose sight has been suddenly restored but who finds the light unbearable," Sheppard "closed his eyes against the revelation." He cannot compromise his hopelessly optimistic humanitarianism to admit that man must acknowledge spiritual lameness to understand his nature. Norton's suicide, then, only reinforces the folly of Sheppard's position, for, ironically, Norton does launch a flight into space—symbolic for Sheppard of the infinite capacity of man's intelligence—but Norton's flight is to his mother and not the moon, and with Jesus and not in a space ship.

In **"Revelation,"** the final story of the cycle as well as the last one written, O'Connor manages to cluster together motifs present in the other stories and to round out themes recurrent throughout the cycle. The assembly of middle-class whites, lower-class whites, and Negroes in the story amounts to a microcosm of the world depicted in the cycle, and their congregating together in a doctor's waiting room reiterates the motif of the lingering, often violent, effects of physical and psychological illness, representative for O'Connor of man's tainted condition: Julian's mother's high blood pressure, Wesley's rheumatic fever, Fortune's heart condition, Asbury's undulant fever, Star Drake's nymphomania, Rufus's club foot, and Claud's ulcerous leg. Ruby Turpin, paralleling the narrow-minded, self-righteous characters of the other stories, is the quintessential egoist, continually thanking Jesus for her superior character:

"If it's one thing I am," Mrs. Turpin said with feeling, "it's grateful. When I think who all I could have been besides myself and what all I got, a little of everything, and a good disposition besides, I just feel like shouting, Thank you, Jesus, for making everything the way it is! It could have been different!!" For one thing, somebody else could have got Claud. At the thought of this, she was flooded with gratitude and a terrible pang of joy ran through her. "Oh thank you, Jesus, Jesus, thank you!" she cried aloud.

Her more-than-coincidental resemblance to Julian's mother of **"Everything That Rises Must Converge"** seems to explain O'Connor's decision to frame the cycle with these two stories. In spite of being middle-aged and overweight, both regard themselves as attractive; just as Julian's mother considers herself the only "lady" who attends the reducing class because no one else wears a hat and gloves, Ruby confirms her socially superior status by noticing the shabbiness and gaudiness of the other patients' shoes; just as Julian's mother enters the bus "as if she were going into a drawing room where everyone had been waiting for her," Ruby enters the doctor's waiting room and is shocked to find no one willing to change seats to accommodate Claud and her; both begin a general conversation for the benefit of all and manage to sustain almost a monologue; just as Julian's mother patronizingly offers the Negro boy a penny, Ruby patronizingly explains to a Negro delivery boy how to push a button to ring for the nurse; and through bland complacency both enrage an adversary who triggers a violent confrontation. The opposite responses to the crisis, however, indicate the distinction between the two and signal the thematic turn in the cycle. The placing of such significance on the final story is characteristic of a short story cycle unified primarily through similarly treated themes, for in another short story cycle structured on this basis, Camus' *Exile and the Kingdom,* the final story, "The Growing Stone," also signals a thematic turn in the cycle. Whereas Julian's mother is only resorting to one of her stock phrases when, describing the disorder of the world, she says "the bottom rail is on the top," Ruby is on the brink of accepting the deflation of her egotistic ordering of the world and the grace concomitant with such an insight moments before her vision when she defiantly shouts, "Put that bottom rail on top."

Ruby also resembles other characters in the cycle. Her habit of naming and ordering the classes of people represents the same obsession with class distinctions Mrs. May and Fortune indulge in and, like them, she feels more hostility for "white trash" than Negroes, commenting "there's a heap of things worse than a nigger." When the "white trash" woman says that all Negroes should be sent back to Africa, Ruby and the stylish lady smugly exchange glances with each other, affirming an enlightened liberalism toward Negroes much like the progressive racial poses Julian and Asbury af-

fect. Ultimately, however, Ruby's paternalism backfires on her as it does on Asbury, for when Asbury in desperation seeks communion with Morgan and Randall and Ruby turns to her Black workers for a candid evaluation of Mary Grace's accusation, both receive only flattery in return. Moreover, Ruby's sense of being pursued by some mysterious force in Mary Grace who "knew her in some intense and personal way, beyond time and place and condition" repeats and advances the pattern throughout the cycle of the intrusion of a figure symbolic of man's tainted nature of God's healing grace: Mrs. May and the bull, Asbury and the bird on the ceiling, Thomas and Star Drake, Sheppard and Rufus.

O'Connor also signals the emphasis **"Revelation"** carries as the climactic story of the cycle by breaking the pattern of the location of her limited omniscient point of view. In the six previous stories the point of view focuses three times on the older member of the generation conflict and three times on the younger member. But in **"Revelation"** O'Connor renders the story through the indirect discourse of Ruby, who observes the conflict between the stylish lady and her daughter, Mary Grace, both of whom through the twinning technique represent the gap between Ruby and her own self-image. Through the non-verbal glances of approval and the Gospel hymn clichés that she exchanges with Mary Grace's mother, Ruby is able to identify with an idealized vision of herself as attractive, slim and fashionable; on the other hand, the persistent staring of the fat, ugly, ill-natured Mary Grace threatens Ruby with the negative self-image she avoids confronting, repeatedly attempting to assure herself that "the girl might be confusing her with somebody else." Mary Grace's violent assault and humiliation of Ruby is motivated by seeing in her a less threatening double of the coercive parent figure who has retarded her independent growth by subtly holding over her pious platitudes demanding gratefulness for all she has received. Like the other young intellectuals of the cycle, especially Asbury who likewise has been educated in the North, Mary Grace arrogantly assumes the task of teaching Ruby and, indirectly, her mother, a lesson. The violent hurling of the book and subsequent physical attack only reinforce the impotence of her rage, though, for after being restrained she rests her head in her mother's lap and her fingers grip her mother's thumb "like a baby's," paralleling Julian's final childlike exclamation of "Mama, Mama" and grotesquely epitomizing the treatment of the profound cruelty involved in the generational struggle of parents and children throughout the cycle.

The significance of the placement of **"Revelation"** as the final story of the cycle is explained by the fact that it does not end at its violent climax like the six previous stories but continues on to show the effects of Ruby's epiphany. The degree to which Ruby's identity has been unsettled is reflected in her surprise upon returning home to find the farm unaltered. When she lies down, only to see the image of a wart hog, her state of shock eases and she begins to realize the implications of her revelation: "she had been singled out for the message, though there was trash in the room to whom it might justly have been applied. The full force of this fact struck her only now. . . . The message had been given to Ruby Turpin, a respectable, hard-working church-going woman." Throughout the afternoon she wrestles with this realization, scowling at the ceiling "as if there were unintelligible handwriting" on it: unlike Asbury, however, she is able to decipher and accept what she sees there. The request that Claud, who previously had amounted to nothing more than her satellite, kiss her demonstrates the dread in which she dwells and the awakened need for love she feels. Not until her vision at the pig parlor, though, does she fully understand and accept the grace offered her. Mary Grace's name suggests her symbolic function as the vehicle through which God's grace intrudes. There in a tree-surrounded, sun-drenched open area reminiscent of the field in which the bull charges Mrs. May and the clearing in which Fortune beats Mary, the spiritual manifestation of Ruby's epiphany is delivered and not aborted.

O'Connor's paralleling of the pig parlor with the doctor's waiting room reinforces the grotesqueness of Ruby's spiritual slothfulness and her need for grace: the pig parlor is described as "a square of concrete as large as a small room"; the same "a-gruntin and a-rootin and a-groanin" sounds are heard in both; Ruby commands the arena of eight hogs before her just as she had attempted to command the attention of the eight patients. In the last fling of defiance at her revelation, Ruby squirts the eyes of the fat, slouching sow with the water hose, demanding to know just how it parallels her and not a slovenly "white trash" person. It is at this moment that the surroundings take on "a mysterious hue" and Ruby gazes down at the hogs "as if through the very heart of mystery":

> A visionary light settled in her eyes. She saw the streak as a vast swinging bridge extending upward from the earth through a field of living fire. Upon it a vast horde of souls were rumbling toward heaven. There were whole companies of white trash, clean for the first time in their lives, and bands of black niggers in white robes, and battalions of freaks and lunatics shouting and clapping and leaping like frogs. And bringing up the end of the procession was a tribe of people whom she recognized at once as those who, like herself and Claud, had always had a little of everything and the God-given wit to use it right. She leaned forward to observe them closer. They were marching behind the others with great dignity, accountable as they had always been for good order and common sense and respectable behavior. They alone were on key. Yet she

could see by their shocked and altered faces that even their virtues were being burned away.

Ironically, Ruby finds herself at the opposite end of the bridge from which her earlier self-satisfied belief in God's approval placed her, for the "bottom rail" is shown to be "on top." The vision serves as the synthesizing vehicle for the cycle, bringing into focus the leveling of the succession of self-righteous hypocrites whose inflated "mental bubbles" obscure their vision, generating a self-conception based less on reality than that of such "white trash" figures as Greenleaf and Pitts, such Negroes as Randall and Morgan, such "lunatics" as Star Drake and Rufus. Unlike the protagonists of the other stories, however, Ruby ultimately accepts her spiritual lameness and converges rather than collides with the grace offered in her moment of epiphany. As she walks away from the pig parlor at the end, the noise of the invisible crickets sounds to her like a hallelujah chorus; she has risen to a new level of consciousness where she can see the world as infused with spirit.

Again and again [O'Connor] dramatizes the violent manifestation of grace to a spiritually empty, narrow-minded egoist, unbalancing him to the point that he cannot regain his equilibrium. The cumulative effect of her ironic leveling of self-righteous figures in varying contexts emphasizes her religious belief in man's spiritual lameness and need for God's grace.

—*Harbour Winn*

The demonstrated interconnectedness of these seven stories culminating with **"Revelation"** establishes that O'Connor intended *Everything That Rises Must Converge* to be much more than a mere collection of randomly selected and arranged stories. A consideration of **"The Partridge Festival,"** the story she decided to exclude from the cycle, as well as **"Parker's Back"** and **"Judgement Day,"** the two stories added by her editor after her death, only reinforces this viewpoint. Since it was written and published during the eight-year period from 1956 to 1964 in which the other seven stories were written and published and originally intended to be part of the cycle, **"The Partridge Festival,"** as might be expected, closely resembles the included stories in character types, point of view, themes, and motifs. In Calhoun, O'Connor maintains her consistently comic and ironic treatment of the would-be intellectual returned home hostile to the materialistic values fostered by his great-grandfather and Partridge. Satirizing Calhoun's elaborate psychological theorizing about Singleton whom he had never met, O'Connor shows that the murderer Calhoun, cast as a scapegoat for the commercialism of the townspeople, is no more than a mentally deranged, lecherous old man. As with Asbury in **"The Enduring Chill,"** O'Connor particularly mocks the inflated, sterile phrases Calhoun as an amateur writer resorts to in his romantic defense of Singleton: "He was an individualist. . . . A man who would not allow himself to be pressed into the mold of his inferiors. A non-conformist. He was a man of depth living among caricatures and they finally drove him mad, unleashed all his violence on themselves. An elaborate paralleling of characters provides the basic technical method for thematic development in this story also: Calhoun consciously identifies with the characterization he superimposes on Singleton, vicariously hoping "to mitigate his own guilt" for the devotion to commercialism his successful salesman's job represents; Because of Mary Elizabeth's similar identification with Singleton and her fledgling attempt at writing, she and Calhoun recognize "that in their common kinship with him [Singleton], a kinship with each other was unavoidable"; and, ultimately, Calhoun sees in his own reflection in Mary Elizabeth's glasses that in spite of his self-righteous attempt to remain aloof from Partridge's commercialism, he ironically resembles the "round, innocent, undistinguished" visage of the master-merchant great-grandfather he had condescendingly repudiated. (Mary Elizabeth's name relates her to the three other Marys of the cycle, all of whom exhibit a similar steadfastness in self-righteously asserting the concept of their own infallibility: Mary Fortune Pitts of **"A View of the Woods,"** Mary George of **"The Enduring Chill,"** and Mary Grace of **"Revelation."**) The concluding moment of epiphany, as in the first six stories of the cycle, is again aborted, for the incorrigible self-image Calhoun sees "fixed him where he was" and foreshadows the future azalea festivals he will never escape from. Clearly, the story as it was intended parallels the other stories in the cycle; moreover, considering the patterned movement of the location of the limited omniscient point of view from parent to child in one story after another, **"The Partridge Festival"** seems to have been intended to contrast with **"A View of the Woods,"** for while the former focuses on the perspective of a great-grandchild, the latter focuses on a grandfather. Any explanation for O'Connor's decision to omit the story from the cycle can only involve speculation; perhaps she made what would seem an appropriately astute aesthetic judgement that **"The Partridge Festival"** simply lacked the suggestive thematic richness of the other stories in its all-too-formulaic working out of related thematic considerations. In any case, the story does bear out the theory that during this eight-year period O'Connor was composing individual stories with a cyclic framework in mind, even when one of them did not perhaps satisfy her aesthetic criteria for inclusion.

Just as the similarity of **"The Partridge Festival"** to theme and technique in the cycle reinforces the interlocking relationship of the seven included stories, so, too, can the differences of **"Parker's Back"** and **"Judgement Day"** further substantiate the structural unity of the collection. Written in the last few months of her life and later added to the cycle by O'Connor's editor, both of these stories resemble the others in the way any works of the same author reflect the stylistic and thematic concerns of a single creator. The particular method and thematic emphasis of the two, however, do not correspond to the stories intended for inclusion in the cycle and, therefore, hinder an understanding of the structural basis of the cycle if considered part of it. **"Parker's Back"** best illustrates this point, for such basic recurring elements in the other stories as sickness, the arrogance of a pseudo-intellectual, the struggle between social classes, the conflict between generations, and the twinning of characters are absent. And although **"Judgement Day"** contains these elements, they are tangential to its development. More importantly, **"Judgement Day"** relates less significantly to the cycle than to O'Connor's favorite story, **"The Geranium,"** for **"Judgement Day"** represents O'Connor's final revision and expansion of the earlier story written ten years before the first story of the cycle was even published.

Considering only the published version of *Everything That Rises Must Converge,* though, **"Parker's Back"** and **"Judgement Day"** differ from the other stories in such cardinal aspects as tone and point of view. Although O'Connor does render the indirect discourse of the main character of each story from a limited omniscient viewpoint, she mixes omniscient commentary with it to a much greater extent than in the others, for the irony in these two does not hinge primarily on the protagonist's unwitting revelation of his own self-righteousness. As a result, O'Connor's tone toward Parker and Tanner is more sympathetic than to the seven protagonists of the cycle: Parker's allegorized search for meaning is motivated by a singular earnestness that leads him ultimately to assume the Christ-like burden—literally, the image of the Byzantine Christ is tattooed on his back—and to accept his Biblical name and the prophetic vision concomitant with it; Tanner's steadfast compassion for Coleman, his desire to return south for burial and his faith in a judgment day lead him at the end to the vision of physical resurrection that overshadows his death. As a result, the brunt of O'Connor's irony falls in **"Parker's Back"** on such minor figures as the commercial artist who desecrates religious images and the fundamentalistic Sarah Ruth who negates the joy of life and in **"Judgement Day"** on Tanner's vain daughter who helps her father only begrudgingly and the dehumanized Black actor who murders Tanner. Clearly, then, **"Parker's Back"** and **"Judgement Day"** differ from the seven stories of the cycle in theme and technique; in addition, their placement as the eighth and ninth stories upsets the placing of **"Revelation"** as the final story and climax of the book. That the two stories O'Connor worked on after completing the cycle diverge from the pattern of the included ones further supports viewing *Everything That Rises Must Converge* as a collection of purposely selected and arranged stories.

Throughout *Everything That Rises Must Converge* O'Connor varies the location of her limited omniscient point of view and interweaves parallel thematic patterns to link together the seven stories. Again and again she dramatizes the violent manifestation of grace to a spiritually empty, narrow-minded egoist, unbalancing him to the point that he cannot regain his equilibrium. The cumulative effect of her ironic leveling of self-righteous figures in varying contexts emphasizes her religious belief in man's spiritual lameness and need for God's grace. Ruby Turpin in **"Revelation"** exemplifies man's capacity to respond to this instant of direct illumination and assume his role in what O'Connor calls "our slow participation" in Christ's redemption. This eschatological view of mankind that she shares with Teilhard finds an apt structural vehicle for expression in the short story cycle, for the repeated exploration of protagonists who collide rather than converge with the grace offered in their moment of epiphany conveys her sense of the continual spiritual upheaval necessary if man's consciousness is to rise to converge with God at Point Omega.

Bryan N. Wyatt (essay date Spring 1992)

SOURCE: "The Domestic Dynamics of Flannery O'Connor: *Everything That Rises Must Converge*," in *Twentieth Century Literature,* Vol. 38, No. 1, Spring, 1992, pp. 66-88.

[*In the following essay, Wyatt discusses the domestic center of O'Connor's* Everything That Rises Must Converge.]

By her own avowal, Flannery O'Connor writes from a fixed perspective of Christian orthodoxy. "I write the way I do," she insists, "because (not though) I am a Catholic" and adds that all her stories "are about the action of grace on a character who is not very willing to accept it."

Her view that her stories are all of a piece clearly is not shared by many of her readers and critics, especially those outside her faith who have interpreted her works in ways that she would consider severe distortions of her materials and aims. For example, a variety of O'Connor's critics have expressed reservations ranging from doubt as to whether *any* religious intent is realized in her writings to the suspicion that her artistry is in fact not theological but demonic.

If O'Connor's fiction fails to resonate sufficiently her spiritual theme, part of the reason may lie in her approach to writing. Discussing this approach, she emphasizes her greater attention to the technical demands of the stories than to other

criteria affecting the formation and portrayal of her characters. Similarly, to the charge that, morally considered, her characters are typically too ambiguous to serve as either heroes or villains, she offers the defense of her affinity for Henry James's concept of felt life, holding that the writer's moral sense and dramatic sense must coincide and that in the best fiction the moral sense will thus emerge intact.

Related to this orientation, in its effect of moderating the religious theme in her works, is the very catholicity, the encompassing embrace, of her outlook. Her protagonists may not be able to support the grace that befalls them, but she loves them nonetheless. Compounding the problem is the fact that she loves the *an*tagonists too and loves them just as much—understandably so, since these are modified into the protagonists of other works and thereby become the objects of the searching grace that finds them lacking. O'Connor confronts a drastically fallen world in which even the remnants of religious belief are vanishing and the instruments and recipients of grace themselves may be as sordid as the damned. She explains:

> I am a Catholic peculiarly possessed of the modern consciousness, that thing Jung describes as unhistorical, solitary, and guilty. To possess this *within* the Church is to bear a burden, the necessary burden for the conscious Catholic. It's to feel the contemporary situation at the ultimate level. I think that the Church is the only thing that is going to make the terrible world we are coming to endurable; the only thing that makes the Church endurable is that it is somehow the body of Christ and that on this we are fed. It seems a fact that you have to suffer as much from the Church as for it but if you believe in the divinity of Christ, you have to cherish the world at the same time that you struggle to endure it. This may explain the lack of bitterness in [my] stories.

To feel *ultimately* the contemporary world, though it is inexorably devolving to an unbearable state, as nonetheless the sole precinct and medium for the teleological realization of mankind's salvation through Christ's redemption is, perhaps inevitably, to possess a concomitant ethos riven with ambivalence—constraining love for the thing despised, cherishing of a world beyond endurance, a world of the spiritually blind, the degenerate, the odious. O'Connor's writings belie neither such an ethos nor her embracing of such a world, the world her fiction limns, one whose future inhabitants, she fears, "will know nothing of mystery or manners."

This paraphrase of the Henry James speculation on the young woman of the future charts the principal dimensions of her fiction, the nonreceptivity toward the mystery of grace by a society ever less mindful of manners (as codified *caritas*), ever less observant of the gestures and rites nourishing social interaction. At the level of realism O'Connor's fiction dramatizes the clashes among her defective characters in the domain of manners, baring their frailties—selfishness, bigotry, pride—and their dubiousness as vessels of grace. It is no wonder that the supernatural action of grace, since it is unrecognized by those it touches, is also too often scarcely detected by her readers, unless O'Connor employs some seemingly obtrusive authorial device to underscore it, thereby accenting the allegorical component of her work, but, more often than not, weakening its artistry. Both her novels are obviously "marred" by this alleged disjunction, as are several of the pieces in her first short-story collection, *A Good Man Is Hard to Find,* including the title story and, to some extent, what well may have been O'Connor's favorite of all her writings, **"The Artificial Nigger."**

In the last-written and most realistic of her books, *Everything That Rises Must Converge,* the disjunction is present but not so pronounced, the supernatural impress not so stark, as in the earlier works. The general domestication of the supernal, its attenuation to an appropriate blend with the "manners" component signaling social decay, is indeed one measure of the greater realism of this posthumous collection. And the central locus for this interplay of mystery and manners, the arena wherein the social skirmishes erupt and find resolution, is unremittingly the *domestic* one: the home, the family.

We may say, parenthetically and with due qualification, that the cohesive and nurturing tendency suggested by the centrality of the domestic theme in her stories is one clear index of the feminine consciousness in O'Connor's canon. Another is her deference to females as protagonists, and if not protagonists, at least stabilizers of the domestic realm, keepers of the house. Feministically viewed, an arguable axiom of O'Connor's works is that male can appear as protagonist or focal character only if he (1) is not the functional (though perhaps titular) family leader or head of household and (2) if head, has no wife alive or physically present.

With a woman, then, established principally as monarch of the domicile (a woman typically bereft, betrayed, despised), the domestic theme in O'Connor's last original collection may be examined, with attention to its sundry functions as medium and catalyst for her characteristic concerns.

The title story, **"Everything That Rises Must Converge,"** is in its consuming secularity the most uniformly realistic of the volume, and as such provides a useful paradigm. Initially there is the conspicuous paradox of *rising descent,* the rising and convergence of a suppressed group (blacks) in so-

ciety, while at the same time the society itself is devolving toward *the terrible world we are coming to*—a spiritual decay signified metaphorically by the themes of physical sordidness, displacement, hostility. This complex of degeneration marks a world "too much with us" today, presaging the irresonant, faithless world of tomorrow. The domestic arena becomes in effect a synecdoche of this transfiguration while providing a resistance to it, a tension affording possibilities for desirable modes of human interaction.

Julian's mother (note how O'Connor's women are typically designated by their *familial* roles—*Mrs.* May, his mother, Parker's *wife,* etc.), displaced from the elegant world of her childhood, suffers for attempting to practice her class-conscious mannerisms in a world that is "in a mess everywhere," where social convergence has blurred class distinctions, where "the bottom rail is on the top." Her displacement is heightened by her present status of living with her son Julian in a modest apartment in a neighborhood once fashionable but now deteriorated and dingy, as contrasted with her sense of her real home, the haven of her childhood, her grandfather's "mansion," toward which she reverts in the confusion of her fatal stroke at the story's end.

It has been said that for O'Connor home is always heaven. This is no doubt true in the light of her ultimate view of present society, but this story conveys no palpable awareness of the celestial home (as does, say, the later **"Judgement Day"**). Here it is only the lost mansion, not heaven, that the mother appears in the end to seek, her heritage—sold, ruined, possessed by Negroes. Significantly, Julian has an obsessive attachment to the house, regularly dreaming about it, assuring himself that only he, not his mother, could have appreciated it, and finally thinking "bitterly of the house that had been lost for him."

Lost *for* him: the symbolic import of the house is enlarged. Of the mother's many sacrifices for Julian, which he rationalizes as demanded in compensation for her ineptness, that of the ancestral home is primal and encompassing. One surmises that the house was lost for Julian's *sake,* that whatever legacy there was to his mother from its sale went to augment the funds scraped together by her in the struggle to better her son's welfare, as her own was largely neglected ("her teeth had gone unfilled so that his could be straightened"). In any case, at another level the house was Julian's link to his mother's world and world view, her manners and values; though decayed when he saw it as a child, "it remained in his mind as his mother had known it."

Clearly her vision determines and controls his own, here as in other respects, despite his professing that he is "not dominated by his mother." His very being, in fact, seems little more than a reaction to his perception of hers. "Everything that gave her pleasure," we are led to believe, "was small and depressed him," and

> in spite of her, he had turned out so well. In spite of going to a third-rate college, he had, on his own initiative, come out with a first-rate education; in spite of growing up dominated by a small mind, he had ended up with a large one; in spite of all her foolish views, he was free of prejudice and unafraid to face facts. Most miraculous of all, instead of being blinded by love for her as she was for him, he had cut himself emotionally free of her and could see her with complete objectivity.

A judicious reading of the story would mitigate these assumptions of Julian's. Consider, for instance, the "miraculous" one that he has severed himself emotionally from his mother and does not return the "blinding" love she has for him. O'Connor is not frivolous in her use of the word *love;* it occurs with startling infrequency in her stories. She asserts,

> I don't think . . . that to be a true Christian you believe that mutual interdependence is a conceit. This is far from Catholic doctrine; in fact it strikes me as highly Protestant, a sort of justification by faith. God became not only a man, but Man. This is the mystery of Redemption and our salvation is worked out on earth according as we love one another, see Christ in one another, etc., by works. This is one reason I am chary of using the word, love, loosely. I prefer to use it in its practical forms, such as prayer, almsgiving, visiting the sick and burying the dead and so forth.

Within the family paradigm, the practical acts that issue from parental bonding, acts of caretaking, sacrificial acts, may be added to O'Connor's list, since those performing such acts (usually mothers who receive no gratitude from the children on whom their parental duties are discharged) are among the characters treated most sympathetically in her scheme of extenuation. Here Julian is correct in concluding that his mother loves him but excessive in contending that she is blinded by such love; and his cultivated ability to see her with complete objectivity looms as one of his severest frailties.

In the end what blinds her to him, beyond any recognition, is his rejection of her (evinced through various gestures, notably his viewing her as a *stranger* and contemplating abandoning her when they reach their bus stop, and culminating symbolically in his rationalized complicity with the contemporary forces that erupt in the black woman's assault on her). Ultimately this rejection is recognized for the evil that it was, and Julian tries to (re)establish genuine familial ties, discard-

ing his conception of her as a child ironically after she has reverted psychically to her childhood, as he cries, "Mamma, Mamma." But it is too late. He has succeeded utterly in his sundering denial, succeeded in making them strangers to each other. Looking gropingly at him in the end, she finds "nothing familiar" about him, finds "nothing." She has returned to *her* world, the matrix of her identity, a world that antedates and excludes him.

Earlier Julian ridicules her contention that "he hadn't even entered the real world." It is true; if her sense of herself is unsuited to the modern temper, his premature world-weariness and arrogant misanthropy insulate him from any genuine relationship, even with his mother. It is his rejection of her, his figurative killing of her, that projects the "real world" that he must enter after her death—"the world of guilt and sorrow."

"Greenleaf" presents another struggling mother with ungrateful offspring, another who is beleaguered and victimized by the changing times. The external antagonists are again placed on the domestic stage, and again the home (homestead) is in danger of being lost. Mrs. May, through industry and perseverance, has succeeded in turning the rundown country property left her by her husband into a viable dairy farm, where she is able to rear and educate her two sons. The Greenleafs, the family of the hired tenant, epitomize for her the inferior order that threatens to supplant the "decent" class of people she represents. Like Julian's mother, she is assured of her social status and character—knows "who she is"—and like Julian, her bachelor sons are peculiarly dependent on her, while mocking her in their cavalier acceptance of, and complicity in, the social change that menaces her. The older, Scofield, takes pride in being "the best nigger-insurance salesman in the county" and taunts her with the professed intent of marrying, after her death, some farm girl to take over the place, someone like Mrs. Greenleaf.

For Mrs. May, Mrs. Greenleaf epitomizes the very dregs of the unsavory Greenleaf clan, a woman who neglects her duties toward her children (e.g., by failing to keep them clean), no mother at all, who directs her attention and energies into a particularly disgusting form of "prayer healing" involving praying and moaning while sprawling on the ground. Of course, for O'Connor Mrs. Greenleaf is a grotesque near-saint, engaged in one of those practical acts—prayer—that manifest Christian love. The prospect of having the place taken over by the likes of *her* repulses Mrs. May, affording an avenue for her son's fiendishly sadistic torment of her.

It is through the Greenleafs that the central themes of the story are realized. In the case of O'Connor's supernatural emphasis, Mrs. Greenleaf and the bull (freighted with symbolism) that finally kills Mrs. May are the principal agents. With respect to the ubiquitous theme of class displacement, the spotlight shifts to the Greenleaf sons, with their foreign wives and progeny. As usual, however, these larger concerns are viewed through the domestic lens, through their impact on the home and family.

The shiftless Greenleafs have managed to produce two sons who, through (in Mrs. May's estimation) their fool's luck, their cunning application of whatever mother wit they possessed, and the largess of the federal government, have begun to rise in the world. Now situated nearby in their own dairy business, with equipment more modern than hers, they seem poised, in their "international" families, for social climbing and likely to become eventually what she calls "Society." In essence, they will be the inheritors. They have been variously successful where her own sons have failed, a fact kept before her by Mr. Greenleaf's harping upon the superior virtues of *his* sons, especially those involving family obligations: "If hit was my boys they would never have allowed their maw to go out after hired help in the middle of the night. They would have did it theirself." Unlike her sons, who are drastically different and forever squabbling, the Greenleaf twins are practically indistinguishable in name, appearance, family constituency, domicile, and disposition. Further, it is *their* bull that threatens to ruin her herd, which represents her sons' future, while the sons seem not at all to care what happens on or to the place. Her conviction that they will marry "trash" after her death and pass her bequest into the lineage of "scrub humans" leads her to entail the property, preventing their leaving it to their wives. The future and her legacy are reified in the homestead, which promises to be lost, ruined, as Julian's was.

The crushing domestic blow in O'Connor is familial rejection or denial. Her much-favored story **"The Artificial Nigger"** reaches its peak of intensity when Mr. Head denies his grandson Nelson, who is reaching out to him for protection in a moment of crisis, by saying to the child's persecutors, "I never seen him before." Perhaps it is because, in the theological tradition, the archetypal denial is yoked to the archetypal betrayal in the primal Christian family group of Christ and his disciples that the willful severing of kinship is so crucial for O'Connor. Clearly in the earlier story the episode of denial is heightened, as the estranged boy refuses thereafter to come near his grandfather; and it reaches resolution, resulting in communion, only through the symbolic influence of the Negro statue, a figure for divine grace and a type of crucifix.

In **"Greenleaf"** there is an arresting involuntary rejection by Mrs. May of her sons when she exclaims that the Greenleaf twins should have been her sons and that *her* boys should have "belonged to that woman!"—Mrs. Greenleaf. (Significantly, this outburst occurs only after one of them declares that he would not milk a cow even to save his mother's soul from hell.) Once uttered, Mrs. May's denial

is so horrible to her that she is blinded by tears. Again, we see the larger, external theme of class conflict, of chauvinism, being subsumed by the more tangible, internal, and affective one of family loyalty.

The rejection of Mrs. May by her sons, especially by the younger Wesley, is cumulative, reiterative, and complete. Complete, at least, within the confines of the story, since in O'Connor's panorama there is no *earthly* closure. If her camera were to continue running after Mrs. May's death on the horn of the bull, for instance, we might see in the sons, as intimated in the case of Julian, and embracing of her as they wake to "the world of guilt and sorrow." But their rejection here progresses through the ghoulish anticipation of her death to Wesley's taunting contention that they are not really her sons. This rejection is heightened by an ensuing outburst between thm that ends in a fight. The rebuff wounds Mrs. May, who wheezes "like an old horse lashed unexpectedly" and runs from the room. Marking the ultimacy of the rejection is the fact that this is the last time the boys appear in the story, the last time they are together. Again the domestic dynamics inform and adumbrate O'Connor's social and religious themes.

"A View of the Woods" at its core presents an internecine clash of family loyalties configuring O'Connor's larger socio-theistic concerns. Thematically, the ecological interests implicit in the destruction of nature for the sake of "progress" merge with the spiritual ones involving the symbolic violation of the divine through the proposed sacrificing of the woods and the concomitant destruction of family unity. Tilman, the up-and-coming businessman to whom the lot fronting the woods is sold, is presented as a palpably Luciferian character who is even a little *ahead* of progress, a representative of The Future. The woods, as described and employed, and as O'Connor herself confirms, are associated with Christ. Old man Fortune allies himself with the new class, with destructive secularism, when he champions Tilman and what he stands for. Tilman's anticipated business enterprises will bring the world's conveniences and travelers of all types from across the nation to the family's door. The sale of the lot in front of their house for the construction of Tilman's gas station will initiate this new era. The sale, in Fortune's estimation, will be a supremely beneficent act, redolent of the highest ideals of patriotism, democracy, egalitarianism:

> If his daughter thought she was better than Tilman, it would be well to take her down a little. All men were created free and equal. When this phrase sounded in his head, his patriotic sense triumphed and he realized that it was his duty to sell the lot, that he must insure the future. He looked out the window at the moon shining over the woods across the road and listened for a while to the hum of the

crickets and treefrogs, and beneath their racket, he could hear the throb of the future town of Fortune.

Of course Mary Fortune Pitts, his granddaughter, knows nothing of these larger significances; *her* responses are domestic, familial: a gas station there would obliterate her family's view of the woods and would replace the "lawn" where her daddy, Pitts, grazes his calves. Daughter of Fortune's daughter who married the despised Pitts, the child becomes a hostage in the battle of wills between Fortune and the Pitts nuclear family. That she is like Fortune—his namesake and a replica in appearance and disposition—makes her his, the only Pitts he has any use for, the designated beneficiary of his total estate. At the same time, her parents suspect that since she is favored by her grandfather (because of her resemblance to him), she is the source of his hostility to *them*. So just as he punishes them through his partiality to her at their expense, they retaliate against him by chastising her for assumed complicity with the old man, for serving as a wedge against her own immediate family. Most remarkably, she is accused of putting him up to selling the lot to Tilman, for which suspected act she is beaten by Pitts.

The periodic beatings given Mary Fortune by Pitts remain rather mysterious and problematical throughout the story. Only within the domestic context, with respect to the issue of family integrity, do they become sufficiently meaningful. At first there is some question of whether they actually occur or are merely imagined by Fortune. When it becomes obvious that they are real, they may be assessed as a kind of bugaboo of Fortune's, enraging him by reason of the girl's acceptance of them, her displaying even "something very like cooperation." What remains baffling is that the child continues to fiercely deny them, proclaiming "Nobody's ever beat me in my life and if anybody did, I'd kill him."

A plausible explanation is that for O'Connor the beatings have a far larger symbolic than literal import, that they are received by the child not as punishment for particular wrongdoing (since from all indication she has done no particular wrong) but as acts of familial bonding, acknowledgment by her father and family that she is indeed one of theirs—a Pitts. They become expressions of acceptance denoting a parental prerogative that Fortune cannot proscribe and that, to his dismay, the child embraces.

It follows then that when Fortune attempts to usurp Pitts's authority and beat her himself for the first time (becoming the *nobody* who has ever beaten her, the *anybody* who ever might beat her), the beating becomes a literal one; and she makes good her pledge by, effectively, killing him.

The most conclusive blow in this homicide is not physical but psychological, and again domestic. Once more it is the ultimate terrestrial rejection: the denial of kin. After the girl pounds the old man to the ground in their mortal combat at the end of the story, she looks down into his eyes and says, "You been whipped by me, and I'm PURE Pitts." There are layers of implications here. Fortune, looking up into her eyes, sees his own image as she announces his vanquishment by pure Pitts. Apart from the evident symbolism of the Pitts clan's finally defeating and supplanting him is the less distinct form betokening his ultimate *self*-defeat. The pride resulting in his rejection of his daughter's family, except for the member he appropriates as his own, is incarnated in Mary Fortune; so that pride is the cause of his final overthrow, at the same time that he is inadvertently extinguishing it, as he slays the granddaughter who has spiritually betrayed and abandoned him in identifying with her father, the detested Pitts.

Fortune, of course, has rejected *her* earlier, in another instance of heightened familial denial. Significantly, it occurs when he belittles her for accepting the beatings from her father:

> "Are you a Fortune," he said, "or are you a Pitts? Make up your mind."
>
> Her voice was loud and positive and belligerent. "I'm Mary—Fortune—Pitts," she said.
>
> "Well I," he shouted, "am PURE Fortune!"
>
> There was nothing she could say to this and she showed it. For an instant she looked completely defeated, and the old man saw with a disturbing clearness that this was the Pitts look. What he saw was the Pitts look, pure and simple, and he felt personally strained by it, as if it had been found on his own face.

The impact of this rejection on the child is telling, and the defeat she suffers associates her thereafter with her father and against Fortune. From this point on in the story, she is deeply morose, glumly unresponsive to all Fortune's efforts to revive their previously communicative banter; "for all the answer he got," "he might have been chauffeuring a small dead body," we are told at one point. She will indeed soon be a small dead body, but already she is dead to him.

Not ignored by O'Connor in her complex of domestic concerns is the dutiful homemaker, Mrs. Pitts, who discharges what she deems her familial obligations to her father in taking care of Fortune in his old age. If her motivation is to be accepted as genuine, against Fortune's conviction of her ulterior motives, she is performing a sacrificial act, being regarded by her father as no more than a tenant while she, apparently against her family's persuasions and with no expectation of reward, stays to care for him. Fortune virtually rejects her when she marries Pitts, concluding that in so doing she has shown that she "preferred Pitts to home"; and a true home is what he has denied her ever since.

"The Enduring Chill" is the first story in the volume that does not end with an actual or imminent death, though Asbury's conviction of his impending demise suffuses the work. Asbury, the intellectual and would-be artist, has renounced his provincial home and family, seeing his mother as the culprit in the utter failure of his life; but, of necessity, it is to *home* that he returns to die.

Though Asbury is the story's protagonist, the one to be touched by O'Connor's "action of grace," as manifested in the conspicuous descent of the symbolized Holy Ghost upon him at the end, it is his mother who is the domestic focus. He blames her for his expected death; she dismisses the notion that she would *allow* him to die under her parental care, and it is through her efforts—deflecting his verbal attacks and stripping away his illusions at every turn—that his life is dispensed to him and he may begin to become a New Man. Mrs. Fox contends to him that he has a home, something his admired Northern associates would wish they had, and forces upon him the services of the local physician he desises, who, she is aware, will take a personal interest in him. The priest she secures for him expects that he will pray—with his family—and, if they do not pray, will pray *for* them. The mother's black dairy workers, with whom Asbury tries to establish an egalitarian rapport, wonder why he disparages his mother and speculate that the reason is her failure to "whup" him enough when he was little. His efforts to have "communion" with them by inducing them to drink with him unpasteurized milk—against his mother's rules, in defiance of the social and racial taboo, but in this instance also a medical taboo—results in his true disease. He drinks the milk (though the workers do not) and contracts undulant fever, which the country doctor, Block, eventually diagnoses, concluding that Asbury must have drunk some unpasteurized milk "up there."

Essentially it is Asbury's assumed realization that his woes have, in the main, resulted not from his mother's values, the values of home, but from his rejection of them that signals the final peeling away of his illusions. His spiritual deficiencies, exposed by the priest, may be most immediately tied to the religious climax at the end, but the realization of his *domestic* failures undergirds it.

"The Comforts of Home," as the title suggests, is anchored in the domestic, and in domestic disruption, since the loss of such comforts eventuates for the story's reflector, Thomas. While treating moral concerns, this work is less recognizably religious than **"The Enduring Chill."** O'Connor's dogma is well insulated by her domestic drama.

What is accentuated in the dramatization is the social theme. Sarah Ham, the "little slut" that Thomas's mother all but adopts and that she obtrudes upon their domain, brings with her the taint of ineffective, perhaps misdirected, institutionalized social services. The mother avers that what she truly needs is a home, though in providing her one she is displacing and alienating her son. A dissembling nymphomaniac who calls herself Star Drake, even Sarah dismisses the woman's do-goodism by labeling her "about seventy-five years behind the times," providing another instance of the ingratitude that frequently greets altruistic efforts in O'Connor's works.

The story illustrates some of the difficulties encountered in O'Connor that inevitably lead to interpretations she would find objectionable. In this regard it is instructive to view it alongside the next story in the collection, **"The Lame Shall Enter First."** Here too, out of the impurely good intentions of the homeowner, a disruptive force is brought into the home. Sheppard, seeing the potential in the clubfooted Rufus, attempts to rescue the boy from the stultifying and corruptive effects of his sordid background and the ineptness of related welfarism and to "reform" the boy himself by providing him a real home, even telling himself also that Rufus's presence will have a salutary, charity-building influence on Norton, Sheppard's young son.

Other parallels abound. Like Sarah Ham, Rufus feels no gratitude for the efforts directed toward his betterment and continues to pursue his usual antisocial, even criminal behavior while in the home of his benefactor, in some sense treacherously desecrating its sanctity. Neither has had a genuine home before, but each seems remarkably indifferent to the one generously provided. Thomas informs his mother that Sarah is "nothing but a slut. She makes fun of you behind your back. She means to get everything she can out of you and you are nothing to her." His mother concedes as much, saying, "I know I'm nothing but an old bag of wind to her." Likewise, when Norton tries to protest to his father about Rufus's breach of domestic ethics—sullying the sanctum of his dead mother's room and her personal effects, dancing, in her corset, with the black cook—Sheppard condemns him for tattling and will brook no denigration of Rufus, who mocks his reform attempts and disparages him for thinking himself Jesus Christ. The "congenital liar" Sarah, having been analyzed and instructed by psychiatrists, "knows" that she is incorrigible, that there is "no hope for her." Rufus flaunts *his* resistance to (Sheppard's) do-goodism, bragging that he persists in committing crimes because he's good at it and that he is in the power of Satan. The similarities go on and on.

A crucial difference is in intended impact; one gathers that O'Connor sanctions the charitable efforts of Thomas's mother. She has written that in **"The Comforts of Home"** "nobody is redeemed" but she explains that

> the old lady is the character whose position is right and the one who is right is usually the victim. If there is any question of a symbolic redemption, it would be through the old lady who brings Thomas face to face with his own evil—which is that of putting his own comfort before charity (however foolish). His doing that destroys the one person his comfort depended on, his mother.

Her opinion of Sheppard's efforts, however, is clarified when she labels him "a man who thought he was good and thought he was doing good when he wasn't."

It may be asked to what extent these contrasting assessments are supported by O'Connor's fictional treatment and realized through her dramatization. Her tenet that the one who is right is usually the victim may be illuminating, but questions are raised concerning her definition of victimization. Does the victim have to die, for example, as Thomas's mother does and O'Connor's characters so often do? If a necessary determinant, is death a *sufficient* determinant of victimization? A case can be made in Thomas's behalf, defending him against the charge of "evil" that O'Connor makes. His analysis of his mother's behavior seems sound enough:

> There was an observable tendency in all her actions. This was, with the best of intentions in the world, to make a mockery of virtue, to pursue it with such mindless intensity that everyone involved was made a fool of and virtue itself became ridiculous.... Had she been in any degree intellectual, he could have proved to her from early Christian history that no excess of virtue is justified.... His own life was made bearable by the fruits of his mother's saner virtues—by the well-regulated house she kept and the excellent meals she served. But when virtue got out of hand with her, as now, a sense of devils grew upon him.

Likewise, Walter Sullivan sees the mother's generosity as representing a "kind of sentimental, self-serving charity" resulting "from a misunderstanding of ultimate truth." Furthermore, Thomas's perception of Sarah's incorrigibility, her being beyond their help and better off in an institution, appears plausible.

The key to his culpability in O'Connor's scheme seems to lie in her rather deterministic revelation that Thomas "had inherited his father's reason without his ruthlessness and his mother's love of good without her tendency to pursue it." In other words, his problem is his very makeup as a family constituent. But in the context of the story this is far from obvious as a problem of culpability. Sarah is such an utterly repulsive character that his stance toward her has merit, and he does wonder, at least, what the attitude of God was to the "moral moron" Sarah—"meaning if possible to adopt it." Moreover, the voice of his dead father impugning the mother's impulsive violation of their home seems a defensible complement to Thomas's own outrage. Additionally, Thomas's mother virtually rejects him, ostensibly a grievous offense in O'Connor's moral scheme. He gives his mother an ultimatum—she must choose between him and Sarah, and she obviously chooses "the little slut" by bringing her back to the house. And on another occasion she allows the girl to stay there longer than just the one night she assures him of; so her credibility as a character is further reduced vis-à-vis his.

The voice of the dead father warrants further consideration. It is one of several components suggesting a mildly feminist strain in the story, wherein the inferior status of female characters is tacitly criticized through the mere highlighting of selected features illustrating their secondary condition. The man, we learn, was ruthless and a hypocrite, a dissembler who, in making the country men regard him as one of them, had "lived his lie" without ever having to tell one. Clearly, while alive he had been at odds with his wife over her "mindless charity" but apparently knew how to "handle her," how to "put his foot down." Thomas lacks his father's attributes in this respect, and to the old man this indicates that Thomas's masculinity is questionable. He belittles Thomas for letting a woman dominate him, proclaiming that she had never driven *him* from his own table. "Show her who's boss," his voice goads Thomas; "[you] let her run over you. You ain't like me. Not enough to be a man."

Extending this strain is Farebrother, the sheriff that Thomas finally goes to see for help, who has known the father and who apparently shares his temperament and tendencies. Farebrother reminds Thomas that the old man would never truckle to a woman and, after agreeing to come to the house and investigate Sarah's taking of the gun, orders him to "keep out of my way—yourself and them two women too."

There are hints of the feminist concern in other stories, e.g., **"Greenleaf,"** where the Greenleaf females seem to be slighted in deference to the male children and to diminish in importance as the action progresses, and where Mrs. May laments that she is the victim, has always been because she is a woman. In **"The Comforts of Home,"** though, as has been suggested, the voice of the dead father may well be taken not merely as a continuation of the battle of wills between the man and his widow but as the force sent to correct the disgraced status of the house resulting from her disruption of its domestic harmony through her "mindless" charity.

The word "mindless" is pertinent, since it fits into the mind-heart dichotomy so prominent in O'Connor's works. (The argument in the title story over the seat of genuine culture—the mind versus the heart—exemplifies the pattern of hyper-rational, unfeeling characters scattered through her fiction.) Here the dichotomy operates most intensely within Thomas himself. Arguably, he may possess the better, or at least less extreme, qualities of both his respective parents—his father's reason, his mother's love of good—without their "worse" ones—ruthlessness and the (excessive) tendency to pursue good. But it is the ruthlessness of the dead father that invades Thomas in the end, signified by the gun (inherited from the old man) and her dead husband's voice that the mother hears issuing from the lips of her son before the trigger is pulled to end her life. The old man evidently triumphs.

Perhaps the strongest feature of the mother's altruism, making it a thing of the heart and therefore blessed for O'Connor, is again domestically based; it is seeing others as her own children. The protagonist of the title story in O'Connor's first volume evinces the action of grace when she recognizes the Misfit as one of her children before he kills her. Thomas's mother demonstrates the radical Christian virtue of loving thy neighbor as thyself, of holding even strangers in no less esteem than one's own kin. This is driven home to us by the reiterated explanation for her avid concern with Sarah's welfare: "I keep thinking it might be you," she repeatedly tells her son. The familial dimension of **"The Comforts of Home"** is vital. In no other of O'Connor's stories is it more deeply based or more multifunctional.

The altruism of Sheppard in **"The Lame Shall Enter First"** is of a different order. His attitude toward his son Norton falls somewhere between condescension and contempt. Hence his benevolence concerning Rufus is hollow—vain, mind-driven, absent of heart. His actions are dictated by self-regard, cold theory, social scientism, as opposed to sincere personal engagement. Rufus succinctly sizes up Sheppard by remarking that he may be good but he "ain't *right*."

Symbolically, because of the emptiness of his motivation, Sheppard is unable to create the family he attempts by positioning Rufus as a prospective brother to (actually a replacement of) his real son, and (the father rationalizes) deflecting Norton's obsessive attachment to his dead mother.

Sheppard stresses the "selfishness" in the child's fixation, but at least the attachment is concrete—to a real person whose death Norton cannot comprehend or accept, which cannot be mitigated (but rather is enhanced) by Sheppard's materialistic denial of a hereafter. And Norton's devotion is necessarily filial, born of a relationship with an integral member of the family and home he has known. Ironically, just as Rufus supplants Norton as Sheppard's son, he also replaces Sheppard as Norton's parent. The latter act is pre-

pared for by Sheppard's rejection of Norton—as usual in highly intensified scenes. After desecrating the dead mother's room, Rufus is given her bed to sleep in; Norton becomes so incensed that his father whips him. Then the utter denial occurs when Sheppard refuses to entertain the thought that Rufus, despite the certainty of the police concerning his guilt, could have left the movie he attended with Norton and broken into a house, as alleged. The captivation is so complete that he misconstrues the words expressing Rufus's enthrallment of him as *thanks* and responds by calling Rufus "son." Immediately thereafter, as he sees Norton beckoning him from across the hall, he decides he cannot go to him without violating Rufus's presumed trust. Norton, of course, would have told him that Rufus *did* leave the theater to commit the break-in, but Sheppard willfully ignores the child's call. He denies his son. We are told that, in response, the child "sat for some time looking at the spot where his father had stood. Finally his gaze became aimless and he lay back down."

After this, we may conclude, the forsaken Norton's central objective is to establish contact with his *one* parent—who resides, according to Rufus, in the sky. Rufus plants the seed of suicide in the child's consciousness through teaching him the Bible, and finally triumphs over Sheppard in their struggle for the boy's soul when Norton hangs himself to join his mother in heaven.

The story shows that rationalized "good works" fail and that human (i.e., familial) sentiment is genuine, *right,* as the ground of altruism. But O'Connor becomes uncharacteristically didactic at the end and restates what has been portrayed, that Sheppard had tried to stuff "his own emptiness with good works" and "had ignored his own child to feed his vision of himself." He at long last feels a rush of love for Norton, vows never to let him suffer again; but the child is gone. With this culmination the religious and domestic themes converge, and, as the story's action illustrates, the domestic configuration is once again a sounding board for the spiritual voice.

In **"Revelation"** the domestic theme is rendered essentially in interfamilial terms. O'Connor again brings to the fore class-consciousness and apprehension regarding the changing times, the new age, connecting the two with her religious component and giving them all about equal emphasis. The most comic of these stories, **"Revelation"** presents the unlikely phenomenon in O'Connor of a female protagonist with a living spouse, a more than incidental feature.

Through Mrs. Turpin's consciousness the gallery of characters is introduced in the doctor's waiting room; the descriptive details individualize each, yet place them all neatly in her pattern of class stratification, as outlined in her pastime of "naming the classes of people":

On the bottom of the heap were most colored people . . . then next to them . . . were the white trash; then above them were the home-owners, and above them the home-and-land-owners, to which she and Claud belonged. Above she and Claud were people with a lot of money and much bigger houses and much more land. But here the complexity of it would begin to bear in on her, for some of the people with a lot of money were common and ought to be below she and Claud and some of the people who had good blood had lost their money and had to rent and then there were colored people who owned their homes and land as well. . . . Usually by the time she had fallen asleep all the classes of people were moiling and roiling around in her head, and she would dream they were all crammed in together in a box car, being ridden off to be put in a gas oven.

Those in the waiting room are delineated by their words, dress, and demeanor, but it is important to note that *domestic* connections form the axis on which the class distinctions revolve and are a principle of character evaluation. Being "white-trashy," for instance, does not inhere simply in lack of possessions or education; it is revealed in the failure to keep one's child clean or teach it proper behavior. Also, the familial focus can serve as a means of *dis*junction. Mary Grace, the ugly girl whose pivotal act of assaulting Mrs. Turpin forms the story's climax, is viewed as an ungrateful family aberration, almost incomprehensible to her mother. A friendly and "stylish" lady, the mother criticizes the girl's thanklessness and failure to appreciate her advantages, i.e., her supportive, loving, sacrificing family and all it has provided for her. In this way the familial theme is dispersed in the story, serving as a generalized elastic device of coherence and emphasis. It is the abstract concept of family that serves functionally as a kind of meta-setting, as opposed to the conventional O'Connor application of the literal and immediate family.

But the immediate familial relationship is not completely neglected. Just before Mary Grace attacks her, Mrs. Turpin is rhapsodically expressing gratitude for her blessings:

"If it's one thing I am," Mrs. Turpin said with feeling, "it's grateful. When I think who all I could have been besides myself and what all I got, a little of everything, and a good disposition besides, I just feel like shouting, 'Thank you, Jesus, for making everything the way it is!' It could have been different!" For one thing, somebody else would have got Claud. At the thought of this, she was flooded with gratitude and a terrible pang of joy ran through her. "Oh thank you Jesus, Jesus, thank you!" she cried aloud.

It is worthy of note that the possibility of someone else's getting her husband Claud is not part of what she says, but something she thinks, realizes—and the realization of her husband as a gift fills her with joy and impels her to shout her thanks; which in turn causes the ugly Mary Grace to hurl the book at her face. Aside from whatever O'Connor's intent may be in having the assault occur on this note, the fact remains that what is set in pointed relief here is the primary domestic relationship—husband and wife.

At this point, with the girl's attack, the dispersed domesticism of the waiting room ends, and the reader is prepared for the Turpins' return to their actual domicile and family context. Emphasis here appears in the fact that Mrs. Turpin cherishes the reality that their home is still there ("she would not have been startled to see a burnt wound between two blackened chimneys"). More appears in the rather peculiar exchange between the spouses later, in bed, when instead of discussing the girl's indictment of her (an "old wart hog" from hell), Mrs. Turpin solicitously asks her husband how his injured leg feels, and later, when he is about to leave to take their workers home, impulsively says, "Kiss me." And, finally, before she has her revelation—of all the classes of people ultimately marching into heaven—there is a signal occurrence. She has just vocally confronted Christ, charging that even if he decrees that the class divisions be erased and the "bottom rail" put on top, there will still be a class system, a hierarchy, "a top and a bottom." Then she sees in the distance Claud's departing truck and realizes that "at any moment a bigger truck might smash into it and scatter Claud's and the niggers' brains all over the road." She remains fixed and anxious until she sees Claud's truck returning, sees it turn into their own road, to safety; only then does the spiritual revelation occur to her. In short, **"Revelation"** stresses social class-consciousness, minimizes *starkly* moral concerns, and follows the expected pattern of rendering the spiritual message in a domestic context.

"Parker's Back" is the least verisimilar, the most biblically allegorical, of all the stories in the collection. It has the least coherence and substance in the mimetic sense, and its characters are seemingly the most manipulated by O'Connor's religious thrust. The religious theme is paramount, even to the extent that it distorts and vitiates the realistic tenor of O'Connor's presentation. Despite all this, however, the domestic theme is discernible in several respects relating to significant events in the title character's life: (1) Parker's *mother* took him to revival, though he ran away and joined the navy; (2) his mother is responsible—paid—for the notable tattoo of his, but insisted that it include her name; (3) against his will Parker gets married, but marriage makes him gloomier than ever; (4) he feels the need for a tattoo on his back, but wants only one his wife would like; (5) he is surprised to be capable of staying with a woman who is pregnant; (6) he is driven to get a strange tattoo on his back (he says) *because* he married a woman who is pregnant; (7) it seems that all along his real desire was to please her (his wife); and so on.

Further, though relatively muted, a pattern of O'Connor's larger domestic concerns is detectable. For example, one senses the theme of displacement when Parker is in the city getting his transforming tattoo. He feels isolated and longs to be home with his wife, Sarah Ruth. And of course there is the theme of rejection—by Parker's cohorts, his "society," when he is thrown out of the pool hall, and by his wife. He has in a sense betrayed her through dissimulation regarding his female employer's attitude toward him and the like. Sarah Ruth rejects him, at least the secular him that has attempted to deceive her, by not responding at last to his preferred name but only to the Testamentary one—Obadiah Elihue.

In this story the domestic theme resonates in other subtle ways. When Parker comes home with his ultimate tattoo and his wife will not admit him until he submits to identifying himself with the name he despises, she has symbolically *named* him. After chastening him for his deception, aware now of the truth of his status with the female employer, she whips him with a broom. At one level of implication, she has become his mother, dominating him as she might a child. Here earlier strains assume related significance—the fact that she had to marry before having children, that he has been repulsed by her pregnancy, that he from all appearances has never known his own motivations, his identity. The story ends with him beaten, standing outside, "crying like a baby." Metaphorically, he *is* a baby, i.e., "born again"—the symbolic fruition of her pregnancy; and whatever implication this episode may carry thematically, it is steeped in domesticity.

The closing story, **"Judgement Day,"** fittingly recapitulates a number of themes sounded in the earlier selections. Not the least of these is that of domestic displacement. As in the title story, the family holdings have been lost, along with the social status they signified. Old Tanner, a former landowner who raised four children, "was somebody when he was somebody," his daughter contends, but now he is decrepit and dispossessed, feebly seeking his Georgia homeland to serve as his final resting place. He, like Julian's mother, is spiritually rebuffed by his offspring and suffers a stroke after being accosted by a Negro who takes offense at a racially insensitive act.

Again the racial encounters illustrate the social phenomenon of rising descent that O'Connor projects. The blacks, as they advance—demonstrating for some the government's inexorable effort to turn society "upsidedown," to put "the bottom rail on top"—grow ever more assertive and testy, consequently engaging in confrontations with those Southern whites continuing to exhibit traditional racial mores.

Sometimes, as in the cases of Julian's mother and Tanner, these confrontations prove deadly.

But the roles of the blacks in **"Judgement Day"** are just as vital to O'Connor's treatment of the story's domestic theme. Coleman, whom Tanner has mentally vanquished with the symbolic aid of the "spectacles" he absently fashions from bark and hay wire, becomes Tanner's domestic servant in their "home"—the shack they construct together as squatters on a plot of vacated land later purchased by a local Negro (only part black, also Indian and white), Doctor Foley. Tanner realizes, as does Foley, that his white skin, with "the government" against him, is no longer a badge of superiority; and Foley gives him the option of becoming *his* servant or being evicted.

Rather than accept such a humiliating role, Tanner goes to live with his daughter in her apartment in New York—which he finds a hellish new world, an impersonal "no-place," inhabited by "all stripes of foreigner, all of them twisted in the tongue." Desmond summarizes its racial and social dynamics:

> The New York world of Tanner's daughter is one ostensibly marked by social progress, at least to the extent that a relative equality exists between whites and Negroes. But underlying this superficial advance is the deeper fact of spiritual alienation, signified by the estrangement from others that characterizes urban life there, the people of each race guardedly "minding their own business." In short, it is a mock community, a perversion of the idea of mystical community, a society which has lost the long view of history because it has turned away from the spiritual roots of such a mystical vision.

Here even Tanner's daughter is a stranger to him, one whose philosophy, too, is non-engagement ("Live and let live"), who shuts him out by conversing with herself, who ridicules his religious beliefs as "Baptist hooey," and who intends to renege on her promise to have him buried at home, in Georgia. This familial betrayal is the unkindest cut of all, and Tanner concludes that he made a colossal mistake in coming to live with her, that Coleman and he constituted a more genuine family, and that now he would gladly be Foley's lackey, his "white nigger," if it meant he could live again in the departed shack that used to be his home.

From this ungodly no-place, symptomatic of that terrible world we are coming to, Tanner must escape. His attempts to do so bring O'Connor's social and theistic themes into panoptic integration with their domestic vehicle. The black actor, whom Tanner has refused to except from his racially stereotypical views, tellingly asserts his difference by proclaiming that he is not any "coal man" before his violent disposal of Tanner as the story draws to a close. The irony in his apparently mistaking Tanner's confused tentative greeting—"Coleman?"—as merely a vocational label, instead of in effect a compounded racial typing, is pronounced. Even more so is the irony suffusing the fatal attack itself on Tanner, in response to the old man's plea for help to get home, an act of hostility that results in sending him not at once to the geographical home, which the old man immediately seeks, but to the otherworldly, eternal one for which he secretly longs. The homicidal act by "Preacher" becomes underhandedly a benevolent rite.

It remains only for the daughter to complete the domestic resolution of the work. She betrays her pledge to Tanner and buries his body there in New York City. But afterward, though herself a professed nonbeliever like the black Northern actor, she is unable to sleep well until she has her father raised and sent home as she had promised—after which her peace and good looks return. We may well see this corrective adjustment in the daughter's attitude as yet another instance of O'Connor's "action of grace." Nonetheless, its resulting gesture, the final and consummating act of the book, is firmly positioned on the clearly *domestic* fulcrum of filial obligation, familial duty.

Michael W. Crocker and Robert C. Evans (essay date June 1993)

SOURCE: "Faulkner's 'Barn Burning' and O'Connor's 'Everything That Rises Must Converge,'" in *CLA Journal*, Vol. XXXVI, No. 4, June, 1993, pp. 371-83.

[*In the following essay, Crocker and Evans outline similarities between O'Connor's "Everything That Rises Must Converge" and Faulkner's "Barn Burning."*]

As two of the most important American writers of this century, William Faulkner and Flannery O'Connor wrote two of the most widely anthologized and widely read short stories of our time—"Barn Burning" and **"Everything That Rises Must Converge."** Although the relationship between the two writers has been a subject of occasional comment, such comment remains largely scattered and difficult to trace. In addition, although the two stories end in basically similar ways, these similarities seem not to have been discussed at any length. The links between the stories may be purely coincidental, or they may have been purposely designed. O'Connor greatly admired Faulkner (although her remarks about him seem not to have been brought together in one place before), and it is possible that her story was influenced—either consciously or unconsciously—by "Barn Burning." In any case, it seems worthwhile to collect O'Connor's comments on Faulkner, to gather some previ-

ous references to the connection between the two writers, and to note a few of the similarities between two of their most significant stories.

Various evidence suggests that O'Connor read and respected Faulkner's writings. For instance, the most recent catalogue of her library shows that she owned at least six different books by Faulkner; Conrad and Mauriac were the only two authors of fiction whose books were more plentiful on her shelves, with ten titles each. In addition, O'Connor's friend Robert Fitzgerald reported that during her brief stay in Connecticut with his family, she persuaded him to read *As I Lay Dying*—one of "only two works of fiction that I can remember her urging on me." Because of this, Fitzgerald surmised that Faulkner's novel was "close to her heart as a writer." Moreover, O'Connor's published correspondence contains several allusions to Faulkner and his works. For example, a letter dated 17 October 1949 refers to "the character in *Sanctuary* who 'had the depthless quality of stamped tin.'" Similarly, a letter dated 1 February 1953 mentions that she had been reading and enjoying a review by Faulkner of Hemingway's *The Old Man and the Sea*. Another letter, dated 13 October 1953, alludes to Quentin Compson of *Absalom, Absalom!* in a way that suggests her familiarity with that novel. Later, in a letter dated 19 May 1957, O'Connor claimed,

> I had never heard of K.A. Porter or Faulkner or Eudora Welty until I got to graduate school, which may have been time enough for me in as much as I got to graduate school, but so many do not; they leave college thinking that literature is anything written before 1900 and that contemporary literature is anything found on the best-seller list. . . .

Two days later, on 21 May 1957, she wrote to another friend: "I haven't seen *The Town* yet. I used to like *The Hamlet*—but for obvious reasons it is better for me to give the Snopes a wide berth." This reference is particularly intriguing, since the incident that is central to "Barn Burning" is alluded to and summarized in the opening pages of *The Hamlet*.

O'Connor's comments about her reading in graduate school suggest that she discovered Faulkner at precisely the same time that she was discovering and most developing her own talents. She was open to Faulkner's influence just when she was most likely to be influenced by him. Years later, after her own schooling was formally finished, she found herself recommending Faulkner to a friend, another young writer. In a letter dated 20 March 1958, she wrote: "Joe Christmas is the hero of Faulkner's book *Light in August* which you better had get and read. It's a real sickmaking book but I guess a classic. I read it a long time ago and only once so I'm in no position to say." Later that year, responding to her friend and fellow writer John Hawkes, who had sent her some Faulkner to read, O'Connor comically reported, "I braved the Faulkner, without tragic results." Her verb suggests some ambivalence in her attitude about Faulkner's possible influence—a point to be discussed more fully later. In general, though, her opinion of him was extremely positive. Once, a visitor, she states,

> said he had a friend who was a writer in Mississippi and I said who was that. He said, His name is Bill Faulkner. I don't know if he's any good or not but he's a mighty nice fellow. I told him he was right good. . . .

In fact, during the same year in which **"Everything That Rises Must Converge"** was first published, O'Connor was reading F.W. Dillistone's *The Novelist and the Passion Story,* a scholarly book focusing largely on Faulkner. A great deal of evidence, then, shows that O'Connor was not only familiar with Faulkner's work but that she also admired it.

O'Connor's admiration for Faulkner seems to have been rooted in several different sources. Her letters, essays, and interviews suggest that she shared many of the same values and attitudes as Faulkner. She also seems to have respected his public persona and private character—the way he lived his life as a writer. For instance, in a letter dated 28 August 1955, she referred to Faulkner as one of "the best Southern writers," and the context (which also mentions Kafka and Joyce) implies that she regarded him as one of the best international writers as well. She considered him, as she considered herself, an author whose works demanded intelligent and insightful reading. For example, in an interview given in the spring of 1963, she remarked that she did not view Faulkner or other modern novelists as "fare for the eighth grade," but she observed that "it is probably better to read Faulkner in the eighth grade than nothing. At the same time, it seems sort of insulting to Faulkner."

Nevertheless, despite her awareness of his fiction's sophistication, O'Connor seems to have respected Faulkner's lack of pretense and his identification with his native region. These were obviously values she also embraced. In an essay written in the winter of 1963, for example, she commented, "It is a great blessing, perhaps the greatest blessing a writer can have, to find at home what others have to go elsewhere seeking. Faulkner was at home in Oxford. . . ." In the same essay, she noted that honest and unpretentious readers in Oxford would have been "more desirable to Faulkner than all the critics in New York City [who were] unreliable [and] incapable of . . . interpreting Southern literature to the world." She mentioned "a story about Faulkner that I like. It may be apocryphal but it's nice anyway." When a local lady asked Faulkner if he thought she would like his latest book, "Faulkner is supposed to have said, 'Yes, I think you'll like that book. It's trash.'" This combination of regionalism,

self-deprecation, self-respect, and wit suggests some of the traits belonging to Faulkner that O'Connor not only admired but also shared. She even seems to have sensed in Faulkner a greater sympathy for Christianity than was common among other modern writers. For instance, in a letter dated 1 February 1953, she mentioned having read a "nice" review by Faulkner of Hemingway's *The Old Man and the Sea:* "He says that Hemingway discovered God the Creator in this one."

However, some of O'Connor's comments about Faulkner suggest a certain ambivalence and sense of intimidation— an understandable "anxiety of influence." For example, in a letter dated 20 March 1958, she claimed to "keep clear of Faulkner so my own little boat won't get swamped." Similarly, in a letter dated 27 July 1958, she suggested, "Probably the real reason I don't read him is because he makes me feel that with my one-cylinder syntax I should quit writing and raise chickens altogether." Of course, the facts already cited show that O'Connor did read Faulkner, but her apprehension about being overpowered by his influence must have been felt by many younger Southern writers at that time. Perhaps the most emphatic evidence of this respectful wariness occurs in an essay written not long before **"Everything That Rises Must Converge."** Discussing the topic of "The Grotesque in Southern Fiction," O'Connor asserted:

> When there are many writers all employing the same idiom, all looking out on more or less the same social scene, the individual writer will have to be more than ever careful that he isn't just doing badly what has already been done to completion. The presence alone of Faulkner in our midst makes a great difference in what a writer can and cannot permit himself to do. Nobody wants his mule and wagon stalled on the same track the Dixie Limited is roaring down.

O'Connor's determination to preserve a sense of her own identity is shown in her remarks during a panel discussion on 28 October 1960, in which she said, "I don't know how either Eudora Welty or Faulkner looks at [the 'Southern community']. I only know how I look at it and I don't feel that I am writing about the community at all." This studied naïveté seems somewhat disingenuous, but it is understandable considering O'Connor's need to think of herself as a distinct and individual talent. In fact, O'Connor was often compared to Faulkner by contemporary critics, especially because of their mutual use of "the grotesque." This tendency among her early critics would seem to have intensified both O'Connor's awareness of Faulkner and her resolution to keep some distance from him. Nonetheless, by the late 1950s, O'Connor was clearly seen as one of Faulkner's heirs. Allen Tate, whose opinion O'Connor respected, maintained in 1959, shortly before **"Everything That Rises"** was written, that

"If the Elizabethan age would still be the glory of English literature without Shakespeare, the new literature of the Southern states would still be formidable without Faulkner." He specifically mentioned the young Flannery O'Connor in his list of "formidable" Southern writers.

Over the years, many other critics have discussed in passing the relationship between O'Connor and Faulkner, although tracing their sometimes brief and scattered comments is often difficult. However, the connection between "Barn Burning" and **"Everything That Rises Must Converge"** seems not to have been considered at any length. Whether O'Connor had ever actually read Faulkner's story is uncertain. It was first published in 1939, so she certainly could have read it, especially during her time in graduate school or shortly thereafter, when she seems to have been reading and enjoying Faulkner. Or she could have read the work when Faulkner's *Collected Stories* were published in 1950. "Barn Burning" was the very first story in that collection, as if Faulkner wished to call special attention to it. It seems unlikely that a short-story writer of O'Connor's time, talent, and Southern background would have dismissed the opportunity to read the collected stories of such a great contemporary. Although there seems no hard proof that O'Connor actually did read the story, the possibility is hardly out of the question. In any case, the similarities and differences between the two stories are so numerous, so striking, and so significant that there seems some value in comparing and contrasting the two works—especially their concluding sections. The resemblances between those conclusions are so remarkable that they hardly seem coincidental.

The similarities between "Barn Burning" and **"Everything That Rises"** are plentiful and varied. Both stories focus on initiation, on the painful growth of maturity, and in both the crucial moment of initiation of the youthful central character is postponed, but abrupt and sudden when it comes. The events in both stories are seen through the eyes of sons struggling for independence from domineering parents, and both works deal with the theme of family heritage, of the influence of the past on the present, and of the inability to break free completely from such ties and memories. Both stories end with the parent figures in conflict with other adults, and in both works the sons see themselves as attracted toward the values represented by those others. Both stories end with suspense and tension caused directly by the conflict between the values of the sons and their parents. In both cases, this conflict leads to tragedy that involves violence being suffered by the parents. Also, circular structures are utilized in both stories: details in the opening paragraph of "Barn Burning" foreshadow ironically details and phrasing from the end of the story, and this is similarly true of **"Everything That Rises."** Both stories depict sons who want to change their circumstances, who want to escape what they regard as the confining strictures of a limited family life. Both sons think

that achieving their own identities involves getting away from their parents, and in both stories the sons do escape in a sense. However, in both cases this escape ultimately involves strong feelings of guilt, loneliness, and loss. Most strikingly, both stories end with the sons running in isolation and in literal and metaphorical darkness, no longer sure of anything except that their futures will differ radically from their pasts, both full of a heavy sense of having lost a connection—however complicated—with someone previously very important to them.

The many similarities between the two stories are also emphasized by several interesting differences. For instance, "Barn Burning" emphasizes final isolation in the midst of a rural setting; **"Everything That Rises"** emphasizes final isolation in the midst of an urban setting. In addition, although both stories focus on the relationship between a son and his parent, in one case the son is still relatively innocent while his father is wholly corrupt, but in the other case the son is far more corrupt than his mother.

Both "Barn Burning" and **"Everything That Rises"** revolve around and explore a central character and his consciousness. Sarty, the central character in Faulkner's story, is a young boy who must break free from an evil father. Julian, the central character of O'Connor's story, is older than Sarty but less mature; he feels the need to break free from his supposedly inferior and old-fashioned mother. However, these are hardly the only similarities between Sarty and Julian. For instance, both sons are fascinated by large, white antebellum houses, which they associate with order, stability, and privilege. Yet while Sarty sees Major de Spain's mansion as a symbol of civility, order, and justice, Julian fantasizes about his family's old homestead and the lost power and social status which it represented. Here, as elsewhere, the differences between the two characters are often as interesting as the similarities. For example, although both sons enter the world of adulthood through a sudden, unexpected, but in some sense inevitable break with their parents, Julian still behaves childishly, especially when he scolds his stricken mother, saying, "I hate to see you behave like this. . . . Just like a child." Ironically, his determination to teach her a lesson is the surest sign that Julian himself needs to learn maturity. Sarty, on the other hand, seems relatively mature from the very beginning of his story. His decision to inform Major de Spain that Abner Snopes intends to burn the Major's barn results not from any desire to teach Abner a lesson, but merely from a decision to prevent any further harm. If Julian's basic motive is to punish, Sarty's basic motive is to protect.

At the ends of the stories, both sons feel personal fear from having broken all family ties; both feel entirely alone in the world. In addition, both Sarty and Julian feel that they have betrayed their parents, and feelings of grief, remorse, sorrow, and guilt quickly flood their minds. However, while Sarty's regret and responsibility are relieved by his knowledge that he has done the right thing, Julian's anguish and self-blame are intensified by his realization that he has behaved shamefully. Even the language the two characters speak is at once strikingly similar and revealingly different. For instance, the final speeches of both characters are dominated by exclamations and repetition. Sarty, standing before Major de Spain, can only cry out, "Barn! . . . Barn!" Similarly, Julian, left alone in darkness, can only exclaim, "Wait here, wait here!" and then, "Help, help!" Both sons seem literally and figuratively tired and out of breath, and both are left almost speechless in the face of tragedy, but young Sarty, significantly, finally seems the more thoughtful and articulate of the two. Interestingly, the transformations that occur in the ways they speak are also quite similar. For example, Sarty goes from shouting "Pap! Pap!" to shouting "Father! Father!"—a change suggesting increased formality, distance, and independence. Julian, on the other hand, goes from shouting "Mother!" to crying (almost melodramatically) "Darling, sweetheart!" to pleading "Mamma! Mamma!"—phrasing that implies belated love, tenderness, and dependence. Paradoxically, although Julian's words insinuate a return to boyhood, they also connote a new maturity. In all these ways, then, both the similarities and differences between the two central characters help emphasize the many parallels as well as the numerous meaningful distinctions that link the two stories.

In fact, the significant differences between "Barn Burning" and **"Everything That Rises"** are so numerous that they do not seem merely accidental. It is almost as if O'Connor had Faulkner's story in mind as she wrote her own. Certainly reading the two stories together helps sharpen our sense of their individual characteristics. For instance, whereas Sarty makes a decision to mature, Julian is much more passive: he is acted upon. Whereas Sarty's consciousness grows and develops during the course of his story, preparing him for the final deliberate decision he makes, Julian's consciousness remains stunted until it is jolted at the end. Whereas Julian seems to enjoy judging his mother and finding faults in her, Sarty seeks to avoid criticizing his father, instead searching for anything positive or good in him, even at the very end of the story.

Both works end by emphasizing the punishment of the parents, but whereas Julian initially gloats about his mother's unexpected fate, Sarty, even though directly responsible for the fate his father suffers, feels genuine conflict and remorse because of his love for his punished parent. Another difference between the two stories involves the ways the two sons face the losses of their parents. Whereas Sarty merely hears the shot that has only possibly injured his father, Julian has to face his mother's death directly. Moreover, Sarty at least can console himself with the thought that he stood for some

higher, impersonal principle, but Julian can not, since he acts mainly from selfishness and pride. While Julian had only pretended to care about the sufferings of victims of injustice, Sarty's fateful decision proves that he does care.

Although Sarty achieves a measure of true personal identity at the end of his story, the achievement of such identity for Julian is left only implicit at the conclusion of **"Everything That Rises."** In fact, the final phrasing of the two works epitomizes their different tones and resolutions. O'Connor's very last words are memorably bleak and grim: "The lights drifted farther away the faster he ran and his feet moved numbly as if they carried him nowhere. The tide of darkness seemed to sweep him back to her, postponing from moment to moment his entry into the world of guilt and sorrow." In contrast, Faulkner's final paragraph is full of details suggesting consolation and hope. A reference to the spinning of "slow constellations" symbolizes a sense of universal order. In addition, Sarty anticipates "dawn and then sun-up after a while"; after briefly falling asleep, "he knew that it was almost dawn, the night almost over. He could tell that from the whipporwills." The growing light and the sounds of the birds singing suggest the beneficence of nature. Although Sarty feels "a little stiff, . . . walking would cure that . . . as it would the cold. . . . He did not look back." Sarty's ability to sleep implies both physical exhaustion and a kind of inner peace. Julian, on the other hand, will definitely look back; he will never forget either the moment of his mother's death or his own preceding behavior. Paradoxically, his inability to forget seems to be the only source of hope that O'Connor provides.

Perhaps it was O'Connor's inability to forget a reading of "Barn Burning" that subtly influenced the writing of her own story. Certainly the many similarities and differences between the two works suggest this possibility. What seems undeniable is O'Connor's admiration for Faulkner—an admiration tinged with ambivalence. When brought together in one place, her many references and allusions to Faulkner and his works confirm what we might have expected: that she often had Faulkner in mind, whether or not she wrote **"Everything That Rises"** under the direct and conscious influence of "Barn Burning."

FURTHER READING

Criticism

Booth, Wayne C. "Ironic Portraits." In his *A Rhetoric of Irony.* Chicago: The University of Chicago Press, 1974, 137-172.

Reprints O'Connor's "Everything That Rises Must Converge," and discusses the irony in the story.

Driskell, Leon V. and Joan T. Brittain. "The Posthumous Collection." *The Eternal Crossroads*. In their *The Eternal Crossroads,* pp. 104-46. The University Press of Kentucky, 1971.

Discusses the significant symbols found in O'Connor's *Everything That Rises Must Converge.*

Esch, Robert M. Review of *Everything That Rises Must Converge,* by Flannery O'Connor. *The Explicator* XXVII, No. 8 (April 1969): p. 8.

Asserts that in O'Connor's "Everything That Rises Must Converge," "the eyes of Julian's mother symbolize the ultimate rejection of Julian."

Hendin, Josephine. "The Enduring Conflict: Parents & Children in *Everything That Rises Must Converge.*" In her *The World of Flannery O'Connor.* Bloomington: Indiana University Press, 1970, 97-130.

Asserts that the stories in O'Connor's *Everything That Rises Must Converge* are about children, even in adulthood, who "are locked in a struggle with a parent they can neither love nor leave."

Russell, Shannon. "Space and the Movement Through Space in *Everything That Rises Must Converge:* A Consideration of Flannery O'Connor's Imaginative Vision." *The Southern Literary Journal* XX, No. 2 (Spring 1988): 81-98.

Discusses space and movement in O'Connor's *Everything That Rises Must Converge* and asserts that "Meaning, for O'Connor, never operates solely on one surface level, but expands into various spatial dimensions."

Additional coverage of O'Connor's life and career is contained in the following sources published by Gale: *Authors and Artists for Young Adults,* **Vol. 7;** *Concise Dictionary of American Literary Biography,* **1941-1968;** *Contemporary Authors,* **Vols. 1-4R;** *Contemporary Authors New Revision Series,* **Vols. 3 and 41;** *Dictionary of Literary Biography,* **Vols. 2 and 152;** *Dictionary of Literary Biography Documentary Series,* **Vol. 12;** *Dictionary of Literary Biography Yearbook,* **Vol. 80;** *DISCovering Authors; DISCovering Authors Modules: Most-Studied Authors* **and** *Novelists; Major Twentieth-Century Writers; Short Story Criticism,* **Vols. 1 and 23; and** *World Literature Criticism.*

Elaine Pagels
1943-

(Full name Elaine Hiesey Pagels) American theologian.

The following entry presents criticism of Pagels's work through 1997.

INTRODUCTION

Pagels is considered one of the foremost contemporary scholars of the early Christian Church. She is known for her ability to write about theoretical and intellectual matters in clear and engaging prose understandable to the layman.

Biographical Information

Pagels was born February 13, 1943 in Palo Alto, California, to William McKinley, a research biologist, and Louise Sophia (van Druten) Hiesey. She received a B.A. from Stanford in 1964, after which she studied at Harvard University, receiving an M.A. in 1965 and a Ph.D. in 1970. In 1969 she married Heinz Pagels, a physicist; the couple had three children. Pagels's husband was killed in a hiking accident in 1988, one year after the death of their son Mark. Pagels worked as a professor of the history of religion at Bernard College from 1970 until 1982, serving as head of the department during her last eight years there. In 1982 she was named the Harrington Spear Paine Professor of Religion at Princeton University, where she continues to teach. Pagels also served as a member of Professor James Robinson's translation team, helping to translate the gnostic texts which were originally found in a cave in Egypt in 1945.

Major Works

Although concerned with disparate subjects, Pagels employs a common structure in her works: the exploration of problems in contemporary society through a consideration of their roots in the early Christian church. She has published widely on the Gnostic church, a group of Christians who splintered from the orthodox faith in the first centuries A.D. While her first books were written primarily for a scholarly audience, her last three books have garnered wider attention. *The Gnostic Gospels* (1979), for which she won the National Book Award, is an account of the early Gnostic faith and the challenges these believers faced. It chronicles the conflict between the smaller gnostic group and the orthodox church which ultimately gained control of the Christian church and suppressed the gnostic tradition. The arguments in *Adam, Eve and the Serpent* (1988) are not based on new data but rather a reworking of existing material in which Pagels considers moral freedom, original sin, and the Genesis creation story. *The Origin of Satan* (1995) explores the historic roots of the concept of Satan. Using anthropological terms, Pagels argues that groups have defined Satan and evil as "other" in conflict with the goodness of "self" and asserts that the urge to demonize others has a long history.

Critical Reception

The reception to Pagels's last three books has been mixed. Some scholars have praised her ability to conceptualize unifying themes from disparate sources. She is also lauded for her ability to present ideas clearly and simply, for her engaging writing style, and for her ability to explain complicated intellectual material clearly to the layperson and to tie the events of the past to contemporary issues. Thomas D'Evelyn wrote that Pagels "not only brings the voices of the early Christians alive, but also presents their lives in sympathetic contexts." Pagels has also been criticized, however, for presenting sensational, opinionated arguments; for ignoring conflicting theories and data; and for promoting questionable scholarship. Raymond Brown challenged her assertion in *The Gnostic Gospels* that she had presented an unbiased argument, declaring that she is clearly sympathetic to the gnostics. Others have suggested that Pagels at times has ignored the latest scholarship in the field. *The Gnostic Gospels* won the 1979 National Book Critics Circle Award and the 1980 National Book Award.

PRINCIPAL WORKS

The Johannine Gospel in Gnostic Exegesis: Heracleon's Commentary on John (nonfiction) 1973
The Gnostic Paul: Gnostic Exegesis of the Pauline Letters (nonfiction) 1975
The Gnostic Gospels (nonfiction) 1979
The Gnostic Jesus and Early Christian Politics (nonfiction) 1981
Adam, Eve and the Serpent (nonfiction) 1988
The Origin of Satan: The New Testament Origins of Christianity's Demonization of the Jews, Pagans & Heretics (nonfiction) 1995

CRITICISM

B. Cobbey Crisler (review date 3 December 1979)

SOURCE: "Gnostic 'Books'," in *The Christian Science Monitor,* December 3, 1979, p. B6.

[*In the following review, Crisler describes* The Gnostic Gospels *as a lucid history of the Gnostic movement.*]

The shattering of two ancient jars, one in December, 1945, near Nag Hammadi in Egypt and the other, almost a year later, in a Dead Sea cave, still reverberates in the alcoves of Biblical scholarship.

Although the extraordinary manuscript discoveries in the Dead Sea area have been widely examined, published, and commented upon (with certain notable exceptions), the "gnostic" library found hidden in the Nag Hammadi jar remained "for eyes only", (except for the "Gospel of Thomas") among scholarly initiates until the end of 1977. Then the 52 tractates in 13 codices appeared in a full facsimile edition and a simultaneous English edition, both under the general supervision and editorship of James M. Robinson, director of the Institute of Antiquity and Christianity at Claremont Graduate School in California. Said Professor Robinson at the time. "The floodgates have just opened."

Random House is in the sluiceway early with this book by Elaine Pagels, a member of Professor Robinson's translation team. As a book, it is the logical and inevitable outcome of her close association with the Nag Hammadi material. She writes for the layman, which is refreshing and she does so lucidly, which is a challenge, especially when "gnosticism" was regarded by its own adherents to be for the initiated only.

But as a title *The Gnostic Gospels* is inappropriate and was probably an editorial choice—the word "gospel" has market appeal. Certainly there is no indication in the introduction or in the text that the author ever intended to isolate the so called "gospels" of truth, of Thomas, Philip, the Egyptians, and Mary, from the rest of the corpus. Nor is any effort made to compare the "gnostic" gospels with the canonical gospels, as would be expected if the title correctly expressed the book's purpose.

Dr. Pagels instead has chosen to examine some of the primary concepts of "gnosticism," its themes and their major challenge to orthodox Christianity, all of which, she thinks should be re-evaluated in the light of the total Nag Hammadi find. In this same light, even the term "gnosticism," like Alice's Cheshire Cat, seems to be losing more of its definition, when it is made to apply to an amorphous collection of sects, loosely related, divergent in many points of view, and allegiant to scattered teachers.

If there is a common denominator that unites all sects called "gnostic," it is not theological concord. For represented in the relevant literature are the monadic and dyadic; the Scriptural and anti-Scriptural; the roots of paganism and source materials both Jewish and Christian; the ascetic and the seducer; the heresy of Simon Magus and the disillusionment of Tertullian.

In her search for a common denominator for a motivation that would and might have linked all these sects, Dr. Pagels writes: "In many churches, the bishop was emerging for the first time, as a 'monarch'—(literally 'sole ruler'). Increasingly, he claimed the power to act as disciplinarian and judge over those he called, 'the laity.' Could certain gnostic movements represent resistance to this process? Could gnostics stand among the critics who oppose the development of church hierarchy? Evidence from Nag Hammadi suggests that they did." This is a prominent thesis in her book.

Dr. Pagels also devotes a full chapter and much detail to the divisive views of the role of women in the church which she thinks may have helped motivate and widen the gap between "gnostics" and orthodox Christians. Some "gnostic" women "were revered as prophets; others acted as teachers, traveling evangelists, healers, priests, perhaps even bishops." Noting the topicality of this issue today, she adds, "The Nag Hammadi sources, discovered at a time of contemporary social crises concerning sexual roles, challenge us to reinterpret history—and to re-evaluate the present situation."

Dr. Pagels is sensitive to the fact that her work might be misinterpreted. Her book practically closes with a disclaimer: "That I have devoted so much of the discussion to gnosticism does not mean, as the casual reader might assume, that I advocate going back to gnosticism—much less that I 'side with it' against orthodox Christianity." For her, there is no question that Christianity would never have survived without the protection of its developing organization and structure, but she also provides the reader with reasons for sympathy with the "gnostic" outlook, not in its phases of wild distortion, but in those phases that offer logical, perhaps even Scriptural, occasion to review inherited ecclesiastical traditions.

Raymond E. Brown (review date 20 January 1980)

SOURCE: "The Christians Who Lost Out," in *The New York Times Book Review,* Vol. 85, January 20, 1980, pp. 3, 33.

[*Below, Brown offers a negative assessment of* The Gnostic Gospels.]

Some 30 years ago, there were two discoveries in the Middle East that have great, even if indirect significance for our knowledge of early Christianity. In 1945, Coptic codices (books) were found at Nag Hammadi, near the Nile, about 300 miles south of Cairo; in 1947, scrolls, mostly Hebrew and Aramaic, were found at Qumran, near the Dead Sea.

These parallel discoveries reflect curiously parallel histories. The Egyptian codices, in fourth-century A.D. script, contain 52 works translated from earlier Greek texts, many of them composed by Christian gnostic sectarians. They contain views of Jesus and God that were condemned by the Fathers of the emerging Catholic Church. Weeded from the library of a nearby monastery, the codices were buried in a jar, probably to prevent their discovery during the anti-heretical purges inaugurated in 367 by Athanasius, the famous bishop of Alexandria. The Dead Sea scrolls came from pre-Christian Jewish sectarians, probably Essenes. They propose legal interpretations and apocalyptic dreams (some shared by Christians) that were anathema to the Pharisees who gave shape to orthodox Judaism. Some of these Hebrew scrolls were also buried in jars, to hide them from advancing Roman armies.

The Dead Sea scrolls got notoriety when Edmund Wilson popularized them in *The New Yorker* and in a subsequent book, unkindly dubbed a novel by some critics. The coptic codices are on their way to notoriety now that Elaine Pagels, chairman of the religion department at Barnard, has popularized them in *The New York Review of Books* and in *The Gnostic Gospels*. Wilson was a littérateur and an amateur scholar of Hebrew, Professor Pagels is a recognized scholar of gnosticism; but her popularization, like his, may well be a controversial success. Both books make important discoveries of antiquity accessible to readers who might otherwise have ignored them, but both are accused by scholars of underlining the sensational.

In her introduction to *The Gnostic Gospels*, Professor Pagels asks why the Nag Hammadi discovery is so little known. She reports that Pahor Labib of the Coptic Museum granted only a few scholars access to the manuscripts and that, as a graduate student at Harvard in 1968, she was "delighted" when she was allowed to study mimeographed transcriptions of the texts. Yet a dozen years before that, it was perfectly possible for me and other graduate students at Johns Hopkins to study a book of photographs, published by the same Pahor Labib, of 13 of the treatises. And the fact that 4,000 studies of varying length have already appeared on the gnostic documents suggests that they have not exactly been neglected.

Without detracting from Professor Pagels's original contribution, let me note another possible confusion in her presentation. She has chosen to call the Coptic library *The Gnostic Gospels*, even though not all the treatises are gnostic

and only about 10 percent are called "Gospels." The title of her book thus might lead us to anticipate new knowledge about the historical Jesus. But from these works we learn not a single verifiable new fact about Jesus' ministry, and only a few new sayings that might plausibly have been his.

Professor Pagels recognizes this, for she does use the Coptic works correctly, not to describe Jesus but to describe the struggle within early Christianity between a smaller group that lost out—i.e., the gnostics—and the larger group that was to become the orthodox Church. Gnosticism is so diverse that it almost defies definition. In general, its Christian proponents claimed special knowledge—about the divine status of human beings—that had been obscured in the Old Testament but was revealed to the elect by Jesus, who was thus regarded as an illuminator rather than a dying savior. Until now we have known the gnostics through the polemics of their adversaries, especially Irenaeus, bishop of Lyons (c. A.D. 180). The importance of the Nag Hammadi find is that it gives us the gnostics' own writings and thoughts. When the Coptic library first appeared, W.F. Albright argued that it proved the Church Fathers were correct in both their analysis of gnostic thought and their aversion to it. Professor Pagels's arguments are more nuanced, but it is noteworthy that *The Gnostic Gospels* contains more references to Irenaeus and the other Fathers than to the Coptic works. The ancient orthodox texts are still the key to the very obscure gnostic writings we now possess.

One can only applaud Professor Pagels's intention to write as a historian of religion, "not to advocate any side, but to explore the evidence." But about nine-tenths of the discussion of each topic in the book consists of her sympathetic effort to understand the gnostics' side, which will leave the reader cheering for them and wishing that the narrow-minded orthodox had not won. Only at the end, nearly buried, comes Professor Pagels's dispassionate statement pointing out the chasm into which gnosticism could lead and hinting that the orthodox, despite their dyspepsia, may have had their heads on straight. Thus she can defend herself against the misinterpretations people will draw from her book.

Indeed, she even anticipates such misunderstandings, Her book, she says, "does not mean, as the casual reader might assume, that I advocate going back to gnosticism—much less that I 'side with it' against orthodox Christianity." But such a one-line disclaimer will not satisfy other scholars who will ask whether she has responsibly executed her duty to the "casual reader." Pheme Perkins, whom Professor Pagels cites for her contribution to gnostic research, will not be alone in her judgment that *The Gnostic Gospels* is "flawed by hasty generalization, over-interpretation of texts to fit a pre-determined scheme, and lack of sympathetic balance."

The scheme into which Professor Pagels seeks to fit the

gnostics is drawn from the sociology of religion, a delicate task for a minority such as the early Christians, and an even more delicate task for the gnostics, who were a minority within that minority. She sees theological differences as reflecting differences in church politics. The orthodox insisted upon the bodily resurrection of Jesus, she argues, because the authority for that claim was a chain of tradition going back to the apostles—a chain that supported the authority of the bishop in the church structure. The gnostics, on the other hand, had a nonphysical view of Christ, based on the spiritual experiences of his presence by the illumined elite; their view lessened the need for an authoritative church teacher and allowed greater freedom.

Yet did not Paul (who did not have a simplistic view of physical resurrection; see I Corinthians 15:44) already emphasize the need for an identifiable chain of witnesses to Jesus raised-from-burial (I Corinthians 15:3-8), long before anyone argued about the authority of bishops? And did not the gnostics develop their own authorities, so that eventually they were as critical of one another as they were of the orthodox? In another chapter of *The Gnostic Gospels*, it becomes clear that the denial of bodily resurrection was less a matter of reliable information than a corollary of the gnostics' denial that Jesus was truly human and really did die.

We are told by Professor Pagels that the orthodox, in order to have a theological analogy for the authority of one bishop, emphasized the one God, while many gnostics downgraded the cruel creator god of the Jews and had a more subtle vision of the Unknown. Here Professor Pagels slips badly by making Clement of Rome, whom she thrice calls bishop, a primary advocate for a church structure ruled by a single bishop. Yet there is no evidence for a single bishop in Rome until well after Clement's time; he never gave himself any title, much less that of bishop; and he clearly advocated an earlier church structure with a plurality of bishops. Moreover, the orthodox insistence on monotheism was surely part of the heritage from Judaism; any relationship of monotheism to monepiscopacy was only a very minor factor.

Professor Pagels presents the orthodox as upholding the distinction between the ordained (male) clergy and the laity—a distinction rejected by gnostics, who often rotated cultic functions, even among women. Yet the discriminating reader of *The Gnostic Gospels* can learn, from material tucked away in the book, that the gnostics' stance reflected neither a laudable democratic instinct nor an anticipation of women's liberation. The gnostics could share the highest clerical functions among themselves because they regarded themselves as the elite and all other Christians as ignorant and (for some gnostics) as the *massa damnata*. It would be a rare orthodox clergyman whose contempt for the laity would be comparable to the gnostic contempt for the non-gnostic.

Similarly, the careful reader can discover that the gnostic texts that praise women do so because these women have rejected the "works of femaleness." One of the most famous gnostic gospels ends with the principle that "Every woman who will make herself male will enter the kingdom of heaven." If some gnostic texts present Mary Magdalene as the great Christian spokesman—as against Peter, the hero of the orthodox—it should not be forgotten that men were probably the authors of such works and that Mary Magdalene was only their mouthpiece. If the gnostics had been victorious, one may suspect sadly that the history of the male manipulation of the female in religion would still be dreary.

A final word on the greening of the gnostics by promoting this book through appeals to sex and daring. On the third page of her introduction, Professor Pagels quotes a passage that has Jesus kissing Mary Magdalene often on her mouth, and that passage is featured in advertisements for the book. It is only fair to warn the prurient that the action goes no further; this book, like the gnostic gospels, rates a PG rather than an X. As for the hint that it would be daring to read such a heterodox book, why not be more daring? Trust neither Professor Pagels nor her possibly suspect detractors, but instead buy the convenient collection of the gnostic works by James M. Robinson. Read the texts themselves and you may emerge "conservative-chic," concluding that crusty old Irenaeus was right, after all, to regard the gnostics as the crazies of the second century.

Hyam Maccoby (review date June 1980)

SOURCE: "Counter-Church," in *Commentary,* Vol. 69, No. 6, June, 1980, pp. 86-88.

[*In the following review, Maccoby argues that while* The Gnostic Gospels *provides the lay reader with an introduction to gnosticism, it is flawed in several crucial areas.*]

Gnosticism, an esoteric movement in ancient religion, has achieved surprising topicality. It may even be regarded as the form of religion most congenial to the modern world. Certain popular sects (such as Scientology) are really modern versions of gnosticism, with their description of earth as a lost, evil planet, containing trapped seeds of divinity, to be redeemed only by intervention of saviors from outer space. Anyone who regards himself as religious but "opposed to organized religion" is liable to gravitate toward the gnostic position.

The drawback of gnosticism is that its adherents turn away from the practical problems of the world. They regard themselves as living on this earth as aliens, having wandered here somehow by mistake. They form small isolated groups devoted to developing the secret knowledge (*gnosis*) of how to link up with their true home. Paupers who have learned that they are really princes, they reject the hovel in which they find themselves, assert their newly-discovered identity, and seek to return to the palace.

This is an attitude that arises in periods when the outward world affords little satisfaction or happiness, and particularly when political expression is stifled by great impersonal forces. Such a time was that of the Greco-Roman world, and such a time is our own. The gnostic movement thus has much to say to troubled, alienated souls of our generation.

The gnostic texts of Nag Hammadi have never received the publicity given to the Dead Sea Scrolls. Elaine Pagels has now written a book for the general reader [*The Gnostic Gospels*] in order to remedy the regrettable public ignorance of this important subject.
—*Hyam Maccoby*

Until quite recently, our knowledge of ancient gnosticism was sparse, being confined to quotations and descriptions embedded in the writings of its Christian opponents, such as Irenaeus and Tertullian, who regarded gnosticism as a Christian heresy. Modern scholars, however, have suggested that gnosticism existed *before* Christianity, and only took a Christian form at a later stage. In the 19th century, some very interesting Christian gnostic documents were brought to light, including the *Gospel of Mary* and the *Apocryphon of John*. Finally, in 1945, a library of gnostic documents (some non-Christian) was discovered at Nag Hammadi in Upper Egypt. They had been hidden in jars, probably by some gnostic-minded monk, at a time when the official Christian church was busily engaged in suppressing all the gnostic writings it could find. These manuscripts were in the Coptic (late Egyptian) language and were written in the 4th century, but were evidently translations of Greek originals dating from the 2nd century and perhaps earlier. From this discovery arose a huge scholarly industry, similar in dimensions to that based on the Dead Sea Scrolls. It will be many years before the full impact of the Nag Hammadi manuscripts can be gauged.

The most interesting questions to which definitive answers are being sought relate to the connections between gnosticism and Christianity. Even though official Christianity persecuted gnosticism in the 2nd and 3rd centuries, its own origins may be very much bound up with this "heresy." Many passages in the New Testament, especially in the Epistles of Paul and the Gospel of John, have a strongly gnostic flavor. The central myth of Pauline Christianity—the rescue of ini-

tiates from a fallen world by a descending and ascending Savior—is essentially gnostic in nature. So the question again presents itself: which came first, gnosticism or Christianity? And why did gnosticism and official Christianity eventually come into conflict? What about Jesus himself? Was he a gnostic teacher, or did gnostic ideas enter Christianity only with Paul? Or was Jesus an essentially Jewish teacher whose career was transformed into a gnostic myth after his death?

There are also some very interesting questions about the relation between gnosticism and Jewish mysticism. There can be no doubt that the vocabulary of Jewish mysticism, from its earliest literary manifestations, is permeated with expressions derived from gnosticism, though these expressions are given a Jewish meaning at variance with the dualism and world-weariness of gnosticism itself. But can it be, as Moritz Friedlander has argued, that the historical origin of gnosticism is actually to be found in heterodox Judaism? Or was gnosticism (as Gershom Scholem has remarked) "conceived in the struggle against Judaism as the conqueror of mythology"? Among the Nag Hammadi manuscripts are some that make no reference to Christianity but are full of Jewish references. Are these the work of heretical Jews, or of non-Jews both fascinated and repelled by Judaism who constructed a mythology from Jewish materials by standing Judaism on its head?

Perhaps we should look for the origins of gnosticism independently of both Christianity and Judaism, in the religiosity of the Hellenistic world. A few of the Nag Hammadi texts are entirely pagan. There are strong similarities between gnosticism and pagan forms of mysticism: Hermetism, which was associated with the worship of the Egyptian god Thoth, and the mystery-religions associated with fertility deities (in their Hellenistic elaborations). Special claims can be made also for a background of Zoroastrianism, or even of Buddhism (which was known in the Hellenistic world). Arguments for a Hellenistic origin of gnosticism were once thought to have been refuted, but the pagan gnostic texts of Nag Hammadi have reopened the debate. And this again revives the question of whether Paul created Christianity by injecting, into a not unusual Jewish messianic group, ideas derived from the pagan mystical sects of his native Tarsus.

The gnostic texts of Nag Hammadi have never received the publicity given to the Dead Sea Scrolls. Elaine Pagels has now written a book for the general reader [*The Gnostic Gospels*] in order to remedy the regrettable public ignorance of this important subject. Professor Pagels's professional work has been concerned with the Nag Hammadi documents, and she has previously written scholarly works on the connections between these documents and the New Testament.

As the only existing guide on the subject for the general

reader, Professor Pagels's book has to be recommended, but it is disappointing. The author does not treat the subject of gnosticism with the breadth it deserves. Her chief topic is the conflict between Christian gnosticism and orthodox Christianity in the 2nd century, and she almost ignores aspects of the Nag Hammadi texts not relevant to this issue. She does, however, provide an introduction of wider scope, describing in readable fashion the history of the Nag Hammadi discovery, including the political and scholarly infighting that took place before the manuscripts were released to the world, and also giving a brief summary of the work that has been done on the manuscripts so far.

In her treatment of the conflict between orthodoxy and gnosticism, Professor Pagels seeks first of all to revise the (allegedly) widely held view of early Christianity as consisting of a central church with a lunatic fringe, and to give us instead a picture of a mass of rival sects of which the so-called orthodox church was only one and not even the most promising. As for the gnostics, she shows that, in contrast to orthodox Christians, they were unconcerned with institutional forms, and their communities were characterized by equality, even extending to the choice of priests and prophets by lot. They narrowed the gap between the human and the divine to such an extent that the initiate was regarded as sharing deity with the Savior, Jesus. She gives an attractive picture of the gnostics, emphasizing the spontaneity and inwardness of their religious approach, and arguing that they were pro-feminist. At the same time, she freely admits that such a religion, by reason of its anti-institutionalism and its tendency to split into innumerable groups, was ill-adapted for survival over a long period.

Her picture of the gnostics is considerably idealized in the interests of recommending them to modern libertarians and anti-authoritarians. The darker side of the gnostics is hardly touched on: their obsession with the evil of this world, their hatred of sex, their elitism, their mystagogic pretension, and at times their "transcendence" of ordinary morality. Still, a valuable description is given of the Valentinians, the one gnostic group that made a serious effort to combine mystical insight with the claims of ordinary communal life.

Professor Pagels, unfortunately, has a tedious bee in her bonnet. This is her idea that doctrinal differences between orthodox and gnostic Christians can often be explained in terms of "politics." She applies this approach, for example, to the orthodox insistence on strict monotheism, as opposed to the gnostic belief that the creator of the world was a minor deity (suffering from megalomania), and that the true, ineffable God was far above him. Professor Pagels argues that this difference of doctrine reflected a difference of political, or organizational, attitude: the orthodox hierarchy, with the Bishop of Rome at its apex, was projected into the heavens in the shape of God and His angels. She does not consider the possibility, exemplified by Judaism, that a religion can insist on strict monotheism while its religious institutions remain unhierarchical and decentralized (there was never any Jewish equivalent to the Pope). Professor Pagels here puts the cart before the horse. For the Church, monotheism was a philosophy of life that included among its consequences the need to take seriously the organization of the community of the faithful. If this world was created by the One God, and not by a limited or flawed underling, then it must be basically good, demanding and repaying efforts to set it in order.

Professor Pagels has very little to say about the personality of the historical Jesus, but her general approach suggests that she thinks he was more like the gnostics than the orthodox, and that his alleged conflict with the Pharisees foreshadowed the gnostic struggle with officialdom. At one point, in a rare direct reference to the historical Jesus, she suggests that the gnostics' free attitude toward women reflected that of Jesus, who "violated Jewish convention by talking openly with women, and . . . included them among his companions." But Jesus did not in fact "violate Jewish convention," since in his easy relationship with women he was following the well-understood pattern of the Jewish prophet (compare Elijah with the widow of Zarephath and Elisha with the woman of Shunem). On the other hand, the feminism of the gnostics can easily be exaggerated; often it only amounted to a contempt for sex and a desire to reduce all mankind to neuter beings.

In general, the role of Judaism in this book is to act as a kind of prototype for the patriarchal, hierarchical structure eventually assumed by the Catholic Church. Opposed to both Judaism and Catholic Christianity is the free individualism of the gnostic sects. This is too simple, not only because it exaggerates the "freedom" of gnosticism but also because the Catholic Church was much more rigid, both doctrinally and institutionally, than Judaism had ever been.

The position of women under Pharisaic Judaism was relatively good: they were allowed to own property even after marriage, to be divorced if ill treated, to refuse an uncongenial marriage. These rights were all lost under Catholic Christianity. The recognition of a female element in the Divine—which Professor Pagels claims as an original achievement of the gnostics—was far from unknown in Judaism, where, for example, one of the divine names, *Shaddai,* means "breast," and another *Rahaman* ("merciful") is derived from a root meaning "womb." The idea of divine femininity is prominent, of course, in Jewish medieval mysticism. The doctrine that Adam was originally hermaphroditic (based on Genesis 1:27, "male and female created He them") is a common-place of the aggadic tradition. The gnostics probably took this idea from the aggada. It is most unlikely that a talmudic rabbi derived it from Plato, as Professor

Pagels asserts, especially as the idea can be traced back to Babylonian literature.

Professor Pagels's simple opposition of gnostics to orthodox Christians will not do. The real problem is the extreme polarization which Christianity underwent. Why did it divide into lawless gnostics on the one hand and rigidly organized "male-chauvinist" Catholics on the other? Why did the Church produce a hierarchy very similar to the pattern falsely attributed to the Pharisees in the (hostile) descriptions of the Gospels? Why was there no middle ground between a complete rejection of human institutions and the formation of a bureaucracy with a penchant for repression? The answer to this, I suggest, lies in the antinomianism of Pauline Christianity—its extremist antagonism to the concept of law. This is what divided Christendom into those trying to capture an impossible spontaneity and those struggling, by an inevitably exaggerated and overstructured reaction, to infuse a commonsense practicality into the business of communal living. Official Christianity has always had to struggle desperately with people who take the original tenets of Pauline Christianity seriously, and so threaten to destroy all continuity and viability in society. The pendulum thus swings between anarchy and repression.

The study of the gnostic texts will continue to throw light both on the origins of Pauline Christianity and on its subsequent struggles. I doubt if it will throw much light on Jesus himself, since he was rooted in Pharisaic Judaism. Professor Pagels's [*The Gnostic Gospels*], on the whole, is a useful but flawed interim report, a guide to the many fascinating possibilities that have been opened up, but a guide that should be consulted with caution.

Kathleen McVey (essay date January 1981)

SOURCE: "Gnosticism, Feminism, and Elaine Pagels," in *Theology Today,* Vol. XXXVII, No. 4, January, 1981, pp. 498-501.

[*In the following essay, McVey explores issues of feminism in Pagels's* The Gnostic Gospels.]

A collection of Coptic documents discovered at Nag Hammadi (Chenoboskion) in Egypt in 1945 has shed important light on early Christianity by increasing our understanding of gnosticism. Gnosticism existed in pagan, Jewish, and Christian forms and was a major competitor with orthodox Christianity during the second century A.D. Christian gnosticism, a complex and varied movement, is nevertheless theologically distinct from Orthodox Christianity because it differentiates between the ineffable true God and the inferior Demiurge who created the material world and who is

essentially identical with the God of the Old Testament. Christian adherents of gnosticism further believed that they, the "pneumatics" or spiritual people, constituted the true church over against the "psychics," ordinary Christians, and the "hylics," the material people.

> **Elaine Pagels . . . is among those who accept [Walter] Bauer's basic understanding of the relationship between orthodoxy and heresy. Her recent book,** *The Gnostic Gospels,* **is therefore a popularization not only of the Coptic gnostic find at Nag Hammadi but also of the Bauer thesis.**
>
> **—*Kathleen McVey***

Accepting the basic thesis of Walter Bauer's *Orthodoxy and Heresy in Earliest Christianity,* some scholars believe that gnosticism represents a form of Christianity, the antiquity and legitimacy of which equals that of orthodox Christianity. Elaine Pagels of Barnard College is among those who accept Bauer's basic understanding of the relationship between orthodoxy and heresy. Her recent book, *The Gnostic Gospels,* is therefore a popularization not only of the Coptic gnostic find at Nag Hammadi but also of the Bauer thesis. As such, it is naturally attractive to certain readers and correspondingly abhorrent to others.

Pagels participated in the preliminary publication of the texts in question (*The Nag Hammadi Library in English,* ed. J. M. Robinson and M.W. Meyer, New York, 1977). She has also written on gnostic biblical exegesis and on other aspects of gnosticism, especially in its Valentinian form. The Gnostic Gospels begins with a lively account of the discovery of the texts, their eventual emergence into availability to scholars, and a general description of the state of research on gnosticism. The book itself consists of six chapters, each of which concentrates on some aspect of theology, contrasts the orthodox with the gnostic view, and seeks sociological explanations for the differences. She considers the theological differences, although real, insufficient to account for the opposition between the two groups., The chapters focus, in turn, on the understanding of Christ's resurrection, on the monarchic episcopacy, on the understanding of the deity in male vs. female terms, on attitudes toward martyrdom, on ecclesiology, and, finally, on "self-knowledge as knowledge of God." Throughout the book she draws out modern parallels to the attitudes of both gnostics and orthodox—with notably greater success in translating the gnostic beliefs into terms attractive to a sophisticated modern audience.

Elaine Pagels' *Gnostic Gospels* is a book calculated to appeal to the liberal intellectual Christian who feels personally religious but who dislikes "institutional religion." In the midst of the resurgence of anti-scientific and anti-intellectual currents throughout American Christianity, Pagels has presented us with an appealing portrayal of the gnostic Christians as a beleaguered minority of creative persons ignorant of their rightful historical role by a well-organized but ignorant lot of literalists. Although in her conclusion the author says she does not, "as the casual reader might assume, . . . advocate going back to gnosticism," she goes on to claim to have presented the gnostic texts "as Christians in the first centuries experienced them—[as] a powerful alternative to what we know as orthodox Christian tradition." Not only the "casual reader" but some careful readers and specialists in early Christian literature have perceived the book as a kind of modern apology for gnosticism.

Rather than repeating the remarks of the reviewers, I propose here to evaluate briefly one of the book's several related theses, that "two very different patterns of sexual attitudes [emerge] in orthodox and gnostic circles." Pagels claims three areas of evidence for these contrasting attitudes: (1) the gnostics describe the deity using both masculine and feminine terms while the orthodox use only masculine images; (2) gnostic exegesis of the creation story focuses on Genesis 1, where humans are created "male and female," while the orthodox emphasize Genesis 2, in which the woman's creation is secondary and for the happiness of the man; (3) the social practice of the two communities differs, the gnostics practicing a "principle of equality" between the sexes, while the orthodox subordinate women to men.

Elaine Pagels' *Gnostic Gospels* is a book calculated to appeal to the liberal intellectual Christian who feels personally religious but who dislikes "institutional religion."
—Kathleen McVey

What is the evidence presented on each of these points? First, on the nature of the deity, the Bible is taken as sufficient evidence of the orthodox use of almost exclusively masculine epithets for God. The few exceptions noted—Deut. 32.11, Hosea 11.1, Isaiah 66.12ff., and Num. 11.12—are insufficient to challenge the overall impression. Without denying the patriarchal framework of the Judaeo-Christian understanding of God, we may ask whether Pagels succeeds in showing that gnostic belief is any less sexist. She notes that "gnostic sources continually use sexual symbolism to describe God. . . . Yet instead of describing a monistic and masculine God, many of these texts speak of God as a dyad who embraces both masculine and feminine elements."

The simple fact that these texts often use "sexual symbol-

ism" to describe God tells us nothing in itself. The relationship between male and female elements in the dyad is the crucial issue. Since the male principle represents the spiritual realm and the female principle at worst the material realm, at best the spiritual elements in the material realm, all the gnostic cosmologies are ultimately patriarchal in conception.

Pagels' citation of excerpts from gnostic writings without their requisite contexts obscures the overall relation of male and female divine powers. For example, when Ialdabaoth boasts (in clear parody of Yahweh) that he is the only God, his Mother reprimands him, "Do not lie, Ialdabaoth." Since nothing of the context is revealed by Pagels, one might imagine that the female divine principle is superior to the male. But the Mother here is herself the "abortion" of Sophia, who is, in turn, the youngest of thirty aeons descended from the ineffable Father. Sophia's fall, caused by her attempt to know the Father apart from Nous, his only-begotten son, is ultimately the cause of the existence of the material world, from which the gnostic must escape.

On the second point, the exegesis of the Genesis creation story, it is simply untrue that orthodox Christians focused exclusively on Genesis 2. In support of her view, Pagels cites only I Corinthians 11.7-9. Other examples could be cited as well, but Pagels is evidently unaware of the Platonic Christian tradition of exegesis from Clement and Origen of Alexandria to the Cappadocians, Ambrose, and Augustine, which concentrates on Genesis 1. Pagels mentions Clement of Alexandria, but as a "striking exception to the orthodox pattern," and she notes that the consensus of orthodoxy "ruled out Clement's position." But Clement was not really so isolated and exceptional as she claims.

On the third point, the social practice of the two communities, our sole sources of information are the orthodox writers. Irenaeus and Tertullian, the only extant sources which describe the behavior of the gnostics, are discounted by Pagels when they describe behavior of which she disapproves but taken literally when the behavior is acceptable to modern feminist views. As Pagels remarks, "no one knows" whether to believe Irenaeus' claim (also, to his mind, an accusation) that Marcus allowed women to celebrate the eucharist with him is simply added without comment to the evidence that "clearly indicates a correlation between religious theory and social practice."

Further, Tertullian functions in this book as the mouthpiece of the "orthodox" view that women should not speak, teach, baptize, or claim any "masculine" function. He was indeed a first-class misogynist as well as one of the most important early Latin Fathers of the church. But Pagels breathes scarcely a word about Tertullian's doctrinal peculiarities, his extreme rigorism, and the fact that he spent more years as a

Montanist than he had as an orthodox Christian. Although early Montanism in Asia Minor provided a context in which women played a prominent role, Tertullian's brand of Montanism, having disposed of the "feminist" elements along with some other less viable eschatological tenets, lived on as a rigorist form of Christianity in North Africa for nearly two centuries, and was known as "Tertullianism."

In short, Heresy and feminism were not such good bedfellows as either Pagels or the modern Christian misogynists would have us believe. While there is some evidence that women may have played a larger role in some heretical communities than in their orthodox counterparts, attempts to link activity with the beliefs of the communities in question have failed.

Insofar as modern proponents of women's rights are concerned, does gnosticism offer a "powerful alternative" to Orthodox Christianity? I think not. Further, I hope that the intellectually curious will refuse to be swept along by Pagels' implicit appeal to see themselves among those "creative persons [who find] themselves at the edges of orthodoxy" but will instead investigate the matter for themselves.

Robin Lane Fox (review date 21 August 1988)

SOURCE: "Sweet Are the Uses of Original Sin," in *The New York Times Book Review,* August 21, 1988, pp. 15-6.

[*In the review below, Fox states that* Adam, Eve, and the Serpent *contains the best elements of Pagels' writing, but contends that Pagels' arguments are not always plausible.*]

The Bible begins with two accounts of the creation, written by different authors at different times. We do not know their dates, but the likeliest guesses are the eighth and seventh centuries B.C. We do know that they were later combined by a third person, the patron saint of relaxed editors. The two stories contradicted each other and each said the bare minimum. The editor did his best, which was next to nothing. He put the stories one after another and left an Eden of unanswered questions, in which posterity has wandered and made its own discoveries ever since.

Elaine Pagels's *Adam, Eve, and the Serpent* is the latest heir to these stories that suggest so much more than they state. Why did God say, "Let *us* make man," if only He existed? Why did He create man twice? Why was Adam given a woman as a helper, not another man? Was it because Adam and Eve were supposed to make love from the start? But if so, was wicked Cain conceived in Paradise? What exactly was the "knowledge" that did such harm: was it carnal, moral or psychedelic? Whatever was bothering the serpent? Ac-

cording to one view, he was jealous because he had seen the human couple making love in the garden. On another, he was disgusted with God's behavior: Why should a single tree be put out of bounds? Why should intelligence be classified as an official secret? One little slip by Adam and Eve, and God appears to weigh in with the death penalty. There were some imaginative early Christians who thought the serpent was the hero of the piece.

Unkind to serpents, the second of the two stories has not been kind to women. In the 17th century, just before the Mayflower sailed, good Englishwomen were still being encouraged to apologize in their prayers for the sin of their grandmother Eve. Speculative unorthodoxy, early Christianity and feminist imagery are a compound that brings the best out of Elaine Pagels, a professor of religion at Princeton University. Her new book takes Genesis 1-3 as the text of its sermon and has the distinctive qualities so many admired in her work on the Gnostic Gospels. It is very clearly written. It has form, moral impetus and direction. The author works with themes and ideas more than facts and historical detail. She sees close connections between contemporary and ancient ways of thinking. She comes across sympathetically and I have greatly enjoyed my dialogue with her argument.

Her book's impact lies in its direction and emphasis, not an any new discoveries that will change future study. The history of Adam and Eve has already been written on a much broader range. Ms. Pagels stops with St. Augustine and his arguments for original sin. This book lacks the luxuriant byways that were traveled only last year by James Turner's "One Flesh," a work that ranged from St. Paul to Milton. Ms. Pagels is less concerned with Jewish speculations on her themes, although books they consider apocryphal do overlap with ideas in early Christian sources. One rabbi even thought Adam had sex with each animal in order to test it before naming it. The idea has a hideous power.

Instead, Ms. Pagels focuses on two ideas, moral freedom and original sin. She admires the former idea as much as she regrets the latter, but I would question several turns in her arguments Christians, she believes, were the first to champion the "absolute moral worth of the individual," although there is more in pagan Greek philosophies about that than she reveals. The Christian "commitment to moral freedom" won converts, she says, and was appealingly radical. It also impelled some early Christians to seek martyrdom. In Ms. Pagels's view, it derived from the text on man's creation in God's image: Genesis inspired Christians to oppose "external domination by the Roman state." The "proclamation of moral freedom grounded in Genesis 1-3 was regarded as effectively synonymous with the Gospel."

I think she exaggerates. A small minority of "knowing," or Gnostic, Christians did make Genesis a battleground with orthodox authors, but the vast majority of Christians were more concerned with redemption by Christ than with possible views of creation by God. They were much less interested in the world's beginning than in its end and their fate afterwards. Christian martyrs and apologists do first voice the idea of "religious liberty," the idea that each person, as Tertullian wrote around 200 A.D., has a "free choice of divinity." That view arose from the position in the martyrs and apologists persecuted nonparticipants in Roman society, not from anything written in Genesis. Rather the martyrs and accounts of them quote Genesis on "bruising the serpent's head," the serpent being Satan over whom the Christian martyr triumphs. The texts on creation were not exploited, not even by the brave Perpetua, the early martyr who wrote an account of her trial and persecution and whom women's histories like to exploit instead.

As for original sin, Ms. Pagels has no truck with St. Augustine's idea and its influence. Her chapters on this lie closest to her title and they make the old issues very clear. When she considers why this doctrine seemed ever more plausible to fellow Christians. I find her case less than plausible. Her particular emphasis is political. By Augustine's day in the fifth century, she argues, the Church was part of a Christian empire under a Christian emperor. The idea that all humans are corrupted by heredity and therefore in need of government made sense of the Christians' new predicament. Why, though, did the doctrine of original sin take root deeply in the West, but much less so in the East, where church and emperor were even more closely intertwined? I think the political view is not much of an answer. Nor, strictly, is the personal one, that original sin made exceptional sense of misfortunes, deaths, illnesses and suffering. To St. Augustine, of course, it did, but why original sin and not just each individual's tendency to sinfulness? Original sin is not an invitation to feel guilt. Original sin and personal guilt are often connected too closely—as they are in this book. We cannot feel guilty for what is not our own fault. The danger in invoking original sin is to take away personal responsibility and open the way to ideas of cheap grace. Grace is not prominent in Ms. Pagels's exposition.

St. Augustine owed much to his wish to explain the great problem of undeserved evil and suffering. He also confronted his own congregations, those groups of stubbornly un-Christian Christians; their sins, more than the Empire's, needed explanation. Above all, he was involved in the particular problems of baptism, especially infant baptism. If babies were sinless, why baptize them? If they were sinful, how had sin entered, except through Adam? Ms. Pagels puts her main emphasis elsewhere. The first part of her book has little to do directly with Genesis; the second half could have advanced on a wider front. Like the serpent, these texts in Genesis offer scope for exceptional subtlety.

Thomas D'Evelyn (review date 14 September 1988)

SOURCE: "Politics in Paradise—the Genesis of 'Original Sin'," in *The Christian Science Monitor,* Vol. 80, No. 203, September 14, 1988, p. 18.

[*In the following review, D'Evelyn finds* Adam, Eve, and the Serpent *an "elegant, well-argued discussion of a bold thesis."*]

Adam, Eve, and the Serpent is an elegant, well-argued discussion of a bold thesis. To cover so much ground—four centuries of the Christian era—in such brief scope (under 200 pages), Elaine Pagels looks at a variety of interpretations of a key biblical text: the first three chapters of Genesis, the creation stories.

Long known to be from two different sources, these chapters cover the beginning of time, and the immediate aftermath. God creates man and woman in his image and gives them dominion over the earth; but Adam and Eve listen to the serpent and disobey God, bringing grief on themselves—Adam must work for a living and Eve must bear children in agony—and the whole race in perpetuity.

Obviously there's a problem here, a contradiction between the two stories, and Pagels manages to account for the range of responses to this text, from Jesus and his witnesses, including the Gnostics and Paul, down to St. Augustine in the fourth century. These responses, she discovers, reflect the position of Christians in the society of the Roman, then Christian, empire.

> ***Adam, Eve, and the Serpent*** is an elegant, well-argued discussion of a bold thesis.
> —*Thomas D'Evelyn*

She begins in the time of Jesus. She sees Jesus as "a firebrand village preacher" whose preaching of the kingdom-at-hand made him a loose cannon in an anxious society watched over by nervous Romans. Jesus' chastity, his advocacy of leaving all for the kingdom of heaven, his astringent, inward view of righteousness: These set the scene for a century of controversy over marriage, family, procreation, and celibacy-indeed, the capacity of men and women to decide how to live their own lives.

Pagels shows how the Apostle Paul's ascetic version of Jesus' message was answered by early church fathers such as the urbane Clement of Alexandria. In the background are the conflicting images in Genesis of sexual equality in the first chapter and the tension-filled, tragic relationship of Adam and Eve.

As the prospects of an early return on the millennial faith of the early Christians grew dim, the issues raised in Genesis became focused on liberty and autonomy. Widely and savagely persecuted, Christians showed remarkable courage, enough to convert pagans like Justin the philosopher, who himself would later become Justin Martyr.

Pagels is a good storyteller and retails these dramatic events-she used some of them in her earlier best-selling book, *The Gnostic Gospels*—to great effect. Her art has been compared to the novelist's: She not only brings the voices of the early Christians alive, but also presents their lives in sympathetic contexts. Her contexts are ultimately ideas, though: the ideas in Genesis-ideas about God's love for men and women, His endowing them with the capacity for righteous, rational action in the face of absurdity and death—meant much to the early Christians, some of whom chose celibacy and martyrdom rather than worship pagan, political gods.

In a neat epigram, Pagels notes that when the church entered the world, the world entered the church. Partly because of their eloquent lives, the Christians won the empire and all the perks that came with high office. A new interpretation of the creation was needed, one that played down autonomy and freedom, and elevated obedience to a high virtue.

In pages that will attract skepticism from Augustine scholars, Pagels argues that the bishop of Hippo filled the bill. His interpretation of Genesis included the concept, now orthodox in many Christian churches, of "original sin." His view implied-he would articulate this in his many debates with old-fashioned Christians, soon to be heretics-that Adam's sin corrupted not only Adam but all mankind, indeed all creation. Christians, like pagans, need empire and emperors!

Pagels carefully shows how useful such an interpretation was to Christians in power. It makes the will to be good impotent; desire is seen as the only autonomous force and must be repressed. Ecclesiastical and political hierarchy are justified because men and women cannot govern their own lives.

As Pagels shows in page after eloquent page, Augustine was opposed by strong arguers like John Chrysostom and Pelagius, the British ascetic whom Paul Johnson, in his "A History of the English People," thinks of as the founder of the English view of life. In our terms, Chrysostom and Pelagius were liberal: They argued for more moderation. Some autonomy, freedom of will, and choice—for Christian liberty. On the strength of Augustinian counterarguments, both were exiled as heretics.

This stunning book opens many questions. It refreshes our view of early Christianity by showing the variety of voices

that rang out in the primitive church. Pagels notes that the early liberal Christians did not articulate the politics of their interpretation of Genesis, but she adds that the American founders did. She does not try to refute Augustine, but rather puts his reading of Genesis in its full context, theological and political.

With wit, grace, profound sympathy for the early Christians, and admirable economy, Pagels has achieved in her little book what miles of biblical commentary have not: She has brought these issues to a white heat and tempered them on the anvil of her historical art.

Judith Ochshorn (review date April 1989)

SOURCE: "The Triumph of Pessimism," in *Women's Review of Books,* Vol. VI, No. 7, April, 1989, pp. 21-2.

[*In the review below, Ochshorn considers* Adam, Eve, and the Serpent *a fascinating account but finds some of Pagels's arguments troubling.*]

Elaine Pagels' new book [*Adam, Eve, and the Serpent*] describes, in rich historical detail, "how certain ideas—in particular, ideas concerning sexuality, moral freedom, and human value—took their definitive form during the first four centuries as interpretations of the Genesis creation stories, and how they have continued to affect our culture and everyone in it, Christian or not, ever since."

Some of these ideas expressed new attitudes toward gender roles, sexuality, marriage, divorce, procreation, family and celibacy, making for "a revolution in sexual attitudes and practices" as Christianity spread. And as Christianity moved from being a dissident, outlawed sect to being Rome's imperial religion in the fourth century, the discussions and disputes over these issues were rooted in diverse, often conflicting interpretations of the Genesis creation story.

The outlook of "orthodox" Christianity was formed during its converts' persecution by Rome and in its disputes with other Christian communities later declared heretical. Pagels devotes more than half her book to arguing that in its reading of Genesis, Chapters 1-3, this early orthodoxy came to be marked by an optimistic view of human nature, a belief in the moral freedom and the infinite worth of the individual. This sets the stage for her description of the later collision between orthodox ideology and Augustine's new, far more pessimistic and punitive, view of human nature. Why, asks Pagels, did the church leadership, then the laity, embrace the Augustinian doctrine?

Adam, Eve and the Serpent is full of the high drama of

women and men who literally staked their lives on their interpretations of the creation text. Pagels' story opens at the beginning of the Common Era, when Jesus broke with his fellow Jews in his attitudes toward divorce, family and procreation, exhorting his followers to abandon family ties and responsibilities and follow him into the new age. When he suggested that celibacy might be preferable to marriage "for the sake of the Kingdom of Heaven," and Paul urged celibacy over marriage in preparation for the imminent endtimes, they fueled a 200-year-long debate that pitted ordinary family and sexual affection against celibacy. Radical, ascetic Christians advocated celibacy as the only way to expunge the sin of Adam and Eve, and because Jesus prohibited divorce, some married converts, women as well as men, even practiced abstinence.

> ***Adam, Eve and the Serpent* is full of the high drama of women and men who literally staked their lives on their interpretations of the creation text.**
> **—*Judith Ochshorn***

Such a life was described in "The Acts of Paul and Thecla," an enormously popular story that circulated widely within a century of Paul's death. Thecla was allegedly a young virgin who deserted her mother, rejected her fiancé and a potentially wealthy marriage, braved rape and the death sentence of the Roman state (from which she was miraculously rescued), all to follow the virginal life preached by Paul. When he refused to baptize her she baptized herself and later became a teacher, holy woman and saint of Eastern churches.

Pagels explains the appeal of Paul's endorsement of asceticism and celibacy for women like Thecla who chose freedom from traditional gender roles:

> she—and thousands like her—welcomed such radical versions of the gospel. . . . Their vows of celibacy served many converts as a declaration of independence from the crushing pressures of tradition and their families, who ordinarily arranged marriages at puberty and so determined the course of their children's lives. As early as the second century of the Christian Era and thereafter, Christian celibates may have invoked Thecla's example to justify the fight of Christian women to baptize and preach. Even two hundred years later, Christian women who chose the way of asceticism, whether living in solitude at home or in monastic communities founded and often financed by wealthy women, called themselves "new Theclas."

In the century following Jesus' death, even while celibacy and asceticism were on the rise, the author of the Gospel According to Matthew qualified Jesus' absolute prohibition of divorce by adding that it is permissible in cases of "immorality." Likewise, he has Jesus enlarge the Christian community, shortly before his call to his followers to abandon earthly ties, by adding the admonition to "honor your father and mother." In effect, Pagels observes, Matthew has Jesus make room for those living ordinary lives with their families as well as those who aspire to spiritual perfection through asceticism. By the second century most Christians agreed with the moderate Clement of Alexandria, who held that Adam's sin consisted essentially of disobedience and was sexual only in form, and that the significance of the story of Adam and Eve was that it showed people were morally responsible for their choices between good and evil—choices, he emphasized, which were freely made.

However, Pagels points out that even Clement, one of the most liberal fathers of the church, established damaging norms for Christian behavior that have endured for two thousand years. Greatly ambivalent about sexuality, he wavered between denunciation and praise of celibacy and he encouraged sex in marriage only if it was without passion and for reproduction alone. He endorsed patriarchal marriage because he believed in male superiority and in the justice of punishing Eve and all women for her sin. Yet he read Genesis 1 as a text showing all people were equal since God formed humanity in his own image. This belief in equality was consistent with what Pagels considers Christianity's two cardinal tenets up to that time: a deep commitment to moral freedom and a belief in the infinite worth of individuals:

> for nearly the first four hundred years of our era, Christians regarded freedom as the primary message of Genesis 1-3—freedom in its many forms, including free will, freedom from demonic powers, freedom from social and sexual obligations, freedom from tyrannical government and from fate; and self-mastery as the source of such freedom.

The Christian martyrs' defiance of Rome in the arena showed their faith in God's assurance of moral freedom. They could battle against wild animals because they were convinced conversion and baptism gave them the power to overcome pain, suffering, evil, even death. Pagels sees this early insistence on individual moral freedom as central in orthodox doctrine, and leading to the suppression of early Christian groups who did not share this belief—Gnostic Christians, for example, who differed fundamentally from the orthodox in their contention that we have some freedom to make moral choice but aren't absolutely free to avoid all suffering, which is built into the structure of the universe.

In the fourth century Augustine entered the debate over human nature and moral freedom. He believed that Adam's sin, freely chosen, was and would forever be transmitted through sexual intercourse (or semen) to all of his progeny; and that from the moment of conception, or the materialization of (shameful) sexual desire, all of us are infected with original sin and deprived of free moral choice. Augustine's contrary interpretation of Genesis argued that suffering, sin, sexuality and death were consequences of human guilt and sin— divinely imposed to punish Adam's original sin—not natural occurrences. God allowed Adam to sin in order to demonstrate that people could not be totally free, and that, poisoned and corrupted by original sin, people needed to be governed by church and state in order to be saved.

Pagels argues that this theory legitimized Christian obedience to Rome, by breaking with the tradition that celebrated moral freedom:

> Augustine says, in simplest terms, . . . [that] human beings cannot be trusted to govern themselves, because our very nature—indeed, all of nature—has become corrupt as the result of Adam's sin. In the late fourth and fifth century, Christianity was no longer a suspect and persecuted movement; now it was the religion of emperors obligated to govern a vast and diffuse population. Under these circumstances . . . Augustine's theory of human depravity—and, correspondingly, the political means to control it—replaced the previous ideology of human freedom.

Thereby, she concludes, Augustine helped establish the hegemony of the Catholic Church (which became the state religion as Rome became a Christian state), excluding those of his Christian rivals who held more traditional, optimistic views of human nature; and his view has held to date.

But why did the church, in the fifth and sixth centuries, choose to adopt what Pagels sees as Augustine's "extraordinary" ideas, rather than discard them as alien to Christian tradition? "People," she conjectures,

> need to find reasons for their sufferings . . . *people often would rather feel guilty than helpless* . . . such guilt, however painful, offers reassurance that such events do not occur at random but follow specific laws of causation; and that their causes, or a significant part of them, lie in the moral sphere, and so within human control.

Her analysis of the triumph of Augustine's views leads Pagels to detect a great paradox at the heart of Christianity, a paradox which becomes the book's main theme. On the one hand the religion adheres to Augustine's doctrine that after Adam no one can choose not to sin. On the other, it is

shaped by its early commitment to moral freedom and human responsibility for moral choices freely made, and by its stress on the infinite worth of each individual created in God's image. Pagels argues that, though eclipsed by the Augustinian view of human nature, Western Christianity's earlier emphasis on individualism and moral freedom has remained influential, with echoes in the American Declaration of Independence, in Jefferson's thinking and in other developments in the modern concepts of individualism and liberty. Her position, then, diverges from that of those feminists who reject Christianity as irredeemably patriarchal, and who believe its patriarchal character derives from its cultural context or male mistranslations and misinterpretations of divine intentions.

There are a number of fascinating things in this book. It is dense with accounts of those who, as martyrs, ascetics, gnostics and fathers of the church, acted out religious beliefs about human nature, defied social conventions, took great personal risks, or participated in fierce controversies over ideas in the focus on Genesis. These few pages in the Hebrew Bible, never again mentioned in the rest of that document and referred to by Jesus only once, have been used ever since to justify male dominance and female subordination. It is striking that, as Pagels notes, when Christianity was in its formative stages, some Christian Gnostic texts portrayed Eve positively as the source of spiritual renewal. Her analysis of Augustine's long battle to impose his theory of original sin both relativizes and demystifies it, especially for women.

Pagels' book [*Adam, Eve, and the Serpent*] is about the power of ideas. She rightly claims that from the time the Church triumphed politically in the fourth century, "Christian attitudes began to transform the consciousness, to say nothing of the moral and legal systems, that continue to form Western society."
—*Judith Ochshorn*

Despite the elegance of Pagels' argument, it has some troublesome elements. She virtually equates the early Christian commitments to human freedom and to the infinite worth of the individual. Certainly there is a basis for this equation in parts of the Gospels, orthodox and gnostic alike, and it is true that part of the attractiveness of Christianity to its many early converts was its emphasis on living the "good life" in Christian community on an everyday basis. But it was precisely in everyday life that the promotion of moral freedom was not necessarily the same as the protection of individual worth. Much of the assessment of Christianity as a champion of moral freedom and human worth depended on who was doing the assessing.

Nowhere in the extensive theological discourse on Genesis 1-3 is slaveholding, for example (cited by Pagels), attacked as oppressive to some individuals (also created in the image of God). Declining to take a position on concrete issues is, of course, a position in itself. That Christianity promoted the moral freedom of slaves in the fourth, as in the nineteenth, century did not affect their material conditions. Similarly, the Christian image of women that identifies us all as daughters of Eve or urges our salvation through emulation of Mary has hardly promoted a belief in the infinite worth of individual women. And while asceticism may have been sexually democratic, it was not the way of life chosen by most who remained within patriarchal marriages.

Pagels' book [*Adam, Eve, and the Serpent*] is about the power of ideas. She rightly claims that from the time the Church triumphed politically in the fourth century, "Christian attitudes began to transform the consciousness, to say nothing of the moral and legal systems, that continue to form Western society." And she credits the early Christian tradition for its influence on later philosophies that championed "the absolute value of the individual." But there is another face to that influence. Just as belief in the universal capacity for moral choice did not guarantee respect for the worth of all individuals, the concept of moral freedom, while important, did not touch issues of oppression, power and powerlessness. Augustine's view, adopted by the Church, has seen women as only instrumental in men's struggles with sex and sin. Historically we have been considered more responsible for and vulnerable to sin than men, dangerous to men's pursuit of righteousness and destabilizing to society (witness the sixteenth-and seventeenth-century witchcraft persecutions). The history of Christianity has been more complex, contradictory, flawed and punitive than Pagels seems to think.

James Finn Cotter (review date Spring 1989)

SOURCE: "Pagels's Paradise Lost," in *The Hudson Review,* Vol. XLII, No. 1, Spring, 1989, pp. 165-70.

[*In the review below, Cotter argues that while* Adam, Eve, and the Serpent *is well-written and persuasive, it contains misleading and inaccurate areas.*]

In the epilogue of her new book [*Adam, Eve, and the Serpent*], Elaine Pagels tells us that, dissatisfied with contemporary Christianity, she turned to the earliest Christians for answers. She assumed that in that era, when the movement was pristine and primitive, things were simpler and purer.

She found the opposite to be true: the movement was diversified, divided by controversy, and complex.

So what else is new?

Well, what Pagels found sounds strangely familiar, a not-so-distant mirror of our own time: martyrs, particularly women, ready to lose their lives rather than surrender their freedom to the will of the State; Gnostics, eager to include women in their services and open-minded in judging moral questions on the basis of situational ethics rather than by precept or authority; leaders like John Chrysostom who opposed wealth and position in ecclesiastical and civil hierarchies; and thinkers like Pelagius who insisted on the goodness of nature and the integrity of free will against Augustine's vision of a world riddled by original sin.

What happened? The martyrs perished, the protesters were silencd, the Gnostics suppressed, Chrysostom exiled, Pelagius condemned, and Augustine canonized. If only things had turned out differently, if only the orthodox had lost and the free spirits had won. Christianity and western civilization would not be the embarrassment they are to enlightened folk today. Certainly, there would have been fewer changes to be made in the contemporary church.

Pagels lets you draw such conclusions for yourself. The danger here, of course, is wishful thinking, history as a series of neatly discovered causes, anachronisms disguised as real ideas or events, and in many instances not history at all. To make freedom the central issue in the first centuries of Christian persecution takes some stretching of the imagination and the texts. The martyrologies tell us the saints died for their faith in Jesus as Lord; they hardly thought of themselves as freedom fighters. If given a choice—except for ardent souls like Ignatius of Antioch—they wanted to go on living. Refusing to sacrifice to the emperor as god, they were put to death for their infidelity. They had no choice but to obey their Lord or deny him. "Freedom," as we know it, hardly existed as "the classical proclamation" Pagels claims. In the texts she quotes it is mentioned in passing, never is it the focus of the Christian message.

The Gnostics are another problem. Pagels treats them as a Christian sect when they may have pre-dated Christianity and existed as an independent syncretic religion. They penetrated Christianity, but seem to have remained on the fringes. Gnostics held so many beliefs that one can find evidence for almost any religious theory in their enigmatic writings. As she did in her *Gnostic Gospels*, which I reviewed in the Summer 1980 issue of *The Hudson Review*, Pagels has a field day manipulating their texts. Here is "an extraordinary poem," called *Thunder: Perfect Mind,* as she quotes it:

I am the first and the last.

I am the honored one and the scorned one.
I am the whore and the holy one.
I am the wife and the virgin.
I am the bride and the bridegroom,
   and it is my husband who begot me.
I am knowledge and ignorance. . . .
I am foolish and I am wise. . . .
I am the one whom they call life [Eve]
and you have called Death. . . .

The subject of this poem, she says, "depicts the spirit, manifested variously as Wisdom and as Eve." George MacRae, in his introduction to it in *The Nag Hammadi Library,* writes: "In terms of religious tradition *Thunder: Perfect Mind* is difficult to classify. It presents no distinctively Jewish, Christian, or Gnostic themes, nor does it seem to presuppose a particular Gnostic myth." To add to the problem of analysis, Pagels has actually quoted as a single conflation five eparate passages scattered over five pages. The name "Eve" does not appear anywhere in the poem; Pagels does put it in square brackets, but the editors also use such brackets in the text. How is the reader to know what is going on?

Again, Pagels quotes *The Secret Book of John* as declaring: I am the intelligence of the pure life," when the original reads "pure light." And she cites the *Gospel of Philip:* "The law was the tree. . . . For when [the law] said, 'Eat this, do not eat that,' it became the beginning of death." In the *Nag Hammadi* text God speaks these lines, not the law. The differences are minor, but they form part of the mosaic portraying the Gnostics as Pagels sees them and not as they really were.

Pagels persists in stereotyping orthodox Christians as law-abiding formalists who believe in a transcendent deity while Gnostics are true-believers open to an immanent divine presence. Jesus' words, "Live on in me and I in you," Paul's claim, "I live now, not I, but Christ lives in me," Augustine's cry, "You are more intimate to me than I am to myself," the Eucharist, interior prayer, the mystics, none of these find a place in Pagels's polemics. For her, no orthodox Christian can say with the Hindu of his God, "I *am* Thou." Why not? What else is Incarnation? "God became man that we may become God," Athanasius and Thomas Aquinas tell us. Meister Eckhart's condemnation, which Pagels naturally drags up, was mired in the politics of its day and proves nothing. Her narrow-minded treatment of "the orthodox" (the name almost hisses in her pages) gives away the game she is playing.

Pagels covers the first five centuries selectively to support her thesis that after Constantine's conversion to Christianity in 313 a "cata—clysmic transformation" occurred. The thesis is hardly new but her examination of commentaries on the first chapters of Genesis does cover fresh ground. The reader learns a good deal about the period; the controversies are vigorously presented, and the martyrdom of Perpetua and Felicitas is especially fascinating in Herbert Musurillo's lively translation. Chrysostom rightly comes across as an admirable bishop and Justin Martyr is an appealing apologist. Jerome and Augustine, however, appear as political opportunists and male chauvinists, which they probably were.

Is the book an accurate picture of the era? Pagels misrepresents Christianity. The Incarnation finds no room in the inn of her thinking; the sacraments, grace, charity, faith have no part in her historical vision. Only doctrines matter and only ideas make things happen. For Pagels the past is a text to be reduced to practical political issues. Jesus himself appears not as the crucified and risen Lord but as the preacher of a new doctrine. His "radical message" undergoes endless revisions at the hands of his followers. Pagels carefully selects her passages and, if one sounds suitably persuasive, she repeats it. She adds emphasis or shifts emphasis to suit her purpose. She magnifies small issues and ignores main ones. She sprinkles her book with terms like "shockingly" and "sadly," as if she too can barely believe what these men are saying about freedom, marriage, sin, and human behavior. She stacks the deck, to make matters work out the way that suits her best. To her innocent readers she is the serpent in the Garden.

In the controversy between Jerome and Jovinian, for example, Pagels makes Jovinian seem like a reasonable monk who, disenchanted with the ascetic life, saw value in a less rigorous way of living. In the debate about the superiority of virginity over marriage, the position which Jerome obstreperously defended, Jovinian appears correct and his subsequent condemnation incredible. Pagels never tells us that Jovinian was condemned for claiming that a person baptized with water and the Spirit cannot commit sin, for holding that all sins are equal, and for denying the virgin birth. In finding no worth in asceticism, Jovinian went against the grain of all religious tradition. Of course he was wrong, but not according to Pagels.

In Augustine's controversy with Pelagius and his follower Julian, Pagels ignores the question of grace, the essential issue for Augustine. She makes the extraordinary statement that Augustine "denied that human beings possess any capacity whatever for free will." Augustine, the author of "On Free Will" and "On Grace and Free will," has been called "the chief exponent of free will in the early church." He is the pastor who told his listeners: "Love, and do what you will." For him the will was not mere choice between good and evil; to do evil meant to lose your power of will. Free will is a love, a pleasure, an impulse and pressure. Sin prevents people from being spontaneous and caring. For Pelagius, the will was self-centered and based on self-control. Pagels is saddened that Pelagius lost the argument and was condemned. But Pelagius has had a long life. As a boy growing up in Irish Catholic Boston, I and everyone else were all semi-Pelagians at heart. Do not believe everything you read.

Of course, Augustine was wrong on a number of counts. He was forever changing his mind and contradicting himself. His *Retractions* reviews his 330 works and repudiates passages or works he no longer agreed with. Such is the prerogative or curse of old age: second thoughts. Thomas Aquinas dismissed his views of nature as contradictory: how can nature be good and utterly depraved? The Council of Trent made it clear that on the question of grace and freedom, Augustine was as fallible as his opponents. The history of the church has not been as monolithic as Pagels would have us believe, and many at the time were troubled by Augustine's exaggerations. He was an existentialist, gloomy, but no life-denier. He was Kierkegaard and Pelagius Norman Vincent Peale. "May nothing horrible happen, nothing inhuman," Augustine says, wanting only good and not bad for himself and others. But good comes from God who became human for our sake, to rescue us from evil. For Pelagius, Christ set a good example and leaves the rest up to us. Older now and no longer living in Boston, I am convinced that Augustine is right—most of the time.

Much of what Pagels writes about the rigorist traditional views of marriage and virginity is probably true, if one-sided. The ideas were not cast in tablets of stone as she seems to think. Surely she exaggerates when she claims that Jesus and Paul never endorsed "procreation in marriage": what does " A man shall cleave to his wife and the two shall be one flesh" imply? In the first century celibacy was a response to an eschatological crisis and not the outcome of a negative attitude toward sex. With the kingdom at hand why worry about sexual fulfillment? The marriage feast at Cana, however, was always seen as a sign of the Lord's blessing on young couples. You find no Cana in Pagels's exegesis.

Augustine's idea that some sin—even if only venial—had to be attached to lovemaking for married couples wanting children seemed harsh then and has seemed so ever since. It never became church teaching. The first church council to deal with sexual morality was Vatican II in 1974; it declared that the actions of marital sexuality "signify and promote that mutual self-giving by which spouses enrich each other with a joyful and thankful will." Augustine himself is ambivalent on the subject. He wrote "On the Good of Marriage" in which he upholds the sacredness of married life as a sacrament and praises fidelity as a source of salvation. He states that the couple should not refuse one another and both partners must agree if they are to abstain from sex. He believed that a humble mother pleases God more than her proud virgin daughter. Augustine is not the harsh marriage-hater Pagels makes him out to be. Jerome, on the other hand,

overstated his case for virginity and made such wild claims that even his friends balked. Without him, however, we would not have had the Wife of Bath.

> **Pagels writes well and argues persuasively. It is easy to see why her books are so popular. She explains so much and makes it clear how down through the centuries we landed in the mess of the present.**
> **—James Finn Cotter**

A lot of water has flowed under the bridge of this topic. Jean Leclerq recently wrote on monastic twelfth-century views in *Monks on Marriage;* monks were sympathetic and had plenty of insights on marital relations. In 1650, the Jesuit theologian Thomas Sanchez attacked Augustine's rigorist views, and much has been written on religion and sex in the past decades. You would know nothing about these developments in reading Pagels. She writes as though she is pioneering some new and sensational discovery about that old story in the Garden. Some terrible secret has been at last revealed! Augustine had sexual hangups and they have darkened the centuries! Read all about it!

The mystery of Christianity here is treated as a whodunit, and Augustine is the villain: "From the fifth century on, Augustine's pessimistic views of sexuality, politics, and human nature would become the dominant influence on western Christianity, both Catholic and Protestant, and color all western culture, Christian or not, ever since." How did this disaster occur? "The eventual triumph of Augustine's theology required, however, the capitulation of all who held the classical proclamation concerning human freedom, once so widely regarded as the heart of the Christian gospel." Regarded by whom? With such sweeping cause-and-effect conclusions, Pagels draws her study to a close. Reader, beware!

Pagels writes well and argues persuasively. It is easy to see why her books are so popular. She explains so much and makes it clear how down through the centuries we landed in the mess of the present. Much is informative, more is shaded and distorted to fit her preconceived thesis. She knows who did it from the start. When she states that her task is "historical investigation" and not "religious inquiry," she sounds sincere, but the statement has to be weighed carefully. Her own confession that "dissatisfied with the representatives of Christianity" she turned to the origins of the early church certainly implies a "religious inquiry" that masks itself, consciously, as objective history.

Pagels answers those who say that she projects her own ideas into the text by first denying it and then admitting it is impossible—and not even desirable—not to make such projections. She quotes Foucault on "the politics of truth" and says that "what each of us perceives and acts upon as true has much to do with our situation, social, political, cultural, religious, or philosophical." "What is truth?" as Pilate asked Jesus, not waiting for an answer. To a colleague who objected that religious ideas cannot be reduced to political agendas, she responds by agreeing and then stating that "moral choices often are political choices." In Boston we called this "talking out of both sides of your mouth." Today it is fashionable as literary and historical theory.

How can you not trust a writer who documents every statement, who seems so fair-handed and scholarly, whose book contains twenty pages of closely written notes with references to French and German as well as English criticism? As compared to *The Gnostic Gospels*, where the notes would not pass the scrutiny of a freshman English instructor, this is a much more carefully researched book. Pagels has learned how to deal with her critics. As the Harrington Spear Paine Professor of Religion at Princeton University and the recipient of a MacArthur Prize Fellowship, Pagels is a formidable academic figure. Whether or not her "brilliant new book," to quote its blurb, is "a work that will prove a landmark of historical thought and profoundly affect all future interpretations of the historical meaning of Christianity" remains to be seen.

Henry Chadwick (review date 21 March 1990)

SOURCE: "The Paths of Heresy," in *Times Literary Supplement,* No. 4017, March 21, 1990, p. 309.

[*In the following review of* The Gnostic Gospels, *Chadwick discusses Pagels's efforts to address modern problems in Christianity by considering the early church.*]

In December 1945, an Egyptian peasant made, with his mattock, an archaeological find that has coe to generate a substantial industry among students of early Christianity and of its pagan environment of high mysticism, low magic, and religious syncretism. The find consisted of a cache of Coptic codices buried in the second half of the fourth century a few miles from Nag Hammadi, containing fifty-two texts most of which were either gnostic in origin or congenial reading in gnostic circles. That is, they represent a broadly theosophical doctrine divergent from and at times severely critical of main-line Christianity as that emerged out of the various second-century groups claiming the Christian name. The spot where the codices were discovered is close to the ruins of a monastery founded in the first half of the fourth century AD by Pachomius. It seems probable that the books once belonged to the library of a monk admitted to that community. Fourth-century Egypt pullulated with Manichees and dual-

istic gnostics of many brands. In the year 367 Archbishop Athanasius of Alexandria issued throughout his jurisdiction a warning against the reading in the church lectionary of books other than the Bible canon and especially deplored the study of "secret books" or apocrypha composed by heretics. Perhaps his instruction led to the hiding of the codices.

The story of the find's zig-zag course towards eventual publication is a mixture of folly, selfishness, generosity, and energy. Some of the original papyri were used as fuel by peasants ignorant of their value. But news came to percolate through to Cairo dealers and so to Western scholars in Egypt with their ear to the ground. One codex was smuggled out of Egypt and, after a journey across the Atlantic and back, was finally bought at a Brussels cafe by Gilles Quispel on behalf of the Jung Institute in Zürich. It was later added, wisely, to the twelve other surviving codices in the Coptic Museum in old Cairo, where the manuscripts now occupy a small room.

A first volume of facsimiles appeared in 1956, a book which is still an essential tool as the codices have not been immune from damage since that time. An initial attempt to restrict access to the new material to a small group of approved scholars was a mistake. Thanks to the energy of James Robinson of Claremont in California and the support of Unesco, the entire set of manuscripts were photographed and English translations made from the transcribed texts! Dr. Robinson and his collaborators produced in 1977 an invaluable volume offering a provisional translation of all the new texts other than the fragments which defy reconstruction. Through an opulent series of facsimiles all the texts are now an open book to scholars able to read Coptic.

Of the fifty-two new documents only three are entitled "Gospels", and one more, because of its opening words. "The gospel of truth . . .", has been accorded that title by modern scholars. The most important of all the new texts is certainly the 114 sayings ascribed to Jesus in the Coptic Gospel of Thomas and this rightly attracted excited attention when the 1956 facsimile text was first translated into European languages in 1959. It remains a matter of scholarly judgment, for each individual saying, whether or not this tradition about Jesus preserves authentic features. Admittedly the proportion of matter with reasonable claims to such respectful treatment may not be large, and the good tradition keeps some pretty bohemian company.

Elaine Pagels teaches at Barnard College, New York, and is a gifted, clever communicator with a lively interest in the new texts and some inclination to think the Christian tradition, in spite of its power and undiminished attraction, sadly responsible for fostering discrimination against women. So she approaches gosticism with very contemporary expectations: notably the hope that in these gnostic documents suppressed by ancient authority we may find an alternative Christianity sympathetic to Eastern and individualist mysticism, unencumbered by historical and miraculous events, emancipated if not from clergymen, at least from the notion that holy orders ought to be a male preserve, and allowing one to be bolder than the main-line Christian tradition in admitting "natural evil" (in contrast to those evils which human beings cause by their actions) to be not only within the purpose but even within the very being of God.

The author's purpose [in *The Gnostic Gospels*] is not to offer a description either of the gnostic systems or of the main-line defence against them, but rather to bring out the social and political implications of some of their characteristic doctrines. The gnostics interpreted Christ's resurrection not as an objective event but as an inward psychological experience in the souls of the apostles and in all who aspire to their vision: She feels that this psychological interpretation undercuts the classic defence of Catholic Christianity to the effect that teaching authority, entrusted by the Lord to the apostles, is then passed on to the churches which their mission founded.

The gnostics also disbelieved in the human reality of Christ's passion, a view which naturally raises the speculative question whether, in the seventh century, Muhammad was influenced towards the same opinion by fringe gnostic sects in Arabia. For many gnostics this disbelief entailed the moral consequence that physical martyrdom could not be something to which they were called.

A feature of gnosticism which seems especially congenial to Elaine Pagels is the large liturgical and teaching role allowed to women in at least some gnostic sects. Admittedly on this point she has to exert gentle pressure on the surviving evidence. The new material from Nag Hammadi offers only few grains of encouragement to liberated women readers, unless it be the gnostic readiness to think the relationship between Jesus and Mary Magdalene erotic. In most of the new Coptic texts the sexuality of woman is an object of fear and contempt. Femininity is interpreted as symbolic of those earthbound appetites which hinder the divine spark in the mind of mankind, of which the symbol is masculinity.

Accordingly, for evidence of gnostic sympathy for feminine emancipation Professor Pagels relies on long familiar texts in Irenaeus and Tertullian. Irenaeus describes Marcus, a seducing heretic addicted to alphabetical magic, as allowing women to prophesy in the community and to minister the chalice in his eucharist. Tertullian knows of heretical women who are allowed to teach argue, exorcise, cure, and even (climax of horrors) baptise. The sentence illustrates little more than Tertullian's unrivalled capacity to manufacture polemic; we may be sure that his climax would have been the exer-

cise of presbyterial or episcopal functions had he known of these being exercised by gnostic women.

Some confusion is introduced here when, to the evidence that in gnostic sects women could exercise liturgical functions, Elaine Pagels adds the Montanist prophetesses Prisca and Maximilla without the least note that their hostility to gnosticism cannot be exaggerated. I am also sorry she allows herself to write that "from the year 200 we have no evidence for women taking prophetic, priestly, or episcopal roles among orthodox churches", a true sentence apparently intended to carry the false suggestion that before the year 200 women are known to have exercised presbyterial or episcopal functions in the great Church. (That they prophesied is of course certain.) When Professor Pagels wants to quote a Christian writer who speaks of women in the Church as she would like, she turns not to any Nag Hammadi text but to the highly anti-gnostic Clement of Alexandria who affirms both a feminine element in God and the equality of men and women. Fourth-century Syrian Fathers would be vexed at her pronouncement that "by 200" virtually all the feminine imagery for God had disappeared from the orthodox Christian tradition. The Odes of Solomon too have something to offer her there. It may be pertinent to her thesis that the first evidence for the invocation of the Virgin Mary comes in the mid-third century.

This book will dissatisfy some learned readers familiar with the new Nag Hammadi material who may feel it to be a pity that so good a scholar has not treated her texts with full rigour. But for most readers that will matter little. Elaine Pagels has an enviable gift for writing easily. Her thesis that the exclusion of gnosticism impoverished the Christian tradition is not convincingly defended here, and it lies in unresolved tension with the recognition that the heretical sects fostered pretentious mumbo-jumbo. They replaced the New Testament affirmations of God's presence in the historical life of Jesus and of his church with a vast fabrication of irrationality that appalled Plotinus and the philosophers. But the bond between the gnostics and the author of this book is perhaps that she and they both share the same basic difficulties about the pattern of main-line Christian tradition.

The trouble with the main-line tradition is no doubt that it speaks the language of paternal authority. Bishops are fathers in God. The minds through whom the tradition took its decisive and irreversible shape have received the honorific title Church Fathers. The authority structure looks unattractive to those who prefer the alternative society or underworld where bearded weirdies are more obviously welcome or at least in evidence. The gnostics expressed an alienation both from this world and from the normal sacramental life of the Christian church.

They expressed their alienation from the world and from the

human condition by attributing it to incompetent or malevo-lent angelic powers. They denied human responsibility by their thoroughgoing determinism. Most of the sects required strict renunciation of sex and marriage, and criticized ortho-doxy for asserting marriage to belong to the divinely in-tended order of creation. A few sects drew the opposite conclusion from the same dualistic premises, and had excit-ing nocturnal ceremonies where men and women prayed to-gether naked or danced in a ring chanting solemn hymns of no clear meaning. One or two had erotic orgies. This heady stuff, however is wholly unrepresented in the Nag Hammadi texts, which sing in unison of their dedication to the radical suppression of sex. Whatever form gnosticism might take, one is still allowed a sigh of relief that the second-century churches succeeded in their life-and-death struggle against it. Elaine Pagels may begin her book with the suggestion that the gnostic defeat was regrettable, but by the end she is ex-plicitly inclined to the opinion that there is a lot to be said for something very like the main-line stuff.

Leslie Houlden (review date 18 June 1995)

SOURCE: "The Prince of Darkness," in *New York Times Book Review,* June 18, 1995, pp. 9-10.

[*In the following review of* The Origin of Satan, *Houlden states that while Pagels's arguments are single-minded and do not always have documentary support, she has written a compelling book that connects the concerns of the early church with contemporary issues.*]

Satan, Elaine Pagels says, has a much more tenacious grip on the world than many people suppose; his power over the human imagination has grown for 22 centuries, and in the West even people who deny his existence, or who have no religion at all, live in a culture in which he is a large pres-ence This demon will not go away

If that sounds like a promotion for fright films, Ms. Pagels, a professor of religion at Princeton University and the au-thor of several volumes on the Gnostics among the early Christians, did not write *The Origin of Satan* as an enter-tainment. By finding out where Satan came from, she thinks, we find out, at least in part, where we came from. That is not to say that some readers of her book will not be shocked, or at least offended.

In ancient Israel, as one sees in early books of the Bible, Satan is hardly a monstrous figure, the dark near-parody of God he later became. In the Book of Job he is the official "opponent" at the heavenly court, his task being to challenge God's assumptions and, with divine permission, to test the fidelity of God's people. But it is no surprise that such a

critic should eventually become a subverter and a wicked tempter; that transformation was complete by the time the First Book of Chronicles took shape, two centuries before Christ.

During the final centuries B.C., divisions appeared among the Jews that were to prove fateful to them. One group de-monized others some Jews might not belong. In the second century B.C. the sect called the Essenes arose, and flourished for several centuries. They taught what they considered a pure form of religious observance, which they charged the majority of Jews had abandoned. Among the Essenes, Ms Pagels thinks, Satan, as ruler of a whole demonic realm, was a necessary evil: "Had Satan not already existed in Jewish tradition, the Essenes would have invented him "She quotes one of their Scriptures, found among the Dead Sea Scrolls, as saying Satan "rules in darkness, and his purpose is to bring about evil and sin" the Essenes envisioned life as a cosmic battle between "sons of light" like themselves and the spawn of darkness, between God and Satan.

The early Christians adopted that view and used much of the same language, she continues, seeing themselves as pro-tected by God and by angels, freed from satanic manipula-tion while their antagonists were under diabolical control. Thus her book moves quickly from the narrow subject of its title, and indeed from Satan as the force behind wicked-ness and misfortune, to become an analysis of how the early Christians used this idea of a cosmic battle in their confron-tations with non-Christians as well as in their own discourse; the book becomes a kind of case study of how people, de-fining difference between themselves and others, find it easy to abandon love and tolerance for a hostility that is licensed, even commanded, by divine decree.

Ms. Pagels concentrates first on the four Gospels in the New Testament. It is generally accepted that they were written in a certain order during the last few decades of the first cen-tury—a time when the early Christians were turning their at-tentions beyond their fellow Jews and beginning to convert gentiles. Ms. Pagels argues that in each succeeding Gospel the Jews are demonized with growing intensity. Increasingly, from the earliest Gospel to the latest, Roman responsibility for the death of Jesus—historically quite clear—is played down, and instead the Jews are blamed. And even though some of the Evangelists perceive widely varied responses to Jesus among the Jews, and write with real sympathy for the Jews, all agree that the community of "God's people" is no longer Israel but the followers of Jesus.

This procss of achieving self-definition by opposing Chris-tians to Jews was soon enough applied to defining the dif-ference between Christians and all non-Christians—though, arguably, its legacy of anti-Semitism has been the most dire of its consequences for everyone. In Ms. Pagels's account, after the Jews, the next people demonized were the pagans, especially when Christianity began to spread and Christians were persecuted for refusing to participate in Roman rites (she reminds us that these, like the ceremonies of virtually all ancient religions, were patriotic rites, and that to reject them was to declare rebellion).

Then, with growing vehemence as the Christian community increased, Christians began to demonize one another, to single out certain people as heretics. After all, who is more intolerable than the traitor within the gates? In many myths, both Jewish and Christian, Satan himself started as a fallen angel, "one of us" become "one of them"—what Ms. Pagels calls "the intimate enemy." In the Second Epistle to the Corinthians, St. Paul, the earliest Christian writer, referred to fellow believers who disagreed with his vision of the Christian mission as agents of Satan. So did the writer of the First Epistle of St. John (whom Ms. Pagels does not cite): to describe such people, and their demonic backer, he coined the word "Antichrist," which was to have quite a future.

Ms. Pagels states her argument—that all four canonical Gospels depict the career of Jesus as a battle between Him as God's agent and the Devil in the visible shape of the Jews or Jewish authorities—with excessive single-mindedness. Such an approach will surely make the book controversial and draw attention to her underlying thesis: that the way in which early Christianity developed is a very troubled heritage. But it also requires one to state some reservations. A minor one is that her adding noncanonical material about Jesus—from Gnostic documents and other writings rejected when the canon of the Bible was formed around the end of the second century A.D.—to what she finds in the New Testament is tendentious with regard to dating, and distracting to readers who are not specialists.

More materially, her theory about demonizing imbalances her reading of the Gospels. It fits the Gospel of St. John, the last one written, fairly well, but the others much less so. Satan is an important presence at both the beginning and the end of Luke, and even Matthew provides a satanic backdrop to the life of Jesus; but there are considerable differences in their treatment of Satan, and of the Jews. In Mark, the earliest Gospel, although Satan's presence makes clear the cosmic significance of Jesus' work, Jesus is involved with devils chiefly as sources of madness: His miraculous power is shown by His exorcisms, done to cure people. Furthermore, in Mark the story of the death of Jesus is told without any reference to invisible evil powers. He is a passive victim and there is virtually no note of a cosmic battle behind His death. Even in the Gospel of Luke, the business of blaming the Jews for the death of Jesus is much less clear-cut than Ms. Pagels makes it seem. Satan instigates the abandonment of Jesus by His disciples at the critical moment, and inspires the as-

sault on Him by the authorities. But the Jews divide over Jesus, some reacting with compassion. Even their leaders act "in ignorance," and Jesus prays they will be forgiven. Demonizing is far from complete here: if this Gospel blames Jews, it also seems to reach out to them.

There is no lack of sympathetic understanding in [*The Origin of Satan*] of the acute dilemmas that led early Christians to reach so readily for the weapon of demonization.
—Leslie Houlden

Altogether, if Ms. Pagels had widened her consideration of how the evangelists account for the death of Jesus, she would have seen that Mark tells the story principally in terms of the fulfillment of biblical prophecies, and that those prophecies are equally prominent in the other Gospels. In a word, testimony from the Bible and cosmic conflict were twin ways in which early Christians could see the death of Jesus as being no mere tragic accident but the climax of God's saving purpose.

Nonetheless, this brief book is thought-provoking—especially effective when it vividly portrays the faith of individual early Christians and of noble pagans. The problem of evil vexed them as it does us; indeed, Ms. Pagels says she was led by the accidental death seven years ago of her husband, Heinz, to search the Scriptures for a clue about how people throughout history have dealt with evil. And that led her to ponder the human tendency to populate the world with invisible presences: controllers, initiators, helpers, hinderers—unseen but all the more potent because they are mysterious. "I began to reflect," she says, "on the ways that various religious traditions give shape to the invisible world, and . . . on the various ways that people from Greek, Jewish and Christian traditions deal with misfortune and loss."

It is when she takes up some of the early Christian fathers and pagans like the Emperor Marcus Aurelius that she writes with greatest feeling about the issues at stake, such as our proper response to the complexities of experience. Should we school ourselves to accept whatever an impersonal fate gives us (as Marcus Aurelius, and some Christian writers, thought we should)? Or should we see ourselves as engaged in a supernatural struggle between good and evil, God and Satan, in which (despite St. Paul's command in the Epistle to the Romans to obey the authorities) even governments and other earthly powers may be on the side of the Devil? Without a strategy of demonization could Christians have seen—as clearly as some did by the third century—that the highest powers in a nation, its legitimate leaders, might be wicked, people to be resisted and even overthrown?

Ms. Pagels also excels in depicting both the strengths and the weaknesses of orthodoxy: how are Christian leaders to resist travesty and mere foolishness by members of their community without stifling vitality of mind and spirit? She gives some samples of both wild speculation and sublime spirituality from Gnostics in the second century, and notes that the church father Tertullian would not discriminate between the two, since the Gnostics were simply heretical to him: good Christians must not ask questions but accept what they are taught by their leaders. One recalls that a great fault of Satan in Milton's *Paradise Lost* is that he insists on asking questions.

There is no lack of sympathetic understanding in [*The Origin of Satan*] of the acute dilemmas that led early Christians to reach so readily for the weapon of demonization. It gave them impetus and assurance, especially when they were new and up against great opposition. But Ms. Pagels believes that demonization of other people tended to accumulate through the centuries, at a terrible cost. It seems almost an afterthought that in the last six pages she points to a powerful tradition in Christianity—represented in the Gospels themselves and by people like St. Francis of Assisi and Martin Luther King Jr.—that rejects a division of the world into followers of light and of darkness. There is a "struggle within Christian tradition," she concludes, "between the profoundly human view that 'otherness' is evil and the words of Jesus that reconciliation is divine."

Mary Gordon (review date 26 June 1995)

SOURCE: "Bedeviling Satan," in *The Nation,* Vol. 260, No. 25, June 26, 1995, pp. 931-33.

[*In the review below, Gordon concludes that* The Origin of Satan *is informative but fails to address some of the questions it raises.*]

Satan may not exist, but there are excellent reasons to invent him. He is called onstage whenever behavior pases our understanding of the limits of the human. To say that something is diabolical means it is inexplicable in ordinary terms. It ruptures the line of measurable cause and effect, or its sheer scope and efficiency seem untraceable. This kind of attribution can be seen as a failure of imagination or a type of species compassion. When we invoke Satan, we are saying that humans can't be that bad; they wouldn't do something like that on their own.

Recently, the temptation to demonize seems stronger than it has for a long time, a fallout, perhaps, of the information age. One intolerable piece of news we all must digest is that whoever *we* are, *we* are a minority, radically outnumbered by *Them,* the *Others.* We must now come to terms with Others who are more other than we'd imagined, therefore more inexplicable, easier to demonize. The readiness with which a term like "demonize" springs even to the lips of the popular media may signal the resurrection of an old habit of mind.

We seem newly in the grip of increasingly numerous, violent and finer-grained xenophobias that encourage those in their thrall to use any means necessary to justify the annihilation of the Other. It seems pandemic, from Islamic fundamentalists' referring to America as "the great Satan" to Pat Robertson's asserting that feminism "encourages women to leave their husbands, kill their children, practice witchcraft" and, even worse, become lesbians. Hindus see the devil in Muslims, African nationalists in Nordic blondes. I myself believe I may have found him in the face of Howard Stern. Who else would have tied up forty blocks of traffic on Fifth Avenue with a book signing?

In such a world, a book about the Origin of Satan, by a scholar of Elaine Pagels's distinction, is awaited with unusual anticipation. An article on Pagels in *The New Yorker* recounting her personal tragedies—the death of her child and the freakish accident that claimed her husband's life just over a year later—and another in *Mirabella* have also generated remarkable advance publicity. And her first two sentences reinforce our expectations: "In 1988, when my husband of twenty years died in a hiking accident, I became aware that, like many people who grieve, I was living in the presence of an invisible being. . . . During the following year, I began to reflect on the ways that various religious traditions give shape to the invisible world, and how our imaginative perceptions of what is invisible relate to the ways we respond to the people around us, to events, and to the natural world."

The Origin of Satan is a fascinating and valuable book, but it is not the book these sentences suggest. Its focus is narrower; it is a philologically trained scholar's book, rather than an intellectual historian's. Pagels, who made her reputation with *The Gnostic Gospels*, a study of radical and dissident early Christian sects, turns her mind here to the history of Satan in the life and texts of the ancient world.

In examining the Hebrew Bible, she notes that whereas certain prophets call upon Canaanite monsters, like the Leviathan, to symbolize Israel's enemies, Satan is not a constant presence, and his role is not the one most familiar to later imaginers. He never appears as "the leader of an 'evil empire,' an army of hostile spirits who make war on God and humankind alike." He is one of God's servants. The biblical term Satan "describes an adversarial role, . . . one of the angels sent by God for the specific purpose of blocking or obstructing human activity." The root means "one who opposes, obstructs, or acts as adversary." He can even act as a kind of messenger of God, as he did with Job.

It is dissident sects like the Essenes and the monastic communiy at Qûmran who begin to invoke Satan to characterize their Jewish opponents, those whom they consider insufficiently observant or pure. "In the process they turned this rather unpleasant angel into a far grander—and far more malevolent—figure. No longer one of God's faithful servants," he begins to become what he is for Christianity, "God's antagonist, his enemy, even his rival." Mark and the other three Evangelists who followed him adopted this radical strain, and Pagels gives us excellent reasons for their choice.

If the leader of your movement has been ignominiously murdered, Pagels suggests, it is helpful to believe that what seems to be disastrous is in fact chimerical; that the real battle is invisible and has, in fact, already been won. What appears to have been Jesus' defeat is actually the sign of a cosmic victory for the forces of God and good. These forces appear as characters in the Gospel narratives, an appearance, Pagels correctly notes, that "many liberal—minded Christians have preferred to ignore." Yet, she says, no one can deny the evidence that Mark (and those who followed him) "intends the presence of angels and demons to address the anguished question that the events of the previous decades had aroused: how could God allow such death and destruction?"

Pagels traces the historical roots of this anti-Semitism, and indeed one of the most valuable contributions of *The Origin of Satan* is its ability to provide coherent and comprehensible historical contexts.
—*Mary Gordon*

By creating such a supernatural and morally charged interpretation of conflict, Christians have created what Pagels calls "fault lines" that have allowed for the demonizing of others throughout Christian history. This tactic has been "effective throughout Western history in consolidating the identity of Christian groups; the same history also shows that it can justify hatred, even mass slaughter." Perhaps the most catastrophic of these fault lines has been a justification for anti-Semitism, which she rightly insists is an inextricable part of the Gospels.

Pagels traces the historical roots of this anti-Semitism, and indeed one of the most valuable contributions of *The Origin of Satan* is its ability to provide coherent and comprehensible historical contexts. She reminds us that "we cannot fully understand the New Testament gospels until we recognize that they are . . . wartime literature." A series of Jewish rebellions in the first century resulted in a vicious attack by the Romans lasting twelve years and ending in the destruction of the Temple in Jerusalem in 70 C.E.

The Jewish community was sharply divided before this war, and in the aftermath of the destruction of the Temple, conflicting sects were eager to cast blame upon one another for the disaster. The followers of Jesus had refused to fight, because of their understanding of the approaching "end." Some, in fact, insisted that the horrors of war actually vindicated his call, "Repent, for the Kingdom of God is near," and that Jesus had predicted the destruction of the Temple and other terrible events.

There were several reasons for the followers of Jesus to dissociate themselves from the Jewish majority. Primary among them was their quarrel with Jews who refused to recognize Jesus as the Messiah, and the majority's insistence upon observation of Jewish law as a prerequisite to salvation. This insistence conflicted with the Christian wish to spread their message among the Gentiles. It also allowed the Christians to justify allying themselves with the stronger power—the Romans. Thus, Pagels tells us, the Evangelists, beginning with Mark, place much greater blame upon the Jews than upon the Romans for the death of Jesus, although there is no historical justification for this. "Mark tells the story of Jesus in the context that matters to him most—within the Jewish community. And here, as in most situations, the more intimate the conflict, the more intense and bitter it becomes."

For Mark, then, the conflict is internecine, among Jews, and his use of the image of Satan reflects the Jewish tradition: Satan is not a hostile power assailing Jews from without; he is a representation of conflict within the community. Matthew, writing in 80-90 C.E., insists that Jesus offers "a universalizing interpretation of Torah . . . so that Gentiles can fulfill it as well as Jews. Matthew in effect encourages people to abandon traditional ethnic identification with Israel." It is one of the tragic paradoxes of Western history that the universal welcome offered by the Gospels is linked with a violent dissociation from, and vilification of, Jews. Followers of Jesus, in insisting that the circumstances of birth were irrelevant to salvation, placed themselves in direct opposition to an idea that had allowed the Jewish community to survive and know itself.

The Gospel of Luke continues the identification of the Jews with Satan and his cohort, but places the accusation in the mouth of Jesus himself. Luke, whom Pagels identifies as a Gentile, is determined to play up the non-Jewish aspects of Christianity, its openness to all believers. John, writing later than the others, around 100 C.E., portrays the struggle between Jesus and his enemies as a struggle between darkness and light. More than any of the other Gospels, Pagels tells us, John's has inspired believers who find themselves in a minority. Another paradox of the history of Christianity arises: The belief that one is the victor in a supernatural war allows for acts of courage that exceed ordinary understanding, and for bloodshed that efies comprehension. The same notion—that the invisible may be more important than the visible, and that one is on the side of the angels—inspired the behavior of both Savonarola and Martin Luther King Jr.

Up to this point in *The Origin of Satan*, Elaine Pagels presents us with fascinating information, and original and thoughtful elucidations. But she loses this lucidity after her analysis of the Gospels. She races through a discussion of Revelation, a book that has been crucial in the imagination of supernatural and cosmic war. And her discussion of the early Christian thinkers seems breathless and cursory. She has encouraged us to understand the Gospels as wartime literature, but neglects to offer a similar context for the early Christians, who were after all a horribly persecuted minority standing up, with superhuman courage, to imperial Rome. She fails to credit the moral value of the "good news" of Christianity, reflected in the marvelous passage of Tatian that she quotes. He is challenging the empire on the practice of gladiatorial combat: "I see people who actually sell themselves to be killed; the destitute sells himself, and the rich man buys someone to kill him; and for this the spectators take their seats, and the fighters meet in single-handed combat for no reason whatever. . . . Just as you slaughter animals to eat their flesh, so you purchase people to supply a cannibal banquet for the soul."

Pagels points out that Christians never gave up any of their old enemies; they just kept on adding new ones. They never abandoned their hatred of Jews even when their focus shifted to pagans and, later, to heretics. She notes that the rancor they directed toward non-Christians shifted when they, like the Essenes, began to see their insufficiently observant or doctrinally impure brethren as the greatest threat to their security. Tertullian, for example, thought that any questioning of any article of faith was the inspiration of the devil.

In the Olympics of Comparative Atrocities, it is tempting to believe that Christianity gets all the gold. But it is perhaps more the case that a love of cruelty and a desire to destroy one's enemies in ways that deny their humanity crosses race, class, ethnic and historical lines. This desire to destroy seems more connected to the possession of secular power than to the shape of belief. The Christians likened their enemies to Satan, and the Romans did not; nevertheless, it would be difficult to defend the behavior of the Romans toward the Christians, or to suggest that the Romans occupied the ethical high ground in this particular confrontation. Pagels tells us that the habit of interpreting the world as a cosmic battleground has its origin in the Gospels; but it is only after the church obtained an inordinate amount of power that it used these ideas to malign effect. The early Christians, with the same or more radical beliefs as their medieval and Renais-sance descendants, were unable to do much harm because they had so little scope for action. They were a minority, and they were poor.

It is churlish of a reviewer to wish that the writer had written a different book from the one she has. But, grateful as I am for the illuminating information in *The Origin of Satan*, I wished for more in the way of interpretation and cross-cultural comparison. Having traced with admirable precision the sources of the Christian habit of placing themselves in the middle of a "cosmic war," Pagels doesn't wonder about the implications of such a belief. It would be fascinating to trace the connection, if any, between the way a particular people describes its enemies and the actions it then takes against them.

The Origin of Satan begs some very large questions. Why do some cultures, like the Greeks, the Romans and the early Hebrews, fail to be taken up by the idea of Satan in an important way? What is the connection between a tendency to Satanize and a taste for ritual and dogmatic purity? In which situations does human behavior cry out for a supernatural explanation, and when doesn't it? If a culture doesn't have a Satan, what does it have in its place?

But the title of her book suggests that Pagels's project is textual rather than interpretive—a task it admirably fulfills. If we forget the somewhat misleading anteor outré-texts and concentrate on the main body of *The Origin of Satan*, we must be grateful to her for not allowing us to forget that embedded in the narrative that tells us to Love Our Enemy and Do Good to Those Who Hate Us is the simultaneous injunction to see them as demons, creatures of darkness dedicated to the destruction of the everlasting light.

John P. Meier (review date 9 July 1995)

SOURCE: "Our Old Enemy," in *Washington Post Book World,* July 9, 1995, p. 2.

[*In the following review, Meier argues that while some of Pagels's assertions are questionable,* The Origin of Satan *reveals Pagels's skill at clearly and concisely developing new theories out of pre-existing facts.*]

Although she has written scholarly works, Elaine Pagels, a professor at Princeton, is perhaps best known as a gifted popularizer. In this example [*The Origin of Satan*], she traces how the idea of Satan as a cosmic power opposed to God developed in early Judaism and Christianity. Pagels is interested in the "social" implications of Satan, i.e., how he was exploited to symbolize human conflict and stigmatize religious enemies as Jews and Christians struggled over their respective identities. Satan served to demonize "the other"— be they Jews of a different persuasion, pagan persecutors or Christian "heretics."

Pagels connects the development of the idea of Satan with Jewish sects in the first centuries B.C. For sectarians, the figure of Satan helped to define "them" (evil Jews) against "us" (righteous Jews). This function already appears in the Jewish Scriptures. From an overzealous member of God's court in the Book of Job, Satan develops into an accuser of the high priest in the Book of Zechariah. This development reflects tensions among Jewish factions after the Babylonian exile (6th century B.C.).

Sectarian strife increased around the time of the Maccabean revolt (mid-second century B.C.), producing a slew of apocalypses, notably *The First Book of Enoch,* in which Satan (under various names) becomes the great rival of God. Once a heavenly prince, the rebellious Satan now leads an army of fallen angels. The message is clear. The most dangerous enemy originates not as an outsider but as one's trusted colleague—the intimate enemy. Satan is the projection into the heavens of the experience of sectarian Jews: Their fellow Jews had apostatized and turned against them and therefore against God.

The underlying question in this struggle was: Who are God's people? While not discarding ethnic identity, the sectarians, notably at Qumran, insisted on moral identity. At Qumran the Essenes defined themselves in terms of the cosmic war between God (and the Essenes) on one side and Satan (and other Jews) on the other. Christians would simply push this definition to the extreme, dispensing ultimately with Jewish identity.

Pagels sees this sectarian ideology of cosmic war in Mark's Gospel. Accordingly she emphasizes the importance in Mark 1 of Satan's temptation of Jesus in the wilderness. This initial struggle sets the stage for the rest of the Gospel: Mark recounts the battle between Jesus and Satan that develops through Jesus's exorcisms up to the final clash in the Passion. This struggle, says Pagels, is a mythological representation of the conflict between Christian Jews and the Jewish majority in 1st-century Palestine.

This tack was then taken up and extended by the later evangelists. Matthew, writing around A.D. 80-90, makes the Pharisees, now ascendant in Judaism, the "intimate enemies" of Jesus (and Christians). About the same time, Luke, writing for Gentiles, claims that his form of Christianity is Israel at its best, virtually the only true Israel. Around A.D. 90-100, John, representing Jewish Christians thrown out of their home synagogue, charges that some Jews are children of the devil. In short, as we move from Gospel to Gospel,

the Jews who reject Jesus are increasingly put on the side of Satan.

As Gentile converts filled up the Church, they in turn began to see Satan in non-Christian Gentiles, especially Roman persecutors. This new stage of the struggle produced some intriguing positions: The pagans objected to Christians severing the traditional bond between religion and nation, while some Christians asserted the rights of conscience and religious liberty. When Gnostic Christians appeared on the scene, they too were seen as agents of Satan by "orthodox" Christians. Some of the Gnostics returned the compliment.

That Pagels can explain tis complicated thesis in a mere 184 pages of text testifies to her skill as a master teacher. Her strength lies not in discovering new facts but in drawing familiar facts into new and meaningful configurations. Her clear, concise exposition rarely bogs down in details. Limited space does not allow her to rehearse classic debates (e.g., the identification of Qumran as Essene, the dating of the Gospels), but she usually accepts consensus positions. One exception involves placing the Coptic Gospel of Thomas after Mark and before Matthew in her chronological survey of the Gospels. Here she reflects the very early dating of Thomas commonly accepted at Harvard and Claremont but questioned by many scholars, American and European.

Though minor errors of fact occur (e.g., *pace* Pagels, Timothy is never called a "bishop" in the Pastoral Epistles), they do not affect Pagels's overall thesis. What, though, of her claim that Satan and demons were at home in Jewish sects like Qumran and Christianity but not in "mainstream Judaism"? There are objections.

First, not all the Jewish intertestamental literature that mentions devils or demons can be assigned to definite sects. In particular, the library at Qumran reflects a wide range of Jewish thought, not all of it sectarian.

> **Pagels's achievement [in *The Origin of Satan*] is both a stimulating intellectual romp and a sobering sermon on the dangers of religious polemic.**
> **—*John P. Meier***

Second, while scholars wrangle over who the historical Jesus was, almost all agree that he was a Jewish exorcist and that some pronouncements on Satan and demons (Matthew 12:28; Mark 3:24-27) go back to him. Now Jesus reflects popular Galilean religion, not elite scribal groups writing apocalypses. Indeed, other Jewish exorcists, not connected with any sect, are also mentioned in the New Testament.

Third, in his *Jewish Antiquities* the historian Josephus gives an eyewitness account of an exorcism performed by a Jew named Eleazar. The way in which Josephus traces this "art" back to Solomon and boasts that this power is prevalent "among us" Jews to this day does not favor a purely sectarian origin for demons. Hence Jesus cannot be antiseptically cordoned off from the idea of cosmic war with Satan. This particular exorcist wound up crucified for something more than his call to reconciliation.

Nonetheless, Pagels's achievement [in *The Origin of Satan*] is both a stimulating intellectual romp and a sobering sermon on the dangers of religious polemic.

Rockwell Gray (review date 30 July 1995)

SOURCE: "A Social History of Satan," in *Chicago Tribune Books,* July 30, 1995, pp. 6-7.

[*In the review below, Gray writes that Pagels's efforts in* The Origin of Satan *to link early Christian ideas to the present are hampered by her failure to include cultural history and psychology in her analysis.*]

In what she terms the social history of Satan, Elaine Pagels, a professor of religion at Princeton University, finds the roots of the need to demonize one's enemies. The practice of explaining adversity or conflict by reference to demons reaches back, Pagels notes, into Old Testament history. But she argues [in *The Origin of Satan*] that it entered a radical phase when the small sect of 1st Century Jews who declared Jesus of Nazareth the Messiah proceeded to demonize their enemies.

In claiming that Satan inspired their opponents—largely the Temple authorities and other established Jewish leaders—those proto-Christians confirmed the truth and solidified the ranks of their new faith. This strategy, while not exactly new, says Pagels, was an intensification of earlier practice. In Old Testament Hebrew, "the Satan" originally designated an adversary and came to refer to a messenger from God who would oppose human design or test human resolution, as with Job. Over time, a more personified figure emerged in the form of a powerful fallen angel—fallen either because his lust for women had drawn him to Earth or because prideful struggle with his Creator had brought expulsion from Heaven. Thus was born the figure of Satan as a great demon or spirit who contended with God and the faithful.

While the earlier Jewish practice of demonizing one's enemies antedated the appearance of Christianity, a crucial turn was given the story between 70 and 100 A.D. by the authors of the New Testament Gospels. Pagels argues that while both Mark and Matthew downplay the role of the Romans and accentuate that of the Jewish authorities in their account of Jesus' arrest and persecution, Luke explicitly links Jewish leaders who were enemies of Jesus to the designs of an evil spirit. John, in turn, implicates "the Jews" in general in the Savior's crucifixion, thus laying the groundwork for Christian anti-Semitism. By the late 2nd Century, when the originally Jewish "Jesus movement" had become the increasingly Gentile religion of Christianity, the practice of demonization had become deeply rooted as a strategy for social and credal cohesion.

Pagels notes that from very early, and across cultures, human groups have divided the world between insiders and outsiders, using the dichotomies human/non-human and us/them. But, she adds, "What may be new in Western Christian tradition . . . is how the use of Satan to represent one's enemies lends to conflict a specific kind of moral and religious interpretation, in which 'we' are God's people and 'they' are God's enemies, and ours as well."

The Israelites had already established the idea of a "chosen people" in covenant with their Lord, and later Christians would universalize this concept to include all believers. The genius of Judaic monotheism had been to replace the many lesser gods, goddesses and demons of the ancient world with a single all-powerful deity. But Jehovah could not stand alone. As the Hebrew adversarial concept of "the Satan" evolved, through internal divisions within the Jewish world, into that of the arch-devil Satan, the scattered emonology of paganism was simplified. Though Pagels does not explicitly say so, the revolutionary advance to monotheism eventually brought with it the counterinvention of what might be called "monodiabolism," setting the stage for strife between the Creator and His powerful rebel angel.

Dissenting Jewish sects before Jesus—notably the Essenes—were already demonizing their enemies, but Pagels argues that the first followers of Jesus used the tactic to defend their precarious place in the larger Jewish community. Historians of religion cite earlier pagan and pre-Christian instances of demonic figures loosely comparable to Satan, but nowhere else, she suggests, has the demonic been as central as in the evolution of Christianity.

If Satan was a Jewish creation, his greatly enlarged role in the Christian church would become fundamental to its dramatic expansion across Europe and, in time, to other continents. The proselytizing thrust of Christendom was much indebted to the dark Tempter whose earthly power must be resisted and overcome.

By late in the 2nd entury, Christians were linking Satan to their new enemies—first, Roman magistrates and pagan worshippers of graven images, and then heretics who threatened the solidarity of nascent orthodoxy. The vigorous Gnostic and Manichean heresies that sprang up in the 3rd Century accorded the realm of darkness an existence independent from divine light. Unlike Satan as conceptualized by orthodox believers, the Gnostic Demiurge, or "creator god" (as distinct from an unknowable higher Being), had actually fashioned a fallen world at odds with the truly spiritual. Seeing in this challenge a limitation on God's omnipotence, early church fathers ruthlessly, if only gradually, suppressed it. The eventually victorious doctrine held that evil, baseless in itself, was merely an absence of good. As an estranged and lapsed angel, then, the devil was only negatively derived from an all-powerful God.

[Pagels'] repeated references to the social uses of demonization cry out for fuller recognition of its psychological aspects, not least because she begins by tracing the genesis of this book to her husband's death in a hiking accident and her subsequent experience of "living . . . with a vivid sense of someone who had died."
—Rockwell Gray

Because Pagels' account is confined to origins, she says nothing of representations of Satan in his later career and full regalia. His highly theatrical incarnations have fascinated visual artists from Hieronymus Bosch to Gustave Dore, great poets like Dante, Milton and Goethe, and many generations of ordinary believers. If, as Tolstoy remarked in favor of suffering and tragedy, "the story of all happy families is the same," then the cosmic struggle of Satan's rebellion and fall is surely the most interesting and original chapter in the family romance of Heaven. Little wonder that popular lore and artistic imagination have been inspired more by the tortures of the damned than by the bliss of those who sit on the Lord's right hand.

One wishes at times in these lucid and closely reasoned pages that Pagels had given us an awesome, full-fledged "prince of this world." But, in fairness, the most dramatic iconography of Satan flourished mainly after the period that concerns her. Moreover, she advises at the outset that she will not duplicate the work of other scholars who have focused on the literary, cultural, theological and psychological implications of the devil. Nonetheless, her repeated references to the social uses of demonization cry out for fuller recognition of its psychological aspects, not least because she begins by tracing the genesis of this book to her husband's death in a hiking accident and her subsequent experience of "living . . . with a vivid sense of someone who had died." In turn, this brought reflection on how many re-

ligions invoke forces from an invisible world to explain and cope with misfortune and loss.

Pagels remains always a lively writer who discerns the human implications of esoteric texts and scholarly disputes. And this book, like her earlier *The Gnostic Gospels* (1979) and *Adam and Eve and the Serpent* (1988), is modest in scale and stays close to materials she knows well. But if her clearly schematized stages in the social history of Satan—Jews against Jews, Christians against pagans and then against heretics—is generally sound, her argument for a progressive demonization of the Jews in the four Gospels seems tendentious and fails to register significant differences in evangelistic references to Satan.

Notwithstanding her larger concern with the dark side of the faith is of great interest. Although restricting herself to the first two centuries of the Christian Era, Pagels makes clear that the original division between Jesus' advocates and his enemies became in time a "supernatural drama" that has allowed believers for "some two thousand years . . . [to identify] their opponents, whether Jews, pagans, or heretics, with forces of evil, and so with Satan." Thus have apostasy, dissent and heresy been met, and holy war and mass conversion justified.

It requires little extrapolation to see that a similar pattern of demonized opposition infests the extremist rhetoric of our public discourse and moral vocabulary. Still given to absolutist, virtually Manichean dramas of Good versus Evil, contemporary American imaginations teem with paranoid visions and prophecies of apocalypse. Rational distinctions and disciplined passions are swallowed up in invective and counterinvective, while lip service paid to a bloodless political correctness only masks our obsession with divisive labels and categories. The intoxicating vision of the other as Antichrist is all too easily adapted to modern uses, both secular and religious.

While the author suggests a link between the early history of Christianity and our present world, her exclusion of cultural history and psychology finally limits her book. Nor does she have much to say for the loving, forgiving face of Christian doctrine. Noting briefly in her closing paragraphs that many Christians have sought reconciliation with rather than damnation of their opponents—one thinks immediately of Martin Luther King's "Letter From Birmingham Jail"—she concludes, "For the most part . . . Christians have taught—and acted upon—the belief that their enemies are evil and beyond redemption."

Pagels' dramatic sense of the tangled social context of early Christianity will constitute her primary appeal to a nonscholarly public, and one does come away from this book with troubling questions about the moral legacy of Christianity. Yet, risking a bit more, Pagels might have delivered more.

After all, the two millennia of Christian history are soaked in the blod shed by crusades, religious wars, expulsions, inquisitions, pogroms and holocaust. And Satan has had a hand in it all. But the author's cool, cogent account only tersely refers to "certain fault lines in Christian tradition that have allowed for the demonizing of others throughout Christian history." It's as though *The Origin of Satan* throws open a window on a vast ideological landscape, only to close it abruptly for the sake of a tighter, closer story.

Norman Cohn (review date 21 September 1995)

SOURCE: "Le Diable au Coeur," in *The New York Review*, Vol. XLII, No. 14, September 21, 1995, pp. 18-20.

[*In the review below, Cohn calls* The Origin of Satan *an important, original, and adventurous work.*]

Whereas in the nineteenth century Satan seldom attracted the attention of serious historians—Gustave Roskoff's two-volume *Geschichte des Teufels* (1869) stands almost alone—of late he has done so repeatedly, and to excellent effect. The collection of essays published in 1948 under the auspices of the French Carmelites, and entitled simply *Satan,* heralded what became in the 1970s and 1980s a flood of scholarly studies. The five-hundred-page *Teufelsglaube* by Herbert Haag and others (1974), Jeffrey Russell's trilogy, *The Devil, Satan, Lucifer* (1977-1984), Henry Ansgar Kelly's *The Devil at Baptism,* Bernard Teyssèdre's *Naissance du Diable* and *Le Diable et l'Enfer* (all 1985), Neil Forsyth's *The Old Enemy: Satan and the Combat Myth* (1987)—all these make up a large contribution to our knowledge and (more importantly) to our understanding. So is there anything left to say? Indeed there is—and Elaine Pagels has made a commendable attempt at saying it.

Hitherto studies of Satan have concentrated on the history of the idea (or concept, or symbol, or myth, or whatever), rather than on its function in society. To learn about that one had to turn to works of a different kind—for instance, to studies of the great European witch-hunts of the sixteenth and seventeenth centuries, notably Robert Muchembled's *Culture populaire et culture des élites* (1978) and Christina Larner's *Enemies of God: The Witchhunt in Scotland* (1981). There one could learn how certain human beings could come to be perceived as servants of the Devil. In its approach Pagels's book belongs with such works, rather than with histories of demonology.

Pagels calls her book [*The Origin of Satan*] "a social his-

tory of Satan." To produce such a history would be beyond the capacities of any one person, however gifted, and what one finds here is in fact a more modest work of scholarship: an account of how, in the first three centuries CE, Christians defamed rival or hostile groups by labeling them servants or allies or worshipers of Satan.

For this purpose the earliest Christian sources are the four canonical gospels. It is true that we have no idea who wrote them (except that it was certainly not the apostles Matthew, Mark, Luke, and John to whom they are ascribed). It is also true that they were granted canonical status only around 200 CE. Nevertheless, as guides to the mentality of at least some early Christian communities these documents are reliable. For all the differences between them, they embody a characteristic world view, and one which has remained potent down to the present day.

As Pagels sees it, a vision of the world as a battleground where the forces of good contend with the forces of evil is integral to all the canonical gospels. All four deal with conflicts between Jesus' followers and groups hostile to them—and in all four those conflicts are interpreted as manifestations of a cosmic struggle between God's spirit and the power of Satan.

Pagels accepts unquestioningly the conventional dating of the gospels. She takes it for granted that all these writings were composed in the wake of the catastrophic Jewish rising against Roman rule in Palestine, 66-70 CE, and builds the first part of her argument around that rather questionable assumption. "We cannot fully understand the New Testament gospels," she writes, "until we recognize that they are, in this sense, wartime literature." Not that they are anti-Roman propaganda. After all, Jesus' followers had taken no part in the war—how could they have done so, since they were convinced that they were living during the last days, when God was about to shatter and transform the existing world? For them, the war against Rome was incidental to the infinitely greater war between God and Satan.

That greater war had moved into its final stage with the appearance of Jesus, whose life and death could be understood in no other terms. Satan had striven to frustrate God's plan by destroying Jesus—but Jesus had struck back, defeating Satan at every turn; and his crucifixion, which superficially seemed to signal the victory of the forces of evil, in reality heralded their ultimate annihilation. In this way the gospels strove to show how a seemingly unsuccessful prophet, who had been betrayed by one of his own fllowers and brutally executed by the Romans, had been, and still was, God's appointed Messiah.

In combating Jesus, Satan had human allies, who were themselves the embodiment of the transcendent forces of evil—

and these monstrous beings were above all Jews. In reality, Jesus' chief enemies seem to have been the Roman governor Pontius Pilate and his soldiers, who, after all, in that same century arrested and crucified thousands of Jews charged with sedition. But Jesus also had enemies among his fellow Jews, especially the Jerusalem priests, and the gospel writers concentrate on them.

Pagels comments, "Had Jesus' followers identified themselves with the majority of Jews rather than with a particular minority, they might have told his story differently—and with considerably more historical plausibility." They could, she suggests, have presented him, in traditional patriotic style, as a Jewish holy man martyred by a foreign oppressor. But that was not to be: in the gospels the ultimate blame for Jesus' death is placed squarely on his Jewish enemies, and it is also made plain that in engineering that death the Jews were consciously serving Satan. Indeed, the link between Satan and the Jews was even closer than that: Mark and Matthew imply, and Luke states explicitly, that in Judas Iscariot Satan returned in person to betray Jesus and cause his arrest and execution. Pagels even suggests that it was because Jesus himself was persuaded of the Satanic nature of the forces arrayed against him that he organized a leadership group of his own—the twelve disciples—as potential leaders of the original twelve tribes of Israel. In giving these men "power to cast out demons," he was declaring war on the Satanic host, including its Jewish wing.

Pagels tries to relate all four gospels to the situations in which she believes them to have been composed, and she gives particular attention to what each gospel in turn has to say about Jews. In her opinion the first gospel, Mark, was probably written in the last year of the war, which was some thirty years after Jesus' death. Even at that tragic moment Mark can insist that Jesus' followers had no quarrel with the Romans, only with the Jewish leaders—the Sanhedrin (council of elders), the Jerusalem priests and scribes. Clearly intent on allaying Roman suspicions, he strives to show that neither Jesus himself nor his followers ever dreamed of undermining Roman order. Matthew and Luke, who wrote some ten to twenty years after Mark, carry this argument further: now Pilate himself is favorably portrayed. This is a large distortion of the facts, for other historical and political sources, both Jewish and Roman, agree in showing Pilate to have been a particularly brutal governor.

In Matthew and Luke the Jewish enemy is also redefined. The Roman victory, with the destruction of the Temple, had deprived the high-priestly dynasty and its aristocratic allies in the Sanhedrin of all power. Leadership of the Jewish community in Judea, and eventually of Jewish communities throughout the world, had passed to a body of teachers and rabbis, most of them Pharisees. These were the people with whom Matthew found himself in competition; for they aimed to set the Torah at the center of Jewish life, as a replacement for the destroyed Temple. It was their intention that a practical interpretation of Jewish law should preserve Jewish groups everywhere as a separate and holy people—which is indeed what happened. Matthew was bound to see this interpretation as a rival to his teachings about Jesus. He responded by presenting the Pharisees of Jesus' time, half a century earlier, as Jesus' main antagonists. Now it is they who are Satan's allies. If Satan tries to seduce Jesus by offering him "all the kingdoms of this world," that means that political success and power are themselves Satanic—and the Pharisees, under Roman patronage, were enjoying political success and power.

Spiritual warfare between God and Satan has a still more important place in the only gospel of Gentile origin, John, which was probably composed around 100 CE. According to John, Jesus sent out seventy apostles to preach the coming of the kingdom and to cast out demons (i.e., to heal the sick, especially the mentally sick). They returned triumphant, claiming that even the demons were subject to them in Jesus' name. This was enough to convince Jesus that the final defeat of Satan was imminent: "I saw Satan fall like lighting from heaven. Behold, I have given you power to tread on snakes and scorpions, upon every power of the enemy."

Pagels argues that, in the gospel of John, Satan is shown to have been incarnate first in the Jewish authorities who organized opposition to Jesus, and finally in all Jews—the overwhelming majority who refused to become Jesus' followers. Jesus is portrayed as fully aware of this, and aware also of what it would lead to. When Jews who had previously believed in him deserted him, he identified them as Satan's brood: "You are of your father, the devil; and you want to accomplish your father's desire. He was a murderer from the beginning." The implication is obvious: it was because they were the spiritual children of the murderer Satan that the Jews killed Jesus.

By the end of the first century CE the Christian movement had become largely Gentile—and now Gentiles began to see Satan at work also among other Gentiles. It was natural that they should see him at work in the Roman authorities, who really did sporadically persecute, torture, and kill Christians—but Christians did not stop there: pagans in general were held to be serving Satan. This was a natural consequence of the Christian view of the pagan gods and goddesses. Such radiant deities as Apollo and Venus were perceived as demons, vessels of Satanic power; so their worshipers, whether consciously or not, were in fact willfully adoring the great supernatural opponent of Jesus.

From the Christian point of view there were in fact only two kinds of people—those belonging to the kingdom of God, and those who were still subjects of Satan. For Christians, the entire universe was a battleground where the struggle between God and Satan was being fought out. Christian martyrs never doubted that by their agony and death they were hastening God's victory in that battle. And this was held to be supremely true of the crucifixion of Jesus himself. For Origen, in the third century CE, it was still quite natural to write that Jesus died "to destroy a great *daimon*—in fact, the ruler of *daimones,* who held in subjection the souls of humanity."

However, the Christian movement-itself was anything but monolithic. In its early days, the apostle Paul already found himself confronted with rival teachers—and he dealt with them by calling them servants of Satan. It was the beginning of a tradition: more damnable even than hostile pagans were Christians with whom one disagreed. As the Christian movement turned into an institutional church, with bishops exercising authority over their congregations, it acquired an orthodoxy. When, around 180 CE, Irenaeus, bishop of the congregation of Lyons, wrote his very influential work *Against Heresies,* he had no hesitation in labeling all dissidents servants of Satan. These people, he claimed, used the name of Christ as a lure; in reality they taught Satanic doctrine, "infecting the hearers with the bitter and malignant poison of the serpent, the great instigator of apostasy."

In describing what these dissidents really believed, Pagels, the author of that celebrated work *The Gnostic Gospels,* speaks with special authority. They did not, of course, think of themselves as servants of Satan but of the only true God. And some went further: it is good to be reminded that in the Gnostic *Testimony of Truth,* which probably dates from the second century CE, the God of the Hebrew Bible is presented as a demon, and his worshipers—i.e., "orthodox" Christians—as demon-worshipers.

Such, in brief, is Pagels's argument. How valid is it? The book has many shortcomings, some small, some not so small. The ones that caught my attention all belong to the earlier part of her book and concern her treatment of relations among Jews and between Jews and Christians.

Pagels's comments on the historical background of the Hebrew Bible take little account of recent scholarship. It is not the case that either the Babylonians or the Persians put pressure on the Jews to assimilate to their ways—they couldn't have cared less. Nor is it now thought that Antiochus Epiphanes rededicated the Temple to "the Greek god Olympian Zeus"; the image he installed was of the god whom he himself worshiped, the Syrian Baal Shamen. These are minor points that do not affect the central argument. More surprising is the absence of any reference to the possibility (which is beginning to look like a probability) that down to the sixth century BCE the normal, traditional religion of the Israelites was polytheistic.

Pagels's attempt to trace the figure of Satan back to the Hebrew Bible is unconvincing. In fact, the "*satan*" who appears from time to time in the Hebrew Bible is an angel of good standing at the heavenly court. Counselor and emissary of God, he owes his title of "satan" (meaning "adversary" or "accuser") solely to the fact that on occasion, at God's bidding, he takes on the role of prosecuting counsel against this or that human being (most famously against Job). Pagels is well aware of this, but nevertheless claims that "when Israelite writers excoriated their fellow Jews in mythological terms . . . most often they identified [them] with an exalted, if treacherous, member of the divine court whom they called the *satan.*" The solitary quotation which she cites from the visions of Zechariah hardly suffices to support so large a claim.

In my view the antecedents of the being who is called by the proper name Satan in the New Testament and in subsequent Christian teachings do not lie in the Hebrew Bible at all. Where do they lie? Pagels points out that relevant material is to be found in those strange Jewish works of the second century BC, the *Book of the Watchers* and the *Book of Jubilees,* and that is true enough. In these works we do indeed meet the fallen angels—former members of the heavenly court who, in one way or another, rebelled against God, came down (or were thrown down) to earth, and there seduced innumerable human beings into sin. The leader of these fallen angels could be regarded as a Jewish prototype of Satan.

Yet he is a very imperfect prototype. If in the *Book of Jubilees* he and some of his followers have God's permission to go on roaming the earth and doing harm, in the *Book of the Watchers* he is quite impotent—buried under-ground, pending the Last Judgment, when he and his followers will be still more grievously punished by being cast into the pit of fire, there to burn forever and ever. There is no denying that the myth of the fallen angels has proved a very enduring one—where would *Paradise Lost* be without it?—but the true origin of Satan, as the mighty and ever-active opponent of God, can hardly be found there.

This conclusion has implications for Pagels's book. If the origins of Satan are not after all to be found in the leader of the fallen angels, one of its central themes collapses: Satan ceases to be an "intimate enemy." An "intimate enemy" Pagels defines as "one's trusted colleague, close associate, brother . . . who turns unexpectedly jealous and hostile." I'm not sure whether it is invariably true even of first-century Jews and Christians that Satan is perceived not as a hostile foreign power, as Pagels writes, but as "the source and representation of conflict *within* the community," i.e., an "intimate enemy." What of the Book of Revelation, where the dragon-Devil who persecutes the Church is doubtless Rome? Certainly the concept of the "intimate enemy" throws little light on the subsequent history of demonization. If Christians have at various times cast near-neighbors—Jews, religious dissidents, "witches"—as servants of Satan, they have done exactly the same to many foreign peoples—the Muslims whom they fought, the pagan peoples whom they colonized throughout the world.

There are other objections to the concept of the "intimate enemy." Satan has always performed a vast number of quite humble, one might say domestic; functions. At various times he has been accused of tempting Christians to fornication, gluttony, vanity, using cosmetics, dressing luxuriously, going to the theater, gambling, avarice, quarreling, spiritual sloth, and much, much more. This side of the Devil's nature, too, can be traced back to early Christianity—and the notion of an "intimate enemy" does nothing to explain it.

Pagels comes near to what I believe to be the true origin of Satan when she turns to the Essenes, some of whom made up the Qûmran community, otherwise known as the Dead Sea Sect. Of them she writes:

> ... the Essenes go much further [than the *Book of the Watchers*] and place at the center of their religious understanding the cosmic war between God and his allies, both angelic and human, against Satan, or Beliar, along with his demonic and human allies. The Essenes place themselves at the very center of this battle between heaven and hell. . . . They invoke Satan—or Beliar—to characterize the irreconcilable opposition between themselves and the "sons of darkness" in the war taking place simultaneously in heaven and on earth. They expect that soon God will come in power, with his holy angels, and finally overthrow the forces of evil and inaugurate the Kingdom of God.

Here, surely, lies the true Jewish origin of the Satan with whom Pagels is concerned. But that said, one must hasten to add that his Jewish origin is not, in all probability, his true origin. On the grounds that others have already "attempted to investigate cross-cultural parallels," and that her own interest is in the social implication of the figure of Satan, Pagels eschews any mention of Zoroastrianism. But it is not a question of mere parallels. Would the members of the Qumran community, or the early Christian movement, ever have imagined themselves as involved in a cosmic struggle between God and Devil—a struggle just nearing its triumphant world-transforming conclusion—if they had not come under strong Zoroastrian influence? For just such a struggle has always been central to the Zoroastrian world view—and current research is showing more and more clearly how close Zoroastrian-Jewish relations were at the relevant time. What has long been suspected is now almost certain: that Satan originated as a Judaized version of the Zoroastrian spirit of

evil, Ahriman. In a book entitled *The Origins of Satan* one might reasonably expect to find more awareness of that research.

These are serious reservations. Despite them, it seems to me that Pagels has achieved something important. She has demonstrated, more fully and convincingly than has been done before, how ancient the demonizing tradition in Christianity is. In particular, she has demonstrated how the authors of the canonical gospels helped—unintentionally and unwittingly, to be sure—to create the stereo-type of the demonic Jew. Thoughtful, scholarly works that are also original and adventurous are not common. *The Origin of Satan* is such a work, and we should be correspondingly grateful.

Mary Troychak (review date September-October 1995)

SOURCE: A review of *The Origin of Satan,* in *The Bloomsbury Review,* September-October, 1995, p. 23.

[*In the review below, Troychak discusses how events in Pagels's life motivated her to explore the dark side of Christianity.*]

Five hundred years ago, Elaine Pagels would have been burned at the stake. She has read the sacred texts of Christianity and become fascinated with the devil. She expresses doubt that Jesus was actually crucified by Jews. She contends that the New Testament gospels—which millions of Christians believe to be the actual word of God set down by his apostles—are polemical tracts written generations later to strengthen the fledgling church against its enemies: the pagans without and the heretics within. Finally, she has gained this knowledge by studying forbidden books, suppressed and deviant gospels that had remained buried until 50 years ago.

The personal tragedies that preceded and inspired *The Origin of Satan* have received almost as much attention as the work itself. For almost 20 years, Pagels was married to physicist Heinz Pagels. In 1987, their six-year-old son Mark died of a lung disease. In a PBS *World of Ideas* interview around that time, she told Bill Moyers that she had become interested in the question of how Christianity interprets bad fortune. Confronted with the death of her child, Pagels admitted that she felt it easier to blame herself, to blame anyone, than to accept the random and meaningless death of someone so beloved. In 1988, when friends perceived that the couple was finally emerging from their mourning, Heinz Pagels fell to his death while hiking in the mountains outside Aspen, Colorado.

Pagels begins her Introduction to *The Origin of Satan* with the observation that, like many people who grieve, she found herself "living in the presence of an invisible being." A historian of the ancient Western world, she began to reflect on how religions have shaped our views of the invisible world, and how those views affect our relationships with other people, with events, and with nature. She assumed she would find that Christianity moralized the universe: Disasters such as she had suffered would be seen as the will of God or a judgment on human sin. What surprised her as she worked was the predominant role of the devil.

Pagels, a professor of religion at Princeton University, has published two books for the general public about the roots of Christianity. She was among the first scholars to translate the Nag Hammadi Library, 13 papyrus books bound in leather that were discovered in 1945 by a man digging for gold in the upper Egyptian desert. Pagels encountered texts that would revolutionize her views on Christianity, direct the course of her future work, and establish her as a creative, intuitive scholar with a gift for making history come alive for the general reader.

The Gnostic Gospels, which concerns a second-century Christian sect, received the National Book Award and has been published in at least 10 languages. *Adam, Eve, and the Serpent* shows how creation as described in Genesis has influenced our culture's beliefs about gender, sex, and reproduction. In her most recent book, Pagels confronts the dark side of Christianity. She peruses ancient manuscripts—the Bible as well as Hebrew, pagan, and heretical Christian texts—to construct what she calls "a social history of Satan." At what point did Satan emerge as a principal player in the Christian drama? How has belief in the devil influenced Western perspectives on ourselves and other people, and affected the course of human history? These are questions Pagels invites the reader to consider in this illuminating and provocative book.

For nearly two millennia, millions of Christian believers have viewed their personal and political struggles as reflections of an eternal cosmic war waged between God and the devil. Many in our culture were raised on this cosmology; the battle continues over whether it should be taught in out public schools. During the Gulf War, Satan was present in the rhetoric of both President Bush and Saddam Hussein. Susan Smith's Methodist pastor told the *New York Times* that when she parked at the lake with her two sleeping children, "God made her a presentation, and Satan made her a beautiful presentation." The importance and the power of Pagel's latest work is her insistence that we scrutinize our dominant mythologies.

Pagels acknowledges that strife between groups is as old as umanity:

> What may be new in Western Christian tradition is how the use of Satan to represent one's enemies lends to conflict a specific kind of moral and religious interpretation, in which "we" are God's people and "they" are God's enemies, and ours as well. Such moral interpretation of conflict has proven extraordinarily effective throughout Western history in consolidating the identity of Christian groups; the same history also shows that it can justify hatred, even mass slaughter.

Pagels concludes [*The Origin of Satan*] with this hope:

> that this research may illuminate the struggle within Christian tradition between the profoundly human view that "otherness" is evil and the words of Jesus that reconciliation is divine.

FURTHER READING

Criticism

Begley, Adam. "The End of Evil." *Los Angeles Times Book Review* (8 October 1995): 1, 11, 13.
> Compares *The Origin of Satan* with several other works on Satan, particularly Robert Fuller's *Naming the Antichrist.*

Review of *The Gnostic Paul: Gnostic Exegesis of the Pauline Letters,* by Elaine Pagels. *Choice* 13, No. 2 (April 1976): 238.
> Calls *The Gnostic Paul* a good comparison between the views of Paul and the Gnostic Christians.

Pagels, Elaine. "The Orthodox Against the Gnostics: Confrontation and Interiority in Early Christianity." In *The Other Side of God: A Polarity in World Religions,* edited by Peter L. Berger, pp. 61-73. Garden City, NY: Anchor Press, 1981.
> Explores what differentiates Gnostic writings from the canonized New Testament.

Salisbury, Joyce. "Sexuality, Freedom, and the Body Politic." *Journal of Social History* 23, No. 4 (Summer 1990): 817-23.
> Discusses theories about historical perceptions of the body and the body politic in several works, including *Adam, Eve, and the Serpent.*

Additional coverage of Pagels's life and career is contained in the following sources published by Gale: *Contemporary Authors,* Vols. 45-48, and *Contemporary Authors New Revision Series,* Vols. 2, 24, and 51.

Henry Roth
1906-1995

American novelist, essayist, and short story writer.

The following entry presents criticism of Roth's work through 1996. For further information on his life and career, see *CLC,* Volumes 2, 6, and 11.

INTRODUCTION

Henry Roth's career has been the subject of intense interest and speculation. After the critical success of his first novel, *Call It Sleep* (1934), Roth suffered from a writer's block that lasted sixty years. When he reconnected with his creative impulse, it gushed forth with a 7,000-page memoir in the form of a novel with several volumes. Due to the autobiographical nature of his work, Roth's controversial life is discussed as often as his fiction.

Biographical Information

Roth was born in Austria circa 1906. When he was eighteen months old his mother brought him to New York where his father had been working to save the money for their passage. There was tension in the Roth family which resulted in Roth's close relationship with his mother and his alienation from his father. In his early childhood, the Roths lived in New York City's Lower East Side. Roth felt a sense of belonging in the Jewish community of this neighborhood that he did not receive at home. He suffered greatly when his family moved to the more threatening and diverse environment of Harlem. His identity as a Jew was shaken at this time in his life. It was his Jewish heritage that marked him as different, and therefore he moved away from his religion to adapt to his Gentile Irish neighborhood. Roth graduated from DeWitt Clinton High School in Manhattan in 1924 and began studying biology at the City College of New York. While a student at City College, Roth became interested in writing and met Eda Lou Walton, a New York University professor and poet. Walton helped Roth with his writing, and in 1928 the two began living together. The two socialized with prominent intellectuals, but Roth still suffered from a sense of alienation. Roth began writing his first novel in 1930. He started recording biographical facts, but then let the literary figures take over. Walton supported Roth both financially and emotionally while he spent the next three and a half years writing *Call It Sleep.* While Roth was still living with her, Walton had an affair with David Mandel, whom she later married. Mandel was a partner in the publishing company Robert O. Ballou, and Walton convinced him to have his company publish Roth's novel in 1934. The book received favorable reviews, but literature of the 1930s was heavily politicized. The Left Wing complained that *Call It Sleep* did not make a strong enough political statement. In an attempt to overcome the guilt of his dependence on Walton and to serve his political impulses, Roth joined the Communist Party. He wanted to feel a part of a larger whole, but later complained that joining the Party hampered his creative skills. He began a never-finished second novel in 1935. The protagonist was a midwestern industrial worker who joins the Communist Party after being injured in an accident at work. Roth felt as though his work had to have some larger political meaning, but he lost his personal connection to his writing. After writing the first 100 pages and having the idea accepted by a publisher, Roth decided he could not write the novel. He eventually burned the manuscript and turned his attention to other pursuits, including a stint as a teacher, a precision grinder, and a raiser of waterfowl. In 1964, *Call It Sleep* was rediscovered and republished. It went on to sell one million copies, which only intensified the mystery of Roth's subsequent silence. Miraculously, after sixty years of writer's block, Roth found his muse again. He began work on a six-volume series of novels that, although fictional, represent a memoir of his life. Roth only lived to see the first volume published, but he did work on the galleys of the second volume before his death in 1995.

Major Works

Call It Sleep is an autobiographical work which traces a young Jewish immigrant's search for belonging in New York City in the 1930s. The protagonist is David Schearl. David suffers from a feeling of alienation—from the father who questions the boy's paternity, from the Gentile neighborhood in which he lives, and from the Jewish religion which he does not understand. The only closeness David feels is with his mother, and the Oedipal aspect of that relationship causes David to pull away from her throughout the novel. The novel is full of symbols which point to the underlying theme: redemption. Roth uses dialect and ethnic speech patterns in the novel to help portray David's isolation. In the end the boy turns to myth and the story of Isaiah for his transfiguration. He touches a milk ladle to the third rail of the trolley tracks, electrocuting himself, and symbolically purifying himself. When David does not die, his father's feelings soften toward him and there is hope that he will transcend his inner conflicts. Roth's return to fiction with *Mercy of a Rude Stream* (1994) was once again autobiographical in nature. Roth strongly denied that the work represented the facts of his life, but the many parallels between himself and the protagonist, Ira, led to speculation about which events the author had actually experienced.

Critical Reception

The critical reception of *Call It Sleep* was favorable on its first release, especially for a first novel. Many reviewers have commented on Roth's skill as a storyteller. Critics were impressed with Roth's use of dialect in the novel, interspersing English with Yiddish and the language of the street. Many reviewers compare Roth to James Joyce in his sensitive portrayal of adolescence. Praise for *Call it Sleep* was even stronger upon its rediscovery in the 1960s after its second release. Many critics asserted that it was the most important work about the Jewish immigrant experience of the twentieth century. Reviews were more mixed for the three volumes of Roth's *Mercy of a Rude Stream.* Critics complained that Roth merely recorded actual events and did not let the story and the characters have their own life. Others praised Roth for the brutal honesty and poignancy of the work.

PRINCIPAL WORKS

Call It Sleep (novel) 1934
Nature's First Green (novel) 1979
Shifting Landscape: A Composite, 1925-1987 (essays and
    short stories) 1991
*Mercy of a Rude Stream, Volume One: A Star Shines Over
    Mt. Morris Park* (novel) 1994
*Mercy of a Rude Stream, Volume Two: A Diving Rock on
    the Hudson* (novel) 1995
Mercy of a Rude Stream, Volume Three: From Bondage
    (novel) 1996

CRITICISM

Fred T. Marsh (review date 17 February 1935)

SOURCE: "A Great Novel About Manhattan Boyhood," in *New York Herald Tribune Books,* Vol. II, No. 24, February 17, 1935, p. 6.

[*In the following review, Marsh praises Roth's* Call It Sleep *and asserts that the novel should win the Pulitzer Prize.*]

This is a novel about a New York childhood, the story of a small boy from the ages of six to nine in Brownsville and Jewish East Side Manhattan. It is a first novel. I believe it to be the most compelling and moving, the most accurate and profound study of an American slum childhood that has yet appeared in this day when, be it said to the credit of our contemporary critics, economic color-lines are no longer drawn in literature.

It has been a long-drawn-out campaign of guerrilla warfare involving the clergy, the law, the press and the academicians; and the young men who bite the hands of the pioneers in the field—from the early Dreiser through the realists of the twenties—show a marble-hearted ingratitude. It is safe to assume that this novel would never have been published if *Ulysses* had not won the decision in our courts. And the law trails enlightened public opinion.

But this book is a novel, a work of superior craftsmanship, more than that, a work of significance, authority and depth. Horace Gregory speaks of it as no mere "human document" and that it seems to me, is one of the first things to be said about it. Michael Gold's autobiographical *Jews Without Money* was a rich human document emerging from the same background; but Henry Roth writing in the third person, has achieved the detachment and universality of the artist.

Curiously, Roth has succeeded in making his David both a more individualized child and a more representative protagonist than most of the boys and girls whom our best younger novelists of metropolitan life have written about. The comparisons here are not invidious, for both Farrell and Dahlberg have concentrated on the years of adolescence and young manhood, rather than on childhood. But the "Studs Lonigan" of Farrell's novels is a product of the extraneous environment of the streets, and the Lorry Lewis of Dahlberg's *Bottom Dogs* and *From Flushing to Calvary* is a waif, egotistic, introspective, unhappy but self-sufficient.

David is bound to his home and to the Father-Mother-Son relationship which here takes the normal turn of the child clinging to the mother while fearing the father. This factor gives the story depth, roots that grow deep into the soil from which human life springs. All three, Studs and Lorry and David, are individuals who are yet representative of thousands of others. And we do not know what happens to David later when the dangerous and rebellious age of puberty is reached. But this novel, within its limited scope, is absolutely true to universals. One thinks immediately of any number of other childhoods—of Vardis Fisher's Vridar, whose boyhood was spent on a remote and impoverished Idaho ranch; of Penrod in his smug suburban town; of the young David Copperfield as a waif on London streets; of Plupy Shute's "Real Diary" of a nineteenth century small-town New England childhood; of Tolstoy's "Boyhood and Youth"; of the boy who was Proust at Combray; of the early chapters of *Sons and Lovers.* David is not like any of these others but this novel has captured more than its share of the essence of boyhood in the rarest and most volatile phases.

But to be more specific, David's father had been in America two years saving money in order to have his wife and son come over and join him. When he meets them at the dock, however, he is in one of his worst moods. And the antagonism between father and child begins there. The father, Albert, is a printer, a powerful man physically but almost unbalanced mentally, complex, a paranoid, suffering from a sense of guilt, violent and moody.

In Brownsville the father goes from one job to another, loses his only man friend, finds in violence the only outlet to his repressed emotions. But he is competent, hard-working and thrifty; would be a good husband and father if he were not ridden by his demons.

The mother is a woman of instinctive grace, resilience and tact, warm and comforting and gentle to her sensitive little boy, managing, providing, pouring oil on troubled waters at all times. The boy and the mother find that vast comfort in each other, that solace for all wounds, that play, full of humor, irony, wit, affection, indulgence, understanding, pathos and beauty, that marks all great fundamental relationships. One sympathizes with the father who remains an outsider. That is owing to his own perverseness; but that perverseness is defensive. To this reader, he stands out as a notable and clean creation. For all the bitterness, David is fortunate in having such a father, rather than a commonplace one.

Of the boy, himself, what can one say! A summary in a review would rob him of that subtlety and those nuances, that unique essential verity which is his, together with his common childishness, which only his creator should be allowed to portray. One must read the novel. But, on the surface, David goes to school, goes to cheder, meets life on the boyhood plane, on the roofs, on the streets, in the alleys, through the neighborhood as many another little boy has done. He runs into dangers, into puppy sex, into and out of boyhood friendships and cruelties. David is an imaginative and clever and sensitive little punk. But he also knows what's what on the realistic plane. Only, he cannot adapt himself to it. And always waiting are his mother's arms, his sovereign remedy against his small world's harshness.

The language of this novel is nothing short of the highest talent. It moves from a kind of transmutation of picturesque, warm, emotional and gentle Yiddish, to the literal English argot of the Ghetto, an ugly, fascinating, and expressive speech. It moves from the delicate attempts at translating refined sentiments from Yiddish into English, into free translations of the coarsest Yiddish into English. Roth has traversed these paths, with a little Hebrew thrown in to perfection. His ear, with all due respect to Arthur Kober, is, I think, the best attuned of all the writers in the field. This, of course is a mere technicality. But it seems to me noteworthy here because it all fits into a serious and outstanding novel. Neither the language nor the license in physical, including sexual, details, nor the various jargons and extraneous incidents with which David comes in contact, are dragged in for the sake of virtuosity. Always they are inci-

dental, natural, implicit, simple and effective. And the next to the last section—where David creates a short-circuit on the trolley line almost to his own destruction—is a little masterpiece, in its asides, of the talk of any congested section in the City of New York. And that talk, except that it is intensified, varies in no way from the talk familiar to every city, large or small, in the United States.

Some will object to the fact that there is a plot running through the novel, that after the plot is resolved one discovers that certain matters have been "planted" anticipating the denouement. I do not think this business adds anything to the story. But this factor is relatively unimportant; and for some readers it will serve as a spur to an already swift-running exciting and tremendously stirring novel.

Expressions used here will shock only because they appear in print. If one had never heard them he would not know what they meant. But, of course, every one has heard them; or almost every one. I learned most of them at the age of eight in the remote little hamlet, twenty houses strong, of Thornton's Ferry, New Hampshire, over thirty years ago. But country children, of course, are more realistic, though less articulate, than the kids I knew when I lived in a big city. Henry Roth's great virtue in this particular field is that he stands aside and lets the whole outpouring of David's emotional reactions, his revulsion, wonder, terror, run its course.

This is a review *about* the book rather than one *of* the book. I have sidestepped the main issues because I have nothing to say about them, beyond what is in the book. To discerning readers, I believe, for its profound intensity, its rare virtuosity, its sensitive realism, its sheer weight, its power, circumference and depth, this first novel of this Mr. Roth will be remembered for some time to come. I should like to see *Call it Sleep* win the Pulitzer prize—which it never will.

Joseph Gollomb (review date 16 March 1935)

SOURCE: "Life in the Ghetto," in *Saturday Review of Literature,* Vol. II, No. 35, March 16, 1935, p. 552.

[*In the following review, Gollomb complains that in* Call It Sleep, *Roth magnifies the foulness of life on the east side of New York instead of accurately portraying it.*]

By this time it is probable that New York's great ghetto of decades ago has been written up as amply as any other equally small segment of the modern world; yet *Call It Sleep* shows once more how rich for the writer has been the yield on New York's lower east side. Here is a novel twice the average length, yet it records only two to three years of a small boy's life down there, and records it with what amounts to a congestion of material.

Part of this is due to the rich soil of the scene itself; it would seem that a writer needs only "tickle it with a hoe, and it laughs with a harvest." But the novel owes most of its plethora of sensation and emotional tension to the author's sensitivity, which is acute to the point of painfulness; and the minutest impact on him seems to him indispensable in his report.

The setting and the people of the novel are by now familiar enough to readers of east side novels; the "stench and throb" of the tenements; tenement Jews writhing in poverty and crowded together beyond endurance; and a central character, a little boy, who bears the brunt of life with only a fine and sensitive mother to help him bear it. But the treatment of all this in the book, for all its wealth of photographic detail, renders Mr. Roth's east side quite an alien, somewhat unreal land, especially to those who have known it at first hand.

Partly the defect is due to reporting. Although poverty, for instance, is the all-embracing, brutally dominating fact in slum tenement life, its climate, so to say, and its very soil, the author in his depiction almost completely ignores its role. What also helps to make the novel seem unreal as a transcript of life is the author's injection of passages and chapters of stylized writing in the ultramodern tradition.

But the distortion of the picture—for, by and large, his picture is distorted—must be laid to the author's temper, which casts over familiar scenes and people a hectic light and creates an atmosphere in which human beings could not long survive. Mr. Roth's east side is an extremely violent and febrile world; rarely a moment of peace there, a breath of respite; nothing but poisonous life goes on. Now anyone who has spent even part of childhood on the lower east side knows how brutal and hectic life can be there even for a youngster of tough fibre, and David, the, boy in the novel, is fragile to an extreme. But a conscientious report of that life would include contrasts to Mr. Roth's picture of it and even triumphs over the undeniable brutalities he depicts. Let anyone who doubts it ask, for example, librarians on the east side how much the children there for generations have found reading almost as much as food a part of life.

There is much, to be sure, that is true in Mr. Roth's novel; he has a sensitive ear for speech; his characters speak from character and in the idioms of their land; he remembers amazingly and reports photographically; still, let me repeat, the book in part and as a whole does violence to the truth. Someone once wished that novels of east side life did not have to be so "excremental." ***Call It Sleep*** is by far the foulest picture of the east side that has yet appeared, in con-

ception and in language. Certainly there was and is foulness down there as in other places; but Mr. Roth treats it not with the discriminating eye of the artist but with a magnifying glass, and if not with a relish, certainly with no effort to see what Emerson saw, that "even in the mud and scum of things there always, always something sings." Whoever omits that something in his picture of east side life omits the very thing which has kept that life so long a fertile field for the creative writer.

Harold V. Ribalow (essay date Fall 1962)

SOURCE: "Henry Roth and His Novel *Call It Sleep*," in *Wisconsin Studies in Contemporary Literature,* Vol. 3, No. 3, Fall, 1962, pp. 5-14.

[*In the following essay, Ribalow asserts the importance of Roth's* Call It Sleep *in a discussion of how it expresses the Jewish immigrant experience in America and how it portrays the pains of adolescence.*]

A phenomenon of contemporary American literature has been the emergence of the "Jewish novel" as a major force on the literary scene in this country.

As recently as a decade ago, novels by American-Jewish writers on Jewish themes were not considered part of the mainstream of American creative activity. Thus the works of Ludwig Lewisohn, Meyer Levin, Maurice Samuel and other significant Jewish writers were overlooked and omitted from the accepted and acknowledged literary histories. This development has been noted previously and is worth stressing at this time only in order to emphasize the radical change that has taken place in the last ten years.

Today, of course, Herman Wouk, Leon Uris and Harry Golden are household names, and even the less "popular" authors, like Bernard Malamud, J.D. Salinger, Herbert Gold, Harvey Swados, Philip Roth and dozens of other young writers, now represent an entire bloc of talented men who have contributed enormously to the fiction of the last decade. Their books are read, bought and widely discussed. Publishers, who used to avoid Jewish subject matter as non-commercial, now seek out Jewish writers and themes.

The current renascence has led publishers and critics to look back in time in order to discover those Jewish novels which had languished in the 1930's. Today, some of these books are being reissued, to the satisfaction of both literary critics and the reading public.

Daniel Fuchs, for example, wrote three novels about Jews in Brooklyn some thirty years ago which were indifferently received in their own time. When they were made available once again, in a single volume and with a new preface by the author, the novels earned long critical appreciations in scores of general and literary periodicals.

It is no wonder, then, that perhaps the best Jewish novel ever written in the United States should have been "rediscovered" in 1960. It is *Call It Sleep* by Henry Roth.

Call It Sleep was published early in 1935, received glowing notices and then fell into complete obscurity for twenty years. From time to time, critics made passing references to it, but the novel itself remained unobtainable while a cult of Henry Roth admirers developed.

Leslie Fiedler and Alfred Kazin were among those who called attention to Henry Roth's novel. They wrote about it and, when they lectured, called attention to it. Marie Syrkin, editor of *The Jewish Frontier,* as long ago as 1940, referred to *Call It Sleep* as the finest Jewish novel produced in America. But Henry Roth had disappeared and it seemed that *Call It Sleep* would remain a fond memory in the minds of a handful of sensitive readers.

As a critic who devotes himself almost entirely to Jewish writing in America, I had been asked time and again by interested readers and lecture audiences about Henry Roth and *Call It Sleep.* It is a book about a young Jewish boy living, at the turn of the century, in New York City, and the sensitivity with which the book was written made a tremendous impact on Jewish readers whose own parents were immigrants and who, themselves, were familiar with the milieu which Henry Roth describes. Accidentally, I had heard from a friend, the novelist and former managing editor of the old *American Mercury,* Charles Angoff, that Roth was alive and living quietly near Augusta, Maine.

I had remembered that early in 1940 I had seen two short stories in *The New Yorker* by someone who signed himself as Henry Roth, but I was not quite sure whether it was the same Roth.

Nevertheless, I wrote to Henry Roth in 1959, and that was the first step taken to bring Roth back into our contemporary world. I have corresponded with him at great length ever since (and learned, almost at the outset, that the two *New Yorker* stories—fragments, he called them—were indeed his). I met him a number of times, both in Maine and in New York City, and was instrumental in the reissuance of *Call It Sleep* by Cooper Square Publishers. The new edition carries a critical introduction of the novel by Maxwell Geismar, a personal appreciation of the book and its author by Meyer Levin, and a biographical essay by the present writer.

It must be stated unhappily that Henry Roth has been a "one-novel" writer. This is his only book and it is unlikely that he shall ever write another.

The crack-up of American novelists from F. Scott Fitzgerald to Ernest Hemingway is not an unusual phenomenon in the United States. Whatever it is that shatters the psyche of sensitive American novelists, assailed Henry Roth as well as Fitzgerald and Hemingway. Ironically, it now develops that Roth was stronger than they. Fitzgerald sought escape in alcohol and Hemingway shot himself. Roth merely retreated to Maine with a loving wife, raised two fine sons and simply stopped writing.

Before analyzing the remarkable qualities of his novel, I think it is instructive to trace the psychology of Henry Roth and perhaps in doing this we may gain some insights into the heart and mind of an extraordinarily talented man who deliberately withdraws from the creative act.

Roth, I discovered, had become a waterfowl farmer five miles south of Augusta, Maine, and when I first wrote to him, in 1959, telling him that I was one of many who admired his novel, he replied:

> It was very kind of you to write. My delay in answering seems to stem from the fact that I apparently have to settle down and become however fleetingly a unified personality, at least during the time of my reply. It's gratifying that *Call It Sleep* still continues to impress people; it is less gratifying, of course, that the author no longer does so. Apparently that flower grew out of a soil that became sterile.
>
> But—one has seen the same thing happen to others in this epoch and previous ones. It's a little painful. I find myself vacillating between an impatience to get the years over with, and a complacency that I got out of it with a whole skin, relatively whole skin, if not a whole soul. Oh, like everyone else, I have illusions, especially when I have the leisure to have them in, but in my most lucid moments I think, or counsel myself, that the less I attempt to write, the better. . . . It would seem as if a personality changes, and what was an attribute of the one is not necessarily an attribute of the other. There is one theme I like above all others, and that is redemption, but I haven't the fable.
>
> I don't know if I have the ability either. Other than that I wondered whether there would be any value, any earthly value; of a literary nature, of communing or communicating with one I know nothing about as a means of getting rid of this huge and hid-

eous cargo I lug about with me. Art is a means of jettison.

Or should I say frequently, or for me?

Outside of this sphere, if you have any curiosity about it, I am merely a waterfowl raiser or farmer, and not a very prosperous one, not that it matters in the least, have two children by a woman who daily retrieves my sanity with her constancy and good sense. I am nominally happy—and curiously enough, when I am in my right mind, which happens a surprising number of times during the day, I accept my own history, and that is perhaps my only inner strength. I would not have it arrive at any other outcome except this, and so I sanction what I lament. I don't imagine that is very unique either, is it?

In his second letter to me, Roth wrote:

I think I'm finished. It's a rather hard thing to say, especially for someone who once felt, or fancied he felt, a truly creative ardor. But one might as well face facts, and try to face them as objectively as possible. I do write occasionally, a kind of protracted reminiscence, but it's not worth much, except psychologically, to discharge some of the potential that would never go anyway. I have rather limited ability; I relied almost entirely on the imagination and when that faded, so did I.

Roth continued his defeatism in later letters as well. Once, he wrote: "Yes, I would like to write, to write as I once wrote, when it had meaning and I seemed to be exploring worlds no one else had before, and the possibility existed for uniqueness and wonder and magnitude. But maybe I was just young. If it doesn't exist, or I can't evoke it, why bother? There's enough pulp in the world."

> **If most of us, passing through only once, can leave behind us a work of art comparable to *Call It Sleep,* we would have every reason to be proud of ourselves.**
> **—*Harold U. Ribalow***

In spite of Roth's nagging feeling of defeat and frustration, he still writes with exceptional brilliance and power, even if only intermittently.

At about the time he learned that ***Call It Sleep*** would be reissued, he was invited to contribute an essay on the last twenty-five years of his life, by the editor of *Commentary.*

Eventually, though reluctantly, he did so. In this essay, he re-echoed the thoughts earlier stated in his letters to me, but here they were more carefully phrased.

"By now," he wrote, "I console myself with the thought that my creative powers, such as they were, even though fully employed, would be on the decline anyway, and by now I would have met myself perhaps with certain volumes published, and conscious of a certain modicum of acclaim, and in possession of certain emoluments, to be sure. What difference does it make? The years would have been over in any event. Poor solace, I know. The mind shuttles and reminds. We go this way only once; and shuttles again and rejoins: once is enough."

If most of us, passing through only once, can leave behind us a work of art comparable to ***Call It Sleep,*** we would have every reason to be proud of ourselves. But it seems to be the fate of many talented writers to see their pride give way to uncertainty, to doubt always that what they are doing is worth doing. Henry Roth carries the heavy burden of the creative writer. He withdraws constantly from society, from his fellow man, and seldom permits us to see him as he truly is. We must, therefore, judge him on his one book.

Call It Sleep describes the inner life of David Schearl, a little Jewish boy who lives with his mother and father in Brownsville Brooklyn, and later, on New York's East Side. David's world is a harsh one, for his father—who is domineering and bitter—jealously harbors a suspicion that his wife has never loved him and that his son David is another man's son. David survives in the nightmare of the big city jungle. He wants desperately to belong, but everywhere, at all corners of life, he finds enemies. Christian boys taunt him; girls flaunt their sex at him; his father, he is convinced, hates him. He has only his mother and her comforting breast, but it is barely enough.

In Hebrew school, David is first praised by his teacher and then tortured. He is deeply aware of the unspoken animosity which shatters the lives of his parents. He exists in a world he never made, but Roth creates of this world a moving series of vignettes, in poetic prose, in experimental language, now tender, now violent.

To the critic in the Jewish field, ***Call It Sleep*** is of special importance. The carefully-phrased dialogue, replete with Yiddishisms brilliantly translated into English to evoke the poetics of the Yiddish language, is only part of Roth's accomplishment. The sounds and smells of the street are here. The give and take between boys and girls, men and women, and the admixture of joy and sorrow, fulfillment and failure, are traced in dozens of pages throughout the narrative.

For example, Roth is particularly observant in tracing the

relationship between David's mother and a man named Luter, a close friend of David's father. The passages involving Luter and David's mother are utilized, in part, to depict David's gradual discovery of sex. Roth offers a keen insight into the attitude of a boy who slowly realizes that his own mother is an object of sexual desire. In a later sequence, the street boys call David to join them in peeping at a naked woman, who, horror of horrors, turns out to be his own mother! But more subtly, this is how Roth suggests jealousy on David's part:

> Luter, his eyes narrowed by a fixed yawn, was staring at his mother, at her hips. For the first time, David was aware of how her flesh, confined by the skirt, formed separate molds against it. He felt suddenly bewildered, struggling with something in his mind that would not become a thought.

David's love for his mother is deep and when Roth writes of the boy's mother, the prose in the novel sings. The book is full of heavy dialect-spelling, but, from time to time, it suddenly becomes clearly and deliberately lucid.

There is the passage where David's mother talks to her little son about Europe and the death of her own grandmother. Recalling the agony of death, David's mother says: "She looked so frail in death, in her shroud—how shall I tell you, my son? Like early winter snow. And I thought to myself even then, let me look deeply into her face for surely she will melt before my eyes."

As he listens to his beloved mother, David thinks: "I was near her. I was part of her. Oh, it was good being here. He watched her every movement hungrily."

But he is not yet done with his probing of her mood and death seems terrible to him.

> "But when do they wake up, mama?" he asks.
>
> Sadly, his mother replies, "There is nothing left to waken."
>
> "But sometime, mama," he persists.

His mother remains the realist and says, "Not here, if anywhere. They say there is a heaven and in heaven they waken. But I myself do not believe it. May God forgive me for telling you this. But it's all I know. I know only that they are buried in the dark earth and names last a few more lifetimes on their gravestones." And the boy listens and thinks, "The dark. In the dark earth. Eternal years. It was a terrible revelation."

The scenes in the cheder, or Hebrew school, are both realistic and idealistic. The aggravated melamed, or teacher, is

irritated and frustrated. The children of the New York immigrant Jews want to tear themselves away from their religious studies, but they fear their teacher. He uses a stick on them, shouts at them, but is delighted when one of them shows an aptitude for study. David is a good boy; he is willing to learn. The letters of the Hebrew alphabet come to him easily, and the blessings and prayers trip from his youthful lips. The teacher likes him for that. But the moment David becomes daring in class, or does something he shouldn't, the teacher—to whom Torah is of paramount importance—becomes a scourge and a tormentor. There is violence in these sketches, but the novelist writes out of love and understanding—and knowledge.

These are elements which have for a long time been missing in American Jewish writing. Where there is knowledge, there too frequently appears cynicism. And love and understanding are usually absent.

The sense of Jewish alienation, too, is captured in *Call It Sleep.* David wants to belong to something. His home is breaking up. The streets are too tough for him. Sex, as it is introduced to him by a sluttish child, frightens him. This is why he is attracted to the rosary of a Catholic street friend. The rosary becomes a symbol of belonging. How he is willing to allow his friend to "woo" his cousin Esther in order to obtain the rosary beads is touching, persuasive and sad at the same time. Just as Roth can describe the Sabbath as "the hushed hour, the hour of tawny beatitude," he can also, within a few swift pages, depict the rawness of life and the cruelty of boys pitted against each other.

It is no wonder that Leslie Fielder has been praising Henry Roth's novel for years. "No one," he has written, "has ever distilled such poetry and wit from the counterpoint between the maimed English and the subtle Yiddish of the immigrant. No one has ever reproduced so sensitively the terror of family life in the imagination of a child caught between two cultures." Fiedler has added that *Call It Sleep* is "a *specifically* Jewish book, the best single book by a Jew about Jewishness written by an American, certainly through the thirties and perhaps ever."

Professor Walter Rideout, author of *The Radical Novel in America,* looks at *Call It Sleep* not as a Jewish book but as an American novel. In an essay in *American Jewish Archives* (October 1959) Professor Rideout stated that:

> *Call It Sleep* is a truly brilliant performance, one of the best first novels which I have ever read. . . . What makes the novel so extraordinary is its seamless web of concrete and abstract, of reality and symbol, of earth and spirit. Many of the events are grossly physical and are described in revolting detail; yet even these become incandescent with the

intensity of a mystic's vision as symbol, in the Transcendentalist phrase, flowers out of fact. The language, too, represents the same unity of opposites; it moves back and forth effortlessly from a precisely heard and rendered everyday speech, complete with oath and obscenity, to the apocalyptic imagery of David's own thoughts. The result is to give the reader the sense of himself experiencing all the levels of a child's inner and outer world and of himself coming to accept the repulsive, the ugly, the horrifying along with the clean, the beautiful, the loving, as necessary parts of life's self-contradictory wholeness.

Maxwell Geismar, in his critical introduction to the new edition of *Call It Sleep,* calls it the definitive novel of a "sidewalk-and-gutter generation" which Roth describes better than anyone else, and he suggests that the descendants of these Jews are to be found in the novels of Herman Wouk. "Yes," Geismar writes, "and what a long distance this branch of our native letters—and our native life—has come in the twenty-five years between Henry Roth's chronicle, and say, a *Marjorie Morningstar.* From the melting pot to the marts of trade and of finance!" Geismar goes further in his analysis and remarks that "in terms of modern psychology the family trio at the center of *Call It Sleep* is a classic example of the oedipal relation—described so beautifully, so completely, that one realizes that the author, too, wrote this classic fable in all innocence of spirit. Oddly enough the novel that we associate today with *Call It Sleep* is William Styron's *Lie Down in Darkness,* another ironic fable of a childhood and adolescence, based on the Electra-complex of father-daughter love, with the same stress of the tragic 'reality' of existence."

Meyer Levin, who himself is a novelist of substance and solidity, remarks that "most of the book tells of David Schearl's life from his sixth to his eighth year. It tells of the life of his mother and father, as seen through the eyes of this child. I know of no more perceptive work in any literature, dealing with a child's conditioning. In this field, *Call It Sleep* is a classic."

Quite apart from Henry Roth's remarkable achievement in recreating the mood, tension and agony of childhood he also has managed to bring off a most unusual final section of the book, in which he borrows from James Joyce's stream-of-consciousness method and concludes his book in crackling, beautiful prose.

David flees his home after a violent fight between his mother and father and he nearly electrocutes himself by placing a piece of iron into the crack of the streetcar tracks, thus calling forth a power flash. Geismar interprets this scene as the young hero finding the "light of God" in the third rail of the trolley-car line. He adds that the "power" which convulses his body makes him a man. There is no question that there is powerful symbolism in the final section of the novel called, quite simply, "The Rail." The reader, however, must submit himself to the cumulative power of the prose to realize how difficult a task Henry Roth set for himself and how well he succeeded.

Here is the final passage of the book, which offers a sample of Roth's prose and demonstrates anew that the skill of Henry Roth has not been surpassed by modern prose masters. David's mother suggests to him that he go to sleep and forget the horrible experience through which he has just lived. He agrees to try:

> He might as well call it sleep. It was only toward sleep that every wink of the eyelids could strike a spark into the cloudy tinder of the dark, kindle out of shadowy corners of the bedroom such myriad and such vivid jets of images—of the glint on tilted beards, of the uneven shine on roller skates, of the dry light on grey stone steps, of the tapering glitter of rails, of the oily sheen on the night-smooth rivers, of the glow on thin blonde hair, red faces, of the glow on the outstretched, open palms of legions upon legions of hands hurtling toward him. He might as well call it sleep. It was only toward sleep that ears had power to cull again and reassemble the shrill cry, the hoarse voice, the scream of fear, the bells, the thick-breathing, the roar of crowds and all sounds that lay fermenting in the vats of silence and the past. It was only toward sleep one knew himself still lying on the cobbles, felt the cobbles under him, and over him and scudding ever toward him like a black foam, the perpetual blur of shod and running feet, the broken shoes, new shoes, stubby, pointed, caked, polished, buniony, pavement-beveled, lumpish, under skirts, under trousers, shoes, over one and through one, and feel them all and feel, not pain, not terror, but strangest triumph, strangest acquiescence. One might as well call it sleep. He shut his eyes.

Call It Sleep is being read avidly by critics in the 1960's, as it was in the 1930's. It is not being overlooked; it is being discussed and analyzed.

Hollywood producers, television personalities, musical comedy writers and paperback publishers are reading it carefully, hoping to find in its pages something which will bring them new fortunes.

Meanwhile Henry Roth continues to live quietly on a byroad in Maine. He is satisfied to have produced his one novel. The rest of us can only regret that he has never given us a second book. But we must be grateful for *Call It Sleep.*

Irving Howe (essay date 25 October 1964)

SOURCE: "Life Never Let Up," in *The New York Times Book Review,* Vol. 69, No. 43, October 25, 1964, pp. 1, 60.

[*In the following essay, Howe asserts that "At the end of a novel like* Call It Sleep, *one has lived through a completeness of rendered life, and all one need do is silently to acknowledge its truth."*]

Thirty years ago a young New Yorker named Henry Roth published his first and thus far, his only novel, *Call It Sleep.* It was a splendid book, one of the few genuinely distinguished novels written by a 20th-century American; and there were critics and readers who recognized this immediately. From the general public, however, the book never won any attention.

In its deepest impress, *Call It Sleep* was alien to the spirit of the times. The politically radical critics then dominating the New York literary scene had enough taste to honor Roth for composing an impressive work, but they did not really know what to make of it. They could not bend the novel to their polemical purposes, and some of them, one suspects, must have felt that the severe detachment with which Roth presented the inner life of a Jewish immigrant boy between the ages of 6 and 8 was an evasion of the social needs of the moment.

Time passed, thousands of cluttering novels came and went each year, and *Call It Sleep* faded from sight. So too did its author, about whom vague rumors arose that he became a hospital attendant in upstate New York and then a duck farmer in Maine. But if most books die and a very few live, some just survive precariously in a kind of underground existence. Copies of *Call It Sleep* became hard to find, but all through the 1940's and 1950's a number of serious critics, writing in such magazines as *Commentary* and *Partisan Review,* remained loyal to the book, and kept insisting that it was a neglected masterpiece which people ought to read and some publisher reprint.

In 1960 a small firm (Pageant Books, Inc., now Cooper Square Publishers) did put out the novel in hardcovers, but to little effect. Now, with some accompanying flourishes, Avon has issued the novel in paperback and this time, one hopes, it will finally gain the public it deserves. As with all belated acts of justice, there is something bitter in the thought of the many years that have had to go by; still, it is an act of justice, and a welcome one.

Call It Sleep is one of those novels—there are not very many—which patiently enter and then wholly exhaust an experience. Taking fierce imaginative possession of its subject, the novel scrutinizes it with an almost unnerving intensity, yet also manages to preserve a sense of distance and dispassion. The central figure is David Schearl, an overwrought, phobic and dangerously imaginative little boy. He has come to New York with his east European Jewish parents, and now, in the years between 1911 and 1913, he is exposed, shock by shock, to the blows of slum life.

Everything is channeled through the child's perceptions. For considerable sections, David's uncorrected apprehensions of the world become the substance of the narrative, a mixture of stony realism and ecstatic phantasmagoria. Yet the book is not at all the kind of precious or narrowing study of a child's sensibility that such a description might suggest; for Henry Roth has taken pains to root it deeply in the external world, in the streets, the tenements, the other children David encounters. We are locked into the experience of a child, but are not limited to his grasp of it.

One of Roth's admirers, the English critic Walter Allen, has elsewhere described this aspect of *Call It Sleep* very well: "David recreates, transmutes, the world he lives in not into any simple fantasy of make-believe—we're a long way here either from Tom Sawyer or the young Studs Lonigan—but with the desperate, compulsive imagination of a poet. He is, indeed, for all the grotesque difference in milieu, much closer to the boy Wordsworth of 'The Prelude.'"

Call It Sleep yields a picture of brutality in the slums quite as oppressive as can be found in any 1930's novel—and because Henry Roth has neither political nor literary preconceptions to advance, neither revolutionary rhetoric nor fatalistic behaviorism, his picture is more authoritative than that of most slum novels. Through the transfiguring imagination of David, *Call It Sleep* also achieves an obbligato of lyricism such as few American novels can match. David Schearl, in his besieged and quavering presence, exemplifies the force of G.M. Doughty's epigram: "The Semites are like to a man sitting in a cloaca to the eyes, and whose brow touches heaven."

". . . *a cloaca to the eyes.*" That is the world of Brownsville and the Lower East Side into which the child is thrust. Quarrelsome grown-ups, marauding toughs, experiments in voyeurism and precocious sex, dark tenements with rat-infested cellars and looming stairways, an overwhelming incident in which David's father, a milkman, whips two derelicts who have stolen a few bottles of milk, the oppressive comedy of Hebrew school where children cower before and learn to torment an enraged rabbi—all these comprise the outer life of the boy, described by Roth with deliberate and gritty detail.

One is reminded of Dickens's evocation of childhood terrors, and Roth certainly shares with Dickens the vision of an unmeditated war between the child and society; but nothing in Dickens is so completely and gravely caught up, as is *Call It Sleep,* with the child's vision of the world as nightmare. Yet—and this seems to me a remarkable achievement—Roth never acquiesces in the child's delusions, never sentimentalizes or quivers over his David. In the economy of psychic life, the book makes abundantly clear, the outer world's vitality and toughness have their claims too.

"*. . . and whose brow touches heaven.*" For David heaven is his mother's lap, the warming banter of her faintly ironic voice. Genya Schearl, immigrant wife who speaks only Yiddish, a tall and pale beauty, fearful of her violent-tempered husband, yet glowing with feminine grace and chastened sexuality—this marvelous figure should some day be honored as one of the great women of American literature, a fit companion to Hawthorne's Hester Prynne. Genya brings radiance and dignity to every page on which she appears. We cannot help share David's craving for her, even as we recognize its morbid elements; we see her most powerfully through the eyes of the child, as the enclosing mother who provides total security, but we also sense what David has begun uneasily to sense, that she has a complex emotional and bodily life beyond the reach of the child.

As we would say in our contemporary glibness, it is a classical Oedipal situation: the troubled delicate boy, the passionate mother, the inflamed father whom the child looks upon as an agent of punishment and who, in turn, feels himself cut off from the household's circle of love. An Oedipal situation indeed—but in our mindless jargon we forget that this phrase refers to one of the most sustaining experiences a human being can know. Henry Roth, who seems to have been happily innocent of Freudian hypotheses, provides in *Call It Sleep* a recognizable "case," but far more important, an experience superbly alive and fluid. He writes:

> "It is summer," she pointed to the window, "the weather grows warm. Whom will you refresh with the icy lips the water lent you?"
>
> "Oh!" he lifted his smiling face.
>
> "You remember nothing," she reproached him, and with a throaty chuckle, lifted him in her arms.
>
> Sinking his fingers in her hair, David kissed her brow. The faint familiar warmth and odor of her skin and hair.
>
> "There!" she laughed, nuzzling his cheek, "but you've waited too long; the sweet chill has dulled.

> Lips for me," she reminded him "must always be cool as the water that wet them." She put him down.

Away from his mother, David is torn by fears: fears of the fingering sexuality he discovers in the street, fears—also hopes—that he is not really the child of his father, fears of the rabbi who curses a fate requiring him to teach the intractable young. At the climax of the book David runs away from home, fleeing the anger of his father who has caught him playing with a rosary and believes him implicated in an act of depravity.

There follows a brilliantly rendered flight through the streets, composed in a Joycean stream-of-consciousness that is broken with fragments of gutter talk, street noise and left-wing oratory. For David, in whose mind a scriptural passage about the fiery coal God put to the lips of Isaiah becomes linked to the terrifying flash of the live rail on a streetcar track, there is now an overmastering urge to sacrifice and cleanse himself. He thrusts the ladle of a milk can into the slot between the car tracks which carries the live rail, suffers a violent shock, and then, recovering, harbors a vision in which all guilts become assuaged and there may yet be a way of containing the terrors of the world.

The writing in *Call It Sleep* is consistently strong. When speaking in his own right, as disciplined narrator, Roth provides a series of powerful urban vignettes: slum kids fishing for pennies through the grate of a cellar, the ghastly little candy store in which David's Aunt Bertha, a red-haired gargoyle, bitterly trades with urchins, the freedom of tenement roofs on which David learns to climb.

Roth is even better at rendering varieties of speech. With a hard impersonality he records the patois of immigrant children several generations back, and because he never condescends to them or tries to exploit them as local color, he transforms their mutilated language into a kind of poetry:

> My ticher calls id Xmas, bod de kids call id Chrizmas. Id's a goyish holiday anyways. Wunst I hanged op a stockin' in Brooklyn. Bod mine fodder pud in eggshells wid terlit paper an' a piece f'om a ol' kendle. So he leffed w'en he seen me.

And here the rabbi curses his "scholars" with a brimstone eloquence:

> "May your skull be dark! . . . and your eyes be dark and your fate be of such dearth and darkness that you will call a poppyseed the sun and a carroway the moon. . . . Away! Or I'll empty my bitter heart upon you."

But when Genya speaks, Roth transposes her Yiddish into a

pure and glowing English, reflecting in prose the ultimate serenity of her character.

Intensely Jewish in tone and setting, *Call It Sleep* rises above all the dangers that beset the usual ghetto novel: it does not deliquesce into nostalgia, nor sentimentalize poverty and parochialism. The Jewish immigrant milieu happens to be its locale, quite as Dublin is Joyce's and Mississippi Faulkner's. A writer possessed by his materials, driven by a need to recapture the world of his youth, does not choose his setting: it chooses him. And to be drawn into Roth's trembling world, the reader need have no special knowledge about Jewish life, just as he need have no special knowledge about the South in order to enjoy Faulkner.

Call It Sleep ends without any explicit moral statement. A human experience scoured to its innermost qualities can take on a value of its own, beyond the convenience of gloss or judgment. At the end of a novel like *Call It Sleep,* one has lived through a completeness of rendered life, and all one need do is silently to acknowledge its truth.

A. Sidney Knowles Jr. (essay date Winter 1965-1966)

SOURCE: "The Fiction of Henry Roth," in *Modern Fiction Studies,* Vol. XI, No. 4, Winter 1965-1966, pp. 393-404.

[*In the following essay, Knowles traces the history of critical discourse about Roth's* Call It Sleep *and briefly analyzes Roth few short pieces of fiction written since the novel.*]

In reviewing the publication history of Henry Roth's *Call It Sleep,* one is struck by the aptness with which its title describes the long period of its obscurity. The novel was first published late in 1934, a year that produced Scott Fitzgerald's *Tender Is the Night,* Graham Greene's *It's a Battlefield,* John O'Hara's *Appointment in Samarra,* William Saroyan's *The Daring Young Man on the Flying Trapeze,* and Evelyn Waugh's *A Handful of Dust.* The same year saw the publication of forty-three other works considered memorable enough to be listed in the second edition of *Annals of English Literature* (1961). *Call It Sleep* is not listed, nor is the novel or its author referred to, in such compendia as Thorp's *American Writing in the Twentieth Century* (1960), Herzberg's *Reader's Encyclopedia of American Literature* (1962), and Burke and Howe's *American Authors and Books* (revised by Weiss, 1962). A search through the numerous paperback cram-books is equally fruitless.

In an afterword to the present widely-circulated edition, Walter Allen praises Alfred Kazin and Leslie Fiedler for calling attention to Roth's novel, "Fiedler notably in his book *Love and Death in the American Novel.*" In reality, Fiedler mentions the novel in part of a parenthetical sentence in *Love and Death* (1960), devotes a short paragraph to it in *No! In Thunder* (1960), and briefly discusses it again in *Waiting for the End* (1964). In the August, 1960, issue of *Commentary,* however, Feidler presents a full treatment of the novel. Kazin contributes a blurb to the latest edition, but does not take up the novel in his essay collections, among them *Contemporaries* (1962), which gathers some seventy-three articles in its 513 pages. In the last ten years there has been a scattering of articles in the literary journals. *Call It Sleep* is discussed in Rideout's *The Radical Novel in the United States* (1956) and by Kazin and Fiedler in a symposium on "The Most Neglected Books of the Past 25 Years" in *The American Scholar* (1956). On the whole, hunting Roth's novel in indexes is useful mainly for reminding the reader that it has been a long time since he looked at Jack London's *Call of the Wild.*

> **Roth is a virtuoso of language; his street dialects are a coarse, dissonant music, rising and falling through the length of the novel.**
> **—A. Sidney Knowles Jr.**

Yet the novel was not treated with indifference when it appeared in December of 1934. F.T. Marsh, in *Books,* called it "the most accurate and profound study of an American slum childhood that has yet appeared," and concluded that he would "like to see **'Call it Sleep'** win the Pulitzer Prize." The Boston *Transcript* termed it an "exceptional book"; Horace Gregory, in *The Nation,* found Roth's novel "an experience which few readers of contemporary fiction can afford to ignore"; *The New Republic* saw "rare powers and densities" in the work; Lewis Gannett, for the New York *Herald Tribune,* thought the novel suggestive of "the great Russians." Reviewers in the New York *Times* and *Saturday Review of Literature* were shocked by the frankness of Roth's language, which, if nothing else, should have given the novel a certain notoriety. Only certain of the leftist press, as Fiedler points out, were able to dismiss *Call It Sleep:* the age required that a novel about the slums invoke the class struggle; Roth offered poetry instead.

In its day *Call It Sleep* did not do badly. The ailing firm of R. O. Ballou gave it two printings; some four thousand copies were put into circulation, a good showing for a first novel in the Depression (but, by comparison, Hemingway's *Winner Take Nothing* was given a first printing of some twenty thousand copies in 1933, his *Green Hills of Africa* a first printing of some ten thousand copies in 1935). In 1960, Pageant Books re-issued the novel in hard covers. This impressive edition, with prefatory essays by Harold U. Ribalow,

Maxwell Geismar, and Meyer Levin, remains in print; at the time of its first appearance, however, it attracted little attention. All the more amazing that Avon's paperback edition, issued in October, 1964, should have brought the great awakening.

Call It Sleep was thirty years, almost to the month, coming into its own with the public. Was it brought in on the tide of reawakened interest in the 'thirties? Did it need a period when competition from established authors was slack? Whatever the answers, the story of Henry Roth suggests that the one-book author can rarely maintain a reputation in a society awash in books; and it forces us to wonder how many other neglected masterpieces are awaiting their miraculous year.

Call It Sleep may seem at first glance to fall into the tradition of urban naturalism. The novel could stand its ground there, rivaling Farrell, Dreiser, and the other recorders of slum life. Roth's account of three years (1911-13) in the life of the immigrant boy David Schearl recreates the qualities of life in the melting pot with remarkable richness. The novel is full of the lore of Jewish life, the clamor of the streets, the stench of the tenements. Roth is a virtuoso of language; his street dialects are a coarse, dissonant music, rising and falling through the length of the novel. He knows the psychology of the city child: David's fear of the cellars, his exhilaration on the rooftops, must strike deep into the memory of any reader who grew up in the tenements and apartments of a big city. Roth knows the city child's sense of the terrible distance between a third-floor apartment and the street, knows his panic at finding himself lost in a "new" neighborhood only two blocks away. Living in the consciousness of David from his sixth to his ninth year, we are uniquely reminded of that chaotic mixture of savagery and beauty that is city life.

II

Equally, *Call It Sleep* belongs in the company of the great *Bildungsroman.* As a document of developing consciousness it is closely related to Joyce's *Portrait of the Artist as a Young Man,* sharing that novel's concern with the peculiar mixture of fascination and revulsion produced by certain types of experience. For David Schearl, sex is such an experience. His lessons at the Hebrew school are a source of both fear and irresistible curiosity. His first real friendship produces both triumph and defeat. His home offers both security (the mother) and rejection (the father). Thus, learning the lessons of experience, growing up, becomes for David—as it does for Stephen Dedalus—a matter of surviving and reconciling the very diversity of existence.

The success of *Call It Sleep,* however, rests ultimately upon factors other than the ease with which it competes with other novels of a certain genre. Something must be said about its extraordinary intensity and about its craftsmanship.

Nineteen thirty-four began with a major event in publishing, the first American edition of Joyce's *Ulysses.* When *Call It Sleep* was published eleven months later, reviewers were struck by similarities between the two novels. Comparison of the two is inevitable: both make massive use of stream-of-consciousness; both are "noisy," their authors fascinated by the sheer clamor of interior and exterior experience. There are certain similarities of characterization. The placid femininity of Genya Schearl relates her to Molly Bloom; there are moments when the rabbi Yidel Pankower conjures up the alienated Leopold.

Certainly both can be called—using the term loosely—Freudian novels, novels based upon the assumption that total character can be revealed only when overt acts and speech are presented in relation to the freely associative flow of psychic experience. Roth's technical handling of this assumption is often highly Joycean: one might guess that both the Sirens and Circe chapters of *Ulysses,* in particular, exercised a strong influence on Roth's presentation of the events in Chapter XXI of *Call It Sleep,* where young David Schearl runs through a wild storm of exterior and interior experience surrounding the climactic act of the novel.

Call It Sleep, however, is technically far less elaborate than *Ulysses,* and it is therefore surprising to find that the experience of reading it is somewhat more intense. The reason, perhaps, is that while *Ulysses* lays bare the complex psychic experience of three characters who may lie in some degree outside ourselves (Leopold, Molly, Stephen), *Call It Sleep,* by focusing on childhood, draws us into an area of intense psychic experience that we have shared in common, and that is at once simpler and more piquant. We confront the basic traumas in *Call It Sleep,* their variant effects in *Ulysses.* We have little choice but to rediscover ourselves in David Schearl; all the terrors, all the joys of childhood seem to dwell in his consciousness. In a very real sense, reading *Call It Sleep* is a psychoanalytic experience, capable of producing an unusual degree of emotional discomfort in the reader.

This awareness of being deeply touched is present in much of the criticism the novel has attracted so far. Walter Allen calls Roth's work "the most powerful evocation of the terrors of childhood ever written." Leslie Fiedler observes that any element of social criticism in the novel is subordinate to "the passion and suffering of Roth's child hero." Harold U. Ribalow mentions "Roth's remarkable achievement in recreating the mood, tension and agony of childhood."

Yet, as appropriate as such reactions are, it would be misleading to suggest that *Call It Sleep* is simply an emotional *tour de force.* While criticism of the novel has been enthusiastic and perceptive (and has, in fact, found much to discuss besides its emotional impact), there is room for further comment on certain subtleties of Roth's craft. It can be suggested, for instance, that the prologue to *Call It Sleep* not only provides a graphic opening but is also a source of basic themes and metaphors for the whole novel. We are taken in the prologue to a steamer leaving Ellis Island in 1907:

> the year that was destined to bring the greatest number of immigrants to the shores of the United States. All that day, as on all the days since spring began, her decks had been thronged by hundreds upon hundreds of foreigners, natives from almost every land in the world, the joweled close-cropped Teuton, the full-bearded Russian, the scraggly-whiskered Jew, and among them Slovack peasants with docile faces, smooth-cheeked and swarthy Armenians, pimply Greeks, Danes with wrinkled eyelids. All day her decks had been colorful, a matrix of the vivid costumes of other lands, the speckled green-and-yellow aprons, the flowered kerchief, embroidered homespun, the silver-braided sheepskin vest, the gaudy scarfs, yellow boots, fur caps, caftans, dull gabardines. All day the guttural, the high-pitched voices, the astonished cries, the gasps of wonder, reiterations of gladness had risen from her decks in a motley billow of sound.

Among the immigrants are David Schearl, then about two years old, and his mother, Genya. Albert, the father, had come to America earlier and the family is now to be reunited. But in Albert's behaviour there is a coldness markedly different from the demonstrativeness of the immigrant families around him. His remarks to his wife and son are contemptuous and accusatory. In a gesture full of shame and pathetic pride, he snatches David's old-country hat and hurls it into the river in order that his boy will not look like an immigrant.

It is a powerful beginning for the novel, and valuable as such, but it is also a scene of considerable resonance. First, it establishes the Schearls as travelers in an alien culture, a circumstance that colors the whole novel. As Marie Syrkin points out, the Schearls are a counterpart of the Holy Family seeking refuge in an inimical land. Second, the prologue establishes the other and more profound kind of alienation existing between mother and son, on one hand, and father on the other. Finally, the prologue suggests a metaphor that underlies the entire work: the voyage that David must take into the alien world of complex experience. In this sense, the sheltering arms of Genya are the old world; David is the immigrant in life who must leave their haven and seek his own meanings in the new culture of maturity. Albert's tearing the hat from David's head and hurling it into the river becomes an abrupt and brutal symbol not only of the father's

pride but of the beginning of David's harrowing journey toward some distant station where he can come to terms with the chaos of experience. The gesture is rounded off at the end of the novel when David, brought home with a burned foot after an experience that has had precisely this reconciling effect, is covered with bedclothes by a gentle interne.

Considering the basic theme of the prologue, it is not surprising to find how often the novel presents David literally in motion: the lost David running through the streets of Brownsville looking for his apartment house; running, after his first encounter with the electrified rail; running, after Leo seduces his cousin Esther; running, after telling the rabbi a fantastic suspicion about his parentage; and, finally, running from the fury of his father toward his second rendezvous with the "fatal glory" of the streetcar track. David's flights are at once a perfectly natural record of childhood behaviour and a metaphor of his chaotic progress toward maturity. It is in the prologue that the basic motion of this metaphor is generated.

The scene in which David touches a milk-ladle to the electrified rail of the streetcar line illustrates the care with which Henry Roth unites his themes at the end of the novel. Throughout *Call It Sleep,* David is perplexed by his growing awareness of sexuality. In an early episode he is uneasily conscious that his mother's body is attractive to Albert's foreman, Luter. In later episodes, David is given a disgusting lesson in the physical mysteries of sex by a crippled girl of the neighborhood; he is horrified to learn that some older boys have been spying on his mother as she bathes; he listens in fascination to the sexual play of Leo and Esther in a coal-bin. Throughout the novel, his days are punctuated by the coarse sexuality of city street-language.

Toward the middle of the novel, David is taken to the Hebrew school, the cheder, where he becomes enthralled by a passage of scripture in which Isaiah is described as having been touched on the lips by a fiery coal, allowing him to speak in the presence of God. In the climactic scene of *Call It Sleep,* as David seeks his own source of all-clarifying light in the streetcar track, the theme of sexuality and the theme of David's quest for the understanding of Isaiah are united. As he moves toward the track, his interior monologue is set against fragments of the sex-obsessed conversations of the surrounding neighborhood. In David's own thoughts, the act of producing light is expressed in terms that have obvious sexual overtones:

> *Now! Now I gotta, In the crack,*
> *remember. In the crack be born.*

When the ladle, thrust between the lips of the track, makes contact with the electrified rail, the result is described in an orgastic explosion of poetic prose:

Power
Power! Power like a paw, titanic power,
ripped through the earth and slammed
against his body and shackled him
where he stood. Power! Incredible,
barbaric power! A blast, a siren of light
within him, rending, quaking, fusing his
brain and blood to a fountain of flame,
vast rockets in a searing spray! Power!
The hawk of radiance raking him with
talons, of fire, battering his skull with
a beak of fire, braying his body with
pinions of intolerable light. And he
writhed without motion in the clutch of
a fatal glory, and his brain swelled
and dilated till it dwarfed the galaxies
in a bubble of refulgence—Recoiled, the
last screaming nerve clawing for survival.
He kicked—once. Terrific rams of darkness
collided; out of their shock space
toppled into havoc. A thin scream wobbled
through the spirals of oblivion, fell like
a brand on water, his-s-s-s-ed—

Thus the two themes are united: the generative touch of the fiery coal upon the lips of Isaiah is equated with the generative act of sex. David's struggles with sexuality, as well as with his total environment, are reconciled in a moment that relates the act of sex to the creative energy of God. The subsidence of action that follows, terminating in sleep, carries these implications to their logical conclusion.

III

Considering the amount of creative energy displayed by *Call It Sleep,* it is astonishing that no major work by Henry Roth has followed it. The pattern of tension and relaxation in the final pages of his novel has, curiously, proved to be prophetic of Roth's literary career.

Yet Roth has not been completely silent over the years. Four short pieces have appeared over his name, two in the *New Yorker* and two in *Commentary.* The first *New Yorker* piece, **"Somebody Always Grabs the Purple,"** appeared sixteen years after *Call It Sleep;* the second, **"Petey and Yotsee and Mario,"** sixteen years after the first. Neither story is of great importance. **"Somebody"** gives us Sammy Farber, "eleven or twelve years old," at a New York branch library. He is looking for the Purple Fairy Book, aware that he might be considered too old for fairy stories. "'Everybody says I'm too big to read fairy books. My mother calls 'em stories with a bear.'" The determined Sammy discovers that another boy is reading the book—"'somebody always grabs the Purple'"—and tries to talk him out of it, without success.

The story ends with a suggestion that Sammy intends to follow the boy home and get "the Purple" one way or another.

"Petey and Yotsee and Mario" is a vignette: the Jewish narrator remembers when, as a child, he almost drowned in the East River, but was saved by three neighborhood boys. His mother baked a "Jewish cake" as a reward for the boys, and the narrator was certain they would laugh at the gesture. Instead, the heroes ate the cake "with gusto," as the mother was confident they would: "'You were afraid they wouldn't like Jewish cake. What kind of people would they be if they didn't like Jewish cake? Would they have even saved you?'"

While both stories draw their materials from essentially the same culture as that of *Call It Sleep,* and are expertly written, they are minor items. It is possible to see in them, of course, some continuing interest in the educative experiences of childhood; in the main, the stories only remind us of a pleasant time when life among ethnic groups in New York was still possible as a subject for gentle humor.

The sixteen-year cycle of Roth's publishing was broken by the two pieces that appeared in 1959 and 1960. Both depart from the world of *Call It Sleep* and are particularly interesting because they attempt, through the medium of the parable, to account for their author's inability (or unwillingness) to go on producing. The first of these, **"At Times in Flight,"** is an impressive piece.

Like Sherwood Anderson's "Death in the Woods," Roth's parable is an attempt to lay bare certain problems of the literary artist. But while Anderson's story suggests the processes through which the artist understands and makes use of his materials, **"At Times in Flight"** reveals why, in Roth's case, his materials became no longer valid. The story begins with a reminiscence of an artists' colony that Roth attended in the summer of 1938 (we must assume that the "I" of the parable is Roth; that the artists' colony, called "Z," was Yaddo, near Saratoga Springs; and that the "Martha" of the story became Roth's wife Muriel). The purpose of the colony was to provide a setting for unhampered creativity, but most of the inmates "loafed or spent a great deal of time in frivolity or idle chatter." Roth was engaged in a second novel: "It had gone badly—aims had become lost, purpose, momentum lost. A profound change seemed to be taking place within me in the way I viewed my craft, in my objectivity."

While there, the parable relates, Roth was courting a young woman "bred and raised in the best traditions of New England and the Middle West, the most wholesome traditions." Around them the essentially trivial life of the colony went on: overeating, playing charades, discussing the civil war in Spain. One diversion Roth and Martha found was going into Saratoga Springs to drink the waters, which bubbled, free, from a fountain at the spa. The water appealed to Roth because it reminded him of the seltzer water his family had bought during his childhood on the East Side. It was "not easily obtainable" then, but here he could have all he wanted. Of those at the colony, only Martha shared his enthusiasm.

Another diversion he and Martha shared was watching the training of horses for the nearby track:

> as we drove past in the early morning, we would see what I suppose was one of the usual sights at race tracks, but to us a novelty: the grooms or trainers bent low over their mounts and urging them on for a longer or shorter gallop. A horse is a beautiful thing. A fleet, running horse, and we would stop sometimes on our way and watch one course along the white railing. Enormously supple and swift, they seemed at times in flight. The dirt beneath their hooves seemed less spurred by their hooves than drawn away beneath them in their magnificent stride.

One afternoon, they decided to watch a horse race, and took a path "not frequently trodden" through the woods to a point beside the track far from the grandstand. "We seemed to be, as we virtually were, in some coign or niche where we could behold the excitement in a remote and almost secret way." The horses seemed "tiny and remote," the whole event an affair of toys. But as the race began and the horses came nearer, Roth realized that his perspective was changing:

> They were no longer toy horses and toy riders. They were very real and growing in reality every second. One could see the utter seriousness of the thing, the supreme effort, the rivalry as horse and man strained every muscle to forge to the front. Oh, it was no toy spectacle; they were in fierce and bitter competition, vying horse and man, even the mounted man, vying for the lead, and the glowing eyeballs and the shrunken jockeys, the quiet, the enormous suppleness and the cry.

As the horses neared the couple, one, with his rider, fell. The jockey rose and limped away, but the horse had broken a leg: "There was something terribly ungainly and grotesque about his motion" as he ran after the pack. A few more steps and the horse fell to the track. Booted men in a truck came to shoot the animal. Martha tried to leave, but Roth restrained her. She was afraid of being shot: "Bullets richochet. I'm afraid." Roth stayed to watch the "grave and dread . . . event."

> I watched them load the carcass aboard the truck, and for some reason a similar scene on the East Side of long ago returned—an image from long-vanished childhood of a cop shooting a horse fallen in the

snow, and the slow, winch of the big green van that hauled the animal aboard later. So that was the end? *Ars brevis, vita longa.*

"'The odd thing is,'" Roth told Martha, "'when I saw him going down, I felt a sense of loss.'" They made their way back to the colony, Martha leading the way because she had a "better sense of direction," Roth musing over the scene they had left, "a horse destroyed when the race became real."

In a note published with the story, Roth says, "The main meaning of the story to me lies in the projection, so to speak, of the inadequacy of a man's art in the face of modern realities, and the implied decision to make a new start." The horse race, then, is life, the fallen horse Roth's art. **Call It Sleep** was a novel about childhood, of events seen far off, as the beginning of the race was seen. As long as he wrote about childhood, there was a certain comfortable distance between Roth and his material. It was an art that was not quite grounded in reality, like the horses in training that "seemed at times in flight." The trips to Saratoga Springs to the bubbling fountain also suggest a continuing attempt to reuse the experiences of childhood. It is a kind of escape; it comes easy, the waters are now "free." But that "path not frequently trodden" leads Roth to a sudden confrontation with present reality. He is no longer viewing events across a distance of time. The track of time, of maturing experience, has brought his art into the present and his art has failed; the only merciful act is to destroy it. Martha, also an artist, flinches and fears a "richochet," but Roth watches, hearing the "oddly insignificant" report of the pistol that dispatches a childhood-centered art that is no longer viable. It is art that is short, life that is long. Roth expressed the problem more simply in a letter to Harold U. Ribalow; "Apparently [**Call It Sleep**] grew out of a soil that became sterile. . . . I haven't the fable."

"The Dun Dakotas" is half a frank expression of Roth's resignation to the failure of his creativity and half a rather enigmatic "yarn." There was something in his era, he asserts, "fatal to creative gusto." He once wondered about what had happened to his art, but he realizes now that "one has to put a term to things." He can accept the fact that there are stages in the continuum of life: "I was a writer once, just as I was an eager East Side kid before that, and a mopey Harlem youth in the interim, who am now a waterfowl farmer." He lives now in present reality. In the parable that follows, Roth tries to express the problem of his generation. He tells of a group of soldiers who went out to map the Bad Lands in the 1870's and were stopped by hostile Indians. To placate the Chief, they gambled with him and lost all their money. When they asked the Chief whether they could pass, he folded his arms and fell silent. Only after "a long dream or a long thought" did he motion them on.

My generation, Roth seems to say, set out to map the Waste Land ("You can imagine the gnarled terrain, or consult an encyclopedia, or consult Mr. Eliot") but were stopped in the process by the hostility of the Waste Landers, or perhaps the hostility of events. We surrendered as much of ourselves as we could, but we still weren't allowed to go on. There was nothing to do but wait:

> That was as far as I got for over twenty-five years, waiting for the decision of the Chief who had turned into stone or into legend, waiting for a man to decide what history was in the dun Dakotas, waiting for a sanction; and oddly enough it would have to be the victim who would provide it, though none could say who was the victim, who the victor. And only now I can tell you, and perhaps it's a good sign—at least for my generation, who waited with me—though perhaps it's too late.

> "Will the Chief let us pass?" the Scout repeated. "Always remember Great Chief."

> "And the Chief unfolded his arms and motioned them the way of their journey. "Go now," he said.

And so the sanction that was denied Roth when he began "a novel about a Communist living in the Midwest" finally came, "though perhaps it's too late."

The story that lies behind these two parables is, in many ways, unique in its revelation of a problem of the American writer. Roth, like so many of his compatriots, started with the myth of childhood, and with the materials of that myth he wrote a remarkable novel. Then he was faced with the problem of where to go next, and the answer seemed to lie in a novel that would deal in some way with adult, political problems of the thirties. He had discovered, as **"At Times in Flight"** reveals, that the myth of childhood was no longer challenging or useful (while the two later *New Yorker* pieces are about childhood, they obviously represent no new inspiration); but he had also discovered that he was unequipped to deal with the present partly because of the failure of his art, partly for extrinsic reasons (**"The Dun Dakotas"**). And so, Roth simply stopped. The themes were there but the embodying fable was not.

While we may lament the virtual retirement of a writer who could produce *Call It Sleep,* it is difficult not to admire his honesty. The path of American literature is strewn with writers who have found themselves in Roth's predicament and have either failed to recognize it or chosen to ignore it. Wolfe kept rewriting himself; Earrell goes on rewriting *Studs Lonigan;* Salinger seems unable to find a fresh perspective. Hemingway's quality declined when he abandoned his early themes and tried to reflect the immediate crises of the present. Faulkner, in mid-career, felt some necessity to abandon his original lyricism; his rhetorical style of the forties produced his least satisfactory work. In short, the American writer seems frequently to encounter some crisis of the imagination that demands a change of theme or style. Some have simply gone on producing embarrassing imitations of themselves. Others have changed but lost their touch. Faced with such a crisis, Henry Roth dropped his pen and found a new occupation.

Sanford Pinsker (essay date July 1966)

SOURCE: "The Re-Awakening of Henry Roth's *Call It Sleep,*" in *Jewish Social Studies,* Vol. XXVIII, No. 3, July, 1966, pp. 148-58.

[*In the following essay, Pinsker provides reasons that the themes contained in Roth's* Call It Sleep *were appropriate for rediscovery in the 1960s.*]

The events which lead to the re-discovery of a previously neglected novel are often as interesting as the conditions which precipitated its original obscurity. In a sense, the recent popularity of *Call it Sleep* is as much a tribute to critics like Alfred Kazin and Leslie Fiedler as it is a triumph for its author Henry Roth. To be sure, *Call it Sleep* is the same novel today that it was when it first appeared in 1934. What has changed, of course, is the way we tend to *read* the novel.

The history of *Call it Sleep* is not so much one of unconcern as it is of misunderstanding. The novel was first published in an era dominated by economic depression, social consciousness, and writers like William Faulkner, James T. Farrell and John Dos Passos. Nevertheless, *Call it Sleep* managed to go through two editions, sell about 4,000 copies, and collect a set of mildly impressive reviews before it slipped quietly into obscurity.

It was not until the publication of Professor Rideout's influential study, *The Radical Novel in the United States* (1956) that *Call it Sleep* was once again brought to the attention of American readers. In that same year, both Alfred Kazin and Leslie Fiedler mentioned the novel in a symposium which appeared in *The American Scholar* under the title, "The Most Neglected Books of the Past 25 Years." Since that time, the popularity of *Call it Sleep* has been growing rapidly. In 1960, the novel was finally re-published and, in 1964, it was issued in paperback edition.

If nothing else, the rather topsy-turvy business of *Call it Sleep*'s popularity seems to suggest that there are other factors besides a lack of merit which may plunge a novel into obscurity. Novels are, after all, written at a particular time and they suffer all the disadvantages thereof. A "first-rate" novelist is very oten determined by the interests and competition of the age in which he happens to have written. For example, we seldom think of Ben Jonson and Christopher Marlowe as "second-rate" playwrights. However, if we compare them with Shakespeare, the results are painfully clear. This is not to imply, of course, that there is something *terrible* about being "second-rate." There are, after all, eighth- and ninth-rate authors too. My point is simply that *everyone* (with the exception of Shakespeare) was at least a "second-rater" during the Elizabethan period.

In the thirties, the really "first-rate" writers were the proletarian novelists who demonstrated a clear and direct social conscience. When we think of the literary scene of the thirties today, the name which looms the largest is certainly Faulkner's: other writers of the period tend to become a bit fuzzy. However, during the thirties themselves, authors like James T. Farrell and John Dos Passos were very much in the running. In a general way, what these authors were reacting against was the Joyce-Proust-Mann notion of putting a great deal of emphasis on the value of an "inner life." For a Farrell or a Dos Passos, the private dilemmas of sensitive souls were not nearly as interesting as where one lived or what job one's father had.

It is, therefore, only natural that Henry Roth's *Call it Sleep* should have been initially considered as simply one more of the many proletarian novels dealing with poverty-stricken Jews on New York's lower East Side. The novel most frequently compared with *Call it Sleep* was Michael Gold's *Jews without Money* (1930) and, as late as 1936, Professor Rideout still felt that the comparison was "an instructive one." According to Rideout, *Call it Sleep* is not only better than *Jews without Money* but it is, in fact, "the most distinguished single proletarian novel."

However, to say that *Call it Sleep* is about poverty on the East Side is to feel that Joyce's *Portrait of the Artist as a Young Man* is about Irish politics or Lawrence's *Sons and Lovers* is about coal mining. There were, of course, reviewers who were sympathetic enough to realize that *Call it Sleep* did not quite fit into the general category of a proletarian novel. As one reviewer commenting for *The New Masses* put it: "It is a pity that so many young writers drawn from the proletariat can make no better use of their working class experience than as material for instrospective and febrile novels." To be sure, the reviewer was unaware that his off-hand remark was anything more than a statement of dissatisfaction about the "unorthodox" way that novels were being written. However, the use of a "proletarian" *milieu* as a backdrop against which an "introspective" novel could be written is at the core of *Call it Sleep*. It is indeed ironic that such a novel should appear at a time when all literature was being read in such a *social* way. It is, I suppose, doubly ironic that the label of "proletarian novel" (which had originally drained the book of its distinctive character) was the very reason Rideout included it in *The Radical Novel in the United States.*

The current critical interest in *Call it Sleep* represents a kind of index to the shifting "hot centers" of literary expression. During the thirties, the Southern agrarians (headed by Faulkner and Co.) had successfully shifted attention from small towns in the Midwest to the post-*bellum* Southerner's tortured quest for identity. The problems of a George Willard, stifled by the lack of possibilities in *Winesburg, Ohio* (1919), began to look almost "trivial" when compared to those of a Quentin Compson in Faulkner's *The Sound and the Fury* (1929).

After World War II, however, the center shifted once again. This time the "city" became the focus of literary attention and, with that shift, the American Jewish novelist finally came into his own. However, the popularity of the Jewish novel was the result of more than a mere change of locale. The Cold War quickly created a situation in which personal insecurity was the rule rather than the exception. The very *size* and increasing complexity of urban life gave rise to a feeling of mass identification on the one hand and the need for individual identity on the other. If the Jew had been the "outsider" or alienated one, now *all* men were Jews. Since it was the Jew who had the longest tradition in the psychodynamics of living on the edge, it was the Jewish novelist who emerged as the spokesman for an entire generation of Jews and non-Jews alike.

The re-discovery of a novel like *Call it Sleep* represents an attempt to discover a distinctly "American-Jewish" identity, by investigating the roots from which we came. Far more than the value of its immediate socio-economic message, the novel projects a world in David Schearl's unconscious which has become a shared condition by 1966. The family unit (treated with warmth in the Yiddish literature of the European ghetto) is now more riddled with the theories of Freud than the practices of writers like Sholom Aleichem. The world of urban New York presents economic opportunities unknown in the *shtetl,* but it also assumes Kafkaesque proportions. In this sense, David's nightmare world of 1934 is not far from the "reality" of our present condition. To be sure, contemporary readers of *Call it Sleep* may be drawn to the novel for the most nostalgic of reasons, but the book has more to say than such "reasons" suggest.

With the exception of a short Prologue, David Schearl is the novel's center of consciousness. However, even the Prologue sets the tone of alienation which is to plague David throughout the novel: "Only the small child in her arms (i.e. David) wore a distinctly foreign costume, an impression one got chiefly from the odd, outlandish, blue straw hat on his head with its polka dot ribbons of the same color dangling over each shoulder." David's "difference" (as symbolized by the "outlandish hat") brings out all of his father's latent paranoia: 'Can't you see that those idiots lying back there are watching us already? They're mocking us! What will the others do on the train? He looks like a clown in it. He's the cause of all this trouble any way!' In the next instant his father "scooped the hat from the child's head" and sent it "sailing over the ship's side to the green waters below." The act is heavy with the psychological symbolism and intensity which characterizes the novel. The symbolic castration which introduces David to both America and his father is quite possibly connected with the family name of "Schearl" or "little scissor" in Yiddish.

In fact, the entire Schearl family adheres (almost *too* perfectly to Freud's notion of what typical families tend to be: David "loves" the mother who will protect and comfort him in adversity and he "hates" the father who is a strict disciplinarian and unbending tyrant. Evidently Roth equated certain movements toward assimilation into American society with Oedipal tension not generally associated with ghetto culture. David's father, after all, had been in America for some time before his wife and son arrive. His hard-boiled cynicism is the result of "golden hopes" which have died only to be replaced by petty jealousies and a variety of psychological fears.

Roth portrays parental roles and emotions in a *leitmotif* of Freudian symbolism. David's mother is continually associated with flowers. When she chooses a picture, for example, it is "a small patch of ground full of tall, green stalks, at the foot of which, tiny blue flowers grew." David's father, on the other hand, is associated with cattle and, particularly, bulls. As if to compete with his wife's romantic penchant for "flowers," he finally places a pair of mounted cow's horns on the wall.

Although David is unable to articulate the *meaning* of these symbols, he is, nevertheless, unconsciously aware of their significance:

> Somehow he couldn't quite believe that it was for memory's sake only that his father had bought the trophy. Somehow looking at the horns, guessing the enormous strength of the beast who must have owned them, there seemed to be another reason. . . . He sensed only that in the horns, in the poised power of them lay a threat, a challenge he must answer, he must meet. But he didn't know how.

The "challenge" is, of course, the inevitable conflict between a father and a son. Albert Schearl is not only an "authority figure" (there are many of *those* in the novel), but he is an authority figure of such magnitude that he nearly frightens David out of his wits. Albert is such a stern disciplinarian that he would rather *beat* his child than understand him. Those of us raised, as it were, "by Spock" may find this hard to swallow. However, if a really first-class rebellion requires a strong Victorian father, Albert certainly fits the bill.

David's mother also represents a "threat" of sorts, but of an entirely different variety. She is characterized by "kisses." In an early section of the novel, she teases him into giving her a kiss with the provocative question, "Whom will you refresh with the icy lips that the water lent you?" Because David's mother feels that "lips for me must always be cool as the water that wet them," David vows he will "eat some ice" so she will like his kisses even more.

However, if David measures his mother by kisses, he measures his father with multi-colored leaves: "He dragged a chair over beneath the calendar on the wall, clambered up, plucked off the outworn leaf, and fingered the remaining ones to see how far off the next red day was. Red days were Sundays, days his father was home. It always gave David a little qualm of dread to watch them draw near." There is no doubt that Albert Schearl is as frightening a character as David imagines him to be. When he loses a job, his excuse is always the same: "They look at me crookedly, with mockery in their eyes!" When David's mother once dared to suggest that such stares might possibly be only his imagination, "his father snarled then. And with one sudden sweep of his arm had sent food and dishes crashing to the floor. . . . He wouldn't speak. His jaws and even his joints seemed to have become fused together by a withering rage."

While David is justifiably afraid of his father, he also complains that "every boy on the street knew where his father worked" except himself because *his* father "had so many jobs." This is, indeed, a curious state of affairs for what critics had thought of as a "proletarian" novel. Albert Schearl's disagreeable disposition (he gets along with his fellow-workers no better than he does with his bosses) merely necessitates a number of job changes. Evidently there is no great problem about getting another job.

However, the change of jobs is often accompanied by a subsequent change of address. Therefore, David tends to live in a fluid community which denies stability at every turn. In *Call it Sleep,* the *economic* condition of the Schearls is of less importance than the Kafkaesque world in which they live. As David's mother so metaphorically points out, theirs is a ghetto founded upon the fear of what might exist beyond the bounds of the familiar:

> "Boddeh Stritt," she resumed apologetically. . . .
> "It's such a strange name—bath street in German. But here I am. I know there is a church on a cer-

tain street to my left, the vegetable market is to my right, behind me are the railroad tracks and the broken rocks, and before me, a few blocks away is a certain store window that has a kind of white-wash on it—and faces in the white-wash, the kind children draw. Within this pale is my America, and if I ventured further I should be lost. In fact," she laughed, "were they even to wash that window, I might never find my way home again."

Of course the mother's fears are merely speculative. It is David, however, who actually experiences all the frightening aspects of being lost in a tangle of streets:

> Which one was it which? Which one was—Long street. Long street, lot of wooden houses. On this side. Yes. Go through the other side. Then other corner. . . . Right away, right away. Be home right away. . . . This one? . . . Didn't look like. . . . Next one bet . . . house . . . giddyap, giddyap. . . . Corner coming, corner coming, corner—here?
>
> . . .
>
> "Mama!" The desolate wail split from his lips. "Mama!" The aloof houses rebuff his woe. "Mama!" his voice trailed off in anguished abandonment. And as if they had been waiting for a signal, the streets through his tear-blurred sight began stealthily to wheel. He could feel them turning under his feet, though never a house changed place—backward to forward, side to side—a sly inexorable carousel.

In Kafka, of course, the physical world tends to become a surrealistic abstraction which helps to carry the allegorical and philosophical aspects of his novels. Other writers, however, have picked up Kafka's notion of alienated terror and blended it into the fabric of a "realistic" novel.

To be sure, there is always a problem with terms like "realistic"; we have lived with the Kafkaesque absurd world for so long that we tend to think of his novels as being very "realistic" indeed. The Kafka novel very successfully portrays the naked anguish of modern man as he confronts the world around him. Although Kafka's descriptions of towns or castles are not likely to be confused with naturalism, the dilemmas of characters like Joseph K. strike us as very *real* indeed. In many respects, Henry Roth imposes such a world upon New York's East Side.

The authors who seem most interesting to us today are the ones who rejected the going beliefs in socio-economic ideologies and, instead, concentrated upon the naked anguish of man in conflict with himself. In this sense, Henry Roth is

more akin to an author like Nathanael West than he is to a Michael Gold. Like West, Henry Roth creates characters whose suffering takes on universal dimensions.

But if *Call it Sleep* in involved with the nightmarish childhood of David Schearl, it is unusual that such a novel *ends* with the protagonist still a child. After all, a character like Stephen Daedalus had a great deal of difficulty in the early portions of Joyce's *Portrait:* he is continually being pushed into ditches by his classmates or punished unfairly by his teachers. However, Stephen really seldom suffers in his difference. If anything, he revels in it for an "artist" is *supposed* to have exactly this kind of childhood.

Call it Sleep, on the other hand, ends with David still only nine years old. He is certainly not ready to make the kind of "arty" proclamations that characterize the Stephen about to launch into a literary career nor is he old enough to join the Communist Party (one of the favorite ploys of the proletarian novelist). Instead of these rather "grand" gestures, David must face a variety of childhood initiations in his journey toward manhood.

One of the most memorable scenes in the novel centers around such an initiation experience. David is introduced to the world of sexuality via a childish "game" suggested by one of his slightly older playmates. The girl is a frightening grotesque who "nudged him gently" into a dark closet with "the iron slat of her brace." Terrified, David accepts her lips (a "muddy spot in vast darkness") and enters into the ritualistic business of playing "bad" for the first time:

> "Yuh must ask me," she said. "G'wan ask me."
>
> "Wot?"
>
> "Yuh must say, Yuh wanna play bad? Say it!"
>
> He trembled. "Yuh wanna play bad?"
>
> "Now *you* said it," she whispered, "Don' forget, you said it."

David is, thus, tricked into accepting a responsibility and a guilt that is really not his. Like Kafka, Roth is fond of presenting such traumatic scenes in settings which suggest claustrophobia. Throughout *Call it Sleep,* the sexual experience is associated with dark, close places such as the closet mentioned above or toilets located in dingy cellars.

However, Roth adds still another dimension to such scenes by his peculiar use of language. As I have already suggested, the sexual confrontation between the innocent David and the more experienced (and perhaps symbolically "crippled") girl is a frightening one. And yet, Roth fills the crucial dialogue with such incongruous terminology that the effect is not only "childish," but almost humorous:

> "Yuh know w'ea babies comm from?"
>
> "N-no."
>
> "From de knish."
>
> —Knish?
>
> "Between de legs. Who puts id in is de poppa. De poppa's god de petzel. Yaw de poppa." She giggled stealthily and took his hand. He could feel her guiding it under her dress, then through a pocket-like flap. Her skin was under his palm. Revolted, he drew back.

The effect which Roth achieved in this scene has become almost a standard one today. Authors like Joseph Heller (*Catch-22*), Ken Kesey (*One Flew Over the Cuckoo's Nest*) and Thomas Pynchon (*V*) mix humor and horror in such rapid succession that the result is a new *genre* of the absurd. In many respects, the revival of interest in Nathanael West and (now) Henry Roth is due, at least in part, to a search by these contemporary authors and their critics for various literary authorities.

Of course sexuality *per se* is not the only terrifying aspect of David's youthful world. "The Cellar" (the title of the novel's first section) finally becomes a metaphor of David's curious descent and initiation into the *dreck* of life. David's characteristic gesture at this point is one of running; he generally runs *from* the nightmarish world of his childhood to the warmth of his mother. As the novel progresses, however, David tends to look for ways to run *out* of his world altogether.

Roth is at his best as a literary artist when he is creating the kind of grotesques that can only be described as Dickensian. These figures usually exert some amount of authority and control over David, and Roth makes them qualify as objects of our disgust and David's rebellion. The Hebrew teacher, Reb Yidel Pankower, is a good case in point. If the Hebrew teacher of Yiddish songs like "Oifn Pripichok" represents a portrait of extreme sentimentality, Pankower has more than made up for him.

Nearly every contemporary Jewish author has a portrait of the "old *heder* teacher" somewhere in the canon of his work. Philip Roth's "Conversion of the Jews" revolves about such a figure as do sections of Bruce Jay Friedman's *Stern.* However, to a very large extent the Hebrew school teacher has dropped out of both modern fiction and life as an influential person. While modern authors continue to use the *heder* teacher as a nostalgic touchstone, their characterizations lack any real intensity because the teacher no longer poses a genuine "threat." Pankower, on the other hand, is a different matter entirely:

> He appeared old and certainly untidy. He wore soft leather shoes like house slippers, that had no place for either laces or buttons. His trousers were baggy and stained, a great area of striped and crumpled shirt intervened between his belt and his bulging vest. The knot of his tie, which was nearer one ear than the other, hung away from his soiled collar.

Pankower is not only physically repulsive, but he is psychologically monstrous. As one of his students describes him, "He's a louser. He hits." Pankower is, in fact, a first-class sadist who gets more joy from *wrong* answers than he does from right ones. His authority symbols are whittled-down popsicle sticks which the boys bring as payment for "special" treatment. Pankower uses the sticks as pointers to keep his place as he goes over the tiny Hebrew letters. When one of his duller students is unable to distinguish between a beth and a veth, [Hebrew letters] he launches into a tirade of very elaborate and characteristic curses:

> "You plaster dunse!" he roared. "When will you learn a byse is a byse and not a vyse. Head of filth, where are your eyes?" He shook a menacing hand at the cringing boy and picked up the pointer.
>
> But a few moments later, again the same error and again the same correction.
>
> "May a demon fly off with your father's father! Won't blows help you? A byse, Esau, pig! A byse! Remember, a byse, even though you die of convulsions!"

Roth's ear for dialect and his ability to capture the flavor of Yiddish in Anglicized forms is one of the great triumphs of ***Call it Sleep.*** However, like Twain's use of the Negro dialect, Roth is more interested in presenting the "illusion" of dialect than the dialect itself. Only a modern author such as Bernard Malamud seems to have more success in conveying a Yiddish dimension through English speech. However, Roth had a number of problems that have gone away as the Anglo-Jewish novel and its audience has grown. Roth, for example, feels compelled to explain whatever Yiddish puns appear in the novel: "Christmas . . . Jesus Crotzmich, the grocery man said and he always laughed. Crotzmich means scratch me. Jesus scratch me. Funny." More often, however, he will simply duplicate the mutilated English of David's immigrant friends by the use of phonetic spellings:

> "My ticher call id Xmas, bod de kids call id Christ-

mas. Id's a goyish holiday anyways. Wunst I hanged up a stockin' in Brooklyn. Bod mine fodder pud in a eggshells wid terlit paper an' a piece f'om a ol' kendle. So he leffed w'en he seen me. Id ain' no Sendy Klaws, didja know?"

The Schearl family, on the other hand, seem to speak English without the slightest trace of an accent. To be sure, Roth keeps reminding us that it is really Yiddish, but the effect, nevertheless, places the Schearls in a curious juxtaposition to the others of their environment. As Mrs. Mink tells David's mother, "Yes, not proud, noble! You always walk with your head in the air—so!"

The major difference, however, between the Schearls and the world surrounding them lies in the area of expressed intensity. Mr. Walter Allen has pointed out that *Call it Sleep* "must be the *noisiest* novel ever written." To be sure, the constant screaming of the Hungarian, Italian and Jewish immigrants who live together in the East Side slums certainly suggests that he is right. However, the Schearls frequently express their most intense moments in silence. Thus, *Call it Sleep* is, in many respects, also the *quietest* novel ever written.

In fact, the only occasions in the Schearl household than inevitably lead to a raised voice are those dealing with David's Aunt Bertha. She is every bit as much a grotesque as Pankower. Like the fiery Hebrew teacher, Bertha has an acid tongue and the courage to wield it. However, unlike Pankower, Bertha is a comic character whose sense of life makes for much of both the humor and pathos in *Call it Sleep*. In many respects, her wit is the only way she *could* cope with such a grotesque physical make-up:

> She had a mass of rebellious, coarse red hair, that was darker than a carrot and lighter than a violin. And the color of her teeth, if one had to decide upon it, *was* green. . . . A single crease divided fat forearm from pudgy hand. Her legs landed into her shoes without benefit of ankles. No matter what she wore, no matter how new or clean, she always managed to look untidy.

If Bertha's "distressingly homely" appearance has caused her moments of anguish, she has, at least, managed to adjust to her condition with a distinctly Jewish shrug. As she puts it, "pearl and cloth of gold would stink on me."

For Bertha, America is a land both cursed and blessed. The factory system has enabled her to buy an incredibly large pair of underpants for only "twenty cents" and, thus, she "can wear what only a baroness in Austria could wear." However, when David's father tears the undergarment in a fit of rage, Bertha changes her tune in a way which must have made the "social reformers" of her day very happy indeed:

Why did I ever set foot on this stinking land? Why did I ever come here? Ten hours a day in a smothering shop—paper flowers! Rag flowers! Ten long hours, afraid to pee too often because the foreman might think I was shirking.

However, no matter how much Bertha may rail against the system in general or David's father in particular, she is still very much aware of her own inadequacies. Although she is still quite young, there is a good possibility that she will not be able to find a husband. When David's mother tries to comfort her with the observation that "New York is full of all kinds of men who would want her," Bertha replies:

> . . . "It's also full of all kinds of glib, limber Jewesses who can play the piano. Go! Go!" she tossed he head petulantly. "By the time I learn to speak this tongue I'll be what? Thirty! Old and dry! Others have money, others can dance, can sing with their hands so—Yuh-Yuh-ruh! All I can do is laugh and eat—my only talents! If I don't get a man now—" She waved her hand as if throwing something away. "Maybe I wont even be able to do that."

The actual threat of the "glib limber Jewesses," however, is more imagined than real. Bertha's role as the "have-not" immigrant who is the economic victim of her surroundings is a decidedly short lived one. In fact, she is ultimately a kind of gastronomic Horatio Alger, who ends up with not only a husband, but a candy store as well.

Therefore, the "threats" in *Call it Sleep* are often more social than economic. David must face the problems of living in a land which puts more premium on "fitting in" than "sticking out." Thus, David's reaction to his first encounter with antisemitism foreshadows the rejection of religious and filial ties which has become a convention in more recent Anglo-Jewish literature:

> "Dat's a sheeny block, Pedey," prompted the second freckled lieutenant with ominous eagerness.
>
> "Yea. Yer a Jew ainchiz?"
>
> "No I ain't!" he protested hotly. "I ain't nod a Jew!"
>
> "Only sheenies live in dat block!" countered Pedey narrowly.
>
> "I'm a Hungarian. My muder 'n' foder's Hungarian. We're de janitors."

The epitome of the freedom to which David aspires is symbolized in his Christian friend, Leo. As David puts it, "There was no end to Leo's blessings—no father, almost no mother, skates." As if these weren't enough, Leo had a Catholic medal which allows its owner to "Johnny-high-dive all yuh wants an' yuh'll never hit bottom." To David, Leo's medal makes him not only "god-like," but gives him the right (as a "superior being") to mock Jewish paraphernalia in a wholesale fashion. Even when Leo describes a mezzuzeh as "full o' Chinee on liddle terlit paper," David remains silent although

> he felt a slight qualm of guilt, yes, guilt because he was betraying all the Jews in his house who had Mezuzehs above their doors; but if Leo thought it was funny, then it was funny and it didn't matter. He even added lamely that the only thing Jews wore around their necks were camphor balls against measles, merely to hear the intoxicating sound of Leo's derisive laughter.

Thus, Leo represents all the glamor and appeal of a world beyond his narrow ghetto and its limited possibilities. David cannot reach this "enchanted land," however, because he lacks the necessary means of transportation:

> Skates. That was the real reason why he had lost Leo—because he lacked them. . . . If he only had a pair of skates! . . . If he had a pair of skates he could leave the hated boys on his block behind him; he could go to Leo's block, to Central Park as Leo said he did.

To be sure, David's almost compulsive desire to escape the shackles of his Jewish environment seems a far cry from the assimilated suburban world of a Philip Roth or a Bruce Jay Friedman. However, the difference between his skates and their station wagons is only one of degree and not of kind. Certainly one of the reasons that *Call it Sleep* has done so well in its re-publication is that it suggested a direction in 1934 which a number of people have taken since. For many people, the novel represents an index of accomplishment and, therefore, it becomes almost fashionable to read about one's ancestors, no matter how poor they might have been.

In the final pages of the novel, David receives "shocks," both literal and figurative. In an extended stream-of-consciousness section which finally widens the social scope until it includes a kind of thirties' panorama, Roth manages to achieve the same effect that John Dos Passos matches in his lengthy trilogies. David is reawakened into both a new life and a new world. Although there have been countless novels which focused on the initiation experience, *Call it Sleep* is one of the very few to *end* with such a young protagonist. However, the intensity of his initiation is not hampered by his youth. David "learns" a variety of lessons and, presumably, he will learn more. However, his childhood nightmare of Oedipal fears finally has been conquered and David can go on with the business of defining himself in an adult world.

In the final analysis *Call it Sleep* is more universal and significant than any critical discussion of the thirties or Anglo-Jewish literature can possibly suggest. Although the Freudian apparatus may strike some contemporary readers as a bit artificial, the bulk of David's initiation experiences are so archetypal in character that they will strike even the most sophisticated reader as "true." And about its neglect, as David's last words suggest, "One might as well call it sleep."

Kenneth Ledbetter (essay date October 1966)

SOURCE: "Henry Roth's *Call It Sleep:* The Revival of a Proletarian Novel," in *Twentieth Century Literature,* Vol. 12, No. 3, October, 1966, pp. 123-30.

[*In the following essay, Ledbetter discusses the relationship between Roth's Call It Sleep and other proletarian novels of the 1930s. He asserts that "Roth's achievement is a novel first, and a proletarian one only secondarily."*]

The recent publication of a paperback edition of Henry Roth's *Call It Sleep* and the prominence afforded a review of it in *The New York Times Book Review* can hardly be construed as a revival of proletarian literature in the United States; our generation remains properly skeptical of the rabid commitment and simple slogans spawned by the confusion of political, economic, and literary values in the 1930s. Such hack work as Mary Heaton Vorse's *Strike!* and Clara Weatherwax's *Marching! Marching!*—indeed, the whole body of proletarian melodramas that once were hailed enthusiastically as weapons in the class struggle—have been mercifully forgotten, and our credulity is strained even to conceive of the high seriousness and religious devotion which characterized the literary controversies of that period. Yet Roth's novel, resurrected now after suffering almost total neglect for thirty years, is perhaps the most authentic and compelling expression the American proletariat has received.

It should be noted, of course, that the qualities of *Call It Sleep* that have given it new life today are the ones most vigorously attacked in the leftist press upon its initial publication in 1934. The Marxist critics of the thirties demanded that proletarian novels meet the immediate needs of the class war, that they be instruments of propaganda containing two-dimensional portrayals of "good guys" and "bad guys" in which the worker-hero discards his petty-bourgeois ideals of virtue and fair play when confronted with the ruthlessness and brutality of capitalist gangsters. To explore the proletarian memory or the consciousness of the worker was to imitate slavishly Proust and Joyce, over-ripe fruits of bougeois decay. Only novels concerned with the proletariat in social relationships (*i.e.,* class conflict) in which the revolutionary movement was portrayed as larger than life and the quickening class-consciousness of the worker anticipated rather than honestly described could expect sympathetic treatment in leftist journals.

> **If the proletarian novel is a novel by and about the proletariat in which it is seen as a separate class with unique experiences and responses, then *Call It Sleep* was the first proletarian novel to be published in the United States.**
> **—Kenneth Ledbetter**

Roth was indignantly chastised by the literary Marxists when they discovered that his talents were introspective rather than bombastic. When first reviewed in the *New Masses, Call It Sleep* was criticized for degenerating into "impression on a rampage," for being too long, for "vile" spelling of dialects, and for over-emphasizing "the sex phobias of this six-year-old Proust." The review concluded: "It is a pity that so many young writers drawn from the proletariat can make no better use of their working class experience than as material for introspective and febrile novels." Favorable comments by John Chamberlain in the New York *Times* and Fred Marsh in the *Herald Tribune* were ignored, as were letters by Kenneth Burke (who wrote that "the great virtue of Roth's book . . . was in the fluent and civilized way in which he found, on our city streets, the new equivalents of the ancient jungle") and Edwin Seaver (who accused the *New Masses* reviewer of suffering from "the infantile disorder of leftism"). After a second printing of 2,500 copies in January, 1935 (1,500 copies had been printed in December, 1934), *Call It Sleep* was virtually forgotten until 1956 when Alfred Kazin and Leslie Fiedler called attention to it in a special issue of *The American Scholar* and Walter Rideout called it "the most distinguished single proletarian novel." It was reprinted from the original plates by Pageant Books, Inc., in 1960, making it possible for readers who had searched unsuccessfully for used copies of the book finally to obtain it, but little critical or popular attention resulted. Now, however, it is available in quantity, and, if the editors of *Life* magazine can be cited as a reliable source, Roth netted $15,000 from the Avon paperback in 1964 alone.

Call It Sleep is the story of the two years between the ages of six and eight in the life of an immigrant Jewish boy named David Schearl, living first in Brownsville, then on New York's East Side. Physically his life is restricted in both neighborhoods by the tenements that surround him; emotionally it is determined by the paranoia of his father an the security of his mother. David lives in a perpetual fear of his father, of the street, of most of his physical environment, finding love and security only when close to his mother. On the surface there is little action and little plot; events have meaning only as they are refracted through David's controlling consciousness. Always introspective and withdrawn, he is intimidated by the other slum children until at the "cheder" he creates and becomes infatuated with a god of fire and power. The only attachment that he ever has for another child ends disastrously when he is forced to arrange a meeting where the friend "plays dirty" with one of the stepdaughters of David's Aunt Bertha. Running from this experience to his mother, he finds that his parents know of the lie he told at the cheder about his "dead mother and goyish father." Hating him because he suspects he is not really his son, David's father threatens to kill him when he discovers David's part in the sex play at his Aunt Bertha's. David runs in terror from the tenement and finds in the street a metal dipper which he drops into the power conduit between the streetcar tracks. The subsequent electrical shock knocks him unconscious, but he revives and is carried home.

Obviously the surface events of the story do not constitute the novel, for essentially it is a symbolic portrayal of the proletarian world and an epitome of the proletarian experience. David Schearl's is a consciousness undergoing orientation and rebirth, and it is through the representative nature and suggestive quality of his experiences that the plight and the hope of the proletariat are conveyed. The error of the more militant Marxist critics who first reviewed the novel was their failure to recognize the complex system of symbols growing organically out of Roth's account of David's childhood, symbols that reflect more accurately and compellingly than any other expression of the period the point of view and the possibilities of the proletariat. If the proletarian novel is a novel by and about the proletariat in which it is seen as a separate class with unique experiences and responses, then ***Call It Sleep*** was the first proletarian novel to be published in the United States.

It is constructed in terms of four major symbols—the cellar, the picture, the coal, and the rail—corresponding to the four parts of the novel. David identifies the cellar with his fear of his father, the terror of the street, bodily corruption, and violence. The picture he associates with his mother, with her warmth and security, and with release. The coal suggests spiritual escape from the physical repulsiveness of his environment, for it is conceived always in terms of the coal with which the angel touched Isaiah's lips so that he might speak with God. The rail, on the other hand, becomes for David the power of God, terrifying in its brilliance, yet comforting in its immensity. In terms of and through these symbols David re-enacts a basically human yet emphatically proletarian pattern of experience—repeated thrusts into the world, each followed by a withdrawal back into the self (in David's case the refuge of his mother's arms, the womb of their tenement flat). Finally, at the end of the novel, cut off from this refuge and unable any longer to retreat, David finds safety—and a new identity—in the power of the rail and in the midst of the proletariat.

The novel begins ironically. The "Prologue," a short scene set four years earlier than the main story, begins with the epigraph, "I pray thee ask no questions / this is that Golden Land," yet the first thing David learns after his journey from Europe and the reunion with his father at Ellis Island is that he is hated and unwanted. To his father he is "the brat," and even the Statue of Liberty is colored by his father's attitude: "the rays of her halo . . . spikes of darkness roweling the air; shadow flattened the torch she bore to a black cross against flawless light—the blackened hilt of a broken sword." At home, David soon realizes that he is not only an unwanted, an insignificant, object to his father, but also a helpless and inconsiderable object in his new world. Contemplating the water faucet, he "again became aware that this world had been created without thought of him. He was thirsty, but the iron hip of the sink rested on legs tall almost as his own body, and by no stretch of arm, no leap, could he ever reach the distant tap." Even at home, where ordinarily there is the security and contentment of his mother, David discovers (although usually only subconsciously) that he remains an alien in a world unconcerned with his existence. Throughout the novel he must fear and try to combat repeated attempts to destroy this haven of home and mother. His father's presence always threatens his security, as do the visits of playmates or neighbors. Luter, the man who befriends his father in order to try unsuccessfully to seduce his mother, is a danger that David only half comprehends and is finally powerless to defy.

It is interesting to observe that as the novel progresses the oedipal attachment that David has for his mother is made more explicit, and one of the dangers from which the power of the rail delivers him is the suffocating extreme to which this relationship might grow. Early in the novel his mother is merely a source of strength and of safety, yet this soon grows into a feeling of identity. Alone with his mother, inside and warm, David watches the cold rain falling outside, and he welcomes his return to a prenatal state: "He was near her now. He was part of her. The rain outside the window set continual seals upon their isolation, upon their intimacy, their identity." Later in the novel, David's dependence on his mother is suddenly united with his hatred for his father, the two impulses blending into a feeling specifically sexual in tone and implication. When his father brings home a pair of huge horns to be mounted on the wall (emblem of his cattle-tending days in Europe before coming to America), David instinctively identifies them with his father's great strength and with his mother's sexual contentment. The horns remind him of the beating his father once gave a man and of the serenity of his mother when confronted unexpectedly

one afternoon as she arose from his father's bed. And although David does not understand how it could be, he immediately sees the horns as a threat that he must somehow meet.

> He was silent. Somehow he couldn't quite believe that it was for memory's sake only that his father had bought this trophy. Somehow looking at the horns, guessing the enormous strength of the beast who must have owned them, there seemed to be another reason. He couldn't quite fathom it though. But why was it that two things so remote from each other seemed to have become firmly coupled in his mind? It was as though the horns lying on the washtub had bridged them, as though one tip pierced one image and one tip the other—that man outstretched on the sidewalk, that mysterious look of repose in his mother's face when he had come in. Why? Why did he think of them at one and the same time. He couldn't tell. He sensed only that in the horns, in the poised power of them lay a threat, a challenge he must answer, he must meet. But he didn't know how.

Outside the peace of his mother's womb lies the street, and David finds himself continually thrust into it by the conditions of his life. Just getting into the street, making the transition from womb to world, requires an almost superhuman effort, for between the safety of home and the insecurity of the street is the cellar, always identified by David with death, corruption, and that part of himself unrelated to his mother, a dark side to his own nature that stems from his father and that occasionally erupts in a burst of temper not unlike the explosive anger of Albert Schearl. The most powerful scene in Part I, and a turning point in David's development, centers around his descent into this darkness of self. Tormented one day by other street urchins until no longer able to endure the frustration, David turns on the one nearest him and knocks him down. As the child falls, his head strikes the pavement and he loses consciousness. David flees, but he cannot go up to his tenement apartment because Luter is there and he is afraid of what he might find Luter and his mother doing. His only refuge from the terror of the street is the terror of the cellar.

> . . . . He sprang to the cellar door and pulled it open—Darkness like a cataract, inexhaustible, monstrous.
>
> "Mama!" he moaned, peering down, "Mama!"
>
> He dipped his foot into night, feeling for the stair, found it, pulled the door shut behind him. . . .
>
> Darkness all about him now, entire and fathomless

night. No single ray threaded it, no flake of light drifted through. From the inpenetrable depths below, the dull marshy stench of surreptitious decay uncurled against his nostrils. . . .

He gritted his teeth with the strain. Minutes had passed while he willed in a rigid pounding trance—willed that Luter would come down, willed that Luter would leave his mother. . . . Exhausted, he slumped back against the edge of the stair. . . . Against his will he sifted the nether dark. It was moving—moving everywhere on a thousand feet. The stealthy horrible dark was climbing the cellar stairs, climbing toward him. . . . His jaws began to chatter. Icy horror swept up and down his spine like a finger scratching a comb. His flesh flowed with terror.—Run! Run!

Escaping from the cellar, David finds momentary deliverance in counting utility poles "marching up the hill" while he loses himself among unfamiliar streets. As he follows the poles he experiences a complete dissociation from self, a release from the bonds of temporal identity:

He stopped counting them. And with them, dwindling in the past, all he feared, all he loathed and fled from: Luter, Annie, the cellar, the boy on the ground. He remembered them still, yes, but they were tiny now, little pictures in his head that no longer writhed into his thoughts and stung him, but stood remote and harmless—something heard about someone else. He felt as if they would vanish from his mind altogether, could he only reach the top of that hill up which all the poles were, striding. He hurried on, skipping sometimes out of sheer deliverance, sometimes waving at a laggard pole, gurgling to himself, giggling at himself, absurdly weary.

After these experiences of viewing the self from deep within its darkest recesses and then from a distance that produces a feeling of separation, David is able to turn his thoughts away from the cellar and toward the picture on the wall, a picture always associated with his mother, yet in its pastoral simplicity suggesting another world, different from the one he knows. He is still acutely aware of his own isolation in an alien world, of which he is vividly reminded when he loses himself among the utility poles, but he can now pass the cellar with a feeling of anger rather than of fear, "as though he defied it, as though he had slammed the door within him and locked it." Initially the picture of the corn with the blue flowers under it is merely a token of his mother's happiness and contentment in which he shares, for "she laughed when she hung it up." Later it becomes the emblem of his mother's youth and of her goyish lover, suggesting to David qualities of peace and simple beauty unknown in his East Side world.

The turning point in David's struggle for identity in a world outside his mother's womb comes when he hears in the cheder the story of Isaiah and the purification through which he passes in order to be judged fit to speak with God. In David's seven-year-old mind, the coal with which the angel touches Isaiah's lips becomes a unifying symbol for all of his experiences, revealing to him in the simple terms of light and dark the antitheses within himself and of his world. His first intimation of this new orientation comes one sunny day as he watches the river, the brilliance of it holding him in a hypnotic trance until "his spirit yielded, melted into light":

In the molten sheen memories and objects overlapped. Smokestacks fused to palings flickering in silence by. Pale lathes grew grey, turned dusky, contracted and in the swimming dimness, he saw sparse teeth that gnawed upon a lip; and ladders on the ground turned into hasty fingers pressing on a thigh and against smokestacks. Straight in air they stood a moment, only to fall on silvered cardboard corrugating brilliance. And he heard the rubbing on a wash-board and the splashing suds, smelled again the acrid soap and a voice speaking words that opened like the bands of a burnished silver accordian—Brighter than day . . . Brighter . . . Sin melted into light. . . .

The peace of the picture and the light of the coal, however, are soon shattered, for as David's vision at the river passes, he is confronted by a group of boys from another block, who, suspecting that he is Jewish, force him to drop a toy zinc sword into the conduit between the streetcar tracks. David is momentarily blinded by the flash and stunned by the power that leaps from the crevice.

Like a paw ripping through all the sable fibres of the earth, power, gigantic, fetterless, thudded into day! And light, unleashed, terrific light bellowed out of iron lips. The street quaked and roared, and like a tortured thing, the sheet zinc sword, leapt writhing, fell back, consumed with radiance.

In the same way the peaceful brilliance of the tenement roof and the release which it seems to promise degenerate into the corruption of sex play in the darkness of the cellar. On the roof David had found what he hoped would be a friend, but the boy whom David begins to trust merely uses him as a means by which he may work his own designs upon the girl to whom David innocently brings him, and the incident terminates in the explosion that seals him off forever from his mother's womb and that finally forces him to find personal identification (and salvation) in something larger than and external to the self.

Two earlier incidents, however, have already forced David to see his world in an altered light. The first is his discovery that the neighborhood urchins have seen his mother naked in her bath, a discovery that arouses in David intense jealousy followed by the fleeting intimation that his mother's pristine (and protective) nature has somehow been tarnished. The second incident concerns a promise to his father that he will not tell his mother that his father beat him because David had allowed two derelicts to steal milk from his father's delivery wagon, and the experience (especially his fancied infidelity to his mother) leaves David with "a globe about his senses" as he sets out for his lesson at the cheder.

> Something had happened! Even Ninth Street, his own familiar Ninth Street was warped, haunted by something he could feel; but perceive with no sense. Faces he had seen so many times he scarcely ever glanced at any more were twisted into secret shadows, smeared, flattened, whorled, grotesque grief and smirking never before revealed.

Confronted finally by an enraged father and a mother no longer able to protect him, David frantically runs from the house that had hitherto been his refuge. The rabbi has told his parents of the lie by which David repudiated his earlier identity; his Aunt Bertha's husband is forced by David's father to reveal David's part in the sex play with his daughter; and his father in turn repudiates David as another man's son and threatens to kill him. Thus with all of the hideous darkness and terror of the cellar closing around him, David flies to the only refuge remaining to him—the rail, the power and light of God by which he must be purified and reborn. Knocked unconscious by the electrical current that leaps through him as he pushes the ladle between the rails, David "sleeps," and through the vision that accompanies this sleep all the disparate elements of his earlier existence are united, so that when he awakes, not so much his world but himself has been changed. He discovers as he awakes that the salvation of those unwanted aliens in a new world will come not through fear and withdrawal, nor by nostalgic yearning for a simpler and more peaceful past, but only through power, the power of the united masses in whose bosom David awakes.

> Humanity. On feet, on crutches, in carts and cars. The ice-vendor. The waffle-wagon. Human voices, motion, seething, throbbing.

In this context David shoves the dipper home, and

> Power! ... titanic power, ripped through the earth and slammed against his body and shackled him

where he stood. . . . A blast, a siren of light within him, rending, quaking, fusing his brain and blood. . . . And he writhed without motion in the clutch of a fatal glory, and his brain swelled and dilated till it dwarfed the galaxies.

As he awakes surrounded by people attracted by the flash, David sees and accepts all of the elements that had previously splintered and terrorized his world (the river, his father, death, corruption, the cheder, God, the cellar) and descends into the cellar of the self until he is nothing, and into nothingness he "would have hidden again," until, attracted by a single ember, he makes the unifying and saving discovery of the novel: in the cellar there is coal. Picking up the coal of his vision he finds it neither cold nor hot, "but as if all eternity's caress were fused and granted in one instant," and "horror and the night fell away. Exalted, he lifted his head." After he awakes, David is carried home where, alone in his bed, he feels the change within him.

> He might as well call it sleep. It was only toward sleep that ears had power to call again and reassemble the shrill cry, the hoarse voice, the scream of fear, the bells, the thick-breathing, the roar of crowds and all sounds that lay fermenting in the vats of silence and the past. It was only toward sleep one knew himself still lying on the cobbles, felt the cobbles under him, and over him and scudding ever toward him like a black foam, the perpetual blur of shod and running feet, the broken shoes, new shoes, stubby, pointed, caked, polished, buniony, pavement-beveled, lumpish, under skirts, under trousers, shoes, over one and through one, and feel them all and feel, not pain, not terror, but strangest triumph, strangest acquiescence.

The agony—and the hope—of the proletariat have never been more powerfully portrayed in an American novel, a fact that makes it ultimately even more revolutionary than the most militant pieces of party propaganda. The principal difference between Roth and other left-wing writers in the 1930s was the place of emphasis in their work. The others stressed the "proletarian" nature of their novels; Roth's achievement is a novel first, and a proletarian one only secondarily. The remarkable reversal in the fortunes of this novel during the past three years indicates that it will soon attract the body of critical commentary that it has so long deserved. Certainly the tentative probings contained here merely suggest the irony in the fact that recognition of the first significant proletarian novel to be published in the United States had to wait until the revolutionary temper that produced it had long grown cold. Our generation, no longer concerned with the distinction between "proletarian" and "bourgeois" or with art as a weapon, can now concentrate on the remarkably natural and unselfconscious symbol-making power displayed by Roth, and on how the theme of *Call It Sleep* is expressed through symbols that grow out of the physical facts of David's world and flower easily into spiritual truths.

Henry Roth with David Bronsen (interview date 1967)

SOURCE: "A Conversation with Henry Roth," in *Partisan Review,* Vol. XXXVI, No. 2, 1967, pp. 265-80.

[*In the following interview, Roth discusses his life and his relationship to writing and creative life.*]

[*Bronsen:*] *I visited Henry Roth on his Farm near Augusta, Maine, and we began to talk. At one point I remarked that he had never lost his command of language. He replied:* "That comes from having talked with myself for twenty-five years."

[Roth:] It's too bad I was not older when I was brought to America, so that I could recall the Old World and the original home of my mother and father. I was born in Tysmenitsa, near Lemberg, Galicia, in 1906, and was only eighteen months old when my mother brought me to this country.

My father had gone to New York and saved up enough money to bring my mother and me over in steerage. This is the material I used in the prologue of *Call It Sleep.* Since there was no birth certificate, there was some doubt about my age. My father said I was two and a half years old when I came, but my mother maintained I was a year younger. As proof she used to point out that my sister, who was conceived in America, was two years younger than I am, so I imagine that her version of my age is correct.

My parents settled down in Brownsville at first, which corresponds to certain passages of the novel. Two years later we moved to Ninth Street on the Lower East Side of Manhattan. When we lived there in the years 1910 to 1914, the East Side represented a very secure enclave. Everyone in our building was Jewish, as were the neighbors to either side of us and the people across the street. Had I thought of it in those terms back them, I would have said that I was surrounded by a homogeneous environment and that I completely identified with it. In that atmosphere of devoutness and orthodoxy it would not have occurred to anyone to question the dietary regulations or the observance of holiday rituals. Those were the years when the huge influx of Eastern Jewish immigration was building the area up. The East Side was helpful, communicative and highly interrelated—in short, a community. It was a place with the promise of opportunities and new horizons, where one could make a new

start in life. And the Jew in those years was optimistic and dynamic, full of the feeling that nothing was holding him back.

We lived in Ninth Street till I was eight years old, and then in the summer of 1914 we moved to Harlem. My mother's parents, along with several uncles and aunts, were brought over just before the outbreak of the First World War and settled by my maternal uncle in a steam-heated, hot-water apartment in Harlem. My mother wanted to be near her parents, which accounted for our moving there too. The move turned out to be crucial for me.

We settled at 108 East 119th Street, near the trestle of the New York-New Haven Railroad. This part of the neighborhood, squeezed in between Little Italy to the east and the more prosperous and predominately Jewish area to the west, was considered the poorer part of Harlem. It was a mixture of Irish, Italians and Jews, and a rough mixture. I was taken from a neighborhood that had been home for me and put in a highly hostile environment. That produced a shock from which I have perhaps never recovered. Until then I had had a natural love of activity and enjoyed the companionship of other children. I had been a good student in school as well as in *cheder.* After the move to Harlem all that changed and I took to avoiding outside contact by staying in the house and near Mama as much as possible, so that I grew fat with the lack of activity. In fact, that is what the children used to call me—"fatty." For weeks I cried and had tantrums, begging to be taken back to Ninth Street. But no one paid any attention to me, nor was there any concern when I received C's for the first time on my report card. I got into fights at the new school for a while, but I soon learned to avoid any provocation. I retreated into myself and stayed out of people's way. Serious psychological damage had been brought about by this uprooting of a naturally conservative child, and it expressed itself after a while in my rejection of Jewish faith and customs, which until then had been a part of me. I felt no anguish over this at the time—I was throwing it all to the winds. My mother, who was the only source of security, did not understand what was going on, although I suppose her example was also influencing my behavior. She herself was reacting against the fanatical orthodoxy of her father, which had oppressed her as a child and a young woman. If her faith had not been tongue in cheek I might have been insulated against the influences of Harlem. But she did not seem to care if I became a Goy or not, and damn it, I became a Goy!

My father was also not particularly orthodox, he merely went through the motions. He did not fail to celebrate Seder and observe Yom Kippur, but at the core true devoutness no longer existed. My father had a pat phrase that he appended to every reference to God, which he continues to use till this day: "*op si doh a Gott*"—"if there is a God."

Looking at it in another way, I suppose my parents went through some of the same dislocation by coming to America that I experienced by moving to Harlem. That kind of change is much more of a trauma for the Eastern Jew than for the Westerner. The Jew coming out of his little Eastern European hamlet, with its insularity and stagnation, is likely to undergo a radical transformation when he gets caught up in the tumult and perpetual change of American life.

In any case, the move in 1914, the Goyish environment and the negative example of my parents threw me into a state of turmoil. I had gone to Harlem with a pronounced Jewish bent and proceeded to take on the conflicting characteristics of my new surroundings. It was as if two valences of the same element were at odds with one another; at the time, of course, I could not intellectualize about the contradictions involved, but I did feel them emotionally, and my response took the form of rebelling against Judaism. I fought as hard as I could against going through with the Bar Mitzvah, even though my parents insisted on it and finally had their way. But only a year later, when I was fourteen, I firmly announced that I was an atheist.

Call It Sleep is set in the East Side, but it violates the truth about what the East Side was like back then. Ninth Street was only a fragmentary model for what I was doing. In reality, I took the violent environment of Harlem—where we lived from 1914 to 1928—and projected it back onto the East Side. It became a montage of milieus, in which I was taking elements of one neighborhood and grafting them onto another. This technique must have grown out of the rage I had been living with all those fourteen years. I was alienated—to use that old hack of a word—and my novel became a picture in metaphors of what had happened to me.

All the rancorous anti-Semitism which Hitler was beginning to epitomize was not limited to Germany alone. To a lesser degree it was being felt everywhere. It may be difficult to explain how such social forces affect the individual psyche, but it is clear that they have powerful behavioral effects. My own experience of being thrown into a neighborhood where anti-Semitism was growing provides an example, and the scene in *Call It Sleep* in which David Schearl lamely denies his being Jewish to the gang that is threatening him is an objectification of the same thing.

> **I was alienated—to use that old hack of a word—and my novel became a picture in metaphors of what had happened to me.**
> **—Henry Roth**

The characters in the novel have a cohesion of their own, but to really understand them you have to go through the characters and back to the author to find out what was motivating and disturbing him. I needed empirical reality for the sake of its plausibility, but I took off from it on a tangent. In other words, I was working with characters, situations and events that had in part been taken from life, but which I molded to give expression to what was oppressing me. To a considerable extent I was drawing on the unconscious to give shape to remembered reality. Things which I could not fully understand but which filled me with apprehension played a critical role in determining the form of the novel. The father in the novel is a powerfully built, menacing person given to uncontrolled violence. My own father, who served as a model for this figure, was basically an impulsive little man with poor judgment, and perhaps a little unbalanced. He did not beat me often, but when he did he went crazy. Because I felt I could be overwhelmed at any time by forces that were constantly threatening me, it became necessary to change this little man into someone capable of real destruction. Violence is associated as a rule with great strength, and to the mind of a child an adult seems to be seven feet tall.

I worked with polarities in expressing the subjective reality of the little boy in the novel. I am referring to the personalities of the mother and father, as well as the characters of the mother and her sister. Actually, my own mother was the source of both of these contrasting female figures. I abstracted one side of my mother, rounded it out and created an aunt who in most respects is the antithesis of David Schearl's mother. The presence of Aunt Bertha seemed to give an aesthetic justification to the character of the mother as well.

My parents were hopelessly mismatched, and their life together was marked by furious quarreling. My mother, who felt profoundly cheated in her husband, could never bring herself to express the full force of her feelings against him until late in life, when an outbreak of paranoia tore down all her reserve. In her earlier years she turned all her attention to me. Since at that age I could hardly have any recourse to depth analysis, the Oedipal fixation that took hold of me was to keep me firmly in its grip.

I made use of a number of incidents out of my childhood experiences, but recast them in a manner that is just as revealing of the author's frame of mind and his hindsight as it is of the character of the little boy. The critical episode in the novel of thrusting the milk dipper into the car track is an example. A couple of boys had enticed me into doing that for the sake of a prank. The author turned the incident into a personal statement: the impressionable boy living in hostile surroundings adopts as his own a destructive act to which he is instigated by outsiders to whom he has no personal relationship.

After publication of *Call It Sleep* a number of critics pointed out what they thought were its social implications. My own feeling was that what I had written was far too private for me to have given much thought to specific social problems. My personal involvement had absorbed my entire consciousness, leaving no room to focus on anything else.

When I force myself to be objective I realize that if I had not moved to Harlem I most likely would never have written the novel. But during the anxieties and hardships of the intervening years I have told myself that I would not hesitate to sacrifice *Call It Sleep* for a happy childhood, adolescence and young manhood. Given the choice, I would have stayed on the East Side until I was at least eighteen years old. Then I would have gone forth.

Of course, I can see that moving to Harlem was a formative experience in its own right. It had the virtue of compelling an enlargement of vision and sympathy. I was presented at an impressionable age, when everything becomes emotionally charged, with the problem of trying to integrate in my mind a much greater diversity and many more contrasting forces than I would have known otherwise. If we had stayed on the East Side and I had gone on to write—two big ifs, because I wanted to become a biology teacher when I was a boy—it is possible that I might have written some honest portrayals of Jewish life on the East Side. Such writing would necessarily have reflected Jewish life *as* Jewish life, which is not the case with my novel; I do not regard *Call It Sleep* as primarily a novel of Jewish life. There is something positive in the writer striving for the broader awareness that enables him to interrelate many more disparate elements in an art form; such an aim, by its very nature, requires the consideration of a much wider world than the one I originally came from.

As an illustration you can take the case of Robert Frost. From my knowledge of his verse, Frost never broke through what might be called the bucolic curtain. Emotionally and ideologically he played it safe by never going out into the larger world to tes his attitudes and views. Had I stayed on the Lower East Side I also would have been spared having to submit my feelings and beliefs to a wider experience and understanding.

During the years in which I devoted myself to writing *Call It Sleep* I came to regard myself as a disciplined writer who could turn his hand to whatever literary task he cut out for himself. I knew that the flow of creativity would not be uniform, and I had come to expect resistance from my material, but I felt that by working at it I could resolve all the difficulties I encountered. My self-confidence approached the point of arrogance in those years. I remember in a moment of introspection reviewing in my mind the authors and literary works that I considered important and that had per-

sonally affected me. At the same time, and with a good deal of pride, I felt that I was consciously fighting literary influences and going my own way.

T.S. Eliot, James Joyce and Eugene O'Neill were the writers of major stature that interested me back then. Eliot's *Waste Land* had a devastating effect on me, I felt stunned by the vastness of its conception. I had been introduced to the work by Eda Lou Walton, a professor of literature at New York University. It was to her that I dedicated *Call It Sleep.* She was a woman twelve years older than I, who was very devoted to me and who for a time supported and sponsored me. Our relationship had certain parallels to that of Thomas Wolfe and Aline Bernstein, although I do not stress the resemblance.

Some of the plays of Eugene O'Neill left a deep imprint. I went to see *The Great God Brown* with Eda Lou and came away feeling that I had been listening to the inner voice of a man.

I had already read Joyce as a freshman in college, and a copy of *Ulysses* which Eda Lou had brought me from France introduced me to an entirely new way of seeing things. I felt I could see doors swinging open on untried possibilities in literature.

But during the time I was writing the novel I was trying to establish a demarcation between myself and other authors. As far as I was concerned, no one could teach me anything and nothing was too big an undertaking.

I started writing *Call It Sleep* in 1929, worked on it for four years and finished it in 1933, when I was twenty-seven. A substantial part of the book was written in Maine, in the small town of Norridgewock, in 1932. I learned of a farmhouse where an elderly widow, a woman of seventy, boarded the local schoolmistress; and since this was summer and the room vacant, she agreed to take me in as a boarder. For seven dollars a week I got room and board—and was fed royally. I had nothing to do but work on my novel, which I did from June till November. It was a happy stay, and years later, when I was casting about for a place in which to settle down, it must have been the memory of those satisfying months that made me decide on Maine.

The book was published in 1934 by Ballou and Company. I paid little attention to the contract at the time and just wondered how the publisher could possibly hope for any financial return on the book in the middle of the Depression. Viewed from today's vantage point, you would think Robert Ballou had a gold mine in his possession. Meyer Levin was one of his authors and John Steinbeck, who was just getting started, was another. But his firm was having difficulties, like so many others; one publisher after another was going on the rocks and selling his writers to the more affluent survivors. Owing to Ballou's rather desperate financial straits, he was relieved when David Mandel, a lawyer, put some money in the firm. That gave Mandel a share of the business and certain rights in deciding policy. Ballou was already favorably inclined to the book, and David Mandel, who subsequently married Eda Lou Walton, submitted to her urging to have the book published.

In later years people would say to me, "You haven't written because you were not given any recognition." That is not true; for a first novel I was given a large measure of acclaim, enough to encourage any writer. And the fact is that I did write, for a time. . . .

Even before the publication of **Call It Sleep** I was at work on a new book. I had met a colorful person around whom I was building my second novel. The man was a tough, second-generation German-American who had been raised on the streets of Cincinnati and relied on his fists and his physical stamina to cope with life. Being an illiterate, he had acquired almost everything he knew through his own experience. I was attracted to him because he always took pride in being able to defend himself, no matter what happened. His build and the way he carried himself made me think of a champion middleweight fighter, and as a matter of fact, he had trained with professionals. When he told me that he had never been beaten I was inclined to believe him. Then suddenly this man who had fought and brawled his way through life lost his right hand in an industrial accident. With that came the terrible shock and realization that he was no longer able to fight the world alone. His personal tragedy and the knowledge that he would have to turn to others for help were terrifying blows that hit him at the depth of the Depression and changed his whole outlook on life.

Like many intellectuals during the Depression, I had become attracted to Marxism and felt the Communist Party to be its true expression. It was as a result of my contact with the Party that I met my German acquaintance and conceived the idea of basing a novel on him. The man and what I learned about him fitted in with what I thought the Party stood for. I carefully gathered the data of his life as well as my observations concerning him, and wrote about a hundred pages of manuscript. He had become an organizer for the Party, and several times I went along with him to distribute leaflets on the waterfront, where I used the Italian I had been studying on my own to make contacts with the longshoreman. There was no CIO at that time, and the Party was espousing the cause of industrial unions on the waterfront, in the same way that Harry Bridges had been doing on the West Coast.

One day while I was accompanying him on his assignment, my "character," whose instincts for danger were better than

mine, warned me, "Better stay close to me." With a hook for a hand he was still a man that no one was likely to cross. But I wandered away from him in the process of handing out the leaflets.

The aims of the Communist Party had been coming into conflict with those of the AFL, which was well entrenched among the longshoremen. I was approached by one of the business agents of the AFL, who asked me for a leaflet. When I held it out to him he belted me across the face, smashed my glasses and proceeded to beat me up, all the time driving me across the highway as he pounded away at me. By the time my friend came running towards me the incident was over, but for a man of sensibility no further lesson was needed about the animosity and antagonism that arise from a struggle over vested interests.

In the meantime, Ballou had gone bankrupt and sold Scribner's the rights to my second book. During the negotiations I had submitted the unfinished manuscript to Scribner's editor, Maxwell Perkins, who was so enthusiastic that he predicted the novel would be one of the outstanding books in contemporary American fiction. The poor man—he died without getting the rest of the manuscript. Once the contract was signed and Ballou was paid, I did not write another word. I had mapped out in detail the course I was to follow in each chapter of the book, but I seemed to have arrived at an utter mpasse.

Only after completing all the rest of **Call It Sleep** did I go back and write the prologue. But after doing the first hundred pages of the second book I changed directions and did the prologue as a pretext for not going on to Section II.

My second book was supposed to be a short but substantial novel, that I was going to follow with a longer one, for which I had been saving myself. This work was to be far more ambitious and of greater scope; in it I would deal with the Jewish intellectual embracing many more elements of the social world. But my second novel was not getting anywhere. For a time I made all kinds of excuses to myself, then I decided I had made a mistake by limiting my perspective to the midwestern proletarian that was turning revolutionary. I wanted the words to come flowing out of me again, and I needed a fresh start; as a physical demonstration of this recognition I burned the manuscript I had shown Perkins and set to work on the next novel. I wrote the opening chapters, which dealt with autobiographical material from Harlem, but I felt I was not reaching the mark. My notes called for bringing together a great many disparate aspects of society and weaving them into an artistic whole. More than anything else I required a sense of unity in the work I did, a unity that could almost be reduced to a metaphor. I struggled with both the style and content, getting only so far before once again running up against immobility and total frustration.

I found myself analyzing my views on progress and indulging for hours and days in mental excursions on the subject of moral righteousness. To my surprise I found myself in sympathy with the South and its myths of tradition and languorous women. I carried on debates with myself in which my intellectual judgment and my sensuous orientation were at odds with each other. Common sense told me that my principles required that I side with the more enlightened North, that my phantasies were ignoring the disadvantaged Negro and the ugliness of racism. To my horror I caught myself musing about the Nazi cult of German brotherhood, and then I would shudder when I stopped to think what they were doing to the Jews in Germany.

I suppose all this was a revulsion from the emphasis on the struggle for social justice. The intellectual decision to identify myself with the proletariat had created a crisis which brought into sharp focus my dichotomy as a human being. I knew that justice was at stake, that Jews were involved, that one had to do something about poverty. But poverty is ugly and the proletarian bored me, with the result that the sensuousness in my nature was pulling me in the opposite direction. The artist in me had never gotten over the appeal of art for art's sake, which had flourished in the twenties. With this war going on inside of me I became immobilized to the point that I found myself incapable of making a narrative decision. All this is subjective evidence that something was knocking the props out from under me, that in spite of my tremendous creative urge something was working against me, stymieing me, preventing me from doing what I desired most. My efforts to get on with the novel petered out and the whole thing gradually shriveled and withered away, until finally I destroyed that manuscript as well. I regret that now. Had I kept the autobiographical material about Harlem it might have provided me at some later time with renewed motivation.

When a writer gives up what is most vital to him, the work in which he has placed his greatest hopes and which was going to be the object of his greatest efforts, he is undercutting his creative gifts and abilities. I was through. For a long time I thought that I was afflicted by some peculiar curse. But I have come to believe that there was something deeper and less personal in my misfortune, that what had happened to me was common to a whole generation of writers in the thirties. One author after another, whether he was Gentile or Jew, stopped writing, became repetitive, ran out of anything new to say or just plain died artistically. I came to this conclusion because I simply could not believe that anyone with as much discipline, creative drive, inbred feeling for the narrative and intense will to write as I had, could, after such rigorous efforts, still be baulked.

Looking about, I saw the same phenomenon manifesting itself in practically every writer I knew. They became barren.

Daniel Fuchs decided after his third novel that he would write for Hollywood. He maintained that he had arrived at his decision clearly and rationally, but I do not believe that. James Farrell is another example. He had exhausted himself by the time he had written his third novel, and everything he wrote after that consisted of variations on played-out themes. Steinbeck is not radically different, as far as his real contribution is concerned; nothing else he ever wrote came up to *The Grapes of Wrath.* And Edward Dahlberg—what did he write after *Bottom Dogs* and *From Flushing to Calvary*? There was Hart Crane and Leonie Adams, both of whom ran into the stone wall of noncreativity. Crane committed suicide, and Nathanael West for his part conveniently died.

I have to get a cigarette—this works me up! [*Mr. Roth lit his cigarette deliberately, abruptly changed the subject and bantered for several minutes before resuming his train of thought.*]

How does one explain this peculiarity? It happened often enough that I began to reflect on it, and I have continued to reflect on it ever since. I do not have the training to make a scientific or sociological analysis, but it seems to me that World War II, which was already in the making, was a dividing line between an era which was coming to an end, namely ours, and another, which was coming into being. I think that we sensed a sharp turn in historic development. How do writers sense these things? We sense it in our prolonged malaise, and in our art—in the fact that, having been fruitful writers, we suddenly grow sterile. The causes are personal, but they are also bigger than any of us. When so many people are affected in the same way and each one is groping for his own diagnosis you have to look for a broader explanation.

To those of us who were committed to the Left, the Soviet Union was the cherished homeland; but that homeland had become an establishment which was interested in consolidating itself. In the Moscow trials the establishment was destroying the revolution, although at the time we were still loudly professing our allegiance. Events often do not become comprehensible until long after they have occurred.

I am throwing out these ideas as possibilities. The scholar who some day will be making a formal study of the question will undoubtedly find other things to single out. One interesting facet he will have to investigate is the influence such historical factors exert on the artist. How do they get into the writer's bloodstream and affect his creative sensibility? How are his potentialities inhibited? The world around him after all remains largely intact, but something inside of him has changed.

In 1938, when I was despairing of ever writing again, my

relationship with Eda Lou Walton deteriorated. We separated, and almost immediately afterwards I met Muriel Parker at Yaddo, an artist's colony at Saratoga Springs. The following year we were married, but the only livelihood we had came from the WPA and relief. They had me working with pick and shovel laying sewer pipes as well as repairing and maintaining streets. In 1940 I wrote **"Somebody Always Grabs the Purple,"** a story of a boy's visit to the public library, which was published in *The New Yorker*. When I notified the relief agency that I had received three hundred dollars for the publication I was reclassified as being no longer indigent, and promptly removed from the rolls.

Shortly after that I obtained a steady job as a substitute teacher at a high school in the Bronx. I decided that jobs offer security, that I would have to accept the obligations and compulsions that came my way and forget I had been a writer. When I discussed this with my wife we both agreed that I would never write again. I told myself I had done so many different things in the meantime that there would be no more suffering, yet there was some hidden reservation that lingered on and continued to crop up in moments of introspection.

By 1940 Europe was at war and the American economy was speeding up. I learned that people were being trained as craftsmen to turn out the immense volume of war material that was beginning to come off the assembly lines, and the thought of a skilled trade appealed to me. Although I had given up being a writer and accepted the idea that I would have to work for a living like everybody else, I still felt that anything remotely touching on my former interest—and that included advertising as well as clerical and office work—was repugnant to me. So I gravitated to machineshop work and became a precision grinder. That entailed doing the high precision finishing work on a variety of cutting tools, dies, fixtures and jigs. The machinists who carried out the earlier parts of the operation left me only a few thousandths of an inch to take off. The ordinary machinist does not care for such slow and demanding work, but I had always been interested in mathematics, which was necessary for the required calculations, and I came to like the work. In time I was classified as A-1 on the basis of the skill I acquired.

For six years I plied that trade and regarded myself as a machinist. During those years, perhaps because it had been the scene of my frustration, I developed a distaste for New York. I wanted to get away from anything that reminded me of my past as a writer. But leaving New York is a two-fold undertaking for a New Yorker. First of all he had to decide to make the break, having always looked upon New York implicitly as the only place in which he could live. Then he has to decide where he is going. In 1945 I finally made the move and took the family to Boston.

Fifteen years passed before I was to return even briefly to New York. I discovered then that it was no longer my New York. I had been so versed in the city, I could see the little detail that spoke for the whole, and had developed an expertise in conning the place. I went back to visit Ninth Street and the East Side, the neighborhood I had known and identified with, and discovered the whole area had become Puerto Rican. The great spirit that had once vitalized that stack of bricks was gone. Nevertheless, I was moved by nostalgia the first time I went back there; perhaps there was a touch of symbolism in my "return." But now I would like to see everything there bulldozed down and some fit habitations erected. My response to prowling through Harlem was markedly different. You experience nostalgia if you are aware of a former identity which has been displaced or replaced. I never had that kind of tie to Harlem, only the feeling that I did not belong.

After working in Boston during 1945 and 1946 I decided that was not the right place for me either. I found an inexpensive farm in Maine, not the one I am living on now, but in Montville, and the price of twelve hundred dollars included the house and barn. The one-hundred-ten acre farm described a ribbon a couple of hundred yards wide and a mile long. I bought the place in March, 1946, and two months later my wife and the two boys came out here to live. After continuing work for six more months in Boston I settled down with my family in Maine.

The years that followed were occupied with making a living and supporting the family. I started out by taking a job as a teacher at a school in which eight grades were all cooped up in one room. I never learned the knack of keeping them all busy; while I was teaching the eighth grade the first and second graders would get restless. I saw myself as a juggler trying to keep up an illusion of perpetual motion.

There followed a variety of odd jobs—from putting in heating insulation to fire fighting in the woods of Maine—whatever offered a livable wage. In 1949, the same year we moved to Augusta, I went to work as an attendant at the Augusta State Hospital and later became a psychiatric aide, a position I held for four years. By then both of my boys were in school and my wife was able to start teaching. From that point on we managed fairly well, although our income never amounted to much. My wife was a wonderful sport and took the ups and downs in her stride. My own attitude was that there was no real meaning outside of writing, so it did not really matter what I did.

Time passed, it became clear that the hospital job had no future, and I turned to something new. Since we were down in a hollow near a brook, I thought the farm would be a good place to raise waterfowl. With the help of my boys that is what I did for a number of years. I used to winter forty breeders each of ducks and geese in order to have fertile eggs in the spring. Then I would incubate the eggs and peddle the ducklings and goslings. I worked up a little trade in feathers too; goose feathers are worth two dollars a pound. When my sons came home from school they ran errands and did chores. That was a happy period for me; I found it wonderful to be working with my own boys.

My life during those years revolved around the family. From time to time I used to wish I could take part in intellectual discussion, but it was pointless to attempt that with the neighbors. There was always my wife, however, and discussion was carried on at home. The area of contact between myself and the natives has been very slight, just as the overlapping of that which is vitally important for them and myself is minimal. The result is that my family and I have lived rather retired lives, to the point where I seem no longer to miss anything in the way of larger human contact. Being a Jew has not provided fellowship either—nor has it been a problem. The Jewish population in Maine is small and I doubt that most of the people I deal with know that I am Jewish.

When my older boy got a scholarship to Phillips Exeter Academy and, a couple of years later, the other one went away to finish high school, my wife and I found ourselves alone. It became necessary to find something less taxing than raising waterfowl by myself, so I took to tutoring Latin and math.

In the summer of 1959 Harold Ribalow, a critic of American-Jewish literature, came out here to talk with me about *Call It Sleep* and its possible republication. That was the first time it occurred to me that anyone might be interested in bringing out the book. I felt that from a business standpoint it would be a foolish venture and would not do any better than it had the first time. I was gratified, however, and hoped that it would result in some needed income. Ribalow pointed out that my copyright was approaching the expiration date, after which the book would become public domain. My obliviousness to that fact shows how divorced I was from literature and writing. As a result of Ribalow's interest the book was brought out by Cooper Square Publishers in 1960, and then in 1964, thirty years after the first publication, it came out as a paperback with Avon Books. After all those years of being out of print the book had become accessible again.

What I had perhaps overlooked is that one grows old and that a book like *Call It Sleep* can gain a certain value as an antiquity. At least I was still alive to see the revival of interest in the novel. I am sure that moving to Maine with its much slower pace of life, giving up the consuming attempt to keep writing at all costs, and the devotion of a steady and sensible wife account for my being alive today. Otherwise

the republication of the book would have been a posthumous event. But as far as literature is concerned, I am in reality no longer alive. The renewed interest in *Call It Sleep* is being witnessed by a dead author who still happens to be ambulatory.

But strangely enough, this dead author may be going through a resurrection. I started writing again in the summer of 1967, simultaneously with the outbreak and conclusion of the Israeli-Arab war. I was in Guadalajara, Mexico, at the time, where I had gone with my wife on the royalties of *Call It Sleep,* and where I followed the daily events of the war in the local newspapers with great avidity. I found myself identifying intensely with the Israelis in their military feats, which repudiated all the anti-Jewish accusations we had been living with in the Diaspora, and I was glorying in their establishment of themselves as a state through their own application and resources. An intellectual excitement seized hold of me that forced me to set down what was going through my mind, to record my thoughts about Israel and my new reservations regarding the Soviet Union. What I wrote seemed to reflect a peculiar adoption. Israel did not adopt me; I adopted my *ex post facto* native land. What seemed important was that I identified with Israel without being a Zionist and without having the least curiosity about Israel as a practical, political entity. Suddenly I had a place in the world and an origin. Having started to write, it seemed natural to go on from there, and I have been writing long hours every day since then. I am not yet sure what it is leading to, but it is necessary and is growing out of a new allegiance, an adhesion that comes from belonging.

I had the need for us to be warriors; I had the need for us to be peasants and farmers, for us to exercise all the callings and trades like any other people. I have become an extreme partisan of Israeli existence—for the first time I have a people. All this made me conscious of a latent conviction—that the individual *per se* disintegrates unless he associates himself with an institution of some sort, with a larger entity. I could not find that kind of bond in religion, and I do not think the Israelis do either. I found it in the existence of a nation. I have not been able to turn for that to America, which is presently committing the folly of destroying itself, so at least for the present I have adopted a people of my own, because they have made it possible for me to do so. And I am further indebted to Israel because I am able to write again.

If there is anything dramatic about all this, I suppose it can be explained as the way a fictioneer does things. Significant for me is that after his vast detour, the once-Orthodox Jewish boy has returned to his own Jewishness. I have reattached myself to part of what I had rejected in 1914. Even before the Israeli-Arab war I was beginning to feel that there might be some path that would lead me back to myself, although I realized there was no returning to the Jews of the East Side of more than a half century ago. Then suddenly I discovered that I could align myself with a people that is forward-looking and engaged in the vital process of its own formation. And with the resumption of writing I find that I myself am reabsorbed into something that is immediately vital. One of the little—or big—projects I have undertaken is a work dealing with the artist responding to his world.

Being a Jew in the Diaspora is basically a state of mind, an attitude of not belonging. In that sense there are also Gentiles who are Jewish. Only two courses remain open to the Jew in America: he assimilates and disappears completely, while giving the best elements of himself to his native culture—and God knows that he has a lot to give; or he goes to Israel and does the same thing there. The emergence of Israel has proved to be the greatest threat to the continued survival of the Jew of the Diaspora. I do not think the Jew in America can exist much longer with a distinct identity, although he continues to make an attempt at it. I myself do not want the Diaspora. I am sick of it. Isn't it time we became a people again? Haven't we suffered enough?

Abruptly the emotional pitch subsided, and an infinite weariness took its place, as Mr. Roth concluded, "This has taken a lot out of me. I don't think I will be giving any more interviews."

The impassioned note on which the long session had ended contrasted with the relaxed, good-natured mood which prevailed at the dinner table. Mrs. Roth had waited patiently until late evening and the conclusion of the interview, at which time this equable woman of Anglo-Saxon stock served us a superb meal consisting of well-known staples and delicacies of the Jewish cuisine. That in turn brought on reminiscences from Henry Roth about his childhood on the Lower East Side. At one point Mrs. Roth spoke of the travels abroad she and her husband have undertaken in the last few years and remarked with a touch of humor, "Henry is a poor traveler. As soon as he gets somewhere he wants to settle down for good."

Daniel Walden (essay date Summer 1979)

SOURCE: "Henry Roth's *Call It Sleep*: Ethnicity, "The Sign," and the Power," in *Modern Fiction Studies*, Vol. 25, No. 2, Summer, 1979, pp. 268-72.

[*In the following essay, Walden discusses David's quest for peace and a sign from God in Roth's* Call It Sleep.]

Henry Roth's *Call It Sleep,* justifiably called one of the great achievements in American writing in this century, was Roth's only novel, a tour de force composed of equal parts of sensitive writing, deep psychological insights, and great ethnic empathy. It was a profound study of an American slum childhood, suggestive of the Great Russians, wrote Lewis Gannett. It revealed more of the actual conditions of living in New York's East Side than any other book extant, said Horace Gregory. Above all, Kenneth Burke said, the book dealt fluently with the psychological phenomena of orientation and rebirth. To me, it is all these, but it is also a book that deals successfully and penetratingly with the traumas of dislocation, the problems of the "New Immigrants" as they were Americanized, and the conditions (especially in the 1920s) of a country tied to industrialism, electricity, energy, power, and disillusionment.

Call It Sleep is very much an autobiographical novel, written in what might have been a state of possession. While working on it from 1929 to 1933 Roth saw that he was in "a sort of general mystical state. I had a sense about the unifying force of some power I neither knew nor had to bother to know," he wrote. "It was part of having been an orthodox Jew," he thought. For at base all he was trying to do was to understand his childhood and what had happened to him. Having felt he was an outcast, having come from a cultural past he felt more than he knew, he had to find relief and release when placed in a present he wanted to understand but could not.

Born in 1906 in a little town in Galicia, to Herman and Leah Roth, Henry was brought to America when he was eighteen months old. His father had arrived earlier to earn money to bring his family over. Unfortunately because Henry's birth date was questioned—it was perfectly natural in the Old Country not to keep records—and Herman was already unhappy in the New World, the intra-familial strife that was to grow was present from that moment. In Henry's eyes his father was a most unadmirable little guy; in a short story in 1969 he called him "a little old dwarf in a baggy pair of pants." His mother, however, who doted on him, was both contemplative and anxiety-ridden, qualities that were given to Genya and Bertha in the book.

At first the Roths lived in Brownsville, but two years later, in 1910, they moved to East Ninth Street, on Manhattan's Lower East Side. Recalling those years, Roth said that he was surrounded by a "homogeneous environment" and "completely identified with it." In that atmosphere of devoutness, orthodoxy, and community, "it would not have occurred to anyone to question the dietary regulations or the observance of holiday rituals." Four years later when the family moved to Harlem it produced an anxiety in him from which he never recovered. The homogeneous environment, in a sense duplicating the life of the shtetl from which they had come, meant a consensus way of living in which almost all the Jews thought alike, dressed alike, ate alike, and reacted alike. Suddenly removed to Harlem, to be near Henry's grandparents, uncles and aunts, he was unceremoniously thrown into a multi-ethnic neighborhood made up of Italians, Irish, and Jews from all over. (In *Call It Sleep,* however, the fictive Lower East Side was made up of a Jewish ghetto that combined the homogeneity of the Lower East Side with the disharmonious elements of Harlem.) The impressionable Henry, who knew he was a Jew but who had progressed in cheder only to the point where he could read Hebrew by pronouncing the letters, was affected by the forces of Americanization. As Roth put it much later, "Continuity was destroyed when [my] family moved from snug, orthodox 9th street, from the homogeneous East Side to rowdy, heterogeneous Harlem. . . . And once continuity was destroyed, there would always be a sense of loss afterward, an insecurity." Like many first and second generation immigrants he badly wanted to blend into the environing fabric. "I wanted to adapt to this gentile Irish neighborhood," he remembered, "in the shortest time possible, and one of the conditions for adapting was to get away from Judaism." A few years later, while at New York University and living with his English teacher Eda Lou Walton, twelve years his senior, he admitted that he had paid a price. "In *Call It Sleep,*" wrote Roth, "I stuck with the child, so I didn't have to mature. And I was being supported by Eda Lou, so I didn't have to mature."

While a freshman at New York University, in 1925, Roth wrote a paper in an English class titled "Impressions of a Plumber." After detailing the events of the day in the life of a plumber's helper, he placed the youth on a subway and then described those parts of the day that were due to the system's influence. As the helper looked around him, he saw that "Grim toil has graven on their faces his trademark." When the factory whistle blew, it made a long "Toooooot." And when the boss came around to check up on the workers, the youth hoped he would trip on the steps of the ladder and hurt himself. In the mind of the helper, "He is the boss; I am the laborer."

Roth, like most immigrants, desperately wanted to be an American but couldn't entirely escape the pull of the past. "Like so many first generation American Jewish youth, I had already come to dissociate from family, Judaism, the whole thing—and to embrace the American scene, the American attitudes." But, he went on, "I couldn't bridge my background. I was able to speak glibly enough at the cocktail party level, but as far as digesting what was going on, especially in the literary world, it just didn't sink in. My whole orientation was to try to understand my own childhood, my own background."

Having written and published this one story, in which the conditions of the working man and the influence of the industrial system were mixed, Roth now began to write *Call*
It Sleep. In the grip of the disillusionment, technocracy, and shattering values of the late 1920s and early 1930s, reminiscent of the traumas, the Social Darwinism, the psychic crisis, and the significance of power at the turn of the century, he sought himself—he sought to find himself—in the tension, problems, and writing of *Call It Sleep.*

It seems obvious that *Call It Sleep* was a novel by a Jew manqué about the Jewish experience early in this century. On a more basic level, however, it was a novel about the travails and neuroses of the immigrant generation in a particular cultural context. It was also a novel about the varieties and persistence of ethnicity in the age of energy.

Let me spell out what I mean. First, here are several examples of ethnicity affected by Americanization. 1) In the beginning, David's speech is pure Yiddish and halting English. By the end of Part One, "The Cellar," his Yiddish is more than half English according to his mother. On the other hand, his father, mother, and Aunt Bertha continue to speak fluent Yiddish, but a heavily accented, ungrammatical English. The forces of acculturation did not work evenly. 2) Although *Call It Sleep* is an American novel it conveys its most important motifs by reference to the past. a) After meeting Genya and David at the boat, it was David's clothes that drew the father's ire. Albert, moving toward becoming an American, picked on the most overt sign of the child's affect. His "distinctly foreign costume" with its "odd, outlandish blue straw hat" marked David a new arrival. b) When Albert, the father, introduced David to his countryman, Luter, he pointed to David, saying, "And that over there is what will pray for me after my death." Albert knew that Luter understood the reference. Albert, unhappy with his son, regretted that the old tradition would be carried out by such a one as "that." c) When Aunt Bertha described her father, she evoked the medieval, Eastern European Jewish past. "His praying," she explained, "was an excuse for his laziness. As long as he prayed he didn't have to do anything else. . . . A pious Jew with a beard—who dared ask more of him? Work? God spare him. He played the lotteries." In the old country, it was enough for a man to study the Torah. In the New World, a man had to work, to achieve, to make a success. d) Lastly, the reference to the past is especially noted in Genya's aside to Albert when she enrolled David in the Hebrew School. As for his learning what it means to be a Jew, she said, "I think he knows how hard that is already." e) Finally, and how with reference to the forces of electricity and efficiency deified in the 1920s, when David, beset by problems too great for a child to either comprehend or overcome, looked for a sign, i.e., a way out, it was in Isaiah that he found it. Told by the Rabbi that an angel had used tongs to place a fiery coal on Isaiah's lips and thus cleansed him, David at first wondered about the story and then was impelled to duplicate it. As he plunged the metal dipper into the car tracks he kept repeating, "I gotta make it come out."

That is, now attempting to fuse the past with the electric present, he had to make the light, the power, the force, the cleansing agent, come to him and cleanse him.

It is this quest for personal peace, and a sign that would lead him to it, that is the driving force of the novel. Seeking his identity, initiated into manhood by Annie, who induced him to "play bad" and then take the blame for it, he was alienated by reason of being a Jew in a Christian multi-ethnic society. At the same time, his father represented terror and irrationality, and the society symbolized hostility and repression. With the coming of spring, however, he felt a new "sense of wary contentment, a curious pause in himself, as though he were waiting for some sign, some seal that would forever relieve him of watchfulness and forever insure his well-being." It was at cheder that he discovered what appeared to be the sign. When the lesson dealt with the pious, unclean Isaiah, who saw God in His majesty and His terrible light, David asked himself: "Why did he want to burn Isaiah's mouth with coal?" Was there some connection with his mother's explanation when he asked her who is God and she said that a pious old woman had once told her that "He was brighter than the day is brighter than the night." Was there a connection with the three antisemitic boys who, in cruelly showing him "magic," forced him to throw a sword into the car tracks? Terror stricken, David remembered, he rammed the sword into the slot, "like a tongue in an iron mouth."

> He stepped back. From open fingers, the blade plunged into darkness. Power. Like a paw ripping through all the stable fibres of the earth, power gigantic, fetterless, thudded into day. And light, unleashed, terrific light bellowed out of iron lips. The street quaked and roared, and like a tortured thing, the sheet zinc sword, leapt writhing, fell back, consumed with radiance. A moment later, he was spurting madly toward Avenue D.

In the Isaiah story God had touched Isaiah's lips with the fiery coal and said you're clean. His mother had said that God "has all power. He can break and rebuild, but He holds." And now out of the iron lips of the car tracks he had witnessed, seen, both light and power.

Soon after, David broke into the cheder to get the Bible; "the blue book with the coal in it! The man and the coal!" was what he was after. Of course, this was all incomprehensible to the Rabbi who caught him. But to David it was another step on the way to the sign, to finding his identity in an ethnic jungle in a technological maze.

At the end of the book, having suffered fear and terror too often, David fled. Instinct guiding him, he headed for the car tracks. Grabbing a metal milk dipper on the way, he kept muttering, "I gotta make it come out" and "in the crack be born." Straddling the sunken rail he braced his legs, held his breath, and "now the wavering point of the dipper's handle found the long, dark grinning lips, scraped, and like a sound in a scabbard—.... Plunged!" But nothing happened. He did it again, this time with his toe crooked into the dipper as into a stirrup. It grated, stirred, slid, and, to the accompaniment of someone else saying "Oy! Machine! Liberty! Revolt! Redeem!, he felt it—

> Power! Power like a paw, titanic power, ripped through the earth and slammed against his body and shackled him where he stood, *Power! Incredible, barbaric power!* A blast, a sren of light within him, rending, quaking, fusing his brain and blood to a fountain of flame, vast rockets in a searing spray! Power! The hawk of radiance raking him with talons of fire, battering his skull with a beak of fire, braying his body with pinions of tolerable light. And he writhed without motion in the clutch of a fatal glory, and his brain swelled and dilated till it dwarfed the galaxies in a bubble of refulgence—Recoiled, the last screaming nerve clawing for survival. He kicked—once. Terrific rams of darkness collided; out of their shock space toppled into havoc. A thin scream wobbled through the spirals of oblivion, fell like a brand on water, his-s-s-s-ed—.

What had happened? After he was revived his mother asked him, what made you go? What made you do it? His only answer, "I don't know, mama," was true. As a child of seven, gripped by fear and terror and guilt, common to so many then, but beyond his comprehension, he sought the "sign," the "light," the force that God touched Isaiah with and made him clean and pure and innocent and burden-free. He sought the sign in order to be reborn. As an outcast, in an age of power, electricity, and industrialism, between 1925 and 1933, he believed that the Biblical image would fuse with the all-powerful symbols of the environing community. Somehow he knew, instinctively, that as darkness met light, it was "only toward sleep that every wink of the eyelids could strike a spark into the cloudy tinder of the dark, kindle out of shadowy corners of the bedroom such myriad and such vivid jets of images," including the "open palms of legions upon legions of hands hurtling toward him." It was only toward sleep that pain and terror were replaced by the "strangest triumph, strangest acquiescence." David had found the sign. David had found a peace.

Henry Roth with William Freedman (interview date Fall 1979)

SOURCE: "Henry Roth in Jerusalem: An Interview," in *The Literary Review,* Vol. 23, No. 1, Fall, 1979, pp. 5-23.

[*In the following interview, Roth discusses the mystical element in* Call It Sleep, *and describes his relationship to Israel.*]

Five years ago, when I first met Henry Roth, it was in the same but in a very different place. He had come to Israel, then as now, on a kind of pilgrimage, an artist's search for the history and possibilities of self, but he had taken a different route. Having turned down a variety of invitations and offers of special treatment in order, as he put it, to avoid commitment and obligation, Roth had attached himself to a charter flight hired for a Hadassah group tour and was staying, when he called me, in Haifa's distinctly second-best hotel. It was a flight from expectation, of self and by others, that in a way, though I neglected to investigate it at the time, threatened the goal.

When I met him in September, 1977, Roth was staying, at the government's invitation, in Mishkenot Shaananim, Jerusalem's fine and fancy guest-artist's residence where Pablo Casals, Saul Bellow, Isaac Stern and Heinrich Böll had stayed before him. Five years ago, when we spoke on the telephone and arranged our meeting, Roth had just returned from an enervating all-day bus tour to the Golan Heights and warned me that I might be wasting my time, that he might have nothing to say. He was wrong then, impressively, thumpingly wrong, and somewhere in that five-year interim he had learned that much about himself and very much more. He seemed more open, better pleased and more comfortable with both of us when he received me at the door to his apartment, and within a quarter hour he suggested we begin taping. He had been interviewed frequently since his arrival at the end of summer and used these interviews for expression and discovery. He had something to say, to himself and others, and would learn what he had to say to himself by speaking to others. I spoke almost as much as he did during our interview in 1972, filling spaces and responding to questions with my own readings, impressions and interpretations. This time my questions were almost interruptions. Roth, who had accepted obligations, had his own.

[*Freedman:*] *I want to begin by working with the contrast between the framework of this visit and that of the last, when we did our first interview five years ago. The last time you came, in '72 if I remember correctly, you turned down offers for a special arrangement and came, oddly I thought, on a Hadassah tour. You insisted on that. You really wanted to do it middle class.*

[Roth:] Middle class, and without any commitments to any institution, person or state whatever. Just as if I were a completely free individual, coming here to see for himself what

it was like and what kind of impression he got out of it, if any. I wanted no sense of being obligated in the least because I felt it might inhibit me, especially if I thought this place was impossible. In the end, I think the impressions of Israel, although they were considerable, were less lasting than that of the Hadassah group itself.

Of course, whether Israel impressed me favorably or not, it's difficult to say. What did we see after all? We saw the great historical sights, the biblical sights, and very little of actual Israeli life. So the first impression is that of a tourist seeing the Church of the Nativity or seeing Masada, etc. But later on I subscribed to the Jerusalem *Post,* so evidently, in the very fact that I did so, the interest per se continued. And then I felt that if I were going to do anything about this revived interest and involvement, I really ought to join the Jewish community in Albuquerque—which was quite a step, I must say. I wanted to see what they were doing about Israel and try to join efforts with them. So ultimately I joined the Israeli subcommittee of the J.C.C.—Jewish Community Council. And it was very Jewish and very diaspora. Muriel [Mrs. Roth] was good enough to come along too; she became the secretary of the subcommittee, the Israeli subcommittee, as it was called. It was the most active of all. Some of the others, subgroups of the public relations committee and such, simply languished and fell apart. The most active was the Israeli subcommittee, which would indicate that it is central to Jewish thinking, even out in far off Albuquerque. At all events, my interest continued.

Did you really get involved in that community, in those activities?

Well, no. No, I didn't, though there was some socializing. Actually, I felt in Albuquerque, in the Jewish and Christian community—let me say it that way and be fair about it—I felt more at home than I'd felt anywhere in all these many years of wandering: Maine, New York, Boston. The west is open still. It still has some of that original openness, so there's a greater degree of friendliness. Through Muriel's music we were able to make friends in the gentile community and through my own efforts, in the Jewish community. We had all the social life we wanted, and it was very satisfactory. But the Israeli thing kept growing.

How about your sense of Jewish identity? Did you feel anything special, that you were making contact with something deep and important in yourself, when you began to make these other contacts?

That's a good question. The Jewish identity was cooking all the time. I think you can say, practically as a verity, that there has always been, for me at all events, in the diaspora, the inner sense that I am different, that there is a reservation, an ambivalence. I can go so far with you, and then I have a different gyroscope in me that orients differently.

What do you mean by "go so far with you"?

Well, I can hardly say what I mean by that, except that I would feel that boundary even with people with whom we enjoy great conviviality. My own interpretations seem always to have extensions in every direction that go beyond theirs. Either it was a compassion that went further than theirs, or it was some sort of introspection that they would stimulate within me, which I knew I couldn't communicate. Those are just two little examples, but there is that reserve, and despite the greatest of friendliness.

But while that was going on, the question and growth of my Jewishness, I was conducting, simultaneously, an interior dialogue between myself and the young man who wrote *Call It Sleep*—essentially a dialogue about what happened. Why didn't you go on, the old man would ask. You wrote a good novel, and obviously you've written what amounted to a self-fulfilling prophecy. You used as one of your chief symbols the short circuit, and you yourself are short-circuited. How did that come about? Why did you choose that theme? This is to give you an example of the kind of inner life you're leading even though outwardly you're married, have work to do, raise a family and so forth. The inner life is continually talking to the youth that was and was created, asking it questions and asking itself: Why can't you continue, and what would it take, or is there any possibility? Muriel and I had agreed there was no possibility, and a divorce, a real divorce took place. I tried to reconcile myself to it, but somehow or other you can't quite reconcile yourself to that. The dialogue goes on, this search for something that would again give you an opportunity to express yourself esthetically, in narrative form or on some level that is of some merit; and you look about for avenues that might allow this. There were none. I can say that very simply.

I recall reading an address that Bellow made to the Anti-Defamation League on the occasion of being awarded a medal for his contribution to democracy in the United States. The title of his piece was, "I Took Myself as I Was." Now there's a fortunate man. He could take himself as he was because he never went through this horrendous business of being an immigrant kid who was tremendously attracted to the Left, a member of the Communist Party who was thereby deflected almost completely and found that the deflection did not pay off in the literary sense. That person has to look for a new avenue which he can't find, having cut himself off from the diaspora which he doesn't want.

You're talking about yourself now.

I'm talking about myself. Bellow wrote his first novel, I think, around 1944. So he never went through that terrible trauma that many of us went through in the thirties, that swept Jewish intellectuals into this messianic, mystical kind of . . . trance (I was about to say) [laughs] . . . out of which *Call It Sleep* was written.

The book has that effect. It reads as though it were written under that kind of special influence.

It's a mystical, messianic grouping, a constellation, if you wish, and it's a constellation that didn't hold out. If you know anything about astronomy you know that in the course of time these various stars move about.

So you do see it as a kind of mystical book. I once began an article on the mysticism of **Call It Sleep** *and abandoned the idea as a bit fanciful.*

Yes. It's a religious continuation despite the individual who protested that he was not religious. It was an efflorescence followed by a wilting. Bellow's a fortunate man because he could take himself as he was. And if you take yourself as you are you can run a tremendous string of literary work. I think it was true of the Elizabethans, some of them. They took themselves as they were. They felt the society was stagnant, was going to stay that way forever, while they went on and on. Not only Shakespeare, but Webster and Turner and Fletcher and the whole caboodle. We were less fortunate. We went through this trauma, and I don't think, and I've said this before, that any of those of use who came of age in the thirties literarily—I can't speak for the whole field of art—seemed to be able to go on. The thirties were disabling, and we were all affected alike.

I can remember Eda Lou Walton saying, "Well, that one's too shallow," or "that one's run out of steam," and so on. But when it happens to you and you know you aren't that shallow, well then, it must be some kind of a social force that's at work. It would really make a good study, and I think some day it will: Jewish writers in the thirties and the proletarian novels they attempted to do.

Can you clarify for me exactly what you think the problem was, what caused the truncation? Was it the deflection into communism? The sense of being cut off from the diaspora? How did these forces work? How did they short-circuit the creative wires?

I can tell you this much—that in going into communism I found a character for a novel, began to write, wrote perhaps a hundred pages, and Scribner's and Maxwell Perkins accepted it. And then I was finished. Apparently I didn't want to go on, and this is part of the dialogue I hold with myself. Why didn't you want to go on? If I understand it correctly, it's a matter of maturity. I didn't want to go through this man's life, although he was a very colorful character. He had lost a hand, he was illiterate, and he had a very colorful way of expressing himself: really made to order. I wanted to do a character who finally realized you can't go it alone. He had once been quite a brawler, and when he was up against it, he didn't hesitate to commit armed robbery. But in the end he would see he wasn't enough, and he would join the Party. It looked good, but I didn't want to go into it. What Scribner's had accepted was the boyhood stage. Now I would have to do a whole section on his life as a young man, and then I'd have to go into his marriage, his kids, his jobs, his strikes, and so forth. That's why I say maturity. All that seemed to be a function of maturity, and I hadn't matured that way. I hadn't matured, period. I think that's an element. The fact that I was dependent on Walton all those years had in a sense been both very beneficial and very harmful.

So now you're offering personal as well as social reasons. You're not really seeing it in exclusively social terms. You also attribute the short-circuiting to your own personal history and composition.

What I'm saying is that they're interrelated and almost inextricable. You just can't take them apart. If I had been made to hit the grit of the Depression, and writing, let's say, was my livelihood, it would have been root, pig, or die, and I might have forced myself through that second novel and maybe gone on from there. Each one might have been worse than the one before, but I'd have gone on anyway—because of the Depression, because I had to.

Have you ever looked at it from the other side of the track, considered the possibility that the flight into communism, into ideology and affiliation, was a form of flight from a literary career that may have frightened you?

Now that's one. A literary career that scared me.

Perhaps something inside you quietly figured: "Maybe I can't do it again," or "It would be a hell of an effort to try it again. If I get myself involved in politics, I'll have an explanation for not going on."

Well, there may have been a subconscious factor there: Now you've become an activist, you don't have to write anymore. That sort of thing. But curiously enough I did attempt to write while being an activist, though I didn't get very far with it. I don't really know whether the deflection into communism was a fatal thing. I don't really know, because I can recall that while I was writing *Call It Sleep* and things seemed to be in a fairly stable state, I would get these promptings: Well, then the next thing you ought to do is take a child, or take a youth (you don't have to go back to childhood) from a ghetto and show his passage from his ghetto associations to a self-consciousness of literary ability, a pas-

sage, in more concrete terms, from the ghetto to Greenwich Village and to somebody like Walton. That seemed to be my next job.

You tried that too, didn't you?

I started it, but it didn't go. And when that didn't go and this other didn't go, then I seemed to be, as far as I was concerned . . . finished.

The failures shook you.

The two failures. They became self-generating, a further cause. The dying out of these things when I had already, I thought, become a disciplined writer, seemed to mark the end of my career. Then I though, well, now wait a minute; you can still force yourself to write small pieces on a high commercial level, for the *New Yorker,* or something. And I did for a while. But it was just too much like work—which is another indication that I was not a pro.

You weren't getting much satisfaction out of it either, were you? It was hack work for you.

Mostly. It was a great thing to get the money the *New Yorker* pays, but as far as that satisfaction a writer gets out of an inspired piece . . .

Which **Call It Sleep** *was; it really was.*

I think that the quality of intellect and analysis and all the rest of it that others had, or that I had, could not have produced *Call It Sleep* without the aid of some kind of inspiration.

Have you ever considered that your emotional roots may really be in childhood and that the electricity from you is somehow linked to, or grounded in, a child's mind or a child's emotional and imaginative life? Have you ever tried to write about a child again?

No, I never did, because I think that even in *Call It Sleep* I was trying to project a scenario of the inner life of the man who was doing the writing via what appealed to me as the most familiar, the easiest, the most accessible instrument, the child, using autobiographical experiences and everything else that goes into *Call It Sleep,* and rearranging them. But of course, at the same time, I was trying to build a structure out of it, an architecture of some kind. The narrative skill I had in abundance, an instinctive sense of narrative. So I drew from that particular period all that I needed, all the narrator wanted to build his particular literary edifice.

You say the book is about the inner life of the narrator, the adult author, yet he doesn't appear in the book at all. Not in that way, not as a character. Let me understand you here. Are you saying you intended the child to be read as a metaphor for the innocent, frightened, intimidated young adult of the thirties, for the author of the book who, like his contemporaries, would be short-circuited by the forces that drove and threatened him? If so, **Call It Sleep** *is not merely a non-proletarian novel. It's an artist's fear of the proletarian novel, of everything that led to its ascendancy and of what those forces and that ascendancy might do to him: the short circuit. I doubt the book has ever been understood in quite that way.*

The narrator of **Call It Sleep** was both naive and complex. Naive as far as recognizing, in ideological terms, the symbolic latency of the central character. He probably wouldn't have written the novel, wouldn't have been capable of it, if he had recognized it. He tried to create with all intensity the yarn of an immigrant childhood, but the factual is at extreme variance with the fable. The author never again experienced the security and happiness of the East Side ghetto. Why then all the anxieties, the fears, the intimations of apocalypse? Because those currents were continually in the author's ambience; they permeated his psyche. Hitler was already on the horizon, together with my own fears which I didn't formulate but which were there nonetheless. And there was a great Depression going on at the same time. Also, before I was through, I developed a fear of communism itself, of the demands it would make on what I regarded as my type of sloppy character and mind, on someone who was impractical and not given to militance or to arousing militance in others: there's always Joe out there with his stern demands. By the time I was through, I realized this was something I had been afraid of, though I'd never told anyone. It was to project those peculiar fears and strains into the novel that I injected Irish or goyish Harlem into the East Side—at the expense of actuality.

How long were you associated with the Party?

I joined at the very beginning of '34 and stayed on a couple of years. And then I dropped out, only to rejoin it when Hitler began to move. Of course I was shaken by the Russo-German pact, but I tried to justify it. That was very important. I knew nothing about the execution of Jewish writers, and whenever I heard anything . . . I mean I was really . . . what's the right word for it?

Insistently naive?

I could justify and defend it on any damn grounds whatever. And as I look back I feel as if I'm as guilty—well, not quite, but that I share in a certain amount of guilt for what happened there to the Jewish writers, because I approved, so to speak, of what was happening in general. And whenever some shocking revelation surfaced, something involving

Jews like Zinoviev, Kamenev and others, people who were really great leaders at one time and who were executed, and when Trotsky was driven out, I applauded it. I condemned "the counter-revolution." I went along with the herd. It's terrible.

Did you feel comfortable with it at the time, or did the guilt accompany the applause?

No, I never felt comfortable with it, but I couldn't create out of it either. I was not only uncreative literarily; I was not creative *in* it, as a political person. I was just one of the inert members who gave his approval.

Then you weren't at home in the Party either?

I wasn't at home. There's a difference between what I felt then and the identification I feel now, with Israel. When I speak of Israel there is always a tendency to bring the identity issue in and a tendency to try to stimulate the non-Jewish community out there in Albuquerque to do more than it does. So there's really quite a difference. In the one I seem to be alive, and in the other I was really inert.

The recurrent biographical theme, as I hear it, is the search for a home.

You asked about the roots in boyhood or childhood. It's very pertinent. I couldn't go back to another childhood. I did one, the one Scribner's accepted, in an entirely different environment, the middle west. I think the key word here is continuity. The roots were there but they had nowhere to continue. I had cut myself off from the diaspora. I disapproved of much, if not most of the diaspora. I cut off the religious aspect of it. The kids I grew up with simply repelled me because they were doing what they were taught to do: drive as hard as possible towards success. It was almost completely mercenary, and most of the diaspora that I came to know, including my own relatives, were doing the same thing. So there was nowhere to go from that childhood. Had I remained on the East Side, there would have been a development. But I was taken away at the age . . . taken away I say; my family moved when I was eight and a half, just short of going into *Chumush* and the other great religious texts. Had I remained there, in that homogeneous society—there again, there's the old man asking the young man, "What would you have done?" And I think that while I probably wouldn't have written **Call It Sleep,** I might have been able to run a string of books, with a less apocalyptic end, had I remained in a Jewish community and seen what the development of a youth is in that kind of community.

How do you talk to that young man when you talk to him? Is it strictly in terms of this one question, or do you have other questions to ask him?

Mostly it's in terms of that one question, since it's such a deep-seated thing. The creativity of the individual is so deep-seated that to cut it off like that creates a profound shock. It's a kind of trauma that sets up a polarity. I began to feel, and I now almost certainly feel, as if we were two individuals.

Do you feel emotionally identified with that person? Is there still an intimate bond of some sort between you, or are you speaking to someone else when you question him?

I don't feel emotionally identified with him. He was cut off, and there's a vast gap and a vast bridge to be crossed. The only continuity between us is this identity I now have with Israel.

I had always missed that, felt the need for the identity and continuity that Eliot, for example, had found in his commitments. As I said in this little article of mine in the January 1977 *Midstream*—and this may represent the first awakening of the literary ability in the new dispensation—Eliot had gone through a transformation by accepting Classicism, Royalism and Anglo-Catholicism; and I thought: the lucky bastard! But that sort of thing was absolutely beyond me, impossible. There was no outlet for me, at least not until the '67 war. But even before that war I was in a way crystallizing. I was beginning to become curious about this place; and then the war seemed to crystallize it. From then on I realized I had bridged this awful chasm, this awful discontinuity, by the identification with Israel. And this continuity made another possible. I could feel, arising again, a kind of literary urge. But it takes quite a while, at least for my slow kind of mind, to move from commitment to its literary expression. I began to write in a rather confused and haphazard way about what I did feel—about what communism meant to me, what I felt about Israel, and so forth. I have the notebook somewhere, and I imagine that will become part of the raw material for what I expect to write.

But what the war and the newly solidified identity did most was to liberate the youthful period. That may be both ambiguous and interesting. It liberated me to examine and write about the whole youthful sexual awakening in relation to Walton, which I had previously felt inadequate for. The kind of thing I did, the kind of person she was—I just felt completely unable to treat that sort of thing. Maybe what I'm representing or attempting to represent is not Walton, but there is a character there.

So that's the book you're working on now?

Yes, and it will be different. I can no longer depend on a linear narrator; too much is happening. But I think I can deal with the diaspora youth leaving his Judaism, or attempting to, trying to get as far away from it as possible. And then,

against that, the old man, in a counter movement, reuniting, because returning is impossible, reuniting with a Judaism in the form it has taken now in the state of Israel.

So the book would span these forty years or so.

Yes. And there would be, I hope, a kind of double movement taking place not quite simultaneously—because you can't do that—but with narrative on the one hand, on the other expositions about the author's views of certain things, or reports of certain conversations. That's the kind of book it will be.

Have you ever thought of writing the story that in effect you just began to tell me, the story of this dialogue itself, the one that centers on the question, Why didn't you go on?

I think that's part of it. You see, you write the narrative, but when you're dealing with the old man again you can treat it as a dialogue then. He can ask the question, What happened? even in the midst of one of these subcommittee meetings. To him all his past, all that he can recall, is contemporaneous.

I was thinking of a book in which the dialogue on that one question would be more central, the focal point and dramatic force in a work of its own.

I really don't know how it's going to come out, but what I see before me is that kind of thing: the intervention in the narrative of the old man and the queries he puts to himself, or what he attempts to do at some particular time, or a letter he may write in protest of, let's say, some editorial. I suppose this may be somewhat Herzogian, but his letters are sent; these things are done in the recognition of his shortcomings, and they have practical consequences.

OK, but one thing is still not quite clear to me. Exactly what is it that Israel has been or done to you to make you feel and respond this way? Where does this re-stimulating power derive from? Can you pin it down?

That's a damn good question. What did Israel do to me? Well, that guy Eliot must have known he was at the end of his rope, that unless he found a way to regenerate himself he was through as a poet. So he found a way.

So you see his political and religious choices as basically literary decisions.

As basically literary decisions. This was what he had to do if he was going to regain his coherence and his literary expression. I had no such vehicle. What I saw was that I had been continually looking for something in the nature of a regeneration, but scarcely realizing it. And then came the '67 war with its preliminary fears, that terrible pall, and then the sense that Israel was holding her own, better; and then the cease-fires, one after another, and what seemed like a total victory evaporating all those fears. So I said to myself, What the hell are you waiting for? This is a people that is regenerating itself, and in battle too, and you'd have to be out of your mind not to go along with this regeneration. Perhaps this is the equivalent of Eliot's regeneration.

And this too you saw as a basically literary decision?

I saw it as a literary decision. I think that is what Israel means to me. I'm not coming here to help Israel in any way or to contribute anything at all, except inadvertently, in cash.

You came here to redeem yourself.

I came here because I feel it is a necessary element in my own writing.

In a letter you wrote to Harold Ribalow, which he printed in his introduction to the Pageant edition of **Call It Sleep** *back around 1960, you said, "I had one theme, redemption, but I haven't the fable." What you're saying now, if I understand you correctly, is, "That is still my theme, but now perhaps I've found a fable to carry it."*

That's a very good point. I think redemption still is my theme; and in this case perhaps not so much the redemption of the individual soul, but of the writer.

Well, how is Israel doing as a redeemer?

I came here with no expectations of utopia. After all, I'd had a look at it before. What I came here for was, again, to get the material that will make for a construct, an edifice. And I think it will. I really think it will.

Where are you getting this literary injection from? From the concept of Israel as a Jewish nation? From the geography? From the people? The military victory?

A little of everything. It's a question of guessing at what you want and then going out to find it. It's not the other way around, where the experiences make for some kind of fusion in literary form. I think the fusion has already taken place, and I think it has something in common with *Call It Sleep.* That was a very Jewish book; all the elements in it are very Jewish, and yet it was written by somebody who no longer felt Jewish. He simply went out and got the material, the components for his architecture. And I think I feel the same way now. It's hardly the sort of thing someone else would come here to look for.

You feel as though you're exploiting Israel a little, don't you?

I'm self-interested. I think that's really a very good sign—that you have a definite self-interest in a particular place, and in a place like Israel in particular. Being here I can see how I can play off one thing against the other—Israel and the youth, his movement towards Greenwich Village and his movement away from it. I can see that. Whether it comes out that way or not I can't say.

I guess that's what I really wanted to know. I know what Eliot got out of Anglo-Catholicism, or at least I think I know some of the benefits he derived from it: authority, tradition, a warehouse of symbols. What are the equivalents here? What are you taking out of Israel that's equivalent to what Eliot mined from orthodoxy?

It probably will not be on that level at all. What I take from here is contrapuntal, a counterpoint between the young man who comes to literary consciousness and who is continually moving away from Judaism and the old man who had to come back, not just to come back but to reunite with it in some way in order to redeem the literary abilities that went to sleep in the youth.

Do you identify a reuniting with Israel with a reunion with Judaism?

I think this is all that Judaism means to me now. I don't think the Judaism of the diaspora is vital anymore. I think Judaism's next stage, whatever it's going to be, is probably here, in this country. Israel, for all its conflicts, inequities, treadmill, errors, and vicissitudes—the quotidian, in short—represents to me both the regeneration of Judaism and its future. And only Israel does. The diaspora may be far more pleasant in creature comfort and such, but only Israel is the state of the Jews. An irreducible value. I've received letters from people in Israel telling me, "You don't have to be religious here. We do the traditional things." But I can't see doing the traditional things unless I'm really communing with some Being or other as I did when I was a child.

The need for miracle again?

Yes, but today they seem to be mainly military. First '67. Then the revival after the first days of the war in '73.

But do you think these wars are anything but postponements? How many wars do you think we can sustain? How many miracles, if that's what they are, can we expect or hope for?

I don't know. I really don't know, and maybe we are doomed in one way or the other. But I know we're damn clever, given the emergency. If we could pull off an Entebbe, and time it to the split second almost, for all I know we could take their oil wells away from them before they woke up to what was happening. So now we're big oil magnates. I don't know. Fantasies go through your mind. You're so identified with the state and its survival you're willing to try anything. That's really what it amounts to. You get a Begin and you say, "O.K., I'm willing to try this guy. If he can get us out of this alive, then I can't deny him even though I don't like his politics. And the same goes for [General Ariel] Sharon. The canal crossing was a marvelous military achievement. So who am I to say this dream of yours is a fruitcake?

Perhaps this all ties in. Perhaps what I'm hearing from you now is a reflection of the same mysticism that energized **Call It Sleep,** *the same belief, the same quest for redemption at a preternatural source.*

Damn it all, I don't know. Apparently that is the one great theme of my life, and nothing else would do. And why is that? I think you put your finger on it. That childhood indoctrination, that childhood formation, the childhood religiosity which nothing will satisfy except a similar, an analogous thing.

So you see Israel being touched by God the way Isaiah was, and you hope somehow to absorb a little of the power by making contact at the other end, with the fingers of Adam's other hand.

I'm a man who proclaims that he's without a religious belief, but when I look at that proclamation I say, "No." Reading Victor Frankel's book, *Man's Search for Meaning,* was really an eye-opener because he adds to the Freudian classification of instincts two more: an artistic instinct and an instinct towards the transcendental. I feel it as a kind of tectonic thing, plates sliding against other plates. I feel the religious urge is part of the intuitive structure.

Yeats described himself as a religious man deprived of his religion, and he became a mystically inclined occultist, if not quite a mystic in the orthodox sense. Does that in any way describe you as well?

I think that's who the author of **Call It Sleep** was: the religious man without a religion who becomes a kind of mystic, with an accretion of communist ideas. And now you have it again, but it's late in the game so I can't guarantee anything. There is the same mysticism, I'm sure, and now it has to tax itself here.

With the same kind of almost magical belief in the power of the state.

Well, I don't know if it's the power of the state or the power of this people in this land. I really don't mean a state. The power of this people in this land is really where it taxes itself. So what you're seeing is what no one has brought out of me before: the continuity of that theme, the stream that still requires a redemptive, mystical association for it to flow. That's what infuses **Call It Sleep** and gives people a kind of religious charge. Some have an almost worshipful attitude towards it.

It has something in common with Invisible Man *in that sense. Ellison also wrote an inspired and a religious book without orthodoxy, and he ran into the same blank wall.*

The same wall. I don't know what his regeneration will be, if he ever achieves it. In my case it's the strain that goes all through Judaism, the prophetic and mystical element. I do think this is what Israel aroused again.

Had you formulated that to yourself before?

No, I think your questions brought it out. That's why I thought I'd like to tape this—because it causes me to attempt to articulate what's happening. And I think you got something here that did not appear and won't appear in any other correspondence: the recognition in me that this is some kind of a conditioning, for lack of a better word. And like other conditionings this alone seems to be able to trigger the profound literary or artistic impulse. When that isn't there, I could probably force myself, and have forced myself to write *New Yorker* stuff, and made some dough. But I was never really involved in that kind of writing.

All right, I'm going to leave this. I want to ask you one other question and change the subject, though perhaps not. Perhaps this too ties in. You seem to me quite different than you were when we met in '72. I mean this very personally and in a very positive way. You seem much more open, more sure of yourself. Accepting the invitation to Mishkenot Shaananim may be a sign of that. Five years ago you didn't want any commitments, partly, I think, because you weren't sure you could meet them. You weren't sure you would live up to expectations. I think you're no longer afraid because you know who you are, what you have to say and what you have to offer. Even honors have become acceptable because, well, you feel you've earned them.

I don't know about deserving honor, but I can now accept it without being thrown off balance or swayed by it or by all the attention I've received. I think you're observing very well. I do feel a much greater certitude. It's too bad it happened so late in life.

What did you say the theme of Bellow's speech was when he was awarded the medal?

He said, "I took myself as I was."

You seem to me to be approaching that kind of acceptance yourself.

I'm taking myself as I am now, but I certainly didn't take myself as I was. I was nothing, so there was nothing for me to take. Bellow took himself as he was and he was satisfied, apparently, with himself. And God knows, why shouldn't he be? He's a Nobel laureate. But being satisfied also has its disadvantages. You can also stop growing in that kind of an attitude, stop that struggle that goes on and on on, I know, in the best of us.

Well, anyway . . . [Muriel enters] . . . HERE COMES ME WIFE, THE IDOL OF ME LIFE!!!

Richard J. Fein (essay date Fall 1984)

SOURCE: "Fear, Fatherhood, and Desire in *Call It Sleep*," in *Yiddish*, Vol. 5, No. 4, Fall, 1984, pp. 49-54.

[*In the following essay, Fein discusses David Schearl's enmity with his father in Roth's* Call It Sleep.]

Call It Sleep is a classic portrayal of the Americanized son who pits himself against the unyielding immigrant father. In an orthodox but dramatic Freudian fashion that never succumbs to a mechanical pattern (and is as moving as Lawrence's rendition of this conflict in *Sons and Lovers*), David Schearl finds his enemy in his father.

Henry Roth's *Call It Sleep* portrays a father who looms as an impregnable tower of energy to his son, the conflict beginning even before the child is conscious of the struggle. David Schearl sees his father as a figure of wrath. He dreams of his father lifting a hammer against people, an image he derives from the knowledge that his father once lost a job for threatening a fellow worker with a hammer. People at the father's former place of employment speak in the boy's presence of his father being crazy, and one man jokingly and sympathetically remarks that the son and the father are like David and Goliath.

The eyes of the father, with their suggestion of uncontrollable energy, haunt the boy throughout the book. David sees those eyes, that "unrelaxed visage," as raging, burning, blazing, glaring, glowering, consuming, smouldering, wrathful, judgmental, and sombre. (Only at the end, significantly, do the father's eyes change.) The father's eyelids are almost always heavy. The eyes of David and his mother Genya, in contrast, are usually described as passively troubled. David's daily encounters with his father are worse than bad dreams; they strike terror into the heart of the child.

The father's body also leaves a powerful impression on the boy. At one point David comes home shortly after his father has risen and concentrates on his father's naked chest while the large man is drying a razor after shaving. David is impressed anew by his father's chest, his muscular arms, and his handsome face. His father is like some powerful local chieftain or god—a god feared and envied but not loved. The father refers to himself as the angel of death and is a force the son cannot conquer or propitiate. Surrounded by the twin fears of the father and darkness, the child seeks a realm of power and light with which he can offset those fears. David Schearl seeks mastery of his soul, control of his world—not to be victim, not to twinge in docility. To exaggerate in terms consonant with remarks made by Roth, David seeks to escape the impotence of his diaspora childhood.

The unpropitiable father in Jewish-American fiction—Anzia Yezierska also offers a dramatic example—gives way to the more sedate father in the fiction of Delmore Schwartz and the other Roth. The authoritarian father of Jewish-American fiction diminishes as the process of embourgeoisement intensifies.

Roth powerfully and delicately registers the boy's sense of the potent-envied-enemy-father in the scene in which David comes home and sees a strange, calm countenance on his mother's face. Her languidness and the quietude of the scene puzzle and frustrate the child. His father is asleep, his new white-handled whip lying near an open package and crisscrossing the handle of the older black whip, broken in a fight with a derelict who stole some bottles from his milkwagon. Genya does not greet her son with outstretched arms as she usually does. David's obvious bewilderment causes his mother to suppose that he wants to ask for the handle of the broken whip. But he shakes off this idea (disturbed by the recent use of the whip against the derelict, an incident his father insists he not reveal to his mother). David is interested in the wooden plaque wrapped in the paper, a plaque on which are mounted the horns of a bull, a token of the time his father raised bulls and cows in Europe, work of which he was manfully proud. The child is struck by the shield-shaped plaque on which

> two magnificent horns curved out and up, pale yellow to the ebony tips. So wide was the span between them he could almost have stretched his arms out on either side, before he could touch them. Though they lay there inertly, their bases solidly fastened to the dark wood, there pulsed from them still a suggestion of terrific power, a power that even while they lay motionless made the breast ache as though they were ever imminent, ever charging.

David then thinks of a picture his mother previously hung

on the wall, a picture of corn flowers that he imperfectly understands is associated in her mind with a love affair she had in Austria before she married and came to America. David ponders both the picture and the plaque, wondering "why was it that two things so remote from each other seemed to have become firmly coupled in his mind?" His thoughts drift back to the derelict "outstretched on the sidewalk, that mysterious look of repose in his mother's face when he had come in. Why? . . . He sensed only that in the horns, in the poised power of them lay a threat, a challenge he must answer, he must meet. But he didn't know how." The sexual and physical prowess of the father vaguely overtakes his mind, making him feel unequal to the father's presence. David is like his biblical counterpart come to live with an angry, unapproachable, and bitterly regal Saul he does not know how to comfort, how to appease, but whose family and power he seeks to be a part of.

The passion for energy goes beyond the boy's relationship to his father. This concern appears in David's fear of the tyrannical melamed and the cheder he attends. Through his experiences there, his fascination for power and energy takes on a religious dimension.

Ultimately it is a religious concern that the book is dealing with, a theme covertly conveyed through the classic conflict of child and father. The father's unassailable strength, the rabbi's vituperative authority, the puzzling arts of gang-freedom so confusingly practiced in the street, the introduction to sex by a lame girl with metal braces in a dark closet, the old fear of dark cellars—all of these swarm through the boy's mind and are suddenly transformed as he hears the rabbi tell the story of the angel who brought a coal of fire to Isaiah's lips in order to make Isaiah clean and worthy of being God's spokesman. David is fascinated by the image of the coal that brings a worthy light and cleansing experience to the prophet. Caught up in his own sense of sin and helplessness and fear, David longs for this state of purity, for this undefiled energy. Suddenly, to the amazed child, God is light, God is power; and perhaps he, David, in imitation of Isaiah, can overcome the sense that he was "hedged in by two fears, the dark and his father."

His sense of God and light is further advanced when, after bringing home a penny from the rabbi for having memorized the Passover song of the goat (a song that culminates in the assertion of a brutal and divine energy in the world), he asks his mother about God. She tells him God is light and he holds the world. In reply to his wondering if God could break the world, Genya explains, "Of course. He has all power. He can break and rebuild, but he holds." Then David's father enters the room, ending all other possible questions. Wondering why they are sitting in the dark, the father calls for more light. Throughout the novel, the child seeks his own

realm of light, as opposed to the realm dominated by the father.

At the docks later, David has a vision that metamorphoses the city landscape. In this vision, the city at the edge of the water is transformed into an environment of light into which, for a moment, the child's sense of sin and fear is suffused.

It is after his risky Isaiah-like vision while looking in the East River that David is forced by some East Side tough to throw a zinc sword into a slot between the trolley car tracks, setting off a flash of light. Frightened and excited, David runs back and sneaks into the cheder, looking for the book that contains the passage about the fiery coal. But when he tells the rabbi that on Tenth Street between the car tracks he has seen a light like that of Isaiah's coal, Reb Pankower (no Hasid, and certainly no reader of Whitman or Blake) only mocks the boy's vision: "Go beat your head on a wall!" he instructs the child, "God's light is not between car-tracks."

The child longs for light, for escape from the dark he associates with the cellar of a previous house in which he lived and that dark closet in which lame Annie introduced him to some obscure flap within her body. He imagines that redeeming light in the coal brought to Isaiah and in the powerful glow between the tracks—and also in a picture of Jesus and the Sacred Heart that he sees on the wall of a friend's house, Leo Dugovka. (Roth is sharp in rendering the fascinating poetic exoticness, especially to a child, of the objects or details of somebody else's religion.) David is impressed both by the dish of light above the bearded figure and the glow from within his exposed heart. "Gee! He's light inside and out, ain' he?" David wonders, his street dialect different in rhythm but not in admiring content from John Milton's praise three centuries earlier: "That glorious Form, that Light unsufferable, and that far-beaming blaze of Majesty." For the innocent and untutored Jewish child, the discovery of a pre-Christian Jesus can be a revelation unappreciated by dulled Christians and impervious Jewish elders. This fascination of Jewish writers with a prelapsarian Jesus (that is, before he fell to the Christians) is an intriguing footnote to modern Jewish thought.

The light of Christ and Isaiah and the flash from the car tracks merge in the boy's mind. These are also related to the rosary beads he gets from Leo as payment for his willingness to lead Leo to the dark cellar of his aunt's candy store, where Leo and Esther play together in the fashion of Annie in the closet. Although he is anxious to receive the beads, David feels guilty over what he has done and longs for the light of redemption, for escape from sin, for escape from the inscrutable darkness of will that others impose upon his weak self.

All of this climaxes with David's escape from his angry father, who has discovered the beads and the story of David's involvement with Leo and Esther—a Lower East Side, juvenile, and vulgar version of the mother's premarital affair—or perhaps even a Lower East Side distortion of an earlier Esther's affair in Shushan. Running away from the turmoil at home, David decides to return to the docks and thrust a milk dipper into the third rail slot between the car tracks so that he can emulate Isaiah's experience with the angels and that startling picture of Christ ("him with the lightguts"). The boy's eyes have defied the dark window of his apartment, an emblem of his father's wrath. In a shifting of imagery that previously belonged to the father, David is pictured with "a shifty steeling glimmer under his eyes."

On the second try, the boy makes contact with the electric current while his toes curl into the handle of the milk dipper, keeping it from falling out. He invokes power, fire, light, and is knocked unconscious from the electrical charge that causes "a quaking splendor . . . a cymbal clash of light." A power drain startles the area and disrupts the conversations and behavior of the people in the neighborhood whom Roth seeks to connect to the boy's act and thoughts through an unsuccessful collage of voices and activities. (Here Joyce and Eliot are no help and invite pretentious difficulties.)

By connecting the boy's actions to the people of the neighborhood, Roth slips from the design of the book. Suddenly, it appears, Roth is looking for a new center for the book's consciousness, a new center for its power. Up to this point the poetry of the novel, its charged awareness, is essentially connected to David. In this ambitious penultimate chapter, Roth switches from a poetry within to the search for a poetry from without, as if he is rendering the proletarian gestures expected of the novel of the thirties. Or perhaps he wishes to place the child's concerns in a larger world, much as Joyce connected Stephen Dedalus to political and social matters simply by having the young man come in contact with the average concerns of an average day in Dublin at the turn of the century. But Roth is unable to do this as his major character is just an eight-year-old boy lost beyond his few blocks of neighborhood. In this attempted climax, Roth tries to put the child's frustrations and urges in some larger social context, but overreaches. This is the least convincing part of the book, the thoughts of the child now appearing as self-conscious italicized prose-poetry paragraphs, and the language tends to get rhetorical. For most of this scene, the book is no longer simply lived; it now appears to be, if I may be allowed the phrase, "pastiched."

During his hallucination as he recovers from the terrific shock he received, David sees his father brandishing a hammer and snapping a whip, but on returning home he sees that his father has been disconcerted by what he has caused his son to do: "His eyes bulged, his jaw dropped, he blanched."

David knew that his father faltered, felt guilty, was shaken. (One price for Roth's misplaced ambitions in the penultimate chapter is that the change of the father is suddenly thrust upon the reader, who does not see that change develop.) For a moment, David feels a sense of power over his father, over all that oppresses him, before he lapses back again into sleep and rest and that dark, rich sense of his mind. Some great passivity accepts him.

In 1960 when the novel was reissued for the first time since its original publication in 1934, Leslie Fiedler made a perceptive remark along the lines I have been tracking: "Roth's book aspires not to sociology but to theology; it is finally and astonishingly a religious book," like all the serious novels of the thirties, "toying with the messianic and the apocalyptic." At its peak, the boy's search is inspired both by a prophetic passage from the Bible and by his desire to override the daily authoritarian forces about him through some luminous self-assertion. Or to weave that religious motif into the linguistic web of the book: Can the inadequately grasped and fragmentary Hebrew offer a magic realm of redemption beyond the street brutalities of English and the family turmoil of Yiddish?

The boy's desire is like the recurring voice of the psalmist that asks for the strength and energetic mercy of God because "fearfulness and trembling are come upon me" and "for man would swallow me up." David's quest may be seen as a childhood version of the idea that God is a punishing God whom the suffering psalmist can appeal to as a force against his enemies. On one level David seeks God's light and power, God's strength and adequacy. But it is only after he is knocked unconscious that he finally attains a mastery over the father and a peace within himself whose price is the sacrifice of the will. The very weakness of this David has unexpectedly subdued the Goliath-father. It is a victory attained by a disarming debility, not by self-assertion. The novel is haunted by the problem of how the child can become reconciled with the powerful father and the unrelenting, harsh forces he comes to represent in the child's imagination. It is a conflict that compelled Roth to write *Call It Sleep* in the first place and that afterwards silenced him. Both David Schearl and his creator desired either a liberating power of their own or a peace that passes conflict. The first is self-assertion; the second you might call sleep.

Morris Dickstein (review date 29 November 1987)

SOURCE: "Call It an Awakening," in *The New York Times Book Review,* November 29, 1987, pp. 1, 33, 35-6.

[*In the following review, Dickstein discusses Roth's* Shifting Landscape *and his journey of self-discovery.*]

I had just finished interviewing Henry Roth, the author of *Call It Sleep,* when as if by some dramatic design, a large, flat package was delivered to his New York hotel room. It was an advance copy of Mr. Roth's first book in 53 years, *Shifting Landscape,* a complete collection of his shorter writings along with many excerpts from letters and interviews, lovingly assembled by his gifted Italian translator, Mario Materassi.

It was a wonderful moment in a singular and enigmatic literary career. Mr. Roth seemed to take it all in stride, as if, by the age of 81, the appearance of a new book were no uncommon event for him. But the book, and my conversation with him, told a different story: five decades of agonizing conflict with crippling writer's block, a career dotted with the signposts of many small victories and defeats, including what he has described as "an equivalent or approximate nervous breakdown" at the end of the 1930's, followed by long years of complete silence.

Call It Sleep, a subjective, almost poetic novel about growing up on the Lower East Side in the early years of the century, was published in 1934 when Mr. Roth was only 28. Influenced by James Joyce and T.S. Eliot, the novel was modernist in method, biblical in cadence, yet intensely personal in its re-creation of family life and street life in the old Jewish ghetto. The book appeared at the height of the Depression when documentary realism, not Proustian recollection, was the latest literary fashion. Speaking of the novel, the Communist journal *The New Masses* said, "It is a pity that so many young writers drawn from the proletariat can make no better use of their working class experience than as material for introspective and febrile novels." Though the book was fiercely defended and favorably reviewed by its admirers, Mr. Roth's publisher went bankrupt and he and his novel were soon totally forgotten until the book was revived to great acclaim and impressive sales in the 1960's.

Henry Roth's appearance today is a study in contrasts. His large, impressive head, crowned by stray tufts of gray hair, rests on a stocky yet fragile-looking frame stiffened by arthritis. His hands speak of years of hard manual labor, and his quietly modulated voice radiates dignity and reserve. Mr. Roth's tall, elegant, gray-haired wife, Muriel, a composer, rarely leaves his side, and she gently cut off our interview when she felt he might be tired. He wouldn't stand out in a group of elderly Jewish pensioners, but he speaks gravely— often in the third person—about the bizarre turns of his life.

Henry Roth is his own severest critic. When we first spoke on the phone he worried that his new book might be "over-sold, overinflated." He found it "a very meager output for 50-some odd years." Searching always for the exact word, he spoke of the book as if it were someone else's case study or dossier: "It impressed me quite objectively with the rather

tragic thread—a trace went through it, I don't know whether it's frustration, a block, or what have you. It's a man fighting or serving his destiny. It had that overtone of a person too obdurate to give up." Ruefully, he added, "I wasn't satisfied. I should have had more wisdom, but I didn't, and the book seems to reflect that kind of tragic struggle."

During a depressed period of complete withdrawal from writing during the 1940's, Mr. Roth worked as a skilled toolmaker and an attendant in a mental hospital, and then, in the 50's and 60's, as a waterfowl farmer in Maine—raising and dressing ducks and geese—returning only gradually to wrest hard-earned sentences from the grasp of his private dybbuk. Meanwhile, his wife worked 17 years as a schoolteacher while caring for their two sons. Since 1968 the Roths have lived in a mobile home in Albuquerque, N.M., even farther from the literary world than Maine. Yet, living in this relative obscurity, he began publishing stories and articles with increasing frequency. *Shifting Landscape* covers this whole terrain, and includes several pieces that till now have appeared only in Italian translation.

In retrospect, Mr. Roth's long-lasting block seems less remarkable than his refusal to yield to it, although he tells us that he once referred to himself as "this dead author," and even burned his journals and the manuscripts of several aborted novels in the 1940's. His first writing in 14 years— in 1954—was a how-to-do-it article on cheap, homemade farm equipment, written for a trade journal. *The Magazine for Ducks and Geese.* Two years later *Call It Sleep* was praised in print by several critics, none of whom knew whether the book's author was still alive.

A chance encounter with Mr. Roth's sister in the late 50's led one critic, Harold Ribalow, to Mr. Roth's doorstep in Maine in the late 50's, and to the resurrection of *Call It Sleep* by a small press in 1960. Picked up by Avon and reissued in paperback in 1964, it went on to sell more than a million copies, permanently disrupting the anonymity of a man who could not write yet could not give up on writing, and who readily describes himself even today as neurotic, obsessive and bullheaded.

Mr. Roth's new literary fame made life on the farm impossible. Life magazine sent a photographer to take a picture of the best-selling author killing ducks and geese. He refused. "They were doing it to make me a freak," he told an interviewer recently, "and I'm freakish enough without that!" The belated success of the book enabled Mr. Roth and his wife to travel, but it also exacerbated the desire to write, as well as what he calls the "counterdrive not to write," which threatened to make life hellish again. A projected novel set in Spain and Mexico never materialized, but in 1966 The New Yorker published **"The Surveyor,"** the story of an American couple in Seville, searching secretly for the site where Jews were burned in public during the Inquisition. It seems clear that Mr. Roth was unconsciously searching for a Judaism—and a writing life—he had left behind many decades earlier.

The turning point in that search, as he now sees it, came the following year during the 1967 Arab-Israeli war, when the Roths were in Mexico. Long ago, almost in another lifetime, Mr. Roth, like many writers who had seen the world break apart in the early years of the Depression, had joined the Communist Party. He was just finishing his novel, and he remembers the woman he lived with, Eda Lou Walton, a poet and English professor nearly 12 years his senior, telling him in anguish, "You are destroying yourself as an artist." Years later, stunned by Khrushchev's revelations about Stalin, Mr. Roth ceased being a party member, but in 1967 he "still adhered very much to party principles," including support for the Arab cause. As the war unfolded in the Middle East, he found himself torn between his political faith, which condemned Israel, and certain buried tribal loyalties that surprised him.

Only four years earlier, Mr. Roth had told the readers of *Midstream,* a Zionist journal, that Jews in America could serve the world best by assimilating and "ceasing to be Jews." Suddenly, as he deciphered the headlines in the Mexican papers, the survival of the Jews deeply mattered to him. He feared a new Holocaust. Mr. Roth's ideological orthodoxy crumbled. "It was with an enormous sense of guilt that I had to *tear* myself away," he told me with great emphasis. "We thought that [Communism] would provide us with the *answer.*" But in the end "it was a sterile move," he said. "It was a disaster."

For the ethnic, working-class writers of his generation who had gone through "a transition from a parochial to a cosmopolitan world," Mr. Roth said quietly, Communism seemed to offer an analysis of society that would "provide us with a method, a technique for being able to portray that transition." It was a way into the larger world. But it also distanced those writers emotionally from their own sources and their most authentic material. Mr. Roth sees the tragic thread of his truncated career as part of the common fate of a whole literary generation.

Shifting Landscape returns again and again to the quandary of writers who could not reconcile the esthetic attitudes of the 20's with the social consciousness of the 30's, and others who could not reorient their work after World War II from the proletarian naturalism of the Depression to more personal forms of expression. These include writers who died early and neglected (like Nathanael West and F. Scott Fitzgerald), who could not continue (like Mr. Roth and Daniel Fuchs), who failed to develop (James T. Farrell and

John Steinbeck), or who simply disappeared, such as the proletarian novelists.

I asked Mr. Roth how much he felt his problems were ingrained in his own makeup and how much they could be traced to the predicament of his generation, the major shifts of sensibility at the beginning and end of the Depression. His answer had weight and cogency like all his comments on his gloomy, destiny as a writer, as if he had spent many years brooding on just this question. "I feel very much that I was caught in the same tide that they were caught in. I couldn't escape it. The way it caught you was at your weakest point. Each one of us succumbed because of a certain weakness in his character."

Mr. Roth doesn't explain what his own weaknesses were, but he makes it clear that he felt a sense of dependency and passivity, a lack of self-assurance. *Call It Sleep* is a classic portrayal of the terrors of childhood, a tenement **"Sons and Lovers"** that sets the sensual warmth of the bond with the mother—and the mother tongue, Yiddish—against the fear and violence associated with the father and the external world. From 1928 to 1938 he lived with Eda Lou Walton, who supported him and encouraged him to write—he dedicated the novel to her. With considerable feeling, he described her to me as "very warm, and very tender, and most maternal." He made an effort to break his dependence on Walton by taking off for the West Coast with a colorful, illiterate working-class character named Bill Clay. But "step by step he assumed a domination over me," Mr. Roth said with astonishment. "As I look back at it I'm amazed. He became my guide, my tutor, my mentor"—exactly what the party itself had already become, the answer to all political and even creative problems.

Mr. Roth now believes the natural successor to *Call It Sleep* would have been a continuation of the boy's story into maturity, showing his discovery of a broader culture in the Greenwich Village ferment of the 1920's. But, as he writes in *Shifting Landscape,* "it was never written because Marxism or Communism fell like a giant shunt across his career." Instead, he tried writing a proletarian novel centering on Bill Clay—there is one surviving excerpt in *Shifting Landscape.* But as Mr. Roth wrote in *The New York Times* in 1971, the "portrayal of proletarian virtue" was not his natural bent. As a writer, he was "no longer at home." His relationship to the world he knew best was ruptured, just as it had been in his childhood by his wrenching departure from the ghetto.

To explain his inability to go on writing, Mr. Roth looks back to his family's move (when he was 8 1/2) from the "Jewish mini-state" on the Lower East Side to "rowdy, heterogeneous Harlem"—from Ninth Street to 119th Street, where he lost his sense of identity and felt like an alien. When Mr. Roth was recapturing those early years in *Call It Sleep,* the book took shape for him with a "pattern of unity and inevitability," a phrase he used more than once in conversation, as if it represents his elusive esthetic ideal. For almost four years when he was writing his novel, he told me, it was really writing him: "I was no longer in control. *It* had taken control. I could not do other, no matter what I wanted."

From a psychological viewpoint, Mr. Roth's unswerving devotion to Israel over the last 20 years could be seen as yet another dependency, replacing his long indenture to Marxism. Mr. Roth's references to Israel are always personal rather than political. They mark his own return to Judaism, his voyage home. As Yeats needed his elaborate system to provide him with "metaphors for poetry." Mr. Roth needs a mythology, including a system of *self*-explanation, to unlock his exceptional creative powers.

Shifting Landscape is not a political document but an engrossing meditation on the creative process. As *Call It Sleep* showed long ago, Mr. Roth's imagination is essentially intimate, sensuous and retrospective. Where Marxism promised him a radiant future, yet made his kind of writing impossible, the unexpected return to Judaism has brought him full circle, restored continuity with the world of his childhood and liberated the conjuror's gift for personal recollection.

"Final Dwarf," one of the best stories in *Shifting Landscape,* chillingly takes up the tense relationship between father and son some 50 years after the conclusion of *Call It Sleep,* Mr. Roth never resolved the conflict with his father, whose reaction to reading *Call It Sleep,* as the author later recalled, was simply, "I shouldn't have beat him so much." When the old man died in the early 70's—Mr. Roth cannot remember the exact year—he left his son exactly one dollar.

Another piece in the new book integrates portions of journals dating from 1938 and 1939, when Mr. Roth left Eda Lou Walton and met his wife, Muriel, at Yaddo, the artists colony—journals that fortuitously survived the Maine bonfire. One remarkable memoir, **"Last Respects,"** recalls a 1970 meeting with Margaret Mead, whom he had known in the 1920's, but it is actually Mr. Roth's oblique tribute to Mead's friend, Walton, who had done so much for him as a man and a writer.

All three pieces show what Mr. Roth does best, conveying the unbearable tension that can lie beneath the surface of ordinary relationships. The last two selections will form a part of a memoir-novel called *Mercy of a Rude Stream* that Mr. Roth has been writing since 1979. In old age, using a word processor, he has been writing this sequel to *Call It Sleep* which he feels be should have written in the 1930's. He has completed four volumes, but because some of them involve people still living he may not release them for publication in his lifetime.

Instead we have this brilliant mosaic constructed by Mr. Materassi, his translator, a book that Mr. Roth, in his self-effacing foreword, describes as "primarily Mario's, not mine," though Mr. Roth wrote or spoke nearly everything in it. It's typical of the ironies of his career that this biographical "composite" should come to us by way of Italy, where Mr. Materassi's translation of *Call It Sleep* won a major literary prize as the best foreign novel of 1985, and where Mr. Roth was mobbed by newspaper reporters and *paparazzi* when he came to collect it.

The collections writers give us *instead* of their long-awaited novels, books like Norman Mailer's *Advertisements for Myself* and Ralph Ellison's *Shadow and Act,* have a special kind of poignancy and appeal. They are holding actions, but also acts of propitiation that lay bare the writer's creative conflicts. As in Mr. Mailer's book (which Mr. Materassi once translated into Italian), many of the selections in *Shifting Landscape* are less remarkable than the personal prose that surrounds them, which Mr. Materassi has culled ingeniously out of letters and taped conversations.

Mr. Roth holds to a notion of art that requires that personal history be transmuted into a text that feels unified, self-contained and inevitable.
—*Morris Dickstein*

If Mr. Mailer rescued a sagging career through a bold act of self-promotion, Mr. Roth, anatomizing his own failures, rivets our attention with almost Kafkaesque gestures of self-accusation. Looking back at some long-lost stories that Mr. Materassi has unearthed, Mr. Roth sees only signs of disintegrating talent and loss of control. After one charming sketch, **"Many Mansions,"** Mr. Roth comments, "what a bit of fluff": "The writer," he says of himself, "was no longer capable of treating, of dealing with and transmitting the wonderful narrative signals, so to speak, that the serious novelist would have been sensitized to." In the book these lines are followed eerily by his 14-year retreat from writing.

One of Mr. Roth's problems may have been the exalted standard he brought to his work, which contributed to the anxiety and self-consciousness that developed with his block. Ulike many fiction writers today, who seem to spill their lives directly onto the page, Mr. Roth holds to a notion of art that requires that personal history be transmuted into a text that feels unified, self-contained and inevitable. The real beginning of *Call It Sleep* came, he told me, when he decided "to leave the realm of strict fact," began treating people and events in his past as "objects that were just mine to use" and grasped the overall fictive shape of his early experiences. For all its human immediacy, *Call It Sleep* is an intricately textured, *literary* novel, each of its four sections woven around key symbols and images. Mr. Roth was a Joycean then, but these unifying devices were "mostly intuitive rather than planned or conscious," he said. "I would continually glimpse elements in it that tied in, and they would gratify me very much, but I wouldn't allow them to interfere with the narrative."

But when he tried writing about the later stages of his life, "I no longer saw, in any of the things I tried to do, that kind of unity," be remarked. "I was not able to integrate the new cosmopolitan world into which I was now plunged." As a result, every project petered out and eventually went dead for him. He was "no longer at home," and his imagination couldn't encompass the larger stage he had entered. His proletarian novel was an attempt at a wholly American project— no Jews in sight—but its style is forced and unconvincing. Thanks to the Communist Party's puritan standards, he didn't feel free to deal with sex, though it haunts the edges of *Call It Sleep* and certainly haunted Mr. Roth himself during this period. "He yearned for the tainted, the perverse, for the pornographic," he wrote in 1971, "and detested himself as degenerate for doing so." "He had a vested interest in the sordid, the squalid, the depraved. He became immobilized."

Today, rediscovered as a classic in America, lionized in Italy where his book is a best seller, Henry Roth is very much a survivor. An Israeli film maker. has taken an option on *Call It Sleep,* and recently drove its author around the Lower East Side to search for remnants of a buried world. Cortisone and hip-replacement surgery have helped in his struggle with arthritis, and the computer has helped him get words on paper. Muriel Roth began composing again as her husband began writing, and for the last four years ("since I was 75," she said), she has been a serious composer for the first time in several decades.

Whether or not Mr. Roth's current project, *Mercy of a Rude Stream,* fulfills its high literary promise, the mere fact of longevity has helped supply a happy turn to the Roths' story. Aside from some of the fine pieces collected in it, *Shifting Landscape* can only excite wonderment as an extraordinary record of an author's stubborn determination to rescue his talent from the clutches of neurosis and the vicissitudes of history.

Robert Alter (review date 25 January 1988)

SOURCE: A review of *Shifting Landscape* and *Call It Sleep,* in *New Republic,* Vol. 198, No. 4, January 25, 1988, pp. 33-7.

[*In the following review, Alter discusses Roth's* Call It Sleep *and asserts that his new volume,* Shifting Landscape *"provides the outlines of a spiritual autobiography."*]

The haunting question about Henry Roth remains his half century of silence after the publication of *Call It Sleep* in 1934. *Call It Sleep,* which, as I have just discovered, is one of those rare books that actually improves with rereading, exhibits the perfect pitch of genius in all the play of its invention and stylistic energy; it clearly belongs among the few great American novels of the 20th century. But this was not a case, as happens frequently enough, of a promising or even brilliant first novel that has no sequel because its author runs out of steam, because he has said the one thing he had to say. If this was Roth's *Portrait of the Artist* (As a Young Boy, for the protagonist, David Schearl, is seven when most of the action occurs), what happened to the *Ulysses* toward which the prodigious imaginative power of the large first novel seems to be moving?

Roth himself—he is now 81—has also been haunted by his own silence, as he repeatedly makes clear in *Shifting Landscape,* a collection of all his published short pieces from 1925 to 1987, assembled by Mario Materassi, his Italian translator and devoted friend. Materassi has helpfully prefaced each of the pieces with generous excerpts from Roth's correspondence, from taped conversations, from the many interviews Roth has given since 1964, when the meteoric success of the paperback reissue of his novel plucked him from the obscurity of his life as a waterfowl farmer in rural Maine. This new volume, then, gives us everything Roth has put into print beyond *Call It Sleep.* It provides the outlines of a spiritual autobiography.

The pieces exhibit the flickerings of an enormous talent, but scarcely any of them transcends the slightness of a fictional sketch or exercise. Between 1935 and 1940, Roth wrote about 100 pages of a proletarian novel, which he subsequently destroyed (one published chapter survives and appears in *Shifting Landscapes*), and three deliberately commercial stories. A state of depression marked the beginning of a total writer's block—even letter-writing, he confesses, became painfully threatening—that continued for a decade and a half.

Roth made his first tentative efforts to write fiction again in the later '50s, and the acclaim and income from the paperback *Call It Sleep* (over a million copies were sold) encouraged him to more sustained work. So far nothing substantial from this later period is visible, though in the last few years Roth has completed a thousand-page manuscript of a book he calls a "memoir-form novel," *Mercy of a Rude Stream.* (The title is from Shakespeare's *Henry VIII.*) He is apparently unwilling to have it published in his lifetime; the two excerpts included in the Materassi volume look intriguing,

ve little sense of what the shape or quality of the
_ _:e.

For the most part, Roth is his own severest critic on the subject of his deflected career. "I am hung with the albatross
of myself," he writes to Materassi in 1964. The one partial
exception to this severity is the attempt, made several times
in interviews and in written remarks, to explain his withdrawal from literature as symptomatic of a whole generation of writers who never realized the brilliance of their
initial promise. The explanation is not altogether persuasive.
There is a big difference between decline and silence; and
it is the former that applies to most of the writers Roth seems
to have in mind. (Among those he mentions are John
Steinbeck, James Farrell, Edward Dahlberg, and Daniel
Fuchs.) And there is an even bigger difference between dis-
sipated talent and the poignant plight (Roth's own) of
aborted genius.

There is one clear and compelling reason for Roth's silence.
It is his joining the Communist Party in 1933, even as he
was completing *Call It Sleep.* That political act very rapidly impaired him as a writer, though its consequences, as I
shall explain, would have certain retrospective complications. His novel's lyric immersion in the experience of childhood soon came to seem to him a throwback to the apolitical
aestheticism of the 1920s, when the book was first conceived; he was made to feel a degree of bad conscience about
his own achievement, earnestly aspiring instead to produce
fiction that would embody revolutionary awareness. This aspiration, as he now says, violated all his inclinations as a
writer, which were to the sensual, the personal, the visionary, the perverse. "Allegiance once deeply inhaled," he notes
grimly in a letter written in 1968, "was as lethal as carbon
monoxide."

Oddly enough, Roth is as vehement about James Joyce as
about the Communist Party. Clearly it was the example of
Joyce that galvanized his talent as a writer. Indeed, *Call It
Sleep* is, together with *The Sound and the Fury,* which appeared five years earlier, the fullest American assimilation
of Joyce; and, unlike Faulkner's novel, it is thematically consonant with Joyce as well as technically imitative of him.
Roth's present quarrel with Joyce is not over technique, but
over an ideal of artistic identity. He now dismisses the
Joycean motto of *silence, exile, cunning* as "specious clap-
trap," and denounces the direction of "monstrous detachment
and artistic autonomy" to which Joyce's enterprise points.
Roth's recent concentration on a large memoir-form novel
is an effort to place his actual life-experience squarely under fictional scrutiny, eschewing all Joycean pretense that the
writer stands outside his work like a god, coolly paring his
fingernails.

The ultimate source of Roth's vehemence toward Joyce,

however, is something he has since discovered about himself—that he is a writer who needs to be deeply rooted in a
particular culture with its distinctive complex of symbols.
Though Joyce's point of departure was just such a connection with Irish culture, he moved toward an ideal of universal art that would integrate all cultures, working from a
condition of self-imposed exile. *Call It Sleep* exhibits a productive tension in this regard. The author's intimate knowledge of the life of Jewish immigrants on the East Side, circa
1913, is masterfully evident on every page. It is a knowledge that is unsparing, affectionate, absolutely unsentimen-
tal. At the same time, the child protagonist pursues an
essentially private visionary prospect (though partly by
means of language and lore made available to him by his
culture); had Roth written the sequel about David Schearl's
adolescence and young manhood, the sequel that he says he
ought to have written, the protagonist would no doubt have
detached himself entirely from the world of his origins and
realized his identity as an American Stephen Dedalus in the
cosmopolitan realm of art.

In fact, this route was not psychologically viable for Roth.
One might even wonder whether the Party's ideal of universal revolutionary solidarity, however illusory, was not an alternative family and culture for him, a substitute for the
Jewish ones he felt he had to put behind him. Now, in the
retrospection of old age, Roth appears to view Joyce as a
kind of mirage that led him out into the wilderness of proudly
autonomous art from which he fled, only to fall into the lethal air of Communist allegiance.

This perspective on his own experience was fixed for him
not by the success of 1964, but, surprisingly, by the Six-Day
War of 1967. Roth had severed all his Jewish ties, even declaring in a symposium in 1963 that the greatest boon that
Jews could now confer on humanity would be to cease being Jews. But in the threat to Israel's survival in the spring
of 1967, Roth suddenly discovered himself profoundly involved in the fate of the Jewish state, despite vestigial radical promptings that he ought to be siding with the Arabs.
He has not, he says, become a Zionist, at least not in any
official sense; but the idea of a new, secular Jewish culture
under the conditions of political autonomy, and the identification with Israel, have become central to his imaginative
life. In 1971 he announced that he had "adopted" Israel "as
a symbolic home, one where symbols can lodge, whatever
it is in actuality." Perhaps we will not be able to understand
what precisely this means until we can read *Mercy of a Rude
Stream* in its entirety, if then; but the identification with Israel seems to have liberated Roth from his sense of crippling
isolation, to have made it possible for him to write again,
after Joyce and contra Joyce.

Yet no reader of *Call It Sleep* will regret its Joycean inspiration. Formally, the novel interweaves the predominant tech-

nique of *Ulysses* with that of *Portrait of the Artist.* There are, that is, brief stream-of-consciousness passages in which staccato sequence of highly elliptical sentences and the repeated tag ends of fragmentary phrases are used to convey the dramatic immediacy, the groping confusion, at times the sheer panic, of a child's inner experience. The more pervasive technique, however, is that of the earlier Joyce. A finely articulate narrator, almost always adhering to the emotional and conceptual viewpoint of the protagonist, conveys that viewpoint in a wrought lyric language that would not be available to the protagonist himself.

Let me illustrate the nature of the connection between the two writers by juxtaposing passages from their novels that deal with similar subjects. Toward the end of *Portrait,* Stephen stands on the steps of the library watching a flock of birds wheel above him, "their dark darting quivering bodies flying clearly against the sky as against a limp hung cloth of tenuous blue." After watching, he listens to the cry of the birds, which sounds to him like the squeaking of mice. The simile, however, is too humble for his taste, as in a moment he will see in the birds a symbol or augury of his own fate:

> But the notes were long and shrill and whirring, un-
> like the cry of vermin, falling a third or a fourth and
> trilled as the flying beaks clove the air. Their cry
> was shrill and clear and fine and falling like threads
> of silken light unwound from whirring spools.

In the last of the four sections of *Call It Sleep,* David daringly climbs to the roof of his tenement building for the first time, and suddenly finds himself in a world of dazzling immensities, under "the blinding whorl of the sun." From the quiet of his lofty vantage he looks all around:

> And about were roof-tops, tarred and red and sun-
> lit and red, roof-tops to the scarred horizon. Flocks
> of pigeons wheeled. Where they flew in lower air,
> they hung like a poised and never-raveling smoke;
> nearer at hand and higher, they glittered like rippling
> water in the sun.

Of course I do not mean to suggest that Roth was specifically imitating Joyce's rendering of bird-flight when he wrote these sentences. But the similarity of the object of description points up the stylistic bond between the two writers. The best literary influence is a kind of alchemy, as here Roth picks up from Joyce a certain incantatory rhythm, the strategic use of simile, and the lyric possibilities of certain kinds of simile (note the intriguing affinity between "a limp hung cloth of tenuous blue" and "they hung like a poised and never-raveling smoke"), and fuses them into the secret cellular structure of his own prose, his own fictional world. For the child David, in contrast to the self-conscious late-adolescent Stephen, the birds are not augury or emblem, they are the immediate objects of wondering attention; and yet Roth could not have made his hero see so well without the example of Joyce.

Technique is not easily separable, however, from literary ideology, and in this regard Roth's sense of vocation, and of the thematic embodiment of vocation, was kindled by Joyce. I have in mind particularly the orientation of fiction toward what Joyce liked to call "epiphany," the revelation of meaning and purpose for the character (and, implicitly, for the reader) in a moment of illuminating vision, when everything comes together. The most spectacular epiphany in *Call It Sleep,* of course, is the awesome moment near the end, when David thrusts a milk dipper into the third rail and experiences a surge of cosmic power through every cell, as he is flung between life and death.

But there are more delicate epiphanies earlier in the novel, including an exquisite one that should be mentioned for its Joycean associations of water and vision. In one of the most famous passages in *Portrait,* Stephen sees a lovely young girl, her skirt hitched up to her waist, wading in the Liffey. He immediately casts her as angel and omen in his privat mythology of a poet in the making, and is inflamed with ecstasy. Near the end of Book III of *Call It Sleep,* David, having been sent out to burn the crumbs of leaven on the morning before Passover, ends up on the wharfs, looking out over the East River. He has been much preoccupied with the passage from the sixth chapter of Isaiah that he has encountered in Hebrew school, in which the Lord appears before the prophet effulgent on his throne and an angel touches the prophet's lips with a livid coal to cleanse them of their impurity. In this case, the writing does not sound much like the corresponding epiphany in *Portrait* (which is a good deal more effusive and pre-Raphaelite in cast), but the Joycean moment might be viewed as a kind of matrix for the vision accorded Roth's protagonist:

> His gaze shifted to the left. As the cloud began to
> pass, a long slim lathe of sunlight burned silver on
> the water—
>
> —Gee, didn't see before!
> Widened to a swath, a lane, widened.
> —Like a ship just went.
> A plain, flawless, sheer as foil to the serried mar-
> gins. His eyes dazzled.
> Fire on the water. White.
> His lids grew heavy.
> —In the water she said. White. Brighter than day.
> Whiter. And He was.
>
> Minutes passed while he stared. The brilliance was
> hypnotic. He could not take his eyes away. His spirit
> yielded, melted into light. In the molten sheen

ries and objects overlapped. Smokestacks
o palings flickering in silence by. Pale lathes
grew gray, turned dusky, contracted and in the
swimming dimness, he saw sparse teeth that gnawed
upon a lip; and ladders on the ground turned into
hasty fingers pressing on a thigh and again smokestacks. Straight in air they stood a moment, only to
fall on silvered corrugating brilliance. And he heard
the rubbing on a wash-board and the splashing suds,
smelled again the acrid soap and a voice speaking
words that opened like the bands of a burnished silver accordion—Brighter than day . . . Brighter . . .
Sin melted into light . . .

Technically, this extraordinary moment could be described
as Joyce doubled back on himself. The thematic juncture of
privileged vision looking out over the water recalls *Portrait.*
The musically lyric narration, with little fragments of stream
of consciousness (typographically marked by introductory
dashes), invokes the opening, or Telemachus, section of
Ulysses. The scattering of crude details of tenement life, including a sexual image, in David's gyrating free associations,
recalls the earthy realism of the Bloom sections of *Ulysses,*
so unlike the vaporous poetic diction and perception of
Stephen's world in *Portrait.* In 1960 Leslie Fiedler sought
to explain this combination in *Call It Sleep* of pungent naturalism and visionary transport by invoking C.M. Doughty's
epigram, "The Semites are like to a man sitting in a cloaca
to the eyes, and whose brows touch heaven." But one hardly
needs such canards about racial imagination to explain the
marriage of opposites in Roth: it is already abundantly
present in *Ulysses,* where Bloom (a Semite, to be sure, but
conceived in a most Hibernian imagination) sits in the privy
dreaming of sunbursts of paradisiacal splendor in a land to
the East.

Roth's alchemic transmutation of Joyce has to do less with
the application of the Irish writer's methods to Jewish materials (David's switchwielding *kheyder* rabbi in place of
Stephen's punitive Jesuit masters) than with the peculiarly
American resonances of his prose, of his whole imaginative
enterprise. At a time when European novelists were creating classics of realism, a central tradition of American literature was producing (as D.H. Lawrence and others came
to recognize) works of a potently mythic character. Joyce's
three novels abound, of course, in mythological elements,
but these are brought into play through an elaborate exercise of learned allsion. What I think Roth draws from an
American matrix is his primary imagination of mythic drama,
even without recourse to allusion, in his handling of realistic materials. He is not a mythological writer, like Joyce, but
a mythographic one, like Melville.

This quality is felt, for a start, in certain recurrent traits of
style. If Roth often displays a mood-painting delicacy remi-

niscent of the earlier Joyce ("The body was aware of a lyric
indolence, a golden lolling within itself"), his language even
more frequently evinces an explosive power of hyperbole
that enlarges and violently transforms the experiences it describes. Here is David falling down a flight of stairs into a
cellar:

> Then darkness, swirling and savage, caught him like
> a wind of stone, pitched him spinning among pal-
> pable drum-beats, engulfed him in a brawling wel-
> ter of ruined shapes—that parted—and he plunged
> down a wailing fathomless shaft. A streak of
> flame—and screaming nothingness.

It does not suffice to say that the language here catches the
immediacy of the tumbling child's terror; what it also does
is to make a fall down a set of stairs into a gripping intimation of the apocalypse. Prose like this ("caught him like a
wind of stone") was scarcely written in English before *Moby
Dick.* Roth, in his novel, does it again, just as well as the
19th-century master. Thus, at the center of David's great vision when he jams the dipper into the third rail are two sentences—like the whole vision, set out in italics as verse—that
are pre-eminently Melvillian in their vigor of metaphoric invention, their muscular rhythm, their insistent force of hyperbole, their cosmic sweep:

> The hawk of radiance raking him with
> talons of fire, battering his skull with
> a beak of fire, braying his body with
> pinions of intolerable light. And he
> writhed without motion in the clutch of a
> fatal glory, and his brain swelled
> and dilated till it dwarfed the galaxies
> in a bubble of refulgence—

There is an obvious Oedipal triangle at the center of *Call It
Sleep,* complete with Freudian Family Romance in the ambiguous suggestion that David may not be his father's child.
What makes this representation of paternal hatred, maternal
love, filial fear and desire utterly compelling is that the stuff
of psychology has been transformed into the drama of myth.
This transformation is in perfect keeping with a child's perspective, in which parents loom as large as the world, and
life and death are at stake in a father's threat, a mother's kiss.

From the very first sentence, the father, with his "grim smouldering face," is like some titanic figure that has surged out
of the archaic imagination, always threatening, never changing. He is repeatedly associated with motifs of upraised hammers, whips, bull's horns, volcanic fury. He is all knotted
muscularity, phallic hardness, a man of stone. David's perception of his father standing over him after whipping him
succinctly illustrates how faithfulness to the child's psychology moves the figure perceived into the realm of myth:

"David's father towered above him, rage billowing from him, shimmering in sunlight almost, like an aura."

Call It Sleep, for all its beautifully limned realistic detail, is a novel that constantly pushes toward an order of meaning beyond the social and historical spheres—another quality that could not have endeared the book to the readers of *The New Masses* in 1934. This movement beyond is perhaps most vividly evident in Roth's English treatment of Yiddish dialogue. It has often been observed that Roth illustrates the linguistic predicament of the immigrants by giving them a finely articulate language when they are speaking in their native tongue, which stands in contrast both to their painfully hobbled, imperfect English and to the crude street-urchin's argot their children speak to each other.

But this is an incomplete description of what Roth accomplishes in the dialogues. The English that Roth lends his characters is more formal, more decorous and elevated, than the Yiddish they would actually have been speaking. A common colloquial expression for feeling sudden despair, *es iz mir finster gevoren oif di oigen*, through a slight modification of diction and word order, assumes a Shakespearean dignity, even falling into an iambic cadence: "The light before my eyes grew black!" The familiar Yiddish reference to a son as a *kadish* is transmuted into something strange and vaguely sinister when the father says, "And that over there is what will pray for me after my death." Above all, the famous Yiddish gift for invective is translated from fishwives' curses into a kind of poetry of resonant wrath—in the mouth of the rabbi, of David's outrageous Aunt Bertha, and, above all, in the mouth of the menacing father: "Curse him and his gifts! . . . May he burn with them! God bray him into bits!" Finally, then, this is not mimetic dialogue, but the speech of a personage in a dramatic prose-poem.

It is not a character in Sholem Aleichem who talks like this, but Melville's Ahab, raging in a state of virtual demonic possession against whale and God and man and life itself. Those cadences, that posture, can be heard again and again in the language of Albert Schearl, which is neither Yiddish nor colloquial English, but, like Melville's, a diction at once tragic and epic: "Nothing fulfills itself with me! It's all doomed!" And in his incandescent fury, when he thinks he has found out David's illegitimacy, he thunders with a 17th-century grandeur: "That's hers! Her spawn! Mark me! Hers! . . . Three years I throttled surmise, I was the beast of burden! Good fortune I never met! Happiness never! Joy never!"

It is possible to think of Albert Schearl in realistic terms as a study in psychopathology. The sweep of his language, however, and its signification, in dialogue and in narration, constantly invite us to see all of the figures in this family constellation, again in keeping with some of the classics of American literature, as images of humanity facing the abso-

lute ultimacy of existence: the father seething with resentment against life, inwardly gnawed at by an unquenchable sense of inadequacy, avenging himself with the brute force of arbitrary authority; the mother dreaming of a lost love that was impossible from the start, and giving herself, like the gift of grace in a doomed world, to her cherished child; the boy lifting his mind toward a horizon of perfect brilliance beyond the grimy existence where fathers whip, other children mock, and tenement cellars swarm with rats and vague unspeakable terrors.

In all this, mastery speaks from every page of *Call It Sleep,* persuading us that its achievement could not have been a fluke. Perhaps we may yet see an answering mastery, in a different fictional mode, when *Mercy of a Rude Stream* is placed before the public. But even if that never happens, this single luminous book will have assured its author a place among the American novelists whose work will not perish.

Lynn Altenbernd (essay date Winter 1989)

SOURCE: "An American Messiah: Myth in Henry Roth's *Call It Sleep,*" in *Modern Fiction Studies,* Vol. 35, No. 4, Winter, 1989, pp. 673-87.

[*In the following essay, Altenbernd asserts that David in Roth's* Call It Sleep *is a messiah figure.*]

Henry Roth's *Call It Sleep* has moved and delighted—and puzzled—two generations of readers. Sometimes regarded as the best of American proletarian novels or as the best novel growing out of the Great Depression, it is in fact neither proletarian in any strict sense nor directly concerned with the economic depression of the 1930s. Since its publication in 1934 and particularly since its reissue in 1960, a succession of commentators have produced something approaching a consensus that the novel is at its core the record of a religious experience and that the novel is a distinctly Jewish work.

I would suggest that the religious theme developed in *Call It Sleep* depicts the birth and childhood of a New-World messiah whose story conflates elements of the Jewish and the Christian traditions and is a version of the birth-of-a-hero myth dealt with by Otto Rank in *The Myth of the Birth of the Hero* and by Joseph Campbell in *The Hero with a Thousand Faces.* Rank derives his hero myth from what Freud identified as the family romance—the widespread tendency of youngsters to reject their biological parents and to imagine themselves the children of other, usually more glamorous, progenitors. Freud sees this tendency as a struggle of the child to break the bonds of the Oedipal relationship and to establish psychological independence. This is the significance of the quarrel over David Schearl's paternity and of his unusually strong and persistent Oedipal bond. His rejection of the hostile father is consonant with both Rank's myth and Freud's romance; his rejection of his mother is less evident but equally important in his struggle to gain mature freedom. Further, although *Call It Sleep* is an intensely Jewish novel, it is also very much an American novel in its depiction of the New York scene and as a part of the major tradition that deals with the supposed exceptional mission and destiny of the American people.

Call It Sleep traces the growth of an immigrant child in Brownsville and the lower East Side of New York City from age six to about age eight. Albert Schearl has come to the New World alone in 1905 and is joined in 1907 by Genya and their son David. From the moment of their reunion at Ellis Island, there is tension between the parents—between the gloomy, threatening, vituperative father and the gentle, submissive, but ardently protective mother. David clings so tenaciously to his mother, and is so fearful—and later so resentful—of his father, that the normal Oedipal relationship is aggravated and prolonged. Albert Schearl has some reason to doubt that he is the child's father; his suspicions poison the atmosphere of the home, while David overhears enough adult talk to suspect that he is not the son of the terrifying god of wrath who rules the family. The child proves to be unusually intelligent and sensitive, so that he suffers more than most of his peers from the rough-and-tumble of city street-life. Enrolled in cheder, he is an eager pupil who quickly earns the approval of the rabbi and who shows an unusual interest in the story of Isaiah. Stimulated even by meager religious instruction, the boy has—or believes that he has—a series of mystic experiences that will ultimately lead him to a terrifying climatic adventure in which he is nearly electrocuted by the current in the slotted rail of a street-car track. He survives to achieve a kind of reconciliation with his father and a sense of triumphant acquiescence in the conditions of his life.

The boy's characteristics and experiences are strikingly like those of the hero-messiah as depicted by Rank, Campbell, and others. David's given name means "the elect of God"; it also identifies him with the Old Testament King David, who, according to Ezekiel, was to return as the messiah and rule eternally over the future united and perfected state (Ezek. 34:23-24). Isaiah had foretold a messiah who would be "a shoot from the stump of Jesse," the father of David (9: 1-6; 11: 1-16; 32: 1-5). Centuries later the gospel writers identified Jesus as that messiah and provided a lineage that derived the Saviour from the house of David (Matt. 1: 1-17; Luke 1: 27). John Gabel and Charles Wheeler note that "When the gospels present Jesus of Nazareth as the Messiah, they are drawing on Jewish tradition. In Hebrew *mashiah* means 'anointed one'; the equivalent in Greek is *christos,* hence 'Christ.' The title refers to the coronation

ceremony: The chosen king is . . . God's choice and reigns with divine backing."

In Hebrew apocalyptic literature, the word *messiah* was applied to persons of unusual perception deemed worthy of receiving the message and mission of God. Like the opening phases of *A Portrait of the Artist as a Young Man* and *The Education of Henry Adams,* (and indeed many a bildungsroman), the earliest passages of *Call It Sleep* depict the awakening of an unusual intelligence. From precise observation of details the five-year-old boy quickly moves to speculation about their meaning and often to reflections of precocious, although not implausible, sophistication. Having observed that a wedding and a funeral used the same carriages, for example, David concludes that "everything belonged to the same dark"—a proposition that he converts into the paradox, implied but unexpressed: everything is at once both light and dark.

Enrolled as a student in the cheder of Rabbi Yidel Pankower, David displays an unusual facility in pronouncing Hebrew. Although among the youngest, he is the one pupil who can remember all of the "Chad Godyah," a traditional Aramaic song usually recited by a child at the end of the Seder service. It is a text appropriate to a novice messiah, for it was once believed to be an allegory promising the redemption of Israel. Obtuse and vulgar though Reb Pankower is in many ways, he is fully able to appreciate David's eager response to the language of God, to commend the boy as "an iron head," and to speculate, "You may be a great rabbi yet—who knows!" Here is a child, then, of exceptional intelligence and aptitude for penetrating the divine mysteries.

Like the prophet-messiahs of history, David sometimes experiences the mystic state. During the Passover season in 1913, David is "content yet strangely nostalgic"—that is, in the mood that enfolds him at each Passover. Sitting on the edge of a dock fronting the East River, he is dazzled by a broad band of sunlight reflected from the water and falls into a trance: "The brilliance was hypnotic. He could not take his eyes away. His spirit yielded, melted into light." Abruptly he is awakened from his reverie by the noise of a tugboat chugging past and by the whistle of a man on board who shouts, "Wake up, Kid . . . 'fore you throw a belly-w'opper!" David is alarmed to find himself in danger of falling into the river and lurches backward to safety. His reflection on this experience further identifies it as a mystic spell: "What was it he had seen? . . . It was as though he had seen it in . . . a world that once left could not be recalled."

At several points late in the novel, usually when David is running and is under the impress of strong emotion or a powerful sense of purpose, he feels impelled by an irresistible force outside himself. As he is breaking into the locked cheder in a desperate effort to learn more about Isaiah, David reflects, "An enormous hand was shoving him forward." Similar language appears elsewhere: "an ineluctable power tore him from the moorings he clutched"; "an act, ordained, foreseen, inevitable at this very moment." These are David's illusions, and they are those of a servant of God.

David Schearl also meets the traditional expectation that the messiah will appear in a time of distress, when the land is "blighted by suffering, death, sin and other evils" and in an era that "has to be changed and superseded by a new age." Without editorializing, Roth depicts that time in the life of the Golden Land when the "huddled masses yearning to breathe free" swarmed into New York to find persistent poverty, discrimination, and cultural blight as their virtually universal fate. The heartbreaking contrast between the promise of the New World and the grim particularity of Roth's picture of New York slum life makes a comment upon the American Dream no less devastating than the parables of Dos Passos, Fitzgerald, or Hemingway.

This theme is introduced by the wry epigraph of the Prologue:

> (*I pray thee ask no questions*
> *this is that Golden Land*)

and by the immigrants' first disconcerting glimpse of the Statue of Liberty, whose welcoming brilliance is ominously darkened and whose guiding beacon becomes the shadow of a sword.

In this blighted land the debility of traditional religious institutions is epitomized in the condition of the cheder David attends. The rebbe, abusive, imaginatively foul-mouthed, greasy, and tobacco-stained, rules a pack of rowdies whose incapacity for the study of Hebrew is exceeded only by their reluctance. The atmosphere is tainted with sweaty bodies, the rebbe's cigarette smoke, and "gollic fahts," while the racket of scuffling boys and their alternating outbursts of glee and quarreling drown out the recitations of the language of God. David has been carried into a waste land where poverty, crowded tenements, stench, and noise, with their consequent pain, fear, and guilt, are the realities that belie the promise of "that Golden Land."

In yet another way, David's experience parallels that of the prophets of history: he has his time in the wilderness. In a rough-and-tumble street game, David knocks down—and knocks out—a boy who has been tormenting him. Frightened by his antagonist's lifeless appearance, David flees along a street that leads him out into the country. Delighted by the row of telephone poles that stretches endlessly "up the hill of distance," he chants, "Hello, Mr. Highwood. . . . Goodbye Mr. Highwood." But soon he is bewildered in a frighteningly unfamiliar area. Later David recognizes a parallel with the experience of biblical prophets when he overhears Rabbi Pankower explaining the circumstances in which Isaiah saw God. The child muses, "—Where did he go to see Him? God? Didn't say. . . . Way, way, way, maybe. Gee! Some place, me too . . . When I—When I—in the street far away. . . . Hello, Mr. Highwood, goodbye Mr. Highwood. Heee! Funny!" (first ellipsis mine). Thus David, like Isaiah—and like Christ—has a sojourn in the wilderness.

Like them he experiences temptation as well. Leo Dugovka, the only major gentile figure in *Call It Sleep,* performs two crucial functions in David's development. As a Roman Catholic, he is the chief source of David's exposure to Christian thought and ritual. In this role he aids David in achieving the ecumenical character that qualifies him as a possible savior of the cosmopolitan American world. But as one who introduces David to the possibilities of sensual delights, he plays the role of tempter, and in this instance is more successful than the devil was in his efforts to corrupt Jesus.

David first encounters Leo on the tenement's roof, "that precinct in the sky, that silent balcony on the pinnacle of turmoil," where they can look out over the neighborhood. With his talk of freedom from a mother's supervision and of kites, roller skates, and distant streets, Leo is, in effect, offering the younger boy "all the kingdoms of the world" (Matt. 4:8). The setting and Leo's street-wise confidence make David eager to learn from the older boy. Recently sensitized by the cheder to things religious, David is especially fascinated by Leo's crude accounts of Catholic doctrine. Leo promises to give him a broken rosary but only at a price. David, eager to obtain the rosary, takes on the role of pander and introduces Leo to his cousin Esther, with whom the older boy "plays bad"—whom, indeed, he rapes, although with the girl's half-willing collusion. This incident in a stinking cellar, as William Freedman has pointed out, is an aspect of David's descent into the underworld—an event that once again places him among the heroes of legend.

The quest of David as hero-messiah is a search for "God's light." Indeed, as a number of critics have observed, the dominant symbol pattern of the novel is the contrast between light and dark, between good and evil. Driven by a child's fear of the dark, David races with pounding heart every time he must pass the cellar door of the Brownsville tenement. Soon he learns that rats, decay, and foul odors as well as the smuttiness of coal belong to the cellar. Again, the darkness and mothball stench of the closet where Annie, the crippled neighbor girl, gives David a crude initiation into the mechanics of sex further extend this set of associations. At a still later stage, Leo's assault upon Esther deepens the evil import of cellar, darkness, stench, and sexual encounter.

But in Book Three, "The Coal," the matter is complicated

by David's discovery that coal—a burning coal—was thrust by an angel against Isaiah's lips to purify him. The coal used as the agent of cleansing can hardly be the filthy substance in the cellar; David postulates an "angel coal" in God's cellar as something bright and purifying. Later he discovers, however, that the two converge and eventually coalesce, so that God's coal—brilliant, burning, and cauterizing—is one with the filthy black coal of the foul cellar. In fact he is recognizing that coal has two aspects, as the carriages used for weddings and funerals have two functions. Both conclusions recognize the moral ambiguity of life.

Light also symbolizes the power of God as well as the blinding divine understanding that engulfs the mystic and takes him out of himself. Gazing out over the river, David sees the essence of divinity in "a plain, flawless, sheer as foil to the serried margins. . . . White. Brighter than day. Whiter. And he was."

Almost immediately after this vision, David is accosted by three Irish toughs who force him to thrust a home-made sheet-metal sword into the crack of the electrified rail on the car-tracks; "power, gigantic, fetterless, thudded into day! And light, unleashed, terrific light bellowed out of the iron lips." Taking refuge in the cheder yard, David muses upon the immanence and power of God and associates them with the river, coal, and whiteness. When the rabbi discovers the boy, David gives a garbled account of his motives for invading the cheder, saying, "'I saw a coal like—like Isaiah. . . . Where the car-tracks run I saw it.'" The rabbi breaks into derisive laughter: "'Fool!' he gasped at length. 'Go beat your head on a wall! God's light is not between car-tracks.'" But Pankower is wrong: "The rabbi didn't know as he knew what the light was, what it meant, what it had done to him." God's light is indeed between car-tracks—as it is everywhere—unknown to the man of God, known to the child.

But if David is seeking purification, he is also seeking salvation—seeking to be saved from the wrath of a father like an angry, irrational god, from the terrors of the streets, from dangers unknown as well as only too well known. With each recurrence of the Passover season, David feels the renewal of life and of hope for serenity and security. But always there is a relapse from whatever sense of confidence he has acquired and a renewed struggle with dangers and fears. Indeed, his crises intensify as he grows and ranges more widely. Ultimately individual salvation eludes him; David reaches at last a scrutiny that is conditioned upon his acceptance of life in the community of his fellows, rather than upon escape from it.

Paramount among David's qualifications as a messiah is the mystery of his parentage. As Otto Rank and others have shown, heroes, including prophets and messiahs, are often the product of a miraculous or mysterious birth. Like Moses, Jesus, and innumerable heroes of myth and fairy tale, David may not be—but then again may be—the child of his nominal father.

The doubt is prompted by the arrival of Genya's younger sister Bertha, who annoys and frightens Genya by probing an old sore spot—the secret surrounding an early love of the older sister. Moved finally by renewed memories of that concealed and cherished episode, Genya pours out to Bertha the tale—or perhaps most of the tale—of her romance with Ludwig, a Christian organist in the old Austrian village. It is a story of youthful passion, of secret meetings, and finally of intervention by the girl's outraged parents and of betrayl by the young man's opportunism.

David, always alert and inquisitive, has hidden himself so as to overhear this enthralling conversation. Even so, he is tantalized by the occasional drift of the talk from Yiddish into Polish, a language unknown to him. The gaps in the account leave room for his imagination to build beyond what he actually hears. David's embellishment of the narrative harmonizes with his at least latent wish to be rid of his putative father; he concludes that he is the son of the shadowy and romantic Ludwig. At a moment of great stress, the child seeks refuge in the cheder and pours out to his rabbi a garbled tale of disaster compounded of fragments of his mother's secret, with some fanciful additions from his own version of what Freud and Rank have called "the family romance": his mother is dead; he is the son of an organist in a remote unidentified country; the people he lives with are his aunt and her husband. Reb Pankower carries this tale to the Schearls. The story reawakens Albert Schearl's secretly nurtured suspicion that David is not his son; in a bitter confrontation after the rabbi leaves, he accuses Genya of having colluded with her parents to deceive him. Most critics have taken the view that Albert's suspicions are the delusions of a maddened mind. In fact, however, a good bit of evidence supports Albert's contentions.

By her own account, Genya has undoubtedly had a love affair with an impoverished Christian youth named Ludwig. Indeed there is little room to doubt that Ludwig and Genya have had sexual intercourse. Her outraged father had no doubt when he shouted, as Genya tells Bertha, "I tell you she'll bring me a 'Benkart' yet, shame me to the dust. How do you know there isn't one in that lewd belly already. . . ?" When Bertha rails against their father at this point in the conversation, Genya concedes, "Well, I wasn't entirely innocent."

However well disposed the reader is toward the gentle, honest, warmly sheltering Genya, the events that have dropped a bitter seed of suspicion into Albert's soul cannot simply be ignored. His theory that Genya was pregnant at the time of their wedding, that the child was well above average size at the alleged age of twenty-two months, that Albert was hustled off to New York with funds provided by his in-laws so that he could not personally ascertain the date of the child's birth, and that the birth certificate was conveniently mislaid so that it could not bear witness to the misdeed— all these circumstances are plausible and perhaps actual. Indeed, the doubts about David's paternity are never satisfactorily resolved. The effect of this measure of doubt is not to establish that David is in fact the son of Ludwig the Christian organist but rather to introduce some doubt, to envelop the child's birth—and particularly his paternity— in a cloud of mystery, and thus to qualify him further as a hero of myth, as a potential messiah.

In adopting an embroidered version of the story of Ludwig as his own history, David abolishes his terrifying natural or nominal father. But he also converts his mother into an aunt, a maneuver that marks an important stage in his escape from the Oedipal embrace.

David's moment of closest attachment to his mother occurs early in the novel in the warmth of home on the sabbath eve in "the hushed hour, the hour of tawny beatitude." "He was near her now. He was part of her. The rain outside the window set continual seals upon their isolation, upon their intimacy, their identity." But before long this intimacy is invaded by the advances of Joe Luter, Albert's friend from the shop, who is for a short time a boarder at the Schearls' table. Observing Luter's ogling of Genya as she moves about the kitchen and noting an insinuating tone in his conversation, David becomes uneasy about his own loving observation of his mother. This uneasiness, although seemingly arising from a desire to protect his mother's virtue, actually marks the beginning of the child's regarding her with growing sexual curiosity and hence of his separation from her. While playing in the street, David sees Luter heading toward the flat at a time when Genya is there alone and surmises that the two are going to "play bad." Subsequently he believes that they have done so, although in fact the reader understands that Genya has repelled her would-be seducer.

Returning to the flat one afternoon from a disastrous episode with his irate father and from a cheder session where he has for once behaved like a dunce, David discovers the neighborhood in an uproar over an escaped canary. In his distress he ignores this excitement and rushes to the flat. Finding the door locked, he raps furiously until his mother appears, just emerged from her bath, and wrapped in a clinging gown. David seeks her embrace and experiences a bliss that is intensified by his father's absence and novel only in being charged with a half-conscious sexual aura. Learning that his father is soon to return, he flees to the street, where he discovers that the boys have pursued the fugitive canary to the roof-top. Across the light well they have spied upon

a woman stepping from her bath in a laundry tub—obviously David's mother, and obviously drawn from her concealment in the tub by his imperious pounding at the door. Outraged at the peepers but tormented by guilt as well, David nevertheless finds a moment to blame his mother: "Why did she let them look. . . . And she let me look at her! Mad at her!" Seeking to hide his tears, David starts toward the flat but is drawn to the pure air and freedom of the rooftop he has never yet visited. Although he cannot peep into the windows of his own flat, and indeed has no conscious intention of doing so, his movements are stealthy.

As he returns to the flat, he takes care to make noises in the hallway that will imply that he has just come up from the street. At home once more, he finds his mother in what the reader recognizes as a state of postcoital lassitude. David does not understand what has happened, but he does recognize that a pair of decorative bullhorns his father has bought connect the image of a man felled by his father's powerful fist and the spectacle of his mother bemused in unwonted contentment. For the first time he feels shut out from intimacy with his mother.

David continues to vacillate between passionate attachment to his mother and rebellion against her, but never again is the sense of intimacy and identity as close as it had been before he began a career of independent adventures. The bitter despair of these childish tragedies is the true dark night of David's soul; like the anguish of classic mystics and prophets it marks a turning toward self-reliance and serenity, toward ultimate escape from the Oedipal bond. As Freud puts the matter, "Every new arrival on this planet is faced by the task of mastering the Oedipus complex; anyone who fails to do so falls a victim to neurosis."

David's second and nearly fatal encounter with the streetcar tracks takes the form of a death-and-resurrection drama. The prelude and stimulus to this catastrophe is the confrontation between Genya and Albert concerning David's paternity. During this quarrel, David stammers out a confession of complicity in Leo's misdeed and asks punishment from his father. At this point Roth explicitly identifies David with Christ: "And the words he spoke were like staggering burdens he bore up a great steep where his own sighs battered him, where he floundered in his own tears." Albert works himself into a frenzy and claims the right to destroy this "goy's get." While Bertha and her husband wrestle with Albert, Genya rescues the child by thrusting him out the door.

Irresistibly impelled by the same external force that he has experienced several times earlier, David heads again toward the car-tracks, bearing a long-handled milk ladle he has found on the street. Now the action emerges from the confines of the Jewish neighborhood into a nearby area where the cast of characters takes on a thoroughly American diversity of nationalities, occupations, and avocations. Their talk, by turns comic, stupid, obscene, or aggressive, includes references to Christ, His ministry, and the events of the Passion. The result is to underscore the juxtaposition of the ordinary and the divine and to identify David unmistakably as a Christ figure.

Although there are procreative overtones in many of these remarks, suggestive of an impending birth, the reference to the Gospel accounts of the Passion is even more important in strengthening the role of David as an ecumenical messiah figure. The sexual reference of "How many times'll your red cock crow, Pete, befaw y' gives up?" is less important in this chapter than its paraphrase of Christ's prediction to Peter that "Before the cock crows, you will deny me three times" (Matt. 26:34). And after the calamity, Pete, the hunchback on crutches, denies aid to the injured David. The phrase "in the crack be born," however, when considered in conjunction with David's posture as he straddles the slotted rail to insert the dipper's handle between "the long, dark, grinning lips. . . . like a sword in a scabbard" clearly suggests an insemination that will assure the rebirth of the self-created creator close upon his symbolic death in a blaze of the light that has come to symbolize divine power. Upon the discovery of the accident, a rapid series of exclamations all add to the identification of David Schearl with Christ: "Jesus!" "Holy Mother o' God!" "Christ, it's a kid!" "A stick, for Jesus sake!" "Bambino! Madre mia!"

As David fades into unconsciousness, his reverie includes a "swirl of broken images," with the tugboatman in his crucified posture hanging among the wires of the Mr. Highwood telegraph poles and with the sugar tongs (*Zwank*) that his mother used to demonstrate the limited human grasp of the infinite fusing with the tongs the angel used to seize the burning coal from the altar to purify Isaiah's lips. Driven downward by his father's thundering voice, he diminishes into darkness and extinction.

But then, as the doctor works to revive the stricken boy, "*out of the darkness, one ember*"; the image that marks his resuscitation is of light emanating from coal. Images of serenity and silence engulf the last glimpse and echo of the terrifying father; finally it is the recollection of the tugboatman who wakened him from his riverside vision—and saved him—that marks his return to consciousness. Thus the David-Christ messiah is resurrected amidst a melange of images drawn from his Jewish background and from the predominantly Christian society in which he is to come of age.

After the melodrama of the immolation-and-resurrection scene, the final chapter of *Call It Sleep* is relaxed and calm. In this conclusion one critic has seen resignation, whereas others have read it as a parable recording the paralysis of Roth's creative powers. I doubt that the novel is prophetic in this way; rather, I take the author's characterization of David's state at the conclusion as literally accurate: "not pain, not terror, but strangest triumph, strangest acquiescence."

The final stages of the hero-messiah myth usually include either the killing of the hero by his father, the killing of the father by the hero, or their reconciliation. According to Freud, the successful outcome of the romantic fantasy that is the individual psychic parallel of the myth is "the liberation of an individual, as he grows up, from the authority of his parents"; the child who masters the Oedipal relationship and thus escapes neurosis learns, by accepting his real parents, to overcome the fear of the presumably hostile father. Joseph Campbell is emphatic in identifying one outcome of the hero's quest as a recognition that "I and the Father are one" (John 10:30).

In the final chapter of *Call It Sleep,* a reconciliation of sorts is achieved. Although he has long believed that he wishes such an outcome, Albert is sobered by the real possibility of David's death. In his chastened mood, though with some residual hesitation about the boy's age, he accepts David as his son, in the one English utterance he makes in the novel: "My sawn. Mine. Yes. Awld eight. Eight en'—en' vun mawnt. He was born in—." After the bitter eloquence that has typified his Yiddish speech throughout the novel, this halting language testifies to his reduced condition. No longer is he for David the avenging Yahweh of the child's infancy.

The final paragraph of *Call It Sleep* is deftly organized. Genya is comforting the injured child, and he is accepting her ministrations, although with the mental reservation that has become characteristic of his attitude toward his mother as he gradually masters his Oedipal connection with her:

> "And then you'll go to sleep and forget it all." She paused. Her dark, unswerving eyes sought his. "Sleepy, beloved?
>
> "Yes, mama."
>
> He might as well call it sleep. It was only toward sleep that every wink of the eyelids could strike a spark. . . .

He might as well *call* it sleep; but it is not sleep and forgetting; it is a state of reverie that lets him recall and evaluate images drawn from all his brief conscious life: images of glitter, sheen, glow—all the varieties of light that have brought his reassurance and delight; scenes from the life of the street; auditory images: "all sounds that lay fermenting in the vats of silence and the past."

All of this reverie leads him to feel, "not pain, not terror, but strangest triumph, strangest acquiescence." The novel ends, then, not in paralysis and defeat, not in the death of the artist, but in serenity, in liberation from the tyranny of a hostile father, the domination of an adoring mother, and the terrors of the unknown. Young though he is, David has come through the worst dangers of an immigrant childhood. After the perils of his quest, according to Campbell, the hero returns to the ordinary world, where as a result of his adventures he can teach his fellow citizens and serve them in a prolonged state of calm. Perhaps David will fulfill Rabbi Pankower's grudging prediction: "You may be a great rabbi yet—who knows!" Having learned the ambiguous moral nature of the world and having accepted life in the less than ideal human community, this obscure child of humblest origins may yet become the teacher, interpreter, examiner, guide, and comforter to the American people. He may become, indeed, the Messiah of the New World.

Roth's novel is a modern redaction of a widely diffused myth, although with significant alterations. The theme of the prince in humble guise is one of the most ubiquitous and enduring motifs in world literature; its usual outcome is the elevation of the apparently lowly to their rightful positions. Often the hero of myth or legend is the scion of wealthy, royal, or divine parents. He has been cast out either by the hostile father or by protectors shielding him from the father and has been adopted by humble parents—servants, peasants, or fishermen. The possible alternate father of David Schearl is neither wealthy, nor aristocratic, nor royal, nor divine, nor otherwise powerful. Roth's attribution of noble qualities to a person of genuinely commonplace origins— that is, one who is not a prince in disguise but who may nevertheless be inspired by the divine afflatus—is fitting in a democracy of common people, whose leaders can emerge from among the most miserable and despised part of its population. In addition, the myth of the messiah in *Call It Sleep* is distinctive in its violation of old xenophobic taboos to produce an American child. In Roth's parable his potential hero may be the child of a Jewish mother and a Christian father, a mixture that will particularly qualify him as the leader of a polyglot nation of nations where "all tribes and people are forming into one federated whole; and there is a future which shall see the estranged children of Adam restored as to the old hearthstone in Eden." Roth has bestowed American citizenship upon traditional materials to develop a myth for a democratic society.

Stephen J. Adams (essay date Spring 1989)

SOURCE: "'The Noisiest Novel Ever Written': The Soundscape of Henry Roth's *Call It Sleep*," in *Twentieth Century Literature*, Vol. 35, No. 1, Spring, 1989, pp. 43-64.

[In the following essay, Adams analyzes the importance of sound as a signifier of power in Roth's Call It Sleep.*]*

"The squalor and filth, the hopelessness and helplessness of slum life are remorselessly presented and the cacophony never ceases—this must be the *noisiest* novel ever written." Walter Allen's remark identifies one of the most striking and unusual features of Henry Roth's novel: this text opens up a world of sound as few others seem to do. Although most fictional imagery is, like our language itself, overwhelmingly visual, *Call It Sleep* offers many lessons in the verbal evocation of "soundscape"—a term coined by the composer R. Murray Schafer in his highly original study of the sonic environment *The Tuning of the World*. Schafer advances many new terms and concepts which, by overturning the visual bias of our language and culture, create a vocabulary that helps to explain the operations of sound in the world of young David Schearl, Roth's central character. Roth's uncanny evocation of David's sonic environment does much to account for the emotional intensity felt by most of the novel's readers.

Call It Sleep is, I am convinced, still undervalued. Though the peculiarities of the novel's publication history—its virtual disappearance in the Thirties, its acclaim after the paperback edition of 1964—are well known to Roth's readers, the book since then seems to have become pigeonholed as a "Jewish novel," rather than the essential American novel that I think it is. There may well be, as Leslie Fiedler has said, "no more Jewish book among American novels," but the impact and significance of this book extend far beyond its Jewish interest, profound as that may be. No other American novel dramatizes so powerfully the trauma of the newly arrived immigrant. It is the classic portrayal, writes Richard J. Fein, "of the Americanized son who pits himself against the unyielding immigrant father." In David's psychological adventure, we experience from the inside a paradigmatic rejection of Old World values and a tentative reaching toward the new. And the novel treats this distinctively American theme with unparalleled richness of implication and technical mastery. Far from being a novel of a particular ethnic group, *Call It Sleep* claims a central place in the canon of American fiction.

Critics of *Call It Sleep* have tended to focus on David's psychology—his oedipal attachment to his mother, Genya, and his fear of his father, Albert. Or they have focused on the novel's spiritual implications, treating it, like Fiedler, as "astonishingly a religious book." On the other hand—still perhaps influenced by the Thirties' controversy in the Marxist *New Masses* over its supposed failure as "proletarian fiction"—they have downplayed the novel's broader social significance. Yet from the immigrant-crowded steamer Peter Stuyvesant sailing past the Statue of Liberty in the prologue, to David's climactic acts of betrayal and atonement, Roth's novel lives through the painful processes of separation and assimilation. Psychologically, David must separate himself from his father's rejection and his mother's emotional hold. Spiritually, he attempts to reach beyond a confining and yet somewhat destabilized Judaism, moving from an Old Testament culture into one defined and controlled by the New. The gradual orientation of a fearful child, and his painful discovery of power, of relative maturity, of freedom from fear—of all the freedoms held out by America—form the core of the novel's experience.

The intensity of this experience derives from Roth's creation of the young boy's point of view, which critics have universally praised. More specifically, it derives, I believe, from Roth's ability to create the sensory world of the child, particularly the sense of sound. Though the text has not entirely traded eyes for ears, it has at least altered the usual ratio. The world of sound, as Schafer insists (taking his cue from Marshall McLuhan), is "loaded with direct personal significance for the hearer. While sight defines objects as separate and distanced from the perceiver, sound seems to enter inside the body. Vision separates objects as distinct things, but the heard object is often unseen and unidentified. For this reason, sound is naturally linked to the disembodied or the supernatural; as Schafer puts it, "God originally came to man through the ear, not the eye." Don Ihde, in *Listening and Voice,* agrees:

> It is the *invisible* which poses a series of almost insurmountable problems for much contemporary philosophy. "Other minds" or persons who fail to disclose themselves in their "inner" invisibility; the "Gods" who remain hidden; my own "self" which constantly eludes a simple visual appearance; the whole realm of spoken and heard language must remain unsolvable so long as our seeing is not also a listening. *It is to the invisible that listening may attend.* . . . The primary presence of the God of the West has been the God of Word, YHWH.

But if sound can acquire a numinous cast, it is also inseparable from the instincts of alarm. As Schafer observes:

> The sense of hearing cannot be closed off at will. There are no earlids. When we go to sleep, our perception of sound is the last door to close and it is also the first to open when we awaken. These facts have prompted McLuhan to write: "Terror is the normal state of any oral society for in it everything affects everything all the time."

If *Call It Sleep* is, as Walter Allen declares, "the most powerful evocation of the terrors of childhood ever written," the reason may be David's heightened sensitivity to sound. And after David's final vision in which his unconscious mind con-

structs a "self" which survives his father's wrath, deliverance from terror of the loud world forms part of the meaning of the ambivalent sleep at the end of the novel.

Roth's text evokes David's soundscape on three levels of awareness. Often it records sound simply as part of the child's general perception. On a second level, David not only registers sounds but reacts to them—often with alarm, but with a range of other emotions as well. On a third level, however, he not only hears and reacts but he interprets as well. David is not the simple passive character that some critics, and even Roth himself, seem to think. As Naomi Diamant has shown, in some of the best criticism written about the novel, *Call It Sleep* is "a semiotic *Bildungsroman*" in which David learns not only to *de*code but to *en*code his environment. (Diamant wisely qualifies this phrase, since the novel covers only three years of David's life and is not technically a *Bildungsroman,* but it raises many issues common to the genre.) I would add furthermore that this process, which Roth quite consciously modeled on Joyce, occurs simultaneously in the character and in the reader; as motifs accumulate, we together with David gradually invest them with symbolic and emotional attributes. The reader's experience fuses with that of the young boy, as he learns not simply to react to his New World but to interpret it and live in it.

On the level of simple perception, David is a remarkably sensitive register of his sonic environment, or to use Schafer's word, he is a reliable "earwitness." After the dry, objective narration of the Prologue, which tonally as well as semantically establishes the family's sense of emotional exile as they enter New York harbor in 1907, the text plunges into David's phenomenal world, creating auditory as well as visual perspective:

> Where did the water come from that lurked so secretly in the curve of the brass? Where did it go, gurgling in the drain? What a strange world must be hidden behind the walls of a house! But he was thirsty. "Mama!" he called, his voice rising above the hiss of sweeping in the frontroom. "Mama, I want a drink." The unseen broom stopped to listen. "I'll be there in a moment," his mother answered. A chair squealed on its castors; a window chuckled down; his mother's approaching tread.

Roth often makes us hear by finding the unexpected phrase: the "slight, spattering sound from the end of her lip," as Genya drinks tea; a "hiss of shoes" on stone outside the door; a door "tittering to and fro in the wind."

And of course, as Bonnie Lyons and others have noted, the text makes us aware of the sounds of languages—Yiddish, Hebrew, Polish, and all the broken English dialects of the street. Roth expertly distinguishes, for example, the Irish brogue of the policemen from the speech of an Italian pea-nut vendor, and with virtuoso flair even endows one of his speakers with both dialect and an almost impenetrable lisp: "Cauthye I wanthyloo, dayuth w'y'." Roth ensures that his text must be read with ears as well as eyes. Such passages may be said to dramatize David's awareness of the difficulty of extracting meaning from an alien language. As Raymond Chapman has noted,

> the primacy of speech over writing can be asserted even through the written text, with humor or with some social purpose. Indeed, the writer may actu-ally draw attention to the difficulty and artificiality of what he is doing. He may emphasize the fact that the nature of language in its two realizations gives him an impossible task.

In "The Cellar," David registers primarily the domestic en-vironment of the apartment in Brownsville: As his mother touches the lock on the door, "the hidden tongue sprang in the groove"; she sets the table, "knives ringing faintly, forks, spoons, side by side"; she talks to her husband, "noisily set-ting the dishes down in the sink." David at this point is in-doors mostly, and on his major venture outdoors, following the telegraph poles, he gets lost. His sleep is disturbed one time by "the frosty ring of a shovel scraping the stony side-walk"; but his awareness of the outdoor soundscape in this setting is dominated by children's play: "So get back in de line. Foller de leader. Boom! Boom! Boom!"

In "The Picture," however, when the Schearls move to the lower East Side, the outdoor soundscape is more insistent:

> Here in 9th Street it wasn't the sun that swamped one as one left the doorway, it was sound—an ava-lanche of sound. There were countless children, there were countless baby carriages, there were countless mothers. And to the screams, rebukes, and bickerings of these, a seemingly endless file of hucksters joined their bawling cries. On Avenue D horse-cars clattered and banged. Avenue D was thronged with beer wagons, garbage carts, and coal trucks. There were many automobiles, some blunt and rangey, some with high straw poops, honking. Beyond Avenue D, at the end of a stunted, ruined block that began with shacks and smithies and selt-zer bottling works and ended in a junk heap, was the East River on which many boat horns sounded. On 10th Street, the 8th Street Crosstown car ground its way toward the switch.

The noises of general humanity invade the indoors as well: "The stairs were of stone and one could hear himself climb. The toilets were in the hall. Sometimes the people in them rattled newspapers, sometimes they hummed, sometimes they groaned. That was cheering." In one scene after another, David's ears register the sound of human crowds:

> Curtains overhead paddled out of open windows. The air had shivered into a thousand shrill, splin-tered cries, wedged here and there by the sudden whoop of a boy or the impatient squawk of a mother.... In the shelter of a doorway, across the gutter, a cluster of children shouted in monotone up at the sky:

> "Rain, rain, go away, come again some oddeh day. Rain, rain...."

> The yard was gloomy. Wash-poles creaked and swayed, pulleys jangled. In a window overhead, a bulky, bare-armed woman shrilled curses at some-one behind her and hastily hauled in the bedding that straddled the sills like bulging sacks.

> "And your guts be plucked!" her words rang out over the yard. "Couldn't you tell me it was raining?"

Even when David, near the beginning of "The Rail," retreats to the freedom of the rooftop—"that silent balcony on the pinnacle of turmoil"—he remains eerily aware of the human-ity below: "What sounds from the street, what voices drifted up the air-shafts, only made his solitude more real." Human crowds provide what Schafer calls the "keynote" sound of the novel, the sound that acts as a constant point of refer-ence like tonality in a piece of music; or to borrow Schafer's figure-ground analogy from visual perception, they provide the ground against which more meaning-laden figures are heard. This crescendo of voices accompanies David through the latter half of the novel to his climactic action at the trol-ley rail. It amply prepares for the daring divided narration of Chapter 21, in which David's self-enclosed consciousness is surrounded by this keynote chorus of human voices, even though he no longer hears them.

Reading ***Call It Sleep*** with Schafer's account of past and present soundscapes in mind, one is struck by the predomi-nance of human over mechanical sounds in Roth's city. If this is in fact the noisiest novel ever written, the reason is the narrating character's sensitivity and the author's vivid aural memory; for the soundscape in the New York of 1907 was hardly as noisy as the modern city's, where the keynote, as Schafer observes, is that of the internal-combustion en-gine. Despite Roth's occasional mention of automobiles, they play little role in the novel; and despite his references to horse-cars, smithies, boat horns, and trolleys—all of which assume important symbolic functions—the human presence dominates; there is a feeling of perspective, of sounds near and far, which is largely obliterated in today's city. Absent from this intensely urban novel too are most natural sounds, apart from the domesticated horses, chickens, parrots, and canaries. And absent, of course, from Roth's indoor settings are modern intrusions like telephone or radio—or any electronic or amplified sound (though curiously enough, Roth's text registers the whine of power lines, the so-called "corona noise" that power companies have just recently begun to study).

In fact, for such a noisy book, there is notably little music of any kind. The music is not set apart as an aesthetic object, but is integrated into the lives of the characters, like the children's game song that arouses David's dim memories of Europe, or the work song that Genya absently sings as she washes windows. Mention is made of a gramophone (Genya had heard one in Europe): "I never heard anything labor so or squawk," she says. "But the peasants were awed. They swore there was devil in the box." The Schearls possess one, but it remains an empty possession, "mute and motionless as the day before creation," as Aunt Bertha chides—though she desires to possess one herself.

But Roth does not treat sonic imagery simply as part of the neutral background of the novelistic world. One cannot consider sound in *Call It Sleep* without quickly becoming entangled in David's emotional responses to it; nor can one consider sound apart from silence. David reacts to both sound and silence at first mainly with aversion, with fear. But gradually in the course of the novel he learns to overcome his fears, to find his place in the apparently hostile environment of the New World. Ultimately, he challenges the noise of power, and he acquiesces in the silence of sleep.

In the important passage near the beginning that establishes David's fear of sudden extinction, symbolized by the dark cellar, critics have noticed Roth's use of darkness and light, but they have failed to comment on his use of sound and silence:

> David never found himself alone on these stairs, but he wished there were not carpet covering them. How could you hear the sound of your own feet in the dark if a carpet muffled every step you took? And if you couldn't hear the sound of your own feet and couldn't see anything either, how could you be sure you were actually there and not dreaming? A few steps from the bottom landing, he paused and stared rigidly at the cellar door. It bulged with darkness. Would it hold? . . . It held! He jumped from the last steps and raced through the narrow hallway to the light of the street.

The incident vividly dramatizes what R.D. Laing would call David's ontological insecurity—his failure to feel secure of his own presence in the world as a real, whole, and continuous person. Thus a few pages later, when David again ventures the same route, he begs his mother, "Mama, will you leave the door open till—till I'm gone—till you hear me downstairs?"

Being heard is assurance of being. As Schafer remarks, silence, in the Western world at least, has mainly negative connotations: "Man likes to make sounds to remind himself that he is not alone. From this point of view total silence is the negation of human personality. Man fears the absence of sound as he fears the absence of life." This fear is observable in other characters as well. Bill Whitney, the watchman who appears briefly in Chapter 21 of "The Rail," mutters to himself—"and this he did not so much to populate the silence with ephemeral, figment selves, but to follow the links of his own, slow thinking, which when he failed to hear, he lost." And the irrepressible Aunt Bertha, perhaps the only character besides David who fully senses the soundscape around her, embraces the turmoil—"I hate quiet and I hate death"—as roundly as she rejects the Old World she has left behind: "But there's life here, isn't there? There's a stir always. Listen! The street! The cars! High laughter! Ha, good! Veljish was still as a fart in company. Who could endure it?"

Many scenes dramatize David's equation of silence with death and sound with life. When he witnesses a passing funeral, he tells himself, frantically:

> Make a noise. Noise. . . . He advanced. What? Noise. Any. "Aaaaah! Ooooh!" he quavered. "My country 'tis of dee!" He began running. The cellar door. Louder. "Sweet land of liberty," he shrilled, and whirled toward the stairs. . . . "Land where our fodders died!" The landing; he dove for the door, flinging himself upon it. . . .

The land where David's forefathers actually died, of course, is not America but the Old World, though his choice of lyrics ironically underlines an oedipal wish for his father's death here. A much later scene again equates silence with nonexistence. David drops a rosary gotten from his Catholic friend Leo on the floor of a different cellar: "At the floor of a vast pit of silence glimmered the rough light, pulsed and glimmered like a coin." He gropes for it: "'I'm gonna get it,' almost audibly. *'I am!'* His teeth gritted, head quivering in such desperate rage, the blood whirred in his ears. . . *'I am.'*" But with the whir of his own life processes in his ears, David's desperation is interrupted by the precocious sexual experimentation of Leo and cousin Polly—sounds that signify not the extinction but the creation of life. At yet another point in the book, David thinks of himself in his mother's womb, a memory, possibly even a prenatal memory, triggered when he overhears the mysterious word "Benkart," Polish for *bastard:* "—Benkart! (Beside the doorway David fastened on the word) What? Know it. No, don't. Heard it. In her belly. Listen!"

David learns early that where there is life there is sound: pure silence is unattainable. Hiding himself in the cellar darkness after a fight with playmates, he discovers

> there was no silence here, but if he dared to listen, he could hear tappings and creakings, patterings and whisperings, all furtive, all malign. It was horrible, the dark. The rats lived there, the hordes of nightmare, the wobbly faces, the crawling and misshapen things.

The composer John Cage similarly learned that there is no such thing as pure silence: when he entered an anechoic chamber and reported two sounds, one high and one low, he was told that one was his nervous system in operation, the other his blood circulating. David likewise experiences sound as part of his most intimate bodily rhythms; his system vibrates with the world around him. Helping with his father's milk deliveries, he is physically oppressed by the jangling bottles: "Louder, louder, nearer, they seemed to clank in David's heart as well. With every step his father took, the breath in his own body became more labored, more suffocating." Sonic metaphors enter Roth's language: "His blood, which a moment before had been chiming in bright abandon, deepened its stress, weighted its rhythm to an ominous tolling." As David flees the violent family confrontation in "The Rail," "every racked fibre in his body screamed out in exhaustion. Each time his foot fell was like a plunger through his skull."

Call It Sleep depicts many scenes in which David detects others by sound, or lurks out of sight eavesdropping on an adult world otherwise closed to him: "He crept to his doorway, stiff ankle-joints cracking like gun-shots. A blur of voices behind the door. . . . Hope clutched at it." David's instinctive recoil from Luter includes a disjunction of sight from sound: "But chiefly he found himself resenting Mr. Luter's eyes. They seemed to be independent of his speech, far outstripping it in fact; for instead of glancing at one, they fixed one and then held on until the voice caught up." Elsewhere, David notes "a short chuckle that pecked like a tiny hammer," or a frown and "a faint smacking sound from the side of his mouth." Indeed throughout the novel, Roth's dialogue is loaded with stage directions in what may seem an excessive way. Within the space of a page we read: "said Luter sympathetically . . . said Luter meditatively . . . she laughed, straightening up . . . said Luter with a sigh . . . she agreed . . . he said warmly . . . said Luter with conviction . . . his mother laughed condoningly . . . he assured her . . . said Luter with the hesitance of careful appraisal." This is a mannerism to be sure, but it is consistent with David's sensitivities. As he constitutes his world through listening, he is alert not just to what is said, but even more to the intonations and intentions behind what is said.

Roth seems unusually aware of the relationship between sound as phenomenon and sound as sign. This is clear in his treatment of languages—such as the Hebrew instilled phonetically before it is joined to "chumish," or translation. And when Genya and Aunt Bertha converse in Polish to close David out of the conversation, he strains to follow: "But though he pried here, there, everywhere among the gutturals and surds striving with all his power so split the stubborn scales of speech, he could not." But nonverbal signals, too, clutter David's world—from the "familiar tinny jangle" of a shopkeeper's bell, to the factory whistles and school bells by which he keeps time.

The factory whistle, however, serves not only as a timekeeper but, to borrow another of Schafer's coinages, a "soundmark" as well. Schafer defines a soundmark as "a community sound which is unique or possesses qualities which make it specially regarded or noticed by the people in that community." In other words, the sound is not merely registered but invested with particular meaning or feeling. During the episode in which David, lost, is taken in by sympathetic policemen, Roth makes it plain that he has learned to orient himself, to interpret his environment, not through his eyes but through his ears. When he loses his way, he first tries to find himself visually: "Though he conned every house on either side of the crossing, no single landmark stirred his memory. They were all alike—wooden houses and narrow sidewalks to his right and left." But when at the police station he hears the familiar whistle, he immediately comprehends the distance he has traveled and panics at the thought of his mother: "Whistles? He raised his head. Factory whistles! The others? None! Too far! So far she was. So far away!—But she heard them—she heard the other whistles that he couldn't hear." The policemen notice, but Genya soon arrives and, as the two walk home, the process of sensory orientation is repeated. David is again deceived by his eyes:

> "That way, Mama?" He started incredulously. "This way!" He pointed to the right. "This way is my school."
>
> "That's why you were lost! It's the other way."

But he knows he has arrived in the right place through the aural and tactile sensations of the wind: "They neared the open lot. He knew where he was now, certain of every step. There was a wind that prowled over that area of rock and dead grass, that would spring up at them when they passed it. And the wind did."

This sonic orientation is repeated in "The Picture," where David again secures his place in the new East Side neighborhood largely through sound:

> He knew his world now. With a kind of meditative

assurance, he singled out the elements of the ever-present din—the far voices, the near, the bells of a junk wagon, the sign-song cry of the I-Cash-clothes-man, waving his truncheon-newspaper, the sloshing jangle of the keys on the huge ring on the back of the tinker.

Indeed throughout the novel, from the bellow of the steamer on the first page to the climactic moment when David regains consciousness at the end, whistles and boat horns—which "set up strange reverberations in the heart"—gather symbolic associations having to do with orientation in time and place.

In *Call It Sleep,* one can observe this process by which a sound signal becomes a sound symbol, or to repeat Naomi Diamant's terms, by which David learns not only to decode but to encode his environment. As Schafer puts it, "a sound event is symbolic when it stirs in us emotions or thoughts beyond its mechanical sensations or signalling function, when it has a numinosity or reverberation that rings through the deeper recesses of the psyche." Whistles and boat horns are the most obvious examples in the novel, but many other sonic motifs are developed and interrelated in complex ways. Furthermore, although the factory whistles suggest David's increasing security in his surroundings, other symbols take on more mysterious overtones. As Walter Allen remarks, Roth's novel captures "better than it has ever been done in English before what might be called a child's magical thinking, which is clearly allied to the thinking of the poet." Like his literary precursor Huck Finn, who hears "an owl, away off, who-whooing about somebody that was dead, and a whippowill and a dog crying about somebody who was going to die," David Schearl hears certain sounds, like the Hebrew words of Isaiah, that trigger feelings of the supernatural.

> All his senses dissolved into the sound. The lines, unknown, dimly surmised, thundered in his heart with limitless meaning, rolled out and flooded the last shores of his being. Unmoored in space, he saw one walking on impalpable pavements that rose with the rising trees. Or were they trees or telegraph-poles, each crossed and leafy, none could say, but forms stood there with footholds in unmitigated light.

Here Isaiah's coal, which purifies his unclean lips and makes him a prophet of God, is associated not only with telegraph poles (and thus with David's earlier venture into the unknown), but also with the cross of the Christian Messiah, the thunder of Yahweh (see below), and the blinding light of unlimited power. It is associations like these, formed in David's mind, that drive him to the apparently irrational but quite explicable act of the penultimate chapter.

Because David, a young boy in a new world, must invent his own symbols, Reb Yiddel Pankower asks himself a key question: "What was going to become of these Yiddish youth? What would become of tis new breed? These Americans?" This process of becoming is what *Call It Sleep* reveals. There may be, as Meyer Levin suggests, "no more perceptive work in any literature dealing with a child's conditioning." But just as the melodramatic convergences of "The Rail" reveal this positive process of conditioning, of encoding and creating new meanings, so do they join them to a mounting series of betrayals—betrayals of his mother's sexual secret and his father's presumed disgrace, of his sympathetic aunt and her stepdaughter's honor, of his religion and his rabbi. The betrayals are psychological, moral, cultural, and religious.

David's climatic act then, is simultaneously an effort to atone for them and an effort to seize power—literally the electric power of the trolley rail, but symbolically the sexual power of his father and the religious power of his private messianic vision. The scene is a confluence of interrelated symbols in which the psychological battle between father and son stands for conflicts on several other levels: it suggests a battle between Old and New Worlds, between Old and New Testaments, between captivity and freedom. As Roth's punning reference to Ahura Mazda suggests ("Vus dere a hura mezda, Morr's?"), it is a Manichaean battle between symbols of light and darkness. To these conflicts, which a number of Roth's critics have explored, I would add that it is a battle between sound and silence.

As Schafer says, "Noise equals Power." The loudest noises in the soundscape are created by those who hold greatest power over it. Thus the factory whistles, boat horns, and trolley noises dominate a society controlled by industry and commerce. It is a society David wishes to enter. This equation of loudness with power is understood instinctively by David's peers:

> "Yuh don' make enough noise, dat's why. Yuh oughta ha' Wildy."

> "Who don' make enough noise? I hollered loud like anyt'ing. Who beats?"

At various points, David's Brownsville playmate Yussie imitates the noise of a gun: "Bing! I'm an Innian"; a firecracker that exploded prematurely in a man's hand: "Kling! Kling! Kling! Jos' like dat! Kling! Kling! Kling! Cauze de fiyuh crecker wen' bang by his ears!"; and the printing press that injures Albert's thumb: "Id don' go boof?" David, whose sensibilities are clearly more delicate, at first recoils from such noisemaking; but when he discovers a source of mystical power between the trolley rails, he experiences it as an overwhelming fusion of light and sound, as Roth's language resorts to the figure of synesthesia:

> From open fingers, the blade plunged into darkness.
>
> Power!
>
> Like a paw ripping through all the stable fibres of the earth, power, gigantic, fetterless, thudded into day! And light, unleashed, terrific light bellowed out of iron lips. The street quaked and roared, and like a tortured thing, the sheet zinc sword, leapt writhing, fell back, consumed with radiance.

This first electric shock has resulted from anti-Semitic hounding by a group of street bullies; that is, it is tied to David's difficulties in making a place for himself in the Gentile-dominated world that he struggles to understand. But after the event, he discovers that his fear of the darkness has been lifted: "Gee. Used to be darker. . . . Ain't really there. Inside my head. Better inside. Can carry it." And soon after, he discovers the relative freedom of the rooftop, where the sunlight again is felt in terms of synesthesia—"a trumpet, triple-trumpet bearing light"—and where he can actually strike up a friendship, though an unequal one, with a kite-flying Christian. (Leo's kite, of course, recalls that prototypical American Ben Franklin, who tapped the sources of electric power directly from the sky.)

The second and climactic electric shock again reaches for the language of synesthesia, but it takes on more intricate symbolic associations, including a fusion of the sexual and the religious. As if to underscore the religious dimension of Roth's sound symbolism, Schafer advances a concept that he calls "sacred noise." "Wherever Noise has been granted immunity from human intervention," he writes, "there will be found a seat of power":

> The association of Noise and power has never really been broken in the human imagination. It descends from God, to the priest, to the industrialist, and more recently to the broadcaster and the aviator. The important thing to realize is this: to have the Sacred Noise is not merely to make the biggest noise; rather it is a matter of having authority to make it without censure.

When David shoves the metal milk dipper—a symbol associated with both his father's penis and his mother's breast—into the trolley track, his quasi-sexual act ("in the crack be born") seems to him "as though he had struck the enormous bell of the very heart of silence." When the circuit is completed, amid allusions to the virgin birth of Jesus and Peter's betrayal, David experiences the shock as "a blast, a siren of light within him . . . braying his body with pinions of intol-

erable light," while onlookers witness "a single cymbal-clash of light" and the milk dipper "consumed in roaring incandescence." Significantly, David seeks this sacred noise not in the cheder but in the power circuit of the commercial world. His privately coded symbolic act brings him into contact, literally, with the true sources of social power.

Roth's cumulative technique builds complex symbolic chains: David's final self-immolation is anticipated in the doll-burning scene of "The Picture," and the incandescent milk dipper by the ritually burned Passover spoon of "The Coal." Likewise, the whistle that brings David back to consciousness is invested with symbolic and magical properties from many earlier scenes; most prominent is the hallucinatory waterfront scene in which David, transfixed by "fire on the water," is saved from falling by the blast of a tugboat:

> Minutes passed while he stared. The brilliance was hypnotic. He could not take his eyes away. . . . And he heard the rubbing on a wash-board and the splashing suds, smelled again the acrid soap and a voice speaking words that opened like the bands of a burnished silver accordion—Brighter than day. . . . Brighter. . . . Sin melted into light. . . .
>
> Uh chug chug, ug chug!
> —Cucka cucka. . . . Is a chicken
> Ug chug, ug chug, ug—TEW WEET!
>
> What! He started as if out of a dream. A tremor shook him from head to foot so violently that his ears whirred and rang. His eyes bulged, staring.

David then sees the man on the tugboat who has saved him, "a man in his undershirt, bare, outstretched arms gripping the doorpost on either side. He whistled again, shrill from mobile lips, grinned, spat, and 'Wake up, Kid!' his sudden amused hail rolled over the water, 'fore you throw a belly-w'opper!'"

This complex scene is mentioned by most of Roth's commentators, but again the auditory imagery has been largely ignored. As Lyons observes, the man's "Wake up, Kid!" links David to the sacrificial kid of the Chadgodya, and the man's pose with outstretched arms suggests the Crucifixion. But this pose also links him to David's father emerging from his bedroom in the previous chapter: "His stretching arms pressed against both sides of the door-frame till it creaked. 'We need some light.'" And the sound of the washboard and splashing suds recalls his mother in the same scene, pronouncing the mystical words "Brighter than day" as she sits in the dark, washing curtains for Passover—surreptitiously breaking the Sabbath after sundown on Friday. The image is thus colored by both oedipal and religious guilt. Furthermore, the "cucka cucka"—a sonic rendition of the chugging tugboat—recalls through a sonic pun an earlier visit with Genya to a chicken market:

> It's a sin. . . . So God told him eat in your own markets. . . . That time with mama in the chicken market when we went. Where all the chickens ran around—cuckacucka—when did I say? Cucka. Gee! Funny. Some place I said. And then the man with a knife went zing! Gee! Blood and wings. And threw him down. Even kosher meat when you see, you don't want to eat—

Although the market was kosher, as David recalls while seated in the cheder, Genya's laxity is disturbing: "Mama don't care except when Bertha was looking." The chicken reference furthermore looks forward to the icon David notices in Leo's apartment, Jesus of the Sacred Heart holding his breast open and pointing to his inner organs: "Guts like a chicken, open. And he's holding them." This scene, in which Leo lectures David on the restrictiveness of the Jewish diet and the superiority of "Christchin light"—"Bigger den Jew light"—is the same in which David also gathers information about the mysterious occupation of Genya's Gentile lover, a church organist. Leo describes a church organ: "Dey looks like pianers, on'y dey w'istles." Chickens, organs, whistles, breaking the Mosaic law, taking a Gentile lover, and the superior power of Christian light—all conspire in the subterranean linkages of Roth's text and David's mind (and the reader's) to drive him to question his own origins and to emulate the freedom of the Christian boy whom he first saw flying a kite and "whistling up at the sky": "*Not afraid! Leo wasn't afraid!*"

Furthermore, in David's hallucinating mind at the waterfront, the tugboat whistle and the whistling man aboard her together fuse with a different bird sound:

> E-e-e. Twee-twee-twee. Tweet! Tweet! Cheep! Eet! R-rawk Gee! Whistle. Thought it was that man. In the tugboat. In the shirt. Whistling. Only birds. Canary. That lady's. Polly too—Polly want a cracker—is out already. On the fire-escape. Whistle.

Behind this stands an episode in which David has heard two caged birds in his East Side neighborhood:

> A parrot and a canary. Awk! Awk! the first cried. Eee-tee-tee—tweet! the other. A smooth and a rusty pulley. He wondered if they understood each other. Maybe it was like Yiddish and English, or Yiddish and Polish, the way his mother and aunt sometimes spoke. Secrets. What?

David clearly associates the bird sounds with the Polish-encoded secrets of his mother, and thus with his own possibly illegitimate origins. The canary, furthermore, looks forward to the escaped canary the boys pursue in Chapter 4 of "The Rail," and thence to the "yellow birds" that symbolize freedom throughout the climactic scene. Though the boys fail to catch the canary in the chapter, they do catch sight of Genya, naked, bathing in the washtub, much to David's anguish. In addition, the parrot bears the name of David's cousin Polly, whom he betrays to Leo's sexual predation in the candy-store cellar, thus repeating the forbidden liaison of Jew and gentile begun by his mother. Leo, in fact being Polish, acts as a double for David, suggesting to the reader and perhaps to his own subconscious the boy he might have been if he were truly the son of Genya's lover. Thus the birds and their sounds are circuitously related to David's awareness of his mother's sexuality and his own, to their mutual need for atonement and purification, and at the same time—even at the cost of betraying his Jewishness—to the desirability of the freedoms allowed to Gentiles.

One other significant though less intricate sound symbol reinforces the association of Leo with freedom of mobility and freedom from fear. Again an early memory is involved. In "The Cellar," David, returning home through the snow with a newspaper for his father, began to run: "He had only taken a few strides forward when his foot suddenly landed on something that was not pavement. The sound of hollow iron warned him too late—A coal-chute cover. He slipped." The ruined paper rouses his father's anger, leading soon after to the brutal beating with a coat hanger. The hollow iron sound of the coal-chute ties together his fear of the cellar with his fear of his father, and relates as well to his desire for Isaiah's purifying coal. Near the end of the novel, the same sound alerts David to Leo's approach behind him—on the coveted roller skates: "The sudden whirr of wheels behind him—now louder on the sidewalk now roaring momentarily over the hollow buckle of a coal-chute—." Leo, the liberated and potent Gentile, flies over coal-chutes as he flies over rooftops. This sound is closely allied to the hollow metallic sound of the phallic milk dipper as David pries it loose: "It bulged, sounded hollow. Again he braced himself, thrust—Clank!" And again when he strikes it against the trolley rail: "Only in his ears, the hollow click of iron lingered. Hollow, vain."

Roth weaves together these sound symbols with many other motifs in the climactic scene to suggest David's reaching out for purification and freedom; but he introduces a number of others, as well, linked with the negative psychological forces embodied in David's father. Bonnie Lyons traces one of these, the *Zwank* motif, and though she concentrates on its semantic meaning—the Yiddish word for tongs, connecting his mother's sugar tongs with those of Isaiah's angel—she recognizes that when the word first appears in the scene at the rail, "the sound itself seems most important"; the word "assumes its semantic and imagistic significance" only gradually, as David's mind recollects. She does not explain, however, why the word appears not with the angelic tongs but together with David's terrifying vision of his father leaping godlike over the rooftops and swinging his hammer. This recollection goes back to a glimpse inside a blacksmith's shop, just before David burns his Passover spoon and becomes hypnotized by the "fire on the water," where tongs and hammer are combined:

> Acrid odor of seared hooves lingered about the place. Now a horse-shoe glowed under the hammer—ong-jonga-ong-jong-joing-jong—ringing on the anvil as the pincers turned it.
>
> —Zwank. Zwank. In a cellar is—
>
> He passed the seltzer bottlery—the rattle and gurgle-passed the stable.

Thus, like the milk dipper, the tongs are associated not only with the mother and her sugar tongs, but also with the father and his hammer, and also therefore with the fear and guilt that both parents arouse. But this passage also links the hammer and tongs to horses and jangling bottles—sounds later invested with terrifying associations in the milk-delivery episode. These sounds at first seem relatively neutral, even positive, since the event promises an adventure into the outer world as his father's helper; but disaster strikes when David first disobeys instructions to wait with the wagon, and then watches helplessly as two bullies steal milk. His father's rage is soon inscribed into the sounds of the wagon, the bottles, the horses—and above all the whip, with which Albert almost beats to death one of the offenders:

> The crunch of heels on the gravel. Terror! His eyes snapped open.
>
> Dwarfed between the huge gas tanks, his father rounded the path. Eyes downcast as always he hurried, jangling the empty grey bottles in their trays. . . .
>
> "Paid yourself again!" he snarled. "Giddap! Giddap, Billy!" He snatched the whip out of the socket, lashed the horse. Stung, the beast plunged forward. The wheels ground against the curb. "Giddap!" Again the whip. Hooves rang out in a pounding, powerful gallop. The wagon lurched, careened around the corner on creaking axle, empty bottles banging in their boxes. . . .

These sounds, incidentally, are among those identified by Schafer as the most aversive in the pre-automotive urban soundscape; but David's response to the cracking whip needs little explication when he presents it to his father for punishment at the end of the violent quarrel in Chapter 19 of

"The Rail." For although David is not physically whipped for the stolen milk, he is verbally disavowed by his raging father—"False son! You, the cause!"—and he is psychologically pressed into silence and nonexistence—"Say anything to your mother . . . and I'll beat you to death! Hear me?" Little wonder, then, that in David's vision the father appears accompanied by jangling milk bottles, a hammer that "snapped like a whip," and the reiterated *Zwank!* as he orders his son to "Go down."

One other archetypal sound attaches to Albert Schearl in this terrible vision: twice we read that his voice "thundered." Lyons quite plausibly identifies this thunder motif with the Germanic hammer-wielding god of wrath, Thor; but oddly enough, she omits reference to the one scene in the novel in which we actually hear "a clap of thunder and a rumbling like a barrel rolling down cellar stairs." It occurs when David, in the cheder, has just successfully recited the Chadgodya. The thunder excites the other children: "Bang! Bang what a bust it gave! I tol' yuh I see a blitz before!" The only characters frightened by the din are David himself and Reb Yiddel Pankower, who ducks his head and exclaims "Shma yisroel. . . . Woe is me!" Both regain composure:

> "Before God," the rabbi interrupted, "none may stand upright."
>
> —Before God
>
> "But what did you think?"
>
> "I thought it was a bed before. Upstairs. But it wasn't."

There is ample precedent in scripture for the rabbi's association of thunder with the wrath of Yahweh. But David's unexpected linking of thunder to the sound of a bed upstairs relates both thunderclap and God's wrath with his oedipal antagonism to his father. The rabbi underlines this association unknowingly, when he derides David's visionary account of Isaiah's coal in the trolley rail: "Oy! Chah! Chah! Chah! I'll split like a herring! Yesterday he heard a bed in the thunder! Today he sees a vision in the crack!" Failing to grasp David's mystical and quasi-sexual symbolic language, the rabbi disqualifies himself in David's mind as an authority: "The rabbi didn't know as he knew what the light was." Thus when the milk dipper makes contact with the rail, it appears (amid cries of "Jesus!," "Schloimee, a blitz like—," and "Holy Mother o' God") as a burst of flame that "growled as if the veil of earth were splitting," and the Old Testament thunder is exchanged for that which rends the veil of the temple at Christ's Crucifixion in the Gospel of Matthew.

The father's appearance in David's vision enacts the psychological conflicts that the boy is struggling to resolve, a life-

and-death struggle partly figured in symbolic language of sound and silence. Before such a God, none may stand upright—and as the visionary father order David to "Go down," his consciousness approaches "nothingness," "oblivion," and "silence." But the sounds of life prevail. We hear the "Kh-r-r-r-f! S-s-s-s" of David's breath, supplied by artificial respiration, but also, certainly, by his will to survive. And we hear the wires that "whined on their crosses" and the groans of the "man in the wires" whose "purple chicken-guts slipped through his fingers," as David's imagination fuses the two episodes in which he is saved by a whistle into a single image of a messianic Savior.

Although the critics are divided, and Roth himself seems uncertain whether the ending of his novel is positive or negative, my own view is close to those of Naomi Diamant, Maxwell Geismar (in his introduction to the Cooper Square edition of the novel), or William Freedman, who writes:

> The myths of redemption and rebirth are implicit in the story of David Schearl, and both are rendered largely by means of symbolic image pattern that is part of David's own conscious awareness and that is viewed symbolically by his own fertile imagination as well as by the reader.

David, whose name allies him to the messianic family of scriptural tradition, clearly emerges from his ordeal as victor, having undergone an almost literal death and rebirth. Though Leslie Fiedler contends that David's "intended sacrifice redeems no one," it does, I think, redeem himself, and by extension the population that he stands for—that of the newly assimilated immigrant. The novel portrays in the intensity of David's vision not a passive sensibility but an emerging poetic imagination capable of shaping an imperfect world to its own uses.

As readers of this climactic scene, we witness David's unconscious mind constitute a "self" in terms of a symbolic narrative woven out of its own experience. This narrative functions, in a paradigmatic Freudian way, to exorcise the parental demons and reassert the unconscious self on new ground; for as Paul Jay has noted, the whole idea of Freudian analysis "depends on the subject's ability to fashion a narrative, a discursive formulation of the meaning of past events identified in the process of analysis as significant." The outcome of this narrative is, to be sure, provisional, for it almost ends in David's death. But his recovery signifies, in psychological terms, a readiness to assert his independent being in the face of his father's rejection, and in social terms, his ability to assume a place in the loud world. At the novel's end, David Schearl is a successful adult and assimilated American *in posse*. Thus he can finally accept the natural rhythm and natural silence of sleep without fear:

> It was only toward sleep that his ears had power to cull again and reassemble the shrill cry, the hoarse voice, the scream of fear, the bells, the thick-breathing, the roar of crowds and all the sounds that lay fermenting in the vats of silence and the past . . . and feel them all and feel, not pain, not terror, but strangest triumph, strangest acquiescence. One might as well call it sleep. He shut his eyes.

Hana Wirth-Neshner (essay date May 1990)

SOURCE: "Between Mother Tongue and Native Language: Multilingualism in Henry Roth's *Call It Sleep*," in *Prooftexts*, Vol. 10, No. 2, May, 1990, pp. 297-312.

[*In the following essay, Wirth-Neshner discusses Roth's use of language in* Call It Sleep *and how the author uses multilingualism to portray David Schearl's experience as an immigrant in America.*]

Henry Roth's ***Call It Sleep*** is a multilingual book, although it is accessible to the American reader who knows none of its languages other than English. In order to portray a world that was both multilingual and multicultural, Roth used a variety of narrative strategies, some designed to simulate the experience of his immigrant child protagonist and others designed to translate these experiences for his general American reader. ***Call It Sleep*** is a classic example of a work in which several cultures interact linguistically, thematically, and symbolically, and it is also an interesting case of ethnic literature, the Jewish-American novel.

Henry Roth offers a classic example as well of the author of a brilliant first novel who keeps the critics speculating as to whether his second work will live up to the first. In his case, the silence that followed that first dazzling performance could be interpreted as a larger cultural phenomenon than a mere individual writer's block. Occasionally what appears to be one artist's dilemma can also be a symptom of a cultural cul-de-sac. Such was the case of Thomas Hardy's last novel, *Jude the Obscure,* which carried the bleakness of the Victorian age and the Victorian novel to its limits, and such was the case of Henry Roth's ***Call It Sleep,*** which embodies the paralysing ambivalence of the Jewish immigrant writer in America, although not every writer's response to this conflict has been silence. Throughout Jewish literary history, writers have developed different narrative strategies for representing the multilingual and multicultural world which they inhabited.

As early as 1918, the Yiddish literary critic Baal Makhshoves argued that the mark of Jewish literature is its bilingualism. Although he was taking this position within the cultural context of the Czernowitz conference and the antagonism between Hebrew and Yiddish, he made claims for the status of Jewish literature from biblical times to the present. In every text that is part of the Jewish tradition, Baal Makhshoves wrote, there existed explicitly or implicitly another language, whether it be Chaldean in the Book of Daniel, Aramaic in the Pentateuch and the prayerbook, Arabic in medieval Jewish philosophical writings, and, in his own day going back as far as the fifteenth century, Yiddish. "Bilingualism accompanied the Jews even in ancient times, even when they had their own land, and they were not as yet wanderers as they are now," he wrote. "We have two languages and a dozen echoes from other foreign languages, but we have only *one* literature." When Baal Makhshoves refers to bilingualism, he means not only the literal presence of two languages, but also the echoes of another language and culture detected in the prose of the one language of which the text is composed. "Don't our finer critics carry within them the spirit of the German language? And among our younger writers, who were educated in the Russian language, isn't it possible to discern the spirit of Russian?"

Bilingualism and diglossia, in their strict linguistic sense and in their broader cultural meanings, have always been distinguishing features of Jewish culture and one major aspect of that enigmatic concept, Jewish literature. By bilingualism, I mean the alternate use of two or more languages by the same individual, which presupposes two different language communities, but does not presuppose the existence of a bilingual community itself. Diglossia, on the other hand, is the existence of complementary varieties of language for intragroup purposes, and therefore it does not necessitate bilingualism, as the linguistic repertoires are limited due to role specialization. In short, as Fishman has pointed out, bilingualism is essentially a characterization of individual linguistic versatility whereas diglossia is a characterization of the societal allocation of functions to different languages. Diglossia is obviously not unique to Jewish civilization. In European culture, for example, the idea that certain languages were specially proper for specific purposes lasted into the sixteenth century, with one of its literary products being macaronic verse. But both bilingualism and diglossia are central concepts in any discussion of Jewish literature, for they presuppose that a truly competent reader of the text must be in command of more than one language, and consequently of more than one culture. When Henry Roth used Hebrew, Yiddish, and Aramaic for specific purposes in his novel, he was employing a device used widely within Jewish literature, and within what has come more generally to be called ethnic literature.

The centrality of both bilingualism and diglossia in Jewish culture has been explored extensively by scholars and literary critics, among them Max Weinreich, Uriel Weinreich, Joshua Fishman, Itamar Even-Zohar, Binyamin Harshav, and

Dan Miron. The extent to which bilingualism is rooted in European Jewish life is expressed by Max Weinreich in his *History of the Yiddish Language*: "a Jew of some scholarly attainment, born around 1870, certainly did not express only his personal opinion when he declared that the Yiddish translation of the Pentateuch had been given to Moses on Mt. Sinai."

Both the diglossia and bilingualism of Jewish literature are particular variants of Bakhtin's concept of heteroglossia in the novel. According to Bakhtin, prose fiction maintains an inner dialogue among different languages, so that a text in one language, from the linguistic perspective, contains within it other languages, which can be social, national, generic, and professional, among others. These languages do not exclude one another, but intersect in a variety of ways. "All languages of heteroglossia, whatever the principle underlying them and making each unique, are specific points of view on the world, forms of conceptualizing the world in words, specific worldviews, each characterized by its own objects, meanings, and values."

Bilingualism and diglossia pose interesting mimetic challenges for the writer who aims for a community of readers beyond those who are competent in all of the language variants employed in his text. Moreover, in the Jewish literary tradition, multilingualism often means allusions, metaphors, and tropes that are derived from at least two widely divergent traditions, the Jewish and the non-Jewish worlds. This cultural situation necessitates various translation strategies for the author, ranging from literal translation from one language to another in the text (sometimes consciously underscoring the differences in world-view of the languages) to the felt sense of translation, as the language of the text contains within it the shades of the other absent language or languages. All authors dealing with a multilingual and multicultural reality have had to devise mimetic strategies for conveying a sense of foreignness, whether it be explicit attribution of speech in "translation," selective reproduction of the source language, or more oblique forms, such as verbal transpositions in the form of poetic or communicative twists. The most challenging for the reader has been the transposition of a different set of values, norms, images, or allusions from an alternative culture.

The strategies for presenting this multicultural reality are varied within Jewish literature. In the case of Jewish-American writing of which Henry Roth is a striking example, those writers who actually have some knowledge of an alternative Jewish literary tradition, in Hebrew or in Yiddish, have located their own works between two traditions, the English and the Yiddish, the Christian and the Jewish. This can express itself not only in linguistic borrowings by incorporation of phrases from the other language, but also by allusions to the other traditions, or to the borrowing of models and types from the other canon. Just as Yiddish poets in America placed themselves in the line of Whitman and Emerson, so writers like Henry Roth, Abraham Cahan, Saul Bellow, and Delmore Schwartz, composing in the English language, often draw on quotations from Jewish sources, intersperse Yiddish words, and turn their characters into types within two cultural frames of reference.

In Abraham Cahan's landmark novel, *The Rise of David Levinsky,* the alternative tradition is the very theme of the work; the central protagonist traces his intellectual assimilation to the English world to his reading of a Dickens novel, but he continues to measure his moral development against the Jewish world that he has abandoned. In the writings of Saul Bellow, for example, this alternative tradition is evident in the intellectual repertoire of his central protagonists, who are repeatedly invoking European figures as predecessors, muses, and mentors. Just as Augie March is clearly a literary grandchild of Huckleberry Finn, so Herzog and Sammler are children of Montaigne and Dostoevsky, of Continental European thought and letters. In some cases it is the other language that haunts the English prose, at times artfully and self-consciously, as in the stories of Delmore Schwartz, when the English reads like a translation from the Yiddish; at other times unself-consciously, as in the Yiddishized English of Anzia Yezierska's fiction, suggesting in the language and syntax a merging of cultures. In one of Cynthia Ozick's works, to cite yet another variation, the imminent extinction of Yiddish language and culture is the very subject of the story, as the Yiddish writer is left wholly dependent on translation itself to assure some precarious survival.

In each of the above works, the emphasis is on a divided identification with more than one culture, and while this is not exclusively a Jewish literary characteristic, it has been one very dominant aspect of Jewish literature and culture.

Henry Roth's novel **Call It Sleep** is a particularly interesting example of the part that multilingualism and translation play in Jewish literature. In that work, Roth uses languages other than English, as well as textual and cultural references outside of the English and American literary tradition. Roth grew up with Yiddish as the language of his home and neighborhood, among the Jewish immigrants on the lower East Side, and along with many of them, he went on to study at City College. There he was introduced to the world of English literature. He obviously created his novel against the entire backdrop of English literature, and more specifically American literature, referring in his interviews to Shakespeare, Joyce, Faulkner, Frost, Steinbeck, Hart Crane, Daniel Fuchs, and James Farrell, among others. Roth writes for an implied reader who is well versed in English literature and the Western Christian tradition; although he has used a number of translation strategies for the non-English

language and culture present in his text, his novel requires that the reader be familiar with some aspects of Jewish tradition. The full artistic scope of his work cannot be comprehended without this multiple cultural grounding. I would like to examine how Roth makes use of multilingualism and translation in his masterful novel as a way of identifying how the book partakes of more than one literary and cultural tradition, and how its artistic strategies express Roth's specific response to the dilemma of the self-consciously Jewish author writing in a language steeped in non-Jewish culture.

The book is almost entirely narrated from the perspective of David Schearl, a boy of eight, with the exception of the Prologue and one short section seen through the eyes of the Hebrew school teacher. It is about an immigrant child's quest for a personal and cultural identity apart from his parents; it traces the arduous and bewildering path of assimilation. It is a book written in the English language but experienced by the reader as if it were a translation, for David's main actions and thoughts are experienced in Yiddish. The original experience in the source language is almost entirely absent. When the original language is reproduced, it is rendered in transliteration, a phonetic transcription, rather than an authentic recording using the actual alphabet, so that from the American reader's perspective, the original language is both irretrievable and incomprehensible. Everything is experienced at a remove linguistically. While the Yiddish language is "home" for David and is associated with his parents, particularly with his mother, it can be an alien language for the reader. Occasionally Roth will provide a translation for the reader who is not familiar with Yiddish, but he will also reproduce the Yiddish for its own sake.

Although one does not have to know Yiddish to understand the book, one does have to be familiar with Jewish culture to understand all of the motifs and to appreciate the artistic pattern. From the point of view of the reader, "foreign" languages intruding on the English text are Yiddish, Hebrew, and Aramaic. While Yiddish is the spoken language of the home, the other two languages are reproduced only as liturgy, as quotations from Jewish textual sources. In other words, Roth treats Hebrew in the Jewish traditional sense of the sacred language or *loshn-koydesh*. As Max Weinreich has noted, for Ashkenazic Jewry Hebrew was the language of the sacred texts, of the immovable basis of study. Just as Yiddish was the language of speech, so Hebrew was the language of whatever had to be committed to writing. Just as Yiddish was the unmediated language, the one that the people used for face-to-face communication, so *loshn-koydesh* (non-modern Hebrew) was the mediated and bookish language. For the central protagonist, Hebrew and Aramaic are also foreign languages, the sounds being as incomprehensible to his ear as they would be to that of the English-speaking reader. Yet they are part of his home culture, because they are central components of his Jewish identity. Thus, David is bilingual and multicultural, his bilingualism consisting of Yiddish and English, and his multiple cultures consisting of Yiddish as home and everyday life, English as the street and the culture to which he is assimilating, and Hebrew and Aramaic as the mysterious languages, the sacred tongues, that represent mystical power to him and that initiate him into the Jewish world. Moreover, Yiddish, Hebrew and Aramaic are all languages of his Jewish culture, while American English, the language of the author's primary literacy, is the language of the "other" in that it is the language of Christianity. Roth's novel charts the struggle with this linguistic and cultural "other," as it speaks through the author and his Jewish child protagonist.

The book maps David's movement outward, away from home both psychologically, as he experiences his oedipal phase, and sociologically as he moves out of his Yiddish environment toward American culture. While Roth's implied reader may not know either Yiddish or Hebrew, he is expected to know the broader cultural significance within Judaeo-Christian civilization of the liturgical passages reproduced in their original, and as a result will be aware of David's location at the nexus of several cultures, far beyond anything that the child can ever comprehend. Furthermore, the book's theme of the irrevocable move away from home, both socially and psychologically, and the concomitant irretrievable losses, is evident in the mimetic strategem as well, for the reader experiences the actions at a linguistic remove, as if it were a translation with a missing original, or from a forgotten language.

Because Yiddish is the absent source language from which the thoughts and actions in English are experienced, it competes with English as the "home" language, or to put it another way, Yiddish is the home culture and English is an everyday language for David, but a foreign culture. Consequently, while actual transliteration from Yiddish is an intrusion in the English text, English intertextual references can also be an intrusion in the cultural context, because the world of English culture is alien to the text's cultural environment. The odd result is that English, the language in which the text is written, can itself be experienced as alien by the reader as well as the characters, as a type of self-distancing or reverse interference. Yiddish reproduction in the English text, in contrast, causes no discomfort to the characters for the selective reproduction is a mimetic device experienced only by the reader, and it brings an alien element to the text for readers unfamiliar with Yiddish. Hebrew reproductions are experienced as alien by the characters and by the American reader, but as less so by the reader who has the cultural background to identify them and to comprehend their cultural implications.

The Prologue, one of the only passages in the book rendered from an omniscient narrator and not through David as focalizer, introduces the main themes as well as the problem of translation, of bilingualism and biculturalism. It begins with a homogenous English text and moves toward Yiddish; it moves inward, from the general description of New York Harbor and the mass immigration as part of the American experience, to the specific characters and their Yiddish world. The Prologue opens with an epigraph in italics: "I pray thee ask no questions / this is that Golden Land." Traditionally, epigraphs provide a motto for a chapter or for an entire work, and they are often quotations from another text. In this case, the epigraph sounds like a quotation, and with its archaic second person singular, it can be associated with English prose of an earlier period. But it is not attributed to any source, nor is it a quotation that is easily recognizable on the part of a literate English reader. Moreover, the capitalizing of "Golden Land" draws attention to that phrase, *di goldene medine,* which in Yiddish is a popular way of referring to America, standard fare on Second Avenue but also echoed in Yiddish poetry as in Moshe-Leyb Halpern's poem, *In goldenem land.* The epigraph is a purely invented quotation, one that *seems* to be part of English literature, but at the same time seems to be a statement from Yiddish, just as the novel itself, written in English and in the modernist experimental tradition of Joyce, also partakes of the world of Eastern European Jewish culture.

Furthermore, the epigraph itself is repeated three pages later as the reported first utterance of David's mother, "And this is the Golden Land." Roth adds, "She spoke in Yiddish." This explicit attribution of a different language to her speech is the first indication, after the general portrait of newly arrived immigrants, that the novel takes place in a Yiddish-speaking environment, and it provides what Sternberg has called "mimetic synechdoche." Once again, after all of the dialogue conveying the miscommunication and tension between the newly arrived immigrant mother and the settled immigrant father who perceives himself to be partly Americanized, there is a further repetition of the golden land motif near the end of the prologue in the narrated interior monologue of Genya, "This was that vast incredible land, the land of freedom, immense opportunity, that Golden Land." But the prologue actually ends with a short dialogue in Yiddish without any translation:

"Albert," she said timidly, "Albert."

"Hm?"

"Gehen vir voinen du? In Nev York?"

"Nein. Bronzeville. Ich hud dir schoin geschriben."

In short, the prologue ends with establishing the literal location of Albert and Genya, not in the golden land, but in a real place called Bronzeville. And it is accessible only to the bilingual reader.

The movement of the prologue is inward, from English to Yiddish, from the general depiction of immigration with the image of the Statue of Liberty and the synoptic view of the couple to the individual characters and their specific plans. It moves from the metaphor of the Golden Land, first appearing in an English epigraph, to identification of the golden land with the dreams of the Jewish immigrant conveyed in English translation, to the final exchange in Yiddish, which displaces the figurative America with a literal geographical location. With each new repetition, the golden land slips into an ironic tone, reinforced by the very tarnished, industrial and demystifying description of the Statue of Liberty marking the entry to America.

The rest of the novel moves in the opposite direction as that of the Prologue, namely outward, from David's mother's kitchen, the realm of Yiddish, to the street and the English world. David's first word, "Mama," rather than "Mommy" or "Mother" marks him as an immigrant. For the first several pages the dialogue between David and his mother takes place in refined, sensitive, and normative language. "'Lips for me,' she reminded him, 'must always be cool as the water that wet them.'" Only when David descends to the street and his speech in English dialect is reproduced—"Kentcha see? Id's coz id's a machine"—does the reader realize that the previous pages were all taking place in Yiddish. The next stage in the movement toward English is the introduction of English folklore in the form of children's street chants, transported onto the streets of New York: "Waltuh, Waltuh, Wiuhlflowuh / Growin' up so high; / So we are all young ladies, / An' so we are ready to die." Not only is the dialect comical, but the refrain is clearly a foreign element in David's world: Walter is not a Jewish name; wildflowers, even figuratively, are not in evidence anywhere in the urban immigrant neighborhood, and the rest of the book demonstrates that romantic love, young ladies ready to die, is a concept alien to David's world. The additional irony in this folklore is that its sexual connotations are not evident to the children who are chanting the rhyme.

Allusion to English sources, whether they be street chants, fairy tales, or songs, are always experienced as foreign, and are always ironic. When David perceives their boarder Luter as an ogre, he places him in the folk tale of Puss in Boots, in a world of a marquis who marries a princess; and when he tries to keep himself from fearing the cellar door, he repeats stanzas from an American patriotic song, "My country 'tis of dee!" only to reach the refuge of his mother's kitchen with the line, "Land where our fodders died!" Quotations or allusions from English culture, despite their being embedded in an English text, appear as something foreign, as translation from another place.

The felt presence of an absent source language, then, which occasionally makes the English text read as if *it* were a translation, is conveyed in a number of ways: by explicit attribution of phrases as Yiddish in "reality"; by selective reproduction of Yiddish phrases; by English rendered in Yiddish dialect; and by references to English culture as if it were an intrusion into the main cultural environment of the text. Before looking at intertextual elements from Jewish culture, we need to examine three other strategies for conveying the multilingualism of the text and its cultural world: interlingual homonyms, self-embedding, single word cultural indicators.

In the first instance, English words are perceived to be homonyms for Yiddish words, and are therefore either accidentally or deliberately misunderstood. When David hears the word "altar," he thinks it means "alter," the Yiddish for old man. When his aunt announces that her dentist is going to relieve her of pain by using cocaine, the others hear "kockin," the Yiddish equivalent for defecating. And Aunt Bertha herself plays on the similarity between the molar which her dentist is going to extract, which she pronounces as "molleh," the Yiddish word for "full," to invent a vulgar pun. "I am going to lose six teeth. And of the six teeth, three he called 'mollehs'. Now isn't this a miracle? He's going to take away a 'molleh' and then he's going to make me 'molleh'." David makes the mental note that "Aunt Bertha was being reckless tonight."

In the case of self-embedding, a word, phrase, symbol, or archetype which is actually in English is imported into the dialogue, rendered as verbal transposition of Yiddish into English, and this English element appears to be foreign, as "other" within the rest of the *English* text. Here is an example in a dialogue between Aunt Bertha and David's mother Genya:

> "I'm not going to the dentist's tomorrow," she said bluntly. "I haven't been going there for weeks—at least not every time I left here. I'm going 'kippin companyih'!"

> "Going what?" His mother knit her brow. "What are you doing?"

> "Kippin companyih! It's time you learned a little more of this tongue. It means I have a suitor."

Finally, occasionally a single word, because it has no referent in the home culture, evokes the entire alien culture. This is true of the word organist when David overhears his mother and aunt speaking in Yiddish. "What was an 'orghaneest'? He was educated, that was clear. And what else, what did he do? He might find out later if he listened. So he was a goy. A Christian. . . .Christian . . . Chrize. Christmas. School parties." The world "altar" also functions as one of these single word indicators, as well as a homonym. In fact, in each of the above three types of bilingual strategies, there is a conflict of cultures, for obviously both the church and romantic courtship are alien to much of the Eastern European Jewish world of the turn of the century.

The absent home language, then, is an exacting and even persecuting presence as it turns David's Americanness, through English, into an agent of the "other." This is developed further in the motifs that accompany the other "Jewish" languages in the text. The most complex and significant instance of diglossia in the book is the infiltration of Hebrew and Aramaic, of *loshn-koydesh,* for David is bilingual when it comes to Yiddish and English, but diglossic when it comes to the sacred languages used only in connection with liturgical texts. In David's heder class he is introduced to Hebrew, first through the learning of the alphabet which is reproduced in the text, and then through the study of a passage from Isaiah recounting the angel's cleansing of the prophet's lips with a burning coal. Roth solves the problem of the reader's incomprehension of the transliterated passage by having the rabbi explain it to the children in Yiddish, which appears in the text in English, thus by translation twice removed: "And when Isaiah saw the Almighty in His majesty and His terrible light—Woe me! he cried, What shall I do? I am lost!" David identifies the fiery coal with an object in his own natural environment, and therefore with the possibility of revelation in his own life. This is communicated in quoted interior monologue: "But where could you get angel-coal? Hee! Hee! In a cellar is coal. But other kind, black coal, not angel coal. Only God had angel-coal. Where is God's cellar I wonder? How light it must be there." As the cellar has previously been the dark place which David fears, particularly because it is associated with the children's sexual games, David is now faced with the sacred and the profane in one image.

Since David does not understand Hebrew, the Aramaic passage is functionally the same as the Hebrew one, another aspect of *loshn-koydesh:* it introduces him to a popular and significat document in Jewish culture, namely one of the concluding songs of the Passover seder, *Had gadya.* Roth gives the reader who is unfamiliar with the Passover liturgy the translation of the song by having the rabbi ask, "Who can render this into Yiddish?" David responds with the last stanza which repeats all of the preceding ones: "And then the Almighty, blessed be He . . . killed the angel of death, who killed the butcher, who killed the ox, who drank the water, that quenched the fire, that burned the stick, that beat the dog, that bit the cat, that ate the kid, that my father bought for two zuzim. One kid, one only kid!"

Although the reader is provided with translations of these two texts, in one case a loose paraphrase and in another an exact translation, the significance of these passages in the novel are clear only when they are perceived within both Jewish and Christian tradition, for they reappear in the final brilliant mosaic, chapter XXI. Both passages are associated with the spring, with Passover, and with the theme of redemption. In *Had gadya* the lyrics are cumulative, as the song runs through a hierarchy of power with each succeeding element overpowering the preceding one, until it reaches an omnipotent god. The kid is purchased for slaughter and ceremonial feasting, to recall the slaughter of the paschal lamb by the Hebrews in ancient Egypt, providing the blood on the doorpost to identify the Hebrew homes for the Angel of Death to pass over during the smiting of the Egyptian first-born. The one only kid about whom David sings is David himself, an innocent sacrifice either for his parents' "sins" (mother's affair with a Gentile and father's passive witness to his father's death) or for those of the tough technological and vulgar city in which he finds himself. But as the languages of the climactic chapter indicate, he is also that other paschal lamb, namely Christ. Two cultural traditions, in some sense complementary and in others oppositional, co-exist in this section, as they do in David's and Roth's world.

The book of Isaiah prophesies redemption through the coming of the Messiah. In Christian hermeneutics, it is read as prefiguring the birth of Christ. Moreover, in Christian tradition, Easter is linked with Passover, with the Crucifixion, with redemption through the sacrificial offering of the one only kid, Christ himself, the sacrificial lamb who takes the sins of the community upon himself. In historical terms, Easter was also when tensions between the Jewish and Gentile communities were at their height in Eastern Europe, often taking the turn of blood libels and pogroms. All of this is eventually evoked in the final scene, when the multilingualism and biculturalism are placed in social, historical, religious, and psychological contexts.

In the last section, David runs from his father's wrath after the rabbi discloses the child's story denying Albert's paternity, insisting that his real father was a Christian organist, his mother's first love. To protect himself, David grabs his father's zinc milk ladle, and rushes to the crack in the trolley car tracks where, in an earlier scene with neighborhood boys, he witnesses the release of electric light from a short circuit. Associating the light between the tracks with God, David seeks refuge from the parents he believes have betrayed him. The electric charge is conducted through his body and he falls unconscious onto the cobblestones.

What follows is the most artistically innovative section of the book, as his loss and subsequent regaining of consciousness, his death and rebirth, are depicted among the cries of urban immigrants in the accents of their native tongues. Here social and spatial boundaries are transcended as a mass of individuals from diverse backgrounds fear and grieve for the prostrate child on the city street. With a minimum of omniscient narration, Roth uses two alternating modes in this climactic scene—reported speech of witnesses to David's suffering, before, during, and after the event and italicized sections which are psycho-narration, rendering David's perceptions in formal and self-consciously poetic language. The former are multi-lingual and multi-dialectical; the latter are self-conscious literary English. The alternation between the styles creates ironic contrasts as one mode spills over into the other. The dialogue of the street is marked by its vulgarity and preoccupation with sex. "Well, I says, you c'n keep yer religion, I says, Shit on de pope," says O'Toole in Callahan's beer-saloon at the start of this section.". . . [w]'en it comes to booze, I says, shove it up yer ass! Cunt for me, ev'y time, I says." When David's thoughts as he runs toward the rail are juxtaposed to O'Toole's declaration, they resonate with sexual as well as religious connotations. "Now! Now I gotta. In the crack, remember. In the crack be born." The italicized report of his consciousness, occurring simultaneously, is marked by its epic and lofty tones.

More than any other section of the book, this final sequence, with its Joycean epiphanies and stream of consciousness and with a collage of disembodied voices reminiscent of Eliot's *Wasteland,* identifies Roth as a modernist writer. The italicized section is very deliberately artistic in the tradition of English and European literature, with languages and constructions that are borrowed from medieval romance quests and from epics. The dipper is like a "sword in a scabbard," "like a dipped metal flag or a grotesque armored head," his father is a mythical figure, "the splendour shrouded in the earth, the titan, dormant in his lair," and his action of inserting the dipper is compared to the end of a romantic quest, "the last smudge of rose, staining the stem of the trembling, jagged chalice of the night-taut stone with the lees of day." The moment of his electrocution is filled with "radiance," "light," "glory," and "galaxies." It is self-consciously literary to the point of even tunneling into the "heart of darkness." In this section of the book, Roth demonstrates clearly his identification with a tradition of English literature. There is only one reference to another culture, and it is to "Chad Gadya" and also to the father's command to "Go down," with Moses clearly implied.

In the reported speech of the bystanders, Roth makes use of dialect: Yiddish, German, Irish, and Italian, and selective reproduction of other languages, namely Yiddish and Italian. But most importantly, he depicts the convergence of the English/Christian tradition and the Yiddish/ Hebrew Jewish tradition, and their equivalents in the social/historical and psychological motifs of the book.

In psychological terms, David's thoughts about the crack between the car tracks where he seeks a spiritual rebirth through contact with a masculine God, also evoke his desire to return to the womb, to the mother and the source of that oceanic oneness that he now seeks in a sublimated form. It is his mother who forces the separation by sending him into the street to escape his father's tyranny, and therefore David is both running away from his actual mother and running toward an image of that mother in the crack between the car tracks. The electric force between the tracks is thus the power of both the male and female principles, his father and his mother, the God of Isaiah and the mother image at once. At the same time, as David flees from his wrathful father brandishing a whip, and he seeks refuge in the divine power between the cracks, in a paternal God who will punish his punitive father, he also imagines his own father as that male God who will punish *him* for his sin of denying his real fatherhood and taking on a Christian past. David dies a symbolic death as he imagines that he no longer sees his own face when he peers into a series of mirrors reflected infinitely. As he is driven out of his home and exposed to the electric charge, he feels himself become "the seed of nothing. And he was not. . . ." Bystanders conclude that he is dead. The first glimmer of regaining consciousness—"and nothingness whimpered being dislodged from night"—occurs as he recalls coal in the cellar below the city streets, the light of God powerful enough to strike down his father, to still "the whirring hammer." Just as David had symbolically killed his father when he invented a story about a Christian father who was an organist, so in his semi-conscious state, a divine power greater than that of his father stills the dread hand and voice and frees him. The psychological dimension of his ordeal is one of a transformation of identity away from the parental and toward the spiritual.

While the social backdrop for this scene of death and rebirth is multilingual, the individual experience as rendered through David's semi-conscious monologue is entirely in a lofty and literary English, as if David dies out of his immigrant life and is born into the world of English literacy and culture, the world of Henry Roth's literary identity, but at the cost of killing both the father and the mother. In traditional Ashkenaz Jewry, Yiddish is referred to as the mother-tongue, *mame-loshn,* and the sacred language Hebrew as the father language or *fotershprakh.* In this case, David abandons both Yiddish and Hebrew, and the multilingual immigrant din of the street, for an English literary language that speaks through him. It is presented as an accident brought on by multiple misunderstandings in a multicultural world. David becomes an emblem of Henry Roth, the bilingual immigrant and Jewish writer, who is cut away from the mother-tongue, whose proficiency in the newly acquired language exceeds that of the mother-tongue, but who cannot transfer his emotional involvement to that acquired language. Furthermore, the loss of the mother-tongue in the process of Americanization carries an additional hazard for the Jewish writer, namely the Christian culture with which English is imbued. This is developed in the liberation from slavery theme which Roth pursues throughout the last section of the novel.

This theme is cast in language beyond the boy's personal plight, language with social, historical, and religious dimensions. The social and historical motifs are conveyed in references to the class struggle, as expressed in the dates of attempted revolutions and periods of worker oppression; recent Jewish history in the form of the pogrom; and the American dream as a form of liberation from bondage for the immigrant. An unidentified voice proclaims the message of socialist ideology: "'They'll betray us!' Above all these voices, the speaker's voice rose. 'In 1789, in 1848, in 1871, in 1905, he who has anything to save will enslave us anew!'" Such passages are often cited as evidence that *Call It Sleep* is truly a proletarian novel. In addition to the class struggle, Roth also refers to the Eastern European background of his characters in the Yiddish calls for rescue, quoted in Yiddish and without translation, "Helftz! Helftz! Helftz Yeedin! 'Rotivit!'" Finally, the same soapbox orator alludes to the national American context in the mocking evocation of the Statue of Liberty, symbol of the Golden Land: "And do you know, you can go all the way up inside her for twenty-five cents. For only twenty-five cents, mind you! Every man, woman and child ought to go up inside her, it's a thrilling experience." That David's oppressive life and near-death run parallel to the lives of these immigrant bystanders is further emphasized by Roth's reference to them as "the masses . . . stricken, huddled, crushed by the pounce of ten-fold night." All of this is rendered in a multilingual collage.

The Christian strain in this entire last section is very bold, with numerous references to the New Testament, and primary focus on the betrayal of Christ. The poker players rejoice "T'ree kings I god. Dey come on huzzbeck"—and vulgar jokes are cast in biblical terms—"How many times'll your red cock crow, Pete, befaw y'gives up? T'ree?" The red cock metaphor condenses the religious and the sexual connotations, and even refers to a historical one, for Emma Lazarus, the Jewish poet whose poem appears on the base of the Statue of Liberty, was the author of a poem entitled "The Crowing of the Red Cock," which reviews the persecution of the Jew by the Christian through the ages. The satiric treatment of these Christian elements is also evident in the reference to the woman Mary who was with child, but had an abortion. In this climactic chapter, David becomes the paschal lamb, the one only kid in *Had gadya,* but also a Christ figure, as the Jewish and Christian traditions are conflated. When he is first noticed by the people, a bystander shouts, "Christ, it's a kid!" When the hospital orderly administers ammonia, a member of the crowd claims that it "Stinks like in the shool on Yom Kippur."

David thinks of himself as the kid in the Passover liturgy, and he seeks the God of the Book of Isaiah in the Jewish scriptures. But he is perceived by the crowd of immigrants, by America's melting poet, as a Christ figure. As he leaves Yiddish behind, the *mame-loshu,* the language of nurture but not literacy for him, and Hebrew and Aramaic, *loshnkoydesh,* the "foreign" languages of his liturgy and his spiritual identity, he is left with English, his genuine native language, which is at the same time the language of the "other," the language of Christianity. At the end, in his semi-conscious state, the English language speaks through him, as it does throughout the book, and it kills the kid who is reborn as Christ. To assimilate, for Roth, is to write in English, to become the "other," and to kill the father. At the time that Roth wrote *Call It Sleep,* he identified as a Communist and he consciously embraced a vision of assimilation into a larger community beyond that of religion and nationality. In 1963, he made his often quoted and later recanted statement that the best thing that Jews could do would be "orienting themselves toward ceasing to be Jews." In *Call It Sleep,* Roth's central protagonist, a Jewish child, is shown to be overly assimilated, to become Christ. This is not what he consciously seeks; it is an imported self-image, an archetype taking root in his consciousness as the English language becomes his sole means of expression. In the climactic linguistic and cultural collage of the last section, David becomes a naturalized American by becoming a Christ symbol, and the English language is experienced as a foreign tongue and a foreign culture inhabiting his psyche. Whether he desires it or not, David is destined to live a life in translation, alienated from the culture of *his* language. It is no wonder that Roth could write no second book.

Among the few stories and sketches that he did write in later years, now collected in *Shifting Landscapes,* are two that further demonstrate this dilemma of the Jewish writer in his relation to his languages and culture. In **"Final Dwarf"** a naive Maine farmer (Roth's occupation at that time) nearly kills his immigrant New York father, but he cannot bring himself to do so. But more significantly, in **"The Surveyor"** an American Jewish tourist to Spain is apprehended for attempting to determine, with precision, the exact site of the *auto da fé* in Seville in order to lay a wreath. When asked by the police about his action, he says, "I was attempting to locate a spot of some sentimental value to myself . . . A place no longer shown on the maps of Seville."

In *Call It Sleep,* Roth's fiction conveys the cultural ethos of immigration, of ethnicity, of living at the nexus of several cultures, of being haunted by missing languages, of being intellectually estranged from the mother-tongue and emotionally estranged from one's native language. He did so by various techniques of translation, linguistic and cultural, woven throughout his novel. But to write another novel, he would have had to kill his father and to embrace the Christian world, the one of the Inquisition in Seville, of the rosary innocently cherished by David. This he could not do. Yet he gave his readers a brilliant artistic document of a cultural dead end. Yiddish has the last word in the street chorus, and it is a disembodied and anonymous voice, "Gott sei dank." It speaks for Roth's readers.

Alfred Kazin (review date 10 October 1991)

SOURCE: "The Art of *Call It Sleep*," in *The New York Review of Books,* Vol. XXXVIII, No. 15, October 10, 1991, p. 15.

[In the following review, Kazin discusses Roth's Call It Sleep *and asserts that it is a story of David's inner growth.]*

Call It Sleep is the most profound novel of Jewish life that I have ever read by an American. It is a work of high art, written with the full resources of modernism, which subtly interweaves an account of the worlds of the city gutter and the tenement cellar with a story of the overwhelming love between a mother and son. It brings together the darkness and light of Jewish immigrant life before the First World War as experienced by a very young boy, really a child, who depends on his imagination alone to fend off a world so immediately hostile that the hostility begins with his own father.

Henry Roth's novel was first published in 1934, at the bottom of the Great Depression. Looking at the date and marveling at this book, which apparently consumed so much of Roth's central experience that he never published another novel, many readers will be astonished. Surely the depressed 1930s produced little else but "proletarian literature" and other forms of left-wing propaganda? A fashionable critic writing in the opulent years after 1945 scorned the 1930s as an "imbecile decade," and explained—with the usual assurance of people who are comfortably off—that the issues in literature are "not political, but moral." Anyone who thinks "political" issues and "moral" ones are unrelated is living in a world very different from the 1930s or the 1990s.

The art fever of the modernist 1920s, in which more first-rate work was produced than in any other single period of American literature, continued well into the 1930s and did not fade until Hitler's war. Henry Roth, twenty-eight when *Call It Sleep* was published, was as open to the many strategies of modernism as he was to political insurgency. (The book owes a great deal to the encouragement of Eda Lou Walton, a remarkable woman who was teaching modern literature at New York University.)

Though *Call It Sleep* was not adequately understood or welcomed until it was reissued in paperback in 1964, it has become popular throughout the world with millions of copies in print. We can see now that the book belongs to the side

of the 1930s that still believed that literature was sacred, whether or not it presumed to change the world. Those who identify the 1930s with works of political protest forget that it was the decade of the best of Faulkner's novels, from *The Sound and the Fury* to *The Wild Palms,* Eliot's *Ash Wednesday,* Hart Crane's *The Bridge,* Dos Passos's *U.S.A.,* Katherine Anne Porter's *Flowering Judas,* Edmund Wilson's *Axel's Castle,* Fitzgerald's *Tender is the Night,* Henry Miller's *Tropic of Cancer,* Steinbeck's *The Grapes of Wrath,* Thornton Wilder's *Our Town,* Nathanael West's *The Day of the Locust,* Richard Wright's *Native Son,* Hemingway's *For Whom the Bell Tolls.*

What *Call It Sleep* has in common with these works is its sense of art sustaining itself in a fallen world, in a time of endless troubles and of political and social fright. The world was visibly shaking under the blows of economic catastrophe, mob hysteria, the fascist domination of much of Europe, fear of another world war. And no one was likely to feel the burden of the times more keenly than a young Jew starting life in a Yiddish-speaking immigrant family and surrounded by the physical and human squalor of the Lower East Side.

That last sentence could describe Michael Gold in his autobiography *Jews Without Money,* an eloquent but primitive outpouring of emotion that concludes with a rousing call to communism as the new Messiah. What from the very beginning makes *Call It Sleep* so different from the usual grim realism of Lower East Side novels is the intractable bitterness of the immigrant father, Albert Schearl, toward his wife, Genya, and their little boy, David. The father is an uncompromisingly hostile workingman, a printer by trade, driven from one shop to another by his ugly temper. "They look at me crookedly, with mockery in their eyes! How much can a man endure? May the fire of God consume them!" Roth makes this complaint sound loftier than it would have in Albert Schearl's Yiddish. He has been driven almost insane by his memory and resentment of his wife's affair with a Gentile back in Austrian Galicia. It pleases him to suspect that David is not his son.

This obsession, the dramatic foundation and background of the novel, may not be enough to explain Albert's unrelenting vituperation of his wife and his rejection, in every small family matter, of the little boy. David is not just unloved; he is violently hated by his father. The father shudderingly regards him as a kind of untouchable. The boy not only depends exclusively and feverishly on his mother but, in the moving story of his inner growth, becomes a determined pilgrim searching for light away from his tenement cellar refuge whose darkness pervades the first section of the novel, away from the dark cave in which the father has imprisoned mother and son.

Albert Schearl is at times so frenzied in his choked-up bitterness and grief that the introspection at the heart of his son's character—the boy wanders the neighborhood and beyond in search of a way out—must be seen as the only rebellion open to him. Whatever the sources of Albert Schearl's madly sustained daily war on his wife and son—he is perhaps less a jealous husband than a crazed immigrant unable to feel at home in the New World—Roth's honesty in putting the man's hatefulness at the center of the book is remarkable. It reminds us that the idealizing of the family in Jewish literature can be far from actual facts. Jews from Eastern Europe did not always emigrate because of anti-Semitism. The enmity sometimes lay within the family itself, as has been known to happen everywhere. Instead of sentimentalizing the family situation, Roth turned husband, wife, and son into the helpless protagonists of an obvious and uncompromising Oedipal situation. I can think of no other novel except D.H. Lawrence's *Sons and Lovers* in which mother and son are so fiercely tied to each other. The father is the outsider he has made of himself, and plainly wants to be.

In *Sons and Lovers* (as in lesser works on the same theme) the father is extraneous because he has lost for the mother the sexual charm that first attracted her. In *Call It Sleep* Genya timidly loves Albert for all his brutality. She is prepared to love him more freely if only he would stop berating her, but he is so unremittingly nasty that he virtually forces mother and son on each other. Albert in his daily rage somehow reflects his unconscious bitterness at being held down in "the Golden Land." But it is also clear that, notwithstanding Albert's dominating airs, Genya married him because she had no other choice. Her father had disowned her for her past infatuation with a Gentile.

Albert's war against his wife and son sounds an alarm at the very opening of the novel that continues to dominate these three lives until the last possible moment, when the shock produced when David is burned in a bizarre accident brings about a necessary but inconclusive pause in Albert's war on his family.

The book begins in 1907, the peak year of immigration to the United States. Wife and son have just been delivered from the immigration station at Ellis Island to be greeted by a somber, frowning Albert. Not in the least prepared to be amiable, he is quickly incensed because his wife doesn't recognize him without his mustache.

> The truth was there was something quite untypical about their behavior. . . . These two stood silent, apart; the man staring with aloof, offended eyes grimly down at the water—or if he turned his face toward his wife at all, it was only to glare in harsh contempt at the blue straw hat worn by the child in her arms, and then his hostile eyes would sweep

about the deck to see if anyone else was observing them. And his wife beside him regarding him uneasily, appealingly. And the child against her breast looking from one to the other with watchful, frightened eyes. . . . The woman, as if driven by the strain into action, tried to smile, and touching her husband's arm said timidly, "And this is the Golden Land." She spoke in Yiddish.

Astonished by her husband's haggard appearance, Genya apologizes for not having known him instantly. With the gentleness that she sustains in all the many crises he creates; she says, "You must have suffered in this land." Indeed he has, and will continue to suffer from himself in a way that turns his harshness into their immediate, their most perilous environment. Albert is his wife's only New York. She never attempts to learn English; she is content just to look after her family and is afraid to move beyond the streets of her neighborhood. Her deepest feeling for Albert is not the passion which unsettles him but a concern that comes from a sense of duty. Anything else would be unthinkable to her. Deprived of actual love, since Albert's quarrelsomeness isolates her, she is free to give her entire soul to her little boy.

David observes, very early, that his mother is attractive to a *Landsman*, "a fellow countryman," of his father's, Luter. Albert notices nothing, finds Luter one of the few people he can talk to, and insists on repeatedly inviting him to dinner. When Luter is alone for a moment and no longer has to keep up his pose of formal amiability, it is little David, studying his face, who realizes without knowing the reason that the man has been playing a part.

> And the eyes themselves, which were always so round and soft, had narrowed now . . . the eyeballs looked charred, remote. It worried David. A faint thrill of disquiet ran through him. He suddenly felt an intense desire to have someone else present in his house. It didn't have to be his mother.

His still unconscious gift of observation will soon provide the way out of the cave in which his father has shut him up.

Call It Sleep is not a naturalist novel, in which character is shaped largely by environment. Jews are generally so conscious of the pressure of history that it was a notable achievement for Henry Roth, coming out of the Lower East Side at a time when it was routine for people to dream of transforming the "conditions" in which they found themselves, to see character as more important than environment. As lower New York in the teens of our century comes alive in David Schearl's anxious but eager consciousness, Roth presents the city not in an external documentary but as formed, instant by instant, out of David's perceptions. David Schearl is portrait of the artist as a very small boy. In this novel we are in the city-world not of *Sister Carrie* but of Joyce's *Ulysses.*

Here is little David groping his way into New York as winter comes:

> The silent white street waited for him, snow-drifts where the curb was. Footfalls silent. Before the houses, the newly swept areas of the sidewalks, black, were greying again. Flakes cold on cheek, quickening. Narrow-eyed, he peered up. Black overhead the flakes were, black till they sank below a housetop. Then suddenly white. Why? A flake settled on his eyelash; he blinked, tearing with the wet chill, lowered his head. Snow trodden down by passing feet into crude, slippery scales. The railings before basements gliding back beside him, white pipes of snow upon them. He scooped one up as he went. Icy, setting the blood tingling, it gathered before the plow of his palm. . . . Voices of children. School a little ways off, on the other side of the street. . . . Must cross. Before him at the corner, children were crossing a beaten path in the snow. Beside him, the untrodden white of the gutter.

The succession of sweet, melodious words recalls Joyce, the most musical of twentieth-century masters. In *Ulysses* Dublin exists through the word-by-word progression of the subliminal consciousness. This is the mental world that is most ourselves, for nothing is so close to us as our inner thinking. Yet in *Ulysses* the sources of this interior world remain mysterious.

Roth never falls into lyrical expansiveness for its own sake, the usual style of romantic autobiographical novels (say, Thomas Wolfe's *Look Homeward, Angel*). Roth's book is always under control. Perhaps the novel is almost too tightly plotted when we come to the seemingly final explosion between the parents which causes David to run away and to seek a burst of light in a trolley barn when he inserts a piece of metal in the third rail. This is meant to be his epiphany, the self-discovery leading to the artist he will become. Roth wishes to show character as fate, character as dominating the most intimate relationships within the family.

He also shows that Genya's enveloping tenderness toward her son is not just "Freudian," theoretical, but a protectiveness that is a part of Jewish history. Its key is the Yiddish that mother and son speak together. David's English is made to sound effortlessly noble, beautifully expressive, almost liturgical, by contrast with the gutteral street English that surrounds him. We are startled to hear him speak a horrible mutilated street dialect when he is away from Mama. Then he is with strangers; and in this novel of New York, English is the stranger, the adopted language, tough and brazen. It

expresses the alienation from the larger world of kids competing with each other in toughness. "Land where our fodders died" becomes a parody of a national hymn that shows how derivative and meaningless the line can be when sung by immigrant street urchins.

The young David, searching for experience beyond his immediate neighborhood, discovers that he is "losted," and he tells a baffled woman who cannot make out where the boy lives, "A hunner 'n' twenny six Boddeh Stritt." Later in the novel David is enchanted by the Polish boy Leo flying a kite from the roof. Like Tom Sawyer encountering Huckleberry Finn, David is astounded by the boy's freedom. Hoping to see this marvel again, David asks, "Yuh gonna comm up hea alluh time?" Leo carelessly explains; "Naw! I hangs out on wes elevent'. Dat's w'ea we lived 'fore we moved."

Maybe street kids once talked this way, maybe not. Roth caricatures the terrible English of the street—a "foreign," external, cold-hearted language—in order to bring out the necessary contrast with the Yiddish spoken at home. This is the language of the heart, of tradition, of intimacy. Just as Roth perhaps overdoes the savage English spoken in the street, so he deliberately exalts the Yiddish that he translates at every point into splendid, almost too splendid, King James English. Even when Albert almost comes to blows with his vulgarly outspoken sister-in-law Bertha, he cries out: "I'm pleading with you as with Death!" Storming at his son, he menacingly demands "Shudder when I speak to you!" The English doesn't convey the routine, insignificant weight of the word for "shudder" in Yiddish. The people speaking Yiddish in this book are not cultivated people carefully choosing their words. They are hard-pressed, keyed-up, deeply emotional. There is nothing about the lives in the "Golden Land" that is not arduous, strange, even threatening. So they talk as extremely vulnerable Yiddish speakers from the immigrant working class have always done. It is a verbal style, even a routine, in which people expostulate with one another as if they were breaking all the windows in order to let a little air into the house.

In Roth's translation, with its implicit meanings, Yiddish often sounds the language of family love and respect for God. The reader from another culture should know that when Albert returns home and, not seeing his son, curtly asks his wife, "Where's the prayer?" he is referring to his son as his "kaddish," the Hebrew prayer over the dead, which is the highest obligation of a son to say in memory of his father.

Yet Albert gives no evidence of being a believer. Genya faithfully lights the Sabbath candles Friday at sundown, but, describing her own grandmother to her son, she admits: "But while my grandfather was very pious, she only pretended to be—just as I pretend, may God forgive us both." That last phrase is entirely characteristic. You don't have to be pious in order to be a faithful Jew—you just have to honor the tradition, as Genya does, with her separate dishes for Passover and the lighting of the Friday-night candles. The Yiddish of such poor immigrants as the Schearls was often quite homely and full of small mistakes. In Roth's text, however, they speak with grace, longing nobility. Yiddish is their real home. When life is fiercest, their language conveys a longing for a better world than this, a longing for spiritual heights that had become customary to people who regard themselves as living under the eye of God.

Yet Roth has no love for the rebbe (teacher) who for twenty-five cents a boy tries to drum the actual language of the Hebrew Bible into his cowed pupils. The "cheder," the primitive Hebrew school in which the boys are pinched, driven, insulted so they will at least pronounce the Hebrew words without necessarily understanding them, is presented with harsh realism as a Dickensian schoolroom of torture. The rebbe is the fat, irascible, ill-smelling Yidel Pankower. Even his first name, meaning "little Jew," brings out Roth's scorn for the place, the practices of the old routine. The rebbe despises his "American idiots." Everything was better in the Old Country. Teacher and pupils talk Yiddish by contrast with the sacred Hebrew text. Throughout *Call It Sleep* the sacred is shown side by side with the profane, as was usual among deeply observant old immigrant Jews. They ignored the actual sordidness of the life surrounding them in their adoration of the holy word itself.

Awful as Reb Yidel Pankower is, he discerns David's abilities. He benevolently brings in an old, kindly sage to hear David recite his lesson. Think of it, he observes, a kid brought up in New York's heathen atmosphere who can come so close to the ancient text! David has his first moment of spiritual illumination when he hears Reb Yidel say the following to another boy:

> "Now I'll tell you a little of what you read, then what it means. Listen to me well that you may remember it. Beshnas mos hamelech." The two nails of his thumb and forefinger met. "In the year that King Uzziah died, Isaiah saw God. And God was sitting on his throne, high in heaven and in his temple—Understand?" He pointed upward . . .

> "Now!" resumed the rabbi. "Around Him stood the angels, God's blessed angels. How beautiful they were you yourself may imagine. And they cried Kadosh! Kadosh! Kadosh!—Holy! Holy! Holy! And the temple rang and quivered with the sound of their voices. So!" He paused, peering into Mendel's face. "Understand?"

David is stimulated by this but he does not find holiness in the Hebrew letters. He is startled by the reluctance of the

other boys to use strips of Yiddish newspaper, written in the Hebrew alphabet, in the communal toilet. What is sacred for him is mother love. Eventually, we can guess, the radiance of this central relation in his life is what he will seek later on by bending the recalcitrant world into words. "Outside" this love, especially in the cellar, is the world of fear he must learn to master. The first section of the book is called "The Cellar" because it deals with the underground side of life—physical, aggressive, sexual. A crippled neighborhood girl wants him to play "bad" with her. She explains that "babies come from de knish."

> *—Knish?*

> "Between de legs. Who puts id in is de poppa. De poppah's god de petzel. Yaw de poppa." She giggled stealthily and took his hand. He could feel her guiding under her dress, then through a pocket-like flap. Her skin under his palm. Revolted, he drew back.

> "Yuh must!" she insisted, tugging his hand, "Yuh ast me!"

> "No!"

> "Put yuh han' in my knish," she coaxed. "Jus'once."

> "No!"

> "I'll hol' yuh petzel." She reached down.

She tells David that they have been playing "bad." "By the emphasis of her words, David knew he had crossed some awful threshold. 'Will yuh tell?' 'No,' he answered weakly." When he is back home with his mother, "she didn't know as he knew how the whole world could break into a thousand little pieces, all buzzing, all whining, and no one hearing them and no one seeing them except himself."

David is now a fallen creature, out of Eden, who must confront the terrible but fascinating city by himself. What had occurred to him in earliest childhood is now a dead certainty: "This world had been created without thought of him." By the same token, he is free. The joy of being a boy in the city is that discoveries are to be made everywhere. In a box kept in the pantry he collects

> whatever striking odds and ends he found in the street. His mother called them his gems and often asked him why he liked things that were worn and old. It would have been hard to tell her. But there was something the way in which the link of a chain was worn or the thread of a bolt or a castor-wheel that gave him a vague feeling of pain when he ran

his fingers over them. . . . You never saw them wear, you only knew they were worn, obscurely aching.

This intense observation of the variety of things around him marks the novelist-to-be. The city becomes the web of life in which, even when he is "lostest," David senses his destiny. It is the writer's city of instant and continuing perception, the Joyce-inspired city of wonders as they come to us through the sensations of the very young David:

> When he had come to the end of the dock, he sat down, and with his feet hanging over the water leaned against the horned and bulbous stanchion to which boats were moored. Out here the wind was fresher. The uncommon quiet excited him. Beneath and under his palms, the dry, splintering timbers radiated warmth. And beneath them, secret, unseen, and always faintly sinister, the tireless lipping of water among the piles. Before him, the river and to the right, the long, grey bridges spanning it—

A bridge makes David think of the sword with the "big middle" that used to appear on the Mecca Turkish cigarettes, of the bridge clipping the plumes of a long ship steaming beneath it, of gulls whose faces are as ugly as their flight is graceful, as they wheel through the wide air on wings that cut like a sickle. A tug on the other side of the river peers at a barge, stolid in the water. After a sluggish time, the tug is yoked to the barge, which gives the barge the look of a mustache. The water is sunlit rhythmic spray sprouting up before the blunt bow of the barge. The spray hangs "whitely" before it falls. Now David associates the blunt heaviness of the barge with a whole house of bricks as "a cloud sheared the sunlight from the wharf." His back feels cooler in the sharpening of the wind, smokestacks on the other bank darken slowly, "fluting filmy distance with iron-grey shadow."

The Polish boy Leo, whom David admires beyond words for his defiant show of independence, carries a rosary. The black beads become "lucky beads" to David. In his Jewish innocence the links of the rosary drive him wild with envy. He is always the outsider. The sight of the boys on the block grabbing a girl makes him feel all the more isolated in his cruelly won sexual "knowledge." "I know . . . I know . . . I know," he repeats to himself. In one of Roth's most telling images, David in sluggish thought resembles "a heavy stone pried half out of its clinging socket of earth." Leo's rosary must belong to him, because the beads give out a light like the marbles which other boys roll along the curb.

As a Jew, David is now transgressing, and there may be no safe place at home in which to hide a rosary. In counterpoint to Leo playing "bad" with David's cousin Esther, David watches Esther, who is afraid of being detected; he hears her squeals at being handled by Leo, and Leo then insists that David "lay chickee" (be a lookout) for him and Esther. Leo pays him off with the rosary David so longs for. The crucifix attached to the rosary frightens him; he recognizes something that may be hostile to him as a Jew. The gold figure on the crucifix swings slowly and David lets the glistening beads fall one by one, in order to see how they light up the dark cellar. Suddenly Esther's sister Polly appears and accuses Esther: "Yuh wuz wit' him in dere!" In the violent dispute between Polly and Leo that follows, the Catholic Leo cries, "Yuh stinkin' sheeny!" The Jewish girl is outraged that her sister not only has been petting, but petting with a Christian! "Her voice trailed off in horrified comprehension. 'Ooh w'en I tell—He's a goy too! Yuh doity Chrischin, get oud f'om my cella'—faw I call my modder. Ged out!'"

David flees the cellar, flees the frightening transposition of sexual taboo into religious taboo. In the streets he wants to get back to his own familiar world. He reaches the *cheder,* performs brilliantly in his Hebrew reading for the visiting rabbi, then in an excited leap of fantasy, owing to his fascination with the rosary, tells Yidel Pankower that his mother is dead and that he is really half-Christian, the son of a European organist who played in a church. The rebbe, alarmed and curious, intrusively carries the strange story to David's parents. There is a violent altercation with his father, who is all too willing to believe that David is someone else's son and beats him.

The scene is mixed with violent humor because it is at this moment that Genya's sister Bertha and her husband have chosen to come by to ask for a loan. As he is shaken by his father, David drops the rosary on the floor. Totally beyond himself now, Albert hysterically takes this as proof of David's supposed Gentile parentage. "God's own hand! A sign! A witness! A proof of another's! A goy's! A cross! A sign of filth!"

David runs away in earnest this time, ending up at the trolley car barns, where at the foot of Tenth Street,

> a quaking splendor dissolved the cobbles, the grimy structures, bleary stables, the dump-heap, river and sky into a single cymbal-clash of light.

David has inserted the metal dipper of a milk can "between the livid jaws of the [third] rail, [where it] twisted and bounced, consumed in roaring radiance, candescent." As a long burst of flame spurts from below, sounding "as if the veil of earth were splitting," David is knocked senseless and the hysterical crowd that gathers around his body thinks he is dead. But only his ankle is partly burnt, and in a rousing conclusion to the book he is brought back to his family. The near-tragedy somehow brings Albert to his senses. As his mother weepingly puts David to bed, David finally has some slight sense of triumph, for he is at last at peace with himself.

> It was only toward sleep that every wink of the eyelids could strike a spark into the cloudy tinder of the dark, kindle out of shadowy corners of the bedroom such vivid jets of images—of the glint on tilted beards, of the uneven shine on roller skates, of the dry light on grey stone stoops, of the tapering glitter of rails, of the oily sheen on the night-smooth rivers, of the glow on thin blonde hair, red faces, of the glow on the outstretched, open palms of legions upon legions of hands hurtling toward him. He might as well call it sleep.

The light he made for himself in the darkness of the cellar was real. David has won his essential first victory. He is on his way to becoming the artist who will write this book.

Robert Alter (review date 16 January 1994)

SOURCE; "The Desolate Breach Between Himself and Himself," in *The New York Times Book Review*, January 16, 1994, p. 3, 29.

[*In the following review, Alter compares Roth's two novels,* Call It Sleep *and* Mercy of a Rude Stream, *complaining that the latter does not have the emotional depth or novelistic tension of the first.*]

There is something utterly improbable about the appearance of a second novel by Henry Roth after 60 years of silence, and the new book can scarcely be read except against the enigmatic background of that silence. The haunting story of Mr. Roth's career has often been told—most recently in these pages by my Berkeley colleague, the novelist Leonard Michaels.

Call It Sleep, Mr. Roth's stunning first novel, was published in 1934, when he was 28. The reviews were mixed, at least in part because the prevailing political climate put some critics out of sympathy with a novel that was so intensely personal and so exquisitely wrought. In any case, by the time it appeared Mr. Roth had, in the phrase of the era, "gone left," and he dutifully undertook as his next project a novel of proletarian life. Working against the grain of his own sensibility, he was soon compelled to abandon the book. He produced three uninspired stories for commercial consumption in the late 1930's. After 1940, he gave up writing entirely, supporting himself, mostly in New England, through a variety of jobs—factory worker, psychiatric hospital attendant, waterfowl farmer. A reissue of *Call It Sleep* in 1960 elicited high praise from a few critics.

Then, in 1964, a paperback edition was brought out, was celebrated on the front page of this review by Irving Howe as a major 20th-century American novel and became a best seller. Mr. Roth, resurrected from what he himself had come to think of as his posthumous existence as a writer, slowly began to turn out short stories again. (All of his stories and interviews, as well as excerpts from his correspondence, were put together by his Italian translator and devoted friend, Mario Materassi, in a 1987 volume, *Shifting Landscape.*) In 1979 Mr. Roth began work on a vast autobiographical novel, *Mercy of a Rude Stream* (the title is taken from Shakespeare's *Henry VIII*). *A Star Shines Over Mt. Morris Park* is the first installment of that novel, of which he has completed five additional volumes.

The new novel is not in the strict sense a sequel to *Call It Sleep,* but it picks up the author's life more or less at the point where the earlier book ended. The family constellation it portrays—irascible father, tender mother, sensitive only son—is basically the same as that of *Call It Sleep.* The child David Schearl of the earlier novel reappears here, with minor modifications, as Ira Stigman. At the beginning of the novel, the family has just moved, precisely as Henry Roth's family did, from the Jewish East Side to East 114th Street in Harlem, then a predominantly Irish neighborhood. The year is 1914 and Ira Stigman is 8 years old. The volume ends in 1920 with the protagonist in junior high school, working part time for a fancy-food provisioner, troubled by his own emergent sexuality and the aggressive sexuality of certain of the adults around him. But he is even more troubled by "the desolate breach opened between himself and himself" through these six years in exile from his old Jewish neighborhood, struggling to define himself in the eyes of the ethnic others surrounding him and thus impelled to reject his own origins.

Mr. Roth remains an admirable craftsman, and the scenes of immigrant life in the second decade of the century are evoked with persuasive concreteness: the clamorous extended Jewish family, the street brawls, the rather grim socialization process in school, a poor child's glimpse of the glitter of Manhattan high living after the war as he delivers a basket of food to an apartment where a party is under way. But in style, mood and conception, all this is very different from the superficially similar *Call It Sleep.*

Mr. Roth's first book was clearly an autobiographical novel emulating Joyce (more *Portrait of the Artist,* I would say, than *Ulysses*). Indeed, it is arguably the most brilliant American adaptation of Joycean techniques outside the novels of Faulkner. *Mercy of a Rude Stream,* by contrast, is less an autobiographical novel than a fictionalized autobiography, and it often seems as though the element of fiction does not go much beyond the substitution of different proper names and whatever invention is required to flesh out memories that lie seven decades back in the receding perspective of the past.

The transparency of the guise of fiction is especially evident in the brief intercut passages in which an aged Ira addresses his computer as he tries to reconstruct his childhood. With his mobile home in New Mexico, his rheumatoid arthritis, his devoted pianist wife, Ira is Henry Roth in all but name. A good many of these intercut passages read more like journal entries than integral elements of a novel. Topics that happened to preoccupy the author from day to day between 1979 and the mid-80's, when he was writing this volume, float up between him and his computer screen: his concern about the Israeli-Egyptian peace treaty, the atrocities of the Khmer Rouge, the medical problems he and his wife face and his son's difficulties with his girlfriend. Some of the aged Ira's musings, however—on his silence as a writer, on the elusive task of writing a life, on his attempt to heal the rupture in identity inflicted on him in his youth—are quite suggestive and do throw light on the narrated events.

One way of defining the difference between *Mercy of a Rude Stream* and *Call It Sleep* is the systematic renunciation of Joyce in the new novel. Mr. Roth has complained several times in interviews that the seductive allure of Joyce's writing had led him on a course that alienated him from himself, encouraging in him an ideal of pure esthetic fulfillment that turned into a dead end. Here he speaks of Joyce as having "stored up creative static for one supreme discharge" and goes on to say that after following that path of the "hermetic ego" Ira "now was left with the realization that the good heart, the kind and affectionate, the discerning, loyal and understanding heart was far more precious than artistic acclaim."

This book, then, is not a novel about a nascent visionary-artist, like *Call It Sleep,* though it does include a few evocative representations of the young Ira's romance with language, his excited sense that "if you could put words to what you felt, it was yours." The gorgeous lyric lambency of the early novel inspired by Joyce, has been rigorously excluded from the prose of the new book. With it, a quality of mythic intensity—perhaps as much Melvillian as Joycean—has also been eliminated.

Thus the child in *Call It Sleep* looks at his father pulsating with anger, whip in hand: "David's father towered above him, rage billowing from him, shimmering in sunlight almost, like an aura." Compare this with a moment early in the new novel when the father ferociously beats his son for supposedly having knocked down Danny True, a smaller child: "Pop had lost all control, and was already treading his son underfoot, stamping on him, so that even Mrs. True's look of satisfaction had turned into one of aversion." The father in the second passage is actually doing something more ter-

rible than the father in the first passage, but the appalling event of an adult tantrum is conveyed as factual report, almost dryly. The hallucinatory sense of the first passage, in which the father looms like some demigod or demon, billowing, shimmering with an aura of incandescent rage, is not intimated in the workaday prose of *Mercy of a Rude Stream.* The Oedipal triangle of *Call It Sleep* is still present in the new novel, but it is not permitted to become an electrified zone from which to view the world startlingly enlarged to the proportions of myth. Even a moment of inadvertent sexual arousal when the boy is sharing his mother's bed while the father is off on a trip is presented not as a cataclysmic event but rather as a kind of hormonal ambush, in which the history of Ira Stigman's pubescence makes its own particular contact with the general history of the male of the species.

Mr. Roth's intention everywhere is to set his protagonist in relation to ethnicity, community, humanity, and to avoid the dramatic heightening of the overweening ego even as the boy harbors dreams of an absolute self free of the constricting world that has shaped him. The abundant use of Yiddish here (sometimes a bit garbled in transliteration) is a reminder of the objective existence of a very particular world outside the self of the protagonist. By contrast, *Call It Sleep* generally renders Yiddish speech as lofty English in keeping with the wrought artifice of the novel.

Mercy of a Rude Stream is absorbing as a meticulous evocation of a now-distant episode of the American experience. The self-critical, self-probing reflections by this author of a single major novel are in themselves quite instructive about the ambiguities of identity and the travails of literary vocation in the American setting. What the book lacks is novelistic tension. Ira Stigman is a focus for experiences without the depth and dynamism of a fully realized fictional character. At one point the aged writer muses over his constant effort "to keep the narrative from falling into separate niches and vignettes," and that seems to me precisely the problem of the book.

One thing comes after another because that is how it happened, or at least that is how the author remembers it, not because there is any inner necessity of imaginative development that drives from beginning to end—as from David Schearl's initial vision of the brass faucets in the tenement sink to his apocalyptic glimpse of the churning fires of the firmament and the dark abyss at the end of *Call It Sleep.* At least in this first volume of the promised six, Henry Roth has not produced another great novel after 60 years of silence. But the narrative he has fashioned from his life has something to offer as both cultural history and personal insight, and there should be much to look forward to in the five volumes to come.

Zachary Leader (review date 25 February 1994)

SOURCE; "An East-Side kid," in *Times Literary Supplement*, No. 4743, February 25, 1994, p. 20.

[*In the following review, Leader proposes that in Roth's* Mercy of a Rude Stream *"The author wishes to recreate a world now lost, one defaced by the earlier novel's 'artistic' distortions, a product of complex personal and political needs."*]

The stream in question is Henry Roth's life: "rude" because materially impoverished as well as harsh, a life of immigrant slums and the coarse intimacies of crowded tenements; "merciful" because by returning to it as a source of art, after decades of "literary desolation", Roth the novelist at last regained his voice, was released from the most striking instance of writer's block in modern American fiction. Roth's block, like Wordsworth's "long continued frost" (a mere blip or glitch in comparison), dissolves in a work of epic autobiography: *A Star Shines over Mt Morris Park* is but the first instalment of *Mercy of a Rude Stream,* a projected six-volume life story. This story, sometimes only perfunctorily fictionalized, was begun in 1979 and is now, its eighty-seven-year-old author assures us, substantially complete, in a manuscript of over 3,000 pages.

Such epic self-absorption, paradoxically, signals a release from selfishness, the sort of writerly selfishness Wordsworth complains of at the beginning of *The Prelude,* that "with a false activity beats off / Simplicity and self-presented truth"—the chief virtues of Roth's new work. "My high blown pride / At length broke under me, and now has left me / Weary and old with service, / To the mercy of a rude stream", declares Cardinal Wolsey in the novel's epigraph, from *Henry VIII.* Wolsey, too, in lines Roth doesn't quote, fell victim to "a killing frost", one that nipped his hopes just when, like Roth, "blushing honours" like "blossoms" grew "thick upon him". But Wolsey's "mercy" is ironic; "mine", Roth declares, "is not. It is literal."

The occluding "selfishness" or "false activity" which blocked Roth was already, he believes, discernible at the end of *Call It Sleep,* the precocious first novel which, after much indirection, made his name. *Call It Sleep* belongs to two distinct traditions: its subject-matter—Jewish immigrant life on the Lower East Side—recalls other "proletarian" works of the 1930s, notably Mike Gold's *Jews Without Money,* Clifford Odets's *Awake and Sing!* and Daniel Fuchs's trilogy of Williamsburg novels. Its manner, though, is high modernist, echoing Joyce, Faulkner, Gertrude Stein, and Hart Crane. Nowhere is this modernist influence clearer than in the novel's penultimate chapter, a sixty-page "chorus" of immigrant and lower-class voices modelled on Crane's *The Bridge* and the "Game of Chess" section of *The Waste Land.*

This chapter Roth has described as the beginning of the end: "an indication that the form of the novel was being broken, along with the creative psyche of the novelist".

The cause of this breakdown or dissolution was partly political. In 1933, while still at work on the novel, Roth joined the Communist Party. Immediately, he began to doubt what he'd written. *Call It Sleep* "didn't strike a posture, didn't locate anywhere, defend anything, or attack anything explicitly . . . and as soon as I realised this 'fact', as soon as I grappled with commitment, I becameimmobilized." Or, as he elsewhere puts it: "it had the effect of making me overly conscious of myself as a writer". Hence the several sorts of discontinuity embodied in the novel's penultimate chapter. Roth had begun to lose his way, under a pressure he saw as historically determined as well as personal: "What had happened to me was common to a whole generation of writers in the thirties. One author after another, whether he was Gentile or Jew, stopped writing, became repetitive, ran out of anything new to say or just plain died artistically."

A Star Shines over Mt Morris Park returns to the world of *Call It Sleep,* but importantly reconceives it. It begins at almost exactly the moment the earlier novel left off, in 1914, a momentous year for Roth's eight-year-old fictional *alter ego,* now called Ira Stigman rather than David Schearl. Though the outbreak of war is immediately recorded (and will eventually effect Ira's larger family), the event that matters most in the opening pages is local: Ira's family moves. The exclusively Jewish Lower East Side of *Call It Sleep* gives way to a tiny enclave of Jewish families within a largely Irish-Catholic neighbourhood in Harlem. The consequences of this removal Roth sees as disastrous: Ira becomes self-conscious about his Jewishness, self-hating, a victim: "he could almost feel the once self-assured East Side kid shrivelling within himself". Hence Ira's embarrassed reaction to the arrival from Europe of his maternal relations, with their "crudity and grimace, their green and carious teeth". Hence, also, Ira's later attraction to goyish strength, as in the choice of a boxer, an Irish-American, as the protagonist of his second, aborted novel—a choice Roth called "the end of my writing life": "after that came the block".

The new novel's rejection of victimhood begins with a more humane and rounded account of Ira/Roth's father, and a less formulaically Freudian conception both of Ira's anchoring mother and of family relations in general. Albert Schearl in *Call It Sleep* was a monster, a crude literalization of Oedipal fears. Chaim Stigman, though still jittery, paranoid, and violent, is less of a caricature, in part because his creator has come to identify with him. When Chaim complains that work on the trolleys has ruined his stomach, his wife asks how the *goyim* stand it:

"Because they're *goyim*", said Pop.

"it's not because they're always on edge like you? It's not because they have a skittish stomach?"

"Why should they have a skittish stomach? . . . Did they have to skimp as I did until I saved enough money for your passage to America?"

This ignoble blame-shifting is like Roth's demonizing father in *Call It Sleep;* or, some would argue, like the metaphor of blockage itself, in which the writer's difficulties are externalized and objectified, are seen as the result not of personal lack or deficiency, but of an alien obstacle or impediment. It is a trait shared also by Ira's *Zaida* or grandfather. "Such a punishment to befall me", Zaida wails when grief and anxiety stop his wife from eating. "If she won't eat, she won't eat. But at least cook. I die of hunger here." Earlier, Zaida offers Ira a "delicacy"; "He picked up a boiled chicken foot from his plate, bit out the one meaty bubble at the base of the toes, and handed his grandson the yellow shank and skimpy talons." That Roth can now find this sort of selfishness comical is a sign of his release from its grip.

The novel's looseness of structure is of a piece with its more relaxed and tolerant eye. The "plot" is the life: in effect, everything the narrator can remember from 1914 to 1920. The only frill in the storytelling is Roth's doubling of narrative voices, in which the main story is periodically interrupted by Ira's adult reflections: on what he's just written, on the causes and cures of his writer's block, on Israel, on characters yet to be introduced, in particular "M" (the composer Muriel Parker, whom Roth met at the artists' colony, Yaddo, in 1938, and who died in 1990). These reflections are addressed to Ira's word processor, named Ecclesias (as in the Biblical book of acceptance and release), which itself sometimes answers back. Though frequently wordy, stilted, repetitive, unsure of tone, and irritatingly enigmatic—easily the weakest sections of the book—they also reinforce central themes, often by virtue of their very artlessness.

For example, when Ira suddenly recognizes an error or misremembering in the main story ("his parents were *not* the first Jews living on 119th Street . . . enticing to the writer as that sort of extreme predicament might be"), he panics and breaks into the main narrative. This panic recalls the "irrational fear" that blocked him long ago and, worse, "unforeseen stretched tentacles into his psyche in the present". Calm down, Ira tells himself: "append the omitted material and go on" which is just what this untidy interruption does.

The impression such moments create is of absolute fidelity to experience. The author wishes to recreate a world now lost, one defaced by the earlier novel's "artistic" distortions, a product of complex personal and political needs. True creation, in Wordsworth's words, is

A balance, an ennobling interchange
Of action from within and from without;
The excellence, pure spirit, and best power
Both of the object seen, and eye that sees.

Though Roth's new work often goes too far in its rejection of "action from within"—is, indeed, insufficiently shaped and worked—the recollections themselves ring true, and make his story utterly absorbing. Here, one feels, is the vanished immigrant world, a world which in turn allows the reader to deduce a prior "old country".

Early in the novel, one of Ira's uncles, newly arrived from Galicia, offers his eight-year-old nephew a bite of raw carrot, something Ira informs him "nobody eats" in America. This moment, the adult narrator recalls, "condensed into the first inference he was ever conscious of as inference. . . . The moist, orangy, peeled carrot at the core of recollection substantiated all that Mom had told him: about the meagreness of rations, about the larder kept under lock and key, about Zaida's autocratic sway, his precedence in being served." Though *Mercy of a Rude Stream* may be something less than art, such moments make two things clear: Henry Roth can write, and his story is still worth listening to.

Robert Towers (review date 3 March 1994)

SOURCE: "Look Homeward, Ira," in *The New York Review of Books,* Vol. XLI, No. 5, pp. 24-5.

[*In the following review, Towers praises the absorbing story in Roth's* Mercy of a Rude Stream, *but complains that the structure is disjointed and the narration of the older Ira is intrusive.*]

The oddity of Henry Roth's career keeps getting in the way as one reads *Mercy of a Rude Stream.* Had he written a number of novels during his eighty-seven years, one could try to place the new work by comparing it with the others. But we have only a single precocious masterpiece, *Call It Sleep,* published sixty years ago, and now generally recognized as the most moving and lyrical novel to come out of the Jewish immigration to America before and after the turn of the century. Even if we take account of the history of Roth's by now famous writing block or the fact that during the last fifteen years, he has, while crippled with arthritis, been able to write no fewer than six volumes of autobiographical fiction (of which the present volume is the first), the power of his first book unavoidably stays in the mind.

The success of *Call it Sleep,* it is clear, has become obsessive for Roth himself: "Ira," in the new novel, in asides to his computer which regularly interrupt the narration, reflects on his failure to follow up on his early triumph. "Ah, how could you have let that life, all that life and configuration and trenchancy and conflict escape you? when it was still accessible, still at hand, retrievable, still close." Groping for an answer, he suggests (simplistically, I suspect) that he felt the need to repudiate both the "Olympian mix" of irony and pity that he associates with Anatole France and the Joycean aesthetic of detachment that had (in his view) informed *Call It Sleep.* He could no longer see himself as "the arrogant, egotistic self-assured author" he had once been—or accept only "a surface perception" of the "Joycean, sordid riches" of the fourteen years that he spent in a Harlem slum after his early childhood on the Lower East Side. What, he asks, made him unable to approach his experience as successfully as he had done in *Call It Sleep?*

> Was it the effect of Marxism? Of the Party's influence? He had to consider, to recognize, somehow to indicate implicitly in his writing the cruel social relations beneath, the cruel class relations, the havoc inflicted by deprivation concealed under the overtly ludicrous.

To write with this new consciousness became impossible for him because of what he calls a "loss of identity," accompanied by a "loss of affirmation," neither of which he fully accounts for. Even in his old age, as he takes up the story where he left off, Ira must still rebel against "Joyce the necromancer himself," his "erstwhile literary liege," and find a different way to deal with the "mountain of copy" he has produced.

Yet despite the comparatively matter-of-fact, more restrained language of the new novel, we are reminded of *Call It Sleep* on almost every page. The family situation is basically the same, with the fearful, imaginative boy Ira Stigman (instead of David Schearl) still caught between an ineffectual but violent father (Albert is now called Chaim) and a generous and seductively protective mother, Leah (instead of Genya). Once again we accompany a small boy as he ventures from his mother's embrace to confront the terrifying but fascinating streets of Harlem, where he must encounter the *goyish* "other"—often in the form of tough Irish kids who jeer at his Jewishness and are likely to beat him up. We are drawn into the lovelessness of his parents' forced marriage and watch with the jealous little boy as a would-be suitor (Luter, Albert's *Landsmann* in *Call It Sleep,* and Chaim's "Americanized" nephew Louie in the new novel) tries to persuade the mother to open herself to the experience of *lyupka* ("love"), which she has renounced. As in the first novel, the "tough" spoken English of the street kids and the heavily accented, stumbling English of the immigrants are rendered phonetically, while the Yiddish spoken at home is translated

(somewhat misleadingly, as Alfred Kazin has pointed out) into exceptionally pure, even poetic English.

But there are significant differences as well. Though in the early chapters of *Mercy of a Rude Stream* he is still capable of viciously beating his son, Chaim is not the ogre that Albert was. Rather, he is unstable, frightened, neurotically incapable of ordinary human give-and-take, doomed to bad luck and failure. (When he gets a decent "jop" as a trolley-car conductor, he must give it up because of bowel spasms—the "cremps" and diarrhea—induced by the lurching of the trolley.) Since Ira is eight at the beginning of the novel in the summer of 1914 and fourteen at the end, school now becomes more important than the streets in his education. Vivid portraits emerge, particularly of the elderly priest-like principal of PS 24, Mr. O'Reilly, who drills his students in "the difference between lay and lie, may and can, who and whom, like and as, . . . as if, Ira reflected afterward, life depended on their correct usage, the life of street urchins, slum adolescents like himself."

Another difference, a major one, becomes apparent at the beginning of *Mercy of a Rude Stream* when, just before Austria and Serbia go to war, the little family of three is joined by Leah's parents and four of her brothers and sisters who arrive from Austrian Galicia and settle into a six-room apartment on 115th Street. Instead of the almost claustrophobic intensity of *Call it Sleep,* the milieu of the new novel is greatly expanded, recalling Irving Howe's memorable account of the Jewish immigration in *World of Our Fathers.* We watch the effort of the younger immigrants to adjust to their harsh new world and eventually rise in it. Initially, Ira is disenchanted by these new relatives. He had imagined that

> they would be somehow charmingly, magically, bountifully pre-Americanized, Instead—they were greenhorns! Greenhorns with uncouth, lopsided and outlandish gestures, . . . speaking "thick" Yiddish, without any English to leaven it . . .

With their "newcomers' crudity and grimace, their green and carious teeth, the sense of oppressive orthodoxy under Zaida's [Grandfather's] sway," they "produce in Ira a sense of unutterable chagrin and disappointment." In one of the novel's many telling vignettes, Ira goes to his grandparents' apartment after Saturday morning services to light the stove—because he is too young to sin he is allowed to break the Sabbath laws—and to look on while his pious but selfish old grandfather eats his dinner:

> Served, Zaida fell to voraciously—halted in midmouthful: "Here, my child, before you go, relish this." He picked up a boiled chicken foot from his plate, bit out the one meaty bubble at the base of

the toes, and handed his grandson the yellow shank and skimpy talons.

"Thanks, Zaida."

One such scene follows another as the years pass and America enters the war and Ira enters puberty. He takes an after-school job with the grocery chain, Park and Tilford, which then had a branch in the highly respectable neighborhood of 126th Street and Lenox Avenue. Uncle Moe is drafted and leaves for overseas duty after a furlough, accompanied to the bus by his father and brother, who break into frenzied lamentations.

> Howling in despair, each one hung onto Moe's arm. And Moe, stalwart, . . . dragged them along like a tug between two barges. . . . Each abandoned himself to extremity of grief: Zaida tore at his beard, tore out bunches of whiskers, wailing at the top of his voice. Saul snatched at his hair, flung himself about, screaming hysterically. Passersby stopped to watch, automobiles slowed down, people leaned out of windows.

Moe gently begs them to stop, while Ira, looking on, cringes with embarrassment, especially when he overhears a cop say to a bystander, "Will yez look at them Jews . . . Didjez ever see the loik? Ye'd think the guy was dead already." Ira announces that he would like to go to West Point and learn to be an officer, but the boy is discouraged by Louie, who tells him, "They don't like Jews at West Point."

There is no conventional plot in the novel, simply a progression of events and encounters. But three preoccupations become clear. One is Ira's feeling of acute estrangement from his heritage. This reaches a climax of sorts at his bar mitzvah, when he realizes "he was only a Jew because he *had* to be a Jew; he hated being a Jew; he didn't want to be one, saw no virtue in being one, and realized he was caught, imprisoned in an identity from which there was no chance of his ever freeing himself." He feels that he is held to his Jewishness by a single bond: "his attachment to Mom, his love for her, for the artless eloquence that imbued so much of her speech, for her martyrdom on his behalf. . . ." What is not made explicit but will seem obvious to most of Roth's readers is that Ira's alienation is not so much the familiar response of the "second generation" in immigrant families (whether Jewish or otherwise) as it is a specific reaction to his cruel father.

> Oh, how different it would be if you loved your father: the Irish kids ran to meet theirs when they came home from work, still daylight in the summer, and hung on to their fathers' hands: "Hey, Dad, how about a nickel? What d'ye say, Dad?" And their fa-

thers smiling, trying not to, but fishing a coin out of their pockets. If *he* tried that, he'd get such a cuff alongside the head, he'd go reeling.

Another preoccupation is Ira's insatiable appetite for reading. The nearest branch of the public library is not only his refuge but the place where he can educate himself and indulge his imagination. At the age of twelve he loves fairy tales, what his mother calls "stories with a bear." There is sadness in this infatuation: "So often the princesses were not only fair, but they were the fairest in Christendom. You couldn't help that. Maybe they wouldn't mind if he was Jewish." Already the boy has intimations of a calling. With his volumes of myths and legends tucked under his arm, he walks past Mt. Morris Park at twilight and sees the evening star in the western sky:

> And so beautiful it was: a rapture to behold. It set him a problem he never dreamed anyone set himself. How do you say it? Before the pale blue twilight left your eyes you had to say it, use words that said it: blue, indigo, blue, indigo. Words that matched, matched that swimming star above the hill and the tower; what words matched it?

Within a short time the boy's taste for the mythic gives way to an even stronger desire for the "true." *Huckleberry Finn* is a revelation. A little later, he weeps "numberless times" over Jean Valjean in *Les Miserables*. He loses himself in "'true' stories" like *The Call of the Wild, The Three Musketeers* and *The Count of Monte Cristo,* Poe's tales and *Riders of the Purple Sage.* In his reading, "Ira submitted to being a Christian. What else could he do when he liked and esteemed the hero?"

Ira's sexuality is, inevitably, another of the novel's concerns. Roth's account of it—much of it in asides to his computer—is enigmatic, confused by incestuous feelings toward his mother. Once, when his father is out of town, Leah invites the surprised Ira to share the parental bed. One night he awakes, horrified, to find himself (in words that echo *Call It Sleep*) "playing bad"—i.e., "pushing, rubbing, squeezing his stiff peg between Mom's thighs." When he wails that he didn't mean it, that he was dreaming, his mother merely laughs indulgently and tells him to go back to sleep. Thereafter he sleeps in his own bed.

An amiable young "bum," Joe, lures Ira to Fort Tryon Park and orders him to take down his pants: when Joe is thwarted by a couple who happen by, he ejaculates against the trunk of a tree—arousing in Ira a profound disgust for what he thinks of as "*lyupka*" or "love." His "faggot" teacher, Mr. Lennard, tries to interest him in mutual masturbation, as do several boys of his own age. Ira resists in every case, but in his dialogue with the computer he suggests that these experiences have had a crippling effect on his sexual development—exactly how a later volume will presumably tell us. No doubt it will include something about his affair with Eda Lou Walton, the NYU English teacher who helped him with his writing and to whom *Call It Sleep* is dedicated.

Roth's addresses to the computer (which he calls "Ecclesias" for reasons never explained) create a wordy and self-conscious diversion from the main narrative. These asides comment on what has just been told, speculate about the future, and ramble on about various "current events" including the difficulties facing Israel. They bewail the lost decades, tell us about Roth's work in progress, about the elderly Ira's suffering from arthritis, and about his strained relationship with his son; above all, they express his devotion to his wife, "M," the composer Muriel Parker whom Roth met at Yaddo and whom he credits with bringing about his sexual salvation and his eventual maturity. In these asides, Ecclesias regularly talks back to Ira, commenting on his comments and often urging him to face matters he would prefer to ignore—particularly matters involving sex.

These passages seem to me unfortunate. Occasionally they are touching in their accounts of the daily struggles of an old and painfully crippled man and of his affection for his elderly but still "girlish" wife. But for the most part, they are slackly written, self-obsessed, and coy, hinting at, and then withholding or obfuscating, what seem to be important revelations. The diction is often stilted, as in the reference to Joyce as his "erstwhile literary liege," or grandiose and obscure, as when he describes himself as "supremely exacerbated, into a veritable virtuosity." The interruptions add to the shapelessness of an already loose-jointed work.

Yet I found myself completely absorbed in the main story being told in *Mercy of a Rude Stream.* Though hardly a novel in any traditional sense, it is a consistently interesting autobiographical document, richly evocative of its time and place. The writing is sometimes slapdash, but on the whole I did not miss the incandescent language and imagery of *Call it Sleep:* the plainer and rather old-fashioned language of the new work is colorful enough in the sections that count. While reading *Mercy of a Rude Stream,* I was often reminded—despite the vast differences in style and ethnic background—of Roth's affinities with Thomas Wolfe and James T. Farrell. It is astonishing to realize that Roth is not much younger than those long-dead and now, I suspect, seldom-read writers and that like them, but at an advanced age, he has been able to tell us vigorously and convincingly what it was like to be a boy living in the first part of this nearly exhausted century.

Paul West (review date 5 February 1995)

SOURCE: "Waves of Memory," in *WP Bookworld,* February 5, 1995, p. 5.

[*In the following review, West discusses the confessional and autobiographical nature of Roth's* A Diving Rock on the Hudson, *pointing out that Roth asserts that the book is a work of fiction.*]

Stationary there on a brown promontory studded with stubs of girder, he has just trudged past us carrying a fishing rod, or he has been there forever. Behind him a tug makes its minor bow-wave in the cobalt blue water, and above him, as if the heavens are rending, a shower of white cloud reaches him. All he has on are dun shorts and a loose-fitting undershirt. This is Ira Stigman, Henry Roth's adolescent Jewish hero drawn by the jacket artist, and the scene—stirring, spacious, rugged—corresponds to a lovely page of writing early on in the novel, when we hear how Ira, a walker in the city, rambled along for a mile or so, "until he came to a painted arrow that marked the entrance to a path downhill whose other end opened on an artificially sandy beach. It was a privately owned swimming area on the Hudson, complete with dressing room, lockers, and a diving platform extending into the river."

Here Ira, a teen of roly-poly build, swims out into the Hudson estuary to "the rusting hulks of the Liberty ships," to anchored pontoon planes, ducking Navy patrol boats, willing the cramp away. A leviathan waits beneath him as he floats. At these times, he thinks of his mother, who said "I let you go because you have to learn about America." The novel is an impasto of romantic and American myths. Rites of passage abound, not least that of the lightning-bolt novel that has to wait a lifetime to be written, Roth making Ira wait just as Roth has. The novel uses two type faces, one for the escapades of Ira's school years (almost like something written by J.G. Farrell), the other for the octogenarian novelist looking back on the book's genesis and the shifting literary fashions among which it lingered, going nowhere.

Readers will have to make up their own minds about a nonbiographical book that seems confessional. Roth says that "although some characters were inspired by people whom the author knew, the narrative is not intended in any way to be a depiction of any real events." So, what we have here is a simulacrum of an artifice or what Plato, if he didn't first toss the book into the sea, might have called a thoughtful deceit. Here is Ira in the New York of the Roaring Twenties, trapped in Bedford Stuyvesant, stealing pens, making love to his sister, incompetently slaving as trolley-car conductor, Yankee Stadium soda-pop hustler and plumber's mate. This part of the novel, matter-of-fact and straightforward, will be easy to translate, but the only section with any real power or magic is that dealing with incest.

On the other hand, the second type of writing in the novel, essayistic or ruminative, rises to impressive heights and informs us that the sometimes pedestrian teller, Henry Roth, has a shiny, agile, well-stocked mind. I caught myself wishing this were the autobiography of a truly Faustian intellect, with teenage mishaps relegated to the role of an almost unheard reveille. After the halfway mark, Roth seems unable to have his narrator keep at bay the book he clearly wants to write—the woof and incidentals of a self-censoring mind—and lets in all his ideas, which are a joy to have, so much more a literary offering than the *de rigueur* postcards of stoical immigrants making do in slum tenements worse than those they came from.

It's a matter of contrast. Roth thinks he needs solid realism to counter his elegant woolgathering, but what he truly needs is a style that can render the lower depths of Ira without textually cutting them off from the novel's intellectual hinterland. To be sure, an ethos comes to life: John McCormick singing "Mavoureen" on the phonograph; "colored" said as "cullud"; the cadences of Yiddish; incessant, clandestine talk of condoms, fried bacon and beans at camp. Ira passes through an alien world in which the women wear picture hats and long white gloves, but his true destination is neither home nor work, neither one school nor the other, neither Cornell (which he turns down without so much as a thought of Ithaca's savage winters) nor City College of New York, where he goes to study biology. His journey is to his imagination, long suppressed.

Ira, who is 16 in 1922, personifies for us the aroma of a long-unopened attic and becomes the incessant mourner of an era gone, a life almost lost. Wanting to be a *fleur du mal,* he ends up ranting against Joyce and his exegetes, taking the diuretic Furosemide, and mentally discussing his novel-in-progress with a guardian-guide he calls Ecclesias. References to T.S. Eliot, S.T. Coleridge, and Thomas de Quincey (misspelled) enliven the text, even though Roth's erratic narrator gives us more information than sensibility.

It is no surprise to receive this time-sliding, constantly interrupted book from Henry Roth, born in 1906, whose first novel, *Call It Sleep,* appeared in 1934, whose second novel, *Mercy of a Rude Stream,* took another 60 years. This second volume of that book will set readers comparing it with a biographical outline of Roth's life—and marveling at the closeness of the two. A portion of the novel appeared in the *Lavender,* a City College of New York journal, in 1925; so too does a portion of Ira's. Roth is the monarch of all he conveys.

Mary Gordon (review date 26 February 1995)

SOURCE: "Confession, Terminable and Interminable," *The New York Times Book Review,* February 26, 1995, p. 5.

[*In the following review, Gordon discusses Roth's complicated relationship with his Jewishness as expressed in his* A Diving Rock on the Hudson.]

The circumstances that surround the writing of Henry Roth's novel *A Diving Rock on the Hudson* are so special that it is impossible to expect a reading untouched by them. At the time of publication of this novel/memoir/journal—a work deliberately hybrid and unfixed—its author is 89 years old. It is the second volume of a series that broke the 60-year silence following the publication of *Call It Sleep,* a masterpiece that told the dark side of the immigrant journey, reminding Americans that their streets were not aved with gold but strewn with victims.

Critics have often marked Joyce's important influence on *Call It Sleep.* But Henry Roth insists, both in this book and in the interviews and essays collected in *Shifting Landscape,* that the looming Joyce has paralyzed him. Mr. Roth maintains that he was forced to reject Joyce's model of the artist's being like God, paring his nails at the border of the universe, in favor of a greater ethical and psychological truth. "I'm no super-verbalist, super-designer of irrelevancies, super-scholastic. I'm just striving to restore one individual to himself."

This project of restoration under the collective title *Mercy of a Rude Stream* centers on a revelation that forms the core of the work. The narrative follows Ira Stigman from his expulsion from Stuyvesant High School in Manhattan in 1922 on to DeWitt Clinton High School in the Bronx. It covers his beginning days at City College and his introduction to the literary world through a New York University professor who is the lover of one of his friends. Although Mr. Roth states in a disclaimer that the novel is not an autobiography, Ira is clearly identified with Mr. Roth by a series of interpolated conversations between him and his computer. He calls his computer Ecclesias, a name that recalls both the author of the Bible's darkest book and Holy Mother Church.

These interruptions—the Old Man and the Machine—are part of the structure of *A Diving Rock on the Hudson,* as they were in the first volume *A Star Shines Over Mt. Morris Park.* The machine allows Mr. Roth to reveal in his ninth decade that as a boy of 14 he began an incestuous relationship with his younger sister that continued for six years, and in addition took up with an even younger cousin.

Not only is incest at the center of the narrative, Mr. Roth believes it is also at the center of his identity as a writer. He tells us that incest is the impetus for breaking the boundaries of conventionality, so the slum boy could become an artist, and the source of the psychic warping that would eventually make the artistic life impossible.

But why after 60 years has the impulse to reveal grown irresistible? Mr. Roth tries to answer this question, but creates only a tenuous web connecting his writing, his sin and his Jewishness. He says that he began to be able to write again after Israel's victory over its Arab enemies in the 1967 war. The connection is never made explicitly. One can only assume that as it became possible for Mr. Roth to stop seeing Jews as the universal victim, he felt free to tell a story in which he himself was not victim but victimizer. In an essay written in 1988, he says that the point of his project, the sequel to *Call It Sleep,* is "to take the ground from under the innocent victim" of *Call It Sleep* and to show him as the "victimizer, but more to the point, all of us as victims—in a degenerative society."

This thought splits in the middle, morally. It seems to take in its teeth the question of individual responsibility, then drop it: something too hot to bear, the coal of Isaiah that burns the lips and tongue. In a degenerate world, all men are inevitably degenerate. But what then of the victims of the victims? The fate of Ira's sister, Minnie, and the effect on her of years of incestuous coupling never trouble her tormented brother. Nor does the effect on his still living sister of the publication of a novel whose very form insists on the connection between the fiction and the life. The octogenarian Roth worries about himself, the fate of the Jews, the State of Israel. He never worries about his sister.

Part of the fascination of *A Diving Rock on the Hudson* is that it is a deliberately unflattering self-portrait of the garrulity and narcissism of old age. This is something we haven't seen before in literature, and if for no other reason, it is valuable as the speech of a tribe until now silenced. Mr. Roth is aware of the position granted him by his infirmity and age: "The journey . . . couldn't contain any more, anyway ought not to. Maybe interesting stuff, but a plethora. Then what? Delete? All that followed? . . . Maybe he ought to delete this intervention too, this bit of Nestorian garrulity. . . . His sense of rightness required this interlude."

Mr. Roth is clear that, this sense of rightness is psychological or spiritual rather than literary. "Would that I had been spared the need to mention these painful events. . . . The story cannot continue without this admission. And I damn near don't give a hoot about the literary quality. . . . Oh, a million billion threads, motes, spirochetes—all of which he had to sweep aside to resume, in acceptable prose . . . the continuity of what be already knew, and knew only too well and grievously, to strive to nurture the masterpiece model he hoped to re-create."

But what is involved in the creation of the masterpiece

model? For the modernist master, the writer must get out of the way of his own work, devote his attention to form rather than content, remain disinterested about the backwash of the work on his own life. The modernist writer is heroic in his self-forgetfulness and in his priestly service to the idea of art. Art is the only redemption, formal beauty the only ideal worth serving.

How does this ideal affect a man in his late 80's? A man who is writing against time, literal time, not the time that is another esthetic device the modernist writer shapes, controls, eventually entraps in the amber of his art? Mr. Roth can't be a modernist master because he has not felt redeemed by the creation of beauty. He insists on another kind of redemption: the redemption of confession, of exposure, of a relentless insistence on his own defilement. But this can only take place through writing: "Writing was all that could in some way gain rehabilitation—without his seeking pardon or absolution, but by employing what he was. . . . He had destroyed, or undermined irreversibly," the central strength of who he was, writing was all there was left to him as justification. . . . The literary path became thus his 'choice.'"

The problem, for Mr. Roth, is that the road that went before him was paved entirely by non-Jews. *In A Star Shines Over Mt. Morris Park,* Mr. Roth says: "Those were the stories he prized above all others, stories he loved: of enchantment and delicacy, of princelings and fair princesses. . . .And King Arthur's knights, they sought the Holy Grail, the radiant vessel like a loving cup out of which Jesus had drunk wine. So everything beautiful was Christian, wasn't it? All that was flawless and pure and bold and courtly and chivalric was *goyish.*"

How then does a Jew, believing what Mr. Roth believes, enter the masterpiece tradition? Particularly the modernist one, with its cult of the priesthood of art, the golden calf to which, rather than to Yahweh, the practitioner must bend the knee? How does he participate in the Eucharist of art? How can be believe himself redeemed by it? Redemption, for a Jew, takes place not through the ritual actions of a priest but through ethical reparations made in the living community by a living soul.

This taste for an ethical dimension might explain Mr. Roth's becoming a Communist after the completion of *Call It Sleep.* It is usually understood that accepting the party's charge to write Socialist Realism was the cause of his writer's block. But it seems to me rather that Mr. Roth was not silenced by his Marxism, he was driven to Marxism by a Jewishness that could not be satisfied with the anti-communal anti-ethical, almost idolatrous tenets of his modernist models, Eliot and Joyce.

An artist does not choose the frequency he or she hears. The frequency is picked up by an inexplicably constructed mesh of miracle and accident. Mr. Roth picked up the frequency of the brooding dream: poetic, darkly lit and full of whispers. For this lyrical mournfulness, he needed his father, Joyce, to show the way. But Joyce, creator of the most famous Jew in modern literature, was not himself a Jew, and so could only be an uneasy foster father. Harold Bloom tells us that all strong writers kill the father before them. But what if the son murders prematurely, before reaching his full strength? Mr. Roth couldn't bear the yoke of the great high priest, Joyce, and killed him. But without Joyce he was unable to move forward into a tale that would accommodate his obsession with what he believed was the vexed state of being a Jew.

What needed to follow *Call It Sleep* was a deep dive into the mire of self-hatred. Mr. Roth says that this is what he's doing now. But he insists that his sense of defilement is personal, connected to nothing larger. "I'm not engaged in a sociological tract, but a rendering . . . of my lamentable past. . . . I feel bound not to mitigate the behavior of this literary scamp, bound to present him as despicable as he was." His prose rings most true when he takes this risk. He describes his sexual adventures with his young cousin: "Boyoboy, his blazing passion could kill this little, oh, fat little heifer, supine, submissive, inviting murderous sacrifice. Jesus. But where? Where freedom for rut to erupt, where a minute of privacy, innocent-seeming privacy? Think Upstairs. Possibly. Try."

Mr. Roth's description of sex with his sister is an unflinching evocation of the sordidness of lust unleavened by any affection or regard.

> "You louse. . . ."
> "You don't get a thrill, too?"
> "You're older, that's why it's your fault. Who started it?"

But Mr. Roth never reaches these heights, or depths, of understanding when he is discussing his Jewishness. A veil comes over his eyes, vital connections aren't made, vital admissions are glossed over. There is a moment when Ira brings sandwiches made of Jewish salami on a picnic with a more genteel Jewish friend and two Christian women professors. Before he meets with the company, however, he throws the sandwiches into the river: they're too heavy, too smelly, too insistent on drawing attention to themselves. But this half-comic scene or metaphor doesn't come to terms with Mr. Roth's conviction that "everything beautiful was Christian." It doesn't sear itself on our memory like the image, in *Call It Sleep,* of the milk dipper dropped onto the third rail.

In a confused and hypercomplicated way, Mr.Roth finds in the Lower East Side (where he lived as a young child before the family move to largely Christian Harlem) the Jewish mother lode that has fed his art and might, if he'd been allowed to stay there, have kept him whole: "I felt at home there shored and stayed by tenets I imagined inhered in the nature of things. I *belonged.* And therefore, everything I did, however wicked, was somehow endemic, indigenous, part of the general scheme." Is Mr. Roth saying that if he'd been allowed to live in an environment of wickedness and madness, because it at least had coherence, he would have been spared the wickedness and madness that later marked his life? That in a world of the wicked and mad he would not have had the pain of knowing himself different? This mysterious passage sheds light, I think on the knot of Mr. Roth's relationship to his Jewishness. It is a knot that, at 89, he has not yet untied.

Mr. Roth circles around the topic of Jewish self-hatred by creating a world of Jewishness without charm or humor. Its warmth is only suffocation; its attentiveness surveillance; its bonds, traps. Judaism provides no poetry for Mr. Roth and no spiritual sustenance. Even the beautiful mother of *Call It Sleep* is replaced by the homely downtrodden mother of *Mercy of a Rude Stream.* The father, less frightening, is perhaps more pathetic. The upper class Jews represented by the family of one of Ira's classmates are materialistic, grasping and limited in their horizons and imaginations.

In the part of *A Diving Rock on the Hudson* that is purely narrative, Mr. Roth gives us an enormous number of details, sometimes so many we can't form a coherent picture. Occasionally, though, the old magic of *Call It Sleep* is there; a street comes alive for us, or a moment. But mostly we are awash in what he has referred to as the "plethora" of details: a pileup of facts rather than concentrated images. Sometimes he lapses into the diction of the "Boys' Own Stories" that must have been his first reading: "the inexorable, irreversible doom that had befallen him—nay, nay, invited to befall him." Boys are referred to as "youths." At moments of stress Ira exclaims "Boyoboy!"

But is this kind of faultfinding appropriate to the enterprise of a man of nearly 90 who says it is part of his goal to include garrulousness, to avoid the trap of beautiful writing? Who says he is doing this, not for literature, but to justify his life? Clearly, this is a different order of work from *Call It Sleep* and must be read with different standards. *Call It Sleep* remains a masterpiece; nothing is lost from it, or added to it, by reading its sequels.

And so, how do we read these new works, trailing behind them both a history and a work of literature? We read them on their own clearly articulated terms and, having agreed to do that, we are wholly taken up by the touching and fascinating record of a marred life that insists on pressing on us its pulsing, painfully relentless vitality.

Frank Kermode (review date 14 July 1996)

SOURCE: "'Holistic Rendering of My Lamentable Past,'" in *The New York Times Book Review,* July 14, 1996, p. 6.

[*In the following review, Kermode states that Roth's* From Bondage *"does what has rarely been done before; it enhances its brilliant youthful original by casting upon it the calmer, contemplative light of old age."*]

There can be few readers of modern American fiction unfamiliar with the extraordinary career of Henry Roth. Born in Galicia in 1906, he arrived in New York with his Yiddish-speaking parents three years later, and lived first on the Lower East Side and then in Harlem. He did many menial jobs and was a not particularly bright student at City College; but in 1934, at the age of 28, he published *Call It Sleep,* a novel dedicated to Eda Lou Walton, who introduced him to the literary world, became his mistress and detected and fostered a talent hardly perceived by anybody else.

Call It Sleep is a truly astonishing achievement. Written almost entirely from the point of view of a young child, it represents with virtuosity the language of the family, giving to its partly Anglicized representation of Yiddish a great richness and an often comic splendor, Roth borrows form James Joyce the technique of internal monologue for vivid accounts of the boy's bewilderment at the mysteries of his parents' marriage, and of the cold world around him, with its vast hostile streets, its ethnic gangs, its harsh employers and its conflicting notions of holiness. Beneath the fascinating surface there lies a powerful, even melodramatic plot involving the beloved mother, suspected by her husband of an infidelity that produced young David, and the terrifying father, almost mythically violent, who in jealous misery hates and persecutes a boy who has trouble enough already with his own day-to-day life.

Having enjoyed a mild success on its first publication, *Call It Sleep* surprisingly dropped from view, but it achieved greater fame when published in paperback in 1964 and now has undisputed classic status. Meanwhile Roth suffered what must be one of the longest bouts of writer's block on record. He made his living in many different trades—toolmaker, waterfowl farmer, math tutor—and delayed his return to fiction for over 40 years. From the work of his old age one deduces that he began to write again in the 1970's, and in the 80's, already in the grip of rheumatoid arthritis (R.A. he calls it, reflecting that *ra* in Hebrew connotes "evil"), reworked the text. He acquired a computer and began to convert the type-

scripts of the previous decade into a very long novel, planned to occupy six volumes. It is not clear whether he progressed beyond the third volume, though the earlier and fuller draft presumably survives.

Mercy of a Rude Stream is the title of the whole project. The first two volumes, *A Star Shines Over Mt. Morris Park* and *A Diving Rock on the Hudson,* were published in 1994 and 1995. Roth died in October 1995, and the posthumously published *From Bondage* is the third in the series. The central figure in these books is Ira Stigman, a boy with a past not unlike that of David Schearl in *Call It Sleep,* though at the outset he is three years older and has a milder (yet still abusive) father. We are warned not to treat these books as autobiography; but with the aid of his trusty word processor the author inserts into the narrative passages about his present condition, his love for his wife, his illness, how he has come to quarrel with his erstwhile master Joyce, how his fears for Israel have changed him from one who, like Joyce, chose silence and exile into a Jew again sure of his loyalties. He looks back rather enviously at what he calls his only novel, *Call It Sleep,* wondering how he was "for five decades . . . well-nigh immobilized," how he "painted himself into the corner of childhood." He chats with his beloved computer about the difficulty of what he has undertaken—his "attempt at holistic rendering of my lamentable past," at "the shedding of his abominable self," with many reflections on the progress of the story, and hints as to what is to come later. The narrative proper ends even before Ira becomes Edith's lover, and long before the writing of *Call It Sleep.*

The computer makes cutting so easy—why not press the delete key and abolish such embarrassing diversions? "Why was he doing this, demeaning himself—and perhaps Jews, the multitude of Jews who had transformed one previous novel into a shrine, a child's shrine at that—to the extent he was?" The commentary, which grows more copious as the story unfolds, is given its own typeface, and has a different tone and status from the rest of the narrative, but in view of what it adds it is hard not to see the entire work as fictionalized autobiography; nor does Roth actively dispute the description.

Indeed this huge second novel has a strong confessional aspect (and there are significant allusions to St. Augustine). The aged Ira brings himself with difficulty to the point of explaining the sense of guilt that partly ruined his life and was a cause of his block: his early incest with an under-age sister, and the sexual exploitation of a young cousin. His encounters with these girls are described with a sort of unrelenting, gritted-teeth dedication to the recording of the deceits, delights and disgust they entail. They are blamed for Ira's ignorance of "how to make a pass at someone refined"—at a woman who didn't belong to the family—as well as for his long silence. We can guess that in still unpublished later parts of the narrative Edith, the character based on Eda Lou Walton, and "M," his wife, Muriel, who died in 1990, will help rid him of this inhibition.

When the dialogue is simply in educated English, as it mostly is when Ira begins to move in literary circles—chattering about T.S. Eliot, discussing a smuggled copy of *Ulysses*—it lacks the vitality and charm of the domestic Yiddish that Roth so beautifully renders in the earlier parts, with its comic lamentation and terrible curses. And the registration of the settings lacks some of the dark, threatening detail of the first book, the old insights into maternal love and into panic, loneliness and lostness.

Yet this third installment of the new one is by no means lacking in energy. The effect is of an old man brooding fruitfully over the details of a youth 70 years past, his memory sharpened by fantasy and enlivened by an apprehension of other personalities now enriched by adult experience. An example is the portrait of his friend Larry, much better off, much smarter, at ease with poets, who in time proves too fragile and too changeable to achieve anything substantial and suffers burnout, atrophy, a fate that almost befell the narrator himself, who lived on ecause, after all, the rude stream proved—to him—merciful.

From Bondage resumes Ira's story at the point where he is closest to Larry, Edith's current lover. He grows more easy in refined company, but he still has to work, especially since his grades at City College aren't good; he has a job in a candy store, hustles soda at the ball park, sweats as a maintenance man or "grease monkey" in a subway repair yard. He does some petty thieving, but also takes his first little steps as a writer and becomes the confidant of Edith.

Ira isn't sure he likes the new direction of his life, but submits almost passively. From what he regards as the dreary company of the poolroom—"the first American-born generation of Jews, the bridge between the poor East European immigrants who landed here and the American Jews their offspring become"—he gradually moves into gentile circles and accepts his vocation as a writer.

It must be said that nothing we learn about Ira in this account by his aged shadow gives much of an explanation of why he became, almost at a stroke, a writer of quite exceptional accomplishment. The impression we are left with is that the chronicler doesn't really know himself. There were, he says, contemporaries much more brilliant and original than he, but he was, in a sense, chosen. He "deserved very little credit. Only that of striving to develop the most preeminent, if not the only gift he had . . . which was what the others did, also . . . those more gifted than he who yet failed to win universal appeal. It was all a Calvinist fluke."

That is a wise saying, even if it borrows the doctrine of election from an alien religion. This latest in the sequence *Mercy of a Rude Stream* does what has rarely been done before; it enhances its brilliant youthful original by casting upon it the calmer, contemplative light of old age. It is clearly indispensable to the appreciation of Roth's unique life and work as a whole.

Marshall Berman (review date 23 September 1996)

SOURCE: "The Bonds of Love," in *The Nation,* Vol. 263, No. 8, September 23, 1996, pp. 25-30.

[*In the following review, Berman discusses how Roth's* From Bondage *was changed and how its impact was lessened when crucial scenes concerning incest were cut from the published edition.*]

Henry Roth, who died last year at age 89, wrote one of the great novels of the century, *Call It Sleep.* It is the story of a poor Jewish boy on the Lower East Side, trying to survive and grow in a world where it was dangerous to go out and maybe even more dangerous to stay in, and yet where life was holy. Roth not only assimilated D.H. Lawrence, James Joyce and William Faulkner but, on his first try, wrote a *Bildungsroman* that was entirely worthy of them. No one has ever written better about how it is to be a child, an immigrant, a Jew. No one has known so well how to use Yiddish and the life of the ghetto to light up the English or the American language.

Then, like a sensational rookie pitcher whose arm just went dead, Roth stopped. For forty years, he and his wife, Muriel Parker, tried everything, or at least everything they could afford, in the hope of getting him writing again. They moved from New York to Boston to Maine to New Mexico—his last address was a trailer on New York Avenue in Albuquerque, where he died. (I met him there in 1980.) Unable to be a writer, he went from being a toolmaker to a farmer to a psychiatric orderly to a schoolteacher, from obscurity to fifteen minutes of fame (in the sixties, when *Call It Sleep* came out in paperback and sold more than a million copies) to a more comfortable obscurity—this time, he said, at least they had hot and cold running water. They never made it to China, where, after the revolution of 1949, they had hoped to dedicate their lives to the Chinese people; their group fell apart and they couldn't learn Chinese. They evolved (that was their word) from communism to psychoanalysis to a liberal from of Jewish chauvinism. They brought up two children together and lived a decent life. But nothing "worked" for him, nothing lit his fire. From time to time he wrote an essay or short story, but he knew no one would remember those pieces if not for *Call It Sleep.* Sometime in the seventies, Roth met Ralph Ellison; they traded grim hypotheses about themselves and each other, and about blacks and Jews, and they laughed.

> **[In *Call It Sleep,*] Roth not only assimilated D.H. Lawrence, James Joyce and William Faulkner but, on his first try, wrote a *Bildungsroman* that was entirely worthy of them.**
> **—*Marshall Berman***

But then, as if to confound all those who say there are no second acts in American lives, Roth resumed his *Bildungsroman* as if it had been only yesterday that he had stopped. He told me in 1980 that he had recently written hundreds of new pages. He now saw *Call It Sleep* as the first part of a trilogy. In the second part the hero would "escape from his family by becoming a rat, a real bastard," and moreover, "a Jewish anti-Semite." In the finale, he would at last "grow up and be reconciled with humanity." Yes, his wife said caustically, "in the arms of Eda Lou Walton"—Roth's first love, and the woman to whom he dedicated *Call It Sleep.*

No one understood the secret of Roth's miraculous renewal, but nobody could deny he was renewed. He poured thousands of new pages down on St. Martin's Press in New York, where editor Robert Weil did a heroic job of transforming them into three roughly coherent volumes (Weil says there are more to come) that Roth anointed with the gloomy Shakespearean title, *Mercy of a Rude Stream.* Their format is a strange one, cutting back and forth between a *Bildungsroman,* written in a narrative voice that seems to come out of a past long before *Call It Sleep,* and (in a different typeface) the author's midrashim and reflections on his characters, his story and himself, composed from the early eighties to the early nineties. Narratologists would probably say it's wrong of me to try to distinguish a "narrator" from an "author," when all the text offers us is two narrators, and neither one should be "privileged" above the other. However, the eighties/nineties narrator discusses many events in his life that are identical with events in Henry Roth's (for example, having a beloved wife, Muriel Parker, a composer who gives up her career for the author of *Call It Sleep,* and who dies in 1990). So I call the eighties/nineties narrator "Neo-Roth." (Neo-Roth composes on a word processor, which he calls "Ecclesias." He talks to Ecclesias with the same irritated reverence my cousins use when they talk to their Harleys and their fast cars.)

The first book, *A Star Shines Over Mt. Morris Park,* appeared in 1994; the second, *A Diving Rock on the Hudson,* came out last fall, just after Roth died (though he did get to work on the galleys); the third, *From Bondage,* was published this June. The hero's name has been changed from David Schearl to Ira Stigman (=stigma, stigmata; get it?); he is a teenager, and he lives with his quarreling parents in East Harlem, where they have moved from the Lower East Side. East Harlem was then a suburb, largely Jewish until after World War II. (It elected both Fiorello LaGuardia and Vito Marcantonio.) Ira's emotions themselves have a postwar ring: the anger of a city child who felt at home in the old neighborhood, which he idealizes, and who sees the suburban move as a personal betrayal. One of the few things that makes the move bearable is that much of his mother's large family has followed her uptown, and Ira can find a fine assortment of interesting and colorful people who love him just a short walk away. Among them is a 14-year-old girl cousin with whom Ira enjoys fast, rough, domineering sex ("Turn around . . . bend over. . .").

It's possible to get into the flow of these narratives, but first you have to reconcile yourself to the fact that Roth's lyrical genius, his visionary gleam, is gone. You will find plenty of fascinating pages here, but you won't find any that will change your life. These new books, especially the first one, read like a midrash (or is it a Monarch Outline?) on The Book. The midrash is full of fascinating background; it may even teach you more about the everyday world of *Call It Sleep* than *Call It Sleep* itself. It's as if Neo-Roth is telling us: "Yeah, I knew that neighborhood, I even knew that family, and sure, things were tough, but it's not like there was thunder and lightning and the earth opening up. Those parents were just *proste menschen,* ordinary people, not mythical gods. There was no big deal about them. Somebody tell that kid to lighten up!"

Ira's life seems to have been written as one work. As a result, the boundaries between *From Bondage* and *Diving Rock* are not so clear. Ira steals fountain pens; is expelled from Stuyvesant High (where the teachers are Dickensian sadists); contemplates suicide (diving off the rock when the currents would engulf and drown him) but chooses life ("the river . . . told him" that he must live and suffer); enrolls at Clinton (where the teachers are slightly less malevolent); forms a friendship with a rich Jewish boy, Larry, who shows him how to be polite and refined; wins a scholarship to Cornell but turns it down because he isn't ready to leave home and goes to C.C.N.Y. instead.

Larry is a poet, and he introduces Ira to the bohemians of downtown, where, for the first time in his life, Ira encounters modern poetry. T.S. Eliot is the star, and the basic idea is "a clean break between what's gone before and now." Downtown is where he meets Larry's girlfriend, Edith, an older (thirtysomething), sophisticated woman, a modern poet, critic and instructor at N.Y.U. She is part of Margaret Mead's circle, and Neo-Roth settles some old scores with

Mead (but neglects to explain the original ball games). He tells us to stay tuned: This is going to be his first love. *From Bondage* features an extended love triangle with Edith/Eda Lou, Ira and Larry, written in an archly comic mode, à la Aldous Huxley. Edith's version of modern love is saturated with modern lit: She examines real and prospective lovers by springing *Ulysses* on them. Larry doesn't get it, and so, unknowingly, flunks body language; but Ira eats it up. So when are they getting into bed together? Not so fast! After 600 pages (*From Bondage* plus half of *Diving Rock*), their love is still unconsummated. Roth draws out the foreplay; if he could wait forty years, we can wait a few hundred more pages. Now there's nothing wrong with these characters or their story, but you have to fight a temptation to call it *Call It Sleep*-Lite.

But there's a theme laid down in *Diving Rock,* and carried on in *From Bondage,* that's unforgettably "heavy": Ira's incestuous affair with his kid sister, Minnie. This affair begins before they even know how to do it (after a while Ira goes to a prostitute, who shows him what to put where and how). It goes on for years; as *From Bondage* ends, we don't know if it's really over. When *Diving Rock* came out last year, there was lots of discussion about whether the real Henry Roth and his real sister had committed incest. I don't see why anyone outside their family should care. What we readers should care about is how he *writes* incest. And he writes it brilliantly, with a remarkable fusion of physical detail and emotional energy. He shows it to us at once from outside, where it's a blatantly disgusting thing to do, and from inside, where it's the one inescapable, perfectly right thing to do. Here his energy level surges up to *Call It Sleep*-like peaks (remember, there was an incestuous love there too); when he does anything else, his prose sags.

Roth's ambivalent incest vision may be part of a larger conflict about sex itself. Sometimes he considers it just plain disgusting and his writing turns clunky: "He had used Edith basely . . . to gratify his sexual urge—and in front of a mirror to intensify his gratification—and she, poor woman, had more than acquiesced—had urged him on." (He drags St. Augustine in to legitimize this way of talking.) It is essentially men who are guilty of this abomination. Women apparently have no desires of their own. But women—even saintly women, even Mom, even his wife—pollute and incriminate themselves by going along.

In spite of this, when Roth focuses on the affair between Ira and Minnie, he portrays sex with great empathy for both of them. The fact that this guy over 80 can write so vividly about sex between people under 20 is a stirring tribute to the power of the imagination. He's best on the details: on the experience of losing control, making too much noise and risking discovery, on learning to put on a condom so it won't fall off, on missing a period, on learning to give your part-

ner pleasure along with your own, on depths of rage and hate that love and pleasure can open up—and on how all these classic sexual risks and terrors explode through the roof if the person whose sweat is mixing with yours is your sister. This is both thrilling and unnerving to read—and not only for those of us who love our sisters. In Roth's best writing, both early and late, sex and incest come to symbolize each other. Stated as a formula it sounds absurd, but his gift as a writer makes it feel right.

Ira and Minnie's incest is the source of the best scene in *From Bondage:* It is the mid-twenties. Ira is a junior at C.C.N.Y.; Minnie, a senior at elite Julia Richmond High School, is planning to go to Hunter and become a teacher. Their affair seems to be winding down, and both are falling in love with people who are not only outside their family (about time!) but outside their people—goyim, non-Jews. One day Minnie bursts into the house sobbing, and throws herself into Ira's arms: "My *s*. . . . The speaking test. I failed. . . . I have a lateral *s*. . . . They don't want me. . . . It was only the Jewish girls."

(Minnie is hysterical, but historically right. Boards of education all over the United States were appalled to find that people who passed their teaching exams were overwhelmingly Jews: They added a speech test designed specifically to keep Jews out. For a couple of decades, this policy kept U.S. school systems effectively *Judenrein.* It was only after World War II and the G.I. Bill that Jews broke through.)

Ira offers brotherly support, and tells how anti-Semites have hurt him, too. But Minnie wants more: She wants him to fuck her, right here, right now. She talks dirty to turn him on; it works, as she knew it would. She says he has ruined her, now she's just a whore. He says she's not ruined. "So do it to me if there's nothing wrong with me." But their parents will be home any minute. She doesn't care, let them see what she is. Her screaming gets louder, more out of control. "So fuck me and I'll shut up. . . . You're my brother, so cure me. . . . You know you can do it in a minute." She lifts her skirt up, and pulls her panties down. "Get your cock out. . . . I want it."

Breathing heavily, Ira reaches to lock the door. But he can't bring himself to do it. "No. For once, no." Instead, he presses her to get dressed, to wash herself, freshen her face, look normal. In a little while, she is grateful. He steers her and himself back to their books. They look like a perfect brother and sister when their parents come home.

Ira looks back on this harrowing scene, and attacks himself: "He had tainted her forever." But readers are likely to disagree. After years of taking advantage of Minnie, he has finally offered her the protective care a sister might expect from an older brother—for once, Ira has acted like a mensch. It's true that, in the past, Minnie herself was always "consenting"; but she was hardly an "adult." Ira wasn't very grown up either; but he may be on his way now. Whatever it might mean to outgrow incest, this dreadful scene could be a start. The nightmarish moment they have just shared might turn out to be a turning point in both their lives, a moment of overcoming and moral growth.

It *might* be—but you won't get a chance to decide, because it's vanished from the published book. I read this scene in a set of galleys that I received at the end of March and took it for granted as I imagined my review. Then, some weeks ago, in the Jewish Museum, a man I'd never met saw me carrying the galleys and asked me if the rumor was true that Roth's sister's lawyers had "forced them to take out all the incest." I laughed, read him a little from the scene I've quoted above, and said not to worry. But then I realized I had never seen the book itself. I called the publisher and spoke to Robert Weil, Roth's editor, and to other people in many departments, and to Larry Fox, Roth's lawyer and literary executor. I spent most of the day on the phone. It was a strange day. (*Dummkopf*, why didn't I at least get it on tape?)

I was told that the rumor was absurd, and apart from typos, there were no changes at all. Still, people were startled to hear I had a set of galleys. *Which* set of galleys? they asked, thus kindly letting me know there was more than one. I tried to find out if Roth's sister or anyone else was suing or threatening to sue. And who actually made the decision that changes had to be made, and on what basis? I was told that nobody was threatening anybody, and Roth's sister was a very nice 90-year-old woman in a nursing home in the Bronx, and she wasn't disturbing anybody, and why should anyone want to hurt her? I asked the lawyer, So where's the pressure coming from? He said, What pressure? I wondered, What *film noir* am I in?

At this point I could sense a process I've seen before: Corporate legal departments win the culture wars. Editors—or, as they are always reminded when there's trouble, editorial employees—are hung out to dry and forced to smile. Writers are forgotten (is that guy dead? alive? or what?) and always the last to know.

In the scene you'll find in print, Minnie comes home distraught and tells her sad story, Ira consoles her in decent normal ways and that's just about all. The publishers haven't exactly "taken out all the incest" but they've done their best to clean it up. When Ira curses the anti-Semites who have done Minnie wrong, she says the real reason for her misfortunes in school is that "I let you lay me." Her guilt and magical thinking are not implausible. What's weird is the way her own desires, so active and volatile in the writer's version, are airbrushed out of the publisher's version. In the galleys,

as Roth wrote them, the sexual bond between brother and sister is fearfully intense. In the book it's redescribed not only as something *he* did to *her* (did they bring in Catharine MacKinnon to rewrite her dialogue?) but as a force that can be eliminated if you simply put it in the past tense. In the galleys, the crosscurrents and contradictions of desire create a harrowing but brilliant scene, a dramatic explosion with transformative power. In the published book, with the woman's desires written out of the script, nothing can happen and there's nothing to remember.

The rewriting is especially sad if we look at it in the light of one of Neo-Roth's most poignant notes to himself. He says he had tried to keep his sister out of his story because he felt guilty toward her. Then he came to see that excluding her would only continue the mistreatment that he felt so guilty about. He asks himself, "When will you admit her to the realm of a legitimate character, acting, active, asserting herself, an individual?" He answers, "I don't know if I'll ever be able to write about her in all the emotional dimensions she deserves. But I have to do something." Roth did do something: He created a compelling girl-woman with inner depth who has grown up too fast and who deserves sympathy and respect. The way in which *From Bondage* was cut suggests that somebody with power wanted to "protect" Roth's sister from him. But also to "protect" the Jewish people from an incest story by one of its most beloved writers, where the girl is not a helpless victim of male lust (there's always room for more women as victims) but an "acting, active, asserting" individual who wants to do it herself.

Does Henry Roth's sister need such protection? Do the Jewish people? (For that matter, do any people?) What we do need is protection from our protectors, breathing space to live and reflect on our lives. Corporate censorship is a crime against the living as well as against the dead. I hope future editions of *From Bondage* will be free enough to let Minnie Stigman come into her own, and I hope we will all be free enough to look her in the face and live with her.

Henry Roth was inspired by the audacious, expansive, world-conquering spirit of twentieth-century Modernism. The world that was his to conquer was the claustral world of the modern ghetto: the street, the block, the house, the apartment, the family. Roth, like many writers, saw the social forces that were pulling the modern family and the modern self apart. Bu, as a Jew living through a Jewish family, he also saw something else: the family imploding, crashing in on itself, with a love so intimate it was incestuous, perishing from its very richness of being. He never freed himself from bondage to this tragic vision, except to fall into something even worse: the feel of not to feel it, a life in death. Roth wandered in a desert of paralysis for 40 years. But then he came back, to wrestle with his angel, to try to make a home in the bonds of love. I think all of us are caught up in his struggle: This is what the words "modern life" mean. But there are people with power who want to paper it over. We need to watch out for them and the desert they have prepared for us all.

FURTHER READING

Criticism

"*Call It Sleep* Author Henry Roth, 89." *Chicago Tribune* (13 October 1995): 11.
    Notice of Roth's death at age 89.

Clark, Eunice. Review of *Call It Sleep*, by Henry Roth. *Common Sense* 4, No. 3 (March 1935): 29.
    Calls Roth's *Call It Sleep* "a gold mine of accurate impressions."

Dickstein, Morris. "No Longer at Home." *Times Literary Supplement*, No. 4840 (5 January 1996): 5.
    Offers a review of Roth's *Shifting Landscape*, asserting that Roth comes through as "the ultimate survivor."

Farber, Frances D. "Encounters with an Alien Culture: Thematic Functions of Dialect in *Call It Sleep*." *Yiddish* 7, No. 4 (1990): 49-56.
    Discusses Roth's use of dialect in his *Call It Sleep*.

Folks, Jeffrey. Review of *Mercy of a Rude Stream*, by Henry Roth. *World Literature Today* 68, No. 4 (August 1994): 813-14.
    Asserts that "*Mercy of a Rude Stream* should be recognized as one of the finest autobiographical fictions of our time."

Greenstone, Maryann D. "The Ghetto Revisited: *Call It Sleep* by Henry Roth." *Studies in Bibliography and Booklore* IX, No. 1 (Spring 1970): 96-100.
    Asserts the importance of Roth's *Call It Sleep* and provides a bibliography of articles about the novel.

Halkin, Hillel. "Henry Roth's Secret." *Commentary* 97, No. 5 (May 1994): 44-7.

Discusses how Roth's homosexual encounters affected his self-image and his work.

Harris, Lis. "A Critic at Large: In the Shadow of the Golden Mountains." *The New Yorker* LXIV, No. 19 (27 June 1988): 84-92.
    Offers an overview of Roth's life and career, and asserts that the alienation found in Roth's *Call It Sleep* came from the author's own experience as an immigrant.

Inge, M. Thomas. "The Ethnic Experience and Aesthetics in Literature: Malamud's *The Assistant* and Roth's *Call It Sleep*." *Journal of Ethnic Studies* 1, No. 4 (Winter 1974): 45-50.
    Discusses how Bernard Malamud's *The Assistant* and Roth's *Call It Sleep* are both about the "struggle for accommodation and survival of an immigrant family in a new world" and how *Call It Sleep* gives "special attention to the strains of the relationship between foreign born parents and American bred children."

Review of *From Bondage*, by Henry Roth. *Kirkus Reviews* LXIV, No. 8 (15 April 1996): 557.
    Criticizes Roth's *From Bondage* as deeply flawed.

Lesser, Wayne. "A Narrative's Revolutionary Energy: The Example of Henry Roth's *Call it Sleep*." *Criticism* XXIII, No. 2 (Spring 1981): 155-176.
    Analyzes Roth's *Call it Sleep* in terms of "how a shared cultural symbolism operates within the text to create an illuminated movement of personal-linguistic history."

Orr, Elaine. "On the Side of the Mother: *Yonnondio* and *Call It Sleep*." *Studies in American Fiction* 21, No. 2 (Autumn 1993): 209-23.
    Compares the role of the mother in Tillie Olsen's *Yonnondio: From the Thirties* and Roth's *Call It Sleep*.

Rosen, Jonathan. "Lost and Found: Remembering Henry Roth." *The New York Times Book Review* (10 December 1995): 47.
    Discusses Roth's exile from and return to writing.

Rosenheim, Andrew. "Growing up absurd in America." *Times Literary Supplement*, No. 4802 (14 April 1995): 20.
    Praises Volume Two of Roth's *Mercy of a Rude Stream* for its credible andvivid characers nd its compelling story.

Additional coverage of Roth's life and career is contained in the following sources published by Gale: *Contemporary Authors*, Vols. 11 and 12; *Contemporary Authors New Revision Series*, Vol. 38; *Contemporary Authors Permanent Series*, Vol. 1; *Dictionary of Literary Biography*, Vol. 28; and *Major Twentieth-Century Writers*.

Hunter S. Thompson
1939-

(Has also written under pseudonyms Raoul Duke and Sebastian Owl) American nonfiction writer, journalist, editor, and scriptwriter.

The following entry presents criticism of Thompson's work. For further information on his life and career, see *CLC,* Volumes 9, 17, and 40.

INTRODUCTION

Thompson is best known as the inventor of "gonzo journalism," a form of outspoken, irreverent commentary. Gonzo journalism grew out of the New Journalism movement of Thomas Wolfe and others who wanted to bring journalism beyond merely reporting facts to a level of literature in which writers bring their creativity to bear on the subject. Thompson's gonzo style parodies current events and satirizes American culture.

Biographical Information

Thompson was born on July 18, 1939, in Louisville, Kentucky. Planning to someday make an impact in the world, Thompson retained carbon copies of all of his correspondence for future publication. These letters were eventually published as *The Proud Highway* (1997). Thompson began his career with a series of jobs at small newspapers, including stints as the sports editor of *The Jersey Shore Herald* and as a reporter for *The Middletown Daily News.* He then moved on to freelance writing, first based in Puerto Rico and then as the South American correspondent for *The National Observer.* During this time he also tried his hand at novel writing, but only fragments of his two novels were ever published. Thompson's unique brand of political writing gained widespread attention through his affiliation with *Rolling Stone* magazine, where the articles that later became *Fear and Loathing in Las Vegas* (1972) and *Fear and Loathing on the Campaign Trail '72* (1973) were originally published. Thompson also worked as a columnist for the *San Francisco Examiner.* He currently lives on a farm in Woody Creek, Colorado, where he continues to write.

Major Works

Thompson is known for his unique perspective and brutal honesty as a writer as well as for his flamboyant lifestyle. As a practitioner of gonzo journalism, Thompson enters a scene—the world of the Hell's Angels, Las Vegas gambling, and Washington politics are examples—and becomes a char-

acter in the story. Far from maintaining the traditional journalistic ideal of impartiality, Thompson interacts with the players and records his impressions, often with scathing irreverence. His first book, *Hell's Angels* (1966), portrays his time on the road with the infamous motorcycle gang. *Fear and Loathing in Las Vegas* collects his articles about five days spent in a drug-induced haze, immersed in the world of casino gambling. *Fear and Loathing on the Campaign Trail '72* includes Thompson's behind-the-scenes impressions of the 1972 presidential campaign and its candidates. Two decades later, *Better Than Sex* (1993) offers the same perspective on the 1992 presidential campaign.

Critical Reception

Thompson's gonzo journalism drew controversy from its inception, and many of the arguments it sparked remain unresolved. One of the points of contention among reviewers is the validity of labeling Thompson's writing "journalism": many believe that since he eschews neutrality, Thompson's writing by definition cannot be categorized as journalism. Beyond the semantics issues, however, critics are divided in their opinions of the quality of Thompson's prose. Some agree with Michael E. Ross, who considers him "one of our most incisive, insightful and hilarious social critics," while others reject his topics as insignificant and unnecessarily offensive. While some critics complain that Thompson's prejudices influence his writing excessively, others praise him for displaying his biases as other journalists attempt to hide theirs. Even some critics who disagree with Thompson's ideas and approach nonetheless comment favorably on the quality of his writing. Some critics in later years, however, have complained that Thompson's recent works do little more than rehash his earlier writings and that the author himself has become his own main subject.

PRINCIPAL WORKS

Hell's Angels: A Strange and Terrible Saga (nonfiction) 1966

Fear and Loathing in Las Vegas: A Savage Journey to the Heart of the American Dream (nonfiction) 1972

Fear and Loathing on the Campaign Trail '72 (nonfiction) 1973

The Great Shark Hunt: Strange Tales from a Strange Time; Gonzo Papers, Volume One (nonfiction) 1979

The Curse of Lono (nonfiction) 1983

Generation of Swine: Tales of Shame and Degradation in the '80s; Gonzo Papers, Volume Two (nonfiction) 1988

Songs of the Doomed: More Notes on the Death of the American Dream; Gonzo Papers, Volume Three (nonfiction) 1990

Silk Road: Thirty-three Years in the Passing Lane (nonfiction) 1990

Untitled Novel (novel) 1992

Better Than Sex: Fear and Loathing on the Campaign Trail, 1992 (nonfiction) 1993

The Proud Highway: Saga of a Desperate Southern Gentleman (nonfiction) 1997

CRITICISM

Herbert Mitgang (review date 11 August 1988)

SOURCE: "The Art of the Insult, or Gonzo Writer Strikes Again," in *The New York Times,* August 11, 1988, p. C23.

[*In the following review, Mitgang asserts that Thompson "takes no prisoners" in his* Generation of Swine: Tales of Shame and Degradation in the 80s.]

Hunter S. Thompson, who gained a fan club with such hand-stitched books as *Fear and Loathing in Las Vegas* and *Fear and Loathing: On the Campaign Trail '72,* is back with a collection of his pieces that appeared in *The San Francisco Examiner* in the last few years. They combine name-calling, bomb-throwing and sardonic humor. He's a little more strident this time out, but if you happen to share his public enemies, Mr. Thompson's your man.

Nearly everything he writes makes yellow journalism pale. With his targets the high rollers, from Sunset Strip to the White House, the former political writer for *Rolling Stone* elevates insult to an art form. He's dead serious and we blink, wondering how he can get away with it.

Gonzo, his own brand of journalism, has even found its way into the new Random House dictionary, which uses such words as bizarre, crazy and eccentric to define it. No one else gets credit for gonzo journalism in the dictionary; but then not many journalists would want it. Timothy Crouse—in his own perceptive book, *The Boys on the Bus,* about the behavior of reporters during the 1972 Presidential campaign—recalled when Mr. Thompson first earned his stripes as a political storm trooper by reporting that he had told Richard M. Nixon, "Go get 'em, Dick, throw the bomb! Fifty years more of the Thousand-Year Reich!"

Mr. Crouse observed, "After the revolution, we'll all write like Thompson." Not quite yet. His train of though often seems stuck at the Finland Station.

Nevertheless, he can be challenging. Mr. Thompson finds Watergate more in the American grain of political corruption than the Iran-contra affair. He writes: "The criminals in Watergate knew they were guilty and so did everybody else; and when the dust cleared the crooked President was gone and so were the others." By contrast, he calls those involved in Iran-contra affair "cheap punks" who have been "strutting every day for the past two months of truly disgraceful testimony." (That column was written July 20, 1987; all the columns have dates at the end but have not been updated by the author.) He finds that the Iran-contra investigation was "a farce and a scam that benefited nobody except Washington lawyers who charge $1,000 an hour for courtroom time."

Swinging for the fences, Mr. Thompson sometimes strikes out in his judgments. Disagreement depends on a reader's own set of assumptions and prejudices. Many of the names in these columns are obscure and require a knowledge of Mr. Thompson's friends and previous books. But he continues to speak up about political candidates for whom he holds more loathing than fear.

Writing about Gov. Michael S. Dukakis of Massachusetts a little over a year ago, Mr. Thompson was half prescient and half wrong. He described Governor Dukakis as "feisty" and possessing impressive credentials and "the style of a mean counterpuncher." Mr. Thompson says of Mr. Dukakis: "He was not in the mood, that night, to be poked and goaded by host/moderator William Buckley, who tried to make Dukakis the butt of his neo-Nazi jokes and left Houston with a rash of fresh teeth marks . . . Buckley has lost speed, in his dotage, but Dukakis is faster and meaner than a bull mongoose . . . But his chances of getting anything except a purple heart out of the 11 Southern States that will vote on 'Super Tuesday' next March are not ripe. The good ole boys will beat him like a gong, and after that he will be little more than a stalking horse for New York Gov. Mario Cuomo, who still insists he's not running."

And assessing Vice President Bush last March, Thompson first quotes a political friend of his about the Republican candidate's intellectual brilliance—"He is smarter than Thomas Jefferson"—and then gonzofies him: "He had no friends and nobody in Washington wanted to be seen with him on the streets at night." Mr. Thompson doesn't think the Vice President has a touch of the poet. He writes: "It was impossible that he could be roaming around Washington or New Orleans at night, jabbering about Dylan Thomas and picking up dead cats."

Mr. Thompson calls the present generation a "Generation of Swine." With that phrase as his title and premise, he takes no prisoners. A reader can go through the 300-plus pages of the book and look in vain for qualifying journalistic words. Mr. Thompson doesn't write measured prose. It's—well, gonzo.

Michael E. Ross (review date 14 August 1988)

SOURCE: A review of *Generation of Swine: Tales of Shame and Degradation in the '80s,* in *The New York Times Book Review,* August 14, 1988, p. 17.

[*In the following review, Ross asserts the value of Thompson's wisdom in* Generation of Swine.]

In the literary free-fire zone of American culture and political commentary, Hunter S. Thompson has always been on point. In his latest book, Mr. Thompson, author of ***Fear and Loathing in Las Vegas*** and ***Fear and Loathing: On the Campaign Trail '72,*** addresses new targets of opportunity— from Muammar el-Qaddafi and Ferdinand Marcos to a Soldier of Fortune trade show, from the George Bush campaign to handicapping the likelihood of a Democratic victory in November. His writing, ever feisty, proves again (as if it were necessary) that he is one of our most incisive, insightful and hilarious social critics. This collection, from his stint as a

columnist for *The San Francisco Examiner,* is vintage Thompson. His celebrated gonzo style is here: facts blended with a savage embroidery of the truth. There are many swings of style and mood, but the heart of the book is disquieting. Mr. Thompson peers into the American future (so far as he is able) and is not happy. Assailing the present Administration, stockbrokers, television, newspapers and various foreign powers, he sees a sobering and profound discontent in American life. With ***Generation of Swine*** Mr. Thompson shows himself to be an outlandish, skeptical Jeremiah. But one harbors a suspicion that his is the kind of unvarnished, crazy wisdom that is valuable in these times. In moderation, of course.

Richard Vigilante (review date 16 September 1988)

SOURCE: "Lost Generation," in *National Review,* Vol. XL, No. 18, September 16, 1988, pp. 52-3.

[*In the following review, Vigilante complains that Thompson's* "Generation of Swine *is no more than the wish-fulfillment of a slightly deranged registered Democrat.*"]

It is hard to admit how bad Hunter Thompson's new book is. To me—as to most of the younger writers I have worked with over the past few years—Thompson, along with Tom Wolfe and a bunch of other now-aging New Journalists and their long-defunct movement, still represents the wild hope that journalism could aspire to the condition of literature, while beating the "just the facts, ma'am" boys at their own game.

It was—heck, it still is—an exciting prospect, even if (especially if?) you were, like us, primarily political journalists at constant risk of being consumed and destroyed by the hack imperative, the insistent demand of the audience to be lied to.

If the audience is made up of political ideologues, the lie they demand is that they are the only ones who see the truth in a sick world and can set things to rights. If they are typical *New York Times* readers, the lie is that everything is under control, or at least would be if the ideologues could be persuaded to sink into that ecstasy of equanimity, that libido of the tedious, that Tiresian torpor of a *Times*-man who has seen it all before and is all too willing to tell it all again, which alone qualifies a man to be an editor of the World's Only (thank heaven) Newspaper of Record—and also if some action could be taken to stabilize worrisome fluctuations in Third World bauxite prices.

The New Journalism offered escape from both lies. It put the pseudo-objective soporifics of the broadsheets to shame by applying to journalism the techniques of the realistic novel. But, at the same time, it required a romance with reality that undermined the ideologues' lust for self-deceit. For all the literary liberties of the most famous New Journalists, their stories, when done right, were more true than traditional journalism.

Thompson was one of the best, though always a high-risk case. The rules of Gonzo, his particular sect, made him a character in every story, and the risk of self-deceit there was high. He succumbed often. The drug stories were about self-deceit, and so was the Hell's Angels book in the end, and even *Fear and Loathing on the Campaign Trail,* which could have been subtitled, "How a Guy as Hip as Me Fell for a Phony like McGovern." But the story was always there: Thompson's illusions were part of it, which come to think of it is pretty classic first-person-narrator novelistic technique and a darned effective story-telling device, which Thompson the devotee of Conrad had obviously thought a lot about.

Unfortunately the only story in *Generation of Swine,* mostly a collection of short pieces from the *San Francisco Examiner,* is how Thompson used to be a real man, and find great stories, but now he's just a worthless political hack who sits up in Aspen all day watching television (huge satellite dish, two hundred stations) and telling himself he is still a pro.

Thompson has become lazy and dishonest. Probably the most revealing story in the book is his great Haitian escapade. When Baby Doc fell, Thompson knew that Haiti was the place the old Hunter Thompson would have been, deep in the heart of a darkness made blacker than anything Conrad ever saw by the admixture of just a drop of civilization, or at least electric lights. And Thompson turned out several Haiti stories sprinkled with life-like details of demonic corruption. But he never went there (as he admits). All of his reporting was done from Miami.

The book is obsessively political. Thompson has always had strong prejudices, but these days that's all he has. Out of three hundred pages, perhaps 250 are consumed by ideological onanism, which he has somehow convinced himself will be as much fun for us as it was for him.

He is unable to demonstrate the slightest sympathy for any of his victims, except occasionally Ronald Reagan, or even to distinguish clearly among them. Reagan is "dumber than three mules" and can "have anybody who bothers him arrested." Robert Bork is a "certified hair-shirt punishment freak." Ed Meese is a "one-eyed hog." George Bush is "a truly evil man, a truthless monster with the brains of a king rat and the soul of a cockroach . . . who will loot the national treasury, warp the laws, mock the rules, and stay awake 22

hours a day looking for at least one reason to declare war, officially, on some hapless tribe in the Sahara or heathen fanatic like the Ayatollah Khomeini." George Bush?

Reagan's denunciations of Qaddafi are a "gaggle of wild charges," the bombing raid was insane, and hardline anti-Communists and born-again Christians are fascist perverts. But just mention selling arms to Iran and our boy goes ballistic with outraged patriotism and righteous anger for the 241 Marines killed by Iranian terrorists.

> *Generation of Swine* is no more than the wish-fulfillment of a slightly deranged registered Democrat.
> —*Richard Vigilante*

The problem here is not that Thompson has strong opinions, or that his opinions differ from mine. It's that it is now possible to predict everything Thompson will say by checking out the party registration of his subject. After all, by the lights of someone who generally regards a hard-line foreign policy as unrealistic (I'm translating), an attempt to uncover a faction of Iranian moderates ought to seem like a sensible idea. But for Thompson, Ollie North and his comrades, including Reagan, Meese, and Bush, are worse than Nixon or Gordon Liddy.

No living Democrat comes in for even mild criticism. But he does have his favorites: Gary Hart and . . . Ted Kennedy. Thompson spends hundreds of pages in outraged moralizing and then breathlessly announces the real moral: "Chappaquiddick was a long time ago. Enough is enough. The time has come."

These are not the judgments of a man who has gotten close enough to the story to "bring the techniques of the realistic novel to journalism," as Wolfe used to say, techniques that require that the author understand his victims' motives if not forgive their crimes. *Generation of Swine* is no more than the wish-fulfillment of a slightly deranged registered Democrat. Hunter Thompson, king of Gonzo Journalism, Hell's Angels outrider, terror of establishment power-worshippers everywhere, is, it turns out, just another party hack, an organization man. He should be sentenced to spend the rest of his life ringing doorbells and collecting kickbacks.

Hunter S. Thompson with Sam Allis (interview date 22 January 1990)

SOURCE: "An Evening (Gasp!) with Hunter Thompson," in *Time,* Vol. 135, No. 4, January 22, 1990, p. 64.

[In the following interview, Allis describes his attempt to interview Thompson.]

Boston correspondent Sam Allis went to Colorado last week to interview Hunter S. Thompson, the inventor of gonzo journalism, author (Hell's Angels, Fear and Loathing in Las Vegas) *and defiant eccentric, at his home in Woody Creek. This is what happened:*

I gave up on the interview and started worrying about my life when Hunter Thompson squirted two cans of fire starter on the Christmas tree he was going to burn in his living-room fireplace, a few feet away from an unopened wooden crate of 9-mm bullets. That the tree was far too large to fit into the fireplace mattered not a whit to Hunter, who was sporting a dime-store wig at the time and resembled Tony Perkins in *Psycho.* Minutes earlier, he had smashed a Polaroid camera on the floor.

Hunter had decided to videotape the Christmas tree burning, and we later heard on the replay the terrified voices of Deborah Fuller, his longtime secretary-baby sitter, and me off-camera pleading with him, "NO, HUNTER, NO! PLEASE, HUNTER, DON'T DO IT!" The original manuscript of *Hell's Angels* was on the table, and there were the bullets. Nothing doing. Thompson was a man possessed by now, full of the Chivas Regal he had been slurping straight from the bottle and the gin he had been mixing with pink lemonade for hours.

But then the whole evening had been like this. It began in late daylight, when Hunter shot his beloved tracer pistol into the air and then started training it at passing cars. One tracer hit a tree and boomeranged back at us. Everyone thought that was really neat.

Then Hunter played his tape of a jackrabbit screaming. I didn't know rabbits even made noise. Hunters apparently use tapes like this to attract coyotes. I thought at first I was listening to a baby crying. Then I realized it was not human.

Then we shot Hunter's Olympic-quality pellet pistol at exploding targets he had mounted over his fireplace. This event was also taped.

Then we watched a tape of a pro-football game and then another of the famous 1971 Ali-Frazier fight. Thompson drank Chivas from the bottle and noshed on desserts he had taken from a fancy restaurant.

Then the fight tape ended, and Hunter decided he didn't want to do the interview with me. He decided he didn't like Q. & A. Deborah reminded him that he had agreed to do it. I reminded him that we had talked on the phone about it. He threw some things on the floor.

Then Hunter decided to try a few questions. But he needed a wig to do the interview, and he couldn't find one. "WHERE IS MY F____ WIG?!" Deborah scurried off and found one. Then we sat down to talk. I began with a soft pitch on the '80s stuff he has written a lot about in his columns. He responded with questions on his views about suicide raised by his lecture audiences.

Then Deborah came in to tell Hunter she was going to bed, and Hunter panicked. Hunter, it became clear, is petrified of being left alone, particularly with *Time* magazine and a tape recorder. Hunter Thompson is a scared little puppy beneath the alcohol, tobacco and firearms. He bawled Deborah out for not briefing him adequately on the interview and said that Sam Allis was not to blame for this. He said this was NOT THE DESIRED EFFECT. That's when he smashed the Polaroid on the floor and decided to burn the Christmas tree.

When Hunter tossed a lit match at the Christmas tree, it exploded into flames. He took a few pulls on the fire extinguisher and then joined us outside. The view from the porch through the window resembled something out of Watts in 1965. The chimney was on fire. His five peacocks, whose roost was separated from the living room by a thin pane of glass, were not happy. Nor was Hunter, who yelled at me, "GET BACK IN THERE, FOOL!" He had given me an iron prodder with which I was to keep pushing the tree into the fireplace. "I'M NOT GOING BACK IN THERE," I yelled back.

The whole room was full of smoke, and flames kicked up onto the mantel and on toward the ceiling. Thompson dashed back in and did battle with the tree. Framed against the fire—his wig askew, his lower lip drooping, his eyes glazed—this 50-year-old man-child was in his element. Meanwhile, a tape of his favorite group, the Cowboy Junkies, played renditions of *Sleep Walk* by Santo and Johnny and then *Blue Moon.*

The video of all this is, quite simply, astonishing. I begged him for a copy, but Hunter only giggled. He knew it could be used in a mental-competency hearing. He was so pleased with it when we watched later in the kitchen that he brought out an earlier video he had made that involves him and an inflated life-size woman doll in a whirlpool bath. It was about then that Hunter called himself the "champion of fun." Deborah was so struck with the line that she immediately wrote it down.

It was now almost 3 a.m. Hunter was calm, his mania temporarily exhausted. He smiled as he walked me to my car and said, "I guess we will never see each other again."

Ron Rosenbaum (review date 25 November 1990)

SOURCE: "Still Gonzo After All These Years," in *The New York Times Book Review,* November 25, 1990, pp. 7-8.

[*In the following review, Rosenbaum asserts that Thompson is at his best in* Songs of the Doomed *when he's on the road after a story, instead of writing from the sidelines of his Woody Creek home.*]

Saigon, May 1975. The city is about to fall to the National Liberation Front. The last American reporters left in the besieged capital are calculating when to fly out before the honorable desire to stay to the bloody end becomes merely suicidal. Meanwhile, Hunter S. Thompson has just flown *in* to the encircled city with $30,000 in cash taped to his body (don't ask). Only to learn he has been fired by *Rolling Stone* (some bitter dispute with its publisher, Jann Wenner, over a book advance) and both his medical insurance and his Telex card link to the outside world have been canceled by the magazine.

No problem. He's got a plan. He's going to convince the enemy that he's their one true friend in American journalism, that he should be the one to cover the final assault on the capital—from behind enemy lines. And so up in his room in Saigon's Hotel Continental Plaza he bangs out a "Confidential Memo to Colonel Giang Vo Don Giang," one of a number of memos, cables, fragments of memoirs and novels, and eviction notices collected in *Songs of the Doomed,* along with some of Mr. Thompson's best work of the past three decades.

In his memo to the Vietcong colonel Mr. Thompson tries heroically to communicate just what kind of writer he is, why he's different from other journalists. It's not an easy job.

"I trust you understand that, as a professional para-journalist, I am in the same position today that you were as a paramilitary professional about three years ago," he tells the colonel, and he offers to send him one of his classic works, *Fear and Loathing: On the Campaign Trail '72.* He tells the colonel that he knows Jane Fonda. And he informs him, "I am one of the best writers currently using the English language as both a musical instrument and a political weapon."

While self-effacement has never been one of Mr. Thompson's strengths, I think he was absolutely right about how good a writer he was then. Fans across the political spectrum from Norman Mailer to Tom Wolfe and William F. Buckley Jr. have said as much in the past.

Is it still true now? Those of us who lack access to the biweekly column he wrote for *The San Francisco Examiner* until earlier this year (Mr. Thompson's chief outlet since his split with *Rolling Stone*) have had to await periodic appearances of these volumes of "The Gonzo Papers." The last one,

Volume Two, cheerfully titled *Generation of Swine,* chiefly concerned itself with Mr. Thompson's jeremiads against the 80's.

This new volume, it should be noted, arrives under something of a cloud, if internal evidence is to be believed.

A peculiar editor's note before the final section informs us, "Our contract allowed us to go to press with whatever sections of the book we already had our hands on—despite the author's objections and bizarre motions filed by his attorneys in courts all over the country."

Reading between the lines one gathers that Mr. Thompson is planning on coming out with an entirely separate book on his recent legal ordeal and vindication—this summer a judge in Aspen, Colo., threw out charges of sexual harassment and drug and weapons possession against Mr. Thompson, which grew out of a dispute that involved a former pornographic film maker and a Jacuzzi. Mr. Thompson is now suing authorities for "malicious prosecution" and general revenge.

Evidently, Mr. Thompson did not want to skim the cream off the forthcoming book (working title: "99 Days: The Trial of Hunter S. Thompson"), but the editors wanted something from him about the celebrated case in this volume. So they have apparently chosen the dubious tactic of appending various clippings, reports and public domain documents on the case to the book, seemingly against the author's wishes.

Of course, this whole business of Mr. Thompson making "bizarre" threats against his own book—indeed the editor's note itself—could be a device concocted by the author.

He is often at his best when he deploys the apparently extraneous detritus of the journalism process as his most expressive vehicle. One of the high points of *Fear and Loathing in Las Vegas,* arguably his best book, is a section introduced by an editor's note declaring that, "in the interests of journalistic purity," the editor is presenting a "verbatim transcript" of a cassette found among Mr. Thompson's effects after he disappeared to escape Vegas debt collectors.

Of course that is the heart of the book—that ostensibly artless but suspiciously artful transcript of a conversation with a waitress in a coffee shop on Paradise Road about the precise location of the American dream.

Indeed, one of the high points of *Songs of the Doomed* is another alleged document, Mr. Thompson's "Secret Cable to Willie Hearst." Subject: his expenses, According to Mr. Thompson, Mr. Hearst's *Examiner* hasn't been paying them.

"I now list my *Examiner* expense bills on my 1040 form as 'uncollectible debts,'" Mr. Thompson writes. "And we now have a column that will never be written from anywhere more than 2.1 miles from the Post Office in Woody Creek," Mr. Thompson's Colorado home.

Mr. Thompson characteristically extracts a profound truth about journalism here from what might seem on the surface to be the standard expense-account memo whine. "The Old Man [William Randolph Hearst Sr.] was a monster," he writes, "but nobody ever accused him of skimming nickels and dimes off his best writers' expense accounts—and it wasn't his cheap-jack *accountants* who made him a legend in American journalism and the highest roller of his time."

The classic Thompson pieces in *Songs of the Doomed,* the kind of stories that have made him a high-rolling legend in journalism, are the ones in which he is out there on the highway running up expenses in search of emblematic weirdness, "Whooping It Up With The War Junkies in Saigon" or pursuing "Bad Craziness in Palm Beach."

But even more interesting than such successes in the book are the self-acknowledged failures: fragments of novels begun in the late 50's and early 60's, before Mr. Thompson burst onto the scene with *Hell's Angels* and his two *Fear and Loathing* books. While not a formal autobiography, the early novels, "Prince Jellyfish" and "The Rum Diary," do give us glimpses of the man behind the maniacal mask, the struggling writer before he attained sacred-monster status.

In the novel fragments we see the young former serviceman, an idealistic good ol' boy from Kentucky who reads Fitzgerald, comes to New York full of wonder hoping to make his mark in journalism by telling The Truth, finds himself rejected and scorned by cynical big-city editors, gets beaten up and disillusioned, and ends up in a kind of self-created hell as a reporter for a bowling magazine in San Juan (don't ask). There he almost self-destructs, stewing in his own bitterness before he catches on with *The National Observer,* the short-lived Dow Jones weekly, and his work starts getting noticed.

One thing you take away from these fragments is a sense of Hunter Thompson as far more complex and, well, sensitive than the cynical Uncle Duke caricature of him in "Doonesbury." All that rage in his work, all that fear and loathing, is the product, it seems, not of the sneering cynic but of a bitterly disillusioned idealist.

Reading *Songs of the Doomed* reminds us how good he was at his best, and how good he still can be when he's given the freedom—and expenses—to hit the road, rather than stewing in his own bitterness in Woody Creek.

Memo to Willie Hearst: Give this man back his expense account.

Louis Menand (review date 7 and 14 January 1991)

SOURCE: "Life in the Stone Age," in *The New Republic,* Vol. 204, Nos. 1 and 2, January 7 and 14, 1991, pp. 38-44.

[*In the following excerpt, Menand reviews Thompson's* Songs of the Doomed, *charging that the author is still living in the counterculture of the 1970s.*]

After the Altamont concert disaster in December 1969, when a fan was killed a few feet from the stage where The Rolling Stones were performing, psychedelia lost its middle-class appeal. More unpleasant news followed in 1970—the Kent State and Jackson State shootings, the Manson Family trials, the deaths by overdose of famous rock stars. And even more quickly than it had sprung up, the media fascination with the counterculture evaporated.

But the counterculture, stripped of its idealism and its sexiness, lingered on. If you drove down the main street of any small city in America in the 1970s, you saw clusters of teenagers standing around, wearing long hair and bell-bottom jeans, listening to Led Zeppelin, furtively getting stoned. This was the massive middle of the baby-boom generation, the remnant of the counterculture—a remnant that was much bigger than the original, but in which the media had lost interest. These people were not activists or dropouts. They had very few public voices. One of them was Hunter Thompson's.

Thompson came to *Rolling Stone* in 1970, an important moment in the magazine's history. [Jann] Wenner had fired Greil Marcus, a music critic with an American studies degree who was then his reviews editor, for running a negative review of an inferior Dylan album called *Self-Portrait* (it is one of Wenner's rules that the big stars must always be hyped); and most of the politically minded members of the staff quit after the "Get Back" episode following Kent State. There were financial problems as well. By the end of 1970, *Rolling Stone* was a quarter million dollars in debt.

Hugh Hefner, who is to testosterone what Wenner is to rock 'n' roll, offered to buy the magazine, but Wenner found other angels. Among them were record companies. Columbia Records and Elektra were delighted to advance their friends at *Rolling Stone* a year's worth of advertising; *Rolling Stone* and the record companies, after all, were in the same business.

The next problem was to sell magazines. (*Rolling Stone* relies heavily on newsstand sales, since its readers are not the sort of people who can be counted on to fill out subscription renewal forms with any degree of regularity.) Here Wenner had two strokes of good fortune. The first was a long interview he obtained with John Lennon, the first time most people had ever heard a Beatle not caring to sound lovable. It sold many magazines. The second was the arrival of Thompson.

Thompson was a well-traveled, free-spirited hack whose résumé included a stint as sports editor of *The Jersey Shore Herald,* a job as general reporter for *The Middletown Daily News,* freelance work out of Puerto Rico for a bowling magazine, a period as South American correspondent for *The National Observer* (during which he suffered some permanent hair loss from stress and drugs), an assignment covering the 1968 presidential campaign for *Pageant,* two unpublished Great American novels, a little male modeling, and a narrowly unsuccessful campaign for sheriff of Aspen, Colorado.

Thompson had actually been discovered for the alternative press by Warren Hinckle, the editor of *Ramparts,* which is when his writing acquired the label "gonzo journalism." But Thompson was interested in *Rolling Stone* because he thought it would help his nascent political career by giving him access to people who had no interest in politics (a good indication of the magazine's political reputation in 1970). A year after signing on, he produced the articles that became *Fear and Loathing in Las Vegas,* a tour de force of pop faction about five days on drugs in Las Vegas. It sold many copies of *Rolling Stone,* and it gave Thompson fortune, celebrity, and a permanent running headline.

Many people who were not young read *Fear and Loathing in Las Vegas* and thought it a witty piece of writing. Wolfe included two selections from Thompson's work in his 1973 anthology *The New Journalism* (everyone else but Wolfe got only one entry); and this has given Thompson the standing of a man identified with an academically recognized Literary Movement. But Thompson is essentially a writer for teenage boys. *Fear and Loathing in Las Vegas* is *The Catcher in the Rye* on speed: the lost weekend of a disaffected loser who tells his story in a mordant style that is addictively appealing to adolescents with a deep and unspecified grudge against life.

Once you understand the target, the thematics make sense. Sexual prowess is part of the Thompson mystique, for example, but the world of his writing is almost entirely male, and sex itself is rarely more than a vague, adult horror; for sex beyond mere bravado is a subject that makes most teenage boys nervous. A vast supply of drugs of every genre and description accompany the Thompson persona and maintain him in a permanent state of dementia; but the drugs have all the verisimilitude of a 14-year-old's secret spy kit: these grown-ups don't realize that the person they are talking to is *completely out of his mind* on dangerous chemicals. The fear and loathing in Thompson's writing is simply Holden Caulfield's fear of growing up—a fear that, in Thompson's case as in Salinger's, is particularly convincing to younger readers because it so clearly runs from the books straight back to the writer himself.

After the Las Vegas book, *Rolling Stone* assigned Thompson to cover the 1972 presidential campaign. His reports were collected in (inevitably) *Fear and Loathing on the Campaign Trail.* The series begins with some astute analysis of primary strategy and the like, salted with irreverent descriptions of the candidates and many personal anecdotes. Thompson's unusual relation to the facts—one piece, which caused a brief stir, reported that Edmund Muskie was addicted to an obscure African drug called Ibogaine—made him the object of some media attention of his own. But eventually the reporting breaks down, and Thompson is reduced at the end of his book to quoting at length from the dispatches of his *Rolling Stone* colleague Timothy Crouse (whose own book about the campaign, *The Boys on the Bus,* became an acclaimed exposé of political journalism).

Since 1972 Thompson has devoted his career to the maintenance of his legend, and his reporting has mostly been reporting about the Thompson style of reporting, which consists largely of unsuccessful attempts to cover his subjects, and of drug misadventures. He doesn't need to report, of course, because reporting is not what his audience cares about. They care about the escapades of their hero, which are recounted obsessively in his writing, and some of which were the basis for an unwatchable movie called *Where the Buffalo Roam,* released in 1980 and starring Bill Murray.

Thompson left *Rolling Stone* around 1975 and eventually became a columnist for the *San Francisco Examiner.* He has been repackaging his pieces in chronicle form regularly since 1979. *Songs of the Doomed* is the third collection, and most of the recent material concerns the author's arrest earlier this year on drug possession and sexual assault charges in Colorado. Having made a fortune portraying himself as a champion consumer of controlled substances, Thompson naturally took the position that the drugs found in his house must have been left there by someone else. (The charges, unfortunately for a writer badly in need of fresh adventures, were dismissed.)

Thompson, in short, is practically the only person in America still living circa 1972. His persona enacts a counterculture sensibility with the utopianism completely leached out. There are no romantic notions about peace and love in his writing, only adolescent paranoia and violence. There is no romanticization of the street, either. Everything disappoints him—an occasionally engaging attitude that is also, of course, romanticism of the very purest sort. Thompson is the eternally bitter elegist of a moment that never really was, and that is why he is the ideal writer for a generation that has always felt that it arrived onstage about five minutes after the audience walked out.

A. Craig Copetas (review date 19 December 1991)

SOURCE: "When the Going Gets Weird," in *London Review of Books,* Vol. 14, No. 23, December 19, 1991.

[*In the following review, Copetas discusses Thompson's* Songs of the Doomed *and offers personal reminiscences of socializing with "Doc" Thompson.*]

The winter of 1978 is full of strange and apocalyptic memories now. Doc and I were weird-betting a college basketball game in the gentrified servants' quarters of a large Georgetown estate house that December. Magic Johnson was playing for Michigan that Saturday night and I'd gambled that three successive baskets would be made by players with odd-numbered jerseys. I was ahead a few bucks when the Ohio State centre put a savage elbow into Magic's young chin and Doc's screams of 'foul' were interrupted by the sight of a White House adviser about to break open a vial of cocaine. Doc slapped me on the shoulder and muttered 'Jeeesus'—a sure sign of impending doom.

Doc always sees things before anyone else. As Magic picked himself up off the court, Doc first glanced quickly at the other fifteen or so people in the spacious loft, and then bored in on the looming White House official. Doc poured two long shots of whisky and offered his prognosis. He said there was venom in the air, a generation of swine were nearing maturity, and life was going to be a whole lot different and a hell of a lot more ominous for anyone who believed in the guarantees of the Constitution of the United States. I remembered that crazy night in Washington a few days ago, right after I heard that Magic had to leave the Lakers because he tested positive for the HIV virus. The tragedy of the Magicman kicked in the memory of that December 1978, the night that I think Doc first started working on the lyrics of what are now his *Songs of the Doomed.*

The American Dream ended bitterly on that cold evening for the nearly seven hundred people who milled around the lower three floors of the townhouse, thrilled that saloonkeeper Fred Moore and CBS heir Bill Paley Jr had convinced Derek and the Dominos to perform live and loud. The food from the Gandy Dancer restaurant was splendid, the wines were vintage and the drugs grown and manufactured by designers with PhDs in botany and chemistry. The acronyms HIV and AIDS were unknown and the only initials to cause anxiety were DEA (Drug Enforcement Administration). The growing voices of America's neoconservative movement would later argue that their interpretation of the American Dream, long deferred because of people like Hunter S. Thompson and the satanic rhythms of rock'n'roll bands like Derek and the Dominos, began that night. The problem was that none of the guests who were downstairs enjoying the largesse of a liberal translation of American Constitutional guarantees knew that a fundamental change in the moral and political tone of their world was taking place upstairs.

It was an eclectic and extremely stoned crowd that had assembled for the annual National Organisation for the Reform of Marijuana Laws (NORML) party in the American capital. Although Ronald Reagan was poised to become the arbiter of the collective conscience of America, Jimmy Carter was still President and social liberalism was in full swing— or so those gathered to celebrate . . . victories for civil liberty in America's courts and legislatures wanted to believe. The house was richly appointed and hotly packed with congressmen, lawyers, physicians, lobbyists, artists, journalists, dope dealers, sports figures and activists of every dogmatic bent, race and biochemical preference. I must be extremely careful in describing what happened next. My attorney Gerry Goldstein of Texas (whose piquant wisdom and expertise in Constitutional law Doc describes in *Songs*) tells me that it's best not to be too detailed about events that might lead to arguing the fine points of a statute of limitation in front of the current US Supreme Court. It's like Doc warns in his new book:

BEWARE

Today: the Doctor Tomorrow: *You.*

Nonetheless, this very senior official in the Carter White House allowed a woman the wires later described as 'the lady from Peru' to stick a half-dozen spoonfuls of Bolivian cocaine up his Oval Office nostrils. It was the snort heard round America and the sound ignited a series of horrible nationwide news reports and twisted political events that led to the total humiliation of Jimmy Carter and his presidency and a national witch hunt for combat liberals. (As the American philosopher Yogi Berra once said to those who want confirmation of the obvious, 'you can look it up.') But what Doc said to me as we watched that scene play out 13 years ago still rings as the most prophetic warning I've heard about the closing decades of the 20th century: 'Jesus, Craig, we're all going to die or be indicted now!'

By the time Ronald Reagan entered his second term, I'd been out of America for nearly four years, writing about events taking place in Europe and points East from the relative safety of the foreign desk. Doc sent a note saying that there was a lot of wreckage piling up in the fast lane. Many of our friends were dead or jailed or in the process of withering away because they couldn't find either an antidote to their own excesses or a remedy for Reagan's toxification of America. There was no melancholy in Doc's words—there never has been any sadness—just the durability and vigour of a sailor trying to repair the torn canvas and shattered spars of his ship during the turmoil of a storm. Doc's a good sailor—and he's always been the champion of the underdog and God bless him for it. It's nothing less than an adventure being on the road with Doc, or even sitting in the Woody Creek Tavern, Doc in his baby wolf hat, sipping whisky and talking about how it's best for writers and journalists to steer a course headlong into the political maelstrom. 'Happy with whatever ripples I caused in the great swamp of history,' he explains. One of the tempests Doc writes about in *Songs* is the Florida criminal trial of dishevelled Palm Beach heiress and cocaine slut Roxanne Pulitzer, and his words on that abominable scene richly echo the gnarled politics that have both paralysed America as a whole and effectively crippled the one thing that Doc holds so dear—the craft of journalism.

Not even the rich feel safe from the wreckage, Doc writes in *Songs,*

> and people are looking for reasons. The smart say they can't understand it, and the dumb snort cocaine in rich discos and stomp to a feverish beat. Which is heard all over the country, or at least felt . . . Journalism is a Ticket to Ride, to get personally involved in the same news other people watch on TV—which is nice, but it won't pay the rent, and people who can't pay their rent in the Eighties are going to be in trouble. We are into a very nasty decade, a brutal Darwinian crunch that will not be a happy time.

Doc's always said that when the going gets weird the weird turn pro. The difference between Doc and the rest of us is that he always sees the strange coming down as reality before anyone else—he first proposed to write a book on the death of the American Dream in 1967, a time when the only place you'd see 'Darwinian crunch' printed was on the cocktail menu at Trader Vic's. Doc's journalism operates on a level that makes the Establishment uneasy and gives its political pronouncements all the congruity of powdered chalk. Every major media outlet claims to report the truth; they must. The whole business of American journalism is based on the certainty of Truth. What Doc realises is that Truth has become a commodity to be bought, sold or spun into whatever clöth the highest bidder decides. The academics call this process intellectual mendacity, the Papists call it Obedience of the Spirit, the politicians call it Conventional Wisdom, and we in journalism call it Objectivity.

American journalism has one rule: a reporter can go as far as he likes so long as he keeps Objectivity and editorial tradition in sight. But Objective political reporting on the American condition over the past twenty years has not had a history of being overwhelmingly accurate. Every reporter lies awake at night knowing that the editorial system that prints his words will not—with rare exceptions—let him write from the gut; that same writer is also trying to figure how best to balance, without getting fired, the Truth he's hearing with the reality he's experiencing. Anyone who has worked on an American newspaper or magazine will tell you, usually no later than the second drink, that reporting and editing events for American consumption during the Reagan-Bush years has turned into a spin-doctoring war between Them & Us, Truth versus Reality.

Now great care must be taken in illuminating this very real political, economic and artistic rift taking place all across America, as well as the problems that go along with reporting on the rupture. It's at this illustrative juncture in the story that the sophists start preaching dogmatics, the out-of-work bricklayers open up with full-auto AK-47s on thirty people in a McDonald's lunch line, and the argument over how to define and apply Constitutional freedoms begins to turn ugly.

Judge Frank M. Johnson Jr, the great liberal Southern jurist on the 11th US Circuit Court of Appeals, who former Alabama Governor George Wallace called an 'integrating, carpet-bagging, scalawagging, bald-faced liar', explained the flammable Constitutional argument over Them v. Us when he wrote:

> Religious differences, race differences, sex differences, age differences and political differences are not the same. It is no mark of intellectual soundness to treat them as if they were. Moreover, if the life of the law has been experience, then the law should be realistic enough to treat certain issues as special: racism is special in American history. A judiciary that cannot declare that is of little value.

The Conventional Wisdom of the American body politic dictates that any distinction between Them & Us or Truth & Reality implies the existence of a Constitutional chasm that creates a crack in the Great American Melting Pot. To write about this abyss with any reality, goes the Conventional Wisdom, smacks of either psychological instability, complex and absurd conspiracy theories, or personal and unpopular political agendas on the part of the individual. Just recall the number of affronted and indignant senators during the Clarence Thomas hearings who refused to believe the reality that women sexually harassed by their bosses don't quit their jobs because they need the money.

The social spark for Constitutional provocation is much simpler than any concocted intrigue: They have their world and We have ours—the two overlap nicely, but they don't completely coincide in some very significant and eruptive areas. 'Gonzo'—which uses phrases such as 'water wit' and 'brain dead' to describe what the *New York Times* national desk referred to as 'the senior senator from Utah' during the Judge Thomas hearings—is the often fatal condition that strikes a reporter when he discovers that reality's hard lump overwhelms the Truths that make up the Conventional Wisdom. 'Gonzo . . . the phrase worked,' Doc explained. 'All of a sudden I had my own standing head.'

As *Songs of the Doomed* so spectacularly illustrates, Doc's the first American writer since John Dos Passos to tap the eroding and elemental fury within the American Dream and make the compost picture of American society in the last quarter of the 20th century work so elegantly on paper. I discovered two curious things about Doc's writing when I was his editor at *Esquire* magazine. His songs require very little (if any) editing, and his words and images are so powerful that they scare the bejesus out of the Conventional Wisdom because his pen seems to have been dipped in the same inkwell used by the hellscribes who wrote the Old Testament. Doc never forgot that the only weapon truly feared by the Philistines is the jawbone of an ass. His philosophy is to never apologise, never explain. Ralph Steadman, who continues to hold the world record for stepping into the fray as Doc's Joshua, sums up the feeling best when he says here: 'Hunter may be the reincarnation of Lono—the God returned after 1500 years of wandering like a lovesick child to save his people—and his beloved American Constitution . . . He is your saviour and he is guardian of all you profess to hold dear. In his weirdness he illuminates the faults in your reason and etches the silhouettes of your antics against a pure white background like Balinese shadow puppets.'

Diagnosing the American condition from his perch at the Owl Farm, screaming at his pet peacocks to shut up or be shot until the dobermans ate them, all Doc had to do during the Eighties was aim his giant satellite receiver toward the heavens to pull down the network news and watch the Great American Dream turn into the Great American Scheme. By the mid-Eighties the age of Fear & Loathing hit America with such a vengeance that it even shocked Doc. Las Vegas—where Hunter had first gone in the summer of 1971 on a busman's vacation that turned into a 'savage journey into the heart of the American Dream'—was now the site of the annual Southern Baptist Convention. Not only had the weird turned pro, but a few thousand holy rollers hauling wooden crosses on their backs were going door-to-door and casino-to-casino to convert their Philistines. Fear & Loathing had turned into a national charismatic anarchy, leaving those who had 'reaped the whirlwind and rode the tiger' of the Seventies to 'dance with the doom' of the Eighties.

When Doc first gained real national attention in the early Seventies for what the Establishment called his bizarre and repulsive views on Richard Nixon and the 1972 Presidential campaign he constituted a real problem for the American press—specifically, those pundits, political tastemakers, and powerbrokers who lived within the pernicious confines of the Beltway that surrounds Washington. Doc had already written two books and served hard time as a New Jersey

sports columnist, Air Force non-com, and Latin American correspondent for the defunct *National Observer* before getting into national politics. And his books, ***Fear & Loathing in Las Vegas*** and ***Hells Angels,*** tapped a nerve in the American psyche so powerful that by the time he hit the campaign trail the Establishment could only portray the realities he wrote about as an example of the level to which public discourse had sunk.

Hunter certainly rode out the Seventies with unimaginable success and, maybe because of it, the manner in which his reputation ('Lear's fool' and 'Washington's hair shirt' are two that come to mind) was misused by others out to make a quick buck in the Eighties smothered the dignity of his words and the exemplary precision of his thought. There's even a guy at a university in Florida who's been given money to write Doc's biography—a great honour to be sure, but such an exchange of cash in these bare-boned times is a sure sign of someone pushing the idea that a literary life is over. A lot of people in the journalism business will tell you that Doc disappeared and that his writing suffered after Nixon resigned as his Baldrick and Hollywood released *Where the buffalo roam,* the wretched and forgettable movie loosely based on Doc's life. Actually, Doc's columns in the *San Francisco Examiner* were so good during the Eighties that his words scared a lot of people; so dead centre in aim that ***Songs*** is an astonishing collection of old newspaper reportage and new personal anecdote; at once so beautiful, horrifying and profound that those reading it will never again see the USA in quite the same way.

Nor should they. Hunter S. Thompson *is* America, and anyone who truly wants a grip on the dread and chaos the Philistines have used for the past 20 years to hoodwink the Land of Liberty and Justice for All needs to read ***Songs of the Doomed:*** part political atlas, part morning paper and part adventure novel, ***Songs*** is three remarkable books on the fatal condition of America. Hunter's a journalist first and foremost, and he's one of the last honest members of a profession blackened and lame from 11 years of Reagan/Bush spin-doctoring. Reporters and social observers of Doc's calibre were not so much forced out of the scene as politically pummelled underground during the Eighties. As usual, Doc ascertained this trend was coming long before anyone else. He first detected the drift on the day he picked Jimmy Carter to be President—the day Doc calls his Leap of Faith.

'I had already picked Carter in '74,' Doc writes in ***Songs:***

> It was a special assignment as everything was after Saigon. I was still on the [*Rolling Stone*] masthead. It was an honour roll of journalists, but the people on it—well, all of them were no longer with *Rolling Stone.* I didn't like that they put on the cover that I endorsed Carter. I picked him as a gambler.

Endorsing isn't something a journalist should do. [*Rolling Stone*] was an Outlaw magazine in California. In New York it became an Establishment magazine and I have never worked well with people like that.

Not only were the 'people like that' beginning to assume control of American journalism: they were taking over the few publications left with the money to bankroll Doc and handle his velocity. By the beginning of 1981, *Esquire* magazine was the last bastion of mass-market independent thought in America with enough money to let Doc loose. The late editor Harold Hayes, who navigated *Esquire's* editorial department through the Sixties and early Seventies, made the monthly periodical into a great American magazine because he refused to allow his editors and writers to perceive any issue as taboo. Every outlaw and political persuasion was welcome in offices still electric with the soul of Ernest Hemingway, the flaming passion of James Baldwin, and the force and animation of Mailer, Wolfe, Vidal, Buckley, Burroughs and Genet. The editors who followed Hayes, men like Byron Dobell and the late Don Erickson, carried on the tradition, ensuring that each new generation of editors understood that *Esquire's* mandate was to remain on the cutting edge of journalism and literature. Although Hayes was long gone from *Esquire* by the time I became an editor at the magazine, shortly after joining the staff he sent me a congratulatory postcard and an invitation to join him for lunch at the Russian Tea Room. Hayes told me that the single most important quality an *Esquire* editor or contributor needed was the ability to smile through the apocalypse. And no one knew how to do that better then Hunter.

But the Generation of Swine, Doc's collective noun for the Wall Street weasels and Beltway bums who managed, manipulated and mauled the American Dream during the money-mad Eighties, had taken over *Esquire* by the time Hunter came back to our pages in 1981. The magazine's new owners were set on turning *Esquire* into a *Cosmopolitan* for men with such exceedingly low testosterone levels that management forced us to run a turgid monthly column in which an *Esquire* editor went on a date with some Hollywood starlet in the hope that a kernel of carnal knowledge could be picked up and transmitted to guys who were having a hard time getting laid. Doc's high-octane prose of the Cuba-to-Key West Freedom Flotilla just didn't fit alongside the smarm stories and columns crafted for no other reason than to keep advertisers content and Reagan Washington impressed. Spiking such stories was as much a difference of style as of philosophy. One camp wanted to publish a consequential magazine, knowing that exciting writing on controversial topics and a robust exchange of ideas had historically cultivated readers and advertisers. But the new management remained intent on publishing a fuzzy/warm consumer guide for the male ego in which political conten-

tion of any sort spelled financial turmoil. Slowly but with precision, management replaced *Esquire's* editors with account executives. The MBAs said this trend made financial sense. 'Why are you spending $5000 in expenses sending Thompson to Key West when the story he's there to write will be covered on television?' a furious *Esquire* ad exec asked me at the time. 'The big money is to be had publishing low-cost advertorials and tying our other coverage into the kinds of stories that we can use as sales tools to get advertisements.' Controversy, courage and passion were out. Money, power and greed were in.

There was no real solution to the baffling problem of editorial integrity without the money to pay for it, and the only certainty that anyone who visited with Doc could agree on was that a lot of voices were being dropped suddenly and too many people who should have known better were grimly accepting the tragedy as the cost of getting a paycheck. Journalists had become the servants of Reagan America, some more willingly than others, but enough had been signed on or shanghaied to persuade the public that any economic ill or social problem facing the country could be fixed by throwing a patriotic parade or giving a Federally-funded abortion clinic counsellor ten years in jail for advising a woman on her legitimate rights. The Constitution had been turned inside out; and, in the process, the American Dream was smothered by a complacent system of social justice based on politically-motivated criminal investigations, by an apathetic system of economic justice which dictated that people be turned away from hospital for lack of insurance, and by a political system so desperate for something to believe in that it needed to legislate an individual's belief in God and a disbelief in any artistic form that suggested otherwise. Doc uses a sly passage to ride down this nasty undercurrent in *Songs.* He says the one problem the rich have never solved is 'how to live in peace with the servants. Sooner or later, the maid has to come into the bedroom, and if you're only paying her $150 a week, she is going to come in hungry, or at least curious, and the time is long past when it was legal to cut their tongues out to keep them from talking.'

They never could cut out Doc's tongue, so They did the next best thing. I was in northern Russia, hunting bear out of Archangel when a colleague from Moscow arrived with the package Gerry Goldstein had sent me from Aspen. The news was not good. Doc had been charged with possession of drugs and dynamite, and sexual assault. 'Hunter S. Thompson, in an episode reminiscent of some of his books, has been charged with sexually assaulting a woman writer who came to his house ostensibly to interview him last week,' read the lead of the news report in the *Aspen Times Daily* dated 28 February 1990. A woman in the business of selling sexual aids and bad lingerie claimed that Doc threatened and beat her after she rebuffed his sexual advances. The ensuing search by police allegedly turned up a variety of drugs and explosives. The whole incident dripped of bad fish wrapped in cheap paper. In ironic spite of a reputation to the contrary and concocted by people who don't know him, Hunter S. Thompson has always been a gentleman. We tacked the news clipping to a tree, blew holes in it, and sent the remains back to Pitkin County Chief Deputy Attorney Chip McCrory.

Gerry Goldstein, Hal Haddon and a top team of attorneys and friends from the National Association of Criminal Defence Lawyers had Doc's hanging 'dismissed without prejudice' by the time I made back to the Owl Farm that Christmas. The Pitkin County DA was also under investigation by a special prosecutor for the felony crime of conspiracy to commit perjury. The bust was a set-up (Doc recounts the events surrounding his 'selective and malicious prosecution' in *Songs*), but Doc had been dragged through the streets and it was too late to stop the fantasy of Gail Palmer-Slater from becoming a part of the Legend of Lono, thereby obfuscating the real story that Doc's victory (and willingness to fight for his rights) was a victory for America, too. Such struggles are always there, but they are rarely acted on.

'There's hysteria running rampant in our nation's capital and our local statehouses,' Gerry Goldstein explains in *Songs.*

> It's accompanied by serious talk of reducing citizen rights in an effort to combat the dreaded plague of drugs. To demagogue about drugs is certainly simpler, and much more popular, than the difficult task of balancing budgets. But escalating the punishment for drug offenders, bankrupting our state and national coffers warehousing these poor souls, will hardly solve our nation's social ills. It's only going to create more poverty. And poverty is a greater root cause of crime than drugs could ever hope to be.

No matter the mess, Doc was in vigorous spirit over the holiday season and Owl Farm was still spearheading the rebellion of the hanged. The old gang was together, the NFL playoffs were in full swing, and there was talk of heading off to the Superbowl, followed by a spring field trip to Moscow and the bear forests north. All that changed after I cabled Doc from Moscow about what I'd discovered about Lenin's brain and how the pre-coup KGB was asking questions about my writing and movements. 'This is a very weird story,' he wrote back, offering Owl Farm as a hideout for me to complete my Russia book, which was already being assailed by American and Soviet officials. 'I will fight to the death for yr *Right* to publish it. We are a free people, Craig, and if anybody tries to muzzle or croak you, or stifle yr song in any way at all, I will stab them in the nuts.'

Steadman's right. Hunter might well be the reincarnation of Lono—at least for those who believe that the social/political order should be prevented from locking men and women into values or rigid forms of consciousness that remain unquestioned. And that ain't preaching. We should feel damned lucky that the Good Doctor is hard at work up in the Woody Creek redoubt. Freedom's fate could not be in more passionate hands. *Res ipsa Loquitur*, Doc.

Thomas Gaughan (review date 1 October 1994)

SOURCE: A review of *Better Than Sex: Confessions of a Political Junkie*, in *Booklist*, Vol. 91, No. 3, October 1, 1994, p. 187.

[*In the following review, Gaughan asserts that although Thompson's* Better Than Sex *is not better than his* Fear and Loathing *books, it is worthy of attention.*]

At some point, people as diverse as John Wayne and the members of Aerosmith appeared to achieve a kind of wisdom when they began to parody themselves. There are hints in **Better Than Sex** that HST is winking—broadly—at us. Sure, he's still a vicious, twisted psychotic thug who can write that Richard Nixon was criminally insane from birth, but he also closes any number of preposterous gonzo screeds with the equally preposterous, "Take my word for it, Bubba. I was there." This is Thompson's take on Clinton's campaign and his first year in office—and its an outrage per page. Nobody escapes the good doctor's wrath: Bush is so guilty he makes Nixon look innocent; Clinton is a swine, but he's our swine; and Hillary is pilloried. Ross Perot, James Carville, Margaret Thatcher, James Baker III, Al Gore, and even Walter Cronkite also get savaged. Along the way, Thompson ruminates, occasionally quite shrewdly, nearly always hilariously, on politics, society, and of course, himself. *Better Than Sex* is not better than Thompson's great *Fear and Loathing on the Campaign Trail* or the gonzo bible *Fear and Loathing in Las Vegas*. Even so, a new book by Thompson is always an event.

Michael E. Ross (review date 23 October 1994)

SOURCE: A review of *Better Than Sex: Confessions of a Political Junkie*, in *The New York Times Book Review*, October 23, 1994, p. 18.

[*In the following review, Ross praises Thompson's style but complains that his* Better Than Sex *is too disjointed.*]

In **Better Than Sex,** Hunter S. Thompson has assembled a

collection of mash notes—faxes to George Stephanopoulos, James Carville and others in the Clinton inner circle, missives that suggest Mr. Thompson's involvement in the Clinton Presidential campaign went beyond that of a mere observer. Mr. Thompson offers pointers on strategy and policy, even instructs the candidate on speaking properly. Mr. Thompson is back in the form we've come to know and love (or at least tolerate), firing at the usual targets, from George Bush and James Baker 3d, the former Secretary of State, to Mr. Thompson's nemesis, Richard M. Nixon, who died just before the book was finished (but not before Mr. Thompson worked up a remembrance that may be charitably described as uncharitable). Such shooting from the hip is Mr. Thompson's forte; what disappoints in this book is its disjointedness. *Better Than Sex* reads like a hodgepodge, a series of dispatches hurriedly lashed together. But in his own cracked, inimitable style, Mr. Thompson proves to be an upbeat Jeremiah, a civic-minded curmudgeon. "It is a very elegant feeling," he writes, "to wake up in the morning and go down to your neighborhood polling place and come away feeling proud of the way you voted." Spoken like true patriot.

Maureen Freely (review date 5 February 1995)

SOURCE: "Rum Days, Acid Nights," in *The Observer Review,* No. 10607, February 5, 1995, p. 22.

[*In the following review, Freely discusses Thompson's* Better Than Sex *and Paul Perry's unauthorized biography of Thompson and asserts that the gonzo journalist has lost his edge.*]

When Peter Cook died, his friends kept apologising for his best comic acts not seeming so shocking anymore. You had to understand how strict the conventions were, and what an exhilarating shock it was to see him break them. To appreciate Hunter S Thompson's humour, as is clear from *Better Than Sex,* you also have to put yourself bak 20 years and remember just how much reverence the silent majority had then for people in office, and just how much faith in the redemptive powers of the party animal.

'Getting assigned to cover Nixon,' said Thompson while covering the '72 election campaign, was 'like being sentenced to six months in a Holiday Inn.' He preferred Wallace: 'The air was electric even before he started talking, and by the time he was five or six minutes into his spiel I had a sense that the bastard had somehow levitated himself and was hovering over us. It reminded me of a Janis Joplin concert.' His political allies were much harder to bear. Of Hubert Humphrey he said: 'He looks like he died in 1959 and has been frozen over ever since.' His least favourite was

Ed Muskie, a 'mushmouth, middle-of-the-road compromiser', with staffers so fat that they had to be helped out of cars and lifts.

Like so many pioneers of the New, but now middle-aged, Journalism, Hunter S Thompson has never given much importance to fact and abhorred objectivity. The point of writing about current events was to explain what they did to his head. If he walked into a situation that was already stranger than fiction and acted badly to make things worse, the story only improved. And if his consciousness was altered by other substances, then so much the better. When he set out to research *Fear and Loathing in Las Vegas,* he claims to have packed 'two bags of grass, 75 pellets of mescalin, five sheets of high-powered blotter acid, a salt shaker half full of cocaine, and a whole galaxy of multi-coloured uppers, downers, screamers, laughers . . . and also a quart of tequila, a quart of rum, a case of Budweiser, a pint of raw ether and two dozen amyls.'

Paul Perry's unauthorised but worryingly deadpan biography suggests that there is not much space between the real man and the self-made caricature. He was a troublemaker and practical joker even when he was a Louisville schoolboy. His first job in journalism was as a copyboy at *Time* magazine, but he quit when they refused to see him as foreign correspondent material.

His heroes were Hemingway, Fitzgerald, Ginsberg and Kerouac—until he read *The Ginger Man.* He seems to have devoted the rest of his life to *being* the Ginger Man. He was horrible to his saintly wife. On a good day this meant cheating on her and telling her she was a bad housewife. On a bad day it meant beating her up in the presence of his publisher and then going out to Ken Kesey's place to witness a Hell's Angels' gang-bang. When she finally left him several decades too late, he was devastated, but had been on controlled-substance autopilot for too long to learn any new tricks.

Friends and fans still can't decide which drug it was that lost him his edge. He still makes plenty of money from his paint-by-numbers paranoia act, but the joy went out of it decades ago, as a quick look at *Better Than Sex* will show. He is too tired and emotional these days to spend much time on the trail itself: what he provides instead are the notes and faxes he wrote while watching CNN on his Colorado farm. He claims to have gone over to Clinton because of Gennifer Flowers, and then renewed his commitment after figuring out Clinton was also seeing the ghost of Marilyn Monroe. But in the end he decides Clinton is the 'Willy Loman of Generation X, a travelling salesman from Arkansas who has the loyalty of a lizard with its tail broken off and the midnight taste of a man who'd double-date with the Rev Jimmy Swaggart.'

He perks up when harking back to the good old days. He confesses to his son that he was the one who killed JFK, and recalls the bitter, farcical end of the McGovern campaign, in which a dingbat named Clinton was held responsible for losing 222 counties in Texas, terminated 'without pay, with prejudice,' and sent back to Arkansas. 'We'll never see *that* bastard again,' one aide is said to have said. 'He'll never work again, not in Washington.'

Rapport (review date 1995)

SOURCE: A review of *Better Than Sex,* in *Rapport,* Vol. 18, No. 5, 1995, p. 30.

[*In the following review, the critic faults Thompson's* Better Than Sex, *saying, "The aim is true but the barbs not quite as lethal as his earlier literary death blows."*]

As irreverent as a T-shirt in church and as illuminating as a wildfire, this Volume 4 of the author's Gonzo Papers is somehow not as focused, nor as forceful as the earlier installments. On any given weekend, this novelist/*Rolling Stone* correspondent is at the forefront of political reporting, but maybe after four consecutive collections on the same subject (not to mention everal earlier works) he needs to change lanes.

President Bill Clinton and his administration is the main target here, and Dr. Thompson does not miss. "Let's face it, Bubba. The main reason I'll vote for Bill Clinton is George Bush, and it has been that way from the start," explains the author about his allegiance to the Democratic camp. And on the President's indiscretions, he writes, "Of course Bill Clinton never inhaled when he put the bong to his lips. Of course he never knew Gennifer Flowers. Never admit anything except when you were born. Why should he? He is, after all, the President. And the President never acts weird."

The aim is true but the barbs not quite as lethal as his earlier literary death blows, particularly when the victim was Richard Nixon. Here, Hunter had prey worthy of his marksmanship, and even Thompson admits that the late President brought out the best (worst?) in him.

Writing with such seeming ease, he makes **Better Than Sex** read like a collection of his scribbled notes rather than the cutting and terse images he's conjured up in earlier political vehicles and his landmark work with *Rolling Stone.* A true Hunterite will enjoy this but not be overwhelmed.

David McCumber (essay date 9 December 1996)

SOURCE: "The Mad Adventure Continues," in *The Los Angeles Times,* December 9, 1996, p. 1.

[*In the following essay, McCumber discusses the impact of Thompson's work and his current projects.*]

"I have weird dreams," Hunter Stockton Thompson says. "I never expected to be looking over my life, page by page. It's like an animal eating its own intestines."

It is 3:45 a.m. on a Tuesday morning, and he is perched like a barn owl on a high stool in his kitchen, eating not innards but a TV dinner, microwaved and then slathered with a hellbroth of mysterious mustards, chutneys and chili sauces. The plate suddenly lows with an unearthly light. I take this at first to be the sign of a chemical reaction, but it is actually the work of Thompson's newest gadget—the man is a gadget freak—a motorized, illuminated pepper grinder. The spotlighted meal is rapidly covered with black flakes, sort of like Pittsburgh in the early 1900s.

This dish alone would probably give most people nightmares for a week, but the famed journalist says the weird dreams he's been having are a byproduct of a gratifying but grueling forced march through his past, caused by the 25th anniversary last month of the publication of his rolling pharmacy classic **Fear and Loathing in Las Vegas** and also by the preparation of the first volume of his collected letters, due in the spring from Villard Books.

Mind you, he's enjoying himself. As he sups, he rolls videotape, and his big-screen TV flickers with images from several stops on the Hunter S. Thompson Fun-Finding Tour of the past few weeks: himself, strolling into Rolling Stone mogul Jann Wenner's office and blasting his longtime editor with a fire extinguisher; a mob scene at the party Wenner and Random House threw for him in New York, commemorating the reissuing of **F&L in Vegas** by the Modern Library; and speaking gigs at such disparate venues as Harvard Law School and Johnny Depp's Sunset Strip hipper-than-thou spot, the Viper Room.

Wait a minute. Rewind the tape. The Modern Library? Hunter S. Thompson, acid-swilling bad boy of American letters, rubbing literary shoulders with Proust and Dos Passos, Faulkner and Fitzgerald?

You bet, bubba. It was inevitable. Not only has Thompson cranked out a stream of bestsellers (**Hell's Angels, Fear and Loathing on the Campaign Trail, The Great Shark Hunt, Generation of Swine, Songs of the Doomed, Better Than Sex**), but along the way he has become revered for his political acuity, personal excesses and utterly inimitable prose style.

Hell's Angels was hailed as a groundbreaking book in 1967, and *Las Vegas* seared the country four years later with what the New York Times called "a kind of mad, corrosive prose poetry that picks up where Norman Mailer . . . left off and explores what Tom Wolfe left out."

So when everybody from Wolfe to Mick Jagger to Matt Dillon to Depp to Ralph Steadman, his illustrator and frequent coconspirator, showed up to honor him in New York, the Modern Library anointing was placed in clear perspective: Thompson has pulled off the difficult trick of being an icon of not only his own generation but of the ones that have followed.

Add to all this adulation the fact that Rhino Films, an offshoot of Rhino Records, has just announced plans to translate *Fear and Loathing in Las Vegas* for the screen (with Depp playing Thompson), and it becomes evident that the Doctor of Gonzo is on a serious roll.

Surprised? So is he, in a way. "I never expected to live this long," Thompson jokes, "and a lot of other people didn't expect me to either."

The rather startling truth is that Thompson, 59, seems to have come out of that crazed quarter of a century in champion form. He has always had the constitution of a moose (he is from stout Kentucky hill country stock), and the poster boy for the drug culture seems poised to continue his craft well into the next century.

For now, there is a book to get to press.

Thompson finishes his late lunch, or early breakfast, or whatever, pours himself a tumbler of Chivas and turns his attention to a mock-up of the dust jacket for *The Proud Highway: Saga of a Desperate Southern Gentleman,* subtitled *The Fear & Loathing Letters,* Volume I, 1955-67. ("Volume II will make some people wish that wolves had stolen them from their cradles," Thompson cracks with glee.) The book features an introduction by the novelist William Kennedy, a longtime Thompson friend and confidant.

It is just one more surprise that throughout Thompson's rather turbulent life, he has kept a carbon of every letter he has written—amounting to several thousand pages of typescript. He is an inveterate correspondent, and the letters provide not only illuminating insights into his development as a literary figure, his personal life and his impressions of the culture of the times, but by sheer volume represent a major percentage of his life's work.

"RED HERE," Thompson scrawls on the proof. "Too Big," "Kill photo on spine" and "Outline with gold here" quickly follow. He is, after all, a visual artist as well as a writer. (His bullet-riddled, paint-spattered images of prominent figures command five-figure prices.)

It is 5 a.m. and Dr. Thompson's workday is progressing nicely. He finishes his design instructions and picks up the telephone, which he is famed for using as a lethal weapon. This time, the target is friendly: Douglas Brinkley, the book's editor.

After a thoroughgoing discussion of the manuscript's status, talk turns to an upcoming tribute to Thompson in his hometown of Louisville. Plans are in place: Warren Zevon will open the show; George McGovern has said he will attend; the venue has been changed to the city's finest concert hall to accommodate an expected crowd of nearly 2,000; he is booked into the presidential suite at the elegant Brown Hotel; his mother will be whisked to the event by limousine; and the same local government that once locked Thompson up as a juvenile delinquent will present him with a key to the city.

At 6:20, things get ugly over the telephone. He is trying to call a friend at the University of Indiana, and the switchboard should have opened 20 minutes earlier, but for some reason the nighttime recorded message is still on.

"I want to know why you people aren't at work," he snarls into the telephone. "You are answerable to the taxpayers, you know. What's the matter with you? I will find out who you are and why you're still asleep. Get a grip on yourself."

He slams down the telephone. The ghost of a little-boy grin flashes, then departs just as quickly. Thompson freshens his drink and moves to the next item on the agenda: a little fun. He cranks a sheet of paper into his typewriter (yes, he plays around with a hopped-up Macintosh, even surfs the Internet, but when it's time for work, it's the Selectric every time) and raps out the following:

Dearest Eric:

This waiting is driving me crazy. I miss you so much I can scream. Soon I will get my hands on you. I have a huge brain tumor. We can get naked and go out to the car. . . . Sweet Dreams—Zan."

A chuckle escapes his throat as he proofreads this horrifying missive (entire contents cannot be included here). He couples it with a photocopied portrait of a woman with an impressive array of body piercings and signs it with a lipsticked, puckered mouth print. Within minutes, it is winging through the fax lines to various people in his Rolodex: several reporters and a network news executive; a White House staffer; the mayor of Aspen, Colo.; and then, for good measure, several randomly selected souls who will get a nasty shock upon waking simply because their numbers happen to be programmed into Thompson's machine. "The fat is in the fire," he says. "The flute is in the wind."

It's no accident that Aspen's mayor is one of the unfortunate recipients. Ever since Thompson ran for Pitkin County Sheriff in 1970 and lost by a handful of votes, he has been deeply involved in local politics and now is by far the most influential political figure in the county. When he takes a position on an issue, it results in front-page headlines in Aspen's newspapers. He proved his power a year ago when he took on the skiing and business establishments, spearheading a fight against expansion of the Aspen airport—and won by a margin of more than a thousand votes.

But the victory carried a price. Just after 2 a.m. that election day, Thompson was returning from the climactic antiairport rally when an Aspen police officer pulled him over. A Breathalyzer test indicated that he wasn't legally drunk, but Thompson was eventually charged with a misdemeanor, driving while impaired. The arresting officer said he stopped Thompson because he had driven six inches over the yellow line for about 40 feet. Thompson could have pleaded guilty and paid a $50 fine, but he charged that the arrest was clearly political, and has been fighting the case ever since.

"I'm spending $30,000 to $40,000 fighting a misdemeanor traffic ticket because this case is about whether a rogue cop has the right to stop people for no good reason," Thompson says. "It's a political bust and I will win."

A trial has been set for March. City officials declined to comment on the case. On this morning, Thompson calls one of his lawyers, criminal defense superstar Gerald Goldstein.

"I don't want them to drop the charges," Thompson tells Goldstein. "I want the cop to go on trial first, then me." He closes with an aphorism straight out of the '60s: "Today's pig is tomorrow's bacon."

You get the feeling that Thompson, a self-confessed political junkie, is getting his fix in the only arena possible. He declined to cover the presidential campaign this year because it was so lackluster. "I don't know if national politics will ever be fun again," he says.

What will he do for fun? Well, there is a novel—working title, "Polo Is My Life"—that Thompson hopes to resume once all the fuss dies down. Thompson has always blurred the lines between journalism and literature, and whether he approaches his work as fiction or nonfiction, the result is sure to be interesting.

The late Edward Abbey, no slouch at both approaches himself, said it succinctly when he commented on *Fear and Loathing in Las Vegas* years ago: "Among journalists I have but one hero, and that is Dr. Hunter S. Thompson. I honor him because he reports the simple facts, in plain language, of what he sees around him. His style is mistaken for fantastic drug-crazed exaggeration, but that was to be expected. As always in this country, they only laugh at you when you tell the truth. He is really much more than a journalist. Not a journalist at all, but one who sees—a seer."

It is 8 a.m. Dr. Thompson's friend at the University of Indiana calls back, unnerved by the message left on the machine. A couple of responses to the fax have also come in. The original faxes were sent anonymously, bearing no return name or number, but it seems that the style is quite unmistakable.

It is daylight now, and a light snow is falling. "Let's gas up the Jeep and go to town," Hunter Thompson says, and the grin returns. "I'll show you where I crossed the yellow line."

Charles Kaiser (review date 13 July 1997)

SOURCE: A review of *The Proud Highway: Saga of a Desperate Southern Gentleman,* in *The New York Times Book Review,* July 13, 1997.

[*In the following review, Kaiser calls Thompson's* The Proud Highway *"neither particularly interesting nor particularly well-written."*]

In the introduction to this nearly 700-page collection of the letters of Hunter S. Thompson, the novelist William J. Kennedy provides a useful definition of the "gonzo journalism" that made Thompson famous. "It was not lunacy defined," Kennedy writes, "but lunacy imagined: in short, a novel." Unfortunately, in these pages Thompson most often cnfines himself to the mundane facts of his everyday life between 1955 (when he was 17 years old) and 1967 (following the publication of *Hell's Angels*), and the results are generally underwhelming. Occasionally we see flashes of humor or intelligence, but for vast stretches we are subjected to observations like these: "I have paid my rent for one month. The apartment seemed horrible at first, but I've been working on it most of the day, and it looks a little better now." Most of the more than 200 letters included in this volume—the first of a projected three—are neither particularly interesting nor particularly well written. There is not enough here to sustain the interest of a Hunter S. Thompson fan—only a fanatic would want to plow through all the way to the end.

Richard Bernstein (review date 25 July 1997)

SOURCE: "Letters of the Young Author (He Saved Them All)," in *The New York Times Book Review,* July 25, 1997.

[*In the following review, Bernstein discusses Thompson's need to record his life and share it with the public in* The Proud Highway.]

One thing that this collection of letters makes clear at the outset is that Hunter S. Thompson, he of the *Fear and Loathing* books, for whom the phrase "gonzo journalist" was invented, has always burned to carve his initials onto the collective awareness. What other kind of person would, beginning in his teen years, make carbon copies of every letter he wrote—to his mother, his Army friends and commanding officers, his girlfriends, his various agents and editors—specifically in the hope that they would be published?

Mr. Thompson, by dint of hard work and enormous talent, has gotten his wish. Edited by Douglas Brinkley and adorned with a sparkling essay by the novelist William J. Kennedy, *The Proud Highway* takes Mr. Thompson's caustic, furious, funny, look-at-me correspondence through 1967, when the author, having arrived on the scene with his book *Hell's Angels,* was 30. It is noteworthy that although just one in seven of the relevant cache of letters was included, this book, labeled *The Fear and Loathing Letters,* Volume I, weighs in at just under 700 pages—and there are still 30 more years to go. Even some of the photographs of Mr. Thompson were taken by the author himself, self-portraits of the writer at work and at play. Manifestly, this is a man who, while anti-snobbish to a fault, abusively contemptuous of self-promotion and pretension, had a powerful need to make a record of himself and to make that record public.

Fortunately, the maverick vibrancy and originality of the record's creator fully redeems what might otherwise have been an act of egomaniacal temerity. The Hunter S. Thompson that emerges in this collection of his letters, complemented by fragments of his other writings, is very much the unrestrained, strenuously nonconformist, Lone Ranger journalist who achieved cult status long ago.

One thinks of Mr. Thompson a bit as one thinks of the hero of George Macdonald Fraser's fictional Flashman books, Flashman rampaging like Don Quixote through the major events of the 19th century, making them his own. Mr. Hunter rampaged through the 60's and 70's of this century, not reporting on them in any conventional sense but using them as raw material for the text that was his own life.

Taken together, as Mr. Brinkley correctly points out in his editor's note, the Thompson correspondence is "an informal and offbeat history of two decades in American life," the two

decades in question having produced the counterculture that Mr. Thompson both chronicled and helped produce. The overriding sensibility, inherited from H.L. Mencken, consists of an eloquent, hyperbolic impatience with the supposed mediocrity of American life, its Rotarian culture, its complacency and its pieties.

"Young people of America, awake from your slumber of indolence and harken the call of the future!" the 18-year-old Mr. Thompson wrote in the first piece reproduced in this book, taken from the yearbook of the Louisville Male High School in Kentucky. "I'm beginning to think you're a phony, Graham," Mr. Hunter writes eight years later in 1963, the Graham in question being Philip L. Graham, president of the *Washington Post* Company. Mr. Hunter, a freelancer writing articles from South America, was moved to a rage by an article in *Newsweek,* owned by *The Washington Post,* that was critical of *The National Observer,* which was publishing his work.

This, evidently, was a guy who took no guff, whose Ayn Rand-influenced determination to do things his way required not only that he make no compromises but that he be seen as making none. Graham invited Mr. Hunter to "write me a somewhat less breathless letter, in which you tell me about yourself," and Mr. Thompson did so. He compliments his correspondent on the "cavalier tone that in some circles would pass for a very high kind of elan" but warns him against interpreting his letter as "a devious means of applying for a job on the assembly line at *Newsweek,* or covering speeches for *The Washington Post.* I sign what I write, and I mean to keep on signing it."

By 1967, Mr. Thompson, who has risen in the world, is blasting others for nincompoopery and knavishness. "I have every honest and serious intention of wreaking a thoroughly personal and honest vengeance on Scott Meredith himself, in the form of cracking his teeth with a knotty stick and rupturing every other bone and organ I can make contact with in the short time I expect will be allotted to me," he writes in a letter to his editor at Random House, speaking of the literary agent whom he has just, in any case, dismissed. "I am probably worse than you think, as a person, but what the hell?" he wrote to Meredith. "When I get hungry for personal judgment on myself, I'll call for a priest."

Mr. Thompson is not always making symbolic threats. This volume shows him as a loyal and clever friend devoted to sporting, high-spirited repartee. It shows him also as a stingingly good stylist as well as a hard-drinking, gun-toting adventurer who never loses his sense of humor even when he is being bitten by South American beetles or stomped on by members of an American motorcycle gang. The letters and other fragments in this collection are invested with the same rugged, outspoken individualism as his more public writings, which make them just as difficult to put down.

What makes them ever more irresistible is that they lend substance to the legend of his life as an ultimate countercultural romance. If books like *Fear and Loathing in Las Vegas* conveyed the image of a handsome young man riding his motorcycle at 100 miles an hour on the defiant highway of the untrammeled life, this collection of his private statements will show that the image was true.

"The most important thing a writer can have," he wrote to a friend when he was 21, is "the ability to live with constant loneliness and a strong sense of revulsion for the banalities of everyday socializing." Evidently, he meant what he said.

FURTHER READING

Criticism

McKeen, William. *Hunter S. Thompson.* Boston: Twayne Publishers, 1991, 120-27.
> Provides information about Thompson's life and career.

"Hunter S. Thompson." *Vanity Fair* 57, No. 9 (September 1994): 214.
> A brief sketch in which Thompson answers questions about his life

---

Additional coverage of Thompson's life and career is contained in the following sources published by Gale: *Bestsellers,* Vol. 89:1; *Contemporary Authors,* Vol. 17-20R; *Contemporary Authors New Revision Series,* Vols. 23 and 46; *DISCovering Authors Modules: Popular Fiction and Genre Authors;* and *Major Twentieth-Century Writers.*

Luisa Valenzuela
1938-

Argentinian novelist, short story writer, journalist, and scriptwriter.

The following entry presents criticism of Valenzuela's work through 1995. For further information on her life and career, see *CLC,* Volume 31.

INTRODUCTION

Recognized as a significant author who has emerged in Argentina since the "boom" in Latin American literature during the 1960s, Valenzuela is one of South America's best known and most widely translated women writers. She has written six novels and six collections of short stories, as well as numerous journalistic essays and a one-act play, each distinguished by a decidedly feminist slant in contrast with the male-dominated world of Hispanic literature. Throughout her writings Valenzuela has focused on contemporary politics, especially those of her native Argentina, and the use, misuse, and abuse of language in order to oppress, control, and censor thought—particularly of women—at both the personal and political level. Critics often have commented on the fantastic, magical elements of her generally realistic fiction, frequently classifying her narrative style as magic realism, a technique used by many writers to reflect the extraordinary qualities of life in Latin America. Although Valenzuela's later works have strayed from personal themes and linear narration toward an emphasis on political concerns and a lyrical, metaphorical style, Cheryl Nimtz has observed that "the personal and the political often reflect each other in Valenzuela's work."

Biographical Information

Valenzuela was born November 26, 1938, in Buenos Aires, to Pablo Franciso Valenzuela, a physician, and Luisa Mercedes Levinson, a novelist and short story writer. Raised by a German governess and English tutor in a household that frequently entertained prominent members of Argentina's literati, among them Jorge Luis Borges and Ernesto Sabato, Valenzuela attended private secondary schools and, as a teenager, began publishing articles in the youth magazine *Quince Abriles.* Instead of entering the university, she pursued journalism full-time, working for several Buenos Aires newspapers and magazines, and served a stint in the Biblioteca Nacional under the direction of Borges. By 1956, Valenzuela had published her first short story, "Ciudad ajena," in the literary magazine *Ficción,* but her first short story collection, *Los heréticos*, didn't appear until 1967. In 1958, she

married Theodore Marjak, a French merchant marine (whom she divorced in 1965), and moved to Paris, where she wrote her first novel, *Hay que sonreír* (1966), and established contacts with the literary groups *Tel Quel* and the "new novel" movement. When Valenzuela returned to Buenos Aires in 1961, she joined the editorial staff of *La Nación* Sunday supplement, assuming the position of assistant editor from 1964 to 1972; thereafter, she freelanced for various publications in Buenos Aires until she settled in the United States in 1979. Since the early 1960s, Valenzuela has traveled and lectured extensively throughout the Americas and Europe, receiving a Fulbright fellowship to the Iowa International Writers' Program in 1969 and a National Arts Foundation grant to study literature at Columbia University in New York City in 1972. Throughout the 1970s and 1980s Valenzuela wrote fiction and conducted many seminars at Columbia, and she taught writing courses at New York University from 1985 to 1990. During the early 1990s, Valenzuela returned to Buenos Aires, where she has continued to travel, lecture, and write, producing works such as the short story collection *Simetrías* (1993) and the novel *Bedside Manners* (1995).

Major Works

Valenzuela's fiction combines the political, the fictional, and the real. Most of her novels take place in the city of Buenos Aires, where lonely inhabitants are victims drowning in their country's violent political history. Valenzuela's works experiment with narrative structure through a constantly shifting point of view and self-conscious language that examines the creative process of art while relating stories. *Clara* depicts the submissive state of women in Argentina as experienced through the urban encounters of Clara, a young prostitute whose innocent dreams conflict with the values and politics of her patriarchal culture. *El gato eficaz* (1972) concerns a female narrator who lets loose "the evils of the world" in the metaphorical form of "the black cats of death," revealing how language itself creates the binary systems that seem to structure Western culture. *Como en la guerra* (1977; *He Who Searches*) hinges on the surreality of Argentine politics as an anonymous male narrator seeks, linguistically and spacially, his female self and the truth. *Cola de lagartija* (1983; *The Lizard's Tail*), widely considered Valenzuela's most important fiction, recounts the rise to power, the fall, the plan to return to power, and the death of a despotic Argentine government official—José López Rega, Isabel Perón's Minister of Social Well-Being—who is a sorcerer and has three testicles. *Novela negra con argentinos* (1990; *Black Novel [with Argentines]*) relates the survival of two Argentine writers in New York City through senseless murders, sexual perversion, and rank cynicism. *Bedside Manners* focuses on a woman who returns to her Latin American homeland to find democracy restored, yet who strangely confines herself to bed at a remote country club, desperately trying to avoid outside events and politics that invade her room. The stories in *Open Door* (1988) feature most of the thematic concerns, artistic methods, and subject matter that characterize Valenzuela's short stories. This collection provides a translated selection of the author's best earlier short fiction, comprising fourteen stories from *Donde viven las águilas* (1983; *Up among the Eagles*), eleven selections from *Aquí pasan cosas raras* (1975; *Strange Things Happen Here*) and seven stories from *Los heréticos*. According to Brooke K. Horvath, "Shamanistic figures, folkloristic superstitions and ritual magic, cultic beliefs and indigenous legends jostle urban settings, café life, state-of-the-art state terrorism, and the amorous doings of vacationing bourgeoisie to yield modern political parables and twice-told (albeit revamped) myths, small comedies of manners and mocking parodies of middle-class conventionality, ironic illuminations of religious realities and secular tales of physical and/or psychological terror. Similarly, traditional narrative techniques combine with a postmodern experimentation (fragmented narration, magical realism, randomness, and linguistic pranksterism) in the service of themes that are as timeless as the search for truth, community, or control over nature's mysteries, and as topical as sexual and political persecution in present-day Argentina or the nature of power relations within and among contemporary social classes."

Critical Reception

Valenzuela has received significant critical attention in the United States. Her fiction is acclaimed for her inventive use of image, metaphor, and symbol in examining themes of violence, political oppression, and cultural repression, especially as the latter relates to women. Commentators have admitted the importance of feminist concerns and Argentine politics in Valenzuela's writings, and others have struggled with her ambiguous narrative structures. However, Caleb Bach remarked that Valenzuela "favors circular, spiral, or even concentric configurations for the passage of events and as to those events themselves, she prefers to describe them with ambiguity." Valenzuela's short stories, on the other hand, have met with a mixed critical response. Critics generally have concluded that her stories appeal mainly to ambitious readers who are willing to search through surreal presentations for meaning. Yet Horvath has suggested that Valenzuela's short stories "explore the boundaries of what is currently thought possible in fiction while reminding us of what must be demanded from fiction in our time." Bach has noted that Valenzuela's ultimate aim in her fiction "is to provoke thoughtfulness, dislodge the apathetic from their comfortable yet fallacious, worn-out assumptions, and see with acuity the disturbing reality within which we live."

PRINCIPAL WORKS

Hay que sonreír (novel) 1966
Los heréticos [The Heretics] (short stories) 1967
†*El gato eficaz* (novel) 1972
‡*Aquí pasan cosas raras [Strange Things Happen Here]* (short stories) 1975
Clara: 13 Short Stories and a Novel (short stories and novel) 1976
‡*Como en la guerra [He Who Searches]* (novel) 1977
Strange Things Happen Here: 26 Short Stories and a Novel (short stories and novel) 1979
§*Libro que no muere* (short stories) 1980
Cambio de armas [Other Weapons] (short stories) 1982
Cola de lagartija [The Lizard's Tail] (novel) 1983
Donde viven las águilas [Up among the Eagles] (short stories) 1983
Open Door (short stories) 1988
Novela negra con argentinos [Black Novel (with Argentines)] (novel) 1990
Realidad nacional desde la cama ["National Reality from the Bed"] (one-act drama) 1990
Simetrías (short stories) 1993
Bedside Manners (novel) 1995

*English translations of these works appear in *Clara.*

†Title means "The Efficient Cat," but portions of this work have appeared in periodicals in English translation under the title *Cat-O-Nine-Deaths.*

‡English translations of these works appear in *Strange Things Happen Here.*

§Title means "The Book that Doesn't Bite" and contains stories from *Aquí pasan cosas raras* and *Los heréticos.*

CRITICISM

Luisa Valenzuela with Evelyn Picon Garfield (interview date 18 July 1978)

SOURCE: An interview in *Women's Voices from Latin America: Interviews with Six Contemporary Authors,* Wayne State University Press, 1985, pp. 141-65.

[*In the following interview conducted in Buenos Aires on July 18, 1978, Valenzuela talks about literary and other influences, the relationship between semiotics and eroticism, the similarities of love and death, her approach to language and politics in her works, the question of gendered writing and themes, and the situation of contemporary Hispanic American women writers.*]

Luisa Valenzuela's narrative is revolutionary in two contradictory acceptations of the word: it reflects a violent break with tradition, future orientation, and change; and it evokes a time, cyclical in nature, like a planet revolving on its axis, a time in which myths are revealed and repeated. Valenzuela praises change and even consecrates herself to opening a breach in the complacent customs of the Western world. In doing this, she continues a modern tradition, born in Europe with Romanticism and in Spanish America of the late nineteenth century with "modernismo": the tradition of revealing society's inadequacies by slapping the middle class in the face—*épater le bourgeois.*

Focusing on eroticism and death in her fiction, Valenzuela transgresses taboos in a challenge to the bulwarks of modern societies in Spanish America: "almighty reason," rampant materialism, stifling social mores, the "fanaticism" of religion and politics, the socioeconomic hierarchies. In the wake of the destruction and desacralization leveled by her critical pen, she erects a universe of constant transformations that forces the reader to shed his self-sufficiency and invites him to confront the precarious nature of life. This existential vision is fused with a surrealistic style that emphasizes physical desire, and is fanned by a playful yet searing humor and irony. Valenzuela's writing becomes a search for identity: at once a carnival of masks that parody life and society and a ritualistic dance of purification and sacrifice.

Her subversive censure of an oppressive society manifests itself in a vitally constructive prose of incessant renovation and re-creation in which she irreverently pokes fun at social institutions. Nothing is spared. She satirizes Gallup polls, the married couple, organized religion, sex (machismo and virginity, the mystical sect of "telecoitus," and instructions for playing the game "fornicopula"), and high and pop cultures (soap operas, doctoral degrees, and semiotics). "Everything livable can be laughable," she explains. With an incisive irony her short stories and novels tackle the political realities of Spanish America—terrorism, persecution, torture, disappearances, dictatorships—and some of their underlying socioeconomic causes, such as hunger, repression, the lack of dignity, and misery. In *El gato eficaz* (*The Efficient Cat*), the protagonist assures us, with tongue in cheek, that "satanism is no longer in vogue. Now the fad is goodness; good people, healthy motives and love-thy-distant-neighbor. It's all right to sigh for those who are starving but that's no reason to let them poke around in our pots. It's good to remind them that rice is healthier with the hull on and to leave them just that, the hull."

Death, a constant in Valenzuela's fiction, stalks the starving masses and persists in every sexual encounter. Valenzuela adheres to many of Georges Bataille's ideas which link orgasm and death to religious experience, taboo and transgression, desire and terror, and pleasure and anguish. Eroticism embodies the violence and violation of death, a temporary negation of individuality on the part of two mortals who aspire to a fleeting union with eternity, the "little death" of an orgasm that erases for a moment their isolated existences: "If love is a little like death (a little death)," says a voice in *Como en la guerra* (*He Who Searches*), "death is pure love, the great cosmic orgasm."

Loss of self in the erotic encounter, in death, or in writing is for Valenzuela the pursuit of otherness which wrenches one free from a spurious "omniscience" to achieve a more truthful polysemic and polymorphic reality. The discourse of her third novel, *Como en la guerra,* is reflected and refracted as if by a mirror into many voices, conscious and subconscious and intimate and collective, whose kaleidoscopic transmutations challenge rational explanation. Her writing constantly responds to a mutable universe and so necessarily subverts language to communicate the only valuable reality, a protean "becoming." Thus, the word is demythified, exposed for its pretense, inadequacy, and incomprehensions: "i want to olev lions i want to hold a scalpel to cut my tongue every day i want i want i want not to belong to anything b cause belonging erases all possibilities for revolution t h atis the olny drue quality in man."

Valenzuela's prose emphasizes free alterations in symbols, characters, structures, and style. Characters undergo corporal transformations or encompass transsexuality, and her language is riddled with puns and word games. The eighteen chapters of Valenzuela's second novel, *El gato eficaz,* form a concatenation of the humorous, violent, and eschatological adventures of the female protagonist, an accomplice of the cats-of-death. She searches for somatic and semantic bliss, an eroticism of body and language, which is a constantly fluctuating state and the only hope for survival and renewal:

> Everything that tries to hold us back and detains us for a while is fatuous. The inalterable is fatuous with pretensions of eternity and not I who am not me myself I am transforming into colors on my retina, I gasify my shapes and keep on calling myself I, me, mine, not because of some old routine but rather for lack of something better and in the hope of a new comrade like you who may discover the keys to this game, line up the pieces—the white dogs-lives, the black cats-of-death—and renew the cycle. Checkmate again, may he smite me from afar. Smite me, imiteme, imitateme: my only hope lies in a rebirth.

Perhaps the title of Valenzuela's second collection of short stories, *Aquí pasan cosas raras* (*Strange Things Happen Here*), best describes her imaginative prose, populated as it is by a gallery of marginal characters—prostitutes, peeping Toms, homosexuals—in an atmosphere of gothic horror or of mythic dimensions. Like her contemporary Julio Cortázar, Valenzuela lashes out to topple moral taboos. The playful quality and surrealistic flair of her fiction, however, do not diminish its social impact. Winking a jaundiced eye at the reader and flashing a great Cheshire cat grin, Valenzuela achieves uncanny, effective combinations in her satires, such as the following erotic parody of capitalist exploitation:

> She, on the other hand, was green like a Lorca poem and combed the vines of her body coursing with sap. Sap with chlorophyll, photosynthesis, a vegetable world decomposing until it becomes oil. And since there is never a scarcity of vampires—I repeat—she, too, met hers in spite of her metamorphoses.

I feel that we usually follow a certain guiding thread which leads us through life. We don't lose that thread but sometimes we lose sight of it. So there could be a relationship between all of my searches because ultimately they are not the pursuit of death but of knowledge.
—*Luisa Valenzuela*

He was a rich Texan with a mighty fine ten-gallon hat who planted his rig deep down and sucked up the heaviest oils instead of irrigating her. A drill, that Texan, a real craftsman of wells even inside her. That's how he managed to extract a high percentage of combustible gases, a little bit of solvent. He could wrench from her a love that also burns, lose himself in petroputrid caresses. . . .

. . . . .

[*Garfield:*] *Do you belong to a specific generation of writers in Argentina?*

[Valenzuela:] I think we are all part of a literary generation and affected by certain influences. But in my time, unfortunately, I don't believe that there is a well-defined literary group. I say unfortunately because I would like to have been part of a group of creative people.

Do you feel an affinity with other Argentinean writers?

We all feel very independent and distant from one another. I don't think we would be the writers we are today if Borges had not existed first and [Julio] Cortázar later. They completely altered our view of literature.

When did you begin to write fiction?

I wrote one solitary poem when I was six, and then when I was seventeen years old I wrote a short story. I had decided it wasn't so difficult to write stories the way a certain fashionable author of that time did. So I gave my story to Juan Goyanarte, who ran the magazine *Ficción*, and he published it. He was impressed and wanted me to write a novel. The revised version of the story called **"Ciudad ajena"** [**"The Foreign City"**] is now part of the book *Los heréticos* [*The Heretics*].

Which literary works have influenced you most in your career as a writer?

I don't know if any writer can answer that question. Personally, I cannot. Influences are so sporadic and aleatory. Everything that surrounds us, that occurs—music, science—influences one's writing.

Do you feel that any particular event in your life has influenced your writing more than another?

Of course. One thing that moved me and definitively transformed my art was my stay in New York. That scared me a great deal. Suddenly *El gato eficaz* was born; it's very different from my other fiction. All of a sudden I touched vibrating passions with my fingertips and discovered that hatred and love are tactile.

The structure of your first novel, **Hay que sonreír (Clara),** *contrasts markedly with your later novels, like* **El gato eficaz.**

I wrote the first one in France when I was twenty-one years old. Later I polished it up a bit. Then I began to realize that the anecdote was less important than a profound philosophy about the subject and the language used to express it. Perhaps what I had been reading influenced me; later, I took the leap with *El gato eficaz.* It was not just the New York experience that motivated it but also a period of extreme solitude. I was in Iowa as a Guggenheim fellow, and all at once, I found myself alone, lonely like a mushroom, abandoned. From that encounter with myself a heap of internal ghosts emerged.

But let's return for a moment to that first novel, **Hay que sonreír.** *Why did you choose the life of a prostitute as the subject?*

There are lots of reasons. I think that all women believe in the prostitute. After all, she's the woman who possesses all men. At that time I lived in Paris, and the prostitutes lived in the same building I did. To my way of thinking they were very brave women because they used to get into cars and go with the men to the Bois de Boulogne Park across the way. It was courageous to get into a car with any old guy just to earn a few meager francs; after all, anything could have happened. I sympathized with those women, and when I heard their footsteps, I used to open the door for them. Sometimes they were running from the police to seek refuge in the building. I never talked with them, but a sort of remote understanding existed between us.

There are several traits in your early short stories, **Los heréticos,** *that evolve in your later novels. For example, the search for the unknown or for roots in the past reappears in* **Como en la guerra (He Who Searches),** *and many of these quests result in death.*

I feel that we usually follow a certain guiding thread which leads us through life. We don't lose that thread but sometimes we lose sight of it. So there could be a relationship between all of my searches because ultimately they are not the pursuit of death but of knowledge. Perhaps in the stories of *Los heréticos* the intent differed from that of the novel *Como en la guerra.* In the latter, one no longer perceives the idea that all religions are heretical simply because they take symbols literally. In *Como en la guerra* symbols *are* taken literally.

Were all the stories in **Los heréticos** *written about the same time?*

No. That's one of the defects of the book; the stories vary

and were written at very different moments of my life. They lack unity. The idea of heresy has always interested me, and I return to it involuntarily. Right now, I'm interested in myths, that is, how myths originate; and I sense that literature may be a form of anthropological exploration (something which never occurred to me in *Los heréticos,* even though the subconscious idea may have been there).

The voyage and quest are fundamental to discovering life's hidden truths in **El gato eficaz** *and in* **Como en la guerra.** *They seem to signify both the flight from and the search for impossible personal love—and by extension death—in a sociopolitical sense. Would you explain the link between the voyage/search and collective societal goals in these two novels?*

There are no individuals who develop outside of their own society; and society is composed of individuals. What seems to be a personal goal is really everyone's battle, a collective quest. The individual search in its egotism is so very human that everyone partakes of it. All personal searches respond to numerous exigencies that many share. So the author may ask himself, "Why am I writing such a personal, egotistical work?" In fact, literature is neither exclusively self-centered nor intimate, for we are answering and formulating new questions that are universal preoccupations.

When you speak of redeeming oneself, what do you mean?

I ask myself that. Redeem oneself from all that has accumulated *against* ourselves or humanity or life. All we do is erect barriers, so possibly we ought not ask for forgiveness for good or bad deeds but rather for those which isolate us from each other.

One of the fundamental elements of **Como en la guerra** *is the mythical archetypical exploration of reality. At times one notes a burlesque treatment of structuralism in the semiotics professor who dedicates himself to psychoanalyzing the prostitute, quotes [Jacques] Lacan, and whose interests are so all-encompassing that his very name, AZ, takes in the whole alphabet. In spite of this parody of a popular modern literary movement in criticism and linguistics, you seem to adhere to theories expounded by Lacan and [Claude] Levi-Strauss, for example. Did you intend such a parody? What are your ideas about structuralism and Lacan's semiotics?*

I read Lacan before I began to write *Como en la guerra.* I spent a sleepless night reading Lacan. It was a great discovery for me. At the same time I joke about my great fascinations. Nothing is serious. I applied what I understood then about Lacan even though later I was to learn much more. That small bite of the Lacan "apple" opened many roads for me. What Lacan and the structuralists say about the subconscious and language, the signifier and signified, seems extraordinary to me. My literary research is based very much on the possibility of multiple significations for a signifier. It is an exploration of the word, the kind of prostituted word we use daily.

Is there no parody then?

Yes, there is a parody of Lacan who speaks in the first person plural form "we." He writes that way; it's a kind of infinite fatuity.

Pseudoscientific?

Yes, but suddenly he pulls your leg. And so do I. I'm not the keeper of truth nor do I pretend to be. That's why I foster ambiguity in my prose. The word is mine and possibly belongs to others, but not to everyone. So I invite you to read into that word whatever you will. Besides, a word has many connotations. Grab a dictionary; sometimes those meanings even contradict each other. I begin a sentence with a word meaning one thing, then all at once, in the middle of the sentence, the word begins to signify something else.

The passion and eroticism in your early stories like "Los heréticos," "La profesora" ("The Professor"), and "Una familia para Clotilde" ("A Family for Clotilde") are also fundamental to your later works. Is there an evolution of these constants?

I believe that eroticism is very closely linked to language, to words laden with our own erotic desires. In the short stories, eroticism is seen from without as sin (that was my fault). Later on, eroticism is viewed more as communication with the divine. It is assumed and accepted by the author. There is an identification with eroticism. In the later works, *Et gato eficaz* and *Como en la guerra,* there is no ethical judgment of eroticism.

In your fiction it appears that love is a synonym for intercourse, for death, sacrifice, and extermination, not only in El gato eficaz but also in Como en la guerra. Would you clarify the source of this eroticism?

I don't know whether or not I can explain that because it is complex. Love is a little death; they call an orgasm a "little death."

And why can't it be a "little bit of life"?

Because there is a contact with pain there, very close to desperation, a need to disintegrate into the other. It is also a vital experience; our way of denying death. Our Western and Judeo-Christian curse is the belief that death is horrible. I don't believe in the integration of souls but rather in the com-

plete dispersion of the self. That is the most important thing one can do. For what reason would we preserve ourselves all tied up with strings? We have a dish in Argentina called *matambre*. It's beef rolled up and tied so the stuffing cannot ooze out. I run across people every day who remind me of *matambre*, all trussed up with strings. We're not *matambre*; we expand, transform, change.

There seems to be a sense of revenge between people in sexual relations, a sort of animal urgency—in the wolf-man, for example. Eroticism encompasses the transgression of taboos; there are peeping Toms, masturbators, lesbians, masochists, playful games, and symbolic sacrifices.

I don't know about the word revenge. Evidently these things happen at a very profound level where one is neither man nor woman. I was going to refer to the female reaction to male aggression. But I don't think that is even certain. Frankly, I don't know.

I'd like to know more about El gato eficaz. Its genesis.

El gato eficaz was a miracle. I was in Iowa as a fellow in the writer's program. In that place full of neurotic authors, I was very lonely. We writers are all neurotic and as individuals we can put up with ourselves; but in a group, it is much worse. We were under terrible stress, yet we were supposed to be creative. Months went by and no one was able to produce a sentence. And there we were, hysterical, playing pinball until about two in the afternoon. We had turned our daily schedules upside down. It was glorious; for example, it was snowing and frightfully cold, so we played "tropics" with the heat blasting as we danced to tropical music. At the same time we switched our routine so that we woke up at two in the afternoon and went to bed at five in the morning. In the midst of all that, at eleven one morning (daybreak for us), I awakened with an idea and a terrible need to write. I said to myself, "No, it can't be. I'll keep sleeping, this is ridiculous." But it persisted until finally that positive impulse won out (usually the negative one wins, the one that doesn't want me to write). So half asleep, I grabbed a notebook and began to write, and as I was writing, I thought, "How strange. This is weird and very interesting." But when one transcribes a dream, I thought, it always seems fascinating until later when you awaken and read it. Then it is a disaster, and you throw it in the trash. But I finished it thinking all along, "How can these ideas be occurring to me?" And sure enough, at two in the afternoon I woke up to discover that what I had written was very odd and interesting, the first three pages of *El gato eficaz.* I figured it was a short story; I read it to my friends who listened enthusiastically. And so the book poured forth like a waterfall, and I allowed it to flow without censoring that awesome relationship between love and death. I had not yet read

[Georges] Bataille. Later on I discovered how profound the material really was.

You wrote it all at once then?

I set it down everywhere. In the elevators of the building where we lived and in hamburger joints.

Did you revise it very much?

A little bit. You see, I have a theory that my subconscious functions very well so the work was already completed. There was some cacophony that needed to be changed. I felt that a certain rhythm had to be maintained and respected.

Is **El gato eficaz** *a novel?*

I consider it to be a novel because everything is a novel.

Everything?

Everything that has a certain form. I believe the word novel now includes many forms, its sense is broader nowadays.

But **El gato eficaz** *has a very fragmented structure. Why?*

We are fragmented; nothing is univocal; there is no unity. God is unity; we are pieces.

Most of the novel is narrated in the first person voice of the protagonist, but every once in a while an omniscient voice, apart from the action, provides a commentary. Why this perspective from beyond?

Every now and then I feel somewhat vain narrating in the first person, saying "*I* think this is *the* truth." The truth is neither here nor there, it is here *and* there. Possibly that perspective of a narrator behind another narrator is my way of setting things straight, but above all, of putting things in their place which is no place at all. Nothing is certain, nothing is a lie; everything is and is not, is outside and inside, and is positive and negative. Possibly it's a search for that "other truth."

The language in **El gato eficaz** *is filled with run-on words, partial words, neologisms,* lunfardo *slang. To what can we attribute your playfulness with language?*

That was an approach to language which was more successful in *Como en la guerra.* It is a certain irreverent stand before language. Words are not so rigid; we have rendered them inflexible and emptied them of internal connotations. Words express much more than we want to say: So, in *El gato eficaz,* there is a sort of respectful disrespect, a need for words to belie their meanings but without allowing complete freedom. Neologisms don't interest me to the extent that simple words do.

As far as **Como en la guerra** *and* El gato eficaz *are concerned, what is your opinion of experimentalism in contemporary prose?*

Nothing should be forced; experimentation must respond to an intimate need. Then, of course, it is no longer experimental for it is simply another search.

Then it is a personal search in the realm of language, as well?

All novels, especially modern ones, question language in order to divest it of its crutches, to rejuvenate it, to make it more flexible, return to it an original vitality. Language communicates the writer's feelings and the reader's. Since I want each reader to undertake his own reading, I infuse language with a good dose of ambiguity.

What of the other games in **El gato eficaz**: *the inclusion of newspaper clippings, poems, outlines. To what extent are you pulling the reader's leg with the use of "pseudo" forms: pseudoscientific, pseudovirgin, pseudo-organized?*

Any jargon is a source of great entertainment. Pulling the reader's leg implies pulling my own; a true sense of humor begins at home with the author who can laugh at herself.

There are many parodies in **El gato eficaz**. *Is a criticism of society implied?*

Yes. It is the only way we are permitted to criticize any number of taboos.

You have written several political short stories. Can you explain to us the importance of politics and the often parodic treatment of it in your work?

With *Como en la guerra* we were seeing a very politicized period in Argentina; the novel captured that intensity. I think there is a message in the novel, and that's one of its defects. You see, we Argentineans feel ourselves to be Europeans, not very Latin American. But we *are* Latin American and we don't want to hear that.

In **El gato eficaz,** *it seems that all vital phenomena which are supposedly contrary to death—the-white-dogs-of-life, the spring, plants—still succumb to destruction like the cats-of-death themselves. The only difference seems to lie in the cyclical nature of life and death where the seasons or plants are concerned. In connection with such resurrections, you refer to "the splendorous fertility after the cataclysm, the primordial power of ashes."*

Of course, in *El gato eficaz* death is vital. That is, accepting death is fatal; the idea of eternity is a kind of constant death.

> **Metamorphosis is a constant, and it is one of the things in life that disturbs me most. I try to instill constant change in those men who approach me. But people fear change. I, too, am afraid of it but cannot avoid it; I know it must be.**
> —*Luisa Valenzuela*

So then, life and death are similar, if not synonymous.

Very similar. It all came about in a strange way. We were discussing the fear of flying, and I boasted that I was not at all afraid of death, that death was of no interest to me. And suddenly this terrible cascade poured forth from me, *El gato eficaz*. Evidently death is the human topic par excellence. But it is the theme of life. Without life there is no death; without death there is no life. By denying death we automatically deny life.

Would you discuss the omnipresent transformations in **El gato eficaz***?*

Metamorphosis is a constant, and it is one of the things in life that disturbs me most. I try to instill constant change in those men who approach me. But people fear change. I, too, am afraid of it but cannot avoid it; I know it must be. Nothing is as it seems, everything is that and something more. So, onward, take heart. That's what Cortázar used to call walking along the edge of an abyss. If we are to walk, let's walk on the edge of a precipice knowing that something else lies beyond. Living is dying a little (so the song goes), but being conscious of death is existing intensely. Forgetting about death is like being a fruit compote in a refrigerator, in suspension, between parentheses.

Living intensely always implies change?

Yes. If we can, to the extent that we can, metamorphosis should persist; but almost always our changes are meager in comparison to our wishes. But it's worth a try.

In **El gato eficaz** *music—especially that of the flute, jazz, and song—bring about metamorphosis and erotic episodes.*

Yes, you see I once went to the village in New York where Herbie Mann was playing jazz flute. And in the middle of a number, all of a sudden I found myself standing on a chair howling with the black musicians who were going crazy. It was an electrifying experience, those notes that erupted from

the vibraphone and the guitar. We all acted very strangely together. I believe that such a magical backdrop exists in literature, too. One reaches a state of the subconscious that [Carl] Jung called collective: That flute moved me then. And many years later, a book appeared by a Bolivian named Taboada Terán, *Manchay Puytu, el amor que quiso ocultar Dios* [Manchay Puytu, the Love that God Tried to Hide]. It's the ancient Bolivian legend (which I never knew before) about a monk, a priest who was in love with an Indian woman and lived with her during the period of the Spanish conquest of America. When the Indian woman died, the priest became desperate. He fashioned a flute from her tibia bone, and with the music it made, he resurrected her. That song is the Manchay Puytu; it has been prohibited in Bolivia for centuries. So you see how everything is linked together. A long time after I had written *El gato eficaz*, I read a book on Shamanism by Mircea Eliade about all kinds of magical rites among the Tibetans. And in *El gato eficaz*, such magical practices appear, too.

In **El gato eficaz** *there are amusing anecdotes, also, based on the exaggeration of the unusual. For example, the couple that must be separated in order to make love ends up founding the mystical sect of "telecoitus."*

I believe that a sense of humor is indispensable in literature, in life, in everything. Besides, there are small incidents that prompt the development of a theme.

In **El gato eficaz,** *alluding to the lame man, you say, "In pain and effort resides triumph." Do you feel one must suffer in order to attain certain ends?*

I don't know. I believe that one ought to take the right road, not always the easiest one. Facility impedes fidelity somehow.

Why is the tendency to corporal disintegration so great in that novel? Sometimes characters divest themselves of bodily parts or end up a bloody mass.

You know, I learned afterwards, while reading Jacques Lacan, about the ghost of the dismembered body. It seems that one of the forms of insanity involves the notion of imaginary anatomy that may be seen as whole, dismembered, or disintegrated. All those who reach beyond the threshold of reason view that imaginary anatomy as if it were foreign to their own bodies. Therefore, to a crazy person, the ghost of the dismembered body is one of the most important visions. I didn't know that when I wrote *El gato eficaz*.

So why did you write that way then?

My subconscious. Evidently we harbor this without realizing it. When I say crazy, I mean illuminated. I believe that religion is closely related to insanity; they are two faces of the same coin.

*The mask and the disguise often play an important role in both **El gato eficaz** and **Como en la guerra**. Would you comment on their significance in relation to transvestism, metamorphosis, and the revelation of death or clairvoyance?*

I cannot comment because I don't know. Whatever I know is in those texts, involuntarily. We wear a series of masks; we're never our deep, true, unique selves.

And transvestism?

Transsexuality as a theme fascinates me. I believe every human being is transsexual and the idea of a perfect, true sex is false. We all harbor both sexes; just as we have many masks, so we are both sexes only because there is no further choice.

What of the revelation of death or clairvoyance behind those masks or disguises?

Perhaps the only truth is death; it is the only moment of re-integration with the cosmos, of removing all masks. It lasts such a short time and afterwards becomes useless. That's its charm; it is a gratuitous act.

*But at the end of **Como en la guerra**, at least, the protagonist doesn't die.*

Well, not everyone has to perish.

Como en la guerra *and* **El gato eficaz** *could be considered surrealistic novels. In them, you esteem chance, exploration, dreams, nighttime, desire, imagination, exceptions to the rules, and that which is illogical, playful, and unusual. Surrealist symbols such as water and masks abound; there are constant metamorphoses; there is the Gothic horror of vampires, the attraction to murderers and the erotic, and woman as the key to the absolute. Some digressions from the surrealist novel can be seen in their fragmented points of view and their political messages.*

The surrealist movement really opened doors, whereas other interesting literary movements have closed doors, like the "new novel" in France. I don't believe in profoundly surrealistic, automatic writing. I believe in structuring prose. That's why Lacan is important to me, for he structures the subconscious. My "other," as Lacan would say, my subconscious, is infinitely more intelligent than I; and I believe that the human race is more intelligent than its individuals. We are social and political animals. And we are surrounded by a dogmatism (which I greatly fear) permitted by politics and religion. People who profess to dogmatic "truths" terrify me.

We are innately political; we need to fight for a cause, an ideal, a hope.

*Does the guerrilla theater in **Como en la guerra** have anything to do with the Escambray group in Cuba?*

I don't know of that Cuban theater. No. It deals with some Argentineans who were putting on productions in the mines and with some Mexican friends whose puppet shows toured small villages exploring the local problems by narrating them in marionette theater. That way the villagers saw themselves mirrored in the productions. So the guerrilla theater in ***Como en la guerra*** is a great mixture of many experiences and my aspiration to create a dialogue with the people, offering them a mirror, the possibility of seeing themselves reflected so they can deduce their own answers.

In your fictional theater, a kind of anthropophagy occurs.

No, it doesn't.

It is suggested, though.

I believe that all love is anthropophagous.

What do you mean?

The problem is that love is anthropophagy.

Why?

There is a need to devour the other, to incorporate him into us. Anthropophagy is not only a form of cruelty but also a ritual form of making someone part of us by taking him into us bodily.

There seems to be an interesting balance between incorporating the other into us and giving of oneself to the other.

Yes. Good.

Because as you mentioned before, the "little death" is giving of oneself or losing isolation to gain continuity with the other for a moment.

But in our primitive villages, above all in the mountainous zones of Peru, the Inca empire regions of the high plateau, when a warrior or a great hunter died, they used to eat pieces of his flesh to recover his magical powers. They didn't kill him to eat him, but when he died, there was a need to physically incorporate his body into theirs in order to perpetuate his virtues. So that ritual anthropophagy conserves the greatness that the hunter represented.

I wonder if we could now turn to your opinion about the most important women authors today in Latin America?

I don't know if "important" is the right word to use because then I could mention the best known authors. But there are those that I esteem within a panorama of Latin America in general. For example, the Brazilian Nélida Piñón. She is a very serious writer who works with a profound literary knowledge. Albalucía Angel in Colombia is highly imaginative, very serious. Usually one believes that women write just to rid themselves of ghosts or other obsessions. But these are full-time authors.

Men also write to exorcise themselves. Why not women?

Because no great author writes just for that reason. Not women nor men. It would be too easy. No one rids himself of those ghosts anyway.

But there is an attempt, nevertheless.

All right. But gossip has it that women write a kind of diary to exorcise themselves, while men write as a kind of quest. It is not so. These women, and many others, write with a serious professionalism. The Colombian Albalucía Angel won a very important national prize (and justifiably so) and engaged in a fierce battle with her male compatriots. *Estaba la pájara pinta sentada en el verde limón* [The Speckled Bird Was Seated in the Green Lemon Tree] is an extraordinary novel. It has no sex. That is to say, it is an absolutely strong novel.

But, do novels have a sex?

Yes. Fortunately. Some are tremendously feminine and glorious.

I don't understand. What makes a novel feminine?

I think there is a feminine voice if a woman assumes her real voice, which can become very strong, very intense. For example, some of my mother's [Luisa Mercedes Levinson] novels are feminine. *La isla de los organilleros* (*The Organ Grinders' Island*) is written from a female perspective and yet has a certain force that many masculine novels would like to have. And there are many masculine novels that are not necessarily better than others because of that.

What characterizes a female novel and a male novel?

The subconscious has no sex, as we all know; it is transsexual. But, evidently all words cross through the barriers of our consciousness and are colored by it. There are men who have explored the feminine soul with a great deal of mastery but, in general, such an exploration into the pro-

foundly aquatic and visceral world of women ... well, I don't believe that a man could have written *El gato eficaz*. It is a view of eroticism from the female point of view. You know men can be tender, also, like women, but men don't allow themselves that trait. I feel sorry for men, at times, because they have to assume a role imposed on them since childhood: a strong man who ought not shed a tear, who should always perform sexually, and be the pillar of the family. Who'd want to do all that all the time? Why can't he be allowed to have weaknesses?

Such roles must be more rigid in Hispanic societies.

I think it's worse in the United States.

Why?

Because there it is a farce. The mask of machismo in Hispanic societies allows for certain weaknesses. But in your society, supposedly egalitarian, the North American business executive has to act like an executive who screws around. We at least have a definition for macho, but you don't, so it must be more difficult for men and for women. We, women, may undertake a complete rebellion but in your country there are many ways to rebel. It is more difficult because the means vary.

Are there certain characteristics, sensitivities, or themes which are more likely attributed to female fiction than to male?

More than themes, it is a question of sensitivities, or perhaps, the angle from which one approaches the same topic of interest to both sexes. I became conscious of this just a short while ago. I thought it was marvelous when they would tell me, "You write like a man." Now it's an insult. I realized that I didn't give a damn whether they said, "You write like a man" or "like a woman" or "like a tortoise." Besides, I believe that real strides will be made when we become more conscious of our true sexuality and write from the womb. I once had an argument with Salvador Elizondo during a radio broadcast in Mexico. While he was interviewing me, he asked, "Do you think there are female and male writers? I mean, feminine writers? Wait. Do you believe that woman write in a feminine way and men in a virile manner?" So I answered him. "Look. Feminine and masculine, as you please. But they're not the same because if a man writes with his balls (scandalous on university radio in Mexico), then women have to write with their ovaries." He was taken aback but interested in the problem, and we did another show on another day. In the last analysis one must offer what one has to offer. We ought not pretend to have what we do not. We have internal reproductive sex organs. Why should we feign an alien form of sexuality, and why should we deny our own sexuality, which is just as strong or perhaps stronger than theirs?

But do you feel that physiological traits influence sociological phenomena?

Yes.

And sociological experience influences writing?

Yes. Absolutely. But I don't feel that we are inferior or less forceful or have fewer possibilities.

You believe, then, that there are some circumstances or situations with which women can deal and men cannot?

Yes. I believe that we are able to approach certain events that men cannot and vice versa.

Physiologically?

No. I'm referring to the exploration of language, of literature. The political power of a word, its ideological importance, is different for a man than for a woman. I feel that words possess power, they are charged with power which we have diluted and filed away so as to render words harmless. Society has done that. For example, the word "revolution" is used indiscriminately—a "revolution" of hairstyles. There are more subtle examples which don't occur to me right now. One of the few duties of a writer is the restoration of the true meaning of words and the search for that which lies behind the myth: the transgression of the myth, its origin. It could be that a man's approach to these problems is not the same as a woman's. Perhaps the truth (I don't know if that's a good word), that is to say, the encounter with a certain form of reality, would be a combination of a man's and a woman's view. Not one or the other but the convergence of the two to render a truth.

Do you have any favorites among the women writers of Latin America?

Those I've already mentioned, and the Costa Rican Carmen Naranjo and the Venezuelan Antonieta Madrid.

And male writers?

One writer opened my eyes, and I continue to esteem him as a novelist: Samuel Beckett. Some of Cortázar's works. [José María] Arguedas interests me a lot right now.

Why?

I imagine because of his search into indigenous myths. Taboada Terán, also, the Bolivian. *Yo el supremo* [*I Reign*

Supreme] by [Augusto] Roa Bastos, the Paraguayan, is an extraordinary novel; and the most important novel of these times is *Terra nostra* [*Terra nostra*] by [Carlos] Fuentes. It seemed to me a cosmogony, a marvelous, subtle, intelligent cosmovision, a game with time, space, and doubles. There is a sense of humor; it is well-written; the characters ring true. You piece together your own novel as you read along, discovering this very strange and complex plot like a puzzle. For me it is the most important novel of the seventies.

What do you think of the "boom" in Latin American literature?

There are marvelous books and very interesting writers who, all of a sudden, made people take note of literature as they never have before. But it was an exaggerated phenomenon.

What are you working on now?

A new novel. I just finished a book of short stories, and I also write for newspapers to stay in touch with life. So the saying goes. But I think that's just another pretense.

> **What society accepts or rejects ought not concern the female writer. What cannot be said even by her because it remains censured in her dark subconscious—that is serious. They are the only truths worth being written.**
> **—Luisa Valenzuela**

Does the situation of the female author in Spanish America differ from that of the male author? Does she have the same opportunities to publish her work and circulate it in her own country? Abroad? In translations? The same opportunities to win national or international literary prizes?

We artists, in general, tend to believe ourselves to be a special race, but this is only one more aspect of our illusions. For that very reason, a woman writer's situation is different from a man's, since it is a matter of one more reflexion of woman's place with respect to man. And I don't want to begin with complaints, that are not always so, about problems concerning publishing or being translated. No. I prefer to circumscribe my comments to a simple fact, which Tillie Olsen points out so well: a woman, who manages a house and raises children, lacks the free time so necessary for writing. And, above all, she lacks a wife to support her in everything and, if necessary, to act as her secretary. I believe that those are the basic problems, besides an undeniable lack of recognition on the part of the publishing house machinery in Hispanic America that separates us most from the Nobel Prize.

Are there certain taboo themes for women writers that would be accepted more easily by society if the author were a man?

What society accepts or rejects ought not concern the female writer. What cannot be said even by her because it remains censured in her dark subconscious—that is serious. They are the only truths worth being written. But women, who until recently were prohibited the use of so-called dirty language or harsh expressions, undoubtedly find it more difficult than men to transgress such barriers.

In your fiction, do you consciously or subconsciously broach themes that specifically pertain to the Spanish American woman? Are you concerned with woman's socioeconomic role in Spanish America?

This first answer to this question would be a flat "no." But since there is always a double game of mirrors, I think that unconsciously, it would be "yes." Undoubtedly, the problems of the Hispanic American woman worry me—not always the problems, many times I am amazed at her enormous fortitude—as do those of others in our countries who have no voice, even though they are so rich in perceptions.

Recently, have you been able to earn a living exclusively by writing fiction?

Let's say yes, but in the least creative aspects of literary tasks. I teach literature; I've been an author-in-residence at important institutions; I'm invited to conferences and write essays. There are very few people in this world who succeed in earning a good living by writing fiction exclusively. Of course, all the other benefits derive unquestionably from the fact that I write fiction, a crazy adventure that's fortunately very respected in this country where I've chosen to live. If I hadn't published books, I'd never be a university professor; I don't even have an Argentinean degree.

What are you writing now? Does it sustain your interests expressed in earlier works? Are there new experiments, directions?

I just finished a book of, let's say novellas. It's difficult to catalogue them, because in this case, though there is a close relationship between the four texts, the form varies and one cannot say if they are really short stories or novels. The title is *Cambio de armas* [*Change of the Guard*], and the theme is the ineffable, all that is not and cannot be said between a man and a woman. I've also written a small collection of poems that would be a new direction for me if it weren't that I consider them prose in truncated lines, as they say, the inverse of poems in prose. The real experiment will be, or perhaps is already, a work I'm planning on masks in which the fiction will be intimately linked to the essay, to the chronicle, or to mere information.

Presently, what kind of readings interest you most?

Scientific ones, as always.

There are many Spanish American writers who do not live or have not lived at some time in their own countries but rather have written from abroad—for political, social, or personal reasons—in voluntary or involuntary exile: Cortázar, [Gabriel] García Márquez, [Mario] Vargas Llosa, [Manuel] Puig, [José] Donoso. Does this situation apply to women writers from Spanish America? Do they feel the need or desire to distance themselves from their social context? Can they do so as easily as male authors?

Woman is the mountain who must go to Muhammed. Therefore, no matter how much she may want or need to emigrate, even in questions of life or death, many times she cannot do so. She cannot leave her children behind, or she must follow her husband, or some other reason that society has invented for anchoring the reproductive uterus. Woman ought to be passive. Right? Of course. Luckily, the list of writers who are away from their respective countries is long and productive: Sara Gallardo, Cristina Perri Rossi, Albalucía Angel, Alicia Dujovne Ortiz, Helena Araújo, me. But this is also known as the diaspora. It would be interesting to be able to meet more often, not only every two or three years during the famous Congress of Inter-American Women Writers. Or, at least, have a publication that would put us in contact with one another.

Since we met for the interview, have you written other books? Would you describe the importance you attach to your recently published fiction?

Libro que no muerde [*A Book That Doesn't Bite*] is really a small anthology of short stories, some from 1966, others from 1976, and some new brief, almost philosophical reflections. As for "La hermana estrella o el señor de Tucuru" (or whatever this novel will ultimately be called), which Gregory Rabassa is now translating, I believe it to be my most ambitious work. They say that after the age of forty, a novelist truly matures. Well, here's the result. I think I've said some important things, but since I said them ironically, completely clothed in black humor, I don't know whether everyone will perceive them. For me, an Argentinean, it was the only way I could touch on a theme which would be too painful otherwise.

Robert Emmet Long (review date 9 July 1979)

SOURCE: "Police State Paranoia," in *Christian Science Monitor*, July 9, 1979, p. 19.

[*Below, Long finds* Strange Things Happen Here *"stranger than strange," noting that fear and paranoia permeate the collection.*]

Strange Things Happen Here, a collection of 22 severely brief stories and a nouvelle by the gifted Argentinean writer Luisa Valenzuela, is stranger than strange. One of the early stories, **"The Best Shod,"** hardly longer than a page, might serve as an example. It recounts the good fortune of beggars in a South American city who are able to find a plentiful plunder—in the shoes of corpses, hidden in vacant lots, sewers, and thickets. The corpses often have bullet holes or have been burned in the course of being tortured by electric cattle prods. The misfortune of these victims of political oppression provides a bountiful harvest.

Valenzuela's landscapes are insistently baroque. Her characters are dehumanized by police-state conditions, under which citizens are encouraged to inform on one another, and innocent people are taken away in the night by the police, or wait to be. Fear permeates her stories, in which the paranoid suspicions of the authorities become everyone's paranoia, and the world seems cut adrift from its moorings of sanity. The bizarre nature of the "real" can be seen at every level of the society Valenzuela depicts. In the title story, two urban cast-abouts find a briefcase in a café and snatch it as an unexpected prize, but are then paralyzed with the fear of what might be in it—counterfeit money or, more likely, a terrorist's bomb. How could they explain to the police if they were found with it?

That night, after returning the briefcase, unopened, to the café, one of them has a dream in which a bomb explodes; but as he awakens he cannot tell if the explosion he has heard is real or part of his dream.

Herbert Gold (review date 11 September 1983)

SOURCE: "Magic and Metaphors of Mystery," in *Los Angeles Times Book Review,* September 11, 1983, p. 12.

[*In the review below, Gold claims that* The Lizard's Tail *suffers from Valenzuela's lack of focus on her subjects, stating that she "broods about making magic too much to be able to make the magic."*]

The notion that a writer can accumulate notes, scenes, assorted peeks at sexy stuff, italicized thoughts, a little dialogue, myth and mystery without numbering the pages, and then perform the work of writing a novel merely by gazing prayerfully and distractedly at this heap of material and adding page numbers—this has done some damage to the art of the novel. Well, not to the art itself, of course, which has

a vigorous tradition of survival despite all assaults, but to the craft as it is occasionally practiced. The no-page-number technique requires a long work table, for spreading out all the material, and perhaps a long weekend of rearranging, but not a long breath, for imagining the lives of important strangers.

The late numbering of pages asks the reader to make a leap of faith: This is so hectic, it must be profound. The horseperson has ridden madly off in so many directions, the bloody fragments must make a superior unity.

Not necessarily so.

Luisa Valenzuela, who comes to us with much praise from South America and Susan Sontag ("There is nothing like *A Lizard's Tail* in contemporary Latin American fiction"), very soon sets our hearts to beating more slowly:

> A serious matter, the drums. They're the strength of the world that lies over the border. Drums, tambours, *gongas*, snares, bongos, *tamborils, marugas, guaguas*, gourds, tambourines, *huehuetes*, tablas. Those. I get strength from the drums and I give strength back to the drums threefold. The drumhead of my skin resounds, Estrella pounds in wild pulsations, I flail about and vibrate as if the hands of ten black drummers were playing me. Twenty hands with cold blue palms stimulating me with the sweet intensity. . . .

And there's more.

The pounding Estrella of this quotation is both the third testicle and the sister of the protagonist of this book. I hate to disagree with the estimable Susan Sontag, but it sometimes seems as if everything in Latin American literature is like this, except for Borges, of course, who writes short. The action takes place, or *perhaps* takes place, in Argentina during the awful time of "disappearances," when the Perons killed and looted their country and Isabella Peron looked with favor on the magic cult in her honor. The Sorcerer who is the protagonist here is based on Isabella Peron's Minister of Public Well-Being. In *Time* magazine, Luisa Valenzuela has been quoted as saying, "Magical realism was a beautiful resting place, but the thing is to go forward."

The pain and anarchy of Argentina drive many a writer up the wall. Witness V. S. Naipaul's cold, brilliant and aloof essay, "The Return of Eva Peron"—but perhaps he had the advantage of not really caring much. Valenzuela shows flashes of wit and brutal cynicism, which at times compensate for the lack of novelistic energy: "I obey a Superior Being who dictates my behavior. I obey Myself." Or, at the end of the book: "Tyrannies are not what they used to be. Now they have replacement parts. One president falls and another is ready to take over."

Throughout the book there are epigrams, flashes of description, exalted moments of Writing. Certain conventional metaphors of mystery and degeneration receive their due: cocaine, ants, magic mushrooms, highfalutin polymorphous sex. (That's going forward from magic realism? The machine is in reverse gear.) "After making love—and there I have no reason to complain, it was always perfect with Navoni—I always put my foot in my mouth." This sounds like some special fancy Latin thing he or she is doing.

Valenzuela goes on to discuss exalted states of mind. There is no doubt about her strong feeling concerning the corruptions and richnesses of Argentine life, the despair and pain, the compulsive dreaming. The problem for her book is expressed in [Fyodor] Dostoevsky's attack on [Ivan] Turgenev: He pays too much attention to the tears on his own cheeks. When he describes a shipwreck, he tells how bad it makes him feel. He should pay attention to the drowning children, not to his own drooping gaze.

Dostoevsky was unfair to Turgenev, but his point about the vanity of writers is a good one. Perhaps a more generous case for Luisa Valenzuela and this book could be made; she is trying for intelligence and trying for magic; but the novelist here points to herself too much, points to the catastrophe—her ostensible subject—not enough. She broods about making magic too much to be able to make the magic. She wants to be wild; that's not the same as wildness. The novelist, as W. H. Auden said, must wear the uniforms of the just and the unjust alike—not just a gaudy motley. A tragedy needs to be placed in time, not in the question, "Your story no longer deserves to be written?"

Luisa Valenzuela has the grace to utter the criticism of herself, to both express the problem of her book and confess it. "I move, I keep on writing, with growing disillusionment and with a certain disgust. Disgust even with myself, for believing that literature can save us, for doubting that literature can save us. . . ."

Ana María Hernández (review date Spring 1984)

SOURCE: A review of *The Lizard's Tail,* in *World Literature Today,* Vol. 58, No. 2, Spring, 1984, p. 247.

[*In the following review, Hernández comments on Valenzuela's verbal wit, black humor, and the Argentine vision of magic realism in* The Lizard's Tail.]

Carlos Fuentes has hailed Luisa Valenzuela as "the heiress of Latin American fiction." That heritage includes the theme of the caudillo and the vision of magic realism, both of which attain new heights in the course of this novel. There is nothing unusual about this combination: both elements appeared in [Alejo] Carpentier's *El recurso del método* and in García Márquez's *El otoño del patriarca*—not to mention [Miguel Angel] Asturias's much earlier masterpiece, *El señor Presidente.* The major difference between Valenzuela's novel and the preceding ones is that ***The Lizard's Tail*** takes place in Argentina, the leader in civilization's battle against *barbarie.* But then, Argentina is no longer seen the way it used to be seen. It appears that Ezequiel Martínez Estrada's prediction in the last lines of *Radiografía de la pampa* comes true with a vengeance in Luisa Valenzuela's novel, just as it came true in the Argentina of the seventies. "The strongholds of civilization were invaded by specters that had been thought to be vanquished," said Don Ezequiel. These resurrected specters of *barbarie* people the pages of Valenzuela's novel and help bring about the necessary catharsis that must precede any lasting reconstruction in Argentina today.

The Sorcerer—the protagonist in the novel—is fashioned after López Rega, Isabel Perón's minister of social welfare, who is said to have ruled Argentina through sorcery and terror. The novel chronicles his rise to power, his overthrow by the military and his plot to return to power. Valenzuela's intricate wit and her sense of (black) humor are evinced in her masterful parodies of Perón (the Generalississimo), his second wife (the Intruder) and the enlightened opposition, who speak about their enemies with terms borrowed from semiotics: "I think we should analyze one by one every link in the chain of signifiers that have been presented to us . . . our duty now consists in dismantling these symbols and interpreting the unconscious discourse of the government." Her appreciation of Evita's still ominous hold on the Latin American imagination is reflected in the sections dealing with the glorious return of The Dead One's embalmed body.

Readers cannot help but be amused by references to rituals in honor of Eshú, Shangó, Iemanjá and other Yoruba deities (in Argentina?) known in the Caribbean as Eleguá, Changó and Yemayá. The differences in spelling remind us that these influences entered Argentina from Brazil, the intermittent enemy where *barbarie* reigned supreme, malgré Sarmiento.

Valenzuela's narrative persona becomes personified halfway through the novel (with the author's own name, or as "The Curly Lady") and engages in a battle of narratives with the Sorcerer for control of the plot. It is not clear who comes out the conqueror. Toward the end the Sorcerer, who had literally inflated himself in a most peculiar manner, explodes from inside his protective pyramid. His blood reaches the capital as a thin streak reminiscent of red ants, those minuscule arch-symbols for the unconscious. Gregory Rabassa, as usual, has elevated translation to the stature of art by pre-serving the puns, the colloquial flavor, the wordplay and the stylistic accomplishments of Valenzuela's text.

Ana M. Fores (essay date Fall 1986)

SOURCE: "Valenzuela's *Cat-O-Nine-Deaths*," in *Review of Contemporary Fiction*, Vol. 6, No. 3, Fall, 1986, pp. 39-47.

[*In the following essay, Fores examines diverse ways language, or the word, performs in* Cat-O-Nine-Deaths.]

The importance of *Cat-O-Nine-Deaths* (*El gato eficaz*) does not rely on setting, theme, or even characters, but on the function of the word, the process that man imposes on language as a communicant. The protagonist of the future is the word; it is the only character that counts in all reality: "I am a trap made of paper and mere printed letters."

> **The importance of *Cat-O-Nine-Deaths* (*El gato eficaz*) does not rely on setting, theme, or even characters, but on the function of the word, the process that man imposes on language as a communicant. The protagoist of the future is the word.**
> **—Ana M. Fores**

The novel itself has no plot. If fragments of a story of a mysterious dark love, or segments of a cripple bitterly descending "a cement stairway" could be called a plot, then there is one. Also, unlike most traditional novels, Valenzuela's includes no characters in *Cat-O-Nine-Deaths*. The protagonist, who at times is a woman, changes always, in a metamorphosis where becoming male is just another phase. The only constancy in this character is that she/he has no constancy. This character/non-character we follow through the mechanical staircases, the mechanized escalators. Margo Glantz, in a Mexican literary newsletter, *Bellas Artes*, explains this elusive writer:

> Maybe one of the keys to Luisa Valenzuela's narrative is not in the difficulty of naming reality but in the impossibility of giing things their true name. As if anything were truth in a reality which in itself is imperfect, always on the eve of destruction and captured from the outside like something ready to explode.

Only in her narrative voice do we see stability. The voice (the writing—the language—which is the body, a body we are never sure of) is the only being which pursues us, even

though, in itself, it also changes into different phases of being.

This novel, filled with a terrorizing surrealism for its readers, is sublime in its unconscious discourse. Valenzuela demonstrates with ferocious ability an automatic and incoherent writing, which simultaneously evokes a poetic lyricism and magic all its own. *Cat-O-Nine-Deaths* is a novel which "takes root at the point where eroticism and death find each other." Valenzuela joins the two with an ability which becomes extremely organized, yet at the same time is poetic and intuitive. This seems to be a paradox. The "montage" which she perfects with language, with the word, becomes obvious upon reading the book. This perfect structural solidity opens doors to other worlds; what makes her most enthusiastic is finding those words, that language, which shocks the audience but at the same time makes that audience think. These hypotheses are exposed in *Cat-O-Nine-Deaths.*

In this novel, Valenzuela uses a variety of methods and their contradictions. Sections which are filled with the most profound thoughts have no punctuation whatsoever:

> I do not want to have fornicons on my face or pimp(el)s on my ass or anything that would bother the free flowing of my beauty I want to ame lions I want to have a scalpel at hand so I can cut my tongue each day I want and I want and I want not to belong to anything ecause belonging erases all possibility of revolution w hi ch is the onyl pruth in man in man and in woman too. . . .

She mixes both—the form with the idea—to give us a fusion of life where the only recognizable truth is eternal chaos. She also joins words together, and invents others; she floods our minds with constant repetitions, and writes each word as if it were an unconscious flow, a being without any form or structure, absolute order without logical synthesis.

Valenzuela not only plays with language, but she also transposes sensations. The senses become interchangeable, until we do not know consciously what is occurring. The novel, to be read as well as to have been written, has to ensnare intuition so that it works in spite of the illogicity of language. This novel cannot be read on a superficial, analytical level; we, as readers, must intuit it: "My musical ear will compose symphonies of flatulences and will arrange the cackling of our empty guts. My acute aesthetic vision will discover the sweet greenish blush of those beings that show their ribs."

The writer, now speaking as a male, consciously voices ideas which are completely revealing; she does not realize she is exposing her authorial self. Language speaks *through* her, and the outlet of that unconscious flow becomes art itself.

As [Erich] Neumann writes in his book, *Art and the Creative Unconscious*:

> The creative individual seems to enjoy such prestige partly because he exemplifies the utmost transformation possible in our time, but above all because the world he creates is an adequate image of the primordial one reality, not yet split by consciousness—a reality that only a personality creating from out of its wholeness is able to create.

That is why, when Valenzuela wrote this work, she could not impose a specific structure. The methodology intuitively formed itself. Because a traditional novel cannot be written with such rigidity, Valenzuela, like many of her colleagues today, has preferred using the method of the New Novel, or the antinovel. This form includes everything; it has no limits; its openness enhances the liberty of the writer, and the word itself.

In *Cat-O-Nine-Deaths,* there are no sexes and all sexes; the woman is not so much a woman, and the man is not a real man. Neither are we so superior, like the hermaphrodites, that we are gods and not animals. We always believe that we belong to that higher spiritual abode where the gods reside and we forget that, in part, we are also bestial. What we have to remember is that in everything we are sublime, whether we are, in essence, a god or a toad. "Frogs are singing, I am singing." Valenzuela, through her ambiguous use of sexuality, establishes a sexual vacuum, eliminating the confusion which genders create. Throughout all the changes, however, the protagonist always returns to the feminine: does that mean, then, that Valenzuela believes woman is superior to man? "This is my confession and also my legacy: future generations will know to what point I approached him to destroy him, how I schemed in elevators to take his soul and to engrave my seal in the depths of his flesh, so that I could retire, dignified, leaving him at the mercy of my fire."

The voice in *Cat-O-Nine-Deaths* is constantly changing. At times, the narrative "I" becomes the undisguised author, Luisa Valenzuela. This narrative voice forms a type of confessional: "I am not writing a novel, but actually only noting with the little life that's left me this major prose which is my testament." Like the protagonist who undergoes various metamorphoses—from woman to cat to tarantula to man/god ("I am a young Apollonian athlete")—language, in its stability, bores her. Because of this, Valenzuela constantly includes stylistic changes throughout *Cat-O-Nine-Deaths.* At times, we see a narcissistic protagonist: "all of myself a cat's paw, a lickable cushion, a bit in love with myself because I am so easygoing . . . I ask myself what compels me—me, so beautiful—to be an accomplice to a cat of death. . . ." We

also see her loving life; even though she may see it as complete chaos, she still celebrates what she encounters: "For a short time I integrate, I sway with his rhythm, let myself be trapped by his self-deception. Most of all when he makes his music, when he becomes the music and his teeth chatter." The only constancy in this vision is that everything that the protagonist feels changes, like everything in life. All appearance is illusory; change is the sole factor which has a static possibility in the reality of being. What, then, is man? "Few recognize that sweet purring of anguish when we don't know where we're going, who we are, or from where we come."

Because she doubts that the true reality of man is a changeless human nature, Valenzuela enjoys manipulating mythology in her writing. In part, she uses it as a joke; everything, in its finality, can be explained through a game with language. She changes one letter for another; Prometheus then becomes Trometheus: "I go about the world spreading the message of the game, just like Trometheus. Flame, game, that is how I am occupying myself with one letter even to its form and I half cut it from an upward path."

Just as the gods were said by Plato to have divided androgynous man in half to punish him, Valenzuela also breaks words in two, or changes them in some way:

This is the enduring	Here, I want
breath	the imperious drum
that has no	to sound
beginning	in time
that reaches	with the brush beats
into eternity	(The drum that makes a racket)
	(The cymbals at the same time)

Gloria in excelsis Deo
Gloria inexcelsisdeo
Gloria in
Gloria inexcelsis
Deo

In this, she becomes the creator, the perfect player. In this, also, she is rising to the heights of the gods. What an absurd game mythology becomes, then, in any human invention which parallels man to god!

We also see an echo of the myth about Orpheus and Euridyce, but Valenzuela manipulates its meaning to suit her ideas about the use of language. Instead of wanting to leave the subterranean world, the protagonist desires to enter its gates, even though she cannot. In *Cat-O-Nine-Deaths,* it is she—not he (the cripple who supposedly parallels Orpheus)—who cannot enter the infernal depths: "I saw his grimace as I turned around. In his pain and in his effort was his triumph: I had chosen the easy path that takes you nowhere, maybe to a subterranean train with glances." What she wants to reach is an infernal life, instead of the life we know in today's world. Does Valenzuela then want to tell us something about this "dogged life"?

We also see the presence of Narcissus, the mythological figure who is in love with himself, and that of Pan, the god of music. Valenzuela combines these sources within the text so that the reader is invaded with paradoxical language. What have the gods to do with man? Does he rise in the comparison? "She caressed his face, grazed the nape of his neck, whispered never let yourself fall in love with a reflection, do not search anymore for pleasure in a solitary flute."

The writer even mixes Greek mythology with Hebrew lore, Sisyphus with Jesus Christ: "the weight of the rocks grinds at my loins, my hands become splinters and all of me becomes flaying stone caused by the effort of creating and destroying the labyrinths." Valenzuela does this purposely so that she can engender, in the reader, not a passive sentiment, but a shocking realization; she wants him to think, to participate in the work. The reader then has no choice. By asking why Valenzuela has chosen these two diverse images, the reader becomes a part of the work itself. She succeeds in making the reader an active participant in her work; her language, as well as her message, come to life through him.

Language, which Valenzuela then saw as an asexual entity, today she views as having a definite sexual identity. She can now view words and feel differences just by examining their syntactical arrangement. From this, we can see that Valenzuela has matured in her thoughts, or at least, what before to her was an unconscious intuition today she has transformed into an articulated theory of writing. The intuitive process, which is said to connote a "feminine" mind, and the masculine, which relies upon rationality and logic, are harmoniously blended in Valenzuela's work. Although she believes herself to be a rational being, she also depends heavily upon her intuitive mind: "I live thinking in aristotelean terms, that is, rational terms. But then, I fall into platonic and pythagoric planes. At the same time, reason deviates, disperses, and scatters in disorder."

Symbolic and mythical language is always a contradiction. Valenzuela wants to show this to the reader, and she does this through games, distinguishing the difference between denotation and connotation, between sign and symbol. She begins with one word, and takes a connotation of that word: "Las excusas semanticas no sirven para nada: que gatillo sea gato chiquito estoy de acuerdo, que el revolver sea gata

paridora de plomo eso si que no, no me parece." She then employs that same word with a different connotation from the first. She, therefore, is saying something else, something completely different. What she wants to form is an ambiguous language in which she may be saying two things, or three, or ten simultaneously. She wants us to see, through the medium of language, the multiplicity of life: "Words have a life of their own. What is said is more important than the characters. I don't care so much for psychological truth but for profound truth of the word, of language."

> **Valenzuela does not want to create the effect of disintegration of the world. In actuality, she believes that reality is an exploited illusion.**
> **—*Ana M. Fores***

Valenzuela even tears away the denotations of words we thought we knew. She wants to say that life is chaotic; through that same language which she explores, she forms, purposely, a labyrinth of confusion. We do not have to read something explicitly; the absurd game in which she forces us to participate has an extremely serious message: "For me, on the other hand, language is a fundamental experience. Verbal games are my weakness, perhaps because through them I realize that it is actually the word that plays with us, and determines our being."

Valenzuela also utilizes the technique employed by the contradiction, making a statement seem paradoxical: "Yes, I want to help man by exposing his faults, denouncing his miseries, cutting his wounds. I am going to destroy him in order to help him, dissole him into particles of aid. I will show him how to die the death of other beings. He will know that there is nothing livelier than the lethal experience of death." To construct a new world, one of perfection, we have to destroy the old one. Of course, we will never reach that utopia, no matter how hard we try. However, evil imposes itself when we destroy the old order without any positive condition to follow. Parallelism, in this sense, is everything, in language, as in life; evil counteracts goodness, purity. With this balance, we can go on living. Valenzuela does not want to create the effect of disintegration of the world. In actuality, she believes that reality is an exploited illusion. This is why she tries to exhaust the parallels in life and death; she wants to present a world that, if not admirable and good, is at least balanced:

> The boys come out with laden arms to distribute smiles. They turn on a switch in the throat and light up their faces; there are red and green ones, there are those with an intermittent smile, and others with illumination that runs along the teeth highlighting

the row. They walk about shedding light on those corners where couples are embraced or a drug addict is shooting up. Their mission is to spread joy to the four winds but they do it halfway: almost always their smile illuminates those in hiding who see darkness and know how to be happy without the neon of good intentions.

The drug addict negates the lovers' embrace; the luminous smiles of the children oppose the darkness of those in hiding. The life of spring (is it ironic that the chapter heading is "The Springtime"?) dies quickly, and again, death triumphs. All is cyclical; with life comes the unalterable opposite, death. The infinite cycle exists; the duty of the writer is to show us this journey without end. In the language itself this language is consumed; all that flows is a river of lyricism, a language so poetic that it cannot be called prose. At the same time, this celebratory prose also expresses crudeness and ugliness: "His foot at times is missing, at times they cut off both his legs so that a good pair of crutches sustain him ten centimeters from the floor. His ass amidst the snow I tell him, but he knows how to laugh, laugh with his ass where his body ends, slightly amputated."

The most important factor is that the writer should not allow himself to fall into a rigid structure. Although he should examine his work constantly, and should always analyze the product in itself, intuition should erase all logical dialectic. Because of this concept, the ideal becomes, then, the incorporation of a reasoned intuition within the work itself. By balancing opposites, Valenzuela attempts to achieve equilibrium. This she does with great success.

The "Fucking Game," a section which is extremely logical and mathematical, like a chess game, instead of producing erotic sensations, succeeds in achieving the opposite. We feel its coldness; we perceive the science of the act. We can do nothing but laugh at the absurdities Valenzuela has juxtaposed:

> It is convenient, though not essential, to have a bed nearby, and to play with dimmed lights . . .

> Because there are neither winners nor losers, "The Fucking Game" hardly ever causes brawls.

> The session comes to its end when one of the two— or more—participants falls exhausted. This does not mean that he has been defeated; actually, the opposite is true. The one who gives more of himself is the better player.

Opposed to this, what is not obviously sexual emerges with a mysterious sensuality. Then, in the lyricism of language, and not in obvious sexuality in pornography—do we find eroticism. Valenzuela triumphs in forming a creation in which the union of opposites is what is principally desired; this she achieves, not with the development of themes or characters, but with the purity of language.

With every word, Valenzuela intends a "double entendre." Like *Cat-O-Nine-Deaths* as a whole, individual passages become metaphors (ah, another metamorphosis!) to symbolize what in reality is the function of this novel—to embody the process of artistic creation. Valenzuela believes that the only positive thing an artist can do to make her creations authentic is to change the form itself. As with all literary achievement, metamorphosis is the supreme value: "Condemned I am to change, to renovation. It is the fault of my cells. With each newborn cell I am someone else. I am in every particle of myself and suffer transformations."

"From Here to There" is the verbal personification of what Valenzuela would like to achieve. It is an intuitive process in which, through the medium of the word, she can find what that exact word really means, and thereby participate in the creation of art, the imaginative process. The chapter called "We Have to Die Wretchedly" portrays the resurrection to a real life. The process of interior development hurts, but suffering consumes all: "If the music pains me, if only the passing of a finger over soft cotton is a laceration, if a smell pierces thorns into my ethnic breasts, what can the feeble beings expect of me? I look at others with eyes of contempt and that gaze grieves me, denudes my essence."

Valenzuela also recognizes that the process of writing is chaotic, it has no logical order, no specific time for development. Although the finished product may seem logical in its completed form, the evolution of a piece may be erratic in its development: "Each time I take a bath that old anguish grips my throat. Finally at the end of the day ideas consume me so that I have to run, grasping the soap between my teeth with an urgency of a long-distance telephone call."

When Valenzuela began *Cat-O-Nine-Deaths,* she could not write; a mental block crippled her, making her feel totally frustrated. Finally, however, from the depths of her subconscious, a radically innovative text began to emerge, one which today surprises even its author: "It was a very unconscious text, one so deep that, even today when I read it, it surprises me." Valenzuela discovered, through this work, that the subconscious discourse—that style exhibited by stream of consciousness—is something which can be extremely organized. Like the cover of the novel, which is geometrically designed but which at the same time shows by a sketch the intuitive process of Valenzuela's mind (two black cats joined in the whiteness of the circle), the novel itself also shows the totality of the mind in collective man. The drawing is one, two cats in one. The two cats are not only resurrected from the unconscious mind of the author but also of complete humanity. The novel transcends specific personal patterns and becomes involved in the Jungian process, where one man/woman represents collective humanity. Also, if the figure is seen as one cat, the observer can discern the masculine and feminine qualities, the yang and yin of one being. Are the cats the blackness, the death, the ugliness and the horrors of our own unconscious? Carl Jung, in his essay "Psychology and Literature," states:

> Human passion falls within the sphere of conscious experience, while the subject of the vision lies beyond it. Through our feelings we experience the known, but our intuitions point to things that are unknown and hidden—that by their very nature are secret. If ever they become conscious, they are intentionally kept back and concealed for which reason they have been regarded from earliest times as mysterious, uncanny, and deceptive.

In *Cat-O-Nine-Deaths,* Valenzuela discovered this great secret: "I am the junction of all contradictions, and as such, I do not exist. I am that point where language converges and at the same time separates." Language is the antenna of those contradictions; it is the mirror image of reality. The medial point between the unconscious and man himself is the word. That word transforms sensory perceptions into a logical process. The word, then; gives synthesis and meaning to the unconscious thought. The writer only has to join these scattered words, these sensory perceptions, to give a vision of reality through written form: "I go out with a net to capture verbal clichés and return home overloaded."

Cat-O-Nine-Deaths, the ultimate concrete realization that a writer can achieve, is a novel of theory about the creative process. Though Valenzuela sees now that when she wrote the novel the ideas were so new and radical that she had to explicitly incorporate them within the body of the "new novel," she says that she would be more subtle today. She would use the theories implicitly: that is to say, she would incorporate them within the body of the novel without saying. In this, her later novel, *He Who Searches,* has more maturity. However, *Cat-O-Nine-Deaths* has its merit; it is a step toward Valenzuela's literary development.

Helena Araújo (essay date Fall 1986)

SOURCE: "Valenzuela's *Other Weapons*," in *Review of Contemporary Fiction,* Vol. 6, No. 3, Fall, 1986, pp. 78-81.

[*In the essay below, Araújo explains the relation between the feminine body and language in terms of the violence and degradation depicted in* Other Weapons.]

The stories, narrations and other works of fiction of Luisa Valenzuela reveal a trajectory that incorporates female identity into social and historical circumstances. *El gato eficaz* and *He Who Searches* are baroque, truculent and multiple novels. With bold rhetoric, the erotic is intermingled with the political, thereby propitiating a textuality bordering on the absurd. Her short-story collections, such as *Aquí pasan cosas raras,* lead to fragmentation with passages of black humor mitigated by frustration-rpression. The more recent and more personal *Other Weapons* describes and punctuates a feminine sexuality which adheres to processes of power. There, subjected to organized and subtle reflexive instances, love corresponds to a subjective interiorized code. While the determinisms are wielded with the vacuous purpose of a game, the superimposition of temporal levels crystallizes desanctifying conflictive processes. In the text, tropes do not derive their effect from their intrinsic value, but from a metonymy that grants them intelligibility within the narrative rhythm. Ever harmonious, this follows the cadences of a discourse directed to the reader as associative agent of processes favorable to the intertextuality. There are times of anguish, cathartic discharges in retrospective introverted monologues. One would say that the conduct of the protagonists implies an exercise of interpretation in the deciphering of psychic phenomena linked to the identity. Oscillations between today and yesterday, the I and the other, impose cycles referring to the woman-being. Feminine and feminist, the existentialist projects paradoxical disencounters, confirming once more [Jean-Paul] Sartre's statement that in the person "the act or the work is what best reveals the secret of conditioning."

Heroism, eroticism . . . she and they vacillate between a disgraceful passivity and an appetite that opens them (as Bataille would say) to the joy of caprice and to the premonition of death. Certainly, representation can be a game of coquetry, a mechanics of vice or a model of licentiousness. Perhaps living certain experiences is not the same as triumphing over them. One more time, embodiment takes itself as an exhaltation of the senses and of the desire for writing. In its unfolding, the theme is intersected by the sexual: one could say that there is an erotic density in the connotations, propitiating transference and reduction. At the level of the amorous process, writing thus becomes, in [Julia] Kristeva's words, a "function of the verbal tension, a between-the-signs." Throughout the text, the amorous propulsion incites and liberates, although it also works destructively. It lives and yet it doesn't; in the same way that memories dissolve into the past, experiences dissolve into this passage of time. Therefore, the efforts to transcend the dichotomy of pleasure and pain in a territory free of guilt.

Masochism, narcissism . . . In five feminine stories the object of desire and the object of sacrifice are confused, lost in reflections that dilute the consciousness of things. A brilliant polysemic textuality draws from the narrative nuclei the multiple dimension of the drama. Captivated by their interior mirrors, the women believe they exist as anti-heroines while trying to enter history. Female-mirrors, idiom-mirrors, mirrors in the production of signs that impose the code of a humiliated, manipulated flesh. In the title story, the protagonist realizes that "the only real problem is that which blossoms forth when one accidentally bumps into it with one's image and spends a long time in front of oneself trying to examine oneself."

Image of images . . . in narratives that deal with an intense life, the discourse repeats an equal watchword, an equal truth. "I am the author, appropriating myself of this material that generates the desperation of writing," says the narrator. Her story is simple: a delicious stranger, a gothic ambassador arrives in a city besieged by terror and torture. When he looks at her, she feels "a wave of heat that creeps up her ribs, one by one, it enters her mouth and thereupon emerges between her legs, forcing her to separate them." They meet. And while passing afternoons and evenings in amorous reunions, guilt and joy brand them in their complicity for the rescue of those destined to "disappear." Beyond the reach of legal forums, asylum is erected in a space of subversion and utopian liberty. And the festival that celebrates it and consecrates it infuses resistance with a surrealist sympathy. Bella is the name of the protagonist who dies beautifully. . . . Suicide? Sacrifice? Here and there, diverse and dispersed, her successors recognize in the task of love a disgrace, but also a "starting point."

If one of them dedicates herself to formulating questions which later leave her "wounded in bare flesh," it is not by accident. Without resting she examines, denounces, and confesses, releasing all to the watchword of manliness, in "the objectivization of the other person, the domination of the other person" (Adrienne Rich). Thus, on her lips the word "murderer" bursts forth like a rebel yell from the utter depths of the soul. However, in her body, a tenuous unfolding could discharge the exorcisms of the possession with rituals of masks, dances and ablutions. At last, for her, the jewels of gallantry turn out to be unfulfilled promises "sketched in the air." An unsatiated hunger for sex, feelings, surrender, which takes its revenge in another anti-heroine, draws her into the revolutionary cause. In the last story, a sordid version of captivity lived by "la llamada Laura" (the so-called Laura), concerns a husband in the military, a shocking torturer. Frightened, wiped out, and amnesiac, the prisoner manages, however, to recover at a given moment her dignity. At that point, her energy transforms into "pure destruction," and she herself into a "loaded weapon" which gives the order to fire from within.

As metaphor-text, hyperbole-text, *Other Weapons* is a landmark in Latin American feminine literature. If at the begin-

ning of the narrative the protagonist pretends to surrender and conform to a relational language, this at once becomes self-referential, transmitting messages in the interchange of language and speech. As [Roland] Barthes said, "The eucratic discourse (employed by those who seek power) never yields to the systematic but rather is opposed to the system." Perhaps the compulsion of submission does not imply a compulsion of dominance. Corresponding to sexist, hierarchical and technified societies, there is a state that imposes structures backed up by an ideology of exploitation. Exploitation called oppression with respect to the feminine condition.

By describing the sordid routines of a woman driven by torture to the limits of autism, Valenzuela's story exceeds any intention of linearity. Oscillating between a function of object and a function of symbol, the feminine body defines and punctuates a text that deals with the degradation of language. The titles of each sequence ("words," "concepts," "voices") denounce a semantics in which signifiers have lost their signifieds, and forms their content. Everything refers to a monstrous powerful situation of fear. And has not fear been the "weaker" sex's response to the "stronger" sex? Victim and paradigm of this fatality, the protagonist conforms to an identity that ignores her free being. Day after day, hour after hour, she must be conditioned to passivity. In her story, the nefariousness of a space consecrated to repetition shatters in the reflection of its own image.

A thing of flesh . . . used, abused. Hispanic tradition consecrates and legalizes an ethic of this use and abuse, an ethic that in Latin America goes very far back, since [Christopher] Columbus, in his second voyage, offered a Carib woman to a member of his retinue; he later enthusiastically relates tying her and whipping her, and enjoying her to such a degree in the sexual sense that "it seemed as if she had been educated in a school of whores" (Todorov). Secular machismo, fantasies of rape, violence. Throughout history the woman's body has been annexed to a phallic order and its trajectory is resolved in the structural organization of an interchange-sign, the same as objects. In this text by Luisa Valenzuela, the interpretation of the feminine embraces an allegorical space and a code of perversity. From terror to fascination, from fascination to terror. Confined in asphyxiating spaces, the prisoner does not conform as such, but neither does she rebel. Upon gaining the control of her body, her intimate interior being has been placed in danger. "Like a fun-house circus mirror, she sees that which has more vitality, more nobility, which is her erotic capacity." However, she adds, "On this side of the door, with its so-called locks and its so-called keys crying out loud that she transgress the limits." Liberty or death. The moment arrives along with this resplendent revelation: the wife-whore-slave glimpses how to cease being so. And she risks a change of weapons.

Dorothy S. Mull (essay date Fall 1986)

SOURCE: "Ritual Transformations in Luisa Valenzuela's 'Rituals of Rejection,'" in *Review of Contemporary Fiction,* Vol. 6, No. 3, Fall, 1986, pp. 88-96.

[*In the following essay, Mull reviews some of Valenzuela's characteristic thematic concerns, motifs, and stylistic techniques through a close reading of "Rituals of Rejection," which demonstrates her "insistence on breaking apart, altering, and/or combining traditional words in untraditional ways."*]

"Rituals of Rejection" (**"Ceremonias de rechazo"**) is the third, and thus in a sense the centerpiece, of the five stories comprising Luisa Valenzuela's highly-acclaimed collection *Other Weapons* (*Cambio de armas,* 1982). Other stories in the volume—notably the first, **"Fourth Version,"** and the last, **"Other Weapons"**—have receved well-deserved critical attention as complex, suggestive narratives offering a multiplicity of interpretations. In contrast, **"Rituals of Rejection"** would appear to require little in the way of critical analysis. The story describes a poignant but all too familiar scenario. A woman, here symbolically named Amanda, is enmeshed in a self-destructive relationship with an unworthy lover, and we witness her attempts, ultimately but perhaps not permanently successful, to free herself.

Yet the very simplicity of the plot—if it can be granted so elevated a name—allows us a clear view of some of Valenzuela's characteristic thematic concerns, motifs, and stylistic techniques. The issue of the locus of power in male-female relationships is obviously central, for example, and this is an issue fundamental to her work as a whole. Elsewhere, as in the story **"Other Weapons,"** it is often linked with the more general question of political struggle; even here, such a link is suggested by words like "torture" and "weapon." We also see in this story an emphasis on violence and mind-body conflict that is typical of Valenzuela's work. In addition, her characteristic preoccupation with cyclic processes and metamorphosis is very prominent; indeed, the situation is archetypal, involving a quest, a symbolic death, and a rebirth.

The multifaceted surface of Valenzuela's prose sparkles with her signature wordplay, powerful rhythmic effects (achieved largely through incremental repetition), and extraordinary imaginative juxtapositions.

—*Dorothy S. Mull*

This concern with transformation is underscored both by the narrative point of view, shifting as it does between third- and first-person, and by dominant Valenzuelan motifs such as the mask, the dance, and the mirror. Further, the story is so enriched by echoes from literature (Dante [Alighieri]), folklore, and ritual language of various kinds, some of it unfortunately lost in translation (incantations, prayers, social pleasantries, rhymes, formulaic speech from children's games), that it calls up responses much deeper than the simple plot would at first seem to warrant. Finally, the multifaceted surface of Valenzuela's prose sparkles with her signature wordplay, powerful rhythmic effects (achieved largely through incremental repetition), and extraordinary imaginative juxtapositios. Although her language is here much less ornate than it is in the more baroque passages of her novels, it provides ample evidence of her marked tendency to "think in metaphor."

The story is divided into four sections. In the first, Amanda waits in solitude for a telephone call from her lover, aptly nicknamed Coyote, who has once again abandoned her to take part in mysterious political activities that he will not explain. Although he insists, with characteristic evasiveness, that he is working for "the cause," Amanda's friends warn her that he could be an informer or even a policeman (the story is set in Buenos Aires). In spite of this possibility—or perhaps, as she says, partly because of it—she continues to make herself completely available to him. As the story opens, she is dancing around the telephone, conjuring it to ring with mock incantations, even resorting to black magic by drawing a chalk pentagram around it on the floor to attract Coyote's attention. When it remains obstinately silent, she finally gives up in disgust, "just barely containing her urge to give the phone a good kick and send it flying far away, where it belongs." The wry humor allows the protagonist to bear the pain of the situation, as often occurs in Valenzuela's work. However, the rest of the story describes Amanda's attempt to deliver just such a rejection to her lover, with whom the telephone is symbolically linked.

In the second section, Coyote has appeared at Amanda's house with no apology or explanation for his absence. They go to a Chinese restaurant, where he wields his fork ravenously while Amanda, equally hungry but for other pleasures, "takes him in delicately" with chopsticks "among bamboo shoots and black mushrooms, morsels of chicken, morsels of words and promises of love." But after the meal, just as she is happily boarding a bus in the belief that they are going home together (the sexual symbolism is obvious), Coyote suddenly tells her good-bye, saying that he will call her the next day, "and Amanda, stepping back down from the bus, descends upon him and the sidewalk." Angrily, she insults him and marches off, but after turning right at the first corner and reaching the second, her fury dissipates and she turns right again so that she ends up going around the block and returning to the very spot where she left him. He embraces her in silence and presents her with a long-stemmed red rose. She accepts it, then tells him good-bye ("forever," Valenzuela adds in parentheses, the punctuation indicating both Amanda's unspoken resolve and Valenzuela's characteristic tendency toward afterthought and amplification).

But as the third and longest section of the story begins, we see that Amanda has by no means won the battle. She has had the telephone disconnected, but she recognizes that she needs to do more, since Coyote represents almost a part of herself, a part that must be ritualistically removed. So, after preparing a bath with perfumed bath salts, she puts on white face cream as the symbolic mask she needs for "exiting from the stage" and stepping into a new and better life. As she waits for this mask to work its magic, overtones of self-denial, masochism, violence, and even death are very prominent: "I'm a fire burning its own flames, the white face says, facing the insane mirror, barely moving its mouth." Rinsing the cream off, Amanda observes that her artificial pallor—the "whitewash" of her "facade"—vanishes down the drain. What returns to her, however, is not only her original skin coloring but also her original suffering. (In the Spanish text, the rhyme "colores"/"dolores" reinforces the parallel.) Not completely satisfied, wanting to do something more drastic to reach her essential self and rid herself of Coyote's influence, she applies another facial mask, a transparent coating that smooths her features until they appear angelic, then violently peels it off and scrubs her face with an abrasive bath mitt.

With her skin now smarting and burning, Amanda decides that she had better proceed "with less fanaticism and more tenderness. One shouldn't erase one's face quite so literally." She paints a mask around her eyes with orange face cream, smears white cream on her forehead and chin, and draws ritualistic patterns on her face with lipstick and eyeliner. Thus "tattooed," she prepares to enter her bath, which has cooled and needs to be refilled, but before doing so, she notices that her legs are unshaven. With kaleidoscopic rapidity, her thoughts shift from a mock invocation ("Protect us, oh Aura, . . . from hairy legs that in moments of true bliss may hinder the hand that caresses") to a reminiscence of childhood to a very real, very anguished sexually charged lament for her lover. As she tries to decide whether her break with Coyote has been an act of bravery or of cowardice, a rejection "so as not to be rejected," Amanda plucks at her legs "with fury and tweezers, a contradictory combination." Finally, in a violent scene bringing to mind witches' cauldrons, she strips the hair off with steaming hot black wax.

Thus "purified"—returned, in a sense, to a hairless prepubescent state—Amanda at last prepares to enter the bath. But it has again cooled off and must again be emptied. Filling it for the third time, she adds pine-scented salts, and the fragrance reminds her of the forests where she spent her summers as a child. As memories flood her mind, she remembers how the tiny toads in the forest used to deposit a few drops of urine in her hand when she attempted to catch them. At first she dismisses this as a "useless defense" but then decides that it may be worth trying. In the end (the passage is an artistic tour de force), she releases her own urine into the bathwater, and Valenzuela describes her as "sumptuously" submerged in a sea permeated by her own fluids, "surrounded by her own self. Ecstatic. Her private inner heat now surrounding her in the pine forest with sunbeams filtering through the branches and giving her a halo of sorts. A golden aura amid the white foam." And the "halo," the "golden aura," now belongs not to some haloed deity that she must invoke, but to herself, now no longer in Coyote's embrace (and grasp), but triumphantly surrounded by a part of her own body.

One thing remains: to dispose of the rose, now withered and dead. The next morning, in the fourth and final section of the story, Amanda picks it up and carries it toward the turbid waters of the River Plate. After walking three blocks—an echo of her earlier three-block walk away from and back toward Coyote, except that she now proceeds "knowing her destination"—she glimpses or envisions a person dressed in white "as in Dante's sonnet" (possibly herself, although the identification is not made explicit in the Spanish text). Amanda observes that this figure looks more like a nurse than like "long-lost Beatrice," and concludes that this is appropriate, since what she wants is to cure herself of her unrequited passion, not to die because of it as the nineteenth-century romantic tradition would dictate.

Nevertheless, she feels that she is committing a subversive act by walking toward the river to throw away the dead rose. In her mind, the rose that Coyote held is not only like a broken mirror that brings bad luck but also a kind of weapon that "makes her run a thousand risks. [Hers would be] an ironic fate: imprisoned for carrying a rose." (And what she is doing *is* subversive, for she is freeing herself, at least for a time, from the dependence of women on men that underpins many social structures.) The rose, of course, has multiple meanings. It was given by Coyote as an "offering" in a gesture that, for Amanda, was an "offense," but at a deeper level it represents a dangerous weapon, sexual passion, and throwing it away is an act of severance. As she herself comments, "*Sic transit,*" the unspoken "*gloria*" being not the "*gloria mundi*" (for that is what she is trying to recapture) but the past glory of Coyote that she hopes to efface from her memory.

As suggested above, the physical paths traced by Amanda in the story reflect her growing independence. In the first scene, her obsessive dance around the telephone is focused on an object identified with Coyote, circumscribed by the walls of the room, circular and thus theoretically never-ending, and ultimately fruitless. In the second scene, her journey around the block begins promisingly but is also ultimately unsuccessful. In this final scene, however, she knows her goal, and the river—unlike her mute telephone and silent lover—receives her with a "lapping of tame, soft waves, a welcoming sigh." Described in a beautiful, memorable metaphor as a vast vicuña poncho "rippled by a secret breath," the river of vicuña, soft and precious, stands in marked contrast to Coyote, an animal of rough coat and rougher ways—a predator, a thief, a devourer of flesh, including carrion. (We recall his greedy attack on the food in the Chinese restaurant, in contrast to Amanda's slow, delicate approach with chopsticks.)

The vicuña has also been on the endangered species list for years, and this leads us—through a metaphorical byway—to an important aspect of the story: although Amanda ends in triumph, she understands that other Coyotes may eventually enter her life. She says that she will try to be "solid within, to stop the game from repeating itself," but the possibility is there, for her name is, after all, Amanda. Although "the Coyotean cycle" may have closed, the phrase itself implies eternal recurrence. Amanda herself identifies Coyote with her unfulfilled desire, and those familiar with Valenzuela's other work may remember Luis Cernuda's observation—reproduced on the cover of the Spanish edition of her 1977 novel *Como en la guerra* (*He Who Searches*)—that "el deseo es una pregunta cuya respuesta no existe" ("desire is a question that has no answer"). Desire is the human condition, and therefore one must assume, however reluctantly, that Amanda's freedom is tenuous and may be transitory.

Nevertheless, it *is* freedom, symbolized by her appropriation of roles formerly held by Coyote. During her walk home from the river, for example, she digs up a plant and brings it back to her garden as he used to do. In the final scene, she is neither entangled in the "jungle" associated with Coyote nor immersed in the comforting but unreal "pine forest" of the bath. Rather, she is surrounded by her own garden, a garden that she herself cultivates and waters. As she dances there, showering herself and the plants with a hose that Coyote has bought and installed, both the phallic symbolism and the regeneration theme are obvious. Whereas before with the telephone she had danced without song and without success and whereas before during the bath scene her mirror had revealed only a death-white face, at the end of the story she is singing and the mirror reflects her whole body—nude, wet, and engaged in that most self-sufficient of activities, calisthenics—and "confirms her song."

The song may also be intended to suggest a renewed ability to write. The metaphor is ancient, writing is a recurrent theme in Valenzuela's work, and Amanda has told us that, once free of Coyote, she will be able to indulge in "more gratifying—albeit solitary—activities: writing, for example, answering all those letters." (Previously, her "writing" has been limited to the chalk pentagram and the bizarre designs that she draws on her own face; and she ultimately destroys them both, stepping on the pentagram and allowing the designs to dissolve in the heat of the bathwater.)

The possibility of a metaphorical equation between singing and renewed creativity is strengthened by the fact that, in the final pages of the story, Valenzuela openly relates the exterior to the interior, the visible to the invisible world. We may have deduced that the beautiful maroon-leaved woodland plant represents the protagonist herself (a similar symbol is used in **"Other Weapons"**), but it is Valenzuela who tells us that the plant is "proof of how Amanda no longer needs the Coyote to tend her outer garden. And the inner one? It may be the same one, inside and out, merging."

This linkage between external acts and internal change is central to the story. What we see is the ritual transformation of a cowed, obsessed woman to a free, self-sufficient one—a symbolic death and rebirth, complete with aspects of purification (entering the bath), renunciation (discarding the rose), and vegetation rites (transplanting the maroon-leaved plant, which, unlike the rose, is rooted in earth and will not wither). Through her own initiative, Amanda has carried out a series of acts that transform her from the meek person whom Coyote addresses as "mamacita" to a goddesslike state approaching that of the archetypal Mother Earth.

What is more, she is a self-sufficient Mother Earth who supplies her own life-giving water so that vegetation can grow. We recall that Coyote, in contrast, has been described as a vampire who sucks out her vital fluids. Water in its many forms—the bath, urine, a golden cup of tea that "tastes like sunlight," the river, and so on—is an organizing metaphor in the story. The message is clear: by acting rather than languidly waiting to be acted upon, Amanda has granted herself new life.

The opposition between waiting and acting—and, implicitly, between death and life—is set up in the quasi-syllogistic opening sentence ("To wait, seated in a chair, is the deadest form of dead anticipation, and waiting [is] the most uninspired form of death, so Amanda finally manages to . . . set her anxiety in motion") and informs the narrative throughout. While circling the telephone, for example, Amanda muses that "the dance helps you forget the rigor mortis of absence and waiting. You shake your hair out, you shake up your thoughts." Later, after she discards the rose, her new, freer motion is linked with a more authentic renovation (a hair image is again glanced at): "Amanda takes off, wandering through the park of Palermo, and the sweet scent of eucalyptus starts combing through her soul, reconstructing it for her and giving her back all she had lost while following the Coyote's tracks."

A related theme is the play between the infernal and the celestial—the violent extremes of experience so prominent in Valenzuela's work as a whole. At the outset, for example, Coyote is described as a "mediator between heaven and hell." Although this phrase may reflect certain Indian legends in which the coyote has positive, even Promethean aspects, at the simplest level it obviously refers to Amanda's ecstasy when she is sexually united with her lover and her despondency when she is not. "When I'm with him, the unconfessable in me runs wild—my darkest desires grow wings, and I can feel angelic, even though it's just the opposite." Coyote controls and guides Amanda's life, but it is a perverse sort of "guidance" that leaves her no room for growth. Later on, we find a passing reference to another powerful guide, Beatrice, Dante's companion in the *Paradiso* and his major source of inspiration. Although, as noted above, Beatrice is here pointedly transformed into a nurselike figure, the allusion stands, and it is important for several reasons.

First, it suggests the possibility that the structure of Valenzuela's narrative reiterates the tripartite structure of the *Divine Comedy*, i.e., that Amanda makes an allegorical journey from a personal Hell (with Coyote either absent from her life, as in the first section of the story, or present but perennially elusive, as in the second), through Purgatory (the cleansing rituals of the third section; the hot wax may even reflect the purifying fire of *Purgatorio* XXVII) to Paradise (the joyous garden scene of the fourth and final section). (We note that the main action of the story takes place on three consecutive days, and that the events of those days correspond to the Hell-Purgatory-Paradise sequence described above.) The reiteration would be partly ironic, of course, in that the culmination of Dante's journey is reunion with Beatrice and a vision of the Celestial Rose in the *Paradiso*, while at the end of **"Rituals of Rejection"** Amanda is alone and triumphantly *free* of the rose, though surrounded by vegetation.

The fact that a female protagonist is implicitly compared with a male, Dante, is also significant, for it suggests Valenzuela's characteristic openness—her resistance to boundaries and categories. (In interviews, she has repeatedly said that she is fascinated by transsexuality, and many of her works touch on this theme.) Still another important facet of the allusion to Dante is the specific mention of his sonnet on Beatrice, especially if, as seems possible, Valenzuela is remembering not only the famous "Tanto gentile" (*Vita Nuova* XXVI) but also "A ciascun' alma presa, e gentil core," which immediately follows Dante's description of Beatrice as dressed in purest white (III). The focus of the latter poem is not on the well-known revitalizing, beneficent

powers of love but on its cruelty. Beatrice is envisioned sitting on the lap of the God of Love, who has a terrifying aspect and who forces her to eat Dante's burning heart, which he holds in his hand. Although the image of the eaten heart was a medieval commonplace, today it shocks. It reminds us of the destructive nature of Amanda's obsession with Coyote before she breaks free through ritual transformation.

The phrase "ritual transformation" is here used advisedly. It has been chosen because its convenient grammatical ambiguity—is the word "ritual" an adjective or a noun?—conveys a fundamental dualism in the story as a whole. Not only do we have the "transformation" of the protagonist, we also have the transformation of ritual itself. For the ceremonies devised by Amanda are not the conventional tribal rites familiar to us all—characteristically public, carried out in groups, and male-dominated. On the contrary, Amanda's are idiosyncratic ("of her own invention") and performed in solitude. Perhaps most important, they represent an ironic inversion of beautification rites that are associated with the enticement rather than the rejection of males in our culture.

Amanda's rituals—applying "practical" cosmetic masks, putting on makeup, removing body hair, taking a scented bath—could all, under different circumstances, have been acts aimed at seduction. Here, however, they are transformed. The cosmetic masks and hair removal are not intended to enhance her skin but to strip away the "old" Amanda, the one addicted to Coyote. The garish, primitive makeup, which is itself a kind of mask, is not designed to compliment her features but to obscure them—or, to put it another way, to allow a previously hidden part of her personality to emerge. (The mask is an extremely important motif in Valenzuela's writing; and she has commented—with her characteristic spirit of contradiction—that what interests her is the *un*masking made possible by the use of the mask.) Finally, Amanda's bath, discussed in detail above, does initially scent her body with the aroma of pine, but this "cosmetic" effect is far overshadowed by the most un-cosmetic addition of urine to the bathwater. The bath is a defense and an assertion of self, not a beautification ritual designed to please someone else.

The ironic inversion (or subversion) of traditional values and associations is, as several critics have pointed out, a fundamental feature of Valenzuela's work. It is related to her radical questioning of constructs often thought of as dominated by males, by logic, and by conventional categorization. One aspect of this questioning is Valenzuela's insistence on breaking apart, altering, and/or combining traditional words in untraditional ways. Her coinage of the appellation *bolastristes* for Coyote in the present story (Spanish text) is a typical example. (Literally "sadballs," and vaguely lyrical as well as sexual, it appears in the English as "little bastard.") As [Sharon] Magnarelli has put it, "Valenzuela seems determined to prove that she is not at the mercy of language, that she does have power and control over that medium."

In **"Rituals of Rejection,"** Valenzuela goes far beyond mere questioning of tradition, whether tradition takes the form of a word, a relationship between unequals, or a beautification rite. Carefully structured, economically but poetically written, the story is not merely a rejection but an affirmation. It is a celebration of the independent self—a self that no longer needs to seek validation in a man's embrace, a self that can rejoice in seeing itself reflected not in a man's eyes, but in a mirror, free and whole and strong. As such, the story is in many ways more positive than any of the rest in **Other Weapons.** Here there is violence, but it is transcended; here there is death, but it is overcome. The protagonist's "weapon" is not merely the written word, or the spoken one, or fantasy, or amnesia, or a revolver. It is her body itself, and what she does with that body.

Brooke K. Horvath (review date Spring 1989)

SOURCE: A review of *Open Door,* in *Review of Contemporary Fiction,* Vol. IX, No. 1, Spring, 1989, p. 243-44.

[*In the following review of* Open Door, *Horvath summarizes the themes and techniques of Valenzuela's short stories.*]

According to Evelyn Picon Garfield, Luisa Valenzuela "has become the most translated contemporary woman author from Latin America"—and for good reason, as readers of this journal's special issue on Valenzuela (Fall 1986) are well aware. The popularity and importance of her work reside both in the themes she dramatizes and in the means she employs to effect this drama, and if Valenzuela reminds one at times of García Márquez or Lydia Cabrera, Donald Barthelme or Paul Bowles, her fiction nonetheless achieves a distinctive voice that allows her o address issues she has clearly made her own.

As Valenzuela's first story collection since **Up among the Eagles** (**Donde viven las águilas**) appeared in Spanish in 1983, **Open Door** provides both something new for American readers and a selection of the author's best earlier short fiction. The book opens with the fourteen stories comprising the '83 collection, gathered together for the first time in translation, and follows with eleven selections from **Strange Things Happen Here** and seven stories from **Clara** (or **Los Heréticos**). As Valenzuela remarks in her Preface, "For the time being, here are my favorite stories from the three collections. But I must hurry, now, and write others: it is the only way I know of jamming a foot in the door so it won't slam in our faces."

Readers familiar with Valenzuela's work will recognize in **Open Door** the author's characteristic heterogeneity of subject matter, artistic method, and thematic concerns. Shamanistic figures, folkloristic superstitions and ritual magic, cultic beliefs and indigenous legends jostle urban settings, café life, state-of-the-art state terrorism, and the amorous doings of vacationing bourgeoisie to yield modern political parables and twice-told (albeit revamped) myths, small comedies of manners and mocking parodies of middle-class conventionality, ironic illuminations of religious realities and secular tales of physical and/or psychological terror. Similarly, traditional narrative techniques combine with a postmodern experimentation (fragmented narration, magical realism, randomness, and linguistic pranksterism) in the service of themes that are as timeless as the search for truth, community, or control over nature's mysteries, and as topical as sexual and political persecution in present-day Argentina or the nature of power relations within and among contemporary social classes. Here, in short, are stories that explore the boundaries of what is currently thought possible in fiction while reminding us of what must be demanded from fiction in our time.

As one moves through this collection, changes in focus are evident. The newest selections are the most artistically adventuresome and, according to their author, speak to "my love for Latin America and my passion for reinventing its myths." Stories gathered from **Strange Things** look most unswervingly at a Buenos Aires given over to violence and government-sanctioned illegalities, whereas those of her first volume "walk in writing the tightrope between religious fanaticism and heresy." Yet different as these stories may be one from another, they all reveal Valenzuela's dislike of "dogmas and certainties" and share her sense of urgency, of knowing something that desperately needs saying. All witness to her efforts to jam that foot in the door, the door of her title, which is also the name, so we are told, "of the most traditional, least threatening lunatic asylum in Argentina."

Patricia Rubio (essay date Spring-Summer 1989)

SOURCE: "Fragmentation in Luisa Valenzuela's Narrative," in *Salmagundi,* Nos. 82-83, Spring-Summer, 1989, pp. 287-96.

[*Below, Rubio discusses the fragmentary nature of Valenzuela's writings, focusing on her narrative procedures, themes, characterizations, discourse, and word-play.*]

Luisa Valenzuela's writing belongs to that class of contemporary works Umberto Eco has called "open works." In them the harmonious representation of reality, supported by logic and syllogism, is replaced by a more ample and complex vision in which the laws of causality cease to operate in a linear fashion. The ordered *Weltanschauung* of the standard realist narrative—the tradition to which **Clara,** Valenzuela's first novel, and [**Los heréticos** (**The Heretics**)], her first collectin of short stories, belong—disintegrates in the face of desire, cruelty, the instinctual, the magical, the fantastic, the sickly. The rules governing ordinary discourse are trampled on. The causality governing the typical realist plot is replaced by association and disjunction. The objective of Valenzuela's writing is not the mimetic representation of reality, but rather the creation of fictive worlds bearing witness to their own process of mutation. Valenzuela's writing, at least in the works I will be referring to, neither affirms nor defines; instead, it questions constantly, interrogating the world and, in the process, also interrogating itself.

One of the central structural units of many of these open texts is the fragment. Because, in Octavio Paz's words, the fragment is an "errant particle," it implies the destruction of linearity, both in the discourse and in the story, and leads to opening or dispersion in multiple directions. The order governing both the enunciation and the enunciated of realist narrative reveals the prevalence of a rational vision of the world; the fragment is by contrast an expression of the irrational and surprising.

The fragment is most especially an essential element in Valenzuela's most ambitious works, including **Cat-O-Nine-Deaths, He Who Searches,** [**Libro que no muerde** (**Book That Doesn't Bite**)], and a great number of the short stories collected in **Strange Things Happen Here.** "We are fragmented," says Valenzuela; "nothing is univocal; there is no unity; God is unity; we are pieces." Such a view is already present in the first novel, **Clara.** In it, as in some of Valenzuela's later texts, fragmentation does not affect the structure of the text, but is present, as a thematic concern. The characters in these stories may be victims of physical dismemberment, as in the case of the main character in **Clara** and **"My daily horse,"** or they may be fragmented by a dualist and mechanistic understanding of the world, as in the case of the protagonist of **"Up Among the Eagles."** In most of the tales in **Strange Things Happen Here** and **Up Among the Eagles,** as in several stories of **Other Weapons,** we find that the fragmentation goes beyond individual experience and is a characteristic of the society at large, a pervasive consequence of political persecution, torture, and fear. The country as a whole may be said to be fragmented, with division between those who live in the city and those who live in the hinterland; between the oppressors who live comfortably, and the others who are underground. These others perceive the "strange things" that reveal the country's fragmentation and understand that the tranquillity of the official order is mere appearance.

But the fragmentation in Valenzuela is extraordinarily vari-

ous. The narrative of **Cat-O-Nine-Deaths** is composed of a series of microstories none of which turns upon ordered causality. Almost none of these texts, furthermore, develops a narrative line from beginning to end. The fragments are pieces of experiences, sensations, bits of dreams, imaginings, sudden occurrences, organized by association or by way of strategic juxtaposition. Between one story and the next, and within the stories themselves, there are spaces that remain unfilled. The following passage characteristically reveals Valenzuela's procedures:

> He told her tomorrow we'll see each other and she, naively, believed him. How could a cat woman fail to see the cat? And how was it that he, who was so much the rat, didn't know how to escape her? This cat had eyes of brass and in the village it was snowing. Beneath the snow a poster declared that God was alive and well in Argentina.

Between the various fragments one finds recurring elements: there are the cats of death and the dogs of life, or the narrator's crippled friend who makes several intermittent appearances. Certain thematic units also recur, such as the relationship between eros and thanatos, or between language and eroticism; other topics include the absurdity of the idea of progress, and an incisive denunciation of Argentinean fascism. These concerns, sometimes mentioned in passing, other times dealt with in depth, give the text a certain unity, while simultaneously dispersing it in several directions at once. There is no specific focus, no center; only fragments which are constantly being further fragmented. No wonder the narrator of **Cat-O-Nine-Deaths,** acknowledging the atomization of the story, says "nothing has happened here and nothing will happen."

In **He Who Searches,** Valenzuela develops a story propelled by the traditional motif of the search. This, however, does not insure the novel's unity; rather, it ironizes it. Although the story progresses, it appears and dissolves like rings of smoke, questioning and undoing itself at every turn. Almost at the center of the novel the university professor, a protagonist in search of the woman with whom he has had many encounters, says: "There has never been anybody here, this room has been deserted for more than a thousand years and if she passed through here a few days ago then my theory is proven: she is nobody." **"Fourth Version,"** in **Other Weapons,** offers a similar, although less radical structure. The text one reads is made up of pre-existent fragments (or pre-texts), and the so-called "fourth version" corresponds to the ordering that the narrative voice has given to these fragments:

> There are so many pages written . . . I read and reread and at times order and reorder them randomly. I stumble across complex components and bump into multiple beginnings. I study, discard and re-

cover them and try to place them appropriately in a furious attempt to revitalize the puzzle.

The writing, then, does not entail developing a story but creating a text which itself becomes the search for new ways of exploring meaning, connectedness, order, disorder.

The fragmentation of the story obviously affects every dimension of the narrative: the categories of time and space are made to inform a new vision of the world in which indeterminacy and discontinuity replace definiteness and certainty, and simultaneity replaces succession. Wandering takes precedence over directedness. "If I am in Buenos Aires how I love to wander at daybreak through the Village," says the narrative voice of *Cat-O-Nine-Deaths,* and in *He Who Searches* we read, "Here I am: traveling the Moebius strip through America because the space where she is to be found is not Euclidean space nor is her time the same time of which we're dimly aware when we see our skin aging." In Luisa Valenzuela's worlds, Euclidean space is but one of several spacial dimensions. The others can only be formulated by non-Euclidean geometry. The fragmented text puts the reader, sometimes dimly, sometimes sharply, in touch with those other, literary geometries, prompting us to seek unexplored pieces of reality and to participate in the destruction of the usual modes of apprehending the world.

Characters also partake in this process of fragmentation which proceeds from the progressive dissolution of their names (Beatriz, Bea, Be, B or AZ, in *He Who Searches,* or Bella, Bel\la, B in **"Fourth Version"**), to their physical obliteration: "I am afraid of falling apart, . . . I am afraid of exploding and spattering all four walls, afraid that a part of me, only a part, may reach her in her image" (*He Who Searches*). In **"Neither the Most Terrifying Nor the Most Memorable,"** a short story in *Strange Things Happen Here,* we find the most radical fragmentation of the character unit. In this story parts of the protagonist's body become city spaces, producing in the end a cubistic image involving the human body and the city: "His mouth is the block between Corrientes and Lavalle, at Anchorena (the produce market) with a little intersecting street that is the Calle Gardel, where sometimes he sings a nostalgic song and sometimes whistles to call the dog." In general, one can say that Valenzuela's characters are mutants, partly human, partly paper figures, who don't, at least in the works we have cited, achieve a definite human configuration. Take for example the following scene from *Cat-O-Nine-Deaths*:

> He has two lively little partridge eyes, the pointy ears of a cub and the teeth of a wild boar—all nicely kept in their little containers in the fridge.

The most radical dissolution occurs in the narrative discourse itself. Logically and normatively ordered discourse yields to one which denies its own capacity to represent. The discourse becomes opaque and diffuse, and in its expansion it seeks to establish itself as the sole "reality." We find in Valenzuela's work an interest in stretching language to its maximum, in affirming its reality as an object of inquiry. Most of her texts possess logomimetic characteristics in the sense that the words on the page establish themselves as signifiers with no evident value or meaning. The intention to destroy the meaning associated with a specific signifier is unmistakable. Valenzuela achieves this either by negating or by affirming—but always to the breaking point—the ambiguity of the linguistic sign. In her narrative, for example, the word "dog" *does* bite, as some of the texts and the title of [*Libro que no muerde* (*Book That Doesn't Bite*)] ironically reveal. The destruction of univocal meaning, on the other hand, is achieved, for example, by accumulating various meanings for one signifier: "Corriendo el albur, corriendo la liebre, corriendo el Amok . . . acabó claro está, estirando la pata" ("Running the risk, running scared, running amok, he ended up croaking"). In this example the meaning of the word "correr" (to run) slides in each expression into another meaning, and in the Spanish, it ends up in "estirando la pata," which literally means "stretching the leg," a colloquial expression akin to "kicking the bucket." Neologisms, the coupling or rupturing of words in order to create new ones, along with the use of "nonsense", also contribute to the dissolution of meaning. This is what Valenzuela is getting at in *Cat-O-Nine-Deaths* when she writes: "that's how my ludicrousidity unfolds to reveal what makes me feel good and well-disposed, it's what's attractive in me, what's fun." ("Mi ludicidad aflora así a revuelo para biendisponerme, es lo pático en mí, lo divertente.") The "exploration of the word, the kind of prostituted word we use daily," as Valenzuela has expressed it, is central to her assault on established systems of meaning and to the unfolding of her writerly temperament.

Other varieties of fragmentation include the abandonment of the paragraph, the destruction of syntax, the fragmented sentence and a punctuation system which introduces disorder rather than order into the sentence. Valenzuela also frequently incorporates literal translations of sayings—usually from English—which in the Spanish version do not evoke their original meaning and thus become nonsensical. The text thus finds itself in continuous metamorphosis and, as Nelly Martínez has indicated, "proclaims the defeat of logos and announces the closure of western episteme."

The fragmentation of the discourse also determines the handling of the narrative voice. Contrary to the narrator in realist fiction, who is easy to characterize, who often possesses total control over the narrated world, and whose word is reliable and of paramount importance for the understanding of the text, Valenzuela's narrator is in constant mutation: s/he is a transvestite, bisexual or hermaphrodite; s/he/it is an animal or an object, both singular and plural, sometimes combining both modes in one instance. In *He Who Searches* the narrator is typically slippery: "He (I shall henceforth call him I) knows (I know) that they will do us no harm; I know(s) many more things. . ." The comments offered by the narrator contribute to the reader's confusion, and rarely orient the reading process. Their function is clearly to underscore the ambiguity, even the mendacity, of the text: "The paper is a trap and nothing coming from it can be remembered. The paper is a trap, I am a trap made out of paper and printed characters." So we read in *Cat-O-Nine-Deaths*. The kaleidoscopic vision of the narrative voice suggests the possibility of multiple readings and interpretations. The reader, lacking elementary guidance, has to penetrate the verbal jungle in order to find possible ways of ordering a puzzle in constant mutation.

> To die . . . to make room for someone else to assume my obligation and attempt to complete puzzles or break the heads s/he loves the most. But always very carefully, apologizing, following my mysteries step by step, making, for example, an apologia for the escape of truth, the escaped-truth.

The image of the text as a puzzle is important, not only because it refers back both to the fragmentary structure of the text and to the fact that it is only a point of departure requiring the reader's complicity for its completion, but also because it contributes to the conception of the text as a space and an object of play. In her texts Valenzuela refers principally to two games: chess, in which a set of rules regulates the moves available to the players; and puzzles, which are not regulated and the execution of which depends exclusively on the individual trying to complete them. There is another opposition between these two games that further emphasizes what I have been saying thus far: in chess, there is a hierarchy determining the value of the pieces, and hence the relative importance of the moves. In a puzzle, all the pieces or fragments are of equal value, and binary oppositions, such as white/black, do not exist. Valenzuela's definition of her narrative as a puzzle affirms its fragmentariness, and also alludes to its iconoclastic intentions.

There is, however, another element of game playing that seems worth mentioning, and that has to do with the very meaning of the term *play*. We are all familiar with the conventional idea of *play* associated with the word "ludens," but to "have play" (in Spanish, "tener juego") also means that two or more pieces are loosely linked together, that there is a space between the pieces which permits flexibility and thus gives the object freedom. This understanding of the word *play* is, I believe, important for the deciphering of the texts I have been considering. In Valenzuela's texts one does not reorder what exists, but rather searches for what is there as well as for what is not, for what needs a space for expres-

sion even though it is nowhere represented. Between one fragment and another there is such a space wherein the fragments may be said to "have play." And it is through this play, within the interstices between fragments, that Valenzuela's texts find their authentic meaning.

Lawrence Thornton (review date 31 May 1992)

SOURCE: "Murder with Mirrors," in *The Washington Post Book World*, May 31, 1992, p. 4.

[*In the following review, Thornton admits that "readers who admire fiction that celebrates its own making will be drawn to* Black Novel.*"*]

Like many contemporary Latin American writers, Luisa Valenzuela delights in pushing language to its limits. ***Black Novel (with Argentines)*** is rich in puns, double entendre, and razor-sharp images. Here, for example, is a description of the habits of one of the main characters: "Roberta had probably popped that question into his head; it was her off-the-cuff kind of remark, jabbed into the listener like a banderilla."

Valenzuela is also fond of theorizing. Roberta Aguliar, like the other protagonist, Augustin Palant, is an Argentine novelist, though unlike him, she does not suffer from writer's block. "Write with the body," she tells him. "The secret is *res, non verba* [things, not words]. Renew, restore, re-create . . . Words lead you by the nose . . . Sure. We're all whores of language. We work for it, feed it, humble ourselves on its account; we brag about it—and in the end, what? Language demands more."

Valenzuela makes similar demands on our attention as well as ou willingness to suspend disbelief in the face of a very self-conscious verbal structure.

Set in New York, ***Black Novel*** opens with the motiveless murder of a young actress by Augustin, whom Roberta helps evade detection as they try to discover the reason behind his act. They begin by exploring the underbelly of the city. Somewhere in this miasma of addicts, killers, thieves and perverts Augustin met his victim, Edwina, after being given a free ticket to a play in a theater whose works are light years from Broadway's.

They visit Roberta's friend and confidant, Ava Taurel, a dominatrix doing a thriving business with chains, whips, and other instruments of degradation. Valenzuela makes it clear that their encounters in Taurel's establishment and other bizarre venues are intended to parallel Harry Haller's lessons in the underground theater of [Hermann] Hesse's

Steppenwolf. These scenes are filled with wonderfully exotic characters, but Valenzuela is too enamored of *nostalgie de la boue*, and allows these scenes to go on longer than they should.

One of the novel's main strategies is to offer feints and diversions to distract us from the ostensible purpose of discovering Augustin's motive. Moreover, the mystery is complicated by suggestions that the murder may not have taken place at all. It appears that the two of them are collaborating on a play whose subject is murder. At one point Roberta's lover, Bill, says: "You two were writing a play."

"Yes. No. On and off, afterward I don't know."

"Tell me about it, if you can."

"There's a murder, I believe. Of a woman. At first I thought the victim was a man, but it turned out to be a woman and then I no longer understood anything. Why she had to be killed, anything. But he insisted. I still don't understand. . . ."

The playwriting motif runs throughout the novel, as do references to [Antonin] Artaud, the theater of cruelty, and Roberta's passionate theory about "writing with the body." There is also passing mention of Argentina's Dirty War, which is elliptically resolved at the end where the various strands of the narrative are brought together in a metacritique of the novel's playful structure.

Everything but the Argentinean motif works to draw us further into the book. While we're given to understand that Augustin's writer's block is related to his inability to confront the horrors of his country's recent past and that he will probably go on to write about it, Valenzuela's summary treatment of this material does not do justice to the tragedy.

Black Novel illustrates the postmodernist's impatience with character and plot. Valenzuela assumes no direct relationship between fiction and external reality, discarding such connections in favor of a narrative that calls attention to its artifice by questioning its own identity. Here is an exchange between Augustin and Roberta:

"Tell me about the novel you're writing."

"I already told you, my novel is the one we're writing together. The other one no longer exists. It's been erased, obliterated, contaminated now because it forms part of this ill-fated novel. How to separate the wheat from the chaff? How to know where one begins and the other ends or vice versa?

Black Novel displays considerable panache; Valenzuela writes with the sure hand of a jazz musician improvising on a theme. But her stylistic virtuosity is achieved at the expense of Augustin and Roberta, who generally strike me more as loci for the author's ideas than as characters I can care about. Their discourse is too often more interesting than who they are.

On the other hand, that is part of what makes this kind of book. Valenzuela teases us with speculations about the truth (or lack of it), delighting in raising questions about the novel she is writing, which may be the novel that Roberta is writing, or a play whose subject is the novel we're reading.

Readers who admire fiction that celebrates its own making will be drawn to ***Black Novel***. Those who prefer believable characters and a clear sense of direction will still find much to admire in the book's pyrotechnics, though it may be a little too self-consciously conceived for their tastes.

Michael Harris (review date 14 June 1992)

SOURCE: "Balloon in the Wind," in *Los Angeles Times Book Review*, June 14, 1992, p. 12.

[*In the following review, Harris emphasizes the theatrical aspect of* Black Novel.]

In New York City, an expatriate Argentine writer named Agustin Palant buys a pistol for protection. One evening he takes a walk on the wild side. Among the pimps and drug pushers lurking in doorways is a mysterious man who gives him a ticket to one of the theaters that honeycomb the slums. An actress in the play he sees invites Palant to her apartment. The script seems to call for seduction, but instead Palant shoots her in the head.

Why? The question, like the echo of the shot, reverberates in Palant's mind and almost shakes it apart. This is murder without a motive. Nothing in his life, he thinks, has led up to it. He takes refuge in the home of his sometime girlfriend, another Argentine writer named Roberta, who doesn't completely believe his story but finds him, if even more preoccupied and distant, more interesting than before.

At first, Luisa Valenzuela (***The Lizard's Tail, Open Door***) seems to be writing a standard psychological novel—and an acute example of the genre, at that—but soon things give her away. Her laguage, for instance. It's as antic and unpredictable as a balloon bobbing in the wind. Also, Palant's search for the truth about the murder, and Roberta's search for the truth about Palant, go off on crazy tangents. This is no meditation on guilt, like Paul Theroux's *Chicago Loop*.

Nor is it an existentialist celebration of a "gratuitous act." It's something else.

Something *theatrical*. "I've completely lost myself," Palant thinks, hiding in Roberta's apartment with his beard shaved, trying out aliases (they settle on Magoo). "Reached the point of not knowing where life begins and theater ends, or even worse, where theater begins and life ends, where life begins to end with all this theater."

For when Palant wearies of playing the fugitive (because nobody seems to be hunting him) and Roberta wearies of playing the gangster's moll, they go out to find all New York in a state of continuous performance. Businessmen playing victims patronize a torture chamber where a spike-heeled friend of Roberta's, playing a sadist, administers carefully calibrated doses of pain. A "sublime old man," a ballet master of [Vaslav] Nijinsky's era, lies dying behind a transparent wall, viewed by party-goers on the other side. Even the homeless in parks and shelters seem to be acting out some half-conscious drama.

Like stage sets taken down and reassembled for the next act, New York keeps on shifting. Palant can't find the warehouse theater he visited on the fatal night. The store where he bought the pistol may have metamorphosed into an antique shop run by a black man who becomes Roberta's next lover. Palant even wonders if the murder itself wasn't elaborately staged, if he wasn't given the ticket and led to kill the actress—or believe that he was killing her—for the secret amusement of some rich and powerful spectator.

At this point, we discover that Valenzuela's balloon, however colorful, however wildly gyrating, is tied by a long string to something as dark and heavy as an anvil. Palant and Roberta are not just expatriates. Like Valenzuela herself, who spent several years in New York, they are self-exiles, haunted by Argentina's "dirty war" of the 1970s and early '80s.

Back home, they know, the rich and powerful *could* arrange murders to their liking. In the torture chambers of the military regime, pain had no limits. New York may be dangerous, but for Argentines its dangers seem somehow unserious, even desirable, "dangers you were looking for because that after all is what it's all about."

> **[*Black Novel*] is a witty, sexy, literary book by a highly sophisticated writer, one who likes to play with male and female stereotypes and themes of dominance and submission, love and creativity.**
> **—*Michael Harris***

Palant experiences New York as theater in part because he got used to play-acting in Buenos Aires, ignoring friends' "disappearances," fearing to speak out. The key to the murder, Valenzuela suggests, isn't a quirk in his individual psychology so much as his infection by the "dirty war" which, like the AIDS virus, can hide for a long time in the system before the delayed trigger clicks.

Yet *Black Novel* isn't standard political fare, either. This is a witty, sexy, literary book by a highly sophisticated writer, one who likes to play with male and female stereotypes and themes of dominance and submission, love and creativity. Some readers will groan: "Not *another* novel about novelists writing (or suffering writer's block) about events that may be real and may just be made up." Those who will enjoy Valenzuela are those who can play along—and follow that bouncing balloon.

Marjorie Agosin (review date 17 June 1992)

SOURCE: "Violence, Politics, and Complex Destinies," in *The Christian Science Monitor,* June 17, 1992, p. 15.

[*In the review below, Agosin focuses on the Argentinian themes of* Black Novel.]

Argentine Luisa Valenzuela and Chilean Isabel Allende are Latin America's best known and most widely translated woen writers. Valenzuela comes from a literary family (her mother, Luisa Mercedes Levinson, was a distinguished writer of prose) and is used to dealing with the intricate complexities of language as well as Argentine politics. She has written five novels and five collections of short stories, as well as numerous journalistic essays. One recurrent theme in Valenzuela's writing is contemporary politics, especially that of her native Argentina. Another is the use, misuse, and abuse of language in order to oppress, control, and censor thought at both the personal and political level.

Valenzuela has been praised for her talent of combining the political, the fictional, and the real. Most of her novels take place in the city of Buenos Aires, where lonely inhabitants are victims drowning in their country's violent political history. But her latest novel, *Black Novel (with Argentines),* takes plac in New York City with all its magnificence, poverty, and violence.

The plot deals with the murder of Edwina, an actress, by an Argentine writer in exile, Agustin Palante. The novel describes Agust's crime, committed apparently for no reason, except perhaps because he owned a gun. Yet, the whole narrative speaks of his consciousness after his crime, his guilt and his seclusion with his friend Roberta Aguilar—another

Argentine writer who only knows the partial truth about the murder and Agust's fabrications of what could happen to him for a crime that has left no traces.

Parallel to Agust's story and the crime he committed is the story of Roberta, who becomes so involved with trying to understand and save Agustin from despair that the novel she is writing becomes his story.

On one level, *Black Novel (with Argentines)* offers a highly provocative plot similar to a detective story. But Valenzuela is also speaking about the recent political history of Argentina, a history of violent dictatorships and the wholesale murder of innocent people. Edwina has disappeared without a trace just as 30,000 people disappeared in Argentina under the dictatorships of the 1970s. One may see Agustin as representing the henchmen of the dictators and Edwina's murder as the story of the disappeared. At one point, Roberta speaks to the question of a writer's task to bear witness and to understand what is happening in their respective nations, yet Agustin replies: "Your country, you mean. I no longer have a country."

The novel concerns the individual's personal and political consciousness. But it also concerns the mysterious nature of humans, which can drive them to commit violent crimes for no apparent reason. Agustin came to New York seeking political asylum and yet committed the same crime he was trying to escape. Once again, Valenzuela has portrayed the complex destinies of human beings as well as that of their nations.

This remarkable, lyrical novel does not allow readers to sit back passively observing the tribulations of Agustin. Rather, it draws them into the plot to share his ordeal, his senseless crime, and his neurotic existence trying to hide the crime. The novel makes clear that life and literature are inexorably woven together.

Amanda Hopkinson (review date 3 July 1992)

SOURCE: "In Flight from the Junta," in *Times Literary Supplement*, No. 4657, July 3, 1992, p. 26.

[*In the review below, Hopkinson briefly recounts the themes, style, and plots of* Open Door.]

Luísa Valenzuela is among Argentina's best-known writers of the "boom" period of the 1970s. Many voices were silenced when military rule returned in 1976 and waged war on "subversives", a category that inevitably included artists and intellectuals. Valenzuela survived by fleeing her coun-

try and spending ten years in exile, mainly in the United States.

Open Door, the latest anthology of her short stories to be published here, is informed by that period. Just as *The Lizard's Tail,* her only novel so far published in England, is based on the hated, strange and sadistic former "Minister for Social Welfare and Head of Paramilitary Organizations", López Rega, so many of these stories of the 1970s and 80s are rooted in the horrors and stupidities of junta dictatorships.

The last stories in this anthology are from the earliest publication, *Clara,* drawing heavily on Valenzuela's time in Normandy and Brittany, at least as magical a part of the world as the ports and pampas of Argentina. Here, in placeswith Celtic names like "Kermaria", cults of the Virgin and of matriarchy reign supreme, along with such tangled family extensions as the boy-with-nine-fathers, a grandfather who kisses the lips of a plaster Madonna, and a wild girl betrothed to a community of fishermen.

The section entitled "Up Among the Eagles" includes the eponymous tale of a fugitive whose solitary possession, a Polaroid camera, evokes not only the inverted images of photography's origins as *camera obscura* but also Plato's cave and a world of shadowed realities. Also here is **"The Censors"**, a moral tale that bears comparison with that of Ariel Dorfman on a theme evidently close to writers' hearts, and which takes the censor's task from an illogical premiss to its ruthlessly logical extreme. Throughout, there is a notable sensitivity to the uses of language—particularly when it has been hijacked by unspecified rulers who, by alternatively appropriating and eliminating terminologies, seek to strip human beings of an essential characteristic.

"Strange Things Happen Here" unpicks "the persecution of man by man" in a cross-over story in which the plot doubles back on itself and what's done forever far outweighs what's said. Language is taken further apart in **"The Verb to Kill"**, in which true heiresses of Jeanne the Strong (in the earlier story, **"The Minstrels"**), devise a new conjugation. This is by far the most overtly feminist section, with such amusing asides on androgyny and misogyny as **"The Blue Car"** and **"Vision out of the Corner of One Eye"**.

The style throughout is terse and taut, often with the staccato immediacy of the present tense and one-word sentences. All the greater achievement, then, to have created a world in which fantasy outweighs fiction and reality remains insidiously pervasive.

Marisa Januzzi (review date Fall 1992)

SOURCE: A review of *Black Novel (with Argentines)*, in *Review of Contemporary Fiction,* Vol. 12, No. 30, Fall, 1992, pp. 175-76.

[*Below, Januzzi offers a favorable review of* Black Novel, *remarking that "the text is so well constructed that it provides a tight alibi for her sense of language as a secretion."*]

From what she terms the "Argentine darkness," from the metaphorical alphabet city of New York's Lower East Side, and from the wild zones of "authority," gender, and language itself, Luisa Valenzuela has won a brilliant, difficult, involving text. In a 1986 interview Valenzuela said she was "stalking" rather than writing this novel, and signs of the five-year struggle for its production are evident in the narrative(s) of its protagonists, who are also authors: "To write about the immediate, almost an impossible task. One's arm must extend way beyond its reach in order to touch what is virtually clinging to one's body." In fact, the story-within-the-story is the recording of what seem to be meditations by the writer-characters, Agustín Palant and Roberta (whose patronymic is not given), on various aspects of its composition.

Originally entitled *The Motive*, the book begins with Agustín losing the door to the apartment of Edwina Irving, an actress he has just murdered, and whose name he has already partially forgotten. In the 1986 interview, Valenzuela described the work as coming out of her desire to write a detective novel: "I began one where the assassin and the victim are known, but not the motive of the crime. Not even the murderer knows it, and he searches because it is absolutely necessary for him to understand himself, of course. He's a writer who finally goes in search of his lover, another writer. Both are Argentines in New York and the search begins with an exchange of identities and all the paraphernalia that I'm interested in. They delve into the darkest regions of the city and of their subconscious. Since they are writers, they are very alert to metaphors, which doesn't mean they find what they are looking for, of course."

The starkness of that final "of course" belies the inference we are allowed to draw at the end, that at least Roberta, by writing and by loving, has been able to transform hers into an instrumental past, but it befits the tone of much of this novel, "extracted," as it reads, "from the folds of one's own sheets, in a clammy speleology of memories." The reinscription of the suppressed is the motive and the political ethos powering this novel, and through the crime of Agustín and Roberta's epic of complicity in concealing it, we get a heightened consideration of suppression, authority, and also of recognition and compassion—all the dynamics, Valenzuela might say, of fiction itself.

Like its characters, the text is preoccupied with traces.

Agustín is concerned about inscriptions of blood on his jacket, the identifiable details in vomit, the traces "which are impossible to erase," which are hidden, appropriated, sublimated. Roberta worries about the evidence in his manuscript, which she hides in an S&M parlor, the suitable submergitory for repressible objects and oblivious encounters. Some traces read like circumstantial evidence, graffiti "left with graphomaniac zeal" in the narrative, and it is difficult to assess their importance to the engine of the novel. In this category I place the references to, and the stylistic or structural autographs of [Alain] Robbe-Grillet, Borges, and Barnes; the gender almost arbitrarily marked in names like Edwina, "Vic" (for victim), and Roberta; and the traces of horror and worship implicit in the Tompkins Square setting, "vortex of the forlorn": Ave. A, Ave. B, and so on. Yet, these tricks with letters retain the occasionally mystifying suggestiveness they held for the characters themselves, as if they were metaphors of great meaning.

There is no question that the novelist, herself an Argentine currently living in New York, deals profoundly with the exiles' burdens of traces of an "other" life. Memories of the past and in particular of the "desaparecidos" in Argentina threaten, particularly in Agustín's dark, incoherent case, to overwhelm attempts at their erasure. Valenzuela's interests in censorship, self-censorship, and objectification of the "other" lead her into an exploration of sado-masochism, where the complicity between agents and customers of pain forms a perverse mirror of the political relationship between dominators and dominated. Thus, she restores the regressive and political subtext to pornography, which is carefully depicted as such in passages rife with casual violence and sinister metonymies ("There are the torturers and the tortured, thought the ear . . ."), and implicitly confirms the obscenity of the wanton exercise of power, as well.

There is a certain postmodern claustrophobia to this enterprise. I have to admit that I wanted to put the book down, as its motives led its characters to visit various urban temples of the desolate—the homeless shelters, surreal soirées, the necrophiliac death chambers of artistic renown, the lengthy confinements in apartments so well described that you can see the cartons of takeout foods rotting in ethnic splendor in the refrigerator. Valenzuela's trademark "way" with secretions and contaminants is evident here, too; but the text is so well constructed that it provides a tight alibi for her sense of language as a secretion, "the most terrifying of all perhaps because of everything it conceals while revealing, or vice versa." One reviewer wrote that you have to wear rubber gloves to read this novel; he or she is striking, possibly unwittingly, at the heart of the author's notion of catharsis. Readerly sweat notwithstanding, I'd say that the source of the novel's grandest question, and Roberta's means of answering it, are unforgettable.

Valenzuela says she likes the translation, but recommends reading **Black Novel** in the original if possible, because the gradations of complexity in the Spanish "spoken" between native speakers and the Spanish-as-English spoken between foreigners are inevitably lost in translation.

Cheryl Nimtz   (review date August-September 1993)

SOURCE: "Enmeshed in Their Own Language," in *American Book Review,* Vol. 15, No. 3, August-September, 1993, p. 8.

[*In the following review, Nimtz details the themes of* Black Novel *and Valenzuela's oeuvre in general, especially in relation to the author's provocative use of language.*]

From the beginning, Luisa Valenzuela's **Black Novel with Argentines** reads like a murder mystery. The first pages set the scene: place, New York City; time, a freezing predawn Saturday. We meet the murderer/protagonist, Agustín Palant, as he creeps, badly shaken, away from the New York apartment where he has just shot and killed a young actress he met only hours before.

We are given the WHO, the WHERE, and the HOW; we must discover the WHY—the motive. Immediately, however, we are presented with an unusual twist on the conventional murder mystery format: the bewildered killer himself does not know the motive for his crime. Agustín, an Argentine writer in New York on a grant to write his new novel, is (or had been up to this point) an ordinary citizen. He is baffled and horrified by his apparently random, arbitrary act of violence, and spends the rest of the novel in a desperate search to find the reasos why. As readers we are drawn into his search as we try to make sense of this novel that is, and is not, a murder mystery. We try to discover the motive and to make sense of the self-referential, multi-layered story. We play the roles of detective, author, and audience to this bizarre crime. In this deflection of expectations typical of her deft writing style, Luisa Valenzuela forces the readers into the story, to struggle to make sense of the novel along with the characters.

Agustín, it turns out, purchased the murder weapon only that day, in a questionable gun shop in a questionable part of town. Emboldened by the gun in his pocket and inspired by the advice of his lover Roberta (also an Argentine novelist) to try to "write with the body," Agustín ventures across the borderline and into the dangerous part of the city. Walking among the many offers for illicit drugs and sex, Agustín accepts an offer of a theater ticket to an underground play where he first meets his victim. After the murder, Agustín confesses his crime to Roberta, who decides to help conceal him and the evidence. Sequestered for months in Roberta's apartment, the two writers enter on a long inner search that ends up powerfully affecting them both.

In committing his crime, Agustín has crossed boundaries. We see him as a person lost, wandering in the bowels of New York City. Valenzuela uses the deteriorated, drug-infested neighborhoods, dark alleys, and rank subway tunnels vividly to evoke the human subconscious. This "subcity" is a zone where anything is possible, society's rules no longer apply, and the dark, foreboding, violent, and bizarre are the norm. Suddenly face to face with his dark side, Agustín is a man no longer capable of self-recognition. He becomes a stranger to himself, going through denial ("No, not me. It wasn't me . . ."), revulsion, and despair. He realizes that "the person he thought he was until the moment of the shot had never existed."

The personal and the political often reflect each other in Luisa Valenzuela's work. In **Black Novel** Agustín's personal struggle with evil becomes a metaphor for humans dealing with acts of horror and violence, specifically for Argentines who witnessed their country's "dirty war" in the late 1970s. Agustín, we are told, is a "typical porteño," and his name even sounds like "Argentine." In his horror and shock, Agustín tries to suppress his memories in a kind of self-imposed blindness. He is a metaphor for his compatriots, who refused to acknowledge the extent of torturings and "disappearances" even after the dirty war was over. In this sense, Valenzuela's art serves as an instrument of instigation or shock. It is meant to startle us into new realizations and make us aware of new connections as we recognize ourselves in her characters. It is a symbolic probe into our individual and collective subconscious, and a struggle with the knowledge of our own fall from innocence.

Roberta is also caught up in Agustín's guilt, fascination, and horror at having crossed the boundary and fallen from grace. She becomes an "accomplice after the fact," cleaning up Agustín's apartment and hiding the murder weapon in her medicine cabinet. She shares his horror and his fascination with the dark side of human nature: that desire to venture into the "mouth of the wolf" without getting swallowed.

Roberta's mingled fascination and revulsion are evident when she visits the workplace of her friend Ava Taurel, a professional dominatrix. Valenzuela achieves a provocative, ironic metaphor in the not-so-underground New York S&M scene. In the spectacles played out in Ava Taurel's theater of pleasure and pain, Roberta encounters a bizarre, distorted reflection of the torture chambers of her country's past. The political resonates and the line between sex and violence blurs as Roberta asks the book's poignant questions: how can some people enjoy voluntary sexual torture when other innocent people are tortured against their will? What makes an ordinary person capable of violence? "What I need is to know why someone becomes a torturer, a murderer, to know why an upright citizen can one day unawares be transformed into a monster."

Along with the blurring of the line between the personal and the political, *Black Novel* includes other topics common in Valenzuela's work: memory, reality versus fiction, and, of course, language.

Memory and self-censorship are two common Valenzuela themes. In her short story **"Cambio de armas,"** Valenzuela portrays Laura, a victim of torture to the point of brainwashing. Although Laura occasionally remembers fragments of who she is and what has happened, she fights her memories because they are too painful for her to bear. In *Black Novel* Agustín also experiences random flashes of memories (of Buenos Aires in the 1970s, when people in his own building "disappeared"), and he too attempts to suppress them. They are too painful; they are "memories to be stifled." But this self-censorship is to Valenzuela the most insidious form of censorship because it comes from within. It means the populace has been frightened into refusing to see. As the homeless woman in the novel explains to Roberta, "What's really yours is always returned." Memories, and the consequences of our actions, will return to haunt us despite our attempts to ignore them. Laura's and Agustín's denial of the truth doesn't change their situation, and in fact hinders their abilities to save themselves. *Black Novel with Argentines* condemns self-censorship and advocates confrontation with the truth—no matter how painful it may be—as a way of dealing with human evils.

Memory is also vital to identity, as Valenzuela shows us in the brainwashed Laura, who can't remember who she is, and in Agustín, who loses all self-recognition when he tries to deny his crime and his experiences in Buenos Aires. An individual without memory has no identity, and a society full of such individuals has no collective memory, no history.

The power of language to shape reality, and the tenuous line between reality and fiction, are two of Valenzuela's most consistent themes. In *Black Novel,* Agustín and Roberta teeter on the border between sanity and madness, and between reality and fiction. The "literariness" of their situation is not lost on the two writers. They refer to the murder/search as the "novel" they're writing together. Fiction seems real ("Do you know this firsthand?" "Yes. I read it in a novel"), and reality takes on the dreamlike quality of a cheap novel, a horror story, or a bad joke. Even as he is leaving the scene of the crime, Agustín feels as if he is trapped—ironically—in the plot of some cheap novel, "so true to the trashy local reading matter."

Valenzuela's work constantly questions language (which is, after all, a *human* creation) and language's ability to reflect "truth" or "reality," which are themselves fluctuating. In *Black Novel,* names reflect the characters' attempts to deny reality. Both Roberta and Agustín attempt to become someone else. Roberta helps Agustín to shave off his beard, then gives him her clothes to wear. She renames him "Gus," then "Magoo" in an effort to help him hide from the truth. As Agustín tries to dissociate himself from his crime and escape his newly discovered capacity for violence, his denial is reflected in his language. When retracing his steps the night of the murder, he refers to himself in the third person. Afraid of making Roberta feel betrayed, he tells her the murder victim was a man. With each lie, Agustín enters "the winding path of someone reciting only half-truths, who at every turn fibs a tiny bit more." Roberta also changes. She cuts and dyes her hair, puts on a man's suit, and is called "Robbie," then "Bobbie," and finally "Bob." Both characters become enmeshed in the web of their own language. Thus, a female murder victim becomes a male, and Roberta and Agustín reverse sex roles. In these transformations, Valenzuela is questioning the assumption that language somehow has a one-to-one correlation with reality. The proliferation of given names, nicknames, pet names, and aliases in the novel poses the question: do names define us and tell us who we are? Or do they just confuse the issue?

> **Valenzuela's work constantly questions language (which is, after all, a *human* creation) and language's ability to reflect "truth" or "reality," which are themselves fluctuating.**
> —*Cheryl Nimtz*

Black Novel with Argentines is not without flaws. There are occasional problems in the novel. Although Roberta and Agustín aren't necessarily meant to be likable characters, at times they come across as overly self-absorbed and writerly. The whole novel is rich in metaphors and multiple levels of meaning. However, this can lead to obscurity in places such as the scenes in the old theater, at the end. Here, theater and theatrical reality, birth and death, motives, and rites of passage references are so dense that it's difficult to navigate. Considering the huge issues that Valenzuela tackles, such as humans' capacity for evil, perhaps it is not surprising that occasionally we feel overwhelmed.

As in much of Valenzuela's work, it is important to notice not just what *Black Novel* says, but what it does. After actively engaging the readers in the search for the motive (for why there is violence in ourselves and our societies), Valenzuela refuses to give us the clear, all-encompassing answers we are looking for. In this sense, the ending of *Black*

Novel completes the detective novel deconstruction. Instead of offering up a final, logical answer to Agustín's/Roberta's/ our search, it compounds the problem. No shrewd detective nters upon the scene to offer us last-minute explanations. It's as if Valenzuela uses the detective novel form to engage us in the search for an answer, then chides us for hoping for a pat answer that would bring order out of the chaos of life. Various possible motives are offered along the way. But none offers the single, complete explanation that allows us the satisfaction of solving the case and putting it to rest so we can go on to other things. This is Valenzuela's point: that the issue of why humans commit violence individually and collectively is one that must be confronted and probed, as the dark face of ourselves. But ultimately what we are exploring is not neat, symmetrical, organized poetry or art, but something far more complicated, where good and bad, reality and fiction are not as clear. It is a cheap, badly written novel, a bad joke, or, as the character Dr. Hector Bravo calls it, "True, harsh, deceptive, gripping, fluctuating, imaginative, exciting, damned reality."

Caleb Bach (essay date January-February 1995)

SOURCE: "Metaphors and Magic Unmask the Soul," in *Américas*, Vol. 47, No. 1, January-February, 1995, pp. 22-7.

[*In the essay below, Bach provides an overview of Valenzuela's life and works.*]

Argentine writer Luisa Valenzuela has defined her country's origins in terms both violent and lyrical. In a 1983 essay penned for the *New York Times*, she referred to the discovery of the Rio de la Plata by Juan Diaz de Solis in 1516: "Poetry was already lurking: on board with Solis was Martin del Barco Centenera, who wrote an ode titled *The Argentina*, . . . a misnomer since there was practically no *argentum*, no silver, there. . . . It was written while the first settlers, surrounded by Indians, were forced to eat their dead. That is why I believe we are descendants of poets and cannibals." At the time, Valenzuela's essay was celebratory and quite specific: "With the return of democracy, the poets' time has come." Still, it reflected an abiding concern that has occupied her during much of her career: why this penchant for self-destruction from a human spirit that also can find expression through peaceful dreaming with words?

In Valenzuela's case, to claim direct descent from poets is accurate Through her mother, Luisa Mercedes Levinson, a well-known author of novels and haunting, ironic short stories, she came to know many other prominent members of Argentina's literary community. "I grew up with all these writers: Jorge Luis Borges, Ernesto Sábato. They came to

our home. That's one thing that probably led me to write. My mother collaborated with Borges on one story ("La hermana de Eloisa"). As a child I thought writing was dreary, drab, but they loved it. They could be quite obnoxious but funny. That impressed me that writing was more lively than one would think."

As a teenager Valenzuela placed her first articles with the youth magazine *Quince Abriles*. Instead of attending the university, she went straight into journalism on a full-time basis, working for several Buenos Aires newspapers and magazines (*La Nación, El Mundo, El Hogar*). At age eighteen she published her first short story, **"Ciudad ajena"** [**"The City of the Unknown"**], a tale suffused with the themes of death, eroticism, and dreams that would endure in much of her later work. For a time Valenzuela also worked at the Biblioteca Nacional, which was directed by Borges and his deputy, José Edmundo Clemente. Valenzuela recalls that she wrote press releases for lectures sponsored by the library. "God knows what I wrote. I didn't even type well. But I was very proud because I knew I was in the presence of someone important. Borges was always pulling some book off the shelf and explaining. He could still see a little bit. The way he related to books was very beautiful."

At one point, Borges complained that rats were eating the books in the Biblioteca Nacional. "My mother had all these cats, sometimes as many as twenty. You thought they might eat you if you didn't feed them. She gave him one which she named Assurbanipal, after the Assyrian king mentioned in a Borges story. Then one day the great writer called very excitedly saying the cat was caught between the roof and cupola of the library, meowing and echoing, and so he realized the fantasy of his life: He called the fire department. My mother thought he would be furious because the cat never caught a mouse and had caused all this commotion. Borges said, 'Oh, no, no. I always dreamed of calling the firemen, but I wasn't permitted to as a child so this was a great opportunity.' Borges was very shy then, much shier than in his later years but sort of wicked you know . . . a *pícaro*."

At age twenty, headstrong and impulsive, Valenzuela left home and headed for France. "Yes, I've been prone to radical shifts in my life," she ruefully admits, "and French sailors!" In rapid succession she married Theodore Marjak, who was in the French merchant marine, resettled in Normandy, and gave birth to her daughter, Anna Lisa. "But I got seasick," she says with a smile, and so the marriage ended in divorce six years later.

While in France Valenzuela continued to write, especially stories that tapped the rich folklore of Normandy and neighboring Brittany, "I was very hooked into the magic. I've always been trying to see that other world." Two memorable (and uncharacteristically gentle) stories came from that period, **"El hijo de Kermaria"** [**"The Son of Kermaria"**] and **"Los Menestrales"** [**"The Minstrels"**]. In the latter, 'a mother named Jeanne the Strong assigns a collective paternity to her son: the traits of nine nomadic musicians who temporarily lived at her farm. This composite identity contrasts strongly with the disagreeable personality of the biological father, a foul-smelling drunkard away at war. The boy feels comforted seeing these likable minstrels mirrored in him, while his mother gives flight to her own fantasy: that she had had an intimate relationship with each of the men. "I meant to do a whole book of stories from the region because I had all these ideas. A distant relative of my ex-husband had a farm in Brittany. He knew all these black magic stories and would tell them as if they were everyday happenings: impressive and fantastic witchcraft. But I couldn't write a word about them. I couldn't write what had been told me. I had to invent everything from scratch. It is a defect I have and at the same time it is my need to surprise myself. If I know where this whole thing is going to take me it's already done. *Escribo lo que no sé.*"

In the early sixties, Valenzuela moved to Paris, where she wrote programs for Radio Television Française. While living in the Bois de Boulogne district she also observed the precarious circumstances of prostitutes living in her building. She used this material for her first novel, **Hay que sonreir** (later translated into English as **Clara**). Not unlike Jeanne the Strong, Clara also attempts to invent a new identity as a foil against the harsh reality of life. Metaphorically, Clara is a headless body at the service of clients in need of sexual gratification. The ingenuous girl exchanges this demeaning life for a job devoid of body, an illusionary act in a circus sideshow. As Aztec Flower, she appears to be just a severed head left from some ancient sacrificial ritual (when in fact her contorted body is concealed in a box beneath the flower). In the end, illusion becomes reality when her new husband turns on her. As he is about to slit her throat—is it a conditioned reflex or in appreciation for her deliverance?—she can only tell herself that she must smile (*"hay que sonreir"*).

Abrupt, even perverse twists in the way a story evolves and culminates characterize many Valenzuela plot lines. This quality may have its roots in her early childhood when her older sister told her bizarre stories with scary endings. Valenzuela was a finicky eater, and when a shocking tale would cause her to open her mouth in astonishment, her sister would be able to get a spoonful of food in. "But I loved them. It wasn't a sort of torture. I loved the horrible stories." Does Valenzuela do that a bit as a writer? "Yes. I like fear. I don't write for little children. At least I try not to. It is one of my pleasures of writing. Suddenly the whole thing comes about in an unexpected way."

In 1964, Valenzuela's wanderings took her back to her homeland where again she worked as a journalist for *La Nación* while completing a screenplay for **Hay que sonreir.** (It later won an award from Argentina's Institución Nacional de Cinematografia.) But she continued to travel throughout Europe and in the United States—always "a tumbleweed, blowing up against a fence somewhere . . . looking for the almost mythic Here-Place, the center of my metaphor" (her words from a 1983 autobiographic sketch). Travel would prove to be the machine behind much of her writing, as if distance made her see things better ("separation sharpens the aim," she has said).

"I have been a traveler all my life," Valenzuela explains. "Even when not on the move I've dreamed of traveling by inventing excursions and adventures, even if it's just around the block. I wanted to be an explorer. I'm a Sagittarius, so that probably has something to do with it." Valenzuela also believes that real home dwells within the person. "I don't know what missing [home] is. When I'm away I'm absolutely there. I'm energized by unpredictability, things coming apart both in my writing and my life. It's uncomfortable, but it makes me go. The moment I feel secure, I get out of the situation."

In 1969 it was wanderlust and a Fulbright grant that took Valenzuela to the United States as a participant in the International Writers Program at the University of Iowa. She disliked Iowa City, "which was neither city nor countryside," but in the solitude of this alien setting and the company of "many other neurotic writers" she wrote her second novel, **El gato eficaz** [**"The Efficient Cat"**]. The feline creature in the title proves to be a "cat-o-nine deaths," a kind of composite of many of the world's evils that accompany a female narrator through a series of strange adventures at once eschatological, violent, erotic, and humorous. Valenzuela abandoned the linear narrative of **Hay que sonreir** and opted for a more daring, subversive, and (as one critic said) "fragmented, respectful disrespect" for language: run-on words, invented terms (like *telecoito*, or long-distance lovemaking), and even words that transform themselves or disintegrate before the reader's eyes (smite me, *imíteme, imitáteme*), much like characters in the novel itself. Outlandish puns and word play, parodies of social taboos, newspaper clippings, diary entries, legal abstracts, operating instructions—all come together in this highly energized yet deeply disturbing novel, which disassembles literature and demythologizes traditional behavior.

As to the role of humor in her writing, Valenzuela responds with a quiet grin: "Humor is serious business, very serious. Because I don't believe there is any life without humor. Of course, not everything is laughable. It's just that it gives you the other face of the same thing. Otherwise you see things unilaterally. The humor that is not always laughing so directly at things also allows you to see more obscure parts. I wouldn't even be looking at certain things if I didn't take a humorous slant to get into it. Sometimes they criticize me seriously. They say, 'You break the climate by making a joke in the middle of this horror,' which I do a lot. Humor is the mortar of life . . . motor of life!"

During the late seventies Valenzuela's writing was strongly shaped by events in her homeland, a military government committed to the "dirty war," which involved persecution, torture, and the disappearances of thousands of persons. *Como en la guerra* [*He Who Searches*], her third novel, employed some of the same kaleidoscopic techniques found in *El gato eficaz* but also mirrored the author's residency first in Barcelona and Mexico and her return to Buenos Aires. As she later wrote in the preface to *Open Door* (a 1988 English-language collection of some of her favorite short stories: "in 1975, upon returning to my city after a long absence . . . it wasn't mine any longer. Buenos Aires belonged then to violence and state terrorism, and I could only sit in cafés and brood. Till I decided a book of short stories could be written in a month, at those same café tables, overhearing scraps of scared conversation, seeping in the general paranoia." And thus *Aquí pasan cosas raras* [*Strange Things Happen Here*] was born, a collection of highly imaginative tales populated with misfits and perverts, Valenzuela's barely disguised portraits of oppressors compensating for their own sense of impotence or inadequacy. In **"A Story About Greenery,"** a thistle manages to prosper despite a municipal edict prohibiting foliage in public places and in the story **"Los mejor calzados"** [**"The Best Shod"**], a city takes pride in its beggars who wear nice shoes. (They have been confiscated from the bodies of those who were tortured and executed.)

[Valenzuela's] rich, descriptive passages detailing rituals and omens, drums and masks also suggest a seasoned anthropologist at work.
—*Caleb Bach*

The oppressive "atmosphere of self-censorship—should I write indecipherably so that nobody could read over my shoulder?" (as she later remembered asking herself)—compelled Valenzuela to find a new place of residence. Thanks to a timely invitation to be a writer-in-residence at Columbia University, she opted for New York City. In 1981 she was named a fellow at the New York Institute for the Humanities, a prestigious multidisciplinary research facility, and the following year she was awarded a Guggenheim Fellowship. Throughout the 1980s Valenzuela conducted many stimulating seminars at Columbia while also teaching writing courses at New York University.

But events unfolding along the shores of the Rio de la Plata continued to attract her attention and ultimately inspire one of her most fascinating novels, *Cola de lagartija* [*The Lizard's Tale*], which refers to a kind of braided whip once used in South America. In the second section of this hallucinatory novel, Valenzuela casts herself in the role of a journalist intent on covering the psychopathic escapades of the book's central figure, a magician gone mad. The author's rich, descriptive passages detailing rituals and omens, drums and masks also suggest a sesoned anthropologist at work. A lifelong student of ethnology, cultural development, and the evolution of myths in different societies, Valenzuela has long held a particular fascination for the mask, both as literary device and art form. She has a sizable collection of masks from Mexico, where she lived on and off during the 1970s. "Once, during that period, I was working in Oaxaca as a journalist. I wanted to go to Huautla, which was forbidden because it was the season of the hallucinogenic mushrooms. They wouldn't let in any foreigners. Eventually a man with a *camioneta* happened by who was leaving for Huautla, and he agreed to take me along. Once there I wanted to meet María Sabina, a famous *curandera*. This young fellow says let's go and so we started climbing, it was like the roof of the world . . . *más arribita, más arribita* . . . forty kilometers [twenty-five miles] on foot, seven hours. Eventually through a nephew who served as interpreter María Sabina offered us mushrooms. I didn't dare. She was a powerful shamaness. It was fantastic!"

That gutsy adventure also gave shape to **"Donde viven las águilas"** [**"Where the Eagles Dwell"**], the title story of a 1983 collection inspired by Valenzuela's adventures in Mexico. In this tale, a female protagonist ascends from the lowlands to a surreal realm high amid the mountaintops, where time seems to stand still. She discovers a village populated by people, a so-called "living" dead who don't age, reproduce, nor decay because the cycle of life is suspended "on a wheel that turns but does not move." The story operates on several levels, but one message clearly reveals itself in a telling line: "Life entails a progression towards death. To remain stagnant is to be already dead." For Valenzuela "life on hold" has absolutely no validity; it must be charged with continual change, risk, and the vitality that comes from actively tasting things firsthand.

During the 1980s Valenzuela purchased a little house in Tepoztlán, a town a couple hours' drive from Mexico City noted for its spectacular cliffs and the otherworldly quality of its setting. Her house was full of spiders, to each of which she gave a name. "I made a *trato* with them that I would leave them alone if they would eat the scorpions and other insects." Events in Tepoztlán proved to be the inspiration for several memorable tales, among them **"El fontanero azul"** [**"Blue Water Man"**], whom Valenzuela describes as "a spider in the middle of a web of plumbing, god of an underground world of sewers." Water in Tepoztlán was rationed, and yet this "vile water man without a doubt, for a hundred pesos, would let the cisterns of the rich overflow while their neighbors could get struck by lightening for all he cared." Against the backdrop of Holy Week, with its traditional papier-mâché figures that are blown apart with fireworks, this latter-day Judas meets his end when an exploding stick of dynamite stuck in his pants splatters his remains upon the clothing of the rich he so unjustly favored. Having vented their resentment, the dancing townsfolk streak their white masks with the "blood of the water man, symbol of water, complete ablution."

In 1988, while writing *Novela negra con argentinos* [*Black Novel (with Argentines)*], Valenzuela decided to leave New York City, which had been her base of operations for nearly ten years. "It was a question of language. I was so invaded by the English language. I was worried because I was dreaming and talking to myself in English. I always wrote in Spanish but if I stayed any longer, I would have to start writing in English." Chillingly faithful to the modern-day reality of many a big city, *Novela negra* features two Argentine writers living a New York existence defined by the basest of circumstances (mindless killings, sexual perversion, foul cynicism at every turn). "My feeling when I was writing was why do I write these horrible things about New York when I really love this city. Then I concluded it was my farewell, my goodbye to New York. I saw the worst part because I was trying to disengage myself."

For the moment, this vagabond storyteller has returned to her homeland and defined her "Here-Place" as an apartment in a quiet, secluded part of the Belgrano district of Buenos Aires. She has continued to travel for conferences, as a lecturer, and to give workshops, but she has still found time to continue writing. In 1990 she issued a polemic on the situation in Argentina entitled *Realidad nacional desde la cama* [**"National Reality from the Bed"**]. In 1993, Editorial Sudamericana issued a new collection of her short stories, *Simetrías* [**"Symmetries"**], among them some fairy tales revised for adults, ghost stories, and personalized accounts set in Venice, Bali, and California's Big Sur.

It had been Valenzuela's intention to do a historical novel based upon the life of Juana Azurduy, a heroine of the nineteenth-century wars of independence from Spain who possessed courageous assertiveness remarkable for those times. "I went to Sucre, Bolivia, in July, 1993, and worked in the archives at the Casa de Libertad. I was there for the anniversary of Azurduy, and so they asked me to speak. They even brought out the urn with her ashes, which I held. It was very moving. But then, after nothing had been published on her here, suddenly a book came out by Paco O'Donnell [former Argentine ambassador to Bolivia] and so . . . well,

I had been speaking too much and not doing it. You have to do things!"

If Valenzuela is hard on herself (and she always is), it is because she feels strongly that one must live what one believes. She demands of herself and those around her the very best kind of thinking—inspired aspirations—and therefore is distressed by the cultural banality so common the world over. "Here in Argentina, our 'postmodernist' government is more interested in bigger shopping centers than better theaters. Buenos Aires used to be more profound. One could sit in a café and talk, and now few can even afford to buy a cup of coffee." Could the tragedy of Argentina's recent past at least be perceived as a catalyst for serious work? "I don't believe that sort of thing. Not at all," Valenzuela states emphatically. "There's no such thing as a placid situation . . . because there's human soul that necessarily is not placid. They used to say to me in the United States: 'You are lucky because you have all these terrible things to fight against and that makes you create.' I thought that a terrible idea. A writer always has to find that force and do things without having to fight because of horrible things you're going through."

Perhaps it is inappropriate to describe Valenzuela's life on the edge with a linear chronology; after, she favors circular, spiral, or even concentric configurations for the passage of events and as to those events themselves, she prefers to describe them with ambiguity. That is to say, her books are not for the "*desocupado lector*," or lazy, uninvolved reader, as her biographer, Sharon Magnarelli, has pointed out. But it also should be noted that she does not intentionally confuse her audience: Her prose is crystalline, and her choice of words precise. It is rather that, like the true teacher, she prefers to trigger self-education by posing questions, not by serving up simplistic solutions. Her goal is to provoke thoughtfulness, dislodge the apathetic from their comfortable yet fallacious, worn-out assumptions, and see with acuity the disturbing reality within which we live. "I write about heresies: when religion ends up falling over the wall which is fascinating, especially dogmatic religions. They are so dogmatic they have to collapse and turn into good things. I also write about power. Now I am asking myself what is love all about. Since I don't have hints of an answer, I might be writing something about it because, as I said, I like to write about that which I don't know."

During our conversation the phone rang, and Valenzuela learned that a close friend's son had just died in a motorcycle accident. Visibly pained by the call, later she nonetheless reflected: "We walk on the edge of death, and there is a certain excitement, it is interesting. It's horrible to say that. But there is strength there too. There's this precarious business but to die has its own strength, validity. He had the right to buy a motorcycle and kill himself. This is not committing suicide. This is some sort of following a destiny that belonged to him. I have no right to deprive him of it. It has a strength that one has to honor. I don't know whether I said it very well, but I have a very strong feeling about that. He did *his* life."

Ilan Stavans (review date 6 March 1995)

SOURCE: "Autumn of the Matriarch?," in *The Nation,* Vol. 260, No. 9, March 6, 1995, pp. 316-19.

[*In the review below, Stavans reads autobiographical aspects of Valenzuela's life into* Bedside Manners.]

Carlos Fuentes once rather pompously referred to Luisa Valenzuela as "the heiress of Latin American fiction" who "wears an opulent, baroque crown, but her feet are naked." That was in the early eighties, when her dislike of dogmas and certainties, her explorations of the uses of ambiguity, her forays into "that reflective field where reality appears at its most real" were the constant subjects of features, book reviews and heavy literary commentary, a time when she could reign unchallenged as the best-known and most-translated contemporary woman writer of the Southern Hemisphere. But things have changed dramatically since then. The region's literature is in crisis today, with luminaries like Valenzuela seemingly unable to find a way out of their artistic quagmire.

Other eloquent female voices have entered the scene on a grand scale, most notably Isabel Allende (*Eva Luna, The House of the Spirits*) and Laura Esquivel (*Like Water for Chocolate*), signaling a variety of alternative styles and themes. Instead of shying away from the kitchen and its gastronomic potentials, and rather than evading melodrama and sentimentality in their work, they have delved into those realms wholeheartedly. The result is a type of women's writing that is commercially successful on levels never experienced by Valenzuela, and that subverts by way of consorting with and exploiting the status quo. And this sort of literary renewal is evident not only among women but also among young, curious writers of both sexes who are devoted to experiments with subgenres like thrillers, science fiction and romance (Luis Sepúlveda's ecological whodunits spring to mind, for example).

One of the causes precipitating a sense of the doldrums in Latin American fiction is the everlasting compulsion to make politics a sine qua non in fiction. The tentacles of tyrannies have been everywhere in the Southern Hemisphere for centuries, and naturally the writer's voice has come to symbolize resistance and rebellion. Valenzuela, who has spent almost as much of her adult life in her native country, Argentina, as she has abroad in Europe and the United States,

believes the primary purpose of lierature is to disturb, to agitate—not by repeating trite political slogans but by questioning our perception of reality. Since her debut in 1966, her literary project has carried on the legacy of astute playfulness of her compatriot and unquestionable tutor, Julio Cortázar, the author of *Hopscotch* and "Blow Up," who died suddenly in 1984. Cortázar's second creative period, from the moment he identified with Fidel Castro's revolution on, was marked by critical barbs aimed at repression and taboos. Less inventive but equally shrewd, Valenzuela roams the same themes and displays similar stylistic pyrotechnics. She enjoys walking the tightrope between religious fanaticism and heresy, deciphering the macabre link between torture and pleasure, and reflecting on the heavy weight of collective history. Even when her topic is sex and superstition, as in her most celebrated novel, *The Lizard's Tail,* its implications are invariably intertwined with politics, cruelty and death. The subject of that 1983 book was José López Rega, the controversial minister of social welfare and personal secretary to Isabel Perón. Rega, a self-proclaimed astrologer who helped rule Argentina through sorcery, had a curious physical abnormality: three testicles. Valenzuela investigated his fanciful life, delivering a demanding, lucidly self-conscious political novel that constantly challenged the reader's expectations. To revolt, then, has been her lifelong activity: She has opposed tyrannical regimes, machismo, bourgeois society and traditional writing styles.

At a time when to accuse meant to unsettle, to unnerve, Valenzuela's much-needed message was quite popular. As the Argentine military junta propagated a dirty war against alternative forces, writers like her became magnets of international attention, and efforts to silence their voices proved ineffective. But now dictatorship has given way to democracy, even if tenuous, throughout Latin America with the exception of Cuba, and the transition to civilian life is proving to be a mammoth challenge to old-guard literati like her. As in Jean-Paul Sartre's theory that Jews need anti-Semites to exist, once Perón, [Alfredo] Stroessner and [Augusto] Pinochet left the spotlight, "oppositional" writers have suddenly found themselves with a limited audience, their prose turned morose, infirm, unappealing. Dissension, as everybody knows, is good literary business.

Valenzuela's youthful bravura has mellowed. Her sharp revolutionary edge seems not tepid but mismatched to current realities, and the role of articulating Argentina's passage to democracy has evaded her. As exemplified by *Bedside Manners,* her latest and probably most evanescent novel to appear in English (originally published in 1990), nostalgia and depression, permanent features of the Argentine psyche, have become somewhat pervasive in her development. The autobiographical plot pertains to a female writer's attempt to understand the drastic, chaotic changes affecting her country since the military regime gave up power. Almost immediately upon her arrival home after a decade-long exile in New York, the Señora, as the protagonist is addressed, accepts an invitation from a new friend to spend time alone in a bungalow at a local country club in an unnamed city (presumably Buenos Aires), where she is to recover and assimilate the heterogeneous stimuli now bombarding her. Her friend tells her: "The club isn't one of those flashy places, it might not seem much to someone like you coming from abroad, but it's actually very private and exclusive. They don't let just anyone in."

She packs a bag with the bare essentials—white sheets, a white nightgown and an empty notebook—and sets off for the "unknown but singularly unthreatening destination." All too soon she finds out that the club is located next to a training camp where extreme-right military forces are planning a coup d'état. As the narrative progresses, TV images, one of Valenzuela's favorite motifs, become ubiquitous and are indistinguishable from reality. Visions keep flying out of the TV set, confusing the Señora even more. Strange encounters and flirtations begin to occur with an eccentric cast of characters, portrayed as vultures and hyenas ready to extort and abuse her. She is first visited by an obnoxiously idiosyncratic maid, María, who keeps turning the TV on and, ironically, while trying to pull her out of depression, never stops repeating that the nation's currency is worthless and inflation is under such fast rhythm that the currency is already lighter than air. Then comes Doctor Alfredi, ready to take sexual advantage of her while diagnosing her melancholic status; Lucho, a miserable, insubordinate soldier often found under the Señora's bed; and the patriotic Major Vento, who justifies his hyperkinetic military actions in the camp by claiming that the country "is plagued with dangerous looters and left-wing agitators who profit from the difficult social situation," and who thinks the army should demoralize and disrupt daily life in order "to crush the malcontents."

The novel has a distinctive Beckett-like atmosphere; its narrative occasionally switches from first to third person and utilizes phrasings that simultaneously employ both philosophical and matter of-fact dimensions. Yet it also reminds me of Anita Brookner's *Hotel du Lac,* in which a woman looks for relaxation in a country home only to find inner perplexity. Valenzuela's entire adventure takes place within the boundaries of the bungalow, where the air is increasingly suffocating, sleep insufficient and the public and domestic spheres constantly collide. (A more accurate, less poetic translation of Valenzuela's title, ***Realidad nacional desde la cama,*** is **"National Reality as Perceived from the Bed"**) The Señora feels alone and aloof. Indeed, at one point she tells Doctor Alfredi: "I feel as if someone was trying to wipe my memory clean, I don't know, obliterate it with new inscriptions. I don't understand it at all." To which he answers: "That happens a lot here. What else is worrying you?" Simi-

lar sarcastic comments on Argentine psychology—like the one suggesting that the country is the best on earth, even if the rest of humankind refuses to accept it—constantly emerge. By the book's end, a military maneuver, at once ridiculous and explosive, shaped to save the nation's collective soul, takes place in the deceptive abyss where imagined and sensory perceptions meet. Talk about a passion for ambiguity. Valenzuela belongs roughly to the generation of Marcos Aguinis, Fernando Sorrentino, Liliana Heer and Ricardo Piglia; most have lived abroad, some permanently, and have taught at American universities. Their fiction is marked by the intense desire to understand the impact of torture, xenophobia and exile on Argentine society.

Valenzuela's literary career began at an early age, writing for periodicals such as *El Hogar,* a women's magazine where Borges had a column. (She is the daughter of writer Luisa Mercedes Levinson, who is responsible for a much-anthologized jungle story, "El abra," and was one of Borges's female collaborators.) Encouraged by her mother, she left Argentina to gain perspective. Paris was her first stop, and in 1965, while working for Radio Television Française, she began to feel attracted to the short story as a literary genre, where I believe, much like Cortázar, she excels. She returned to Argentina and worked as a journalist, only to leave again in 1969, this time for the United States. Interest here in the Latin American literary boom was in its early stages: Cortázar's *Hopscotch* had appeared a few years before; *One Hundred Years of Solitude* was soon selling like hot cakes; and Borges, thanks to the International Publisher's Prize he shared with Samuel Beckett, was newly translated into a dozen languages and quickly becoming a classic. Valenzuela dreamed of entering this male club, and succeeded in a bit more than a decade.

> **Valenzuela's opulent, baroque crown and naked feet can be interpreted in numerous ways, including, prophetically, the one suggesting that her adorned style hides a certain vulnerability to new terrain.**
> **—Ilan Stavans**

The existence she led finally disturbed Valenzuela, though. Much like the Señora, she found herself in New York, dreaming in English, and felt unhappy. She returned to Buenos Aires but soon realized the city belonged to her no more. It now belonged "to violence and state terrorism," and she "could only sit in cafés and brood." She would spend hours with a cup of coffee, "responding to the general paranoia and fear, and thinking that I should write indecipherably so that nobody could read over my shoulder. (The writer as witness? The writer as antenna?)" *Bedside Manners* mirrors that troublesome return home. Whereas elsewhere in her work, including *Other Weapons, The Lizard's Tail* and *Open Door,* violence and death are linked to myth and erotic rituals, here the plot is straightforward and doesn't call for deep interpretations. In Margaret Jull Costa's remarkably smooth translation (with British spellings left intact by the publisher), the novel reads like a diary on the struggle to adapt to life in a new milieu. "This new city isn't the one I used to know, they've changed everything," she tells Lucho. "Now I don't know who the enemy is, I don't know who to fight against. Before I went away I did, now the enemy's no longer there, or at least he says he isn't, but he is and I just don't know where I stand."

Indeed, the quote embodies Valenzuela's present existential dilemma, and that of many members of her generation. While she's already part of an essential chapter in Latin American letters, one in which politics and repression, metamorphosed into magical fiction, brought world attention, her current standing poses a challenge she's struggling to meet: How to address political issues in the Southern Hemisphere at a time when, happily, they are less than life-threatening? Should the region's writers become sheer entertainers, as are the majority of U.S. literati? Her younger peers such as Ana María Shúa, also influenced by Cortázar, are already exploring and exploiting new venues, signaling a way out of the current literary crisis. Which brings me back to Fuentes's cryptic metaphor at the outset of this review: Valenzuela's opulent, baroque crown and naked feet can be interpreted in numerous ways, including, prophetically, the one suggesting that her adorned style hides a certain vulnerability to new terrain. This onetime heiress of Latin American fiction appears disorientd, perhaps no longer certain who the enemy is or what to fight against—or indeed, what literature is to be if not a fight.

D. Quentin Miller (review date Summer 1995)

SOURCE: A review of *Bedside Manners,* in *Review of Contemporary Fiction,* Vol. 15, No. 2, Summer, 1995, p. 201.

[*In the following review, Miller maintains that the "overlapping of military and personal struggles is what makes* Bedside Manners *so appealing."*]

Luisa Valenzuela's short novel *Bedside Manners* offers a fresh perspective on the difficulties of facing reality, specifically the reality of economic and political instability in an unnamed Latin American country. Valenzuela somehow manages to communicate this theme while creating a landscape that evades realism at every turn. The result is a playful account of one woman's quest to come to terms with her changing homeland and her fractured identity.

The protagonist, referred to only as the Señora, returns from New York to the country of her birth "in search of refuge" from the spiritually destructive world she inhabits. She takes up residence in a country club, where she is to rest and recuperate, but finds that her bed becomes "a boat adrift on troubled waters." The country club is supposed to be sheltered from the world surrounding it, but the changed landscape of her country penetrates her room relentlessly. The invasion of the Señora's world, specifically by her chambermaid María, a psychologist/cab driver named Alfredi, and Lucho, one of a number of soldiers on military maneuvers outside the country club, comprises the primary action of the novel.

The world that cannot be kept out is characterized by hyperinflation; María charges the Señora more for services rendered even as they haggle over prices, since the currency is devalued so often. The government has created a cheery version of present conditions on television to placate its citizens, and María does her best to isolate the Señora from the world outside by refusing to bring her a newspaper and drawing her curtains against her will. Yet the intrusion of reality is inevitable, and it affects the Señora's quest to make sense of her life, which begins to overlap with the military's struggle for governmental control: "She's learned counterinsurgency and non-conventional warfare techniques." Defense mechanisms become literal as well as figurative, as the Señora takes part in a military offensive called Operation Identity, which parallels her own struggle to recover her ability to think and to remember.

This overlpping of military and personal struggles is what makes *Bedside Manners* so appealing. The reader may be like the protagonist, who is initially described as "suspecting nothing of the superimposition of different planes of reality," yet once we have accepted the way the author is superimposing these planes, we can begin to share her vision of the Señora's all-too-familiar world.

Lucille Kerr (essay date Autumn 1995)

SOURCE: "Novels and 'Noir' in New York," in *World Literature Today,* Vol. 69, No. 4, Autumn, 1995, pp. 733-39.

[*In the essay below, Kerr explicates the narrative features of* Black Novel *in terms of conventional crime fiction and its relation to the* novela negra *genre.*]

Near the end of part 1 of *Novela negra con argentinos,* one of the novel's protagonists, Roberta Aguilar, an Argentine writer living in New York, considers how to deal with a potentially significant set of papers—more specifically, an unfinished novel manuscript and some of its author's notebooks, which Roberta has removed from the apartment of Agustín Palant, also an Argentine writer in New York. Agustín is the author of the pages with which Roberta is preoccupied and also the apparent perpetrator of the crime (a murder) around which Valenzuela's *novela negra* and its investigations revolve. The narrator presents Roberta's dilemma as follows: "Pensar en alguien conquien dejar esos manuscritos, alguien ni hispano-hablante ni curioso de literatura capaz de descifrar el secreto antes que ella" (Think up someone . . . to leave the manuscripts with. Someone neither Spanish-speaking nor curious about literature, who wouldn't try to decipher the secret before she did). While the pages in question may or may not play a prominent role in the novel's story, they do have an emblematic function within its text. These pages appear and disappear at significant moments. They circulate like a set of "purloined letters" whose meaning may well be found not in what they literally say but in what they implicitly signal within the conventional framework of Valenzuela's novel.

Roberta's thoughts, if not the novel's narrative, suggest that these texts could, and perhaps should, play a critical role in reading. Her reflection on the situation implies that Agustín's papers may hold some kind of "secret" which is susceptible to being deciphered by readers with the appropriate linguistic and literary competence, and who, in addition, are capable of seeing through Roberta's efforts to keep the pages' possible secrets from being seen. Roberta virtually plots to keep the papers from being read properly (that is, by a competing competent reader) as she decides on a fitting locale for their sequestration; her plan aims to foreclose as much as forestall reading (including, of course, the reading tat might be attempted by the reader of *Novela negra con argentinos*). The novel implements such foreclosure as the papers disappear from both story and text, and into a drawer in the S&M establishment where Roberta's friend Ava Taurel works. They reappear only near the end of the novel, when Roberta reclaims and returns them to their original owner and author.

The suggestion that these pages may contain a secret which one of the novel's characters, if not also its readers, may attempt to discover is not an innocent proposition. Indeed, the apparently criminal circumstances surrounding the appearance and disappearance of these texts, if not the possibility of answering various questions about them, are such that one cannot fail to consider these papers as potentially significant. That one has such expectations derives not only from Roberta's characterization of these pages and her own relation to them—that is, not only from her indications that the texts encode some secret she wishes to decipher prior to any other reader (perhaps the motive, the hidden explanation of Agustín's seemingly gratuitous criminal act). The suggested significance also derives from the narrative and generic frames within which these elusive manuscripts are presented.

The reading model Roberta presupposes through her plot figures different routes around, and several possible entries into, the familiar and foreign territories of *Novela negra con argentinos.* We are reminded of the critical frames through which Roberta's dilemma can be read and around which a reading of the novel might develop when we recall that the texts to which the passage refers actually belong to Agustín, the supposed murderer with whom Roberta finds herself conspiring and living, if not writing, some sort of *noir* tale in Valenzuela's novel. Roberta's conundrum can be read as one of the moments in which the novel demands from its reader a performance that is at once at odds with and faithful to its own reading poetics, which in the end is more or less consistent with that of criminal fiction generally and the *novela negra* in particular. As contrary as it might seem, Roberta's preferred reader—the reader incapable of reading things correctly or completely—is, within the criminal fiction genre, precisely the figure required for a proper reading of such a text. Indeed, in mystery or criminal fiction the reader is supposed to remain virtually in the dark, until the revelation of a correct reading is provided at the end of the text. To read criminal fiction correctly, it could be argued, is to agree to read incorrectly, to occupy a position of ignorance for the duration of reading.

The reader Roberta would appear to seek, however, is not so much a reader who would agree to the reading contract associated with criminal fiction, but rather a reader virtually innocent of what, more generally, it means to read, a reader not only unfamiliar with these texts' linguistic codes but also unschooled in their literary conventions. The reader to whom Roberta would entrust Agustín's texts is a reader with lesser interpretive or investigative skills than herself, a reader who would function as a blind repository for writing rather than as an astute decoder of any sense that these written pages might make. The writing that Roberta holds within her possession—and which she herself reads only partially—must, she decides, be kept from the eyes of anyone capable of competing with her for their potential significance.

Roberta's plan to forestall closure on reading emanates not only from her character but from the whole text of *Novela negra con argentinos,* whose titular and narrative gestures of adherence to a crime fiction genre could be read as explaining everything about reading in Valenzuela's novel. Readers familiar with the history of crime fiction can readily see that *Novela negra con argentinos* is positioned in a provocative relation to the principles and practices of the *novela negra*—or *roman noir*—tradition to which its title alludes. In the text authored by Valenzuela, as well as in the traditions recalled by the novel's title and narrative features, the question of reading—as well as reading how one reads—can hardly be ignored.

As convention would have it, the novel begins with an apparently criminal scene. A scene of murder—a murder that seems to have just been committed as the first chapter begins—propels the actions of the two protagonists throughout the text, which ends without confirming that this crime has occurred and without meting out punishment to any culpable figure. The narrative focuses on Agustín, the apparently motiveless though self-confessed murderer (he supposedly kills a woman he barely knows and then confesses the essence, but not all the facts, of his deed to Roberta), and on Roberta, his lover and after-the-fact accomplice (she disposes of his gun and other evidence, and initiates their attempt to investigate the murderous event remembered and recounted by Agustín).

However, their attempt to examine and explain this undocumented crime, by retracing the criminal steps apparently taken by Agustín, becomes the virtual writing of another kind of story. The story of *Novela negra con argentinos* is also a story tied up with the theory and practice of writing—the protagonists are, after all, literary figures. Roberta and Agustín are writers, whose talk about writing, and especially Roberta's notion of "writing with the body," should sound familiar to readers acquainted with currents in modern (and especially feminist) literary criticism and theory. It is at the same time a story that calls up images of the recent history of Latin America, in particular Argentina: the main characters make sporadic but persistent references to the *desaparecidos* and Argentina's recent era of military rule. And it is a story that presents a view of New York around the 1980s—or rather a view of the city's recent cultural geography, as the characters go from the Upper West Side to the Lower East Side, from a secondhand clothing shop to the Salvation Army, from an S&M establishment to an artist's loft or a writer's apartment; in all, from the artsy to the kinky, from the literary and the laughable to the seedy and the sinister, and back again.

> **[*Novela negra con argentinos*] develops a meditation on the relations between criminal fictions and murderous facts— that is, between the conventions of a literary genre such as crime fiction and the *novela negra* and the practices of a political regime such as military dictatorship (and more specifically the *guerra sucia* in Argentina).**
>
> **—*Lucille Kerr***

Let us recall the novel's textual trajectory around those sites and its narrative organization. *Novela negra con argentinos* is divided into four parts of unequal length; its story covers a period of perhaps two months, during which time the protagonists Roberta and Agustín live and write their *noir* tale

in New York (the action moves from a Friday night/early Saturday morning in October to just after Christmas). The first part moves from Agustín's exit from the apparent murder scene to Roberta's dilemma about what to do with his manuscripts. In between, the narrative follows Agustín to his apartment and then to Roberta's, where he continues to live for the duration of the novel; then out into the Lower East Side, where, together, the two unsuccessfully try to return to the scene of the crime; then back to Roberta's apartment, where Agustín remains and from which Roberta later exits on her own to continue their "investigation." The second part presents Roberta and Agustín living a kind of self-imprisonment, in her apartment, for approximately one month. The third part begins with their emergence from their self-imposed "arresto domiciliario" (house arrest) and follows them back into the outside world, again into New York streets and local sites and shops, and back to Roberta's apartment. The fourth and final section is centered on a Saturday-night party at a friend's downtown loft, and ends with Roberta's foray outside to retrieve Agustín's papers from Ava's S&M shop and her return to her own apartment, where she remains with Bill (one of the owners of the secondhand clothing shop), her new lover.

In the course of this movement between Roberta's apartment and other sites, and also around the area of New York where she and Agustín live, the original generic frame named by the title might seem to disappear. The story of Agustín's crime recedes into the background—behind the scenes, as it were, of the theater of actions and meditations, if not also sights and sounds, that define the interior spaces as well as the exterior scenes of the city where the novel's characters are situated. However, criminally violent and potentially murderous scenes and stories continually erupt into the text, into the thoughts and conversations of its main characters. Violence is figured not only directly, in overt actions and statements, but also obliquely, in the violent reframing of innocent sights and sounds everywhere. But as in criminal fiction more generally, in *Novela negra con argentinos* what appears innocent may come to look like it is murderous and criminal, and what looks like it is potentially murderous and criminal may be revealed to be essentially innocent.

In fact, that the novel develops a meditation on the relations between criminal fictions and murderous facts—that is, between the conventions of a literary genre such as crime fiction and the *novela negra* and the practices of a political regime such as military dictatorship (and more specifically the *guerra sucia* in Argentina)—is quite obvious. The characters' ruminations about such connections, in Agustín's intermittent memories of scenes from the "dirty war" or in Roberta's explicit comparisons of the scenes of torture played out in Ava's S&M establishment and those lived by victims of the *guerra sucia*, underscore the route from one criminal scene to another, from one notion of "the simple art of murder" to another or from one kind of "murder for pleasure" to another.

These highlighted references to two well-known titles from crime fiction criticism—that is, Raymond Chandler's essay "The Simple Art of Murder" (1944) and Howard Haycraft's collection of essays *Murder for Pleasure: The Life and Times of the Detective Story* (1941)—are meant to recall a network of texts that inevitably frame Valenzuela's novel, and especially the American settings (both generic and geographic) that are engaged by her text. Indeed, Chandler's essay about "the simple art of murder" returns us to a critical criminal frame: that of the hard-boiled genre of which he is considered to be one of the founders. As we recall, Chandler's essay is a kind of manifesto, which explains the art of the hard-boiled American genre in opposition to that of the classic British murder mystery. To mention it, and the texts he and other hard-boiled writers produced in the early days of the hard-boiled tradition (most particularly, Dashiell Hammett, the exemplary and originary figure for Chandler), is also to recall the territory through which **Novela negra con argentinos** travels, and which it reinscribes in familiar and foreign ways.

The insistence on this specific literary frame and affiliation derives from the blatant generic marker contained in the novel's title. As we know, *novela negra* is the phrase used to identify and classify Hispanic texts whose origins are precisely in the Chandler and Hammett—that is, the hard-boiled—model of detective or criminal fiction. This phrase leaves an irrevocable mark on Valenzuela's text, a kind of black mark that demarcates certain cultural and generic territories where several foreign and familiar currents converge to map out a potentially new terrain.

As we recall, the history of detective fiction generally in Latin America is a history marked first by foreign authors and titles, and by translated texts, and more recently (in the 1970s and 1980s) by more "native" works. The early models that traveled to Latin America were principally of the classic English model (also called *novela enigma*), whose circulation grew in the 1940s. While the introduction of the American model, and the translations of Hammett and Chandler and others, also began in the 1940s, the American genre apparently was not to find a wide readership, or become a preferred model within the Latin American context, until the late 1960s and beyond. The reasons for this preference on the part of writers and readers, it has been pointed out, lie precisely in the "dark" settings and ideological frame of the Chandler and Hammett texts, which, we recall, also served as the primary source of the cinematic form called *film noir*. That is, the world of the hard-boiled detectives—the *duros*—presented by *noir* texts, whether written or filmed, involves the depiction of the "dark" underside of society, where corruption and violence, sex and death, go hand in hand. (It has

been suggested, moreover, that this depiction reflects more accurately than the classic murder mystery the realities recognizable to American readers in both the northern and southern hemispheres)

While the term *duros* directly connects the Hispanic detectives of the *negra* genre to their American models, the term *novela negra* calls up paths of affiliation perhaps more European than American, complex paths that confound the dark settings and scenes of a whole network of texts and traditions. Indeed, if one were to look for the origins of the term *novela negra*, it seems that one would have to turn to foreign territories. While it isn't entirely clear how, exactly, this term was first used within the Hispanic tradition—that is, how the generic phrase first left its "black mark" in that literary and cultural terrain—the phrase is certainly affiliated with, if not in some way derived through, the term *roman noir* from the French tradition. But *roman noir* has had its own history. In the eighteenth and nineteenth centuries it seems to have served as both a general and a generic term (an apparent alternate tag for "dark genre," "novel of terror," and "gothic novel"). In the twentieth century the term was popularized by the surrealists, who seemed to favor a confusion among generic categories while also privileging its association with the gothic novel and its "official" forms, which flourished until the middle of the nineteenth century. During the 1920s a new form of *noir* fiction was introduced by popular mystery serials in France, and these texts, in turn, led the way to the *séries noires* publications of detective fiction.

It is precisely with the *noir* detective series that the American hard-boiled genre comes to take the place of the British enigma novel in France, and also later in Latin America. (One might note, parenthetically, that while the American literary genre was translated and published in France, where detective fiction was substantially Americanized as writers began to adapt and produce their own versions of the hard-boiled works, the film genre based on the texts of Chandler and Hammett and others—what has been called officially *film noir*—was in fact both identified and named from a foreign territory, that is, by the French, as the term *film noir* plainly recalls.)

That the decade of the twenties is a critical period for the modern *roman noir* is not so much suggested by this detail about the introduction of a hard-boiled direction within the French arena during that time, as it is established by the contemporaneous publication of the American texts that founded this branch of criminal fiction and that, we can already see, frame the reading of Valenzuela's novel in odd but fitting ways. As we recollect, the first works by Hammett and Chandler, and others of their ilk, are published in the U.S., and the "new" American genre is virtually founded, during the period of the so-called golden age of detective fiction (that is, during the period when Agatha Christie, Dorothy Sayers, S. S. Van Dine, and others wrote and achieved great success—that is, during the 1920s to the 1930s).

Moreover, the hard-boiled genre has its origins in a pulp magazine called *Black Mask*, which began publication in 1920 and was dedicated to crime fiction. Shortly after its debut, the magazine broke with the classic deductive model and began to create what would become the hard-boiled genre, which focused not on pristine settings but on the grimy underside of American political, social, and economic realities. As early as 1922, in fact, *Black Mask* began to publish precisely those writers who would later be identified as having founded the hard-boiled genre (specifically Hammett).

The hard-boiled texts are credited with having introduced into the crime fiction genre the sort of realism that Chandler would later praise in his crisp—if not hard-boiled—assessment of Hammett, whom he credits with "[taking] murder out of the Venetian vase and [dropping] it into the alley." This description pithily describes the American model's departure from the classic British model, and the shift in the social and political frames for this sort of fiction. The new American form's cultural and ideological parameters are clearly implicated in the production of the modern French *roman noir* and the Latin American *novela negra*, following on the American hard-boiled models transported to Europe and Latin America, where crime fiction writers and readers, as well as filmmakers, have been influenced by the current. The signature setting of such texts, as we know, is "the seamy side of things," the dark underside of society, whose darkness is ostensibly exposed by the light that the hard-boiled genre, or the *novela negra*, throws on it. (This darkness is of course a visually literal feature and one of the signature truisms of *film noir*). Moreover, the name of the genre in Spanish recalls that some sort of dark frame, or even black figure, informs the genre, regardless of the tradition within which it is cultivated. Through its chromatic adjective, the generic phrase (and subsequently Valenzuela's title as well) metonymically acquires a criminal sense. The phrase and the title, as well as the name "Black Mask" that originally marked this literary current, metonymically take on the meaning of the genre as a whole. Furthermore, in all these names and titles, the term *black* eventually acquires a connotative as well as a denotative value; it becomes the sign, or mark, of crime, or more generally of an evil that is also criminal.

The term *novela negra*, then, marks a genre that appears naturally, as it were, to both cultivate and illuminate a kind of black mark, and to wear the mark of genre as both a dark mask and a transparent design. The hard-boiled genre, which, we recall, is originally foreign rather than native or intrinsic to Latin American soil, is adapted and adopted such that its foreignness, while ineradicable, becomes utterly familiar through the *novela negra*—a genre that naturally, as it were, masks its origins while also unmasking the dark settings and black scenes that its stories aim to expose. While Luisa Valenzuela's *Novela negra con argentinos* may not have originally aimed to situate itself so squarely within this generic frame—indeed, the novel might seem to offer its "black" title as something of a red herring (we recall that the text also seems to abandon its generic markers, as noted above), its text and story are generically marked in provocative, and instructive, ways. Moreover, her text inevitably winds up leaving its own idiosyncratic mark on the *novela negra* model.

There are, of course, a number of ways to read Valenzuela's novel's generic affiliations, and the different literary and cultural frames (both European and American) with which it associates and disassociates itself. Through its two initial words, *Novela negra con argentinos*'s self-conscious title tells the reader to which family it supposedly belongs; then, with its prepositional phrase, it declares that the novel is perhaps but a distant, or foreign, cousin, since its characters appear to come from a cultural frame different from that of the original genre. (This separation, or mapped hierarchy, of phrases and frames, as well as cultural and literary territories, is further emphasized by the English title, where the phrase "with Argentines" is set off in parentheses.)

Novela negra con argentinos straddles different generic borders and disparate, though possibly contiguous, cultural as well as geographic territories. As it moves among several of those terrains, one might argue, the novel also remains engaged with the "black" model from which it departs. *Novela negra con argentinos* relocates the *novela negra* to a foreign site that is also the genre's original national setting. That is, set in New York (the quintessential American urban site, though not the original city of the hard-boiled genre) and revolving around foreign figures (the Argentines Roberta and Agustín are foreign to the New York scene, though in a sense familiar to Latin American readers and to the *novela negra* frame), Valenzuela's novel confounds the borders of the foreign and familiar within an urban setting that is at once idiosyncratic and international, and where cultural, as well as generic, borders are erased as much as erected. The novel roots its characters in a city whose own sights and sounds are second nature to the native-born but which, in a way, become just as familiar to Valenzuela's foreign figures living so far from home.

Roberta and Agustín, both Argentine exiles, bring the *novela negra* to New York, a city whose dark sites and scenes, naturally it seems, become the stage upon which the story of Agustín's crime circulates and from underneath which another—a Latin American—criminal tale erupts to declare its familiar and foreign presence. We recall that the dark—indeed, also "dirty"—story to which the novel persistently refers, and whose violent eruption into the thoughts of Roberta and especially Agustín cannot be ignored, is the story of the *guerra sucia*. This foreign story is of course all too familiar to the Argentine protagonists, who find in New York's shadowy settings, as well as in their own criminal scenario, persistent and powerful affiliations.

The text abounds not only with references to scenes from Argentina's recent dark history—for instance, in fleeting images and recollections of Agustín, as noted above (for example, garbage bags in New York's streets become body bags in Buenos Aires). It also resonates, as noted above, with Roberta's analytic meditations on the nexus of pleasure and pain, sex and death, which in one frame may well appear playfully frivolous (i.e., the New York subculture of Ava's S&M shop) but in another are deadly serious (the Argentine story of violence and torture and the *desaparecidos*). That these topics are at home in such different frames, that stories of crime are familiar to these disparate but not disconnected literary and historical settings, are points acknowledged more or less openly by Valenzuela's novel. The work is, in the end, perhaps all too conscious of these connections and of the literary, if not theoretical, underpinnings of their formulations.

Moreover, *Novela negra con argentinos* not only produces a dialogue with recent Argentine history by calling up a host of horrible images of historical violence from beneath the surface of its own quasi-criminal text. It also calls forward a wide family of literary and cultural texts from which, one might argue, a variety of figures and fictions, if not narrative structures and strategies—or even pages or papers—appear to be purloined, if not parodied, in the novel. This reference to textual borrowings—if not to purloined papers—returns us, of course, to the reading dilemma described at the beginning of this discussion of Valenzuela's novel.

To finish reading *Novela negra con argentinos* is to see the text repeat in a way Roberta's gesture of placing a kind of veil—if not a black mask—over an apparent secret while also calling attention to its own closing, conventional gesture. The text's refusal to display any such secret plays on the expectation that explanations will appear at the end, where generic conventions dictate they should. While Valenzuela's novel exposes, by thematizing, such conventions (i.e., questions about literary endings and solutions . . .) and thus might appear to renounce them, it also dramatizes its engagement with the principles that govern how things end in a *novela negra* as well as in other forms of criminal fiction.

Valenzuela's novel recalls that the ends of criminal texts—whether of the classic enigma type or the hard-boiled variety—are the conventional sites not just for criminal solutions but also for criminal repetitions. That is, solutions are always displayed through repetition, through the retelling of the initially enigmatic criminal scenes which are finally restaged to include all the causes and consequences originally kept from view. Such texts conventionally end as well as begin with displays of crime, if not with scenes of death; the appearance of those scenes signals that the end is near and that "secrets" and solutions will soon be revealed.

This criminal frame reasserts itself near the end of Valenzuela's novel, where the telling of stories of death, if not the solution to crime, is incorporated into the ending of Roberta's and Agustín's *noir* New York tale. Near the novel's end, and in a series of dialogues involving Agustín and Héctor Bravo, a Uruguayan doctor whom Agustín meets at the Saturday-night party he attends with Roberta and who, it has been rumored, may have been a doctor who tortured rather than a physician who treated military prisoners before coming to the U.S., there are recountings of scenes of death (if not crimes) by figures about whose guilt or innocence the novel has already speculated. Agustín retells the story of his crime in what appears to be a final confession and thus confirmation of his guilt. But his narration remains uncorroborated. Although his criminal identity is suggested if not stated at times, it is finally never definitively determined, since no objective evidence or authoritative narrative is presented by the text as certification of his criminal deed. Héctor Bravo describes the death offstage, as it were, of Edouard, the old man for whom he works as a personal physician, and he also talks about his medical work. But his narration never answers questions about his activities before coming to the U.S., referring as it does to only one of the circulated versions of his story (that of his role as medical figure treating patients not only in Latin America but also in the U.S.). He thus presents himself as an instrument for medical rather than criminal ends.

The encounter between these two characters and their exchange of descriptions and narratives is a meeting of potentially criminal figures that neither resolves questions of crime nor dispels issues of guilt in the novel. Like the purloined pages partially read by Roberta but closed off from further reading, or like the phrase of a song that both Roberta and Agustín seek to interpret but whose solution she finally keeps to herself, the conversational confessions of these characters lead in several directions at once, directions not unfamiliar to the literary currents and forms with which *Novela negra con argentinos* frames itself. In the recounting of two deaths by figures potentially identified as criminal, and in the resurfacing and return of the purloined pages hidden away earlier by Roberta, near the end of the novel, Valenzuela's text recalls the conventional and controversial territories it traverses and perhaps transforms.

The return of papers purloined from Agustín at the novel's end marks the moment where, in classic and also hard-boiled criminal fiction, some sort of secret or solution would usually be revealed. Valenzuela's novel makes a point, however, of refusing to follow those rules, not only by staging the finally inconclusive conversation between Agustín and Héctor Bravo, but also by having Roberta both claim to have knowledge of a secret (a word or phrase) that both she and Agustín had sought and retrieve Agustín's "secret" papers only to have them returned to him (Roberta gives them to Lara, who returns them to Agustín) without revealing to the reader what they contain. Just as Roberta seems to leave Agustín on his own, if not in the dark, having drawn a black mask, as it were, over him, the novel leaves its reader with the powerful clues and possible conclusions that inevitably mark the text in conventional ways. That is, this apparent masking of final truth is familiar rather than foreign to criminal fiction. Arguably, such plays upon convention are themselves some of the most identifiable conventions of the genre, which has been revived, if not renewed, by texts such as Valenzuela's. In the end, then, while this literary frame may not define precisely what *Novela negra con argentinos* is, in its refusal to disappear completely beneath this text, the generic market—the black mark or mask of the *novela negra*—naturally frames reading as a conventional problem. This problem persists, Valenzuela reminds us, around every text we read, but especially, perhaps, around a "novela negra con argentinos."

FURTHER READING

Criticism

Garcia-Moreno, Laura. "Other Weapons, Other Words: Literary and Political Reconsiderations in Luisa Valenzuela's *Other Weapons.*" *Latin American Literary Review* XIX, No. 38 (July-December 1991): 7-22.

Explores forms of oppression of Latin American women in *Other Weapons,* with reference to the theories of French feminism.

Gerrard, Nicci. "Beauty and the Beasts." *The Observer,* No. 10240 (10 January 1988): 20.

Briefly mentions *The Lizard's Tail* as "an extraordinary novel whose thematic ferocity and baroque images explore a political situation too exotically appalling for reportage."

Magnarelli, Sharon. "The New Novel / A New Novel: Spider's Webs and Detectives in Luisa Valenzuela's *Black Novel (with Argentines)*." *Studies in Twentieth-Century Literature* 19, No. 1 (Winter 1995): 43-60.

Analyzes *Black Novel* in terms of theatricality and the visual as both theme and technique.

March, Kathleen N. Review of *Novela negra con argentinos,* by Luisa Valenzuela. *World Literature Today* 66, No. 1 (Winter 1992): 100.

Examines the diverse levels of meaning and structure in *Black Novel,* demonstrating their effects on the writing and reading the novel.

Taylor, Erika. Review of *Bedside Manners,* by Luisa Valenzuela. *Los Angeles Times Book Review* (5 February 1995): 6.

Feels that "somewhere inside this novel, a really wonderful one-act play is dying to be seen."

World Literature Today 69, No. 4 (Autumn 1995).

Special issue devoted exclusively to criticism of Valenzuela's works through *Simetrías.*

Additional coverage of Valenzuela's life and career is contained in the following sources published by Gale: *Contemporary Authors,* Vol. 101; *Contemporary Authors New Revision Series,* Vol. 32; *Dictionary of Literary Biography,* Vol. 113; *DISCovering Authors Modules: Multicultural Authors*; *Hispanic Writers*; and *Short Story Criticism,* Vol. 14.

☐ Contemporary Literary Criticism

Indexes

Literary Criticism Series
Cumulative Author Index
Cumulative Topic Index
Cumulative Nationality Index
Title Index, Volume 104

How to Use This Index

The main references

Camus, Albert
1913-1960 ...... **CLC 1, 2, 4, 9, 11, 14,
32, 69; DA; DAB; DAC; DAM DRAM,
MST, NOV; DC2; SSC 9; WLC**

list all author entries in the following Gale Literary Criticism series:

BLC = Black Literature Criticism
CLC = Contemporary Literary Criticism
CLR = Children's Literature Review
CMLC = Classical and Medieval Literature Criticism
DA = DISCovering Authors
DAB = DISCovering Authors: British
DAC = DISCovering Authors: Canadian
DAM = DISCovering Authors Modules
  DRAM = dramatists; **MST** = most-studied
  authors; **MULT** = multicultural authors; **NOV** =
  novelists; **POET** = poets; **POP** = popular/genre
  writers; **DC** = Drama Criticism
HLC = Hispanic Literature Criticism
LC = Literature Criticism from 1400 to 1800
NCLC = Nineteenth-Century Literature Criticism
PC = Poetry Criticism
SSC = Short Story Criticism
TCLC = Twentieth-Century Literary Criticism
WLC = World Literature Criticism, 1500 to the Present

The cross-references

See also CA 89-92; DLB 72; MTCW

list all author entries in the following Gale biographical and literary sources:

AAYA = Authors & Artists for Young Adults
AITN = Authors in the News
BEST = Bestsellers
BW = Black Writers
CA = Contemporary Authors
CAAS = Contemporary Authors Autobiography Series
CABS = Contemporary Authors Bibliographical Series
CANR = Contemporary Authors New Revision Series
CAP = Contemporary Authors Permanent Series
CDALB = Concise Dictionary of American Literary Biography
CDBLB = Concise Dictionary of British Literary Biography

DLB = Dictionary of Literary Biography
DLBD = Dictionary of Literary Biography Documentary Series
DLBY = Dictionary of Literary Biography Yearbook
HW = Hispanic Writers
JRDA = Junior DISCovering Authors
MAICYA = Major Authors and Illustrators for Children and Young Adults
MTCW = Major 20th-Century Writers
NNAL = Native North American Literature
SAAS = Something about the Author Autobiography Series
SATA = Something about the Author
YABC = Yesterday's Authors of Books for Children

Literary Criticism Series
Cumulative Author Index

See Elytis, Odysseus

Aleshkovsky, Joseph 1929-
See Aleshkovsky, Yuz
See also CA 121; 128

Aleshkovsky, Yuz .... **CLC 44**
See also Aleshkovsky, Joseph

Alexander, Lloyd (Chudley) 1924- .. **CLC 35**
See also AAYA 1; CA 1-4R; CANR 1, 24, 38,
55; CLR 1, 5; DLB 52; JRDA; MAICYA;
MTCW; SAAS 19; SATA 3, 49, 81

Alexie, Sherman (Joseph, Jr.) 1966- **CLC 96;
DAM MULT**
See also CA 138; DLB 175; NNAL

Alfau, Felipe 1902- .... **CLC 66**
See also CA 137

Alger, Horatio, Jr. 1832-1899 .... **NCLC 8**
See also DLB 42; SATA 16

Algren, Nelson 1909-1981 .... **CLC 4, 10, 33**
See also CA 13-16R; 103; CANR 20, 61;
CDALB 1941-1968; DLB 9; DLBY 81, 82;
MTCW

Ali, Ahmed 1910- .... **CLC 69**
See also CA 25-28R; CANR 15, 34

Alighieri, Dante 1265-1321 ...... **CMLC 3, 18;
WLCS**

Allan, John B.
See Westlake, Donald E(dwin)

Allan, Sidney
See Hartmann, Sadakichi

Allan, Sydney
See Hartmann, Sadakichi

Allen, Edward 1948- .... **CLC 59**

Allen, Paula Gunn 1939- .... **CLC 84; DAM
MULT**
See also CA 112; 143; DLB 175; NNAL

Allen, Roland
See Ayckbourn, Alan

Allen, Sarah A.
See Hopkins, Pauline Elizabeth

Allen, Sidney H.
See Hartmann, Sadakichi

Allen, Woody 1935- **CLC 16, 52; DAM POP**
See also AAYA 10; CA 33-36R; CANR 27, 38;
DLB 44; MTCW

Allende, Isabel 1942- . **CLC 39, 57, 97; DAM
MULT, NOV; HLC; WLCS**
See also AAYA 18; CA 125; 130; CANR 51;
DLB 145; HW; INT 130; MTCW

Alleyn, Ellen
See Rossetti, Christina (Georgina)

Allingham, Margery (Louise) 1904-1966 **C L C
19**
See also CA 5-8R; 25-28R; CANR 4, 58; DLB
77; MTCW

Allingham, William 1824-1889 ...... **NCLC 25**
See also DLB 35

Allison, Dorothy E. 1949- .... **CLC 78**
See also CA 140

Allston, Washington 1779-1843 .... **NCLC 2**
See also DLB 1

Almedingen, E. M. .... **CLC 12**
See also Almedingen, Martha Edith von
See also SATA 3

Almedingen, Martha Edith von 1898-1971
See Almedingen, E. M.
See also CA 1-4R; CANR 1

Almqvist, Carl Jonas Love 1793-1866 **N C L C
42**

Alonso, Damaso 1898-1990 .... **CLC 14**
See also CA 110; 131; 130; DLB 108; HW

Alov
See Gogol, Nikolai (Vasilyevich)

Alta 1942- .... **CLC 19**

See also CA 57-60

Alter, Robert B(ernard) 1935- .... **CLC 34**
See also CA 49-52; CANR 1, 47

Alther, Lisa 1944- .... **CLC 7, 41**
See also CA 65-68; CANR 12, 30, 51; MTCW

Altman, Robert 1925- .... **CLC 16**
See also CA 73-76; CANR 43

Alvarez, A(lfred) 1929- .... **CLC 5, 13**
See also CA 1-4R; CANR 3, 33; DLB 14, 40

Alvarez, Alejandro Rodriguez 1903-1965
See Casona, Alejandro
See also CA 131; 93-96; HW

Alvarez, Julia 1950- .... **CLC 93**
See also CA 147

Alvaro, Corrado 1896-1956 .... **TCLC 60**

Amado, Jorge 1912- **CLC 13, 40; DAM MULT,
NOV; HLC**
See also CA 77-80; CANR 35; DLB 113;
MTCW

Ambler, Eric 1909- .... **CLC 4, 6, 9**
See also CA 9-12R; CANR 7, 38; DLB 77;
MTCW

Amichai, Yehuda 1924- .... **CLC 9, 22, 57**
See also CA 85-88; CANR 46, 60; MTCW

Amichai, Yehudah
See Amichai, Yehuda

Amiel, Henri Frederic 1821-1881 .... **NCLC 4**

Amis, Kingsley (William) 1922-1995 **CLC 1, 2,
3, 5, 8, 13, 40, 44; DA; DAB; DAC; DAM
MST, NOV**
See also AITN 2; CA 9-12R; 150; CANR 8, 28,
54; CDBLB 1945-1960; DLB 15, 27, 100,
139; DLBY 96; INT CANR-8; MTCW

Amis, Martin (Louis) 1949- **CLC 4, 9, 38, 62,
101**
See also BEST 90:3; CA 65-68; CANR 8, 27,
54; DLB 14; INT CANR-27

Ammons, A(rchie) R(andolph) 1926- **CLC 2, 3,
5, 8, 9, 25, 57; DAM POET; PC 16**
See also AITN 1; CA 9-12R; CANR 6, 36, 51;
DLB 5, 165; MTCW

Amo, Tauraatua i
See Adams, Henry (Brooks)

Anand, Mulk Raj 1905- .. **CLC 23, 93; DAM
NOV**
See also CA 65-68; CANR 32; MTCW

Anatol
See Schnitzler, Arthur

Anaximander c. 610B.C.-c. 546B.C. **CMLC 22**

Anaya, Rudolfo A(lfonso) 1937- ..... **CLC 23;
DAM MULT, NOV; HLC**
See also AAYA 20; CA 45-48; CAAS 4; CANR
1, 32, 51; DLB 82; HW 1; MTCW

Andersen, Hans Christian 1805-1875 **NCLC 7;
DA; DAB; DAC; DAM MST, POP; SSC
6; WLC**
See also CLR 6; MAICYA; YABC 1

Anderson, C. Farley
See Mencken, H(enry) L(ouis); Nathan, George
Jean

Anderson, Jessica (Margaret) Queale **CLC 37**
See also CA 9-12R; CANR 4

Anderson, Jon (Victor) 1940- .. **CLC 9; DAM
POET**
See also CA 25-28R; CANR 20

Anderson, Lindsay (Gordon) 1923-1994 **C L C
20**
See also CA 125; 128; 146

Anderson, Maxwell 1888-1959 **TCLC 2; DAM
DRAM**
See also CA 105; 152; DLB 7

Anderson, Poul (William) 1926- .... **CLC 15**
See also AAYA 5; CA 1-4R; CAAS 2; CANR

2, 15, 34; DLB 8; INT CANR-15; MTCW;
SATA 90; SATA-Brief 39

Anderson, Robert (Woodruff) 1917- **CLC 23;
DAM DRAM**
See also AITN 1; CA 21-24R; CANR 32; DLB
7

Anderson, Sherwood 1876-1941 **TCLC 1, 10,
24; DA; DAB; DAC; DAM MST, NOV;
SSC 1; WLC**
See also CA 104; 121; CANR 61; CDALB
1917-1929; DLB 4, 9, 86; DLBD 1; MTCW

Andier, Pierre
See Desnos, Robert

Andouard
See Giraudoux, (Hippolyte) Jean

Andrade, Carlos Drummond de .... **CLC 18**
See also Drummond de Andrade, Carlos

Andrade, Mario de 1893-1945 .... **TCLC 43**

Andreae, Johann V(alentin) 1586-1654 **LC 32**
See also DLB 164

Andreas-Salome, Lou 1861-1937 ... **TCLC 56**
See also DLB 66

Andrewes, Lancelot 1555-1626 .... **LC 5**
See also DLB 151, 172

Andrews, Cicily Fairfield
See West, Rebecca

Andrews, Elton V.
See Pohl, Frederik

Andreyev, Leonid (Nikolaevich) 1871-1919
TCLC 3
See also CA 104

Andric, Ivo 1892-1975 .... **CLC 8**
See also CA 81-84; 57-60; CANR 43, 60; DLB
147; MTCW

Angelique, Pierre
See Bataille, Georges

Angell, Roger 1920- .... **CLC 26**
See also CA 57-60; CANR 13, 44; DLB 171

Angelou, Maya 1928- **CLC 12, 35, 64, 77; BLC;
DA; DAB; DAC; DAM MST, MULT,
POET, POP; WLCS**
See also AAYA 7, 20; BW 2; CA 65-68; CANR
19, 42; DLB 38; MTCW; SATA 49

Annensky, Innokenty (Fyodorovich) 1856-1909
TCLC 14
See also CA 110; 155

Annunzio, Gabriele d'
See D'Annunzio, Gabriele

Anodos
See Coleridge, Mary E(lizabeth)

Anon, Charles Robert
See Pessoa, Fernando (Antonio Nogueira)

Anouilh, Jean (Marie Lucien Pierre) 1910-1987
CLC 1, 3, 8, 13, 40, 50; DAM DRAM
See also CA 17-20R; 123; CANR 32; MTCW

Anthony, Florence
See Ai

Anthony, John
See Ciardi, John (Anthony)

Anthony, Peter
See Shaffer, Anthony (Joshua); Shaffer, Peter
(Levin)

Anthony, Piers 1934- ..... **CLC 35; DAM POP**
See also AAYA 11; CA 21-24R; CANR 28, 56;
DLB 8; MTCW; SAAS 22; SATA 84

Antoine, Marc
See Proust, (Valentin-Louis-George-Eugene-)
Marcel

Antoninus, Brother
See Everson, William (Oliver)

Antonioni, Michelangelo 1912- .... **CLC 20**
See also CA 73-76; CANR 45

Antschel, Paul 1920-1970

2; DAB; DAM DRAM
See also CA 104; 136; CDBLB 1890-1914;
CLR 16; DLB 10, 141, 156; MAICYA;
YABC 1
Barrington, Michael
See Moorcock, Michael (John)
Barrol, Grady
See Bograd, Larry
Barry, Mike
See Malzberg, Barry N(athaniel)
Barry, Philip 1896-1949 .... **TCLC 11**
See also CA 109; DLB 7
Bart, Andre Schwarz
See Schwarz-Bart, Andre
Barth, John (Simmons) 1930-**CLC 1, 2, 3, 5, 7,
9, 10, 14, 27, 51, 89; DAM NOV; SSC 10**
See also AITN 1, 2; CA 1-4R; CABS 1; CANR
5, 23, 49; DLB 2; MTCW
Barthelme, Donald 1931-1989**CLC 1, 2, 3, 5, 6,
8, 13, 23, 46, 59; DAM NOV; SSC 2**
See also CA 21-24R; 129; CANR 20, 58; DLB
2; DLBY 80, 89; MTCW; SATA 7; SATA-
Obit 62
Barthelme, Frederick 1943- .... **CLC 36**
See also CA 114; 122; DLBY 85; INT 122
Barthes, Roland (Gerard) 1915-1980**CLC 24,
83**
See also CA 130; 97-100; MTCW
Barzun, Jacques (Martin) 1907- ...... **CLC 51**
See also CA 61-64; CANR 22
Bashevis, Isaac
See Singer, Isaac Bashevis
Bashkirtseff, Marie 1859-1884 .... **NCLC 27**
Basho
See Matsuo Basho
Bass, Kingsley B., Jr.
See Bullins, Ed
Bass, Rick 1958-................................ **CLC 79**
See also CA 126; CANR 53
Bassani, Giorgio 1916-......................... **CLC 9**
See also CA 65-68; CANR 33; DLB 128, 177;
MTCW
Bastos, Augusto (Antonio) Roa
See Roa Bastos, Augusto (Antonio)
Bataille, Georges 1897-1962 .... **CLC 29**
See also CA 101; 89-92
Bates, H(erbert) E(rnest) 1905-1974**CLC 46;
DAB; DAM POP; SSC 10**
See also CA 93-96; 45-48; CANR 34; DLB 162;
MTCW
Bauchart
See Camus, Albert
Baudelaire, Charles 1821-1867 **NCLC 6, 29,
55; DA; DAB; DAC; DAM MST, POET;
PC 1; SSC 18; WLC**
Baudrillard, Jean 1929-.................... **CLC 60**
Baum, L(yman) Frank 1856-1919 ... **TCLC 7**
See also CA 108; 133; CLR 15; DLB 22; JRDA;
MAICYA; MTCW; SATA 18
Baum, Louis F.
See Baum, L(yman) Frank
Baumbach, Jonathan 1933-.......... **CLC 6, 23**
See also CA 13-16R; CAAS 5; CANR 12;
DLBY 80; INT CANR-12; MTCW
Bausch, Richard (Carl) 1945- .... **CLC 51**
See also CA 101; CAAS 14; CANR 43, 61; DLB
130
Baxter, Charles 1947-**CLC 45, 78; DAM POP**
See also CA 57-60; CANR 40; DLB 130
Baxter, George Owen
See Faust, Frederick (Schiller)
Baxter, James K(eir) 1926-1972 .... **CLC 14**
See also CA 77-80

Baxter, John
See Hunt, E(verette) Howard, (Jr.)
Bayer, Sylvia
See Glassco, John
Baynton, Barbara 1857-1929 .... **TCLC 57**
Beagle, Peter S(oyer) 1939- .... **CLC 7, 104**
See also CA 9-12R; CANR 4, 51; DLBY 80;
INT CANR-4; SATA 60
Bean, Normal
See Burroughs, Edgar Rice
Beard, Charles A(ustin) 1874-1948 **TCLC 15**
See also CA 115; DLB 17; SATA 18
Beardsley, Aubrey 1872-1898 .... **NCLC 6**
Beattie, Ann 1947-**CLC 8, 13, 18, 40, 63; DAM
NOV, POP; SSC 11**
See also BEST 90:2; CA 81-84; CANR 53;
DLBY 82; MTCW
Beattie, James 1735-1803 .... **NCLC 25**
See also DLB 109
Beauchamp, Kathleen Mansfield 1888-1923
See Mansfield, Katherine
See also CA 104; 134; DA; DAC; DAM MST
Beaumarchais, Pierre-Augustin Caron de 1732-
1799 .... **DC 4**
See also DAM DRAM
Beaumont, Francis 1584(?)-1616**LC 33; DC 6**
See also CDBLB Before 1660; DLB 58, 121
**Beauvoir, Simone (Lucie Ernestine Marie
Bertrand) de** 1908-1986**CLC 1, 2, 4, 8, 14,
31, 44, 50, 71; DA; DAB; DAC; DAM MST,
NOV; WLC**
See also CA 9-12R; 118; CANR 28, 61; DLB
72; DLBY 86; MTCW
Becker, Carl (Lotus) 1873-1945 ..... **TCLC 63**
See also CA 157; DLB 17
Becker, Jurek 1937-1997 .... **CLC 7, 19**
See also CA 85-88; 157; CANR 60; DLB 75
Becker, Walter 1950- .... **CLC 26**
Beckett, Samuel (Barclay) 1906-1989 **CLC 1,
2, 3, 4, 6, 9, 10, 11, 14, 18, 29, 57, 59, 83;
DA; DAB; DAC; DAM DRAM, MST,
NOV; SSC 16; WLC**
See also CA 5-8R; 130; CANR 33, 61; CDBLB
1945-1960; DLB 13, 15; DLBY 90; MTCW
Beckford, William 1760-1844 .... **NCLC 16**
See also DLB 39
Beckman, Gunnel 1910- .... **CLC 26**
See also CA 33-36R; CANR 15; CLR 25;
MAICYA; SAAS 9; SATA 6
Becque, Henri 1837-1899.................. **NCLC 3**
Beddoes, Thomas Lovell 1803-1849 **NCLC 3**
See also DLB 96
Bede c. 673-735 .... **CMLC 20**
See also DLB 146
Bedford, Donald F.
See Fearing, Kenneth (Flexner)
Beecher, Catharine Esther 1800-1878 **N C L C
30**
See also DLB 1
Beecher, John 1904-1980 .... **CLC 6**
See also AITN 1; CA 5-8R; 105; CANR 8
Beer, Johann 1655-1700 .... **LC 5**
See also DLB 168
Beer, Patricia 1924- .... **CLC 58**
See also CA 61-64; CANR 13, 46; DLB 40
Beerbohm, Max
See Beerbohm, (Henry) Max(imilian)
Beerbohm, (Henry) Max(imilian) 1872-1956
TCLC 1, 24
See also CA 104; 154; DLB 34, 100
Beer-Hofmann, Richard 1866-1945**TCLC 60**
See also DLB 81
Begiebing, Robert J(ohn) 1946- .... **CLC 70**

See also CA 122; CANR 40
Behan, Brendan 1923-1964 **CLC 1, 8, 11, 15,
79; DAM DRAM**
See also CA 73-76; CANR 33; CDBLB 1945-
1960; DLB 13; MTCW
Behn, Aphra 1640(?)-1689**LC 1, 30; DA; DAB;
DAC; DAM DRAM, MST, NOV, POET;
DC 4; PC 13; WLC**
See also DLB 39, 80, 131
Behrman, S(amuel) N(athaniel) 1893-1973
CLC 40
See also CA 13-16; 45-48; CAP 1; DLB 7, 44
Belasco, David 1853-1931 .... **TCLC 3**
See also CA 104; DLB 7
Belcheva, Elisaveta 1893- .... **CLC 10**
See also Bagryana, Elisaveta
Beldone, Phil "Cheech"
See Ellison, Harlan (Jay)
Beleno
See Azuela, Mariano
Belinski, Vissarion Grigoryevich 1811-1848
NCLC 5
Belitt, Ben 1911- .... **CLC 22**
See also CA 13-16R; CAAS 4; CANR 7; DLB
5
Bell, Gertrude 1868-1926 .... **TCLC 67**
See also DLB 174
Bell, James Madison 1826-1902 ... **TCLC 43;
BLC; DAM MULT**
See also BW 1; CA 122; 124; DLB 50
Bell, Madison Smartt 1957-...... **CLC 41, 102**
See also CA 111; CANR 28, 54
Bell, Marvin (Hartley) 1937-**CLC 8, 31; DAM
POET**
See also CA 21-24R; CAAS 14; CANR 59; DLB
5; MTCW
Bell, W. L. D.
See Mencken, H(enry) L(ouis)
Bellamy, Atwood C.
See Mencken, H(enry) L(ouis)
Bellamy, Edward 1850-1898 .... **NCLC 4**
See also DLB 12
Bellin, Edward J.
See Kuttner, Henry
**Belloc, (Joseph) Hilaire (Pierre Sebastien Rene
Swanton)** 1870-1953 **TCLC 7, 18; DAM
POET**
See also CA 106; 152; DLB 19, 100, 141, 174;
YABC 1
Belloc, Joseph Peter Rene Hilaire
See Belloc, (Joseph) Hilaire (Pierre Sebastien
Rene Swanton)
Belloc, Joseph Pierre Hilaire
See Belloc, (Joseph) Hilaire (Pierre Sebastien
Rene Swanton)
Belloc, M. A.
See Lowndes, Marie Adelaide (Belloc)
Bellow, Saul 1915-**CLC 1, 2, 3, 6, 8, 10, 13, 15,
25, 33, 34, 63, 79; DA; DAB; DAC; DAM
MST, NOV, POP; SSC 14; WLC**
See also AITN 2; BEST 89:3; CA 5-8R; CABS
1; CANR 29, 53; CDALB 1941-1968; DLB
2, 28; DLBD 3; DLBY 82; MTCW
Belser, Reimond Karel Maria de 1929-
See Ruyslinck, Ward
See also CA 152
Bely, Andrey .... **TCLC 7; PC 11**
See also Bugayev, Boris Nikolayevich
Benary, Margot
See Benary-Isbert, Margot
Benary-Isbert, Margot 1889-1979 ....**CLC 12**
See also CA 5-8R; 89-92; CANR 4; CLR 12;
MAICYA; SATA 2; SATA-Obit 21

Benavente (y Martinez), Jacinto 1866-1954
TCLC 3; DAM DRAM, MULT
See also CA 106; 131; HW; MTCW
Benchley, Peter (Bradford) 1940- . CLC 4, 8;
DAM NOV, POP
See also AAYA 14; AITN 2; CA 17-20R; CANR
12, 35; MTCW; SATA 3, 89
Benchley, Robert (Charles) 1889-1945T C L C
1, 55
See also CA 105; 153; DLB 11
Benda, Julien 1867-1956 .... TCLC 60
See also CA 120; 154
Benedict, Ruth (Fulton) 1887-1948 TCLC 60
See also CA 158
Benedikt, Michael 1935- .... CLC 4, 14
See also CA 13-16R; CANR 7; DLB 5
Benet, Juan 1927- .... CLC 28
See also CA 143
Benet, Stephen Vincent 1898-1943 . TCLC 7;
DAM POET; SSC 10
See also CA 104; 152; DLB 4, 48, 102; YABC
1
Benet, William Rose 1886-1950 ... TCLC 28;
DAM POET
See also CA 118; 152; DLB 45
Benford, Gregory (Albert) 1941- ..... CLC 52
See also CA 69-72; CAAS 27; CANR 12, 24,
49; DLBY 82
Bengtsson, Frans (Gunnar) 1894-1954T C L C
48
Benjamin, David
See Slavitt, David R(ytman)
Benjamin, Lois
See Gould, Lois
Benjamin, Walter 1892-1940 .... TCLC 39
Benn, Gottfried 1886-1956 .... TCLC 3
See also CA 106; 153; DLB 56
Bennett, Alan 1934-CLC 45, 77; DAB; DAM
MST
See also CA 103; CANR 35, 55; MTCW
Bennett, (Enoch) Arnold 1867-1931 TCLC 5,
20
See also CA 106; 155; CDBLB 1890-1914;
DLB 10, 34, 98, 135
Bennett, Elizabeth
See Mitchell, Margaret (Munnerlyn)
Bennett, George Harold 1930-
See Bennett, Hal
See also BW 1; CA 97-100
Bennett, Hal .... CLC 5
See also Bennett, George Harold
See also DLB 33
Bennett, Jay 1912- .... CLC 35
See also AAYA 10; CA 69-72; CANR 11, 42;
JRDA; SAAS 4; SATA 41, 87; SATA-Brief
27
Bennett, Louise (Simone) 1919-CLC 28; BLC;
DAM MULT
See also BW 2; CA 151; DLB 117
Benson, E(dward) F(rederic) 1867-1940
TCLC 27
See also CA 114; 157; DLB 135, 153
Benson, Jackson J. 1930- .... CLC 34
See also CA 25-28R; DLB 111
Benson, Sally 1900-1972 .... CLC 17
See also CA 19-20; 37-40R; CAP 1; SATA 1,
35; SATA-Obit 27
Benson, Stella 1892-1933 .... TCLC 17
See also CA 117; 155; DLB 36, 162
Bentham, Jeremy 1748-1832 .... NCLC 38
See also DLB 107, 158
Bentley, E(dmund) C(lerihew) 1875-1956
TCLC 12

See also CA 108; DLB 70
Bentley, Eric (Russell) 1916- .... CLC 24
See also CA 5-8R; CANR 6; INT CANR-6
Beranger, Pierre Jean de 1780-1857NCLC 34
Berdyaev, Nicolas
See Berdyaev, Nikolai (Aleksandrovich)
Berdyaev, Nikolai (Aleksandrovich) 1874-1948
TCLC 67
See also CA 120; 157
Berdyayev, Nikolai (Aleksandrovich)
See Berdyaev, Nikolai (Aleksandrovich)
Berendt, John (Lawrence) 1939- ...... CLC 86
See also CA 146
Berger, Colonel
See Malraux, (Georges-)Andre
Berger, John (Peter) 1926- .... CLC 2, 19
See also CA 81-84; CANR 51; DLB 14
Berger, Melvin H. 1927- .... CLC 12
See also CA 5-8R; CANR 4; CLR 32; SAAS 2;
SATA 5, 88
Berger, Thomas (Louis) 1924-CLC 3, 5, 8, 11,
18, 38; DAM NOV
See also CA 1-4R; CANR 5, 28, 51; DLB 2;
DLBY 80; INT CANR-28; MTCW
Bergman, (Ernst) Ingmar 1918- CLC 16, 72
See also CA 81-84; CANR 33
Bergson, Henri 1859-1941 .... TCLC 32
Bergstein, Eleanor 1938- .... CLC 4
See also CA 53-56; CANR 5
Berkoff, Steven 1937- .... CLC 56
See also CA 104
Bermant, Chaim (Icyk) 1929- .... CLC 40
See also CA 57-60; CANR 6, 31, 57
Bern, Victoria
See Fisher, M(ary) F(rances) K(ennedy)
Bernanos, (Paul Louis) Georges 1888-1948
TCLC 3
See also CA 104; 130; DLB 72
Bernard, April 1956- .... CLC 59
See also CA 131
Berne, Victoria
See Fisher, M(ary) F(rances) K(ennedy)
Bernhard, Thomas 1931-1989 CLC 3, 32, 61
See also CA 85-88; 127; CANR 32, 57; DLB
85, 124; MTCW
Berriault, Gina 1926- .... CLC 54
See also CA 116; 129; DLB 130
Berrigan, Daniel 1921- .... CLC 4
See also CA 33-36R; CAAS 1; CANR 11, 43;
DLB 5
Berrigan, Edmund Joseph Michael, Jr. 1934-
1983
See Berrigan, Ted
See also CA 61-64; 110; CANR 14
Berrigan, Ted .... CLC 37
See also Berrigan, Edmund Joseph Michael, Jr.
See also DLB 5, 169
Berry, Charles Edward Anderson 1931-
See Berry, Chuck
See also CA 115
Berry, Chuck .... CLC 17
See also Berry, Charles Edward Anderson
Berry, Jonas
See Ashbery, John (Lawrence)
Berry, Wendell (Erdman) 1934- CLC 4, 6, 8,
27, 46; DAM POET
See also AITN 1; CA 73-76; CANR 50; DLB 5,
6
Berryman, John 1914-1972CLC 1, 2, 3, 4, 6, 8,
10, 13, 25, 62; DAM POET
See also CA 13-16; 33-36R; CABS 2; CANR
35; CAP 1; CDALB 1941-1968; DLB 48;
MTCW

Bertolucci, Bernardo 1940- .... CLC 16
See also CA 106
Berton, Pierre (Francis De Marigny) 1920-
CLC 104
See also CA 1-4R; CANR 2, 56; DLB 68
Bertrand, Aloysius 1807-1841 .... NCLC 31
Bertran de Born c. 1140-1215 .... CMLC 5
Besant, Annie (Wood) 1847-1933 ..... TCLC 9
See also CA 105
Bessie, Alvah 1904-1985 .... CLC 23
See also CA 5-8R; 116; CANR 2; DLB 26
Bethlen, T. D.
See Silverberg, Robert
Beti, Mongo ...... CLC 27; BLC; DAM MULT
See also Biyidi, Alexandre
Betjeman, John 1906-1984 CLC 2, 6, 10, 34,
43; DAB; DAM MST, POET
See also CA 9-12R; 112; CANR 33, 56; CDBLB
1945-1960; DLB 20; DLBY 84; MTCW
Bettelheim, Bruno 1903-1990 .... CLC 79
See also CA 81-84; 131; CANR 23, 61; MTCW
Betti, Ugo 1892-1953 .... TCLC 5
See also CA 104; 155
Betts, Doris (Waugh) 1932- ...... CLC 3, 6, 28
See also CA 13-16R; CANR 9; DLBY 82; INT
CANR-9
Bevan, Alistair
See Roberts, Keith (John Kingston)
Bialik, Chaim Nachman 1873-1934 TCLC 25
Bickerstaff, Isaac
See Swift, Jonathan
Bidart, Frank 1939- .... CLC 33
See also CA 140
Bienek, Horst 1930- .... CLC 7, 11
See also CA 73-76; DLB 75
Bierce, Ambrose (Gwinett) 1842-1914(?)
TCLC 1, 7, 44; DA; DAC; DAM MST; SSC
9; WLC
See also CA 104; 139; CDALB 1865-1917;
DLB 11, 12, 23, 71, 74
Biggers, Earl Derr 1884-1933 .... TCLC 65
See also CA 108; 153
Billings, Josh
See Shaw, Henry Wheeler
Billington, (Lady) Rachel (Mary) 1942- C L C
43
See also AITN 2; CA 33-36R; CANR 44
Binyon, T(imothy) J(ohn) 1936- ...... CLC 34
See also CA 111; CANR 28
Bioy Casares, Adolfo 1914- CLC 4, 8, 13, 88;
DAM MULT; HLC; SSC 17
See also CA 29-32R; CANR 19, 43; DLB 113;
HW; MTCW
Bird, Cordwainer
See Ellison, Harlan (Jay)
Bird, Robert Montgomery 1806-1854NCLC 1
Birney, (Alfred) Earle 1904- CLC 1, 4, 6, 11;
DAC; DAM MST, POET
See also CA 1-4R; CANR 5, 20; DLB 88;
MTCW
Bishop, Elizabeth 1911-1979 CLC 1, 4, 9, 13,
15, 32; DA; DAC; DAM MST, POET; PC
3
See also CA 5-8R; 89-92; CABS 2; CANR 26,
61; CDALB 1968-1988; DLB 5, 169;
MTCW; SATA-Obit 24
Bishop, John 1935- .... CLC 10
See also CA 105
Bissett, Bill 1939- .... CLC 18; PC 14
See also CA 69-72; CAAS 19; CANR 15; DLB
53; MTCW
Bitov, Andrei (Georgievich) 1937- ... CLC 57
See also CA 142

See also CA 13-16R; CANR 58; DLB 14

Brookner, Anita 1928-**CLC 32, 34, 51; DAB; DAM POP**
See also CA 114; 120; CANR 37, 56; DLBY 87; MTCW

Brooks, Cleanth 1906-1994 .... **CLC 24, 86**
See also CA 17-20R; 145; CANR 33, 35; DLB 63; DLBY 94; INT CANR-35; MTCW

Brooks, George
See Baum, L(yman) Frank

Brooks, Gwendolyn 1917- **CLC 1, 2, 4, 5, 15, 49; BLC; DA; DAC; DAM MST, MULT, POET; PC 7; WLC**
See also AAYA 20; AITN 1; BW 2; CA 1-4R; CANR 1, 27, 52; CDALB 1941-1968; CLR 27; DLB 5, 76, 165; MTCW; SATA 6

Brooks, Mel .... **CLC 12**
See also Kaminsky, Melvin
See also AAYA 13; DLB 26

Brooks, Peter 1938- .... **CLC 34**
See also CA 45-48; CANR 1

Brooks, Van Wyck 1886-1963 .... **CLC 29**
See also CA 1-4R; CANR 6; DLB 45, 63, 103

Brophy, Brigid (Antonia) 1929-1995 . **CLC 6, 11, 29**
See also CA 5-8R; 149; CAAS 4; CANR 25, 53; DLB 14; MTCW

Brosman, Catharine Savage 1934- ..... **CLC 9**
See also CA 61-64; CANR 21, 46

Brother Antoninus
See Everson, William (Oliver)

Broughton, T(homas) Alan 1936- .... **CLC 19**
See also CA 45-48; CANR 2, 23, 48

Broumas, Olga 1949- .... **CLC 10, 73**
See also CA 85-88; CANR 20

Brown, Alan 1951- .... **CLC 99**

Brown, Charles Brockden 1771-1810 **N C L C 22**
See also CDALB 1640-1865; DLB 37, 59, 73

Brown, Christy 1932-1981 .... **CLC 63**
See also CA 105; 104; DLB 14

Brown, Claude 1937- .. **CLC 30; BLC; DAM MULT**
See also AAYA 7; BW 1; CA 73-76

Brown, Dee (Alexander) 1908-.. **CLC 18, 47; DAM POP**
See also CA 13-16R; CAAS 6; CANR 11, 45, 60; DLBY 80; MTCW; SATA 5

Brown, George
See Wertmueller, Lina

Brown, George Douglas 1869-1902 **TCLC 28**

Brown, George Mackay 1921-1996**CLC 5, 48, 100**
See also CA 21-24R; 151; CAAS 6; CANR 12, 37; DLB 14, 27, 139; MTCW; SATA 35

Brown, (William) Larry 1951- .... **CLC 73**
See also CA 130; 134; INT 133

Brown, Moses
See Barrett, William (Christopher)

Brown, Rita Mae 1944-**CLC 18, 43, 79; DAM NOV, POP**
See also CA 45-48; CANR 2, 11, 35; INT CANR-11; MTCW

Brown, Roderick (Langmere) Haig-
See Haig-Brown, Roderick (Langmere)

Brown, Rosellen 1939- .... **CLC 32**
See also CA 77-80; CAAS 10; CANR 14, 44

Brown, Sterling Allen 1901-1989 **CLC 1, 23, 59; BLC; DAM MULT, POET**
See also BW 1; CA 85-88; 127; CANR 26; DLB 48, 51, 63; MTCW

Brown, Will
See Ainsworth, William Harrison

Brown, William Wells 1813-1884 .. **NCLC 2; BLC; DAM MULT; DC 1**
See also DLB 3, 50

Browne, (Clyde) Jackson 1948(?)- .... **CLC 21**
See also CA 120

Browning, Elizabeth Barrett 1806-1861 **NCLC 1, 16, 61; DA; DAB; DAC; DAM MST, POET; PC 6; WLC**
See also CDBLB 1832-1890; DLB 32

Browning, Robert 1812-1889 **NCLC 19; DA; DAB; DAC; DAM MST, POET; PC 2; WLCS**
See also CDBLB 1832-1890; DLB 32, 163; YABC 1

Browning, Tod 1882-1962 .... **CLC 16**
See also CA 141; 117

Brownson, Orestes (Augustus) 1803-1876 **NCLC 50**

Bruccoli, Matthew J(oseph) 1931-.... **CLC 34**
See also CA 9-12R; CANR 7; DLB 103

Bruce, Lenny .... **CLC 21**
See also Schneider, Leonard Alfred

Bruin, John
See Brutus, Dennis

Brulard, Henri
See Stendhal

Brulls, Christian
See Simenon, Georges (Jacques Christian)

Brunner, John (Kilian Houston) 1934-1995 **CLC 8, 10; DAM POP**
See also CA 1-4R; 149; CAAS 8; CANR 2, 37; MTCW

Bruno, Giordano 1548-1600 .... **LC 27**

Brutus, Dennis 1924-... **CLC 43; BLC; DAM MULT, POET**
See also BW 2; CA 49-52; CAAS 14; CANR 2, 27, 42; DLB 117

Bryan, C(ourtlandt) D(ixon) B(arnes) 1936- **CLC 29**
See also CA 73-76; CANR 13; INT CANR-13

Bryan, Michael
See Moore, Brian

Bryant, William Cullen 1794-1878 . **NCLC 6, 46; DA; DAB; DAC; DAM MST, POET**
See also CDALB 1640-1865; DLB 3, 43, 59

Bryusov, Valery Yakovlevich 1873-1924 **TCLC 10**
See also CA 107; 155

Buchan, John 1875-1940 .... **TCLC 41; DAB; DAM POP**
See also CA 108; 145; DLB 34, 70, 156; YABC 2

Buchanan, George 1506-1582 .... **LC 4**

Buchheim, Lothar-Guenther 1918- .... **CLC 6**
See also CA 85-88

Buchner, (Karl) Georg 1813-1837 . **NCLC 26**

Buchwald, Art(hur) 1925- .... **CLC 33**
See also AITN 1; CA 5-8R; CANR 21; MTCW; SATA 10

Buck, Pearl S(ydenstricker) 1892-1973**CLC 7, 11, 18; DA; DAB; DAC; DAM MST, NOV**
See also AITN 1; CA 1-4R; 41-44R; CANR 1, 34; DLB 9, 102; MTCW; SATA 1, 25

Buckler, Ernest 1908-1984 .... **CLC 13; DAC; DAM MST**
See also CA 11-12; 114; CAP 1; DLB 68; SATA 47

Buckley, Vincent (Thomas) 1925-1988**CLC 57**
See also CA 101

Buckley, William F(rank), Jr. 1925-**CLC 7, 18, 37; DAM POP**
See also AITN 1; CA 1-4R; CANR 1, 24, 53; DLB 137; DLBY 80; INT CANR-24; MTCW

Buechner, (Carl) Frederick 1926-**CLC 2, 4, 6, 9; DAM NOV**
See also CA 13-16R; CANR 11, 39; DLBY 80; INT CANR-11; MTCW

Buell, John (Edward) 1927- .... **CLC 10**
See also CA 1-4R; DLB 53

Buero Vallejo, Antonio 1916- ..... **CLC 15, 46**
See also CA 106; CANR 24, 49; HW; MTCW

Bufalino, Gesualdo 1920(?)- .... **CLC 74**

Bugayev, Boris Nikolayevich 1880-1934
See Bely, Andrey
See also CA 104

Bukowski, Charles 1920-1994**CLC 2, 5, 9, 41, 82; DAM NOV, POET; PC 18**
See also CA 17-20R; 144; CANR 40; DLB 5, 130, 169; MTCW

Bulgakov, Mikhail (Afanas'evich) 1891-1940 **TCLC 2, 16; DAM DRAM, NOV; SSC 18**
See also CA 105; 152

Bulgya, Alexander Alexandrovich 1901-1956 **TCLC 53**
See also Fadeyev, Alexander
See also CA 117

Bullins, Ed 1935- ... **CLC 1, 5, 7; BLC; DAM DRAM, MULT; DC 6**
See also BW 2; CA 49-52; CAAS 16; CANR 24, 46; DLB 7, 38; MTCW

Bulwer-Lytton, Edward (George Earle Lytton) 1803-1873 .... **NCLC 1, 45**
See also DLB 21

Bunin, Ivan Alexeyevich 1870-1953 **TCLC 6; SSC 5**
See also CA 104

Bunting, Basil 1900-1985 ..... **CLC 10, 39, 47; DAM POET**
See also CA 53-56; 115; CANR 7; DLB 20

Bunuel, Luis 1900-1983 .. **CLC 16, 80; DAM MULT; HLC**
See also CA 101; 110; CANR 32; HW

Bunyan, John 1628-1688 ... **LC 4; DA; DAB; DAC; DAM MST; WLC**
See also CDBLB 1660-1789; DLB 39

Burckhardt, Jacob (Christoph) 1818-1897 **NCLC 49**

Burford, Eleanor
See Hibbert, Eleanor Alice Burford

Burgess, AnthonyCLC 1, 2, 4, 5, 8, 10, 13, 15, 22, 40, 62, 81, 94; DAB
See also Wilson, John (Anthony) Burgess
See also AITN 1; CDBLB 1960 to Present; DLB 14

Burke, Edmund 1729(?)-1797 **LC 7, 36; DA; DAB; DAC; DAM MST; WLC**
See also DLB 104

Burke, Kenneth (Duva) 1897-1993**CLC 2, 24**
See also CA 5-8R; 143; CANR 39; DLB 45, 63; MTCW

Burke, Leda
See Garnett, David

Burke, Ralph
See Silverberg, Robert

Burke, Thomas 1886-1945 .... **TCLC 63**
See also CA 113; 155

Burney, Fanny 1752-1840 .... **NCLC 12, 54**
See also DLB 39

Burns, Robert 1759-1796 .... **PC 6**
See also CDBLB 1789-1832; DA; DAB; DAC; DAM MST, POET; DLB 109; WLC

Burns, Tex
See L'Amour, Louis (Dearborn)

Burnshaw, Stanley 1906- .... **CLC 3, 13, 44**
See also CA 9-12R; DLB 48

Burr, Anne 1937- .... **CLC 6**

See also CA 25-28R

Burroughs, Edgar Rice 1875-1950 . **TCLC 2, 32; DAM NOV**
See also AAYA 11; CA 104; 132; DLB 8; MTCW; SATA 41

Burroughs, William S(eward) 1914-**CLC 1, 2, 5, 15, 22, 42, 75; DA; DAB; DAC; DAM MST, NOV, POP; WLC**
See also AITN 2; CA 9-12R; CANR 20, 52; DLB 2, 8, 16, 152; DLBY 81; MTCW

Burton, Richard F. 1821-1890 .... **NCLC 42**
See also DLB 55

Busch, Frederick 1941- ..... **CLC 7, 10, 18, 47**
See also CA 33-36R; CAAS 1; CANR 45; DLB 6

Bush, Ronald 1946- .... **CLC 34**
See also CA 136

Bustos, F(rancisco)
See Borges, Jorge Luis

Bustos Domecq, H(onorio)
See Bioy Casares, Adolfo; Borges, Jorge Luis

Butler, Octavia E(stelle) 1947-**CLC 38; DAM MULT, POP**
See also AAYA 18; BW 2; CA 73-76; CANR 12, 24, 38; DLB 33; MTCW; SATA 84

Butler, Robert Olen (Jr.) 1945-**CLC 81; DAM POP**
See also CA 112; DLB 173; INT 112

Butler, Samuel 1612-1680 .... **LC 16**
See also DLB 101, 126

Butler, Samuel 1835-1902 . **TCLC 1, 33; DA; DAB; DAC; DAM MST, NOV; WLC**
See also CA 143; CDBLB 1890-1914; DLB 18, 57, 174

Butler, Walter C.
See Faust, Frederick (Schiller)

Butor, Michel (Marie Francois) 1926-**CLC 1, 3, 8, 11, 15**
See also CA 9-12R; CANR 33; DLB 83; MTCW

Buzo, Alexander (John) 1944- .... **CLC 61**
See also CA 97-100; CANR 17, 39

Buzzati, Dino 1906-1972 .... **CLC 36**
See also CA 33-36R; DLB 177

Byars, Betsy (Cromer) 1928-............ **CLC 35**
See also AAYA 19; CA 33-36R; CANR 18, 36, 57; CLR 1, 16; DLB 52; INT CANR-18; JRDA; MAICYA; MTCW; SAAS 1; SATA 4, 46, 80

Byatt, A(ntonia) S(usan Drabble) 1936-**C L C 19, 65; DAM NOV, POP**
See also CA 13-16R; CANR 13, 33, 50; DLB 14; MTCW

Byrne, David 1952-........................... **CLC 26**
See also CA 127

Byrne, John Keyes 1926-
See Leonard, Hugh
See also CA 102; INT 102

Byron, George Gordon (Noel) 1788-1824 **NCLC 2, 12; DA; DAB; DAC; DAM MST, POET; PC 16; WLC**
See also CDBLB 1789-1832; DLB 96, 110

Byron, Robert 1905-1941 .... **TCLC 67**

C. 3. 3.
See Wilde, Oscar (Fingal O'Flahertie Wills)

Caballero, Fernan 1796-1877 .... **NCLC 10**

Cabell, Branch
See Cabell, James Branch

Cabell, James Branch 1879-1958 .... **TCLC 6**
See also CA 105; 152; DLB 9, 78

Cable, George Washington 1844-1925 **T C L C 4; SSC 4**
See also CA 104; 155; DLB 12, 74; DLBD 13

Cabral de Melo Neto, Joao 1920- ... **CLC 76;**

DAM MULT
See also CA 151

Cabrera Infante, G(uillermo) 1929-**CLC 5, 25, 45; DAM MULT; HLC**
See also CA 85-88; CANR 29; DLB 113; HW; MTCW

Cade, Toni
See Bambara, Toni Cade

Cadmus and Harmonia
See Buchan, John

Caedmon fl. 658-680 .... **CMLC 7**
See also DLB 146

Caeiro, Alberto
See Pessoa, Fernando (Antonio Nogueira)

Cage, John (Milton, Jr.) 1912- .... **CLC 41**
See also CA 13-16R; CANR 9; INT CANR-9

Cahan, Abraham 1860-1951 .... **TCLC 71**
See also CA 108; 154; DLB 9, 25, 28

Cain, G.
See Cabrera Infante, G(uillermo)

Cain, Guillermo
See Cabrera Infante, G(uillermo)

Cain, James M(allahan) 1892-1977**CLC 3, 11, 28**
See also AITN 1; CA 17-20R; 73-76; CANR 8, 34, 61; MTCW

Caine, Mark
See Raphael, Frederic (Michael)

Calasso, Roberto 1941- .... **CLC 81**
See also CA 143

Calderon de la Barca, Pedro 1600-1681 ..**L C 23; DC 3**

Caldwell, Erskine (Preston) 1903-1987**CLC 1, 8, 14, 50, 60; DAM NOV; SSC 19**
See also AITN 1; CA 1-4R; 121; CAAS 1; CANR 2, 33; DLB 9, 86; MTCW

Caldwell, (Janet Miriam) Taylor (Holland) 1900-1985**CLC 2, 28, 39; DAM NOV, POP**
See also CA 5-8R; 116; CANR 5

Calhoun, John Caldwell 1782-1850**NCLC 15**
See also DLB 3

Calisher, Hortense 1911-**CLC 2, 4, 8, 38; DAM NOV; SSC 15**
See also CA 1-4R; CANR 1, 22; DLB 2; INT CANR-22; MTCW

Callaghan, Morley Edward 1903-1990**CLC 3, 14, 41, 65; DAC; DAM MST**
See also CA 9-12R; 132; CANR 33; DLB 68; MTCW

Callimachus c. 305B.C.-c. 240B.C. **CMLC 18**
See also DLB 176

Calvin, John 1509-1564 .... **LC 37**

Calvino, Italo 1923-1985**CLC 5, 8, 11, 22, 33, 39, 73; DAM NOV; SSC 3**
See also CA 85-88; 116; CANR 23, 61; MTCW

Cameron, Carey 1952-...................... **CLC 59**
See also CA 135

Cameron, Peter 1959- .... **CLC 44**
See also CA 125; CANR 50

Campana, Dino 1885-1932 .... **TCLC 20**
See also CA 117; DLB 114

Campanella, Tommaso 1568-1639 ...... **LC 32**

Campbell, John W(ood, Jr.) 1910-1971 **C L C 32**
See also CA 21-22; 29-32R; CANR 34; CAP 2; DLB 8; MTCW

Campbell, Joseph 1904-1987 .... **CLC 69**
See also AAYA 3; BEST 89:2; CA 1-4R; 124; CANR 3, 28, 61; MTCW

Campbell, Maria 1940-........... **CLC 85; DAC**
See also CA 102; CANR 54; NNAL

Campbell, (John) Ramsey 1946-**CLC 42; SSC 19**

See also CA 57-60; CANR 7; INT CANR-7

Campbell, (Ignatius) Roy (Dunnachie) 1901-1957 .... **TCLC 5**
See also CA 104; 155; DLB 20

Campbell, Thomas 1777-1844 .... **NCLC 19**
See also DLB 93; 144

Campbell, Wilfred .... **TCLC 9**
See also Campbell, William

Campbell, William 1858(?)-1918
See Campbell, Wilfred
See also CA 106; DLB 92

Campion, Jane .... **CLC 95**
See also CA 138

Campos, Alvaro de
See Pessoa, Fernando (Antonio Nogueira)

Camus, Albert 1913-1960**CLC 1, 2, 4, 9, 11, 14, 32, 63, 69; DA; DAB; DAC; DAM DRAM, MST, NOV; DC 2; SSC 9; WLC**
See also CA 89-92; DLB 72; MTCW

Canby, Vincent 1924- .... **CLC 13**
See also CA 81-84

Cancale
See Desnos, Robert

Canetti, Elias 1905-1994**CLC 3, 14, 25, 75, 86**
See also CA 21-24R; 146; CANR 23, 61; DLB 85, 124; MTCW

Canin, Ethan 1960- .... **CLC 55**
See also CA 131; 135

Cannon, Curt
See Hunter, Evan

Cape, Judith
See Page, P(atricia) K(athleen)

Capek, Karel 1890-1938 ... **TCLC 6, 37; DA; DAB; DAC; DAM DRAM, MST, NOV; DC 1; WLC**
See also CA 104; 140

Capote, Truman 1924-1984**CLC 1, 3, 8, 13, 19, 34, 38, 58; DA; DAB; DAC; DAM MST, NOV, POP; SSC 2; WLC**
See also CA 5-8R; 113; CANR 18; CDALB 1941-1968; DLB 2; DLBY 80, 84; MTCW; SATA 91

Capra, Frank 1897-1991 .... **CLC 16**
See also CA 61-64; 135

Caputo, Philip 1941- .... **CLC 32**
See also CA 73-76; CANR 40

Card, Orson Scott 1951-**CLC 44, 47, 50; DAM POP**
See also AAYA 11; CA 102; CANR 27, 47; INT CANR-27; MTCW; SATA 83

Cardenal, Ernesto 1925- .... **CLC 31; DAM MULT, POET; HLC**
See also CA 49-52; CANR 2, 32; HW; MTCW

Cardozo, Benjamin N(athan) 1870-1938 **TCLC 65**
See also CA 117

Carducci, Giosue 1835-1907 .... **TCLC 32**

Carew, Thomas 1595(?)-1640 .... **LC 13**
See also DLB 126

Carey, Ernestine Gilbreth 1908-...... **CLC 17**
See also CA 5-8R; SATA 2

Carey, Peter 1943- .... **CLC 40, 55, 96**
See also CA 123; 127; CANR 53; INT 127; MTCW; SATA 94

Carleton, William 1794-1869 .... **NCLC 3**
See also DLB 159

Carlisle, Henry (Coffin) 1926- .... **CLC 33**
See also CA 13-16R; CANR 15

Carlsen, Chris
See Holdstock, Robert P.

Carlson, Ron(ald F.) 1947- .... **CLC 54**
See also CA 105; CANR 27

Carlyle, Thomas 1795-1881 .. **NCLC 22; DA;**

Clarke, Gillian 1937- .... **CLC 61**
See also CA 106; DLB 40
Clarke, Marcus (Andrew Hislop) 1846-1881
NCLC 19
Clarke, Shirley 1925- .... **CLC 16**
Clash, The
See Headon, (Nicky) Topper; Jones, Mick;
Simonon, Paul; Strummer, Joe
Claudel, Paul (Louis Charles Marie) 1868-1955
TCLC 2, 10
See also CA 104
Clavell, James (duMaresq) 1925-1994**CLC 6,
25, 87; DAM NOV, POP**
See also CA 25-28R; 146; CANR 26, 48;
MTCW
Cleaver, (Leroy) Eldridge 1935- ..... **CLC 30;
BLC; DAM MULT**
See also BW 1; CA 21-24R; CANR 16
Cleese, John (Marwood) 1939- .... **CLC 21**
See also Monty Python
See also CA 112; 116; CANR 35; MTCW
Cleishbotham, Jebediah
See Scott, Walter
Cleland, John 1710-1789 .... **LC 2**
See also DLB 39
Clemens, Samuel Langhorne 1835-1910
See Twain, Mark
See also CA 104; 135; CDALB 1865-1917; DA;
DAB; DAC; DAM MST, NOV; DLB 11, 12,
23, 64, 74; JRDA; MAICYA; YABC 2
Cleophil
See Congreve, William
Clerihew, E.
See Bentley, E(dmund) C(lerihew)
Clerk, N. W.
See Lewis, C(live) S(taples)
Cliff, Jimmy .... **CLC 21**
See also Chambers, James
Clifton, (Thelma) Lucille 1936- **CLC 19, 66;
BLC; DAM MULT, POET; PC 17**
See also BW 2; CA 49-52; CANR 2, 24, 42;
CLR 5; DLB 5, 41; MAICYA; MTCW; SATA
20, 69
Clinton, Dirk
See Silverberg, Robert
Clough, Arthur Hugh 1819-1861 ...**NCLC 27**
See also DLB 32
Clutha, Janet Paterson Frame 1924-
See Frame, Janet
See also CA 1-4R; CANR 2, 36; MTCW
Clyne, Terence
See Blatty, William Peter
Cobalt, Martin
See Mayne, William (James Carter)
Cobbett, William 1763-1835 ....**NCLC 49**
See also DLB 43, 107, 158
Coburn, D(onald) L(ee) 1938- .... **CLC 10**
See also CA 89-92
Cocteau, Jean (Maurice Eugene Clement) 1889-
1963**CLC 1, 8, 15, 16, 43; DA; DAB; DAC;
DAM DRAM, MST, NOV; WLC**
See also CA 25-28; CANR 40; CAP 2; DLB
65; MTCW
Codrescu, Andrei 1946-**CLC 46; DAM POET**
See also CA 33-36R; CAAS 19; CANR 13, 34,
53
Coe, Max
See Bourne, Randolph S(illiman)
Coe, Tucker
See Westlake, Donald E(dwin)
Coetzee, J(ohn) M(ichael) 1940- **CLC 23, 33,
66; DAM NOV**
See also CA 77-80; CANR 41, 54; MTCW

Coffey, Brian
See Koontz, Dean R(ay)
Cohan, George M. 1878-1942 .... **TCLC 60**
See also CA 157
Cohen, Arthur A(llen) 1928-1986 **CLC 7, 31**
See also CA 1-4R; 120; CANR 1, 17, 42; DLB
28
Cohen, Leonard (Norman) 1934- **CLC 3, 38;
DAC; DAM MST**
See also CA 21-24R; CANR 14; DLB 53;
MTCW
Cohen, Matt 1942- .... **CLC 19; DAC**
See also CA 61-64; CAAS 18; CANR 40; DLB
53
Cohen-Solal, Annie 19(?)- .... **CLC 50**
Colegate, Isabel 1931- .... **CLC 36**
See also CA 17-20R; CANR 8, 22; DLB 14;
INT CANR-22; MTCW
Coleman, Emmett
See Reed, Ishmael
Coleridge, M. E.
See Coleridge, Mary E(lizabeth)
Coleridge, Mary E(lizabeth) 1861-1907**TCLC
73**
See also CA 116; DLB 19, 98
Coleridge, Samuel Taylor 1772-1834**NCLC 9,
54; DA; DAB; DAC; DAM MST, POET;
PC 11; WLC**
See also CDBLB 1789-1832; DLB 93, 107
Coleridge, Sara 1802-1852 ....**NCLC 31**
Coles, Don 1928- ....**CLC 46**
See also CA 115; CANR 38
Colette, (Sidonie-Gabrielle) 1873-1954**T C L C
1, 5, 16; DAM NOV; SSC 10**
See also CA 104; 131; DLB 65; MTCW
Collett, (Jacobine) Camilla (Wergeland) 1813-
1895 ....**NCLC 22**
Collier, Christopher 1930- ....**CLC 30**
See also AAYA 13; CA 33-36R; CANR 13, 33;
JRDA; MAICYA; SATA 16, 70
Collier, James L(incoln) 1928-**CLC 30; DAM
POP**
See also AAYA 13; CA 9-12R; CANR 4, 33,
60; CLR 3; JRDA; MAICYA; SAAS 21;
SATA 8, 70
Collier, Jeremy 1650-1726 .... **LC 6**
Collier, John 1901-1980 .... **SSC 19**
See also CA 65-68; 97-100; CANR 10; DLB
77
Collingwood, R(obin) G(eorge) 1889(?)-1943
TCLC 67
See also CA 117; 155
Collins, Hunt
See Hunter, Evan
Collins, Linda 1931- ....**CLC 44**
See also CA 125
Collins, (William) Wilkie 1824-1889**NCLC 1,
18**
See also CDBLB 1832-1890; DLB 18, 70, 159
Collins, William 1721-1759**LC 4; DAM POET**
See also DLB 109
Collodi, Carlo 1826-1890 ....**NCLC 54**
See also Lorenzini, Carlo
See also CLR 5
Colman, George
See Glassco, John
Colt, Winchester Remington
See Hubbard, L(afayette) Ron(ald)
Colter, Cyrus 1910- ....**CLC 58**
See also BW 1; CA 65-68; CANR 10; DLB 33
Colton, James
See Hansen, Joseph
Colum, Padraic 1881-1972 ....**CLC 28**

See also CA 73-76; 33-36R; CANR 35; CLR
36; MAICYA; MTCW; SATA 15
Colvin, James
See Moorcock, Michael (John)
Colwin, Laurie (E.) 1944-1992**CLC 5, 13, 23,
84**
See also CA 89-92; 139; CANR 20, 46; DLBY
80; MTCW
Comfort, Alex(ander) 1920-**CLC 7; DAM POP**
See also CA 1-4R; CANR 1, 45
Comfort, Montgomery
See Campbell, (John) Ramsey
Compton-Burnett, I(vy) 1884(?)-1969**CLC 1,
3, 10, 15, 34; DAM NOV**
See also CA 1-4R; 25-28R; CANR 4; DLB 36;
MTCW
Comstock, Anthony 1844-1915 ...... **TCLC 13**
See also CA 110
Comte, Auguste 1798-1857 ....**NCLC 54**
Conan Doyle, Arthur
See Doyle, Arthur Conan
Conde, Maryse 1937- ...... **CLC 52, 92; DAM
MULT**
See also Boucolon, Maryse
See also BW 2
Condillac, Etienne Bonnot de 1714-1780 **L C
26**
Condon, Richard (Thomas) 1915-1996**CLC 4,
6, 8, 10, 45, 100; DAM NOV**
See also BEST 90:3; CA 1-4R; 151; CAAS 1;
CANR 2, 23; INT CANR-23; MTCW
Confucius 551B.C.-479B.C. . **CMLC 19; DA;
DAB; DAC; DAM MST; WLCS**
Congreve, William 1670-1729 **LC 5, 21; DA;
DAB; DAC; DAM DRAM, MST, POET;
DC 2; WLC**
See also CDBLB 1660-1789; DLB 39, 84
Connell, Evan S(helby), Jr. 1924-**CLC 4, 6, 45;
DAM NOV**
See also AAYA 7; CA 1-4R; CAAS 2; CANR
2, 39; DLB 2; DLBY 81; MTCW
Connelly, Marc(us Cook) 1890-1980 ..**CLC 7**
See also CA 85-88; 102; CANR 30; DLB 7;
DLBY 80; SATA-Obit 25
Connor, Ralph .... **TCLC 31**
See also Gordon, Charles William
See also DLB 92
Conrad, Joseph 1857-1924**TCLC 1, 6, 13, 25,
43, 57; DA; DAB; DAC; DAM MST, NOV;
SSC 9; WLC**
See also CA 104; 131; CANR 60; CDBLB
1890-1914; DLB 10, 34, 98, 156; MTCW;
SATA 27
Conrad, Robert Arnold
See Hart, Moss
Conroy, Donald Pat(rick) 1945- **CLC 30, 74;
DAM NOV, POP**
See also AAYA 8; AITN 1; CA 85-88; CANR
24, 53; DLB 6; MTCW
Constant (de Rebecque), (Henri) Benjamin
1767-1830 .... **NCLC 6**
See also DLB 119
Conybeare, Charles Augustus
See Eliot, T(homas) S(tearns)
Cook, Michael 1933- ....**CLC 58**
See also CA 93-96; DLB 53
Cook, Robin 1940- .... **CLC 14; DAM POP**
See also BEST 90:2; CA 108; 111; CANR 41;
INT 111
Cook, Roy
See Silverberg, Robert
Cooke, Elizabeth 1948- .... **CLC 55**
See also CA 129

See also Crowley, Edward Alexander
Crowley, Edward Alexander 1875-1947
    See Crowley, Aleister
    See also CA 104
Crowley, John 1942- .... **CLC 57**
    See also CA 61-64; CANR 43; DLBY 82; SATA 65
Crud
    See Crumb, R(obert)
Crumarums
    See Crumb, R(obert)
Crumb, R(obert) 1943- .... **CLC 17**
    See also CA 106
Crumbum
    See Crumb, R(obert)
Crumski
    See Crumb, R(obert)
Crum the Bum
    See Crumb, R(obert)
Crunk
    See Crumb, R(obert)
Crustt
    See Crumb, R(obert)
Cryer, Gretchen (Kiger) 1935- .... **CLC 21**
    See also CA 114; 123
Csath, Geza 1887-1919 .... **TCLC 13**
    See also CA 111
Cudlip, David 1933- .... **CLC 34**
Cullen, Countee 1903-1946**TCLC 4, 37; BLC; DA; DAC; DAM MST, MULT, POET; WLCS**
    See also BW 1; CA 108; 124; CDALB 1917-1929; DLB 4, 48, 51; MTCW; SATA 18
Cum, R.
    See Crumb, R(obert)
Cummings, Bruce F(rederick) 1889-1919
    See Barbellion, W. N. P.
    See also CA 123
Cummings, E(dward) E(stlin) 1894-1962**CLC 1, 3, 8, 12, 15, 68; DA; DAB; DAC; DAM MST, POET; PC 5; WLC 2**
    See also CA 73-76; CANR 31; CDALB 1929-1941; DLB 4, 48; MTCW
Cunha, Euclides (Rodrigues Pimenta) da 1866-1909 .... **TCLC 24**
    See also CA 123
Cunningham, E. V.
    See Fast, Howard (Melvin)
Cunningham, J(ames) V(incent) 1911-1985 **CLC 3, 31**
    See also CA 1-4R; 115; CANR 1; DLB 5
Cunningham, Julia (Woolfolk) 1916-**CLC 12**
    See also CA 9-12R; CANR 4, 19, 36; JRDA; MAICYA; SAAS 2; SATA 1, 26
Cunningham, Michael 1952- .... **CLC 34**
    See also CA 136
Cunninghame Graham, R(obert) B(ontine) 1852-1936 .... **TCLC 19**
    See also Graham, R(obert) B(ontine) Cunninghame
    See also CA 119; DLB 98
Currie, Ellen 19(?)- .... **CLC 44**
Curtin, Philip
    See Lowndes, Marie Adelaide (Belloc)
Curtis, Price
    See Ellison, Harlan (Jay)
Cutrate, Joe
    See Spiegelman, Art
Cynewulf c. 770-c. 840 .... **CMLC 23**
Czaczkes, Shmuel Yosef
    See Agnon, S(hmuel) Y(osef Halevi)
Dabrowska, Maria (Szumska) 1889-1965**CLC 15**

See also CA 106
Dabydeen, David 1955- .... **CLC 34**
    See also BW 1; CA 125; CANR 56
Dacey, Philip 1939-............................ **CLC 51**
    See also CA 37-40R; CAAS 17; CANR 14, 32; DLB 105
Dagerman, Stig (Halvard) 1923-1954 **T C L C 17**
    See also CA 117; 155
Dahl, Roald 1916-1990**CLC 1, 6, 18, 79; DAB; DAC; DAM MST, NOV, POP**
    See also AAYA 15; CA 1-4R; 133; CANR 6, 32, 37; CLR 1, 7, 41; DLB 139; JRDA; MAICYA; MTCW; SATA 1, 26, 73; SATA-Obit 65
Dahlberg, Edward 1900-1977 .. **CLC 1, 7, 14**
    See also CA 9-12R; 69-72; CANR 31; DLB 48; MTCW
Daitch, Susan 1954-......................... **CLC 103**
Dale, Colin .... **TCLC 18**
    See also Lawrence, T(homas) E(dward)
Dale, George E.
    See Asimov, Isaac
Daly, Elizabeth 1878-1967 .... **CLC 52**
    See also CA 23-24; 25-28R; CANR 60; CAP 2
Daly, Maureen 1921-......................... **CLC 17**
    See also AAYA 5; CANR 37; JRDA; MAICYA; SAAS 1; SATA 2
Damas, Leon-Gontran 1912-1978 ..... **CLC 84**
    See also BW 1; CA 125; 73-76
Dana, Richard Henry Sr. 1787-1879**NCLC 53**
Daniel, Samuel 1562(?)-1619 .... **LC 24**
    See also DLB 62
Daniels, Brett
    See Adler, Renata
Dannay, Frederic 1905-1982 . **CLC 11; DAM POP**
    See also Queen, Ellery
    See also CA 1-4R; 107; CANR 1, 39; DLB 137; MTCW
D'Annunzio, Gabriele 1863-1938**TCLC 6, 40**
    See also CA 104; 155
Danois, N. le
    See Gourmont, Remy (-Marie-Charles) de
d'Antibes, Germain
    See Simenon, Georges (Jacques Christian)
Danticat, Edwidge 1969- .... **CLC 94**
    See also CA 152
Danvers, Dennis 1947- .... **CLC 70**
Danziger, Paula 1944- .... **CLC 21**
    See also AAYA 4; CA 112; 115; CANR 37; CLR 20; JRDA; MAICYA; SATA 36, 63; SATA-Brief 30
Da Ponte, Lorenzo 1749-1838 .... **NCLC 50**
Dario, Ruben 1867-1916 .... **TCLC 4; DAM MULT; HLC; PC 15**
    See also CA 131; HW; MTCW
Darley, George 1795-1846 .... **NCLC 2**
    See also DLB 96
Darwin, Charles 1809-1882 .... **NCLC 57**
    See also DLB 57, 166
Daryush, Elizabeth 1887-1977 ..... **CLC 6, 19**
    See also CA 49-52; CANR 3; DLB 20
Dashwood, Edmee Elizabeth Monica de la Pasture 1890-1943
    See Delafield, E. M.
    See also CA 119; 154
Daudet, (Louis Marie) Alphonse 1840-1897 **NCLC 1**
    See also DLB 123
Daumal, Rene 1908-1944 .... **TCLC 14**
    See also CA 114
Davenport, Guy (Mattison, Jr.) 1927-**CLC 6,**

14, 38; SSC 16
    See also CA 33-36R; CANR 23; DLB 130
Davidson, Avram 1923-
    See Queen, Ellery
    See also CA 101; CANR 26; DLB 8
Davidson, Donald (Grady) 1893-1968**CLC 2, 13, 19**
    See also CA 5-8R; 25-28R; CANR 4; DLB 45
Davidson, Hugh
    See Hamilton, Edmond
Davidson, John 1857-1909 .... **TCLC 24**
    See also CA 118; DLB 19
Davidson, Sara 1943- .... **CLC 9**
    See also CA 81-84; CANR 44
Davie, Donald (Alfred) 1922-1995 **CLC 5, 8, 10, 31**
    See also CA 1-4R; 149; CAAS 3; CANR 1, 44; DLB 27; MTCW
Davies, Ray(mond Douglas) 1944- .... **CLC 21**
    See also CA 116; 146
Davies, Rhys 1903-1978 .... **CLC 23**
    See also CA 9-12R; 81-84; CANR 4; DLB 139
Davies, (William) Robertson 1913-1995 **C L C 2, 7, 13, 25, 42, 75, 91; DA; DAB; DAC; DAM MST, NOV, POP; WLC**
    See also BEST 89:2; CA 33-36R; 150; CANR 17, 42; DLB 68; INT CANR-17; MTCW
Davies, W(illiam) H(enry) 1871-1940**TCLC 5**
    See also CA 104; DLB 19, 174
Davies, Walter C.
    See Kornbluth, C(yril) M.
Davis, Angela (Yvonne) 1944- **CLC 77; DAM MULT**
    See also BW 2; CA 57-60; CANR 10
Davis, B. Lynch
    See Bioy Casares, Adolfo; Borges, Jorge Luis
Davis, Gordon
    See Hunt, E(verette) Howard, (Jr.)
Davis, Harold Lenoir 1896-1960 ...... **CLC 49**
    See also CA 89-92; DLB 9
Davis, Rebecca (Blaine) Harding 1831-1910 **TCLC 6**
    See also CA 104; DLB 74
Davis, Richard Harding 1864-1916**TCLC 24**
    See also CA 114; DLB 12, 23, 78, 79; DLBD 13
Davison, Frank Dalby 1893-1970 ..... **CLC 15**
    See also CA 116
Davison, Lawrence H.
    See Lawrence, D(avid) H(erbert Richards)
Davison, Peter (Hubert) 1928- .... **CLC 28**
    See also CA 9-12R; CAAS 4; CANR 3, 43; DLB 5
Davys, Mary 1674-1732 .... **LC 1**
    See also DLB 39
Dawson, Fielding 1930- .... **CLC 6**
    See also CA 85-88; DLB 130
Dawson, Peter
    See Faust, Frederick (Schiller)
Day, Clarence (Shepard, Jr.) 1874-1935 **TCLC 25**
    See also CA 108; DLB 11
Day, Thomas 1748-1789 .... **LC 1**
    See also DLB 39; YABC 1
Day Lewis, C(ecil) 1904-1972 .. **CLC 1, 6, 10; DAM POET; PC 11**
    See also Blake, Nicholas
    See also CA 13-16; 33-36R; CANR 34; CAP 1; DLB 15, 20; MTCW
Dazai, Osamu .... **TCLC 11**
    See also Tsushima, Shuji
    See also DLB 182
de Andrade, Carlos Drummond

See Drummond de Andrade, Carlos
Deane, Norman
  See Creasey, John
de Beauvoir, Simone (Lucie Ernestine Marie Bertrand)
  See Beauvoir, Simone (Lucie Ernestine Marie Bertrand) de
de Brissac, Malcolm
  See Dickinson, Peter (Malcolm)
de Chardin, Pierre Teilhard
  See Teilhard de Chardin, (Marie Joseph) Pierre
Dee, John 1527-1608 .... **LC 20**
Deer, Sandra 1940- .... **CLC 45**
De Ferrari, Gabriella 1941- .... **CLC 65**
  See also CA 146
Defoe, Daniel 1660(?)-1731 **LC 1; DA; DAB; DAC; DAM MST, NOV; WLC**
  See also CDBLB 1660-1789; DLB 39, 95, 101; JRDA; MAICYA; SATA 22
de Gourmont, Remy(-Marie-Charles)
  See Gourmont, Remy (-Marie-Charles) de
de Hartog, Jan 1914- .... **CLC 19**
  See also CA 1-4R; CANR 1
de Hostos, E. M.
  See Hostos (y Bonilla), Eugenio Maria de
de Hostos, Eugenio M.
  See Hostos (y Bonilla), Eugenio Maria de
Deighton, Len .... **CLC 4, 7, 22, 46**
  See also Deighton, Leonard Cyril
  See also AAYA 6; BEST 89:2; CDBLB 1960 to Present; DLB 87
Deighton, Leonard Cyril 1929-
  See Deighton, Len
  See also CA 9-12R; CANR 19, 33; DAM NOV, POP; MTCW
Dekker, Thomas 1572(?)-1632 ..**LC 22; DAM DRAM**
  See also CDBLB Before 1660; DLB 62, 172
Delafield, E. M. 1890-1943 .... **TCLC 61**
  See also Dashwood, Edmee Elizabeth Monica de la Pasture
  See also DLB 34
de la Mare, Walter (John) 1873-1956**TCLC 4, 53; DAB; DAC; DAM MST, POET; SSC 14; WLC**
  See also CDBLB 1914-1945; CLR 23; DLB 162; SATA 16
Delaney, Franey
  See O'Hara, John (Henry)
Delaney, Shelagh 1939-**CLC 29; DAM DRAM**
  See also CA 17-20R; CANR 30; CDBLB 1960 to Present; DLB 13; MTCW
Delany, Mary (Granville Pendarves) 1700-1788 **LC 12**
Delany, Samuel R(ay, Jr.) 1942-**CLC 8, 14, 38; BLC; DAM MULT**
  See also BW 2; CA 81-84; CANR 27, 43; DLB 8, 33; MTCW
De La Ramee, (Marie) Louise 1839-1908
  See Ouida
  See also SATA 20
de la Roche, Mazo 1879-1961 .... **CLC 14**
  See also CA 85-88; CANR 30; DLB 68; SATA 64
De La Salle, Innocent
  See Hartmann, Sadakichi
Delbanco, Nicholas (Franklin) 1942- **CLC 6, 13**
  See also CA 17-20R; CAAS 2; CANR 29, 55; DLB 6
del Castillo, Michel 1933- .... **CLC 38**
  See also CA 109
Deledda, Grazia (Cosima) 1875(?)-1936

TCLC 23
  See also CA 123
Delibes, Miguel .... **CLC 8, 18**
  See also Delibes Setien, Miguel
Delibes Setien, Miguel 1920-
  See Delibes, Miguel
  See also CA 45-48; CANR 1, 32; HW; MTCW
DeLillo, Don 1936- **CLC 8, 10, 13, 27, 39, 54, 76; DAM NOV, POP**
  See also BEST 89:1; CA 81-84; CANR 21; DLB 6, 173; MTCW
de Lisser, H. G.
  See De Lisser, H(erbert) G(eorge)
  See also DLB 117
De Lisser, H(erbert) G(eorge) 1878-1944 **TCLC 12**
  See also de Lisser, H. G.
  See also BW 2; CA 109; 152
Deloria, Vine (Victor), Jr. 1933- ..... **CLC 21; DAM MULT**
  See also CA 53-56; CANR 5, 20, 48; DLB 175; MTCW; NNAL; SATA 21
Del Vecchio, John M(ichael) 1947- ...**CLC 29**
  See also CA 110; DLBD 9
de Man, Paul (Adolph Michel) 1919-1983 **CLC 55**
  See also CA 128; 111; CANR 61; DLB 67; MTCW
De Marinis, Rick 1934- .... **CLC 54**
  See also CA 57-60; CAAS 24; CANR 9, 25, 50
Dembry, R. Emmet
  See Murfree, Mary Noailles
Demby, William 1922- **CLC 53; BLC; DAM MULT**
  See also BW 1; CA 81-84; DLB 33
de Menton, Francisco
  See Chin, Frank (Chew, Jr.)
Demijohn, Thom
  See Disch, Thomas M(ichael)
de Montherlant, Henry (Milon)
  See Montherlant, Henry (Milon) de
Demosthenes 384B.C.-322B.C. ...... **CMLC 13**
  See also DLB 176
de Natale, Francine
  See Malzberg, Barry N(athaniel)
Denby, Edwin (Orr) 1903-1983 ....**CLC 48**
  See also CA 138; 110
Denis, Julio
  See Cortazar, Julio
Denmark, Harrison
  See Zelazny, Roger (Joseph)
Dennis, John 1658-1734 ....**LC 11**
  See also DLB 101
Dennis, Nigel (Forbes) 1912-1989 ....**CLC 8**
  See also CA 25-28R; 129; DLB 13, 15; MTCW
Dent, Lester 1904(?)-1959 ....**TCLC 72**
  See also CA 112
De Palma, Brian (Russell) 1940- ....**CLC 20**
  See also CA 109
De Quincey, Thomas 1785-1859 ....**NCLC 4**
  See also CDBLB 1789-1832; DLB 110; 144
Deren, Eleanora 1908(?)-1961
  See Deren, Maya
  See also CA 111
Deren, Maya 1917-1961 .... **CLC 16, 102**
  See also Deren, Eleanora
Derleth, August (William) 1909-1971**CLC 31**
  See also CA 1-4R; 29-32R; CANR 4; DLB 9; SATA 5
Der Nister 1884-1950 .... **TCLC 56**
de Routisie, Albert
  See Aragon, Louis
Derrida, Jacques 1930- .... **CLC 24, 87**

See also CA 124; 127
Derry Down Derry
  See Lear, Edward
Dersonnes, Jacques
  See Simenon, Georges (Jacques Christian)
Desai, Anita 1937-**CLC 19, 37, 97; DAB; DAM NOV**
  See also CA 81-84; CANR 33, 53; MTCW; SATA 63
de Saint-Luc, Jean
  See Glassco, John
de Saint Roman, Arnaud
  See Aragon, Louis
Descartes, Rene 1596-1650 .... **LC 20, 35**
De Sica, Vittorio 1901(?)-1974 .... **CLC 20**
  See also CA 117
Desnos, Robert 1900-1945 .... **TCLC 22**
  See also CA 121; 151
Destouches, Louis-Ferdinand 1894-1961**CLC 9, 15**
  See also Celine, Louis-Ferdinand
  See also CA 85-88; CANR 28; MTCW
de Tolignac, Gaston
  See Griffith, D(avid Lewelyn) W(ark)
Deutsch, Babette 1895-1982 .... **CLC 18**
  See also CA 1-4R; 108; CANR 4; DLB 45; SATA 1; SATA-Obit 33
Devenant, William 1606-1649 .... **LC 13**
Devkota, Laxmiprasad 1909-1959 . **TCLC 23**
  See also CA 123
De Voto, Bernard (Augustine) 1897-1955 **TCLC 29**
  See also CA 113; DLB 9
De Vries, Peter 1910-1993 **CLC 1, 2, 3, 7, 10, 28, 46; DAM NOV**
  See also CA 17-20R; 142; CANR 41; DLB 6; DLBY 82; MTCW
Dexter, John
  See Bradley, Marion Zimmer
Dexter, Martin
  See Faust, Frederick (Schiller)
Dexter, Pete 1943- ... **CLC 34, 55; DAM POP**
  See also BEST 89:2; CA 127; 131; INT 131; MTCW
Diamano, Silmang
  See Senghor, Leopold Sedar
Diamond, Neil 1941- .... **CLC 30**
  See also CA 108
Diaz del Castillo, Bernal 1496-1584 ... **LC 31**
di Bassetto, Corno
  See Shaw, George Bernard
Dick, Philip K(indred) 1928-1982**CLC 10, 30, 72; DAM NOV, POP**
  See also CA 49-52; 106; CANR 2, 16; DLB 8; MTCW
Dickens, Charles (John Huffam) 1812-1870 **NCLC 3, 8, 18, 26, 37, 50; DA; DAB; DAC; DAM MST, NOV; SSC 17; WLC**
  See also CDBLB 1832-1890; DLB 21, 55, 70, 159, 166; JRDA; MAICYA; SATA 15
Dickey, James (Lafayette) 1923-1997 **CLC 1, 2, 4, 7, 10, 15, 47; DAM NOV, POET, POP**
  See also AITN 1, 2; CA 9-12R; 156; CABS 2; CANR 10, 48, 61; CDALB 1968-1988; DLB 5; DLBD 7; DLBY 82, 93, 96; INT CANR-10; MTCW
Dickey, William 1928-1994 .... **CLC 3, 28**
  See also CA 9-12R; 145; CANR 24; DLB 5
Dickinson, Charles 1951- .... **CLC 49**
  See also CA 128
Dickinson, Emily (Elizabeth) 1830-1886 **NCLC 21; DA; DAB; DAC; DAM MST, POET; PC 1; WLC**

See also AAYA 22; CDALB 1865-1917; DLB 1; SATA 29

Dickinson, Peter (Malcolm) 1927-CLC **12, 35**
See also AAYA 9; CA 41-44R; CANR 31, 58; CLR 29; DLB 87, 161; JRDA; MAICYA; SATA 5, 62, 95

Dickson, Carr
See Carr, John Dickson

Dickson, Carter
See Carr, John Dickson

Diderot, Denis 1713-1784 .... LC **26**

Didion, Joan 1934-CLC **1, 3, 8, 14, 32; DAM NOV**
See also AITN 1; CA 5-8R; CANR 14, 52; CDALB 1968-1988; DLB 2, 173; DLBY 81, 86; MTCW

Dietrich, Robert
See Hunt, E(verette) Howard, (Jr.)

Dillard, Annie 1945- . CLC **9, 60; DAM NOV**
See also AAYA 6; CA 49-52; CANR 3, 43; DLBY 80; MTCW; SATA 10

Dillard, R(ichard) H(enry) W(ilde) 1937-
CLC **5**
See also CA 21-24R; CAAS 7; CANR 10; DLB 5

Dillon, Eilis 1920-1994 .... CLC **17**
See also CA 9-12R; 147; CAAS 3; CANR 4, 38; CLR 26; MAICYA; SATA 2, 74; SATA-Obit 83

Dimont, Penelope
See Mortimer, Penelope (Ruth)

Dinesen, Isak .... CLC **10, 29, 95; SSC 7**
See also Blixen, Karen (Christentze Dinesen)

Ding Ling .... CLC **68**
See also Chiang Pin-chin

Disch, Thomas M(ichael) 1940- ... CLC **7, 36**
See also AAYA 17; CA 21-24R; CAAS 4; CANR 17, 36, 54; CLR 18; DLB 8; MAICYA; MTCW; SAAS 15; SATA 92

Disch, Tom
See Disch, Thomas M(ichael)

d'Isly, Georges
See Simenon, Georges (Jacques Christian)

Disraeli, Benjamin 1804-1881 .... NCLC **2, 39**
See also DLB 21, 55

Ditcum, Steve
See Crumb, R(obert)

Dixon, Paige
See Corcoran, Barbara

Dixon, Stephen 1936- .... CLC **52; SSC 16**
See also CA 89-92; CANR 17, 40, 54; DLB 130

Dobell, Sydney Thompson 1824-1874 N C L C
43
See also DLB 32

Doblin, Alfred .... TCLC **13**
See also Doeblin, Alfred

Dobrolyubov, Nikolai Alexandrovich 1836-1861
NCLC **5**

Dobyns, Stephen 1941- .... CLC **37**
See also CA 45-48; CANR 2, 18

Doctorow, E(dgar) L(aurence) 1931- CLC **6, 11, 15, 18, 37, 44, 65; DAM NOV, POP**
See also AAYA 22; AITN 2; BEST 89:3; CA 45-48; CANR 2, 33, 51; CDALB 1968-1988; DLB 2, 28, 173; DLBY 80; MTCW

Dodgson, Charles Lutwidge 1832-1898
See Carroll, Lewis
See also CLR 2; DA; DAB; DAC; DAM MST, NOV, POET; MAICYA; YABC 2

Dodson, Owen (Vincent) 1914-1983 CLC **79; BLC; DAM MULT**
See also BW 1; CA 65-68; 110; CANR 24; DLB 76

Doeblin, Alfred 1878-1957 .... TCLC **13**
See also Doblin, Alfred
See also CA 110; 141; DLB 66

Doerr, Harriet 1910- .... CLC **34**
See also CA 117; 122; CANR 47; INT 122

Domecq, H(onorio) Bustos
See Bioy Casares, Adolfo; Borges, Jorge Luis

Domini, Rey
See Lorde, Audre (Geraldine)

Dominique
See Proust, (Valentin-Louis-George-Eugene-) Marcel

Don, A
See Stephen, Leslie

Donaldson, Stephen R. 1947- CLC **46; DAM POP**
See also CA 89-92; CANR 13, 55; INT CANR-13

Donleavy, J(ames) P(atrick) 1926-CLC **1, 4, 6, 10, 45**
See also AITN 2; CA 9-12R; CANR 24, 49; DLB 6, 173; INT CANR-24; MTCW

Donne, John 1572-1631LC **10, 24; DA; DAB; DAC; DAM MST, POET; PC 1**
See also CDBLB Before 1660; DLB 121, 151

Donnell, David 1939(?)- .... CLC **34**

Donoghue, P. S.
See Hunt, E(verette) Howard, (Jr.)

Donoso (Yanez), Jose 1924-1996CLC **4, 8, 11, 32, 99; DAM MULT; HLC**
See also CA 81-84; 155; CANR 32; DLB 113; HW; MTCW

Donovan, John 1928-1992 .... CLC **35**
See also AAYA 20; CA 97-100; 137; CLR 3; MAICYA; SATA 72; SATA-Brief 29

Don Roberto
See Cunninghame Graham, R(obert) B(ontine)

Doolittle, Hilda 1886-1961CLC **3, 8, 14, 31, 34, 73; DA; DAC; DAM MST, POET; PC 5; WLC**
See also H. D.
See also CA 97-100; CANR 35; DLB 4, 45; MTCW

Dorfman, Ariel 1942- .... CLC **48, 77; DAM MULT; HLC**
See also CA 124; 130; HW; INT 130

Dorn, Edward (Merton) 1929- ... CLC **10, 18**
See also CA 93-96; CANR 42; DLB 5; INT 93-96

Dorsan, Luc
See Simenon, Georges (Jacques Christian)

Dorsange, Jean
See Simenon, Georges (Jacques Christian)

Dos Passos, John (Roderigo) 1896-1970 C L C
1, 4, 8, 11, 15, 25, 34, 82; DA; DAB; DAC; DAM MST, NOV; WLC
See also CA 1-4R; 29-32R; CANR 3; CDALB 1929-1941; DLB 4, 9; DLBD 1, 15; DLBY 96; MTCW

Dossage, Jean
See Simenon, Georges (Jacques Christian)

Dostoevsky, Fedor Mikhailovich 1821-1881
NCLC **2, 7, 21, 33, 43; DA; DAB; DAC; DAM MST, NOV; SSC 2; WLC**

Doughty, Charles M(ontagu) 1843-1926
TCLC **27**
See also CA 115; DLB 19, 57, 174

Douglas, Ellen .... CLC **73**
See also Haxton, Josephine Ayres; Williamson, Ellen Douglas

Douglas, Gavin 1475(?)-1522 .... LC **20**

Douglas, Keith 1920-1944 .... TCLC **40**
See also DLB 27

Douglas, Leonard
See Bradbury, Ray (Douglas)

Douglas, Michael
See Crichton, (John) Michael

Douglas, Norman 1868-1952 .... TCLC **68**

Douglass, Frederick 1817(?)-1895NCLC **7, 55; BLC; DA; DAC; DAM MST, MULT; WLC**
See also CDALB 1640-1865; DLB 1, 43, 50, 79; SATA 29

Dourado, (Waldomiro Freitas) Autran 1926-
CLC **23, 60**
See also CA 25-28R; CANR 34

Dourado, Waldomiro Autran
See Dourado, (Waldomiro Freitas) Autran

Dove, Rita (Frances) 1952-CLC **50, 81; DAM MULT, POET; PC 6**
See also BW 2; CA 109; CAAS 19; CANR 27, 42; DLB 120

Dowell, Coleman 1925-1985 .... CLC **60**
See also CA 25-28R; 117; CANR 10; DLB 130

Dowson, Ernest (Christopher) 1867-1900
TCLC **4**
See also CA 105; 150; DLB 19, 135

Doyle, A. Conan
See Doyle, Arthur Conan

Doyle, Arthur Conan 1859-1930TCLC **7; DA; DAB; DAC; DAM MST, NOV; SSC 12; WLC**
See also AAYA 14; CA 104; 122; CDBLB 1890-1914; DLB 18, 70, 156, 178; MTCW; SATA 24

Doyle, Conan
See Doyle, Arthur Conan

Doyle, John
See Graves, Robert (von Ranke)

Doyle, Roddy 1958(?)- .... CLC **81**
See also AAYA 14; CA 143

Doyle, Sir A. Conan
See Doyle, Arthur Conan

Doyle, Sir Arthur Conan
See Doyle, Arthur Conan

Dr. A
See Asimov, Isaac; Silverstein, Alvin

Drabble, Margaret 1939-CLC **2, 3, 5, 8, 10, 22, 53; DAB; DAC; DAM MST, NOV, POP**
See also CA 13-16R; CANR 18, 35; CDBLB 1960 to Present; DLB 14, 155; MTCW; SATA 48

Drapier, M. B.
See Swift, Jonathan

Drayham, James
See Mencken, H(enry) L(ouis)

Drayton, Michael 1563-1631 .... LC **8**

Dreadstone, Carl
See Campbell, (John) Ramsey

Dreiser, Theodore (Herman Albert) 1871-1945
TCLC **10, 18, 35; DA; DAC; DAM MST, NOV; WLC**
See also CA 106; 132; CDALB 1865-1917; DLB 9, 12, 102, 137; DLBD 1; MTCW

Drexler, Rosalyn 1926- .... CLC **2, 6**
See also CA 81-84

Dreyer, Carl Theodor 1889-1968 ...... CLC **16**
See also CA 116

Drieu la Rochelle, Pierre(-Eugene) 1893-1945
TCLC **21**
See also CA 117; DLB 72

Drinkwater, John 1882-1937 .... TCLC **57**
See also CA 109; 149; DLB 10, 19, 149

Drop Shot
See Cable, George Washington

Droste-Hulshoff, Annette Freiin von 1797-1848
NCLC **3**

See also CA 65-68

Franklin, Benjamin
See Hasek, Jaroslav (Matej Frantisek)

Franklin, Benjamin 1706-1790 .. **LC 25; DA; DAB; DAC; DAM MST; WLCS**
See also CDALB 1640-1865; DLB 24, 43, 73

Franklin, (Stella Maraia Sarah) Miles 1879-1954 .... **TCLC 7**
See also CA 104

Fraser, (Lady) Antonia (Pakenham) 1932-**CLC 32**
See also CA 85-88; CANR 44; MTCW; SATA-Brief 32

Fraser, George MacDonald 1925- ...... **CLC 7**
See also CA 45-48; CANR 2, 48

Fraser, Sylvia 1935- .... **CLC 64**
See also CA 45-48; CANR 1, 16, 60

Frayn, Michael 1933-**CLC 3, 7, 31, 47; DAM DRAM, NOV**
See also CA 5-8R; CANR 30; DLB 13, 14; MTCW

Fraze, Candida (Merrill) 1945- .... **CLC 50**
See also CA 126

Frazer, J(ames) G(eorge) 1854-1941**TCLC 32**
See also CA 118

Frazer, Robert Caine
See Creasey, John

Frazer, Sir James George
See Frazer, J(ames) G(eorge)

Frazier, Ian 1951- .... **CLC 46**
See also CA 130; CANR 54

Frederic, Harold 1856-1898 .... **NCLC 10**
See also DLB 12, 23; DLBD 13

Frederick, John
See Faust, Frederick (Schiller)

Frederick the Great 1712-1786 .... **LC 14**

Fredro, Aleksander 1793-1876 .... **NCLC 8**

Freeling, Nicolas 1927- .... **CLC 38**
See also CA 49-52; CAAS 12; CANR 1, 17, 50; DLB 87

Freeman, Douglas Southall 1886-1953**T C L C 11**
See also CA 109; DLB 17

Freeman, Judith 1946- .... **CLC 55**
See also CA 148

Freeman, Mary Eleanor Wilkins 1852-1930 **TCLC 9; SSC 1**
See also CA 106; DLB 12, 78

Freeman, R(ichard) Austin 1862-1943**T C L C 21**
See also CA 113; DLB 70

French, Albert 1943- .... **CLC 86**

French, Marilyn 1929-**CLC 10, 18, 60; DAM DRAM, NOV, POP**
See also CA 69-72; CANR 3, 31; INT CANR-31; MTCW

French, Paul
See Asimov, Isaac

Freneau, Philip Morin 1752-1832 .... **NCLC 1**
See also DLB 37, 43

Freud, Sigmund 1856-1939 .... **TCLC 52**
See also CA 115; 133; MTCW

Friedan, Betty (Naomi) 1921- .... **CLC 74**
See also CA 65-68; CANR 18, 45; MTCW

Friedlander, Saul 1932- .... **CLC 90**
See also CA 117; 130

Friedman, B(ernard) H(arper) 1926- . **CLC 7**
See also CA 1-4R; CANR 3, 48

Friedman, Bruce Jay 1930- ...... **CLC 3, 5, 56**
See also CA 9-12R; CANR 25, 52; DLB 2, 28; INT CANR-25

Friel, Brian 1929- .... **CLC 5, 42, 59**
See also CA 21-24R; CANR 33; DLB 13;

MTCW

Friis-Baastad, Babbis Ellinor 1921-1970**C L C 12**
See also CA 17-20R; 134; SATA 7

Frisch, Max (Rudolf) 1911-1991**CLC 3, 9, 14, 18, 32, 44; DAM DRAM, NOV**
See also CA 85-88; 134; CANR 32; DLB 69, 124; MTCW

Fromentin, Eugene (Samuel Auguste) 1820-1876 .... **NCLC 10**
See also DLB 123

Frost, Frederick
See Faust, Frederick (Schiller)

Frost, Robert (Lee) 1874-1963**CLC 1, 3, 4, 9, 10, 13, 15, 26, 34, 44; DA; DAB; DAC; DAM MST, POET; PC 1; WLC**
See also AAYA 21; CA 89-92; CANR 33; CDALB 1917-1929; DLB 54; DLBD 7; MTCW; SATA 14

Froude, James Anthony 1818-1894**NCLC 43**
See also DLB 18, 57, 144

Froy, Herald
See Waterhouse, Keith (Spencer)

Fry, Christopher 1907- **CLC 2, 10, 14; DAM DRAM**
See also CA 17-20R; CAAS 23; CANR 9, 30; DLB 13; MTCW; SATA 66

Frye, (Herman) Northrop 1912-1991**CLC 24, 70**
See also CA 5-8R; 133; CANR 8, 37; DLB 67, 68; MTCW

Fuchs, Daniel 1909-1993 .... **CLC 8, 22**
See also CA 81-84; 142; CAAS 5; CANR 40; DLB 9, 26, 28; DLBY 93

Fuchs, Daniel 1934- .... **CLC 34**
See also CA 37-40R; CANR 14, 48

Fuentes, Carlos 1928-**CLC 3, 8, 10, 13, 22, 41, 60; DA; DAB; DAC; DAM MST, MULT, NOV; HLC; SSC 24; WLC**
See also AAYA 4; AITN 2; CA 69-72; CANR 10, 32; DLB 113; HW; MTCW

Fuentes, Gregorio Lopez y
See Lopez y Fuentes, Gregorio

Fugard, (Harold) Athol 1932-**CLC 5, 9, 14, 25, 40, 80; DAM DRAM; DC 3**
See also AAYA 17; CA 85-88; CANR 32, 54; MTCW

Fugard, Sheila 1932- .... **CLC 48**
See also CA 125

Fuller, Charles (H., Jr.) 1939-**CLC 25; BLC; DAM DRAM, MULT; DC 1**
See also BW 2; CA 108; 112; DLB 38; INT 112; MTCW

Fuller, John (Leopold) 1937- .... **CLC 62**
See also CA 21-24R; CANR 9, 44; DLB 40

Fuller, Margaret .... **NCLC 5, 50**
See also Ossoli, Sarah Margaret (Fuller marchesa d')

Fuller, Roy (Broadbent) 1912-1991**CLC 4, 28**
See also CA 5-8R; 135; CAAS 10; CANR 53; DLB 15, 20; SATA 87

Fulton, Alice 1952- .... **CLC 52**
See also CA 116; CANR 57

Furphy, Joseph 1843-1912 .... **TCLC 25**

Fussell, Paul 1924- .... **CLC 74**
See also BEST 90:1; CA 17-20R; CANR 8, 21, 35; INT CANR-21; MTCW

Futabatei, Shimei 1864-1909 .... **TCLC 44**
See also DLB 180

Futrelle, Jacques 1875-1912 .... **TCLC 19**
See also CA 113; 155

Gaboriau, Emile 1835-1873 .... **NCLC 14**

Gadda, Carlo Emilio 1893-1973 .... **CLC 11**

See also CA 89-92; DLB 177

Gaddis, William 1922- **CLC 1, 3, 6, 8, 10, 19, 43, 86**
See also CA 17-20R; CANR 21, 48; DLB 2; MTCW

Gage, Walter
See Inge, William (Motter)

Gaines, Ernest J(ames) 1933- **CLC 3, 11, 18, 86; BLC; DAM MULT**
See also AAYA 18; AITN 1; BW 2; CA 9-12R; CANR 6, 24, 42; CDALB 1968-1988; DLB 2, 33, 152; DLBY 80; MTCW; SATA 86

Gaitskill, Mary 1954- .... **CLC 69**
See also CA 128; CANR 61

Galdos, Benito Perez
See Perez Galdos, Benito

Gale, Zona 1874-1938**TCLC 7; DAM DRAM**
See also CA 105; 153; DLB 9, 78

Galeano, Eduardo (Hughes) 1940- .. **CLC 72**
See also CA 29-32R; CANR 13, 32; HW

Galiano, Juan Valera y Alcala
See Valera y Alcala-Galiano, Juan

Gallagher, Tess 1943- ...... **CLC 18, 63; DAM POET; PC 9**
See also CA 106; DLB 120

Gallant, Mavis 1922- ... **CLC 7, 18, 38; DAC; DAM MST; SSC 5**
See also CA 69-72; CANR 29; DLB 53; MTCW

Gallant, Roy A(rthur) 1924- .... **CLC 17**
See also CA 5-8R; CANR 4, 29, 54; CLR 30; MAICYA; SATA 4, 68

Gallico, Paul (William) 1897-1976 ..... **CLC 2**
See also AITN 1; CA 5-8R; 69-72; CANR 23; DLB 9, 171; MAICYA; SATA 13

Gallo, Max Louis 1932- .... **CLC 95**
See also CA 85-88

Gallois, Lucien
See Desnos, Robert

Gallup, Ralph
See Whitemore, Hugh (John)

Galsworthy, John 1867-1933**TCLC 1, 45; DA; DAB; DAC; DAM DRAM, MST, NOV; SSC 22; WLC 2**
See also CA 104; 141; CDBLB 1890-1914; DLB 10, 34, 98, 162

Galt, John 1779-1839 .... **NCLC 1**
See also DLB 99, 116, 159

Galvin, James 1951- .... **CLC 38**
See also CA 108; CANR 26

Gamboa, Federico 1864-1939 .... **TCLC 36**

Gandhi, M. K.
See Gandhi, Mohandas Karamchand

Gandhi, Mahatma
See Gandhi, Mohandas Karamchand

Gandhi, Mohandas Karamchand 1869-1948 **TCLC 59; DAM MULT**
See also CA 121; 132; MTCW

Gann, Ernest Kellogg 1910-1991 ..... **CLC 23**
See also AITN 1; CA 1-4R; 136; CANR 1

Garcia, Cristina 1958- .... **CLC 76**
See also CA 141

Garcia Lorca, Federico 1898-1936**TCLC 1, 7, 49; DA; DAB; DAC; DAM DRAM, MST, MULT, POET; DC 2; HLC; PC 3; WLC**
See also CA 104; 131; DLB 108; HW; MTCW

Garcia Marquez, Gabriel (Jose) 1928-**CLC 2, 3, 8, 10, 15, 27, 47, 55, 68; DA; DAB; DAC; DAM MST, MULT, NOV, POP; HLC; SSC 8; WLC**
See also AAYA 3; BEST 89:1, 90:4; CA 33-36R; CANR 10, 28, 50; DLB 113; HW; MTCW

Gard, Janice

See Latham, Jean Lee
Gard, Roger Martin du
See Martin du Gard, Roger
Gardam, Jane 1928- .... **CLC 43**
See also CA 49-52; CANR 2, 18, 33, 54; CLR 12; DLB 14, 161; MAICYA; MTCW; SAAS 9; SATA 39, 76; SATA-Brief 28
Gardner, Herb(ert) 1934- .... **CLC 44**
See also CA 149
Gardner, John (Champlin), Jr. 1933-1982
CLC 2, 3, 5, 7, 8, 10, 18, 28, 34; DAM NOV, POP; SSC 7
See also AITN 1; CA 65-68; 107; CANR 33; DLB 2; DLBY 82; MTCW; SATA 40; SATA-Obit 31
Gardner, John (Edmund) 1926-CLC 30; DAM POP
See also CA 103; CANR 15; MTCW
Gardner, Miriam
See Bradley, Marion Zimmer
Gardner, Noel
See Kuttner, Henry
Gardons, S. S.
See Snodgrass, W(illiam) D(e Witt)
Garfield, Leon 1921-1996 .... **CLC 12**
See also AAYA 8; CA 17-20R; 152; CANR 38, 41; CLR 21; DLB 161; JRDA; MAICYA; SATA 1, 32, 76; SATA-Obit 90
Garland, (Hannibal) Hamlin 1860-1940
TCLC 3; SSC 18
See also CA 104; DLB 12, 71, 78
Garneau, (Hector de) Saint-Denys 1912-1943
TCLC 13
See also CA 111; DLB 88
Garner, Alan 1934-CLC 17; DAB; DAM POP
See also AAYA 18; CA 73-76; CANR 15; CLR 20; DLB 161; MAICYA; MTCW; SATA 18, 69
Garner, Hugh 1913-1979 .... **CLC 13**
See also CA 69-72; CANR 31; DLB 68
Garnett, David 1892-1981 .... **CLC 3**
See also CA 5-8R; 103; CANR 17; DLB 34
Garos, Stephanie
See Katz, Steve
Garrett, George (Palmer) 1929-CLC 3, 11, 51
See also CA 1-4R; CAAS 5; CANR 1, 42; DLB 2, 5, 130, 152; DLBY 83
Garrick, David 1717-1779 ....**LC 15; DAM DRAM**
See also DLB 84
Garrigue, Jean 1914-1972 .... **CLC 2, 8**
See also CA 5-8R; 37-40R; CANR 20
Garrison, Frederick
See Sinclair, Upton (Beall)
Garth, Will
See Hamilton, Edmond; Kuttner, Henry
Garvey, Marcus (Moziah, Jr.) 1887-1940
TCLC 41; BLC; DAM MULT
See also BW 1; CA 120; 124
Gary, Romain .... **CLC 25**
See also Kacew, Romain
See also DLB 83
Gascar, Pierre .... **CLC 11**
See also Fournier, Pierre
Gascoyne, David (Emery) 1916- ...... **CLC 45**
See also CA 65-68; CANR 10, 28, 54; DLB 20; MTCW
Gaskell, Elizabeth Cleghorn 1810-1865NCLC 5; DAB; DAM MST; SSC 25
See also CDBLB 1832-1890; DLB 21, 144, 159
Gass, William H(oward) 1924-CLC 1, 2, 8, 11, 15, 39; SSC 12
See also CA 17-20R; CANR 30; DLB 2; MTCW

Gasset, Jose Ortega y
See Ortega y Gasset, Jose
Gates, Henry Louis, Jr. 1950- CLC 65; DAM MULT
See also BW 2; CA 109; CANR 25, 53; DLB 67
Gautier, Theophile 1811-1872 .. NCLC 1, 59; DAM POET; PC 18; SSC 20
See also DLB 119
Gawsworth, John
See Bates, H(erbert) E(rnest)
Gay, Oliver
See Gogarty, Oliver St. John
Gaye, Marvin (Penze) 1939-1984 ..... **CLC 26**
See also CA 112
Gebler, Carlo (Ernest) 1954- .... **CLC 39**
See also CA 119; 133
Gee, Maggie (Mary) 1948- .... **CLC 57**
See also CA 130
Gee, Maurice (Gough) 1931- .... **CLC 29**
See also CA 97-100; SATA 46
Gelbart, Larry (Simon) 1923- .... **CLC 21, 61**
See also CA 73-76; CANR 45
Gelber, Jack 1932- .... **CLC 1, 6, 14, 79**
See also CA 1-4R; CANR 2; DLB 7
Gellhorn, Martha (Ellis) 1908- .. **CLC 14, 60**
See also CA 77-80; CANR 44; DLBY 82
Genet, Jean 1910-1986CLC 1, 2, 5, 10, 14, 44, 46; DAM DRAM
See also CA 13-16R; CANR 18; DLB 72; DLBY 86; MTCW
Gent, Peter 1942- .... **CLC 29**
See also AITN 1; CA 89-92; DLBY 82
Gentlewoman in New England, A
See Bradstreet, Anne
Gentlewoman in Those Parts, A
See Bradstreet, Anne
George, Jean Craighead 1919- .... **CLC 35**
See also AAYA 8; CA 5-8R; CANR 25; CLR 1; DLB 52; JRDA; MAICYA; SATA 2, 68
George, Stefan (Anton) 1868-1933TCLC 2, 14
See also CA 104
Georges, Georges Martin
See Simenon, Georges (Jacques Christian)
Gerhardi, William Alexander
See Gerhardie, William Alexander
Gerhardie, William Alexander 1895-1977
CLC 5
See also CA 25-28R; 73-76; CANR 18; DLB 36
Gerstler, Amy 1956- .... **CLC 70**
See also CA 146
Gertler, T. .... **CLC 34**
See also CA 116; 121; INT 121
Ghalib .... **NCLC 39**
See also Ghalib, Hsadullah Khan
Ghalib, Hsadullah Khan 1797-1869
See Ghalib
See also DAM POET
Ghelderode, Michel de 1898-1962CLC 6, 11; DAM DRAM
See also CA 85-88; CANR 40
Ghiselin, Brewster 1903- .... **CLC 23**
See also CA 13-16R; CAAS 10; CANR 13
Ghose, Zulfikar 1935- .... **CLC 42**
See also CA 65-68
Ghosh, Amitav 1956- .... **CLC 44**
See also CA 147
Giacosa, Giuseppe 1847-1906 .... **TCLC 7**
See also CA 104
Gibb, Lee
See Waterhouse, Keith (Spencer)
Gibbon, Lewis Grassic .... **TCLC 4**

See also Mitchell, James Leslie
Gibbons, Kaye 1960-CLC 50, 88; DAM POP
See also CA 151
Gibran, Kahlil 1883-1931 . TCLC 1, 9; DAM POET, POP; PC 9
See also CA 104; 150
Gibran, Khalil
See Gibran, Kahlil
Gibson, William 1914- .. CLC 23; DA; DAB; DAC; DAM DRAM, MST
See also CA 9-12R; CANR 9, 42; DLB 7; SATA 66
Gibson, William (Ford) 1948- ... CLC 39, 63; DAM POP
See also AAYA 12; CA 126; 133; CANR 52
Gide, Andre (Paul Guillaume) 1869-1951
TCLC 5, 12, 36; DA; DAB; DAC; DAM MST, NOV; SSC 13; WLC
See also CA 104; 124; DLB 65; MTCW
Gifford, Barry (Colby) 1946- .... **CLC 34**
See also CA 65-68; CANR 9, 30, 40
Gilbert, W(illiam) S(chwenck) 1836-1911
TCLC 3; DAM DRAM, POET
See also CA 104; SATA 36
Gilbreth, Frank B., Jr. 1911- .... **CLC 17**
See also CA 9-12R; SATA 2
Gilchrist, Ellen 1935-CLC 34, 48; DAM POP; SSC 14
See also CA 113; 116; CANR 41, 61; DLB 130; MTCW
Giles, Molly 1942- .... **CLC 39**
See also CA 126
Gill, Patrick
See Creasey, John
Gilliam, Terry (Vance) 1940- .... **CLC 21**
See also Monty Python
See also AAYA 19; CA 108; 113; CANR 35; INT 113
Gillian, Jerry
See Gilliam, Terry (Vance)
Gilliatt, Penelope (Ann Douglass) 1932-1993
CLC 2, 10, 13, 53
See also AITN 2; CA 13-16R; 141; CANR 49; DLB 14
Gilman, Charlotte (Anna) Perkins (Stetson)
1860-1935 .... **TCLC 9, 37; SSC 13**
See also CA 106; 150
Gilmour, David 1949- .... **CLC 35**
See also CA 138, 147
Gilpin, William 1724-1804 .... **NCLC 30**
Gilray, J. D.
See Mencken, H(enry) L(ouis)
Gilroy, Frank D(aniel) 1925- .... **CLC 2**
See also CA 81-84; CANR 32; DLB 7
Gilstrap, John 1957(?)- .... **CLC 99**
Ginsberg, Allen (Irwin) 1926-1997 CLC 1, 2, 3, 4, 6, 13, 36, 69; DA; DAB; DAC; DAM MST, POET; PC 4; WLC 3
See also AITN 1; CA 1-4R; 157; CANR 2, 41; CDALB 1941-1968; DLB 5, 16, 169; MTCW
Ginzburg, Natalia 1916-1991CLC 5, 11, 54, 70
See also CA 85-88; 135; CANR 33; DLB 177; MTCW
Giono, Jean 1895-1970 .... **CLC 4, 11**
See also CA 45-48; 29-32R; CANR 2, 35; DLB 72; MTCW
Giovanni, Nikki 1943-CLC 2, 4, 19, 64; BLC; DA; DAB; DAC; DAM MST, MULT, POET; PC 19; WLCS
See also AAYA 22; AITN 1; BW 2; CA 29-32R; CAAS 6; CANR 18, 41, 60; CLR 6; DLB 5, 41; INT CANR-18; MAICYA; MTCW; SATA 24

See also CA 49-52; CANR 2, 22, 45; DLB 77

Grahame, Kenneth 1859-1932 **TCLC 64; DAB**
See also CA 108; 136; CLR 5; DLB 34, 141, 178; MAICYA; YABC 1

Grant, Skeeter
See Spiegelman, Art

Granville-Barker, Harley 1877-1946 **TCLC 2; DAM DRAM**
See also Barker, Harley Granville
See also CA 104

Grass, Guenter (Wilhelm) 1927- **CLC 1, 2, 4, 6, 11, 15, 22, 32, 49, 88; DA; DAB; DAC; DAM MST, NOV; WLC**
See also CA 13-16R; CANR 20; DLB 75, 124; MTCW

Gratton, Thomas
See Hulme, T(homas) E(rnest)

Grau, Shirley Ann 1929- .. **CLC 4, 9; SSC 15**
See also CA 89-92; CANR 22; DLB 2; INT CANR-22; MTCW

Gravel, Fern
See Hall, James Norman

Graver, Elizabeth 1964- .... **CLC 70**
See also CA 135

Graves, Richard Perceval 1945- ...... **CLC 44**
See also CA 65-68; CANR 9, 26, 51

Graves, Robert (von Ranke) 1895-1985 **C L C 1, 2, 6, 11, 39, 44, 45; DAB; DAC; DAM MST, POET; PC 6**
See also CA 5-8R; 117; CANR 5, 36; CDBLB 1914-1945; DLB 20, 100; DLBY 85; MTCW; SATA 45

Graves, Valerie
See Bradley, Marion Zimmer

Gray, Alasdair (James) 1934- .... **CLC 41**
See also CA 126; CANR 47; INT 126; MTCW

Gray, Amlin 1946- .... **CLC 29**
See also CA 138

Gray, Francine du Plessix 1930- ..... **CLC 22; DAM NOV**
See also BEST 90:3; CA 61-64; CAAS 2; CANR 11, 33; INT CANR-11; MTCW

Gray, John (Henry) 1866-1934 ...... **TCLC 19**
See also CA 119

Gray, Simon (James Holliday) 1936- **CLC 9, 14, 36**
See also AITN 1; CA 21-24R; CAAS 3; CANR 32; DLB 13; MTCW

Gray, Spalding 1941- **CLC 49; DAM POP; DC 7**
See also CA 128

Gray, Thomas 1716-1771 ... **LC 4; DA; DAB; DAC; DAM MST; PC 2; WLC**
See also CDBLB 1660-1789; DLB 109

Grayson, David
See Baker, Ray Stannard

Grayson, Richard (A.) 1951- .... **CLC 38**
See also CA 85-88; CANR 14, 31, 57

Greeley, Andrew M(oran) 1928- ..... **CLC 28; DAM POP**
See also CA 5-8R; CAAS 7; CANR 7, 43; MTCW

Green, Anna Katharine 1846-1935 **TCLC 63**
See also CA 112; 159

Green, Brian
See Card, Orson Scott

Green, Hannah
See Greenberg, Joanne (Goldenberg)

Green, Hannah 1927(?)-1996 .... **CLC 3**
See also CA 73-76; CANR 59

Green, Henry 1905-1973 .... **CLC 2, 13, 97**
See also Yorke, Henry Vincent
See also DLB 15

Green, Julian (Hartridge) 1900-
See Green, Julien
See also CA 21-24R; CANR 33; DLB 4, 72; MTCW

Green, Julien .... **CLC 3, 11, 77**
See also Green, Julian (Hartridge)

Green, Paul (Eliot) 1894-1981 **CLC 25; DAM DRAM**
See also AITN 1; CA 5-8R; 103; CANR 3; DLB 7, 9; DLBY 81

Greenberg, Ivan 1908-1973
See Rahv, Philip
See also CA 85-88

Greenberg, Joanne (Goldenberg) 1932- **C L C 7, 30**
See also AAYA 12; CA 5-8R; CANR 14, 32; SATA 25

Greenberg, Richard 1959(?)- .... **CLC 57**
See also CA 138

Greene, Bette 1934- .... **CLC 30**
See also AAYA 7; CA 53-56; CANR 4; CLR 2; JRDA; MAICYA; SAAS 16; SATA 8

Greene, Gael .... **CLC 8**
See also CA 13-16R; CANR 10

Greene, Graham Henry 1904-1991 **CLC 1, 3, 6, 9, 14, 18, 27, 37, 70, 72; DA; DAB; DAC; DAM MST, NOV; SSC 29; WLC**
See also AITN 2; CA 13-16R; 133; CANR 35, 61; CDBLB 1945-1960; DLB 13, 15, 77, 100, 162; DLBY 91; MTCW; SATA 20

Greer, Richard
See Silverberg, Robert

Gregor, Arthur 1923- .... **CLC 9**
See also CA 25-28R; CAAS 10; CANR 11; SATA 36

Gregor, Lee
See Pohl, Frederik

Gregory, Isabella Augusta (Persse) 1852-1932 **TCLC 1**
See also CA 104; DLB 10

Gregory, J. Dennis
See Williams, John A(lfred)

Grendon, Stephen
See Derleth, August (William)

Grenville, Kate 1950- .... **CLC 61**
See also CA 118; CANR 53

Grenville, Pelham
See Wodehouse, P(elham) G(renville)

Greve, Felix Paul (Berthold Friedrich) 1879-1948
See Grove, Frederick Philip
See also CA 104; 141; DAC; DAM MST

Grey, Zane 1872-1939 .. **TCLC 6; DAM POP**
See also CA 104; 132; DLB 9; MTCW

Grieg, (Johan) Nordahl (Brun) 1902-1943 **TCLC 10**
See also CA 107

Grieve, C(hristopher) M(urray) 1892-1978 **CLC 11, 19; DAM POET**
See also MacDiarmid, Hugh; Pteleon
See also CA 5-8R; 85-88; CANR 33; MTCW

Griffin, Gerald 1803-1840 .... **NCLC 7**
See also DLB 159

Griffin, John Howard 1920-1980 ..... **CLC 68**
See also AITN 1; CA 1-4R; 101; CANR 2

Griffin, Peter 1942- .... **CLC 39**
See also CA 136

Griffith, D(avid Lewelyn) W(ark) 1875(?)-1948 **TCLC 68**
See also CA 119; 150

Griffith, Lawrence
See Griffith, D(avid Lewelyn) W(ark)

Griffiths, Trevor 1935- .... **CLC 13, 52**

See also CA 97-100; CANR 45; DLB 13

Grigson, Geoffrey (Edward Harvey) 1905-1985 **CLC 7, 39**
See also CA 25-28R; 118; CANR 20, 33; DLB 27; MTCW

Grillparzer, Franz 1791-1872 .... **NCLC 1**
See also DLB 133

Grimble, Reverend Charles James
See Eliot, T(homas) S(tearns)

Grimke, Charlotte L(ottie) Forten 1837(?)-1914
See Forten, Charlotte L.
See also BW 1; CA 117; 124; DAM MULT, POET

Grimm, Jacob Ludwig Karl 1785-1863 **NCLC 3**
See also DLB 90; MAICYA; SATA 22

Grimm, Wilhelm Karl 1786-1859 .... **NCLC 3**
See also DLB 90; MAICYA; SATA 22

Grimmelshausen, Johann Jakob Christoffel von 1621-1676 .... **LC 6**
See also DLB 168

Grindel, Eugene 1895-1952
See Eluard, Paul
See also CA 104

Grisham, John 1955- ..... **CLC 84; DAM POP**
See also AAYA 14; CA 138; CANR 47

Grossman, David 1954- .... **CLC 67**
See also CA 138

Grossman, Vasily (Semenovich) 1905-1964 **CLC 41**
See also CA 124; 130; MTCW

Grove, Frederick Philip .... **TCLC 4**
See also Greve, Felix Paul (Berthold Friedrich)
See also DLB 92

Grubb
See Crumb, R(obert)

Grumbach, Doris (Isaac) 1918- **CLC 13, 22, 64**
See also CA 5-8R; CAAS 2; CANR 9, 42; INT CANR-9

Grundtvig, Nicolai Frederik Severin 1783-1872 **NCLC 1**

Grunge
See Crumb, R(obert)

Grunwald, Lisa 1959- .... **CLC 44**
See also CA 120

Guare, John 1938- . **CLC 8, 14, 29, 67; DAM DRAM**
See also CA 73-76; CANR 21; DLB 7; MTCW

Gudjonsson, Halldor Kiljan 1902-
See Laxness, Halldor
See also CA 103

Guenter, Erich
See Eich, Guenter

Guest, Barbara 1920- .... **CLC 34**
See also CA 25-28R; CANR 11, 44; DLB 5

Guest, Judith (Ann) 1936- . **CLC 8, 30; DAM NOV, POP**
See also AAYA 7; CA 77-80; CANR 15; INT CANR-15; MTCW

Guevara, Che .... **CLC 87; HLC**
See also Guevara (Serna), Ernesto

Guevara (Serna), Ernesto 1928-1967
See Guevara, Che
See also CA 127; 111; CANR 56; DAM MULT; HW

Guild, Nicholas M. 1944- .... **CLC 33**
See also CA 93-96

Guillemin, Jacques
See Sartre, Jean-Paul

Guillen, Jorge 1893-1984 .... **CLC 11; DAM MULT, POET**
See also CA 89-92; 112; DLB 108; HW

Guillen, Nicolas (Cristobal) 1902-1989 . **C L C**

48, 79; BLC; DAM MST, MULT, POET; HLC
See also BW 2; CA 116; 125; 129; HW
Guillevic, (Eugene) 1907- .... CLC 33
See also CA 93-96
Guillois
See Desnos, Robert
Guillois, Valentin
See Desnos, Robert
Guiney, Louise Imogen 1861-1920 TCLC 41
See also DLB 54
Guiraldes, Ricardo (Guillermo) 1886-1927 TCLC 39
See also CA 131; HW; MTCW
Gumilev, Nikolai Stephanovich 1886-1921 TCLC 60
Gunesekera, Romesh 1954- .... CLC 91
See also CA 159
Gunn, Bill .... CLC 5
See also Gunn, William Harrison
See also DLB 38
Gunn, Thom(son William) 1929-CLC 3, 6, 18, 32, 81; DAM POET
See also CA 17-20R; CANR 9, 33; CDBLB 1960 to Present; DLB 27; INT CANR-33; MTCW
Gunn, William Harrison 1934(?)-1989
See Gunn, Bill
See also AITN 1; BW 1; CA 13-16R; 128; CANR 12, 25
Gunnars, Kristjana 1948- .... CLC 69
See also CA 113; DLB 60
Gurdjieff, G(eorgei) I(vanovich) 1877(?)-1949 TCLC 71
See also CA 157
Gurganus, Allan 1947-.. CLC 70; DAM POP
See also BEST 90:1; CA 135
Gurney, A(lbert) R(amsdell), Jr. 1930- .C L C 32, 50, 54; DAM DRAM
See also CA 77-80; CANR 32
Gurney, Ivor (Bertie) 1890-1937 ... TCLC 33
Gurney, Peter
See Gurney, A(lbert) R(amsdell), Jr.
Guro, Elena 1877-1913 .... TCLC 56
Gustafson, James M(oody) 1925- .. CLC 100
See also CA 25-28R; CANR 37
Gustafson, Ralph (Barker) 1909- .... CLC 36
See also CA 21-24R; CANR 8, 45; DLB 88
Gut, Gom
See Simenon, Georges (Jacques Christian)
Guterson, David 1956- .... CLC 91
See also CA 132
Guthrie, A(lfred) B(ertram), Jr. 1901-1991 CLC 23
See also CA 57-60; 134; CANR 24; DLB 6; SATA 62; SATA-Obit 67
Guthrie, Isobel
See Grieve, C(hristopher) M(urray)
Guthrie, Woodrow Wilson 1912-1967
See Guthrie, Woody
See also CA 113; 93-96
Guthrie, Woody .... CLC 35
See also Guthrie, Woodrow Wilson
Guy, Rosa (Cuthbert) 1928- .... CLC 26
See also AAYA 4; BW 2; CA 17-20R; CANR 14, 34; CLR 13; DLB 33; JRDA; MAICYA; SATA 14, 62
Gwendolyn
See Bennett, (Enoch) Arnold
H. D. .... CLC 3, 8, 14, 31, 34, 73; PC 5
See also Doolittle, Hilda
H. de V.
See Buchan, John

Haavikko, Paavo Juhani 1931-`.. CLC 18, 34
See also CA 106
Habbema, Koos
See Heijermans, Herman
Habermas, Juergen 1929-............... CLC 104
See also CA 109
Habermas, Jurgen
See Habermas, Juergen
Hacker, Marilyn 1942-.CLC 5, 9, 23, 72, 91; DAM POET
See also CA 77-80; DLB 120
Haggard, H(enry) Rider 1856-1925TCLC 11
See also CA 108; 148; DLB 70, 156, 174, 178; SATA 16
Hagiosy, L.
See Larbaud, Valery (Nicolas)
Hagiwara Sakutaro 1886-1942TCLC 60; PC 18
Haig, Fenil
See Ford, Ford Madox
Haig-Brown, Roderick (Langmere) 1908-1976 CLC 21
See also CA 5-8R; 69-72; CANR 4, 38; CLR 31; DLB 88; MAICYA; SATA 12
Hailey, Arthur 1920-CLC 5; DAM NOV, POP
See also AITN 2; BEST 90:3; CA 1-4R; CANR 2, 36; DLB 88; DLBY 82; MTCW
Hailey, Elizabeth Forsythe 1938- ..... CLC 40
See also CA 93-96; CAAS 1; CANR 15, 48; INT CANR-15
Haines, John (Meade) 1924-.............. CLC 58
See also CA 17-20R; CANR 13, 34; DLB 5
Hakluyt, Richard 1552-1616 .... LC 31
Haldeman, Joe (William) 1943- ....CLC 61
See also CA 53-56; CAAS 25; CANR 6; DLB 8; INT CANR-6
Haley, Alex(ander Murray Palmer) 1921-1992 CLC 8, 12, 76; BLC; DA; DAB; DAC; DAM MST, MULT, POP
See also BW 2; CA 77-80; 136; CANR 61; DLB 38; MTCW
Haliburton, Thomas Chandler 1796-1865 NCLC 15
See also DLB 11, 99
Hall, Donald (Andrew, Jr.) 1928- CLC 1, 13, 37, 59; DAM POET
See also CA 5-8R; CAAS 7; CANR 2, 44; DLB 5; SATA 23
Hall, Frederic Sauser
See Sauser-Hall, Frederic
Hall, James
See Kuttner, Henry
Hall, James Norman 1887-1951 ..... TCLC 23
See also CA 123; SATA 21
Hall, (Marguerite) Radclyffe 1886-1943 TCLC 12
See also CA 110; 150
Hall, Rodney 1935-............................CLC 51
See also CA 109
Halleck, Fitz-Greene 1790-1867 ....NCLC 47
See also DLB 3
Halliday, Michael
See Creasey, John
Halpern, Daniel 1945-........................CLC 14
See also CA 33-36R
Hamburger, Michael (Peter Leopold) 1924- CLC 5, 14
See also CA 5-8R; CAAS 4; CANR 2, 47; DLB 27
Hamill, Pete 1935- ....CLC 10
See also CA 25-28R; CANR 18
Hamilton, Alexander 1755(?)-1804 NCLC 49
See also DLB 37

Hamilton, Clive
See Lewis, C(live) S(taples)
Hamilton, Edmond 1904-1977 ....CLC 1
See also CA 1-4R; CANR 3; DLB 8
Hamilton, Eugene (Jacob) Lee
See Lee-Hamilton, Eugene (Jacob)
Hamilton, Franklin
See Silverberg, Robert
Hamilton, Gail
See Corcoran, Barbara
Hamilton, Mollie
See Kaye, M(ary) M(argaret)
Hamilton, (Anthony Walter) Patrick 1904-1962 CLC 51
See also CA 113; DLB 10
Hamilton, Virginia 1936-.......CLC 26; DAM MULT
See also AAYA 2, 21; BW 2; CA 25-28R; CANR 20, 37; CLR 1, 11, 40; DLB 33, 52; INT CANR-20; JRDA; MAICYA; MTCW; SATA 4, 56, 79
Hammett, (Samuel) Dashiell 1894-1961 C L C 3, 5, 10, 19, 47; SSC 17
See also AITN 1; CA 81-84; CANR 42; CDALB 1929-1941; DLBD 6; DLBY 96; MTCW
Hammon, Jupiter 1711(?)-1800(?) . NCLC 5; BLC; DAM MULT, POET; PC 16
See also DLB 31, 50
Hammond, Keith
See Kuttner, Henry
Hamner, Earl (Henry), Jr. 1923-...... CLC 12
See also AITN 2; CA 73-76; DLB 6
Hampton, Christopher (James) 1946- CLC 4
See also CA 25-28R; DLB 13; MTCW
Hamsun, Knut .... TCLC 2, 14, 49
See also Pedersen, Knut
Handke, Peter 1942-CLC 5, 8, 10, 15, 38; DAM DRAM, NOV
See also CA 77-80; CANR 33; DLB 85, 124; MTCW
Hanley, James 1901-1985 ..... CLC 3, 5, 8, 13
See also CA 73-76; 117; CANR 36; MTCW
Hannah, Barry 1942- .... CLC 23, 38, 90
See also CA 108; 110; CANR 43; DLB 6; INT 110; MTCW
Hannon, Ezra
See Hunter, Evan
Hansberry, Lorraine (Vivian) 1930-1965CLC 17, 62; BLC; DA; DAB; DAC; DAM DRAM, MST, MULT; DC 2
See also BW 1; CA 109; 25-28R; CABS 3; CANR 58; CDALB 1941-1968; DLB 7, 38; MTCW
Hansen, Joseph 1923-........................ CLC 38
See also CA 29-32R; CAAS 17; CANR 16, 44; INT CANR-16
Hansen, Martin A. 1909-1955 .... TCLC 32
Hanson, Kenneth O(stlin) 1922- ...... CLC 13
See also CA 53-56; CANR 7
Hardwick, Elizabeth 1916-....CLC 13; DAM NOV
See also CA 5-8R; CANR 3, 32; DLB 6; MTCW
Hardy, Thomas 1840-1928TCLC 4, 10, 18, 32, 48, 53, 72; DA; DAB; DAC; DAM MST, NOV, POET; PC 8; SSC 2; WLC
See also CA 104; 123; CDBLB 1890-1914; DLB 18, 19, 135; MTCW
Hare, David 1947- .... CLC 29, 58
See also CA 97-100; CANR 39; DLB 13; MTCW
Harford, Henry
See Hudson, W(illiam) H(enry)
Hargrave, Leonie

See Disch, Thomas M(ichael)

Harjo, Joy 1951- .... **CLC 83; DAM MULT**
See also CA 114; CANR 35; DLB 120, 175;
NNAL

Harlan, Louis R(udolph) 1922- .... **CLC 34**
See also CA 21-24R; CANR 25, 55

Harling, Robert 1951(?)- .... **CLC 53**
See also CA 147

Harmon, William (Ruth) 1938- .... **CLC 38**
See also CA 33-36R; CANR 14, 32, 35; SATA
65

Harper, F. E. W.
See Harper, Frances Ellen Watkins

Harper, Frances E. W.
See Harper, Frances Ellen Watkins

Harper, Frances E. Watkins
See Harper, Frances Ellen Watkins

Harper, Frances Ellen
See Harper, Frances Ellen Watkins

Harper, Frances Ellen Watkins 1825-1911
TCLC 14; BLC; DAM MULT, POET
See also BW 1; CA 111; 125; DLB 50

Harper, Michael S(teven) 1938- ... **CLC 7, 22**
See also BW 1; CA 33-36R; CANR 24; DLB
41

Harper, Mrs. F. E. W.
See Harper, Frances Ellen Watkins

Harris, Christie (Lucy) Irwin 1907- **CLC 12**
See also CA 5-8R; CANR 6; DLB 88; JRDA;
MAICYA; SAAS 10; SATA 6, 74

Harris, Frank 1856-1931 .... **TCLC 24**
See also CA 109; 150; DLB 156

Harris, George Washington 1814-1869 **NCLC
23**
See also DLB 3, 11

Harris, Joel Chandler 1848-1908 ...**TCLC 2;
SSC 19**
See also CA 104; 137; DLB 11, 23, 42, 78, 91;
MAICYA; YABC 1

Harris, John (Wyndham Parkes Lucas) Beynon
1903-1969
See Wyndham, John
See also CA 102; 89-92

Harris, MacDonald .... **CLC 9**
See also Heiney, Donald (William)

Harris, Mark 1922- .... **CLC 19**
See also CA 5-8R; CAAS 3; CANR 2, 55; DLB
2; DLBY 80

Harris, (Theodore) Wilson 1921- ..... **CLC 25**
See also BW 2; CA 65-68; CAAS 16; CANR
11, 27; DLB 117; MTCW

Harrison, Elizabeth Cavanna 1909-
See Cavanna, Betty
See also CA 9-12R; CANR 6, 27

Harrison, Harry (Max) 1925- .... **CLC 42**
See also CA 1-4R; CANR 5, 21; DLB 8; SATA
4

Harrison, James (Thomas) 1937- **CLC 6, 14,
33, 66; SSC 19**
See also CA 13-16R; CANR 8, 51; DLBY 82;
INT CANR-8

Harrison, Jim
See Harrison, James (Thomas)

Harrison, Kathryn 1961- .... **CLC 70**
See also CA 144

Harrison, Tony 1937- .... **CLC 43**
See also CA 65-68; CANR 44; DLB 40; MTCW

Harriss, Will(ard Irvin) 1922- .... **CLC 34**
See also CA 111

Harson, Sley
See Ellison, Harlan (Jay)

Hart, Ellis
See Ellison, Harlan (Jay)

Hart, Josephine 1942(?)-**CLC 70; DAM POP**
See also CA 138

Hart, Moss 1904-1961**CLC 66; DAM DRAM**
See also CA 109; 89-92; DLB 7

Harte, (Francis) Bret(t) 1836(?)-1902**TCLC 1,
25; DA; DAC; DAM MST; SSC 8; WLC**
See also CA 104; 140; CDALB 1865-1917;
DLB 12, 64, 74, 79; SATA 26

Hartley, L(eslie) P(oles) 1895-1972**CLC 2, 22**
See also CA 45-48; 37-40R; CANR 33; DLB
15, 139; MTCW

Hartman, Geoffrey H. 1929- .... **CLC 27**
See also CA 117; 125; DLB 67

Hartmann, Sadakichi 1867-1944 ... **TCLC 73**
See also CA 157; DLB 54

Hartmann von Aue c. 1160-c. 1205**CMLC 15**
See also DLB 138

Hartmann von Aue 1170-1210 ...... **CMLC 15**

Haruf, Kent 1943- ....**CLC 34**
See also CA 149

Harwood, Ronald 1934-......... **CLC 32; DAM
DRAM, MST**
See also CA 1-4R; CANR 4, 55; DLB 13

Hasek, Jaroslav (Matej Frantisek) 1883-1923
TCLC 4
See also CA 104; 129; MTCW

Hass, Robert 1941- ... **CLC 18, 39, 99; PC 16**
See also CA 111; CANR 30, 50; DLB 105;
SATA 94

Hastings, Hudson
See Kuttner, Henry

Hastings, Selina ....**CLC 44**

Hathorne, John 1641-1717 .... **LC 38**

Hatteras, Amelia
See Mencken, H(enry) L(ouis)

Hatteras, Owen .... **TCLC 18**
See also Mencken, H(enry) L(ouis); Nathan,
George Jean

Hauptmann, Gerhart (Johann Robert) 1862-
1946 .... **TCLC 4; DAM DRAM**
See also CA 104; 153; DLB 66, 118

Havel, Vaclav 1936-... **CLC 25, 58, 65; DAM
DRAM; DC 6**
See also CA 104; CANR 36; MTCW

Haviaras, Stratis ....**CLC 33**
See also Chaviaras, Strates

Hawes, Stephen 1475(?)-1523(?) .... **LC 17**

Hawkes, John (Clendennin Burne, Jr.) 1925-
CLC 1, 2, 3, 4, 7, 9, 14, 15, 27, 49
See also CA 1-4R; CANR 2, 47; DLB 2, 7;
DLBY 80; MTCW

Hawking, S. W.
See Hawking, Stephen W(illiam)

Hawking, Stephen W(illiam) 1942- ..**CLC 63**
See also AAYA 13; BEST 89:1; CA 126; 129;
CANR 48

Hawthorne, Julian 1846-1934 .... **TCLC 25**

Hawthorne, Nathaniel 1804-1864 **NCLC 39;
DA; DAB; DAC; DAM MST, NOV; SSC
29; WLC**
See also AAYA 18; CDALB 1640-1865; DLB
1, 74; YABC 2

Haxton, Josephine Ayres 1921-
See Douglas, Ellen
See also CA 115; CANR 41

Hayaseca y Eizaguirre, Jorge
See Echegaray (y Eizaguirre), Jose (Maria
Waldo)

Hayashi Fumiko 1904-1951 .... **TCLC 27**
See also DLB 180

Haycraft, Anna
See Ellis, Alice Thomas
See also CA 122

Hayden, Robert E(arl) 1913-1980 **CLC 5, 9,
14, 37; BLC; DA; DAC; DAM MST,
MULT, POET; PC 6**
See also BW 1; CA 69-72; 97-100; CABS 2;
CANR 24; CDALB 1941-1968; DLB 5, 76;
MTCW; SATA 19; SATA-Obit 26

Hayford, J(oseph) E(phraim) Casely
See Casely-Hayford, J(oseph) E(phraim)

Hayman, Ronald 1932- ....:.......... **CLC 44**
See also CA 25-28R; CANR 18, 50; DLB 155

Haywood, Eliza (Fowler) 1693(?)-1756 **LC 1**

Hazlitt, William 1778-1830 .... **NCLC 29**
See also DLB 110, 158

Hazzard, Shirley 1931- ....**CLC 18**
See also CA 9-12R; CANR 4; DLBY 82;
MTCW

Head, Bessie 1937-1986 .. **CLC 25, 67; BLC;
DAM MULT**
See also BW 2; CA 29-32R; 119; CANR 25;
DLB 117; MTCW

Headon, (Nicky) Topper 1956(?)- ..... **CLC 30**

Heaney, Seamus (Justin) 1939- **CLC 5, 7, 14,
25, 37, 74, 91; DAB; DAM POET; PC 18;
WLCS**
See also CA 85-88; CANR 25, 48; CDBLB
1960 to Present; DLB 40; DLBY 95; MTCW

Hearn, (Patricio) Lafcadio (Tessima Carlos)
1850-1904 .... **TCLC 9**
See also CA 105; DLB 12, 78

Hearne, Vicki 1946- ....**CLC 56**
See also CA 139

Hearon, Shelby 1931- ....**CLC 63**
See also AITN 2; CA 25-28R; CANR 18, 48

Heat-Moon, William Least ....**CLC 29**
See also Trogdon, William (Lewis)
See also AAYA 9

Hebbel, Friedrich 1813-1863**NCLC 43; DAM
DRAM**
See also DLB 129

Hebert, Anne 1916-**CLC 4, 13, 29; DAC; DAM
MST, POET**
See also CA 85-88; DLB 68; MTCW

Hecht, Anthony (Evan) 1923- **CLC 8, 13, 19;
DAM POET**
See also CA 9-12R; CANR 6; DLB 5, 169

Hecht, Ben 1894-1964 ....**CLC 8**
See also CA 85-88; DLB 7, 9, 25, 26, 28, 86

Hedayat, Sadeq 1903-1951 .... **TCLC 21**
See also CA 120

Hegel, Georg Wilhelm Friedrich 1770-1831
NCLC 46
See also DLB 90

Heidegger, Martin 1889-1976 ....**CLC 24**
See also CA 81-84; 65-68; CANR 34; MTCW

Heidenstam, (Carl Gustaf) Verner von 1859-
1940 .... **TCLC 5**
See also CA 104

Heifner, Jack 1946- ....**CLC 11**
See also CA 105; CANR 47

Heijermans, Herman 1864-1924 .... **TCLC 24**
See also CA 123

Heilbrun, Carolyn G(old) 1926- ....**CLC 25**
See also CA 45-48; CANR 1, 28, 58

Heine, Heinrich 1797-1856 ....**NCLC 4, 54**
See also DLB 90

Heinemann, Larry (Curtiss) 1944- ...**CLC 50**
See also CA 110; CAAS 21; CANR 31; DLBD
9; INT CANR-31

Heiney, Donald (William) 1921-1993
See Harris, MacDonald
See also CA 1-4R; 142; CANR 3, 58

Heinlein, Robert A(nson) 1907-1988**CLC 1, 3,
8, 14, 26, 55; DAM POP**

See also AAYA 17; CA 1-4R; 125; CANR 1, 20, 53; DLB 8; JRDA; MAICYA; MTCW; SATA 9, 69; SATA-Obit 56

Helforth, John
See Doolittle, Hilda

Hellenhofferu, Vojtech Kapristian z
See Hasek, Jaroslav (Matej Frantisek)

Heller, Joseph 1923-CLC **1, 3, 5, 8, 11, 36, 63; DA; DAB; DAC; DAM MST, NOV, POP; WLC**
See also AITN 1; CA 5-8R; CABS 1; CANR 8, 42; DLB 2, 28; DLBY 80; INT CANR-8; MTCW

Hellman, Lillian (Florence) 1906-1984CLC **2, 4, 8, 14, 18, 34, 44, 52; DAM DRAM; DC 1**
See also AITN 1, 2; CA 13-16R; 112; CANR 33; DLB 7; DLBY 84; MTCW

Helprin, Mark 1947-CLC **7, 10, 22, 32; DAM NOV, POP**
See also CA 81-84; CANR 47; DLBY 85; MTCW

Helvetius, Claude-Adrien 1715-1771 . LC **26**

Helyar, Jane Penelope Josephine 1933-
See Poole, Josephine
See also CA 21-24R; CANR 10, 26; SATA 82

Hemans, Felicia 1793-1835 .... NCLC **29**
See also DLB 96

Hemingway, Ernest (Miller) 1899-1961 C L C **1, 3, 6, 8, 10, 13, 19, 30, 34, 39, 41, 44, 50, 61, 80; DA; DAB; DAC; DAM MST, NOV; SSC 25; WLC**
See also AAYA 19; CA 77-80; CANR 34; CDALB 1917-1929; DLB 4, 9, 102; DLBD 1, 15; DLBY 81, 87, 96; MTCW

Hempel, Amy 1951- .... CLC **39**
See also CA 118; 137

Henderson, F. C.
See Mencken, H(enry) L(ouis)

Henderson, Sylvia
See Ashton-Warner, Sylvia (Constance)

Henderson, Zenna (Chlarson) 1917-1983S S C **29**
See also CA 1-4R; 133; CANR 1; DLB 8; SATA 5

Henley, Beth .... CLC **23; DC 6**
See also Henley, Elizabeth Becker
See also CABS 3; DLBY 86

Henley, Elizabeth Becker 1952-
See Henley, Beth
See also CA 107; CANR 32; DAM DRAM, MST; MTCW

Henley, William Ernest 1849-1903 .. TCLC **8**
See also CA 105; DLB 19

Hennissart, Martha
See Lathen, Emma
See also CA 85-88

Henry, O. .... TCLC **1, 19; SSC 5; WLC**
See also Porter, William Sydney

Henry, Patrick 1736-1799 .... LC **25**

Henryson, Robert 1430(?)-1506(?) ..... LC **20**
See also DLB 146

Henry VIII 1491-1547 .... LC **10**

Henschke, Alfred
See Klabund

Hentoff, Nat(han Irving) 1925- .... CLC **26**
See also AAYA 4; CA 1-4R; CAAS 6; CANR 5, 25; CLR 1; INT CANR-25; JRDA; MAICYA; SATA 42, 69; SATA-Brief 27

Heppenstall, (John) Rayner 1911-1981 . C L C **10**
See also CA 1-4R; 103; CANR 29

Heraclitus c. 540B.C.-c. 450B.C. .... CMLC **22**
See also DLB 176

Herbert, Frank (Patrick) 1920-1986 CLC **12, 23, 35, 44, 85; DAM POP**
See also AAYA 21; CA 53-56; 118; CANR 5, 43; DLB 8; INT CANR-5; MTCW; SATA 9, 37; SATA-Obit 47

Herbert, George 1593-1633 ..... LC **24; DAB; DAM POET; PC 4**
See also CDBLB Before 1660; DLB 126

Herbert, Zbigniew 1924- ...CLC **9, 43; DAM POET**
See also CA 89-92; CANR 36; MTCW

Herbst, Josephine (Frey) 1897-1969 . CLC **34**
See also CA 5-8R; 25-28R; DLB 9

Hergesheimer, Joseph 1880-1954 .. TCLC **11**
See also CA 109; DLB 102, 9

Herlihy, James Leo 1927-1993 .... CLC **6**
See also CA 1-4R; 143; CANR 2

Hermogenes fl. c. 175- .... CMLC **6**

Hernandez, Jose 1834-1886 .... NCLC **17**

Herodotus c. 484B.C.-429B.C. ...... CMLC **17**
See also DLB 176

Herrick, Robert 1591-1674LC **13; DA; DAB; DAC; DAM MST, POP; PC 9**
See also DLB 126

Herring, Guilles
See Somerville, Edith

Herriot, James 1916-1995CLC **12; DAM POP**
See also Wight, James Alfred
See also AAYA 1; CA 148; CANR 40; SATA 86

Herrmann, Dorothy 1941- .... CLC **44**
See also CA 107

Herrmann, Taffy
See Herrmann, Dorothy

Hersey, John (Richard) 1914-1993CLC **1, 2, 7, 9, 40, 81, 97; DAM POP**
See also CA 17-20R; 140; CANR 33; DLB 6; MTCW; SATA 25; SATA-Obit 76

Herzen, Aleksandr Ivanovich 1812-1870 NCLC **10, 61**

Herzl, Theodor 1860-1904 .... TCLC **36**

Herzog, Werner 1942- .... CLC **16**
See also CA 89-92

Hesiod c. 8th cent. B.C.- .... CMLC **5**
See also DLB 176

Hesse, Hermann 1877-1962CLC **1, 2, 3, 6, 11, 17, 25, 69; DA; DAB; DAC; DAM MST, NOV; SSC 9; WLC**
See also CA 17-18; CAP 2; DLB 66; MTCW; SATA 50

Hewes, Cady
See De Voto, Bernard (Augustine)

Heyen, William 1940- .... CLC **13, 18**
See also CA 33-36R; CAAS 9; DLB 5

Heyerdahl, Thor 1914- .... CLC **26**
See also CA 5-8R; CANR 5, 22; MTCW; SATA 2, 52

Heym, Georg (Theodor Franz Arthur) 1887-1912 .... TCLC **9**
See also CA 106

Heym, Stefan 1913- .... CLC **41**
See also CA 9-12R; CANR 4; DLB 69

Heyse, Paul (Johann Ludwig von) 1830-1914 TCLC **8**
See also CA 104; DLB 129

Heyward, (Edwin) DuBose 1885-1940 T C L C **59**
See also CA 108; 157; DLB 7, 9, 45; SATA 21

Hibbert, Eleanor Alice Burford 1906-1993 CLC **7; DAM POP**
See also BEST 90:4; CA 17-20R; 140; CANR 9, 28, 59; SATA 2; SATA-Obit 74

Hichens, Robert S. 1864-1950 .... TCLC **64**

See also DLB 153

Higgins, George V(incent) 1939-CLC **4, 7, 10, 18**
See also CA 77-80; CAAS 5; CANR 17, 51; DLB 2; DLBY 81; INT CANR-17; MTCW

Higginson, Thomas Wentworth 1823-1911 TCLC **36**
See also DLB 1, 64

Highet, Helen
See MacInnes, Helen (Clark)

Highsmith, (Mary) Patricia 1921-1995CLC **2, 4, 14, 42, 102; DAM NOV, POP**
See also CA 1-4R; 147; CANR 1, 20, 48; MTCW

Highwater, Jamake (Mamake) 1942(?)- C L C **12**
See also AAYA 7; CA 65-68; CAAS 7; CANR 10, 34; CLR 17; DLB 52; DLBY 85; JRDA; MAICYA; SATA 32, 69; SATA-Brief 30

Highway, Tomson 1951-CLC **92; DAC; DAM MULT**
See also CA 151; NNAL

Higuchi, Ichiyo 1872-1896 .... NCLC **49**

Hijuelos, Oscar 1951- CLC **65; DAM MULT, POP; HLC**
See also BEST 90:1; CA 123; CANR 50; DLB 145; HW

Hikmet, Nazim 1902(?)-1963 .... CLC **40**
See also CA 141; 93-96

Hildegard von Bingen 1098-1179 . CMLC **20**
See also DLB 148

Hildesheimer, Wolfgang 1916-1991 . CLC **49**
See also CA 101; 135; DLB 69, 124

Hill, Geoffrey (William) 1932- CLC **5, 8, 18, 45; DAM POET**
See also CA 81-84; CANR 21; CDBLB 1960 to Present; DLB 40; MTCW

Hill, George Roy 1921- .... CLC **26**
See also CA 110; 122

Hill, John
See Koontz, Dean R(ay)

Hill, Susan (Elizabeth) 1942- . CLC **4; DAB; DAM MST, NOV**
See also CA 33-36R; CANR 29; DLB 14, 139; MTCW

Hillerman, Tony 1925- ..CLC **62; DAM POP**
See also AAYA 6; BEST 89:1; CA 29-32R; CANR 21, 42; SATA 6

Hillesum, Etty 1914-1943 .... TCLC **49**
See also CA 137

Hilliard, Noel (Harvey) 1929- .... CLC **15**
See also CA 9-12R; CANR 7

Hillis, Rick 1956- .... CLC **66**
See also CA 134

Hilton, James 1900-1954 .... TCLC **21**
See also CA 108; DLB 34, 77; SATA 34

Himes, Chester (Bomar) 1909-1984CLC **2, 4, 7, 18, 58; BLC; DAM MULT**
See also BW 2; CA 25-28R; 114; CANR 22; DLB 2, 76, 143; MTCW

Hinde, Thomas ....CLC **6, 11**
See also Chitty, Thomas Willes

Hindin, Nathan
See Bloch, Robert (Albert)

Hine, (William) Daryl 1936-............. CLC **15**
See also CA 1-4R; CAAS 15; CANR 1, 20; DLB 60

Hinkson, Katharine Tynan
See Tynan, Katharine

Hinton, S(usan) E(loise) 1950- CLC **30; DA; DAB; DAC; DAM MST, NOV**
See also AAYA 2; CA 81-84; CANR 32; CLR 3, 23; JRDA; MAICYA; MTCW; SATA 19,

1929; CLR 32; DLB 51; MTCW; SATA 31

Johnson, Joyce 1935- .... CLC 58
See also CA 125; 129

Johnson, Lionel (Pigot) 1867-1902 **TCLC 19**
See also CA 117; DLB 19

Johnson, Mel
See Malzberg, Barry N(athaniel)

Johnson, Pamela Hansford 1912-1981CLC 1,
7, 27
See also CA 1-4R; 104; CANR 2, 28; DLB 15;
MTCW

Johnson, Robert 1911(?)-1938 .... TCLC 69

Johnson, Samuel 1709-1784LC 15; DA; DAB;
DAC; DAM MST; WLC
See also CDBLB 1660-1789; DLB 39, 95, 104,
142

Johnson, Uwe 1934-1984 .. CLC 5, 10, 15, 40
See also CA 1-4R; 112; CANR 1, 39; DLB 75;
MTCW

Johnston, George (Benson) 1913- .... CLC 51
See also CA 1-4R; CANR 5, 20; DLB 88

Johnston, Jennifer 1930- .... CLC 7
See also CA 85-88; DLB 14

Jolley, (Monica) Elizabeth 1923-CLC 46; SSC
19
See also CA 127; CAAS 13; CANR 59

Jones, Arthur Llewellyn 1863-1947
See Machen, Arthur
See also CA 104

Jones, D(ouglas) G(ordon) 1929- ..... CLC 10
See also CA 29-32R; CANR 13; DLB 53

Jones, David (Michael) 1895-1974CLC 2, 4, 7,
13, 42
See also CA 9-12R; 53-56; CANR 28; CDBLB
1945-1960; DLB 20, 100; MTCW

Jones, David Robert 1947-
See Bowie, David
See also CA 103

Jones, Diana Wynne 1934- .... CLC 26
See also AAYA 12; CA 49-52; CANR 4, 26,
56; CLR 23; DLB 161; JRDA; MAICYA;
SAAS 7; SATA 9, 70

Jones, Edward P. 1950-..................... CLC 76
See also BW 2; CA 142

Jones, Gayl 1949- ...... CLC 6, 9; BLC; DAM
MULT
See also BW 2; CA 77-80; CANR 27; DLB 33;
MTCW

Jones, James 1921-1977 ...... CLC 1, 3, 10, 39
See also AITN 1, 2; CA 1-4R; 69-72; CANR 6;
DLB 2, 143; MTCW

Jones, John J.
See Lovecraft, H(oward) P(hillips)

Jones, LeRoi .... CLC 1, 2, 3, 5, 10, 14
See also Baraka, Amiri

Jones, Louis B. .... CLC 65
See also CA 141

Jones, Madison (Percy, Jr.) 1925- ....CLC 4
See also CA 13-16R; CAAS 11; CANR 7, 54;
DLB 152

Jones, Mervyn 1922- .... CLC 10, 52
See also CA 45-48; CAAS 5; CANR 1; MTCW

Jones, Mick 1956(?)- .... CLC 30

Jones, Nettie (Pearl) 1941- .... CLC 34
See also BW 2; CA 137; CAAS 20

Jones, Preston 1936-1979 .... CLC 10
See also CA 73-76; 89-92; DLB 7

Jones, Robert F(rancis) 1934- ....CLC 7
See also CA 49-52; CANR 2, 61

Jones, Rod 1953-................................ CLC 50
See also CA 128

Jones, Terence Graham Parry 1942- CLC 21
See also Jones, Terry; Monty Python

See also CA 112; 116; CANR 35; INT 116

Jones, Terry
See Jones, Terence Graham Parry
See also SATA 67; SATA-Brief 51

Jones, Thom 1945(?)- .... CLC 81
See also CA 157

Jong, Erica 1942- CLC 4, 6, 8, 18, 83; DAM
NOV, POP
See also AITN 1; BEST 90:2; CA 73-76; CANR
26, 52; DLB 2, 5, 28, 152; INT CANR-26;
MTCW

Jonson, Ben(jamin) 1572(?)-1637 .. LC 6, 33;
DA; DAB; DAC; DAM DRAM, MST,
POET; DC 4; PC 17; WLC
See also CDBLB Before 1660; DLB 62, 121

Jordan, June 1936-........ CLC 5, 11, 23; DAM
MULT, POET
See also AAYA 2; BW 2; CA 33-36R; CANR
25; CLR 10; DLB 38; MAICYA; MTCW;
SATA 4

Jordan, Pat(rick M.) 1941- .... CLC 37
See also CA 33-36R

Jorgensen, Ivar
See Ellison, Harlan (Jay)

Jorgenson, Ivar
See Silverberg, Robert

Josephus, Flavius c. 37-100 .... CMLC 13

Josipovici, Gabriel 1940- .... CLC 6, 43
See also CA 37-40R; CAAS 8; CANR 47; DLB
14

Joubert, Joseph 1754-1824 .... NCLC 9

Jouve, Pierre Jean 1887-1976 ....CLC 47
See also CA 65-68

Joyce, James (Augustine Aloysius) 1882-1941
TCLC 3, 8, 16, 35, 52; DA; DAB; DAC;
DAM MST, NOV, POET; SSC 26; WLC
See also CA 104; 126; CDBLB 1914-1945;
DLB 10, 19, 36, 162; MTCW

Jozsef, Attila 1905-1937 .... TCLC 22
See also CA 116

Juana Ines de la Cruz 1651(?)-1695 ..... LC 5

Judd, Cyril
See Kornbluth, C(yril) M.; Pohl, Frederik

Julian of Norwich 1342(?)-1416(?) .... LC 6
See also DLB 146

Juniper, Alex
See Hospital, Janette Turner

Junius
See Luxemburg, Rosa

Just, Ward (Swift) 1935-............... CLC 4, 27
See also CA 25-28R; CANR 32; INT CANR-
32

Justice, Donald (Rodney) 1925- .. CLC 6, 19,
102; DAM POET
See also CA 5-8R; CANR 26, 54; DLBY 83;
INT CANR-26

Juvenal c. 55-c. 127 .... CMLC 8

Juvenis
See Bourne, Randolph S(illiman)

Kacew, Romain 1914-1980
See Gary, Romain
See also CA 108; 102

Kadare, Ismail 1936-.......................... CLC 52

Kadohata, Cynthia .... CLC 59
See also CA 140

Kafka, Franz 1883-1924TCLC 2, 6, 13, 29, 47,
53; DA; DAB; DAC; DAM MST, NOV;
SSC 29; WLC
See also CA 105; 126; DLB 81; MTCW

Kahanovitsch, Pinkhes
See Der Nister

Kahn, Roger 1927- .... CLC 30
See also CA 25-28R; CANR 44; DLB 171;

SATA 37

Kain, Saul
See Sassoon, Siegfried (Lorraine)

Kaiser, Georg 1878-1945 .... TCLC 9
See also CA 106; DLB 124

Kaletski, Alexander 1946- .... CLC 39
See also CA 118; 143

Kalidasa fl. c. 400- .... CMLC 9

Kallman, Chester (Simon) 1921-1975 CLC 2
See also CA 45-48; 53-56; CANR 3

Kaminsky, Melvin 1926-
See Brooks, Mel
See also CA 65-68; CANR 16

Kaminsky, Stuart M(elvin) 1934- .... CLC 59
See also CA 73-76; CANR 29, 53

Kane, Francis
See Robbins, Harold

Kane, Paul
See Simon, Paul (Frederick)

Kane, Wilson
See Bloch, Robert (Albert)

Kanin, Garson 1912-........................ CLC 22
See also AITN 1; CA 5-8R; CANR 7; DLB 7

Kaniuk, Yoram 1930- .... CLC 19
See also CA 134

Kant, Immanuel 1724-1804 .... NCLC 27
See also DLB 94

Kantor, MacKinlay 1904-1977 ....CLC 7
See also CA 61-64; 73-76; CANR 60; DLB 9,
102

Kaplan, David Michael 1946- .... CLC 50

Kaplan, James 1951- .... CLC 59
See also CA 135

Karageorge, Michael
See Anderson, Poul (William)

Karamzin, Nikolai Mikhailovich 1766-1826
NCLC 3
See also DLB 150

Karapanou, Margarita 1946-........... CLC 13
See also CA 101

Karinthy, Frigyes 1887-1938 .... TCLC 47

Karl, Frederick R(obert) 1927-........ CLC 34
See also CA 5-8R; CANR 3, 44

Kastel, Warren
See Silverberg, Robert

Kataev, Evgeny Petrovich 1903-1942
See Petrov, Evgeny
See also CA 120

Kataphusin
See Ruskin, John

Katz, Steve 1935-.............................. CLC 47
See also CA 25-28R; CAAS 14; CANR 12;
DLBY 83

Kauffman, Janet 1945- .... CLC 42
See also CA 117; CANR 43; DLBY 86

Kaufman, Bob (Garnell) 1925-1986 CLC 49
See also BW 1; CA 41-44R; 118; CANR 22;
DLB 16, 41

Kaufman, George S. 1889-1961CLC 38; DAM
DRAM
See also CA 108; 93-96; DLB 7; INT 108

Kaufman, Sue .... CLC 3, 8
See also Barondess, Sue K(aufman)

Kavafis, Konstantinos Petrou 1863-1933
See Cavafy, C(onstantine) P(eter)
See also CA 104

Kavan, Anna 1901-1968 .... CLC 5, 13, 82
See also CA 5-8R; CANR 6, 57; MTCW

Kavanagh, Dan
See Barnes, Julian (Patrick)

Kavanagh, Patrick (Joseph) 1904-1967 C L C
22
See also CA 123; 25-28R; DLB 15, 20; MTCW

Kawabata, Yasunari 1899-1972 **CLC 2, 5, 9, 18; DAM MULT; SSC 17**
See also CA 93-96; 33-36R; DLB 180

Kaye, M(ary) M(argaret) 1909- .... **CLC 28**
See also CA 89-92; CANR 24, 60; MTCW; SATA 62

Kaye, Mollie
See Kaye, M(ary) M(argaret)

Kaye-Smith, Sheila 1887-1956 .... **TCLC 20**
See also CA 118; DLB 36

Kaymor, Patrice Maguilene
See Senghor, Leopold Sedar

Kazan, Elia 1909- .... **CLC 6, 16, 63**
See also CA 21-24R; CANR 32

Kazantzakis, Nikos 1883(?)-1957 **TCLC 2, 5, 33**
See also CA 105; 132; MTCW

Kazin, Alfred 1915- .... **CLC 34, 38**
See also CA 1-4R; CAAS 7; CANR 1, 45; DLB 67

Keane, Mary Nesta (Skrine) 1904-1996
See Keane, Molly
See also CA 108; 114; 151

Keane, Molly .... **CLC 31**
See also Keane, Mary Nesta (Skrine)
See also INT 114

Keates, Jonathan 19(?)- .... **CLC 34**

Keaton, Buster 1895-1966 .... **CLC 20**

Keats, John 1795-1821 . **NCLC 8; DA; DAB; DAC; DAM MST, POET; PC 1; WLC**
See also CDBLB 1789-1832; DLB 96, 110

Keene, Donald 1922- .... **CLC 34**
See also CA 1-4R; CANR 5

Keillor, Garrison .... **CLC 40**
See also Keillor, Gary (Edward)
See also AAYA 2; BEST 89:3; DLBY 87; SATA 58

Keillor, Gary (Edward) 1942-
See Keillor, Garrison
See also CA 111; 117; CANR 36, 59; DAM POP; MTCW

Keith, Michael
See Hubbard, L(afayette) Ron(ald)

Keller, Gottfried 1819-1890 **NCLC 2; SSC 26**
See also DLB 129

Kellerman, Jonathan 1949- ... **CLC 44; DAM POP**
See also BEST 90:1; CA 106; CANR 29, 51; INT CANR-29

Kelley, William Melvin 1937- .... **CLC 22**
See also BW 1; CA 77-80; CANR 27; DLB 33

Kellogg, Marjorie 1922- .... **CLC 2**
See also CA 81-84

Kellow, Kathleen
See Hibbert, Eleanor Alice Burford

Kelly, M(ilton) T(erry) 1947- .... **CLC 55**
See also CA 97-100; CAAS 22; CANR 19, 43

Kelman, James 1946- .... **CLC 58, 86**
See also CA 148

Kemal, Yashar 1923- .... **CLC 14, 29**
See also CA 89-92; CANR 44

Kemble, Fanny 1809-1893 .... **NCLC 18**
See also DLB 32

Kemelman, Harry 1908-1996 .... **CLC 2**
See also AITN 1; CA 9-12R; 155; CANR 6; DLB 28

Kempe, Margery 1373(?)-1440(?) .... **LC 6**
See also DLB 146

Kempis, Thomas a 1380-1471 .... **LC 11**

Kendall, Henry 1839-1882 .... **NCLC 12**

Keneally, Thomas (Michael) 1935- **CLC 5, 8, 10, 14, 19, 27, 43; DAM NOV**
See also CA 85-88; CANR 10, 50; MTCW

Kennedy, Adrienne (Lita) 1931- ..... **CLC 66; BLC; DAM MULT; DC 5**
See also BW 2; CA 103; CAAS 20; CABS 3; CANR 26, 53; DLB 38

Kennedy, John Pendleton 1795-1870 **NCLC 2**
See also DLB 3

Kennedy, Joseph Charles 1929-
See Kennedy, X. J.
See also CA 1-4R; CANR 4, 30, 40; SATA 14, 86

Kennedy, William 1928- .. **CLC 6, 28, 34, 53; DAM NOV**
See also AAYA 1; CA 85-88; CANR 14, 31; DLB 143; DLBY 85; INT CANR-31; MTCW; SATA 57

Kennedy, X. J. .... **CLC 8, 42**
See also Kennedy, Joseph Charles
See also CAAS 9; CLR 27; DLB 5; SAAS 22

Kenny, Maurice (Francis) 1929- ..... **CLC 87; DAM MULT**
See also CA 144; CAAS 22; DLB 175; NNAL

Kent, Kelvin
See Kuttner, Henry

Kenton, Maxwell
See Southern, Terry

Kenyon, Robert O.
See Kuttner, Henry

Kerouac, Jack .... **CLC 1, 2, 3, 5, 14, 29, 61**
See also Kerouac, Jean-Louis Lebris de
See also CDALB 1941-1968; DLB 2, 16; DLBD 3; DLBY 95

Kerouac, Jean-Louis Lebris de 1922-1969
See Kerouac, Jack
See also AITN 1; CA 5-8R; 25-28R; CANR 26, 54; DA; DAB; DAC; DAM MST, NOV, POET, POP; MTCW; WLC

Kerr, Jean 1923- .... **CLC 22**
See also CA 5-8R; CANR 7; INT CANR-7

Kerr, M. E. .... **CLC 12, 35**
See also Meaker, Marijane (Agnes)
See also AAYA 2; CLR 29; SAAS 1

Kerr, Robert .... **CLC 55**

Kerrigan, (Thomas) Anthony 1918- **CLC 4, 6**
See also CA 49-52; CAAS 11; CANR 4

Kerry, Lois
See Duncan, Lois

Kesey, Ken (Elton) 1935- **CLC 1, 3, 6, 11, 46, 64; DA; DAB; DAC; DAM MST, NOV, POP; WLC**
See also CA 1-4R; CANR 22, 38; CDALB 1968-1988; DLB 2, 16; MTCW; SATA 66

Kesselring, Joseph (Otto) 1902-1967 **CLC 45; DAM DRAM, MST**
See also CA 150

Kessler, Jascha (Frederick) 1929- .... **CLC 4**
See also CA 17-20R; CANR 8, 48

Kettelkamp, Larry (Dale) 1933- .... **CLC 12**
See also CA 29-32R; CANR 16; SAAS 3; SATA 2

Key, Ellen 1849-1926 .... **TCLC 65**

Keyber, Conny
See Fielding, Henry

Keyes, Daniel 1927- **CLC 80; DA; DAC; DAM MST, NOV**
See also CA 17-20R; CANR 10, 26, 54; SATA 37

Keynes, John Maynard 1883-1946 **TCLC 64**
See also CA 114; DLBD 10

Khanshendel, Chiron
See Rose, Wendy

Khayyam, Omar 1048-1131 **CMLC 11; DAM POET; PC 8**

Kherdian, David 1931- .... **CLC 6, 9**

See also CA 21-24R; CAAS 2; CANR 39; CLR 24; JRDA; MAICYA; SATA 16, 74

Khlebnikov, Velimir .... **TCLC 20**
See also Khlebnikov, Viktor Vladimirovich

Khlebnikov, Viktor Vladimirovich 1885-1922
See Khlebnikov, Velimir
See also CA 117

Khodasevich, Vladislav (Felitsianovich) 1886-1939 .... **TCLC 15**
See also CA 115

Kielland, Alexander Lange 1849-1906 **TCLC 5**
See also CA 104

Kiely, Benedict 1919- .... **CLC 23, 43**
See also CA 1-4R; CANR 2; DLB 15

Kienzle, William X(avier) 1928- ..... **CLC 25; DAM POP**
See also CA 93-96; CAAS 1; CANR 9, 31, 59; INT CANR-31; MTCW

Kierkegaard, Soren 1813-1855 ...... **NCLC 34**

Killens, John Oliver 1916-1987 .... **CLC 10**
See also BW 2; CA 77-80; 123; CAAS 2; CANR 26; DLB 33

Killigrew, Anne 1660-1685 .... **LC 4**
See also DLB 131

Kim
See Simenon, Georges (Jacques Christian)

Kincaid, Jamaica 1949- .. **CLC 43, 68; BLC; DAM MULT, NOV**
See also AAYA 13; BW 2; CA 125; CANR 47, 59; DLB 157

King, Francis (Henry) 1923- **CLC 8, 53; DAM NOV**
See also CA 1-4R; CANR 1, 33; DLB 15, 139; MTCW

King, Martin Luther, Jr. 1929-1968 **CLC 83; BLC; DA; DAB; DAC; DAM MST, MULT; WLCS**
See also BW 2; CA 25-28; CANR 27, 44; CAP 2; MTCW; SATA 14

King, Stephen (Edwin) 1947- **CLC 12, 26, 37, 61; DAM NOV, POP; SSC 17**
See also AAYA 1, 17; BEST 90:1; CA 61-64; CANR 1, 30, 52; DLB 143; DLBY 80; JRDA; MTCW; SATA 9, 55

King, Steve
See King, Stephen (Edwin)

King, Thomas 1943- .... **CLC 89; DAC; DAM MULT**
See also CA 144; DLB 175; NNAL

Kingman, Lee .... **CLC 17**
See also Natti, (Mary) Lee
See also SAAS 3; SATA 1, 67

Kingsley, Charles 1819-1875 .... **NCLC 35**
See also DLB 21, 32, 163; YABC 2

Kingsley, Sidney 1906-1995 .... **CLC 44**
See also CA 85-88; 147; DLB 7

Kingsolver, Barbara 1955- **CLC 55, 81; DAM POP**
See also AAYA 15; CA 129; 134; CANR 60; INT 134

Kingston, Maxine (Ting Ting) Hong 1940- **CLC 12, 19, 58; DAM MULT, NOV; WLCS**
See also AAYA 8; CA 69-72; CANR 13, 38; DLB 173; DLBY 80; INT CANR-13; MTCW; SATA 53

Kinnell, Galway 1927- **CLC 1, 2, 3, 5, 13, 29**
See also CA 9-12R; CANR 10, 34; DLB 5; DLBY 87; INT CANR-34; MTCW

Kinsella, Thomas 1928- .... **CLC 4, 19**
See also CA 17-20R; CANR 15; DLB 27; MTCW

See also DLB 36, 156, 178

Machiavelli, Niccolo 1469-1527**LC 8, 36; DA; DAB; DAC; DAM MST; WLCS**

MacInnes, Colin 1914-1976 .... **CLC 4, 23**
See also CA 69-72; 65-68; CANR 21; DLB 14; MTCW

MacInnes, Helen (Clark) 1907-1985 **CLC 27, 39; DAM POP**
See also CA 1-4R; 117; CANR 1, 28, 58; DLB 87; MTCW; SATA 22; SATA-Obit 44

Mackay, Mary 1855-1924
See Corelli, Marie
See also CA 118

Mackenzie, Compton (Edward Montague) 1883-1972 .... **CLC 18**
See also CA 21-22; 37-40R; CAP 2; DLB 34, 100

Mackenzie, Henry 1745-1831 .... **NCLC 41**
See also DLB 39

Mackintosh, Elizabeth 1896(?)-1952
See Tey, Josephine
Sce also CA 110

MacLaren, James
See Grieve, C(hristopher) M(urray)

Mac Laverty, Bernard 1942- .... **CLC 31**
See also CA 116; 118; CANR 43; INT 118

MacLean, Alistair (Stuart) 1922(?)-1987**CLC 3, 13, 50, 63; DAM POP**
See also CA 57-60; 121; CANR 28, 61; MTCW; SATA 23; SATA-Obit 50

Maclean, Norman (Fitzroy) 1902-1990 . **CLC 78; DAM POP; SSC 13**
See also CA 102; 132; CANR 49

MacLeish, Archibald 1892-1982**CLC 3, 8, 14, 68; DAM POET**
See also CA 9-12R; 106; CANR 33; DLB 4, 7, 45; DLBY 82; MTCW

MacLennan, (John) Hugh 1907-1990 **CLC 2, 14, 92; DAC; DAM MST**
See also CA 5-8R; 142; CANR 33; DLB 68; MTCW

MacLeod, Alistair 1936-**CLC 56; DAC; DAM MST**
See also CA 123; DLB 60

MacNeice, (Frederick) Louis 1907-1963 **C L C 1, 4, 10, 53; DAB; DAM POET**
See also CA 85-88; CANR 61; DLB 10, 20; MTCW

MacNeill, Dand
See Fraser, George MacDonald

Macpherson, James 1736-1796 .... **LC 29**
See also DLB 109

Macpherson, (Jean) Jay 1931- .... **CLC 14**
See also CA 5-8R; DLB 53

MacShane, Frank 1927- .... **CLC 39**
See also CA 9-12R; CANR 3, 33; DLB 111

Macumber, Mari
See Sandoz, Mari(e Susette)

Madach, Imre 1823-1864 .... **NCLC 19**

Madden, (Jerry) David 1933- .... **CLC 5, 15**
See also CA 1-4R; CAAS 3; CANR 4, 45; DLB 6; MTCW

Maddern, Al(an)
See Ellison, Harlan (Jay)

Madhubuti, Haki R. 1942- **CLC 6, 73; BLC; DAM MULT, POET; PC 5**
See also Lee, Don L.
See also BW 2; CA 73-76; CANR 24, 51; DLB 5, 41; DLBD 8

Maepenn, Hugh
See Kuttner, Henry

Maepenn, K. H.
See Kuttner, Henry

Maeterlinck, Maurice 1862-1949 .... **TCLC 3; DAM DRAM**
See also CA 104; 136; SATA 66

Maginn, William 1794-1842 .... **NCLC 8**
See also DLB 110, 159

Mahapatra, Jayanta 1928- .... **CLC 33; DAM MULT**
See also CA 73-76; CAAS 9; CANR 15, 33

Mahfouz, Naguib (Abdel Aziz Al-Sabilgi) 1911(?)-
See Mahfuz, Najib
See also BEST 89:2; CA 128; CANR 55; DAM NOV; MTCW

Mahfuz, Najib .... **CLC 52, 55**
See also Mahfouz, Naguib (Abdel Aziz Al-Sabilgi)
See also DLBY 88

Mahon, Derek 1941- .... **CLC 27**
See also CA 113; 128; DLB 40

Mailer, Norman 1923-**CLC 1, 2, 3, 4, 5, 8, 11, 14, 28, 39, 74; DA; DAB; DAC; DAM MST, NOV, POP**
See also AITN 2; CA 9-12R; CABS 1; CANR 28; CDALB 1968-1988; DLB 2, 16, 28; DLBD 3; DLBY 80, 83; MTCW

Maillet, Antonine 1929- .... **CLC 54; DAC**
See also CA 115; 120; CANR 46; DLB 60; INT 120

Mais, Roger 1905-1955 .... **TCLC 8**
See also BW 1; CA 105; 124; DLB 125; MTCW

Maistre, Joseph de 1753-1821 .... **NCLC 37**

Maitland, Frederic 1850-1906 .... **TCLC 65**

Maitland, Sara (Louise) 1950- .... **CLC 49**
See also CA 69-72; CANR 13, 59

Major, Clarence 1936- **CLC 3, 19, 48; BLC; DAM MULT**
See also BW 2; CA 21-24R; CAAS 6; CANR 13, 25, 53; DLB 33

Major, Kevin (Gerald) 1949- .. **CLC 26; DAC**
See also AAYA 16; CA 97-100; CANR 21, 38; CLR 11; DLB 60; INT CANR-21; JRDA; MAICYA; SATA 32, 82

Maki, James
See Ozu, Yasujiro

Malabaila, Damiano
See Levi, Primo

Malamud, Bernard 1914-1986**CLC 1, 2, 3, 5, 8, 9, 11, 18, 27, 44, 78, 85; DA; DAB; DAC; DAM MST, NOV, POP; SSC 15; WLC**
See also AAYA 16; CA 5-8R; 118; CABS 1; CANR 28; CDALB 1941-1968; DLB 2, 28, 152; DLBY 80, 86; MTCW

Malaparte, Curzio 1898-1957 .... **TCLC 52**

Malcolm, Dan
See Silverberg, Robert

Malcolm X .... **CLC 82; BLC; WLCS**
See also Little, Malcolm

Malherbe, Francois de 1555-1628 .... **LC 5**

Mallarme, Stephane 1842-1898 **NCLC 4, 41; DAM POET; PC 4**

Mallet-Joris, Francoise 1930- .... **CLC 11**
See also CA 65-68; CANR 17; DLB 83

Malley, Ern
See McAuley, James Phillip

Mallowan, Agatha Christie
See Christie, Agatha (Mary Clarissa)

Maloff, Saul 1922- .... **CLC 5**
See also CA 33-36R

Malone, Louis
See MacNeice, (Frederick) Louis

Malone, Michael (Christopher) 1942-**CLC 43**
See also CA 77-80; CANR 14, 32, 57

Malory, (Sir) Thomas 1410(?)-1471(?)**LC 11;**

DA; DAB; DAC; DAM MST; WLCS
See also CDBLB Before 1660; DLB 146; SATA 59; SATA-Brief 33

Malouf, (George Joseph) David 1934-**CLC 28, 86**
See also CA 124; CANR 50

Malraux, (Georges-)Andre 1901-1976**CLC 1, 4, 9, 13, 15, 57; DAM NOV**
See also CA 21-22; 69-72; CANR 34, 58; CAP 2; DLB 72; MTCW

Malzberg, Barry N(athaniel) 1939- .... **CLC 7**
See also CA 61-64; CAAS 4; CANR 16; DLB 8

Mamet, David (Alan) 1947-**CLC 9, 15, 34, 46, 91; DAM DRAM; DC 4**
See also AAYA 3; CA 81-84; CABS 3; CANR 15, 41; DLB 7; MTCW

Mamoulian, Rouben (Zachary) 1897-1987 **CLC 16**
See also CA 25-28R; 124

Mandelstam, Osip (Emilievich) 1891(?)-1938(?) **TCLC 2, 6; PC 14**
See also CA 104; 150

Mander, (Mary) Jane 1877-1949 ... **TCLC 31**

Mandeville, John fl. 1350- .... **CMLC 19**
See also DLB 146

Mandiargues, Andre Pieyre de .... **CLC 41**
See also Pieyre de Mandiargues, Andre
See also DLB 83

Mandrake, Ethel Belle
See Thurman, Wallace (Henry)

Mangan, James Clarence 1803-1849**NCLC 27**

Maniere, J.-E.
See Giraudoux, (Hippolyte) Jean

Manley, (Mary) Delariviere 1672(?)-1724 **L C 1**
See also DLB 39, 80

Mann, Abel
See Creasey, John

Mann, Emily 1952- .... **DC 7**
See also CA 130; CANR 55

Mann, (Luiz) Heinrich 1871-1950 ... **TCLC 9**
See also CA 106; DLB 66

Mann, (Paul) Thomas 1875-1955 **TCLC 2, 8, 14, 21, 35, 44, 60; DA; DAB; DAC; DAM MST, NOV; SSC 5; WLC**
See also CA 104; 128; DLB 66; MTCW

Mannheim, Karl 1893-1947 .... **TCLC 65**

Manning, David
See Faust, Frederick (Schiller)

Manning, Frederic 1887(?)-1935 ... **TCLC 25**
See also CA 124

Manning, Olivia 1915-1980 .... **CLC 5, 19**
See also CA 5-8R; 101; CANR 29; MTCW

Mano, D. Keith 1942- .... **CLC 2, 10**
See also CA 25-28R; CAAS 6; CANR 26, 57; DLB 6

Mansfield, KatherineTCLC 2, 8, 39; DAB; SSC 9, 23; WLC
See also Beauchamp, Kathleen Mansfield
See also DLB 162

Manso, Peter 1940-............................**CLC 39**
See also CA 29-32R; CANR 44

Mantecon, Juan Jimenez
See Jimenez (Mantecon), Juan Ramon

Manton, Peter
See Creasey, John

Man Without a Spleen, A
See Chekhov, Anton (Pavlovich)

Manzoni, Alessandro 1785-1873 ....**NCLC 29**

Mapu, Abraham (ben Jekutiel) 1808-1867 **NCLC 18**

Mara, Sally

See also CA 89-92; 152; DLB 83

Mauriac, Francois (Charles) 1885-1970 **C L C 4, 9, 56; SSC 24**
See also CA 25-28; CAP 2; DLB 65; MTCW

Mavor, Osborne Henry 1888-1951
See Bridie, James
See also CA 104

Maxwell, William (Keepers, Jr.) 1908-**CLC 19**
See also CA 93-96; CANR 54; DLBY 80; INT 93-96

May, Elaine 1932- .... **CLC 16**
See also CA 124; 142; DLB 44

Mayakovski, Vladimir (Vladimirovich) 1893-1930 .... **TCLC 4, 18**
See also CA 104; 158

Mayhew, Henry 1812-1887 .... **NCLC 31**
See also DLB 18, 55

Mayle, Peter 1939(?)- .... **CLC 89**
See also CA 139

Maynard, Joyce 1953- .... **CLC 23**
See also CA 111; 129

Mayne, William (James Carter) 1928-**CLC 12**
See also AAYA 20; CA 9-12R; CANR 37; CLR 25; JRDA; MAICYA; SAAS 11; SATA 6, 68

Mayo, Jim
See L'Amour, Louis (Dearborn)

Maysles, Albert 1926- .... **CLC 16**
See also CA 29-32R

Maysles, David 1932- .... **CLC 16**

Mazer, Norma Fox 1931- .... **CLC 26**
See also AAYA 5; CA 69-72; CANR 12, 32; CLR 23; JRDA; MAICYA; SAAS 1; SATA 24, 67

Mazzini, Guiseppe 1805-1872 .... **NCLC 34**

McAuley, James Phillip 1917-1976 . **CLC 45**
See also CA 97-100

McBain, Ed
See Hunter, Evan

McBrien, William Augustine 1930- . **CLC 44**
See also CA 107

McCaffrey, Anne (Inez) 1926-**CLC 17; DAM NOV, POP**
See also AAYA 6; AITN 2; BEST 89:2; CA 25-28R; CANR 15, 35, 55; DLB 8; JRDA; MAICYA; MTCW; SAAS 11; SATA 8, 70

McCall, Nathan 1955(?)- .... **CLC 86**
See also CA 146

McCann, Arthur
See Campbell, John W(ood, Jr.)

McCann, Edson
See Pohl, Frederik

McCarthy, Charles, Jr. 1933-
See McCarthy, Cormac
See also CANR 42; DAM POP

McCarthy, Cormac 1933- **CLC 4, 57, 59, 101**
See also McCarthy, Charles, Jr.
See also DLB 6, 143

McCarthy, Mary (Therese) 1912-1989**CLC 1, 3, 5, 14, 24, 39, 59; SSC 24**
See also CA 5-8R; 129; CANR 16, 50; DLB 2; DLBY 81; INT CANR-16; MTCW

McCartney, (James) Paul 1942-. **CLC 12, 35**
See also CA 146

McCauley, Stephen (D.) 1955- .... **CLC 50**
See also CA 141

McClure, Michael (Thomas) 1932-**CLC 6, 10**
See also CA 21-24R; CANR 17, 46; DLB 16

McCorkle, Jill (Collins) 1958- .... **CLC 51**
See also CA 121; DLBY 87

McCourt, James 1941- .... **CLC 5**
See also CA 57-60

McCoy, Horace (Stanley) 1897-1955**TCLC 28**
See also CA 108; 155; DLB 9

McCrae, John 1872-1918 .... **TCLC 12**
See also CA 109; DLB 92

McCreigh, James
See Pohl, Frederik

McCullers, (Lula) Carson (Smith) 1917-1967 **CLC 1, 4, 10, 12, 48, 100; DA; DAB; DAC; DAM MST, NOV; SSC 9, 24; WLC**
See also AAYA 21; CA 5-8R; 25-28R; CABS 1, 3; CANR 18; CDALB 1941-1968; DLB 2, 7, 173; MTCW; SATA 27

McCulloch, John Tyler
See Burroughs, Edgar Rice

McCullough, Colleen 1938(?)-**CLC 27; DAM NOV, POP**
See also CA 81-84; CANR 17, 46; MTCW

McDermott, Alice 1953- .... **CLC 90**
See also CA 109; CANR 40

McElroy, Joseph 1930- .... **CLC 5, 47**
See also CA 17-20R

McEwan, Ian (Russell) 1948- .... **CLC 13, 66; DAM NOV**
See also BEST 90:4; CA 61-64; CANR 14, 41; DLB 14; MTCW

McFadden, David 1940- .... **CLC 48**
See also CA 104; DLB 60; INT 104

McFarland, Dennis 1950- .... **CLC 65**

McGahern, John 1934-**CLC 5, 9, 48; SSC 17**
See also CA 17-20R; CANR 29; DLB 14; MTCW

McGinley, Patrick (Anthony) 1937- .**CLC 41**
See also CA 120; 127; CANR 56; INT 127

McGinley, Phyllis 1905-1978 .... **CLC 14**
See also CA 9-12R; 77-80; CANR 19; DLB 11, 48; SATA 2, 44; SATA-Obit 24

McGinniss, Joe 1942- .... **CLC 32**
See also AITN 2; BEST 89:2; CA 25-28R; CANR 26; INT CANR-26

McGivern, Maureen Daly
See Daly, Maureen

McGrath, Patrick 1950- .... **CLC 55**
See also CA 136

McGrath, Thomas (Matthew) 1916-1990**CLC 28, 59; DAM POET**
See also CA 9-12R; 132; CANR 6, 33; MTCW; SATA 41; SATA-Obit 66

McGuane, Thomas (Francis III) 1939-**CLC 3, 7, 18, 45**
See also AITN 2; CA 49-52; CANR 5, 24, 49; DLB 2; DLBY 80; INT CANR-24; MTCW

McGuckian, Medbh 1950- ..... **CLC 48; DAM POET**
See also CA 143; DLB 40

McHale, Tom 1942(?)-1982 .... **CLC 3, 5**
See also AITN 1; CA 77-80; 106

McIlvanney, William 1936- .... **CLC 42**
See also CA 25-28R; CANR 61; DLB 14

McIlwraith, Maureen Mollie Hunter
See Hunter, Mollie
See also SATA 2

McInerney, Jay 1955- ... **CLC 34; DAM POP**
See also AAYA 18; CA 116; 123; CANR 45; INT 123

McIntyre, Vonda N(eel) 1948- .... **CLC 18**
See also CA 81-84; CANR 17, 34; MTCW

McKay, ClaudeTCLC 7, 41; BLC; DAB; PC 2
See also McKay, Festus Claudius
See also DLB 4, 45, 51, 117

McKay, Festus Claudius 1889-1948
See McKay, Claude
See also BW 1; CA 104; 124; DA; DAC; DAM MST, MULT, NOV, POET; MTCW; WLC

McKuen, Rod 1933- .... **CLC 1, 3**
See also AITN 1; CA 41-44R; CANR 40

McLoughlin, R. B.
See Mencken, H(enry) L(ouis)

McLuhan, (Herbert) Marshall 1911-1980 **CLC 37, 83**
See also CA 9-12R; 102; CANR 12, 34, 61; DLB 88; INT CANR-12; MTCW

McMillan, Terry (L.) 1951-**CLC 50, 61; DAM MULT, NOV, POP**
See also AAYA 21; BW 2; CA 140; CANR 60

McMurtry, Larry (Jeff) 1936-**CLC 2, 3, 7, 11, 27, 44; DAM NOV, POP**
See also AAYA 15; AITN 2; BEST 89:2; CA 5-8R; CANR 19, 43; CDALB 1968-1988; DLB 2, 143; DLBY 80, 87; MTCW

McNally, T. M. 1961- .... **CLC 82**

McNally, Terrence 1939- ... **CLC 4, 7, 41, 91; DAM DRAM**
See also CA 45-48; CANR 2, 56; DLB 7

McNamer, Deirdre 1950- .... **CLC 70**

McNeile, Herman Cyril 1888-1937
See Sapper
See also DLB 77

McNickle, (William) D'Arcy 1904-1977 **C L C 89; DAM MULT**
See also CA 9-12R; 85-88; CANR 5, 45; DLB 175; NNAL; SATA-Obit 22

McPhee, John (Angus) 1931- ....**CLC 36**
See also BEST 90:1; CA 65-68; CANR 20, 46; MTCW

McPherson, James Alan 1943- ... **CLC 19, 77**
See also BW 1; CA 25-28R; CAAS 17; CANR 24; DLB 38; MTCW

McPherson, William (Alexander) 1933- **C L C 34**
See also CA 69-72; CANR 28; INT CANR-28

Mead, Margaret 1901-1978 ....**CLC 37**
See also AITN 1; CA 1-4R; 81-84; CANR 4; MTCW; SATA-Obit 20

Meaker, Marijane (Agnes) 1927-
See Kerr, M. E.
See also CA 107; CANR 37; INT 107; JRDA; MAICYA; MTCW; SATA 20, 61

Medoff, Mark (Howard) 1940- ... **CLC 6, 23; DAM DRAM**
See also AITN 1; CA 53-56; CANR 5; DLB 7; INT CANR-5

Medvedev, P. N.
See Bakhtin, Mikhail Mikhailovich

Meged, Aharon
See Megged, Aharon

Meged, Aron
See Megged, Aharon

Megged, Aharon 1920-........................ **CLC 9**
See also CA 49-52; CAAS 13; CANR 1

Mehta, Ved (Parkash) 1934-..............**CLC 37**
See also CA 1-4R; CANR 2, 23; MTCW

Melanter
See Blackmore, R(ichard) D(oddridge)

Melikow, Loris
See Hofmannsthal, Hugo von

Melmoth, Sebastian
See Wilde, Oscar (Fingal O'Flahertie Wills)

Meltzer, Milton 1915-........................**CLC 26**
See also AAYA 8; CA 13-16R; CANR 38; CLR 13; DLB 61; JRDA; MAICYA; SAAS 1; SATA 1, 50, 80

Melville, Herman 1819-1891**NCLC 3, 12, 29, 45, 49; DA; DAB; DAC; DAM MST, NOV; SSC 1, 17; WLC**
See also CDALB 1640-1865; DLB 3, 74; SATA 59

Menander c. 342B.C.-c. 292B.C. .... **CMLC 9; DAM DRAM; DC 3**

See also AAYA 1; CA 1-4R; CANR 4, 24, 42; CLR 20; DLB 68; INT CANAR-24; JRDA; MAICYA; MTCW; SATA 3, 55
Moyers, Bill 1934- .... **CLC 74**
See also AITN 2; CA 61-64; CANR 31, 52
Mphahlele, Es'kia
See Mphahlele, Ezekiel
See also DLB 125
Mphahlele, Ezekiel 1919-**CLC 25; BLC; DAM MULT**
See also Mphahlele, Es'kia
See also BW 2; CA 81-84; CANR 26
Mqhayi, S(amuel) E(dward) K(rune Loliwe) 1875-1945**TCLC 25; BLC; DAM MULT**
See also CA 153
Mrozek, Slawomir 1930- .... **CLC 3, 13**
See also CA 13-16R; CAAS 10; CANR 29; MTCW
Mrs. Belloc-Lowndes
See Lowndes, Marie Adelaide (Belloc)
Mtwa, Percy (?)- .... **CLC 47**
Mueller, Lisel 1924- .... **CLC 13, 51**
See also CA 93-96; DLB 105
Muir, Edwin 1887-1959 .... **TCLC 2**
See also CA 104; DLB 20, 100
Muir, John 1838-1914 .... **TCLC 28**
Mujica Lainez, Manuel 1910-1984 .. **CLC 31**
See also Lainez, Manuel Mujica
See also CA 81-84; 112; CANR 32; HW
Mukherjee, Bharati 1940-**CLC 53; DAM NOV**
See also BEST 89:2; CA 107; CANR 45; DLB 60; MTCW
Muldoon, Paul 1951-**CLC 32, 72; DAM POET**
See also CA 113; 129; CANR 52; DLB 40; INT 129
Mulisch, Harry 1927- .... **CLC 42**
See also CA 9-12R; CANR 6, 26, 56
Mull, Martin 1943- .... **CLC 17**
See also CA 105
Mulock, Dinah Maria
See Craik, Dinah Maria (Mulock)
Munford, Robert 1737(?)-1783 .... **LC 5**
See also DLB 31
Mungo, Raymond 1946- .... **CLC 72**
See also CA 49-52; CANR 2
Munro, Alice 1931- .... **CLC 6, 10, 19, 50, 95; DAC; DAM MST, NOV; SSC 3; WLCS**
See also AITN 2; CA 33-36R; CANR 33, 53; DLB 53; MTCW; SATA 29
Munro, H(ector) H(ugh) 1870-1916
See Saki
See also CA 104; 130; CDBLB 1890-1914; DA; DAB; DAC; DAM MST, NOV; DLB 34, 162; MTCW; WLC
Murasaki, Lady .... **CMLC 1**
Murdoch, (Jean) Iris 1919-**CLC 1, 2, 3, 4, 6, 8, 11, 15, 22, 31, 51; DAB; DAC; DAM MST, NOV**
See also CA 13-16R; CANR 8, 43; CDBLB 1960 to Present; DLB 14; INT CANR-8; MTCW
Murfree, Mary Noailles 1850-1922 ... **SSC 22**
See also CA 122; DLB 12, 74
Murnau, Friedrich Wilhelm
See Plumpe, Friedrich Wilhelm
Murphy, Richard 1927- .... **CLC 41**
See also CA 29-32R; DLB 40
Murphy, Sylvia 1937- .... **CLC 34**
See also CA 121
Murphy, Thomas (Bernard) 1935- .. **CLC 51**
See also CA 101
Murray, Albert L. 1916- .... **CLC 73**
See also BW 2; CA 49-52; CANR 26, 52; DLB

38
Murray, Judith Sargent 1751-1820**NCLC 63**
See also DLB 37
Murray, Les(lie) A(llan) 1938-**CLC 40; DAM POET**
See also CA 21-24R; CANR 11, 27, 56
Murry, J. Middleton
See Murry, John Middleton
Murry, John Middleton 1889-1957 **TCLC 16**
See also CA 118; DLB 149
Musgrave, Susan 1951- .... **CLC 13, 54**
See also CA 69-72; CANR 45
Musil, Robert (Edler von) 1880-1942 . **T C L C 12, 68; SSC 18**
See also CA 109; CANR 55; DLB 81, 124
Muske, Carol 1945- ....**CLC 90**
See also Muske-Dukes, Carol (Anne)
Muske-Dukes, Carol (Anne) 1945-
See Muske, Carol
See also CA 65-68; CANR 32
Musset, (Louis Charles) Alfred de 1810-1857 **NCLC 7**
My Brother's Brother
See Chekhov, Anton (Pavlovich)
Myers, L(eopold) H(amilton) 1881-1944 **TCLC 59**
See also CA 157; DLB 15
Myers, Walter Dean 1937- ..... **CLC 35; BLC; DAM MULT, NOV**
See also AAYA 4; BW 2; CA 33-36R; CANR 20, 42; CLR 4, 16, 35; DLB 33; INT CANR-20; JRDA; MAICYA; SAAS 2; SATA 41, 71; SATA-Brief 27
Myers, Walter M.
See Myers, Walter Dean
Myles, Symon
See Follett, Ken(neth Martin)
Nabokov, Vladimir (Vladimirovich) 1899-1977 **CLC 1, 2, 3, 6, 8, 11, 15, 23, 44, 46, 64; DA; DAB; DAC; DAM MST, NOV; SSC 11; WLC**
See also CA 5-8R; 69-72; CANR 20; CDALB 1941-1968; DLB 2; DLBD 3; DLBY 80, 91; MTCW
Nagai Kafu 1879-1959 .... **TCLC 51**
See also Nagai Sokichi
See also DLB 180
Nagai Sokichi 1879-1959
See Nagai Kafu
See also CA 117
Nagy, Laszlo 1925-1978 ....**CLC 7**
See also CA 129; 112
Naipaul, Shiva(dhar Srinivasa) 1945-1985 **CLC 32, 39; DAM NOV**
See also CA 110; 112; 116; CANR 33; DLB 157; DLBY 85; MTCW
Naipaul, V(idiadhar) S(urajprasad) 1932-**CLC 4, 7, 9, 13, 18, 37; DAB; DAC; DAM MST, NOV**
See also CA 1-4R; CANR 1, 33, 51; CDBLB 1960 to Present; DLB 125; DLBY 85; MTCW
Nakos, Lilika 1899(?)- ....**CLC 29**
Narayan, R(asipuram) K(rishnaswami) 1906-**CLC 7, 28, 47; DAM NOV; SSC 25**
See also CA 81-84; CANR 33, 61; MTCW; SATA 62
Nash, (Frediric) Ogden 1902-1971 . **CLC 23; DAM POET**
See also CA 13-14; 29-32R; CANR 34, 61; CAP 1; DLB 11; MAICYA; MTCW; SATA 2, 46
Nathan, Daniel
See Dannay, Frederic

Nathan, George Jean 1882-1958 .... **TCLC 18**
See also Hatteras, Owen
See also CA 114; DLB 137
Natsume, Kinnosuke 1867-1916
See Natsume, Soseki
See also CA 104
Natsume, Soseki 1867-1916 .... **TCLC 2, 10**
See also Natsume, Kinnosuke
See also DLB 180
Natti, (Mary) Lee 1919-
See Kingman, Lee
See also CA 5-8R; CANR 2
Naylor, Gloria 1950- **CLC 28, 52; BLC; DA; DAC; DAM MST, MULT, NOV, POP; WLCS**
See also AAYA 6; BW 2; CA 107; CANR 27, 51; DLB 173; MTCW
Neihardt, John Gneisenau 1881-1973**CLC 32**
See also CA 13-14; CAP 1; DLB 9, 54
Nekrasov, Nikolai Alekseevich 1821-1878 **NCLC 11**
Nelligan, Emile 1879-1941 .... **TCLC 14**
See also CA 114; DLB 92
Nelson, Willie 1933- .... **CLC 17**
See also CA 107
Nemerov, Howard (Stanley) 1920-1991**CLC 2, 6, 9, 36; DAM POET**
See also CA 1-4R; 134; CABS 2; CANR 1, 27, 53; DLB 5, 6; DLBY 83; INT CANR-27; MTCW
Neruda, Pablo 1904-1973**CLC 1, 2, 5, 7, 9, 28, 62; DA; DAB; DAC; DAM MST, MULT, POET; HLC; PC 4; WLC**
See also CA 19-20; 45-48; CAP 2; HW; MTCW
Nerval, Gerard de 1808-1855**NCLC 1; PC 13; SSC 18**
Nervo, (Jose) Amado (Ruiz de) 1870-1919 **TCLC 11**
See also CA 109; 131; HW
Nessi, Pio Baroja y
See Baroja (y Nessi), Pio
Nestroy, Johann 1801-1862 ....**NCLC 42**
See also DLB 133
Netterville, Luke
See O'Grady, Standish (James)
Neufeld, John (Arthur) 1938- .... **CLC 17**
See also AAYA 11; CA 25-28R; CANR 11, 37, 56; MAICYA; SAAS 3; SATA 6, 81
Neville, Emily Cheney 1919- .... **CLC 12**
See also CA 5-8R; CANR 3, 37; JRDA; MAICYA; SAAS 2; SATA 1
Newbound, Bernard Slade 1930-
See Slade, Bernard
See also CA 81-84; CANR 49; DAM DRAM
Newby, P(ercy) H(oward) 1918- . **CLC 2, 13; DAM NOV**
See also CA 5-8R; CANR 32; DLB 15; MTCW
Newlove, Donald 1928- ....**CLC 6**
See also CA 29-32R; CANR 25
Newlove, John (Herbert) 1938- .... **CLC 14**
See also CA 21-24R; CANR 9, 25
Newman, Charles 1938- .... **CLC 2, 8**
See also CA 21-24R
Newman, Edwin (Harold) 1919- ...... **CLC 14**
See also AITN 1; CA 69-72; CANR 5
Newman, John Henry 1801-1890 ...**NCLC 38**
See also DLB 18, 32, 55
Newton, Suzanne 1936- .... **CLC 35**
See also CA 41-44R; CANR 14; JRDA; SATA 5, 77
Nexo, Martin Andersen 1869-1954 **TCLC 43**
Nezval, Vitezslav 1900-1958 .... **TCLC 44**
See also CA 123

Philips, Katherine 1632-1664 .... **LC 30**
See also DLB 131
Philipson, Morris H. 1926- .... **CLC 53**
See also CA 1-4R; CANR 4
Phillips, Caryl 1958- . **CLC 96; DAM MULT**
See also BW 2; CA 141; DLB 157
Phillips, David Graham 1867-1911 **TCLC 44**
See also CA 108; DLB 9, 12
Phillips, Jack
See Sandburg, Carl (August)
Phillips, Jayne Anne 1952-**CLC 15, 33; SSC 16**
See also CA 101; CANR 24, 50; DLBY 80; INT CANR-24; MTCW
Phillips, Richard
See Dick, Philip K(indred)
Phillips, Robert (Schaeffer) 1938- ... **CLC 28**
See also CA 17-20R; CAAS 13; CANR 8; DLB 105
Phillips, Ward
See Lovecraft, H(oward) P(hillips)
Piccolo, Lucio 1901-1969 .... **CLC 13**
See also CA 97-100; DLB 114
Pickthall, Marjorie L(owry) C(hristie) 1883-1922 .... **TCLC 21**
See also CA 107; DLB 92
Pico della Mirandola, Giovanni 1463-1494**LC 15**
Piercy, Marge 1936- **CLC 3, 6, 14, 18, 27, 62**
See also CA 21-24R; CAAS 1; CANR 13, 43; DLB 120; MTCW
Piers, Robert
See Anthony, Piers
Pieyre de Mandiargues, Andre 1909-1991
See Mandiargues, Andre Pieyre de
See also CA 103; 136; CANR 22
Pilnyak, Boris.....................................**TCLC 23**
See also Vogau, Boris Andreyevich
Pincherle, Alberto 1907-1990.... **CLC 11, 18; DAM NOV**
See also Moravia, Alberto
See also CA 25-28R; 132; CANR 33; MTCW
Pinckney, Darryl 1953- .... **CLC 76**
See also BW 2; CA 143
Pindar 518B.C.-446B.C..... **CMLC 12; PC 19**
See also DLB 176
Pineda, Cecile 1942- .... **CLC 39**
See also CA 118
Pinero, Arthur Wing 1855-1934 .. **TCLC 32; DAM DRAM**
See also CA 110; 153; DLB 10
Pinero, Miguel (Antonio Gomez) 1946-1988 **CLC 4, 55**
See also CA 61-64; 125; CANR 29; HW
Pinget, Robert 1919- .... **CLC 7, 13, 37**
See also CA 85-88; DLB 83
Pink Floyd
See Barrett, (Roger) Syd; Gilmour, David; Mason, Nick; Waters, Roger; Wright, Rick
Pinkney, Edward 1802-1828........... **NCLC 31**
Pinkwater, Daniel Manus 1941- .... **CLC 35**
See also Pinkwater, Manus
See also AAYA 1; CA 29-32R; CANR 12, 38; CLR 4; JRDA; MAICYA; SAAS 3; SATA 46, 76
Pinkwater, Manus
See Pinkwater, Daniel Manus
See also SATA 8
Pinsky, Robert 1940-**CLC 9, 19, 38, 94; DAM POET**
See also CA 29-32R; CAAS 4; CANR 58; DLBY 82
Pinta, Harold
See Pinter, Harold

Pinter, Harold 1930-**CLC 1, 3, 6, 9, 11, 15, 27, 58, 73; DA; DAB; DAC; DAM DRAM, MST; WLC**
See also CA 5-8R; CANR 33; CDBLB 1960 to Present; DLB 13; MTCW
Piozzi, Hester Lynch (Thrale) 1741-1821 **NCLC 57**
See also DLB 104, 142
Pirandello, Luigi 1867-1936**TCLC 4, 29; DA; DAB; DAC; DAM DRAM, MST; DC 5; SSC 22; WLC**
See also CA 104; 153
Pirsig, Robert M(aynard) 1928-**CLC 4, 6, 73; DAM POP**
See also CA 53-56; CANR 42; MTCW; SATA 39
Pisarev, Dmitry Ivanovich 1840-1868 **N C L C 25**
Pix, Mary (Griffith) 1666-1709 .... **LC 8**
See also DLB 80
Pixerecourt, Guilbert de 1773-1844**NCLC 39**
Plaatje, Sol(omon) T(shekisho) 1876-1932 **TCLC 73**
See also BW 2; CA 141
Plaidy, Jean
See Hibbert, Eleanor Alice Burford
Planche, James Robinson 1796-1880**NCLC 42**
Plant, Robert 1948- ....**CLC 12**
Plante, David (Robert) 1940- **CLC 7, 23, 38; DAM NOV**
See also CA 37-40R; CANR 12, 36, 58; DLBY 83; INT CANR-12; MTCW
Plath, Sylvia 1932-1963 **CLC 1, 2, 3, 5, 9, 11, 14, 17, 50, 51, 62; DA; DAB; DAC; DAM MST, POET; PC 1; WLC**
See also AAYA 13; CA 19-20; CANR 34; CAP 2; CDALB 1941-1968; DLB 5, 6, 152; MTCW
Plato 428(?)B.C.-348(?)B.C.... **CMLC 8; DA; DAB; DAC; DAM MST; WLCS**
See also DLB 176
Platonov, Andrei ....**TCLC 14**
See also Klimentov, Andrei Platonovich
Platt, Kin 1911-.................................**CLC 26**
See also AAYA 11; CA 17-20R; CANR 11; JRDA; SAAS 17; SATA 21, 86
Plautus c. 251B.C.-184B.C..................... **DC 6**
Plick et Plock
See Simenon, Georges (Jacques Christian)
Plimpton, George (Ames) 1927-........**CLC 36**
See also AITN 1; CA 21-24R; CANR 32; MTCW; SATA 10
Pliny the Elder c. 23-79 .... **CMLC 23**
Plomer, William Charles Franklin 1903-1973 **CLC 4, 8**
See also CA 21-22; CANR 34; CAP 2; DLB 20, 162; MTCW; SATA 24
Plowman, Piers
See Kavanagh, Patrick (Joseph)
Plum, J.
See Wodehouse, P(elham) G(renville)
Plumly, Stanley (Ross) 1939- ....**CLC 33**
See also CA 108; 110; DLB 5; INT 110
Plumpe, Friedrich Wilhelm 1888-1931**T C L C 53**
See also CA 112
Poe, Edgar Allan 1809-1849**NCLC 1, 16, 55; DA; DAB; DAC; DAM MST, POET; PC 1; SSC 1, 22; WLC**
See also AAYA 14; CDALB 1640-1865; DLB 3, 59, 73, 74; SATA 23
Poet of Titchfield Street, The
See Pound, Ezra (Weston Loomis)

Pohl, Frederik 1919- .... **CLC 18; SSC 25**
See also CA 61-64; CAAS 1; CANR 11, 37; DLB 8; INT CANR-11; MTCW; SATA 24
Poirier, Louis 1910-
See Gracq, Julien
See also CA 122; 126
Poitier, Sidney 1927- .... **CLC 26**
See also BW 1; CA 117
Polanski, Roman 1933- .... **CLC 16**
See also CA 77-80
Poliakoff, Stephen 1952- .... **CLC 38**
See also CA 106; DLB 13
Police, The
See Copeland, Stewart (Armstrong); Summers, Andrew James; Sumner, Gordon Matthew
Polidori, John William 1795-1821 .**NCLC 51**
See also DLB 116
Pollitt, Katha 1949- .... **CLC 28**
See also CA 120; 122; MTCW
Pollock, (Mary) Sharon 1936-**CLC 50; DAC; DAM DRAM, MST**
See also CA 141; DLB 60
Polo, Marco 1254-1324 .... **CMLC 15**
Polonsky, Abraham (Lincoln) 1910- **CLC 92**
See also CA 104; DLB 26; INT 104
Polybius c. 200B.C.-c. 118B.C. .... **CMLC 17**
See also DLB 176
Pomerance, Bernard 1940-....**CLC 13; DAM DRAM**
See also CA 101; CANR 49
Ponge, Francis (Jean Gaston Alfred) 1899-1988 **CLC 6, 18; DAM POET**
See also CA 85-88; 126; CANR 40
Pontoppidan, Henrik 1857-1943 .... **TCLC 29**
Poole, Josephine .... **CLC 17**
See also Helyar, Jane Penelope Josephine
See also SAAS 2; SATA 5
Popa, Vasko 1922-1991 .... **CLC 19**
See also CA 112; 148; DLB 181
Pope, Alexander 1688-1744 **LC 3; DA; DAB; DAC; DAM MST, POET; WLC**
See also CDBLB 1660-1789; DLB 95, 101
Porter, Connie (Rose) 1959(?)- .... **CLC 70**
See also BW 2; CA 142; SATA 81
Porter, Gene(va Grace) Stratton 1863(?)-1924 **TCLC 21**
See also CA 112
Porter, Katherine Anne 1890-1980**CLC 1, 3, 7, 10, 13, 15, 27, 101; DA; DAB; DAC; DAM MST, NOV; SSC 4**
See also AITN 2; CA 1-4R; 101; CANR 1; DLB 4, 9, 102; DLBD 12; DLBY 80; MTCW; SATA 39; SATA-Obit 23
Porter, Peter (Neville Frederick) 1929-**CLC 5, 13, 33**
See also CA 85-88; DLB 40
Porter, William Sydney 1862-1910
See Henry, O.
See also CA 104; 131; CDALB 1865-1917; DA; DAB; DAC; DAM MST; DLB 12, 78, 79; MTCW; YABC 2
Portillo (y Pacheco), Jose Lopez
See Lopez Portillo (y Pacheco), Jose
Post, Melville Davisson 1869-1930 **TCLC 39**
See also CA 110
Potok, Chaim 1929- . **CLC 2, 7, 14, 26; DAM NOV**
See also AAYA 15; AITN 1, 2; CA 17-20R; CANR 19, 35; DLB 28, 152; INT CANR-19; MTCW; SATA 33
Potter, (Helen) Beatrix 1866-1943
See Webb, (Martha) Beatrice (Potter)
See also MAICYA

See also CA 9-12R; CANR 20, 53; DLB 5, 67;
MTCW
Rich, Barbara
See Graves, Robert (von Ranke)
Rich, Robert
See Trumbo, Dalton
Richard, Keith .... **CLC 17**
See also Richards, Keith
Richards, David Adams 1950- **CLC 59; DAC**
See also CA 93-96; CANR 60; DLB 53
Richards, I(vor) A(rmstrong) 1893-1979**C L C
14, 24**
See also CA 41-44R; 89-92; CANR 34; DLB
27
Richards, Keith 1943-
See Richard, Keith
See also CA 107
Richardson, Anne
See Roiphe, Anne (Richardson)
Richardson, Dorothy Miller 1873-1957**TCLC
3**
See also CA 104; DLB 36
Richardson, Ethel Florence (Lindesay) 1870-
1946
See Richardson, Henry Handel
See also CA 105
Richardson, Henry Handel .... **TCLC 4**
See also Richardson, Ethel Florence (Lindesay)
Richardson, John 1796-1852**NCLC 55; DAC**
See also DLB 99
Richardson, Samuel 1689-1761 .... **LC 1; DA;
DAB; DAC; DAM MST, NOV; WLC**
See also CDBLB 1660-1789; DLB 39
Richler, Mordecai 1931-**CLC 3, 5, 9, 13, 18, 46,
70; DAC; DAM MST, NOV**
See also AITN 1; CA 65-68; CANR 31; CLR
17; DLB 53; MAICYA; MTCW; SATA 44;
SATA-Brief 27
Richter, Conrad (Michael) 1890-1968**CLC 30**
See also AAYA 21; CA 5-8R; 25-28R; CANR
23; DLB 9; MTCW; SATA 3
Ricostranza, Tom
See Ellis, Trey
Riddell, J. H. 1832-1906 .... **TCLC 40**
Riding, Laura .... **CLC 3, 7**
See also Jackson, Laura (Riding)
Riefenstahl, Berta Helene Amalia 1902-
See Riefenstahl, Leni
See also CA 108
Riefenstahl, Leni .... **CLC 16**
See also Riefenstah!, Berta Helene Amalia
Riffe, Ernest
See Bergman, (Ernst) Ingmar
Riggs, (Rolla) Lynn 1899-1954 ..... **TCLC 56;
DAM MULT**
See also CA 144; DLB 175; NNAL
Riley, James Whitcomb 1849-1916**TCLC 51;
DAM POET**
See also CA 118; 137; MAICYA; SATA 17
Riley, Tex
See Creasey, John
Rilke, Rainer Maria 1875-1926**TCLC 1, 6, 19;
DAM POET; PC 2**
See also CA 104; 132; DLB 81; MTCW
Rimbaud, (Jean Nicolas) Arthur 1854-1891
**NCLC 4, 35; DA; DAB; DAC; DAM MST,
POET; PC 3; WLC**
Rinehart, Mary Roberts 1876-1958**TCLC 52**
See also CA 108
Ringmaster, The
See Mencken, H(enry) L(ouis)
Ringwood, Gwen(dolyn Margaret) Pharis
1910-1984 .... **CLC 48**

See also CA 148; 112; DLB 88
Rio, Michel 19(?)- .... **CLC 43**
Ritsos, Giannes
See Ritsos, Yannis
Ritsos, Yannis 1909-1990 .... **CLC 6, 13, 31**
See also CA 77-80; 133; CANR 39, 61; MTCW
Ritter, Erika 1948(?)- .... **CLC 52**
Rivera, Jose Eustasio 1889-1928 ... **TCLC 35**
See also HW
Rivers, Conrad Kent 1933-1968 .... **CLC 1**
See also BW 1; CA 85-88; DLB 41
Rivers, Elfrida
See Bradley, Marion Zimmer
Riverside, John
See Heinlein, Robert A(nson)
Rizal, Jose 1861-1896 .... **NCLC 27**
Roa Bastos, Augusto (Antonio) 1917-**CLC 45;
DAM MULT; HLC**
See also CA 131; DLB 113; HW
Robbe-Grillet, Alain 1922-**CLC 1, 2, 4, 6, 8, 10,
14, 43**
See also CA 9-12R; CANR 33; DLB 83; MTCW
Robbins, Harold 1916- ... **CLC 5; DAM NOV**
See also CA 73-76; CANR 26, 54; MTCW
Robbins, Thomas Eugene 1936-
See Robbins, Tom
See also CA 81-84; CANR 29, 59; DAM NOV,
POP; MTCW
Robbins, Tom .... **CLC 9, 32, 64**
See also Robbins, Thomas Eugene
See also BEST 90:3; DLBY 80
Robbins, Trina 1938- .... **CLC 21**
See also CA 128
Roberts, Charles G(eorge) D(ouglas) 1860-1943
TCLC 8
See also CA 105; CLR 33; DLB 92; SATA 88;
SATA-Brief 29
Roberts, Elizabeth Madox 1886-1941 **T C L C
68**
See also CA 111; DLB 9, 54, 102; SATA 33;
SATA-Brief 27
Roberts, Kate 1891-1985 .... **CLC 15**
See also CA 107; 116
Roberts, Keith (John Kingston) 1935-**CLC 14**
See also CA 25-28R; CANR 46
Roberts, Kenneth (Lewis) 1885-1957**TCLC 23**
See also CA 109; DLB 9
Roberts, Michele (B.) 1949- .... **CLC 48**
See also CA 115; CANR 58
Robertson, Ellis
See Ellison, Harlan (Jay); Silverberg, Robert
Robertson, Thomas William 1829-1871**NCLC
35; DAM DRAM**
Robeson, Kenneth
See Dent, Lester
Robinson, Edwin Arlington 1869-1935**T C L C
5; DA; DAC; DAM MST, POET; PC 1**
See also CA 104; 133; CDALB 1865-1917;
DLB 54; MTCW
Robinson, Henry Crabb 1775-1867**NCLC 15**
See also DLB 107
Robinson, Jill 1936- .... **CLC 10**
See also CA 102; INT 102
Robinson, Kim Stanley 1952-............ **CLC 34**
See also CA 126
Robinson, Lloyd
See Silverberg, Robert
Robinson, Marilynne 1944- .... **CLC 25**
See also CA 116
Robinson, Smokey .... **CLC 21**
See also Robinson, William, Jr.
Robinson, William, Jr. 1940-
See Robinson, Smokey

See also CA 116
Robison, Mary 1949-................... **CLC 42, 98**
See also CA 113; 116; DLB 130; INT 116
Rod, Edouard 1857-1910 .... **TCLC 52**
Roddenberry, Eugene Wesley 1921-1991
See Roddenberry, Gene
See also CA 110; 135; CANR 37; SATA 45;
SATA-Obit 69
Roddenberry, Gene .... **CLC 17**
See also Roddenberry, Eugene Wesley
See also AAYA 5; SATA-Obit 69
Rodgers, Mary 1931- .... **CLC 12**
See also CA 49-52; CANR 8, 55; CLR 20; INT
CANR-8; JRDA; MAICYA; SATA 8
Rodgers, W(illiam) R(obert) 1909-1969**CLC 7**
See also CA 85-88; DLB 20
Rodman, Eric
See Silverberg, Robert
Rodman, Howard 1920(?)-1985 .... **CLC 65**
See also CA 118
Rodman, Maia
See Wojciechowska, Maia (Teresa)
Rodriguez, Claudio 1934- .... **CLC 10**
See also DLB 134
Roelvaag, O(le) E(dvart) 1876-1931**TCLC 17**
See also CA 117; DLB 9
Roethke, Theodore (Huebner) 1908-1963**CLC
1, 3, 8, 11, 19, 46, 101; DAM POET; PC 15**
See also CA 81-84; CABS 2; CDALB 1941-
1968; DLB 5; MTCW
Rogers, Thomas Hunter 1927- .... **CLC 57**
See also CA 89-92; INT 89-92
Rogers, Will(iam Penn Adair) 1879-1935
TCLC 8, 71; DAM MULT
See also CA 105; 144; DLB 11; NNAL
Rogin, Gilbert 1929- .... **CLC 18**
See also CA 65-68; CANR 15
Rohan, Koda .... **TCLC 22**
See also Koda Shigeyuki
Rohlfs, Anna Katharine Green
See Green, Anna Katharine
Rohmer, Eric .... **CLC 16**
See also Scherer, Jean-Marie Maurice
Rohmer, Sax .... **TCLC 28**
See also Ward, Arthur Henry Sarsfield
See also DLB 70
Roiphe, Anne (Richardson) 1935- . **CLC 3, 9**
See also CA 89-92; CANR 45; DLBY 80; INT
89-92
Rojas, Fernando de 1465-1541 .... **LC 23**
**Rolfe, Frederick (William Serafino Austin
Lewis Mary)** 1860-1913 .... **TCLC 12**
See also CA 107; DLB 34, 156
Rolland, Romain 1866-1944 .... **TCLC 23**
See also CA 118; DLB 65
Rolle, Richard c. 1300-c. 1349 ...... **CMLC 21**
See also DLB 146
Rolvaag, O(le) E(dvart)
See Roelvaag, O(le) E(dvart)
Romain Arnaud, Saint
See Aragon, Louis
Romains, Jules 1885-1972 .... **CLC 7**
See also CA 85-88; CANR 34; DLB 65; MTCW
Romero, Jose Ruben 1890-1952 ..... **TCLC 14**
See also CA 114; 131; HW
Ronsard, Pierre de 1524-1585 ... **LC 6; PC 11**
Rooke, Leon 1934-.. **CLC 25, 34; DAM POP**
See also CA 25-28R; CANR 23, 53
Roosevelt, Theodore 1858-1919 ..... **TCLC 69**
See also CA 115; DLB 47
Roper, William 1498-1578 .... **LC 10**
Roquelaure, A. N.
See Rice, Anne

Rosa, Joao Guimaraes 1908-1967 ... **CLC 23**
See also CA 89-92; DLB 113

Rose, Wendy 1948-**CLC 85; DAM MULT; PC 13**
See also CA 53-56; CANR 5, 51; DLB 175; NNAL; SATA 12

Rosen, Richard (Dean) 1949- .... **CLC 39**
See also CA 77-80; INT CANR-30

Rosenberg, Isaac 1890-1918 .... **TCLC 12**
See also CA 107; DLB 20

Rosenblatt, Joe .... **CLC 15**
See also Rosenblatt, Joseph

Rosenblatt, Joseph 1933-
See Rosenblatt, Joe
See also CA 89-92; INT 89-92

Rosenfeld, Samuel 1896-1963
See Tzara, Tristan
See also CA 89-92

Rosenstock, Sami
See Tzara, Tristan

Rosenstock, Samuel
See Tzara, Tristan

Rosenthal, M(acha) L(ouis) 1917-1996 . **C L C 28**
See also CA 1-4R; 152; CAAS 6; CANR 4, 51; DLB 5; SATA 59

Ross, Barnaby
See Dannay, Frederic

Ross, Bernard L.
See Follett, Ken(neth Martin)

Ross, J. H.
See Lawrence, T(homas) E(dward)

Ross, Martin
See Martin, Violet Florence
See also DLB 135

Ross, (James) Sinclair 1908- **CLC 13; DAC; DAM MST; SSC 24**
See also CA 73-76; DLB 88

Rossetti, Christina (Georgina) 1830-1894 **NCLC 2, 50; DA; DAB; DAC; DAM MST, POET; PC 7; WLC**
See also DLB 35, 163; MAICYA; SATA 20

Rossetti, Dante Gabriel 1828-1882 **NCLC 4; DA; DAB; DAC; DAM MST, POET; WLC**
See also CDBLB 1832-1890; DLB 35

Rossner, Judith (Perelman) 1935-**CLC 6, 9, 29**
See also AITN 2; BEST 90:3; CA 17-20R; CANR 18, 51; DLB 6; INT CANR-18; MTCW

Rostand, Edmond (Eugene Alexis) 1868-1918 **TCLC 6, 37; DA; DAB; DAC; DAM DRAM, MST**
See also CA 104; 126; MTCW

Roth, Henry 1906-1995 ..... **CLC 2, 6, 11, 104**
See also CA 11-12; 149; CANR 38; CAP 1; DLB 28; MTCW

Roth, Philip (Milton) 1933-**CLC 1, 2, 3, 4, 6, 9, 15, 22, 31, 47, 66, 86; DA; DAB; DAC; DAM MST, NOV, POP; SSC 26; WLC**
See also BEST 90:3; CA 1-4R; CANR 1, 22, 36, 55; CDALB 1968-1988; DLB 2, 28, 173; DLBY 82; MTCW

Rothenberg, Jerome 1931- .... **CLC 6, 57**
See also CA 45-48; CANR 1; DLB 5

Roumain, Jacques (Jean Baptiste) 1907-1944 **TCLC 19; BLC; DAM MULT**
See also BW 1; CA 117; 125

Rourke, Constance (Mayfield) 1885-1941 **TCLC 12**
See also CA 107; YABC 1

Rousseau, Jean-Baptiste 1671-1741 ..... **LC 9**

Rousseau, Jean-Jacques 1712-1778**LC 14, 36; DA; DAB; DAC; DAM MST; WLC**

Roussel, Raymond 1877-1933 .... **TCLC 20**
See also CA 117

Rovit, Earl (Herbert) 1927-................. **CLC 7**
See also CA 5-8R; CANR 12

Rowe, Nicholas 1674-1718 .... **LC 8**
See also DLB 84

Rowley, Ames Dorrance
See Lovecraft, H(oward) P(hillips)

Rowson, Susanna Haswell 1762(?)-1824 **NCLC 5**
See also DLB 37

Roy, Gabrielle 1909-1983 **CLC 10, 14; DAB; DAC; DAM MST**
See also CA 53-56; 110; CANR 5, 61; DLB 68; MTCW

Rozewicz, Tadeusz 1921- ...**CLC 9, 23; DAM POET**
See also CA 108; CANR 36; MTCW

Ruark, Gibbons 1941- ....**CLC 3**
See also CA 33-36R; CAAS 23; CANR 14, 31, 57; DLB 120

Rubens, Bernice (Ruth) 1923-.... **CLC 19, 31**
See also CA 25-28R; CANR 33; DLB 14; MTCW

Rubin, Harold
See Robbins, Harold

Rudkin, (James) David 1936- ....**CLC 14**
See also CA 89-92; DLB 13

Rudnik, Raphael 1933- ....**CLC 7**
See also CA 29-32R

Ruffian, M.
See Hasek, Jaroslav (Matej Frantisek)

Ruiz, Jose Martinez............................**CLC 11**
See also Martinez Ruiz, Jose

Rukeyser, Muriel 1913-1980**CLC 6, 10, 15, 27; DAM POET; PC 12**
See also CA 5-8R; 93-96; CANR 26, 60; DLB 48; MTCW; SATA-Obit 22

Rule, Jane (Vance) 1931- ....**CLC 27**
See also CA 25-28R; CAAS 18; CANR 12; DLB 60

Rulfo, Juan 1918-1986 ....**CLC 8, 80; DAM MULT; HLC; SSC 25**
See also CA 85-88; 118; CANR 26; DLB 113; HW; MTCW

Rumi, Jalal al-Din 1297-1373 .... **CMLC 20**

Runeberg, Johan 1804-1877 ....**NCLC 41**

Runyon, (Alfred) Damon 1884(?)-1946**T C L C 10**
See also CA 107; DLB 11, 86, 171

Rush, Norman 1933- ....**CLC 44**
See also CA 121; 126; INT 126

Rushdie, (Ahmed) Salman 1947-**CLC 23, 31, 55, 100; DAB; DAC; DAM MST, NOV, POP; WLCS**
See also BEST 89:3; CA 108; 111; CANR 33, 56; INT 111; MTCW

Rushforth, Peter (Scott) 1945- ....**CLC 19**
See also CA 101

Ruskin, John 1819-1900 .... **TCLC 63**
See also CA 114; 129; CDBLB 1832-1890; DLB 55, 163; SATA 24

Russ, Joanna 1937-............................**CLC 15**
See also CA 25-28R; CANR 11, 31; DLB 8; MTCW

Russell, George William 1867-1935
See Baker, Jean H.
See also CA 104; 153; CDBLB 1890-1914; DAM POET

Russell, (Henry) Ken(neth Alfred) 1927-**C L C 16**
See also CA 105

Russell, Willy 1947-...........................**CLC 60**

Rutherford, Mark ....**TCLC 25**
See also White, William Hale
See also DLB 18

Ruyslinck, Ward 1929- ....**CLC 14**
See also Belser, Reimond Karel Maria de

Ryan, Cornelius (John) 1920-1974 .....**CLC 7**
See also CA 69-72; 53-56; CANR 38

Ryan, Michael 1946- ....**CLC 65**
See also CA 49-52; DLBY 82

Ryan, Tim
See Dent, Lester

Rybakov, Anatoli (Naumovich) 1911-**CLC 23, 53**
See also CA 126; 135; SATA 79

Ryder, Jonathan
See Ludlum, Robert

Ryga, George 1932-1987**CLC 14; DAC; DAM MST**
See also CA 101; 124; CANR 43; DLB 60

S. H.
See Hartmann, Sadakichi

S. S.
See Sassoon, Siegfried (Lorraine)

Saba, Umberto 1883-1957 .... **TCLC 33**
See also CA 144; DLB 114

Sabatini, Rafael 1875-1950 .... **TCLC 47**

Sabato, Ernesto (R.) 1911-**CLC 10, 23; DAM MULT; HLC**
See also CA 97-100; CANR 32; DLB 145; HW; MTCW

Sacastru, Martin
See Bioy Casares, Adolfo

Sacher-Masoch, Leopold von 1836(?)-1895 **NCLC 31**

Sachs, Marilyn (Stickle) 1927- ....**CLC 35**
See also AAYA 2; CA 17-20R; CANR 13, 47; CLR 2; JRDA; MAICYA; SAAS 2; SATA 3, 68

Sachs, Nelly 1891-1970 .... **CLC 14, 98**
See also CA 17-18; 25-28R; CAP 2

Sackler, Howard (Oliver) 1929-1982 **CLC 14**
See also CA 61-64; 108; CANR 30; DLB 7

Sacks, Oliver (Wolf) 1933-...............**CLC 67**
See also CA 53-56; CANR 28, 50; INT CANR-28; MTCW

Sadakichi
See Hartmann, Sadakichi

Sade, Donatien Alphonse Francois Comte 1740-1814 ....**NCLC 47**

Sadoff, Ira 1945-.................................**CLC 9**
See also CA 53-56; CANR 5, 21; DLB 120

Saetone
See Camus, Albert

Safire, William 1929- ....**CLC 10**
See also CA 17-20R; CANR 31, 54

Sagan, Carl (Edward) 1934-1996 ....**CLC 30**
See also AAYA 2; CA 25-28R; 155; CANR 11, 36; MTCW; SATA 58; SATA-Obit 94

Sagan, Francoise ....**CLC 3, 6, 9, 17, 36**
See also Quoirez, Francoise
See also DLB 83

Sahgal, Nayantara (Pandit) 1927- ... **CLC 41**
See also CA 9-12R; CANR 11

Saint, H(arry) F. 1941- ....**CLC 50**
See also CA 127

St. Aubin de Teran, Lisa 1953-
See Teran, Lisa St. Aubin de
See also CA 118; 126; INT 126

Sainte-Beuve, Charles Augustin 1804-1869 **NCLC 5**

Saint-Exupery, Antoine (Jean Baptiste Marie Roger) de 1900-1944**TCLC 2, 56; DAM NOV; WLC**

See Sharpe, Tom
See also CA 114; 122; INT 122
Sharpe, Tom .... **CLC 36**
See also Sharpe, Thomas Ridley
See also DLB 14
Shaw, Bernard .... **TCLC 45**
See also Shaw, George Bernard
See also BW 1
Shaw, G. Bernard
See Shaw, George Bernard
Shaw, George Bernard 1856-1950**TCLC 3, 9, 21; DA; DAB; DAC; DAM DRAM, MST; WLC**
See also Shaw, Bernard
See also CA 104; 128; CDBLB 1914-1945; DLB 10, 57; MTCW
Shaw, Henry Wheeler 1818-1885 ..**NCLC 15**
See also DLB 11
Shaw, Irwin 1913-1984 **CLC 7, 23, 34; DAM DRAM, POP**
See also AITN 1; CA 13-16R; 112; CANR 21; CDALB 1941-1968; DLB 6, 102; DLBY 84; MTCW
Shaw, Robert 1927-1978 .... **CLC 5**
See also AITN 1; CA 1-4R; 81-84; CANR 4; DLB 13, 14
Shaw, T. E.
See Lawrence, T(homas) E(dward)
Shawn, Wallace 1943- .... **CLC 41**
See also CA 112
Shea, Lisa 1953-.............................. **CLC 86**
See also CA 147
Sheed, Wilfrid (John Joseph) 1930-**CLC 2, 4, 10, 53**
See also CA 65-68; CANR 30; DLB 6; MTCW
Sheldon, Alice Hastings Bradley 1915(?)-1987
See Tiptree, James, Jr.
See also CA 108; 122; CANR 34; INT 108; MTCW
Sheldon, John
See Bloch, Robert (Albert)
Shelley, Mary Wollstonecraft (Godwin) 1797-1851**NCLC 14, 59; DA; DAB; DAC; DAM MST, NOV; WLC**
See also AAYA 20; CDBLB 1789-1832; DLB 110, 116, 159, 178; SATA 29
Shelley, Percy Bysshe 1792-1822 . **NCLC 18; DA; DAB; DAC; DAM MST, POET; PC 14; WLC**
See also CDBLB 1789-1832; DLB 96, 110, 158
Shepard, Jim 1956- .... **CLC 36**
See also CA 137; CANR 59; SATA 90
Shepard, Lucius 1947- .... **CLC 34**
See also CA 128; 141
Shepard, Sam 1943-**CLC 4, 6, 17, 34, 41, 44; DAM DRAM; DC 5**
See also AAYA 1; CA 69-72; CABS 3; CANR 22; DLB 7; MTCW
Shepherd, Michael
See Ludlum, Robert
Sherburne, Zoa (Morin) 1912- .... **CLC 30**
See also AAYA 13; CA 1-4R; CANR 3, 37; MAICYA; SAAS 18; SATA 3
Sheridan, Frances 1724-1766 .... **LC 7**
See also DLB 39, 84
Sheridan, Richard Brinsley 1751-1816**NCLC 5; DA; DAB; DAC; DAM DRAM, MST; DC 1; WLC**
See also CDBLB 1660-1789; DLB 89
Sherman, Jonathan Marc .... **CLC 55**
Sherman, Martin 1941(?)- .... **CLC 19**
See also CA 116; 123
Sherwin, Judith Johnson 1936- ... **CLC 7, 15**

See also CA 25-28R; CANR 34
Sherwood, Frances 1940- .... **CLC 81**
See also CA 146
Sherwood, Robert E(mmet) 1896-1955**TCLC 3; DAM DRAM**
See also CA 104; 153; DLB 7, 26
Shestov, Lev 1866-1938 .... **TCLC 56**
Shevchenko, Taras 1814-1861 .... **NCLC 54**
Shiel, M(atthew) P(hipps) 1865-1947**TCLC 8**
See also CA 106; DLB 153
Shields, Carol 1935- ....**CLC 91; DAC**
See also CA 81-84; CANR 51
Shields, David 1956-........................... **CLC 97**
See also CA 124; CANR 48
Shiga, Naoya 1883-1971 .... **CLC 33; SSC 23**
See also CA 101; 33-36R; DLB 180
Shilts, Randy 1951-1994 .... **CLC 85**
See also AAYA 19; CA 115; 127; 144; CANR 45; INT 127
Shimazaki, Haruki 1872-1943
See Shimazaki Toson
See also CA 105; 134
Shimazaki Toson 1872-1943 .... **TCLC 5**
See also Shimazaki, Haruki
See also DLB 180
Sholokhov, Mikhail (Aleksandrovich) 1905-1984 .... **CLC 7, 15**
See also CA 101; 112; MTCW; SATA-Obit 36
Shone, Patric
See Hanley, James
Shreve, Susan Richards 1939-........... **CLC 23**
See also CA 49-52; CAAS 5; CANR 5, 38; MAICYA; SATA 46, 95; SATA-Brief 41
Shue, Larry 1946-1985**CLC 52; DAM DRAM**
See also CA 145; 117
Shu-Jen, Chou 1881-1936
See Lu Hsun
See also CA 104
Shulman, Alix Kates 1932- .... **CLC 2, 10**
See also CA 29-32R; CANR 43; SATA 7
Shuster, Joe 1914- .... **CLC 21**
Shute, Nevil .... **CLC 30**
See also Norway, Nevil Shute
Shuttle, Penelope (Diane) 1947- .... **CLC 7**
See also CA 93-96; CANR 39; DLB 14, 40
Sidney, Mary 1561-1621 .... **LC 19, 39**
Sidney, Sir Philip 1554-1586 **LC 19, 39; DA; DAB; DAC; DAM MST, POET**
See also CDBLB Before 1660; DLB 167
Siegel, Jerome 1914-1996 .... **CLC 21**
See also CA 116; 151
Siegel, Jerry
See Siegel, Jerome
Sienkiewicz, Henryk (Adam Alexander Pius) 1846-1916.................................. **TCLC 3**
See also CA 104; 134
Sierra, Gregorio Martinez
See Martinez Sierra, Gregorio
Sierra, Maria (de la O'LeJarraga) Martinez
See Martinez Sierra, Maria (de la O'LeJarraga)
Sigal, Clancy 1926-............................... **CLC 7**
See also CA 1-4R
Sigourney, Lydia Howard (Huntley) 1791-1865 **NCLC 21**
See also DLB 1, 42, 73
Siguenza y Gongora, Carlos de 1645-1700**LC 8**
Sigurjonsson, Johann 1880-1919 ... **TCLC 27**
Sikelianos, Angelos 1884-1951 .... **TCLC 39**
Silkin, Jon 1930- .... **CLC 2, 6, 43**
See also CA 5-8R; CAAS 5; DLB 27
Silko, Leslie (Marmon) 1948-**CLC 23, 74; DA; DAC; DAM MST, MULT, POP; WLCS**

See also AAYA 14; CA 115; 122; CANR 45; DLB 143, 175; NNAL
Sillanpaa, Frans Eemil 1888-1964 ....**CLC 19**
See also CA 129; 93-96; MTCW
Sillitoe, Alan 1928- .... **CLC 1, 3, 6, 10, 19, 57**
See also AITN 1; CA 9-12R; CAAS 2; CANR 8, 26, 55; CDBLB 1960 to Present; DLB 14, 139; MTCW; SATA 61
Silone, Ignazio 1900-1978 .... **CLC 4**
See also CA 25-28; 81-84; CANR 34; CAP 2; MTCW
Silver, Joan Micklin 1935- .... **CLC 20**
See also CA 114; 121; INT 121
Silver, Nicholas
See Faust, Frederick (Schiller)
Silverberg, Robert 1935- **CLC 7; DAM POP**
See also CA 1-4R; CAAS 3; CANR 1, 20, 36; DLB 8; INT CANR-20; MAICYA; MTCW; SATA 13, 91
Silverstein, Alvin 1933- .... **CLC 17**
See also CA 49-52; CANR 2; CLR 25; JRDA; MAICYA; SATA 8, 69
Silverstein, Virginia B(arbara Opshelor) 1937-**CLC 17**
See also CA 49-52; CANR 2; CLR 25; JRDA; MAICYA; SATA 8, 69
Sim, Georges
See Simenon, Georges (Jacques Christian)
Simak, Clifford D(onald) 1904-1988**CLC 1, 55**
See also CA 1-4R; 125; CANR 1, 35; DLB 8; MTCW; SATA-Obit 56
Simenon, Georges (Jacques Christian) 1903-1989 .. **CLC 1, 2, 3, 8, 18, 47; DAM POP**
See also CA 85-88; 129; CANR 35; DLB 72; DLBY 89; MTCW
Simic, Charles 1938- ....**CLC 6, 9, 22, 49, 68; DAM POET**
See also CA 29-32R; CAAS 4; CANR 12, 33, 52, 61; DLB 105
Simmel, Georg 1858-1918 .... **TCLC 64**
See also CA 157
Simmons, Charles (Paul) 1924-......... **CLC 57**
See also CA 89-92; INT 89-92
Simmons, Dan 1948-...... **CLC 44; DAM POP**
See also AAYA 16; CA 138; CANR 53
Simmons, James (Stewart Alexander) 1933-**CLC 43**
See also CA 105; CAAS 21; DLB 40
Simms, William Gilmore 1806-1870 **NCLC 3**
See also DLB 3, 30, 59, 73
Simon, Carly 1945-........................... **CLC 26**
See also CA 105
Simon, Claude 1913- **CLC 4, 9, 15, 39; DAM NOV**
See also CA 89-92; CANR 33; DLB 83; MTCW
Simon, (Marvin) Neil 1927-**CLC 6, 11, 31, 39, 70; DAM DRAM**
See also AITN 1; CA 21-24R; CANR 26, 54; DLB 7; MTCW
Simon, Paul (Frederick) 1941(?)- ...... **CLC 17**
See also CA 116; 153
Simonon, Paul 1956(?)- .... **CLC 30**
Simpson, Harriette
See Arnow, Harriette (Louisa) Simpson
Simpson, Louis (Aston Marantz) 1923-**CLC 4, 7, 9, 32; DAM POET**
See also CA 1-4R; CAAS 4; CANR 1, 61; DLB 5; MTCW
Simpson, Mona (Elizabeth) 1957- ....**CLC 44**
See also CA 122; 135
Simpson, N(orman) F(rederick) 1919-**CLC 29**
See also CA 13-16R; DLB 13
Sinclair, Andrew (Annandale) 1935- .**CLC 2,**

Sophocles 496(?)B.C.-406(?)B.C.... **CMLC 2; DA; DAB; DAC; DAM DRAM, MST; DC 1; WLCS**
See also DLB 176
Sordello 1189-1269 .... **CMLC 15**
Sorel, Julia
See Drexler, Rosalyn
Sorrentino, Gilbert 1929-**CLC 3, 7, 14, 22, 40**
See also CA 77-80; CANR 14, 33; DLB 5, 173; DLBY 80; INT CANR-14
Soto, Gary 1952-. **CLC 32, 80; DAM MULT; HLC**
See also AAYA 10; CA 119; 125; CANR 50; CLR 38; DLB 82; HW; INT 125; JRDA; SATA 80
Soupault, Philippe 1897-1990 .... **CLC 68**
See also CA 116; 147; 131
Souster, (Holmes) Raymond 1921-**CLC 5, 14; DAC; DAM POET**
See also CA 13-16R; CAAS 14; CANR 13, 29, 53; DLB 88; SATA 63
Southern, Terry 1924(?)-1995 .... **CLC 7**
See also CA 1-4R; 150; CANR 1, 55; DLB 2
Southey, Robert 1774-1843 .... **NCLC 8**
See also DLB 93, 107, 142; SATA 54
Southworth, Emma Dorothy Eliza Nevitte 1819-1899 .... **NCLC 26**
Souza, Ernest
See Scott, Evelyn
Soyinka, Wole 1934-**CLC 3, 5, 14, 36, 44; BLC; DA; DAB; DAC; DAM DRAM, MST, MULT; DC 2; WLC**
See also BW 2; CA 13-16R; CANR 27, 39; DLB 125; MTCW
Spackman, W(illiam) M(ode) 1905-1990**CLC 46**
See also CA 81-84; 132
Spacks, Barry (Bernard) 1931- .... **CLC 14**
See also CA 154; CANR 33; DLB 105
Spanidou, Irini 1946- .... **CLC 44**
Spark, Muriel (Sarah) 1918-**CLC 2, 3, 5, 8, 13, 18, 40, 94; DAB; DAC; DAM MST, NOV; SSC 10**
See also CA 5-8R; CANR 12, 36; CDBLB 1945-1960; DLB 15, 139; INT CANR-12; MTCW
Spaulding, Douglas
See Bradbury, Ray (Douglas)
Spaulding, Leonard
See Bradbury, Ray (Douglas)
Spence, J. A. D.
See Eliot, T(homas) S(tearns)
Spencer, Elizabeth 1921- .... **CLC 22**
See also CA 13-16R; CANR 32; DLB 6; MTCW; SATA 14
Spencer, Leonard G.
See Silverberg, Robert
Spencer, Scott 1945- .... **CLC 30**
See also CA 113; CANR 51; DLBY 86
Spender, Stephen (Harold) 1909-1995**CLC 1, 2, 5, 10, 41, 91; DAM POET**
See also CA 9-12R; 149; CANR 31, 54; CDBLB 1945-1960; DLB 20; MTCW
Spengler, Oswald (Arnold Gottfried) 1880-1936 **TCLC 25**
See also CA 118
Spenser, Edmund 1552(?)-1599**LC 5, 39; DA; DAB; DAC; DAM MST, POET; PC 8; WLC**
See also CDBLB Before 1660; DLB 167
Spicer, Jack 1925-1965 **CLC 8, 18, 72; DAM POET**
See also CA 85-88; DLB 5, 16
Spiegelman, Art 1948- .... **CLC 76**

See also AAYA 10; CA 125; CANR 41, 55
Spielberg, Peter 1929-......................... **CLC 6**
See also CA 5-8R; CANR 4, 48; DLBY 81
Spielberg, Steven 1947-...................... **CLC 20**
See also AAYA 8; CA 77-80; CANR 32; SATA 32
Spillane, Frank Morrison 1918-
See Spillane, Mickey
See also CA 25-28R; CANR 28; MTCW; SATA 66
Spillane, Mickey .... **CLC 3, 13**
See also Spillane, Frank Morrison
Spinoza, Benedictus de 1632-1677 .... **LC 9**
Spinrad, Norman (Richard) 1940- ...**CLC 46**
See also CA 37-40R; CAAS 19; CANR 20; DLB 8; INT CANR-20
Spitteler, Carl (Friedrich Georg) 1845-1924 **TCLC 12**
See also CA 109; DLB 129
Spivack, Kathleen (Romola Drucker) 1938-**CLC 6**
See also CA 49-52
Spoto, Donald 1941- .... **CLC 39**
See also CA 65-68; CANR 11, 57
Springsteen, Bruce (F.) 1949- .... **CLC 17**
See also CA 111
Spurling, Hilary 1940- .... **CLC 34**
See also CA 104; CANR 25, 52
Spyker, John Howland
See Elman, Richard
Squires, (James) Radcliffe 1917-1993**CLC 51**
See also CA 1-4R; 140; CANR 6, 21
Srivastava, Dhanpat Rai 1880(?)-1936
See Premchand
See also CA 118
Stacy, Donald
See Pohl, Frederik
Stael, Germaine de
See Stael-Holstein, Anne Louise Germaine Necker Baronn
See also DLB 119
Stael-Holstein, Anne Louise Germaine Necker Baronn 1766-1817 .... **NCLC 3**
See also Stael, Germaine de
Stafford, Jean 1915-1979**CLC 4, 7, 19, 68; SSC 26**
See also CA 1-4R; 85-88; CANR 3; DLB 2, 173; MTCW; SATA-Obit 22
Stafford, William (Edgar) 1914-1993 **CLC 4, 7, 29; DAM POET**
See also CA 5-8R; 142; CAAS 3; CANR 5, 22; DLB 5; INT CANR-22
Stagnelius, Eric Johan 1793-1823 . **NCLC 61**
Staines, Trevor
See Brunner, John (Kilian Houston)
Stairs, Gordon
See Austin, Mary (Hunter)
Stannard, Martin 1947- .... **CLC 44**
See also CA 142; DLB 155
Stanton, Elizabeth Cady 1815-1902**TCLC 73**
See also DLB 79
Stanton, Maura 1946- .... **CLC 9**
See also CA 89-92; CANR 15; DLB 120
Stanton, Schuyler
See Baum, L(yman) Frank
Stapledon, (William) Olaf 1886-1950 . **TCLC 22**
See also CA 111; DLB 15
Starbuck, George (Edwin) 1931-1996**CLC 53; DAM POET**
See also CA 21-24R; 153; CANR 23
Stark, Richard
See Westlake, Donald E(dwin)

Staunton, Schuyler
See Baum, L(yman) Frank
Stead, Christina (Ellen) 1902-1983 **CLC 2, 5, 8, 32, 80**
See also CA 13-16R; 109; CANR 33, 40; MTCW
Stead, William Thomas 1849-1912 **TCLC 48**
Steele, Richard 1672-1729 .... **LC 18**
See also CDBLB 1660-1789; DLB 84, 101
Steele, Timothy (Reid) 1948- .... **CLC 45**
See also CA 93-96; CANR 16, 50; DLB 120
Steffens, (Joseph) Lincoln 1866-1936 . **T C L C 20**
See also CA 117
Stegner, Wallace (Earle) 1909-1993**CLC 9, 49, 81; DAM NOV; SSC 27**
See also AITN 1; BEST 90:3; CA 1-4R; 141; CAAS 9; CANR 1, 21, 46; DLB 9; DLBY 93; MTCW
Stein, Gertrude 1874-1946**TCLC 1, 6, 28, 48; DA; DAB; DAC; DAM MST, NOV, POET; PC 18; WLC**
See also CA 104; 132; CDALB 1917-1929; DLB 4, 54, 86; DLBD 15; MTCW
Steinbeck, John (Ernst) 1902-1968 **CLC 1, 5, 9, 13, 21, 34, 45, 75; DA; DAB; DAC; DAM DRAM, MST, NOV; SSC 11; WLC**
See also AAYA 12; CA 1-4R; 25-28R; CANR 1, 35; CDALB 1929-1941; DLB 7, 9; DLBD 2; MTCW; SATA 9
Steinem, Gloria 1934- .... **CLC 63**
See also CA 53-56; CANR 28, 51; MTCW
Steiner, George 1929- ... **CLC 24; DAM NOV**
See also CA 73-76; CANR 31; DLB 67; MTCW; SATA 62
Steiner, K. Leslie
See Delany, Samuel R(ay, Jr.)
Steiner, Rudolf 1861-1925 .... **TCLC 13**
See also CA 107
Stendhal 1783-1842**NCLC 23, 46; DA; DAB; DAC; DAM MST, NOV; SSC 27; WLC**
See also DLB 119
Stephen, Leslie 1832-1904 .... **TCLC 23**
See also CA 123; DLB 57, 144
Stephen, Sir Leslie
See Stephen, Leslie
Stephen, Virginia
See Woolf, (Adeline) Virginia
Stephens, James 1882(?)-1950 .... **TCLC 4**
See also CA 104; DLB 19, 153, 162
Stephens, Reed
See Donaldson, Stephen R.
Steptoe, Lydia
See Barnes, Djuna
Sterchi, Beat 1949- .... **CLC 65**
Sterling, Brett
See Bradbury, Ray (Douglas); Hamilton, Edmond
Sterling, Bruce 1954- .... **CLC 72**
See also CA 119; CANR 44
Sterling, George 1869-1926 .... **TCLC 20**
See also CA 117; DLB 54
Stern, Gerald 1925- .... **CLC 40, 100**
See also CA 81-84; CANR 28; DLB 105
Stern, Richard (Gustave) 1928- ... **CLC 4, 39**
See also CA 1-4R; CANR 1, 25, 52; DLBY 87; INT CANR-25
Sternberg, Josef von 1894-1969 .... **CLC 20**
See also CA 81-84
Sterne, Laurence 1713-1768**LC 2; DA; DAB; DAC; DAM MST, NOV; WLC**
See also CDBLB 1660-1789; DLB 39
Sternheim, (William Adolf) Carl 1878-1942

TCLC 8
See also CA 105; DLB 56, 118
Stevens, Mark 1951- .... **CLC 34**
See also CA 122
Stevens, Wallace 1879-1955 **TCLC 3, 12, 45;
DA; DAB; DAC; DAM MST, POET; PC
6; WLC**
See also CA 104; 124; CDALB 1929-1941;
DLB 54; MTCW
Stevenson, Anne (Katharine) 1933-**CLC 7, 33**
See also CA 17-20R; CAAS 9; CANR 9, 33;
DLB 40; MTCW
Stevenson, Robert Louis (Balfour) 1850-1894
**NCLC 5, 14, 63; DA; DAB; DAC; DAM
MST, NOV; SSC 11; WLC**
See also CDBLB 1890-1914; CLR 10, 11; DLB
18, 57, 141, 156, 174; DLBD 13; JRDA;
MAICYA; YABC 2
Stewart, J(ohn) I(nnes) M(ackintosh) 1906-
1994 .... **CLC 7, 14, 32**
See also CA 85-88; 147; CAAS 3; CANR 47;
MTCW
Stewart, Mary (Florence Elinor) 1916-**CLC 7,
35; DAB**
See also CA 1-4R; CANR 1, 59; SATA 12
Stewart, Mary Rainbow
See Stewart, Mary (Florence Elinor)
Stifle, June
See Campbell, Maria
Stifter, Adalbert 1805-1868 .... **NCLC 41**
See also DLB 133
Still, James 1906-............................... **CLC 49**
See also CA 65-68; CAAS 17; CANR 10, 26;
DLB 9; SATA 29
Sting
See Sumner, Gordon Matthew
Stirling, Arthur
See Sinclair, Upton (Beall)
Stitt, Milan 1941-............................... **CLC 29**
See also CA 69-72
Stockton, Francis Richard 1834-1902
See Stockton, Frank R.
See also CA 108; 137; MAICYA; SATA 44
Stockton, Frank R. .... **TCLC 47**
See also Stockton, Francis Richard
See also DLB 42, 74; DLBD 13; SATA-Brief
32
Stoddard, Charles
See Kuttner, Henry
Stoker, Abraham 1847-1912
See Stoker, Bram
See also CA 105; DA; DAC; DAM MST, NOV;
SATA 29
Stoker, Bram 1847-1912**TCLC 8; DAB; WLC**
See also Stoker, Abraham
See also CA 150; CDBLB 1890-1914; DLB 36,
70, 178
Stolz, Mary (Slattery) 1920-............. **CLC 12**
See also AAYA 8; AITN 1; CA 5-8R; CANR
13, 41; JRDA; MAICYA; SAAS 3; SATA 10,
71
Stone, Irving 1903-1989 .. **CLC 7; DAM POP**
See also AITN 1; CA 1-4R; 129; CAAS 3;
CANR 1, 23; INT CANR-23; MTCW; SATA
3; SATA-Obit 64
Stone, Oliver (William) 1946- .... **CLC 73**
See also AAYA 15; CA 110; CANR 55
Stone, Robert (Anthony) 1937-**CLC 5, 23, 42**
See also CA 85-88; CANR 23; DLB 152; INT
CANR-23; MTCW
Stone, Zachary
See Follett, Ken(neth Martin)
Stoppard, Tom 1937-**CLC 1, 3, 4, 5, 8, 15, 29,**

34, 63, 91; **DA; DAB; DAC; DAM DRAM,
MST; DC 6; WLC**
See also CA 81-84; CANR 39; CDBLB 1960
to Present; DLB 13; DLBY 85; MTCW
Storey, David (Malcolm) 1933-**CLC 2, 4, 5, 8;
DAM DRAM**
See also CA 81-84; CANR 36; DLB 13, 14;
MTCW
Storm, Hyemeyohsts 1935- ...... **CLC 3; DAM
MULT**
See also CA 81-84; CANR 45; NNAL
Storm, (Hans) Theodor (Woldsen) 1817-1888
NCLC 1; SSC 27
Storni, Alfonsina 1892-1938 . **TCLC 5; DAM
MULT; HLC**
See also CA 104; 131; HW
Stoughton, William 1631-1701 .... **LC 38**
See also DLB 24
Stout, Rex (Todhunter) 1886-1975 ..... **CLC 3**
See also AITN 2; CA 61-64
Stow, (Julian) Randolph 1935- .. **CLC 23, 48**
See also CA 13-16R; CANR 33; MTCW
Stowe, Harriet (Elizabeth) Beecher 1811-1896
**NCLC 3, 50; DA; DAB; DAC; DAM MST,
NOV; WLC**
See also CDALB 1865-1917; DLB 1, 12, 42,
74; JRDA; MAICYA; YABC 1
Strachey, (Giles) Lytton 1880-1932 **TCLC 12**
See also CA 110; DLB 149; DLBD 10
Strand, Mark 1934- **CLC 6, 18, 41, 71; DAM
POET**
See also CA 21-24R; CANR 40; DLB 5; SATA
41
Straub, Peter (Francis) 1943- **CLC 28; DAM
POP**
See also BEST 89:1; CA 85-88; CANR 28;
DLBY 84; MTCW
Strauss, Botho 1944- .... **CLC 22**
See also CA 157; DLB 124
Streatfeild, (Mary) Noel 1895(?)-1986**CLC 21**
See also CA 81-84; 120; CANR 31; CLR 17;
DLB 160; MAICYA; SATA 20; SATA-Obit
48
Stribling, T(homas) S(igismund) 1881-1965
CLC 23
See also CA 107; DLB 9
Strindberg, (Johan) August 1849-1912**T C L C
1, 8, 21, 47; DA; DAB; DAC; DAM DRAM,
MST; WLC**
See also CA 104; 135
Stringer, Arthur 1874-1950 .... **TCLC 37**
See also DLB 92
Stringer, David
See Roberts, Keith (John Kingston)
Stroheim, Erich von 1885-1957 ..... **TCLC 71**
Strugatskii, Arkadii (Natanovich) 1925-1991
CLC 27
See also CA 106; 135
Strugatskii, Boris (Natanovich) 1933-**CLC 27**
See also CA 106
Strummer, Joe 1953(?)- .... **CLC 30**
Stuart, Don A.
See Campbell, John W(ood, Jr.)
Stuart, Ian
See MacLean, Alistair (Stuart)
Stuart, Jesse (Hilton) 1906-1984**CLC 1, 8, 11,
14, 34**
See also CA 5-8R; 112; CANR 31; DLB 9, 48,
102; DLBY 84; SATA 2; SATA-Obit 36
Sturgeon, Theodore (Hamilton) 1918-1985
CLC 22, 39
See also Queen, Ellery
See also CA 81-84; 116; CANR 32; DLB 8;

DLBY 85; MTCW
Sturges, Preston 1898-1959 .... **TCLC 48**
See also CA 114; 149; DLB 26
Styron, William 1925-**CLC 1, 3, 5, 11, 15, 60;
DAM NOV, POP; SSC 25**
See also BEST 90:4; CA 5-8R; CANR 6, 33;
CDALB 1968-1988; DLB 2, 143; DLBY 80;
INT CANR-6; MTCW
Suarez Lynch, B.
See Bioy Casares, Adolfo; Borges, Jorge Luis
Su Chien 1884-1918
See Su Man-shu
See also CA 123
Suckow, Ruth 1892-1960 .... **SSC 18**
See also CA 113; DLB 9, 102
Sudermann, Hermann 1857-1928 .. **TCLC 15**
See also CA 107; DLB 118
Sue, Eugene 1804-1857 .... **NCLC 1**
See also DLB 119
Sueskind, Patrick 1949- .... **CLC 44**
See also Suskind, Patrick
Sukenick, Ronald 1932- .... **CLC 3, 4, 6, 48**
See also CA 25-28R; CAAS 8; CANR 32; DLB
173; DLBY 81
Suknaski, Andrew 1942- .... **CLC 19**
See also CA 101; DLB 53
Sullivan, Vernon
See Vian, Boris
Sully Prudhomme 1839-1907 .... **TCLC 31**
Su Man-shu .... **TCLC 24**
See also Su Chien
Summerforest, Ivy B.
See Kirkup, James
Summers, Andrew James 1942- .... **CLC 26**
Summers, Andy
See Summers, Andrew James
Summers, Hollis (Spurgeon, Jr.) 1916-**CLC 10**
See also CA 5-8R; CANR 3; DLB 6
**Summers, (Alphonsus Joseph-Mary Augustus)
Montague** 1880-1948 .... **TCLC 16**
See also CA 118
Sumner, Gordon Matthew 1951- ..... **CLC 26**
Surtees, Robert Smith 1803-1864 .. **NCLC 14**
See also DLB 21
Susann, Jacqueline 1921-1974 .... **CLC 3**
See also AITN 1; CA 65-68; 53-56; MTCW
Su Shih 1036-1101 .... **CMLC 15**
Suskind, Patrick
See Sueskind, Patrick
See also CA 145
Sutcliff, Rosemary 1920-1992**CLC 26; DAB;
DAC; DAM MST, POP**
See also AAYA 10; CA 5-8R; 139; CANR 37;
CLR 1, 37; JRDA; MAICYA; SATA 6, 44,
78; SATA-Obit 73
Sutro, Alfred 1863-1933 .... **TCLC 6**
See also CA 105; DLB 10
Sutton, Henry
See Slavitt, David R(ytman)
Svevo, Italo 1861-1928 . **TCLC 2, 35; SSC 25**
See also Schmitz, Aron Hector
Swados, Elizabeth (A.) 1951- .... **CLC 12**
See also CA 97-100; CANR 49; INT 97-100
Swados, Harvey 1920-1972 .... **CLC 5**
See also CA 5-8R; 37-40R; CANR 6; DLB 2
Swan, Gladys 1934-.......................... **CLC 69**
See also CA 101; CANR 17, 39
Swarthout, Glendon (Fred) 1918-1992**CLC 35**
See also CA 1-4R; 139; CANR 1, 47; SATA 26
Sweet, Sarah C.
See Jewett, (Theodora) Sarah Orne
Swenson, May 1919-1989**CLC 4, 14, 61; DA;
DAB; DAC; DAM MST, POET; PC 14**

See also CA 5-8R; 130; CANR 36, 61; DLB 5;
MTCW; SATA 15

Swift, Augustus
See Lovecraft, H(oward) P(hillips)

Swift, Graham (Colin) 1949- ...... CLC 41, 88
See also CA 117; 122; CANR 46

**Swift, Jonathan 1667-1745 LC 1; DA; DAB;
DAC; DAM MST, NOV, POET; PC 9;
WLC**
See also CDBLB 1660-1789; DLB 39, 95, 101;
SATA 19

**Swinburne, Algernon Charles 1837-1909
TCLC 8, 36; DA; DAB; DAC; DAM MST,
POET; WLC**
See also CA 105; 140; CDBLB 1832-1890;
DLB 35, 57

Swinfen, Ann .... CLC 34

Swinnerton, Frank Arthur 1884-1982CLC 31
See also CA 108; DLB 34

Swithen, John
See King, Stephen (Edwin)

Sylvia
See Ashton-Warner, Sylvia (Constance)

Symmes, Robert Edward
See Duncan, Robert (Edward)

**Symonds, John Addington 1840-1893 N C L C
34**
See also DLB 57, 144

Symons, Arthur 1865-1945 .... TCLC 11
See also CA 107; DLB 19, 57, 149

**Symons, Julian (Gustave) 1912-1994 CLC 2,
14, 32**
See also CA 49-52; 147; CAAS 3; CANR 3,
33, 59; DLB 87, 155; DLBY 92; MTCW

**Synge, (Edmund) J(ohn) M(illington) 1871-
1909 .. TCLC 6, 37; DAM DRAM; DC 2**
See also CA 104; 141; CDBLB 1890-1914;
DLB 10, 19

Syruc, J.
See Milosz, Czeslaw

Szirtes, George 1948- .... CLC 46
See also CA 109; CANR 27, 61

Szymborska, Wislawa 1923-............. CLC 99
See also CA 154; DLBY 96

T. O., Nik
See Annensky, Innokenty (Fyodorovich)

Tabori, George 1914- .... CLC 19
See also CA 49-52; CANR 4

**Tagore, Rabindranath 1861-1941TCLC 3, 53;
DAM DRAM, POET; PC 8**
See also CA 104; 120; MTCW

**Taine, Hippolyte Adolphe 1828-1893 . N C L C
15**

Talese, Gay 1932- .... CLC 37
See also AITN 1; CA 1-4R; CANR 9, 58; INT
CANR-9; MTCW

Tallent, Elizabeth (Ann) 1954- .... CLC 45
See also CA 117; DLB 130

Tally, Ted 1952-............................... CLC 42
See also CA 120; 124; INT 124

Tamayo y Baus, Manuel 1829-1898 . NCLC 1

**Tammsaare, A(nton) H(ansen) 1878-1940
TCLC 27**

Tam'si, Tchicaya U
See Tchicaya, Gerald Felix

**Tan, Amy (Ruth) 1952-CLC 59; DAM MULT,
NOV, POP**
See also AAYA 9; BEST 89:3; CA 136; CANR
54; DLB 173; SATA 75

Tandem, Felix
See Spitteler, Carl (Friedrich Georg)

**Tanizaki, Jun'ichiro 1886-1965CLC 8, 14, 28;
SSC 21**

See also CA 93-96; 25-28R; DLB 180

Tanner, William
See Amis, Kingsley (William)

Tao Lao
See Storni, Alfonsina

Tarassoff, Lev
See Troyat, Henri

Tarbell, Ida M(inerva) 1857-1944 . TCLC 40
See also CA 122; DLB 47

**Tarkington, (Newton) Booth 1869-1946TCLC
9**
See also CA 110; 143; DLB 9, 102; SATA 17

**Tarkovsky, Andrei (Arsenyevich) 1932-1986
CLC 75**
See also CA 127

Tartt, Donna 1964(?)- .... CLC 76
See also CA 142

Tasso, Torquato 1544-1595 .... LC 5

**Tate, (John Orley) Allen 1899-1979CLC 2, 4,
6, 9, 11, 14, 24**
See also CA 5-8R; 85-88; CANR 32; DLB 4,
45, 63; MTCW

Tate, Ellalice
See Hibbert, Eleanor Alice Burford

Tate, James (Vincent) 1943- ..... CLC 2, 6, 25
See also CA 21-24R; CANR 29, 57; DLB 5,
169

Tavel, Ronald 1940- .... CLC 6
See also CA 21-24R; CANR 33

Taylor, C(ecil) P(hilip) 1929-1981 ..... CLC 27
See also CA 25-28R; 105; CANR 47

**Taylor, Edward 1642(?)-1729 ..... LC 11; DA;
DAB; DAC; DAM MST, POET**
See also DLB 24

Taylor, Eleanor Ross 1920- .... CLC 5
See also CA 81-84

Taylor, Elizabeth 1912-1975 ..... CLC 2, 4, 29
See also CA 13-16R; CANR 9; DLB 139;
MTCW; SATA 13

Taylor, Henry (Splawn) 1942- .... CLC 44
See also CA 33-36R; CAAS 7; CANR 31; DLB
5

Taylor, Kamala (Purnaiya) 1924-
See Markandaya, Kamala
See also CA 77-80

Taylor, Mildred D. .... CLC 21
See also AAYA 10; BW 1; CA 85-88; CANR
25; CLR 9; DLB 52; JRDA; MAICYA; SAAS
5; SATA 15, 70

**Taylor, Peter (Hillsman) 1917-1994CLC 1, 4,
18, 37, 44, 50, 71; SSC 10**
See also CA 13-16R; 147; CANR 9, 50; DLBY
81, 94; INT CANR-9; MTCW

Taylor, Robert Lewis 1912- .... CLC 14
See also CA 1-4R; CANR 3; SATA 10

Tchekhov, Anton
See Chekhov, Anton (Pavlovich)

Tchicaya, Gerald Felix 1931-1988 . CLC 101
See also CA 129; 125

Tchicaya U Tam'si
See Tchicaya, Gerald Felix

Teasdale, Sara 1884-1933 .... TCLC 4
See also CA 104; DLB 45; SATA 32

Tegner, Esaias 1782-1846 .... NCLC 2

**Teilhard de Chardin, (Marie Joseph) Pierre
1881-1955................................... TCLC 9**
See also CA 105

Temple, Ann
See Mortimer, Penelope (Ruth)

Tennant, Emma (Christina) 1937-CLC 13, 52
See also CA 65-68; CAAS 9; CANR 10, 38,
59; DLB 14

Tenneshaw, S. M.

See Silverberg, Robert

**Tennyson, Alfred 1809-1892 . NCLC 30; DA;
DAB; DAC; DAM MST, POET; PC 6;
WLC**
See also CDBLB 1832-1890; DLB 32

Teran, Lisa St. Aubin de .... CLC 36
See also St. Aubin de Teran, Lisa

Terence 195(?)B.C.-159B.C. CMLC 14; DC 7

Teresa de Jesus, St. 1515-1582 .... LC 18

Terkel, Louis 1912-
See Terkel, Studs
See also CA 57-60; CANR 18, 45; MTCW

Terkel, Studs .... CLC 38
See also Terkel, Louis
See also AITN 1

Terry, C. V.
See Slaughter, Frank G(ill)

Terry, Megan 1932- .... CLC 19
See also CA 77-80; CABS 3; CANR 43; DLB 7

Tertz, Abram
See Sinyavsky, Andrei (Donatevich)

Tesich, Steve 1943(?)-1996 .... CLC 40, 69
See also CA 105; 152; DLBY 83

Teternikov, Fyodor Kuzmich 1863-1927
See Sologub, Fyodor
See also CA 104

Tevis, Walter 1928-1984 .... CLC 42
See also CA 113

Tey, Josephine .... TCLC 14
See also Mackintosh, Elizabeth
See also DLB 77

**Thackeray, William Makepeace 1811-1863
NCLC 5, 14, 22, 43; DA; DAB; DAC; DAM
MST, NOV; WLC**
See also CDBLB 1832-1890; DLB 21, 55, 159,
163; SATA 23

Thakura, Ravindranatha
See Tagore, Rabindranath

Tharoor, Shashi 1956- .... CLC 70
See also CA 141

Thelwell, Michael Miles 1939- .... CLC 22
See also BW 2; CA 101

Theobald, Lewis, Jr.
See Lovecraft, H(oward) P(hillips)

Theodorescu, Ion N. 1880-1967
See Arghezi, Tudor
See also CA 116

**Theriault, Yves 1915-1983 .... CLC 79; DAC;
DAM MST**
See also CA 102; DLB 88

Theroux, Alexander (Louis) 1939-CLC 2, 25
See also CA 85-88; CANR 20

**Theroux, Paul (Edward) 1941- CLC 5, 8, 11,
15, 28, 46; DAM POP**
See also BEST 89:4; CA 33-36R; CANR 20,
45; DLB 2; MTCW; SATA 44

Thesen, Sharon 1946-........................ CLC 56

Thevenin, Denis
See Duhamel, Georges

Thibault, Jacques Anatole Francois 1844-1924
See France, Anatole
See also CA 106; 127; DAM NOV; MTCW

Thiele, Colin (Milton) 1920-.............. CLC 17
See also CA 29-32R; CANR 12, 28, 53; CLR
27; MAICYA; SAAS 2; SATA 14, 72

**Thomas, Audrey (Callahan) 1935-CLC 7, 13,
37; SSC 20**
See also AITN 2; CA 21-24R; CAAS 19; CANR
36, 58; DLB 60; MTCW

**Thomas, D(onald) M(ichael) 1935-. CLC 13,
22, 31**
See also CA 61-64; CAAS 11; CANR 17, 45;
CDBLB 1960 to Present; DLB 40; INT

CANR-17; MTCW

Thomas, Dylan (Marlais) 1914-1953 **TCLC 1, 8, 45; DA; DAB; DAC; DAM DRAM, MST, POET; PC 2; SSC 3; WLC**
See also CA 104; 120; CDBLB 1945-1960; DLB 13, 20, 139; MTCW; SATA 60

Thomas, (Philip) Edward 1878-1917 . **T C L C 10; DAM POET**
See also CA 106; 153; DLB 19

Thomas, Joyce Carol 1938- .... **CLC 35**
See also AAYA 12; BW 2; CA 113; 116; CANR 48; CLR 19; DLB 33; INT 116; JRDA; MAICYA; MTCW; SAAS 7; SATA 40, 78

Thomas, Lewis 1913-1993 .... **CLC 35**
See also CA 85-88; 143; CANR 38, 60; MTCW

Thomas, Paul
See Mann, (Paul) Thomas

Thomas, Piri 1928- .... **CLC 17**
See also CA 73-76; HW

Thomas, R(onald) S(tuart) 1913- **CLC 6, 13, 48; DAB; DAM POET**
See also CA 89-92; CAAS 4; CANR 30; CDBLB 1960 to Present; DLB 27; MTCW

Thomas, Ross (Elmore) 1926-1995 .. **CLC 39**
See also CA 33-36R; 150; CANR 22

Thompson, Francis Clegg
See Mencken, H(enry) L(ouis)

Thompson, Francis Joseph 1859-1907 **TCLC 4**
See also CA 104; CDBLB 1890-1914; DLB 19

Thompson, Hunter S(tockton) 1939- **CLC 9, 17, 40, 104; DAM POP**
See also BEST 89:1; CA 17-20R; CANR 23, 46; MTCW

Thompson, James Myers
See Thompson, Jim (Myers)

Thompson, Jim (Myers) 1906-1977(?) **CLC 69**
See also CA 140

Thompson, Judith .... **CLC 39**

Thomson, James 1700-1748 **LC 16, 29; DAM POET**
See also DLB 95

Thomson, James 1834-1882 **NCLC 18; DAM POET**
See also DLB 35

Thoreau, Henry David 1817-1862 **NCLC 7, 21, 61; DA; DAB; DAC; DAM MST; WLC**
See also CDALB 1640-1865; DLB 1

Thornton, Hall
See Silverberg, Robert

Thucydides c. 455B.C.-399B.C. ...... **CMLC 17**
See also DLB 176

Thurber, James (Grover) 1894-1961 **CLC 5, 11, 25; DA; DAB; DAC; DAM DRAM, MST, NOV; SSC 1**
See also CA 73-76; CANR 17, 39; CDALB 1929-1941; DLB 4, 11, 22, 102; MAICYA; MTCW; SATA 13

Thurman, Wallace (Henry) 1902-1934 **T C L C 6; BLC; DAM MULT**
See also BW 1; CA 104; 124; DLB 51

Ticheburn, Cheviot
See Ainsworth, William Harrison

Tieck, (Johann) Ludwig 1773-1853 **NCLC 5, 46**
See also DLB 90

Tiger, Derry
See Ellison, Harlan (Jay)

Tilghman, Christopher 1948(?)- ...... **CLC 65**
See also CA 159

Tillinghast, Richard (Williford) 1940- **CLC 29**
See also CA 29-32R; CAAS 23; CANR 26, 51

Timrod, Henry 1828-1867 .... **NCLC 25**
See also DLB 3

Tindall, Gillian 1938- .... **CLC 7**
See also CA 21-24R; CANR 11

Tiptree, James, Jr. .... **CLC 48, 50**
See also Sheldon, Alice Hastings Bradley
See also DLB 8

Titmarsh, Michael Angelo
See Thackeray, William Makepeace

Tocqueville, Alexis (Charles Henri Maurice Clerel Comte) 1805-1859 ... **NCLC 7, 63**

Tolkien, J(ohn) R(onald) R(euel) 1892-1973 **CLC 1, 2, 3, 8, 12, 38; DA; DAB; DAC; DAM MST, NOV, POP; WLC**
See also AAYA 10; AITN 1; CA 17-18; 45-48; CANR 36; CAP 2; CDBLB 1914-1945; DLB 15, 160; JRDA; MAICYA; MTCW; SATA 2, 32; SATA-Obit 24

Toller, Ernst 1893-1939 .... **TCLC 10**
See also CA 107; DLB 124

Tolson, M. B.
See Tolson, Melvin B(eaunorus)

Tolson, Melvin B(eaunorus) 1898(?)-1966 **CLC 36; BLC; DAM MULT, POET**
See also BW 1; CA 124; 89-92; DLB 48, 76

Tolstoi, Aleksei Nikolaevich
See Tolstoy, Alexey Nikolaevich

Tolstoy, Alexey Nikolaevich 1882-1945 **T C L C 18**
See also CA 107; 158

Tolstoy, Count Leo
See Tolstoy, Leo (Nikolaevich)

Tolstoy, Leo (Nikolaevich) 1828-1910 **TCLC 4, 11, 17, 28, 44; DA; DAB; DAC; DAM MST, NOV; SSC 9; WLC**
See also CA 104; 123; SATA 26

Tomasi di Lampedusa, Giuseppe 1896-1957
See Lampedusa, Giuseppe (Tomasi) di
See also CA 111

Tomlin, Lily .... **CLC 17**
See also Tomlin, Mary Jean

Tomlin, Mary Jean 1939(?)-
See Tomlin, Lily
See also CA 117

Tomlinson, (Alfred) Charles 1927- **CLC 2, 4, 6, 13, 45; DAM POET; PC 17**
See also CA 5-8R; CANR 33; DLB 40

Tomlinson, H(enry) M(ajor) 1873-1958 **TCLC 71**
See also CA 118; DLB 36, 100

Tonson, Jacob
See Bennett, (Enoch) Arnold

Toole, John Kennedy 1937-1969 **CLC 19, 64**
See also CA 104; DLBY 81

Toomer, Jean 1894-1967 .... **CLC 1, 4, 13, 22; BLC; DAM MULT; PC 7; SSC 1; WLCS**
See also BW 1; CA 85-88; CDALB 1917-1929; DLB 45, 51; MTCW

Torley, Luke
See Blish, James (Benjamin)

Tornimparte, Alessandra
See Ginzburg, Natalia

Torre, Raoul della
See Mencken, H(enry) L(ouis)

Torrey, E(dwin) Fuller 1937- .... **CLC 34**
See also CA 119

Torsvan, Ben Traven
See Traven, B.

Torsvan, Benno Traven
See Traven, B.

Torsvan, Berick Traven
See Traven, B.

Torsvan, Berwick Traven
See Traven, B.

Torsvan, Bruno Traven

See Traven, B.

Torsvan, Traven
See Traven, B.

Tournier, Michel (Edouard) 1924- **CLC 6, 23, 36, 95**
See also CA 49-52; CANR 3, 36; DLB 83; MTCW; SATA 23

Tournimparte, Alessandra
See Ginzburg, Natalia

Towers, Ivar
See Kornbluth, C(yril) M.

Towne, Robert (Burton) 1936(?)- ..... **CLC 87**
See also CA 108; DLB 44

Townsend, Sue 1946- .... **CLC 61; DAB; DAC**
See also CA 119; 127; INT 127; MTCW; SATA 55, 93; SATA-Brief 48

Townshend, Peter (Dennis Blandford) 1945- **CLC 17, 42**
See also CA 107

Tozzi, Federigo 1883-1920 .... **TCLC 31**

Traill, Catharine Parr 1802-1899 .. **NCLC 31**
See also DLB 99

Trakl, Georg 1887-1914 .... **TCLC 5**
See also CA 104

Transtroemer, Tomas (Goesta) 1931- **CLC 52, 65; DAM POET**
See also CA 117; 129; CAAS 17

Transtromer, Tomas Gosta
See Transtroemer, Tomas (Goesta)

Traven, B. (?)-1969 .... **CLC 8, 11**
See also CA 19-20; 25-28R; CAP 2; DLB 9, 56; MTCW

Treitel, Jonathan 1959- .... **CLC 70**

Tremain, Rose 1943- .... **CLC 42**
See also CA 97-100; CANR 44; DLB 14

Tremblay, Michel 1942- **CLC 29, 102; DAC; DAM MST**
See also CA 116; 128; DLB 60; MTCW

Trevanian .... **CLC 29**
See also Whitaker, Rod(ney)

Trevor, Glen
See Hilton, James

Trevor, William 1928- .. **CLC 7, 9, 14, 25, 71; SSC 21**
See also Cox, William Trevor
See also DLB 14, 139

Trifonov, Yuri (Valentinovich) 1925-1981 **CLC 45**
See also CA 126; 103; MTCW

Trilling, Lionel 1905-1975 ...... **CLC 9, 11, 24**
See also CA 9-12R; 61-64; CANR 10; DLB 28, 63; INT CANR-10; MTCW

Trimball, W. H.
See Mencken, H(enry) L(ouis)

Tristan
See Gomez de la Serna, Ramon

Tristram
See Housman, A(lfred) E(dward)

Trogdon, William (Lewis) 1939-
See Heat-Moon, William Least
See also CA 115; 119; CANR 47; INT 119

Trollope, Anthony 1815-1882 **NCLC 6, 33; DA; DAB; DAC; DAM MST, NOV; WLC**
See also CDBLB 1832-1890; DLB 21, 57, 159; SATA 22

Trollope, Frances 1779-1863 .... **NCLC 30**
See also DLB 21, 166

Trotsky, Leon 1879-1940 .... **TCLC 22**
See also CA 118

Trotter (Cockburn), Catharine 1679-1749 **L C 8**
See also DLB 84

Trout, Kilgore

See Farmer, Philip Jose
Trow, George W. S. 1943- .... **CLC 52**
   See also CA 126
Troyat, Henri 1911- .... **CLC 23**
   See also CA 45-48; CANR 2, 33; MTCW
Trudeau, G(arretson) B(eekman) 1948-
   See Trudeau, Garry B.
   See also CA 81-84; CANR 31; SATA 35
Trudeau, Garry B. .... **CLC 12**
   See also Trudeau, G(arretson) B(eekman)
   See also AAYA 10; AITN 2
Truffaut, Francois 1932-1984 .. **CLC 20, 101**
   See also CA 81-84; 113; CANR 34
Trumbo, Dalton 1905-1976 .... **CLC 19**
   See also CA 21-24R; 69-72; CANR 10; DLB
   26
Trumbull, John 1750-1831 .... **NCLC 30**
   See also DLB 31
Trundlett, Helen B.
   See Eliot, T(homas) S(tearns)
Tryon, Thomas 1926-1991 . **CLC 3, 11; DAM
   POP**
   See also AITN 1; CA 29-32R; 135; CANR 32;
   MTCW
Tryon, Tom
   See Tryon, Thomas
Ts'ao Hsueh-ch'in 1715(?)-1763 .... **LC 1**
Tsushima, Shuji 1909-1948
   See Dazai, Osamu
   See also CA 107
Tsvetaeva (Efron), Marina (Ivanovna) 1892-
   1941 .... **TCLC 7, 35; PC 14**
   See also CA 104; 128; MTCW
Tuck, Lily 1938- .... **CLC 70**
   See also CA 139
Tu Fu 712-770 .... **PC 9**
   See also DAM MULT
Tunis, John R(oberts) 1889-1975 ..... **CLC 12**
   See also CA 61-64; DLB 22, 171; JRDA;
   MAICYA; SATA 37; SATA-Brief 30
Tuohy, Frank .... **CLC 37**
   See also Tuohy, John Francis
   See also DLB 14, 139
Tuohy, John Francis 1925-
   See Tuohy, Frank
   See also CA 5-8R; CANR 3, 47
Turco, Lewis (Putnam) 1934- ...... **CLC 11, 63**
   See also CA 13-16R; CAAS 22; CANR 24, 51;
   DLBY 84
Turgenev, Ivan 1818-1883 .... **NCLC 21; DA;
   DAB; DAC; DAM MST, NOV; DC 7; SSC
   7; WLC**
Turgot, Anne-Robert-Jacques 1727-1781 **L C
   26**
Turner, Frederick 1943- .... **CLC 48**
   See also CA 73-76; CAAS 10; CANR 12, 30,
   56; DLB 40
Tutu, Desmond M(pilo) 1931- **CLC 80; BLC;
   DAM MULT**
   See also BW 1; CA 125
Tutuola, Amos 1920-1997 **CLC 5, 14, 29; BLC;
   DAM MULT**
   See also BW 2; CA 9-12R; 159; CANR 27; DLB
   125; MTCW
**Twain, Mark TCLC 6, 12, 19, 36, 48, 59; SSC
   26; WLC**
   See also Clemens, Samuel Langhorne
   See also AAYA 20; DLB 11, 12, 23, 64, 74
Tyler, Anne 1941- . **CLC 7, 11, 18, 28, 44, 59,
   103; DAM NOV, POP**
   See also AAYA 18; BEST 89:1; CA 9-12R;
   CANR 11, 33, 53; DLB 6, 143; DLBY 82;
   MTCW; SATA 7, 90

Tyler, Royall 1757-1826 .... **NCLC 3**
   See also DLB 37
Tynan, Katharine 1861-1931 .... **TCLC 3**
   See also CA 104; DLB 153
Tyutchev, Fyodor 1803-1873 .... **NCLC 34**
Tzara, Tristan 1896-1963 ...... **CLC 47; DAM
   POET**
   See also Rosenfeld, Samuel; Rosenstock, Sami;
   Rosenstock, Samuel
   See also CA 153
Uhry, Alfred 1936- .. **CLC 55; DAM DRAM,
   POP**
   See also CA 127; 133; INT 133
Ulf, Haerved
   See Strindberg, (Johan) August
Ulf, Harved
   See Strindberg, (Johan) August
Ulibarri, Sabine R(eyes) 1919- **CLC 83; DAM
   MULT**
   See also CA 131; DLB 82; HW
Unamuno (y Jugo), Miguel de 1864-1936
   **TCLC 2, 9; DAM MULT, NOV; HLC; SSC
   11**
   See also CA 104; 131; DLB 108; HW; MTCW
Undercliffe, Errol
   See Campbell, (John) Ramsey
Underwood, Miles
   See Glassco, John
Undset, Sigrid 1882-1949 **TCLC 3; DA; DAB;
   DAC; DAM MST, NOV; WLC**
   See also CA 104; 129; MTCW
Ungaretti, Giuseppe 1888-1970 **CLC 7, 11, 15**
   See also CA 19-20; 25-28R; CAP 2; DLB 114
Unger, Douglas 1952- .... **CLC 34**
   See also CA 130
Unsworth, Barry (Forster) 1930- ..... **CLC 76**
   See also CA 25-28R; CANR 30, 54
Updike, John (Hoyer) 1932- **CLC 1, 2, 3, 5, 7,
   9, 13, 15, 23, 34, 43, 70; DA; DAB; DAC;
   DAM MST, NOV, POET, POP; SSC 13, 27;
   WLC**
   See also CA 1-4R; CABS 1; CANR 4, 33, 51;
   CDALB 1968-1988; DLB 2, 5, 143; DLBD
   3; DLBY 80, 82; MTCW
Upshaw, Margaret Mitchell
   See Mitchell, Margaret (Munnerlyn)
Upton, Mark
   See Sanders, Lawrence
Urdang, Constance (Henriette) 1922- **CLC 47**
   See also CA 21-24R; CANR 9, 24
Uriel, Henry
   See Faust, Frederick (Schiller)
Uris, Leon (Marcus) 1924- **CLC 7, 32; DAM
   NOV, POP**
   See also AITN 1, 2; BEST 89:2; CA 1-4R;
   CANR 1, 40; MTCW; SATA 49
Urmuz
   See Codrescu, Andrei
Urquhart, Jane 1949- .... **CLC 90; DAC**
   See also CA 113; CANR 32
Ustinov, Peter (Alexander) 1921- .... **CLC 1**
   See also AITN 1; CA 13-16R; CANR 25, 51;
   DLB 13
U Tam'si, Gerald Felix Tchicaya
   See Tchicaya, Gerald Felix
U Tam'si, Tchicaya
   See Tchicaya, Gerald Felix
Vaculik, Ludvik 1926- .... **CLC 7**
   See also CA 53-56
Vaihinger, Hans 1852-1933 .... **TCLC 71**
   See also CA 116
Valdez, Luis (Miguel) 1940- .. **CLC 84; DAM
   MULT; HLC**

   See also CA 101; CANR 32; DLB 122; HW
Valenzuela, Luisa 1938- **CLC 31, 104; DAM
   MULT; SSC 14**
   See also CA 101; CANR 32; DLB 113; HW
Valera y Alcala-Galiano, Juan 1824-1905
   TCLC 10
   See also CA 106
Valery, (Ambroise) Paul (Toussaint Jules) 1871-
   1945 .... **TCLC 4, 15; DAM POET; PC 9**
   See also CA 104; 122; MTCW
Valle-Inclan, Ramon (Maria) del 1866-1936
   TCLC 5; DAM MULT; HLC
   See also CA 106; 153; DLB 134
Vallejo, Antonio Buero
   See Buero Vallejo, Antonio
Vallejo, Cesar (Abraham) 1892-1938 **TCLC 3,
   56; DAM MULT; HLC**
   See also CA 105; 153; HW
Vallette, Marguerite Eymery
   See Rachilde
Valle Y Pena, Ramon del
   See Valle-Inclan, Ramon (Maria) del
Van Ash, Cay 1918- .... **CLC 34**
Vanbrugh, Sir John 1664-1726 **LC 21; DAM
   DRAM**
   See also DLB 80
Van Campen, Karl
   See Campbell, John W(ood, Jr.)
Vance, Gerald
   See Silverberg, Robert
Vance, Jack .... **CLC 35**
   See also Kuttner, Henry; Vance, John Holbrook
   See also DLB 8
Vance, John Holbrook 1916-
   See Queen, Ellery; Vance, Jack
   See also CA 29-32R; CANR 17; MTCW
**Van Den Bogarde, Derek Jules Gaspard Ulric
   Niven** 1921-
   See Bogarde, Dirk
   See also CA 77-80
Vandenburgh, Jane .... **CLC 59**
Vanderhaeghe, Guy 1951- .... **CLC 41**
   See also CA 113
van der Post, Laurens (Jan) 1906-1996 **CLC 5**
   See also CA 5-8R; 155; CANR 35
van de Wetering, Janwillem 1931- ... **CLC 47**
   See also CA 49-52; CANR 4
Van Dine, S. S. .... **TCLC 23**
   See also Wright, Willard Huntington
Van Doren, Carl (Clinton) 1885-1950 **T C L C
   18**
   See also CA 111
Van Doren, Mark 1894-1972 .... **CLC 6, 10**
   See also CA 1-4R; 37-40R; CANR 3; DLB 45;
   MTCW
Van Druten, John (William) 1901-1957 **T C L C
   2**
   See also CA 104; DLB 10
Van Duyn, Mona (Jane) 1921- **CLC 3, 7, 63;
   DAM POET**
   See also CA 9-12R; CANR 7, 38, 60; DLB 5
Van Dyne, Edith
   See Baum, L(yman) Frank
van Itallie, Jean-Claude 1936- .... **CLC 3**
   See also CA 45-48; CAAS 2; CANR 1, 48; DLB
   7
van Ostaijen, Paul 1896-1928 .... **TCLC 33**
Van Peebles, Melvin 1932- . **CLC 2, 20; DAM
   MULT**
   See also BW 2; CA 85-88; CANR 27
Vansittart, Peter 1920- .... **CLC 42**
   See also CA 1-4R; CANR 3, 49
Van Vechten, Carl 1880-1964 .... **CLC 33**

Walker, Joseph A. 1935- .... **CLC 19; DAM DRAM, MST**
See also BW 1; CA 89-92; CANR 26; DLB 38

Walker, Margaret (Abigail) 1915- **CLC 1, 6; BLC; DAM MULT**
See also BW 2; CA 73-76; CANR 26, 54; DLB 76, 152; MTCW

Walker, Ted .... **CLC 13**
See also Walker, Edward Joseph
See also DLB 40

Wallace, David Foster 1962- .... **CLC 50**
See also CA 132; CANR 59

Wallace, Dexter
See Masters, Edgar Lee

Wallace, (Richard Horatio) Edgar 1875-1932
TCLC 57
See also CA 115; DLB 70

Wallace, Irving 1916-1990 . **CLC 7, 13; DAM NOV, POP**
See also AITN 1; CA 1-4R; 132; CAAS 1; CANR 1, 27; INT CANR-27; MTCW

Wallant, Edward Lewis 1926-1962 **CLC 5, 10**
See also CA 1-4R; CANR 22; DLB 2, 28, 143; MTCW

Walley, Byron
See Card, Orson Scott

Walpole, Horace 1717-1797 .... **LC 2**
See also DLB 39, 104

Walpole, Hugh (Seymour) 1884-1941 **TCLC 5**
See also CA 104; DLB 34

Walser, Martin 1927- .... **CLC 27**
See also CA 57-60; CANR 8, 46; DLB 75, 124

Walser, Robert 1878-1956 **TCLC 18; SSC 20**
See also CA 118; DLB 66

Walsh, Jill Paton .... **CLC 35**
See also Paton Walsh, Gillian
See also AAYA 11; CLR 2; DLB 161; SAAS 3

Walter, Villiam Christian
See Andersen, Hans Christian

Wambaugh, Joseph (Aloysius, Jr.) 1937- **CLC 3, 18; DAM NOV, POP**
See also AITN 1; BEST 89:3; CA 33-36R; CANR 42; DLB 6; DLBY 83; MTCW

Wang Wei 699(?)-761(?) .... **PC 18**

Ward, Arthur Henry Sarsfield 1883-1959
See Rohmer, Sax
See also CA 108

Ward, Douglas Turner 1930- .... **CLC 19**
See also BW 1; CA 81-84; CANR 27; DLB 7, 38

Ward, Mary Augusta
See Ward, Mrs. Humphry

Ward, Mrs. Humphry 1851-1920 .. **TCLC 55**
See also DLB 18

Ward, Peter
See Faust, Frederick (Schiller)

Warhol, Andy 1928(?)-1987 .... **CLC 20**
See also AAYA 12; BEST 89:4; CA 89-92; 121; CANR 34

Warner, Francis (Robert le Plastrier) 1937-
CLC 14
See also CA 53-56; CANR 11

Warner, Marina 1946- .... **CLC 59**
See also CA 65-68; CANR 21, 55

Warner, Rex (Ernest) 1905-1986 ..... **CLC 45**
See also CA 89-92; 119; DLB 15

Warner, Susan (Bogert) 1819-1885 **NCLC 31**
See also DLB 3, 42

Warner, Sylvia (Constance) Ashton
See Ashton-Warner, Sylvia (Constance)

Warner, Sylvia Townsend 1893-1978 **CLC 7, 19; SSC 23**
See also CA 61-64; 77-80; CANR 16, 60; DLB 34, 139; MTCW

Warren, Mercy Otis 1728-1814 ...... **NCLC 13**
See also DLB 31

Warren, Robert Penn 1905-1989 **CLC 1, 4, 6, 8, 10, 13, 18, 39, 53, 59; DA; DAB; DAC; DAM MST, NOV, POET; SSC 4; WLC**
See also AITN 1; CA 13-16R; 129; CANR 10, 47; CDALB 1968-1988; DLB 2, 48, 152; DLBY 80, 89; INT CANR-10; MTCW; SATA 46; SATA-Obit 63

Warshofsky, Isaac
See Singer, Isaac Bashevis

Warton, Thomas 1728-1790 ..... **LC 15; DAM POET**
See also DLB 104, 109

Waruk, Kona
See Harris, (Theodore) Wilson

Warung, Price 1855-1911 .... **TCLC 45**

Warwick, Jarvis
See Garner, Hugh

Washington, Alex
See Harris, Mark

Washington, Booker T(aliaferro) 1856-1915
TCLC 10; BLC; DAM MULT
See also BW 1; CA 114; 125; SATA 28

Washington, George 1732-1799 .... **LC 25**
See also DLB 31

Wassermann, (Karl) Jakob 1873-1934 **TCLC 6**
See also CA 104; DLB 66

Wasserstein, Wendy 1950- ... **CLC 32, 59, 90; DAM DRAM; DC 4**
See also CA 121; 129; CABS 3; CANR 53; INT 129; SATA 94

Waterhouse, Keith (Spencer) 1929- .. **CLC 47**
See also CA 5-8R; CANR 38; DLB 13, 15; MTCW

Waters, Frank (Joseph) 1902-1995 ... **CLC 88**
See also CA 5-8R; 149; CAAS 13; CANR 3, 18; DLBY 86

Waters, Roger 1944- .... **CLC 35**

Watkins, Frances Ellen
See Harper, Frances Ellen Watkins

Watkins, Gerrold
See Malzberg, Barry N(athaniel)

Watkins, Gloria 1955(?)-
See hooks, bell
See also BW 2; CA 143

Watkins, Paul 1964- .... **CLC 55**
See also CA 132

Watkins, Vernon Phillips 1906-1967 **CLC 43**
See also CA 9-10; 25-28R; CAP 1; DLB 20

Watson, Irving S.
See Mencken, H(enry) L(ouis)

Watson, John H.
See Farmer, Philip Jose

Watson, Richard F.
See Silverberg, Robert

Waugh, Auberon (Alexander) 1939- .. **CLC 7**
See also CA 45-48; CANR 6, 22; DLB 14

Waugh, Evelyn (Arthur St. John) 1903-1966
CLC 1, 3, 8, 13, 19, 27, 44; DA; DAB; DAC; DAM MST, NOV, POP; WLC
See also CA 85-88; 25-28R; CANR 22; CDBLB 1914-1945; DLB 15, 162; MTCW

Waugh, Harriet 1944- .... **CLC 6**
See also CA 85-88; CANR 22

Ways, C. R.
See Blount, Roy (Alton), Jr.

Waystaff, Simon
See Swift, Jonathan

Webb, (Martha) Beatrice (Potter) 1858-1943
TCLC 22
See also Potter, (Helen) Beatrix
See also CA 117

Webb, Charles (Richard) 1939- .... **CLC 7**
See also CA 25-28R

Webb, James H(enry), Jr. 1946- .... **CLC 22**
See also CA 81-84

Webb, Mary (Gladys Meredith) 1881-1927
TCLC 24
See also CA 123; DLB 34

Webb, Mrs. Sidney
See Webb, (Martha) Beatrice (Potter)

Webb, Phyllis 1927- .... **CLC 18**
See also CA 104; CANR 23; DLB 53

Webb, Sidney (James) 1859-1947 .. **TCLC 22**
See also CA 117

Webber, Andrew Lloyd .... **CLC 21**
See also Lloyd Webber, Andrew

Weber, Lenora Mattingly 1895-1971 **CLC 12**
See also CA 19-20; 29-32R; CAP 1; SATA 2; SATA-Obit 26

Weber, Max 1864-1920 .... **TCLC 69**
See also CA 109

Webster, John 1579(?)-1634(?) ... **LC 33; DA; DAB; DAC; DAM DRAM, MST; DC 2; WLC**
See also CDBLB Before 1660; DLB 58

Webster, Noah 1758-1843 .... **NCLC 30**

Wedekind, (Benjamin) Frank(lin) 1864-1918
TCLC 7; DAM DRAM
See also CA 104; 153; DLB 118

Weidman, Jerome 1913- .... **CLC 7**
See also AITN 2; CA 1-4R; CANR 1; DLB 28

Weil, Simone (Adolphine) 1909-1943 **TCLC 23**
See also CA 117; 159

Weinstein, Nathan
See West, Nathanael

Weinstein, Nathan von Wallenstein
See West, Nathanael

Weir, Peter (Lindsay) 1944- .... **CLC 20**
See also CA 113; 123

Weiss, Peter (Ulrich) 1916-1982 **CLC 3, 15, 51; DAM DRAM**
See also CA 45-48; 106; CANR 3; DLB 69, 124

Weiss, Theodore (Russell) 1916- **CLC 3, 8, 14**
See also CA 9-12R; CAAS 2; CANR 46; DLB 5

Welch, (Maurice) Denton 1915-1948 **TCLC 22**
See also CA 121; 148

Welch, James 1940- ..... **CLC 6, 14, 52; DAM MULT, POP**
See also CA 85-88; CANR 42; DLB 175; NNAL

Weldon, Fay 1933- .. **CLC 6, 9, 11, 19, 36, 59; DAM POP**
See also CA 21-24R; CANR 16, 46; CDBLB 1960 to Present; DLB 14; INT CANR-16; MTCW

Wellek, Rene 1903-1995 .... **CLC 28**
See also CA 5-8R; 150; CAAS 7; CANR 8; DLB 63; INT CANR-8

Weller, Michael 1942- .... **CLC 10, 53**
See also CA 85-88

Weller, Paul 1958- .... **CLC 26**

Wellershoff, Dieter 1925- .... **CLC 46**
See also CA 89-92; CANR 16, 37

Welles, (George) Orson 1915-1985 **CLC 20, 80**
See also CA 93-96; 117

Wellman, Mac 1945- .... **CLC 65**

Wellman, Manly Wade 1903-1986 .... **CLC 49**
See also CA 1-4R; 118; CANR 6, 16, 44; SATA 6; SATA-Obit 47

Wells, Carolyn 1869(?)-1942 .... **TCLC 35**
See also CA 113; DLB 11

Wells, H(erbert) G(eorge) 1866-1946 **TCLC 6,**

12, 19; DA; DAB; DAC; DAM MST, NOV; SSC 6; WLC
See also AAYA 18; CA 110; 121; CDBLB 1914-1945; DLB 34, 70, 156, 178; MTCW; SATA 20

Wells, Rosemary 1943- .... **CLC 12**
See also AAYA 13; CA 85-88; CANR 48; CLR 16; MAICYA; SAAS 1; SATA 18, 69

Welty, Eudora 1909- **CLC 1, 2, 5, 14, 22, 33; DA; DAB; DAC; DAM MST, NOV; SSC 1, 27; WLC**
See also CA 9-12R; CABS 1; CANR 32; CDALB 1941-1968; DLB 2, 102, 143; DLBD 12; DLBY 87; MTCW

Wen I-to 1899-1946 .... **TCLC 28**

Wentworth, Robert
See Hamilton, Edmond

Werfel, Franz (V.) 1890-1945 .... **TCLC 8**
See also CA 104; DLB 81, 124

Wergeland, Henrik Arnold 1808-1845 **N C L C 5**

Wersba, Barbara 1932- .... **CLC 30**
See also AAYA 2; CA 29-32R; CANR 16, 38; CLR 3; DLB 52; JRDA; MAICYA; SAAS 2; SATA 1, 58

Wertmueller, Lina 1928- .... **CLC 16**
See also CA 97-100; CANR 39

Wescott, Glenway 1901-1987 .... **CLC 13**
See also CA 13-16R; 121; CANR 23; DLB 4, 9, 102

Wesker, Arnold 1932- .... **CLC 3, 5, 42; DAB; DAM DRAM**
See also CA 1-4R; CAAS 7; CANR 1, 33; CDBLB 1960 to Present; DLB 13; MTCW

Wesley, Richard (Errol) 1945- .... **CLC 7**
See also BW 1; CA 57-60; CANR 27; DLB 38

Wessel, Johan Herman 1742-1785 .... **LC 7**

West, Anthony (Panther) 1914-1987 **CLC 50**
See also CA 45-48; 124; CANR 3, 19; DLB 15

West, C. P.
See Wodehouse, P(elham) G(renville)

West, (Mary) Jessamyn 1902-1984 **CLC 7, 17**
See also CA 9-12R; 112; CANR 27; DLB 6; DLBY 84; MTCW; SATA-Obit 37

West, Morris L(anglo) 1916- .... **CLC 6, 33**
See also CA 5-8R; CANR 24, 49; MTCW

West, Nathanael 1903-1940 **TCLC 1, 14, 44; SSC 16**
See also CA 104; 125; CDALB 1929-1941; DLB 4, 9, 28; MTCW

West, Owen
See Koontz, Dean R(ay)

West, Paul 1930- .... **CLC 7, 14, 96**
See also CA 13-16R; CAAS 7; CANR 22, 53; DLB 14; INT CANR-22

West, Rebecca 1892-1983 ... **CLC 7, 9, 31, 50**
See also CA 5-8R; 109; CANR 19; DLB 36; DLBY 83; MTCW

Westall, Robert (Atkinson) 1929-1993 **CLC 17**
See also AAYA 12; CA 69-72; 141; CANR 18; CLR 13; JRDA; MAICYA; SAAS 2; SATA 23, 69; SATA-Obit 75

Westlake, Donald E(dwin) 1933- **CLC 7, 33; DAM POP**
See also CA 17-20R; CAAS 13; CANR 16, 44; INT CANR-16

Westmacott, Mary
See Christie, Agatha (Mary Clarissa)

Weston, Allen
See Norton, Andre

Wetcheek, J. L.
See Feuchtwanger, Lion

Wetering, Janwillem van de

See van de Wetering, Janwillem

Wetherell, Elizabeth
See Warner, Susan (Bogert)

Whale, James 1889-1957 .... **TCLC 63**

Whalen, Philip 1923- .... **CLC 6, 29**
See also CA 9-12R; CANR 5, 39; DLB 16

Wharton, Edith (Newbold Jones) 1862-1937 **TCLC 3, 9, 27, 53; DA; DAB; DAC; DAM MST, NOV; SSC 6; WLC**
See also CA 104; 132; CDALB 1865-1917; DLB 4, 9, 12, 78; DLBD 13; MTCW

Wharton, James
See Mencken, H(enry) L(ouis)

Wharton, William (a pseudonym)CLC 18, 37
See also CA 93-96; DLBY 80; INT 93-96

Wheatley (Peters), Phillis 1754(?)-1784**LC 3; BLC; DA; DAC; DAM MST, MULT, POET; PC 3; WLC**
See also CDALB 1640-1865; DLB 31, 50

Wheelock, John Hall 1886-1978 .... **CLC 14**
See also CA 13-16R; 77-80; CANR 14; DLB 45

White, E(lwyn) B(rooks) 1899-1985 **CLC 10, 34, 39; DAM POP**
See also AITN 2; CA 13-16R; 116; CANR 16, 37; CLR 1, 21; DLB 11, 22; MAICYA; MTCW; SATA 2, 29; SATA-Obit 44

White, Edmund (Valentine III) 1940-**CLC 27; DAM POP**
See also AAYA 7; CA 45-48; CANR 3, 19, 36; MTCW

White, Patrick (Victor Martindale) 1912-1990 **CLC 3, 4, 5, 7, 9, 18, 65, 69**
See also CA 81-84; 132; CANR 43; MTCW

White, Phyllis Dorothy James 1920-
See James, P. D.
See also CA 21-24R; CANR 17, 43; DAM POP; MTCW

White, T(erence) H(anbury) 1906-1964 **C L C 30**
See also AAYA 22; CA 73-76; CANR 37; DLB 160; JRDA; MAICYA; SATA 12

White, Terence de Vere 1912-1994 ... **CLC 49**
See also CA 49-52; 145; CANR 3

White, Walter F(rancis) 1893-1955 **TCLC 15**
See also White, Walter
See also BW 1; CA 115; 124; DLB 51

White, William Hale 1831-1913
See Rutherford, Mark
See also CA 121

Whitehead, E(dward) A(nthony) 1933-**CLC 5**
See also CA 65-68; CANR 58

Whitemore, Hugh (John) 1936- .... **CLC 37**
See also CA 132; INT 132

Whitman, Sarah Helen (Power) 1803-1878 **NCLC 19**
See also DLB 1

Whitman, Walt(er) 1819-1892 .. **NCLC 4, 31; DA; DAB; DAC; DAM MST, POET; PC 3; WLC**
See also CDALB 1640-1865; DLB 3, 64; SATA 20

Whitney, Phyllis A(yame) 1903- ..... **CLC 42; DAM POP**
See also AITN 2; BEST 90:3; CA 1-4R; CANR 3, 25, 38, 60; JRDA; MAICYA; SATA 1, 30

Whittemore, (Edward) Reed (Jr.) 1919-**CLC 4**
See also CA 9-12R; CAAS 8; CANR 4; DLB 5

Whittier, John Greenleaf 1807-1892**NCLC 8, 59**
See also DLB 1

Whittlebot, Hernia
See Coward, Noel (Peirce)

Wicker, Thomas Grey 1926-
See Wicker, Tom
See also CA 65-68; CANR 21, 46

Wicker, Tom .... **CLC 7**
See also Wicker, Thomas Grey

Wideman, John Edgar 1941- **CLC 5, 34, 36, 67; BLC; DAM MULT**
See also BW 2; CA 85-88; CANR 14, 42; DLB 33, 143

Wiebe, Rudy (Henry) 1934-... **CLC 6, 11, 14; DAC; DAM MST**
See also CA 37-40R; CANR 42; DLB 60

Wieland, Christoph Martin 1733-1813**N C L C 17**
See also DLB 97

Wiene, Robert 1881-1938 .... **TCLC 56**

Wieners, John 1934- .... **CLC 7**
See also CA 13-16R; DLB 16

Wiesel, Elie(zer) 1928- **CLC 3, 5, 11, 37; DA; DAB; DAC; DAM MST, NOV; WLCS 2:855-57, 854**
See also AAYA 7; AITN 1; CA 5-8R; CAAS 4; CANR 8, 40; DLB 83; DLBY 87; INT CANR-8; MTCW; SATA 56

Wiggins, Marianne 1947- .... **CLC 57**
See also BEST 89:3; CA 130; CANR 60

Wight, James Alfred 1916-
See Herriot, James
See also CA 77-80; SATA 55; SATA-Brief 44

Wilbur, Richard (Purdy) 1921-**CLC 3, 6, 9, 14, 53; DA; DAB; DAC; DAM MST, POET**
See also CA 1-4R; CABS 2; CANR 2, 29; DLB 5, 169; INT CANR-29; MTCW; SATA 9

Wild, Peter 1940- .... **CLC 14**
See also CA 37-40R; DLB 5

Wilde, Oscar (Fingal O'Flahertie Wills) 1854(?)-1900**TCLC 1, 8, 23, 41; DA; DAB; DAC; DAM DRAM, MST, NOV; SSC 11; WLC**
See also CA 104; 119; CDBLB 1890-1914; DLB 10, 19, 34, 57, 141, 156; SATA 24

Wilder, Billy .... **CLC 20**
See also Wilder, Samuel
See also DLB 26

Wilder, Samuel 1906-
See Wilder, Billy
See also CA 89-92

Wilder, Thornton (Niven) 1897-1975**CLC 1, 5, 6, 10, 15, 35, 82; DA; DAB; DAC; DAM DRAM, MST, NOV; DC 1; WLC**
See also AITN 2; CA 13-16R; 61-64; CANR 40; DLB 4, 7, 9; MTCW

Wilding, Michael 1942- .... **CLC 73**
See also CA 104; CANR 24, 49

Wiley, Richard 1944- .... **CLC 44**
See also CA 121; 129

Wilhelm, Kate .... **CLC 7**
See also Wilhelm, Katie Gertrude
See also AAYA 20; CAAS 5; DLB 8; INT CANR-17

Wilhelm, Katie Gertrude 1928-
See Wilhelm, Kate
See also CA 37-40R; CANR 17, 36, 60; MTCW

Wilkins, Mary
See Freeman, Mary Eleanor Wilkins

Willard, Nancy 1936- .... **CLC 7, 37**
See also CA 89-92; CANR 10, 39; CLR 5; DLB 5, 52; MAICYA; MTCW; SATA 37, 71; SATA-Brief 30

Williams, C(harles) K(enneth) 1936-**CLC 33, 56; DAM POET**
See also CA 37-40R; CAAS 26; CANR 57; DLB 5

Williams, Charles
See Collier, James L(incoln)
Williams, Charles (Walter Stansby) 1886-1945
TCLC 1, 11
See also CA 104; DLB 100, 153
Williams, (George) Emlyn 1905-1987CLC 15;
DAM DRAM
See also CA 104; 123; CANR 36; DLB 10, 77;
MTCW
Williams, Hugo 1942- .... **CLC 42**
See also CA 17-20R; CANR 45; DLB 40
Williams, J. Walker
See Wodehouse, P(elham) G(renville)
Williams, John A(lfred) 1925- ..... **CLC 5, 13;**
BLC; DAM MULT
See also BW 2; CA 53-56; CAAS 3; CANR 6,
26, 51; DLB 2, 33; INT CANR-6
Williams, Jonathan (Chamberlain) 1929-
CLC 13
See also CA 9-12R; CAAS 12; CANR 8; DLB
5
Williams, Joy 1944- .... **CLC 31**
See also CA 41-44R; CANR 22, 48
Williams, Norman 1952- .... **CLC 39**
See also CA 118
Williams, Sherley Anne 1944-CLC 89; BLC;
DAM MULT, POET
See also BW 2; CA 73-76; CANR 25; DLB 41;
INT CANR-25; SATA 78
Williams, Shirley
See Williams, Sherley Anne
Williams, Tennessee 1911-1983CLC 1, 2, 5, 7,
8, 11, 15, 19, 30, 39, 45, 71; DA; DAB;
DAC; DAM DRAM, MST; DC 4; WLC
See also AITN 1, 2; CA 5-8R; 108; CABS 3;
CANR 31; CDALB 1941-1968; DLB 7;
DLBD 4; DLBY 83; MTCW
Williams, Thomas (Alonzo) 1926-1990CLC 14
See also CA 1-4R; 132; CANR 2
Williams, William C.
See Williams, William Carlos
Williams, William Carlos 1883-1963CLC 1, 2,
5, 9, 13, 22, 42, 67; DA; DAB; DAC; DAM
MST, POET; PC 7
See also CA 89-92; CANR 34; CDALB 1917-
1929; DLB 4, 16, 54, 86; MTCW
Williamson, David (Keith) 1942- ..... **CLC 56**
See also CA 103; CANR 41
Williamson, Ellen Douglas 1905-1984
See Douglas, Ellen
See also CA 17-20R; 114; CANR 39
Williamson, Jack .... **CLC 29**
See also Williamson, John Stewart
See also CAAS 8; DLB 8
Williamson, John Stewart 1908-
See Williamson, Jack
See also CA 17-20R; CANR 23
Willie, Frederick
See Lovecraft, H(oward) P(hillips)
Willingham, Calder (Baynard, Jr.) 1922-1995
CLC 5, 51
See also CA 5-8R; 147; CANR 3; DLB 2, 44;
MTCW
Willis, Charles
See Clarke, Arthur C(harles)
Willy
See Colette, (Sidonie-Gabrielle)
Willy, Colette
See Colette, (Sidonie-Gabrielle)
Wilson, A(ndrew) N(orman) 1950- .. **CLC 33**
See also CA 112; 122; DLB 14, 155
Wilson, Angus (Frank Johnstone) 1913-1991
CLC 2, 3, 5, 25, 34; SSC 21

See also CA 5-8R; 134; CANR 21; DLB 15,
139, 155; MTCW
Wilson, August 1945- CLC 39, 50, 63; BLC;
DA; DAB; DAC; DAM DRAM, MST,
MULT; DC 2; WLCS
See also AAYA 16; BW 2; CA 115; 122; CANR
42, 54; MTCW
Wilson, Brian 1942- .... **CLC 12**
Wilson, Colin 1931- .... **CLC 3, 14**
See also CA 1-4R; CAAS 5; CANR 1, 22, 33;
DLB 14; MTCW
Wilson, Dirk
See Pohl, Frederik
Wilson, Edmund 1895-1972CLC 1, 2, 3, 8, 24
See also CA 1-4R; 37-40R; CANR 1, 46; DLB
63; MTCW
Wilson, Ethel Davis (Bryant) 1888(?)-1980
CLC 13; DAC; DAM POET
See also CA 102; DLB 68; MTCW
Wilson, John 1785-1854 .... **NCLC 5**
Wilson, John (Anthony) Burgess 1917-1993
See Burgess, Anthony
See also CA 1-4R; 143; CANR 2, 46; DAC;
DAM NOV; MTCW
Wilson, Lanford 1937- CLC 7, 14, 36; DAM
DRAM
See also CA 17-20R; CABS 3; CANR 45; DLB
7
Wilson, Robert M. 1944- .... **CLC 7, 9**
See also CA 49-52; CANR 2, 41; MTCW
Wilson, Robert McLiam 1964- .... **CLC 59**
See also CA 132
Wilson, Sloan 1920- .... **CLC 32**
See also CA 1-4R; CANR 1, 44
Wilson, Snoo 1948- .... **CLC 33**
See also CA 69-72
Wilson, William S(mith) 1932- .... **CLC 49**
See also CA 81-84
Wilson, Woodrow 1856-1924 .... **TCLC 73**
See also DLB 47
Winchilsea, Anne (Kingsmill) Finch Counte
1661-1720 .... **LC 3**
Windham, Basil
See Wodehouse, P(elham) G(renville)
Wingrove, David (John) 1954- .... **CLC 68**
See also CA 133
Wintergreen, Jane
See Duncan, Sara Jeannette
Winters, Janet Lewis .... **CLC 41**
See also Lewis, Janet
See also DLBY 87
Winters, (Arthur) Yvor 1900-1968 CLC 4, 8,
32
See also CA 11-12; 25-28R; CAP 1; DLB 48;
MTCW
Winterson, Jeanette 1959-CLC 64; DAM POP
See also CA 136; CANR 58
Winthrop, John 1588-1649 .... **LC 31**
See also DLB 24, 30
Wiseman, Frederick 1930- .... **CLC 20**
See also CA 159
Wister, Owen 1860-1938 .... **TCLC 21**
See also CA 108; DLB 9, 78; SATA 62
Witkacy
See Witkiewicz, Stanislaw Ignacy
Witkiewicz, Stanislaw Ignacy 1885-1939
TCLC 8
See also CA 105
Wittgenstein, Ludwig (Josef Johann) 1889-1951
TCLC 59
See also CA 113
Wittig, Monique 1935(?)- .... **CLC 22**
See also CA 116; 135; DLB 83

Wittlin, Jozef 1896-1976 .... **CLC 25**
See also CA 49-52; 65-68; CANR 3
Wodehouse, P(elham) G(renville) 1881-1975
CLC 1, 2, 5, 10, 22; DAB; DAC; DAM
NOV; SSC 2
See also AITN 2; CA 45-48; 57-60; CANR 3,
33; CDBLB 1914-1945; DLB 34, 162;
MTCW; SATA 22
Woiwode, L.
See Woiwode, Larry (Alfred)
Woiwode, Larry (Alfred) 1941- ... **CLC 6, 10**
See also CA 73-76; CANR 16; DLB 6; INT
CANR-16
Wojciechowska, Maia (Teresa) 1927-CLC 26
See also AAYA 8; CA 9-12R; CANR 4, 41; CLR
1; JRDA; MAICYA; SAAS 1; SATA 1, 28,
83
Wolf, Christa 1929- .... **CLC 14, 29, 58**
See also CA 85-88; CANR 45; DLB 75; MTCW
Wolfe, Gene (Rodman) 1931- CLC 25; DAM
POP
See also CA 57-60; CAAS 9; CANR 6, 32, 60;
DLB 8
Wolfe, George C. 1954- .... **CLC 49**
See also CA 149
Wolfe, Thomas (Clayton) 1900-1938TCLC 4,
13, 29, 61; DA; DAB; DAC; DAM MST,
NOV; WLC
See also CA 104; 132; CDALB 1929-1941;
DLB 9, 102; DLBD 2; DLBY 85; MTCW
Wolfe, Thomas Kennerly, Jr. 1931-
See Wolfe, Tom
See also CA 13-16R; CANR 9, 33; DAM POP;
INT CANR-9; MTCW
Wolfe, Tom .... **CLC 1, 2, 9, 15, 35, 51**
See also Wolfe, Thomas Kennerly, Jr.
See also AAYA 8; AITN 2; BEST 89:1; DLB
152
Wolff, Geoffrey (Ansell) 1937- .... **CLC 41**
See also CA 29-32R; CANR 29, 43
Wolff, Sonia
See Levitin, Sonia (Wolff)
Wolff, Tobias (Jonathan Ansell) 1945-.. C L C
39, 64
See also AAYA 16; BEST 90:2; CA 114; 117;
CAAS 22; CANR 54; DLB 130; INT 117
Wolfram von Eschenbach c. 1170-c. 1220
CMLC 5
See also DLB 138
Wolitzer, Hilma 1930- .... **CLC 17**
See also CA 65-68; CANR 18, 40; INT CANR-
18; SATA 31
Wollstonecraft, Mary 1759-1797 .... **LC 5**
See also CDBLB 1789-1832; DLB 39, 104, 158
Wonder, Stevie .... **CLC 12**
See also Morris, Steveland Judkins
Wong, Jade Snow 1922- .... **CLC 17**
See also CA 109
Woodberry, George Edward 1855-1930
TCLC 73
See also DLB 71, 103
Woodcott, Keith
See Brunner, John (Kilian Houston)
Woodruff, Robert W.
See Mencken, H(enry) L(ouis)
Woolf, (Adeline) Virginia 1882-1941TCLC 1,
5, 20, 43, 56; DA; DAB; DAC; DAM MST,
NOV; SSC 7; WLC
See also CA 104; 130; CDBLB 1914-1945;
DLB 36, 100, 162; DLBD 10; MTCW
Woollcott, Alexander (Humphreys) 1887-1943
TCLC 5
See also CA 105; DLB 29

Literary Criticism Series
Cumulative Topic Index

This index lists all topic entries in Gale's *Classical and Medieval Literature Criticism, Contemporary Literary Criticism, Literature Criticism from 1400 to 1800, Nineteenth-Century Literature Criticism,* and *Twentieth-Century Literary Criticism.*

Topic Index

Contemporary Literary Criticism
Cumulative Nationality Index

Nationality Index

Nationality Index

Nationality Index

CLC-104 Title Index